Crossword Puzzle
Name Finder

SOLVER SERIES

Crossword Puzzle Name Finder

Compiled and edited by
TERRY G. FALCONER

FIREFLY BOOKS

A FIREFLY BOOK

Published by Firefly Books Ltd. 2007

First Firefly Books printing

Publisher Cataloging-in-Publication Data (U.S.)
Falconer, Terry G.
    Crossword puzzle name finder : solver series / compiled and edited by Terry G. Falconer.
[608] p. : cm.
Summary: A crossword puzzle dictionary of names to help with solving clues related to names. Names are listed alphabetically by last name, first name and category. Entries also include information on country and fame of each individual.
ISBN-13: 978-1-55407-288-0 (pbk.)
ISBN-10: 1-55407-288-3 (pbk.)
1. Crossword puzzles -- Glossaries, vocabularies, etc. I. Title.
793.73/203 dc22   GV1507.F353   2007

Library and Archives Canada Cataloguing in Publication
Falconer, Terry G. (Terry George), 1942-
    Crossword puzzle name finder / Terry G. Falconer.
(Solver series)
Includes index.
ISBN-13: 978-1-55407-288-0
ISBN-10: 1-55407-288-3
    1. Crossword puzzles--Glossaries, vocabularies, etc. 2. Names,
Personal--Dictionaries. I. Title. II. Series.
GV1507.C7F24 2007   793.73'203   C2007-900794-5

Published in the United States by
Firefly Books (U.S.) Inc.
P.O. Box 1338, Ellicott Station
Buffalo, New York 14205

Published in Canada by
Firefly Books Ltd.
66 Leek Crescent
Richmond Hill, Ontario L4B 1H1

Cover design by Lindsay Munro Smail; interior design by Relish Design Studio Ltd.

The publisher gratefully acknowledges the financial support for our publishing program by the Government of Canada through the Book Publishing Industry Development Program.

Printed in Canada

Author's website: www.solverseries.com

CONTENTS

Introduction   1

Explanatory Notes   3

Categorical Inclusions   5

SECTION 1   All names listed alphabetically by the last name
and then by category, fame and country.   11

SECTION 2   All names listed alphabetically by the first name
and then by category, fame and country.   191

SECTION 3   All names listed alphabetically by category and
then by last name, fame and country.   371

SECTION 4   All gods and goddesses listed alphabetically
by name.   567

SECTION 5   All gods and goddesses listed alphabetically
by category.   579

SECTION 6   All gods and goddesses listed alphabetically
by origin.   591

INTRODUCTION

This book has been compiled to meet an important need in solving modern crossword puzzles. Over the years, crossword puzzles have increased in complexity and to meet this demand many crossword puzzle dictionaries have been researched, published and made available to the general public. The quality of these publications varies substantially, some being very poor and while others are excellent. However, the one major shortcoming of the vast majority of these dictionaries is that they tend to direct little attention to solving clues related to names. This publication has been designed to fill this significant gap.

Obviously, there are millions of names that could be put into a publication such as this one. The challenge was to create a reference source that was relevant and easy to use. To address this challenge the most important names in all categories were researched and categorized in a manner that those who solve crosswords would find easy to use. The categories used in this book were designed to cover a broad spectrum of famous individuals and his or her claim to fame. The book has been organized using this information so that it is easy to use.

Few people would have a broad enough knowledge that would include the vast array of names in this publication and when crossword designers use many names in a puzzle most individuals find themselves in need of a reliable reference source. Apart from common words found in most dictionaries, the second most used words in crossword clues are related to names. To my knowledge, this is the first such publication that addresses this specific need in detail.

As one reviewer noted, "Most folks either do crosswords or know someone that does. Give this book to the ones that you know. They will be forever thankful." I would just add one note to that observation which is, "Each time they use the book gives them the opportunity to think of you."

I have been doing crosswords since the tender age of eleven. I have seen the need for this reference work growing over the years. The creation of this book has been a labor of love. I wish to acknowledge the many hours of assistance and understanding provided to me by my dedicated spouse Irene.

—Terry Falconer

EXPLANATORY NOTES

1. This compilation has been prepared exclusively to assist those interested in solving crossword puzzles. Others may also find the information of value.
2. Where a country is indicated against a name, this will normally be the country of birth. In some cases, this entry will represent the country of citizenship or the country where the individual spent the most time or the country in which the individual gained recognition.
3. It is impossible to provide an exhaustive list of names. This compilation is intended to provide the most important names in each category. For instance, all the Academy Award nominations are included within the Performing Arts category. It also is intended to include names which are commonly found in crossword puzzles.
4. Gods and goddesses number in the hundreds of thousand. There are many variations in spelling. Those included within this publication are more common or their names are commonly used in crossword puzzle clues.
5. Parenthetical information indicates nick names, commonly used names or variations on the original name.
6. The last name may be the assumed name. In cases such as this where there is also a parenthetical last name; the name in parenthesis will be the real name.

CATEGORICAL INCLUSIONS

Architecture	Architects AIA Gold Medal Winners Jefferson Gold Medal Winners Pritzker Laureates
Arts	Anthropologists Archaeologists Biographers Clergymen/Theologians Economists (Nobel Laureates) Educators Historians Lexicographers Linguists Philosophers Psychologists Socialists
Aviation	Astronauts Inventors Pilots
Business	Designers

Business (cont.)	-	Entrepreneurs
		Financiers
		Industrialists
		Labor Leaders
		Publishers
		Retailers
Creative Works	-	Authors (Pulitzers)
		Cartoonists
		Composers
		Dramatists (Pulitzers)
		Humorists
		Journalists (Pulitzers)
		Literature (Nobel Laureates)
		Novelists (Pulitzers)
		Playwrights
		Poets (Pulitzers)
		Writers
Exploration	-	Explorers
		Frontiersmen
Games	-	Bridge Experts
		Chess Experts
Law & Order	-	Justices
		Lawmen
		Mafia
		Outlaws
		Serial Killers
Movie Production	-	Directors (Academy Award Nominees)
Performing Arts	-	Actors (Academy Award Nominees)
		Actresses (Academy Award Nominees)

Performing Arts (cont.)	-	Band Leaders
		Comedians
		Conductors
		Dancers
		Musicians
		Singers
		Show Hosts
		Super Models
Politics	-	Activists
		Chancellors
		Congressmen
		First Ladies
		Kings/Queens
		Politicians
		Premiers
		Presidents
		Prime Ministers
		Secretaries of State
		Senators
		Statespersons
		Vice-Presidents
Science	-	Astronomers
		Biologists
		Chemists (Nobel Laureates)
		Engineers
		Inventors
		Mathematicians
		Medical Professionals (Nobel Laureates)
		Physicists (Nobel Laureates)
		Psychiatrists
Sports	-	Baseball Players
		Basketball Players
		Boxers

Sports (cont.)	Football Players
	Golfers
	Hall of Fame Inductees
	Hockey Players
	Olympians
	Race Car Drivers
	Soccer Players
	Tennis Players
War & Peace	Army Officers
	Naval Officers
	Peace Advocates (Nobel Laureates)
	Revolutionists
Works of Art	Artists
	Painters
	Photographers
	Sculptors

NAME
FINDER

LAST NAME	FIRST NAME	CATEGORY	COUNTRY	FAME
Aalto	Alvar	Architecture	Finland	Architect - AIA/Jefferson Gold Medal
Aaron	Henry Louis (Hank)	Sports	USA	Baseball Player - HF
Abbot	Charles Greeley	Science	USA	Astrophysicist
Abbott	Bud	Performing Arts	USA	Comedian
	George Francis	Creative Works	USA	Dramatist - Pulitzer
	Jacob	Creative Works	USA	Author
	John Joseph Caldwell	Politics	Canada	Prime Minister
	Lyman	Creative Works	USA	Author
Abd al-Raziq	Ali	Arts	Egypt	Philosopher
Abdallah	Nia Nicole	Sports	USA	Olympic Taekwondo
Abduh	Muhammad	Arts	Egypt	Philosopher
Abdul	Paula	Performing Arts	USA	Singer/Choreographer
Abdul-Jabbar	Kareem	Sports	USA	Basketball Player - HF
Abdur	Rahman Khan	Politics	Afghanistan	Amir
Abel	Sidney Gerald (Sid)	Sports	Canada	Hockey Player - HF
Abelard	Pierre	Arts	France	Theologian/Philosopher
Abercrombie	James	Business	USA	Oil Industry
	Patrick	Architecture	England	Architect - AIA Gold Medal
Abraham	Fahrid Murray	Performing Arts	USA	Actor - Academy Award
Abramovitz	Max	Architecture	USA	Architect
Abrams	Elliott	Politics	USA	Assistant Secretary of State
Abrams Jr.	Creighton Williams	War & Peace	USA	General - Army
Abrikosov	Alexei A.	Science	USA	Physics - Nobel Laureate
Abul	Kasim	Science	Saudi Arabia	Surgeon
Abzug	Bella Savitsky	Politics	USA	Stateswoman
Acheson	Dean Gooderham	Creative Works	USA	Author - Pulitzer
	Dean Gooderham	Politics	USA	Secretary of State
Acton	John Edward Dalberg	Arts	England	Philosopher/Historian
	Loren Wilbur	Aviation	USA	Astronaut
Acuff	Roy	Performing Arts	USA	Singer - Country Music - HF
Adair	Deborah	Performing Arts	USA	Actress
Adams	Abigail	Politics	USA	First Lady
	Alice Boyd	Creative Works	USA	Novelist/Short Story Writer
	Ansel	Works of Art	USA	Photography
	Brooke	Performing Arts	USA	Actress
	Bryan	Performing Arts	Canada	Singer
	Charles Benjamin (Babe)	Sports	USA	Baseball Player
	Charles Francis	Politics	USA	Statesman

SOLVER SERIES: NAME FINDER

LAST NAME	FIRST NAME	CATEGORY	COUNTRY	FAME
Adams	Don	Performing Arts	USA	Actor
	Douglas Noël	Creative Works	England	Author
	Edie	Performing Arts	USA	Actress
	George Plimpton	Arts	USA	Philosopher
	Henry Brooks	Creative Works	USA	Author - Pulitzer
	James Truslow	Creative Works	USA	Author - Pulitzer
	John	Politics	USA	President
	John James (Jack)	Sports	Canada	Hockey Player - HF
	John Quincy	Politics	USA	President
	Louise Catherine	Politics	USA	First Lady
	Mason	Performing Arts	USA	Actor
	Maude	Performing Arts	Sweden	Actress
	Nick	Performing Arts	USA	Actor - Acad Award Nom
	Samuel	Politics	USA	Statesman
	Sarah Flower	Creative Works	England	Author/Poet
Adamson	James Craig	Aviation	USA	Astronaut
Addams	Charles	Creative Works	USA	Cartoonist - Addams Family
	Jane	Creative Works	USA	Social Worker
	Jane	War & Peace	USA	Peace - Nobel Laureate
Adderley	Julian (Cannonball)	Performing Arts	USA	Jazz Saxophonist - Big Band/Jazz - HF
	Nat	Performing Arts	USA	Jazz Trumpeter
Adderly	Herbert A. (Herb)	Sports	USA	Football Player - HF
Addison	Joseph	Creative Works	England	Essayist/Poet
	Thomas	Science	England	Physician
Ade	George	Creative Works	USA	Humorist
Adee	George Townsend	Sports	USA	Tennis Player - HF
Adenauer	Konrad	Politics	Germany	Chancellor
Adjani	Isabelle	Performing Arts	France	Actress - Acad Award Nom
Adler	Alfred	Science	Austria	Psychiatrist
	Cyrus	Creative Works	USA	Writer
	Felix	Arts	USA	Philosopher/Educator
	Jerry	Performing Arts	USA	Harmonica Musician - Classical Soloist
	Larry	Performing Arts	USA	Harmonica Musician
	Mortimer Jerome	Arts	USA	Philosopher
Adolphus	Gustavus	War & Peace	Sweden	Military Leader - King
Adoree	Renee	Performing Arts	France	Actress
Adorno	Theodor Ludwig Wiesengrund	Arts	Germany	Philosopher/Sociologist
Adrian	Edgar Douglas	Science	USA	Medicine - Nobel Laureate
Ady	Endre	Creative Works	Hungary	Poet
Agar	Herbert Sebastian	Creative Works	England	Author - Pulitzer
	John	Performing Arts	USA	Actor
Agassi	André	Sports	USA	Tennis Player
Agee	James	Creative Works	USA	Novelist/Poet - Pulitzer
Ager	Milton	Creative Works	USA	Composer/Pianist/Songwriter
Aghdashloo	Shohreh	Performing Arts	Iran	Actress - Acad Award Nom
Agnew	Spiro T.	Politics	USA	Vice-President
Agnon	Shmuel Yosef	Creative Works	Israel	Literature - Nobel Laureate
Agre	Peter	Science	USA	Chemistry - Nobel Laureate
Agricola	Georgius	Science	Germany	Scholar
Agutter	Jenny	Performing Arts	England	Actress
Ahern	Bertie	Politics	Ireland	Prime Minster
Aherne	Brian	Performing Arts	England	Actor - Acad Award Nom
Aiello	Danny	Performing Arts	USA	Actor - Acad Award Nom
Aiken	Conrad Potter	Creative Works	USA	Poet - Pulitzer
Aikman	Troy	Sports	USA	Football Player
Ailey	Alvin	Performing Arts	USA	Actor
Ailing	Liu	Sports	China	Soccer Player
Aimee	Anouk	Performing Arts	France	Actress - Acad Award Nom
Ain	Gregory	Architecture	USA	Architect
Ainge	Danny	Sports	USA	Basketball Player
Aitken	William Maxwell	Business	England	Publishing
Akerlof	George A.	Arts	USA	Economics - Nobel Laureate
Akermann	Rudolf	Business	England	Publishing

LAST NAME	FIRST NAME	CATEGORY	COUNTRY	FAME
Akers	Michelle	Sports	USA	Soccer Player - HF
	Thomas Dale	Aviation	USA	Astronaut
Akins	Zoe	Creative Works	USA	Dramatist - Pulitzer
Akiyoshi	Toshiko	Performing Arts	Manchuria	Jazz Pianist - Big Band/Jazz - HF
al Assad	Hafez	Politics	Syria	President
Albanese	Licia	Performing Arts	USA	Singer - Opera
Albee	Edward	Creative Works	USA	Dramatist - Pulitzer
Albéniz	Isaac	Creative Works	Spain	Composer/Pianist
Alberghetti	Anna Maria	Performing Arts	Italy	Actress
Albert	Al	Creative Works	USA	Journalist - Television
	Eddie	Performing Arts	USA	Actor - Acad Award Nom
	Marv Philip	Creative Works	USA	Journalist - Television
	Steve	Creative Works	USA	Journalist - Television
Alberti	Leon Battista	Architecture	Italy	Architect/Painter/Sculptor
Albertson	Jack	Performing Arts	USA	Actor - Academy Award
Albertus	Magnus	Arts	Germany	Philosopher
Albini	Franco	Architecture	Italy	Architect/Furniture Designer
Albuquerque	Alphonso de	Exploration	Portugal	Explorer - Spice Islands
Alcott	Amos Bronson	Arts	USA	Philosopher
	Amy	Sports	USA	Golfer - HF
	Louisa May	Creative Works	USA	Novelist
Alda	Alan	Performing Arts	USA	Actor - Acad Award Nom
	Frances	Performing Arts	USA	Singer - Opera
	Robert	Performing Arts	USA	Actor
Alder	Kurt	Science	Germany	Chemistry - Nobel Laureate
Aldiss	Brian Wilson	Creative Works	England	Author - SciFi
Aldrich	Thomas Bailey	Creative Works	USA	Poet/Novelist
Aldrin	Edwin Eugene (Buzz)	Aviation	USA	Astronaut
Aleandro	Norma	Performing Arts	Argentina	Actress - Acad Award Nom
Aleixandre	Vincente	Creative Works	Spain	Literature - Nobel Laureate
Alekhine	Alexander	Games	Russia	Chess Player
Alekseyvich	Pyotr (Peter the Great)	Politics	Russia	Emperor
Alemán	Mateo	Creative Works	Spain	Novelist
	Miguel	Politics	Mexico	President
Alen	James Henry Van (Tie-Breaker)	Sports	USA	Tennis Player - HF
Alexander	Christopher	Architecture	Austria	Architect/Writer/Teacher
	Frederick Beasley	Sports	USA	Tennis Player - HF
	Grover Cleveland (Pete)	Sports	USA	Baseball Player - HF
	Harold Rupert	Politics	England	Statesman
	Jane	Performing Arts	USA	Actress - Acad Award Nom
	Jason	Performing Arts	USA	Actor
	Shana	Creative Works	USA	Journalist - Magazine
Alexis	Kim	Performing Arts	USA	Super Model
Alferov	Zhores I.	Science	Russia	Physics - Nobel Laureate
Alfieri	Vittorio	Creative Works	Italy	Dramatist/Poet
Alfvén	Hannes Olof Gösta	Science	Sweden	Physics - Nobel Laureate
Alger	Horatio	Creative Works	USA	Writer
Ali	Muhammad (Casius Clay)	Sports	USA	Boxer - HF
	Pasha	Politics	Turkey	Governor
Alicia	Ana	Performing Arts	Mexico	Actress
Alighieri	Dante	Creative Works	Italy	Poet
Allais	Maurice	Arts	France	Economics - Nobel Laureate
Allen	Andrew Michael	Aviation	USA	Astronaut
	Arlo	Performing Arts	USA	Pianist/Trombonist
	Debbie	Performing Arts	USA	Actress
	Ethan	War & Peace	USA	Revolutionist
	Fred	Performing Arts	USA	Actor/Comedian
	George Herbert	Sports	USA	Football Player - HF
	Gracie	Performing Arts	USA	Actress/Comedian
	Henry (Red)	Performing Arts	USA	Jazz Trumpeter - Big Band/Jazz - HF
	James A. Van	Science	USA	Physicist
	Joan	Performing Arts	USA	Actress - Acad Award Nom
	Joseph Percival	Aviation	USA	Astronaut

SOLVER SERIES: NAME FINDER

LAST NAME	FIRST NAME	CATEGORY	COUNTRY	FAME
Allen	Karen	Performing Arts	USA	Actress
	Marcus LeMarr	Sports	USA	Football Player - HF
	Mel	Creative Works	USA	Journalist - Television
	Nancy	Performing Arts	USA	Actress
	Steve	Performing Arts	USA	Actor/Comedian
	Woody	Movie Production	USA	Director - Academy Award
	Woody	Performing Arts	USA	Actor - Acad Award Nom
Allenby	Edmund Henry Hynman	War & Peace	England	Commander
Alley	Kirstie	Performing Arts	USA	Actress
Allgood	Sara	Performing Arts	Ireland	Actress - Acad Award Nom
Allinson	Thomas	Business	England	Entrepreneur
Allison	Bobby	Sports	USA	Race Car Driver - HF
	Davey	Sports	USA	Race Car Driver - HF
	Laverne	Performing Arts	USA	Rock & Roll - HF - The Dells
Allison Jr.	Wilmer Lawson	Sports	USA	Tennis Player - HF
Allman	Duane	Performing Arts	USA	Singer/Guitarist
Allmann	Gregg	Performing Arts	USA	Rock & Roll - HF - Allmann Brothers Band
	Howard (Duane)	Performing Arts	USA	Rock & Roll - HF - Allmann Brothers Band
Allport	Gordon Willard	Arts	USA	Psychologist
Allyson	June	Performing Arts	USA	Actress
Alma-Tadema	Lawrence	Works of Art	England	Painter
Almodovar	Pedro	Movie Production	Spain	Director - Acad Award Nom
Alomar	Roberto	Sports	USA	Baseball Player
	Sandy	Sports	USA	Baseball Player
Alonso	Manolo (Manuel)	Sports	Spain	Tennis Player - HF
	Maria Conchita	Performing Arts	Cuba	Actress
Alou	Felipe	Sports	USA	Baseball Player
	Jesus	Sports	USA	Baseball Player
	Matty	Sports	USA	Baseball Player
Alpert	Herb	Performing Arts	USA	Band Leader/Trumpeter
Al-Saud	Salman Abdel-Aziz	Aviation	Saudi Arabia	Astronaut
Alston	Walter Emmonds	Sports	USA	Baseball Manager - HF
	William Payne	Arts	USA	Philosopher
Alt	Carol	Performing Arts	USA	Super Model
Altgeld	John Peter	Politics	USA	Governor
Alther	Lisa	Creative Works	USA	Author
Althusser	Louis	Arts	Algeria	Philosopher
Altman	Robert	Movie Production	USA	Director - Acad Award Nom
	Sidney	Science	Canada	Chemistry - Nobel Laureate
Alva	Luigi Ernesto	Performing Arts	Peru	Singer - Opera
Alvarado	Pedro de	War & Peace	Spain	General
	Trini	Performing Arts	USA	Actress
Alvarez	Luis Walter	Science	USA	Physics - Nobel Laureate
Alvarez Quintero	Joaquin	Creative Works	Spain	Playwright
	Serafin	Creative Works	Spain	Playwright
Alworth	Lance Dwight	Sports	USA	Football Player - HF
Amado	Jorge	Creative Works	Brazil	Author
Amara	Lucine	Performing Arts	USA	Singer - Opera
Amati	Niccolo	Arts	Italy	Violin Maker
Amato	Joe	Sports	USA	Race Car Driver - HF
Ambasz	Emilio	Architecture	USA	Architect
Ambler	Eric	Creative Works	England	Author
Ameche	Don	Performing Arts	USA	Actor - Academy Award
Ameling	Elly	Performing Arts	Netherlands	Singer - Opera
Ames	Ed	Performing Arts	USA	Singer/Actor
	Leon	Performing Arts	USA	Actor
Amherst	Jeffrey	War & Peace	England	General
Amiel	Henri Frédéric	Creative Works	Switzerland	Writer
Amin	Idi	Politics	Uganda	President
Amis	Kingsley	Creative Works	England	Author
	Martin	Creative Works	England	Novelist
Amory	Cleveland	Creative Works	USA	Author
Amos	John	Performing Arts	USA	Actor

LAST NAME	FIRST NAME	CATEGORY	COUNTRY	FAME
Amos	Tori	Performing Arts	USA	Singer/Song Writer
Ampere	André Marie	Science	France	Physicist
Amsterdam	Morey	Performing Arts	USA	Comedian
Amunsden	Roald	Exploration	Norway	Explorer - Polar
Anaïs	Nin	Creative Works	France	Novelist/Short Story Writer
Anand	Viswanathan	Games	India	Chess Player
Anastasia	Albert	Law & Order	Italy	Mafia
Anden	Mini (Susanna)	Performing Arts	Sweden	Super Model
Anders	William Alison	Aviation	USA	Astronaut
Andersen	Hans Christian	Creative Works	Denmark	Writer/Poet
Anderson	Bill	Performing Arts	USA	Singer - Country Music - HF
	Carl David	Science	USA	Physics - Nobel Laureate
	George Lee (Sparky)	Sports	USA	Baseball Manager - HF
	Harry	Performing Arts	USA	Actor
	Ian	Performing Arts	Scotland	Flutist
	Jack	Creative Works	USA	Journalist - Newspaper - Pulitzer
	John	Arts	Scotland	Philosopher
	Jon	Performing Arts	England	Singer
	Judith	Performing Arts	Australia	Actress - Acad Award Nom
	Leroy	Creative Works	USA	Composer
	Lindsay	Movie Production	India	Director
	Loni	Performing Arts	USA	Actress
	Lynn	Performing Arts	USA	Actress
	Malcolm (Mal)	Sports	USA	Tennis Player - HF
	Marian	Performing Arts	USA	Singer
	Maxwell	Creative Works	USA	Dramatist - Pulitzer
	Michael	Movie Production	England	Director - Acad Award Nom
	Michael Phillip	Aviation	USA	Astronaut
	Ottis	Sports	USA	Football Player
	Philip Warren	Science	USA	Physics - Nobel Laureate
	Richard Dean	Performing Arts	USA	Actor
	Sherwood	Creative Works	USA	Novelist
	Willie	Sports	Scotland	Golfer - HF
Andersson	Bibi	Performing Arts	Sweden	Actress
Ando	Tadao	Architecture	Japan	Architect - Pritzker/ AIA Gold
Andrássy	Gyula	Politics	Hungary	Prime Minister
Andre	John	War & Peace	England	Major
Andress	Ursula	Performing Arts	Switzerland	Actress
Andretti	Mario	Sports	Italy	Race Car Driver - HF
Andrewes	Lancelot	Arts	England	Theologian
Andrews	Anthony	Performing Arts	England	Actor
	Charles McLean	Creative Works	USA	Author - Pulitzer
	Dana	Performing Arts	USA	Actor
	Julie	Performing Arts	England	Actress - Academy Award
	LaVerne	Performing Arts	USA	Singer
	Maxene	Performing Arts	USA	Singer
	Patti	Performing Arts	USA	Singer
	Roy Chapman	Exploration	USA	Explorer - Mongolia
	Tige	Performing Arts	USA	Actor
Andreyev	Leonid Nikolayevich	Creative Works	Russia	Playwright/Novelist
Andric	Ivo	Creative Works	Yugoslavia	Literature - Nobel Laureate
Anfinsen	Christian B.	Science	USA	Chemistry - Nobel Laureate
Angelico	Fra	Works of Art	Italy	Painter
Angell	James Rowland	Arts	USA	Psychologist
	Norman	Creative Works	England	Economist/Writer
	Norman	War & Peace	England	Peace - Nobel Laureate
Angelou	Maya	Creative Works	USA	Poet/Historian
Angott	Sammy (The Clutch)	Sports	USA	Boxer - HF
Angström	Anders Jöns	Science	Sweden	Physicist
Anka	Paul	Performing Arts	Canada	Singer/Composer - Canadian Music - HF
Annan	Kofi Atta	War & Peace	Ghana	Peace - Nobel Laureate
Annenberg	Walter Hubert	Business	USA	Media Magnate
Annis	Robert Joseph	Sports	USA	Soccer Player - HF

SOLVER SERIES: NAME FINDER

LAST NAME	FIRST NAME	CATEGORY	COUNTRY	FAME
Anouilh	Jean	Creative Works	France	Playwright
Ansara	Michael	Performing Arts	Syria	Actor
Anson	Adrian Constantine (Cap)	Sports	USA	Baseball Player - HF
Anspach	Susan	Performing Arts	USA	Actress
Ant	Adam	Performing Arts	England	Singer
Anthony	Susan B.	Politics	USA	Women's Rights Proponent
Anton	Susan	Performing Arts	USA	Actress
Antonelli	Alessandro	Architecture	Italy	Architect
Antonioni	Michaelangelo	Movie Production	Italy	Director - Acad Award Nom
Anza	Juan Bautista de	Exploration	Mexico	Explorer - California
Aoki	Isao	Sports	Japan	Golfer - HF
Aparicio	Luis Ernesto	Sports	Venezuela	Baseball Player - HF
Applebaum	Anne	Creative Works	USA	Author - Pulitzer
Applegate	Christina	Performing Arts	USA	Actress
Appleton	Edward Victor	Science	England	Physics - Nobel Laureate
Appling	Lucius Benjamin (Luke)	Sports	USA	Baseball Player - HF
Appollinaire	Guillaume	Creative Works	France	Poet/Essayist
Apps	Charles Joseph Sylvanus (Syl)	Sports	Canada	Hockey Player - HF
Apt III	Jerome Jay	Aviation	USA	Astronaut
Aquinas	Thomas	Arts	Italy	Philosopher
Arafat	Yasir	Politics	Palestine	President
	Yasir	War & Peace	Palestine	Peace - Nobel Laureate
Arber	Werner	Science	Switzerland	Medicine - Nobel Laureate
Arbuckle	Fatty	Performing Arts	USA	Comedian
Arbus	Diane	Works of Art	USA	Photographer
Arbuthnot	John	Creative Works	Scotland	Writer/Physician
Archer	Anne	Performing Arts	USA	Actress - Acad Award Nom
	George	Sports	USA	Golfer
	William	Creative Works	Scotland	Playwright
Archibald	Nathaniel (Nate) (Tiny)	Sports	USA	Basketball Player - HF
Archipenko	Alexander	Works of Art	USA	Sculptor
Arden	Elizabeth	Business	USA	Designing
	Eve	Performing Arts	USA	Actress - Acad Award Nom
Arendt	Hannah	Politics	Germany	Philosopher/Political Theorist
Arens	Moshe	Politics	Israel	Foreign Minister
Aretino	Pietro	Creative Works	Italy	Writer
Ariosto	Lodovico	Creative Works	Italy	Poet/Author
Arizin	Paul J.	Sports	USA	Basketball Player - HF
Ark	Joan Van	Performing Arts	USA	Actress
Arkin	Adam	Performing Arts	USA	Actor
	Alan	Performing Arts	USA	Actor - Acad Award Nom
Arkwright	Richard	Business	England	Textile Industry
	Richard	Science	England	Inventor
Arledge	Roone	Business	USA	Television
Arlen	Harold	Creative Works	USA	Composer
Arliss	George	Performing Arts	England	Actor - Academy Award
Armani	Georgio	Business	Italy	Fashion Designer
Arminius	Jacobus	Arts	Netherlands	Theologian
Armour	Tommy	Sports	Scotland	Golfer - HF
Armstrong	Bess	Performing Arts	USA	Actress
	George Edward (Chief)	Sports	Canada	Hockey Player - HF
	Louis (Satchmo)	Performing Arts	USA	Jazz Trumpeter - Big Band/Jazz -HF
	Neil Alden	Aviation	USA	Astronaut
	Satchmo (Louis Daniel)	Performing Arts	USA	Singer - Rock & Roll - HF
Armstrong (Hardin)	Lillian	Performing Arts	USA	Jazz Pianist/Composer - Big Band/Jazz - HF
Arnaz	Desi	Performing Arts	Cuba	Actor/Musician
	Lucie	Performing Arts	USA	Actress
Arne	Thomas Augustine	Creative Works	England	Composer/Violinist
Arness	James	Performing Arts	USA	Actor
Arno	Peter	Creative Works	USA	Cartoonist - New Yorker
Arnold	Benedict	War & Peace	USA	Revolutionist
	Eddy (Richard Edward)	Performing Arts	USA	Singer - Country Music - HF
	Edwin	Creative Works	England	Poet/Journalist

LAST NAME	FIRST NAME	CATEGORY	COUNTRY	FAME
Arnold	James (Jimmy)	Performing Arts	Canada	Canadian Music - HF - The Four Lads
	Matthew	Creative Works	England	Poet/Essayist
	Roseanne	Performing Arts	USA	Actress/Comedian
	Thomas	Arts	England	Educator
	Tom	Performing Arts	USA	Actor
Arnoldson	Klas Pontus	War & Peace	Sweden	Peace - Nobel Laureate
Arosio	Ana Paula	Performing Arts	Brazil	Super Model
Arp	Jean (Hans)	Works of Art	France	Painter/Sculptor
Arquette	Cliff	Performing Arts	USA	Actor/Comedian
	Rosanna	Performing Arts	USA	Actress
Arrau	Claudio	Performing Arts	Chile	Pianist
Arrhenius	Svante August	Science	Sweden	Chemistry - Nobel Laureate
Arrol	William	Business	England	Railway Magnate
Arrow	Kenneth J.	Arts	USA	Economics - Nobel Laureate
Arroyo	Martina	Performing Arts	USA	Singer - Opera
Artevelde	Jacob Van	Politics	USA	Statesman
	Phillip Van	Politics	USA	Statesman
Arthur	Beatrice	Performing Arts	USA	Actress/Comedian
	Chester Alan	Politics	USA	President
	Ellen Lewis	Politics	USA	First Lady
	Jean	Performing Arts	USA	Actress - Acad Award Nom
Artigas	João Batista Villanova	Architecture	Brazil	Architect
Arturi	Mike	Performing Arts	USA	Rock & Roll - HF - Lovin' Spoonful
Asbury	Francis	Arts	USA	Bishop
Ascari	Alberto	Sports	Italy	Race Car Driver - HF
Asch	Sholem	Creative Works	USA	Playwright/Novelist
Ascham	Roger	Creative Works	England	Writer
Ashbery	John	Creative Works	USA	Poet - Pulitzer
Ashburn	Don Richard (Richie)	Sports	USA	Baseball Player - HF
Ashby	Hal	Movie Production	USA	Director - Acad Award Nom
Ashcroft	Peggy	Performing Arts	England	Actress - Academy Award
Ashe Jr.	Arthur Robert	Sports	USA	Tennis Player - HF
Asher	Peter	Performing Arts	England	Singer
Ashford	Evelyn	Sports	USA	Olympic Runner
	Rosalind	Performing Arts	USA	Rock & Roll - HF - Martha & The Vandellas
Ashley	Elizabeth	Performing Arts	USA	Actress
	Laura	Business	England	Designing
Ashton	Thomas	Business	England	Textile Industry
Asimov	Isaac	Creative Works	Russia	Author - SciFi
Asnago	Mario	Architecture	Italy	Architect
Asner	Ed	Performing Arts	USA	Actor
Asper	Israel Harold (Izzy)	Business	Canada	Communications
Aspin	Leslie (Les)	Politics	USA	Secretary of Defense
Asplund	Erik Gunnar	Architecture	Sweden	Architect
Asquith	Herbert Henry	Politics	England	Prime Minister
Assante	Armand	Performing Arts	USA	Actor
Asser	Tobias Michael Carl	War & Peace	Netherlands	Peace - Nobel Laureate
Assuras	Thalia	Creative Works	Canada	Journalist - Television
Astaire	Adele	Performing Arts	USA	Dancer
	Fred	Performing Arts	USA	Actor - Acad Award Nom
Astin	John	Performing Arts	USA	Actor
	Sean	Performing Arts	USA	Actor
Aston	Francis William	Science	England	Chemistry - Nobel Laureate
Astor	Brooke Russell	Creative Works	USA	Writer/Philanthropist
	Gertrude	Performing Arts	USA	Actress
	John Jacob	Business	USA	Financier
	Mary	Performing Arts	USA	Actress - Academy Award
Asturias	Miguel Angel	Creative Works	Guatemala	Literature - Nobel Laureate
Ates	Roscoe	Performing Arts	USA	Actor
Atherton	William	Performing Arts	USA	Actor
Atkins	Chester Burton (Chet)	Performing Arts	USA	Singer/Guitarist - Country Music - HF
	Chester Burton (Chet)	Performing Arts	USA	Singer/Guitarist - Rock & Roll - HF
	Douglas Leon (Doug)	Sports	USA	Football Player - HF

SOLVER SERIES: NAME FINDER

LAST NAME	FIRST NAME	CATEGORY	COUNTRY	FAME
Atkinson	Juliette Paxton	Sports	USA	Tennis Player - HF
	Justin Brooks	Creative Works	USA	Journalist
	Rick	Creative Works	USA	Author - Pulitzer
Attenborough	David Frederick	Arts	England	Anthropologist
	Richard	Movie Production	England	Director - Academy Award
Attlee	Clement Richard	Politics	England	Prime Minster
Atwill	Lionel	Performing Arts	England	Actor
Atwood	Margaret	Creative Works	Canada	Author
Auber	Daniel Francois Esprit	Creative Works	France	Composer/Opera
Auberjonois	René	Performing Arts	USA	Actor
Auburn	David	Creative Works	USA	Dramatist - Pulitzer
Auchincloss	Louis	Creative Works	USA	Novelist
Auden	Wystan Hugh	Creative Works	England	Poet - Pulitzer
Audubon	John James	Science	USA	Ornithologist
	John James	Works of Art	USA	Painter
Auel	Jean	Creative Works	USA	Author
Auer	Leopold	Performing Arts	Hungary	Violinist
	Mischa	Performing Arts	Russia	Actor - Acad Award Nom
Auerbach	Red	Sports	USA	Basketball Player
Auermann	Nadja	Performing Arts	Germany	Super Model
Augier	Guillaume Victor Emile	Creative Works	France	Playwright
Auld	Andrew (Andy)	Sports	Scotland	Soccer Player - HF
Aulenti	Gae	Architecture	Italy	Architect
Aulin	Ewa	Performing Arts	Sweden	Actress
Aumann	Robert J.	Arts	Germany	Economics - Nobel Laureate
Aumont	Jean-Pierre	Performing Arts	France	Actor
Aurobindo	Sri	Arts	India	Philosopher
Austen	Jane	Creative Works	England	Novelist
Austin	Alfred	Creative Works	England	Poet
	Henry W. (Bunny)	Sports	England	Tennis Player - HF
	John	Arts	England	Legal Philosopher
	Patti	Performing Arts	USA	Singer
	Stephen Fuller	Exploration	USA	Frontiersman - America
	Tracy Ann	Sports	USA	Tennis Player - HF
Autry	Gene (Orvon)	Performing Arts	USA	Actor/Singer - Country Music - HF
Avalon	Frankie	Performing Arts	USA	Singer/Actor
Averill	Howard Earl	Sports	USA	Baseball Player - HF
Averroes	Ibn-Rusjd	Arts	Spain	Philosopher
Avery	Frederick Bean (Tex)	Creative Works	USA	Cartoonist - Animated Movies
	Margaret	Performing Arts	USA	Actress - Acad Award Nom
Avildsen	John G.	Movie Production	USA	Director - Academy Award
Aviles	Pedro Menendez de	Exploration	Spain	Explorer - Florida
Avogadro	Amedeo	Science	Italy	Chemist/Physicist
Avory	Mick	Performing Arts	England	Rock & Roll - HF - The Kinks
Axel	Richard	Science	USA	Medicine - Nobel Laureate
Axelrod	Julius	Science	USA	Medicine - Nobel Laureate
Axton	Hoyt	Performing Arts	USA	Singer/Composer
Ayer	Alfred Jules	Arts	England	Philosopher
Aykroyd	Dan	Performing Arts	Canada	Actor - Acad Award Nom
Ayllón	Lucas Vázquez de	Exploration	Spain	Explorer - North Carolina
Aymonino	Carlo	Architecture	Italy	Architect
Ayres	Lew	Performing Arts	USA	Actor - Acad Award Nom
Aznavour	Charles	Performing Arts	France	Singer
Babbitt	Irving	Arts	USA	Educator/Critic
Babel	Isaac	Creative Works	Russia	Writer
Babenco	Hector	Movie Production	Argentina	Director - Acad Award Nom
Babilonia	Tai	Sports	USA	Olympic Skater
Bacall	Lauren	Performing Arts	USA	Actress - Acad Award Nom
Bach	Johann Christian	Creative Works	Germany	Composer/Organist
	Johann Sebastian	Creative Works	Germany	Composer/Organist
	Karl Phillipp Emanuel	Creative Works	Germany	Composer
Bacharach	Burt	Creative Works	USA	Composer/Pianist
Bachelard	Gaston	Arts	France	Philosopher

LAST NAME	FIRST NAME	CATEGORY	COUNTRY	FAME
Bachmeier	Adolph	Sports	Romania	Soccer Player - HF
Backus	Jim	Performing Arts	USA	Actor
Bacon	Francis	Politics	England	Essayist/Statesman/Philosopher
	Henry	Architecture	USA	Architect - AIA Gold Medal
	Henry	Works of Art	USA	Painter
	Kevin	Performing Arts	USA	Actor
	Leonard	Creative Works	USA	Poet - Pulitzer
	Nathaniel	Exploration	USA	Colonist - Virginia
	Roger	Arts	England	Philosopher
Baddeley	Hermione	Performing Arts	England	Actress - Acad Award Nom
Baden-Powell	Robert Stephenson Smyth	War & Peace	England	General
Badgro	Morris Hiram (Red)	Sports	USA	Football Player - HF
Badham	Mary	Performing Arts	USA	Actress - Acad Award Nom
Baer	Max	Sports	USA	Boxer - HF
Baeyer	Johann Friedrich Adolf von	Science	Germany	Chemistry - Nobel Laureate
Baez	Joan	Performing Arts	USA	Singer/Composer
Baffin	William	Exploration	England	Explorer - Arctic
Bagehot	Walter	Arts	England	Economist/Journalist
Baggio	Roberto	Sports	Brazil	Soccer Player
Bagian	James Philip	Aviation	USA	Astronaut
Bagnold	Enid	Creative Works	England	Novelist
Bahr	Matt	Sports	USA	Football Player
	Walter Alfred	Sports	USA	Soccer Player - HF
Bailer	Mildred	Performing Arts	USA	Singer - Big Band/Jazz - HF
	De Ford	Performing Arts	USA	Singer - Country Music - HF
	Irvine Wallace (Ace)	Sports	Canada	Hockey Player - HF
	Nathaniel	Creative Works	England	Lexicographer
	Pearl	Performing Arts	USA	Singer/Composer
Bailyn	Bernard	Creative Works	USA	Author - Pulitzer
Bain	Alexander	Arts	Scotland	Philosopher
	Conrad	Performing Arts	Canada	Actor
	Donald Henderson (Dan)	Sports	Canada	Hockey Player - HF
Baines	Edward	Business	England	Publishing
Bainter	Fay	Performing Arts	USA	Actress - Academy Award
Baio	Scott	Performing Arts	USA	Actor
Baird	Bil	Performing Arts	USA	Puppeteer
	Cora	Performing Arts	USA	Puppeteer
Bajer	Fredrik	War & Peace	Denmark	Peace - Nobel Laureate
Baker	Amery Hare (Hobey)	Sports	USA	Hockey Player - HF
	Anita	Performing Arts	USA	Singer
	Carroll	Performing Arts	USA	Actress - Acad Award Nom
	George	Creative Works	USA	Cartoonist - Sad Sack
	George Pierce	Creative Works	USA	Author
	Ginger	Performing Arts	England	Rock & Roll - HF - Cream
	James A.	Politics	USA	Secretary of State
	Joe Don	Performing Arts	USA	Actor
	John Franklin (Frank)	Sports	USA	Baseball Player - HF
	Josephine	Performing Arts	USA	Actress
	LaVern	Performing Arts	USA	Singer - Rock & Roll - HF
	Leonard	Creative Works	USA	Author - Pulitzer
	Newton Diehl	Politics	USA	Statesman
	Ray Stannard	Creative Works	USA	Author - Pulitzer
	Robby	Performing Arts	Canada	Canadian Music - HF - The Tragically Hip
	Russell	Creative Works	USA	Journalist/Author - Pulitzer
	Wylie (Buddy)	Sports	USA	Race Car Driver - HF
Baker Jr.	Howard Henry	Politics	USA	Senator
	Chet (Chesney Henry)	Performing Arts	USA	Jazz Trumpeter - Big Band/Jazz - HF
Baker Sr.	Elzie Wylie (Buck)	Sports	USA	Race Car Driver - HF
	Lawrence Adams	Sports	USA	Tennis Player - HF
Baker-Finch	Ian	Sports	Australia	Golfer
Bakr	Abu	Politics	Saudi Arabia	Calif
Bakst	Leon Nikolaevich	Works of Art	Russia	Painter
Bakula	Scott	Performing Arts	USA	Actor

SOLVER SERIES: NAME FINDER

LAST NAME	FIRST NAME	CATEGORY	COUNTRY	FAME
Bakunin	Mikhail Aleksandrovich	Politics	Russia	Philosopher/Anarchist
Balanchine	George	Creative Works	USA	Choreographer
Balboa	Marcelo (Iron Man)	Sports	USA	Soccer Player - HF
	Vasco Núñez de	Exploration	Spain	Explorer - Panama
Balche	Emily Greene	War & Peace	USA	Peace - Nobel Laureate
Baldessari	Luciano	Architecture	Italy	Architect
Baldeweg	Juan Navarro	Architecture	Spain	Architect
Baldwin	Alec	Performing Arts	USA	Actor - Acad Award Nom
	James Mark	Arts	USA	Psychologist
	Stanley	Politics	England	Prime Minster
	William	Performing Arts	USA	Actor
Balfe	Michael William	Creative Works	England	Composer/Opera
Balfour	Arthur	Politics	England	Prime Minster
Balin	Ina	Performing Arts	USA	Actress
Balin (Buckwald)	Marty (Martyn)	Performing Arts	USA	Rock & Roll - HF - Jefferson Airplane
Ball	John	Arts	England	Priest
	John	Sports	England	Golfer - HF
	Kenneth (Kenny)	Performing Arts	England	Jazz Trumpeter/Band Leader
Ball (Arnaz)	Lucille	Performing Arts	USA	Comedian/Actress
Ballard	Florence Glenda (Flo)	Performing Arts	USA	Rock & Roll - HF - The Supremes
	James Graham	Creative Works	England	Novelist
	Robert	Exploration	USA	Explorer - Marine/Titanic
	Kaye	Performing Arts	USA	Singer
Ballard (Kendricks)	John Henry (Hank)	Performing Arts	USA	Singer - Rock & Roll - HF
Ballesteros	Seve	Sports	Spain	Golfer - HF
Bally	Carl Franz	Business	Switzerland	Fashion Designer
Balsam	Martin	Performing Arts	USA	Actor - Academy Award
Baltimore	David	Science	USA	Medicine - Nobel Laureate
Balzac	Honoré de	Creative Works	France	Novelist
Ban	Shigeru	Architecture	Japan	Architect - Jefferson Medal
Bancroft	Anne	Performing Arts	USA	Actress - Academy Award
	David James (Dave)	Sports	USA	Baseball Player - HF
	George	Performing Arts	USA	Actor - Acad Award Nom
	George	Politics	USA	Statesman
Bando	Sal	Sports	USA	Baseball Player
Bankhead	Tallulah	Performing Arts	USA	Actress
Banks	Ernest (Ernie)	Sports	USA	Baseball Player - HF
	Gordon	Sports	England	Soccer Player - HF
	Joseph	Science	England	Botanist
	Tony	Creative Works	England	Song Writer/Keyboarder
	Tyra	Performing Arts	USA	Super Model
Bannen	Ian	Performing Arts	Scotland	Actor - Acad Award Nom
Bannister	Roger	Sports	USA	Olympic Runner
Banting	Frederick Grant	Science	Canada	Medicine - Nobel Laureate
Bara	Theda	Performing Arts	USA	Actress
Baradei	Mohammed El	War & Peace	Egypt	Peace - Nobel Laureate
Barak	Ehud	Politics	Israel	Prime Minister
Bárány	Robert	Science	Austria	Medicine - Nobel Laureate
Barbeau	Adrienne	Performing Arts	USA	Actress
Barber	Samuel	Creative Works	USA	Composer
	Walter (Red)	Creative Works	USA	Journalist - Television
	William Charles (Bill)	Sports	Canada	Hockey Player - HF
Barbera	Joe	Creative Works	USA	Cartoonist
Barbusse	Henri	Creative Works	France	Novelist/Journalist
Barca	Hannibal	War & Peace	Carthage	Military Commander
Bardeen	John	Science	USA	Physics - Nobel Laureate
Bardem	Javier	Performing Arts	Spain	Actor - Acad Award Nom
Bardot	Brigitte	Performing Arts	France	Actress
Barenboim	Daniel	Performing Arts	Argentina	Conductor/Pianist
Barge	Eldra De	Performing Arts	USA	Singer
Barger-Wallach	Maud	Sports	USA	Tennis Player - HF
Barker	Clive	Creative Works	England	Author
	Clive	Movie Production	England	Director

LAST NAME	FIRST NAME	CATEGORY	COUNTRY	FAME
Barkin	Ellen	Performing Arts	USA	Actress
Barkla	Charles Glover	Science	England	Physics - Nobel Laureate
Barkley	Alben W.	Politics	USA	Vice-President
	Charles	Sports	USA	Basketball Player
Barksdale	Chuck	Performing Arts	USA	Rock & Roll - HF - The Dells
Barlick	Albert Joseph (Al)	Sports	USA	Baseball Umpire - HF
Barlow	Joel	Creative Works	USA	Poet/Diplomat
	Thomas B.	Sports	USA	Basketball Player - HF
Barnard	George Gray	Works of Art	USA	Sculptor
	Robert	Creative Works	England	Author
Barnes	Clive	Creative Works	USA	Journalist - Newspaper
	Edward Larrabee	Architecture	USA	Architect - Jefferson Medal
	Henry Elmer	Arts	USA	Historian/Sociologist
	Jim (Long Jim)	Sports	England	Golfer - HF
	Magaret Ayer	Creative Works	USA	Novelist - Pulitzer
	Prentiss	Performing Arts	USA	Rock & Roll - HF - Moonglows
Barnet	Charles Daly	Performing Arts	USA	Band Leader - Big Band/Jazz - HF
Barneveldt	Jan van Olden	Politics	Netherlands	Statesman/Patriot
Barney	Lemuel Jackson (Lem)	Sports	USA	Football Player - HF
Barnum	Phineas Taylor	Arts	USA	Showman
Baroja	Pio	Creative Works	Spain	Novelist
Barr	George	Sports	Scotland	Soccer Player - HF
Barragan	Luis	Architecture	Mexico	Architect - Pritzker Laureate
Barrault	Marie-Christine	Performing Arts	France	Actress - Acad Award Nom
Barrett	Pat	Performing Arts	Canada	Canadian Music - HF - The Crew Cuts
	Roger Keith (Syd)	Performing Arts	England	Rock & Roll - HF - Pink Floyd
Barrie	Barbara	Performing Arts	USA	Actress - Acad Award Nom
	James Matthew	Creative Works	England	Playwright/Novelist
Barrow	Clyde Champion	Law & Order	USA	Outlaw
	Edward Grant	Sports	USA	Baseball Executive - HF
Barry	Charles	Architecture	England	Architect/Designer
	Dave	Creative Works	USA	Journalist - Newspaper
	Gene	Performing Arts	USA	Actor
	Martin A. (Marty)	Sports	Canada	Hockey Player - HF
	Richard F. (Rick)	Sports	USA	Basketball Player - HF
Barry (Borisoff)	Leonard (Len)	Performing Arts	USA	Singer
Barrymore	Drew	Performing Arts	USA	Actress
	Ethel	Performing Arts	USA	Actress - Academy Award
	John	Performing Arts	USA	Actor
	Lionel	Movie Production	USA	Director - Acad Award Nom
	Lionel	Performing Arts	USA	Actor - Academy Award
	Maurice	Performing Arts	USA	Actor
Barsalona	Frank	Performing Arts	USA	Promoter - Rock & Roll - HF
Barstow	Stanley (Stan)	Creative Works	England	Author
Barth	Carl	Arts	Switzerland	Theologian
	John Simmons	Creative Works	USA	Novelist/Short Story Writer
Barthelmess	Richard	Performing Arts	USA	Actor - Acad Award Nom
Bartholdi	Frédéric Auguste	Works of Art	France	Sculptor
Bartlett	John	Creative Works	USA	Editor/Publisher
Bartoe	John David Francis	Aviation	USA	Astronaut
Bartók	Bela	Creative Works	Hungary	Composer
Bartolomé	Murillo	Works of Art	Spain	Painter
Barton	Clara	Business	USA	Philanthropist - Red Cross
	Derek H.R.	Science	England	Chemistry - Nobel Laureate
Bartowski	Steve	Sports	USA	Football Player
Barty	Billy	Performing Arts	USA	Actor
Baruch	Bernard Mannes	Business	USA	Financier/Statesman
Baryshnikov	Mikhail	Performing Arts	Latvia	Actor - Acad Award Nom
	Mikhail	Performing Arts	Latvia	Dancer
Basehart	Richard	Performing Arts	USA	Actor
Basekett	James	Performing Arts	USA	Actor - Academy Award
Basie	Count (William)	Performing Arts	USA	Band Leader - Big Band/Jazz - HF
Basile	Ernesto	Architecture	Italy	Architect

SOLVER SERIES: NAME FINDER

LAST NAME	FIRST NAME	CATEGORY	COUNTRY	FAME
Basinger	Kim	Performing Arts	USA	Actress - Academy Award
Baskerville	John	Arts	England	Printer/Designer
Basov	Nicolay Gennadiyevich	Science	Russia	Physics - Nobel Laureate
Bass	Michael	Business	England	Retail Trade
Basserman	Albert	Performing Arts	Germany	Actor - Acad Award Nom
Bassett	Angela	Performing Arts	USA	Actress - Acad Award Nom
	Angela	Performing Arts	USA	Singer
Bassett II	Charles Arthur	Aviation	USA	Astronaut
Bassey	Shirley	Performing Arts	Wales	Singer
Basten	Marco Van	Sports	Netherlands	Soccer Player - HF
Bate	Walter Jackson	Creative Works	USA	Author - Pulitzer
Bateman	Jason	Performing Arts	USA	Actor
	Justine	Performing Arts	USA	Actress
	Robert	Works of Art	Canada	Painter
Bates	Alan	Performing Arts	England	Actor - Acad Award Nom
	Kathy	Performing Arts	USA	Actress - Academy Award
Bathgate	Andrew James (Andy)	Sports	Canada	Hockey Player - HF
Batistutu	Gabriel	Sports	Argentina	Soccer Player
Battles	Clifford Franklin (Cliff)	Sports	USA	Football Player - HF
Battuta	Abu Abdulla Ibn	Exploration	Morocco	Explorer - Africa
Baudelaire	Pierre Charles	Creative Works	France	Poet
Baudin	Nicholas	Exploration	France	Explorer - Tasmania
Baudrillard	Jean	Arts	France	Philosopher/Sociologist
Baudry	Patrick Pierre Roger	Aviation	France	Astronaut
Bauer	Harold	Performing Arts	USA	Pianist
	Robert Theodore (Bobby)	Sports	Canada	Hockey Player - HF
Baugh	Sammy Adrian	Sports	USA	Football Player - HF
Baum	Lyman Frank	Creative Works	USA	Writer
Bausch	John Jacob	Business	USA	Optical Industry
Baxter	Anne	Performing Arts	USA	Actress - Academy Award
	Meridith	Performing Arts	USA	Actress
	Warner	Performing Arts	USA	Actor - Academy Award
Baxter III	James Phinney	Creative Works	USA	Author - Pulitzer
Bayes	Thomas	Science	England	Mathematician/Clergyman
Bayes (Goldberg)	Nora (Dora)	Performing Arts	USA	Actress
Bayh III	Birch Evans (Evan)	Politics	USA	Senator
Bayle	Pierre	Arts	France	Philosopher/Critic
Baylor	Elgin	Sports	USA	Basketball Player - HF
Beadle	George Wells	Science	USA	Medicine - Nobel Laureate
Beals	Jennifer	Performing Arts	USA	Actress
Beamon	Bob	Sports	USA	Olympic Long Jumper
Bean	Alan LaVerne	Aviation	USA	Astronaut
	Orson	Performing Arts	USA	Actor
Beane	Roy	Law & Order	USA	Judge
Beard	Frank	Performing Arts	USA	Rock & Roll - HF - ZZ Top
Beardsley	Aubrey Vincent	Works of Art	England	Painter
Deardsworth	Fred	Sports	England	Soccer Player - HF
Beasley	Allyce	Performing Arts	USA	Actress
Beaton	Cecil	Arts	England	Photographer
Beattie	Ann	Creative Works	USA	Author
Beatty	David	War & Peace	England	Admiral
	Ned	Performing Arts	USA	Actor - Acad Award Nom
	Warren	Performing Arts	USA	Actor - Acad Award Nom
	Warren	Movie Production	USA	Director - Academy Award
Beaumont	Francis	Creative Works	England	Dramatist
	Harry	Movie Production	USA	Director - Acad Award Nom
Beauregard	Pierre Gustave Toutant de	War & Peace	USA	General
Beauvoir	Simone de	Creative Works	France	Novelist/Essayist/Philosopher
Beaverbrook	William Maxwell Aitkin	Creative Works	England	Publisher
Bebel	Ferdinand August	Arts	Germany	Socialist/Writer
Bechet	Sidney	Performing Arts	USA	Jazz Saxaphonist - Big Band/Jazz - HF
Beck	Clarence Charles	Creative Works	USA	Cartoonist - Captain Marvel
	Jeff	Performing Arts	England	Guitarist

LAST NAME	FIRST NAME	CATEGORY	COUNTRY	FAME
Beckenbauer	Franz	Sports	Germany	Soccer Player - HF
Becker	Boris	Sports	Germany	Tennis Player - HF
	Ernest	Creative Works	USA	Author - Pulitzer
	Gary S.	Arts	USA	Economics - Nobel Laureate
	Stephen	Creative Works	USA	Novelist
	Walter Carl	Performing Arts	USA	Rock & Roll - HF - Steely Dan
Beckett	Samuel	Creative Works	Ireland	Literature - Nobel Laureate
Beckham	David	Sports	England	Soccer Player
Beckley	Jacob Peter (Jake)	Sports	USA	Baseball Player - HF
Beckman	John	Sports	USA	Basketball Player - HF
Beckmann	Max	Works of Art	Germany	Painter - Expressionist
Becquerel	Alexandre Edmond	Science	France	Physicist
	Antoine César	Science	France	Physicist
	Antoine Henri	Science	France	Physics - Nobel Laureate
Beddoes	Thomas Lovell	Creative Works	England	Poet/Playwright
Bednarik	Charles Philip (Chuck)	Sports	USA	Football Player - HF
Bednorz	Johannes Georg	Science	Germany	Physics - Nobel Laureate
Beebe	Charles William	Creative Works	USA	Writer/Naturalist
	William	Exploration	USA	Explorer - Deep Sea
Beecham	Thomas	Performing Arts	England	Conductor
Beecher	Henry Ward	Arts	USA	Clergyman
	Lyman	Arts	USA	Theologian/Clergyman
Beerbohm	Max	Creative Works	England	Essayist/Novelist
Beernaert	Auguste Marie François	War & Peace	Belgium	Peace - Nobel Laureate
Beery	Noah	Performing Arts	USA	Actor
	Wallace	Performing Arts	USA	Actor - Academy Award
Beethoven	Ludwig van	Creative Works	Germany	Composer
	Ludwig Van	Creative Works	Austria	Composer
Begin	Menachem	Politics	Israel	Prime Minister
	Menachem	War & Peace	Israel	Peace - Nobel Laureate
Begley	Ed	Performing Arts	USA	Actor - Academy Award
Begley, Jr.	Ed	Performing Arts	USA	Actor
Behaim	Martin	Exploration	Portugal	Explorer - West Africa
Behan	Brendan	Creative Works	Ireland	Playwright/Author
Behennah	Michelle	Performing Arts	Singapore	Super Model
Behr	Karl Howell	Sports	USA	Tennis Player - HF
Behrens	Peter	Architecture	Germany	Architect
Behring	Emil Adolf von	Science	Germany	Medicine - Nobel Laureate
Beiderbecke	Leon (Bix)	Performing Arts	USA	Jazz Cornetist - Big Band/Jazz - HF
Béjart	Maurice	Creative Works	France	Composer
Békésy	Georg von	Science	USA	Medicine - Nobel Laureate
Bel Geddes	Barbara	Performing Arts	USA	Actress - Acad Award Nom
Belafonte	Harry	Performing Arts	USA	Singer
	Shari	Performing Arts	USA	Actress
Belasco	David	Creative Works	USA	Playwright/Actor
Beliveau	Jean Arthur	Sports	Canada	Hockey Player - HF
Bell	Alexander Graham	Business	USA	Telephones
	Alexander Graham	Science	USA	Inventor - Telephone
	De Benneville (Bert)	Sports	USA	Football Commissioner - HF
	Gus	Sports	USA	Baseball Player
	James Thomas (Cool Papa)	Sports	USA	Baseball Player - HF
	Judy	Sports	USA	Golfer - HF
	Lawrence Dale	Business	USA	Aviation - Helecopters
	Ricky	Sports	USA	Football Player
	Robert "Kool"	Performing Arts	USA	Singer/Composer
Bell Jr.	Robert Lee (Bobby)	Sports	USA	Football Player - HF
Bellamy	Edward	Creative Works	USA	Writer/Theorist
	Ralph	Performing Arts	USA	Actor - Acad Award Nom
	Walter (Walt)	Sports	USA	Basketball Player - HF
Belle	Patti La	Performing Arts	USA	Singer
Bellini	Gentile	Works of Art	Italy	Painter
	Giovanni	Works of Art	Italy	Painter
	Jacopo	Works of Art	Italy	Painter

SOLVER SERIES: NAME FINDER

LAST NAME	FIRST NAME	CATEGORY	COUNTRY	FAME
Bellini	Vincenzo	Creative Works	Italy	Composer/Opera
Belloc	Joseph Hillaire Pierre	Creative Works	England	Writer
Bellow	Saul	Creative Works	USA	Literature - Nobel/Pulitzer
Bellows	George Wesley	Works of Art	USA	Painter
Bellson (Balassoni)	Louie (Luigi Paulino)	Performing Arts	USA	Jazz Drummer - Big Band/Jazz - HF
Bellucci	Monica	Performing Arts	Italy	Super Model
Belluschi	Pietro	Architecture	Italy	Architect - AIA Gold Medal
Belmondo	Jean-Paul	Performing Arts	France	Actor
Belmont	August	Business	USA	Banking
Belmonte	Juan	Sports	Spain	Bull Fighter
Belo	Carlos Filipe Ximenes	War & Peace	East Timor	Peace - Nobel Laureate
Belov	Sergei	Sports	Russia	Basketball Player - HF
Belushi	James	Performing Arts	USA	Actor
	John	Performing Arts	USA	Actor
Belyayev	Pavel Ivanovich	Aviation	Russia	Astronaut
Beman	Deane	Sports	USA	Golfer - HF
Bemini	Gian Lorenzo	Works of Art	Italy	Artist
Bemis	Samuel Flagg	Creative Works	USA	Author - Pulitzer
Benacerraf	Baruj	Science	USA	Medicine - Nobel Laureate
Benaderet	Bea	Performing Arts	USA	Actress
Benatar	Pat	Performing Arts	USA	Singer
Benavente	Jacinto	Creative Works	Spain	Literature - Nobel Laureate
Benben	Brian	Performing Arts	USA	Actor
Bench	Johnny Lee	Sports	USA	Baseball Player - HF
Benchley	Peter	Creative Works	USA	Author - Jaws
	Robert Charles	Creative Works	USA	Humorist
Bender	Charles Albert (Chief)	Sports	USA	Baseball Player - HF
Bendix	William	Performing Arts	USA	Actor - Acad Award Nom
Benedict	Clinton S. (Clint)	Sports	Canada	Hockey Player - HF
	Dirk	Performing Arts	USA	Actor
	Ruth Fulton	Arts	USA	Anthropologist
Beneke	Gordon (Tex)	Performing Arts	USA	Band Leader/Saxophonist
Beneš	Eduard	Politics	Czechoslovakia	President
Benét	Stephen Vincent	Creative Works	USA	Poet - Pulitzer
	William Rose	Creative Works	USA	Poet - Pulitzer
Ben-Gurion	David	Politics	Israel	Prime Minster
Benigni	Roberto	Movie Production	Italy	Director - Acad Award Nom
	Roberto	Performing Arts	Italy	Actor - Academy Award
Bening	Annette	Performing Arts	USA	Actress - Acad Award Nom
Benitez	Elsa	Performing Arts	Mexico	Super Model
Benjamin	Richard	Movie Production	USA	Director
	Richard	Performing Arts	USA	Actor
	Walter	Creative Works	Germany	Writer/Critic
	Benny (Papa Zita) (William)	Performing Arts	USA	Drummer - Rock & Roll - HF
Bennett	Constance	Performing Arts	USA	Actress
	Enoch Arnold	Creative Works	England	Novelist
	James Gordon	Creative Works	USA	Journalist
	Joan	Performing Arts	USA	Actress
	Richard Bedford	Politics	Canada	Prime Minster
Bennett (Benedetto)	Anthony Dominick (Tony)	Performing Arts	USA	Singer - Big Band/Jazz - HF
Benny	Jack	Performing Arts	USA	Comedian
Benoit	Joan	Sports	USA	Olympic Marathoner
Benson	Ezra Taft	Politics	USA	Secretary of Agriculture
	George	Performing Arts	USA	Jazz Guitarist/Singer
	Renaldo	Performing Arts	USA	Rock & Roll - HF - The Four Tops
	Robby	Performing Arts	USA	Actor
Bentham	Jeremy	Arts	England	Philosopher/Economist
Bentley	Douglas Wagner (Doug)	Sports	Canada	Hockey Player - HF
	Eric Russell	Creative Works	USA	Drama Critic/Director
	Maxwell Herbert Lloyd	Sports	Canada	Hockey Player - HF
	Richard	Creative Works	England	Scholar/Critic
Benton	Brook	Performing Arts	USA	Singer
	Robert	Movie Production	USA	Director - Academy Award

LAST NAME	FIRST NAME	CATEGORY	COUNTRY	FAME
Benton	Thomas Hart	Politics	USA	Senator
	Thomas Hart	Works of Art	USA	Painter
	William	Business	USA	Advertising
Bentsen Jr.	Lloyd Millard	Politics	USA	Senator
Benvenuti	Nino	Sports	USA	Boxer - HF
Béranger	Pierre Jean de	Creative Works	France	Lyric Poet
Berdyaev	Nikolai Alexsandrovich	Arts	Russia	Philosopher
Beregovoi	Georgi Timofeyevich	Aviation	Russia	Astronaut
Berenger	Tom	Performing Arts	USA	Actor - Acad Award Nom
Berenson	Bernard	Creative Works	USA	Art Critic
Beresford	Bruce	Movie Production	Australia	Director - Acad Award Nom
Berg	Alan Scott	Creative Works	USA	Author - Pulitzer
	Alban Maria Johannes	Creative Works	Austria	Composer/Opera
	Gertrude	Performing Arts	USA	Comedian
	Lodewijk Van Den	Aviation	USA	Astronaut
	Moe	Sports	USA	Baseball Player/Spy
	Patty	Sports	USA	Golfer - HF
	Paul	Science	USA	Chemistry - Nobel Laureate
	Steve De	Sports	USA	Football Player
Bergen	Candice	Performing Arts	USA	Actress - Acad Award Nom
	Edgar	Performing Arts	USA	Comedian
	Polly	Performing Arts	USA	Actress
Berger	Nadine	Creative Works	Canada	Journalist - Television
	Senta	Performing Arts	Austria	Actress
	Thomas	Creative Works	USA	Novelist
Bergerac	Cyrano de	Creative Works	France	Writer/Soldier
Bergius	Friedrich	Science	Germany	Chemistry - Nobel Laureate
Bergkamp	Dennis	Sports	Netherlands	Soccer Player
Bergman	Ingmar	Movie Production	Sweden	Director - Acad Award Nom
	Ingrid	Performing Arts	Sweden	Actress - Academy Award
Bergner	Elisabeth	Performing Arts	Ukraine	Actress - Acad Award Nom
Bergson	Henri	Arts	France	Literature - Nobel Laureate
Bergström	Sune K.	Science	Sweden	Medicine - Nobel Laureate
Berigan (Bernart)	Rowland (Bunny)	Performing Arts	USA	Jazz Trumpeter - Big Band/Jazz -HF
Bering	Vitus Jonassen	Exploration	Denmark	Explorer - Siberia
Berkely	Busby	Movie Production	USA	Director
	George	Arts	Ireland	Philosopher
Berkely	William	Politics	England	Governor
Berkowitz	David (Son of Sam)	Law & Order	USA	Serial Killer
Berlage	Hendrick Petrus	Architecture	Netherlands	Architect
Berle	Milton	Performing Arts	USA	Comedian
Berlin	Irving	Creative Works	USA	Composer Music
	Isaiah	Arts	England	Philosopher
	Jeannie	Performing Arts	USA	Actress - Acad Award Nom
Berlin (Baline)	Israel Isidore (Irving)	Performing Arts	Siberia	Composer/Lyricist - Big Band/Jazz - HF
Berlioz	Hector	Creative Works	France	Composer Classical
Berman	Chris	Creative Works	USA	Journalist - Television
	Len	Creative Works	USA	Journalist - Television
	Shelley	Performing Arts	USA	Comedian
Bernabei	Raymond	Sports	USA	Soccer Player - HF
Bernadotte	Jean Baptiste Jules	War & Peace	France	Marshall
Bernard	Claude	Science	France	Physiologist
Bernardi	Herschel	Performing Arts	USA	Actor
Bernardin de Saint-Pierre	Jacques Henri	Creative Works	France	Writer
Bernhard	Sandra	Performing Arts	USA	Comedian
Bernhardt	Sarah	Performing Arts	France	Actress
Bernini	Gian Lorenzo	Architecture	Italy	Architect
	Giovanni Lorenzo	Works of Art	Italy	Sculptor/Painter
Bernoulli	Daniel	Science	Switzerland	Physicist
	Hans	Architecture	Switzerland	Architect
	Jacques	Science	Switzerland	Mathematician
	Jean	Science	Switzerland	Mathematician
Bernsen	Corbin	Performing Arts	USA	Actor

SOLVER SERIES: NAME FINDER

LAST NAME	FIRST NAME	CATEGORY	COUNTRY	FAME
Bernstein	Carl	Creative Works	USA	Journalist - Newspaper
	Elmer	Creative Works	USA	Composer/Movie Music
	Leonard	Creative Works	USA	Composer/Conductor
Berra	Lawrence Peter (Yogi)	Sports	USA	Baseball Player - HF
Berry	Charles Edward (Chuck)	Performing Arts	USA	Singer - Rock & Roll - HF
	Halle	Performing Arts	USA	Actress - Academy Award
	Jim	Creative Works	USA	Cartoonist - Berry's World
	Ken	Performing Arts	USA	Actor
	Raymond Emmett	Sports	USA	Football Player - HF
Berryman	John	Creative Works	USA	Poet - Pulitzer
Bertinelli	Valerie	Performing Arts	USA	Actress
Bertolucci	Bernardo	Movie Production	Italy	Director - Acad Award Nom
Berzelius	Jons	Science	Sweden	Chemist
Besant	Annie	Politics	England	Theosophist
Besch	Bibi	Performing Arts	Austria	Actress
Bessemer	Henry	Science	England	Engineer
Best	George	Sports	Northern Ireland	Soccer Player - HF
Bethe	Hans Albrecht	Science	USA	Physics - Nobel Laureate
Bethea	Elvin Lamont	Sports	USA	Football Player - HF
Bethmann-Hollweg	Theobald von	Politics	Germany	Chancellor
Betjeman	John	Creative Works	England	Poet Laureate
Bettelheim	Bruno	Arts	USA	Psychologist
Bettenhausen	Melvin (Tony)	Sports	USA	Race Car Driver - HF
Betterton	Thomas	Performing Arts	England	Actor
Betts	Dickey (Forrest Richard)	Performing Arts	USA	Rock & Roll - HF - Allmann Brothers Band
Betz	Carl	Performing Arts	USA	Actor
Betz-Addie	Pauline May	Sports	USA	Tennis Player - HF
Bevan	Aneurin	Politics	Wales	Minister
Beveridge	Albert Jeremiah	Creative Works	USA	Author - Pulitzer
	Albert Jeremiah	Politics	USA	Statesman/Historian
	William Henry	Science	England	Economist
Bevin	Ernest	Politics	England	Labor Leader
Beyle	Marie Henri	Creative Works	France	Novelist/Essayist
Bianchi	Kenneth	Law & Order	USA	Serial Killer - Hillside Strangler
Biao	Lin	War & Peace	China	General - Communist
Bickford	Charles	Performing Arts	USA	Actor - Acad Award Nom
Biddle	John	Arts	England	Theologian
	Nicholas	Business	USA	Financier
Biden Jr.	Joseph Robinette	Politics	USA	Senator
Bidwell Sr.	Charles W.	Sports	USA	Football Owner - HF
Bierce	Ambrose Gwinett	Creative Works	USA	Writer/Satire
Biggars	Earl Derr	Creative Works	USA	Writer - Mystery
Bignotti	George	Sports	USA	Race Car Driver - HF
Bikel	Theodore	Performing Arts	Austria	Actor - Acad Award Nom
Biletnikoff	Frederick S. (Fred)	Sports	USA	Football Player - HF
Billings	Josh	Performing Arts	USA	Humorist
Bing	David (Dave)	Sports	USA	Basketball Player - HF
	Rudolf	Performing Arts	Austria	Singer - Opera
Bingham	George Caleb	Works of Art	USA	Painter - Realist
	Traci	Performing Arts	USA	Actress/Model
Binnig	Gerd	Science	Germany	Physics - Nobel Laureate
Binoche	Juliette	Performing Arts	France	Actress - Academy Award
Biondi	Matt	Sports	USA	Olympic Swimmer
Bird	Larry	Sports	USA	Basketball Player - HF
Birdsong	Cindy	Performing Arts	USA	Rock & Roll - HF - The Supremes
Birkerts	Gunnar	Architecture	USA	Architect
Birney	David	Performing Arts	USA	Actor
Bishop	Elizabeth	Creative Works	USA	Poet - Pulitzer
	Joey	Performing Arts	USA	Actor/Comedian
	John Michael	Science	USA	Medicine - Nobel Laureate
	Stephen	Performing Arts	USA	Singer/Composer
Bismarck	Otto Eduard Leopold von	Politics	Germany	Chancellor
Bisset	Jacqueline	Performing Arts	England	Actress

LAST NAME	FIRST NAME	CATEGORY	COUNTRY	FAME
Bix	Herbert P.	Creative Works	USA	Author - Pulitzer
Bixby	Bill	Performing Arts	USA	Actor
Bizet	Georges	Creative Works	France	Composer/Opera
Björnson	Björnstjerne Martinus	Creative Works	Norway	Literature - Nobel Laureate
Black	Cilla	Performing Arts	England	Singer
	Clint	Performing Arts	USA	Singer
	Conrad	Business	Canada	Media Magnate
	Fred	Business	USA	Aviation Industry
	Hugo La Fayette	Law & Order	USA	Jurist
	James W.	Science	England	Medicine - Nobel Laureate
	Karen	Performing Arts	USA	Actress - Acad Award Nom
Blackett	Patrick Maynard Stuart	Science	England	Physics - Nobel Laureate
Blackman	Honor	Performing Arts	England	Actress
Blackmun	Harry Andrew	Law & Order	USA	Justice/Supreme Court
Blackstone	William	Law & Order	England	Jurist
Blackwell	Elizabeth	Science	USA	Physician
Blades	Ruben	Performing Arts	Panama	Actor/Composer
Blaha	John Elmer	Aviation	USA	Astronaut
Blaine	James Gillespie	Politics	USA	Secretary of State
	Vivian	Performing Arts	USA	Singer/Comedian
Blair	Betsy	Performing Arts	USA	Actress - Acad Award Nom
	Linda	Performing Arts	USA	Actress - Acad Award Nom
	Tony	Politics	England	Prime Minster
Blake	Hector (Toe)	Sports	Canada	Hockey Player - HF
	James Herbert (Eubie)	Performing Arts	USA	Jazz Pianist/Composer - Big Band/Jazz - HF
	Robert	Performing Arts	USA	Actor
	Robert	War & Peace	England	Admiral
	William	Creative Works	England	Poet/Artist
Blakely	Ronee	Performing Arts	USA	Singer - Country & Western
	Susan	Performing Arts	Germany	Actress
	Arthur (Art)	Performing Arts	USA	Jazz Drummer - Big Band/Jazz - HF
	Ronee	Performing Arts	USA	Actress - Acad Award Nom
Blanc	Jean Joseph Charles Louis	Arts	France	Socialist/Historian
	Matt Le	Performing Arts	USA	Actor
	Mel	Performing Arts	USA	Comedian
Blanchett	Cate	Performing Arts	Australia	Actress - Academy Award
Blanco	Raül Gonzalez	Sports	Spain	Soccer Player
Bland	Robert Calvin (Bobby) (Blue)	Performing Arts	USA	Singer - Rock & Roll - HF
Blanda	George Frederick	Sports	USA	Football Player - HF
Blanton	Jimmy	Performing Arts	USA	Jazz Bassist - Big Band/Jazz - HF
Blasco Ibáñez	Vincente	Creative Works	Spain	Novelist
Blass	William Ralph	Business	USA	Fashion Designer
Blavatsky	Helena	Arts	Russia	Theosophist
Blazejowski	Carol	Sports	USA	Basketball Player - HF
Bledsoe	Tempestt	Performing Arts	USA	Actress
Blériot	Louis	Aviation	France	Aeronautical Engineer
Blethyn	Brenda	Performing Arts	England	Actress - Acad Award Nom
Bligh	William	War & Peace	England	Commander
Blitzer	Wolf	Creative Works	USA	Journalist - Television
Blobel	Günter	Science	USA	Medicine - Nobel Laureate
Bloch	Ernest	Creative Works	USA	Composer Classical
	Ernst	Arts	Germany	Philosopher
	Felix	Science	USA	Physics - Nobel Laureate
	Konrad	Science	USA	Medicine - Nobel Laureate
	Herb	Creative Works	USA	Cartoonist - Pulitzer
Blocker	Dan	Performing Arts	USA	Actor
Bloembergen	Nicolaas	Science	USA	Physics - Nobel Laureate
Blok	Alexandr Alexandrovich	Creative Works	Russia	Poet
Blondell	Joan	Performing Arts	USA	Actress - Acad Award Nom
Bloom	Claire	Performing Arts	England	Actress
Bloomer	Amelia Jenks	Politics	USA	Social Reformist
Bloomfield	Leonard	Arts	USA	Linguist
Blore	Eric	Performing Arts	England	Actor

SOLVER SERIES: NAME FINDER

LAST NAME	FIRST NAME	CATEGORY	COUNTRY	FAME
Blount	Melvin Cornell (Mel)	Sports	USA	Football Player - HF
Blücher	Gebhard Leberecht von	War & Peace	Germany	Field Marshall
Blue	Ben	Performing Arts	Canada	Comedian
	Vida	Sports	USA	Baseball Player
Bluford	Guion Steward	Aviation	USA	Astronaut
Blumberg	Baruch S.	Science	USA	Medicine - Nobel Laureate
Blume	Judy	Creative Works	USA	Author
Bly	Nellie	Creative Works	USA	Journalist - Newspaper
	Robert	Creative Works	USA	Author/Poet
Blyleven	Bert	Sports	USA	Baseball Player
Blyth	Ann	Performing Arts	USA	Actress - Acad Award Nom
Blyton	Enid Mary	Creative Works	England	Author
Bo Bardi	Lina	Architecture	Brazil	Architect/Furniture Designer
Boas	Franz	Arts	USA	Anthropologist
Bobko	Karol Joseph	Aviation	USA	Astronaut
Boccaccio	Giovanni	Creative Works	Italy	Author/Poet
Boccherini	Luigi	Creative Works	Italy	Composer
Boccioni	Umberto	Works of Art	Italy	Painter/Sculptor
Bock	Jerry	Creative Works	USA	Composer - Musicals
Bodenheim	Maxwell	Creative Works	USA	Poet/Novelist
Bodin	Jean	Arts	France	Philosopher/Jurist
Bodley	Thomas	Politics	England	Statesman/Scholar
Bodnar	Roberta Lynn	Aviation	Canada	Astronaut
Bodoni	Giambattista	Arts	Italy	Print Designer
Boehm	Gottfried	Architecture	Germany	Architect - Pritzker Laureate
Boeyinga	Berend Tobia	Architecture	Netherlands	Architect - Churches
Bofill	Riccardo	Architecture	Spain	Architect
Bogarde	Dirk	Performing Arts	England	Actor
Bogart	Humphrey	Performing Arts	USA	Actor - Academy Award
Bogdanovich	Peter	Movie Production	USA	Director - Acad Award Nom
Boggs	Wade	Sports	USA	Baseball Player - HF
Bogicevic	Vladislav (Bogie)	Sports	Yugoslavia	Soccer Player - HF
Bohay	Heidi	Performing Arts	USA	Actress
Böhme	Jakob	Arts	Germany	Philosopher/Mystic
Bohr	Aage Niels Henrik David	Science	Denmark	Physics - Nobel Laureate
Boiardo	Matteo Maria	Creative Works	Italy	Poet
Boileau-Despréaux	Nicholas	Creative Works	France	Poet/Critic
Bois	Guy Pene du	Works of Art	USA	Painter/Art Critic
	William Edward Burghardt du	Arts	USA	Historian/Educator
Boitano	Brian	Sports	USA	Olympic Skater
Boivin	Leo Joseph	Sports	Canada	Hockey Player - HF
Bojer	Johan	Creative Works	Norway	Novelist/Playwright
Bok	Edward William	Creative Works	USA	Author - Pulitzer
	Sissela	Arts	Sweden	Philosopher
Bolden	Buddy	Performing Arts	USA	Jazz Trumpeter - Big Band/Jazz - HF
Bolden Jr.	Charles Frank	Aviation	USA	Astronaut
Bolet	Jorge	Performing Arts	Cuba	Conductor/Pianist
Boleyn	Anne	Politics	England	King's Wife
Bolger	Ray	Performing Arts	USA	Actor
Bolivar	Simón José	War & Peace	Venezuela	General/Revolutionary
Böll	Heinrich	Creative Works	Germany	Literature - Nobel Laureate
Bolt	Tommy	Sports	USA	Golfer - HF
Bombeck	Erma	Creative Works	USA	Journalist - Newspaper
Bon	Simon Le	Performing Arts	England	Singer
	Yasmin Le	Performing Arts	England	Super Model
Bon Jovi	Jon	Performing Arts	USA	Singer/Composer
Bonallack	Michael	Sports	England	Golfer - HF
Bonaparte	Napoléon	War & Peace	France	General
Bonatz	Paul Michael Nikolaus	Architecture	Germany	Architect
Bond	Johnny (Cyrus Whitfield)	Performing Arts	USA	Singer - Country Music - HF
	Ward	Performing Arts	USA	Actor
Bondi	Beulah	Performing Arts	USA	Actress - Acad Award Nom
Bonds	Barry	Sports	USA	Baseball Player

LAST NAME	FIRST NAME	CATEGORY	COUNTRY	FAME
Bonds	Bobby	Sports	USA	Baseball Player
Bonet	Lisa	Performing Arts	USA	Actress
Bonham	John Henry	Performing Arts	England	Rock & Roll - HF - Led Zepplin
Bonham-Carter	Helena	Performing Arts	England	Actress - Acad Award Nom
Bonheur	Rosa	Works of Art	France	Painter
Bonnano	Joseph (Bananas)	Law & Order	Sicily	Mafia
	Salvatore (Bill)	Law & Order	USA	Mafia
Bonnard	Pierre	Works of Art	France	Painter
Bonnett	Neil	Sports	USA	Race Car Driver - HF
Bonney	William H. (Billy the Kid)	Law & Order	USA	Outlaw
Bono	Sonny	Performing Arts	USA	Singer
Bonsal	Stephen	Creative Works	USA	Author - Pulitzer
Bookie	Mike	Sports	USA	Soccer Player - HF
Boon	Richard R. (Dickie)	Sports	Canada	Hockey Player - HF
Boone	Daniel	Exploration	USA	Frontiersman - Kentucky
	Debby	Performing Arts	USA	Singer
	Pat	Performing Arts	USA	Singer/Actor
	Richard	Performing Arts	USA	Actor
	Steve	Performing Arts	USA	Rock & Roll - HF - Lovin' Spoonful
Boorman	John	Movie Production	England	Director - Acad Award Nom
Boorstein	Daniel J.	Creative Works	USA	Author - Pulitzer
Boosler	Elayne	Performing Arts	USA	Comedian
Booth	Ballington	Arts	England	Revivalist
	EdwinThomas	Performing Arts	USA	Actor
	Evangeline Cory	Arts	England	Revivalist
	Henry	Business	England	Railway Magnate
	Jessie	Business	England	Retail Trade
	John Wilkes	Performing Arts	USA	Actor/Assassin
	Junius Brutus	Performing Arts	USA	Actor
	Shirley	Performing Arts	USA	Actress - Academy Award
	William	Arts	England	Revivalist
Bopp	Franz	Arts	Germany	Philologist
Borden	Robert Laird	Politics	Canada	Prime Minster
Bordet	Jules	Science	Belgium	Medicine - Nobel Laureate
Borg	Björn Rune	Sports	Sweden	Tennis Player - HF
Borge	Victor	Performing Arts	Denmark	Pianist/Entertainer
Borges	Jorge Luis	Creative Works	Argentina	Poet/Writer
Borghi	Frank	Sports	USA	Soccer Player - HF
Borgia	Cesare	War & Peace	Italy	Cardinal
	Lucretia	Politics	Italy	Duchess
Borglum	John Gutzon	Works of Art	USA	Sculptor/Painter
Borgman	Bernard (Bennie)	Sports	USA	Basketball Player - HF
Borgnine	Ernest	Performing Arts	USA	Actor - Academy Award
Bori	Lucretia	Performing Arts	USA	Singer - Opera
Borlaug	Norman E.	War & Peace	USA	Peace - Nobel Laureate
Borman	Frank Frederick	Aviation	USA	Astronaut
Born	Max	Science	Germany	Physics - Nobel Laureate
Borodin	Aleksandr Porfirevich	Creative Works	Russia	Composer
Boros	Julius	Sports	USA	Golfer - HF
Borotra	Jean Robert	Sports	France	Tennis Player - HF
Borromini	Francesco	Architecture	Italy	Architect
Borrow	George Henry	Creative Works	England	Writer/Linguist
Boru	Brian	Politics	Ireland	King
Borzage	Frank	Movie Production	USA	Director - Academy Award
Borzov	Valery	Sports	Russia	Olympic Runner
Bosch	Carl	Science	Germany	Chemistry - Nobel Laureate
	Hieronymus	Works of Art	Netherlands	Painter
Bose	Jagadis Chandra	Science	India	Physicist
Bosley	Tom	Performing Arts	USA	Actor
Boss	Hugo	Business	Germany	Fashion Designer
Bosson	Barbara	Performing Arts	USA	Actress
Bossuet	Jacques Bénigne	Arts	France	Bishop/Orator
Bossy	Michael (Mike)	Sports	Canada	Hockey Player - HF

SOLVER SERIES: NAME FINDER

LAST NAME	FIRST NAME	CATEGORY	COUNTRY	FAME
Bostwick	Barry	Performing Arts	USA	Actor - Musical
Boswell	James	Creative Works	Scotland	Writer/Lawyer
Botha	Louis	Politics	South Africa	Prime Minister
Bothe	Walther	Science	Germany	Physics - Nobel Laureate
Botta	Mario	Architecture	Switzerland	Architect
Botticelli	Sandro	Works of Art	Italy	Painter
Bottomley	James Leroy (Jim)	Sports	USA	Baseball Player - HF
Bottoms	Timothy	Performing Arts	USA	Actor
Bottoni	Archivio Piero	Architecture	Italy	Architect
Botvinnik	Mikhail	Games	Russia	Chess Player
Bouchard	Emil (Butch)	Sports	Canada	Hockey Player - HF
Boucher	François	Works of Art	France	Painter
	Francois X. (Frank)	Sports	Canada	Hockey Player - HF
	George (Buck)	Sports	Canada	Hockey Player - HF
Boucicault	Dion	Performing Arts	England	Actor/Playwright
Boudreau	Louis (Lou)	Sports	USA	Baseball Player - HF
Bougainville	Louis Antoinne de	Exploration	France	Explorer - Falkland Islands
Boulanger	Nadia Juliette	Performing Arts	France	Conductor/Teacher
Boulée	Etienne Louis	Architecture	France	Architect
Boulos	John (Frenchy)	Sports	Haiti	Soccer Player - HF
Bourgeois	Léon Victor Auguste	War & Peace	France	Peace - Nobel Laureate
Bourget	Paul Charles Joseph	Creative Works	France	Novelist/Essayist
Bourguiba	Habib ben Ali	Politics	Tunisia	President
Bourke-White	Margaret	Works of Art	USA	Photographer
Bourque	Raymond Jean (Ray)	Sports	Canada	Hockey Player - HF
Bovet	Daniel	Science	Italy	Medicine - Nobel Laureate
Bow	Clara	Performing Arts	USA	Actress
Bowditch	Nathaniel	Science	USA	Mathematician/Astronomer
Bowe	Riddick	Sports	USA	Boxer
Bowell	Mackenzie	Politics	Canada	Prime Minister
Bower	John William (Johnny)	Sports	Canada	Hockey Player - HF
Bowie	Russell (Dubbie)	Sports	Canada	Hockey Player - HF
Bowie (Hayward-Jones)	David (Robert David)	Performing Arts	England	Singer - Rock & Roll - HF
Bowrey	Lesley Rosemary Turner	Sports	Australia	Tennis Player - HF
Boxer	Barbara Levy	Politics	USA	Senator
Boxleitner	Bruce	Performing Arts	USA	Actor
Boyd	Louise Arner	Exploration	USA	Explorer - Arctic
	Stephen	Performing Arts	Northern Ireland	Actor
Boyer	Charles	Performing Arts	France	Actor - Acad Award Nom
	Clete	Sports	USA	Baseball Player
	Paul D.	Science	USA	Chemistry - Nobel Laureate
Boyle	Lara Flynn	Performing Arts	USA	Actress
	Peter	Performing Arts	USA	Actor
	Robert	Science	England	Chemist/Physicist
Brabham	John Arthur (Black Jack)	Sports	Australia	Race Car Driver - HF
Bracco	Lorraine	Performing Arts	USA	Actress - Acad Award Nom
Bracken	Eddie	Performing Arts	USA	Actor
Bradbury	Ray	Creative Works	USA	Author - SciFi
Braddock	Edward	War & Peace	England	General
Bradford	Gamaliel	Arts	USA	Biographer
	William	Politics	USA	Governor
Bradlee	Ben	Creative Works	USA	Journalist - Newspaper
Bradley	Andrew Cecil	Arts	England	Educator/Critic
	Ed	Creative Works	USA	Journalist - Television
	Henry	Arts	England	Lexicographer
	Omar Nelson	War & Peace	USA	General
	Pat	Sports	USA	Golfer - HF
	William Owen	Performing Arts	USA	Singer - Country Music - HF
	William W. (Bill)	Sports	USA	Basketball Player - HF
	William Warren (Bill)	Politics	USA	Senator
Bradley (Schwichtenberg)	Wilbur (Will)	Performing Arts	USA	Band Leader - Big Band/Jazz - HF
Bradshaw	George	Business	England	Railway Magnate
	John	Arts	USA	Philosopher/Lecturer/Author

LAST NAME	FIRST NAME	CATEGORY	COUNTRY	FAME
Bradshaw	Terry Paxton	Sports	USA	Football Player - HF
Bradstreet	Anne	Creative Works	USA	Poet
Brady	Alice	Performing Arts	USA	Actress - Academy Award
	James (Diamond Jim)	Business	USA	Financier/Philanthropy
	Matthew B.	Works of Art	USA	Photographer
Brady Jr.	Charles Eldon	Aviation	USA	Astronaut
Braga	Sonia	Performing Arts	Brazil	Actress
Bragdon	Claude Fayette	Architecture	USA	Architect/Painter/Author
Bragg	Braxton	War & Peace	USA	General
	William Henry	Science	England	Physics - Nobel Laureate
	William Lawrence	Science	England	Physics - Nobel Laureate
Brahe	Tycho	Science	Denmark	Astronomer
Brahms	Johannes	Creative Works	Germany	Composer
Braid	James	Sports	Scotland	Golfer - HF
Braille	Louis	Arts	France	Printing/Writing
Bramante	Donato d'Agnolo	Architecture	Italy	Architect/Painter
Branagh	Kenneth	Movie Production	Ireland	Director - Acad Award Nom
	Kenneth	Performing Arts	Ireland	Actor - Acad Award Nom
Branch	Taylor	Creative Works	USA	Author - Pulitzer
Brancusi	Constantin	Works of Art	Romania	Sculptor
Brandauer	Klaus Maria	Performing Arts	Austria	Actor - Acad Award Nom
Brandeis	Louis Dembitz	Law & Order	USA	Justice/Supreme Court
Brandenstein	Daniel Charles	Aviation	USA	Astronaut
Brandes	Georg Morris	Arts	Denmark	Literary Critic
Brando	Marlon	Performing Arts	USA	Actor - Academy Award
Brandt	Herbert Ernst (Willy)	Politics	Germany	Chancellor
	Willy	War & Peace	Germany	Peace - Nobel Laureate
Branigan	Laura	Performing Arts	USA	Singer
Branson	Richard	Business	England	Aviation - Virgin Blue
Brant	Joseph	War & Peace	USA	Mowhawk Chief
Branting	Karl Hjalmar	War & Peace	Sweden	Peace - Nobel Laureate
Braque	Georges	Works of Art	France	Painter
Brasfield	Rodney Leon	Performing Arts	USA	Comedian - Country Music - HF
Brasini	Armando	Architecture	Italy	Architect
Brassey	Thomas	Business	England	Railway Magnate
Brattain	Walter Houser	Science	USA	Physics - Nobel Laureate
Braun	Karl Ferdinand	Science	Germany	Physics - Nobel Laureate
	Wernher von	Aviation	USA	Engineer - Rocket
Brazzi	Rossano	Performing Arts	Italy	Actor
Breame	Sid	Sports	USA	Baseball Player
Breathed	Berke	Creative Works	USA	Cartoonist - Pulitzer
Breau	Lenny	Performing Arts	USA	Guitarist - Canadian Music - HF
Brecht	Bertolt	Creative Works	Germany	Playwright
Breckenridge	John Cabell	Politics	USA	Vice-President
Breedlove	Craig	Sports	USA	Race Car Driver - HF
Brennan	Eileen	Performing Arts	USA	Actress - Acad Award Nom
	Joseph R.	Sports	USA	Basketball Player - HF
	Walter	Performing Arts	USA	Actor - Academy Award
	William Joseph	Law & Order	USA	Justice/Supreme Court
Brenner	David	Performing Arts	USA	Comedian
	Sydney	Science	England	Medicine - Nobel Laureate
Brenon	Herbert	Movie Production	Ireland	Director - Acad Award Nom
Brent	George	Creative Works	France	Poet/Art Critic
Breslin	Jimmy	Creative Works	USA	Journalist - Newspaper - Pulitzer
Bresnahan	Roger Philip	Sports	USA	Baseball Player - HF
Brest	Martin	Movie Production	USA	Director - Acad Award Nom
Breton	André	Creative Works	France	Poet/Critic
Brett	George Howard	Sports	USA	Baseball Player - HF
Breuer	Marcel	Architecture	USA	Architect - AIA/Jefferson Gold Medal
Brewer	Teresa	Performing Arts	USA	Singer
Brewster	William	Exploration	England	Pilgrim - Plymounth
Brezhnev	Leonid	Politics	Russia	General Secretary
Briand	Aristide	Politics	France	Statesman

SOLVER SERIES: NAME FINDER

LAST NAME	FIRST NAME	CATEGORY	COUNTRY	FAME
Briand	Aristide	War & Peace	France	Peace - Nobel Laureate
Brice	Fanny	Performing Arts	USA	Comedian
Brickell	Edie	Performing Arts	USA	Singer
Bridges	Alicia	Performing Arts	USA	Singer
	Beau	Performing Arts	USA	Actor
	Harry	Business	USA	Labor Leader
	Jeff	Performing Arts	USA	Actor - Acad Award Nom
	Lloyd	Performing Arts	USA	Actor
	Robert Seymour	Creative Works	England	Poet Laureate
Bridgman	Percy Williams	Science	USA	Physics - Nobel Laureate
Brigati	Eddie	Performing Arts	USA	Rock & Roll - HF - The Young Rascals
Bright	John	Politics	England	Statesman
	Richard	Performing Arts	USA	Actor
Brill	Abraham Arden	Arts	USA	Psychoanalyst
Brillat-Savarin	Anthelme	Arts	France	Food Expert
Brimley	Wilford	Performing Arts	USA	Actor
Brimsek	Frances Charles (Frank)	Sports	Canada	Hockey Player - HF
Brinkley	Christie	Performing Arts	USA	Super Model
	David McClure	Creative Works	USA	Journalist - Television
Brittan	Harold Pemberton	Sports	England	Soccer Player - HF
Britten	Edward Benjamin	Creative Works	England	Composer
Brix	Adolf F.	Science	Germany	Chemist
Broadbent	Harry L. (Punch)	Sports	Canada	Hockey Player - HF
	Jimmy	Performing Arts	England	Actor - Academy Award
Brock	Isaac	Politics	Canada	Lieutenant Governor
	Louis Clark (Lou)	Sports	USA	Baseball Player - HF
Brockhouse	Bertram N.	Science	Canada	Physics - Nobel Laureate
Brocklin	Norman Mack Van (Norm)	Sports	USA	Football Player - HF
Broda	Walter Edward (Turk)	Sports	Canada	Hockey Player - HF
Broder	David	Creative Works	USA	Journalist - Newspaper
Broderick	James	Performing Arts	USA	Actor
	Matthew	Performing Arts	USA	Actor
Brodie	John	Sports	USA	Football Player
Brodsky	Joseph	Creative Works	USA	Literature - Nobel Laureate
Brody	Adrien	Performing Arts	USA	Actor - Academy Award
	Jane	Creative Works	USA	Journalist - Newspaper
Broglie	Achille Charles Léonce	Politics	France	Statesman
	Louis César Victor Maurice	Science	France	Physicist
	Louis Victor Pierre Raymond de	Science	France	Physics - Nobel Laureate
Brokaw	Tom	Creative Works	USA	Journalist - Television
Brolin	James	Performing Arts	USA	Actor
Bromfield	Louis	Creative Works	USA	Author - Pulitzer
Bromwich	John Edward	Sports	Australia	Tennis Player - HF
Bronson	Charles	Performing Arts	USA	Actor
Brontë	Anne	Creative Works	England	Novelist
	Charlotte	Creative Works	England	Novelist
	Emily	Creative Works	England	Novelist/Poet
Brook	Peter	Movie Production	England	Director
Brooke	Rupert	Creative Works	England	Poet
Brooke III	Edward William	Politics	USA	Senator
Brookes	Norman Everard	Sports	Australia	Tennis Player - HF
Brookmeyer	Robert (Bob)	Performing Arts	USA	Jazz Trombonist - Big Band/Jazz - HF
Brookner	Anita	Creative Works	England	Writer/Art Critic
Brooks	Albert	Performing Arts	USA	Actor - Acad Award Nom
	Arthur	Performing Arts	USA	Rock & Roll - HF - The Impressions
	Garth	Performing Arts	USA	Singer/Composer
	Gwendolyn	Creative Works	USA	Poet - Pulitzer
	James L.	Movie Production	USA	Director - Academy Award
	Mel	Movie Production	USA	Director
	Mel	Performing Arts	USA	Actor
	Ned	Creative Works	USA	Author
	Phillips	Creative Works	USA	Writer/Clergyman
	Richard	Movie Production	USA	Director - Acad Award Nom

LAST NAME	FIRST NAME	CATEGORY	COUNTRY	FAME
Brooks	Richard	Performing Arts	USA	Rock & Roll - HF - The Impressions
	Van Wyck	Creative Works	USA	Author - Pulitzer
Brosh	Nina	Performing Arts	Israel	Super Model
Brosnan	Pierce	Performing Arts	Ireland	Actor
Brothers	Joyce	Creative Works	USA	Journalist/Psychologist - Newspaper
Brough	Althea Louise	Sports	USA	Tennis Player - HF
Brouthers	Dennis Joseph (Dan)	Sports	USA	Baseball Player - HF
Brown	Blair	Performing Arts	USA	Actress
	Bryan	Performing Arts	Australia	Actor
	Charles	Performing Arts	USA	Singer - Rock & Roll - HF
	Charles Brockden	Creative Works	USA	Novelist
	Clifford	Performing Arts	USA	Jazz Trumpeter - Big Band/Jazz - HF
	Davey	Sports	USA	Soccer Player - HF
	David McDowell	Aviation	USA	Astronaut
	Denise Scott	Architecture	USA	Architect
	George	Business	USA	Ship Building
	George	Sports	Scotland	Soccer Player - HF
	Helen Gurley	Creative Works	USA	Journalist - Magazine
	Herbert C.	Science	USA	Chemistry - Nobel Laureate
	Herman	Business	USA	Ship Building
	James (Jim)	Sports	Scotland	Soccer Player - HF
	James Nathaniel (Jim)	Sports	USA	Football Player - HF
	Joe E.	Performing Arts	USA	Comedian
	John	Politics	USA	Abolitionist
	Lawrence	Performing Arts	USA	Jazz Trombonist - Big Band/Jazz HF
	Lester (Les) Raymond	Performing Arts	USA	Band Leader - Big Band/Jazz - HF
	Mark Neil	Aviation	USA	Astronaut
	Michael S.	Science	USA	Medicine - Nobel Laureate
	Mordecai Peter Centennial	Sports	USA	Baseball Player - HF
	Paul Eugene	Sports	USA	Football Coach - HF
	Ray (Raymond Matthews)	Performing Arts	USA	Jazz Bassist - Big Band/Jazz - HF
	Robert	Science	England	Botanist
	Robert Stanford (Bob Boomer)	Sports	USA	Football Player - HF
	Ronald Harmon (Ron)	Politics	USA	Secretary of Commerce
	Ruth	Performing Arts	USA	Singer - Rock & Roll - HF
	William Ferdie (Willie)	Sports	USA	Football Player - HF
	Clarence	Movie Production	USA	Director - Acad Award Nom
Brown Jr.	Curtis Lee	Aviation	USA	Astronaut
	Roosevelt	Sports	USA	Football Player - HF
Browne	Charles Farrar	Creative Works	USA	Humorist
	Clyde Jackson	Performing Arts	Germany	Singer - Rock & Roll - HF
	Leslie	Performing Arts	USA	Actress - Acad Award Nom
	Mary Kendall	Sports	USA	Tennis Player - HF
	Richard Arthur (Dik)	Creative Works	USA	Cartoonist - Hagar
	Roscoe Lee	Performing Arts	USA	Actor
	Thomas	Science	England	Physician/Writer
Browning	Elizabeth Barrett	Creative Works	England	Poet
	John Moses	Science	USA	Inventor - Firearms
	Robert	Creative Works	England	Poet
	Tod	Movie Production	USA	Director
Brubeck	Dave	Performing Arts	USA	Jazz Pianist - Big Band/Jazz - HF
Bruce	Jack	Performing Arts	Scotland	Rock & Roll - HF - Cream
	Lenny	Performing Arts	USA	Comedian
	Nigel	Performing Arts	Mexico	Actor
	Robert	Creative Works	USA	Author - Pulitzer
	Robert	Politics	Scotland	King
	Stanley Melbourne	Politics	Australia	Prime Minister
	Virginia	Performing Arts	USA	Actress
	William Cabell	Creative Works	USA	Author - Pulitzer
Bruch	Max	Creative Works	Germany	Composer
Bruckner	Anton	Creative Works	Austria	Composer
Bruder	William	Architecture	USA	Architect
Bruegel	Jan	Works of Art	Italy	Painter

LAST NAME	FIRST NAME	CATEGORY	COUNTRY	FAME
Bruegel	Pieter	Works of Art	Italy	Painter
Brugnon	Jacques (Toto)	Sports	France	Tennis Player - HF
Brunelleschi	Fillipo	Architecture	Italy	Architect
Bruni	Carla	Performing Arts	Italy	Super Model
Brunner	John Kilian Houston	Creative Works	England	Novelist
Bruno	Giordano	Arts	Italy	Philosopher
Bruton	John	Politics	Ireland	Prime Minister
Bruyère	Jean de La	Creative Works	France	Essayist/Moralist
Bryan	Jimmy (Cowboy)	Sports	USA	Race Car Driver - HF
	William Jennings	Politics	USA	Politician/Orator
Bryant	Bondleaux	Performing Arts	USA	Violinist - Country Music - HF
	William Cullen	Creative Works	USA	Poet
Brynner	Yul	Performing Arts	USA	Actor - Academy Award
Bryson	Peabo	Performing Arts	USA	Singer
Buber	Martin	Arts	Israel	Philosopher/Theologian
Buchan	John	Creative Works	Scotland	Novelist/Statesman
Buchanan	Edgar	Performing Arts	USA	Actor
	James	Politics	USA	President
	Junious (Buck)	Sports	USA	Football Player - HF
	Kenneth (Ken)	Sports	Scotland	Boxer - HF
	Pat	Creative Works	USA	Journalist - Newspaper
Buchanan Jr.	James M.	Arts	USA	Economics - Nobel Laureate
Buchholz	Horst	Performing Arts	Germany	Actor
Buchholz Jr.	Earl (Butch)	Sports	USA	Tennis Player - HF
Buchli	James Frederick	Aviation	USA	Astronaut
Buchner	Eduard	Science	Germany	Chemistry - Nobel Laureate
Buchwald	Arthur	Creative Works	USA	Journalist - Newspaper
Buck	Linda B.	Science	USA	Medicine - Nobel Laureate
	Paul Herman	Creative Works	USA	Author - Pulitzer
	Pearl Sydenstricker	Creative Works	USA	Literature - Nobel/Pulitzer
Buckey Jr.	Jay Clark	Aviation	USA	Astronaut
Buckingham	Lindsey	Performing Arts	USA	Rock & Roll - HF - Fleetwood Mac
Buckle	Henry Thomas	Arts	England	Historian
Buckley	Betty	Performing Arts	USA	Actress
	William F.	Creative Works	USA	Journalist - Newspaper
Bucyk	John Paul (Johnny)	Sports	Canada	Hockey Player - HF
Budd	Zola	Sports	South Africa	Olympic Runner
Budge	John Donald (Don)	Sports	USA	Tennis Player - HF
Bueno	Maria Esther Andion	Sports	Brazil	Tennis Player - HF
Buffett	Jimmy	Performing Arts	USA	Singer/Composer
Buffon	Georges Louis Leclerc	Arts	France	Naturalist
Bugatti	Ettore	Sports	Italy	Race Car Designer - HF
Buisson	Ferdinand	War & Peace	France	Peace - Nobel Laureate
Bujold	Genevieve	Performing Arts	Canada	Actress - Acad Award Nom
Buley	Oscar Carlyle	Creative Works	USA	Author - Pulitzer
Bulfinch	Charles	Architecture	USA	Architect - Government Buildings
Bulfinch	Thomas	Creative Works	USA	Writer/Mythologist
Bulkeley	Morgan Gardner	Sports	USA	Baseball Executive - HF
Bull	John Sumter	Aviation	USA	Astronaut
	Ole	Performing Arts	Norway	Violinist
Bülow	Bernhard von	Politics	Germany	Chancellor
Bultmann	Rudolf Karl	Arts	Germany	Theologian
Bulwer	Edward Robert	Creative Works	England	Poet
Bulwer-Lytton	Edward George Earl	Creative Works	England	Playwright/Novelist
Bumpers	Dale Leon	Politics	USA	Senator
Bunche	Ralph Johnson	Politics	USA	Statesman/Educator
	Ralph Johnson	War & Peace	USA	Peace - Nobel Laureate
Bundchen	Gisele	Performing Arts	Brazil	Super Model
Bundy	Theodore Robert (Ted)	Law & Order	USA	Serial Killer
Bunin	Ivan Alekseyevich	Creative Works	Russia	Literature - Nobel Laureate
Bunning	James Paul David (Jim)	Sports	USA	Baseball Player - HF
Bunsen	Robert Wilhelm	Science	Germany	Chemist/Inventor
Bunshaft	Gordon	Architecture	USA	Architect - Pritzker Laureate

LAST NAME	FIRST NAME	CATEGORY	COUNTRY	FAME
Bunuel	Luis	Movie Production	France	Director
Bunyan	John	Creative Works	England	Writer/Preacher
Buonarroti	Michelangelo	Works of Art	Italy	Sculptor/Painter/Poet/Architect
Buoniconti	Nicholas Anthony (Nick)	Sports	USA	Football Player - HF
Buono	Angelo	Law & Order	USA	Serial Killer - Hillside Strangler
	Victor	Performing Arts	USA	Actor - Acad Award Nom
Burbank	Luther	Science	USA	Horticulturalist
Burberry	Thomas	Business	England	Fashion Designer
Burch	William (Billy)	Sports	USA	Hockey Player - HF
Burchard	John Ely	Architecture	USA	Architect - Jefferson Medal
Burckhardt	Jacob	Arts	Switzerland	Historian/Critic
Burden	Eric	Performing Arts	England	Rock & Roll - HF - The Animals
Burelli	Augusto Romano	Architecture	Italy	Architect
Buren	Abigail Van	Creative Works	USA	Journalist - Newspaper
	Hannah Van	Politics	USA	First Lady
	Martin Van	Politics	USA	President
	Stephen W. Van (Steve)	Sports	USA	Football Player - HF
Burger	Warren Earl	Law & Order	USA	Chief Justice
Burgess	Frank Gelett	Creative Works	USA	Humorist/Illustrator
	John Anthony	Creative Works	England	Author
Burghoff	Gary	Performing Arts	USA	Actor
Burgoyne	John	War & Peace	England	General
Burke	Billie	Performing Arts	USA	Actress - Acad Award Nom
	Delta	Performing Arts	USA	Actress
	Edmund	Arts	England	Philosopher/Writer/Statesman
	Robert O'Hara	Exploration	Australia	Explorer - Central Australia
	Solomon	Performing Arts	USA	Singer - Rock & Roll - HF
Burke Jr.	Jack	Sports	USA	Golfer - HF
Burkett	Jesse Cail	Sports	USA	Baseball Player - HF
Burne-Jones	Edwar Coley	Works of Art	England	Painter/Designer
Burnet	Frank Macfarlane	Science	Australia	Medicine - Nobel Laureate
Burnett	Carol	Performing Arts	USA	Comedian
	Frances Hodgson	Creative Works	USA	Writer
	Howlin Wolf (Chester)	Performing Arts	USA	Singer - Rock & Roll - HF
Burney	Fanny	Creative Works	England	Novelist/Diarist
Burnham	Daniel Hudson	Architecture	USA	Architect
Burns	Catherine	Performing Arts	USA	Actress - Acad Award Nom
	George	Performing Arts	USA	Actor - Academy Award
	James MacGregor	Creative Works	USA	Author - Pulitzer
	Jethro (Kenneth)	Performing Arts	USA	Country Music - HF - Homer & Jethro
	Robert	Creative Works	Scotland	Poet
Burnside	Ambrose Everett	War & Peace	USA	General
Burr	Aaron	Politics	USA	Vice-President
	Raymond	Performing Arts	Canada	Actor
Burroughs	Edgar Rice	Creative Works	USA	Writer
	John	Creative Works	USA	Writer/Naturalist
Burrows	Abram S. (Abe)	Creative Works	USA	Dramatist - Pulitzer
	Edwin G.	Creative Works	USA	Author - Pulitzer
Burrrell	Kenneth Earl (Kenny)	Performing Arts	USA	Jazz Guitarist - Big Band/Jazz - HF
Burstyn	Ellen	Performing Arts	USA	Actress - Academy Award
Burton	Levar	Performing Arts	Germany	Actor
	Richard	Performing Arts	Wales	Actor - Acad Award Nom
	Richard Francis	Exploration	England	Explorer/Writer - Africa
	Robert	Creative Works	England	Writer/Clergyman
	Timothy (Tim)	Movie Production	USA	Director
Busch	Adolphus	Business	USA	Breweries
Busey	Gary	Performing Arts	USA	Actor - Acad Award Nom
Busfield	Timothy	Performing Arts	USA	Actor
Bush	Barbara	Politics	USA	First Lady
Bush	George Herbert Walker	Politics	USA	President
	George W.	Politics	USA	President
	Laura	Politics	USA	First Lady
	Vannevar	Science	USA	Engineer/Administrator

SOLVER SERIES: NAME FINDER

LAST NAME	FIRST NAME	CATEGORY	COUNTRY	FAME
Bushman	Francis X.	Performing Arts	USA	Actor
Bushmiller	Ernie	Creative Works	USA	Cartoonist - Nancy
Busoni	Ferruccido Benvenuto	Creative Works	Italy	Composer
Busseri	Frank	Performing Arts	Canada	Canadian Music - HF - The Four Lads
Butenandt	Adolf Friedrich Johann	Science	Germany	Chemistry - Nobel Laureate
Butkus	Richard Marvin (Dick)	Sports	USA	Football Player - HF
Butler	Jerry	Performing Arts	USA	Rock & Roll - HF - The Impressions
	Joe	Performing Arts	USA	Rock & Roll - HF - Lovin' Spoonful
	Nicholas Murray	War & Peace	USA	Peace - Nobel Laureate
	Robert N.	Creative Works	USA	Author - Pulitzer
	Robert Olen	Creative Works	USA	Author - Pulitzer
	Samuel	Creative Works	England	Author
	Samuel	Creative Works	England	Composer
	Samuel	Works of Art	England	Painter
Button	Dick	Sports	USA	Olympic Skater
Buttons	Red	Performing Arts	USA	Actor - Academy Award
Buxtehude	Diderik	Creative Works	Denmark	Composer/Organist
Buzzi	Ruth	Performing Arts	USA	Comedian
Byington	Spring	Performing Arts	USA	Actress - Acad Award Nom
Bykovskiy	Valeri Fyodorovich	Aviation	Russia	Astronaut
Byner	Earnest	Sports	USA	Football Player
Byng	Julian Hedworth George	Politics	England	General
	Richard Evelyn	Exploration	USA	Explorer - Antarctic
	William	Creative Works	England	Composer
Byrne	David	Performing Arts	Scotland	Rock & Roll - HF - The Talking Heads
Caan	James	Performing Arts	USA	Actor - Acad Award Nom
Cabell	Enos	Sports	USA	Baseball Player
	James Branch	Creative Works	USA	Novelist
Cable	George Washington	Creative Works	USA	Novelist
Cabot	Bruce	Performing Arts	USA	Actor
	John	Exploration	England	Explorer - Canada
	Sebastian	Exploration	England	Explorer - North West Passage
	Sebastian	Performing Arts	England	Actor
Cabral	Pedro Alvares	Exploration	Portugal	Explorer - Brazil
Cabrillo	Juan Rodriguez	Exploration	Spain	Explorer - California
Cabrini	Frances Xavier	Arts	USA	Nun
Cacoyannis	Michael	Movie Production	Cyprus	Director - Acad Award Nom
Cadamosto	Alvise Da	Exploration	Italy	Explorer - West Africa
Cadbury	George	Business	England	Confection Industry
Cadillac	Antoine de la Mothe	Exploration	France	Explorer - Detroit
Cadman	Charles Wakefield	Creative Works	USA	Composer
Caen	Herb	Creative Works	USA	Journalist
Caesar	Adolph	Performing Arts	USA	Actor - Acad Award Nom
	Gaius Julius	War & Peace	Italy	Dictator/Military Leader
	Sid	Performing Arts	USA	Comedian
Cage	John Milton	Creative Works	USA	Composer
	Nicolas	Performing Arts	USA	Actor - Academy Award
Cagliostro	Alesandro di	Science	Sicily	Alchemist
Cagney	James	Performing Arts	USA	Actor - Academy Award
Cahill	Mabel Esmonde	Sports	Ireland	Tennis Player - HF
Cain	Bob	Creative Works	USA	Journalist - Radio
	James Mallahan	Creative Works	USA	Novelist - Crime Fiction
Caine	Michael	Performing Arts	England	Actor - Academy Award
Cajal	Santiago Ramón y	Science	Spain	Medicine - Nobel Laureate
Calatrava	Santiago	Architecture	Spain	Architect
Calcavecchia	Mark	Sports	USA	Golfer
Calder	Alexander	Works of Art	USA	Abstract Sculptor
	Alexander Stirling	Works of Art	USA	Sculptor
Caldwell	Erskine	Creative Works	USA	Novelist
	Sarah	Creative Works	USA	Screenwriter
	Zoe	Performing Arts	Australia	Actress
Cale	John	Performing Arts	Wales	Rock & Roll - HF - Velvet Underground
Calhern	Louis	Performing Arts	USA	Actor - Acad Award Nom

LAST NAME	FIRST NAME	CATEGORY	COUNTRY	FAME
Calhoun	John Caldwell	Politics	USA	Vice-President
	Rory	Performing Arts	USA	Actor
Caligiuri	Paul	Sports	USA	Soccer Player - HF
Calisher	Hortense	Creative Works	USA	Author
Callaghan	James	Politics	England	Prime Minister
Callas	Maria Meneghini	Performing Arts	Germany	Singer - Opera
Calles	Plutarco Elías	Politics	Mexico	President
Calloway III	Cabell (Cab)	Performing Arts	USA	Band Leader - Big Band/Jazz - HF
Calvé	Emma	Performing Arts	France	Singer - Opera
Calvin	Melvin	Science	USA	Chemistry - Nobel Laureate
Calvino	Italo	Creative Works	Italy	Author
Camacho	Hector	Sports	USA	Boxer
Cambio	Arnolfo di	Architecture	Italy	Architect/Sculptor
Cameron	Harold Hugh (Harry)	Sports	Canada	Hockey Player - HF
	James	Movie Production	Canada	Director - Academy Award
	Kirk	Performing Arts	USA	Actor
	Richard	Arts	Scotland	Minister/Covenanter
Cammaerts	Émile Léon	Creative Works	Belgium	Poet
Camões	Luiz Vaz de	Creative Works	England	Poet
Camp	Hamilton	Performing Arts	England	Actor
	Rosemary De	Performing Arts	USA	Actress
	Walter Chauncey	Sports	USA	Football Coach
Campanella	Joseph	Performing Arts	USA	Actor
	Roy	Sports	USA	Baseball Player - HF
Campbell	Alexander	Arts	USA	Clergyman
	Avril Phaedra Douglas (Kim)	Politics	Canada	Prime Minister
	Beatrice	Performing Arts	England	Actress
	Ben Nighthorse	Politics	USA	Senator
	Earl Christian	Sports	USA	Football Player - HF
	Glen	Performing Arts	USA	Singer - Country Music - HF
	Joseph	Arts	USA	Philosopher/Author/Editor
	Malcolm	Sports	USA	Race Car Driver - HF
	Mike	Performing Arts	USA	Rock & Roll - HF - Heart Breakers
	Naomi	Performing Arts	England	Super Model
	Neve	Performing Arts	Canada	Actress
	Thomas	Creative Works	Scotland	Poet
	William C. (Bill)	Sports	USA	Golfer - HF
	Oliver Samuel	Sports	USA	Tennis Player - HF
Campbell-Bannerman	Henry	Politics	England	Prime Minister
Campion	Jane	Movie Production	New Zealand	Director - Acad Award Nom
	Thomas	Creative Works	England	Poet/Composer
Camus	Albert	Creative Works	France	Literature - Nobel Laureate
Canadeo	Anthony Robert (Tony)	Sports	USA	Football Player - HF
Canaletto	Antonio	Works of Art	Italy	Painter
Canarray	Martha (Calamity) Jane	Law & Order	USA	Hunter
Canby	Vincent	Creative Works	USA	Journalist - Newspaper
Candela	Felix	Architecture	Spain	Architect
Candler	Asa Griggs	Business	USA	Coca Cola Founder
Candy	John	Performing Arts	Canada	Actor/Comedian
Canella	Guido	Architecture	Italy	Architect
Canetti	Elias	Creative Works	Bulgaria	Literature - Nobel Laureate
Caniff	Milton	Creative Works	USA	Cartoonist - Terry and the Pirates
Canning	Edward	Creative Works	USA	Author - Pulitzer
	George	Politics	England	Prime Minister
Cannon	Dyan	Performing Arts	USA	Actress - Acad Award Nom
	Freddy	Performing Arts	USA	Singer
	Joseph Gurney	Politics	USA	Congressman
Canova	Antonio	Works of Art	Italy	Sculptor
Canseco	José	Sports	USA	Baseball Player
Canto	Miguel	Sports	USA	Boxer - HF
Cantoni	Simone	Architecture	Switzerland	Architect
Cantor	Eddie	Performing Arts	USA	Singer/Actor
Cantrell	Lana	Performing Arts	Australia	Singer

SOLVER SERIES: NAME FINDER

LAST NAME	FIRST NAME	CATEGORY	COUNTRY	FAME
Capablanca	José Raúl	Games	Cuba	Chess Player
Capaldi (Traffic)	Jim	Performing Arts	England	Rock & Roll - HF - Traffic
Čapek	Karel	Creative Works	Czechoslovakia	Playwright/Novelist
Capet	Hugh	Politics	France	King
Capone	Al (Scarface)	Law & Order	USA	Mafia
	Ralph	Law & Order	Italy	Mafia
	Salvatore (Frank)	Law & Order	USA	Mafia
Caponi	Donna	Sports	USA	Golfer - HF
Capote	Truman	Creative Works	USA	Author
Capp	Al	Creative Works	USA	Cartoonist - Lil Abner
Cappelletti	Gino	Sports	USA	Football Player
Capra	Frank	Movie Production	Italy	Director - Academy Award
Capriati	Jennifer	Sports	USA	Tennis Player
Caprio	Leonardo Di	Performing Arts	USA	Actor - Acad Award Nom
Cara	Irene	Performing Arts	USA	Singer/Actress
Caracciola	Rudolf (Rudi)	Sports	Germany	Race Car Driver - HF
Caravaggio	Michaelangelo Amerighi da	Works of Art	Italy	Painter
Cárdenas	Lázaro	Politics	Mexico	President
Cardiff	Jack	Movie Production	England	Director - Acad Award Nom
Cardin	Pierre	Business	France	Fashion Designer
Cardozo	Benjamin Nathan	Law & Order	USA	Justice/Supreme Court
Carducci	Giosuè	Creative Works	Italy	Literature - Nobel Laureate
Carenza	Joseph	Sports	USA	Soccer Player - HF
Carew	Rodney Cline (Rod)	Sports	Panama	Baseball Player - HF
	Thomas	Creative Works	England	Poet
Carey	Duane Gene (Digger)	Aviation	USA	Astronaut
	Ezekiel	Performing Arts	USA	Rock & Roll - HF - The Flamingos
	Harry	Performing Arts	USA	Actor - Acad Award Nom
	Jacob	Performing Arts	USA	Rock & Roll - HF - The Flamingos
	MacDonald	Performing Arts	USA	Actor
	Mariah	Performing Arts	USA	Singer
	Max George	Sports	USA	Baseball Player - HF
Cariou	Len	Performing Arts	Canada	Actor/Singer
Carlile	Richard	Business	England	Publishing
Carlin	George	Performing Arts	USA	Comedian
	Lynn	Performing Arts	USA	Actress - Acad Award Nom
Carlisle	Belinda	Performing Arts	USA	Singer
	Kitty	Performing Arts	USA	Singer
	William Toliver (Bill)	Performing Arts	USA	Singer - Country Music - HF
Carlo	Giancarlo de	Architecture	Italy	Architect
	Yvonne De	Performing Arts	Canada	Actress
Carlos	Don	Politics	Spain	Pretender to Throne
	Roberto	Sports	Brazil	Soccer Player
Carlsson	Arvid	Science	Sweden	Medicine - Nobel Laureate
Carlton	Steven Norman (Steve)	Sports	USA	Baseball Player - HF
Carlyle	Thomas	Creative Works	England	Writer
Carman	William Bliss	Creative Works	Canada	Poet/Journalist
Carmen	Eric	Performing Arts	USA	Singer/Composer
Carmichael	Hoagland Howard (Hoagy)	Creative Works	USA	Composer
	Ian	Performing Arts	England	Actor
Carnap	Rudolf	Arts	Germany	Philosopher
Carne	Judy	Performing Arts	USA	Comedian
Carnegie	Andrew	Business	USA	Industrialist/Philanthropist
Carner	Joanne Gunderson	Sports	USA	Golfer - HF
Carnera	Primo	Sports	Italy	Boxer
Carnes	Kim	Performing Arts	USA	Singer
Carney	Art	Performing Arts	USA	Actor - Academy Award
	Harry	Performing Arts	USA	Jazz Saxophonist - Big Band/Jazz - HF
Carnot	Lazare Nicolas Marguerite	Politics	France	Statesman
	Marie Francois Sadi	Politics	France	President
	Nicolas Léonard Sadi	Science	France	Physicist
Caro	Robert Allan	Creative Works	USA	Author - Pulitzer
Caron	Leslie	Performing Arts	France	Actress - Acad Award Nom

LAST NAME	FIRST NAME	CATEGORY	COUNTRY	FAME
Carpenter	John Alden	Creative Works	USA	Composer
	Karen	Performing Arts	USA	Singer
	Malcolm Scott	Aviation	USA	Astronaut
Carr	Gerald Paul	Aviation	USA	Astronaut
	John Dickson	Creative Works	USA	Novelist - Crime Fiction
	Joseph F. (Joe)	Sports	USA	Football League Administrator - HF
	Vikki	Performing Arts	USA	Singer
Carradine	David	Performing Arts	USA	Actor
	John	Performing Arts	USA	Actor
	Keith	Performing Arts	USA	Actor
Carrafi	Ralph	Sports	USA	Soccer Player - HF
Carranza	Venustiano	Politics	Mexico	President
Carré	John Le	Creative Works	England	Author
	Otis	Performing Arts	USA	Super Model
Carrel	Alexis	Science	France	Medicine - Nobel Laureate
Carreras	José	Performing Arts	Spain	Singer - Opera
Carrere	Tia	Performing Arts	USA	Actress
Carrier	Mark	Sports	USA	Football Player
Carrilo	Leo	Performing Arts	USA	Actor
Carroll	Charles	War & Peace	USA	Revolutionary Leader
	Diahann	Performing Arts	USA	Actress - Acad Award Nom
	John Alexander	Creative Works	USA	Author - Pulitzer
	Leo G.	Performing Arts	England	Actor
	Lewis	Creative Works	England	Author/Mathematician
	Nancy	Performing Arts	USA	Actress - Acad Award Nom
	Pat	Performing Arts	USA	Actress
Carson	Christopher Houston (Kit)	Exploration	USA	Frontiersman - America
	Jack	Performing Arts	Canada	Actor
	Johnny	Performing Arts	USA	Show Host/Comedian
	Rachel Louise	Science	USA	Biologist/Writer
Carter	Alvin Pleasant (A.P.)	Performing Arts	USA	Country Music - HF - Carter Family
	Bennett Lester (Benny)	Performing Arts	USA	Band Leader - Big Band/Jazz - HF
	Gary Edmund	Sports	USA	Baseball Player - HF
	Jack	Performing Arts	USA	Comedian
	James (Jimmy) Earl	Politics	USA	President
	James (Jimmy) Earl	War & Peace	USA	Peace - Nobel Laureate
	Jimmy	Sports	USA	Boxer - HF
	Joe	Sports	USA	Baseball Player
	John E.	Performing Arts	USA	"Rock & Roll - HF - The Flamingos,The Dells"
	June	Performing Arts	USA	Singer
	Lynda	Performing Arts	USA	Actress
	Maybelle Addington	Performing Arts	USA	Country Music - HF - Carter Family
	Nell	Performing Arts	USA	Actress
	Ron	Performing Arts	USA	Jazz Bassist - Big Band/Jazz - HF
	Rosalynn	Politics	USA	First Lady
	Sara Dougherty	Performing Arts	USA	Country Music - HF - Carter Family
	Wilf (Montana Slim)	Performing Arts	Canada	Singer - Canadian Music - HF
Carter (Jones)	Lillie Mae (Betty)	Performing Arts	USA	Jazz Singer - Big Band/Jazz - HF
Carter Jr.	Manley Lanier (Sonny)	Aviation	USA	Astronaut
Carteret	John	Politics	England	Statesman/Diplomat
Cartier	Jacques	Exploration	France	Explorer - St. Lawrence River
Cartwright	Alexander Joy	Sports	USA	Baseball Pioneer - HF
	Edmund	Science	England	Inventor - Power Loom
	John	Politics	England	Reformer
Caruso	Enrico	Performing Arts	Italy	Singer - Opera
Carvel	Tom	Business	USA	Confection Industry - Soft Ice Cream
Carver	George Washington	Science	USA	Botanist/Chemist
	John	Politics	USA	Governor - Plymouth Colony
Carvey	Dana	Performing Arts	USA	Comedian
Casady	Jack	Performing Arts	USA	Rock & Roll - HF - Jefferson Airplane
Casals	Pablo	Creative Works	Spain	Composer/Cellist
	Rosemary (Rosie)	Sports	USA	Tennis Player - HF
Casanova	Giovanni Jacopo	Arts	Italy	Adventurer

LAST NAME	FIRST NAME	CATEGORY	COUNTRY	FAME
Casaubon	Isaac	Arts	France	Theologian
Casement	Roger David	Politics	Ireland	Nationalist
Cash	Fred	Performing Arts	USA	Rock & Roll - HF - The Impressions
	Johnny (John R.)	Performing Arts	USA	Singer - Country Music - HF
	Johnny (John R.)	Performing Arts	USA	Singer - Rock & Roll - HF
	Rosanne	Performing Arts	USA	Singer
Caslon	William	Arts	England	Type Designer
Casper	Billy	Sports	USA	Golfer - HF
	David John (Dave)	Sports	USA	Football Player - HF
Cass	Gilbert	Architecture	USA	Architect - Skyscraper
	Lewis	Politics	USA	Statesman
	Peggy	Performing Arts	USA	Actress - Acad Award Nom
Cassatt	Mary	Works of Art	USA	Painter
Cassavetes	John	Movie Production	USA	Director - Acad Award Nom
	John	Performing Arts	USA	Actor - Acad Award Nom
Cassel	Seymour	Performing Arts	USA	Actor - Acad Award Nom
Cassidy	David	Performing Arts	USA	Singer/Actor
	Shaun	Performing Arts	USA	Actor
Cassidy (Boyd)	William (Hopalong)	Performing Arts	USA	Actor
Cassin	René	War & Peace	France	Peace - Nobel Laureate
Cassini	Oleg	Business	USA	Designer - Fashions
Cassirer	Ernst	Arts	Germany	Philosopher
Casta	Laetitia	Performing Arts	France	Super Model
Castellano	Paul (Big Pauly)	Law & Order	USA	Mafia
	Richard	Performing Arts	USA	Actor - Acad Award Nom
Castiglione	Baldassare	Creative Works	Italy	Writer/Diplomat
Castillo	Bernal Diaz Del	Exploration	Spain	Explorer - Mexico
Castle	Irene	Performing Arts	USA	Actress
	Vernon	Creative Works	England	Writer
Castle-Hughes	Keisha	Performing Arts	Australia	Actress - Acad Award Nom
Castro	Fidel Alejandro	War & Peace	Cuba	Revolutionary Leader - President
Cates	Phoebe	Performing Arts	USA	Actress
Cather	Willa Sibert	Creative Works	USA	Novelist - Pulitzer
Catlin	George	Works of Art	USA	Artist/Ethnologist
Catt	Carrie Chapman	Politics	USA	Leader - Women's Suffrage
Cattaneo	Peter	Movie Production	England	Director - Acad Award Nom
Catton	Bruce (Charles)	Creative Works	USA	Author - Pulitzer
Caudill	William Wayne	Architecture	USA	Architect - AIA Gold Medal
Cava	Gregory La	Movie Production	USA	Director - Acad Award Nom
Cavaliere	Felix	Performing Arts	USA	Rock & Roll - HF - The Young Rascals
Cavell	Edith Louisa	Science	England	Nurse
Cavendish	Henry	Science	England	Physicist/Chemist
Cavett	Dick	Performing Arts	USA	Show Host/Comedian
Caxton	William	Arts	England	Printer
Cech	Thomas R.	Science	USA	Chemistry - Nobel Laureate
Cecil	Robert Gascoyne	War & Peace	England	Peace - Nobel Laureate
Cela	Camilo José	Creative Works	Spain	Literature - Nobel Laureate
Cellini	Benvenuto	Works of Art	Italy	Sculpture/Goldsmith
	Francesco	Architecture	Italy	Architect
Celsius	Anders	Science	Sweden	Inventor - Astronomer
Cenker	Robert Joseph	Aviation	USA	Astronaut
Cepeda	Orlando Manuel	Sports	Puerto Rico	Baseball Player - HF
Cerdan	Marcel (Casablanca Clouter)	Sports	Algeria	Boxer - HF
Cerf	Bennett Alfred	Business	USA	Publishing
	Bennett Alfred	Creative Works	USA	Author
Cermenho	Sebastian	Exploration	Spain	Explorer - California
Cernan	Eugene Andrew	Aviation	USA	Astronaut
Cerruti	Nino	Business	Italy	Fashion Designer
Cervantes	Antonio	Sports	Columbia	Boxer - HF
	Miguel de	Creative Works	Spain	Poet/Novelist/Playwright
Cervi	Alfred N. (Al)	Sports	USA	Basketball Player - HF
Cesariano	Cesare di Lorenzo	Architecture	Italy	Architect
Cetera	Peter	Performing Arts	USA	Singer

LAST NAME	FIRST NAME	CATEGORY	COUNTRY	FAME
Cézanne	Paul	Works of Art	France	Painter - Impressionist
Chabon	Michael	Creative Works	USA	Author - Pulitzer
Chacon	Bobby	Sports	USA	Boxer - HF
Chacurian	Efrain (Chico)	Sports	Argentina	Soccer Player - HF
Chadwick	George White	Creative Works	USA	Composer
	Henry	Sports	England	Baseball Pioneer - HF
	James	Science	England	Physics - Nobel Laureate
Chaffee	Roger Bruce	Aviation	USA	Astronaut
Chagall	Marc	Works of Art	France	Painter/Stained Glass Artist
Chain	Ernst Boris	Science	England	Medicine - Nobel Laureate
Chakiris	George	Performing Arts	USA	Actor - Academy Award
Chaliapin	Feodor Ivanovich	Performing Arts	Russia	Singer - Opera
Chamberlain	Arthur Neville	Politics	England	Prime Minister
	Joseph Austen	Politics	England	Statesman
	Joseph Austen	War & Peace	England	Peace - Nobel Laureate
	Owen	Science	USA	Physics - Nobel Laureate
	Richard	Performing Arts	USA	Actor
	Wilton M. (Wilt)	Sports	USA	Basketball Player - HF
Chamberlin	Berlin Guy	Sports	USA	Football Player - HF
	Thomas Chrowder	Science	USA	Geologist
Chambers	Martin	Performing Arts	England	Rock & Roll - HF - The Pretenders
	Paul Laurence	Performing Arts	USA	Jazz Bassist - Big Band/Jazz - HF
Champion	Gower	Creative Works	USA	Choreographer
	Marge	Performing Arts	USA	Actress/Dancer
Champlain	Samuel de	Exploration	France	Explorer - Quebec
Champollion	Jean François	Arts	France	Egyptologist
Chance	Dean	Sports	USA	Baseball Player
	Frank Leroy	Sports	USA	Baseball Player - HF
	Malcolm Greene	Sports	USA	Tennis Player - HF
Chancellor	John	Creative Works	USA	Journalist - Television
Chandler	Albert Benjamin (Happy)	Sports	USA	Baseball Commissioner - HF
	Alfred D.	Creative Works	USA	Author - Pulitzer
	Bryan James (Chas)	Performing Arts	England	Rock & Roll - HF - The Animals
	Gene	Performing Arts	USA	Singer
	Jeff	Performing Arts	USA	Actor - Academy Award
	Jeff	Sports	USA	Boxer - HF
	Raymond	Creative Works	USA	Novelist - Crime Fiction
Chandrasekhar	Subramanyan	Science	USA	Physics - Nobel Laureate
Chanel	Coco	Business	France	Fashion Designer
	Gabrielle	Business	France	Fashion Designer
Chaney	Lon	Performing Arts	USA	Actor
Chaney Jr.	Lon	Performing Arts	USA	Actor
Chang	Michael	Sports	USA	Tennis Player
Channing	Carol	Performing Arts	USA	Actress - Acad Award Nom
	Stockard	Performing Arts	USA	Actress - Acad Award Nom
	William Ellery	Politics	USA	Social Critic
Chao	Rosalind	Performing Arts	USA	Actress
Chapin	Harry	Performing Arts	USA	Singer
Chaplin	Charles	Movie Production	England	Director - Academy Award
	Charly (Charles)	Performing Arts	England	Actor - Academy Award
Chaplin (O'Neill)	Oona	Performing Arts	USA	Actress
Chapman	Anthony Colin Bruce	Sports	England	Race Car Designer - HF
	George	Creative Works	England	Playwright
	Graham	Performing Arts	England	Comedian
	John (Johnny Appleseed)	Exploration	USA	Frontiersman - America
	Philip Kenyon	Aviation	USA	Astronaut
	Tracy	Performing Arts	USA	Singer
Charcot	Jean Martin	Science	France	Neurologist
Chardin	Jean Baptiste Siméon	Works of Art	France	Painter
	Pierre Teilhard de	Arts	France	Philosopher/Geologist/Jesuit
Charen	Mona	Creative Works	USA	Jounalist - Newspaper
Charisse	Cyd	Performing Arts	USA	Actress/Dancer
Charles	Bob	Sports	New Zealand	Golfer

SOLVER SERIES: NAME FINDER

LAST NAME	FIRST NAME	CATEGORY	COUNTRY	FAME
Charles	Ezzard	Sports	USA	Boxer - HF
	John	Sports	Wales	Soccer Player - HF
Charles (Robinson)	Ray	Performing Arts	USA	Singer - Rock & Roll - HF
	Ray	Performing Arts	USA	Singer/Pianist - Big Band/Jazz - HF
Charleston	Oscar McKinley	Sports	USA	Baseball Player - HF
Charlevoix	Pierre François-Xavier	Exploration	France	Explorer - Mississippi River
Charlton	Bobby	Sports	England	Soccer Player - HF
Charo	Maria	Performing Arts	Spain	Singer
Charpak	Georges	Science	France	Physics - Nobel Laureate
Charpentier	Gustave	Creative Works	France	Composer
Chartrier	Philippe	Sports	France	Tennis Player - HF
Chase	Chevy	Performing Arts	USA	Actor/Comedian
	Ilka	Performing Arts	USA	Actress
	Mary	Creative Works	USA	Dramatist - Pulitzer
	Salmon Portland	Law & Order	USA	Chief Justice
	Samuel	Law & Order	USA	Justice/Supreme Court
Chast	Roz	Creative Works	USA	Cartoonist - New Yorker
Chatterton	Ruth	Performing Arts	USA	Actress - Acad Award Nom
	Thomas	Creative Works	England	Poet
Chaucer	Geoffrey	Creative Works	England	Poet
Chauvin	Yves	Science	France	Chemistry - Nobel Laureate
Chavannes	Pierre Puvis de	Works of Art	France	Painter
Chavez	Cesar Estrada	Business	USA	Union Leader
	Julio Cesar	Sports	USA	Boxer
Chawla	Kalpana	Aviation	USA	Astronaut
Cheadle	Don	Performing Arts	USA	Actor - Acad Award Nom
Checker	Chubby	Performing Arts	USA	Singer
Cheever	John	Creative Works	USA	Author - Pulitzer
Cheevers	Gerald Michael (Gerry)	Sports	Canada	Hockey Player - HF
Chekhov	Anton Pavlovich	Creative Works	Russia	Writer/Dramatist
	Michael	Performing Arts	Russia	Actor - Acad Award Nom
Cheli	Maurizio	Aviation	Italy	Astronaut
Cheney	Dorothy (Dodo)	Sports	USA	Tennis Player - HF
	Richard	Politics	USA	Vice-President
Chénier	André	Creative Works	France	Poet
Cherenkov	Pavel Aleksevevich	Science	Russia	Physics - Nobel Laureate
Cherry	Don	Performing Arts	USA	Jazz Trumpeter - Big Band/Jazz - HF
Cherubini	Luigi	Creative Works	Italy	Composer
Chesbro	John Dwight (Happy Jack)	Sports	USA	Baseball Player - HF
Chesney	Stanley	Sports	USA	Soccer Player - HF
Chesterton	Gilbert Keith	Creative Works	England	Writer
Chevalier	Maurice	Performing Arts	France	Actor - Acad Award Nom
Chevrolet	Louis	Sports	Switzerland	Race Car Driver - HF
Chiang Kaishek	Chung Chen	Politics	China	Head of Government
Chiattone	Mario	Architecture	Switzerland	Architect/Painter
Ch'ien	Chang	Exploration	China	Explorer - Central Asia
Chikatilo	Andrei Romanovich	Law & Order	Ukraine	Serial Killer
Child	Paul	Sports	England	Soccer Player - HF
Childers	Erskine Hamilton	Politics	Ireland	President
	Francis James	Arts	USA	Scholar
Chiles	Lois	Performing Arts	USA	Actress
Chilton	Kevin Patrick (Chili)	Aviation	USA	Astronaut
Chimes	Terry	Performing Arts	England	Rock & Roll - HF - The Clash
Chinaglia	Giorgio	Sports	Italy	Soccer Player - HF
Chippendale	Thomas	Arts	England	Furniture Designer
Chirico	Giorgio	Works of Art	Italy	Painter
Choate	Rufus	Law & Order	USA	Lawyer
Chomsky	Avram Noam	Arts	USA	Linguist
Chong	Rae Dawn	Performing Arts	Canada	Actress
	Tommy	Performing Arts	Canada	Comedian
Chopin	Frederic François	Creative Works	Poland	Composer
Chou	En-Lai	Politics	China	Prime Minister
Chouteau	August	Business	USA	Fur Trade

LAST NAME	FIRST NAME	CATEGORY	COUNTRY	FAME
Chrétien	Jean Joseph Jacques	Politics	Canada	Prime Minister
	Jean-Loup Jacques Marie	Aviation	France	Astronaut
Christensen	Helena	Performing Arts	Denmark	Super Model
	Todd	Sports	USA	Football Player
Christian	Charles Henry (Charlie)	Performing Arts	USA	Jazz Guitarist - Big Band/Jazz - HF
	Charles Henry (Charlie)	Performing Arts	USA	Singer - Rock & Roll - HF
Christiansen	John Leroy (Jack)	Sports	USA	Football Player - HF
Christie	Agatha	Creative Works	England	Writer
	Julie	Performing Arts	India	Actress - Academy Award
	Lou	Performing Arts	USA	Singer
Christophe	Henri	Politics	Haiti	King
Christopher	Warren	Politics	USA	Secretary of State
	William	Performing Arts	USA	Actor
Christy	Howard Chandler	Works of Art	USA	Painter/Illustrator
Chu	Steven	Science	USA	Physics - Nobel Laureate
Chung	Connie	Creative Works	USA	Journalist - Television
Church	Frederick	Works of Art	USA	Painter - Landscape
	Thomas Haden	Performing Arts	USA	Actor - Acad Award Nom
Churchill	John	Politics	England	Duke
	Randolph Henry Spencer	Politics	England	Statesman
	Winston	Creative Works	USA	Novelist
	Winston Leonard Spencer	Creative Works	England	Literature - Nobel Laureate
	Winston Leonard Spencer	Politics	England	Prime Minister
Chylak Jr.	Nestor	Sports	USA	Baseball Umpire - HF
Ciardi	John	Creative Works	USA	Poet
Ciechanover	Aaron	Science	Israel	Chemistry - Nobel Laureate
Cierpinski	Waldemar	Sports	Germany	Olympic Marathoner
Cilea	Francesco	Performing Arts	Italy	Singer/Composer
Cilento	Diane	Performing Arts	New Guinea	Actress - Acad Award Nom
Cimabue	Giovanni	Works of Art	Italy	Painter/Artist
Cimino	Michael	Movie Production	USA	Director - Academy Award
Cioran	Émile Michel	Arts	France	Philosopher
Claiborne	Liz	Business	USA	Fashion Designer
Clair	René	Movie Production	France	Director
Claire	Ina	Performing Arts	USA	Actress
Clancy	Francis M. (King)	Sports	Canada	Hockey Player - HF
Clancy Jr.	Thomas L. (Tom)	Creative Works	USA	Author
Clapp	Margaret	Creative Works	USA	Author - Pulitzer
Clapper	Aubrey V. (Dit)	Sports	Canada	Hockey Player - HF
Clapton	Eric Patrick	Performing Arts	England	"Rock & Roll - HF - Cream,Yardbirds"
Clark	Candy	Performing Arts	USA	Actress - Acad Award Nom
	Charles Joseph	Politics	Canada	Prime Minister
	Clarence Munroe	Sports	USA	Tennis Player - HF
	Cyrus	Business	USA	Entrepreneur
	Dane	Performing Arts	USA	Actor
	Dick	Performing Arts	USA	Producer
	Earl Harry (Dutch)	Sports	USA	Football Player - HF
	Gary	Sports	USA	Football Player
	Gene (Harold Eugene)	Performing Arts	USA	Rock & Roll - HF - The Bryds
	George Rogers	War & Peace	USA	Revolutionary Leader
	Joseph Sill	Sports	USA	Tennis Player - HF
	Laurel Blair Salton	Aviation	USA	Astronaut
	Mary Higgins	Creative Works	USA	Novelist
	Petula	Performing Arts	England	Singer
	Roy	Performing Arts	USA	Singer
	Susan	Performing Arts	Canada	Actress
	Terri	Performing Arts	Canada	Singer - Country Music
	Tom Campbell	Law & Order	USA	Justice/Supreme Court
	Will	Sports	USA	Baseball Player
	William	Exploration	USA	Explorer - Missouri River
Clark Jr.	James (Jimmy)	Sports	Scotland	Race Car Driver - HF
Clarke	Arthur Charles	Creative Works	England	Author - SciFi
	Fred Clifford	Sports	USA	Baseball Player - HF

SOLVER SERIES: NAME FINDER

LAST NAME	FIRST NAME	CATEGORY	COUNTRY	FAME
Clarke	Mae	Performing Arts	USA	Actress
	Michael (Mike)	Performing Arts	USA	Rock & Roll - HF - The Bryds
	Robert Earle (Bobby)	Sports	Canada	Hockey Player - HF
Clarke (Spearman)	Kenny (Kenneth)	Performing Arts	USA	Band Leader - Big Band/Jazz - HF
Clarkson	John Gibson	Sports	USA	Baseball Player - HF
	Patricia	Performing Arts	USA	Actress - Acad Award Nom
Clary	Robert	Performing Arts	France	Actor
Claude	Albert	Science	Belgium	Medicine - Nobel Laureate
Claudel	Aurelie	Performing Arts	France	Super Model
	Paul Louis Charles	Creative Works	France	Poet/Playwright
Clavell	James du Maresqu	Creative Works	Australia	Author
Clavijo	Fernando	Sports	Uruguay	Soccer Player - HF
Clay	Henry	Politics	USA	Statesman/Orator
Clayburgh	Jill	Performing Arts	USA	Actress - Acad Award Nom
Clayton	Adam	Performing Arts	England	Rock & Roll - HF - U2
	Jack	Movie Production	England	Director - Acad Award Nom
	Mark	Sports	USA	Football Player
Clayton-Thomas	David Henry	Performing Arts	England	Singer - Canadian Music - HF
Cleave	John	Business	England	Publishing
Cleese	John	Performing Arts	England	Actor
Cleghorn	Sprague	Sports	Canada	Hockey Player - HF
Clemenceau	Georges Benjamin Eugéne	Politics	France	Premier
Clemens	Roger	Sports	USA	Baseball Player
	Samuel Langhorne	Creative Works	USA	Writer/Humorist
Clemente	Roberto	Sports	Puerto Rico	Baseball Player - HF
Clervoy	Jean-François André	Aviation	France	Astronaut
Cleveland	Frances	Politics	USA	First Lady
	Stephen Grover	Politics	USA	President
Clews	Henry	Business	USA	Financier
Cliburn	Van	Performing Arts	USA	Pianist
Clifford	Michael Richard Uram	Aviation	USA	Astronaut
	William K.	Arts	England	Philosopher/Mathematician
Clift	Montgomery	Performing Arts	USA	Actor - Acad Award Nom
Cline (Hensley)	Virginia Patterson (Patsy)	Performing Arts	USA	Singer - Country Music - HF
Clinton	DeWitt	Politics	USA	Governor - New York
	George	Politics	USA	Vice-President
	Hillary	Politics	USA	First Lady
	William Jefferson	Politics	USA	President
Clive	Robert	Politics	England	Statesman
Clooney	George	Performing Arts	USA	Actor
	Rosemary	Performing Arts	USA	Singer/Actress
Close	Glenn	Performing Arts	USA	Actress - Acad Award Nom
Clothier	William Jackson	Sports	USA	Tennis Player - HF
Clouet	François	Works of Art	France	Painter - Portraits
	Jean	Works of Art	France	Painter - Portraits
Clough	Arthur Hugh	Creative Works	England	Poet
Coase	Ronald H.	Arts	England	Economics - Nobel Laureate
Coates	Eric	Creative Works	England	Composer
Coats	Michael Lloyd	Aviation	USA	Astronaut
Cobb	Lee J.	Performing Arts	USA	Actor - Acad Award Nom
	Tyrus Raymond (Ty)	Sports	USA	Baseball Player - HF
Cobbett	William	Business	England	Publishing
	William	Creative Works	England	Journalist/Reformer
Coburn	Charles	Performing Arts	England	Actor - Academy Award
	Donald L.	Creative Works	USA	Dramatist - Pulitzer
	James	Performing Arts	USA	Actor - Academy Award
Coca	Imogene	Performing Arts	USA	Actress
Cochet	Henri Jean	Sports	France	Tennis Player - HF
Cochran	Edward Ray (Eddie)	Performing Arts	USA	Singer - Rock & Roll - HF
Cochrane	Gordon Stanley (Mickey)	Sports	USA	Baseball Player - HF
	Tom	Performing Arts	Canada	Singer/Song Writer - Canadian Music - HF
Cockburn	Bruce	Performing Arts	Canada	Singer/Guitarist - Canadian Music - HF
Cockcroft	John Douglas	Science	England	Physics - Nobel Laureate

LAST NAME	FIRST NAME	CATEGORY	COUNTRY	FAME
Cocker	Joe	Performing Arts	England	Singer
Cockerham	Chuck	Performing Arts	USA	Rock & Roll - HF - The Drifters
Coco	James	Performing Arts	USA	Actor - Acad Award Nom
Cocteau	Jean	Creative Works	France	Poet/Novelist/Playwright
	Jean	Movie Production	France	Director
Codarini	Corrado (Connie)	Performing Arts	Canada	Canadian Music - HF - The Four Lads
Cody	William (Buffalo Bill)	Law & Order	USA	Hunter/Scout/Indian Fighter
	William Frederick	Exploration	USA	Frontiersman - America
Coe	Sebastian Newbold	Sports	England	Olympic Runner
Coen	Ethan	Movie Production	USA	Director
	Joel	Movie Production	USA	Director - Acad Award Nom
Coetzee	John M.	Creative Works	South Africa	Literature - Nobel Laureate
Coffey	Paul Douglas	Sports	Canada	Hockey Player - HF
Coffin	Robert P. Tristram	Creative Works	USA	Poet - Pulitzer
Cohan	George Michael	Performing Arts	USA	Actor/Playwright/Producer
Cohen	Andrew	Arts	USA	Philosopher
	Leonard	Creative Works	Canada	Poet/Song Writer
	Leonard	Performing Arts	Canada	Singer/Composer - Canadian Music - HF
	Morris Raphael	Arts	USA	Philosopher
	Myron	Performing Arts	Poland	Comedian
	Sasha	Sports	USA	Olympic Skater
	Stanley	Science	USA	Medicine - Nobel Laureate
	William S.	Politics	USA	Secretary of Defense
Cohen-Tannoudji	Claude	Science	France	Physics - Nobel Laureate
Cohn	Ferdinand Julius	Science	Germany	Botanist/Bacteriologist
	Marc	Performing Arts	USA	Singer/Song Writer
	Roy	Law & Order	USA	Lawyer - Mafia
Coimbra	Artur Antunes (Zico)	Sports	Brazil	Soccer Player - HF
Coit	Margaret Louise	Creative Works	USA	Author - Pulitzer
Coke	Edward	Politics	England	Statesman/Jurist
Cokes	Curtis	Sports	USA	Boxer - HF
Colbert	Caudette	Performing Arts	France	Actress - Academy Award
	Jean Baptiste	Politics	France	Statesman
	Jim	Sports	USA	Golfer
Cole	Cozy	Performing Arts	USA	Jazz Drummer
	Kenneth	Business	USA	Fashion Designer
	Natalie	Performing Arts	USA	Singer
	Nathaniel (Nat King)	Performing Arts	USA	Singer - Rock & Roll - HF
	Nathaniel (Nat King)	Performing Arts	USA	Singer/Musician - Big Band/Jazz - HF
	Thomas	Works of Art	USA	Painter
Coleman	Cy	Creative Works	USA	Composer
	Dabney	Performing Arts	USA	Actor
	Gary	Performing Arts	USA	Actor
	Ornette	Performing Arts	USA	Jazz Saxophonist - Big Band/Jazz - HF
Coleridge	Samuel Taylor	Arts	England	Philosopher/Lyrical Poet/Critic
Coles	Neil	Sports	England	Golfer - HF
	Robert	Creative Works	USA	Author - Pulitzer
Colette	John	Arts	England	Theologian
	Sidonie Gabrielle Claudine	Creative Works	France	Novelist
Colfax	Schuyler	Politics	USA	Vice-President
Colgate	William	Business	USA	Industrialist - Soap
Coligny	Gaspard de	War & Peace	France	Admiral
Coll	Steve	Creative Works	USA	Novelist - Pulitzer
Collette	Toni	Performing Arts	Australia	Actress - Acad Award Nom
Collinge	Patricia	Performing Arts	Ireland	Actress - Acad Award Nom
Collingwood	Robin George	Arts	England	Philosopher/Historian
Collins	Jackie	Creative Works	England	Novelist
	James Joseph (Jimmy)	Sports	USA	Baseball Player - HF
	Joan	Performing Arts	England	Actress
	Judy	Performing Arts	USA	Singer
	Michael	Aviation	USA	Astronaut
	Michael	War & Peace	Ireland	Revolutionary Leader
	Pauline	Performing Arts	England	Actress - Acad Award Nom

SOLVER SERIES: NAME FINDER

LAST NAME	FIRST NAME	CATEGORY	COUNTRY	FAME
Collins	Phil	Performing Arts	England	Singer/Composer
	William	Creative Works	England	Poet
	William Wilkie	Creative Works	England	Novelist
Collins Jr.	Arthur Worth (Bud)	Sports	USA	Tennis Player - HF
Collins Sr.	Edward Trowbridge (Eddie)	Sports	USA	Baseball Player - HF
Colman	Ronald	Performing Arts	England	Actor - Academy Award
Colombo	Charles Martin (Charlie)	Sports	USA	Soccer Player - HF
	Joseph	Law & Order	USA	Mafia
Colt	Samuel	Science	USA	Inventor - Revolver
Colter	Jessi	Performing Arts	USA	Actor
Coltrane	John	Performing Arts	USA	Jazz Saxophonist - Big Band/Jazz - HF
Columbo	Padraic	Creative Works	Ireland	Poet/Playwright
	Russ	Performing Arts	USA	Singer/Violinist/Actor
Columbus	Christopher	Exploration	Italy	Explorer - Caribbean
Colville	Neil McNeil	Sports	Canada	Hockey Player - HF
Colvin	Douglas Glenn (Dee Dee)	Performing Arts	Germany	Rock & Roll - HF - The Ramones
Comaneci	Nadia	Sports	Romania	Olympic Gymnast
Combs	Earle Bryan	Sports	USA	Baseball Player - HF
Comines	Phillipe de	Arts	France	Historian/Diplomat
Comiskey	Charles Albert (Charlie)	Sports	USA	Baseball Executive -HF
Como	Pierino Ronald (Perry)	Performing Arts	USA	Singer - Big Band/Jazz - HF
Compson	Betty	Performing Arts	USA	Actress - Acad Award Nom
Compton	Arthur Holly	Science	USA	Physics - Nobel Laureate
	Karl Taylor	Science	USA	Physicist
Compton-Burnett	Ivy	Creative Works	England	Novelist
Comte	Auguste	Arts	France	Philosopher
Conacher	Charles William (Charlie)	Sports	Canada	Hockey Player - HF
	Lionel Pretoria	Sports	Canada	Hockey Player - HF
	Roy Gordon	Sports	Canada	Hockey Player - HF
Conant	James Bryant	Science	USA	Chemist/Educator
Condamine	Charles Marie de la	Exploration	France	Explorer - Amazon Region
Condillac	Étienne Bonnot de	Arts	France	Philosopher
Condon	Albert Edwin (Eddie)	Performing Arts	USA	Band Leader - Big Band/Jazz - HF
	Edward Uhler	Science	USA	Physicist
Cone	David	Sports	USA	Baseball Player
Congreve	William	Creative Works	England	Playwright
Conlan	John Bertrand (Jocko)	Sports	USA	Baseball Umpire - HF
Conn	Billy	Sports	USA	Boxer - HF
	Didi	Performing Arts	USA	Actress
Connell	Alex	Sports	Canada	Hockey Player - HF
Connelly	Jennifer	Performing Arts	USA	Actress - Academy Award
	Markus Cook (Marc)	Creative Works	USA	Dramatist - Pulitzer
Conner	Bart	Sports	USA	Olympic Gymnast
Connery	Sean	Performing Arts	Scotland	Actor - Academy Award
Connick Jr.	Harry	Performing Arts	USA	Singer
Conniff	Ray	Performing Arts	USA	Band Leader/Trombonist
Connolly	Maureen Catherine (Little Mo)	Sports	USA	Tennis Player - HF
	Thomas Henry (Tom)	Sports	USA	Baseball Umpire - HF
	William (Billy)	Performing Arts	Scotland	Comedian
Connor	George Leo	Sports	USA	Football Player - HF
	Roger	Sports	USA	Baseball Player - HF
Connors	Chuck	Performing Arts	USA	Actor
	James Scott (Jimmy)	Sports	USA	Tennis Player - HF
	Mike	Performing Arts	USA	Actor
Conrad	Joseph	Creative Works	Ukraine	Novelist/Short Story Writer
	Robert	Performing Arts	USA	Actor
	William	Performing Arts	USA	Actor
Conrad Jr.	Charles Peter	Aviation	USA	Astronaut
Conried	Hans	Performing Arts	USA	Actor
Conroy	Pat	Creative Works	USA	Novelist
Constable	John	Works of Art	England	Painter - Landscapes
Constant	Benjamin	Creative Works	France	Writer/Politician
	Paul Henri d'Estournelles de	War & Peace	France	Peace - Nobel Laureate

LAST NAME	FIRST NAME	CATEGORY	COUNTRY	FAME
Conte	Richard	Performing Arts	USA	Actor
Conti	Tom	Performing Arts	Scotland	Actor - Acad Award Nom
Conway	Tim	Performing Arts	USA	Comedian
Conzelman	James Gleason (Jimmy)	Sports	USA	Football Player - HF
Coogan	Jackie	Performing Arts	USA	Actor
Cook	Frederick Joseph (Bun)	Sports	Canada	Hockey Player - HF
	James	Exploration	England	Explorer - Arctic/Australia
	Jeff	Performing Arts	USA	Country Music - HF - Alabama
	John	Sports	USA	Golfer
	Peter	Performing Arts	England	Comedian
	Thomas	Business	England	Travel Industry
	William (Bill)	Sports	Canada	Hockey Player - HF
Cooke	Alistair	Creative Works	England	Journalist - Television
	Samuel	Performing Arts	USA	Singer - Rock & Roll - HF
Coolidge	Grace Anna	Politics	USA	First Lady
	John Calvin	Politics	USA	President
	Rita	Performing Arts	USA	Singer
Coombes	Geoff	Sports	England	Soccer Player - HF
Coombs	Earle	Sports	USA	Baseball Player
Cooper	Alice	Performing Arts	USA	Singer
	Ashley John	Sports	Australia	Tennis Player - HF
	Charles T. (Tarzan)	Sports	USA	Basketball Player - HF
	Chris	Performing Arts	USA	Actor - Academy Award
	Gary	Performing Arts	USA	Actor - Academy Award
	Gladys	Performing Arts	England	Actress - Acad Award Nom
	Harry	Sports	England	Golfer - HF
	Jackie	Performing Arts	USA	Actor - Acad Award Nom
	James Fenimore	Creative Works	USA	Novelist
	Leon Neil	Science	USA	Physics - Nobel Laureate
	Leroy Gordon	Aviation	USA	Astronaut
	Peter	Business	USA	Steel Industry/Philanthropy
Copeland	Stewart	Performing Arts	USA	Rock & Roll - HF - The Police
Copernicus	Nicholas	Science	Poland	Astronomer
Copland	Aaron	Creative Works	USA	Composer
Copley	John Singleton	Works of Art	USA	Painter
Coppola	Francis Ford	Movie Production	USA	Director - Academy Award
	Sofia	Movie Production	USA	Director - Acad Award Nom
Coquelin	Benoit Constant	Performing Arts	France	Actor
Corbett	James J.	Sports	USA	Boxer - HF
Corbusier	Charles Edouard le	Architecture	Switzerland	Architect - AIA Gold Medal
Corby	Ellen	Performing Arts	USA	Actress - Acad Award Nom
Corcoran	Fred	Sports	USA	Golfer - HF
Cord	Alex	Performing Arts	USA	Actor
Corday	Marie Anne Charlotte	Politics	France	Girondist
Córdoba	Francisco Fernández de	Exploration	Spain	Explorer - Mexico
Corea	Armando Anthony (Chick)	Performing Arts	USA	Jazz Pianist
Corelli	Arcangelo	Creative Works	Italy	Composer/Violinist
Corey	Elias James	Science	USA	Chemistry - Nobel Laureate
	Wendell	Performing Arts	USA	Actor
Cori	Carl Ferdinand	Science	USA	Medicine - Nobel Laureate
	Gerty	Science	USA	Medicine - Nobel Laureate
Cormack	Allan M.	Science	USA	Medicine - Nobel Laureate
Corman	Roger	Movie Production	USA	Director
Corneille	Pierre	Creative Works	France	Dramatist
Cornell	Eric A.	Science	USA	Physics - Nobel Laureate
	Ezra	Business	USA	Capitalist/Philanthropist
	Katharine	Performing Arts	USA	Actress
Cornforth	John Warcup	Science	Australia	Chemistry - Nobel Laureate
Cornish	Gene	Performing Arts	Canada	Rock & Roll - HF - The Young Rascals
Cornwallis	Charles	War & Peace	England	General
Coronado	Francisco Vásquez de	Exploration	Spain	Explorer - Mexico
Corot	Jean-Baptiste Camille	Works of Art	France	Painter
Correggio	Antonio Allegri de	Works of Art	Italy	Painter

SOLVER SERIES: NAME FINDER

LAST NAME	FIRST NAME	CATEGORY	COUNTRY	FAME
Corrigan	Mairead	War & Peace	England	Peace - Nobel Laureate
Corte Real	Gaspar	Exploration	Portugal	Explorer - Greenland
Cortés	Hernán	Exploration	Spain	Explorer - Mexico
	Hernando	War & Peace	Spain	Military Leader
Cortese	Valentina	Performing Arts	Italy	Actress - Acad Award Nom
Cortona	Domenico da	Architecture	Italy	Architect
	Pietro da	Architecture	Italy	Architect
Coryate	Thomas	Creative Works	England	Writer
Cosby	Bill	Performing Arts	USA	Comedian
Cosell	Howard	Creative Works	USA	Journalist - Television
Cosgrave	Liam	Politics	Ireland	Prime Minister
Cosic	Kresimir	Sports	Croatia	Basketball Player - HF
Costa	Lucio	Architecture	Brazil	Architect/Planner/Author
Costain	Thomas	Creative Works	Canada	Novelist - Historical
Costas	Bob	Creative Works	USA	Journalist - Television
Costello	Francesco (Frank)	Law & Order	Italy	Mafia
	Lou	Performing Arts	USA	Comedian
	Murray	Sports	Canada	Hockey Player - HF
Costello (MacManus)	Declan Patrick (Elvis)	Performing Arts	England	Rock & Roll - HF - The Attractions
Costner	Kevin	Movie Production	USA	Director - Academy Award
	Kevin	Performing Arts	USA	Actor - Acad Award Nom
Cotton	Henry	Sports	England	Golfer - HF
	John	Arts	USA	Clergyman - Puritan
	Joseph	Performing Arts	USA	Actor
Coty	René	Politics	France	President
Coulter	Arthur Edmund (Art)	Sports	Canada	Hockey Player - HF
Couperin	François	Creative Works	France	Composer/Organist
Couples	Fred	Sports	USA	Golfer
Courbet	Gustave	Works of Art	France	Painter
Couric	Katie	Creative Works	USA	Journalist - Television
Courier	Jim	Sports	USA	Tennis Player - HF
Cournand	Andre Frédéric	Science	USA	Medicine - Nobel Laureate
Cournoyer	Yvan Serge (Roadrunner)	Sports	Canada	Hockey Player - HF
Court	Margaret Smith	Sports	Australia	Tennis Player
Courtauld	George	Business	England	Textile Industry
	Samuel	Business	England	Textile Industry
Courtenay	Bryce	Creative Works	South Africa	Author
	Tom	Performing Arts	England	Actor - Acad Award Nom
Cousin	Victor	Arts	France	Philosopher
Cousins	Norman	Creative Works	USA	Journalist - Magazine
Cousteau	Jaques	Exploration	France	Explorer - Marine
Cousy	Robert J. (Bob)	Sports	USA	Basketball Player - HF
Coutts	Thomas	Business	England	Entrepreneur
Coveleski	Stanley Anthony (Stan)	Sports	USA	Baseball Player - HF
Coverdale	Miles	Arts	England	Clergyman - Translator
Covey	Richard Oswalt	Aviation	USA	Astronaut
Coward	Noel	Performing Arts	England	Actor/Playwright
Cowell	Henry Dixon	Creative Works	USA	Composer
Cowens	David W. (Dave)	Sports	USA	Basketball Player - HF
Cowley	Abraham	Creative Works	England	Poet/Essayist
	William Mailes (Bill)	Sports	Canada	Hockey Player - HF
Cowper	William	Creative Works	England	Poet
Cox	Courtenay	Performing Arts	USA	Actress
	Wally	Performing Arts	USA	Comedian
Cozzens	James Gould	Creative Works	USA	Novelist - Pulitzer
Crabbe	Buster	Performing Arts	USA	Actor
	George	Creative Works	England	Poet
Craddock	Robert W.	Sports	USA	Soccer Player - HF
Craig	Roger	Sports	USA	Football Player
Craigie	William Alexander	Arts	England	Lexicographer
Crain	Jeanne	Performing Arts	USA	Actress - Acad Award Nom
Cram	Donald J.	Science	USA	Chemistry - Nobel Laureate
	Ralph Adams	Architecture	USA	Architect/Writer

LAST NAME	FIRST NAME	CATEGORY	COUNTRY	FAME
Cramer	Floyd	Performing Arts	USA	Singer - Country Music - HF
	Floyd	Performing Arts	USA	Singer - Rock & Roll - HF
Cramm	Gottfried Von (The Baron)	Sports	Germany	Tennis Player - HF
Crampton	Bruce	Sports	Australia	Golfer
Cranach	Lucas	Works of Art	Germany	Painter/Engraver
Crane	Bob	Performing Arts	USA	Actor
	Harold Hart	Creative Works	USA	Poet
	Stephen	Creative Works	USA	Novelist
Cranmer	Thomas	Arts	England	Archbishop
Cranston	Alan	Politics	USA	Senator
Crashaw	Richard	Creative Works	England	Poet - Religion
Craven	Wes	Creative Works	USA	Novelist
Crawford	Broderick	Performing Arts	USA	Actor - Academy Award
	Cindy	Performing Arts	USA	Super Model
	Joan	Performing Arts	USA	Actress - Academy Award
	John Herbert (Gentleman Jack)	Sports	Australia	Tennis Player - HF
	Michael	Performing Arts	England	Actor
	Samuel Earl (Sam)	Sports	USA	Baseball Player - HF
	Samuel Russell (Rusty)	Sports	Canada	Hockey Player - HF
	Joan	Sports	USA	Basketball Player - HF
Creach	John (Papa)	Performing Arts	USA	Rock & Roll - HF - Jefferson Airplane
Creekmur	Louis (Lou)	Sports	USA	Football Player - HF
Creighton	John Oliver	Aviation	USA	Astronaut
Cremer	William Randal	War & Peace	England	Peace - Nobel Laureate
Cremin	Lawrence A.	Creative Works	USA	Author - Pulitzer
Crenna	Richard	Performing Arts	USA	Actor
Crenshaw	Ben	Sports	USA	Golfer - HF
Cret	Paul Phillippe	Architecture	USA	Architect - AIA Gold Medal
Crèvecoeur	Michel Guillaume Jean de	Creative Works	France	Essayist
Crewe	Bob	Performing Arts	USA	Rock & Roll - HF - The Four Seasons
Crichton	Charles	Movie Production	England	Director - Acad Award Nom
	Michael	Creative Works	USA	Author
Crick	Francis Harry Compton	Science	England	Medicine - Nobel Laureate
Crippen	Robert Laurel	Aviation	USA	Astronaut
Crisp	Donald	Performing Arts	England	Actor - Academy Award
	Quentin	Creative Works	England	Author
Crispi	Francesco	Politics	Italy	Prime Minister
Crist	Judith	Creative Works	USA	Journalist - Newspaper
Cristofer	Michael	Creative Works	USA	Dramatist - Pulitzer
Croce	Benedetto	Arts	Italy	Philosopher/Critic
	Jim	Performing Arts	USA	Singer
Croci	Antonio	Architecture	Switzerland	Architect
Crockett	David (Davie)	Exploration	USA	Frontiersman - America
Crompton	Samuel	Science	England	Inventor - Spinning Mule
Cromwell	James	Performing Arts	USA	Actor - Acad Award Nom
	Oliver	Politics	England	Revolutionary Leader
	Oliver	War & Peace	England	Military Leader
	Richard	Politics	England	Protector - Commonwealth
	Thomas	Politics	England	Statesman
Cronin	James Watson	Science	USA	Physics - Nobel Laureate
	Joseph Edward (Joe)	Sports	USA	Baseball Player - HF
Cronkite	Walter	Creative Works	USA	Journalist - Newspaper
Cronyn	Hume	Performing Arts	Canada	Actor - Acad Award Nom
Crookes	William	Science	England	Chemist/Physicist
Cropper	Steve	Performing Arts	USA	Rock & Roll - HF - Booker T & The Mg's
Crosby	Bing	Sports	USA	Golfer - HF
	David	Performing Arts	USA	Rock & Roll - HF - Crosby Stills & Nash
	David	Performing Arts	USA	Rock & Roll - HF - The Bryds
	Norm	Performing Arts	USA	Comedian
	Harry Lillis (Bing)	Performing Arts	USA	Actor/Singer - Academy Award
	Harry Lillis (Bing)	Performing Arts	USA	Singer - Big Band/Jazz - HF
Cross	Ben	Performing Arts	England	Actor
	Christopher	Performing Arts	USA	Singer/Composer

SOLVER SERIES: NAME FINDER

LAST NAME	FIRST NAME	CATEGORY	COUNTRY	FAME
Crosse	Rupert	Performing Arts	West Indies	Actor - Acad Award Nom
Crothers	Rachel	Creative Works	USA	Playwright
	Scatman	Performing Arts	USA	Singer/Composer
Crouch	Roger Keith	Aviation	USA	Astronaut
Crouse	Lindsay	Performing Arts	USA	Actress - Acad Award Nom
Crouse	Russell	Creative Works	USA	Dramatist - Pulitzer
Crowe	Russell	Performing Arts	New Zealand	Actor - Academy Award
Crowell	Rodney	Creative Works	USA	Composer
Crowley	Aleister	Science	England	Writer/Poet/Occultist
Cruikshank	George	Creative Works	England	Caricaturist/Illustrator
Cruise	Tom	Performing Arts	USA	Actor - Acad Award Nom
Crumb	Robert	Creative Works	USA	Cartoonist - Fritz the Cat
Crutzen	Paul J.	Science	Netherlands	Chemistry - Nobel Laureate
Cruyff	Johan	Sports	Netherlands	Soccer Player - HF
Cruz	Nilo	Creative Works	USA	Dramatist - Pulitzer
Crystal	Billy	Performing Arts	USA	Actor/Comedian
Csonka	Lawrence Richard (Larry)	Sports	USA	Football Player - HF
Cudahy	Michael	Business	USA	Livestock
Cuevas	Pipino	Sports	Mexico	Boxer - HF
Cugat	Xavier	Performing Arts	Cuba	Band Leader
Cukor	George	Movie Production	USA	Director - Academy Award
Culbertson	Ely	Games	USA	Bridge Expert
Culbertson Jr.	Frank Lee	Aviation	USA	Astronaut
Culkin	Macaulay	Performing Arts	USA	Actor
Cullen	Countee	Creative Works	USA	Poet
	Hugh Roy	Business	USA	Oil Industry
Cullman III	Joseph Frederick	Sports	USA	Tennis Player - HF
Culp	Robert	Performing Arts	USA	Actor
Cumberland	Richard	Arts	England	Philosopher/Bishop
Cummings	Burton	Performing Arts	Canada	Canadian Music - HF - The Guess Who
	Edward Estlin	Creative Works	USA	Poet
	Irving	Movie Production	USA	Director - Acad Award Nom
	Quinn	Performing Arts	USA	Actress - Acad Award Nom
	Robert	Performing Arts	USA	Actor
	William Arthur (Candy)	Sports	USA	Baseball Executive - HF
Cunanan	Andrew Philip	Law & Order	USA	Serial Killer
Cunard	Samuel	Business	Canada	Shipping Magnate
Cunningham	Allan	Exploration	England	Explorer - Brazil/Australia
	Merce	Creative Works	USA	Choreographer
	Michael	Creative Works	USA	Novelist - Pulitzer
	Ronnie Walter	Aviation	USA	Astronaut
	William J. (Billy)	Sports	USA	Basketball Player - HF
Cunningham Jr.	Briggs Swift	Sports	USA	Race Car Driver - HF
Cuomo	Mario	Politics	USA	Governor - New York
Curie	Marie	Science	France	Chemistry - Nobel Laureate
	Marie	Science	France	Physics - Nobel Laureate
	Pierre	Science	France	Physics - Nobel Laureate
Curl Jr.	Robert F.	Science	USA	Chemistry - Nobel Laureate
Currier	Nathaniel	Works of Art	USA	Lithographer
Curry	Denise	Sports	USA	Basketball Player - HF
	John Steuart	Works of Art	USA	Painter - Regionalist
	Tim	Performing Arts	England	Actor
Curti	Merle E.	Creative Works	USA	Author - Pulitzer
Curtin	Jane	Performing Arts	USA	Actress
Curtis	Charles	Politics	USA	Vice-President
	Glenn Hammond	Aviation	USA	Aircraft Construction
	Jamie Lee	Performing Arts	USA	Actress
	Keene	Performing Arts	USA	Actor
	Tony	Performing Arts	USA	Actor - Acad Award Nom
Curtiz	Michael	Movie Production	Hungary	Director - Academy Award
Curzon	George Nathaniel	Politics	England	Viceroy
Cusack	Cyril	Performing Arts	South Africa	Actor
	Joan	Performing Arts	USA	Actress - Acad Award Nom

LAST NAME	FIRST NAME	CATEGORY	COUNTRY	FAME
Cusack	John	Performing Arts	USA	Actor
Cushing	Caleb	Politics	USA	Diplomat
	Harvey	Creative Works	USA	Author - Pulitzer
	Harvey Williams	Science	USA	Neurosurgeon
	Peter	Performing Arts	England	Actor
Custer	George Armstrong	War & Peace	USA	Army Officer
Cuvier	Georges Léopold	Arts	France	Naturalist
Cuyler	Hazen Shirley (Kiki)	Sports	USA	Baseball Player - HF
Cuyp	Aalbert	Works of Art	Netherlands	Painter
Czerny	Karl	Creative Works	Austria	Composer
Da Silva	Eusebio Ferreria	Sports	Mozambique	Soccer Player - HF
Dae-jung	Kim	War & Peace	South Korea	Peace - Nobel Laureate
Dafoe	Willem	Performing Arts	USA	Actor - Acad Award Nom
Dahl	Arlene	Performing Arts	USA	Actress
	Roald	Creative Works	Wales	Writer
Dahmer	Jeffrey	Law & Order	USA	Serial Killer
Dailey	Dan	Performing Arts	USA	Actor - Acad Award Nom
Daimler	Gottlieb	Business	Germany	Automobile Industy
Dakin	Henry D.	Science	USA	Chemist
Daldry	Stephen	Movie Production	England	Director - Acad Award Nom
Dale	David	Business	England	Textile Industry
	Henry Hallett	Science	England	Medicine - Nobel Laureate
	Jim	Performing Arts	England	Actor
	Thomas	Politics	England	Governor - Virginia
Dalén	Nils Gustaf	Science	Sweden	Physics - Nobel Laureate
Daley	Richard Joseph	Politics	USA	Mayor - Chicago
	Richard Michael	Politics	USA	Mayor - Chicago
Dalglish	Kenny	Sports	Scotland	Soccer Player - HF
Dalhart (Slaughter)	Vernon (Marion Try)	Performing Arts	USA	Singer - Country Music - HF
Dali	Salvador	Works of Art	Spain	Painter
Dalipagic	Drazen	Sports	Yugoslavia	Basketball Player - HF
Dall	John	Performing Arts	USA	Actor - Acad Award Nom
Dallas	George M.	Politics	USA	Vice-President
Dalton	Abby	Performing Arts	USA	Actress
	Bob	Law & Order	USA	Outlaw
	Emmett	Law & Order	USA	Outlaw
	Gratton	Law & Order	USA	Outlaw
	John	Science	England	Chemist/Physicist
	Timothy	Performing Arts	Wales	Actor
Daltrey	Roger	Performing Arts	England	Rock & Roll - HF - The Who
Daly	John	Sports	USA	Golfer
	John Augustin	Creative Works	USA	Playwright
	Tyne	Performing Arts	USA	Actress
Dalziel	George Henry	Business	England	Publishing
Dam	Henri Carl Peter	Science	Denmark	Medicine - Nobel Laureate
D'Amato	Alfonse	Politics	USA	Senator
Dameron (Peake)	Tadd (Tadley Ewing)	Performing Arts	USA	Jazz Pianist/Composer - Big Band/Jazz - HF
Damien	Joseph	Arts	Belgium	Priest/Missionary
Damme	Jean-Claude Van	Performing Arts	Belgium	Actor
Damon	Matt	Performing Arts	USA	Actor - Acad Award Nom
Damone	Vic	Performing Arts	USA	Singer
Dampier	William	Exploration	England	Explorer - Caribbean
Damrosch	Walter Johannes	Creative Works	USA	Composer/Conductor
Dana	Charles Anderson	Arts	USA	Newspaper Editor
	James Dwight	Science	USA	Geologist/Mineralogist
	Leora	Performing Arts	USA	Actress
	Richard Henry	Creative Works	USA	Writer/Lawyer
	Victor (Vic)	Performing Arts	USA	Singer
	William (Bill)	Performing Arts	USA	Actor
Dance	Helen Oakley	Performing Arts	USA	Arranger - Big Band/Jazz - HF
Dandridge	Dorothy	Performing Arts	USA	Actress - Acad Award Nom
	Raymond Emmitt (Ray)	Sports	USA	Baseball Player - HF
Danelli	Dino	Performing Arts	USA	Rock & Roll - HF - The Young Rascals

SOLVER SERIES: NAME FINDER

LAST NAME	FIRST NAME	CATEGORY	COUNTRY	FAME
D'Angelo	Beverly	Performing Arts	USA	Actress
Dangerfield	George	Creative Works	USA	Author - Pulitzer
	Rodney	Performing Arts	USA	Comedian
D'Angers	Pierre-Jean David	Works of Art	France	Sculptor
Daniel	Beth	Sports	USA	Golfer - HF
Daniels	Bebe	Performing Arts	USA	Actress
	Billy	Performing Arts	USA	Singer
	Charlie	Performing Arts	USA	Singer
	Jeff	Performing Arts	USA	Actor
	Josephus	Politics	USA	Statesman
	William	Performing Arts	USA	Actor
Danilo	Paul (Duts)	Sports	USA	Soccer Player - HF
Danko	Rick	Performing Arts	Canada	Rock & Roll - HF - The Band
Danner	Blythe	Performing Arts	USA	Actress
D'Annunzio	Gabriele	Creative Works	Italy	Poet
Danson	Ted	Performing Arts	USA	Actor
Dante	Nicholas	Creative Works	USA	Dramatist - Pulitzer
Dantley	Adrian	Sports	USA	Basketball Player
Danton	Georges Jacques	Politics	France	Revolutionary Leader
Danza	Tony	Performing Arts	USA	Actor
Danzig	Allison (Al)	Sports	USA	Tennis Player - HF
Darby	Kim	Performing Arts	USA	Actress
D'Arc	Jeanne (Joan of Arc)	War & Peace	France	Heroine/Military Leader
Dare	Virginia	Arts	USA	First American Child
d'Arezzo	Guido	Arts	Italy	Musical Theorist
Darin (Cossotto)	Walden Roberto (Bobby)	Performing Arts	USA	Actor - Acad Award Nom
	Walden Roberto (Bobby)	Performing Arts	USA	Singer - Rock & Roll - HF
Darnell	Linda	Performing Arts	USA	Actress
Darragh	John Proctor (Jack)	Sports	Canada	Hockey Player - HF
Darrow	Clarence Seward	Law & Order	USA	Lawyer
Darwell	Jane	Performing Arts	USA	Actress - Academy Award
Darwin	Charles Robert	Science	England	Naturalist
	Erasmus	Science	England	Naturalist/Physician
Dash	Stacey	Performing Arts	USA	Actress
Dassin	Jules	Movie Production	USA	Director - Acad Award Nom
Daubigny	Charles François	Works of Art	France	Painter - Landscapes
Daudet	Aphonse	Creative Works	France	Novelist
	Léon	Politics	France	Politician/Journalist
Daumier	Honore	Works of Art	France	Painter/Lithographer
Dausset	Jean	Science	France	Medicine - Nobel Laureate
D'Avenant	William	Creative Works	England	Poet/Playwright
David	Herman Francis	Sports	England	Tennis Player - HF
	Jacques-Louis	Works of Art	France	Painter
Davidson	Allan M. (Scotty)	Sports	Canada	Hockey Player - HF
	Jaye	Performing Arts	USA	Actor - Acad Award Nom
	John	Performing Arts	USA	Singer
	Joseph	Works of Art	USA	Sculptor
Davies	David Russell Gordon (Dave)	Performing Arts	England	Rock & Roll - HF - The Kinks
	Laura	Sports	England	Golfer
	Raymond Douglas (Ray)	Performing Arts	England	Rock & Roll - HF - The Kinks
	Robert E.	Sports	USA	Basketball Player - HF
Davis	Allen	Sports	USA	Football Commissioner - HF
	Angela Yvonne	Politics	USA	Activist/Abolutionist
	Ann B	Performing Arts	USA	Singer
	Bette	Performing Arts	USA	Actress - Academy Award
	David Brion	Creative Works	USA	Author - Pulitzer
	Dwight Filley	Sports	USA	Tennis Player - HF
	Geena	Performing Arts	USA	Actress - Academy Award
	George Stacey	Sports	USA	Baseball Player - HF
	Harold Lenoir	Creative Works	USA	Novelist - Pulitzer
	Jefferson	Politics	USA	President - Confederacy
	Jim	Creative Works	USA	Cartoonist - Garfield
	Jimmie (James Houston)	Performing Arts	USA	Singer - Country Music - HF

LAST NAME	FIRST NAME	CATEGORY	COUNTRY	FAME
Davis	Joan	Performing Arts	USA	Actress
	Judy	Performing Arts	Australia	Actress - Acad Award Nom
	Mac	Performing Arts	USA	Singer
	Miles	Performing Arts	USA	Jazz Trumpeter - Big Band/Jazz - HF
	Ossie	Performing Arts	USA	Actor
	Owen	Creative Works	USA	Dramatist - Pulitzer
	Richard Harding	Creative Works	USA	Novelist/Journalist/Editor
	Rick (Ricky)	Sports	USA	Soccer Player - HF
	Skeeter	Performing Arts	USA	Singer
	William Delford (Willie)	Sports	USA	Football Player - HF
Davis Jr.	Raymond	Science	USA	Physics - Nobel Laureate
	Sammy	Performing Arts	USA	Singer
Davison	Bruce	Performing Arts	USA	Actor - Acad Award Nom
Davisson	Clinton Joseph	Science	USA	Physics - Nobel Laureate
Davy	Humphry	Science	England	Chemist
Dawber	Pam	Performing Arts	USA	Actress
Dawes	Charles Gates	Politics	USA	Vice-President
	Charles Gates	War & Peace	USA	Peace - Nobel Laureate
Dawson	André	Sports	USA	Baseball Player
	John William	Arts	Canada	Geologist/Naturalist
	Leonard Ray (Len)	Sports	USA	Football Player - HF
	Richard	Performing Arts	England	Actor
Day	Clarence (Happy)	Sports	Canada	Hockey Player - HF
	Doris	Performing Arts	USA	Actress - Acad Award Nom
	Doris	Performing Arts	USA	Singer
	Laraine	Performing Arts	USA	Actress
	Leon	Sports	USA	Baseball Player - HF
Dayan	Moshe	War & Peace	Israel	Military Leader
Day-Lewis	Daniel	Performing Arts	England	Actor - Academy Award
Deacon	John	Performing Arts	England	Rock & Roll - HF - Queen
Dean	James	Performing Arts	USA	Actor - Acad Award Nom
	Jay Hanna (Dizzy)	Sports	USA	Baseball Player - HF
Deane	Silas	Politics	USA	Revolutionary Patriot
Debernardy	Forrest S. (Red)	Sports	USA	Basketball Player - HF
Debreu	Gerard	Arts	USA	Economics - Nobel Laureate
Debs	Eugene Victor	Business	USA	Labor Leader
Debusschere	David (Dave)	Sports	USA	Basketball Player - HF
Debussy	Claude	Creative Works	France	Composer
Debye	Peter Joseph William	Science	USA	Chemistry - Nobel Laureate
Decatur	Stephen	War & Peace	USA	Naval Officer
Dee	Joey	Performing Arts	USA	Rock & Roll - HF - The Young Rascals
	Kiki	Performing Arts	England	Singer
	Ruby	Performing Arts	USA	Actress
	Sandra	Performing Arts	USA	Actress
Defoe	Daniel	Creative Works	England	Writer
Deford	Frank	Creative Works	USA	Journalist - Newspaper
Defore	Don	Performing Arts	USA	Actor
Degas	Hilaire Germain Edgar	Works of Art	France	Painter
Degler	Carl N.	Creative Works	USA	Author - Pulitzer
Dehmelt	Hans G.	Science	USA	Physics - Nobel Laureate
Dehnert	Henry J. (Dutch)	Sports	USA	Basketball Player - HF
Deighton	Len	Creative Works	England	Author
Deisenhofer	Johann	Science	Germany	Chemistry - Nobel Laureate
Dekker	Thomas	Creative Works	England	Playwright
Delacorte	George T.	Business	USA	Publishing - Dell
Delacroix	Ferdinand Victor Eugene	Works of Art	France	Painter
Delahanty	Edward James (Ed)	Sports	USA	Baseball Player - HF
Delamair	Pierre Antoine	Architecture	France	Architect
Delaney	Jack	Sports	Canada	Boxer - HF
Delano	William Adams	Architecture	USA	Architect - AIA Gold Medal
Delany	Dana	Performing Arts	USA	Actress
	Samuel Ray	Creative Works	USA	Author - SciFi
Delaroche	Hippolyte Paul	Works of Art	France	Painter

SOLVER SERIES: NAME FINDER

LAST NAME	FIRST NAME	CATEGORY	COUNTRY	FAME
Delavigne	Jean François Casimir	Creative Works	France	Poet/Playwright
Delbrück	Max	Science	USA	Medicine - Nobel Laureate
Deledda	Grazia	Creative Works	Italy	Literature - Nobel Laureate
Delibes	Clément Philibert Léo	Creative Works	France	Composer
Delius	Frederick	Creative Works	England	Composer
Dellacroce	Aniello (The Hat)	Law & Order	USA	Mafia
Dellums	Ronald Vernie (Ron)	Politics	USA	Senator
Delmore	Alton	Performing Arts	USA	Country Music - HF - Delmore Brothers
	Rabon	Performing Arts	USA	Country Music - HF - Delmore Brothers
Delon	Alain	Performing Arts	France	Actor
Delorme	Philibert	Architecture	France	Architect - Renaissance
Delucas	Lawrence James	Aviation	USA	Astronaut
Deluise	Dom	Performing Arts	USA	Actor
Delvecchio	Alexander Peter (Alex)	Sports	Canada	Hockey Player - HF
Demarest	William	Performing Arts	USA	Actor - Acad Award Nom
Demaret	Jimmy	Sports	USA	Golfer - HF
Demme	Jonathan	Movie Production	USA	Director - Academy Award
Dempsey	Jack	Sports	USA	Boxer - HF
Dench	Judi	Performing Arts	England	Actress - Academy Award
Deneuve	Catherine	Performing Arts	France	Actress - Acad Award Nom
Dennehy	Brian	Performing Arts	USA	Actor
	Cyril Joseph (Cy)	Sports	Canada	Hockey Player - HF
Dennett	Tyler	Creative Works	USA	Author - Pulitzer
Dennis	Carl	Creative Works	USA	Poet - Pulitzer
	Sandy	Performing Arts	USA	Actress - Academy Award
Denny	Reginald	Performing Arts	England	Actor
	Sandy	Performing Arts	England	Singer
Densmore	John	Performing Arts	USA	Rock & Roll - HF - The Doors
Dent	Jim	Sports	USA	Golfer
	Richard	Sports	USA	Football Player
Denver	Bob	Performing Arts	USA	Actor
Denver	John	Performing Arts	USA	Singer
Depardieu	Gerard	Performing Arts	France	Actor - Acad Award Nom
Depp	Johnny	Performing Arts	USA	Actor - Acad Award Nom
Derain	André	Works of Art	France	Painter
Derek	Bo	Performing Arts	USA	Actress
	John	Performing Arts	USA	Actor
Dern	Bruce	Performing Arts	USA	Actor - Acad Award Nom
	Laura	Performing Arts	USA	Actress - Acad Award Nom
Descartes	René	Arts	France	Philosopher/Mathematician
Desmond	Paul	Performing Arts	USA	Jazz Saxophonist - Big Band/Jazz - HF
Desmoulins	Lucie Simplice Camille	Creative Works	France	Journalist/Pamphleteer
Destinn	Emmy	Performing Arts	Czechoslovakia	Singer - Opera
Devane	William	Performing Arts	USA	Actor
Devere	Trish Van	Performing Arts	USA	Actress
Devers	Gail	Sports	USA	Olympic Runner
Devine	Andy	Performing Arts	USA	Actor
Dewey	George	War & Peace	USA	Admiral
	John	Arts	USA	Philosopher/Educator
	Melville	Arts	USA	Educator/Librarian
	Thomas Edmund	Law & Order	USA	Lawyer
	Thomas Edmund	Politics	USA	Governor - New York
Dexter	Norman Colin	Creative Works	England	Author
Dey	Joseph C.	Sports	USA	Golf Promoter - HF
	Susan	Performing Arts	USA	Actress
Diaghilev	Sergei Pavlovich	Performing Arts	Russia	Ballet Producer
Diamond	Jared	Creative Works	USA	Author - Pulitzer
	Neil	Performing Arts	USA	Singer
	Selma	Performing Arts	Canada	Actress
Dias	Bartolomeu	Exploration	Portugal	Explorer - Africa West Coast
	Diogo	Exploration	Portugal	Explorer - Madagascar
Diaz	Yamila	Performing Arts	Argentina	Super Model
	José de la Cruz Porfirio	Politics	Mexico	President

LAST NAME	FIRST NAME	CATEGORY	COUNTRY	FAME
Dick	Walter	Sports	Scotland	Soccer Player - HF
Dickens	Charles	Creative Works	England	Novelist
	James Cecil (Little Jimmy)	Performing Arts	USA	Singer - Country Music - HF
Dickerson	Eric Demetric	Sports	USA	Football Player - HF
Dickey	James	Creative Works	USA	Poet
	William Malcolm	Sports	USA	Baseball Player - HF
Dickinson	Angie	Performing Arts	USA	Actress
	Emily Elizabeth	Creative Works	USA	Poet
	John	Politics	USA	Statesman
Diddley	Bo	Performing Arts	USA	Singer/Song Writer
Diderot	Denis	Arts	France	Philosopher/Encylopedist
Didion	Joan	Creative Works	USA	Journalist - Magazine
Didley (Bates)	Ellis (Bo)	Performing Arts	USA	Singer - Rock & Roll - HF
Didrikson	Mildred (Babe)	Sports	USA	Olympic Javelin/Hurdles
Diefenbaker	John George	Politics	Canada	Prime Minister
Diegel	Leo	Sports	USA	Golfer - HF
Diels	Otto Paul Hermann	Science	Germany	Chemistry - Nobel Laureate
Diem	Ngo Dinh	Politics	South Vietnam	President
Diener	Marcus	Architecture	Switzerland	Architect
	Roger	Architecture	Switzerland	Architect
Dierdorf	Daniel Lee (Dan)	Sports	USA	Football Player - HF
Diesel	Rudolph	Science	Germany	Inventor - Diesel Engine
	Vin	Performing Arts	USA	Actor
Dieste	Eladio	Architecture	Uruguay	Architect
Dieterle	William	Movie Production	Germany	Director - Acad Award Nom
Dietrich	Marlene	Performing Arts	Germany	Actress - Acad Award Nom
Dihigo	Martín Magdaleno	Sports	Cuba	Baseball Player - HF
Dillard	Annie	Creative Works	USA	Author - Pulitzer
Diller	Phyllis	Performing Arts	USA	Comedian
Dillman	Bradford	Performing Arts	USA	Actor
Dillon	George	Creative Works	USA	Poet - Pulitzer
	Matt	Performing Arts	USA	Actor
	Melinda	Performing Arts	USA	Actress - Acad Award Nom
Dinesen	Isak	Creative Works	Denmark	Author
Dinkeloo	John Gerard	Architecture	USA	Architect
Dinkins	David Norman	Politics	USA	Mayor - New York City
Dinwiddle	Robert	Politics	England	Governor - Virginia
Dionne	Marcel Elphege	Sports	Canada	Hockey Player - HF
Dior	Christian	Business	France	Fashion Designer
Dirac	Paul Adrien Maurice	Science	England	Physics - Nobel Laureate
Dirksen	Everett McKinley	Politics	USA	Senator
Disch	Thomas Michael	Creative Works	USA	Author - SciFi
Disney	Walter Elias	Movie Production	USA	Producer
Disraeli	Benjamin	Politics	England	Prime Minister
Ditka	Michael Keller (Mike)	Sports	USA	Football Player - HF
Ditmars	Raymond Lee	Arts	USA	Naturalist/Zoo Curator
Dix	Richard	Performing Arts	USA	Actor - Acad Award Nom
Dixon	Donna	Performing Arts	USA	Actress
	Ivan	Performing Arts	USA	Director
	William James (Willie)	Performing Arts	USA	Singer - Rock & Roll - HF
Dmytryk	Edward	Movie Production	Canada	Director - Acad Award Nom
Dobie	James Frank	Creative Works	USA	Writer/Scholar
Dobson	Henry Austin	Creative Works	England	Poet
	Kevin	Performing Arts	USA	Actor
Doby	Lawrence Eugene (Larry)	Sports	USA	Baseball Player - HF
Dobzhansky	Theodosius Grigorievich	Science	USA	Geneticist
Doctorow	Edgar Lawrence	Creative Works	USA	Novelist
Dod	Charlotte (Lottie)	Sports	England	Tennis Player - HF
Dodd	Alice	Performing Arts	England	Super Model
	Christopher J. (Chris)	Politics	USA	Senator - Connecticut
Dodds	Johnny	Performing Arts	USA	Jazz Clarinetist - Big Band/Jazz - HF
	Warren (Baby)	Performing Arts	USA	Jazz Drummer - Big Band/Jazz - HF
Dodgson	Charles Lutwidge	Creative Works	England	Author/Mathematician

SOLVER SERIES: NAME FINDER

LAST NAME	FIRST NAME	CATEGORY	COUNTRY	FAME
Doeg	John Thomas Godfray Hope	Sports	USA	Tennis Player - HF
Doenitz	Karl	War & Peace	Germany	Grand Admiral
Doerr	Robert Pershing (Bobby)	Sports	USA	Baseball Player - HF
Doesburg	Theo van	Architecture	Netherlands	Architect
Doherty	Dennis (Denny) Gerrard	Performing Arts	Canada	Canadian Music - HF - Mamas & Papas
	Dennis (Denny) Gerrard	Performing Arts	Canada	Rock & Roll - HF - Mamas & Papas
	Hugh Laurence (Little Do)	Sports	England	Tennis Player - HF
	Peter C.	Science	Australia	Medicine - Nobel Laureate
	Reginald Frank (Reggie)	Sports	England	Tennis Player - HF
Dohnányi	Ernö	Creative Works	Hungary	Composer/Pianist
Doi	Takao	Aviation	Japan	Astronaut
Doisy	Edward Adelbert	Science	USA	Medicine - Nobel Laureate
Dolce	Domenico	Business	Italy	Fashion Designer
Dole	Elizabeth Hanford (Liddy)	Politics	USA	Senator - North Carolina
	Robert Joseph (Bob)	Politics	USA	Senator - Kansas
Dollond	Peter	Business	England	Retail Trade
Dolphy	Eric Allan	Performing Arts	USA	Jazz Saxophonist - Big Band/Jazz - HF
Domagk	Gerhard	Science	Germany	Medicine - Nobel Laureate
Domingo	Placido	Performing Arts	Spain	Singer - Opera
Dominick	Peter	Architecture	USA	Architect
Domino	Antoine (Fats)	Performing Arts	USA	Singer - Rock & Roll - HF
Donahue	Elinor	Performing Arts	USA	Actress
	Phil	Creative Works	USA	Journalist - Television
	Troy	Performing Arts	USA	Actor
Donald	David Herbert	Creative Works	USA	Author - Pulitzer
Donaldson	Sam	Creative Works	USA	Journalist - Television
Donat	Robert	Performing Arts	England	Actor - Academy Award
Donegan	Lonnie	Performing Arts	Scotland	Singer
Donelli	Aldo Teo (Buff)	Sports	USA	Soccer Player - HF
Donizetti	Gaetano	Creative Works	Italy	Composer - Opera
Donleavy	James Patrick	Creative Works	USA	Novelist
Donlevy	Brian	Performing Arts	Northern Ireland	Actor - Acad Award Nom
Donne	John	Creative Works	England	Poet
Donohue	Mark	Sports	USA	Race Car Driver - HF
Donovan	Anne	Sports	USA	Basketball Player - HF
Donovan Jr.	Arthur James (Art)	Sports	USA	Football Player - HF
Dooley	Thomas Anthony	Science	USA	Medical Doctor
Doppler	Christian	Science	Austria	Physicist/Mathematician
Dorati	Anatal	Performing Arts	USA	Conductor
Doré	Paul Gustave	Works of Art	France	Painter/Illustrator
Doren	Carl Clinton Van	Creative Works	USA	Author - Pulitzer
	Mamie Van	Performing Arts	USA	Actress
	Mark Albert Van	Creative Works	USA	Poet - Pulitzer
Doria	Andrea	War & Peace	Italy	Admiral
Dorn	Michael	Performing Arts	USA	Actor
Dors	Diana	Performing Arts	England	Actress
Dorsett Sr.	Anthony Drew (Tony)	Sports	USA	Football Player - HF
Dorsey	James (Jimmy)	Performing Arts	USA	Band Leader - Big Band/Jazz - HF
	Thomas (Tommy)	Performing Arts	USA	Band Leader - Big Band/Jazz - HF
Dostoyevsky	Feodor Mikhailovich	Creative Works	Russia	Novelist
Dotrice	Roy	Performing Arts	England	Actor
Dou	Gerard	Works of Art	Netherlands	Painter
Doubleday	Abner	Sports	USA	Inventor - Baseball
Doughty	Charles Montagu	Creative Works	England	Poet/Travel Writer
Douglas	George Norman	Creative Works	England	Novelist/Essayist
	James	War & Peace	Scotland	Military Leader
	Jimmy	Sports	USA	Soccer Player - HF
	Kirk	Performing Arts	USA	Actor - Acad Award Nom
	Melvyn	Performing Arts	USA	Actor - Academy Award
	Michael	Performing Arts	USA	Actor - Academy Award
	Mike	Performing Arts	Canada	Canadian Music - HF - The Diamonds
	Paul	Performing Arts	USA	Actor
	Stephen Arnold	Politics	USA	Politician

LAST NAME	FIRST NAME	CATEGORY	COUNTRY	FAME
Douglas	William Orville	Law & Order	USA	Justice - Supreme Court
	Steve	Performing Arts	USA	Singer - Rock & Roll - HF
Douglas-Home	Alec	Politics	England	Prime Minister
Douglass	Dale	Sports	USA	Golfer
	Frederick	Creative Works	USA	Journalist - Newspaper
	Frederick	Politics	USA	Statesman/Journalist
Douglass-Chambers	Dorthea Katherine	Sports	USA	Tennis Player - HF
Dourif	Brad	Performing Arts	USA	Actor - Acad Award Nom
Dove	Rita	Creative Works	USA	Poet - Pulitzer
Dow	Tony	Performing Arts	USA	Actor
Dowden	Edward	Arts	Ireland	Biographer/Critic
Dower	John W.	Creative Works	USA	Author - Pulitzer
Dowland	John	Creative Works	England	Composer/Lutanist
Down	John L.H.	Science	England	Physician - Down's Syndrome
	Lesley-Anne	Performing Arts	England	Actress
Downey	John	Business	USA	Oil Industry
	Robert	Movie Production	USA	Director
	Rosemary (Roma)	Performing Arts	Ireland	Actress
"Downey, Jr"	Robert	Performing Arts	USA	Actor - Acad Award Nom
Downie	Gordon	Performing Arts	Canada	Canadian Music - HF - The Tragically Hip
Downs	Hugh	Creative Works	USA	Journalist - Television
Dowson	Ernest Christopher	Creative Works	England	Poet - Lyric
Doxiadis	Constantinos Apostolou	Architecture	Greece	Architect
Doyle	Arthur Conan	Creative Works	England	Novelist/Physician
	David	Performing Arts	USA	Actor
Dozier	Lamont	Creative Works	USA	Composer
Drabble	Margaret	Creative Works	England	Novelist
Drabowsky	Moe	Sports	Poland	Baseball Player
Drake	Alfred	Performing Arts	USA	Actor - Musical
	Francis	Exploration	England	Explorer - Circumnavigation
	Larry	Performing Arts	USA	Actor
Draper	Henry	Science	USA	Astronomer
	John William	Science	USA	Scientist/Historian
Drayton	Michael	Creative Works	England	Poet
Dreiser	Theodore Herman Albert	Creative Works	USA	Novelist
Dreja	Chris	Performing Arts	England	Rock & Roll - HF - The Yardbirds
Dresser	Louise	Performing Arts	USA	Actress - Acad Award Nom
	Marie	Performing Arts	Canada	Actress - Academy Award
Drew	Ellen	Performing Arts	USA	Actress
	John	Performing Arts	USA	Actor
Drexler	Clyde	Sports	USA	Basketball Player - HF
Dreyfus	Alfred	War & Peace	France	Army Officer
Dreyfuss	Richard	Performing Arts	USA	Actor - Academy Award
Drillon	Gordon Arthur	Sports	Canada	Hockey Player - HF
Drinkwater	Charles Graham	Sports	Canada	Hockey Player - HF
Driscoll	Bobby	Performing Arts	USA	Actor - Academy Award
Driver	Minnie	Performing Arts	England	Actress - Acad Award Nom
Drobny	Jaroslav	Sports	Czechoslovakia	Tennis Player - HF
Dru	Joanne	Performing Arts	USA	Actress
Drucker	Mort	Creative Works	USA	Cartoonist - Mad Magazine
Drury	Allen	Creative Works	USA	Author - Pulitzer
Dryden	John	Creative Works	England	Poet Laureate
	Kenneth Wayne (Ken)	Sports	Canada	Hockey Player - HF
Dryer	Fred	Performing Arts	USA	Actor
	Fred	Sports	USA	Football Player
Drysdale	Cliff	Sports	South Africa	Tennis Player
	Donald Scott (Don)	Sports	USA	Baseball Player - HF
Duany	Andres	Architecture	USA	Architect - Jefferson Medal
Dubos	René Jules	Creative Works	USA	Author - Pulitzer
Dubuque	Julian	Exploration	France	Explorer - Mississippi River
Duchamp	Marcel	Works of Art	USA	Painter
Duchin	Edwin Frank (Eddy)	Performing Arts	USA	Pianist
Ducommun	Elie	War & Peace	Switzerland	Peace - Nobel Laureate

SOLVER SERIES: NAME FINDER

LAST NAME	FIRST NAME	CATEGORY	COUNTRY	FAME
Dudley	Robert	Politics	England	Courtier
	William McGarvey	Sports	USA	Football Player - HF
Duer	William	Politics	USA	Statesman
Duffy	Brian	Aviation	USA	Astronaut
	Hugh	Sports	USA	Baseball Player - HF
	Julia	Performing Arts	USA	Actress
	Patrick	Performing Arts	USA	Actor
	Raoul Ernest Joseph	Works of Art	France	Painter
Dugan	Alan	Creative Works	USA	Poet - Pulitzer
Duggan	Thomas	Sports	England	Soccer Player - HF
Duhamel	Georges	Creative Works	France	Poet/Novelist/Dramatist
Dukakis	Michael Stanley	Politics	USA	Governor - Massachusetts
	Olympia	Performing Arts	USA	Actress - Academy Award
Duke	Patty	Performing Arts	USA	Actress - Academy Award
Duke Jr.	Charles Moss	Aviation	USA	Astronaut
Dukes	David	Performing Arts	USA	Actor
Dulbecco	Renato	Science	USA	Medicine - Nobel Laureate
Dullea	Keir	Performing Arts	USA	Actor
Dulles	John Foster	Politics	USA	Secretary of State
Dumars	Joe	Sports	USA	Basketball Player
Dumart	Woodrow Clarence (Woody)	Sports	Canada	Hockey Player - HF
Dumas	Alexandre	Creative Works	France	Novelist/Dramatist/Playwright
Dumont	Margaret	Performing Arts	USA	Actress
Dunant	Jean Henry	Business	Switzerland	Philanthropist - Red Cross
	Jean Henry	War & Peace	Switzerland	Peace - Nobel Laureate
Dunaway	Faye	Performing Arts	USA	Actress - Academy Award
Dunbar	Paul Laurence	Creative Works	USA	Poet
	Richard	Performing Arts	USA	Rock & Roll - HF - The Drifters
	William	Creative Works	Scotland	Poet
Duncan	Isadora	Performing Arts	USA	Dancer
	Michael Clarke	Performing Arts	USA	Actor - Acad Award Nom
	Sandy	Performing Arts	USA	Actress
Dunderdale	Thomas (Tommy)	Sports	Australia	Hockey Player - HF
Dunn	Donald	Performing Arts	USA	Rock & Roll - HF - Booker T & The Mg's
	James	Performing Arts	USA	Actor - Acad Award Nom
	Jimmy	Sports	USA	Soccer Player - HF
	Michael	Performing Arts	USA	Actor - Acad Award Nom
	Stephen	Creative Works	USA	Poet - Pulitzer
Dunn (Dunhill)	Lawrence (Larry)	Performing Arts	USA	Rock & Roll - HF - Earth Wind & Fire
Dunne	Finley Peter	Creative Works	USA	Humorist/Journalist
	Griffin	Performing Arts	USA	Actor
	Irene	Performing Arts	USA	Actress - Acad Award Nom
	John Gregory	Creative Works	USA	Novelist
Dunnock	Mildred	Performing Arts	USA	Actress - Acad Award Nom
Dunsany	Edward John Moreton	Creative Works	Ireland	Poet/Playwright
Duper	Mark	Sports	USA	Football Player
Dupré	Marcel	Creative Works	France	Composer
Duque	Pedro Francisco	Aviation	Spain	Astronaut
Duran	Roberto	Sports	USA	Boxer
Durand	Asher Brown	Works of Art	USA	Painter
	Jean Nicolas Louis	Architecture	France	Architect
Durant	Ariel	Creative Works	USA	Author - Pulitzer
	Will	Creative Works	USA	Author - Pulitzer
Durante	Jimmy	Performing Arts	USA	Comedian
Durbin	Deanna	Performing Arts	Canada	Actress - Academy Award
Dürer	Albrecht	Works of Art	Germany	Painter/Engraver
Durnan	William Ronald (Bill)	Sports	Canada	Hockey Player - HF
Durning	Charles	Performing Arts	USA	Actor - Acad Award Nom
Durocher	Leo Ernest (The Lip)	Sports	USA	Baseball Manager - HF
Durr	Francoise (Frankie)	Sports	France	Tennis Player - HF
Durrance	Samuel Thorton	Aviation	USA	Astronaut
Durrell	Lawrence	Creative Works	England	Author
Duryea	Dan	Performing Arts	USA	Actor

LAST NAME	FIRST NAME	CATEGORY	COUNTRY	FAME
Duse	Eleonora	Performing Arts	Italy	Actress
Dussault	Nancy	Performing Arts	USA	Actress - Musical
Dutra	Olin	Sports	USA	Golfer
Dutton	Mervyn (Red)	Sports	Canada	Hockey Player - HF
Duval	David	Sports	USA	Golfer
Duvalier	François (Papa Doc)	Politics	Haiti	President
Duvall	Robert	Performing Arts	USA	Actor - Academy Award
	Shelley	Performing Arts	USA	Actress
Duve	Christian de	Science	Belgium	Medicine - Nobel Laureate
Duyn	Mona Jane Van	Creative Works	USA	Poet - Pulitzer
Dvořák	Antonín	Creative Works	Czechoslovakia	Composer
Dwight	James	Sports	France	Tennis Player - HF
Dyck	Anthony Van	Works of Art	Italy	Painter
Dye	Cecil Henry (Babe)	Sports	Canada	Hockey Player - HF
Dyke	Dick Van	Performing Arts	USA	Actor
	Jerry Van	Performing Arts	USA	Actor
	Woodbridge Strong Van	Movie Production	USA	Director - Acad Award Nom
Dykstra	Len	Sports	USA	Baseball Player
Dylan (Zimmerman)	Robert Alan (Bob)	Performing Arts	USA	Singer - Rock & Roll - HF
Dysart	Richard	Performing Arts	USA	Actor
Dzundza	George	Performing Arts	Germany	Actor
Eads	James Buchanan	Science	USA	Engineer
Eagels	Jeanne	Performing Arts	USA	Actress - Acad Award Nom
Eakins	Thomas	Works of Art	USA	Painter/Sculptor
Eames Jr.	Charles Ormond	Business	USA	Designer - Chairs
Eannes	Gil	Exploration	Portugal	Explorer - North Africa
Earhart	Amelia	Aviation	USA	Pioneer Aviator
Earle	Sylvia Alice	Exploration	USA	Explorer - Marine
Early	Jubal Anderson	War & Peace	USA	Confederate General
Earnhardt	Dale	Sports	USA	Race Car Driver - HF
	Ralph	Sports	USA	Race Car Driver - HF
Earp	Wyatt	Law & Order	USA	Lawman
Eastman	George	Business	USA	Kodak Film Company
Easton	Sheena	Performing Arts	Scotland	Singer
Eastwood	Clint	Performing Arts	USA	Actor - Acad Award Nom
	Clint	Movie Production	USA	Director - Academy Award
Eaton	Cyrus	Business	USA	Industrialist
	Shirley	Performing Arts	England	Actress
	Timothy	Business	Canada	Retail Trade
Ebadi	Shirin	War & Peace	Iran	Peace - Nobel Laureate
Eberhardt	Isabella	Exploration	Switzerland	Explorer - North Africa
Eberhart	Richard	Creative Works	USA	Poet - Pulitzer
Ebert	Roger	Creative Works	USA	Journalist - Newspaper
Ebsen	Buddy	Performing Arts	USA	Actor
Eccles	John Carew	Science	Australia	Medicine - Nobel Laureate
Echegaray	José	Creative Works	Spain	Literature - Nobel Laureate
Eck	Johann Maier von	Arts	Germany	Theologian
Eckersley	Dennis Lee	Sports	USA	Baseball Player - HF
Eckhart	Johannes	Arts	Germany	Theologian/Mystic
Eckstine	Billy	Performing Arts	USA	Band Leader - Big Band/Jazz - HF
Eco	Umberto	Creative Works	Italy	Author
Edberg	Stefan	Sports	Sweden	Tennis Player - HF
Eddington	Arthur Stanley	Science	England	Astronomer/Astrophysicist
Eddy	Duane	Performing Arts	USA	Guitarist
	Mary Baker	Arts	USA	Founder - Christian Science
	Nelson	Performing Arts	USA	Singer
Eddy (Colter)	Jessi (Duane)	Performing Arts	USA	Singer - Rock & Roll - HF
Edel	Leon	Creative Works	USA	Author - Pulitzer
Edelman	Gerald M.	Science	USA	Medicine - Nobel Laureate
Eden	Barbara	Performing Arts	USA	Actress
	Robert Anthony	Politics	England	Prime Minister
Ederle	Gertrude	Sports	USA	Swimmer - English Channel
Edgeworth	Maria	Creative Works	England	Novelist

SOLVER SERIES: NAME FINDER

LAST NAME	FIRST NAME	CATEGORY	COUNTRY	FAME
Edison	Harry (Sweets)	Performing Arts	USA	Trumpeter - Big Band/Jazz - HF
	Thomas Alva	Science	USA	Inventor - Electrical Devices
Edman	Irwin	Arts	USA	Philosopher
Edson	Margaret	Creative Works	USA	Dramatist - Pulitzer
Edwards	Albert Glen (Turk)	Sports	USA	Football Player - HF
	Anthony	Performing Arts	USA	Actor
	Blake	Movie Production	USA	Director
	Dennis	Performing Arts	USA	Rock & Roll - HF - The Temptations
	Duncan	Sports	England	Soccer Player - HF
	Johnathon	Arts	USA	Philosopher/Theologian
Edwards Jr.	Joe Frank	Aviation	USA	Astronaut
Eggar	Samantha	Performing Arts	England	Actress - Acad Award Nom
Eggleston	Edward	Creative Works	USA	Novelist/Historian
Egmont	Lamoral	Politics	Italy	Statesman
Egoyan	Atom	Movie Production	Egypt	Director - Acad Award Nom
Ehrenburg	Ilya Grigorievich	Creative Works	Russia	Writer
Ehrlich	Paul	Science	Germany	Medicine - Nobel Laureate
Eichhorn	Lisa	Performing Arts	USA	Actress
Eichler	Joseph	Architecture	USA	Architect/Developer
Eijkman	Christiaan	Science	Netherlands	Medicine - Nobel Laureate
Eikenberry	Jill	Performing Arts	USA	Actress
Einstein	Albert	Science	USA	Physics - Nobel Laureate
Einthoven	Willem	Science	Netherlands	Medicine - Nobel Laureate
Eisele	Donn Fulton	Aviation	USA	Astronaut
Eiseley	Loren Corey	Arts	USA	Philosopher/Essayist/Naturalist
Eisenhower	Dwight David (Ike)	Politics	USA	President
	Dwight David (Ike)	War & Peace	USA	General - Army
	Mamie Geneva	Politics	USA	First Lady
Eisenstein	Sergei Mikhailovich	Movie Production	Russia	Director/Producer
Eisner	Michael Dammann	Business	USA	Disney Film Head
	Will	Creative Works	USA	Cartoonist
Ekberg	Anita	Performing Arts	Sweden	Actress
Ekland	Britt	Performing Arts	Sweden	Actress
Elam	Jack	Performing Arts	USA	Actor
Elders	Minnie Jocelyn	Politics	USA	Surgeon General
Eldridge	Roy (David)	Performing Arts	USA	Jazz Trumpeter - Big Band/Jazz -HF
Elfman	Jenna	Performing Arts	USA	Actress
Elg	Taina	Performing Arts	Finland	Actress
Elgar	Edward William	Creative Works	England	Composer
Elyen	Manfred	Science	Germany	Chemistry - Nobel Laureate
Eliade	Mircea	Arts	USA	Theologian
Elion	Gertrude B.	Science	USA	Medicine - Nobel Laureate
Eliot	Charles William	Arts	USA	Educator
	John	Arts	USA	Clergyman
	Thomas Stearns	Creative Works	England	Literature - Nobel Laureate
Eliot (Marian Evans)	George	Creative Works	England	Novelist
Elkin	James	Business	USA	Oil Industry
Elkington	Steve	Sports	Australia	Golfer
Eller	Carl Lee	Sports	USA	Football Player - HF
Elliman	Yvonne	Performing Arts	USA	Singer
Ellington	Edward Kennedy (Duke)	Performing Arts	USA	Band Leader - Big Band/Jazz - HF
Elliot	Cass	Performing Arts	USA	Singer
Elliott	Bill	Sports	USA	Race Car Driver
	Bob	Performing Arts	USA	Comedian
	Chris	Performing Arts	USA	Comedian
	Denholm	Performing Arts	England	Actor - Acad Award Nom
	Helene	Sports	USA	Hockey Journalist - HF
	Maude Howe	Creative Works	USA	Author - Pulitzer
	Sam	Performing Arts	USA	Actor
Elliott (Cohen)	Ellen Naomi (Mama Cass)	Performing Arts	USA	Rock & Roll - HF - Mamas & Papas
Ellis	Albert	Arts	USA	Psychologist
	Henry Havelock	Creative Works	England	Writer/Psychologist
	Perry	Business	USA	Fashion Designer

LAST NAME	FIRST NAME	CATEGORY	COUNTRY	FAME
Ellis	Shirley	Performing Arts	USA	Singer
	Joseph J.	Creative Works	USA	Author - Pulitzer
Ellison	Harlan	Creative Works	USA	Author
	Ralph	Creative Works	USA	Author
Ellmann	Richard	Creative Works	USA	Author - Pulitzer
Ellsworth	Lincoln	Exploration	USA	Explorer - Polar
	Oliver	Law & Order	USA	Justice - Supreme Court
Elman	Mischa	Performing Arts	USA	Violinist
Elorde	Gabriel (Flash)	Sports	Philippines	Boxer - HF
Els	Ernie	Sports	South Africa	Golfer
Éluard	Paul	Creative Works	France	Poet
Elway	John Albert	Sports	USA	Football Player - HF
Elwes	Cary	Performing Arts	England	Actor
Ely	Alex	Sports	Brazil	Soccer Player - HF
	Ron	Performing Arts	USA	Actor
Elyot	Thomas	Creative Works	England	Writer/Diplomat
Elytis	Odysseus	Creative Works	Greece	Literature - Nobel Laureate
Elzevir	Bonaventure	Arts	Netherlands	Printer
	Louis	Arts	Netherlands	Printer
Emerson	Hope	Performing Arts	USA	Actress - Acad Award Nom
	Ralph Waldo	Creative Works	USA	Poet/Essayist/Philosopher
	Roy Stanley	Sports	Australia	Tennis Player - HF
Emilio	Aguinaldo	Politics	Philippines	Leader
Endacott	Paul	Sports	USA	Basketball Player - HF
Endecott	John	Politics	England	Governor - Massachusetts
Enders	John Franklin	Science	USA	Medicine - Nobel Laureate
Endo	Akira	Performing Arts	Japan	Conductor
Enesco	Georges	Creative Works	Romania	Composer/Violinist/Conductor
Engel	Howard	Creative Works	Canada	Author
	Lehmen	Creative Works	USA	Author
Engels	Friedrich	Arts	Germany	Philosopher/Socialist/Writer
England	Anthony Wayne	Aviation	USA	Astronaut
Engle	Joe Henry	Aviation	USA	Astronaut
Engle III	Robert F.	Arts	USA	Economics - Nobel Laureate
English	Alex	Sports	USA	Basketball Player - HF
Englund	Robert	Performing Arts	USA	Actor
En-Lai	Zhou	Politics	China	Premier
Eno	Brian	Creative Works	England	Composer/Producer
Entwistle	John	Performing Arts	England	Rock & Roll - HF - The Who
Epee	Michel de l'	Creative Works	France	Writer - Sign Language
Ephraim	Gotthold	Creative Works	Germany	Dramatist/Critic
Ephron	Delia	Performing Arts	USA	Actress
	Nora	Creative Works	USA	Novelist
Epps	Omar Hashim	Performing Arts	USA	Actor
Epstein	Howie	Performing Arts	USA	Rock & Roll - HF - Heart Breakers
	Jacog	Works of Art	England	Sculptor
Erasmus	Desiderius	Arts	Netherlands	Humanist/Theologian
Erastus	Thomas	Arts	Germany	Theologian
Erede	Alberto	Performing Arts	Italy	Conductor
Erickson	Arthur Charles	Architecture	Canada	Architect - AIA Gold Medal
Ericson	John	War & Peace	USA	Naval Engineer
	Leif	Exploration	Iceland	Explorer - East Coast America
Erigena	Johannes Scotus	Arts	Ireland	Theologian/Philosopher
Erikson	Erik Homburger	Creative Works	USA	Author - Pulitzer
Erlanger	Joseph	Science	USA	Medicine - Nobel Laureate
Ernst	Max	Works of Art	Germany	Painter - Surrealist
	Richard R.	Science	Switzerland	Chemistry - Nobel Laureate
Errol	Leon	Performing Arts	Australia	Comedian
Erskine	John	Arts	Scotland	Religious Reformer
	John	Creative Works	USA	Writer/Educator
	John	Law & Order	Scotland	Jurist
Ervine	John Greer	Creative Works	England	Novelist/Playwright
Erving	Julius W.	Sports	USA	Basketball Player - HF

SOLVER SERIES: NAME FINDER

LAST NAME	FIRST NAME	CATEGORY	COUNTRY	FAME
Erwin	Stu	Performing Arts	USA	Actor - Acad Award Nom
Esaki	Leo	Science	Japan	Physics - Nobel Laureate
Escher	Maurits Cornelis	Works of Art	Netherlands	Illustrator
Escoffier	Auguste	Creative Works	France	Writer - Cooking
Esherick	Joseph	Architecture	USA	Architect - AIA Gold Medal
Esiason	Boomer	Sports	USA	Football Player
Esposito	Anthony James (Tony)	Sports	Canada	Hockey Player - HF
	Philip Anthony (Phil)	Sports	Canada	Hockey Player - HF
Esquivel	Adolfo Pérez	War & Peace	Argentina	Peace - Nobel Laureate
Essex	David	Performing Arts	England	Singer
Estefan	Gloria	Performing Arts	Cuba	Singer
Estes	Billy Sol	Business	USA	Cotton Industry
	Bob	Sports	USA	Golfer
	Simon	Performing Arts	USA	Singer - Opera
Estevez	Emilio	Performing Arts	USA	Actor
Estleman	Loren D.	Creative Works	USA	Author
Estrada	Erik	Performing Arts	USA	Actor
Etchebaster	Pierre	Sports	France	Tennis Player - HF
Etherege	George	Creative Works	England	Playwright
Eucken	Rudolf Christoph	Creative Works	Germany	Literature - Nobel Laureate
Eugenides	Jeffrey	Creative Works	USA	Novelist - Pulitzer
Euler	Leonhard	Science	Switzerland	Mathematician
	Ulf von	Science	Sweden	Medicine - Nobel Laureate
Euler-Chelpin	Hans Karl August Simon von	Science	Sweden	Chemistry - Nobel Laureate
Euwe	Max	Games	Netherlands	Chess Player
Evangelista	Linda	Performing Arts	Canada	Super Model
Evans	Arthur John	Arts	England	Archaeologist
	Bill	Performing Arts	USA	Jazz Pianist - Big Band/Jazz - HF
	Charles (Chick)	Sports	USA	Golfer - HF
	Dale	Performing Arts	USA	Actress
	Darrell	Sports	USA	Baseball Player
	Dave (The Edge)	Performing Arts	Ireland	Rock & Roll - HF - U2
	Dwight	Sports	USA	Baseball Player
	Edith	Performing Arts	England	Actress - Acad Award Nom
	Geraint	Performing Arts	Wales	Singer - Opera
	Janet	Sports	USA	Olympic Swimmer
	Linda	Performing Arts	USA	Actress
	Mary Ann	Performing Arts	USA	Actress
	Richie	Sports	USA	Race Car Driver - HF
	Robert	Creative Works	USA	Journalist - Television
	Ronald Ellwin	Aviation	USA	Astronaut
	William George	Sports	USA	Baseball Umpire - HF
Evans (Green)	Ian Ernest Gilmore (Gil)	Performing Arts	Canada	Jazz Pianist - Big Band/Jazz - HF
Evans (Green)	Ian Ernest Gilmore (Gil)	Performing Arts	Canada	Jazz Pianist - Canadian Music - HF
Evans-Pritchard	Edward Evan	Arts	England	Anthropologist
Everett	Chad	Performing Arts	USA	Actor
	Edward	Politics	USA	Statesman/Orator
Everhart	Angie	Performing Arts	USA	Super Model
Everly	Isaac Donald (Don)	Performing Arts	USA	Country Music - HF - Everly Brothers
	Isaac Donald (Don)	Performing Arts	USA	Rock & Roll - HF - Everly Brothers
	Phillip (Phil)	Performing Arts	USA	Country Music - HF - Everly Brothers
	Phillip (Phil)	Performing Arts	USA	Rock & Roll - HF - Everly Brothers
Evers	John Joseph (Johnny)	Sports	USA	Baseball Player - HF
Evert	Christine Marie (Chris)	Sports	USA	Tennis Player - HF
Evinrude	Ole	Business	USA	Outboard Engine Designer
Ewbank	Wilbur Charles (Weeb)	Sports	USA	Football Coach - HF
Ewell	Richard Stoddert	War & Peace	USA	Confederate General
	Tom	Performing Arts	USA	Actor
Ewing	Patrick	Sports	USA	Basketball Player
	William (Buck)	Sports	USA	Baseball Player - HF
Eyck	Aldo van	Architecture	Netherlands	Architect
	Huybrecht Van	Works of Art	Belgium	Painter
	Jan Van	Works of Art	Belgium	Painter

LAST NAME	FIRST NAME	CATEGORY	COUNTRY	FAME
Eyharts	Léopold	Aviation	France	Astronaut
Eyre	Edward John	Exploration	Australia	Explorer - South Australia
Ezekiel	Moses Jacob	Works of Art	USA	Sculptor
Ezrin	Bob	Performing Arts	Canada	Musician/Producer - Canadian Music - HF
Fabares	Shelley	Performing Arts	USA	Actress/Singer
Faber	Urban Charles (Red)	Sports	USA	Baseball Player - HF
Fabian	John McCreary	Aviation	USA	Astronaut
Fabray	Nanette	Performing Arts	USA	Actress
Fabre	Jean Henri	Science	France	Entomologist
Fagen	Donald	Performing Arts	USA	Rock & Roll - HF - Steely Dan
Fahey	Jeff	Performing Arts	USA	Actor
Fahrenheit	Gabriel	Science	Germany	Physicist
Fain	Samuel (Sammy)	Creative Works	USA	Composer
Fairbairn	Bruce	Performing Arts	Canada	Musician/Producer - Canadian Music - HF
Fairbanks	Charles W.	Politics	USA	Vice-President
	Douglas	Performing Arts	USA	Actor
Fairbanks Jr.	Douglas	Performing Arts	USA	Actor
Fairchild	Morgan	Performing Arts	USA	Actress
Faith	Adam	Performing Arts	England	Singer/Actor
Faithful	Marianne	Performing Arts	England	Singer
Fakir	Abdul (Duke)	Performing Arts	USA	Rock & Roll - HF - The Four Tops
Falana	Lola	Performing Arts	USA	Singer
Falco	Edie	Performing Arts	USA	Actress
Faldo	Nick	Sports	England	Golfer - HF
Falk	Peter	Performing Arts	USA	Actor - Acad Award Nom
Falkenburg	Robert (Bob)	Sports	USA	Tennis Player - HF
Falla	Manuel	Creative Works	Spain	Composer
	Manuel De	Creative Works	Spain	Composer - Classical
Fallaci	Oriana	Creative Works	Italy	Author/Journalist
Fangio	Juan-Manuel	Sports	Argentina	Race Car Driver - HF
Fanon	Frantz	Science	France	Psychiatrist
Faraday	Michael	Science	England	Scientist - Electricity
Faraj	Abd al-Salam	Creative Works	Egypt	Writer
Farentino	James	Performing Arts	USA	Actor
Farge	John La	Works of Art	USA	Artist/Writer
	Oliver La	Creative Works	USA	Novelist - Pulitzer
Fargo	Donna	Performing Arts	USA	Singer
Faria	Romario Da Souza	Sports	Brazil	Soccer Player
Farmer	Arthur Stewart (Art)	Performing Arts	USA	Jazz Trumpeter - Big Band/Jazz - HF
	Charles (Red)	Sports	USA	Race Car Driver - HF
	Frances	Performing Arts	USA	Actress
	Philip José	Creative Works	USA	Author
Farndon	Pete	Performing Arts	England	Rock & Roll - HF - The Pretenders
Farnsworth	Richard	Performing Arts	USA	Actor - Acad Award Nom
Faro	Rocco Scott La	Performing Arts	USA	Jazz Bassist - Big Band/Jazz - HF
Farquar	George	Creative Works	England	Playwright
Farr	Hugh	Performing Arts	USA	Country Music - HF - Sons of the Pioneers
	Jamie	Performing Arts	USA	Actor
	Karl	Performing Arts	USA	Country Music - HF - Sons of the Pioneers
Farragut	David	War & Peace	USA	Naval Commander
Farrar	Geraldine	Performing Arts	USA	Singer - Opera
Farrel	Arthur F.	Sports	Canada	Hockey Player - HF
Farrell	James Thomas	Creative Works	USA	Novelist
	Mike	Performing Arts	USA	Actor
Farrow	John	Movie Production	Australia	Director - Acad Award Nom
	Mia	Performing Arts	USA	Actress
	Tal	Performing Arts	USA	Jazz Guitarist - Big Band/Jazz - HF
	Tisa	Performing Arts	USA	Actress
Fathy	Hassan	Architecture	Egypt	Architect
Faulkner	William	Creative Works	USA	Literature - Nobel/Pulitzer
Fauré	Gabriel Urbain	Creative Works	France	Composer
Favier	Jean-Jacques	Aviation	France	Astronaut
Fawcett	Farrah	Performing Arts	USA	Actress

SOLVER SERIES: NAME FINDER

LAST NAME	FIRST NAME	CATEGORY	COUNTRY	FAME
Fawkes	Guy	War & Peace	England	Conspirator
Faxon	Brad	Sports	USA	Golfer
Faye	Alice	Performing Arts	USA	Actress
	Johnny	Performing Arts	Canada	Canadian Music - HF - The Tragically Hip
Fears	Thomas Jesse (Tom)	Sports	USA	Football Player - HF
Fechner	Gustav Theodor	Science	Germany	Physicist/Philosopher
Federko	Bernard Allan	Sports	Canada	Hockey Player - HF
Fehn	Sverre	Architecture	Norway	Architect - Pritzker Laureate
Fehrenbacher	Don E.	Creative Works	USA	Author - Pulitzer
Feibleman	James	Creative Works	USA	Author/Philosopher
Feiffer	Jules	Creative Works	USA	Cartoonist - Political
Feininger	Lyonel Charles Adrian	Works of Art	USA	Painter
Feinstein	Dianne Goldman Berman	Politics	USA	Senator - California
Feis	Herbert	Creative Works	USA	Author - Pulitzer
Felder	Don	Performing Arts	USA	Rock & Roll - HF - The Eagles
Feldman	Corey	Performing Arts	USA	Actor
	Marty	Performing Arts	England	Comedian
Feldon	Barbara	Performing Arts	USA	Actress
Feliciano	José	Performing Arts	Puerto Rico	Singer
Fell	Norman	Performing Arts	USA	Actor
Feller	Robert William Andrew (Bob)	Sports	USA	Baseball Player - HF
Fellini	Federico	Movie Production	Italy	Director - Acad Award Nom
Felton	John	Performing Arts	USA	Canadian Music - HF - The Diamonds
Fender	Freddy	Performing Arts	USA	Singer
Fenech	Jeff	Sports	Australia	Boxer - HF
Fénelon	François de Salignac	Arts	France	Clergyman/Writer
Fenn	John B.	Science	USA	Chemistry - Nobel Laureate
Feoktistov	Konstantin Petrovich	Aviation	Russia	Astronaut
Ferber	Edna	Creative Works	USA	Author - Pulitzer
Ferguson	John (Jock)	Sports	Scotland	Soccer Player - HF
Ferguson	Maynarad	Performing Arts	Canada	Jazz Trumpeter - Canadian Music - HF
Fermi	Enrico	Science	Italy	Physics - Nobel Laureate
Fernandes	Almudena	Performing Arts	Spain	Super Model
Fernandez	Gigi	Sports	USA	Tennis Player
Fernandez	Mary Joe	Sports	USA	Tennis Player
Ferrari	Enzo Anselmo	Sports	Italy	Race Car Driver - HF
Ferrel	Tyra	Performing Arts	USA	Actress
Ferrell	Conchata	Performing Arts	USA	Actress
	Richard Benjamin (Rick)	Sports	USA	Baseball Player - HF
Ferrer	José	Performing Arts	Puerto Rico	Actor - Academy Award
	Mel	Performing Arts	USA	Actor
Ferreria	Rivaldo Vito Barbosa	Sports	Brazil	Soccer Player
Ferrigno	Lou	Performing Arts	USA	Actor
Ferrone	Steve	Performing Arts	England	Rock & Roll - HF - Heart Breakers
Ferry	Bryan	Performing Arts	England	Singer
Fetchit	Stepin	Performing Arts	USA	Comedian
Fetisov	Viacheslav	Sports	Russia	Hockey Player - HF
Fettman	Martin Joseph	Aviation	USA	Astronaut
Feuchtwanger	Lion	Creative Works	Germany	Novelist
Feuerbach	Ludwig Andreas	Arts	Germany	Philosopher/Materialist
Feynman	Richard P.	Science	USA	Physics - Nobel Laureate
Fibiger	Julius Andreas Grib	Science	Denmark	Medicine - Nobel Laureate
Fichte	Immanuel Hermass von	Arts	Germany	Philosopher
Fichte	Johann Gottlieb	Arts	Germany	Philosopher
Fiedler	Arthur	Performing Arts	USA	Conductor
Field	Cyrus West	Business	USA	Industrialist
	Eugene	Creative Works	USA	Poet/Journalist
	Sally	Performing Arts	USA	Actress - Academy Award
Fielden	John	Business	England	Textile Industry
Fielden	Joshua	Business	England	Textile Industry
	Samuel	Business	England	Textile Industry
	Thomas	Business	England	Textile Industry
Fielder	Cecil	Sports	USA	Baseball Player

LAST NAME	FIRST NAME	CATEGORY	COUNTRY	FAME
Fielding	Henry	Creative Works	England	Novelist
Fields	Gracie	Performing Arts	England	Singer
	Totie	Performing Arts	USA	Comedian
Fields (Dukenfield)	William Claude (WC)	Performing Arts	USA	Comedian
Fiennes	Ralph	Performing Arts	England	Actor - Acad Award Nom
	Ranulf	Exploration	England	Explorer - Polar Explorer
Fiesole	Giovanni da	Works of Art	Italy	Painter
Figgis	Mike	Movie Production	England	Director - Acad Award Nom
Figo	Luis	Sports	Portugal	Soccer Player
Filho	Jair Ventura Jairzinho	Sports	Brazil	Soccer Player - HF
Filipchenko	Anatoli Vassilyevich	Aviation	Russia	Astronaut
Fillmore	Abigail	Politics	USA	First Lady
	Caroline Carmichael	Politics	USA	First Lady
	Millard	Politics	USA	President
Finch	Peter	Performing Arts	England	Actor - Academy Award
Fine	Larry	Performing Arts	USA	Comedian
Fingers	Roland Glen (Rollie)	Sports	USA	Baseball Player - HF
Finks	James Edward (Jim)	Sports	USA	Football Administrator - HF
Finlay	Frank	Performing Arts	England	Actor - Acad Award Nom
Finney	Albert	Performing Arts	England	Actor - Acad Award Nom
	Tom	Sports	England	Soccer Player - HF
Finsen	Niels Ryberg	Science	Denmark	Medicine - Nobel Laureate
Fiorucci	Elio	Business	Italy	Fashion Designer
Firth	Peter	Performing Arts	England	Actor - Acad Award Nom
Fischer	Bobby	Games	USA	Chess Player
	David Hackett	Creative Works	USA	Author - Pulitzer
	Edmond H.	Science	Switzerland	Medicine - Nobel Laureate
	Ernst Otto	Science	Germany	Chemistry - Nobel Laureate
	Evan	Performing Arts	USA	Canadian Music - HF - The Diamonds
	Hans	Science	Germany	Chemistry - Nobel Laureate
	Hermann Emil	Science	Germany	Chemistry - Nobel Laureate
Fischer von Erlach	Johan Bernhard	Architecture	Austria	Architect
Fish	Albert	Law & Order	USA	Serial Killer - Hannibal Lector
	Hamilton	Politics	USA	Statesman
Fishburne	Lawrence	Performing Arts	USA	Actor - Acad Award Nom
Fisher	Carrie	Performing Arts	USA	Actress
	Dorothy Canfield	Creative Works	USA	Writer
	Eddie	Performing Arts	USA	Singer
	William Frederick	Aviation	USA	Astronaut
Fisk	Carlton Ernest	Sports	USA	Baseball Player - HF
Fiske	John	Arts	USA	Philosopher/Historian
	Minnie Maddern	Performing Arts	USA	Actress
Fitch	John	Science	USA	Inventor - Steam Boat
	Val Logsdon	Science	USA	Physics - Nobel Laureate
	William Clyde	Creative Works	USA	Playwright
Fittipaldi	Emerson	Sports	Brazil	Race Car Driver - HF
Fitzgerald	Barry	Performing Arts	Ireland	Actor - Academy Award
	Edward	Creative Works	England	Poet/Translator
	Ella Jane	Performing Arts	USA	Singer - Big Band/Jazz - HF
	Francis Scott Ley	Creative Works	USA	Author - Pulitzer
	Garrett	Politics	Ireland	Prime Minister
	Geraldine	Performing Arts	Ireland	Actress - Acad Award Nom
Fitzmaurice	Deanne	Creative Works	USA	Photographer - Pulitzer
Flack	Roberta	Performing Arts	USA	Singer
Flagg	James Montgomery	Creative Works	USA	Illustrator
Flagstad	Kirsten	Performing Arts	Norway	Singer - Opera
Flaherty	Raymond Paul (Ray)	Sports	USA	Football Coach - HF
	Robert Joseph	Movie Production	USA	Director - Documentaries
Flaman	Ferdinand Charles (Fernie)	Sports	Canada	Hockey Player - HF
Flammarion	Camille	Science	France	Astronomer
Flatt	Lester Raymond	Performing Arts	USA	Country Music - HF - Foggy Mountain Boys
Flaubert	Gustave	Creative Works	France	Novelist
Flavin	Martin	Creative Works	USA	Novelist - Pulitzer

LAST NAME	FIRST NAME	CATEGORY	COUNTRY	FAME
Flaxman	John	Arts	England	Sculptor
Fleck	Béla	Performing Arts	USA	Band Leader
Fleet	Jo Van	Performing Arts	USA	Actress - Academy Award
Fleetwood	Michael John (Mike)	Performing Arts	England	Rock & Roll - HF - Fleetwood Mac
	Mick	Performing Arts	England	Band Leader/Drummer
Fleischer	Lawrence Ari	Politics	USA	Federal Press Secretary
Fleming	Alexander	Science	England	Medicine - Nobel Laureate
	Ian	Creative Works	England	Author
	Peggy	Sports	USA	Olympic Skater
	Renée	Performing Arts	USA	Singer - Opera
	Rhonda	Performing Arts	USA	Actress
	Tom (Whitey)	Sports	Scotland	Soccer Player - HF
	Victor	Movie Production	USA	Director - Academy Award
Fletcher	John Gould	Creative Works	England	Poet/Playwright - Pulitzer
	Louise	Performing Arts	USA	Actress - Academy Award
Fleur	Guy Damien La	Sports	Canada	Hockey Player - HF
Fleury	André Hercule	Politics	France	Statesman/Cardinal
Flexner	Abraham	Arts	USA	Educator
	Simon	Science	USA	Pathologist
Flick	Elmer Harrison	Sports	USA	Baseball Player - HF
Flinders	Matthew	Exploration	England	Explorer - Australia
Flock	Julius Timothy (Tim)	Sports	USA	Race Car Driver - HF
Flockhart	Calista	Performing Arts	USA	Actress
Florey	Howard Walter	Science	Australia	Medicine - Nobel Laureate
Florie	Thomas (Tom)	Sports	USA	Soccer Player - HF
Florio	John	Creative Works	England	Writer/Lexicographer
Floris de Vriend	Cornelis	Architecture	Belgium	Architect
Flory	Paul J.	Science	USA	Chemistry - Nobel Laureate
Flotow	Friedrich von	Creative Works	Germany	Composer - Opera
Floyd	Raymond	Sports	USA	Golfer - HF
Flynn	Errol	Performing Arts	Australia	Actor
	Joe	Performing Arts	USA	Actor
Fo	Dario	Creative Works	Italy	Literature - Nobel Laureate
Foch	Ferdinand	War & Peace	France	Marshall
	Nina	Performing Arts	Netherlands	Actress - Acad Award Nom
Fogel	Robert W.	Arts	USA	Economics - Nobel Laureate
Fogelberg	Dan	Performing Arts	USA	Singer
Fogerty	John Cameron	Performing Arts	USA	Rock & Roll - HF - Creed. Clearwater Revival
	Tom	Performing Arts	USA	Rock & Roll - HF - Creed. Clearwater Revival
Fokine	Michel	Creative Works	USA	Choreographer
Fokker	Anthony Herman Gerard	Aviation	USA	Aircraft Designer
Foley	Clyde Julian (Red)	Performing Arts	USA	Singer - Country Music - HF
	Thomas Stephen	Politics	USA	Congressman
Follette	Robert Marion La	Politics	USA	Legislator/Reformer
Follows	Megan	Performing Arts	Canada	Actress
Fonda	Bridget	Performing Arts	USA	Actress
	Henry	Performing Arts	USA	Actor - Academy Award
	Jane	Performing Arts	USA	Actress - Academy Award
	Peter	Performing Arts	USA	Actor - Acad Award Nom
Fontaine	Henry La	War & Peace	Belgium	Peace - Nobel Laureate
	Jean de La	Creative Works	France	Poet/Writer
	Joan	Performing Arts	Japan	Actress - Academy Award
	Pat La	Sports	USA	Hockey Player - HF
Fontanne	Lynn	Performing Arts	England	Actress - Acad Award Nom
Fonteyn	Margot	Performing Arts	England	Dancer - Ballerina
Foote	Horton	Creative Works	USA	Dramatist - Pulitzer
Forbes	Esther	Creative Works	USA	Author - Pulitzer
	Malcolm	Business	USA	Publishing
Forbes-Robertson	Johnston	Performing Arts	England	Actor
Ford	Edward Charles (Whitey)	Sports	USA	Baseball Player - HF
	Elizabeth Ann (Betty)	Politics	USA	First Lady
	Ernest (Tennessee Ernie)	Performing Arts	USA	Singer - Country Music - HF
	Ford Madox	Creative Works	England	Writer/Editor

LAST NAME	FIRST NAME	CATEGORY	COUNTRY	FAME
Ford	Gerald Rudolph	Politics	USA	President
	Glenn	Performing Arts	USA	Actor
	Harrison	Performing Arts	USA	Actor - Acad Award Nom
	Henry	Business	USA	Manufacturer - Automobiles
	Henry	Sports	USA	Race Car Designer - HF
	John	Creative Works	England	Dramatist
	John	Movie Production	USA	Director - Academy Award
	Lita	Performing Arts	England	Singer
	Richard	Creative Works	USA	Author - Pulitzer
Ford (Duke of Palucah)	Benjamin (Whitey)	Performing Arts	USA	Comedian - Country Music - HF
Ford Jr.	Leonard Guy (Len)	Sports	USA	Football Player - HF
Foreman	George Edward	Sports	USA	Boxer - HF
Forest	Lee De	Science	USA	Inventor - Radio Equipment
Forester	Cecil Scott	Creative Works	England	Novelist
Forget	Guy	Sports	Morocco	Tennis Player
Forman	Milos	Movie Production	Czechoslovakia	Director - Academy Award
Forrest	Frederic	Performing Arts	USA	Actor - Acad Award Nom
Forrester	Maureen	Performing Arts	Canada	Singer - Opera - Canadian Music - HF
Forssmann	Werner	Science	Germany	Medicine - Nobel Laureate
Forster	Edward Morgan	Creative Works	England	Novelist
	Robert	Performing Arts	USA	Actor - Acad Award Nom
Forsythe	John	Performing Arts	USA	Actor
Fortas	Abe	Law & Order	USA	Justice - Supreme Court
Fortmann	Daniel John	Sports	USA	Football Player - HF
Fosbury	Dick	Sports	USA	Olympic High Jumper
Foscolo	Ugo	Creative Works	Italy	Poet
Foss	Lukas	Creative Works	USA	Composer
Fosse	Bob	Movie Production	USA	Director - Academy Award
Fossey	Dian	Science	USA	Ethologist
Foster	Andrew (Rube)	Sports	USA	Baseball Executive - HF
	Bob	Sports	USA	Boxer - HF
	David	Performing Arts	Canada	Musician/Composer - Canadian Music - HF
	George Murphy	Performing Arts	USA	Jazz Bassist - Big Band/Jazz - HF
	Harold E.	Sports	USA	Basketball Player - HF
	Jodie	Performing Arts	USA	Actress - Academy Award
	Norman	Architecture	England	Architect - Pritzker/ AIA Gold
	Preston	Performing Arts	USA	Actor
	Stephen Collins	Creative Works	USA	Composer - Songs
	William Hendrick (Bill)	Sports	USA	Baseball Player - HF
	William Zebulon	Politics	USA	Political Leader - Communist
Foucault	Jean Bernard Léon	Science	France	Physicist
	Michel	Arts	France	Philosopher
Fountain Jr.	Peter Dewey (Pete)	Performing Arts	USA	Jazz Clarinetist - Big Band/Jazz - HF
Fourier	François Marie Charles	Politics	France	Socialist Reformer
	Jean Baptiste Joseph	Science	France	Physicist/Mathematician
Fouts	Daniel Francis (Dan)	Sports	USA	Football Player - HF
Fowler	Henry Watson	Arts	England	Lexicographer/Arbiter
	William Alfred	Science	USA	Physics - Nobel Laureate
Fowles	John	Creative Works	England	Author
Fox	Charles James	Politics	England	Statesman/Orator
	Edward	Performing Arts	England	Actor
	George	Arts	England	Religious Leader
	Jacob Nelson (Nellie)	Sports	USA	Baseball Player - HF
	James	Performing Arts	England	Actor
	Michael J.	Performing Arts	Canada	Actor
	Ray	Sports	USA	Race Car Designer - HF
Foxworth	Robert	Performing Arts	USA	Actor
Foxx	Charlie	Performing Arts	USA	Singer
	Inez	Performing Arts	USA	Singer
	James Emory (Jimmy)	Sports	USA	Baseball Player - HF
	Jamie	Performing Arts	USA	Actor - Academy Award
	Redd	Performing Arts	USA	Comedian
Foy	Eddie	Performing Arts	USA	Actor

SOLVER SERIES: NAME FINDER

LAST NAME	FIRST NAME	CATEGORY	COUNTRY	FAME
Foy Jr	Eddie	Performing Arts	USA	Actor
Foyston	Frank C.	Sports	Canada	Hockey Player - HF
Foyt	Anthony Joseph (AJ)	Sports	USA	Race Car Driver - HF
Frakes	Jonathon	Performing Arts	USA	Actor
Frampton	Peter	Performing Arts	England	Singer
France	Anatole	Creative Works	France	Literature - Nobel Laureate
France Jr.	William (Bill)	Sports	USA	Race Car Promoter - HF
France Sr.	William Henry Getty (Bill)	Sports	USA	Race Car Promoter - HF
Franciosa	Anthony	Performing Arts	USA	Actor - Acad Award Nom
Francis	Anne	Performing Arts	USA	Actress
	Arlene	Performing Arts	USA	Actress
	Connie	Performing Arts	USA	Singer
	Emile Percy (The Cat)	Sports	Canada	Hockey Player
	Richard Stanley (Dick)	Creative Works	Wales	Author
Franck	César	Creative Works	France	Composer/Organist
	James	Science	Germany	Physics - Nobel Laureate
Franco	Ani Di	Performing Arts	USA	Singer
	Buddy De	Performing Arts	USA	Jazz Clarinetist - Big Band/Jazz - HF
	Francisco	Politics	Spain	Dictator
Frank	Elizabeth	Creative Works	USA	Author - Pulitzer
	Il'ja Mikhailovich	Science	Russia	Physics - Nobel Laureate
Frankenheimer	John	Movie Production	USA	Director
Frankfurter	Felix	Law & Order	USA	Justice - Supreme Court
Franklin	Aretha Louise	Performing Arts	USA	Singer - Rock & Roll - HF
	Benjamin	Science	USA	Inventor/Statesman/Writer
	Bonnie	Performing Arts	USA	Actress
	Joe	Creative Works	USA	Journalist - Television
	John	Exploration	England	Explorer - Arctic
	Sidney	Movie Production	USA	Director - Acad Award Nom
Franklin (English)	Melvin (Donald Melvin)	Performing Arts	USA	Rock & Roll - HF - The Temptations
Frann	Mary	Performing Arts	USA	Actress
Frantz	Charlton Christopher	Performing Arts	USA	Rock & Roll - HF - The Talking Heads
Fraser	Dawn	Sports	Australia	Olympic Swimmer
	Neale Andrew	Sports	Australia	Tennis Player - HF
	Simon	Exploration	Canada	Explorer - Alberta
Fraunhofer	Joseph von	Science	Bavaria	Optician
Frawley	William	Performing Arts	USA	Actor
Frazer	James George	Arts	Scotland	Antropologist
	Joe (Smokin Joe)	Sports	USA	Boxer - HF
	Walter	Sports	USA	Basketball Player - HF
Frears	Stephen	Movie Production	England	Director - Acad Award Nom
Fredrickson	Frank	Sports	Canada	Hockey Player - HF
Freeman	Douglas S.	Creative Works	USA	Author - Pulitzer
	Morgan	Performing Arts	USA	Actor - Academy Award
	Theodore Cordy	Aviation	USA	Astronaut
Freleng	Isadore (Friz)	Creative Works	USA	Cartoonist - Warner Bros.
Frémont	John Charles	War & Peace	USA	Union General
French	Daniel Chester	Works of Art	USA	Sculptor
	Marilyn	Creative Works	USA	Author
Freneau	Phillip Morin	Creative Works	USA	Poet/Journalist
Freni	Mirella	Performing Arts	Italy	Singer - Opera
Fresnel	Augustin Jean	Science	France	Physicist
Freud	Anna	Science	Austria	Psychiatrist
	Sigmund	Science	Austria	Psychiatrist/Physician
Frey	Glenn	Performing Arts	USA	Rock & Roll - HF - The Eagles
	Leonard	Performing Arts	USA	Actor - Acad Award Nom
Frick	Ford Christopher	Sports	USA	Baseball Commissioner - HF
	Henry Clay	Business	USA	Industrialist
Fricker	Brenda	Performing Arts	Ireland	Actress - Academy Award
	Werner	Sports	Yugoslavia	Soccer Player - HF
Frid	John Herbert (Johnathan)	Performing Arts	Canada	Actor
Fried	Alfred Hermann	War & Peace	Austria	Peace - Nobel Laureate
Friedan	Betty	Creative Works	USA	Writer

LAST NAME	FIRST NAME	CATEGORY	COUNTRY	FAME
Friedkin	Wlliam	Movie Production	USA	Director - Academy Award
Friedman	Benjamin (Benny)	Sports	USA	Football Player - HF
	Jerome I.	Science	USA	Physics - Nobel Laureate
	Max (Marty)	Sports	USA	Basketball Player - HF
	Milton	Arts	USA	Economics - Nobel Laureate
Friesz	Achille Émile Othon	Works of Art	France	Painter
Friml	Charles Rudolf	Creative Works	USA	Composer
Frimout	Dirk Dries David Damian	Aviation	Belgium	Astronaut
Frings	Ketti	Creative Works	USA	Dramatist - Pulitzer
Frisch	Frank Francis (Frankie)	Sports	USA	Baseball Player - HF
	Karl von	Science	Germany	Medicine - Nobel Laureate
	Ragnar	Arts	Norway	Economics - Nobel Laureate
Frizzell	William Orville (Lefty)	Performing Arts	USA	Singer - Country Music - HF
Froben	Johann	Arts	Germany	Printer
Frobisher	Martin	Exploration	England	Explorer - North West Passage
Froebel	Friedrich Wilhelm August	Arts	Germany	Educator
Frohman	Charles	Movie Production	USA	Producer/Theatrical Manager
Froissart	Jean	Creative Works	France	Poet/Chronicler
Fromm	Erich	Arts	Germany	Philosopher/Psychologist
Frontenac	Louis de Buade	Politics	France	Colonial Governor
Frost	David	Creative Works	England	Journalist - Television
	Robert Lee	Creative Works	USA	Poet - Pulitzer
Froude	James Anthony	Arts	England	Historian
Fry	Christopher	Creative Works	England	Playwright
	Joseph	Business	England	Confection Industry
	Roger Eliot	Works of Art	England	Art Critic
Fryer	William (Tucker)	Sports	England	Soccer Player - HF
Fry-Irvin	Shirley June	Sports	USA	Tennis Player - HF
Fuca	Juan de	Exploration	Greece	Explorer - West America
Fugard	Athol	Creative Works	South Africa	Playwright
Fuglesang	Arne Christer	Aviation	Sweden	Astronaut
Fuhr	Grant	Sports	Canada	Hockey Player - HF
Fuksas	Massimiliano	Architecture	Italy	Architect
Fukui	Kenichi	Science	Japan	Chemistry - Nobel Laureate
Fulbright	James William	Politics	USA	Senator
Fulks	Joseph F.	Sports	USA	Basketball Player - HF
Fuller	Charles	Creative Works	USA	Dramatist - Pulitzer
	Melville Weston	Law & Order	USA	Justice - Supreme Court
	Richard Buckminster	Architecture	USA	Architect - AIA Gold Medal
	Sarah Margaret	Creative Works	USA	Writer/Social Reformer
Fullmer	Gene	Sports	USA	Boxer - HF
Fulton	Robert	Science	USA	Inventor - Steam Boat
Funicello	Annette	Performing Arts	USA	Actress
Fuqua	Charles	Performing Arts	USA	Rock & Roll - HF - The Ink Spots
	Harvey	Performing Arts	USA	Rock & Roll - HF - The Moonglows
Furay	Richie	Performing Arts	USA	Rock & Roll - HF - Buffalo Springfield
Furchgott	Robert F.	Science	USA	Medicine - Nobel Laureate
Furness	Horace Howard	Arts	USA	Scholar - Shakespear
Furnivall	Frederick James	Arts	England	Philologist/Editor
Furrer	Reinhard Alfred	Aviation	Germany	Astronaut
Gabbana	Stefano	Business	Italy	Fashion Designer
Gable	Clark	Performing Arts	USA	Actor - Academy Award
Gabor	Dennis	Science	England	Physics - Nobel Laureate
	Eva	Performing Arts	Hungary	Actress
	Magda	Performing Arts	Hungary	Actress
	Zsa Zsa	Performing Arts	Hungary	Actress
Gaboriau	Émile	Creative Works	France	Writer - Detective Stories
Gaboury	Étienne	Architecture	Canada	Architect
Gabriel	Peter	Performing Arts	England	Singer
Gacy	John Wayne	Law & Order	USA	Serial Killer - Killer Clown
Gaddis	William	Creative Works	USA	Novelist
Gadsby	William (Bill)	Sports	Canada	Hockey Player - HF
Gadsden	James	Politics	USA	Diplomat

SOLVER SERIES: NAME FINDER

LAST NAME	FIRST NAME	CATEGORY	COUNTRY	FAME
Gaetjens	Joseph Eduard (Joe)	Sports	Haiti	Soccer Player - HF
Gaffney	Francis Andrew	Aviation	USA	Astronaut
Gagarin	Yuri Alekseyevich	Aviation	Russia	Cosmonaut
Gage	Nicholas	Creative Works	Greece	Author
	Thomas	War & Peace	England	General
Gail	Max	Performing Arts	USA	Actor
Gaines	Andrew	Arts	USA	Philosopher
Gainey	Robert Michael (Bob)	Sports	Canada	Hockey Player - HF
Gainsborough	Thomas	Works of Art	England	Painter
Gaither	Tommy	Performing Arts	USA	Rock & Roll - HF - The Orioles
Gajdusek	Daniel Carleton	Science	USA	Medicine - Nobel Laureate
Galante	Carmine (The Cigar)	Law & Order	Sicily	Mafia
Galaxy	Khaosai (The Thai Tyson)	Sports	Thailand	Boxer - HF
Galbraith	John Kenneth	Creative Works	Canada	Economist
Gale	Lauren (Laddie)	Sports	USA	Basketball Player - HF
	Zona	Creative Works	USA	Dramatist - Pulitzer
Galen	Claudius	Science	Greece	Writer/Physician
Galfetti	Aurelio	Architecture	Switzerland	Architect
Galilei	Galileo	Science	Italy	Astronomer/Physicist
Galindez	Victor	Sports	Argentina	Boxer - HF
Gallagher	James (Jimmy)	Sports	Scotland	Soccer Player - HF
	Megan	Performing Arts	USA	Actress
	Noel	Performing Arts	England	Rock & Roll - Oasis
Gallatin	Abraham Alfonse	Business	USA	Financier/Statesman
	Harry J.	Sports	USA	Basketball Player - HF
Galli-Curci	Amelita	Performing Arts	USA	Singer - Opera
Gallienne	Eva Le	Performing Arts	England	Actress
	Eva Le	Performing Arts	England	Actress - Acad Award Nom
Galois	Evariste	Science	France	Mathametician
Galsworthy	John	Creative Works	England	Literature - Nobel Laureate
Galton	Francis	Science	England	Writer/Pioneer - Eugenics
Galvani	Luigi	Science	Italy	Physicist/Physiologist
Galvin	James Francis (Pud)	Sports	USA	Baseball Player - HF
Galway	James	Performing Arts	Ireland	Flutist
Gam	Rita	Performing Arts	USA	Actress
Gama	Vasco da	Exploration	Portugal	Explorer - Africa Coast
Gambetta	Léon	Politics	France	Premier
Gambino	Carlo	Law & Order	Sicily	Mafia
Gandi	Indira Nehru	Politics	India	Prime Minister
	Mohandas Karamchand	Politics	India	Leader - Hindu Nationalist
Gant	Harry	Sports	USA	Race Car Driver - HF
Garagiola	Joseph Henry	Creative Works	USA	Journalist - Television
Garbo	Greta	Performing Arts	Sweden	Actress - Acad Award Nom
Garcés	Francisco Tomás	Exploration	Spain	Explorer - South/West America
Garcia	Andy	Performing Arts	Cuba	Actor - Acad Award Nom
	Jerome John	Performing Arts	USA	Rock & Roll - HF - Grateful Dead
Garcia Lorca	Federico	Creative Works	Spain	Poet/Playwright
Gard	Roger Martin du	Creative Works	France	Literature - Nobel Laureate
Gard (Gardassanich)	Gino	Sports	Croatia	Soccer Player - HF
Gardella	Ignazio	Architecture	Italy	Architect
Gardenia	Vincent	Performing Arts	Italy	Actor - Acad Award Nom
Gardiner	Charles Robert (Chuck)	Sports	Scotland	Hockey Player - HF
	Herbert Martin (Herb)	Sports	Canada	Hockey Player - HF
	Samuel Rawson	Arts	England	Historian
Gardner	Ava	Performing Arts	USA	Actress - Acad Award Nom
	Dale Allan	Aviation	USA	Astronaut
	Erle Stanley	Creative Works	USA	Author
	Guy Spencer	Aviation	USA	Astronaut
	James Henry (Jimmy)	Sports	Canada	Hockey Player - HF
Garfield	Brian Francis Wynne	Creative Works	USA	Author
	James Abram	Politics	USA	President
	John	Performing Arts	USA	Actor - Acad Award Nom
	Lucretia	Politics	USA	First Lady

LAST NAME	FIRST NAME	CATEGORY	COUNTRY	FAME
Garfunkel	Arthur Ira (Art)	Performing Arts	USA	Rock & Roll - HF - Simon & Garfunkel
Gargan	William	Performing Arts	USA	Actor - Acad Award Nom
Garibaldi	Giuseppe	War & Peace	Italy	General/Patriot
Garland	Charles Stedman (Chuck)	Sports	USA	Tennis Player - HF
	Hannibal Hamlin	Creative Works	USA	Author - Pulitzer
	Judy	Performing Arts	USA	Actress/Singer - Acad Award
Garlits	Don	Sports	USA	Race Car Driver - HF
Garn	Edwin Jacob (Jake)	Aviation	USA	Astronaut
	Edwin Jacob (Jake)	Politics	USA	Senator - Utah
Garneau	Joseph Jean-Pierre Marc	Aviation	Canada	Astronaut
Garner	Erroll Louis	Performing Arts	USA	Jazz Pianist - Big Band/Jazz - HF
	James	Performing Arts	USA	Actor - Acad Award Nom
	John Nance	Politics	USA	Vice-President
	Peggy Ann	Performing Arts	USA	Actress - Academy Award
Garnett	Constance	Arts	England	Translator
Garnier	Charles	Architecture	France	Architect
	Tony	Architecture	France	Architect
Garr	Teri	Performing Arts	USA	Actress - Acad Award Nom
Garrett	Pat	Law & Order	USA	Lawman
Garrick	David	Performing Arts	England	Actor/Theatrical Manager
Garriott	Owen Kay	Aviation	USA	Astronaut
Garrison	William Lloyd	Arts	USA	Editor/Lecturer/Abolitionist
Garrow	David J.	Creative Works	USA	Author - Pulitzer
Garson	Greer	Performing Arts	England	Actress - Academy Award
Gartner	Michael Alfred	Sports	Canada	Hockey Player - HF
Garvey	Marcus	Politics	West Indies	Leader - Negro
	Steve	Sports	USA	Baseball Player
Gascoyne-Cecil	Robert Arthur Talbot	Politics	England	Prime Minister
Gaskell	Elizabeth Cleghorn	Creative Works	England	Novelist
Gasser	Herbert Spencer	Science	USA	Medicine - Nobel Laureate
Gasset	José Ortega y	Arts	Spain	Philosopher/Essayist
Gastineau	Mark	Sports	USA	Football Player
Gates	Bill	Business	USA	Microsoft
	David	Performing Arts	USA	Singer
	Horatio	War & Peace	USA	General
	William (Pop)	Sports	USA	Basketball Player - HF
Gatling	Richard Jordan	Business	USA	Firearms
Gatski	Frank	Sports	USA	Football Player - HF
Gaudi	Antoni	Architecture	Spain	Architect
Gauguin	Eugène Henri Paul	Works of Art	France	Painter
Gaulle	Charles Andre Joseph de	Politics	France	President
	Charles André Marie de	War & Peace	France	General
Gaultier	Jean-Paul	Business	France	Fashion Designer
	Théophile	Creative Works	France	Poet/Novelist
Gavilan	Gerardo (Kid)	Sports	Cuba	Boxer - HF
Gavras	Costa	Movie Production	Greece	Director - Acad Award Nom
Gay	John	Creative Works	England	Dramatist/Poet
	John	Creative Works	England	Poet/Playwright
Gaye Jr.	Marvin Pentz	Performing Arts	USA	Singer - Rock & Roll - HF
Gayle	Crystal	Performing Arts	USA	Singer
Gay-Lussac	Joseph Louis	Science	France	Chemist/Physicist
Gaynor	Janet	Performing Arts	USA	Actress - Acad Award Nom
	Mitzi	Performing Arts	USA	Actress - Musical
Gazzara	Ben	Performing Arts	USA	Actor
Gazzo	Michael V.	Performing Arts	USA	Actor - Acad Award Nom
Gedda	Nicolai	Performing Arts	Sweden	Singer - Opera
Geddes	Norman Bel	Arts	USA	"Designer - Theatrical, Industrial"
Geer	Will	Performing Arts	USA	Actor
Gehrig	Henry Louis (Lou)	Sports	USA	Baseball Player - HF
Gehringer	Charles Leonard (Charlie)	Sports	USA	Baseball Player - HF
Gehry	Frank O.	Architecture	USA	Architect - Pritzker/ AIA Gold
Geiberger	Al	Sports	USA	Golfer
Geikie	Archibald	Science	Scotland	Geologist

SOLVER SERIES: NAME FINDER

LAST NAME	FIRST NAME	CATEGORY	COUNTRY	FAME
Gein	Edward Theodore (Ed)	Law & Order	USA	Serial Killer
Geller	Uri	Performing Arts	Israel	Magician
Gell-Mann	Murray	Science	USA	Physics - Nobel Laureate
Gemar	Charles Donald	Aviation	USA	Astronaut
Genêt	Edmond Charles Edouard	Politics	France	Diplomat
	Jean	Creative Works	France	Novelist/Playwright
Genn	Leo	Performing Arts	England	Actor - Acad Award Nom
Gennes	Pierre-Gilles de	Science	France	Physics - Nobel Laureate
Genovese	Don Vitone (Vito)	Law & Order	Italy	Mafia
Gentle	James	Sports	USA	Soccer Player - HF
Gentry	Teddy Wayne	Performing Arts	USA	Country Music - HF - Alabama
Geoffrion	Bernard Joseph Andre (Bernie)	Sports	Canada	Hockey Player - HF
George	Dan (Chief)	Performing Arts	Canada	Actor - Acad Award Nom
	David Lloyd	Politics	England	Prime Minister
	Gladys	Performing Arts	USA	Actress - Acad Award Nom
	William J. (Bill)	Sports	USA	Football Player - HF
Gephardt	Richard Andrew	Politics	USA	Congressman - Missouri
Gerard	Edward George (Eddie)	Sports	Canada	Hockey Player - HF
Gere	Richard	Performing Arts	USA	Actor
Gerhardt	Elena	Performing Arts	Germany	Singer - Opera
Gerkan	Manon von	Performing Arts	Germany	Super Model
	Meinhard von	Architecture	Germany	Architect
Germany	Eugene Benjamin	Business	USA	Oil Industry
Germi	Pietro	Movie Production	Italy	Director - Acad Award Nom
Germond	Jack W.	Creative Works	USA	Journalist - Newspaper
Gernreich	Rudi	Business	Austria	Designer - Fashions
Gerry	Elbridge	Politics	USA	Vice-President
Gershon	Gina	Performing Arts	USA	Actress
Gershwin	George	Creative Works	USA	Composer
	Ira	Creative Works	USA	Dramatist - Pulitzer
	Israel (Ira)	Creative Works	USA	Composer
Gerulaitis	Vitas	Sports	USA	Tennis Player
Gervin	George	Sports	USA	Basketball Player - HF
Gesell	Arnold Lucius	Arts	USA	Psychologist
Getty	Estelle	Performing Arts	USA	Actress
	Jean Paul	Business	USA	Oil Industry
Getz (Gayetzby)	Stanley (Stan)	Performing Arts	USA	Jazz Saxophonist - Big Band/Jazz - HF
Getzinger	Rudy	Sports	Yugoslavia	Soccer Player - HF
Ghandi	Rajiv	Politics	India	Prime Minister
Ghauri	Yasmeen	Performing Arts	Canada	Super Model
Ghiberti	Lorenzo	Architecture	Italy	Architect
	Lorenzo	Works of Art	Italy	Sculptor
Ghirlandaio	Domenico	Works of Art	Italy	Painter
Ghostley	Alice	Performing Arts	USA	Actress
Giacconi	Riccardo	Science	USA	Physics - Nobel Laureate
Giacometti	Alberto	Works of Art	Switzerland	Painter/Sculptor
Giacomin	Edward (Fast Eddie)	Sports	Canada	Hockey Player - HF
Giaever	Ivar	Science	USA	Physics - Nobel Laureate
Giancana	Gilorma (Sam) (Momo)	Law & Order	USA	Mafia
Giannini	Giancarlo	Performing Arts	Italy	Actor - Acad Award Nom
Giap	Vo Nguyen	War & Peace	Vietnam	General - Four Star
Giauque	William Francis	Science	USA	Chemistry - Nobel Laureate
Gibb	Andy	Performing Arts	England	Singer
	Barry	Performing Arts	England	Rock & Roll - HF - The Bee Gees
	Maurice	Performing Arts	England	Rock & Roll - HF - The Bee Gees
	Robin	Performing Arts	England	Rock & Roll - HF - The Bee Gees
Gibbon	Edward	Arts	England	Historian
Gibbons	Billy	Performing Arts	USA	Rock & Roll - HF - ZZ Top
	Orlando	Creative Works	England	Composer/Organist
Gibbs	James	Architecture	England	Architect
	Joe Jackson	Sports	USA	Football Coach - HF
	Josiah Willard	Science	USA	Physicist/Mathematician
	Marla	Performing Arts	USA	Actress

LAST NAME	FIRST NAME	CATEGORY	COUNTRY	FAME
Gibbs	Terry	Performing Arts	USA	Jazz Vibraphonist - Big Band/Jazz - HF
Gibran	Kahlil	Creative Works	Lebanon	Poet
Gibson	Althea	Sports	USA	Tennis Player - HF
	Charles Dana	Creative Works	USA	Journalist - Newspaper
	Debbie	Performing Arts	USA	Singer
	Donald Eugene (Don)	Performing Arts	USA	Singer - Country Music - HF
	Edward George	Aviation	USA	Astronaut
	Henry	Performing Arts	USA	Comedian
	Hoot	Performing Arts	USA	Actor
	Joshua (Josh)	Sports	USA	Baseball Player - HF
	Lawrence H.	Creative Works	USA	Author - Pulitzer
	Mel	Movie Production	USA	Director - Academy Award
	Mel	Performing Arts	USA	Actor
	Robert (Bob)	Sports	USA	Baseball Player - HF
	Robert Lee (Hoot)	Aviation	USA	Astronaut
Gide	André Paul Guillaume	Creative Works	France	Literature - Nobel Laureate
Gielgud	John	Performing Arts	England	Actor - Academy Award
Gifford	Frank Newton	Sports	USA	Football Player - HF
Gigli	Beniamino	Performing Arts	Italy	Singer - Opera
Gilbert	Cass	Architecture	USA	Architect
	Humphrey	Exploration	England	Explorer - Canada East Coast
	John	Performing Arts	USA	Actor
	Melissa	Performing Arts	USA	Actress
	Rodriquez Gabriel (Rod)	Sports	Canada	Hockey Player
	Sara	Performing Arts	USA	Actress
	Walter	Science	USA	Chemistry - Nobel Laureate
	William Schwenck	Creative Works	England	Poet/Librettist
Gilberto	Astrud	Performing Arts	Brazil	Singer
Gilels	Emil Grigoryevich	Performing Arts	Ukraine	Pianist - Classical
Giles	Warren Crandall	Sports	USA	Baseball Executive - HF
Gilford	Jack	Performing Arts	USA	Actor - Acad Award Nom
Gillespie	John Birks (Dizzy)	Performing Arts	USA	Band Leader - Big Band/Jazz - HF
Gillette	Anita	Performing Arts	USA	Actress
	William Hooker	Performing Arts	USA	Actor
Gilley	Mickey	Performing Arts	USA	Singer
Gilliam	Terry	Performing Arts	USA	Actor
Gillies	Clark	Sports	Canada	Hockey Player - HF
Gillman	Sidney (Sid)	Sports	USA	Football Coach - HF
Gilly	David Friedrich	Architecture	Germany	Architect
Gilman	Alfred G.	Science	USA	Medicine - Nobel Laureate
Gilmore	Artis	Sports	USA	Basketball Player
Gilmour	David John	Performing Arts	England	Rock & Roll - HF - Pink Floyd
	Hamilton Livingston (Billy)	Sports	Canada	Hockey Player - HF
Gilroy	Frank Daniel	Creative Works	USA	Dramatist - Pulitzer
Gingold	Hermione	Performing Arts	England	Actress
Gingrich	Newton Leroy (Newt)	Politics	USA	Speaker of the House
Ginsberg	Allen	Creative Works	USA	Poet
Ginsburg	Ruth Joan Bader	Law & Order	USA	Justice - Supreme Court
Ginzburg	Moisej	Architecture	Russia	Architect
	Vitaly L.	Science	Russia	Physics - Nobel Laureate
Giorgione	Il	Works of Art	Italy	Painter
Giovanni	Cimabue	Works of Art	Italy	Painter
Girard	Stephen	Business	USA	Financier/Philanthropist
Giraudoux	Hippolyte Jean	Creative Works	France	Novelist/Playwright
Gish	Dorothy	Performing Arts	USA	Actress
	Lillian	Performing Arts	USA	Actress - Acad Award Nom
Gissing	George Robert	Creative Works	England	Novelist
Giurgola	Romaldo	Architecture	USA	Architect - AIA/Jefferson Gold Medal
Givenchy	Hubert de	Business	France	Fashion Designer
Givens	Robin	Performing Arts	USA	Actress
Givens Jr.	Edward Galen	Aviation	USA	Astronaut
Gjellerup	Karl Adolph	Creative Works	Denmark	Literature - Nobel Laureate
Gladstone	William Ewart	Politics	England	Prime Minister

SOLVER SERIES: NAME FINDER

LAST NAME	FIRST NAME	CATEGORY	COUNTRY	FAME
Glaser	Donald Arthur	Science	USA	Physics - Nobel Laureate
Glasgow	Ellen Anderson Gholson	Creative Works	USA	Novelist - Pulitzer
Glashow	Sheldon Lee	Science	USA	Physics - Nobel Laureate
Glaspell	Susan	Creative Works	USA	Dramatist - Pulitzer
Glass	Philip	Creative Works	USA	Composer
Glauber	Roy J.	Science	USA	Physics - Nobel Laureate
Glavine	Tom	Sports	USA	Baseball Player
Glazunov	Aleksandr Konstantinovich	Creative Works	Russia	Composer
Gleason	Jackie	Performing Arts	USA	Actor - Acad Award Nom
	James	Performing Arts	USA	Actor - Acad Award Nom
Glendower	Owen	War & Peace	Wales	Chieftain
Glenn	John Herschel	Aviation	USA	Astronaut
	Scott	Performing Arts	USA	Actor
Glenn Jr.	John Herschel	Politics	USA	Senator - Ohio
Glenville	Peter	Movie Production	England	Director - Acad Award Nom
Gless	Sharon	Performing Arts	USA	Actress
Glidden	Bob	Sports	USA	Race Car Driver - HF
Glinka	Mikhail Ivanovich	Creative Works	Russia	Composer
Glover	Danny	Performing Arts	USA	Actor
	Edward (Teddy)	Sports	England	Soccer Player - HF
Gluck	Alma	Performing Arts	USA	Singer - Opera
	Christoph Willibald	Creative Works	Germany	Composer
	Louise	Creative Works	USA	Poet - Pulitzer
Glyn	Elinor	Creative Works	England	Novelist
Gobat	Albert	War & Peace	Switzerland	Peace - Nobel Laureate
Godard	Jean-Luc	Movie Production	France	Director
Godchaux	Donna	Performing Arts	USA	Rock & Roll - HF - Grateful Dead
	Keith	Performing Arts	USA	Rock & Roll - HF - Grateful Dead
Goddard	Paulette	Performing Arts	USA	Actress - Acad Award Nom
Godden	Margaret Rumer	Creative Works	England	Novelist
Gödel	Kurt	Arts	USA	Philosopher/Mathematician
Godfrey	Arthur	Performing Arts	USA	Comedian
Godunov	Boris Fëdorovich	Politics	Russia	Czar
Godwin	Gail	Creative Works	USA	Novelist
	William	Creative Works	England	Writer/Political Philosopher
Goebbels	Joseph Paul	Politics	Germany	Nazi Propagandist
Goeppert-Mayer	Maria	Science	USA	Physics - Nobel Laureate
Goering	Hermann Wilhelm	War & Peace	Germany	Nazi Field Marshall
Goethals	George Washington	War & Peace	USA	Army Officer/Engineer
Goethe	Johann	Creative Works	Germany	Poet/Dramatist
Goetzmann	William H.	Creative Works	USA	Author - Pulitzer
Goff	Bruce	Architecture	USA	Architect
Gogh	Vincent Van	Works of Art	Netherlands	Painter
Gogol	Nikolai Vasillevich	Creative Works	Russia	Novelist/Dramatist
Goheen	Frank Xavier (Moose)	Sports	USA	Hockey Player - HF
Gola	Thomas J.	Sports	USA	Basketball Player - HF
Goldberg	Caryn Elaine (Whoopi)	Performing Arts	USA	Actress - Academy Award
	Reuben Lucius (Rube)	Creative Works	USA	Cartoonist - Pulitzer
Goldblum	Jeff	Performing Arts	USA	Actor
Golding	William	Creative Works	England	Literature - Nobel Laureate
Goldman	James	Creative Works	USA	Playwright/Novelist
Goldmark	Karl	Creative Works	Hungary	Composer
Goldoni	Carlo	Creative Works	Italy	Dramatist
Goldsboro	Bobby	Performing Arts	USA	Singer
Goldsmith	Oliver	Creative Works	Ireland	Poet/Playwright/Novelist
Goldstein	Joseph L.	Science	USA	Medicine - Nobel Laureate
Goldwater	Barry Morris	Politics	USA	Senator - Arizona
Goldwyn	Samuel	Movie Production	Poland	Director
Golgi	Camillo	Science	Italy	Medicine - Nobel Laureate
Gomez	Thomas	Performing Arts	USA	Actor - Acad Award Nom
Gómez	Vernon Louis (Lefty)	Sports	USA	Baseball Player - HF
	Wilfredo	Sports	Puerto Rico	Boxer - HF
Goncourt	Edmond Louis Huot de	Creative Works	France	Novelist/Art Critic

LAST NAME	FIRST NAME	CATEGORY	COUNTRY	FAME
Goncourt	Jules Alfred Huot de	Creative Works	France	Novelist/Art Critic
Gonsalves	Adelino (Billy)	Sports	USA	Soccer Player - HF
	Paul	Performing Arts	USA	Jazz Saxophonist - Big Band/Jazz - HF
Gonzales	Richard Alonzo (Pancho)	Sports	USA	Tennis Player - HF
Gooden	Dwight	Sports	USA	Baseball Player
	Samuel	Performing Arts	USA	Rock & Roll - HF - The Impressions
Goodfellow	Ebenezer Ralston (Ebbie)	Sports	Canada	Hockey Player - HF
Goodhue	Bertram	Architecture	USA	Architect - AIA Gold Medal
Gooding Jr.	Cuba	Performing Arts	USA	Actor - Academy Award
Goodman	Benjamin David (Benny)	Performing Arts	USA	Band Leader - Big Band/Jazz - HF
	Dody	Performing Arts	USA	Actress
	John	Performing Arts	USA	Actor
Goodrich	Frances	Creative Works	USA	Dramatist - Pulitzer
	Gail	Sports	USA	Basketball Player - HF
Goodwin	Doris Kearns	Creative Works	USA	Author - Pulitzer
Goodyear	Charles	Science	USA	Inventor - Vulcanizing Rubber
Goolagong	Evonne Fay	Sports	Australia	Tennis Player - HF
Gorbachev	Mikhail Sergeyevich	Politics	Russia	Head of State
	Mikhail Sergeyevich	War & Peace	Russia	Peace - Nobel Laureate
	Raisa	Politics	Russia	First Lady
Gorbatko	Viktor Vassilyevich	Aviation	Russia	Astronaut
Gorcey	Leo	Performing Arts	USA	Comedian
Gordimer	Nadine	Creative Works	South Africa	Literature - Nobel Laureate
Gordon	Charles George	War & Peace	England	General
	Dexter	Performing Arts	USA	Actor - Acad Award Nom
	Dexter	Performing Arts	USA	Jazz Saxophonist - Big Band/Jazz - HF
	Gale	Performing Arts	USA	Actor
	Ruth	Performing Arts	USA	Actress - Academy Award
Gordon Jr.	Richard Francis	Aviation	USA	Astronaut
Gordone	Charles	Creative Works	USA	Dramatist - Pulitzer
Gore	Albert	Politics	USA	Vice-President
	Lesley	Performing Arts	USA	Singer
	Mary Elizabeth (Tipper)	Politics	USA	Second Lady
Goren	Charles Henry	Games	USA	Bridge Expert
Gorki	Maxim	Creative Works	Russia	Novelist/Playwright
Gorky	Arshile	Works of Art	USA	Painter - Abstract Expressionist
Gorme	Eydie	Performing Arts	USA	Singer
Gormley	Robert (Bob)	Sports	USA	Soccer Player - HF
Gorshin	Frank	Performing Arts	USA	Comedian
Gosden	Freeman	Performing Arts	USA	Comedian
Goslin	Leon Allen (Goose)	Sports	USA	Baseball Player - HF
Gosse	Edmund William	Creative Works	England	Poet/Critic/Biographer
Gossett Jr.	Louis	Performing Arts	USA	Actor - Academy Award
Gotti	Irving (Irv)	Performing Arts	USA	Music Producer
	John (Dapper Don)	Law & Order	USA	Mafia
Goudy	Frederic William	Arts	USA	Print Designer
Gould	Chester	Creative Works	USA	Cartoonist - Dick Tracy
	Elliott	Performing Arts	USA	Actor - Acad Award Nom
	Glenn Herbert	Performing Arts	Canada	Pianist - Canadian Music - HF
	Jay	Business	USA	Financier
	Lois	Creative Works	USA	Author
	Shane	Sports	Australia	Olympic Swimmer
Goulet	Michel	Sports	Canada	Hockey Player - HF
	Robert	Performing Arts	USA	Singer
Gounod	Charles François	Creative Works	France	Composer
Gourmont	Rémy de	Arts	France	Philosopher/Poet/Novelist/Critic
Govier	Sheldon	Sports	Scotland	Soccer Player - HF
Gowdy	Curt	Creative Works	USA	Journalist - Television
Gowen	Franklin	Business	USA	Railway Magnate
Gower	John	Creative Works	England	Poet
Goya	Francisco José de	Works of Art	Spain	Painter
Graaff	Robert J. Van de	Science	USA	Physicist
Grabe	Ronald John	Aviation	USA	Astronaut

SOLVER SERIES: NAME FINDER

LAST NAME	FIRST NAME	CATEGORY	COUNTRY	FAME
Grable	Betty	Performing Arts	USA	Actor
Grace	William	Business	USA	Shipping Magnate
Gracián	Baltasar	Arts	Spain	Philosopher/Jesuit
Grady Jr.	Michael	Performing Arts	USA	Rock & Roll - HF - The Soul Stirrers
Graf	Steffi	Sports	Germany	Tennis Player - HF
Graff	Ilene	Performing Arts	USA	Actress/Singer
Graffis	Herb	Sports	USA	Golf Promoter - HF
Grafton	Sue	Creative Works	USA	Author
Graham	Bruce	Architecture	USA	Architect - High Rise
	Daniel Robert (Bob)	Politics	USA	Senator - Florida
	David	Sports	Australia	Golfer
	Johnny	Performing Arts	USA	Rock & Roll - HF - Earth Wind & Fire
	Jorie	Creative Works	USA	Poet - Pulitzer
	Katharine	Creative Works	USA	Author - Pulitzer
	Martha	Performing Arts	USA	Dancer
	Virginia	Performing Arts	USA	Actress
Graham Jr.	Otto Everett	Sports	USA	Football Player - HF
Grahame	Gloria	Performing Arts	USA	Actress - Academy Award
Grainger	Percy Aldridge	Creative Works	USA	Composer/Pianist
Gramm	Lou	Performing Arts	USA	Singer
	William Philip (Phil)	Politics	USA	Senator - Texas
Grammer	Kelsey	Performing Arts	Virgin Islands	Actor
Granatelli	Andy	Sports	USA	Race Car Driver - HF
Grange	Harold Edward (Red)	Sports	USA	Football Player - HF
Granger	Clive W.J.	Arts	England	Economics - Nobel Laureate
	Farley	Performing Arts	USA	Actor
	Stewart	Performing Arts	England	Actor
Granit	Ragnar	Science	Sweden	Medicine - Nobel Laureate
Granitza	Karl-Heinz	Sports	Germany	Soccer Player - HF
Grant	Amy	Performing Arts	USA	Singer
	Cary	Performing Arts	England	Actor - Acad Award Nom
	Eric Nolan	Performing Arts	USA	Rock & Roll - HF - The O'Jays
	Julia	Politics	USA	First Lady
	Lee	Performing Arts	USA	Actress - Academy Award
	Michael (Mike)	Sports	Canada	Hockey Player - HF
	Ulysses Simpson	Politics	USA	President
	Ulysses Simpson	War & Peace	USA	General
Grant Jr.	Bryan Moral (Bitsy)	Sports	USA	Tennis Player - HF
	Harold Peter (Bud)	Sports	USA	Football Coach - HF
Granville	Bonita	Performing Arts	USA	Actress - Acad Award Nom
Granville-Barker	Harley	Creative Works	England	Playwright/Critic/Actor
Granz	Norman	Performing Arts	Switzerland	Jazz Impresario - Big Band/Jazz - HF
Grappelli	Stephane	Performing Arts	France	Jazz Violinist - Big Band/Jazz - HF
Grass	Günter	Creative Works	Germany	Literature - Nobel Laureate
Grassi	Giorgio	Architecture	Italy	Architect
Grasso	Ella Rose Tambussi	Politics	USA	Governor - Connecticut
Gratton	Henry	Politics	Ireland	Statesman
Grau	Shirley Ann	Creative Works	USA	Author - Pulitzer
Gravano	Salvatore (Sammy the Bull)	Law & Order	USA	Mafia
Graveline	Duane Edgar	Aviation	USA	Astronaut
Graves	Alexander	Performing Arts	USA	Rock & Roll - HF - The Moonglows
	Michael	Architecture	USA	Architect - AIA Gold Medal
	Peter	Performing Arts	USA	Actor
	Robert Ranke	Creative Works	England	Poet/Novelist/Critic
	Teressa	Performing Arts	USA	Actress
Gray	Asa	Science	USA	Botanist
	David	Sports	England	Tennis Reporter - HF
	Erin	Performing Arts	USA	Actress
	Linda	Performing Arts	USA	Actress
	Robert	Exploration	USA	Explorer - Circumnavigation
	Thomas	Creative Works	England	Poet
Grayson	David	Creative Works	USA	Author
	Kathryn	Performing Arts	USA	Actress

LAST NAME	FIRST NAME	CATEGORY	COUNTRY	FAME
Grazia	Sebastian de	Creative Works	USA	Author - Pulitzer
Graziano	Thomas Rocco (Rocky)	Sports	USA	Boxer - HF
Greco	Buddy	Performing Arts	USA	Singer
	Domenikos El	Works of Art	Italy	Painter
Greco	El	Works of Art	Spain	Painter
Greeley	Horace	Politics	USA	Political Leader/Journalist
Greely	Horace	Creative Works	USA	Journalist - Newspaper
Green	Adolph	Creative Works	USA	Composer
	Albert (Al)	Performing Arts	USA	Singer - Rock & Roll - HF
	Constance McLaughlin	Creative Works	USA	Author - Pulitzer
	Hubert	Sports	USA	Golfer
	John Richard	Arts	England	Historian
	Paul Eliot	Creative Works	USA	Dramatist - Pulitzer
	Wilfred Thomas (Shorty)	Sports	Canada	Hockey Player - HF
	William	Business	USA	Labor Leader
Green (Greenbaum)	Peter Allan	Performing Arts	England	Rock & Roll - HF - Fleetwood Mac
Greenberg	Henry Benjamin (Hank)	Sports	USA	Baseball Player - HF
	Jay	Creative Works	USA	Composer Pianist
Greene	Bob	Creative Works	USA	Journalist - Newspaper
	Charles Edward (Joe)	Sports	USA	Football Player - HF
	Graham	Creative Works	England	Novelist
	Graham	Performing Arts	Canada	Actor - Acad Award Nom
	Lorne	Performing Arts	Canada	Actor
	Michele	Performing Arts	USA	Actress
	Nathanael	War & Peace	USA	General - Revolutionary War
	Robert	Creative Works	England	Poet/Dramatist/Pamphleteer
	Shecky	Performing Arts	USA	Comedian
Greenfield	Jeff	Creative Works	USA	Journalist - Television
Greengard	Paul	Science	USA	Medicine - Nobel Laureate
Greenough	Horatio	Works of Art	USA	Sculptor
Greenstreet	Sydney	Performing Arts	England	Actor - Acad Award Nom
Greenwich	Ellie	Performing Arts	USA	Singer
Greer	Harold E. (Hal)	Sports	USA	Basketball Player - HF
Greg	Robert Hyde	Business	England	Textile Industry
	Samuel	Business	England	Textile Industry
Gregg	Alvis Forrest	Sports	USA	Football Player - HF
	Peter Holden	Sports	USA	Race Car Driver - HF
Gregory	Augusta	Creative Works	Ireland	Playwright
	Dick	Performing Arts	USA	Comedian/Politician
	William George	Aviation	USA	Astronaut
Gregotti	Vittorio	Architecture	Italy	Architect
Grenfell	Wifred	Science	England	Physician/Writer
Grenville	George	Politics	England	Prime Minister
	Georgina	Performing Arts	South Africa	Super Model
	Richard	War & Peace	England	Naval Commander
Gretzky	Wayne Douglas (Great One)	Sports	Canada	Hockey Player - HF
Greuze	Jean Baptiste	Works of Art	France	Painter
Grey	Charles	Politics	England	Prime Minister
	Earl	Politics	England	Prime Minister
	Edward	Politics	England	Statesman
	Jane	Politics	England	Queen
	Jennifer	Performing Arts	USA	Actress
	Joel	Performing Arts	USA	Actor - Academy Award
	Lita	Performing Arts	USA	Actress
	Zane	Creative Works	USA	Novelist
Grieg	Edvard Hagerup	Creative Works	Norway	Composer
Grier	Pam	Performing Arts	USA	Actress
	Rosie	Sports	USA	Football Player
Griese	Robert Allen (Bob)	Sports	USA	Football Player - HF
Griffin	Clarence James (Peck)	Sports	USA	Tennis Player - HF
	Merv	Performing Arts	USA	Show Host/Singer
Griffis	Silas Seth (Si)	Sports	USA	Hockey Player - HF
Griffith	Andy	Performing Arts	USA	Actor

SOLVER SERIES: NAME FINDER

LAST NAME	FIRST NAME	CATEGORY	COUNTRY	FAME
Griffith	Clark Calvin	Sports	USA	Baseball Executive -HF
	Corinne	Performing Arts	USA	Actress - Acad Award Nom
	David Lewelyn	Movie Production	USA	Director/Producer
	Emile	Sports	USA	Boxer - HF
	Hugh	Performing Arts	Wales	Actor - Academy Award
	Melanie	Performing Arts	USA	Actress - Acad Award Nom
Griffiths	Rachael	Performing Arts	Australia	Actress - Acad Award Nom
Griggs	Stanley David	Aviation	USA	Astronaut
Grignard	Victor	Science	France	Chemistry - Nobel Laureate
Grillparzer	Franz	Creative Works	Austria	Dramatist
Grimes	Burleigh Arland	Sports	USA	Baseball Player - HF
	Martha	Creative Works	USA	Author
	Tammy	Performing Arts	USA	Actress
Grimm	Jakob	Creative Works	Germany	Philologist - Fairy Tales
	Wilhelm	Creative Works	Germany	Philologist - Fairy Tales
Gris	Juan	Works of Art	Spain	Painter
Grisham	John	Creative Works	USA	Author
Grissom	Virgil Ivan (Gus)	Aviation	USA	Astronaut
Grist	Reri	Performing Arts	USA	Singer - Opera
Grizzard	George	Performing Arts	USA	Actor
Grodin	Charles	Performing Arts	USA	Actor
Groening	Matt	Creative Works	USA	Cartoonist - The Simpsons
Grofé	Ferde	Creative Works	USA	Composer/Pianist
Grogas	William Crawford	War & Peace	USA	Medical Officer
Groh	David	Performing Arts	USA	Actor
Gromyko	Andrei Andreevich	Politics	Russia	Diplomat
Gropius	Walter	Architecture	Germany	Architect - AIA Gold Medal
Gros	Antoine Jean	Works of Art	France	Painter
Grosbard	Ulu	Movie Production	Belgium	Director
Gross	David J.	Science	USA	Physics - Nobel Laureate
Gross	Mary	Performing Arts	USA	Comedian
	Michael	Performing Arts	USA	Actor
Grosz	George	Works of Art	USA	Painter/Caricaturist
Grote	George	Arts	England	Historian
Grotius	Hugo	Politics	Netherlands	Statesman/Jurist/Scholar
Grove	Robert Moses (Lefty)	Sports	USA	Baseball Player - HF
Groza	Louis Roy (Lou)	Sports	USA	Football Player - HF
Grubbs	Robert H.	Science	USA	Chemistry - Nobel Laureate
Gruberova	Edita	Performing Arts	Slovakia	Singer - Opera
Gruenig	Robert F. (Ace)	Sports	USA	Basketball Player - HF
Grünewald	Matthias	Works of Art	Germany	Painter
Gryzik	Joseph (Joe)	Sports	Poland	Soccer Player - HF
Guadio	Bob	Performing Arts	USA	Rock & Roll - HF - The Four Seasons
Guardia	Fiorello Henry La	Politics	USA	Lawyer/Political Leader
Guardino	Harry	Performing Arts	USA	Actor
Guarini	Guarino	Architecture	Italy	Architect
Guarneri	Giuseppe Antonio	Arts	Italy	Violin Maker
Gucci	Guccio	Business	Italy	Fashion Designer
Gudahl	Ralph	Sports	USA	Golfer - HF
Guderian	Heinz Wilhelm	War & Peace	Germany	General
Guest	Edgar	Creative Works	England	Poet
Guevara	Ernesto Rafael (Che)	War & Peace	Cuba	Revolutionist/Guerilla Leader
Guggenheim	Daniel	Business	USA	Industrialist/Philanthropist
	Myer	Business	USA	Mining Industry
	Simon	Business	USA	Industrialist/Philanthropist
	Solomon R.	Business	USA	Industrialist/Philanthropist
Guidoni	Umberto	Aviation	Italy	Astronaut
Guillaume	Charles Edouard	Science	Switzerland	Physics - Nobel Laureate
	Robert	Performing Arts	USA	Actor - Musical
Guillemin	Roger	Science	USA	Medicine - Nobel Laureate
Guimard	Hector	Architecture	France	Architect
Guin	Ursula Kroeber Le	Creative Works	USA	Novelist
Guiness	Alec	Performing Arts	England	Actor - Academy Award

LAST NAME	FIRST NAME	CATEGORY	COUNTRY	FAME
Guinier	Lani	Politics	USA	Proponent - Civil Rights
Guise	François de Lorraine	Politics	France	Statesman/General
	Henri de Lorranine	Politics	France	Statesman/General
Guisewite	Cathy	Creative Works	USA	Cartoonist - Cathy
Guitry	Sacha	Creative Works	France	Playwright/Actor
Guizot	François Pierre Guillaume	Politics	France	Statesman/Historian
Gulager	Clu	Performing Arts	USA	Actor
Gullstrand	Allvar	Science	Sweden	Medicine - Nobel Laureate
Gumble	Bryant	Creative Works	USA	Journalist - Television
Gunter	Edmund	Science	England	Mathematician
Gurney	Daniel Sexton (Dan)	Sports	USA	Race Car Driver - HF
Gurney	Joseph	Business	USA	Railway Magnate
Gustav V	King (Mr.G)	Sports	Sweden	Tennis Player - HF
Gutenberg	Johann	Arts	Germany	Printer
Guthrie	Alfred Bertram	Creative Works	USA	Novelist - Pulitzer
	Arlo	Performing Arts	USA	Singer
	Janet	Sports	USA	Race Car Driver - HF
	William Tyrone	Movie Production	England	Director
	Woodrow Wilson (Woody)	Performing Arts	USA	Singer - Rock & Roll - HF
Gutierrez	Sidney McNeil	Aviation	USA	Astronaut
Guttenberg	Steve	Performing Arts	USA	Actor
Guy	Buddy	Performing Arts	USA	Guitarist - Rock & Roll - HF
	Jasmine	Performing Arts	USA	Actress
Guyon	Joseph Napoleon (Joe)	Sports	USA	Football Player - HF
Guzik	Jake (Greasy Thumb)	Law & Order	Russia	Mafia
Gwathmey	Charles	Architecture	USA	Architect
Gwenn	Edmund	Performing Arts	Wales	Actor - Academy Award
Gwinett	Button	Politics	USA	Patriot
Gwyn	Nell	Performing Arts	England	Actress
Gwynn	Tony	Sports	USA	Baseball Player
Gwynne	Fred	Performing Arts	USA	Actor
Gyatso	Tenzin	War & Peace	Tibet	Peace - Nobel Laureate
Haavelmo	Trygve	Arts	Norway	Economics - Nobel Laureate
Haber	Fritz	Science	Germany	Chemistry - Nobel Laureate
Habermas	Jürgen	Arts	Germany	Philosopher/Social Theorist
Hackett	Albert	Creative Works	USA	Dramatist - Pulitzer
	Buddy	Performing Arts	USA	Comedian
	Harold Humphrey	Sports	USA	Tennis Player - HF
	Joan	Performing Arts	USA	Actress - Acad Award Nom
	Robert Leo (Bobby)	Performing Arts	USA	Cornetist/Guitarist - Big Band/Jazz - HF
Hackford	Taylor	Movie Production	USA	Director - Acad Award Nom
Hackman	Gene	Performing Arts	USA	Actor - Academy Award
Hadfield	Chris Austin	Aviation	Canada	Astronaut
Hadid	Zaha	Architecture	England	Architect - Pritzker Laureate
Haeckel	Ernst Heinrich	Science	Germany	Biologist/Philosopher
Hafey	Charles James (Chick)	Sports	USA	Baseball Player - HF
Hagar	Sammy	Performing Arts	USA	Singer
Hagen	Cifford O.	Sports	USA	Basketball Player - HF
	Jean	Performing Arts	USA	Actress - Acad Award Nom
	Uta	Performing Arts	Germany	Actress
	Walter	Sports	USA	Golfer - HF
Haggard	Henry Ryder	Creative Works	England	Novelist
	Merle Ronald	Performing Arts	USA	Singer - Country Music - HF
Hagge	Marlene Bauer	Sports	USA	Golfer - HF
Hagler	Marvin	Sports	USA	Boxer - HF
Hagman	Larry	Performing Arts	USA	Actor
Hahn	Otto	Science	Germany	Chemistry - Nobel Laureate
	Steven	Creative Works	USA	Author - Pulitzer
Hahnemann	Christian Friedrich Samuel	Science	Germany	Physician - Homeopathy
Haid	Charles	Performing Arts	USA	Actor
Haig	Douglas	War & Peace	England	Commander in Chief
Haig Jr.	Alexander Meigs	War & Peace	USA	General - Army
Haile	Selassie	Politics	Ethiopia	Emperor

SOLVER SERIES: NAME FINDER

LAST NAME	FIRST NAME	CATEGORY	COUNTRY	FAME
Hailey	Arthur	Creative Works	England	Author
Hailwood	Mike (The Bike)	Sports	England	Race Car Driver - HF
Haim	Corey	Performing Arts	Canada	Actor
Haines	Jesse Joseph	Sports	USA	Baseball Player - HF
Hainsworth	George	Sports	Canada	Hockey Player - HF
Haise Jr.	Fred Wallace	Aviation	USA	Astronaut
Hakluyt	Richard	Arts	England	Geographer/Chronicler
Halas	George Stanley	Sports	USA	Football Coach - HF
Halberstam	David	Creative Works	USA	Journalist - Pulitzer
Haldane	John Burdon	Science	England	Biologist/Writer
	Richard Burdon	Politics	Scotland	Statesman/Philosopher
Hale	Barbara	Performing Arts	USA	Actress
	Edward Everett	Arts	USA	Clergyman/Writer
	Nathan	War & Peace	USA	Soldier - Revolutionary War
Hale Jr	Alan	Performing Arts	USA	Actor
Halévy	Jacques	Creative Works	France	Composer
Haley	Alex	Creative Works	USA	Author
	Jack	Performing Arts	USA	Actor
	William John Clifton (Bill)	Performing Arts	USA	Band Leader - Rock & Roll - HF
	William John Clifton (Bill)	Performing Arts	USA	Singer - Rock & Roll - HF
Hall	Alexander	Movie Production	USA	Director - Acad Award Nom
	Arsenio	Performing Arts	USA	Comedian
	Bridget	Performing Arts	USA	Super Model
	Charles Martin	Science	USA	Chemist
	Daryl	Performing Arts	USA	Singer
	Deidre	Performing Arts	USA	Actress
	Glenn Henry	Sports	Canada	Hockey Player - HF
	Granville Stanley	Arts	USA	Psychologist/Educator
	Grayson	Performing Arts	USA	Actress - Acad Award Nom
	Huntz	Performing Arts	USA	Actor
	James Stanley (Jim)	Performing Arts	USA	Jazz Guitarist - Big Band/Jazz - HF
	Jim	Sports	USA	Race Car Driver - HF
	John	Performing Arts	USA	Singer
	John L.	Science	USA	Physics - Nobel Laureate
	Joseph	Arts	England	Philosopher/Theologian
	Joseph Henry (Joe)	Sports	England	Hockey Player - HF
	Manly Palmer	Arts	Canada	Philosopher
	Monty	Performing Arts	Canada	Show Host
	Tom T.	Performing Arts	USA	Singer
Hall (Weir)	Robert (Bob)	Performing Arts	USA	Rock & Roll - HF - Grateful Dead
Hallam	Henry	Arts	England	Historian
Halley	Edmund	Science	England	Astronomer/Mathematician
Halliwell	Geri (Ginger)	Performing Arts	England	Rock & Roll - Spice Girls
Hallstrom	Lasse	Movie Production	Sweden	Director - Acad Award Nom
Halprin	Lawrence	Architecture	USA	Architect - Jefferson Medal
Hals	Frans	Works of Art	Netherlands	Painter
Ham Jr.	Jack Raphael	Sports	USA	Football Player - HF
Hamel	Veronica	Performing Arts	USA	Actress
Hamill	Mark	Performing Arts	USA	Actor
Hamilton	Alexander	Politics	USA	Statesman
	George	Performing Arts	USA	Actor
	Linda	Performing Arts	USA	Actress
	Margaret	Performing Arts	USA	Actress
	Scott	Sports	USA	Olympic Skater
	William Robert (Billy)	Sports	USA	Baseball Player - HF
	Thomas (Tom)	Performing Arts	USA	Rock & Roll - HF - Aerosmith
Hamlin	Hannibal	Politics	USA	Vice-President
	Harry	Performing Arts	USA	Actor
	Talbot Faulkner	Creative Works	USA	Author - Pulitzer
Hamlisch	Marvin	Creative Works	USA	Composer
Hamm	Mia	Sports	USA	Soccer
Hammarskjöld	Dag Hjalmar Agne Carl	Politics	Sweden	Secretary - United Nations
	Dag Hjalmar Agne Carl	War & Peace	Sweden	Peace - Nobel Laureate

LAST NAME	FIRST NAME	CATEGORY	COUNTRY	FAME
Hammer	Armand	Business	USA	Oil Industry
	Jan	Creative Works	Czechoslovakia	Composer
Hammerstein	Oscar	Business	USA	Tobacco Industry
	Oscar	Creative Works	USA	Librettist/Lyricist
Hammerstein II	Oscar	Creative Works	USA	Dramatist - Pulitzer
Hammett	Dashiell	Creative Works	USA	Author
Hammond	Bray	Creative Works	USA	Author - Pulitzer
Hammond Jr.	Lloyd Blaine	Aviation	USA	Astronaut
Hampden	John	Politics	England	Statesman/Parlimentarian
	Walter	Performing Arts	USA	Actor
Hampton	Daniel Oliver (Dan)	Sports	USA	Football Player - HF
	Lionel (Hamps)	Performing Arts	USA	Band Leader - Big Band/Jazz - HF
Hamsun	Knut Pedersen	Creative Works	Norway	Literature - Nobel Laureate
Hanauer	Chip	Sports	USA	Hydro Plane Driver - HF
Hancock	Herbert Jeffrey (Herbie)	Performing Arts	USA	Jazz Pianist/Composer - Big Band/Jazz - HF
	John	Politics	USA	President - Continental Congress
	Winfield Scott	War & Peace	USA	Union General
Hand	Billings Learned	Law & Order	USA	Jurist
Handel	George Frederick	Creative Works	England	Composer
Handlin	Oscar	Creative Works	USA	Author - Pulitzer
Handy	William Christopher	Performing Arts	USA	Band Leader - Big Band/Jazz - HF
Hankar	Paul	Architecture	Belgium	Architect
Hanks	Tom	Performing Arts	USA	Actor - Academy Award
Hanlon	Edward Hugh (Ned)	Sports	USA	Baseball Manager - HF
Hanna	Marcus	Business	USA	Financier/Politician
	William (Bill)	Creative Works	USA	Cartoonist - Tom and Jerry
Hannah	Daryl	Performing Arts	USA	Actress
	John Allen	Sports	USA	Football Player - HF
Hänsch	Theodore	Science	Germany	Physics - Nobel Laureate
Hansell	Ellen Forde	Sports	USA	Tennis Player - HF
Hansen	Marcus Lee	Creative Works	USA	Author - Pulitzer
	Victor A.	Sports	USA	Basketball Player - HF
Hanson	Curtis	Movie Production	USA	Director - Acad Award Nom
	Howard	Creative Works	USA	Composer
Harada	Masahiko (Fighting)	Sports	Japan	Boxer - HF
Harbach	Otto	Creative Works	USA	Lyricist
Harbaugh	Gregory Jordan	Aviation	USA	Astronaut
Hard	Darlene Ruth	Sports	USA	Tennis Player - HF
Harden	Arthur	Science	England	Chemistry - Nobel Laureate
	Marcia Gay	Performing Arts	USA	Actress - Academy Award
Harding	Ann	Performing Arts	USA	Actress - Acad Award Nom
	Florence Kling	Politics	USA	First Lady
	Warren Gamaliel	Politics	USA	President
Hardison	Kadeem	Performing Arts	USA	Actor
Hardwicke	Cedric	Performing Arts	England	Actor
Hardy	Oliver	Performing Arts	USA	Comedian
	Thomas	Creative Works	England	Poet/Novelist
Hare	Richard Mervyn	Arts	England	Philosopher
Harewood	Dorian	Performing Arts	USA	Actor
Hargreaves	James	Science	England	Inventor - Spinning Jenny
Haring	Keith	Works of Art	USA	Painter
	Hugo	Architecture	Germany	Architect
Harker	Albert (Al)	Sports	USA	Soccer Player - HF
Harkes	John	Sports	USA	Soccer Player - HF
Harlan	John Marshall	Law & Order	USA	Justice - Supreme Court
	Louis R.	Creative Works	USA	Author - Pulitzer
Harlow	Jean	Performing Arts	USA	Actress
	Robert (Bob)	Sports	USA	Golf Promoter - HF
	Shalom	Performing Arts	Canada	Super Model
Harmon	Mark	Performing Arts	USA	Actor
	Tom	Sports	USA	Football Player
Harmsworth	Alfred Charles William	Arts	England	Newspaper Publisher
	Harold	Business	England	Publishing

SOLVER SERIES: NAME FINDER

LAST NAME	FIRST NAME	CATEGORY	COUNTRY	FAME
Harpe	Jean Baptiste de la	Exploration	France	Explorer - America South
Harper	Harry	Sports	USA	Baseball Player
	Jessica	Performing Arts	USA	Actress
	Lee	Creative Works	USA	Author
	Tess	Performing Arts	USA	Actress - Acad Award Nom
	Valerie	Performing Arts	USA	Actress
Harrelson	Woody	Performing Arts	USA	Actor - Acad Award Nom
Harridge	William (Will)	Sports	USA	Baseball Executive - HF
Harriman	Edward Henry	Business	USA	Financier/Railroad Magnate
	William Averell	Business	USA	Financier/Industrialist
Harrington Jr.	Pat	Performing Arts	USA	Actor
Harris	Barbara	Performing Arts	USA	Actress - Acad Award Nom
	Ed	Performing Arts	USA	Actor - Acad Award Nom
	Emmylou	Performing Arts	USA	Singer
	Franco	Sports	USA	Football Player - HF
	Joel Chandler	Creative Works	USA	Author
	Julie	Performing Arts	USA	Actress - Acad Award Nom
	Micki	Performing Arts	USA	Rock & Roll - HF - The Shirelles
	Phil	Performing Arts	USA	Comedian
	Richard	Performing Arts	Ireland	Actor - Acad Award Nom
	Rosemary	Performing Arts	England	Actress - Acad Award Nom
	Roy Ellsworth	Creative Works	USA	Composer
	Stanley Raymond (Bucky)	Sports	USA	Baseball Manager - HF
Harris Jr.	Bernard Andrew	Aviation	USA	Astronaut
Harrison	Anna	Politics	USA	First Lady
	Benjamin	Politics	USA	President
	Caroline Lavinia	Politics	USA	First Lady
	George	Performing Arts	England	Rock & Roll - HF - The Beatles
	Gregory	Performing Arts	USA	Actor
	Jeremiah (Jerry)	Performing Arts	USA	Rock & Roll - HF - The Talking Heads
	Mary Scott Lord	Politics	USA	First Lady
	Noel	Performing Arts	England	Singer
	Rex	Performing Arts	England	Actor - Academy Award
	Wallace Kirkman	Architecture	USA	Architect - AIA Gold Medal
	William Henry	Politics	USA	President
Harris-Stewart	Lusia	Sports	USA	Basketball Player - HF
Harrod	Charles	Business	England	Retail Trade
Harry	Deborah	Performing Arts	USA	Singer
Harsanyi	John C.	Arts	USA	Economics - Nobel Laureate
Hart	Doris Jane	Sports	USA	Tennis Player - HF
	Gary Warren	Politics	USA	Senator - Colorado
	Johnny	Creative Works	USA	Cartoonist - BC
	Mickey	Performing Arts	USA	Rock & Roll - HF - Grateful Dead
	Moss	Creative Works	USA	Dramatist - Pulitzer
	Terry Jonathon	Aviation	USA	Astronaut
	William S.	Performing Arts	USA	Actor
Harte	Bret	Creative Works	USA	Writer - Short Stories
Hartley	Mariette	Performing Arts	USA	Actress
Hartline	Haldan Keffer	Science	USA	Medicine - Nobel Laureate
Hartman	David	Creative Works	USA	Journalist - Television
	Elizabeth	Performing Arts	USA	Actress - Acad Award Nom
	Lisa	Performing Arts	USA	Actress
	Phil	Performing Arts	Canada	Comedian
Hartnett	Charles Leo (Gabby)	Sports	USA	Baseball Player - HF
Hartog	Dirck	Exploration	Netherlands	Explorer - Australia West Coast
Hartsfield Jr.	Henry Warren	Aviation	USA	Astronaut
Hartwell	Leland H.	Science	USA	Medicine - Nobel Laureate
Harvard	John	Arts	England	Clergyman
Harvey	Anthony	Movie Production	England	Director - Acad Award Nom
	Douglas Norman (Doug)	Sports	Canada	Hockey Player - HF
	Laurence	Performing Arts	Lithuania	Actor - Acad Award Nom
	Paul	Creative Works	USA	Journalist - Radio
	William	Science	England	Physician

LAST NAME	FIRST NAME	CATEGORY	COUNTRY	FAME
Haskell	Peter	Performing Arts	USA	Actor
Hassam	Frederick Childe	Works of Art	USA	Painter/Etcher
Hassel	Odd	Science	Norway	Chemistry - Nobel Laureate
Hässler	Thomas	Sports	Germany	Soccer Player
Hasso	Signe	Performing Arts	Sweden	Actress
Hastings	Warren	Politics	England	Statesman
Hatch	Orrin Grant	Politics	USA	Senator - Utah
Hatfield	Robert Lee (Bobby)	Performing Arts	USA	Rock & Roll - HF - Righteous Brothers
Hathaway	Henry	Movie Production	USA	Director - Acad Award Nom
Hauck	Frederick Hamilton	Aviation	USA	Astronaut
Hauer	Rutger	Performing Arts	Netherlands	Actor
Haughey	Charles James	Politics	Ireland	Prime Minister
Hauptman	Herbert	Science	USA	Chemistry - Nobel Laureate
Hauptmann	Gerhart Johann Robert	Creative Works	Germany	Literature - Nobel Laureate
Haussmann	George Eugène	Architecture	France	Architect
Havelock	Ellis	Creative Works	England	Author
Haven	Gloria De	Performing Arts	USA	Actress
Havens	Richie	Performing Arts	USA	Singer
Haver	June	Performing Arts	USA	Actress
Havers	Nigel	Performing Arts	England	Actor
Havilland	Olivia De	Performing Arts	Japan	Actress - Academy Award
Havlicek	John (Hondo)	Sports	USA	Basketball Player - HF
Havoc	June	Performing Arts	Canada	Actress
Hawerchuk	Dale (Ducky)	Sports	Canada	Hockey Player - HF
Hawke	Ethan	Performing Arts	USA	Actor - Acad Award Nom
Hawking	Stephen William	Science	England	Physicist
Hawkings	Hoyt	Performing Arts	USA	Country Music - HF - The Jordanaires
Hawkins	Coleman Randolph	Performing Arts	USA	Jazz Saxophonist - Big Band/Jazz - HF
	"Cornelius (Connie, The Hawk)"	Sports	USA	Basketball Player - HF
	Jack	Performing Arts	England	Actor
	John	Exploration	England	Explorer - Caribbean
	John	War & Peace	England	Naval Officer/Slave Trader
Hawks	Howard	Movie Production	USA	Director - Acad Award Nom
Hawn	Goldie	Performing Arts	USA	Actress - Acad Award Nom
Haworth	Walter Norman	Science	England	Chemistry - Nobel Laureate
Hawthorne	Nathaniel	Creative Works	USA	Novelist/Short Story Writer
	Nigel	Performing Arts	England	Actor - Acad Award Nom
Hay	George William	Sports	Canada	Hockey Player - HF
	John Milton	Politics	USA	Statesman/Writer
Hayakawa	Sessue	Performing Arts	Japan	Actor - Acad Award Nom
Hayden-Jones	Adrianne Shirley Ann	Sports	England	Tennis Player - HF
Haydn	Franz Joseph	Creative Works	Austria	Composer
Hayek	Friedrich August von	Arts	Austria	Economics - Nobel Laureate
	Salma	Performing Arts	Mexico	Actress - Acad Award Nom
Hayes	Bob (Bullet)	Sports	USA	Olympic Sprinter
	Carlton Joseph Huntley	Arts	USA	Historian
	Elvin E.	Sports	USA	Basketball Player - HF
	Gabby	Performing Arts	USA	Actor
	Helen	Performing Arts	USA	Actress - Academy Award
	Isaac	Performing Arts	USA	Singer - Rock & Roll - HF
	Lucy Ware	Politics	USA	First Lady
	Rutherford Birchard	Politics	USA	President
Haynes	Henry Doyle (Homer)	Performing Arts	USA	Country Music - HF - Homer & Jethro
	Marques	Sports	USA	Basketball Player - HF
	Michael James (Mike)	Sports	USA	Football Player - HF
Haynie	Sandra	Sports	USA	Golfer - HF
Hays	Arthur Garfield	Law & Order	USA	Lawyer/Civil Libertarian
	Robert	Performing Arts	USA	Actor
Hayward	Justin	Performing Arts	England	Singer
	Susan	Performing Arts	USA	Actress - Academy Award
Hayworth	Rita	Performing Arts	USA	Actress
Hazlitt	William	Creative Works	England	Essayist
Headon	Nicky	Performing Arts	England	Rock & Roll - HF - The Clash

SOLVER SERIES: NAME FINDER

LAST NAME	FIRST NAME	CATEGORY	COUNTRY	FAME
Healey	Donald Mitchell	Sports	England	Race Car Driver - HF
	Edward Francis (Ed)	Sports	USA	Football Player - HF
Heaney	Seamus	Creative Works	Ireland	Literature - Nobel Laureate
Hearn	Lafcadio	Creative Works	USA	Writer
Hearns	Thomas	Sports	USA	Boxer
Hearst	William Randolph	Business	USA	Newspaper Publisher
Heath	Edward Richard George	Politics	England	Prime Minister
Heaviside	Oliver	Science	England	Physicist
Hebbel	Christian Friedrich	Creative Works	Germany	Poet/Playwright
Hebert	Bobby	Sports	USA	Football Player
Hébert	Jacques René	War & Peace	France	Revolutionary Leader
Hecht	Anthony	Creative Works	USA	Poet - Pulitzer
	Ben	Creative Works	USA	Screenwriter
Heckart	Eileen	Performing Arts	USA	Actress - Academy Award
Heckman	James J.	Arts	USA	Economics - Nobel Laureate
Hedin	Sven Anders	Exploration	Sweden	Explorer- Central Asia
Hedren	Tippi	Performing Arts	USA	Actress
Heeger	Alan	Science	USA	Chemistry - Nobel Laureate
Heflin	Van	Performing Arts	USA	Actor - Academy Award
Hefner	Hugh Marston	Business	USA	Publishing
Hefti	Neal	Performing Arts	USA	Jazz Trumpeter
Hegel	Georg Wilhelm Frederich	Arts	Germany	Philosopher
Heidegger	Martin	Arts	Germany	Philosopher/Existentialist
Heiden	Eric	Sports	USA	Olympic Speed Skater
Heidenstam	Carl Gustaf Verner von	Creative Works	Sweden	Literature - Nobel Laureate
Heifetz	Jascha	Performing Arts	USA	Violinist
Heilmann	Harry Edwin	Sports	USA	Baseball Player - HF
Hein	Melvin Jack (Mel)	Sports	USA	Football Player - HF
Heine	Heinrich	Creative Works	Germany	Poet/Essayist
Heinlein	Robert Anson	Creative Works	USA	Author - SciFi
Heinrichs	April	Sports	USA	Soccer Player - HF
Heinsohn	Thomas W. (Tom)	Sports	USA	Basketball Player - HF
Heisenberg	Werner Karl	Science	Germany	Physics - Nobel Laureate
Heiss	Carol	Sports	USA	Olympic Skater
Hejduk	John	Architecture	USA	Architect
Heldman	Gladys Medalie	Sports	USA	Tennis Player - HF
Helgenberger	Marg	Performing Arts	USA	Actress
Heller	Joseph	Creative Works	USA	Novelist
Hellman	Lillian	Creative Works	USA	Playwright
Helm	Mark Levon	Performing Arts	USA	Rock & Roll - HF - The Band
Helmholtz	Hermann Ludwig Ferdinand von	Science	Germany	Physicist/Physiologist
Helmond	Katherine	Performing Arts	USA	Actress
Helms	Jesse Alexander	Politics	USA	Senator - North Carolina
	Susan Jane	Aviation	USA	Astronaut
Helmsley	Harry Edwin	Law & Order	USA	Fraud Artist
	Leona	Law & Order	USA	Fraud Artist
Helvétius	Claude Adrien	Arts	France	Philosopher
Hemingway	Ernest Miller	Creative Works	USA	Literature - Nobel/Pulitzer
	Margaux	Performing Arts	USA	Actress
	Mariel	Performing Arts	USA	Actress - Acad Award Nom
Hemmings	David	Performing Arts	England	Actor
Hemsley	Sherman	Performing Arts	USA	Comedian
Hench	Philip Showalter	Science	USA	Medicine - Nobel Laureate
Henderson	Arthur	War & Peace	England	Peace - Nobel Laureate
	Fletcher	Performing Arts	USA	Band Leader - Big Band/Jazz - HF
	Florence	Performing Arts	USA	Actress
	Lyle Russell Cedric (Skitch)	Performing Arts	USA	Conductor/Composer/Pianist
	Rickey	Sports	USA	Baseball Player
Hendrick	Burton J.	Creative Works	USA	Author - Pulitzer
Hendricks	Theodore Paul (Ted)	Sports	Guatemala	Football Player - HF
	Thomas	Politics	USA	Vice-President
Hendrix	Jimi	Performing Arts	USA	Singer - Rock & Roll - HF
Henie	Sonja	Sports	Norway	Olympic Skater

LAST NAME	FIRST NAME	CATEGORY	COUNTRY	FAME
Henize	Karl Gordon	Aviation	USA	Astronaut
Henley	Beth	Creative Works	USA	Dramatist - Pulitzer
	Don	Performing Arts	USA	Rock & Roll - HF - The Eagles
	William Ernest	Creative Works	England	Poet/Editor/Critic
Hennen	Thomas John	Aviation	USA	Astronaut
Henner	Marilu	Performing Arts	USA	Actress
Henning	Doug	Performing Arts	Canada	Magician
Henricks	Terence Thomas	Aviation	USA	Astronaut
Henry	Buck	Movie Production	USA	Director - Acad Award Nom
	Buck	Performing Arts	USA	Comedian
	Justin	Performing Arts	USA	Actor - Acad Award Nom
	Patrick	Politics	USA	Statesman/Orator
	Wilbur Francis (Pete)	Sports	USA	Football Player - HF
Henslowe	Phillip	Arts	England	Theater Manager
Henson	Matthew Alexander	Exploration	USA	Explorer - Arctic
Henty	George Alfred	Creative Works	England	Writer
Hepburn	Audrey	Performing Arts	Belgium	Actress - Academy Award
	Katharine	Performing Arts	USA	Actress - Academy Award
Hepplewhite	George	Arts	England	Cabinetmaker
Herbart	Johann Fredrich	Arts	Germany	Philosopher/Educator
Herber	Arnold Charles (Arnie)	Sports	USA	Football Player - HF
Herbert	Frank	Creative Works	USA	Author
	Victor	Creative Works	Ireland	Composer - Light Opera
Herder	Johann Gottfried von	Arts	Germany	Philosopher/Poet
Herdon	Mark Joel	Performing Arts	USA	Country Music - HF - Alabama
Herjulfsson	Bjarni	Exploration	Iceland	Explorer - America East Coast
Herman	Gerald (Jerry)	Creative Works	USA	Composer
	Pee Wee	Performing Arts	USA	Comedian
	William Jennings Bryan (Billy)	Sports	USA	Baseball Player - HF
Herman (Wilson)	Woodrow Charles (Woody)	Performing Arts	USA	Band Leader - Big Band/Jazz - HF
Hermes	Thierry	Business	France	Fashion Designer
Hern	William Milton (Riley)	Sports	Canada	Hockey Player - HF
Hernandez	Keith	Sports	USA	Baseball Player
Herrera	Francisco de	Works of Art	Spain	Painter
Herrick	Robert	Creative Works	England	Poet
Herrmann	Edward	Performing Arts	USA	Actor
Herschbach	Dudley R.	Science	USA	Chemistry - Nobel Laureate
Herschel	John Frederick William	Science	England	Physicist/Chemist/Astronomer
	William	Science	England	Astronomer
Hersey	John	Creative Works	USA	Author - Pulitzer
Hershey	Alfred D.	Science	USA	Medicine - Nobel Laureate
	Barbara	Performing Arts	USA	Actress - Acad Award Nom
Hershiser	Orel	Sports	USA	Baseball Player
Hershko	Avram	Science	Israel	Chemistry - Nobel Laureate
Hertz	Gustav Ludwig	Science	Germany	Physics - Nobel Laureate
	Heinrich Rudolph	Science	Germany	Physicist
Herzberg	Gerhard	Science	Canada	Chemistry - Nobel Laureate
Herzigova	Eva	Performing Arts	Czechoslovakia	Super Model
Herzl	Theodor	Creative Works	Austria	Writer
Herzog	Chaim	Politics	Israel	President
	Jacques	Architecture	Switzerland	Architect - Pritzker Laureate
	Werner	Movie Production	Germany	Director
Heschel	Abraham Joshua	Arts	USA	Philosopher/Scholar/Rabbi
Hess	Myra	Performing Arts	England	Pianist
	Victor Franz	Science	Austria	Physics - Nobel Laureate
	Walter Rudolf	Science	Switzerland	Medicine - Nobel Laureate
Hesse	Hermann	Creative Works	Switzerland	Literature - Nobel Laureate
Hesseman	Howard	Performing Arts	USA	Actor
Hester	William Ewing (Slew)	Sports	USA	Tennis Player - HF
Heston	Charlton	Performing Arts	USA	Actor - Academy Award
Hetherington	Henry	Business	England	Publishing
Hevesy	George de	Science	Hungary	Chemistry - Nobel Laureate
Hewish	Antony	Science	England	Physics - Nobel Laureate

SOLVER SERIES: NAME FINDER

LAST NAME	FIRST NAME	CATEGORY	COUNTRY	FAME
Hewitt	Robert Anthony (Bob)	Sports	Australia	Tennis Player - HF
	William Ernest	Sports	USA	Football Player - HF
Hewson	Paul David (Bono)	Performing Arts	Ireland	Rock & Roll - HF - U2
Hextall	Bryan Aldwyn	Sports	Canada	Hockey Player - HF
Heyerdahl	Thor	Exploration	Norway	Explorer - South Pacific
Heymans	Corneille Jean François	Science	Belgium	Medicine - Nobel Laureate
Heyrovsky	Jaroslav	Science	Czechoslovakia	Chemistry - Nobel Laureate
Heyse	Paul Johann Ludwig	Creative Works	Germany	Literature - Nobel Laureate
Hiberseimer	Ludwig	Architecture	Germany	Architect
Hickey	William	Performing Arts	USA	Actor - Acad Award Nom
Hickok	James Butler (Wild Bill)	Law & Order	USA	Lawman
Hicks	John R.	Arts	England	Economics - Nobel Laureate
	Scott	Movie Production	Uganda	Director - Acad Award Nom
Hieb	Richard James	Aviation	USA	Astronaut
Higgins-Cirovski	Shannon	Sports	USA	Soccer Player - HF
Higginson	Thomas Wentworth	Creative Works	USA	Writer/Social Reformer
Higinbotham	Jack (JC)	Performing Arts	USA	Jazz Trombonist - Big Band/Jazz - HF
Higuchi	Hisako (Chako)	Sports	Japan	Golfer - HF
Hijuelos	Oscar	Creative Works	USA	Author - Pulitzer
Hilfiger	Thomas Jacob	Business	USA	Fashion Designer
Hill	Archibald Vivian	Science	England	Medicine - Nobel Laureate
	Dan	Performing Arts	Canada	Singer
	Dave	Sports	USA	Golfer
	Dusty	Performing Arts	USA	Rock & Roll - HF - ZZ Top
	George Roy	Movie Production	USA	Director - Academy Award
	James Jerome	Business	USA	Railway Magnate
	Mike	Sports	USA	Golfer
	Norman Graham	Sports	England	Race Car Driver - HF
	Phil	Sports	USA	Race Car Driver - HF
Hillary	Edmund Percival	Exploration	New Zealand	Explorer - Antarctic
	Patrick John	Politics	Ireland	President
Hiller	Arthur	Movie Production	Canada	Director - Acad Award Nom
	Wendy	Performing Arts	England	Actress - Academy Award
Hillerman	John	Performing Arts	USA	Actor
Hillman	Chris	Performing Arts	USA	Rock & Roll - HF - The Bryds
Hills	Carla Anderson	Politics	USA	Assistant Attorney-General
Hillyer	Robert	Creative Works	USA	Poet - Pulitzer
Hilmers	David Carl	Aviation	USA	Astronaut
Hilton	Conrad	Business	USA	Hotelier
	Harold	Sports	England	Golfer - HF
Hilversum	William Marinus Dudok	Architecture	Netherlands	Architect - AIA Gold Medal
Hindemith	Paul	Creative Works	USA	Composer
Hindenburg	Paul von	War & Peace	Germany	Field Marshall
Hines	Earl Kenneth (Fatha)	Performing Arts	USA	Jazz Pianist - Big Band/Jazz - HF
	Gregory	Performing Arts	USA	Actor/Dancer
	Jerome	Performing Arts	USA	Singer - Opera
Hinkle	William Clarke	Sports	USA	Football Player - HF
Hinshelwood	Cyril Norman	Science	England	Chemistry - Nobel Laureate
Hinton	Susan Eloise	Creative Works	USA	Author
Hiroshige	Ando	Works of Art	Japan	Painter
Hirsch	Elroy Leon (Crazy Legs)	Sports	USA	Football Player - HF
	Judd	Performing Arts	USA	Actor - Acad Award Nom
Hirschfeld	Al	Creative Works	USA	Cartoonist - NY Times
Hiss	Alger	Politics	USA	Government Official/Lawyer
Hitchcock	Alfred	Movie Production	England	Director - Acad Award Nom
Hitchings	George H.	Science	USA	Medicine - Nobel Laureate
Hite	Shere	Creative Works	USA	Author
Hitler	Adolf	War & Peace	Germany	Military Leader
Ho	Don	Performing Arts	USA	Singer
Ho Chi Minh	Nguyen Van	Politics	North Vietnam	President
Hoad	Lewis Alan (Lew)	Sports	Australia	Tennis Player - HF
Hoban	James	Architecture	USA	Architect
Hobart	Garret A.	Politics	USA	Vice-President

LAST NAME	FIRST NAME	CATEGORY	COUNTRY	FAME
Hobbema	Meindert	Works of Art	Netherlands	Painter
Hobbes	Thomas	Arts	England	Philosopher/Author
Hobby	William	Business	USA	Newspaper Industry
Hocking	William Ernest	Arts	USA	Philosopher
Hockney	David	Works of Art	England	Painter/Photographer
Hodges	Gil	Sports	USA	Baseball Player
	John Cornelius (Johnny)	Performing Arts	USA	Saxophonist - Big Band/Jazz - HF
Hodgkin	Alan Lloyd	Science	England	Medicine - Nobel Laureate
	Dorothy Crowfoot	Science	England	Chemistry - Nobel Laureate
	Thomas	Science	England	Physician
Hodiak	John	Performing Arts	USA	Actor
Hoff	Jacobus Henricus Van't	Science	Netherlands	Chemistry - Nobel Laureate
Hoffa	James Riddle (Jimmy)	Business	USA	Labor Leader
Hoffer	Eric	Arts	USA	Philosopher
Hoffman	Abbie	Creative Works	USA	Journalist - Magazine
	Dustin	Performing Arts	USA	Actor - Academy Award
	Jeffrey Alan	Aviation	USA	Astronaut
	Joseph	Architecture	Austria	Architect
Hoffmann	Ernst Theodor Amadeus	Creative Works	Germany	Composer/Writer
	Roald	Science	USA	Chemistry - Nobel Laureate
Hofmann	Hans	Works of Art	Germany	Painter
	Josef	Creative Works	USA	Composer/Pianist
Hofmannsthal	Hugo von	Creative Works	Austria	Poet/Playwright
Hofstadter	Douglas Richard	Creative Works	USA	Author - Pulitzer
	Robert	Science	USA	Physics - Nobel Laureate
Hoften	James Douglas Van (Ox)	Aviation	USA	Astronaut
Hogan	Ben	Sports	USA	Golfer - HF
	Paul	Performing Arts	Australia	Actor
Hogarth	William	Works of Art	England	Painter/Engraver
Hogg	Ima	Business	USA	Philanthropist/Pianist
	James	Creative Works	Scotland	Poet
Hokusai	Katsushika	Works of Art	Japan	Painter/Engraver
Holabird	William	Architecture	USA	Architect - Skyscraper
Holbein	Hans	Works of Art	Germany	Painter - Portrait
Holbert	Al	Sports	USA	Race Car Driver - HF
Holbrook	Hal	Performing Arts	USA	Actor
Holden	Amanda	Performing Arts	England	Actress
	William	Performing Arts	USA	Actor - Academy Award
Holder	Geoffrey	Performing Arts	Trinidad	Actor
Holiday (Fagan)	Eleanora (Billie)	Performing Arts	USA	Singer - Big Band/Jazz - HF
	Eleanora (Billie)	Performing Arts	USA	Singer - Rock & Roll - HF
Holinshed	Raphael	Arts	England	Chronicler
Holl	Elias	Architecture	Germany	Architect
	Steven	Architecture	USA	Architect
Holland	Brian	Creative Works	USA	Composer
	Edward (Eddie)	Creative Works	USA	Composer
Holldobler	Bert	Creative Works	Germany	Author - Pulitzer
Hollein	Hans	Architecture	Austria	Architect - Pritzker Laureate
Holley	Robert W.	Science	USA	Medicine - Nobel Laureate
Holliday	John H. (Doc)	Law & Order	USA	Outlaw
	Judy	Performing Arts	USA	Actress - Academy Award
	Polly	Performing Arts	USA	Actress
Holliman	Earl	Performing Arts	USA	Actor
Holloway	Emory	Creative Works	USA	Author - Pulitzer
	Stanley	Performing Arts	England	Actor - Acad Award Nom
	Sterling	Performing Arts	USA	Actor
Holly (Holley)	Charles Hardin (Buddy)	Performing Arts	USA	Singer - Rock & Roll - HF
Holm	Celeste	Performing Arts	USA	Actress - Academy Award
	Ian	Performing Arts	England	Actor - Acad Award Nom
Holman	Nat	Sports	USA	Basketball Player - HF
Holmes	Harry (Hap)	Sports	Canada	Hockey Player - HF
	John Haynes	Arts	USA	Clergyman/Reformer
	Larry	Sports	USA	Boxer

SOLVER SERIES: NAME FINDER

LAST NAME	FIRST NAME	CATEGORY	COUNTRY	FAME
Holmes	Oliver Wendell	Science	USA	Physician/Writer
Holmquest	Donald Lee	Aviation	USA	Astronaut
Holst	Gustavus Theodore Von	Creative Works	England	Composer
Holt	Jack	Performing Arts	USA	Actor
	Lester	Creative Works	USA	Journalist - Television
	Tim	Performing Arts	USA	Actor
Holyfield	Evander	Sports	USA	Boxer
Homer	Winslow	Works of Art	USA	Painter
Homolka	Oskar	Performing Arts	Austria	Actor - Acad Award Nom
Hone	William	Business	England	Publishing
Honegger	Arthur	Creative Works	Switzerland	Composer
Honeyman-Scott	James	Performing Arts	England	Rock & Roll - HF - The Pretenders
Hong	Gao	Sports	China	Soccer Player
Hooch	Pieter de	Works of Art	Netherlands	Painter
Hood	John Bell	War & Peace	USA	Confederate General
	Thomas	Creative Works	England	Poet/Humorist
Hooft	Gerhardus 't	Science	Netherlands	Physics - Nobel Laureate
Hook	Sidney	Arts	USA	Philosopher
Hooke	Robert	Science	England	Inventor/Physicist
Hooker	Johnny Lee	Performing Arts	USA	Singer - Rock & Roll - HF
	Joseph	War & Peace	USA	Union General
	Richard	Arts	England	Clergyman/Writer
	Thomas	Arts	England	Clergyman
Hooks	Jan	Performing Arts	USA	Comedian
	Robert	Performing Arts	USA	Actor
Hooper	Charles Thomas (Tom)	Sports	Canada	Hockey Player - HF
	Harry Bartholomew	Sports	USA	Baseball Player - HF
	Tobe	Movie Production	USA	Director
Hoover	Herbert Clark	Politics	USA	President
	John Edgar	Law & Order	USA	Director - FBI
	Lou	Politics	USA	First Lady
Hope	Anthony	Creative Works	England	Novelist
	Bob	Performing Arts	England	Comedian
	Bob	Sports	USA	Golfer - HF
Hopkins	Anthony	Performing Arts	Wales	Actor - Academy Award
	Claude Driskett	Performing Arts	USA	Band Leader - Big Band/Jazz - HF
	Frederick Gowland	Science	England	Medicine - Nobel Laureate
	Gerard Manley	Creative Works	England	Poet/Jesuit Priest
	Johns	Creative Works	USA	Financier/Philanthropist
	Mark	Arts	USA	Educator
	Michael	Architecture	England	Architect
	Miriam	Performing Arts	USA	Actress - Acad Award Nom
Hopman	Henry Christian (Harry)	Sports	Australia	Tennis Player - HF
Hopper	Dennis	Performing Arts	USA	Actor - Acad Award Nom
	Edward	Works of Art	USA	Painter - Realist
Horgan	Paul	Creative Works	USA	Author - Pulitzer
Horkheimer	Max	Arts	Germany	Philosopher
Horne	Lena	Performing Arts	USA	Singer - Big Band/Jazz - HF
	Marilyn	Performing Arts	USA	Singer
	Shirley	Performing Arts	USA	Singer/Pianist - Big Band/Jazz - HF
	William Cornelius Van	Business	Canada	Railway Magnate
Horner	George Reginald (Red)	Sports	Canada	Hockey Player - HF
Horney	Karen	Science	Germany	Psychoanalyist
Hornsby	Rogers	Sports	USA	Baseball Player - HF
Hornung	Paul Vernon	Sports	USA	Football Player - HF
Horowitz	Scott Jay (Doc)	Aviation	USA	Astronaut
	Vladimir	Performing Arts	Russia	Pianist
Horrocks	John	Business	England	Textile Industry
Horsley	Lee	Performing Arts	USA	Actor
Horta	Victor	Architecture	Belgium	Architect
Horton	Edward Everett	Performing Arts	USA	Comedian
	Miles Gilbert (Tim)	Sports	Canada	Hockey Player - HF
Horvitz	Robert	Science	USA	Medicine - Nobel Laureate

LAST NAME	FIRST NAME	CATEGORY	COUNTRY	FAME
Hoskins	Bob	Performing Arts	England	Actor - Acad Award Nom
Hotchkis	Benjamin	Business	USA	Firearms
Hotchkiss-Wightman	Hazel Virginia (Lady Tennis)	Sports	USA	Tennis Player - HF
Houbregs	Robert J. (Bob)	Sports	Canada	Basketball Player - HF
Houdini	Harry	Performing Arts	USA	Magician
Hounsfield	Godfrey N.	Science	England	Medicine - Nobel Laureate
Hounsou	Djimon	Performing Arts	Africa	Actor - Acad Award Nom
House	Edward Mandell	Politics	USA	Diplomat
Houseman	John	Performing Arts	Romania	Actor - Academy Award
Housman	Alfred Edward	Creative Works	England	Poet
Houssay	Bernardo Alberto	Science	Argentina	Medicine - Nobel Laureate
Houston	Cissy	Performing Arts	USA	Singer
	Kenneth Ray (Ken)	Sports	USA	Football Player - HF
	Samuel	Politics	USA	Senator
	Samuel	War & Peace	USA	General - Texas Army
	Whitney	Performing Arts	USA	Singer
Hovell	William	Exploration	England	Explorer - Australia
Hovey	Frederick Howard (Fred)	Sports	USA	Tennis Player - HF
Howard	Curly	Performing Arts	USA	Comedian
	Frank	Sports	USA	Baseball Player
	Ken	Performing Arts	USA	Actor
	Leslie	Performing Arts	England	Actor - Acad Award Nom
	Moe	Performing Arts	USA	Comedian
	Richard	Creative Works	USA	Poet - Pulitzer
	Ron	Movie Production	USA	Director - Academy Award
	Ron	Performing Arts	USA	Actor
	Roy Wilson	Arts	USA	Newspaper Publisher/Editor
	Shemp	Performing Arts	USA	Comedian
	Sidney	Creative Works	USA	Dramatist - Pulitzer
	Trevor	Performing Arts	England	Actor - Acad Award Nom
Howe	Dorothy Campbell Hurd	Sports	Scotland	Golfer - HF
	Elias	Science	USA	Inventor - Sewing Machine
	Gordon (Gordie) (Mr. Hockey)	Sports	Canada	Hockey Player - HF
	Julia Ward	Creative Works	USA	Poet/Social Reformer
	Mark Antony DeWolfe	Creative Works	USA	Author - Pulitzer
	Stephen James (Steve)	Performing Arts	England	Guitarist
	Sydney Harris (Syd)	Sports	Canada	Hockey Player - HF
	William	War & Peace	England	Commander in Chief
Howell	Bailey	Sports	USA	Basketball Player - HF
	C. Thomas	Performing Arts	USA	Actor
	Henry Vernon (Harry)	Sports	Canada	Hockey Player - HF
Howells	William Dean	Creative Works	USA	Novelist/Critic/Editor
Howes	Sally Ann	Performing Arts	England	Actress
Hoyt	Waite Charles	Sports	USA	Baseball Player - HF
Hubbard	Freddie (Frederick DeWayne)	Performing Arts	USA	Jazz Trumpeter - Big Band/Jazz -HF
	Lafayette Ronald	Creative Works	USA	Author - SciFi
	Robert (Cal)	Sports	USA	Baseball Umpire - HF
	Robert Calvin (Cal)	Sports	USA	Football Player - HF
Hubbell	Carl Owen	Sports	USA	Baseball Player - HF
Hubble	Edwin Powell	Science	USA	Astronomer
Hubel	David H.	Science	USA	Medicine - Nobel Laureate
Huber	Robert	Science	Germany	Chemistry - Nobel Laureate
Hudson	Garth (Eric)	Performing Arts	Canada	Rock & Roll - HF - The Band
	George	Business	England	Railway Magnate
	Henry	Exploration	England	Explorer - America
	Hugh	Movie Production	England	Director - Acad Award Nom
	Kate	Performing Arts	USA	Actress - Acad Award Nom
	Rock	Performing Arts	USA	Actor - Acad Award Nom
	William Henry	Arts	England	Naturalist/Writer
Huff	Robert Lee (Sam)	Sports	USA	Football Player - HF
Huggins	Charles Brenton	Science	USA	Medicine - Nobel Laureate
	Miller James (Mighty Mite)	Sports	USA	Baseball Manager - HF
Hughes	Barnard	Performing Arts	USA	Actor

SOLVER SERIES: NAME FINDER

LAST NAME	FIRST NAME	CATEGORY	COUNTRY	FAME
Hughes	Charles Evans	Law & Order	USA	Jurist/Statesman
	Edward James (Ted)	Creative Works	England	Poet
	Hatcher	Creative Works	USA	Dramatist - Pulitzer
	Howard Robard	Business	USA	Industrialist
	James Langston	Creative Works	USA	Poet/Writer
	Thomas	Creative Works	England	Writer/Social Reformer
Hughes-Fulford	Millie Elizabeth	Aviation	USA	Astronaut
Hugo	Victor Marie	Creative Works	England	Poet/Novelist/Playwright
Hulbert	Mike	Sports	USA	Golfer
	William Ambrose	Sports	USA	Baseball Executive - HF
Hulce	Tom	Performing Arts	USA	Actor - Acad Award Nom
Hull	Brett	Sports	Canada	Hockey Player
	Cordell	Politics	USA	Statesman
	Cordell	War & Peace	USA	Peace - Nobel Laureate
	Josephine	Performing Arts	USA	Actress - Academy Award
	Robert Marvin (Bobby)	Sports	Canada	Hockey Player - HF
Hulman Jr.	Anton (Tony)	Sports	USA	Race Car Promoter - HF
Hulme	Denis	Sports	New Zealand	Race Car Driver - HF
Hulse	Russell A.	Science	USA	Physics - Nobel Laureate
Hulton	Edward	Business	England	Publishing
	William	Business	England	Railway Magnate
Humboldt	Alexander Von	Exploration	Prussia	Explorer - South America
	Friedrich Heinrich	Exploration	Germany	Explorer- Orinoco River
Hume	David	Arts	Scotland	Philosopher/Historian
	Hamilton	Exploration	Australia	Explorer - Australia
	John	War & Peace	England	Peace - Nobel Laureate
	Kirsty	Performing Arts	Scotland	Super Model
Humperdinck	Engelbert	Creative Works	Germany	Composer
Humperdink	Engelbert	Performing Arts	India	Singer
Humphrey	Hubert H.	Politics	USA	Vice-President
Hundertwasser	Friedensreich	Architecture	Austria	Architect
Hunnicutt	Arthur	Performing Arts	USA	Actor - Acad Award Nom
Hunt	Haroldson L.	Business	USA	Oil Industry
	Helen	Performing Arts	USA	Actress - Academy Award
	James Henry Leigh	Creative Works	England	Poet/Essayist/Critic
	Joseph Raphael	Sports	USA	Tennis Player - HF
	Lamar	Sports	USA	Football Owner - HF
	Lamar	Sports	USA	Tennis Founder - HF
	Leigh	Business	England	Publishing
	Linda	Performing Arts	USA	Actress - Academy Award
	Richard Morris	Architecture	USA	Architect
	Tim	Science	England	Medicine - Nobel Laureate
	Tommy	Performing Arts	USA	Rock & Roll - HF - The Flamingos
Hunt	William Holman	Works of Art	England	Painter
Hunter	Alberta	Performing Arts	USA	Singer - Big Band/Jazz - HF
	Evan	Creative Works	USA	Author
	Francis Townsend (Frank)	Sports	USA	Tennis Player - HF
	Holly	Performing Arts	USA	Actress - Acad Award Nom
	Ian	Performing Arts	England	Singer
	James Augustus (Catfish)	Sports	USA	Baseball Player - HF
	Jeffrey	Performing Arts	USA	Actor
	John	Science	England	Surgeon/Physiologist
	Kim	Performing Arts	USA	Actress - Academy Award
	Rachel	Performing Arts	New Zealand	Super Model
	Ross	Movie Production	USA	Director
	Tab	Performing Arts	USA	Singer
Huntington	Collis Potter	Business	USA	Railway Magnate
	Samuel	Politics	USA	Statesman
Huntley	Chet	Creative Works	USA	Journalist - Television
Hunyadi	János	War & Peace	Hungary	General
Hurley	Elizabeth	Performing Arts	England	Super Model
Hurok	Sol	Movie Production	USA	Impresario
Hurt	John	Performing Arts	England	Actor - Acad Award Nom

LAST NAME	FIRST NAME	CATEGORY	COUNTRY	FAME
Hurt	Mary Beth	Performing Arts	USA	Actress
	William	Performing Arts	USA	Actor - Academy Award
Husband	Rick Douglas	Aviation	USA	Astronaut
Hussein	King	Politics	Jordan	King
	Saddam	Politics	Iraq	President/Military Leader
Husserl	Edmund Gustav Albrecht	Arts	Germany	Philosopher
Hussey	Ruth	Performing Arts	USA	Actress - Acad Award Nom
Huston	Anjelica	Performing Arts	USA	Actress - Academy Award
	John	Movie Production	USA	Director - Academy Award
	John	Performing Arts	USA	Actor - Acad Award Nom
	Walter	Performing Arts	Canada	Actor - Academy Award
Hutcheson	Francis	Arts	Ireland	Philosopher
Hutchins	Robert Maynard	Arts	USA	Educator
Hutchinson	Anne	Arts	USA	Founder of Rhode Island
	Thomas	Politics	USA	Governor of Massachusetts
Hutson	Donald Montgomery (Don)	Sports	USA	Football Player - HF
Hutton	Betty	Performing Arts	USA	Actress
	Jim	Performing Arts	USA	Actor
	John Bower (Bouse)	Sports	Canada	Hockey Player - HF
	Lauren	Performing Arts	USA	Actress
	Timothy	Performing Arts	USA	Actor - Academy Award
Huxley	Aldous Leonard	Creative Works	England	Novelist/Essayist
	Andrew Fielding	Science	England	Medicine - Nobel Laureate
	Julian Sorrell	Science	England	Biologist/Writer
	Thomas Henry	Science	England	Biologist/Writer
Huxtable	Ada Louise	Architecture	USA	Architect - Jefferson Medal
Huygens	Christian	Science	Netherlands	Physicist/Astronomer
Hyatt	Charles D.	Sports	USA	Basketball Player - HF
Hyde	Douglas	Politics	Ireland	President
	Harry	Sports	USA	Race Car Promoter - HF
Hyer	Martha	Performing Arts	USA	Actress - Acad Award Nom
Hyland	Brian	Performing Arts	USA	Singer
	Harrold M. (Harry)	Sports	Canada	Hockey Player - HF
Hynde	Chrissie	Performing Arts	USA	Rock & Roll - HF - The Pretenders
	John (Jackie)	Sports	Scotland	Soccer Player - HF
Iacocca	Lee A.	Business	USA	Automobile Industy
Ian	Janis	Performing Arts	USA	Singer
Ibsen	Henrik	Creative Works	Norway	Poet/Playwright
Ichan	Carl	Business	USA	Entrepreneur
Ickx	Jackie	Sports	Belgium	Race Car Driver - HF
Idle	Eric	Performing Arts	England	Comedian
Idol	Billy	Performing Arts	England	Singer
Iglesias	Enrico	Performing Arts	Spain	Singer
	Julio	Performing Arts	Spain	Singer
Ignarro	Louis J.	Science	USA	Medicine - Nobel Laureate
Inge	William	Creative Works	Ireland	Dramatist - Pulitzer
	William Ralph	Arts	England	Theologian
Ingersoll	Robert Green	Law & Order	USA	Lawyer/Lecturer
Ingram	James	Performing Arts	USA	Singer
Ingres	Jean Auguste Dominique	Works of Art	France	Painter
Inkster	Juli	Sports	USA	Golfer - HF
Inness	George	Works of Art	USA	Painter
Inönü	Ismet	Politics	Turkey	Prime Minister
Inouye	Daniel Ken	Politics	USA	Senator - Hawaii
Ionesco	Eugene	Creative Works	France	Playwright
Ireland	John	Performing Arts	Canada	Actor - Acad Award Nom
	Kathy	Performing Arts	USA	Super Model
Irons	Jeremy	Performing Arts	England	Actor - Academy Award
Irvan	Ernie	Sports	USA	Race Car Driver
Irvin	James Dickenson (Dick)	Sports	Canada	Hockey Player - HF
	Monford (Monte)	Sports	USA	Baseball Player - HF
Irving	Amy	Performing Arts	USA	Actress - Acad Award Nom
	John	Creative Works	USA	Writer

SOLVER SERIES: NAME FINDER

LAST NAME	FIRST NAME	CATEGORY	COUNTRY	FAME
Irving	Washington	Creative Works	USA	Author
Irwin	Hale	Sports	USA	Golfer - HF
	James Benson	Aviation	USA	Astronaut
Isaac	Bobby	Sports	USA	Race Car Driver - HF
	Rhys L.	Creative Works	USA	Author - Pulitzer
Isherwood	Christopher William Bradshaw	Creative Works	USA	Writer
Isley	Ernie	Performing Arts	USA	Rock & Roll - HF - Isley Brothers
	Marvin	Performing Arts	USA	Rock & Roll - HF - Isley Brothers
	O'Kelly	Performing Arts	USA	Rock & Roll - HF - Isley Brothers
	Ronald	Performing Arts	USA	Rock & Roll - HF - Isley Brothers
	Rudolph	Performing Arts	USA	Rock & Roll - HF - Isley Brothers
Isozaki	Arata	Architecture	Japan	Architect
Israel	Frank	Architecture	USA	Architect
Issel	Daniel P. (Dan)	Sports	USA	Basketball Player - HF
Ito	Lance	Law & Order	USA	Judge - Simpson Case
	Robert	Performing Arts	Canada	Actor
	Toyo	Architecture	Japan	Architect
Ives	Burl	Performing Arts	USA	Actor/Singer - Academy Award
	Charles Edward	Creative Works	USA	Composer
	James M.	Works of Art	USA	Lithographer
Ivey	Judith	Performing Arts	USA	Actress
Ivory	James	Movie Production	USA	Director - Acad Award Nom
Iwamatsu	Makoto "Mako"	Performing Arts	Japan	Actor - Acad Award Nom
Izzard	Eddie	Performing Arts	Ireland	Comedian
Jack	Sidney (Beau)	Sports	USA	Boxer - HF
Jacklin	Tony	Sports	England	Golfer - HF
Jackson	Andrew	Politics	USA	President
	Anne	Performing Arts	USA	Actress
	Bo	Sports	USA	Football Player
	Glenda	Performing Arts	England	Actress - Academy Award
	Harvey (Busher)	Sports	Canada	Hockey Player - HF
	Jackie	Performing Arts	USA	Rock & Roll - HF - The Jackson Five
	Janet	Performing Arts	USA	Singer
	Jermaine	Performing Arts	USA	Rock & Roll - HF - The Jackson Five
	Joe	Performing Arts	England	Singer
	Kate	Performing Arts	USA	Actress
	Mahalia	Performing Arts	USA	Singer - Rock & Roll - HF
	Marlon	Performing Arts	USA	Rock & Roll - HF - The Jackson Five
	Michael	Performing Arts	USA	Rock & Roll - HF - The Jackson Five
	Michael	Performing Arts	USA	Singer - Rock & Roll - HF
	Milton (Milt)	Performing Arts	USA	Jazz Vibraphonist - Big Band/Jazz - HF
	Peter	Movie Production	New Zealand	Director - Academy Award
	Rachel Donelson	Politics	USA	First Lady
	Reginald Martinez (Reggie)	Sports	USA	Baseball Player - HF
	Robert Houghwout	Law & Order	USA	Justice - Supreme Court
	Samuel L.	Performing Arts	USA	Actor - Acad Award Nom
	Thomas Jonathon (Stonewall)	War & Peace	USA	Confederate General
	Tito	Performing Arts	USA	Rock & Roll - HF - The Jackson Five
	Travis Calvin	Sports	USA	Baseball Player - HF
	Victoria	Performing Arts	USA	Comedian
Jackson Sr.	Jesse Louis	Politics	USA	Activist - Civil Rights
Jacob	François	Science	France	Medicine - Nobel Laureate
Jacobi	Derek	Performing Arts	England	Actor
Jacobs	Helen Hull	Sports	USA	Tennis Player - HF
	Jane	Architecture	Canada	Architect - Jefferson Medal
	John	Sports	England	Golfer - HF
Jacobsen	Arne	Architecture	Denmark	Architect
Jacquet	Jean-Baptiste (Illinois)	Performing Arts	USA	Jazz Saxophonist - Big Band/Jazz - HF
Jaeckel	Richard	Performing Arts	USA	Actor - Acad Award Nom
Jaffe	Rona	Creative Works	USA	Author
	Sam	Performing Arts	USA	Actor - Acad Award Nom
Jagger	Dean	Performing Arts	USA	Actor - Academy Award
	Michael Phillip (Mick)	Performing Arts	England	Rock & Roll - HF - Rolling Stones

LAST NAME	FIRST NAME	CATEGORY	COUNTRY	FAME
Jahn	Helmut	Architecture	Germany	Architect
James	Alexander Franklin (Frank)	Law & Order	USA	Outlaw
	Elmore	Performing Arts	USA	Singer - Rock & Roll - HF
	Harry Haag	Performing Arts	USA	Band Leader - Big Band/Jazz - HF
	Henry	Creative Works	USA	Author - Pulitzer
	Jesse Woodson	Law & Order	USA	Outlaw
	Marquis	Creative Works	USA	Author - Pulitzer
	Tommy	Performing Arts	USA	Singer
	William	Arts	USA	Philosopher/Psychologist
	William	Business	England	Railway Magnate
James (Hawkins)	Jamesetta (Etta)	Performing Arts	USA	Singer - Rock & Roll - HF
Jameson	Betty	Sports	USA	Golfer - HF
Janáček	Leoš	Creative Works	Czechoslovakia	Composer
Jandl	Ivan	Performing Arts	Czechoslovakia	Actor - Academy Award
Janet	Pierre Marie Félix	Arts	France	Psychologist
Janis	Elsie	Performing Arts	USA	Actress
Jannings	Emil	Performing Arts	Switzerland	Actor - Academy Award
Jano	Vittorio	Sports	Italy	Race Car Driver - HF
Jansen	Cornelis	Arts	Netherlands	Theologian
Janssen	David	Performing Arts	USA	Actor
Jantszoon	Willem	Exploration	Netherlands	Explorer - Australia
January	Don	Sports	USA	Golfer
Japp	John	Sports	Scotland	Soccer Player - HF
Jaques-Dalcroze	Émile	Creative Works	Switzerland	Composer
Jarman Jr	Claude	Performing Arts	USA	Actor - Academy Award
Jarreau	Al	Performing Arts	USA	Singer
Jarrett	Keith	Performing Arts	USA	Jazz Pianist
	Ned (Gentleman)	Sports	USA	Race Car Driver - HF
Jarvis	Gregory Bruce	Aviation	USA	Astronaut
Jasper	Chris	Performing Arts	USA	Rock & Roll - HF - Isley Brothers
	John	Arts	USA	Philosopher/Clergyman
Jaspers	Karl	Arts	Germany	Philosopher
Jaurès	Jean Léon	Politics	France	Socialist Leader/Journalist
Jay	John	Politics	USA	Justice - Supreme Court
Jean-Baptiste	Marianne	Performing Arts	England	Actress - Acad Award Nom
Jeanette	Harry (Buddy)	Sports	USA	Basketball Player - HF
Jeans	James Hopwood	Science	England	Physicist/Astronomer
Jefferson	Joseph	Performing Arts	USA	Actor
	Martha Wayles	Politics	USA	First Lady
	Thomas	Architecture	USA	Architect - AIA Gold Medal
	Thomas	Politics	USA	President
Jeffreys	Anne	Performing Arts	USA	Actress
Jelinek	Elfriede	Creative Works	Austria	Literature - Nobel Laureate
Jellicoe	John Rushworth	War & Peace	England	Admiral
Jemison	Mae Carol	Aviation	USA	Astronaut
Jenkins	Allen	Performing Arts	USA	Actor
	Ferguson Arthur (Fergie)	Sports	Canada	Baseball Player - HF
	Lew	Sports	USA	Boxer - HF
Jenner	Bruce	Sports	USA	Olympic Decathlete
	Edward	Science	England	Physician
	William	Science	England	Physician
Jenney	William le Baron	Architecture	USA	Architect - Skyscraper
Jennings	Hugh Ambrose (Hughie)	Sports	USA	Baseball Player - HF
	Peter	Creative Works	Canada	Journalist - Television
	Waylon	Performing Arts	USA	Singer - Country Music - HF
Jennings-Gabarra	Carin	Sports	USA	Soccer Player - HF
Jensen	Johannes Hans Daniel	Science	Germany	Physics - Nobel Laureate
	Johannes Vilhelm	Creative Works	Denmark	Literature - Nobel Laureate
Jerne	Niels K.	Science	Denmark	Medicine - Nobel Laureate
Jernigan	Tamara Elizabeth	Aviation	USA	Astronaut
Jesperson	Jens Otto Harry	Arts	Denmark	Linguist
Jessel	George	Performing Arts	USA	Comedian
Jett	Joan	Performing Arts	USA	Singer

SOLVER SERIES: NAME FINDER

LAST NAME	FIRST NAME	CATEGORY	COUNTRY	FAME
Jewett	Sarah Orne	Creative Works	USA	Writer
Jewison	Norman	Movie Production	Canada	Director - Acad Award Nom
Jillian	Ann	Performing Arts	USA	Actress
Jiménez	Juan Ramón	Creative Works	Spain	Literature - Nobel Laureate
Joachim	Joseph	Creative Works	Hungary	Composer/Violinist
Joel	William Martin (Billy)	Performing Arts	USA	Singer - Rock & Roll - HF
Joffe	Roland	Movie Production	England	Director - Acad Award Nom
Joffre	Joseph Jacques Césaire	War & Peace	France	Commander in Chief
Joffrey	Robert	Performing Arts	USA	Dancer - Ballet
Jofre	Eder	Sports	Brazil	Boxer - HF
Johansson	Ingemar	Sports	Sweden	Boxer - HF
John	William (Little Willie John)	Performing Arts	USA	Singer - Rock & Roll - HF
John (Dwight)	Reginald K. (Elton)	Performing Arts	England	Singer - Rock & Roll - HF
Johncock	Gordon (Gordie)	Sports	USA	Race Car Driver - HF
Johns	Glynis	Performing Arts	South Africa	Actress - Acad Award Nom
	Jasper	Works of Art	USA	Painter/Sculptor
Johnson	Andrew	Politics	USA	President
	Arte	Performing Arts	USA	Comedian
	Ben	Performing Arts	USA	Actor - Academy Award
	Betsey	Business	USA	Fashion Designer
	Billy	Performing Arts	USA	Rock & Roll - HF - The Moonglows
	Brian	Performing Arts	England	Rock & Roll - HF - AC/DC
	Buck	Performing Arts	USA	Jazz Trumpeter - Big Band/Jazz - HF
	Byron Bancroft (Ban)	Sports	USA	Baseball Executive - HF
	Celia	Performing Arts	England	Actress - Acad Award Nom
	Claudia (Ladybird) Alta	Politics	USA	First Lady
	Davey	Sports	USA	Baseball Player
	Don	Performing Arts	USA	Actor
	Earvin (Magic)	Sports	USA	Basketball Player - HF
	Eliza	Politics	USA	First Lady
	Ernest (Moose)	Sports	Canada	Hockey Player - HF
	Eyvind	Creative Works	Sweden	Literature - Nobel Laureate
	Harold	Sports	USA	Boxer - HF
	Howard	Business	USA	Hotelier
	Howard	Sports	USA	Baseball Player
	Ivan Wilfred (Ching)	Sports	Canada	Hockey Player - HF
	James Earl (Jimmy)	Sports	USA	Football Player - HF
	James Louis (JJ)	Performing Arts	USA	Jazz Trombonist - Big Band/Jazz - HF
	James P.	Performing Arts	USA	Jazz Pianist - Big Band/Jazz - HF
	James Weldon	Creative Works	USA	Writer/Diplomat
	John Henry	Sports	USA	Football Player - HF
	Joseph	Business	England	Publishing
	Josephine Winslow	Creative Works	USA	Novelist - Pulitzer
	Lyndon Baines	Politics	USA	President
	Philip Cortelyou	Architecture	USA	Architect - Pritzker/ AIA Gold
	Rafer Lewis	Sports	USA	Olympic Runner
	Richard M.	Politics	USA	Vice-President
	Robert	Performing Arts	USA	Singer - Rock & Roll - HF
	Robert Glenn (Junior)	Sports	USA	Race Car Driver - HF
	Samuel	Creative Works	England	Writer/Lexicographer/Critic
	Terry	Performing Arts	USA	Rock & Roll - HF - The Flamingos
	Thomas Christian (Tom)	Sports	Canada	Hockey Player - HF
	Van	Performing Arts	USA	Actor
	Walter Perry	Sports	USA	Baseball Player - HF
	William C. (Skinny)	Sports	USA	Basketball Player - HF
	William Jullius (Judy)	Sports	USA	Baseball Player - HF
Johnston	Albert Sidney	War & Peace	USA	Confederate General
	Donald Neil	Sports	USA	Basketball Player - HF
	Joseph Eggleston	War & Peace	USA	Confederate General
	Lynn	Creative Works	Canada	Cartoonist
	William M. (Little Bill)	Sports	USA	Tennis Player - HF
Joiner Jr.	Charles (Charlie)	Sports	USA	Football Player - HF
Joinville	Jean de	Arts	France	Chronicler

LAST NAME	FIRST NAME	CATEGORY	COUNTRY	FAME
Jókai	Maurus	Creative Works	Hungary	Novelist
Joliat	Aurel Emile	Sports	Canada	Hockey Player - HF
Jolie	Angelina	Performing Arts	USA	Actress - Academy Award
Joliet	Louis	Exploration	Canada	Explorer - Mississippi River
Joliot-Curie	Irène	Science	France	Chemistry - Nobel Laureate
	Jean Frédéric	Science	France	Chemistry - Nobel Laureate
Jolson (Yoelson)	Asa (Al)	Performing Arts	Lithuania	Singer
Jones	Booker T.	Performing Arts	USA	Rock & Roll - HF - Booker T & The Mg's
	Brian	Performing Arts	England	Rock & Roll - HF - Rolling Stones
	Carolyn	Performing Arts	USA	Actress - Acad Award Nom
	Charles Marting (Chuck)	Creative Works	USA	Cartoonist - Road Runner
	Daniel	Arts	England	Phonetician
	David D. (Deacon)	Sports	USA	Football Player - HF
	Davy	Performing Arts	England	Singer
	Dean	Performing Arts	USA	Actor
	Ed (Too Tall)	Sports	USA	Football Player
	Edward P.	Creative Works	USA	Novelist - Pulitzer
	Ernest	Arts	England	Psychoanalyst
	Euine Fay	Architecture	USA	Architect - AIA Gold Medal
	George Glen	Performing Arts	USA	Singer - Country Music - HF
	Grace	Performing Arts	Jamaica	Singer/Model
	Grandpa (Louis Marshall)	Performing Arts	USA	Singer - Country Music - HF
	Hank	Performing Arts	USA	Pianist - Big Band/Jazz -HF
	Hoppy (Orville)	Performing Arts	USA	Rock & Roll - HF - The Ink Spots
	Howard	Performing Arts	England	Singer
	Howard Mumford	Arts	USA	Educator/Critic
	Howard Mumford	Creative Works	USA	Author - Pulitzer
	Inigo	Architecture	England	Architect/Stage Designer
	Isham	Performing Arts	USA	Band Leader - Big Band/Jazz - HF
	Isola	Performing Arts	USA	Singer - Opera
	Jack	Performing Arts	USA	Singer
	James	Creative Works	USA	Author
	James Earl	Performing Arts	USA	Actor - Acad Award Nom
	Jennifer	Performing Arts	USA	Actress - Academy Award
	Jesse Holman	Business	USA	Construction Industry
	John Paul	War & Peace	USA	Naval Officer - Revoltionary War
	KC	Sports	USA	Basketball Player - HF
	Lindley Armstrong (Spike)	Performing Arts	USA	Drummer/Comedian
	Michael (Mick)	Performing Arts	England	Rock & Roll - HF - The Clash
	Perry Thomas (Mr. Tennis)	Sports	USA	Tennis Promoter - HF
	Quincy Delight	Performing Arts	USA	Musician/Producer - Big Band/Jazz - HF
	Rickie Lee	Performing Arts	USA	Singer
	Rufus Parnell (Parnelli)	Sports	USA	Race Car Driver - HF
	Samuel (Sam)	Sports	USA	Basketball Player - HF
	Samuel Milton	Business	USA	Manufacturing Industry
	Shirley	Performing Arts	USA	Actress - Academy Award
	Stanley Paul (Stan)	Sports	USA	Football Player - HF
	Terry	Performing Arts	Wales	Comedian
	Thaddeus Joseph (Thad)	Performing Arts	USA	Jazz Trumpeter - Big Band/Jazz - HF
	Thomas David	Aviation	USA	Astronaut
	Tom	Performing Arts	Wales	Singer
	Tommy Lee	Performing Arts	USA	Actor - Academy Award
Jones Jr.	Robert Tyre (Bobby)	Sports	USA	Golfer - HF
Jones Sr.	Robert Trent	Sports	England	Golf Course Designer - HF
Jong	Erica	Creative Works	USA	Author
Jonson	BenJamin (Ben)	Creative Works	England	Poet/Dramatist
Jonze	Spike	Movie Production	USA	Director - Acad Award Nom
Joplin	Janis Lyn	Performing Arts	USA	Singer - Rock & Roll - HF
	Scott	Performing Arts	USA	Pianist/Composer - Big Band/Jazz - HF
Jordan	Henry Wendell	Sports	USA	Football Player - HF
	Louis Thomas	Performing Arts	USA	Singer - Rock & Roll - HF
	Michael	Sports	USA	Basketball Player
	Neil	Movie Production	England	Director - Acad Award Nom

SOLVER SERIES: NAME FINDER

LAST NAME	FIRST NAME	CATEGORY	COUNTRY	FAME
Jordan	Richard	Performing Arts	USA	Actor
Jory	Victor	Performing Arts	Canada	Actor
Josephson	Brian David	Science	England	Physics - Nobel Laureate
Joss	Adrian (Addie)	Sports	USA	Baseball Player - HF
Jouhaux	Léon	War & Peace	France	Peace - Nobel Laureate
Jourdan	Louis	Performing Arts	USA	Actor
Jovovich	Milla	Performing Arts	Ukraine	Super Model
Jowett	Benjamin	Arts	England	Classical Scholar
Joyce	James Augustine Aloysius	Creative Works	Ireland	Poet/Novelist
Juárez	Benito Pablo	Politics	Mexico	President
Judaeus	Philo	Arts	Greece	Philosopher
Judd	Naomi	Performing Arts	USA	Singer
	Wynonna	Performing Arts	USA	Singer
Julia	Raul	Performing Arts	Puerto Rico	Actor
Jump	Gordon	Performing Arts	USA	Actor
Jung	Carl Gustav	Science	Switzerland	Psychiatrist/Psychologist
	Kim Dae	Politics	South Korea	President
Junior	Marvin	Performing Arts	USA	Rock & Roll - HF - The Dells
Jurado	Katy	Performing Arts	Mexico	Actress - Acad Award Nom
Jurgensen III	Christian Adolph (Sonny)	Sports	USA	Football Player - HF
Jusserand	Jean Jules	Creative Works	USA	Author - Pulitzer
Justice	Donald	Creative Works	USA	Poet - Pulitzer
Juvarra	Fillippo	Architecture	Italy	Architect
Kaat	Jim	Sports	USA	Baseball Player
Kadenyuk	Leonid Konstantinovich	Aviation	Ukraine	Astronaut
Kael	Pauline	Creative Works	USA	Journalist - Newspaper
Kafka	Franz	Creative Works	Austria	Writer
Kagawa	Toyohiko	Politics	Japan	Social Reformer/Writer
Kahn	Albert	Architecture	USA	Architect
	Chaka	Performing Arts	USA	Singer
	Louis Isadore	Architecture	USA	Architect - AIA Gold Medal
	Madeline	Performing Arts	USA	Actress - Acad Award Nom
	Oliver	Sports	Germany	Soccer Player
	Otto	Business	USA	Financier
	Sammy	Performing Arts	USA	Actor
Kahneman	Daniel	Arts	USA	Economics - Nobel Laureate
Kaiser	Henry John	Business	USA	Industrialist
Kai-shek	Chaing	War & Peace	China	Military Leader
Kalb	Johann De	War & Peace	France	General
Kaline	Albert William (Al)	Sports	USA	Baseball Player - HF
Kaminska	Ida	Performing Arts	Ukraine	Actress - Acad Award Nom
Kammen	Michael	Creative Works	USA	Author - Pulitzer
Kanaly	Steve	Performing Arts	USA	Actor
Kanawa	Kiri Te	Performing Arts	New Zealand	Singer - Opera
Kandel	Eric R.	Science	USA	Medicine - Nobel Laureate
Kander	John	Creative Works	USA	Composer
Kandinsky	Wassily	Works of Art	Russia	Painter
Kane	Carol	Performing Arts	USA	Actress - Acad Award Nom
Kant	Immanuel	Arts	Germany	Philosopher
Kantner	Paul	Creative Works	USA	Song Writer/Guitarist
	Paul	Performing Arts	USA	Rock & Roll - HF - Jefferson Airplane
Kantor	Mackinlay	Creative Works	USA	Novelist - Pulitzer
Kantorovich	Leonid Vitaliyevich	Arts	Russia	Economics - Nobel Laureate
Kapitza	Pëtr Leonidovich	Science	Russia	Physics - Nobel Laureate
Kaplan	Gabe	Performing Arts	USA	Comedian
	Justin	Creative Works	USA	Author - Pulitzer
Karan	Donna	Business	USA	Fashion Designer
Karembeu	Adriana	Performing Arts	Czechoslovakia	Super Model
Karle	Jerome	Science	USA	Chemistry - Nobel Laureate
Karlfeldt	Erik Axel	Creative Works	Sweden	Literature - Nobel Laureate
Karloff	Boris	Performing Arts	England	Actor
Karnow	Stanley	Creative Works	USA	Author - Pulitzer
Karoly	Bella	Sports	Romania	Olympic Gymnast Coach

LAST NAME	FIRST NAME	CATEGORY	COUNTRY	FAME
Károlyi	Mihály	Politics	Hungary	President
Karpov	Anatoly	Games	Russia	Chess Player
Karrer	Paul	Science	Switzerland	Chemistry - Nobel Laureate
Kasdan	Lawrence	Movie Production	USA	Director
Kasem	Casey	Performing Arts	USA	Show Host - Radio
Kasimdzhanov	Rustam	Games	Uzbekistan	Chess Player
Kasparov	Gary	Games	Russia	Chess Player
Kastler	Alfred	Science	France	Physics - Nobel Laureate
Katz	Bernard	Science	England	Medicine - Nobel Laureate
Kaufman	Bel	Creative Works	Russia	Author
	George Simon	Creative Works	USA	Dramatist - Pulitzer
Kaukonen	Jorma	Performing Arts	USA	Rock & Roll - HF - Jefferson Airplane
Kavner	Julie	Performing Arts	USA	Actor
Kawabata	Yasunari	Creative Works	Japan	Literature - Nobel Laureate
Kay (Krauledat)	Joachim Fritz (John)	Performing Arts	Germany	Singer - Canadian Music - HF
Kaye	Danny	Performing Arts	USA	Actor
	Nora	Performing Arts	USA	Dancer - Ballerina
	Stubby	Performing Arts	USA	Actor - Musical
Kaye (Zarnokay)	Samuel (Sammy)	Performing Arts	USA	Band Leader - Big Band/Jazz - HF
Kazan	Elia	Creative Works	Turkey	Screenwriter
	Elia	Movie Production	Turkey	Director - Academy Award
	Lainie	Performing Arts	USA	Singer
Kazantzakis	Nikos	Creative Works	Greece	Novelist
Keach	Stacey	Performing Arts	USA	Actor
Kean	Edmund	Performing Arts	England	Actor
Keane	Bil	Creative Works	USA	Cartoonist - Family Circle
Keaton	Buster	Performing Arts	USA	Actor
	Diane	Performing Arts	USA	Actress - Academy Award
	Michael	Performing Arts	USA	Actor
Keats	Gordon Blanchard (Duke)	Sports	Canada	Hockey Player - HF
	John	Creative Works	England	Poet
Kedrova	Lila	Performing Arts	Russia	Actress - Academy Award
Keefe	Timothy John (Tim)	Sports	USA	Baseball Player - HF
Keel	Howard	Performing Arts	USA	Actor - Musical
Keeler	Ruby	Performing Arts	Canada	Actress
	William Henry (Willie)	Sports	USA	Baseball Player - HF
Keener	Catherine	Performing Arts	USA	Actress - Acad Award Nom
Keeshan	Bob	Performing Arts	USA	Show Host
Kefauver	Estes	Politics	USA	Senator - Tennessee
Keillor	Garrison	Creative Works	USA	Journalist - Radio
Keitel	Harvey	Performing Arts	USA	Actor - Acad Award Nom
Keith	Arthur	Arts	England	Antropologist/Writer
	Brian	Performing Arts	USA	Actor
	David	Performing Arts	USA	Actor
Kell	George Clyde	Sports	USA	Baseball Player - HF
Kellaway	Cecil	Performing Arts	South Africa	Actor - Acad Award Nom
Kelleher	Robert J.	Sports	USA	Tennis Player - HF
Keller	Helen Adams	Creative Works	USA	Writer/Lecturer
Kellerman	Sally	Performing Arts	USA	Actress - Acad Award Nom
Kelley	Betty	Performing Arts	USA	Rock & Roll - HF - Martha & The Vandellas
	DeForest	Performing Arts	USA	Actor
	Donna	Creative Works	USA	Journalist - Television
	Joseph James (Joe)	Sports	USA	Baseball Player - HF
Kellogg	Frank Billings	War & Peace	USA	Peace - Nobel Laureate
Kelly	Emmett	Performing Arts	USA	Comedian
	Gene	Performing Arts	USA	Actor - Acad Award Nom
	George	Creative Works	USA	Dramatist - Pulitzer
	George Lange	Sports	USA	Baseball Player - HF
	Grace	Performing Arts	USA	Actress - Academy Award
	James Edward (Jim)	Sports	USA	Football Player - HF
	Leonard Patrick (Red)	Sports	Canada	Hockey Player - HF
	Leroy	Sports	USA	Football Player - HF
	Michael Joseph (King)	Sports	USA	Baseball Player - HF

SOLVER SERIES: NAME FINDER

LAST NAME	FIRST NAME	CATEGORY	COUNTRY	FAME
Kelly	Nancy	Performing Arts	USA	Actress - Acad Award Nom
	Walt	Creative Works	USA	Animator
Kelsey	Henry	Exploration	England	Explorer - Canada Inland
Kemal	Mustafa	Politics	Egypt	Patriot - Revolutionary
Kemble	Fanny	Performing Arts	England	Actress
	John Phillip	Performing Arts	England	Actor
Kemp	Jack French	Politics	USA	Congressman
Kemper	Edmund	Law & Order	USA	Serial Killer
Kempis	Thomas à	Arts	Germany	Scholar/Monk
Kendall	Edward Calvin	Science	USA	Medicine - Nobel Laureate
	Henry W.	Science	USA	Physics - Nobel Laureate
Kendrew	John Cowdery	Science	England	Chemistry - Nobel Laureate
Kendricks	Eddie James	Performing Arts	USA	Rock & Roll - HF - The Temptations
Kennan	George Frost	Creative Works	USA	Author - Pulitzer
Kennedy	Anthony McLeod	Law & Order	USA	Justice - Supreme Court
	Arthur	Performing Arts	USA	Actor - Acad Award Nom
	David Matthew	Creative Works	USA	Author - Pulitzer
	Edmund	Exploration	Australia	Explorer - Australia
	Edward Moore (Ted)	Politics	USA	Senator - Massachusetts
	Ethel Skakel	Politics	USA	Wife - Robert Kennedy
	George	Performing Arts	USA	Actor - Academy Award
	Jacqueline Lee	Politics	USA	First Lady
	Jayne	Performing Arts	USA	Actress
	John F.	Creative Works	USA	Author - Pulitzer
	John Fitzgerald	Politics	USA	President
	Patrick Joseph	Business	USA	Importer
	Robert Francis (Bobby)	Politics	USA	Senator - New York
	Theodre Samuel (Ted Teeter)	Sports	Canada	Hockey Player - HF
	William	Creative Works	USA	Novelist - Pulitzer
Kenner-Jackson	Doris	Performing Arts	USA	Rock & Roll - HF - The Shirelles
Kenny	Bill	Performing Arts	USA	Rock & Roll - HF - The Ink Spots
Kent	Arthur	Creative Works	Canada	Journalist - Television
	James	Law & Order	USA	Jurist
	Peter	Creative Works	Canada	Journalist - Television
	Rockwell	Works of Art	USA	Artist
Kenton	Stan	Performing Arts	USA	Jazz Pianist
	Stanley Newcomb (Stan)	Performing Arts	USA	Band Leader - Big Band/Jazz - HF
Kenyatta	Jomo	Politics	Africa	President/Kenya
Kenyon	John Samuel	Arts	USA	Phonetician/Educator
	Mel	Sports	USA	Race Car Driver - HF
Keon	David Michael (Dave)	Sports	Canada	Hockey Player - HF
Keough	Harry Joseph	Sports	USA	Soccer Player - HF
Kepler	Johannes	Science	Germany	Astronomer/Mathematician
Keppard	Freddie	Performing Arts	USA	Jazz Cornetist - Big Band/Jazz - HF
Kercheval	Ken	Performing Arts	USA	Actor
Kerensky	Aleksandr Feodorovich	Politics	Russia	Prime Minister
Kern	Jerome David	Creative Works	USA	Composer
Kerns	Joanna	Performing Arts	USA	Actress
Kerouac	Jack	Creative Works	USA	Novelist/Poet
Kerr	Deborah	Performing Arts	Scotland	Actress - Acad Award Nom
	John	Performing Arts	USA	Actor
	Robert Samuel	Business	USA	Oil Industry
Kertész	Imre	Creative Works	Hungary	Literature - Nobel Laureate
Kerwin	Joseph Peter	Aviation	USA	Astronaut
Kesey	Ken	Creative Works	USA	Author
Kessell	Barney	Performing Arts	USA	Jazz Guitarist - Big Band/Jazz - HF
Ketterie	Wolfgang	Science	Germany	Physics - Nobel Laureate
Kettering	Charles Franklin	Science	USA	Inventor/Electrical Engineer
Key	Francis Scott	Creative Works	USA	Poet
	Ted	Creative Works	USA	Cartoonist - Political
Keyes	Evelyn	Performing Arts	USA	Actress
	John Maynard	Creative Works	England	Writer/Economist
Keynes	John Maynard	Arts	England	Economist

LAST NAME	FIRST NAME	CATEGORY	COUNTRY	FAME
Khachaturian	Aram	Creative Works	Russia	Composer
Khalifman	Alexander	Games	Russia	Chess Player
Khan	Aga	Architecture	France	Architect - Jefferson Medal
	Genghis	War & Peace	Mongolia	Military Leader
Kharlamov	Valeri	Sports	Russia	Hockey Player - HF
Khayyám	Omar	Creative Works	Persia	Poet
Khorana	Har Gobind	Science	USA	Medicine - Nobel Laureate
Khrunov	Yeugeni Vassilyevich	Aviation	Russia	Astronaut
Khrushchev	Nikita Sergeyevich	Politics	Russia	Premier
Kibbee	Guy	Performing Arts	USA	Actor
Kidd	William	Law & Order	England	Privateer/Pirate
Kidder	Margot	Performing Arts	Canada	Actress
	Tracy	Creative Works	USA	Author - Pulitzer
Kidman	Nicole	Performing Arts	USA	Actress - Academy Award
Kiepura	Jan	Performing Arts	Poland	Singer - Opera
Kierkegaard	Soren Aabye	Arts	Denmark	Philosopher/Theologian
Kiesling	Walter Andrew (Walt)	Sports	USA	Football Player - HF
Kieslowski	Krzysztof	Movie Production	Poland	Director - Acad Award Nom
Kiker	Douglas	Creative Works	USA	Journalist - Television
Kilbride	Percy	Performing Arts	USA	Actor
Kilby	Jack S.	Science	USA	Physics - Nobel Laureate
	Dan	Architecture	USA	Architect - Jefferson Medal
	Richard	Performing Arts	USA	Singer
Killebrew	Harmon Clayton	Sports	USA	Baseball Player - HF
Killy	Jean-Claude	Sports	France	Olympic - Skier
Kilmer	Alfred Joyce	Creative Works	USA	Poet
	Val	Performing Arts	USA	Actor
Kilrain	Susan Leigh	Aviation	USA	Astronaut
Kinard	Frank Manning (Bruiser)	Sports	USA	Football Player - HF
Kiner	Ralph McPherran	Sports	USA	Baseball Player - HF
King	Alan	Performing Arts	USA	Comedian
	Bernard	Sports	USA	Basketball Player
	Betsy	Sports	USA	Golfer - HF
	Billie Jean Moffitt	Sports	USA	Tennis Player - HF
	Carole	Performing Arts	USA	Singer
	Cecil	Business	England	Publishing
	Coretta Scott	Politics	USA	Wife - Martin Luther King
	Henry	Movie Production	USA	Director - Acad Award Nom
	Jaime	Performing Arts	USA	Super Model
	Larry	Creative Works	USA	Journalist - Television
	Perry	Performing Arts	USA	Actor
	Regina	Performing Arts	USA	Actress
	Riley B. (BB)	Performing Arts	USA	Guitarist/Songwriter - Big Band/Jazz - HF
	Riley B. (BB)	Performing Arts	USA	Singer - Rock & Roll - HF
	Stephen Edwin	Creative Works	USA	Novelist - Horror
	William Lyon Mackenzie	Politics	Canada	Prime Minister
	William R.	Politics	USA	Vice-President
King (Kuczynski)	Frank Julius (Pee Wee)	Performing Arts	USA	Musician - Country Music - HF
King Jr.	Martin Luther	Politics	USA	Clergyman
	Martin Luther	War & Peace	USA	Peace - Nobel Laureate
Kingdom	Roger	Sports	USA	Olympic Hurdler
Kingman	Dave	Sports	USA	Baseball Player
Kingsley	Ben	Performing Arts	England	Actor - Academy Award
	Charles	Creative Works	England	Novelist/Clergyman
	Mary Henrietta	Exploration	England	Explorer - Africa West/North
	Sidney	Creative Works	USA	Dramatist - Pulitzer
Kinnear	Greg	Performing Arts	USA	Actor - Acad Award Nom
Kinnell	Galway	Creative Works	USA	Poet - Pulitzer
Kino	Eusebio Francisco	Exploration	Spain	Explorer - Mexico
Kinsey	Alfred Charles	Science	USA	Zoologist - Sexual Behavior
Kinski	Nastassia	Performing Arts	Germany	Actress
Kinsley	Mike	Creative Works	USA	Journalist - Newspaper
Kipling	Joseph Rudyard	Creative Works	England	Literature - Nobel Laureate

SOLVER SERIES: NAME FINDER

LAST NAME	FIRST NAME	CATEGORY	COUNTRY	FAME
Kirby	Bruno	Performing Arts	USA	Actor
	Durward	Performing Arts	USA	Actor
Kirchhoff	Gustav Robert	Science	Germany	Physicist
Kirk	Andy	Performing Arts	USA	Jazz Saxophonist - Big Band/Jazz - HF
Kirkland	Joseph Lane	Business	USA	Labor Leader
	Sally	Performing Arts	USA	Actress - Acad Award Nom
Kirkpatrick	Jeane Jordan	Politics	USA	Politician
Kirkwood	James	Creative Works	USA	Dramatist - Pulitzer
Kirwan	Danny	Performing Arts	England	Rock & Roll - HF - Fleetwood Mac
Kissinger	Henry Alfred	Politics	USA	Secretary of State
	Henry Alfred	War & Peace	USA	Peace - Nobel Laureate
Kitchener	Horatio Herbert	War & Peace	England	Statesman/Military Officer
Kite	Thomas O. (Tom)	Sports	USA	Golfer - HF
Kitt	Eartha	Performing Arts	USA	Singer
Kittredge	George Lyman	Arts	USA	Scholar/Educator
Kizer	Carolyn	Creative Works	USA	Poet - Pulitzer
Klee	Paul	Works of Art	Switzerland	Painter - Abstract
Klein	Alexander	Architecture	USA	Architect
	Anne	Business	USA	Fashion Designer
	Calvin	Business	USA	Fashion Designer
	Charles Herbert (Chuck)	Sports	USA	Baseball Player - HF
	Lawrence R.	Arts	USA	Economics - Nobel Laureate
	Martina	Performing Arts	Argentina	Super Model
	Robert	Performing Arts	USA	Actor - Musical
Klem	William (Bill)	Sports	USA	Baseball Umpire - HF
Klemperer	Otto	Performing Arts	Germany	Conductor/Composer
	Werner	Performing Arts	Germany	Actor
Klenze	Leo von	Architecture	Germany	Architect/Painter/Writer
Klerk	Frederik Willem de	War & Peace	South Africa	Peace - Nobel Laureate
	Michel de	Architecture	Netherlands	Architect
Kliban	Bernard	Creative Works	USA	Cartoonist - Playboy
Klimt	Gustav	Works of Art	Austria	Painter - Art Nouveau
Kline	Benjamin S.	Science	USA	Pathologist
	Franz	Works of Art	USA	Painter - Abstract Expressionist
	Kevin	Performing Arts	USA	Actor - Academy Award
Klinsman	Jürgen	Sports	Germany	Soccer Player
Klitzing	Klaus von	Science	Germany	Physics - Nobel Laureate
Klug	Aaron	Science	England	Chemistry - Nobel Laureate
Kluger	Richard	Creative Works	USA	Author - Pulitzer
Klugman	Jack	Performing Arts	USA	Actor
Klum	Heidi	Performing Arts	Germany	Super Model
Knight	Gladys Marie	Performing Arts	USA	Rock & Roll - HF - The Pips
	Shirley	Performing Arts	USA	Actress - Acad Award Nom
	Ted	Performing Arts	USA	Actor
Knopf	Alfred Abraham	Business	USA	Publishing
Knopfler	Mark	Performing Arts	Scotland	Singer
Knotts	Don	Performing Arts	USA	Comedian
Knowles	John	Creative Works	USA	Novelist
	William S.	Science	USA	Chemistry - Nobel Laureate
Knox	Alexander	Performing Arts	Canada	Actor - Acad Award Nom
	John	Arts	Scotland	Clergyman/Religious Reformer
	Ronald Arbuthnott	Arts	England	Priest/Translator
Knudsen	Martin	Science	Denmark	Chemist
Kobo	Abe	Creative Works	Japan	Novelist/Playwright
Koch	Edward Irving (Ed)	Politics	USA	Mayor - New York City
	Robert	Science	Germany	Medicine - Nobel Laureate
Kocher	Emil Theodor	Science	Switzerland	Medicine - Nobel Laureate
Kodály	Zoltan	Creative Works	Hungary	Composer
Kodes	Jan	Sports	Czechoslovakia	Tennis Player - HF
Koffka	Kurt	Arts	USA	Psychologist
Koffman	Morris (Moe)	Performing Arts	Canada	Jazz Flutist - Canadian Music - HF
Kohl	Helmut	Politics	Germany	Chancellor
Köhler	Georges J.F.	Science	Germany	Medicine - Nobel Laureate

LAST NAME	FIRST NAME	CATEGORY	COUNTRY	FAME
Köhler	Wolfgang	Arts	Germany	Psychologist
Kohn	Walter	Science	USA	Chemistry - Nobel Laureate
Kohner	Susan	Performing Arts	USA	Actress - Acad Award Nom
Kokoschka	Oskar	Works of Art	England	Painter
Kollhoff	Hans	Architecture	Germany	Architect
Kollwitz	Käthe	Works of Art	Germany	Painter/Etcher/Lithographer
Komarov	Vladimir Mikhailovich	Aviation	Russia	Astronaut
Komunyakaa	Yusef	Creative Works	USA	Poet - Pulitzer
Koolhaas	Rem	Architecture	Netherlands	Architect - Pritzker Laureate
Kooning	Willem de	Works of Art	USA	Painter
Koontz	Dean Ray	Creative Works	USA	Author
Koop	Charles Everett	Politics	USA	Surgeon General
Koopmans	Tjalling C.	Arts	USA	Economics - Nobel Laureate
Kooser	Ted	Creative Works	USA	Poet - Pulitzer
Kopell	Bernie	Performing Arts	USA	Actor
Koppel	Ted	Creative Works	USA	Journalist - Television
Korbut	Olga	Sports	Russia	Olympic Gymnast
Korjus	Miliza	Performing Arts	Poland	Actress - Acad Award Nom
Korman	Harvey	Performing Arts	USA	Actor
Kornberg	Arthur	Science	USA	Medicine - Nobel Laureate
Korth	Fred	Business	USA	Banking
Korzybski	Alfred Habdank	Creative Works	USA	Writer/Semanticist
Kosciusko	Thadeus	War & Peace	Poland	General/Patriot
Koshiba	Masatoshi	Science	Japan	Physics - Nobel Laureate
Kossel	Albrecht	Science	Germany	Medicine - Nobel Laureate
Kostelanetz	André	Performing Arts	Russia	Conductor/Arranger
Koster	Henry	Movie Production	Germany	Director - Acad Award Nom
Kosygin	Aleksei Nikolaevich	Politics	Russia	Premier - U.S.S.R.
Kotto	Yaphet	Performing Arts	USA	Actor
Kotzebue	August Friedrich Ferdinand	Creative Works	Germany	Playwright
Koufax	Sanford (Sandy)	Sports	USA	Baseball Player - HF
Koussevitzky	Serge	Performing Arts	Russia	Conductor
Kovacs	Ernie	Performing Arts	USA	Comedian
Kovalev	Alexei	Sports	Russia	Hockey Player
Kraepelin	Emil	Science	Germany	Psychiatrist
Kramer	Erik	Sports	USA	Football Player
	Joey (Joseph)	Performing Arts	USA	Rock & Roll - HF - Aerosmith
	John Albert (Jack)	Sports	USA	Tennis Player - HF
	Pieter Lodewijk	Architecture	Netherlands	Architect
	Stanley	Movie Production	USA	Director - Acad Award Nom
Kramm	Joseph	Creative Works	USA	Dramatist - Pulitzer
Kramnik	Vladimir	Games	Russia	Chess Player
Krantz	Judith	Creative Works	USA	Novelist
Krause	Edward W. (Moose)	Sports	USA	Basketball Player - HF
	Paul James	Sports	USA	Football Player - HF
Krebs	Edwin G.	Science	USA	Medicine - Nobel Laureate
	Hans Adolf	Science	England	Medicine - Nobel Laureate
Kregel	Kevin Richard	Aviation	USA	Astronaut
Kreisler	Fritz	Creative Works	USA	Composer/Violinist
Kreutzmann	Bill	Performing Arts	USA	Rock & Roll - HF - Grateful Dead
Krieger	Robby	Performing Arts	USA	Rock & Roll - HF - The Doors
Krier	Leon	Architecture	England	Architect - Jefferson Medal
Kristofferson	Kris	Performing Arts	USA	Actor/Singer - Country Music - HF
Kroc	Joan	Business	USA	Philanthropy
	Ray	Business	USA	McDonalds Restaurants
Kroeber	Alfred Louis	Arts	USA	Anthropologist
Kroemer	Herbert	Science	Germany	Physics - Nobel Laureate
Krogh	Schack August Steenberg	Science	Denmark	Medicine - Nobel Laureate
Kropfelder	Nicholas	Sports	USA	Soccer Player - HF
Kroto	Harold	Science	England	Chemistry - Nobel Laureate
Kruger	Alma	Performing Arts	USA	Actress
	Otto	Performing Arts	USA	Actor
	Paul	Politics	South Africa	President

LAST NAME	FIRST NAME	CATEGORY	COUNTRY	FAME
Kruif	Paul Henry de	Science	USA	Bacteriologist/Writer
Krupa	Gene	Performing Arts	USA	Jazz Drummer - Big Band/Jazz - HF
Krupp	Alfred	Business	Germany	Industrialist
Kruschen	Jack	Performing Arts	Canada	Actor - Acad Award Nom
Krutch	Joseph Wood	Creative Works	USA	Essayist/Naturalist/Critic
Kubasov	Valeri Nikolayevich	Aviation	Russia	Astronaut
Kubek	Tony	Sports	USA	Baseball Player
Kubelik	Rafaël	Performing Arts	Czechoslovakia	Orchestra Conductor
Kubrick	Stanley	Movie Production	USA	Director - Acad Award Nom
Kuhn	Bowie Kent	Sports	USA	Baseball Commissioner
	Richard	Science	Germany	Chemistry - Nobel Laureate
	Thomas	Arts	USA	Philosopher/Historian
Kulp	Nancy	Performing Arts	USA	Actress
Kulwicki	Alan	Sports	USA	Race Car Driver - HF
Kumin	Maxine	Creative Works	USA	Poet - Pulitzer
Kun	Béla	Politics	Hungary	Communist Leader
Kundera	Milan	Creative Works	Czechoslovakia	Author
Kunitz	Stanley	Creative Works	USA	Poet - Pulitzer
Kuntner	Rudolph (Rudy)	Sports	Vienna	Soccer Player - HF
Kuralt	Charles	Creative Works	USA	Journalist - Television
Kurkova	Karolina	Performing Arts	Czechoslovakia	Super Model
Kurland	Robert A. (Bob)	Sports	USA	Basketball Player - HF
Kurokawa	Kisho	Architecture	Japan	Architect
Kurosawa	Akira	Movie Production	Japan	Director - Acad Award Nom
Kurri	Jari Pekka	Sports	Finland	Hockey Player - HF
Kurten	Peter	Law & Order	Germany	Serial Killer - Dusseldorf Vampire
Kurtz	Swoosie	Performing Arts	USA	Actress
Kusch	Polykarp	Science	USA	Physics - Nobel Laureate
Kushner	Tony	Creative Works	USA	Dramatist - Pulitzer
Kutuzov	Mikhail Ilarionovich	War & Peace	Russia	Field Marshall
Kuznets	Simon	Arts	USA	Economics - Nobel Laureate
Kyd	Thomas	Creative Works	England	Dramatist
Kydland	Finn E.	Arts	Norway	Economics - Nobel Laureate
Kyi	Aung San Suu	War & Peace	Burma	Peace - Nobel Laureate
Kyser	Kay	Performing Arts	USA	Band Leader
Laan	Hans Dom van der	Architecture	Netherlands	Architect
Labatut	Jean	Architecture	USA	Architect - Jefferson Medal
Labrouste	Henri	Architecture	France	Architect
Lach	Elmer James	Sports	Canada	Hockey Player - HF
Lachaise	Gaston	Works of Art	USA	Sculptor
Lacoste	Jean René (The Crocodile)	Sports	France	Tennis Player - HF
Lacroix	Christian	Business	France	Fashion Designer
Ladd	Alan	Performing Arts	USA	Actor
	Cheryl	Performing Arts	USA	Actress
	Diane	Performing Arts	USA	Actress - Acad Award Nom
Lafitte	Jean	Law & Order	France	Pirate
Lagarde	Jocelyne	Performing Arts	Tahiti	Actress - Acad Award Nom
Lagasse	Emeril	Performing Arts	USA	Actor - Chef
Lagerfeld	Karl	Business	Germany	Fashion Designer
Lagerkvist	Pär Fabian	Creative Works	Sweden	Literature - Nobel Laureate
Lagerlöf	Selma Ottilana Lovisa	Creative Works	Sweden	Literature - Nobel Laureate
Lagrange	Joseph Louis	Science	France	Astronomer/Mathematician
Laguna	Ismael	Sports	Panama	Boxer - HF
Lahiri	Jhumpa	Creative Works	USA	Novelist - Pulitzer
Lahr	Bert	Performing Arts	USA	Actor
Lahti	Christine	Performing Arts	USA	Actress - Acad Award Nom
Lai	Francis	Performing Arts	France	Singer
Laine	Cleo	Performing Arts	England	Singer
	Frankie	Performing Arts	USA	Singer
Laing	Ronald David	Science	Scotland	Psychiatrist
	Samuel	Business	England	Railway Magnate
Lajoie	Napoleon (Nap)	Sports	USA	Baseball Player - HF
Lakatos	Imre	Arts	Hungary	Philosopher/Mathematician

LAST NAME	FIRST NAME	CATEGORY	COUNTRY	FAME
Lake	Greg	Performing Arts	England	Singer
	Veronica	Performing Arts	USA	Actress
Lalo	Édouard Victor Antoine	Creative Works	France	Composer
Lalonde	Edouard (Newsy)	Sports	Canada	Hockey Player - HF
Laloux	Victor	Architecture	France	Architect - AIA Gold Medal
Lamarr	Hedy	Performing Arts	Austria	Actress
Lamartine	Alphonse Marie Louis de	Creative Works	France	Poet
Lamas	Carlos Saavedra	War & Peace	Argentina	Peace - Nobel Laureate
	Fernando	Performing Arts	Argentina	Actor
	Lorenzo	Performing Arts	USA	Actor
Lamb	Charles	Creative Works	England	Essayist/Critic
	Mary Ann	Creative Works	England	Writer
	Willis Eugene	Science	USA	Physics - Nobel Laureate
Lambeau	Earl Louis (Curly)	Sports	USA	Football Coach - HF
Lambert	John Harold (Jack)	Sports	USA	Football Player - HF
Lamielleure	Joseph Michael De (Joe)	Sports	USA	Football Player - HF
Lamour	Dorothy	Performing Arts	USA	Actress
Lancaster	Burt	Performing Arts	USA	Actor - Academy Award
	Elsa	Performing Arts	England	Actress - Acad Award Nom
Land	Edwin Herbert	Science	USA	Inventor - Land Camera
Landau	Lev Davidivich	Science	Russia	Physics - Nobel Laureate
	Martin	Performing Arts	USA	Actor - Academy Award
Landers	Ann	Creative Works	USA	Journalist - Newspaper
	Richard Lemon	Exploration	England	Explorer - Africa West
Landi	Elissa	Performing Arts	Italy	Actress/Author
Landis	Carole	Performing Arts	USA	Actress
	John	Movie Production	USA	Director
	Kenesaw Mountain	Law & Order	USA	Jurist
	Kenesaw Mountain	Sports	USA	Baseball Commissioner - HF
Lando	Joseph (Joe)	Performing Arts	USA	Actor
Landon	Alfred Mossman (Alf)	Politics	USA	Governor - Kansas
	Michael	Performing Arts	USA	Actor
Landor	Walter Savage	Creative Works	England	Poet/Writer
Landowska	Wanda	Performing Arts	Poland	Harpsichordist
Landry	Thomas Wade (Tom)	Sports	USA	Football Player - HF
Landseer	Edwin Henry	Works of Art	England	Painter - Animals
Landsteiner	Karl	Science	Austria	Medicine - Nobel Laureate
Lane	Diane	Performing Arts	USA	Actress - Acad Award Nom
	Richard (Dick) (Night Train)	Sports	USA	Football Player - HF
Laney	Albert Gillis	Sports	USA	Tennis Writer - HF
Lang	Fritz	Movie Production	Austria	Director
	K.D.	Performing Arts	Canada	Singer
	Millard Tuttle (Millar)	Sports	USA	Soccer Player - HF
	Timur (Tamerlane)	War & Peace	Mongolia	Military Leader
	Walter	Movie Production	USA	Director - Acad Award Nom
Lang (Massaro)	Salvatore (Eddie)	Performing Arts	USA	Jazz Guitarist - Big Band/Jazz - HF
Langdon	Sue Ane	Performing Arts	USA	Actress
Lange	Christian Lous	War & Peace	Norway	Peace - Nobel Laureate
	Hope	Performing Arts	USA	Actress - Acad Award Nom
	Jessica	Performing Arts	USA	Actress - Academy Award
Langella	Frank	Performing Arts	USA	Actor
Langer	Bernhard	Sports	Germany	Golfer - HF
	James John (Jim)	Sports	USA	Football Player - HF
	Susan Katherina	Arts	USA	Philosopher
Langhans	Carl Gotthard	Architecture	Germany	Architect
Langland	William	Creative Works	England	Poet
Langley	Samuel Pierpoint	Science	USA	Physicist/Astronomer
Langmuir	Irving	Science	USA	Chemistry - Nobel Laureate
Langois	Paul	Performing Arts	Canada	Canadian Music - HF - The Tragically Hip
Langtry	Lillie	Performing Arts	England	Actress
Langway	Rod Corry	Sports	Taiwan	Hockey Player - HF
Lanier	Robert J. (Bob)	Sports	USA	Basketball Player - HF
	Sidney	Creative Works	USA	Poet

SOLVER SERIES: NAME FINDER

LAST NAME	FIRST NAME	CATEGORY	COUNTRY	FAME
Lanier	Willie Edward	Sports	USA	Football Player - HF
Lanin	Lester	Performing Arts	USA	Band Leader
Lanois	Daniel	Performing Arts	Canada	Musician/Producer - Canadian Music - HF
Lansbury	Angela	Performing Arts	England	Actress - Acad Award Nom
Lansing	John	Law & Order	USA	Jurist
	Robert	Performing Arts	USA	Actor
Lansky	Meyer (The Brain)	Law & Order	Russia	Mafia
Lanz	Walter	Creative Works	USA	Cartoonist - Woody Woodpecker
Lanza	Mario	Performing Arts	USA	Singer
Lapchick	Joe	Sports	USA	Basketball Player - HF
Laperriere	Joseph Jacques Hughes	Sports	Canada	Hockey Player - HF
Lapidus	Ted	Business	France	Designer - Fashion/Fragrances
LaPierre	Cherilyn (Cher)	Performing Arts	USA	Actress/Singer - Acad Award
Lapine	James	Creative Works	USA	Dramatist - Pulitzer
Laplace	Pierre Simon de	Science	France	Astronomer/Mathematician
Lapointe	Guy Gerard	Sports	Canada	Hockey Player - HF
Laprade	Edgar Louis	Sports	Canada	Hockey Player - HF
Lardner	Ringgold Wilmer	Creative Works	USA	Humorist/Sports Reporter
Largent	Stephen Michael (Steve)	Sports	USA	Football Player - HF
Larkin	Oliver Waterman	Creative Works	USA	Author - Pulitzer
	Philip	Creative Works	England	Poet/Novelist
Larned	William Augustus (Bill)	Sports	USA	Tennis Player - HF
Laroche	Guy	Business	France	Fashion Designer
LaRosa	Julius	Performing Arts	USA	Singer
Larroquette	John	Performing Arts	USA	Actor
Larsen	Arthur David (Tappy)	Sports	USA	Tennis Player - HF
	Don	Sports	USA	Baseball Player
Larson	Edward J.	Creative Works	USA	Author - Pulitzer
	Gary	Creative Works	USA	Cartoonist - Far Side
	Jonathan	Creative Works	USA	Dramatist - Pulitzer
Lary Jr.	Robert Yale	Sports	USA	Football Player - HF
Las Casas	Bartolomé	Arts	Spain	Historian/Missionary
Lash	Joseph P.	Creative Works	USA	Author - Pulitzer
Lasker	Emanuel	Games	Germany	Chess Player
Laski	Harold Joseph	Politics	England	Political Scientist/Socialist
Lasorda	Thomas Charles (Tommy)	Sports	USA	Baseball Manager - HF
Lassalle	Ferdinand	Arts	Germany	Socialist/Writer
Lasser	Louise	Performing Arts	USA	Actress
Latifah	Queen	Performing Arts	USA	Actress - Acad Award Nom
Latimer	Hugh	Arts	England	Protestant Bishop/Reformer
Latrobe	Benjamin Henry	Architecture	USA	Architect
Laud	William	Arts	England	Prelate/Archbishop
Lauda	Niki van	Sports	Austria	Race Car Driver - HF
Lauder	Estee	Business	USA	Cosmetics Industry
	Harry	Performing Arts	Scotland	Comedian/Singer
Laue	Max von	Science	Germany	Physics - Nobel Laureate
Laughlin	Robert B.	Science	USA	Physics - Nobel Laureate
Laughton	Charles	Performing Arts	England	Actor - Academy Award
Laugier	Marc Antoine	Architecture	France	Architect
Lauper	Cyndi	Performing Arts	USA	Singer
Laurel	Stan	Performing Arts	England	Comedian
Lauren	Ralph	Business	USA	Fashion Designer
Laurie	Piper	Performing Arts	USA	Actress - Acad Award Nom
Laurier	Wilfred	Politics	Canada	Prime Minister
Lauterbur	Paul C.	Science	USA	Medicine - Nobel Laureate
Laval	Pierre	Politics	France	Premier
Lavelli	Dante Bert Joseph	Sports	USA	Football Player - HF
Laver	Rodney George (Rocket)	Sports	Australia	Tennis Player - HF
Laveran	Charles Louis Alphonse	Science	France	Medicine - Nobel Laureate
Lavin	Linda	Performing Arts	USA	Actress
Laviolette	Jean Baptiste (Jack)	Sports	Canada	Hockey Player - HF
Lavoisier	Antoine-Laurent de	Science	France	Chemist
Law	Andrew Bonar	Politics	England	Prime Minister

LAST NAME	FIRST NAME	CATEGORY	COUNTRY	FAME
Law	Jude	Performing Arts	England	Actor - Acad Award Nom
Lawford	Peter	Performing Arts	England	Actor
Lawrence	Carol	Performing Arts	USA	Actress
	David Herbert	Creative Works	England	Poet/Novelist
	Ernest Orlando	Science	USA	Physics - Nobel Laureate
	Gertrude	Performing Arts	England	Actress
	Martin	Performing Arts	Germany	Comedian
	Steve	Performing Arts	USA	Singer
	Thomas	Works of Art	England	Painter - Portrait
	Thomas Edward	Creative Works	England	Writer/Adventurer
	Vicki	Performing Arts	USA	Actress
Laws	Hubert	Performing Arts	USA	Jazz Flutist
Lawson	Edward Levy	Business	England	Publishing
Lawton	Henry W.	War & Peace	USA	Major General
Laxness	Halldór Kiljan	Creative Works	Iceland	Literature - Nobel Laureate
Layne	Robert Lawrence (Bobby)	Sports	USA	Football Player - HF
Lazarus	Emma	Creative Works	USA	Poet
Lazzeri	Anthony Michael (Tony)	Sports	USA	Baseball Player - HF
Leach	Robin	Creative Works	England	Journalist - Television
Leachman	Cloris	Performing Arts	USA	Actress - Academy Award
Leacock	Stephen Butler	Arts	Canada	Humorist/Political Economist
Leadon	Bernie	Performing Arts	USA	Rock & Roll - HF - The Eagles
Leakey	Louis Seymour Bazett	Arts	England	Anthropologist
Lean	David	Movie Production	England	Director - Academy Award
Lear	Edward	Works of Art	England	Painter/Illustrator/Humorist
Learned	Michael	Performing Arts	USA	Actress
Lebrun	Albert	Politics	France	President
	Charles	Works of Art	France	Painter - Historical
Lecky	William Edward Hartpole	Arts	England	Historian
Leconte de Lisle	Charles Marie René	Creative Works	England	Poet
Ledbetter	Huddie William	Performing Arts	USA	Rock & Roll - HF - Lead Belly
Lederberg	Joshua	Science	USA	Medicine - Nobel Laureate
Lederman	Leon M.	Science	USA	Physics - Nobel Laureate
Ledoux	Claude Nicholas	Architecture	France	Architect
Lee	Ang	Movie Production	Taiwan	Director - Acad Award Nom
	Ann	Arts	England	Mystic - Shakers Founder
	Beverley	Performing Arts	USA	Rock & Roll - HF - The Shirelles
	Bruce	Performing Arts	USA	Actor
	Charles	War & Peace	USA	General - Revolutionary War
	Christopher	Performing Arts	England	Actor
	David M.	Science	USA	Physics - Nobel Laureate
	Geddy	Performing Arts	Canada	Canadian Music - HF - Rush
	Gypsy Rose	Performing Arts	USA	Dancer
	Harper	Creative Works	USA	Novelist - Pulitzer
	Henry	War & Peace	USA	General - Revolutionary War
	Mark Charles	Aviation	USA	Astronaut
	Michele	Performing Arts	USA	Actress
	Robert Edward	War & Peace	USA	Commander in Chief
	Spike	Movie Production	USA	Director
	Stanley Martin (Stan)	Creative Works	USA	Cartoonist - Spiderman
	Tsung-Dao	Science	China	Physics - Nobel Laureate
	Yuan T.	Science	USA	Chemistry - Nobel Laureate
Lee (Engstrom)	Norma Delores (Peggy)	Performing Arts	USA	Actress/Singer - Acad Award Nom
	Norma Delores (Peggy)	Performing Arts	USA	Singer - Big Band/Jazz - HF
Lee (Tarpley)	Brenda Mae	Performing Arts	USA	Singer - Country Music - HF
	Brenda Mae	Performing Arts	USA	Singer - Rock & Roll - HF
Leech	Margaret	Creative Works	USA	Author - Pulitzer
Leeds	Andrea	Performing Arts	USA	Actress - Acad Award Nom
Leek	Sybil	Science	England	Astrologer/Witch
Leemans	Alphonse Emil (Tuffy)	Sports	USA	Football Player - HF
Leeuwenhoek	Anton van	Arts	Netherlands	Naturalist
Legendre	Adrien Marie	Science	France	Mathematician
Léger	Fernand	Works of Art	France	Painter

SOLVER SERIES: NAME FINDER

LAST NAME	FIRST NAME	CATEGORY	COUNTRY	FAME
Leggett	Anthony J.	Science	England	Physics - Nobel Laureate
Legorreta	Ricardo	Architecture	Mexico	Architect - AIA Gold Medal
Legrand	Michel	Performing Arts	France	Jazz Pianist
Leguizamo	John	Performing Arts	Colombia	Actor
Lehár	Franz	Creative Works	Hungary	Composer - Operettas
Lehman	Frederick Hugh (Hughie)	Sports	Canada	Hockey Player - HF
	Tom	Sports	USA	Golfer
Lehmann	Lilli	Performing Arts	Germany	Singer - Opera
	Lotte	Performing Arts	Germany	Singer - Opera
Lehn	Jean-Marie	Science	France	Chemistry - Nobel Laureate
Lehr	Lew	Performing Arts	USA	Comedian
Lehrer	Jim	Creative Works	USA	Journalist - Television
Leiber Jr.	Fritz Reuter	Creative Works	USA	Author - SciFi
Leibman	Ron	Performing Arts	USA	Actor
Leibniz	Gottfried Wilhelm von	Arts	Germany	Philosopher/Mathematician
Leicester	Robert Dudley	Arts	England	Courtier
Leigh	Janet	Performing Arts	USA	Actress - Acad Award Nom
	Jennifer Jason	Performing Arts	USA	Actress
	Mike	Movie Production	England	Director - Acad Award Nom
	Vivien	Performing Arts	India	Actress - Academy Award
Leighton	Margaret	Performing Arts	England	Actress - Acad Award Nom
Leinsdorf	Erich	Performing Arts	Austria	Conductor
Leisure	David	Performing Arts	USA	Comedian
Leloir	Luis F.	Science	Argentina	Chemistry - Nobel Laureate
Lelouch	Claude	Movie Production	France	Director - Acad Award Nom
Lelyveld	Joseph	Creative Works	USA	Author - Pulitzer
Lema	Tony	Sports	USA	Golfer
Lemaire	Jacques Gerard	Sports	Canada	Hockey Player - HF
Lemieux	Mario	Sports	Canada	Hockey Player - HF
Lemmon	Jack	Performing Arts	USA	Actor - Academy Award
Lemon	Mark	Business	USA	Publishing
	Robert Granville (Bob)	Sports	USA	Baseball Player - HF
Lenard	Phillipp Eduard Anton von	Science	Germany	Physics - Nobel Laureate
Lenarduzzi	Bobby	Sports	Canada	Soccer Player - HF
Lendl	Ivan	Sports	Czechoslovakia	Tennis Player - HF
L'Enfant	Pierre Charles	Architecture	France	Architect/Engineer
Lenglen	Suzanne Rachel Flore	Sports	France	Tennis Player - HF
Lenin	Vladimir Ilyich	Politics	Russia	Premier - U.S.S.R.
Lenné	Peter Josef	Architecture	Germany	Architect - Landscape Design
Lennon	John Winston	Performing Arts	England	Rock & Roll - HF - The Beatles
	Julian	Performing Arts	England	Singer
Lennox	Annie	Performing Arts	Scotland	Singer
Leno	Jay	Performing Arts	USA	Show Host/Comedian
Lenoir	William Benjamin	Aviation	USA	Astronaut
Lenska	Rula	Performing Arts	England	Actress
Lenya	Lotte	Performing Arts	Austria	Actress - Acad Award Nom
Lenz	Kay	Performing Arts	USA	Actress
Lcon	Juan Ponce de	Exploration	Spain	Explorer - Florida
León	Juan Ponce de	Exploration	Spain	Explorer - Florida
Leonard	Elmore	Creative Works	USA	Novelist
	Raymond (Sugar Ray)	Sports	USA	Boxer - HF
	Robert	Movie Production	USA	Director - Acad Award Nom
	Sheldon	Performing Arts	USA	Actor/Comedian
	Walter Fenner (Buck)	Sports	USA	Baseball Player - HF
Leoncavallo	Ruggiero	Creative Works	Italy	Composer - Opera
Leone	Sergio	Movie Production	Italy	Director
Leoni	Tea	Performing Arts	USA	Actress
Leonidov	Ivan	Architecture	Russia	Architect
Leonov	Alexei Arkhipovich	Aviation	Russia	Astronaut
Leontief	Wassily	Arts	USA	Economics - Nobel Laureate
Leopardi	Conte Giacomo	Arts	Italy	Philosopher/Poet
Lequeu	Jean Jacques	Architecture	France	Architect
Lermontov	Mikhail Yurievich	Creative Works	Russia	Poet/Novelist

LAST NAME	FIRST NAME	CATEGORY	COUNTRY	FAME
Lerner	Jaime	Architecture	Brazil	Architect - Jefferson Medal
	Michael	Performing Arts	USA	Actor - Acad Award Nom
Leroy	Mervyn	Movie Production	USA	Director - Acad Award Nom
Lesage	Alain René	Creative Works	France	Novelist/Dramatist
Leschetizky	Theodor	Creative Works	Poland	Composer/Pianist/Teacher
Lescot	Pierre	Architecture	France	Architect
Lesh (Chapman)	Phillip	Performing Arts	USA	Rock & Roll - HF - Grateful Dead
Leslie	Fred Weldon	Aviation	USA	Astronaut
Lesseps	Ferdinand Marie de	Politics	France	Diplomat/Engineer - Suez
Lessing	Doris May	Creative Works	Iran	Novelist
Lester	Bobby	Performing Arts	USA	Rock & Roll - HF - The Moonglows
LeSueur	Percy	Sports	Canada	Hockey Player - HF
Leto	Jared	Performing Arts	USA	Actor
Letterman	David	Performing Arts	USA	Show Host/Comedian
Levant	Oscar	Performing Arts	USA	Pianist/Composer
Lever	William	Business	England	Entrepreneur
Levert	Eddie	Performing Arts	USA	Rock & Roll - HF - The O'Jays
Levi-Montalcini	Rtia	Science	Italy	Medicine - Nobel Laureate
Levin	Ira	Creative Works	USA	Author/Playwright
Levine	David	Creative Works	USA	Cartoonist - Political
	Irving R.	Creative Works	USA	Journalist - Television
	James	Performing Arts	USA	Conductor
	Philip	Creative Works	USA	Poet - Pulitzer
	Ted	Performing Arts	USA	Actor
Levinson	Barry	Movie Production	USA	Director - Academy Award
Levi-Strauss	Claude	Arts	France	Anthropologist
Levy	Leonard Williams	Creative Works	USA	Author - Pulitzer
	Marvin Daniel (Marv)	Sports	USA	Football Coach - HF
Lewes	George Henry	Creative Works	England	Writer/Critic
Lewis	Arthur	Arts	England	Economics - Nobel Laureate
	Carl	Sports	USA	Olympic Runner
	Cecil Day	Creative Works	England	Poet Laureate/Novelist
	Clea	Performing Arts	USA	Actress
	Clive Staples	Creative Works	England	Writer
	David Levering	Creative Works	USA	Author - Pulitzer
	Edward B.	Science	USA	Medicine - Nobel Laureate
	Herbert (Herbie)	Sports	Canada	Hockey Player - HF
	Huey	Performing Arts	USA	Singer
	Jerry	Performing Arts	USA	Comedian
	Jerry Lee	Performing Arts	USA	Singer - Rock & Roll - HF
	Joe E.	Performing Arts	USA	Singer
	John Llewellyn	Business	USA	Labor Leader
	John Aaron	Performing Arts	USA	Jazz Pianist/Composer - Big Band/Jazz - HF
	Juliette	Performing Arts	USA	Actress - Acad Award Nom
	Meade Anderson (Lux)	Performing Arts	USA	Pianist/Composer - Big Band/Jazz - HF
	Meriwether	Exploration	USA	Explorer - Missouri River
	Percy Wyndham	Creative Works	England	Author/Painter
	Ramsey	Creative Works	USA	Composer/Pianist
	Richard	Performing Arts	USA	Comedian
	Richard Warrington Baldwin	Creative Works	USA	Author - Pulitzer
	Shari	Performing Arts	USA	Puppeteer
	Sinclair	Creative Works	USA	Literature - Nobel Laureate
	Ted	Performing Arts	USA	Clarinetist/Jazz Musician
	Ted	Performing Arts	USA	Comedian
Li	Hung-chang	Politics	China	Prime Minister
Libby	Willard Frank	Science	USA	Chemistry - Nobel Laureate
Libera	Adalberto	Architecture	Italy	Architect
Liberty	Arthur	Business	England	Retail Trade
Libeskind	Daniel	Architecture	Poland	Architect
Lichtenberg	Byron Kurt	Aviation	USA	Astronaut
Lieber	Francis	Arts	USA	Philosopher
Lieberman	Nancy	Sports	USA	Basketball Player - HF
Liebig	Justus von	Science	Germany	Chemist

LAST NAME	FIRST NAME	CATEGORY	COUNTRY	FAME
Liebknecht	Karl	Politics	Germany	Socialist Leader
Lifeson	Alexander	Performing Arts	Canada	Canadian Music - HF - Rush
Light	Judith	Performing Arts	USA	Actress
Lightfoot	Gordon	Performing Arts	Canada	Singer - Folk - Canadian Music - HF
Liliuokalani	Lydia Kamekeha	Politics	USA	Queen - Hawaiian Islands
Lillie	Beatrice	Performing Arts	Canada	Comedian
Lilly	Robert Lewis (Bob)	Sports	USA	Football Player - HF
Lima	Adriana	Performing Arts	Brazil	Super Model
Limón	José	Performing Arts	Mexico	Dancer
Lin	Maya	Architecture	Thailand	Architect
Lincoln	Abraham	Politics	USA	President
	Elmo	Performing Arts	USA	Actor
	Mary	Politics	USA	First Lady
Lind	Don Leslie	Aviation	USA	Astronaut
	Jenny	Performing Arts	Sweden	Singer - Opera
Lindbergh	Anne Morrow	Creative Works	USA	Author
	Charles	Aviation	USA	Aviator
	Charles A.	Creative Works	USA	Author - Pulitzer
Linden	Hal	Performing Arts	USA	Actor
Lindfors	Viveca	Performing Arts	Sweden	Actress
Lindsay	Howard	Creative Works	USA	Dramatist - Pulitzer
	John V.	Architecture	USA	Architect - Jefferson Medal
	Nicholas Vachel	Creative Works	USA	Poet
	Robert Blake Theodore (Ted)	Sports	Canada	Hockey Player - HF
Lindstrom	Frederick Charles (Fred)	Sports	USA	Baseball Player - HF
	Pia	Performing Arts	Sweden	Actress
Lindvall	Angela	Performing Arts	USA	Super Model
Lineker	Gary	Sports	England	Soccer Player
Linenger	Jerry Michael	Aviation	USA	Astronaut
Link	Theodore	Architecture	USA	Architect
Linkletter	Art	Performing Arts	Canada	Comedian
Linnaeus	Carolus	Science	Sweden	Botanist
Linn-Baker	Mark	Performing Arts	USA	Actor
Linney	Laura	Performing Arts	USA	Actress - Acad Award Nom
Linteris	Gregory Thomas	Aviation	USA	Astronaut
Lion	Richard Couer de	War & Peace	England	Military Leader
Liotta	Ray	Performing Arts	USA	Actor
Lipchitz	Jacques	Works of Art	USA	Sculptor
Lipinski	Tara	Sports	USA	Olympic Skater
Lipmann	Fritz Albert	Science	USA	Medicine - Nobel Laureate
Lippi	Filippino	Works of Art	Italy	Painter
	Fra Filippo	Works of Art	Italy	Painter
Lippmann	Gabriel	Science	France	Physics - Nobel Laureate
	Walter	Arts	USA	Journalist
Lipscomb	William N.	Science	USA	Chemistry - Nobel Laureate
Lisi	Virna	Performing Arts	Italy	Actress
Lisle	Claude Joseph Rouget de	Creative Works	France	Composer/Army Officer
Lister	Joseph	Science	England	Surgeon
Liston	Sonny	Sports	USA	Boxer - HF
Liszt	Franz	Creative Works	Hungary	Composer/Pianist
Lithgow	John	Performing Arts	USA	Actor - Acad Award Nom
Little	Cleavon	Performing Arts	USA	Actor
	Lawrence Chatmon (Larry)	Sports	USA	Football Player - HF
	Lawson	Sports	USA	Golfer - HF
	Malcolm X.	Politics	USA	Activist
	Rich	Performing Arts	Canada	Comedian
Littler	Gene	Sports	USA	Golfer - HF
Litvak	Anatole	Movie Production	Ukraine	Director - Acad Award Nom
Litvinov	Maximovitch	Politics	Russia	Statesman
Litwack	Leon F.	Creative Works	USA	Author - Pulitzer
Livingston	Robert R.	Politics	USA	Statesman
Livingstone	David	Exploration	Scotland	Explorer - Africa
Llewellyn	John Anthony	Aviation	USA	Astronaut

LAST NAME	FIRST NAME	CATEGORY	COUNTRY	FAME
Lloyd	Christopher	Performing Arts	USA	Actor
	Edward	Business	England	Publishing
	Frank	Movie Production	Scotland	Director - Academy Award
	Harold	Performing Arts	USA	Comedian
	John Henry (Pop)	Sports	USA	Baseball Player - HF
Lloyd George	David	Politics	England	Prime Minister
Lloyd II	Sampson	Business	England	Entrepreneur
Loach	Joseph Nathaniel De (Joe)	Sports	USA	Olympic - Sprinter
Lobachevski	Nikolai Ivanovich	Science	Russia	Mathematician
Lobkowitz	Juan Caramuel de	Architecture	Italy	Architect
Locche	Nicolino	Sports	Argentina	Boxer - HF
Locke	Arthur Darcy (Bobby)	Sports	South Africa	Golfer - HF
	John	Arts	England	Philosopher
	Sondra	Performing Arts	USA	Actress - Acad Award Nom
Lockhart	Gene	Performing Arts	Canada	Actor - Acad Award Nom
	June	Performing Arts	USA	Actress
Locklear	Heather	Performing Arts	USA	Actress
Lodge	Henry Cabot	Politics	USA	Senator
	Oliver Joseph	Science	England	Physicist/Writer
Loeb	Jacques	Science	USA	Biologist/Physiologist
	James	Business	USA	Banking/Philanthropist
	Solomon	Business	USA	Drygoods
Loesser	Frank	Creative Works	USA	Dramatist - Pulitzer
Loewi	Otto	Science	Austria	Medicine - Nobel Laureate
Loewy	Raymond Ferdinand	Business	USA	Industrial Designer
Lofting	Hugh John	Creative Works	USA	Writer/Illustrator
Lofton	James David	Sports	USA	Football Player - HF
Logan	Ella	Performing Arts	Scotland	Singer
	Joshua	Creative Works	USA	Dramatist - Pulitzer
	Joshua	Movie Production	USA	Director - Acad Award Nom
Loggia	Robert	Performing Arts	USA	Actor - Acad Award Nom
Loggins	Kenny	Performing Arts	USA	Singer
Loi	Duilio	Sports	Italy	Boxer - HF
Lollobrigida	Gina	Performing Arts	Italy	Actress
Lom	Herbert	Performing Arts	Hungary	Actor
Lomax	Alan	Arts	USA	Collector - American Folk Songs
Lomb	Henry	Business	USA	Optical Industry
Lombard	Alain	Performing Arts	USA	Conductor
	Carole	Performing Arts	USA	Actress - Acad Award Nom
Lombardi	Ernesto Natali (Ernie)	Sports	USA	Baseball Player - HF
	Vincent Thomas (Vince)	Sports	USA	Football Coach - HF
Lombardo	Gaetano Alberto (Guy)	Performing Arts	Canada	Band Leader - Big Band/Jazz - HF
	Gaetano Alberto (Guy)	Performing Arts	Canada	Band Leader - Canadian Music - HF
Lombroso	Cesare	Science	Italy	Physician/Criminologist
London	Jack	Creative Works	USA	Novelist/Short Story Writer
	Julie	Performing Arts	USA	Singer
Long	Howard Michael (Howie)	Sports	USA	Football Coach - HF
	Huey Pierce (The Kingfish)	Politics	USA	Senator - Louisiana
	Nia	Performing Arts	USA	Actress
	Richard	Performing Arts	USA	Actor
	Shelley	Performing Arts	USA	Actress
Longabaugh	Harry Alonzo (Sundance Kid)	Law & Order	USA	Outlaw
Longfellow	Henry Wadsworth	Creative Works	USA	Poet
Longhair (Byrd)	Henry (Professor Roy)	Performing Arts	USA	Singer - Rock & Roll - HF
Longhena	Baldassarre	Architecture	Italy	Architect
Longstreet	James	War & Peace	USA	Confederate General
Looby	William (Bill)	Sports	USA	Soccer Player - HF
Loos	Adolf	Architecture	Austria	Architect
	Anita	Creative Works	USA	Screenwriter/Playwright
Lopez	Nancy	Sports	USA	Golfer - HF
	Trini	Performing Arts	USA	Singer
	Alphonso Ramón (Al)	Sports	USA	Baseball Manager - HF
Lorca	Federico Garcia	Creative Works	Spain	Poet

SOLVER SERIES: NAME FINDER

LAST NAME	FIRST NAME	CATEGORY	COUNTRY	FAME
Lord	Jack	Performing Arts	USA	Actor
Loren	Sophia	Performing Arts	Italy	Actress - Academy Award
Lorentz	Hendrik Antoon	Science	Netherlands	Physics - Nobel Laureate
Lorenz	Konrad Zacharias	Science	Austria	Medicine - Nobel Laureate
Lorenzen	Fred	Sports	USA	Race Car Driver - HF
Lorenzo	Frank	Business	USA	Aviation Industry
	Vanessa	Performing Arts	Spain	Super Model
Loring	Gloria	Performing Arts	USA	Actress/Singer
Lorre	Peter	Performing Arts	Slovakia	Actor
Lorring	Joan	Performing Arts	China	Actress - Acad Award Nom
Loti	Pierre	Creative Works	France	Novelist
Lott	George Martin	Sports	USA	Tennis Player - HF
	Ronald Mandel (Ronnie)	Sports	USA	Football Player - HF
Lotte Jr.	Chester Trent	Politics	USA	Senator - Mississippi
Loudermilk	Charlie Elzer	Performing Arts	USA	Country Music - HF - Louvin Brothers
	Ira Lonnie	Performing Arts	USA	Country Music - HF - Louvin Brothers
Loudon	Dorothy	Performing Arts	USA	Actress
Louganis	Greg	Sports	USA	Olympic
Louis	Joseph (Joe)	Sports	USA	Boxer - HF
Louis-Dreyfus	Julia	Performing Arts	USA	Actress
Louise	Tina	Performing Arts	USA	Actress
Lounge	John Michael	Aviation	USA	Astronaut
Lourenco	Teresa	Performing Arts	Trinidad	Super Model
Lousma	Jack Robert	Aviation	USA	Astronaut
Louÿs	Pierre	Creative Works	France	Poet/Novelist
Love	Bessie	Performing Arts	USA	Actress - Acad Award Nom
	Darlene	Performing Arts	USA	Singer
Love 111	Davis	Sports	USA	Golfer
Lovelace	Richard	Creative Works	England	Poet
Lovell	Alfred Charles Bernard	Science	England	Astronomer
Lovell Jr.	James Arthur	Aviation	USA	Astronaut
Lovellette	Clyde E.	Sports	USA	Basketball Player
Lovett	Lyle	Performing Arts	USA	Singer
Lovitz	Jon	Performing Arts	USA	Comedian
Low	David	Creative Works	England	Cartoonist - Political
	George David	Aviation	USA	Astronaut
	Juliette	Arts	USA	Founder - Girl Scouts
	Seth	Business	USA	Importer
Lowe	Edmund	Performing Arts	USA	Actor
	Mundell	Performing Arts	USA	Jazz Guitarist - Big Band/Jazz - HF
	Nick	Performing Arts	England	Singer
	Rob	Performing Arts	USA	Actor
Lowell	Abbott Lawrence	Arts	USA	Educator
	Amy	Creative Works	USA	Poet - Pulitzer
	James Russell	Creative Works	USA	Poet/Essayist
	Percival	Science	USA	Astronomer
	Robert Trail Spence Jr.	Creative Works	USA	Poet - Pulitzer
Lowcs	John Livingston	Arts	USA	Educator/Scholar/Critic
Loy	Myrna	Performing Arts	USA	Actress
Lubitsch	Ernst	Movie Production	Germany	Director - Acad Award Nom
Lucas	George	Movie Production	USA	Director - Acad Award Nom
	Henry Lee	Law & Order	USA	Serial Killer
	Jerry R.	Sports	USA	Basketball Player - HF
Lucas Jr.	Robert E.	Arts	USA	Economics - Nobel Laureate
Lucci	Susan	Performing Arts	USA	Actress
Luce	Henry Robinson	Business	USA	Publisher/Editor
Luciano	Charles (Lucky)	Law & Order	Sicily	Mafia
Luckman	Sidney (Sid)	Sports	USA	Football Player - HF
Lucretius	Titus Lucretius Carus	Arts	Italy	Philosopher
Ludlum	Robert	Creative Works	USA	Author - Spy Novels
Luft	Lorna	Performing Arts	USA	Singer
Lugar	Richard Green (Dick)	Politics	USA	Senator - Indiana
Lugosi	Bela	Performing Arts	Hungary	Actor

LAST NAME	FIRST NAME	CATEGORY	COUNTRY	FAME
Luisetti	Angelo (Hank)	Sports	USA	Basketball Player - HF
Lukas	Jay Anthony	Creative Works	USA	Author - Pulitzer
	Paul	Performing Arts	Hungary	Actor - Academy Award
Lully	Jean Baptiste	Creative Works	France	Composer - Opera
Lumet	Sidney	Movie Production	USA	Director - Acad Award Nom
Lumley	Harry (Apple Cheeks)	Sports	Canada	Hockey Player - HF
Lunceford	James Melvin (Jimmie)	Performing Arts	USA	Band Leader - Big Band/Jazz - HF
Lund	DeWayne Louis (Tiny)	Sports	USA	Race Car Driver - HF
Lunt	Alfred	Performing Arts	USA	Actor - Acad Award Nom
Lupino	Ida	Performing Arts	England	Actress
Lupone	Patti	Performing Arts	USA	Actress
Lupu	Radu	Performing Arts	Romania	Pianist
Luria	Salvador E.	Science	USA	Medicine - Nobel Laureate
Lurie	Alison	Creative Works	USA	Author - Pulitzer
Luther	Martin	Arts	Germany	Theologian
Lutuli	Albert John	War & Peace	South Africa	Peace - Nobel Laureate
Lutyens	Edwin Landseer	Architecture	England	Architect - AIA Gold Medal
Luyendyk	Arie	Sports	Netherlands	Race Car Driver
Lwoff	André	Science	France	Medicine - Nobel Laureate
Lyell	Charles	Science	England	Geologist
Lyle	Alexander Walter (Sandy)	Sports	England	Golfer
	Sparky	Sports	USA	Baseball Player
Lyly	John	Creative Works	England	Author/Dramatist
Lyman	Abe	Performing Arts	USA	Orchestra Leader
	William Roy (Link)	Sports	USA	Football Player - HF
Lymon	Franklin (Frankie)	Performing Arts	USA	Singer - Rock & Roll - HF
Lynch	David	Movie Production	USA	Director - Acad Award Nom
	David	Performing Arts	USA	Rock & Roll - HF - The Platters
	John Mary	Politics	Ireland	Prime Minister
Lynde	Paul	Performing Arts	USA	Comedian
Lyne	Adrian	Movie Production	England	Director - Acad Award Nom
Lynen	Feodor	Science	Germany	Medicine - Nobel Laureate
Lynn(Webb)	Loretta	Performing Arts	USA	Singer - Country Music - HF
Lynne	Jeff	Performing Arts	England	Singer/Guitarist
Lyon	Mary	Arts	USA	Educator
Lyons	Theodore Amar (Ted)	Sports	USA	Baseball Player - HF
Maas	Peter	Creative Works	USA	Novelist
Maathai	Wangari	War & Peace	Kenya	Peace - Nobel Laureate
Maazel	Lorin	Performing Arts	France	Conductor - Orchestra
Mabee	Carlton	Creative Works	USA	Author - Pulitzer
Mac (Brunning)	Bob (Fleetwood)	Performing Arts	England	Rock & Roll - HF - Fleetwood Mac
Maca	Joseph	Sports	Belgium	Soccer Player - HF
MacArthur	Douglas	War & Peace	USA	Commander in Chief
Macaulay	Rose	Creative Works	England	Novelist
	Thomas Babington	Politics	England	Statesman/Essayist
	Edward C. (Ed)	Sports	USA	Basketball Player - HF
MacBride	Sean	War & Peace	Ireland	Peace - Nobel Laureate
Macchio	Ralph	Performing Arts	USA	Actor
MacDiarmid	Alan G.	Science	New Zealand	Chemistry - Nobel Laureate
Macdonald	George	Creative Works	Scotland	Poet/Novelist
	John Alexander	Politics	Canada	Prime Minister
	Ross	Creative Works	USA	Author
MacDonald	James Ramsay	Politics	England	Prime Minister
	Jeanette	Performing Arts	USA	Actress - Musical
	John Dann	Creative Works	USA	Author
MacDowell	Andie	Performing Arts	USA	Actress
	Edward Alexander	Creative Works	USA	Composer/Pianist
MacGraw	Ali	Performing Arts	USA	Actress - Acad Award Nom
Mach	Ernst	Arts	Austria	Philosopher/Physicist
Machiavelli	Niccolo	Creative Works	Italy	Writer/Statesman
Mack	Cornelius Alexander (Connie)	Sports	USA	Baseball Manager - HF
	John E.	Creative Works	USA	Author - Pulitzer
	Ted	Performing Arts	USA	Show Host - Television

SOLVER SERIES: NAME FINDER

LAST NAME	FIRST NAME	CATEGORY	COUNTRY	FAME
Mack	Thomas Lee (Tom)	Sports	USA	Football Player - HF
MacKay	Duncan McMillan (Mickey)	Sports	Canada	Hockey Player - HF
Mackenzie	Alexander	Exploration	Canada	Explorer - Canada West
	Alexander	Politics	Canada	Prime Minister
	Gisele	Performing Arts	Canada	Singer
Mackey	John	Sports	USA	Football Player - HF
Mackie	Bob	Business	USA	Fashion Designer
MacKinnon	Roderick	Science	USA	Chemistry - Nobel Laureate
Mackintosh	Charles Rennie	Architecture	England	Architect
MacLachlan	Kyle	Performing Arts	USA	Actor
MacLaine	Shirley	Performing Arts	USA	Actress - Academy Award
MacLean	Steven Glenwood	Aviation	Canada	Astronaut
MacLeish	Archibald	Creative Works	USA	Dramatist - Pulitzer
	Archibald	Creative Works	USA	Poet - Pulitzer
MacLeod	Gavin	Performing Arts	USA	Actor
	John James Richard	Science	Canada	Medicine - Nobel Laureate
MacMahon	Aline	Performing Arts	USA	Actress - Acad Award Nom
	Marie Edmé Maurice de	Politics	France	President
MacMillan	Donald Baxter	Exploration	USA	Explorer - Arctic
	Harold	Politics	England	Prime Minister
MacMurray	Fred	Performing Arts	USA	Actor
MacNee	Patrick	Performing Arts	England	Actor
MacNeice	Louis	Creative Works	England	Poet/Classical Scholar
MacNeil	Robert	Creative Works	Canada	Journalist - Television
MacNelly	Jeffery Kenneth (Jeff)	Creative Works	USA	Cartoonist - Editorial
Macon	Uncle Dave (David)	Performing Arts	USA	Singer - Country Music - HF
MacPhail	Leland Standford (Larry) Sr.	Sports	USA	Baseball Pioneer - HF
	Leland Standford (Lee) Jr.	Sports	USA	Baseball Executive - HF
MacPherson	Elle	Performing Arts	Australia	Super Model
	James	Creative Works	Scotland	Poet
MacRae	Gordon	Performing Arts	USA	Singer
Macready	William Charles	Performing Arts	England	Actor
Macy	William H.	Performing Arts	USA	Actor - Acad Award Nom
Madden	John	Movie Production	England	Director - Acad Award Nom
	John	Sports	USA	Football Player/Coach/Commentator
Maderno	Carlo	Architecture	Italy	Architect
Madero	Francisco Indalecio	Politics	Mexico	President
Madigan	Amy	Performing Arts	USA	Actress - Acad Award Nom
Madison	Dorothea (Dolley) Payne	Politics	USA	First Lady
Madison	James	Politics	USA	President
Madsen	Virginia	Performing Arts	USA	Actress - Acad Award Nom
Mae	Vanessa	Performing Arts	China	Violinist
Maeterlinck	Maurice Polidore Bernhard	Creative Works	Belgium	Literature - Nobel Laureate
Magellan	Ferdinand	Exploration	Spain	Explorer - Circumnavigation
Maggio	Dom Di	Sports	USA	Baseball Player
	Joseph Paul Di(Joe)	Sports	USA	Baseball Player - HF
Maginnis	Charles Donagh	Architecture	USA	Architect - AIA Gold Medal
Magistretti	Vico	Architecture	Italy	Architect
Magnani	Anna	Performing Arts	Italy	Actress - Academy Award
Magritte	René	Works of Art	Belgium	Painter - Surrealist
Mahan	Alfred Thayer	War & Peace	USA	Naval Officer/Historian
Maharidge	Dale	Works of Art	USA	Photographer - Pulitzer
Maharshi	Ramana	Arts	India	Philosopher /Sage
Mahfouz	Naguib	Creative Works	Egypt	Literature - Nobel Laureate
Mahler	Gustav	Creative Works	Austria	Composer
Mahon	Jackie	Creative Works	Canada	Journalist - Television
	Michael C.	Performing Arts	USA	Actor
Mahovolich	Francis William (Frank)	Sports	Canada	Hockey Player - HF
Mahre	Phil	Sports	USA	Olympic Skier
Mailer	Norman Kingsley	Creative Works	USA	Author - Pulitzer
Maillart	Robert	Architecture	Switzerland	Architect
Maillol	Aristide Joseph Bonaventure	Works of Art	France	Sculptor
Main	Marjorie	Performing Arts	USA	Actress - Acad Award Nom

LAST NAME	FIRST NAME	CATEGORY	COUNTRY	FAME
Maistre	Joseph Marie de	Arts	France	Philosopher/Writer
Maitland	Frederic William	Law & Order	England	Jurist/Legal Historian
Major	John	Politics	England	Prime Minister
Majors	Lee	Performing Arts	USA	Actor
Makeba	Miriam	Performing Arts	South Africa	Singer
Maki	Fumihiko	Architecture	Japan	Architect - Pritzker/Jefferson Medal
Mako	Constantine Gene	Sports	Hungary	Tennis Player - HF
Makovecz	Imre	Architecture	Hungary	Architect
Malamud	Bernard	Creative Works	USA	Novelist - Pulitzer
Malden	Karl	Performing Arts	USA	Actor - Academy Award
Maldini	Paolo	Sports	Italy	Soccer Player
Malebranche	Nicolas	Arts	France	Philosopher
Malerba	Franco Egidio	Aviation	France	Astronaut
Malick	Terrence	Movie Production	USA	Director - Acad Award Nom
Malinowski	Bronislaw Kaspar	Arts	Poland	Anthropologist
Malkovich	John	Performing Arts	USA	Actor - Acad Award Nom
Mallarmé	Stéphane	Creative Works	France	Poet - Symbolist
Malle	Louis	Movie Production	France	Director - Acad Award Nom
Mallon	Meg	Sports	USA	Golfer
Mallory	Anna Margarethe (Molla)	Sports	Norway	Tennis Player - HF
Malone	Dorothy	Performing Arts	USA	Actress - Academy Award
	Dumas	Creative Works	USA	Author - Pulitzer
	Edmund	Arts	Ireland	Literary Critic/Editor
	Karl	Sports	USA	Basketball Player
	Maurice Joseph (Joe)	Sports	Canada	Hockey Player - HF
	Moses	Sports	USA	Basketball Player - HF
Malory	Thomas	Creative Works	England	Compiler - Arthurian Tales
Malpighi	Marcello	Science	Italy	Physiologist - Micro Anatomy
Malraux	André	Creative Works	France	Writer/Politician
Malthus	Thomas Robert	Arts	England	Political Economist
Maltin	Leonard	Creative Works	Canada	Journalist - Television
Mamet	David	Creative Works	USA	Dramatist - Pulitzer
Manchester	Melissa	Performing Arts	USA	Singer
Mancini	Henry	Performing Arts	USA	Conductor/Composer
Mandel	Howie	Performing Arts	Canada	Comedian
Mandela	Nelson	War & Peace	South Africa	Peace - Nobel Laureate
Mandeville	Bernard de	Creative Works	England	Satirist
	John	Creative Works	England	Author
Mandlíková	Hana	Sports	Czechoslovakia	Tennis Player - HF
Mandrell	Barbara	Performing Arts	USA	Singer
Manet	Edouard	Works of Art	France	Painter - Impressionist
Mangione	Chuck	Performing Arts	USA	Jazz Flugel Horn
Mangrum	Lloyd	Sports	USA	Golfer - HF
Manilow	Barry	Performing Arts	USA	Singer
Mankiewicz	Joseph L.	Movie Production	USA	Director - Academy Award
Mann	Barry	Creative Works	USA	Song Writer
	Carol	Sports	USA	Golfer - HF
	Delbert	Movie Production	USA	Director - Academy Award
	Herbert Jay (Herbie)	Performing Arts	USA	Jazz Flutist
	Horace	Arts	USA	Educator
	James Robert	Politics	USA	Congressman
	Michael	Movie Production	USA	Director - Acad Award Nom
	Thomas	Creative Works	Germany	Literature - Nobel Laureate
Manne	Sheldon (Shelly)	Performing Arts	USA	Jazz Drummer - Big Band/Jazz - HF
Manolete	Manuel Rodriguez	Sports	Spain	Matador
Mansart	Jules Hardouin	Architecture	France	Architect
Mansbridge	Peter	Creative Works	Canada	Journalist - Television
Mansell	Nigel	Sports	England	Race Car Driver - HF
Mansfield	Jayne	Performing Arts	USA	Actress
	Katherine	Creative Works	England	Writer - Short Stories
	Peter	Science	England	Medicine - Nobel Laureate
	Richard	Performing Arts	USA	Actor
Manship	Paul	Works of Art	USA	Sculptor

SOLVER SERIES: NAME FINDER

LAST NAME	FIRST NAME	CATEGORY	COUNTRY	FAME
Manson	Charles Milles	Law & Order	USA	Serial Killer
Mantegna	Andrea	Works of Art	Italy	Painter/Engraver
Mantell	Joe	Performing Arts	USA	Actor - Acad Award Nom
Mantha	Sylvio	Sports	Canada	Hockey Player - HF
Mantle	Mickey Charles	Sports	USA	Baseball Player - HF
Mantoux	Charles	Science	France	Physician
Mantovani	Annunzio	Performing Arts	England	Conductor/Composer
Manuel	Richard	Performing Arts	Canada	Rock & Roll - HF - The Band
Manush	Henry Emmett (Heinie)	Sports	USA	Baseball Player - HF
Manzarek	Ray	Performing Arts	USA	Rock & Roll - HF - The Doors
Manzoni	Alessandro	Creative Works	Italy	Poet/Novelist
Map	Walter	Creative Works	Wales	Poet/Satirist
Maplethorpe	Robert	Works of Art	USA	Photographer
Mara	Timothy James (Tim)	Sports	USA	Football Founder - HF
Mara	Wellington Timothy	Sports	USA	Football Owner - HF
Maradona	Diego Armando	Sports	Italy	Soccer Player
Maran	Josie	Performing Arts	USA	Super Model
Maranville	Walter James (Rabbit)	Sports	USA	Baseball Player - HF
Marat	Jean Paul	Politics	France	Revolutionary Leader
Maravich	Peter P. (Pete)	Sports	USA	Basketball Player - HF
Marble	Alice	Sports	USA	Tennis Player - HF
Marc	Franz	Works of Art	Germany	Painter
Marceau	Marcel	Performing Arts	France	Pantomimist
Marcel	Gabriel	Arts	France	Philosopher
March	Fredric	Performing Arts	USA	Actor - Academy Award
Marchand	Colette	Performing Arts	France	Actress - Acad Award Nom
	Nancy	Performing Arts	USA	Actress
Marchetti	Gino John	Sports	USA	Football Player - HF
Marciano	Rocky	Sports	USA	Boxer - HF
Marconi	Guglielmo	Science	Italy	Physics - Nobel Laureate
Marcos	Ferdinand	Politics	Philippines	President
	Imelda	Politics	Philippines	First Lady
Marcum	John	Sports	USA	Race Car Driver - HF
Marcus	Rudolph A.	Science	USA	Chemistry - Nobel Laureate
Marcuse	Herbert	Arts	Germany	Philosopher
Mare	Walter de la	Creative Works	England	Poet/Novelist
Maresca	Ernie	Performing Arts	USA	Singer/Composer
Margolin	Janet	Performing Arts	USA	Actress
Margulies	Donald	Creative Works	USA	Dramatist - Pulitzer
Marichal	Juan Antonio	Sports	Dominican Rep	Baseball Player - HF
Marie	Teena	Performing Arts	USA	Singer
Marin	Cheech	Performing Arts	USA	Comedian
	John	Works of Art	USA	Painter
Marino Jr.	Daniel Constantine (Dan)	Sports	USA	Football Player - HF
Marion	Francis	War & Peace	USA	General - Revolutionary War
Maris	Ada	Performing Arts	USA	Actress
	Roger	Sports	USA	Baseball Player
Maritain	Jacques	Arts	France	Philosopher
Markey	Enid	Performing Arts	USA	Actress
Markham	Charles Edwin	Creative Works	USA	Poet
Markowitz	Harry M.	Arts	USA	Economics - Nobel Laureate
Marks	Michael	Business	England	Retail Trade
Marley	John	Performing Arts	USA	Actor - Acad Award Nom
	Nesta Robert (Bob)	Performing Arts	Jamaica	Singer - Rock & Roll - HF
Marlowe	Christopher	Creative Works	England	Poet/Dramatist
	Julia	Performing Arts	USA	Actress
Marquand	John Phillips	Creative Works	USA	Novelist - Pulitzer
	Richard William (Rube)	Sports	USA	Baseball Player - HF
Marquette	Jacques	Exploration	France	Explorer - Mississippi River
Márquez	Gabriel Garcia	Creative Works	Colombia	Literature - Nobel Laureate
Marquis	Donald Robert Perry	Creative Works	USA	Humorist/Journalist
Marr	Dave	Sports	USA	Golfer
Marriner	Neville	Performing Arts	England	Conductor/Violinist

LAST NAME	FIRST NAME	CATEGORY	COUNTRY	FAME
Marryat	Frederick	Creative Works	England	Novelist/Naval Officer
Marsalis	Branford	Performing Arts	USA	Jazz Saxaphonist
	Wynton	Performing Arts	USA	Jazz Trumpeter - Big Band/Jazz - HF
Marsh	Jean	Performing Arts	England	Actress
	Ngaio	Creative Works	New Zealand	Novelist - Crime Fiction
	Reginald	Works of Art	USA	Painter
Marshall	Barry J.	Science	Australia	Medicine - Nobel Laureate
	Everett Grunz	Performing Arts	USA	Actor
	George Catlett	Politics	USA	Statesman/General
	George Catlett	War & Peace	USA	Peace - Nobel Laureate
	George Preston	Sports	USA	Football Founder - HF
	Herbert	Performing Arts	England	Actor
	John	Business	England	Textile Industry
	John	Law & Order	USA	Chief Justice
	John C. (Jack)	Sports	Canada	Hockey Player - HF
	Penny	Performing Arts	USA	Actress
	Peter	Performing Arts	USA	Comedian
	Rob	Movie Production	USA	Director - Acad Award Nom
	Thomas R.	Politics	USA	Vice-President
	Thurgood	Politics	USA	Justice - Supreme Court
Marston	John	Creative Works	England	Dramatist/Satirist
Martí	José Julian	Creative Works	Cuba	Poet/Essayist/Revolutionary
Martin	Alastair Bradley	Sports	USA	Tennis Player - HF
	Andrea	Performing Arts	USA	Actress
	Archer John Porter	Science	England	Chemistry - Nobel Laureate
	Dean	Performing Arts	USA	Singer
	Dewey	Performing Arts	Canada	Rock & Roll - HF - Buffalo Springfield
	Dick	Performing Arts	USA	Comedian
	Lynn Morley	Politics	USA	Congressman
	Mary	Performing Arts	USA	Actress
	Pamela Sue	Performing Arts	USA	Actress
	Paul Edgar Phillipe	Politics	Canada	Prime Minister
	Ramon Grau San	Politics	Cuba	President
	Ross	Performing Arts	Poland	Actor
	Slater N. (Dugie)	Sports	USA	Basketball Player - HF
	Steve	Performing Arts	USA	Actor
	Tony	Performing Arts	USA	Singer
	William McChesney	Sports	USA	Tennis Promoter - HF
Martineau	Harriet	Arts	England	Theologian
	James	Arts	England	Philosopher/Theologian
Martinelli	Elsa	Performing Arts	Italy	Actress
	Giovanni	Performing Arts	USA	Singer - Opera
Martinez	Tino	Sports	USA	Baseball Player
Martini	Francesco di Giorgio	Architecture	Italy	Architect
Martino	Al	Performing Arts	USA	Singer
Martinson	Harry	Creative Works	Sweden	Literature - Nobel Laureate
Marton	Eva	Performing Arts	Hungary	Singer - Opera
Marvell	Andrew	Creative Works	England	Poet
Marvin	Lee	Performing Arts	USA	Actor - Academy Award
Marx	Arthur (Harpo)	Performing Arts	USA	Comedian
	Herbert (Zeppo)	Performing Arts	USA	Comedian
	Julius (Groucho)	Performing Arts	USA	Comedian
	Karl Heirich	Politics	Germany	Revolutionary Leader
	Leonard (Chico)	Performing Arts	USA	Comedian
	Milton (Gummo)	Performing Arts	USA	Comedian
Masaryk	Jan	Politics	Czechoslovakia	Statesman
	Tomáš Garogue	Politics	Czechoslovakia	President
Mascagni	Pietro	Creative Works	Italy	Composer - Opera
Masefield	John	Creative Works	England	Poet Laureate/Writer
Masekela	Hugh	Performing Arts	South Africa	Flugel Horn Player
Maskell	Dan	Sports	England	Tennis Player - HF
Maslow	Abraham Harold	Arts	USA	Philosopher
Mason	Jackie	Performing Arts	USA	Comedian

SOLVER SERIES: NAME FINDER

LAST NAME	FIRST NAME	CATEGORY	COUNTRY	FAME
Mason	James	Performing Arts	England	Actor - Acad Award Nom
	Marsha	Performing Arts	USA	Actress - Acad Award Nom
	Nicolas (Nick)	Performing Arts	England	Rock & Roll - HF - Pink Floyd
Massen	Osa	Performing Arts	Denmark	Actress
Masséna	André	War & Peace	France	Marshall
Massenet	Jules Émile Frédéric	Creative Works	France	Composer
Massey	Bobby	Performing Arts	USA	Rock & Roll - HF - The O'Jays
	Daniel	Performing Arts	England	Actor - Acad Award Nom
	Ilona	Performing Arts	Hungary	Actress/Singer
	Raymond	Performing Arts	Canada	Actor - Acad Award Nom
Massi (Macioci)	Nicholas (Nick)	Performing Arts	USA	Rock & Roll - HF - The Four Seasons
Massie	Robert K.	Creative Works	USA	Author - Pulitzer
Massine	Léonide	Performing Arts	USA	Ballet Dancer/Choreographer
Massinger	Phillip	Creative Works	England	Dramatist
Masters	Edgar Lee	Creative Works	USA	Poet
Masterson	Mary Stuart	Performing Arts	USA	Actress
	William Barclay	Law & Order	USA	Lawman
Mastrantonio	Mary Elizabeth	Performing Arts	USA	Actress - Acad Award Nom
Mastroianni	Marcello	Performing Arts	Italy	Actor - Acad Award Nom
Mat	Paul Le	Performing Arts	USA	Actor
Mather	Cotton	Creative Works	USA	Writer/Clergyman
	Increase	Creative Works	USA	Writer/Clergyman
Matheson	Tim	Performing Arts	USA	Actor
Mathews	Edwin Lee (Eddie)	Sports	USA	Baseball Player
	Mitford McLeod	Arts	USA	Lexicographer/Educator
Mathewson	Christopher (Christy)	Sports	USA	Baseball Player - HF
Mathias	Bob	Sports	USA	Olympic Decathlon
Mathis	Johnny	Performing Arts	USA	Singer
Matisse	Henri	Works of Art	France	Painter
Matlin	Marlee	Performing Arts	USA	Actress - Academy Award
Matson	Ollie Genoa	Sports	USA	Football Player - HF
Mattea	Kathy	Performing Arts	USA	Singer
Matthau	Walter	Performing Arts	USA	Actor - Academy Award
Matthäus	Lothar	Sports	Germany	Soccer Player
Matthews	Dave	Performing Arts	South Africa	Singer/Guitarist
	Edwin Keith (Banjo)	Sports	USA	Race Car Driver - HF
	James Brander	Creative Works	USA	Writer/Scholar/Critic
	Stanley	Sports	England	Soccer Player - HF
Matthews Jr.	Neal	Performing Arts	USA	Country Music - HF - The Jordonaires
Mattingly	Don	Sports	USA	Baseball Player
Mattingly II	Thomas Kenneth	Aviation	USA	Astronaut
Mature	Victor	Performing Arts	USA	Actor
Maugeri	Rudi	Performing Arts	Canada	Canadian Music - HF - The Crew Cuts
Maugham	William Somerset	Creative Works	England	Novelist/Playwright
Maupassant	Henri René Albert Guy de	Creative Works	France	Novelist/Short Story Writer
Mauriac	François	Creative Works	France	Literature - Nobel Laureate
Maurier	Daphne du	Creative Works	England	Author/Playwright
	George Louis Palmella du	Creative Works	England	Novelist/Illustrator
Maurois	André	Arts	France	Biographer
Mausser	Arnie	Sports	USA	Soccer Player - HF
Mawson	Douglas	Exploration	Australia	Explorer - Antarctica
Maxim	Hiram Stevens	Business	England	Engineer/Inventor - Firearms
	Hudson	Science	USA	Chemist/Inventor - Explosives
	Joey	Sports	USA	Boxer - HF
Maxwell	Fred G. (Steamer)	Sports	Canada	Hockey Player - HF
	James Clerk	Science	Scotland	Physicist
May	Brian Harold	Performing Arts	England	Rock & Roll - HF - Queen
	Curtis Emerson Le	War & Peace	USA	General - Air Force
	Elaine	Performing Arts	USA	Actress/Director
	Ernst	Architecture	Germany	Architect
	William E. (Billy)	Performing Arts	USA	Composer/Arranger - Big Band/Jazz - HF
Mayakovsky	Vladimirovich	Creative Works	Russia	Poet
Maybeck	Bernard Ralph	Architecture	USA	Architect - AIA Gold Medal

LAST NAME	FIRST NAME	CATEGORY	COUNTRY	FAME
Mayer	Louis B.	Movie Production	Russia	Director
Mayfield	Curtis	Performing Arts	USA	Rock & Roll - HF - The Impressions
Maynard	Donald Rogers (Don)	Sports	USA	Football Player - HF
Mayne	Thom	Architecture	USA	Architect
Mayo	Charles Horace	Science	USA	Physician
	Virginia	Performing Arts	USA	Actress
	William James	Science	USA	Physician
Mayron	Melanie	Performing Arts	USA	Actress
Mays	David J.	Creative Works	USA	Author - Pulitzer
	Rex	Sports	USA	Race Car Driver - HF
	Willie Howard	Sports	USA	Baseball Player - HF
Mazarin	Jules	Politics	France	Statesman/Prelate
Mazeroski	William Stanley (Bill)	Sports	USA	Baseball Player - HF
Mazursky	Paul	Movie Production	USA	Director
Mazza	Valeria	Performing Arts	Argentina	Super Model
Mazzini	Giuseppe	Politics	Italy	Patriot/Revolutionist
McAdoo	Robert (Bob)	Sports	USA	Basketball Player - HF
McAfee	George Anderson	Sports	USA	Football Player - HF
McAleese	Mary	Politics	Ireland	President
McArdle	Andrea	Performing Arts	USA	Actress
McAuliffe	Sharon Christa Corrigan	Aviation	USA	Astronaut
McBain	Diane	Performing Arts	USA	Actress
	Ed	Creative Works	USA	Novelist - Crime Fiction
McBride	Jon Andrew	Aviation	USA	Astronaut
	Pat	Sports	USA	Soccer Player - HF
McCallum	David	Performing Arts	Scotland	Actor
	Michael McKenzie (Mike)	Sports	Jamaica	Boxer - HF
McCambridge	Mercedes	Performing Arts	USA	Actress - Academy Award
McCandless II	Bruce	Aviation	USA	Astronaut
McCarey	Leo	Movie Production	USA	Director - Academy Award
McCarthy	Andrew	Performing Arts	USA	Actor
	Eugene Joseph (Gene)	Politics	USA	Senator - Minnesota
	Glenn	Business	USA	Oil Industry
	Joseph Raymond	Politics	USA	Senator - Wisconsin
	Joseph Vincent (Joe)	Sports	USA	Baseball Manager - HF
	Kevin	Performing Arts	USA	Actor - Acad Award Nom
	Mary	Creative Works	USA	Novelist
	Thomas Michael (Tommy)	Sports	USA	Baseball Player - HF
McCartney	James Paul	Performing Arts	England	Rock & Roll - HF - The Beatles
	Stella	Business	England	Fashion Designer
McCarty	Jim	Performing Arts	England	Rock & Roll - HF - The Yardbirds
McCarver	Tim	Sports	USA	Baseball Player
McClanahan	Rue	Performing Arts	USA	Actress
McClellan	George Brinton	War & Peace	USA	General - Civil War
McClintock	Barbara	Science	USA	Medicine - Nobel Laureate
McClure	Doug	Performing Arts	USA	Actor
	Samuel	Business	USA	Publishing
McClurg	Edie	Performing Arts	USA	Actress
McConnell	Rob	Performing Arts	Canada	Trombonist/Arranger - Canadian Music - HF
McCool	William Cameron	Aviation	USA	Astronaut
McCormack	John	Performing Arts	USA	Singer - Opera
	Patty	Performing Arts	USA	Actress - Acad Award Nom
McCormack Jr.	Michael Joseph (Mike)	Sports	USA	Football Player - HF
McCormick	Cyrus Hall	Science	USA	Inventor - Reaping Machine
McCourt	Frank	Creative Works	USA	Author - Pulitzer
McCovey	Willie Lee	Sports	USA	Baseball Player - HF
McCracken	Branch	Sports	USA	Basketball Player - HF
	Jack (Jumping Jack)	Sports	USA	Basketball Player - HF
McCrea	Joel	Performing Arts	USA	Actor
McCullers	Carson	Creative Works	USA	Novelist
McCulley	Michael James	Aviation	USA	Astronaut
McCullough	David	Creative Works	USA	Author - Pulitzer
McDaniel	Hattie	Performing Arts	USA	Actress - Academy Award

SOLVER SERIES: NAME FINDER

LAST NAME	FIRST NAME	CATEGORY	COUNTRY	FAME
McDermott	Robert (Bobby)	Sports	USA	Basketball Player - HF
McDivitt	James Alton	Aviation	USA	Astronaut
McDonald	Lanny King	Sports	Canada	Hockey Player - HF
	Michael	Performing Arts	USA	Singer
	Michael James	Performing Arts	USA	Comedian
	Thomas Franklin (Tommy)	Sports	USA	Football Player - HF
McDonnell	Mary	Performing Arts	USA	Actress - Acad Award Nom
McDormand	Frances	Performing Arts	USA	Actress - Academy Award
McDougall	Walter A.	Creative Works	USA	Author - Pulitzer
McDowall	Roddy	Performing Arts	England	Actor
McDowell	Malcolm	Performing Arts	England	Actor
McElhenny Jr.	Hug Edward (The king)	Sports	USA	Football Player - HF
McElroy	Sollie	Performing Arts	USA	Rock & Roll - HF - The Flamingos
McEnroe	John Patrick	Sports	USA	Tennis Player - HF
McEntire	Reba	Performing Arts	USA	Singer
McFadden	Daniel L.	Arts	USA	Economics - Nobel Laureate
	Gates	Performing Arts	USA	Actress
McFarland	George (Spanky)	Performing Arts	USA	Actor
McFeely	William S.	Creative Works	USA	Author - Pulitzer
McFerrin	Bobby	Performing Arts	USA	Singer
McGavin	Darren	Performing Arts	USA	Actor
McGee	Francis (Frank)	Sports	Canada	Hockey Player - HF
	Willie	Sports	USA	Baseball Player
McGhee	Bart	Sports	Scotland	Soccer Player - HF
McGill	Michael	Performing Arts	USA	Rock & Roll - HF - The Dells
McGillis	Kelly	Performing Arts	USA	Actress
McGimsie	William George (Bill)	Sports	Canada	Hockey Player - HF
McGinley	Phyllis	Creative Works	USA	Poet - Pulitzer
McGinnity	Joseph Jerome (Joe)	Sports	USA	Baseball Player - HF
McGoohan	Patrick	Performing Arts	USA	Actor
McGovern	Elizabeth	Performing Arts	USA	Actress - Acad Award Nom
	George Stanley	Politics	USA	Senator - South Dakota
	Maureen	Performing Arts	USA	Singer
	William Aloysius (Bill)	Sports	USA	Baseball Umpire - HF
McGraw	John Joseph	Sports	USA	Baseball Manager - HF
	Thomas K.	Creative Works	USA	Author - Pulitzer
	Tug	Sports	USA	Baseball Player
McGregor	Ewan	Performing Arts	Scotland	Actor
	Ken	Sports	Australia	Tennis Player - HF
McGriff	Fred	Sports	USA	Baseball Player
McGuffey	William Holmes	Arts	USA	Educator/Editor
McGuigan	Finbar Patrick (Barry)	Sports	Ireland	Boxer - HF
McGuinn	James Joseph (Roger)	Performing Arts	USA	Rock & Roll - HF - The Bryds
McGuire	Dorothy	Performing Arts	USA	Actress - Acad Award Nom
	John	Sports	Scotland	Soccer Player - HF
	Richard S. (Dick)	Sports	USA	Basketball Player - HF
McGwire	Mark	Sports	USA	Baseball Player
McHale	Kevin	Sports	USA	Basketball Player - HF
McHarg	Ian	Architecture	USA	Architect - Jefferson Medal
McIlvenny	Edward John (Ed)	Sports	Scotland	Soccer Player - HF
McIlwain	Charles Howard	Creative Works	USA	Author - Pulitzer
McIntosh	John	Science	Canada	Inventor - McIntosh Apple
	Robbie	Performing Arts	England	Rock & Roll - HF - The Pretenders
McKane-Godfree	Kathleen (Kitty)	Sports	England	Tennis Player - HF
McKay	Albert Phillip	Performing Arts	USA	Rock & Roll - HF - Earth Wind & Fire
McKean	Michael	Performing Arts	USA	Actor
McKechnie	William Boyd (Bill)	Sports	USA	Baseball Manager - HF
McKellen	Ian	Performing Arts	England	Actor - Acad Award Nom
McKenna	Lori	Performing Arts	USA	Singer
McKennitt	Loreena	Performing Arts	Canada	Singer
McKernan	Ron	Performing Arts	USA	Rock & Roll - HF - Grateful Dead
McKim	Charles Follen	Architecture	USA	Architect - AIA Gold Medal
McKinley	Charles Robert (Chuck)	Sports	USA	Tennis Player - HF

LAST NAME	FIRST NAME	CATEGORY	COUNTRY	FAME
McKinley	Ida	Politics	USA	First Lady
	William	Politics	USA	President
	William	Performing Arts	USA	Jazz Drummer - Big Band/Jazz - HF
McLaglen	Victor	Performing Arts	England	Actor - Academy Award
McLaren	Bruce	Sports	New Zealand	Race Car Driver - HF
McLaughlin	Andrew Cunningham	Creative Works	USA	Author - Pulitzer
	Bernard (Benny)	Sports	USA	Soccer Player - HF
McLean	Don	Performing Arts	USA	Singer
McLoughlin	Maurice Evans (Red)	Sports	USA	Tennis Player - HF
McLuhan	Herbert Marshall	Creative Works	Canada	Writer/Educator
McMahon	Ed	Performing Arts	USA	Show Host/Comedian
	Jim	Sports	USA	Football Player
McMillan	Edwin Mattison	Science	USA	Chemistry - Nobel Laureate
	Frew Donald	Sports	South Africa	Tennis Player - HF
McMonagle	Donald Ray	Aviation	USA	Astronaut
McMurtry	Larry	Creative Works	USA	Novelist - Pulitzer
McNab	Alex	Sports	Scotland	Soccer Player - HF
McNair	Ronald Erwin	Aviation	USA	Astronaut
McNally	John Victor (Blood)	Sports	USA	Football Player - HF
McNamara	George	Sports	Canada	Hockey Player - HF
McNamara	Maggie	Performing Arts	USA	Actress - Acad Award Nom
McNeill	William Donald (Don)	Sports	USA	Tennis Player - HF
McNichol	Kristy	Performing Arts	USA	Actress
McPartland (Turner)	Margaret Marian	Performing Arts	England	Jazz Pianist - Big Band/Jazz - HF
McPhatter	Clyde Lensley	Performing Arts	USA	Singer - Rock & Roll - HF
	Ron	Performing Arts	USA	Rock & Roll - HF - The Drifters
McPhee	John	Creative Works	USA	Author - Pulitzer
	John Alexander (Bid)	Sports	USA	Baseball Player - HF
McPherson	James Alan	Creative Works	USA	Novelist - Pulitzer
	James M.	Creative Works	USA	Author - Pulitzer
McQueen	Butterfly	Performing Arts	USA	Actress
	Steve	Performing Arts	USA	Actor - Acad Award Nom
McRaney	Gerald	Performing Arts	USA	Actor
McShane	Ian	Performing Arts	England	Actor
McShann	James Columbus (Jay)	Performing Arts	USA	Band Leader - Big Band/Jazz - HF
McTeer	Janet	Performing Arts	England	Actress - Acad Award Nom
McVie	John Graham	Performing Arts	England	Rock & Roll - HF - Fleetwood Mac
McVie (Perfect)	Christine Ann	Performing Arts	England	Rock & Roll - HF - Fleetwood Mac
McWhorter	Diane	Creative Works	USA	Author - Pulitzer
Mead	Margaret	Arts	USA	Anthropologist/Writer
Meade	Carl Joseph	Aviation	USA	Astronaut
	George Gordon	War & Peace	USA	General - Civil War
	James E.	Arts	England	Economics - Nobel Laureate
Meadows	Audrey	Performing Arts	China	Actress
	Jayne	Performing Arts	China	Actress
Meany	Colm	Performing Arts	Ireland	Actor
	George	Business	USA	Labor Leader
Meara	Anne	Performing Arts	USA	Actress
Mears	Rick	Sports	USA	Race Car Driver - HF
Mechnikov	Ilya Ilyich	Science	Russia	Medicine - Nobel Laureate
Medary	Milton Bennett	Architecture	USA	Architect - AIA Gold Medal
Medawar	Peter Brian	Science	England	Medicine - Nobel Laureate
Medford	Kay	Performing Arts	USA	Actress - Acad Award Nom
Medley	William Thomas (Bill)	Performing Arts	USA	Rock & Roll - HF - Righteous Brothers
Medwick	Joseph Michael (Joe)	Sports	USA	Baseball Player - HF
Meek	Donald	Performing Arts	Scotland	Actor
Meer	Simon van der	Science	Netherlands	Physics - Nobel Laureate
Mehemet	Ali	Politics	Egypt	Viceroy
Mehta	Zubin	Performing Arts	India	Conductor
Meier	Richard	Architecture	USA	Architect - Pritzker/ AIA Gold
Meighen	Arthur	Politics	Canada	Prime Minister
Meiklejohn	Alexander	Arts	USA	Philosopher
Meir	Golda	Politics	Israel	Prime Minister

SOLVER SERIES: NAME FINDER

LAST NAME	FIRST NAME	CATEGORY	COUNTRY	FAME
Meirelles	Fernando	Movie Production	Brazil	Director - Acad Award Nom
Meisner	Randy	Performing Arts	USA	Rock & Roll - HF - The Eagles
Meissonier	Jean Louis Ernest	Works of Art	France	Painter
Meitner	Lise	Science	Austria	Nuclear Physicist
Melanchthon	Phillip	Politics	Germany	Reformer - Protestant
Melba	Nellie	Performing Arts	Australia	Singer - Opera
Melbourne	William Lamb	Politics	England	Prime Minister
Melchior	Lauritz Lebrecht Hommel	Performing Arts	USA	Singer - Opera
Mellencamp	John Cougar	Performing Arts	USA	Singer
Mellon	Andrew William	Business	USA	Financier/Mining Industry
	Paul	Architecture	USA	Architect - Jefferson Medal
Melnick	Bruce Edward	Aviation	USA	Astronaut
Melnikov	Konstantin	Architecture	Austria	Architect
Melville	Herman	Creative Works	USA	Novelist
Melvin	Harold	Performing Arts	USA	Singer (Blue Notes)
Memling	Hans	Works of Art	Germany	Painter
Menand	Louis	Creative Works	USA	Author - Pulitzer
Mencken	Henry Louis	Creative Works	USA	Journalist - Newspaper
Mendel	Gregor Johann	Science	Austria	Botanist - Founder of Genetics
Mendeleev	Dmitri Ivanovich	Science	Russia	Chemist
Mendelsohn	Erich	Architecture	USA	Architect
Mendelssohn	Felix	Creative Works	Germany	Composer
	Moses	Arts	Germany	Philosopher - Jewish
Mendes	Sam	Movie Production	England	Director - Academy Award
	Sergio	Performing Arts	Brazil	Jazz Pianist/Arranger
Mendini	Alessandro	Architecture	Italy	Architect
Meneghin	Dino	Sports	Italy	Basketball Player - HF
Ménière	Prosper	Science	France	Physician
Menjou	Adolphe	Performing Arts	USA	Actor - Acad Award Nom
Menken	Adah Isaacs	Performing Arts	USA	Actress/Poet
	Helen	Performing Arts	USA	Actress
Menn	Christian	Architecture	Switzerland	Architect
Menninger	Karl Augustus	Science	USA	Psychiatrist
Menotti	Gian-Carlo	Creative Works	USA	Composer - Opera
Menuhin	Yehudl	Performing Arts	USA	Violinist
Menzies	John	Business	England	Retail Trade
	Robert Gordon	Politics	Australia	Prime Minister
Merbold	Ulf Dietrich	Aviation	Germany	Astronaut
Mercator	Gerhardus	Arts	Italy	Geographer/Cartographer
Mercer	Marian	Performing Arts	USA	Actress
	Ray	Sports	USA	Boxer
Merchant	Vivien	Performing Arts	England	Actress - Acad Award Nom
Mercouri	Melina	Performing Arts	Greece	Actress - Acad Award Nom
Mercury (Bulsara)	Farrokh (Freddie)	Performing Arts	Tanzania	Rock & Roll - HF - Queen
Meredith	Burgess	Performing Arts	USA	Actor - Acad Award Nom
	George	Creative Works	England	Poet/Novelist
	Owen	Creative Works	England	Poet/Diplomat
	William	Creative Works	USA	Poet - Pulitzer
Mergenthaler	Ottmar	Science	USA	Inventor - Linotype
Mérimée	Prosper	Creative Works	France	Novelist/Essayist/Historian
Merkel	Una	Performing Arts	USA	Actress - Acad Award Nom
Merman	Ethel	Performing Arts	USA	Singer
Merrick	David	Movie Production	USA	Director
Merrifield	Bruce	Science	USA	Chemistry - Nobel Laureate
Merrill	Dina	Performing Arts	USA	Actress
	Gary	Performing Arts	USA	Actor
	James	Creative Works	USA	Poet - Pulitzer
	Robert	Performing Arts	USA	Singer - Opera
Merriman	Nan	Performing Arts	USA	Singer - Opera
Merriweather	Allison Lee	Works of Art	USA	Painter
Merton	Robert C.	Arts	USA	Economics - Nobel Laureate
Merwin	William Stanley	Creative Works	USA	Poet - Pulitzer
Messerschmid	Ernst Willi	Aviation	Germany	Astronaut

LAST NAME	FIRST NAME	CATEGORY	COUNTRY	FAME
Messier	Mark	Sports	Canada	Hockey Player
Messina	Jim	Performing Arts	USA	Rock & Roll - HF - Buffalo Springfield
	Sal	Sports	USA	Hockey Broadcaster - HF
Messing	Debra	Performing Arts	USA	Actress
Mesta	Perle	Politics	USA	Political Supporter
Meštrovic	Ivan	Works of Art	Yugoslavia	Sculptor
Metcalf	Laurie	Performing Arts	USA	Actress
Metchnikoff	Élie	Science	Russia	Biologist/Bacteriologist
Metternich	Klemens Wenzel von	Politics	Austria	Statesman/Diplomat
Meuron	Pierre de	Architecture	Switzerland	Architect - Pritzker Laureate
Meyer	Adolf	Architecture	Germany	Architect
	Hannes	Architecture	Switzerland	Architect
	Louis	Sports	USA	Race Car Driver - HF
	Nathan	Business	Germany	Banking
Meyerbeer	Giacomo	Creative Works	Germany	Composer - Opera
Meyerhof	Otto Fritz	Science	Germany	Medicine - Nobel Laureate
Meyers	Anne E.	Sports	USA	Basketball Player - HF
	Ari	Performing Arts	Puerto Rico	Actress
Michael	George	Performing Arts	England	Singer
Michaels	Alan Richard	Creative Works	USA	Journalist - Television
	Lorne	Movie Production	Canada	Director
Michalske	August Mike	Sports	USA	Football Player - HF
Michel	Frank Curtis	Aviation	USA	Astronaut
	Hartmut	Science	Germany	Chemistry - Nobel Laureate
Michelangelo	Buonarroti	Architecture	Italy	Architect/Sculptor/Painter/Author
Michelet	Jules	Arts	France	Historian
Michelozzi	Michelozzo di Bartolomeo	Architecture	Italy	Architect
Michels	Ana Claudia	Performing Arts	Brazil	Super Model
Michelson	Albert Abraham	Science	USA	Physics - Nobel Laureate
Michener	James A.	Creative Works	USA	Author - Pulitzer
Mickiewicz	Adam	Creative Works	Poland	Poet
Middlecoff	Cary	Sports	USA	Golfer - HF
Middleton	Thomas	Creative Works	England	Dramatist
Midler	Bette	Performing Arts	USA	Actress - Acad Award Nom
	Bette	Performing Arts	USA	Singer
Midori	Ito	Sports	Japan	Olympic Skater
Mieth	Werner E.	Sports	Germany	Soccer Player - HF
Mifune	Toshiro	Performing Arts	China	Actor
Mikan	George L.	Sports	USA	Basketball Player - HF
Mikita	Stanley (Stan)	Sports	Czechoslovakia	Hockey Player - HF
Mikkelsen	Vern	Sports	USA	Basketball Player - HF
Miles	Jack	Creative Works	USA	Author - Pulitzer
	Sarah	Performing Arts	England	Actress - Acad Award Nom
	Sylvia	Performing Arts	USA	Actress
	Vera	Performing Arts	USA	Actress
Milestone	Lewis	Movie Production	Russia	Director - Academy Award
Mileto	Isidoro di	Architecture	Italy	Architect
Milford	Penelope	Performing Arts	USA	Actress - Acad Award Nom
Milgram	Stanley	Arts	USA	Philosopher
Milhaud	Darius	Creative Works	France	Composer
Mill	James	Arts	Scotland	Philosoper/Historian
	John Stuart	Arts	England	Philosopher/Political Economist
Millais	John Everett	Works of Art	England	Painter
Milland	Ray	Performing Arts	Wales	Actor - Academy Award
Millar	Robert (Bob)	Sports	Scotland	Soccer Player - HF
Millay	Edna St. Vincent	Creative Works	USA	Poet - Pulitzer
Mille	Agnes George De	Performing Arts	USA	Dancer/Choreographer
	Cecil Blount De	Movie Production	USA	Director - Acad Award Nom
	Nelson De	Creative Works	USA	Author
Miller	Alton Glenn	Performing Arts	USA	Band Leader - Big Band/Jazz - HF
	Ann	Performing Arts	USA	Actress/Dancer
	Arthur	Creative Works	USA	Dramatist - Pulitzer
	Caroline	Creative Works	USA	Novelist - Pulitzer

SOLVER SERIES: NAME FINDER

LAST NAME	FIRST NAME	CATEGORY	COUNTRY	FAME
Miller	Cheryl	Sports	USA	Basketball Player - HF
	Dennis	Performing Arts	USA	Comedian
	Henry	Creative Works	USA	Writer
	Jason	Creative Works	USA	Dramatist - Pulitzer
	Jason	Performing Arts	USA	Actor - Acad Award Nom
	Joaquin	Creative Works	USA	Poet
	Joe	Performing Arts	England	Comedian
	Johnny	Sports	USA	Golfer - HF
	Jonathon	Creative Works	England	Producer/Author
	Jonathon	Movie Production	England	Director
	Merton H.	Arts	USA	Economics - Nobel Laureate
	Mitchell William (Mitch)	Performing Arts	USA	Choir Leader
	Nicole	Business	USA	Fashion Designer
	Perry	Creative Works	USA	Author - Pulitzer
	Roger Dean	Performing Arts	USA	Singer - Country Music - HF
	Steve	Performing Arts	USA	Band Leader/Guitarist
	Sue	Creative Works	USA	Author
Milles	Carl	Works of Art	USA	Sculptor
Millet	Jean François	Works of Art	France	Painter
Millhauser	Steven	Creative Works	USA	Novelist - Pulitzer
Millikan	Robert Andrews	Science	USA	Physics - Nobel Laureate
Millinder	Lucius Venable (Lucky)	Performing Arts	USA	Band Leader - Big Band/Jazz - HF
Millner	Wayne Vernal	Sports	USA	Football Player - HF
Mills	Donna	Performing Arts	USA	Actress
	Erie	Performing Arts	USA	Singer - Opera
	Hayley	Performing Arts	England	Actress - Academy Award
	John	Performing Arts	England	Actor - Academy Award
Milne	Alan Alexander	Creative Works	England	Playwright/Novelist/Writer
Milner	Martin	Performing Arts	USA	Actor
Milosz	Czeslaw	Creative Works	Poland	Literature - Nobel Laureate
Milsap	Ronnie	Performing Arts	USA	Singer
Milstein	César	Science	England	Medicine - Nobel Laureate
	Nathan	Performing Arts	USA	Violinist
Milton	John	Creative Works	England	Poet
Mimieux	Yvette	Performing Arts	USA	Actress
Minardi	Bruno	Architecture	Italy	Architect
Mineo	Sal	Performing Arts	USA	Actor - Acad Award Nom
Minghella	Anthony	Movie Production	England	Director - Academy Award
Mingus	Charlie	Performing Arts	USA	Band Leader - Big Band/Jazz - HF
Minnelli	Liza	Performing Arts	USA	Actress - Academy Award
	Liza	Performing Arts	USA	Singer
	Vincente	Movie Production	USA	Director - Academy Award
Minot	George Richards	Science	USA	Medicine - Nobel Laureate
Minuit	Peter	Exploration	Netherlands	Explorer - Manhattan
	Peter	Politics	Netherlands	Director General
Mirabeau	Honoré Gabriel Riqueti	Politics	France	Revolutionist/Statesman
Miranda	Carmen	Performing Arts	Portugal	Actress
Mirandola	Giovanni Pico della	Arts	Italy	Philosopher/Humanist
Miró	Joan	Works of Art	Spain	Painter/Sculptor - Surrealist
Mirren	Helen	Performing Arts	England	Actress - Acad Award Nom
Mirrlees	James A.	Arts	England	Economics - Nobel Laureate
Mishima	Yukio	Creative Works	Japan	Author
Mistral	Frédéric	Creative Works	France	Literature - Nobel Laureate
	Gabriela	Creative Works	Chile	Literature - Nobel Laureate
Mitchell	Andrea	Creative Works	USA	Journalist - Television
	Cameron	Performing Arts	USA	Actor
	Edgar Dean	Aviation	USA	Astronaut
	Kevin	Sports	USA	Baseball Player
	Leona	Performing Arts	USA	Singer - Opera
	Margaret Munnerlyn	Creative Works	USA	Author - Pulitzer
	Maria	Science	USA	Astronomer
	Peter	Science	England	Chemistry - Nobel Laureate
	Robert Cornelius (Bobby)	Sports	USA	Football Player - HF

LAST NAME	FIRST NAME	CATEGORY	COUNTRY	FAME
Mitchell	Roberta Joan (Joni)	Performing Arts	Canada	Singer - Rock & Roll - Canadian Music HF
	Roberta Joan (Joni)	Performing Arts	Canada	Singer - Rock & Roll - HF
	Thomas	Performing Arts	USA	Actor - Academy Award
	Thomas Livingstone	Exploration	Australia	Explorer - Australia South East
	William	War & Peace	USA	Army Officer/Aviation Pioneer
Mitchum	Robert	Performing Arts	USA	Actor - Acad Award Nom
Mitford	Jessica	Creative Works	England	Author
	Nancy	Creative Works	England	Novelist
Mitterrand	Francois	Politics	France	President
Mix	Ronald Jack (Ron)	Sports	USA	Football Player - HF
	Tom	Performing Arts	USA	Actor
Mize	John Robert (Johnny)	Sports	USA	Baseball Player - HF
	Larry	Sports	USA	Golfer
Mizner	Addison	Architecture	USA	Architect
Mizrahi	Isaak	Business	USA	Fashion Designer
Mochrie	Dottie (Pepper)	Sports	USA	Golfer
Mockbee	Samuel (Sambo)	Architecture	USA	Architect - AIA Gold Medal
Modigliani	Amedeo	Works of Art	Italy	Painter
	Franco	Arts	USA	Economics - Nobel Laureate
Modine	Matthew	Performing Arts	USA	Actor
Modjeska	Helena	Performing Arts	Poland	Actress
Moffo	Anna	Performing Arts	Italy	Singer - Opera
Mohammad	Matthew Saad	Sports	USA	Boxer - HF
Mohri	Mamoru	Aviation	Japan	Astronaut
Moissan	Henri	Science	France	Chemistry - Nobel Laureate
Molière	Jean Baptiste	Creative Works	France	Dramatist
Molina	Gabriel Tirso de	Creative Works	Spain	Dramatist
	Mario J.	Science	USA	Chemistry - Nobel Laureate
Molinaro	Al	Performing Arts	USA	Actor
	Edouard	Movie Production	France	Director - Acad Award Nom
Molitor	Paul Leo	Sports	USA	Baseball Player - HF
Moll	Richard	Performing Arts	USA	Actor
Mollino	Carlo	Architecture	Italy	Architect
Mollweide	Karl B.	Science	Germany	Mathematician
Molnár	Ferenc	Creative Works	Hungary	Playwright/Novelist
Molotov	Vyacheslav Mikhailovich	Politics	Russia	Statesman
Moltke	Helmuth Johannes Ludwig von	War & Peace	Germany	General
	Helmuth Karl Bernard	War & Peace	Germany	Field Marshall
Momaday	Navarre Scott	Creative Works	USA	Novelist - Pulitzer
Mommsen	Christian Matthias	Creative Works	Germany	Literature - Nobel Laureate
Mondale	Walter	Politics	USA	Vice-President
Mondrian	Piet	Works of Art	Netherlands	Painter
Moneo	Rafael	Architecture	Spain	Architect - Pritzker Laureate
Monet	Claude	Works of Art	France	Painter
Moneta	Ernesto Teodoro	War & Peace	Italy	Peace - Nobel Laureate
Money	Eddie	Performing Arts	USA	Singer
Moniz	Antonio Caetano Egas	Science	Portugal	Medicine - Nobel Laureate
Monk	Art	Sports	USA	Football Player
	George	War & Peace	England	General/Politician
	Thelonious Sphere	Performing Arts	USA	Jazz Pianist - Big Band/Jazz - HF
Monod	Jacques	Science	France	Medicine - Nobel Laureate
Monroe	Elizabeth	Politics	USA	First Lady
	James	Politics	USA	President
	Marilyn	Performing Arts	USA	Actress
	Vaughn	Performing Arts	USA	Singer
	Vernon Earl (The Pearl)	Sports	USA	Basketball Player - HF
	William Smith (Bill)	Performing Arts	USA	Country Music - HF - Blue Grass Boys
Monsen	Lloyd	Sports	USA	Soccer Player - HF
Montagu	Mary Wortley	Creative Works	England	Writer
Montaigne	Michel Eyquem de	Arts	France	Philosopher/Writer
Montalban	Ricardo	Performing Arts	Mexico	Actor
Montale	Eugenio	Creative Works	Italy	Literature - Nobel Laureate
Montana	Bob	Creative Works	USA	Cartoonist - Archie

SOLVER SERIES: NAME FINDER

LAST NAME	FIRST NAME	CATEGORY	COUNTRY	FAME
Montana	Joseph Clifford (Joe)	Sports	USA	Football Player - HF
Montana (Blevins)	Patsy (Ruby)	Performing Arts	USA	Singer - Country Music - HF
Montcalm	Louis Joseph de	War & Peace	France	General
Montenegro	Fernanda	Performing Arts	Brazil	Actress - Acad Award Nom
Montesquieu	Charles de	Arts	France	Philosopher
Montessori	Maria	Arts	Italy	Educator
Monteux	Pierre	Performing Arts	USA	Conductor - Orchestra
Monteverdi	Claudio Giovanni Antonio	Creative Works	Italy	Composer
Montfort	Simon de	War & Peace	France	Crusader
Montgomery	Bernard Law	War & Peace	England	Field Marshall
	Bob	Sports	USA	Boxer - HF
	Elizabeth	Performing Arts	USA	Actress
	John Wesley (Wes)	Performing Arts	USA	Jazz Guitarist - Big Band/Jazz - HF
	Robert	Performing Arts	USA	Actor - Acad Award Nom
Montherlant	Henri Millon de	Creative Works	France	Novelist/Playwright
Montreuil	Pierre de	Architecture	France	Architect
Monzon	Carlos	Sports	Argentina	Boxer - HF
Moody	Dwight Lyman	Arts	USA	Evangelist
	James	Performing Arts	USA	Jazz Saxophonist - Big Band/Jazz - HF
	Orville	Sports	USA	Golfer
	Ron	Performing Arts	England	Actor - Acad Award Nom
	William Vaughn	Creative Works	USA	Poet/Playwright
Moody Jr.	Ralph	Sports	USA	Race Car Driver - HF
Moon	Keith	Performing Arts	England	Rock & Roll - HF - The Who
	Warren	Sports	USA	Football Player
Moore	Archie	Sports	USA	Boxer - HF
	Bobby	Sports	England	Soccer Player - HF
	Charles Willard	Architecture	USA	Architect - AIA Gold Medal
	Clayton	Performing Arts	USA	Actor
	Clement Clarke	Creative Works	USA	Poet
	Demi	Performing Arts	USA	Actress
	Dudley	Performing Arts	England	Actor - Acad Award Nom
	Elisabeth Holmes (Bessie)	Sports	USA	Tennis Player - HF
	George Augustus	Creative Works	Ireland	Novelist/Playwright/Critic
	George Edward	Arts	England	Philosopher
	Grace	Performing Arts	USA	Actress - Acad Award Nom
	Henry	Works of Art	England	Sculptor
	Johnny	Sports	Scotland	Soccer Player - HF
	Juanita	Performing Arts	USA	Actress - Acad Award Nom
	Julianne	Performing Arts	USA	Actress - Acad Award Nom
	Leonard Edward (Lenny)	Sports	USA	Football Player - HF
	Lloyd (Big Finger)	Performing Arts	USA	Rock & Roll - HF - The Soul Stirrers
	Marianne Craig	Creative Works	USA	Poet - Pulitzer
	Mary Tyler	Performing Arts	USA	Actress - Acad Award Nom
	Melba	Performing Arts	USA	Singer
	Richard Winston (Dickie)	Sports	Canada	Hockey Player - HF
	Roger	Performing Arts	England	Actor
	Sam	Performing Arts	USA	Rock & Roll - HF - Sam & Dave
	Stanford	Science	USA	Chemistry - Nobel Laureate
	Terry	Performing Arts	USA	Actress - Acad Award Nom
	Thomas	Creative Works	Ireland	Poet
Moorehead	Agnes	Performing Arts	USA	Actress - Acad Award Nom
Moorhouse	George	Sports	England	Soccer Player - HF
Moraglia	Giacomo	Architecture	Italy	Architect
Morales	Esai	Performing Arts	USA	Actor
Moran	Erin	Performing Arts	USA	Actress
	Patrick Joseph (Paddy)	Sports	Canada	Hockey Player - HF
Moranis	Rick	Performing Arts	Canada	Actor
Moravia	Alberto	Creative Works	Italy	Novelist
More	Hannah	Creative Works	England	Writer - Religious Tracts
	Thomas	Creative Works	England	Writer/Statesman
Moreau	Jean Victor	War & Peace	France	General
	Jeanne	Performing Arts	France	Actress

LAST NAME	FIRST NAME	CATEGORY	COUNTRY	FAME
Moreira	Ronaldo de Assis (Ronaldinho)	Sports	Brazil	Soccer Player
Moreno	Catalina Sandino	Performing Arts	Columbia	Actress - Acad Award Nom
	Rita	Performing Arts	Puerto Rico	Actress - Academy Award
Morenz	Howarth William (Howie)	Sports	Canada	Hockey Player - HF
Moretti	Luigi	Architecture	Italy	Architect
Morgan	Daniel	War & Peace	USA	Revolutionary General
	Frank	Performing Arts	USA	Actor - Acad Award Nom
	Harry	Performing Arts	USA	Actor
	Henry	Performing Arts	USA	Comedian
	Henry	War & Peace	Wales	Buccaneer
	Joe Leonard	Sports	USA	Baseball Player - HF
	John Hunt	War & Peace	USA	Confederate General
	John Pierpont	Business	USA	Financier
	John Thomas	Performing Arts	USA	Singer - Country Music - HF
	Julia	Architecture	USA	Architect
	Lewis Henry	Arts	USA	Anthropologist
	Thomas Hunt	Science	USA	Medicine - Nobel Laureate
Morgenthau	Henry	Politics	USA	Secretary of the Treasury
Moriarty	Cathy	Performing Arts	USA	Actress
	Michael	Performing Arts	USA	Actor
Morini	Erica	Performing Arts	Austria	Violinist
Morison	Samuel Eliot	Creative Works	USA	Author - Pulitzer
Morita	Noriyuki (Pat)	Performing Arts	USA	Actor - Acad Award Nom
Morley	Robert	Performing Arts	England	Actor - Acad Award Nom
Mornay	Phillipe de	Politics	France	Diplomat
	Rebecca De	Performing Arts	USA	Actress
Moro	Aldo	Politics	Italy	Head of State
	Antonio	Works of Art	Netherlands	Painter - Portrait
Morrall	Earl	Sports	USA	Football Player
Morris	Aldo	Movie Production	USA	Director
	Chester	Performing Arts	USA	Actor - Acad Award Nom
	Edmund	Creative Works	USA	Author - Pulitzer
	Gouverneur	Politics	USA	Statesman/Diplomat
	Greg	Performing Arts	USA	Actor
	Robert	Business	USA	Financier/Patriot
	William	Architecture	England	Architect
	William	Business	England	Entrepreneur
	William	Works of Art	England	Artist/Craftsman/Poet
Morris Jr.	Tom	Sports	Scotland	Golfer - HF
Morris Sr.	Tom	Sports	Scotland	Golfer - HF
Morrison	Holmes Sterling	Performing Arts	USA	Rock & Roll - HF - Velvet Underground
	James (Jim) Douglas	Performing Arts	USA	Rock & Roll - HF - The Doors
	Robert	Sports	Scotland	Soccer Player - HF
	Toni	Creative Works	USA	Literature - Nobel/Pulitzer
	Van	Performing Arts	Northern Ireland	Singer
Morrow	Vic	Performing Arts	USA	Actor
Morse	Robert	Performing Arts	USA	Actor
	Samuel Finley Breese	Science	USA	Inventor - Telegraph
Mortimer-Barrett	Florence Angela Margaret	Sports	England	Tennis Player - HF
Morton	Levi P.	Politics	USA	Vice-President
	Samantha	Performing Arts	England	Actress - Acad Award Nom
	William Thomas Green	Science	USA	Dentist
Morton (Lemothe)	Ferdinand (Jelly Roll)	Performing Arts	USA	Singer - Big Band/Jazz - HF
	Ferdinand (Jelly Roll)	Performing Arts	USA	Singer - Rock & Roll - HF
Mosel	Tad	Creative Works	USA	Dramatist - Pulitzer
Moser	Karl	Architecture	Switzerland	Architect
Moses	Anna Mary Robertson	Works of Art	USA	Painter - Primitive
	Edwin C.	Sports	USA	Olympic Hurdler
Mosienko	William (Bill)	Sports	Canada	Hockey Player - HF
Moss	Eric Owen	Architecture	USA	Architect
	Hart	Creative Works	USA	Playwright
	Kate	Performing Arts	England	Super Model
	Stirling	Sports	England	Race Car Driver - HF

SOLVER SERIES: NAME FINDER

LAST NAME	FIRST NAME	CATEGORY	COUNTRY	FAME
Mössbauer	Rudolf Ludwig	Science	Germany	Physics - Nobel Laureate
Mostel	Josh	Performing Arts	USA	Actor
	Zero	Performing Arts	USA	Actor
Motherwell	Robert	Works of Art	USA	Painter - Abstract Expressionist
Motley	John Lothrop	Politics	USA	Diplomat/Historian
	Marion	Sports	USA	Football Player - HF
Mott	Frank Luther	Creative Works	USA	Author - Pulitzer
	John Raleigh	War & Peace	USA	Peace - Nobel Laureate
	Lucretia	Politics	USA	Abolitionist/Rights Advocate
	Nevill Francis	Science	England	Physics - Nobel Laureate
Motta	Jack La(Jake)	Sports	USA	Boxer - HF
Mottelson	Ben Roy	Science	Denmark	Physics - Nobel Laureate
Mountbatten	Louis	War & Peace	England	Admiral
Moura	Eduardo Souto de	Architecture	Portugal	Architect
Mourning	Alonzo	Sports	USA	Basketball Player
Moussorgsky	Modest Petrovich	Creative Works	Russia	Composer
Mowbray	Alan	Performing Arts	England	Actor
Mowry	Tia Dashon	Performing Arts	Germany	Actress
Moyers	William (Bill)	Creative Works	USA	Journalist - Television
Moynihan	Daniel Patrick	Architecture	USA	Architect - Jefferson Medal
	Daniel Patrick (Pat)	Politics	USA	Senator - New York
Mozart	Wolfgang Amadeus	Creative Works	Austria	Composer
Mubarak	Muhammad Hosni Said	Politics	Egypt	President
Mucci	Dion Di	Performing Arts	USA	Singer - Rock & Roll - HF
Mudd	Roger	Creative Works	USA	Journalist - Television
Mueller	Lisel	Creative Works	Germany	Poet - Pulitzer
Mueller-Stahl	Armin	Performing Arts	Russia	Actor - Acad Award Nom
Muggenast	Josef	Architecture	Austria	Architect
Muir	Frank	Creative Works	England	Writer - Comedy
	Jean	Business	England	Fashion Designer
	John	Science	USA	Naturalist/Writer
Muldaur	Diana	Performing Arts	USA	Actress
Mulder	Karen	Performing Arts	Netherlands	Super Model
Muldoon	Paul	Creative Works	Ireland	Poet - Pulitzer
Muldowney	Shirley	Sports	USA	Race Car Driver - HF
Mulgrew	Kate	Performing Arts	USA	Actress
Mull	Martin	Performing Arts	USA	Comedian
Mullane	Richard Michael	Aviation	USA	Astronaut
Mullen	Joseph (Joe)	Sports	USA	Hockey Player - HF
Mullen Jr.	Larry	Performing Arts	Ireland	Rock & Roll - HF - U2
Muller	Gerd	Sports	Germany	Soccer Player - HF
	Hermann Joseph	Science	USA	Medicine - Nobel Laureate
	Friedrich Max	Arts	England	Philologist/Mythologist
	Karl Alex	Science	Switzerland	Physics - Nobel Laureate
	Paul Hermann	Science	Switzerland	Medicine - Nobel Laureate
Mulligan	Gerald Joseph (Gerry)	Performing Arts	USA	Jazz Saxophonist - Big Band/Jazz - HF
	Richard	Performing Arts	USA	Actor
	Robert	Movie Production	USA	Director - Acad Award Nom
Mulliken	Robert S.	Science	USA	Chemistry - Nobel Laureate
Mullin	Chris	Sports	USA	Basketball Player
Mullis	Kary B.	Science	USA	Chemistry - Nobel Laureate
Mulloy	Gardnar Putnam (Gar)	Sports	USA	Tennis Player - HF
Mulroney	Martin Brian	Politics	Canada	Prime Minister
Mumford	Lewis	Architecture	USA	Architect - Jefferson Medal
	Lewis	Arts	USA	Philosopher - Social
	Thad	Creative Works	USA	Screenwriter - Mash
Muncey	William (Bill)	Sports	USA	Hydroplane Race Driver - HF
Munch	Edvard	Works of Art	Norway	Painter/Print Maker
Munchak	Michael Anthony (Mike)	Sports	USA	Football Player - HF
Mundell	Robert A.	Arts	Canada	Economics - Nobel Laureate
Muni	Paul	Performing Arts	Ukraine	Actor - Academy Award
Munoz	Astrid	Performing Arts	Puerto Rico	Super Model
Muñoz	Michael Anthony	Sports	USA	Football Player - HF

LAST NAME	FIRST NAME	CATEGORY	COUNTRY	FAME
Munro	Hector Hugh (Saki)	Creative Works	England	Author
Munson	Ona	Performing Arts	USA	Actress
Murad	Ferid	Science	USA	Medicine - Nobel Laureate
Murasaki	Shikibu	Creative Works	Japan	Poet/Novelist
Murat	Joachim	War & Peace	France	Marshal
Muratori	Saverio	Architecture	Italy	Architect
Murchison	Clint	Business	USA	Publishing/Oil Industry
Murcutt	Glenn	Architecture	Australia	Architect - Pritzker/Jefferson Medal
Murdoch	Iris	Creative Works	England	Author
	Keith Rupert	Business	USA	Media Magnate
Murillo	Bartolomé Esteban	Works of Art	Spain	Painter
Murphy	Audie	Performing Arts	USA	Actor
	Calvin J.	Sports	USA	Basketball Player - HF
	Charles C. (Stretch)	Sports	USA	Basketball Player - HF
	Dale	Sports	USA	Baseball Player
	Eddie	Performing Arts	USA	Comedian
	Edward (Ed)	Sports	Scotland	Soccer Player - HF
	George	Performing Arts	USA	Actor
	Larry Thomas	Sports	Canada	Hockey Player - HF
	William Parry	Science	USA	Medicine - Nobel Laureate
Murray	Anne	Performing Arts	Canada	Singer - Canadian Music - HF
	Bill	Performing Arts	USA	Actor - Acad Award Nom
	Bill	Performing Arts	USA	Comedian
	Brian Doyle	Performing Arts	USA	Comedian
	Don	Performing Arts	USA	Actor - Acad Award Nom
	Eddie Clarence	Sports	USA	Baseball Player - HF
	George Gilbert	Arts	England	Scholar - Classical
	James Augustus Henry	Arts	England	Lexicographer
	Joseph E.	Science	USA	Medicine - Nobel Laureate
	Lindley	Arts	England	Grammarian
	Mae	Performing Arts	USA	Actress
	Robert Lindley	Sports	USA	Tennis Player - HF
Murrow	Edward Roscoe	Creative Works	USA	Journalist - Radio
Musante	Tony	Performing Arts	USA	Actor
Musburger	Brent	Creative Works	USA	Journalist - Television
Musgrave	Franklin Story	Aviation	USA	Astronaut
Musial	Stanley Frank (Stan)	Sports	USA	Baseball Player - HF
Muskie	Edmund Sixtus	Politics	USA	Senator - Maine
Musset	Louis Charles Alfred de	Creative Works	France	Poet/Writer
Musso	George Francis	Sports	USA	Football Player - HF
Mussolini	Benito	Politics	Italy	Dictator
Mussorgsky	Modest Petrovich	Creative Works	Russia	Composer
Muti	Ricardo	Performing Arts	Italy	Conductor
Mydland	Brent	Performing Arts	Germany	Rock & Roll - HF - Grateful Dead
Myers	Mike	Performing Arts	Canada	Comedian
Myerson	Bess	Performing Arts	USA	Actress
Myrdal	Alva	War & Peace	Sweden	Peace - Nobel Laureate
	Karl Gunner	Arts	Sweden	Economics - Nobel Laureate
Myrick	Don	Performing Arts	USA	Rock & Roll - HF - Earth Wind & Fire
	Julian Southall (Uncle Mike)	Sports	USA	Tennis Promoter - HF
Nabokov	Vladimir	Creative Works	USA	Writer/Teacher
Nabors	Jim	Performing Arts	USA	Actor
Nader	Michael	Performing Arts	USA	Actor
	Ralph	Politics	USA	Lawyer/Reformer
Nagel	Conrad	Performing Arts	USA	Actor
	Ernest	Arts	USA	Philosopher
Nagurski	Bronislaw (Bronko)	Sports	Canada	Football Player - HF
Nagy	Imre	Politics	Hungary	Prime Minister
	Ivan	Performing Arts	Hungary	Dancer/Composer - Ballet
Naifeh	Steven	Creative Works	USA	Author - Pulitzer
Naipaul	Vidiadhar Surajprasad	Creative Works	England	Literature - Nobel Laureate
Nair	Mira	Movie Production	India	Director
Naish	Joseph Carrol	Performing Arts	USA	Actor - Acad Award Nom

SOLVER SERIES: NAME FINDER

LAST NAME	FIRST NAME	CATEGORY	COUNTRY	FAME
Naito-Mukai	Chiaki	Aviation	Japan	Astronaut
Naldi	Nita	Performing Arts	USA	Actor
Namath	Joseph William (Joe)	Sports	USA	Football Player - HF
Namier	Lewis Bernstein	Arts	England	Historian
Nance	James (Jim)	Creative Works	USA	Journalist - Television
	Jim	Sports	USA	Football Player
	Ray Willis	Performing Arts	USA	Jazz Trumpeter - Big Band/Jazz - HF
Nanoski	John (Jukey)	Sports	USA	Soccer Player - HF
Nansen	Fridtjof	Exploration	Norway	Explorer - Arctic
	Fridtjof	War & Peace	Norway	Peace - Nobel Laureate
Napier	Charles James	War & Peace	England	General
	John	Science	Scotland	Mathematician - Logarithms
Napoles	Jose	Sports	Cuba	Boxer - HF
Narvaez	Panfilo de	Exploration	Spain	Explorer - Cuba
Nasby	Petroleum V.	Creative Works	USA	Humorist
Nash	Graham	Performing Arts	England	Rock & Roll - HF - Crosby Stills & Nash
	John	Architecture	England	Architect
	John F.	Arts	USA	Economics - Nobel Laureate
	Ogden	Creative Works	USA	Poet
Nashe	Thomas	Creative Works	England	Satirist/Pamphleteer
Nasser	Gamal Abdel	Politics	Saudi Arabia	President
Nast	Condé Montrose	Business	USA	Publishing/Magazine
	Thomas	Creative Works	USA	Cartoonist - Newspaper
Nastase	Ilie (Bucharest Bufoon)	Sports	Romania	Tennis Player - HF
Nater	Sven	Sports	USA	Basketball Player
Nathans	Daniel	Science	USA	Medicine - Nobel Laureate
Nation	Carry	Politics	USA	Agitator - Temperance
Natta	Giulio	Science	Italy	Chemistry - Nobel Laureate
Natwick	Mildred	Performing Arts	USA	Actress - Acad Award Nom
Navarro	Theodore (Fats)	Performing Arts	USA	Jazz Trumpeter - Big Band/Jazz - HF
Navrátilová	Martina	Sports	Czechoslovakia	Tennis Player - HF
Nazimova	Alla	Performing Arts	Ukraine	Actress
Neagle	Anna	Performing Arts	USA	Actress
Neal	Patricia	Performing Arts	USA	Actress - Academy Award
Neale	Alfred Earle (Greasy)	Sports	USA	Football Coach - HF
Nealon	Kevin	Performing Arts	USA	Comedian
Necker	Jacques	Business	France	Financier/Statesman
Néel	Louis Eugène Félix	Science	France	Physics - Nobel Laureate
Neely	Cam	Sports	Canada	Hockey Player - HF
Neely Jr.	Mark E.	Creative Works	USA	Author - Pulitzer
Neeson	Liam	Performing Arts	Northern Ireland	Actor - Acad Award Nom
Negri	Pola	Performing Arts	Poland	Actress
Negulesco	Jean	Movie Production	Romania	Director - Acad Award Nom
Neher	Erwin	Science	Germany	Medicine - Nobel Laureate
Nehru	Jawaharlal	Politics	India	Prime Minister
Neill	Sam	Performing Arts	Northern Ireland	Actor
Neilson	William Allan	Arts	USA	Educator/Editor
Neiman	LeRoy	Works of Art	USA	Artist
Nelligan	Kate	Performing Arts	Canada	Actress - Acad Award Nom
Nelson	Azumah	Sports	Ghana	Boxer - HF
	Byron	Sports	USA	Golfer - HF
	Clarens William	Aviation	USA	Astronaut
	David	Performing Arts	USA	Actor/Producer
	Ed	Performing Arts	USA	Actor
	Eric Hilliard (Ricky)	Performing Arts	USA	Singer - Rock & Roll - HF
	George	Performing Arts	USA	Rock & Roll - HF - The Orioles
	George Driver (Pinky)	Aviation	USA	Astronaut
	Gunnar	Performing Arts	USA	Singer
	Harriet	Performing Arts	USA	Actress
	Horatio	War & Peace	England	Admiral
	John	Sports	Scotland	Soccer Player - HF
	Judd	Performing Arts	USA	Actor
	Nathaniel	Performing Arts	USA	Rock & Roll - HF - The Flamingos

LAST NAME	FIRST NAME	CATEGORY	COUNTRY	FAME
Nelson	Ozzie	Performing Arts	USA	Actor
	Prince Rogers	Performing Arts	USA	Singer - Rock & Roll - HF
	Willie Hugh	Performing Arts	USA	Singer - Country Music - HF
Nemerov	Howard	Creative Works	USA	Poet - Pulitzer
Nen	Robb	Sports	USA	Baseball Player
Neri Vela	Rodolfo	Aviation	Mexico	Astronaut
Nernst	Walter Hermann	Science	Germany	Chemistry - Nobel Laureate
Neruda	Jan Nepomuk	Creative Works	Czechoslovakia	Poet/Writer
	Pablo	Creative Works	Chile	Literature - Nobel Laureate
Nervi	Pier Luigi	Architecture	Italy	Architect - AIA Gold Medal
Nesmith	Michael	Creative Works	USA	Song Writer
Nespoli	Paolo Angelo	Aviation	Italy	Astronaut
Ness	Eliot	Law & Order	USA	Treasury Agent
Nesselrode	Karl Robert	Politics	Russia	Statesman/Diplomat
Nessen	Ron	Creative Works	USA	Journalist - Newspaper
Nestico	Sammy	Performing Arts	USA	Composer/Arranger - Big Band/Jazz - HF
Nettles	Graig	Sports	USA	Baseball Player
Nettleton	Lois	Performing Arts	USA	Actress
Neubauer	Alfred	Sports	Czechoslovakia	Race Car Driver - HF
Neumann	Balthasar Johann	Architecture	Germany	Architect
Neutra	Richard Joseph	Architecture	Austria	Architect - AIA Gold Medal
Neuwirth	Bebe	Performing Arts	USA	Actress
Nevers	Ernest Alonzo (Ernie)	Sports	USA	Football Player - HF
Nevins	Allan	Creative Works	USA	Author - Pulitzer
Newcombe	John David	Sports	Australia	Tennis Player - HF
Newhart	Bob	Performing Arts	USA	Comedian
Newhouser	Harold (Hal)	Sports	USA	Baseball Player - HF
Newly	Anthony	Performing Arts	England	Singer
Newman	John Henry	Arts	England	Theologian/Writer
	Paul	Performing Arts	USA	Actor - Academy Award
	Randy	Creative Works	USA	Composer
Newport	Christopher	Exploration	England	Explorer - Jamestown
Newsome Jr.	Ozzie	Sports	USA	Football Player - HF
Newton	Isaac	Science	England	Mathematician/Philosopher
	Juice	Performing Arts	USA	Singer
	Wayne	Performing Arts	USA	Singer
Newton-John	Olivia	Performing Arts	England	Singer
Nexo	Martin Andersen	Creative Works	Denmark	Novelist
Ney	Michel	War & Peace	France	Military Leader
Ngor	Haing .S	Performing Arts	Cambodia	Actor - Academy Award
Nichols	Charles Augustus (Kid)	Sports	USA	Baseball Player - HF
	Ernest Loring (Red)	Performing Arts	USA	Jazz Cornetist - Big Band/Jazz - HF
	Mike	Movie Production	Germany	Director - Academy Award
	Roy Franklin	Creative Works	USA	Author - Pulitzer
Nicholson	Jack	Performing Arts	USA	Actor - Academy Award
Nicklaus	Jack	Sports	USA	Golfer - HF
Nicks	Stephanie Lynn (Stevie)	Performing Arts	USA	Rock & Roll - HF - Fleetwood Mac
Nicolle	Charles Jules Henri	Science	France	Medicine - Nobel Laureate
Nicollet	Jean	Exploration	France	Explorer - Great Lakes
Nicollier	Claude	Aviation	Switzerland	Astronaut
Nicolosi	Dick	Arts	USA	Philosopher
Niekro	Philip Henry (Phil)	Sports	USA	Baseball Player - HF
Nielson	Arthur Charles	Sports	USA	Tennis Player - HF
	Asta	Performing Arts	Germany	Actress
	Brigitte	Performing Arts	Denmark	Actress
	Leslie	Performing Arts	Canada	Actor
Niemeyer	Oscar	Architecture	Brazil	Architect - Pritzker Laureate
Niemöller	Friedrich Gustav Emil Martin	Arts	Germany	Protestant Leader
Nietzsche	Friedrich Wilhelm	Arts	Germany	Philosopher
Nieve(Nason)	Steven (Steve)	Performing Arts	England	Rock & Roll - HF- Costello & The Attractions
Nighbor	Frank	Sports	Canada	Hockey Player - HF
Nightingale	Florence	Science	England	Nurse - Crimean War
Nijinsky	Vaslav	Performing Arts	Russia	Dancer - Ballet

SOLVER SERIES: NAME FINDER

LAST NAME	FIRST NAME	CATEGORY	COUNTRY	FAME
Nikolaev	Andrian Grigoryevich	Aviation	Russia	Astronaut
Nikolaidi	Elena	Performing Arts	Greece	Singer - Opera
Nilsen	Werner	Sports	Norway	Soccer Player - HF
Nilsson	Birgit	Performing Arts	Sweden	Singer - Opera
	Harry	Performing Arts	USA	Singer
Nimitz	Chester William	War & Peace	USA	Admiral
Nimoy	Leonard	Performing Arts	USA	Actor
Niro	Robert De	Performing Arts	USA	Actor - Academy Award
Nitschke	Raymond Ernest (Ray)	Sports	USA	Football Player - HF
Nitti	Frank (The Enforcer)	Law & Order	Italy	Mafia
Niven	David	Performing Arts	England	Actor - Academy Award
	Larry	Creative Works	USA	Author - SciFi
Nixon	Otis	Sports	USA	Baseball Player
	Richard Milhous	Politics	USA	President
	Thelma Catherine Patricia	Politics	USA	First Lady
Niza	Marcos de	Exploration	Italy	Explorer - Mexico/New Mexico
Noah	Yannick	Sports	France	Tennis Player - HF
Nobel	Alfred Bernhard	Business	Sweden	Industrialist/Philanthropist
Noble	Edward Reginald (Reg)	Sports	Canada	Hockey Player - HF
	Ray	Performing Arts	England	Band Leader - Big Band/Jazz - HF
Noel-Baker	Philip J.	War & Peace	England	Peace - Nobel Laureate
Noguchi	Hideyo	Science	Japan	Bacteriologist
	Isamu	Works of Art	Japan	Sculptor
	Soichi	Aviation	Japan	Astronaut
Nol	Lon	War & Peace	Vietnam	Cambodian General
Nolan	Bob	Performing Arts	Canada	Country Music - HF - Sons of the Pioneers
	Gena Lee	Performing Arts	USA	Actress
	Lloyd	Performing Arts	USA	Actor
Noll	Charles Henry (Chuck)	Sports	USA	Football Coach - HF
Nolte	Nick	Performing Arts	USA	Actor - Acad Award Nom
Nomellini	Leo Joseph	Sports	Italy	Football Player - HF
Noonan	Chris	Movie Production	Australia	Director - Acad Award Nom
Noone	Jimmie	Performing Arts	USA	Jazz Clarinetist - Big Band/Jazz - HF
	Peter	Performing Arts	England	Singer
Noor	Lisa	Politics	Jordan	Queen
Nordau	Max Simon	Science	Germany	Physician/Writer
Nordenskjöld	Nils Adolf Erik	Exploration	Sweden	Explorer - Arctic
Norgay	Tenzing	Exploration	Nepal	Explorer - Mount Everest
Norman	Greg	Sports	Australia	Golfer - HF
	Marsha	Creative Works	USA	Dramatist - Pulitzer
Normand	Mabel	Performing Arts	USA	Actress
Norris	Chuck	Performing Arts	USA	Actor
	Frank	Creative Works	USA	Novelist
	George William	Politics	USA	Senator
	Terry Wayne	Sports	USA	Boxer - HF
Norrish	Ronald George Wreyford	Science	England	Chemistry - Nobel Laureate
North	Andy	Sports	USA	Golfer
	Douglass C.	Arts	USA	Economics - Nobel Laureate
	Frederick	Politics	England	Prime Minister
	Oliver Laurence	War & Peace	USA	Colonel
	Sheree	Performing Arts	USA	Actress
Northcliffe	Alfred Charles William	Arts	England	Publisher - Newspaper
Northrop	John Howard	Science	USA	Chemistry - Nobel Laureate
Norton	André Alice	Creative Works	USA	Author - SciFi
	Edward	Performing Arts	USA	Actor - Acad Award Nom
	Ken	Sports	USA	Boxer - HF
Norville (Norvo)	Kenneth (Red)	Performing Arts	USA	Jazz Vibraphonist - Big Band/Jazz - HF
Nôtre	André le	Architecture	France	Architect - Landscape Design
Nouvel	Jean	Architecture	France	Architect
Novak	Kim	Performing Arts	USA	Actress
	Robert	Creative Works	USA	Journalist - Newspaper
Novarro	Ramon	Performing Arts	Mexico	Actor
Novello	Don	Performing Arts	USA	Comedian

LAST NAME	FIRST NAME	CATEGORY	COUNTRY	FAME
Novello	Ivor	Performing Arts	Wales	Actor
Novotna	Jana	Sports	Czechoslovakia	Tennis Player - HF
Noyes	Alfred	Creative Works	England	Poet
Noyori	Ryoji	Science	Japan	Chemistry - Nobel Laureate
Nozick	Robert	Arts	USA	Philosopher
Ntsoelengoe	Patrick (Ace)	Sports	South Africa	Soccer Player - HF
Nugent	Ted (The Nuge)	Performing Arts	USA	Band Leader/Guitarist
Nunn	Samuel Augustus (Sam)	Politics	USA	Senator - Georgia
Nureyev	Rudolph	Performing Arts	Russia	Dancer - Ballet
Nurmi	Paavo	Sports	Finland	Olympic Runner
Nurse	Paul M.	Science	England	Medicine - Nobel Laureate
Nüsslein-Volhard	Christiane	Science	Germany	Medicine - Nobel Laureate
Nuthall-Shoemaker	Betty Kay	Sports	England	Tennis Player - HF
Nuvolari	Tazio	Sports	Italy	Race Car Driver - HF
Nye	Edgar Wilson	Creative Works	USA	Humorist
	Louis	Performing Arts	USA	Actor
	Russell Blaine	Creative Works	USA	Author - Pulitzer
Oakie	Jack	Performing Arts	USA	Actor - Acad Award Nom
Oakley	Annie	Law & Order	USA	Hunter/Sure Shot
	Berry	Performing Arts	USA	Rock & Roll - HF - Allmann Brothers Band
Oates	John	Performing Arts	USA	Singer
	Joyce Carol	Creative Works	USA	Novelist
	Titus	Politics	England	Conspirator
	Warren	Performing Arts	USA	Actor
O'Banion	Charles Dion (Deanie)	Law & Order	USA	Mafia
Oberon	Merle	Performing Arts	India	Actress - Acad Award Nom
Obregón	Alvaro	Politics	Mexico	President
O'Brian	Hugh	Performing Arts	USA	Actor
O'Brien	Edmond	Performing Arts	USA	Actor - Academy Award
	Edna	Creative Works	Ireland	Author
	Margaret	Performing Arts	USA	Actress - Academy Award
	Pat	Performing Arts	USA	Actor
	William Shamus	Sports	Scotland	Soccer Player - HF
Ocasek	Ric	Performing Arts	USA	Singer
O'Casey	Sean	Creative Works	Ireland	Playwright
Ocean	Billy	Performing Arts	West Indies	Singer
Ochoa	Severo	Science	USA	Medicine - Nobel Laureate
Ochs	Adolph Simon	Creative Works	USA	Publisher - Newspaper
	Phil	Performing Arts	USA	Singer
Ockels	Wubbo Johannes	Aviation	Netherlands	Astronaut
Ockham	William	Arts	England	Philosopher
O'Connell	Arthur	Performing Arts	USA	Actor - Acad Award Nom
	Daniel	Politics	Ireland	Nationalist Leader
O'Connor	Carroll	Performing Arts	USA	Actor
	Des	Performing Arts	England	Singer
	Donald	Performing Arts	USA	Actor
	Edwin	Creative Works	USA	Novelist/Journalist - Pulitzer
	Herbert William (Buddy)	Sports	Canada	Hockey Player - HF
	Mary Flannery	Creative Works	USA	Author
	Sandra Day	Law & Order	USA	Justice - Supreme Court
	Sinead	Performing Arts	Ireland	Singer
	Thomas Power	Politics	Ireland	Nationalist Leader
	Una	Performing Arts	Northern Ireland	Actress
O'Dalaigh	Cearbhall	Politics	Ireland	President
O'Day	Anita	Performing Arts	USA	Singer
Odets	Clifford	Creative Works	USA	Playwright
Odom	Benjamin	Performing Arts	USA	Rock & Roll - HF - The Soul Stirrers
Oe	Kenzaburo	Creative Works	Japan	Literature - Nobel Laureate
Oerter	Al	Sports	USA	Olympic Runner
Offenbach	Jacques	Creative Works	France	Composer - Operettas
Offenhauser	Fred	Sports	USA	Race Car Designer - HF
O'Flaherty	Liam	Creative Works	Ireland	Author
Ogden	Charles Kay	Arts	England	Educator/Linguist

SOLVER SERIES: NAME FINDER

LAST NAME	FIRST NAME	CATEGORY	COUNTRY	FAME
Ogilvie	Heneage	Science	England	Physician/Surgeon
	John	Arts	Scotland	Lexicographer
Ogle	Brett	Sports	Australia	Golfer
O'Grady	Sean	Sports	USA	Boxer
O'Hara	John Henry	Creative Works	USA	Author
	Maureen	Performing Arts	Ireland	Actress
O'Hare	Sarah	Performing Arts	England	Super Model
O'Herlihy	Dan	Performing Arts	Ireland	Actor - Acad Award Nom
O'Higgins	Bernardo	Politics	Chile	President
Ohlin	Bertil	Arts	Sweden	Economics - Nobel Laureate
Ohm	Georg Simon	Science	Germany	Physicist
Oistrakh	David Fyodorovich	Performing Arts	Russia	Violinist
	Igor Davidovich	Performing Arts	Russia	Violinist
O'Keefe	Dennis	Performing Arts	USA	Actor
	Georgia	Works of Art	USA	Painter
	Michael	Performing Arts	USA	Actor - Acad Award Nom
O'Kelly	Sean Thomas	Politics	Ireland	President
Okker	Tom	Sports	Netherlands	Tennis Player
Okonedo	Sophie	Performing Arts	England	Actress - Acad Award Nom
Olaff	Gene	Sports	USA	Soccer Player - HF
Olah	George A.	Science	USA	Chemistry - Nobel Laureate
Olajuwon	Hakeem	Sports	USA	Basketball Player
Oland	Warner	Performing Arts	Sweden	Actor
Olbrick	Joseph Maria	Architecture	Germany	Architect
Oldcastle	John	Politics	England	Lollard Leader
Oldenburg	Claes	Works of Art	Sweden	Sculptor - Pop
Oldfield	Bern Eli (Bernie)	Sports	USA	Race Car Driver - HF
	Michael Gordon (Mike)	Performing Arts	England	Musician/Composer
Oldman	Gary	Performing Arts	England	Actor
Olds	Ransom Eli	Business	USA	Automobile Industy
O'Leary	Brian Todd	Aviation	USA	Astronaut
Olerud	John	Sports	USA	Baseball Player
Olin	Ken	Performing Arts	USA	Actor
	Lena	Performing Arts	Sweden	Actress - Acad Award Nom
Oliva	Tony	Sports	USA	Baseball Player
Olivares	Omar Palqu	Sports	Puerto Rico	Baseball Player
	Ruben	Sports	Mexico	Boxer - HF
Oliver	Arnold (Arnie)	Sports	USA	Soccer Player - HF
	Edna May	Performing Arts	USA	Actress - Acad Award Nom
	Harold (Harry)	Sports	Canada	Hockey Player - HF
	Joe (King)	Performing Arts	USA	Band Leader - Big Band/Jazz - HF
	Len	Sports	USA	Soccer Player - HF
	Mary	Creative Works	USA	Poet - Pulitzer
	Melvin (Sy)	Performing Arts	USA	Arranger - Big Band/Jazz - HF
Olivier	Laurence	Movie Production	England	Director - Acad Award Nom
	Laurence	Performing Arts	England	Actor - Academy Award
Olmedo	Alejandre Rodrigues (Alex)	Sports	Peru	Tennis Player - HF
Olmos	Edward James	Performing Arts	USA	Actor - Acad Award Nom
Olmstead	Murray Bert	Sports	Canada	Hockey Player - HF
Olmsted	Frederick Law	Architecture	USA	Architect - Landscape Design
Olsen	Merlin Jay	Sports	USA	Football Player - HF
	Ole	Performing Arts	USA	Comedian
Olson	Carl (Bobo)	Sports	USA	Boxer - HF
	Charles	Creative Works	USA	Poet
	Nancy	Performing Arts	USA	Actress - Acad Award Nom
Olsson	Ann-Margret	Performing Arts	Sweden	Actress - Acad Award Nom
O'Mara	Kate	Performing Arts	England	Actress
O'Meara	Mark	Sports	USA	Golfer
Onassis	Aristotle	Business	Greece	Shipping Magnate
Oñate	Juan de	Exploration	Spain	Explorer - New Mexico
O'Neal	Patrick	Performing Arts	USA	Actor
	Ryan	Performing Arts	USA	Actor - Acad Award Nom
	Shaquille	Sports	USA	Basketball Player

LAST NAME	FIRST NAME	CATEGORY	COUNTRY	FAME
O'Neal	Tatum	Performing Arts	USA	Actress - Academy Award
O'Neil	Barbara	Performing Arts	USA	Actress - Acad Award Nom
	Ed	Performing Arts	USA	Actor
	Eugene Gladstone	Creative Works	USA	Literature - Nobel/Pulitzer
	Jennifer	Performing Arts	Brazil	Actress
Onetti	Juan Carlos	Creative Works	Paraguay	Novelist/Short Story Writer
Onions	Charles Talbut	Arts	England	Lexicographer
Onizuka	Ellison Shoji	Aviation	USA	Astronaut
Onnes	Heike Kamerlingh	Science	Netherlands	Physics - Nobel Laureate
Ono	Yoko	Performing Arts	Japan	Singer
	Yoko	Works of Art	Japan	Painter
Onsager	Lars	Science	USA	Chemistry - Nobel Laureate
Ontkean	Michael	Performing Arts	Canada	Actor
Oppen	George	Creative Works	USA	Poet - Pulitzer
Oppenheim	Edward Phillips	Creative Works	England	Novelist
Oppenheimer	Julius Robert	Science	USA	Physicist - Nuclear
Orbach	Jerry	Performing Arts	USA	Actor
Orbison	Roy Kelton	Performing Arts	USA	Singer - Rock & Roll - HF
Orff	Carl	Creative Works	Germany	Composer
Orio	Nicholas Di (Nick)	Sports	USA	Soccer Player - HF
Orlando	Tony	Performing Arts	USA	Singer
	Vittorio Emanuele	Politics	Italy	Premier
Orléans	Louis Phillipe Joseph	Politics	France	Revolutionist
Ormandy	Eugene	Performing Arts	Hungary	Conductor/Violinist
Ormond	Julia	Performing Arts	England	Actress
O'Rourke	James Henry (Jim)	Sports	USA	Baseball Player - HF
Orozco	José Clemente	Works of Art	Mexico	Painter
Orr	John Boyd	War & Peace	England	Peace - Nobel Laureate
	Robert Gordon (Bobby)	Sports	Canada	Hockey Player - HF
Orr (Orzechowski)	Benjamin	Performing Arts	USA	Bassist - The Cars
Ortega y Gasset	José	Creative Works	Spain	Essayist/Philosopher
Ortiz	Carlos	Sports	Puerto Rico	Boxer - HF
	Manuel	Sports	USA	Boxer - HF
	Roberto	Sports	USA	Baseball Player
Orton	John Kingsley (Joe)	Creative Works	England	Playwright
Orwell	George	Creative Works	England	Writer
Ory	Edward (Kid)	Performing Arts	USA	Band Leader - Big Band/Jazz - HF
Osborn	Henry Fairfield	Science	USA	Paleontologist/Biologist
Osborne	John James	Creative Works	England	Playwright
	Thomas Mott	Law & Order	USA	Reformer - Prison
Osbourne	Ozzy	Performing Arts	England	Singer
O'Shea	Milo	Performing Arts	Ireland	Actor
	Tessie	Performing Arts	Wales	Actress
Osheroff	Douglas D.	Science	USA	Physics - Nobel Laureate
Osler	William	Science	Canada	Physician
Oslin	Kay Toinette (KT)	Performing Arts	USA	Singer
Osment	Haley Joel	Performing Arts	USA	Actor - Acad Award Nom
Osmond	Alan	Performing Arts	USA	Singer
	Donny	Performing Arts	USA	Singer
	Jay	Performing Arts	USA	Singer
	Jimmy	Performing Arts	USA	Singer
	Ken	Performing Arts	USA	Actor
	Marie	Performing Arts	USA	Singer
	Merrill	Performing Arts	USA	Singer
	Wayne	Performing Arts	USA	Singer
Ossietzky	Carl von	Creative Works	Germany	Journalist/Pacifist
	Carl von	War & Peace	Germany	Peace - Nobel Laureate
Ostberg	Ragnar	Architecture	Sweden	Architect - AIA Gold Medal
Ostwald	Wilhelm	Science	Germany	Chemistry - Nobel Laureate
O'Sullivan	Maureen	Performing Arts	Ireland	Actress
Osuna	Rafael Herrera (Rafe)	Sports	Mexico	Tennis Player - HF
Oswald	Stephen Scott	Aviation	USA	Astronaut
Oteri	Cheri	Performing Arts	USA	Actress

SOLVER SERIES: NAME FINDER

LAST NAME	FIRST NAME	CATEGORY	COUNTRY	FAME
Otis	Carre	Performing Arts	USA	Super Model
	Elisha Graves	Science	USA	Inventor - Elevator
	James	Politics	USA	Advocate - Civil Rights
O'Toole	Annette	Performing Arts	USA	Actress
	Peter	Performing Arts	Ireland	Actor - Acad Award Nom
Ott	Melvin Thomas (Mel)	Sports	USA	Baseball Player - HF
Otto	Frei	Architecture	Germany	Architect - Jefferson Medal
	James Edwin (Jim)	Sports	USA	Football Player - HF
	Rudolph	Arts	Germany	Philosopher/Theologian
Ottorino	Respighi	Creative Works	Italy	Composer
Otway	Thomas	Creative Works	England	Dramatist
Oud	Jacobus Johannes Pieter	Architecture	Netherlands	Architect
Ouimet	Francis	Sports	USA	Golfer - HF
Ouspenskaya	Maria	Performing Arts	Russia	Actress - Acad Award Nom
Outerbridge	Mary Ewing (Mother of Tennis)	Sports	USA	Tennis Player - HF
Overmyer	Robert Franklin	Aviation	USA	Astronaut
Ovett	Steven Michael James (Steve)	Sports	England	Olympic Runner
Owen	Clive	Performing Arts	England	Actor - Acad Award Nom
	Randy Yeuell	Performing Arts	USA	Country Music - HF - Alabama
	Reginald	Performing Arts	England	Actor
	Robert	Architecture	England	Architect
	Robert	Business	England	Textile Industry
	Stephen Joseph (Steve)	Sports	USA	Football Player - HF
	Wilfred	Creative Works	England	Poet
Owens	Alvis Edgar (Buck)	Performing Arts	USA	Singer - Country Music - HF
	James (Jesse)	Sports	USA	Olympic
	John	Business	England	Textile Industry
Owings	Nathaniel Alexander	Architecture	USA	Architect - AIA Gold Medal
Oxley	John Joseph Molesworth	Exploration	Australia	Explorer - Tasmania
Oz	Amos	Creative Works	Israel	Journalist/Novelist
Ozawa	Seiji	Performing Arts	Japan	Conductor
Paar	Jack	Performing Arts	USA	Show Host
Pacino	Al	Performing Arts	USA	Actor - Academy Award
Packwood	Robert William (Bob)	Politics	USA	Senator - Oregon
Paderewski	Ignace Jan	Creative Works	Poland	Composer/Pianist
	Ignace Jan	Politics	Poland	Prime Minister
Paganini	Niccolò	Creative Works	Italy	Composer/Violinist
Pagano	Giuseppe	Architecture	Austria	Architect
Page	Alan Cedric	Sports	USA	Football Player - HF
	Geraldine	Performing Arts	USA	Actress - Academy Award
	Harlan O.	Sports	USA	Basketball Player - HF
	James Patrick (Jimmy)	Performing Arts	England	Rock & Roll - HF - Led Zepplin
	Patti	Performing Arts	USA	Singer
	Walter Hines	Creative Works	USA	Journalist/Editor/Diplomat
Pagliara	Nicola	Architecture	Italy	Architect
Pahlavi	Mohammed Reza	Politics	Iran	Shah
	Shabanu Farah	Politics	Iran	Empress
Paige	Janis	Performing Arts	USA	Actress
	Leroy Robert (Satchel)	Sports	USA	Baseball Player - HF
Pailes	William Arthur	Aviation	USA	Astronaut
Paine	Robert Treat	Politics	USA	Jurist/Statesman
	Thomas	Creative Works	USA	Writer/Revolutionary Patriot
Pakula	Alan J.	Movie Production	USA	Director - Acad Award Nom
Palade	George E.	Science	USA	Medicine - Nobel Laureate
Palance	Jack	Performing Arts	USA	Actor - Academy Award
Paley	William	Arts	England	Theologian/Philosopher
	William Samuel	Business	USA	Media Magnate
Palfrey	Sarah Hammond	Sports	USA	Tennis Player - HF
Palgrave	Francis Turner	Creative Works	England	Poet/Anthologist
Palin	Michael	Performing Arts	England	Comedian
Palladio	Andrea	Architecture	Italy	Architect
Palma	Brian De	Movie Production	USA	Director
	Ralph De	Sports	Italy	Race Car Driver - HF

LAST NAME	FIRST NAME	CATEGORY	COUNTRY	FAME
Palme	Sven Olof Joachim	Politics	Sweden	Prime Minister
Palmer	Arnold (Arnie)	Sports	USA	Golfer - HF
	Betsy	Performing Arts	USA	Actress
	Bruce	Performing Arts	Canada	Rock & Roll - HF - Buffalo Springfield
	James Alvin (Jim)	Sports	USA	Baseball Player - HF
	Lilli	Performing Arts	Poland	Actress
	Robert	Performing Arts	England	Singer
	Sandra	Sports	USA	Golfer
Palmerston	Henry John Temple	Politics	England	Prime Minister
Palminteri	Chazz	Performing Arts	USA	Actor - Acad Award Nom
Palomino	Carlos	Sports	USA	Boxer - HF
Paltrow	Gwyneth	Performing Arts	USA	Actress - Academy Award
Pániker	Salvador	Arts	Spain	Philosopher/Writer
Pankhurst	Emmeline	Politics	England	Suffragist
Panzram	Carl	Law & Order	USA	Serial Killer
Papas	Irene	Performing Arts	Greece	Actress
Papp	Joseph	Movie Production	USA	Director
	Laszlo	Sports	Hungary	Boxer - HF
Paquin	Anna	Performing Arts	Canada	Actress - Academy Award
Paracelsus	Philippus Aurelus	Science	Switzerland	Physician/Alchemist
Paré	Ambroise	Science	France	Surgeon
Parent	Bernard Marcel (Bernie)	Sports	Canada	Hockey Player - HF
Pares	Bernard	Arts	England	Historian
Pareto	Vilfredo	Arts	Switzerland	Economist/Sociologist
Paretsky	Sara	Creative Works	USA	Author - Crime Fiction
Pariani	Gino	Sports	USA	Soccer Player - HF
Parise	Ronald Anthony	Aviation	USA	Astronaut
Parish	Robert	Sports	USA	Basketball Player - HF
Park	Douglas Bradford (Brad)	Sports	Canada	Hockey Player - HF
	Mungo	Exploration	Scotland	Explorer - Africa
Parker	Alan J.	Movie Production	England	Director - Acad Award Nom
	Bonnie	Law & Order	USA	Outlaw
	Charlie	Performing Arts	USA	Jazz Saxophonist - Big Band/Jazz - HF
	Charlie Bird	Performing Arts	USA	Jazz Saxophonist
	Clarence McKay (Ace)	Sports	USA	Football Player - HF
	Dorothy	Creative Works	USA	Poet/Writer
	Eleanor	Performing Arts	USA	Actress - Acad Award Nom
	Fess	Performing Arts	USA	Actor
	Franciszek Andrew (Frank)	Sports	USA	Tennis Player - HF
	Gilbert	Creative Works	Canada	Novelist
	Graham	Performing Arts	England	Singer
	James Thomas (Jim)	Sports	USA	Football Player - HF
	Jameson	Performing Arts	USA	Actor
	Robert Leroy	Law & Order	USA	Outlaw - Butch Cassidy
	Sarah Jessica	Performing Arts	USA	Actress
	Wes	Sports	USA	Baseball Player
Parkinson	James	Science	England	Physician
Parkman	Francis	Arts	USA	Historian
Parks	Bert	Performing Arts	USA	Actor
	Larry	Performing Arts	USA	Actor - Acad Award Nom
	Suzan-Lori	Creative Works	USA	Dramatist - Pulitzer
	Wally	Sports	USA	Race Car Promoter - HF
Parnell	Charles Stewart	Politics	Ireland	Nationalist Leader
Parrington	Vernon Louis	Creative Works	USA	Author - Pulitzer
Parrish	Maxfield	Works of Art	USA	Painter/Illustrator
Parry	William Edward	Exploration	England	Explorer - Arctic
Parseghian	Ara	Sports	USA	Football Player
Parsons	Benny	Sports	USA	Race Car Driver - HF
	Estelle	Performing Arts	USA	Actress - Academy Award
	Talcott	Arts	USA	Sociologist
Parton	Dolly Rebecca	Performing Arts	USA	Singer - Country Music - HF
Partridge	Eric Honeywood	Arts	England	Lexicographer/Writer
Pascal	Blaise	Science	France	Mathematician/Philsopher

SOLVER SERIES: NAME FINDER

LAST NAME	FIRST NAME	CATEGORY	COUNTRY	FAME
Pascal	Blaise	Science	France	Physicist/Mathematician
	Jean Louis	Architecture	France	Architect - AIA Gold Medal
Pasolini	Pier Paolo	Movie Production	Italy	Director
Pass (Passalaqua)	Joseph Anthony (Joe)	Performing Arts	USA	Jazz Guitarist - Big Band/Jazz - HF
Passos	John Roderigo Dos	Creative Works	USA	Novelist/Artist
	John Roderigo Dos	Creative Works	USA	Writer
Passy	Frédéric	Arts	France	Economist
	Frédéric	War & Peace	France	Peace - Nobel Laureate
	Paul Édouard	Arts	France	Phonetician
Pasternak	Boris Leonidovich	Creative Works	Russia	Literature - Nobel Laureate
Pasteur	Louis	Science	France	Chemist/Bacteriologist
Pastrano	Willie	Sports	USA	Boxer - HF
Pate	Jerry	Sports	USA	Golfer
	Steve	Sports	USA	Golfer
Patenaude	Bertram Albert (Bert)	Sports	USA	Soccer Player - HF
Pater	Walter Horatio	Creative Works	England	Essayist/Critic
Pathé	Charles	Movie Production	France	Director
Patinkin	Mandy	Performing Arts	USA	Actor
Patitz	Tatjana	Performing Arts	Sweden	Super Model
Patmore	Coventry Kersey Dighton	Creative Works	England	Poet
Paton	Alan Stewart	Creative Works	South Africa	Author
Patou	Jean	Business	France	Fragrance Designer
Patrick	John	Creative Works	USA	Dramatist - Pulitzer
	Joseph Lynn	Sports	Canada	Hockey Player - HF
	Lester	Sports	Canada	Hockey Player - HF
Patterson	Floyd	Sports	USA	Boxer - HF
	Gerald Leighton	Sports	Australia	Tennis Player - HF
	James	Creative Works	USA	Author
Patti	Adelina	Performing Arts	Italy	Singer - Opera
	Carlotta	Performing Arts	Italy	Singer - Opera
Patton	George S	War & Peace	USA	General
Patty	John Edward (Budge)	Sports	USA	Tennis Player - HF
Paul	Wolfgang	Science	Germany	Physics - Nobel Laureate
Paul (Polfuss)	Lester William (Les)	Performing Arts	USA	Guitarist - Big Band/Jazz - HF
	Lester William (Les)	Performing Arts	USA	Rock & Roll - HF - Les Paul & Mary Ford
Pauley	Margaret Jane	Creative Works	USA	Journalist - Television
Pauli	Wolfgang	Science	Austria	Physics - Nobel Laureate
Pauling	Linus Carl	Science	USA	Chemistry - Nobel Laureate
	Linus Carl	War & Peace	USA	Peace - Nobel Laureate
Pavan	Marisa	Performing Arts	Italy	Actress - Acad Award Nom
Pavarotti	Luciano	Performing Arts	Italy	Singer - Opera
Pavin	Corey	Sports	USA	Golfer
Pavlov	Ivan Petrovich	Science	Russia	Medicine - Nobel Laureate
Pavlova	Anna	Performing Arts	Russia	Dancer - Ballerina
Pawelczyk	James Anthony	Aviation	USA	Astronaut
Pawley	William	Business	USA	Transportation Industry
Paxinou	Katina	Performing Arts	Greece	Actress - Academy Award
Paxson	Frederic L.	Creative Works	USA	Author - Pulitzer
Paxton	Joseph	Architecture	England	Architect
Paycheck	Johnny	Performing Arts	USA	Singer
Payette	Julie	Aviation	Canada	Astronaut
Paymer	David	Performing Arts	USA	Actor - Acad Award Nom
Payne	Alexander	Movie Production	USA	Director - Acad Award Nom
	Freda	Performing Arts	USA	Singer
Payton	Gary Eugene	Aviation	USA	Astronaut
	Lawrence	Performing Arts	USA	Rock & Roll - HF - The Four Tops
	Walter Jerry	Sports	USA	Football Player - HF
Paz	Octavio	Creative Works	Mexico	Literature - Nobel Laureate
Peabody	George	Business	USA	Merchant/Philanthropist
Peacock	Thomas Love	Creative Works	England	Poet/Novelist
Peale	Charles Willson	Works of Art	USA	Painter - Portrait
	Rembrandt	Works of Art	USA	Painter - Neoclassical
Pearl (Colley)	Sarah Ophelia (Minnie)	Performing Arts	USA	Comedian - Country Music - HF

LAST NAME	FIRST NAME	CATEGORY	COUNTRY	FAME
Pears	Peter	Performing Arts	England	Singer - Opera
Pearson	Cyril	Business	England	Publishing
	David	Sports	USA	Race Car Driver - HF
	Lester Bowles	Politics	Canada	Prime Minister
	Lester Bowles	War & Peace	Canada	Peace - Nobel Laureate
Peart	Neil	Performing Arts	Canada	Canadian Music - HF - Rush
Peary	Robert Edwin	Exploration	USA	Explorer - North Pole
Pease	Edward	Business	England	Railway Magnate
Peck	Gregory	Performing Arts	USA	Actor - Academy Award
Pedersen	Charles J.	Science	USA	Chemistry - Nobel Laureate
Pedroza	Eusebio	Sports	Panama	Boxer - HF
Peebles	Mario Van	Performing Arts	Mexico	Actor
Peel	Robert	Politics	England	Prime Minister
Peel Sr.	Robert	Business	England	Textile Industry
Peele	George	Creative Works	England	Dramatist
Peeples	Nia	Performing Arts	USA	Actress
Peerce	Jan	Performing Arts	USA	Singer - Opera
Peete	Calvin	Sports	USA	Golfer
Pei	Ieoh Ming	Architecture	USA	Architect - Pritzker/ AIA Gold
Peirce	Charles Sanders	Science	USA	Mathematician/Philosopher
Pelé	Edson Arantes	Sports	Brazil	Soccer Player - HF
Pell	Claiborne de Borda	Politics	USA	Senator - Rhode Island
	Theodore Roosevelt	Sports	USA	Tennis Player - HF
Pelli	César	Architecture	Argentina	Architect - AIA Gold Medal
Peltier	Jean	Science	France	Physicist
Peña	Tony	Sports	USA	Baseball Player
Pendergrass	Teddy	Performing Arts	USA	Singer
Penick	Harvey	Sports	USA	Golf Teacher - HF
Penn	Arthur	Movie Production	USA	Director - Acad Award Nom
	Sean	Performing Arts	USA	Actor - Academy Award
	William	Exploration	England	Leader - Quakers
Pennel	Joseph	Works of Art	USA	Etcher/Illustrator/Writer
Pennock	Herbert Jefferis (Herb)	Sports	USA	Baseball Player - HF
Penrose	Roger	Science	England	Physicist/Mathematician
Penske	Roger	Sports	USA	Race Car Driver - HF
Penzias	Arno Allan	Science	USA	Physics - Nobel Laureate
Pep	Willie (Will O' the Wisp)	Sports	USA	Boxer - HF
Pepin	Jean-Pierre	Sports	France	Soccer Player
Peppard	George	Performing Arts	USA	Actor
Pepper Jr.	Arthur Edward (Art)	Performing Arts	USA	Jazz Saxophonist - Big Band/Jazz - HF
Pepys	Samuel	Creative Works	England	Writer - Diary
Percy	Henry	War & Peace	England	Soldier/Rebel
	Thomas	Arts	England	Collector - Ballads
	Walker	Creative Works	USA	Author
Perelman	Sidney Joseph	Creative Works	USA	Humorist
Peres	Shimon	Politics	Israel	Prime Minister
	Shimon	War & Peace	Israel	Peace - Nobel Laureate
Peretti	Elsa	Business	Italy	Designer - Jewelery
Perez	Juan	Exploration	Spain	Explorer - America East Coast
	Pascual	Sports	Argentina	Boxer - HF
	Rosie	Performing Arts	USA	Actress - Acad Award Nom
Pérez	Antanasio (Tony)	Sports	Cuba	Baseball Player - HF
Pergolesi	Giovanni Battista	Creative Works	Italy	Composer
Perkins	Anthony	Performing Arts	USA	Actor - Acad Award Nom
	Elizabeth	Performing Arts	USA	Actress
	Frances	Arts	USA	Social Worker
	John	Performing Arts	Canada	Canadian Music - HF - The Crew Cuts
	Ray	Performing Arts	Canada	Canadian Music - HF - The Crew Cuts
Perkins (Perkings)	Carl Lee	Performing Arts	USA	Singer - Rock & Roll - HF
Perl	Martin L.	Science	USA	Physics - Nobel Laureate
Perlman	Itzhak	Performing Arts	Israel	Violinist
	Rhea	Performing Arts	USA	Actress
	Ron	Performing Arts	USA	Actor

SOLVER SERIES: NAME FINDER

LAST NAME	FIRST NAME	CATEGORY	COUNTRY	FAME
Peron	Evita (Eva)	Politics	Argentina	First Lady
Perón Sosa	Juan Domingo	Politics	Argentina	President
Perot	Henry Ross	Business	USA	Computer Industry
	Henry Ross	Politics	USA	Presidential Candidate
Perouse	Jean-François de la	Exploration	France	Explorer - Hawaii
Perrault	Charles	Creative Works	France	Writer/Compiler - Fairy Tales
Perreault	Gilbert (Gil)	Sports	Canada	Hockey Player - HF
Perret	Auguste	Architecture	France	Architect - AIA Gold Medal
Perrin	Jean Baptiste	Science	France	Physics - Nobel Laureate
	Philippe	Aviation	France	Astronaut
Perrine	Valerie	Performing Arts	USA	Actress - Acad Award Nom
Perry	Fletcher Joseph (Joe)	Sports	USA	Football Player - HF
	Frank	Movie Production	USA	Director - Acad Award Nom
	Frederick John (Fred)	Sports	England	Tennis Player - HF
	Gaylord Jackson	Sports	USA	Baseball Player - HF
	Luke	Performing Arts	USA	Actor
	Matthew	War & Peace	USA	Naval Officer
	Oliver Hazard	War & Peace	USA	Naval Officer
	Ralph Barton	Creative Works	USA	Author - Pulitzer
	Steve	Performing Arts	USA	Singer
Perry (Pereira)	Anthony Joseph (Joe)	Performing Arts	USA	Rock & Roll - HF - Aerosmith
Perse	Saint-John	Creative Works	France	Literature - Nobel Laureate
Pershing	John Joseph	Creative Works	USA	Author - Pulitzer
	John Joseph	War & Peace	USA	General
Persico	Edoardo	Architecture	Italy	Architect
Persoff	Nehemiah	Performing Arts	Israel	Actor
Perugino	Il	Works of Art	Italy	Painter
Perutz	Max Ferdinand	Science	England	Chemistry - Nobel Laureate
Peruzzi	Baldassarre	Architecture	Italy	Architect
Pesci	Joe	Performing Arts	USA	Actor - Academy Award
Pestalozzi	Johann Heinrich	Arts	Switzerland	Educational Reformer
Pestova	Daniela	Performing Arts	Czechoslovakia	Super Model
Pétain	Henri Philippe	Politics	France	Premier
Peterkin	Julia	Creative Works	USA	Novelist - Pulitzer
Peters	Bernadette	Performing Arts	USA	Singer
	Roberta	Performing Arts	USA	Singer - Opera
	Susan	Performing Arts	USA	Actress - Acad Award Nom
Peterson	Donald Herod	Aviation	USA	Astronaut
	Oscar Emmanuel	Performing Arts	Canada	Jazz Pianist - Big Band/Jazz - HF -
	Oscar Emmanuel	Performing Arts	Canada	Jazz Pianist - Canadian Music - HF
	Ronnie	Sports	Sweden	Race Car Driver - HF
	Wolfgang	Movie Production	Germany	Director - Acad Award Nom
Petit	Roland	Creative Works	France	Choreographer
Petöfi	Sándor	Creative Works	Hungary	Poet/Patriot
Petrarch	Francesco	Creative Works	Italy	Poet/Scholar
Petrie	William Matthew Flinders	Arts	England	Archaeologist/Egyptologist
Petrosian	Tigran	Games	Armenia	Chess Player
Petrovic	Drazen	Sports	Croatia	Basketball Player - HF
Pettiford	Oscar	Performing Arts	USA	Bassist/Cellist - Big Band/Jazz - HF
Pettit	Robert L.	Sports	USA	Basketball Player - HF
Pettitt	Thomas (Tom)	Sports	England	Tennis Player - HF
Petty	Kyle	Sports	USA	Race Car Driver
	Lee	Sports	USA	Race Car Driver - HF
	Lori	Performing Arts	USA	Actress
	Richard (The King)	Sports	USA	Race Car Driver - HF
	Tom	Performing Arts	USA	Rock & Roll - HF - Heart Breakers
Pevsner	Antoine	Works of Art	Russia	Sculptor/Painter
	Nikolaus	Architecture	England	Architect - Jefferson Medal
Pfeiffer	Michelle	Performing Arts	USA	Actress - Acad Award Nom
Phelan	James	Business	USA	Banking
Phillip	Andy	Sports	USA	Basketball Player - HF
	Arthur	Exploration	England	Explorer - Australia
Phillips	Emo	Performing Arts	USA	Comedian

LAST NAME	FIRST NAME	CATEGORY	COUNTRY	FAME
Phillips	Holly Michelle	Performing Arts	USA	Rock & Roll - HF - Mamas & Papas
	Jayne Anne	Creative Works	USA	Author
	John Edmund	Performing Arts	USA	Rock & Roll - HF - Mamas & Papas
	Lou Diamond	Performing Arts	Philippines	Actor
	MacKenzie	Performing Arts	USA	Singer
	Stephen	Creative Works	England	Dramatist - Poetic
	Thomas N. (Tommy)	Sports	Canada	Hockey Player - HF
	Wendell	Politics	USA	Abolitionist
	William D.	Science	USA	Physics - Nobel Laureate
Phoenix	Joaquin	Performing Arts	Puerto Rico	Actor - Acad Award Nom
	River	Performing Arts	USA	Actor - Acad Award Nom
Piacentini	Marcello	Architecture	Italy	Architect
Piaf	Edith	Performing Arts	France	Singer
Piaget	Jean	Arts	Switzerland	Psychologist
Piano	Renzo	Architecture	Italy	Architect - Pritzker Laureate
Picasso	Pablo	Works of Art	Spain	Sculptor/Painter - Cubist
Piccard	Auguste	Science	Switzerland	Physicist
	Jacques	Exploration	Switzerland	Explorer - Marine
	Jean Félix	Science	Switzerland	Physicist
Pickens	Thomas Boone	Business	USA	Oil Industry
Pickering	Edward Charles	Science	USA	Physicist/Astronomer
	William Henry	Science	USA	Astronomer
Pickett	George Edward	War & Peace	USA	Confederate General
	Wilson	Performing Arts	USA	Singer - Rock & Roll - HF
Pickford	Mary	Performing Arts	Canada	Actress - Academy Award
Pidgeon	Walter	Performing Arts	Canada	Actor - Acad Award Nom
Pierce	Charles Sanders	Arts	USA	Philosopher
	Franklin	Politics	USA	President
	Jane Mears	Politics	USA	First Lady
	Michael Webb	Performing Arts	USA	Singer - Country Music - HF
Piercy	Marge	Creative Works	USA	Poet
Pietilä	Reima	Architecture	Finland	Architect
Pietrangeli	Nicola (Nicky)	Sports	Italy	Tennis Player - HF
Pihos	Peter Louis (Pete)	Sports	USA	Football Player - HF
Pike	Zebulon Montgomery	Exploration	USA	Explorer - Mississippi River
Pikionis	Dimitris	Architecture	Greece	Architect
Pilote	Pierre Paul	Sports	Canada	Hockey Player - HF
Pinchot	Bronson	Performing Arts	USA	Actor
Pinckney	Charles Cotes-worth	Politics	USA	Statesman/Diplomat
Pineda	Alonso Alvarez de	Exploration	Spain	Explorer - Gulf of Mexico
Pinero	Arthur Wing	Creative Works	England	Playwright
Pingree	Hazen	Business	USA	Manufacturing Industry
Pinkerton	Allan	Law & Order	USA	Private Detective
Pinkett-Smith	Jada	Performing Arts	USA	Actress
Pinkney	Bill	Performing Arts	USA	Rock & Roll - HF - The Drifters
Pinsent	Gordon	Performing Arts	Canada	Actor
Pinter	Harold	Creative Works	England	Literature - Nobel Laureate
	Harold	Movie Production	England	Director
Pinza	Ezio	Performing Arts	Italy	Singer - Opera
Pinzón	Martin Alonso	Exploration	Spain	Explorer - Caribbean
	Vincente Yáñez	Exploration	Spain	Explorer - Caribbean
Pippen	Scottie	Sports	USA	Basketball Player
Piquet	Nelson	Sports	Brazil	Race Car Driver - HF
Pirandello	Luigi	Creative Works	Italy	Literature - Nobel Laureate
Piranesi	Giovanni Battista	Architecture	Italy	Architect
Pire	Georges	War & Peace	Belgium	Peace - Nobel Laureate
Pisano	Nicola	Works of Art	Italy	Sculptor/Architect
Piscator	Erwin	Movie Production	USA	Director/Producer- Theatrical
Piscopo	Joe	Performing Arts	USA	Comedian
Pissarro	Camille	Works of Art	France	Painter
Piston	Walter	Creative Works	USA	Composer
Pitman	Isaac	Science	England	Inventor - Shorthand
Pitney	Gene	Performing Arts	USA	Singer - Rock & Roll - HF

SOLVER SERIES: NAME FINDER

LAST NAME	FIRST NAME	CATEGORY	COUNTRY	FAME
Pitre	Didier	Sports	Canada	Hockey Player - HF
Pitt	Brad	Performing Arts	USA	Actor - Acad Award Nom
	William	Politics	England	Prime Minister
Pitts	Zasu	Performing Arts	USA	Actress
Pizarro	Francisco	Exploration	Spain	Explorer - South America
	Francisco	War & Peace	Spain	Conquistador
Plamondon	Luciano	Performing Arts	Canada	Francophone Lyricist - Canadian Music - HF
Planck	Max Karl Ernst Ludwig	Science	Germany	Physicist - Nobel Prize
Plank	Edward Stewart (Eddie)	Sports	USA	Baseball Player - HF
Plant	Robert Anthony	Performing Arts	England	Rock & Roll - HF - Led Zepplin
Plante	Joseph Jacques	Sports	Canada	Hockey Player - HF
Plater-Zyberk	Elizabeth	Architecture	USA	Architect - Jefferson Medal
Plath	Sylvia	Creative Works	USA	Poet - Pulitzer
Platini	Michel	Sports	France	Soccer Player - HF
Player	Gary	Sports	South Africa	Golfer - HF
Pleasence	Donald	Performing Arts	England	Actor
Plecnik	Joze	Architecture	Slovenia	Architect
Pleshette	Suzanne	Performing Arts	USA	Actress
Plowright	Joan	Performing Arts	England	Actress - Acad Award Nom
Plumb	Eve	Performing Arts	USA	Actress
Plummer	Amanda	Performing Arts	USA	Actress
	Christopher	Performing Arts	Canada	Actor
Plunkett	Jim	Sports	USA	Football Player
Podrecca	Boris	Architecture	Yugoslavia	Architect
Poe	Edgar Allan	Creative Works	USA	Poet/Short Story Writer/Critic
Poelzig	Hans	Architecture	Germany	Architect
Pogue	William Reid	Aviation	USA	Astronaut
Pohl	Frederick	Creative Works	USA	Author - SciFi
Poincaré	Jules Henri	Science	France	Mathematician
	Raymond	Politics	France	President
Pointer	Anita	Performing Arts	USA	Singer
	Bonnie	Performing Arts	USA	Singer
	June	Performing Arts	USA	Singer
	Ruth	Performing Arts	USA	Singer
Poitier	Sidney	Performing Arts	USA	Actor - Academy Award
Polanski	Roman	Movie Production	France	Director - Academy Award
Polanyi	John C.	Science	Canada	Chemistry - Nobel Laureate
Pole	Reginald	Arts	England	Archbishop of Canterbury
Politzer	Hugh David	Science	USA	Physics - Nobel Laureate
Polk	James	Politics	USA	President
	Sarah	Politics	USA	First Lady
Pollack	Ben	Performing Arts	USA	Band Leader - Big Band/Jazz - HF
	Sydney	Movie Production	USA	Director - Acad Award Nom
Pollard	Frederick Douglass (Fritz)	Sports	USA	Football Player - HF
	James C.	Sports	USA	Basketball Player - HF
	Michael J.	Performing Arts	USA	Actor - Acad Award Nom
Pollock	Frederick	Law & Order	England	Jurist/Writer
	Jackson	Works of Art	USA	Painter - Abstract
Polo	Marco	Exploration	Italy	Explorer - East Asia
Ponchielli	Amilcare	Creative Works	Italy	Composer - Opera
Ponicsan	Darryl	Creative Works	USA	Screenwriter
Ponomariov	Ruslan	Games	Ukraine	Chess Player
Pons	Lily	Performing Arts	France	Singer - Opera
Ponselle	Rosa	Performing Arts	USA	Singer - Opera
Pont	Éleuthère Irénée du	Business	USA	Industrialist
	Margaret Evelyn Osborne du	Sports	USA	Tennis Player - HF
Ponte	Laura	Performing Arts	Spain	Super Model
	Lorenzo da	Creative Works	Italy	Poet/Librettist
Pontecorvo	Gillo	Movie Production	Italy	Director - Acad Award Nom
Pontes	Marcos	Aviation	Brazil	Astronaut
Ponti	Carlo	Movie Production	Italy	Director
	Franco	Architecture	Switzerland	Architect
	Gio	Architecture	Italy	Architect

LAST NAME	FIRST NAME	CATEGORY	COUNTRY	FAME
Pontoppidan	Henrik	Creative Works	Denmark	Literature - Nobel Laureate
Poole	Ernest	Creative Works	USA	Novelist - Pulitzer
Pope	Alexander	Creative Works	England	Poet
	John	War & Peace	USA	Union General - Civil War
Pople	John A.	Science	England	Chemistry - Nobel Laureate
Popovich	Pavel Romanovich	Aviation	Russia	Astronaut
Popper	Karl Raimund	Arts	Austria	Philosopher
Porphyrios	Demetri	Architecture	Greece	Architect
Porro	Ricardo	Architecture	Cuba	Architect
Porsche	Ferdinand	Sports	Bohemia	Race Car Designer - HF
Porson	Richard	Arts	England	Scholar - Classical
Portaluppi	Piero	Architecture	Italy	Architect
Porter	Cole	Creative Works	USA	Composer - Popular Songs
	David Dixon	War & Peace	USA	Union Admiral - Civil War
	George	Science	England	Chemistry - Nobel Laureate
	Katherine Anne	Creative Works	USA	Novelist - Pulitzer
	Rodney	Science	England	Medicine - Nobel Laureate
Portman	Natalie	Performing Arts	Israel	Actress - Acad Award Nom
Portoghesi	Paolo	Architecture	Italy	Architect
Portolá	Gaspar de	Exploration	Spain	Explorer - California
Portzamparc	Christian de	Architecture	France	Architect - Pritzker Laureate
Posada	Jorge	Sports	Puerto Rica	Baseball Player
Post	Emily	Creative Works	USA	Author
	George Brown	Architecture	USA	Architect - AIA Gold Medal
	Markie	Performing Arts	USA	Actress
	Mike	Creative Works	USA	Composer
	Wiley	Aviation	USA	Pilot - Around the World
Postlethwaite	Pete	Performing Arts	England	Actor - Acad Award Nom
Poston	Tom	Performing Arts	USA	Comedian
Potok	Chaim	Creative Works	USA	Author
Potter	Beatrix	Creative Works	England	Writer/Illustrator - Children's Books
	David M.	Creative Works	USA	Author - Pulitzer
	Paul	Works of Art	Netherlands	Painter
Potts	Annie	Performing Arts	USA	Actress
Potvin	Denis Charles	Sports	Canada	Hockey Player - HF
Pouillon	Fernand	Architecture	France	Architect
Poulenc	Francis Jean Marcel	Creative Works	France	Composer
Pound	Ezra Loomis	Creative Works	USA	Poet
	Louise	Arts	USA	Linguist/Folklorist
	Roscoe	Arts	USA	Educator/Legal Scholar
Poundstone	Paula	Performing Arts	USA	Comedian
Poussin	Nicolas	Works of Art	France	Painter
Powell	Bud	Performing Arts	USA	Jazz Pianist - Big Band/Jazz - HF
	Cecil Frank	Science	England	Physics - Nobel Laureate
	Colin Luther	Politics	USA	Secretary of State
	Colin Luther	War & Peace	USA	General
	Dick	Performing Arts	USA	Actor
	Eleanor	Performing Arts	USA	Actress/Dancer
	Gordon (Specs)	Performing Arts	USA	Jazz Trombonist - Big Band/Jazz - HF
	Jane	Performing Arts	USA	Actress
	John Wesley	Exploration	USA	Explorer - America Deserts
	Lewis Franklin	Law & Order	USA	Justice - Supreme Court
	Sumner Chilton	Creative Works	USA	Author - Pulitzer
	William	Performing Arts	USA	Actor - Acad Award Nom
	William	Performing Arts	USA	Rock & Roll - HF - The O'Jays
	William	Performing Arts	USA	Rock & Roll - HF - The O'Jays
Powell (Epstein)	Melvin (Mel)	Performing Arts	USA	Jazz Pianist - Big Band/Jazz - HF
Power	Samantha	Creative Works	Ireland	Author - Pulitzer
	Tyrone	Performing Arts	USA	Actor
Powers	Stefannie	Performing Arts	USA	Actress
Powys	John Cowper	Creative Works	England	Novelist/Critic
	Llewelyn	Creative Works	England	Author
	Theodore Francis	Creative Works	England	Novelist

SOLVER SERIES: NAME FINDER

LAST NAME	FIRST NAME	CATEGORY	COUNTRY	FAME
Prado	Dámaso Peréz (Mambo King)	Performing Arts	Cuba	Pianist
Prandtauer	Jakob	Architecture	Austria	Architect
Prater	Dave	Performing Arts	USA	Rock & Roll - HF - Sam & Dave
Pratt	Walter (Babe)	Sports	Canada	Hockey Player - HF
Predock	Antoine	Architecture	USA	Architect
Pregl	Fritz	Science	Austria	Chemistry - Nobel Laureate
Prelog	Vladimir	Science	Switzerland	Chemistry - Nobel Laureate
Preminger	Otto	Movie Production	Austria	Director - Acad Award Nom
Prentice	Archibald	Business	England	Publishing
Prentiss	Paula	Performing Arts	USA	Actress
Prescott	Edward C.	Arts	USA	Economics - Nobel Laureate
	William Hickling	Arts	USA	Historian
Presley	Elvis Aaron	Performing Arts	USA	Singer - Country Music - HF
	Elvis Aaron	Performing Arts	USA	Singer - Rock & Roll - HF
	Priscilla	Performing Arts	USA	Actress
Preston	Billy	Performing Arts	USA	Pianist/Writer
	Robert	Performing Arts	USA	Actor - Acad Award Nom
Previn	André	Performing Arts	Germany	Conductor/Composer
Prey	Hermann	Performing Arts	Germany	Singer - Opera
Price	Alan	Performing Arts	England	Rock & Roll - HF - The Animals
	Lloyd	Performing Arts	USA	Singer - Rock & Roll - HF
	Mary Leontyne	Performing Arts	USA	Singer - Opera
	Nick	Sports	South Africa	Golfer - HF
	Ray Noble	Performing Arts	USA	Singer - Country Music - HF
	Vincent	Performing Arts	USA	Actor
Pride	Charley Frank	Performing Arts	USA	Singer - Country Music - HF
	Thomas	War & Peace	England	Army Officer
Priestley	John Boynton	Creative Works	England	Novelist/Playwright/Critic
	Joseph	Science	England	Scientist/Theologian
Prigogine	Ilya	Science	Belgium	Chemistry - Nobel Laureate
Prima	Louis	Performing Arts	USA	Band Leader - Big Band/Jazz - HF
Primeau	Joseph (Joe)	Sports	Canada	Hockey Player - HF
Prince	Hal	Movie Production	USA	Director
Principal	Victoria	Performing Arts	Japan	Actress
Pringle	Henry F.	Creative Works	USA	Author - Pulitzer
Prinze	Freddie	Performing Arts	USA	Actor
Prinze Jr.	Freddie	Performing Arts	USA	Actor
Prior	Matthew	Creative Works	England	Poet
Profaci	Joseph (Hammer)	Law & Order	Italy	Mafia
Prokhorov	Aleksandr Mikhailovich	Science	Russia	Physics - Nobel Laureate
Prokofiev	Sergei	Creative Works	Russia	Composer
Pronovost	Marcel	Sports	Canada	Hockey Player - HF
Prosky	Robert	Performing Arts	USA	Actor
Prost	Alain (The Professor)	Sports	France	Race Car Driver - HF
Proudhon	Pierre Joseph	Arts	France	Socialist/Writer
Proulx	Edna Annie	Creative Works	USA	Author - Novelist
Proust	Marcel	Creative Works	France	Novelist
Prudhomme	Don (The Snake)	Sports	USA	Race Car Driver - HF
	Sully	Creative Works	France	Literature - Nobel Laureate
Prud'hon	Pierre Paul	Works of Art	France	Painter/Draftsman
Prusiner	Stanley B.	Science	USA	Medicine - Nobel Laureate
Pryce	Jonathon	Performing Arts	Wales	Actor
Pryor	Aaron	Sports	USA	Boxer - HF
	Richard	Performing Arts	USA	Comedian
Pucci	Emilio	Business	Italy	Fashion Designer
Puccini	Giacomo	Creative Works	Italy	Composer - Opera
Puckett	Kirby	Sports	USA	Baseball Player - HF
Puente	Tito	Performing Arts	Puerto Rica	Jazz Drummer - Big Band/Jazz - HF
Pulaski	Casimir	War & Peace	Poland	General - Am. Revolutionary Army
Pulford	Harvey	Sports	Canada	Hockey Player - HF
	Robert Jesse (Bob)	Sports	Canada	Hockey Player - HF
Pulitzer	Joseph	Business	USA	Publishing/Philanthropist
	Joseph	Creative Works	USA	Journalist - Newspaper

LAST NAME	FIRST NAME	CATEGORY	COUNTRY	FAME
Puller Jr.	Lewis Burwell	Creative Works	USA	Author - Pulitzer
Pullman	George Mortimer	Business	USA	Manufacturing - Pullman Car
Pupin	Michael Idvorsky	Creative Works	USA	Author - Pulitzer
	Michael Idvorsky	Science	USA	Physicist/Inventor
Purcell	Edward Mills	Science	USA	Physics - Nobel Laureate
	Henry	Creative Works	England	Composer
	Sarah	Performing Arts	USA	Actress
Purini	Franco	Architecture	Italy	Architect
Pusey	Merlo J.	Creative Works	USA	Author - Pulitzer
Pushkin	Aleksandr Sergeyevich	Creative Works	Russia	Poet
Puskas	Ferenc	Sports	Hungary	Soccer Player - HF
Putnam	Israel	War & Peace	USA	General - Revolutionary War
Puzo	Mario	Creative Works	USA	Author
Pyle	Ernest Taylor (Ernie)	Creative Works	USA	Journalist - Newspaper
	Howard	Creative Works	USA	Writer/Illustrator
Pym	John	Politics	England	Parliamentary Leader
Pynchon Jr.	Thomas Ruggles	Creative Works	USA	Novelist
Qaddafi	Muammar Abu Minyar al	Politics	Libya	Head of State
Qawi	Dwight Muhammad	Sports	USA	Boxer - HF
Quackenbush	Hubert George (Bill)	Sports	Canada	Hockey Player - HF
Quadrio	Giovanni Battista	Architecture	Italy	Architect
Quaid	Dennis	Performing Arts	USA	Actor
	Randy	Performing Arts	USA	Actor - Acad Award Nom
Quaife (The Kinks)	Peter	Performing Arts	England	Rock & Roll - HF - The Kinks
Quarles	Francis	Creative Works	England	Poet
Quaroni	Ludovico	Architecture	Italy	Architect
Quasimodo	Salvatore	Creative Works	Italy	Literature - Nobel Laureate
Quayle	Anthony	Performing Arts	England	Actor - Acad Award Nom
	James Danforth	Politics	USA	Vice-President
Queler	Eve Rabin	Performing Arts	USA	Conductor
Quesnay	François	Science	France	Physician/Economist
Questel	Mae	Performing Arts	USA	Singer
Quezon	Manuel Luis	Politics	Philippines	President
Quian	Zhang	Exploration	China	Explorer - Central Asia
Quidde	Ludwig	War & Peace	Germany	Peace - Nobel Laureate
Quiller-Couch	Arthur Thomas	Creative Works	England	Writer
Quincey	Thomas De	Creative Works	England	Essayist/Critic
Quincy	Antoine Quatremère de	Architecture	France	Architect
	Josiah	War & Peace	USA	Patriot - Revolutionary
Quindland	Anna	Creative Works	USA	Author
Quine	Willard Van Orman	Arts	USA	Philosopher
Quinet	Edgar	Arts	France	Philosopher/Poet/Historian
Quinlan	Kathlees	Performing Arts	USA	Actress - Acad Award Nom
Quinn	Aidan	Performing Arts	USA	Actor
	Aileen	Performing Arts	USA	Actress
	Anthony	Performing Arts	Mexico	Actor - Academy Award
	Jane Bryant	Creative Works	USA	Journalist - Newspaper
Quiros	Pedro Fernandez de	Exploration	Portugal	Explorer - South Pacific
Quist	Adrian Karl	Sports	Australia	Tennis Player - HF
Ra (Blount)	Herman Poole (Sun)	Performing Arts	USA	Band Leader - Big Band/Jazz - HF
Rabanne	Paco	Business	France	Fashion Designer
Rabbitt	Eddie	Performing Arts	USA	Singer
Rabe	David	Creative Works	USA	Screenwriter/Playwright
Rabelais	François	Creative Works	France	Satirist/Humorist
Rabi	Isidor Isaac	Science	USA	Physics - Nobel Laureate
Rabin	Yitzhak	Politics	Israel	Prime Minister
	Yitzhak	War & Peace	Israel	Peace - Nobel Laureate
Rachins	Alan	Performing Arts	USA	Actor
Rachmaninoff	Sergi Vassilievich	Creative Works	Russia	Composer/Conductor/Violinist
Racine	Jean Baptiste	Creative Works	France	Poet/Dramatist
Rackham	Arthur	Creative Works	England	Illustrator
Radbourn	Charles Gardner (Old Hoss)	Sports	USA	Baseball Player - HF
Radcliffe	Ann	Creative Works	England	Author

SOLVER SERIES: NAME FINDER

LAST NAME	FIRST NAME	CATEGORY	COUNTRY	FAME
Radcliffe	William	Business	England	Textile Industry
Radford	Michael	Movie Production	India	Director - Acad Award Nom
Radisson	Pierre Esprit	Exploration	France	Explorer - Minnesota
Radner	Gilda	Performing Arts	USA	Comedian
Rae	Cassidy	Performing Arts	USA	Actress
	Charlotte	Performing Arts	USA	Actress
	John	Exploration	Scotland	Explorer - Arctic
Raeburn	Henry	Works of Art	Scotland	Painter
Raffaello	Sanzio	Architecture	Italy	Architect
Rafferty	Gerry	Performing Arts	Scotland	Singer
Raft	George	Performing Arts	USA	Actor
Rahal	Bobby	Sports	USA	Race Car Driver - HF
Rainer	Luise	Performing Arts	Germany	Actress - Academy Award
Raines	Tim	Sports	USA	Baseball Player
Rainey (Pridgett)	Gertrude (Ma)	Performing Arts	USA	Singer - Big Band/Jazz - HF
	Gertrude (Ma)	Performing Arts	USA	Singer - Rock & Roll - HF
Rains	Claude	Performing Arts	England	Actor - Acad Award Nom
Rainwater	Leo James	Science	USA	Physics - Nobel Laureate
Raitt	Bonnie	Performing Arts	USA	Singer - Rock & Roll - HF
	John	Performing Arts	USA	Singer
Rakove	Jack N.	Creative Works	USA	Author - Pulitzer
Raleigh	Walter	Politics	England	Statesman/Explorer/Poet
Ralston	Richard Dennis (Denny)	Sports	USA	Tennis Player - HF
	Vera Helena Hruba	Sports	Czechoslovakia	Olympic Skater
Raman	Chandrasekhara Venkata	Science	India	Physics - Nobel Laureate
Rambeau	Marjorie	Performing Arts	USA	Actress - Acad Award Nom
Rameau	Jean Philippe	Creative Works	France	Composer/Organist
Ramie	Jacques la	Exploration	Canada	Explorer - Colorado River
Ramirez	Richard	Law & Order	USA	Serial Killer - Night Stalker
Ramis	Harold	Performing Arts	USA	Actor
Ramon	Ilan	Aviation	Israel	Astronaut
Ramone (Bell)	Mark (Marky)	Performing Arts	USA	Rock & Roll - HF - The Ramones
Ramone (Cummings)	John (Johnny)	Performing Arts	USA	Rock & Roll - HF - The Ramones
Ramone (Hyman)	Jeffry Ross (Joey)	Performing Arts	USA	Rock & Roll - HF - The Ramones
Ramos	Tab	Sports	Uruguay	Soccer Player - HF
	Ultiminio (Sugar)	Sports	Cuba	Boxer - HF
Ramos-Horta	José	War & Peace	East Timor	Peace - Nobel Laureate
Rampal	Jean-Pierre	Performing Arts	France	Flutist
Ramsay	Allen	Creative Works	Scotland	Poet/Bookseller
	William	Science	England	Chemistry - Nobel Laureate
Ramsey	Anne	Performing Arts	USA	Actress - Acad Award Nom
	Frank V.	Sports	USA	Basketball Player - HF
	Norman F.	Science	USA	Physics - Nobel Laureate
Rand	Ayn	Creative Works	USA	Novelist/Philosopher
	Sally	Performing Arts	USA	Actress
Randall	Tony	Performing Arts	USA	Actor
Randolph	John	Politics	USA	Statesman/Orator
	Joyce	Performing Arts	USA	Actress
Ranke	Leopold von	Arts	Germany	Historian
Rankin	Frank	Sports	Canada	Hockey Player - HF
	Judy	Sports	USA	Golfer - HF
Ransom	John Crowe	Creative Works	USA	Poet/Critic
Rapée	Erno	Performing Arts	Hungary	Band Leader/Composer
Rashad	Ahmad	Sports	USA	Football Player
	Phylicia	Performing Arts	USA	Actress
Rasht	Rasmus Christian	Arts	Denmark	Philologist
Rasmussen	Knud Johan Victor	Exploration	Denmark	Explorer - Arctic
Rasputin	Grigori Efimovich	Science	Russia	Faith Healer/Religious Mystic
Rasser	Max	Architecture	Germany	Architect
Ratelle	Joseph Gilbert Yvon (Jean)	Sports	Canada	Hockey Player - HF
Rathbone	Basil	Performing Arts	South Africa	Actor - Acad Award Nom
Rathenau	Walther	Business	Germany	Industrialist/Statesman
Rather	Daniel Irving (Dan)	Creative Works	USA	Journalist - Television

LAST NAME	FIRST NAME	CATEGORY	COUNTRY	FAME
Ratican	Henry (Harry)	Sports	USA	Soccer Player - HF
Ratzenberger	John	Performing Arts	USA	Actor
Rauschenberg	Robert	Works of Art	USA	Painter - Pop
Ravel	Maurice Joseph	Creative Works	France	Composer
Rawlings	Marjorie Kinnan	Creative Works	USA	Novelist - Pulitzer
Rawlinson	George	Arts	England	Historian/Orientalist
	Henry Creswicke	Arts	England	Orientalist/Statesman
Rawls	Betsy	Sports	USA	Golfer - HF
	John	Arts	USA	Philosopher
	Lou	Performing Arts	USA	Singer
Ray	Aldo	Performing Arts	USA	Actor
	Hugh L. (Shorty)	Sports	USA	Football Advisor - HF
	Johnnie	Performing Arts	USA	Singer
	Man	Works of Art	USA	Painter/Photographer
Rayburn	Samuel Taliaferro (Sam)	Politics	USA	Congressman
Rayder	Frankie	Performing Arts	USA	Super Model
Raye	Matha	Performing Arts	USA	Comedian
Rayleigh	John William Strutt	Science	England	Physicist
Raymond	Alex	Creative Works	USA	Cartoonist - Blondie
Rayner	Claude Earl (Chuck)	Sports	Canada	Hockey Player - HF
Rea	Chris	Performing Arts	England	Singer
	Gardner	Creative Works	USA	Cartoonist
	Peggy	Performing Arts	USA	Actress
	Stephen	Performing Arts	Northern Ireland	Actor - Acad Award Nom
Read	Herbert Edward	Creative Works	England	Poet/Art Critic
Reade	Charles	Creative Works	England	Novelist
Reagan	Anne Frances Robbins	Politics	USA	First Lady
	Ronald	Politics	USA	President
Reagan (Davis)	Patti	Performing Arts	USA	Actress
Reardon	Kenneth Joseph (Kenny)	Sports	Canada	Hockey Player - HF
Reasoner	Harry	Creative Works	USA	Journalist - Television
Récamier	Jean Françoise Julie	Politics	France	Social Leader
Redding	Otis	Performing Arts	USA	Singer - Rock & Roll -HF
Reddy	Helen	Performing Arts	Australia	Singer
Redford	Robert	Movie Production	USA	Director - Academy Award
	Robert	Performing Arts	USA	Actor - Acad Award Nom
Redgrave	Lynn	Performing Arts	England	Actress - Acad Award Nom
	Michael	Performing Arts	England	Actor - Acad Award Nom
	Vanessa	Performing Arts	England	Actress - Academy Award
Redman	Donald Matthew (Don)	Performing Arts	USA	Jazz Clarinetist - Big Band/Jazz - HF
	Joyce	Performing Arts	Ireland	Actress - Acad Award Nom
Redon	Odilon	Works of Art	France	Painter/Lithographer
Reed	Carol	Movie Production	England	Director - Academy Award
	Donna	Performing Arts	USA	Actress - Academy Award
	Herb	Performing Arts	USA	Rock & Roll - HF - The Platters
	Jerry	Performing Arts	USA	Singer
	John	Creative Works	USA	Journalist/Radical
	Johnny	Performing Arts	USA	Rock & Roll - HF - The Orioles
	Lewis Allan (Lou)	Performing Arts	USA	Rock & Roll - HF - Velvet Underground
	Mathis James (Jimmy)	Performing Arts	USA	Singer - Rock & Roll - HF
	Oliver	Performing Arts	England	Actor
	Rex	Creative Works	USA	Journalist - Newspaper
	Robert	Performing Arts	USA	Actor
	Walter	Science	USA	Surgeon/Bacteriologist
Reed Jr.	Willis	Sports	USA	Basketball Player - HF
Rees	Roger	Performing Arts	Wales	Actor
Reese	Della	Performing Arts	USA	Actress/Singer
	Harold Henry (Pee Wee)	Sports	USA	Baseball Player - HF
Reeve	Christopher	Performing Arts	USA	Actor
Reeves	Daniel Farrell (Dan)	Sports	USA	Football Owner - HF
	George	Performing Arts	USA	Actor
	James Travis	Performing Arts	USA	Singer - Country Music - HF
	Keanu	Performing Arts	Lebanon	Actor

LAST NAME	FIRST NAME	CATEGORY	COUNTRY	FAME
Reeves	Martha	Performing Arts	USA	Rock & Roll - HF - Martha & The Vandellas
Rehan	Ada	Performing Arts	Ireland	Actress
Rehnquist	William Hubbs	Politics	USA	Chief Justice
Reich	Lilly	Architecture	Germany	Architect
Reichlin	Bruno	Architecture	Switzerland	Architect
Reichman	Albert	Business	Canada	Real Estate
	Paul	Business	Canada	Real Estate
	Ralph	Business	Canada	Real Estate
Reichstein	Tadeus	Science	Switzerland	Medicine - Nobel Laureate
Reid	Benjamin Lawrence	Creative Works	USA	Author - Pulitzer
	Kate	Performing Arts	England	Actress
	Tara	Performing Arts	USA	Actress
	Tim	Performing Arts	USA	Actor
	Whitelaw	Creative Works	USA	Journalist - Newspaper
Reightler	Kenneth Stanley	Aviation	USA	Astronaut
Reilly	John C.	Performing Arts	USA	Actor - Acad Award Nom
Reiner	Carl	Performing Arts	USA	Comedian
	Rob	Movie Production	USA	Director
	Rob	Performing Arts	USA	Comedian
Reinhardt	Django	Performing Arts	Belgium	Jazz Guitarist - Big Band/Jazz - HF
Reinhart	Fabio	Architecture	Switzerland	Architect
Reinhold	Judge	Performing Arts	USA	Actor
Reinking	Ann	Performing Arts	USA	Actress
Reins	Frederick	Science	USA	Physics - Nobel Laureate
Reitman	Ivan	Movie Production	Czechoslovakia	Director
Relf	Keith	Performing Arts	England	Rock & Roll - HF - The Yardbirds
Remarque	Erich Maria	Creative Works	USA	Novelist
Rembrandt	Harmensz van Rijn	Works of Art	Netherlands	Painter/Etcher
Remick	Lee	Performing Arts	USA	Actress - Acad Award Nom
Remington	Frederic	Works of Art	USA	Painter/Sculptor/Illustrator
Remnick	David	Creative Works	USA	Author - Pulitzer
Renan	Joseph Ernest	Arts	France	Historian/Essayist
Renault	Louis	War & Peace	France	Peace - Nobel Laureate
Rendell	Ruth Barbara	Creative Works	England	Author - Crime Fiction
Renfro	Melvin Lacy (Mel)	Sports	USA	Football Player - HF
Reni	Guido	Works of Art	Italy	Painter - Baroque
Rennie	Michael	Performing Arts	England	Actor
Reno	Janet	Politics	USA	Attorney General
Renoir	Jean	Movie Production	France	Director - Acad Award Nom
	Pierre Auguste	Works of Art	France	Painter
Renshaw	James Ernest	Sports	England	Tennis Player - HF
	William Charles (Willie)	Sports	England	Tennis Player - HF
Rensselaer	Stephen Van	Politics	USA	Politician/General
Renta	Oscar de la	Business	France	Fashion Designer
Renzulli	Peter	Sports	USA	Soccer Player - HF
Resnik	Regina	Performing Arts	USA	Singer
Respighi	Ottorino	Creative Works	Italy	Composer
Reston	James Barrett	Creative Works	USA	Journalist - Newspaper
Reszke	Jean de	Performing Arts	Poland	Singer - Opera
Retton	Mary Lou	Sports	USA	Olympic Gymnast
Reuchlin	Johann	Arts	Germany	Scholar - Humanist
Reuther	Walter	Business	USA	Labor Leader
Revere	Anne	Performing Arts	USA	Actress - Academy Award
	Paul	Politics	USA	Patriot/Silversmith
Reville	Alma	Creative Works	England	Writer
Rey	Alejandro	Performing Arts	Argentina	Actor
	Alvino	Performing Arts	USA	Guitarist/Singer
	Fernando	Performing Arts	Spain	Actor
Reyes	Alfonso	Creative Works	Mexico	Author
Reymont	Wladyslaw Stanislaw	Creative Works	Poland	Literature - Nobel Laureate
Reynaud	Paul	Politics	France	Premier
Reynolds	Albert	Politics	Ireland	Prime Minister
	Burt	Performing Arts	USA	Actor - Acad Award Nom

LAST NAME	FIRST NAME	CATEGORY	COUNTRY	FAME
Reynolds	Debbie	Performing Arts	USA	Actress - Acad Award Nom
	Joshua	Works of Art	England	Painter - Portrait
Rhee	Syngman	Politics	South Korea	President
Rhodes	Cecil John	Business	England	Financier/Administrator
	James Ford	Creative Works	USA	Author - Pulitzer
	Richard	Creative Works	USA	Author - Pulitzer
Ribera	José	Works of Art	Spain	Painter
Ricardo	David	Arts	England	Economist
Ricci	Nina	Business	France	Fashion Designer
Rice	Edgar Charles (Sam)	Sports	USA	Baseball Player - HF
	Elmer L.	Creative Works	USA	Dramatist - Pulitzer
	Jerry	Sports	USA	Football Player
	Jim	Sports	USA	Baseball Player
Rich	Bernard (Buddy)	Performing Arts	USA	Band Leader - Big Band/Jazz - HF
	Charlie	Performing Arts	USA	Singer
Richard	Cliff	Performing Arts	India	Singer
	Joseph Henri (Pocket Rocket)	Sports	Canada	Hockey Player - HF
	Joseph Henri Maurice (Rocket)	Sports	Canada	Hockey Player - HF
Richard (Penniman)	Richard Wayne (Little Richard)	Performing Arts	USA	Singer - Rock & Roll - HF
Richards	Ann Willis	Politics	USA	Governor - Texas
	Beah	Performing Arts	USA	Actress - Acad Award Nom
	Bob	Sports	USA	Olympic Pole Vaulter
	Dickinson W.	Science	USA	Medicine - Nobel Laureate
	Ivor Armstrong	Arts	England	Critic - Literary
	Keith	Performing Arts	England	Rock & Roll - HF - Rolling Stones
	Laura Elizabeth	Creative Works	USA	Author - Pulitzer
	Michael	Performing Arts	USA	Actor
	Richard Noel	Aviation	USA	Astronaut
	Theodore William	Science	USA	Chemistry - Nobel Laureate
	Vincent (Vinnie)	Sports	USA	Tennis Player - HF
Richardson	Elliot Lee	Politics	USA	Politician
	George	Sports	Canada	Hockey Player - HF
	Henry Handel	Creative Works	Australia	Novelist
	Henry Hobson	Architecture	USA	Architect
	Ian	Performing Arts	Scotland	Actor
	Miranda	Performing Arts	England	Actress - Acad Award Nom
	Owen Willans	Science	England	Physics - Nobel Laureate
	Ralph	Performing Arts	England	Actor - Acad Award Nom
	Robert C.	Science	USA	Physics - Nobel Laureate
	Samuel	Creative Works	England	Novelist
	Sid Williams	Business	USA	Oil Industry
	Tony	Movie Production	England	Director - Academy Award
Richelieu	Armand Jean du Plessis	Politics	France	Statesman
Richet	Charles Robert	Science	France	Medicine - Nobel Laureate
Richey	Nancy	Sports	USA	Tennis Player - HF
Richie	Lionel	Performing Arts	USA	Singer
Richmond	Tim	Sports	USA	Race Car Driver - HF
Richter	Burton	Science	USA	Physics - Nobel Laureate
	Conrad	Creative Works	USA	Novelist - Pulitzer
	Jean Paul	Creative Works	Germany	Writer
	Paul Andrew (Andy)	Performing Arts	USA	Comedian
Rickenbacker	Edward (Eddie)	Sports	USA	Race Car Driver - HF
	Edward Vernon	Aviation	USA	Aviator/Aviation Executive
Rickey	Wesley Branch	Sports	USA	Baseball Executive -HF
Rickles	Don	Performing Arts	USA	Comedian
Rickover	Hyman George	War & Peace	USA	Admiral
Riddle	Nelson	Performing Arts	USA	Conductor/Composer
Ride	Sally Kristen	Aviation	USA	Astronaut
Ridley	Nicholas	Arts	England	Bishop/Protestant Reformer
Ridolfi	Mario	Architecture	Italy	Architect
Rienzi	Cola di	Politics	Italy	Patriot/Political Reformer
Rietveld	Gerrit	Architecture	Netherlands	Architect
Rigby	Cathy	Sports	USA	Olympic Gymnast

SOLVER SERIES: NAME FINDER

LAST NAME	FIRST NAME	CATEGORY	COUNTRY	FAME
Rigg	Diana	Performing Arts	England	Actress
Riggins	Robert John	Sports	USA	Football Player - HF
Riggs	Robert Larimore (Bobby)	Sports	USA	Tennis Player - HF
Riis	Jacob	Creative Works	USA	Journalist/Social Reformer
Rijn	Rembrandt Van	Works of Art	Netherlands	Painter/Engraver
Riley	James Whitcomb	Creative Works	USA	Poet
	Pat	Sports	USA	Basketball Player
Rilke	Rainer Maria	Creative Works	Austria	Poet - Lyric
Rimbaud	Jean Nicolas Arthur	Creative Works	France	Poet
Rimes	Leanne	Performing Arts	USA	Singer - Country Music
Rimsky-Korsakov	Nikolai Andreyevich	Creative Works	Russia	Composer
Rindt	Jochen	Sports	Germany	Race Car Driver - HF
Rinehart	Mary Roberts	Creative Works	USA	Playwright/Writer - Mysteries
Ringer	Sydney	Science	England	Physiologist
Ringo	James Stephen (Jim)	Sports	USA	Football Player - HF
Ringwald	Molly	Performing Arts	USA	Actress
Rio	Dolores Del	Performing Arts	Mexico	Actress
Riperton	Minnie	Performing Arts	USA	Singer
Ripken	Bill	Sports	USA	Baseball Player
Ripken Jr.	Cal	Sports	USA	Baseball Player
Risen	Arnold (Arnie)	Sports	USA	Basketball Player - HF
Ritchard	Cyril	Performing Arts	Australia	Comedian
Ritenour	Lee Mack	Performing Arts	USA	Jazz Guitarist
Ritt	Martin	Movie Production	USA	Director - Acad Award Nom
Ritter	John	Performing Arts	USA	Comedian
	Thelma	Performing Arts	USA	Actress - Acad Award Nom
	Woodward Morris (Tex)	Performing Arts	USA	Singer - Country Music - HF
Ritz	Al	Performing Arts	USA	Comedian
	Harry	Performing Arts	USA	Comedian
	Jimmy	Performing Arts	USA	Comedian
Rivelino	Roberto	Sports	Brazil	Soccer Player - HF
Rivera	Chita	Performing Arts	USA	Singer
	Diego	Works of Art	Mexico	Painter
	Geraldo	Creative Works	USA	Journalist - Television
Rivero	Inez	Performing Arts	Argentina	Super Model
Rivers	Joan	Performing Arts	USA	Comedian
	Johnny	Performing Arts	USA	Singer
Rixey	Eppa	Sports	USA	Baseball Player - HF
Rizal	José Mercado	Creative Works	Philippines	Poet/Novelist/Patriot
Rizzio	David	Performing Arts	Italy	Violinist
Rizzuto	Philip Francis (Phil)	Sports	USA	Baseball Player - HF
Roach	Max	Performing Arts	USA	Jazz Drummer - Big Band/Jazz - HF
Robards Jr.	Jason	Performing Arts	USA	Actor - Academy Award
Robb	Charles Spittal (Chuck)	Politics	USA	Senator - Virginia
Robbia	Luca della	Works of Art	Italy	Sculptor - Early Renaissance
Robbins	Frederick Chapman	Science	USA	Medicine - Nobel Laureate
	Jerome	Movie Production	USA	Director - Academy Award
	Tim	Movie Production	USA	Director - Acad Award Nom
	Tim	Performing Arts	USA	Actor - Academy Award
Robbins(Robinson)	Martin David (Marty)	Performing Arts	USA	Singer - Country Music - HF
Roberts	Clifford	Sports	USA	Golf Promoter - HF
	Cokie	Creative Works	USA	Journalist - Television
	Doris	Performing Arts	USA	Actress
	Eric	Performing Arts	USA	Actor - Acad Award Nom
	Glenn (Fireball)	Sports	USA	Race Car Driver - HF
	Gordon	Sports	Canada	Hockey Player - HF
	John	Creative Works	Canada	Journalist - Television
	Julia	Performing Arts	USA	Actress - Acad Award Nom
	Kenny	Sports	USA	Motor Cycle Race Driver - HF
	Pernell	Performing Arts	USA	Actor
	Rachel	Performing Arts	Wales	Actress - Acad Award Nom
	Richard J.	Science	England	Medicine - Nobel Laureate
	Robin Evan	Sports	USA	Baseball Player - HF

LAST NAME	FIRST NAME	CATEGORY	COUNTRY	FAME
Roberts	Tanya	Performing Arts	USA	Actress
	Tony	Performing Arts	USA	Actor
Robertson	Allan	Sports	Scotland	Golfer - HF
	Cliff	Performing Arts	USA	Actor - Academy Award
	Dale	Performing Arts	USA	Actor
	Jaime Robert (Robbie)	Performing Arts	Canada	Rock & Roll - HF - The Band
	Jaquelin T.	Architecture	USA	Architect - Jefferson Medal
	Lloyd	Creative Works	Canada	Journalist - Television
	Oscar P.	Sports	USA	Basketball Player - HF
	Patricia Consolatrix Hilliard	Aviation	USA	Astronaut
Robeson	Paul	Performing Arts	USA	Actor/Singer
Robespierre	Maxmilien	War & Peace	France	Revolutionist
Robi (Roby)	Paul	Performing Arts	USA	Rock & Roll - HF - The Platters
Robinson	Brooks Calbert	Sports	USA	Baseball Player - HF
	Edward G.	Performing Arts	Romania	Actor
	Edwin Arlington	Creative Works	USA	Poet - Pulitzer
	Frank	Sports	USA	Baseball Player - HF
	Jack Roosevelt (Jackie)	Sports	USA	Baseball Player - HF
	James Harvey	Arts	USA	Historian
	Larry	Sports	Canada	Hockey Player - HF
	Marilynne	Creative Works	USA	Novelist - Pulitzer
	Mary	Politics	Ireland	President
	Raymond (Sugar Ray)	Sports	USA	Boxer - HF
	Robert	Science	England	Chemistry - Nobel Laureate
	Wilbert	Sports	USA	Baseball Manager - HF
	William (Smokey)	Performing Arts	USA	Singer - Rock & Roll - HF
Robles	Alfonso Garcia	War & Peace	Mexico	Peace - Nobel Laureate
Robson	Flora	Performing Arts	England	Actress - Acad Award Nom
	Mark	Movie Production	Canada	Director - Acad Award Nom
	May	Performing Arts	Australia	Actress - Acad Award Nom
Robustelli	Andrew Richard (Andy)	Sports	USA	Football Player - HF
Roby	Reggie	Sports	USA	Football Player
Rochambeau	Jean Baptiste de	War & Peace	France	General - Revolutionary War
Roche	Anthony Dalton (Tony)	Sports	Australia	Tennis Player - HF
	Kevin	Architecture	USA	Architect - Pritzker/ AIA Gold
Rochefoucauld	François de La	Arts	France	Moralist/Writer
Rochelle	Pierre Athanase La	Arts	France	Lexicographer/Grammarian
Rock	Chris	Performing Arts	USA	Comedian
Rockefeller	John Davison	Business	USA	Industrialist/Philanthropist
	John Davison Jr.	Business	USA	Industrialist/Philanthropist
	Nelson Aldrich	Politics	USA	Vice-President
Rockne	Kenneth (Knute)	Sports	USA	Football Coach
Rockwell	Norman	Works of Art	USA	Illustrator
Rodbell	Martin	Science	USA	Medicine - Nobel Laureate
Rodgers	James Charles (Jimmie)	Performing Arts	USA	Country Music - HF - Singing Brakeman
	Jimmie	Performing Arts	USA	Singer - Rock & Roll - HF
	Paul	Performing Arts	England	Singer
	Richard	Creative Works	USA	Composer - Musicals
	Richard	Creative Works	USA	Dramatist - Pulitzer
Rodin	François Auguste René	Works of Art	France	Sculptor
Rodman	Dennis	Sports	USA	Basketball Player
Rodriquez	Juan (Chi Chi)	Sports	Puerto Rico	Golfer - HF
	Luis	Sports	Cuba	Boxer - HF
Roe	Jimmy	Sports	USA	Soccer Player - HF
Roebling	John Augustus	Architecture	USA	Bridge Designer/Civil Engineer
Roeg	Nicolas	Movie Production	England	Director
Roentgen	Wilhelm Konrad	Science	Germany	Physicist - X-Ray Discoverer
Roethke	Theodore	Creative Works	USA	Poet - Pulitzer
Rogan	Wilber Joe (Bullet)	Sports	USA	Baseball Player - HF
Rogers	Bruce	Arts	USA	Typographer/Book Designer
	Fred	Performing Arts	USA	Show Host
	Ginger	Performing Arts	USA	Actress - Academy Award
	Kenny	Performing Arts	USA	Singer

SOLVER SERIES: NAME FINDER

LAST NAME	FIRST NAME	CATEGORY	COUNTRY	FAME
Rogers	Mimi	Performing Arts	USA	Actress
	Nathan Ernesto	Architecture	Italy	Architect
	Richard	Architecture	England	Architect - Jefferson Medal
	Will	Performing Arts	USA	Actor/Humorist
	Willie	Performing Arts	USA	Rock & Roll - HF - The Soul Stirrers
Rogers (Slye)	Leonard (Roy)	Performing Arts	USA	Country Music - HF - Sons of the Pioneers
Roget	Peter Mark	Science	England	Physician/Compiler - Thesaurus
Rohe	Ludwig Miës van der Rohe	Architecture	USA	Architect - AIA/Jefferson Gold Medal
Rohmer	Eric	Movie Production	France	Director
Rohrer	Heinrich	Science	Switzerland	Physics - Nobel Laureate
Roland	Gilbert	Performing Arts	Mexico	Actor
	Romain	Creative Works	France	Literature - Nobel Laureate
Rolle	Esther	Performing Arts	USA	Actress
Rollini	Adrian Francis	Performing Arts	USA	Jazz Saxophonist - Big Band/Jazz - HF
Rollins	Sonny	Performing Arts	USA	Jazz Saxophonist - Big Band/Jazz - HF
Rollins Jr.	Howard E.	Performing Arts	USA	Actor - Acad Award Nom
Rolvaag	Ole Edvart	Creative Works	USA	Novelist
Romains	John	Creative Works	France	Poet/Novelist/Playwright
Roman	Ruth	Performing Arts	USA	Actress
Romano	Giulio	Architecture	Italy	Architect
Romanov	Mikhail Feodorovich	Politics	Russia	Czar
Rome	Harold Jacob	Creative Works	USA	Composer/Songwriter
Romero	Cesar	Performing Arts	USA	Actor
Romijn-Stamos	Rebecca	Performing Arts	USA	Actress/Super Model
Rommel	Erwin Johannes Eugen	War & Peace	Germany	Field Marshall
Ronaldo	Cristiano	Sports	Brazil	Soccer Player
Ronsard	Pierre de	Creative Works	France	Poet
Ronstadt	Linda	Performing Arts	USA	Singer
Röntgen	Wilhelm Conrad	Science	Germany	Physics - Nobel Laureate
Rooney	Andy	Creative Works	USA	Journalist - Newspaper
	Daniel M. (Dan)	Sports	USA	Football Team President
	Mickey	Performing Arts	USA	Actor - Academy Award
Rooney Sr.	Arthur Joseph (Art)	Sports	USA	Football Founder - HF
Roosa	Stuart Allen	Aviation	USA	Astronaut
Roosevelt	Alice Hathaway	Politics	USA	First Lady
	Anna Eleanor	Politics	USA	First Lady
	Edith Kermit	Politics	USA	First Lady
	Ellen Crosby	Sports	USA	Tennis Player - HF
	Franklin Delano	Politics	USA	President
	Theodore	Politics	USA	President
	Theodore	War & Peace	USA	Peace - Nobel Laureate
Roosma	John S.	Sports	USA	Basketball Player - HF
Root	Elihu	Politics	USA	Statesman
	Elihu	War & Peace	USA	Peace - Nobel Laureate
	John Wellborn	Architecture	USA	Architect - AIA Gold Medal
Rorem	Ned	Creative Works	USA	Composer/Pianist
Rorschach	Hermann	Arts	Switzerland	Psychologist
Rorty	Richard	Arts	USA	Philosopher
Rosar	Buddy	Sports	USA	Baseball Player
Rose	Charlie	Creative Works	USA	Journalist - Television
	Irwin	Science	USA	Chemistry - Nobel Laureate
	Mauri	Sports	USA	Race Car Driver - HF
	Mervyn	Sports	Australia	Tennis Player - HF
	Pete	Sports	USA	Baseball Player
Rosecrans	William Starke	War & Peace	USA	General - Civil War
Rosemeyer	Bernd	Sports	Netherlands	Race Car Driver - HF
Rosenberg	Harold	Arts	USA	Philosopher/Writer/Educator
Rosenberg	Tina	Creative Works	USA	Author - Pulitzer
Rosenbloom	Maxey	Sports	USA	Boxer - HF
Rosewall	Kenneth Robert (Ken)	Sports	Australia	Tennis Player - HF
Ross	Arthur Howie (Art)	Sports	Canada	Hockey Player - HF
	Betsy	Arts	USA	Flag Maker
	Diane Ersnastine (Diana)	Performing Arts	USA	Actress - Acad Award Nom

LAST NAME	FIRST NAME	CATEGORY	COUNTRY	FAME
Ross	Diane Ersnastine (Diana)	Performing Arts	USA	Rock & Roll - HF - The Supremes
	Donald	Sports	Scotland	Golfer/Course Designer - HF
	Harold Wallace	Business	USA	Magazine Editor
	Herbert	Movie Production	USA	Director - Acad Award Nom
	James Clark	Exploration	England	Explorer - Polar
	John	Exploration	England	Explorer - Arctic
	Katharine	Performing Arts	USA	Actress - Acad Award Nom
	Marion	Performing Arts	USA	Actress
	Ronald	Science	England	Medicine - Nobel Laureate
Rossellini	Isabella	Performing Arts	Italy	Actress
	Roberto	Movie Production	Italy	Director
Rossen	Robert	Movie Production	USA	Director - Acad Award Nom
Rossetti	Christina Georgina	Creative Works	England	Poet
	Dante Gabriel	Creative Works	England	Poet/Painter
Rossi	Aldo	Architecture	Italy	Architect - Pritzker/Jefferson Medal
Rossini	Gioacchino Antonio	Creative Works	Italy	Composer
Rostand	Edmond	Creative Works	France	Poet/Dramatist
Rosten	Leo	Creative Works	USA	Writer
Rostenkowski	Dan	Politics	USA	Congressman - Illinois
Rostovtzeff	Michael Ivanovich	Arts	USA	Historian
Rota	Nino	Creative Works	Italy	Composer
Rotblat	Joseph Ernest	War & Peace	England	Peace - Nobel Laureate
Rote	Kyle	Sports	USA	Football Player
Roth	David Lee	Performing Arts	USA	Singer
	Philip	Creative Works	USA	Novelist - Pulitzer
	Tim	Performing Arts	England	Actor - Acad Award Nom
	Werner	Sports	Yugoslavia	Soccer Player - HF
Rothko	Mark	Works of Art	Latvia	Painter - Abstract Expressionist
Rothschild	Meyer Anselm	Business	Germany	Founder - Bank
Rothstein	Arnold	Law & Order	USA	Underworld - Jewish
Rouault	Georges	Works of Art	France	Painter - Fauvist Expressionist
Round-Little	Dorothy Edith	Sports	England	Tennis Player - HF
Rourke	Mickey	Performing Arts	USA	Actor
Rous	Peyton	Science	USA	Medicine - Nobel Laureate
Roush	Edd J.	Sports	USA	Baseball Player - HF
Roush	Jack	Sports	USA	Race Car Designer - HF
Rousseau	Henri	Works of Art	France	Painter - Primitive
	Jean Jacques	Arts	France	Philosopher/Writer
	Pierre ÉtienneThéodore	Works of Art	France	Painter - Landscape
Rowan	Dan	Performing Arts	USA	Comedian
	Rena	Business	Poland	Fashion Designer
Rowe	Misty	Performing Arts	USA	Actress
	Nicholas	Performing Arts	Scotland	Actor
Rowland	Frank Sherwood	Science	USA	Chemistry - Nobel Laureate
Rowlands	Gena	Performing Arts	USA	Actress - Acad Award Nom
Rowlandson	Thomas	Works of Art	England	Painter/Caricaturist
Rowntree	Joseph	Business	England	Confection Industry
Rowntree	Seebohm	Business	England	Confection Industry
Roy	Willy	Sports	Germany	Soccer Player - HF
Royce	Josiah	Arts	USA	Philosopher/Educator
Rozelle	Alvin Ray (Pete)	Sports	USA	Football Commissioner - HF
Rroethke	Theodore	Creative Works	USA	Poet
Rubbia	Carlo	Science	Italy	Physics - Nobel Laureate
Rubens	Peter Paul	Works of Art	Netherlands	Painter
Rubik	Ernö	Science	Hungary	Inventor/Sculptor - Rubik's Cube
Rubinstein	Anton Grigorevich	Creative Works	Russia	Composer/Pianist
	Arthur	Performing Arts	USA	Pianist
Rudd (Norman)	Phillip (Phil)	Performing Arts	Australia	Rock & Roll - HF - AC/DC
Rudner	Rita	Performing Arts	USA	Comedian
Rudolph	Paul	Architecture	USA	Architect
	Wilma Glodean	Sports	USA	Olympic Runner
Ruehl	Mercedes	Performing Arts	USA	Actress - Academy Award
Ruffin	Davis Eli (David)	Performing Arts	USA	Rock & Roll - HF - The Temptations

SOLVER SERIES: NAME FINDER

LAST NAME	FIRST NAME	CATEGORY	COUNTRY	FAME
Ruffing	Charles Herbert (Red)	Sports	USA	Baseball Player - HF
Ruggles	Charlie	Performing Arts	USA	Actor
	Wesley	Movie Production	USA	Director - Acad Award Nom
Ruisdael	Jacob van	Works of Art	Netherlands	Painter - Landscape
Rukeyser	Louis	Creative Works	USA	Journalist - Television
Rundgren	Todd Harry	Performing Arts	USA	Singer/Guitarist
Runyan	Paul (Little Poison)	Sports	USA	Golfer - HF
Runyon	Alfred Damon	Creative Works	USA	Journalist/Short Story Writer
Rush	Barbara	Performing Arts	USA	Actress
	Benjamin	Science	USA	Physician
	Geoffrey	Performing Arts	Australia	Actor - Academy Award
	Richard	Movie Production	USA	Director - Acad Award Nom
Rushing	James Andrew (Jimmy)	Performing Arts	USA	Singer - Big Band/Jazz - HF
Rusie	Amos Wilson	Sports	USA	Baseball Player - HF
Rusk	David Dean	Politics	USA	Secretary of State
Ruska	Ernst	Science	Germany	Physics - Nobel Laureate
Ruskin	John	Architecture	England	Architect/Writer/Poet/Artist
	John	Creative Works	England	Writer/Art Critic/Social Reformer
Russel	Blair	Sports	Canada	Hockey Player - HF
Russell	Cazzie	Sports	USA	Basketball Player
	Charles Edward	Creative Works	USA	Author - Pulitzer
	Charles Elsworth (PeeWee)	Performing Arts	USA	Jazz Clarinetist - Big Band/Jazz - HF
	Earl Bertrand Arthur William	Creative Works	England	Literature - Nobel Laureate
	Ernest (Ernie)	Sports	Canada	Hockey Player - HF
	George William	Creative Works	Ireland	Poet/Essayist
	Harold	Performing Arts	Canada	Actor - Academy Award
	Jane	Performing Arts	USA	Actress
	John	Politics	England	Prime Minister
	John D. (Honey)	Sports	USA	Basketball Player - HF
	Ken	Movie Production	England	Director - Acad Award Nom
	Kurt	Performing Arts	USA	Actor
	Leon	Performing Arts	USA	Singer
	Lillian	Performing Arts	USA	Actress/Singer
	Mark	Performing Arts	USA	Comedian/Pianist
	Nipsey	Performing Arts	USA	Comedian
	Rosalind	Performing Arts	USA	Actress - Acad Award Nom
	Theresa	Performing Arts	USA	Actress
	William F. (Bill)	Sports	USA	Basketball Player - HF
Russert	Tim	Performing Arts	USA	Show Host/Political Analyst
Russo	Rene	Performing Arts	USA	Actress
	Richard	Creative Works	USA	Novelist - Pulitzer
Ruth	George Herman (Babe)	Sports	USA	Baseball Player - HF
Rutherford	Ernest	Science	England	Chemistry - Nobel Laureate
	Johnny	Sports	USA	Race Car Driver - HF
	Margaret	Performing Arts	England	Actress - Academy Award
	Michael John (Mike)	Performing Arts	England	Singer/Guitarist
Rutledge	Edward	Politics	USA	Statesman
	John	Politics	USA	Statesman
Ruttan	Jack D.	Sports	Canada	Hockey Player - HF
	Susan	Performing Arts	USA	Actress
Ruysdael	Michiel Adriaanszoon de	War & Peace	Netherlands	Admiral
Ruzicka	Leopold	Science	Switzerland	Chemistry - Nobel Laureate
Ryan	Elizabeth Montague (Bunny)	Sports	USA	Tennis Player - HF
	Francis John (Hun)	Sports	USA	Soccer Player - HF
	Irene	Performing Arts	USA	Actress
	Lynn Nolan	Sports	USA	Baseball Player - HF
	Meg	Performing Arts	USA	Actress
	Robert	Performing Arts	USA	Actor - Acad Award Nom
	Thomas	Business	USA	Railway Magnate
Rydell	Bobby	Performing Arts	USA	Singer
	Mark	Movie Production	USA	Director - Acad Award Nom
Ryder	Albert Pinkham	Works of Art	USA	Painter
	William Levise (Mitch)	Performing Arts	USA	Singer

LAST NAME	FIRST NAME	CATEGORY	COUNTRY	FAME
Ryder	Winona	Performing Arts	USA	Actress - Acad Award Nom
Ryle	Gilbert	Arts	England	Philosopher
	Martin	Science	England	Physics - Nobel Laureate
Ryn	John Van	Sports	USA	Tennis Player - HF
Rypien	Mark	Sports	USA	Football Player
Rysanek	Leonie	Performing Arts	Austria	Singer - Opera
Ryskind	Morrie	Creative Works	USA	Dramatist - Pulitzer
Ryun	James Ronald (Jim)	Sports	USA	Olympic Runner
Saarinen	Eero	Architecture	USA	Architect - AIA Gold Medal
	Gottlieb Eliel	Architecture	Finland	Architect - AIA Gold Medal
Sabatier	Paul	Science	France	Chemistry - Nobel Laureate
Sabatini	Gabriela	Sports	Argentina	Tennis Player
Sabato	Ernesto	Creative Works	Argentina	Author
Saberhagen	Bret	Sports	USA	Baseball Player
Sabin	Albert Bruce	Science	USA	Physician - Polio Vaccine
Sable	Jean-Baptiste-Point du	Exploration	France	Explorer - Chicago
Sacco	Nicola	Politics	Italy	Anarchist
Sacco Jr.	Albert	Aviation	USA	Astronaut
Sachs	Hans	Performing Arts	Germany	Singer - Meister
	Nellie	Creative Works	Sweden	Literature - Nobel Laureate
Sackler	Howard	Creative Works	USA	Dramatist - Pulitzer
Sackville	Thomas	Creative Works	England	Poet/Statesman
Sadat	Anwar al	Politics	Egypt	Head of State
	Anwar al	War & Peace	Egypt	Peace - Nobel Laureate
Saddler	Sandy	Sports	USA	Boxer - HF
Sade	Alponse François de	Creative Works	France	Novelist/Soldier
Safdie	Moshe	Architecture	Israel	Architect
Safer	Morley	Creative Works	Canada	Journalist - Television
Safire	William	Creative Works	USA	Journalist - Newspaper - Pulitzer
Sagan	Carl	Science	USA	Astronomer
	Carl Edward	Creative Works	USA	Author - Pulitzer
Sage	Alain René Le	Creative Works	France	Novelist
	Russell	Business	USA	Financier
Saget	Bob	Performing Arts	USA	Actor
Sahl	Mort	Performing Arts	Canada	Comedian
Sainsbury	John	Business	England	Confection Industry
Saint	Eva Marie	Performing Arts	USA	Actress - Academy Award
Saint Laurent	Yves	Business	France	Fashion Designer
Sainte-Beuve	Charles Augustin	Creative Works	France	Writer/Literary Critic
Sainte-Exupéry	Antoine de	Creative Works	France	Writer/Aviator
Sainte-Gaudens	Augustus	Works of Art	USA	Sculptor
Sainte-Just	Louis Antoine Léon de	War & Peace	France	Revolutionist
Sainte-Marie	Buffy	Performing Arts	Canada	Singer - Canadian Music - HF
Saint-Saëns	Charles Camille	Creative Works	France	Composer
Saintsbury	George Edward Bateman	Arts	England	Critic - Literary
Saint-Simon	Charles Henri de Rouvroy	Politics	France	Reformer - Social
Sajak	Pat	Performing Arts	USA	Show Host
Sakharov	Andrei Dmitrievich	War & Peace	Russia	Peace - Nobel Laureate
Sakmann	Bert	Science	Germany	Medicine - Nobel Laureate
Saks	Gene	Movie Production	USA	Director
Salam	Abdus	Science	Pakistan	Physics - Nobel Laureate
Salamanca	Jack R	Creative Works	USA	Author
Salazar	Antonio de Oliveira	Politics	Portugal	Prime Minister
Salcedo	Fabri	Sports	Spain	Soccer Player - HF
Saldivar	Vincente	Sports	Mexico	Boxer - HF
Sales	Soupy	Performing Arts	USA	Comedian
Salieri	Antonio	Creative Works	Austria	Composer
Salinger	Jerome David	Creative Works	USA	Novelist/Short Story Writer
	Pierre Emil George	Politics	USA	Senator/Press Secretary
Salk	Jonas Edward	Science	USA	Physician - Polio Vaccine
	Lee	Arts	USA	Psychologist
Salle	Réne-Robert Cavelier de la	Exploration	France	Explorer - Mississippi River
Salming	Anders Borje	Sports	Sweden	Hockey Player - HF

SOLVER SERIES: NAME FINDER

LAST NAME	FIRST NAME	CATEGORY	COUNTRY	FAME
Salomon	Haym	Business	USA	Financier
Salt	Titus	Business	England	Textile Industry
Salvo	Albert De	Law & Order	USA	Serial Killer - Boston Strangler
	Ann De	Performing Arts	USA	Actress
Samms	Emma	Performing Arts	England	Actress
Samonà	Giuseppe	Architecture	Italy	Architect
Sampras	Pete	Sports	USA	Tennis Player
Samuels	Ernest	Creative Works	USA	Author - Pulitzer
Samuelson	Paul A.	Arts	USA	Economics - Nobel Laureate
Samuelsson	Bengt I.	Science	Sweden	Medicine - Nobel Laureate
San Martín	José de	War & Peace	Argentina	Revolutionary Leader
Sanchez	Salvadore	Sports	Mexico	Boxer - HF
Sánchez	Oscar Arias	Politics	Costa Rica	President
	Oscar Arias	War & Peace	Costa Rica	Peace - Nobel Laureate
Sandars	Joseph	Business	England	Railway Magnate
Sandberg	Ryne	Sports	USA	Baseball Player - HF
Sandburg	Carl	Creative Works	USA	Author - Pulitzer
	Carl	Creative Works	USA	Poet - Pulitzer
Sanders	Barry David	Sports	USA	Football Player - HF
	Deion	Sports	USA	Baseball Player
	George	Performing Arts	Russia	Actor - Academy Award
	Lawrence	Creative Works	USA	Author
Sandy	Gary	Performing Arts	USA	Actor
Sanford	Isabel	Performing Arts	USA	Actress
Sangallo	Antonio da il Giovane	Architecture	Italy	Architect
	Antonio da il Vecchio	Architecture	Italy	Architect
	Giuliano da	Architecture	Italy	Architect
Sanger	Frederick	Science	England	Chemistry - Nobel Laureate
	Margaret	Science	USA	Nurse
Sansovino	Jacopo Tatti	Architecture	Italy	Architect
Sant	Gus Van	Movie Production	USA	Director - Acad Award Nom
Santa Anna	Antonio López de	Politics	Mexico	President
Santana	Carlos	Performing Arts	Mexico	Guitarist
	Carlos	Performing Arts	Mexico	Singer - Rock & Roll - HF
	Manuel Martinez (Manolo)	Sports	Spain	Tennis Player - HF
Santayana	George	Arts	Spain	Philosopher/Writer
Sant'Elia	Antonio	Architecture	Italy	Architect
Santi	Nello	Performing Arts	Italy	Conductor
	Raphael	Works of Art	Italy	Painter/Architect
Santos	Manuel Dos (Garrincha)	Sports	Brazil	Soccer Player - HF
Sapir	Edward	Arts	USA	Linguist/Anthropologist
Sara	Mia	Performing Arts	USA	Actress
Saramago	José	Creative Works	Portugal	Literature - Nobel Laureate
Sarandon	Chris	Performing Arts	USA	Actor - Acad Award Nom
	Susan	Performing Arts	USA	Actress - Academy Award
Sarazen	Gene	Sports	USA	Golfer - HF
Sardou	Victorien	Creative Works	France	Dramatist
Sarg	Tony	Performing Arts	Guatemala	Puppeteer
Sargent	John Singer	Works of Art	USA	Painter
Saroyan	William	Creative Works	USA	Dramatist - Pulitzer
Sarto	Andrea del	Works of Art	Italy	Painter
	Andrea del	Works of Art	Italy	Painter
Sartoris	Alberto	Architecture	Italy	Architect
Sartre	Jean-Paul	Creative Works	France	Literature - Nobel Laureate
Sassoon	Siegfried Lorraine	Creative Works	England	Poet/Writer
Sastre	Inez	Performing Arts	Spain	Super Model
Satie	Erik Alfred Leslie	Creative Works	France	Composer
Sato	Eisaku	War & Peace	Japan	Peace - Nobel Laureate
Satyajit	Ray	Movie Production	India	Director
Saussure	Ferdinand de	Arts	Switzerland	Linguist
Sauvage	Henri	Architecture	France	Architect
Savage	Fred	Performing Arts	USA	Actor
Savalas	Telly	Performing Arts	USA	Actor - Acad Award Nom

LAST NAME	FIRST NAME	CATEGORY	COUNTRY	FAME
Savard	Denis	Sports	Canada	Hockey Player - HF
	Serger Aubrey	Sports	Canada	Hockey Player - HF
Savitt	Richard (Dick)	Sports	USA	Tennis Player - HF
Sawchuk	Terrance Gordon (Terry)	Sports	Canada	Hockey Player - HF
Sawyer	Diane	Creative Works	USA	Journalist - Television
Saxon	John	Performing Arts	USA	Actor
	Steve	Sports	USA	Base Ball Player
Sayer	Leo	Performing Arts	England	Singer
Sayers	Dorothy L.	Creative Works	England	Author
	Gale Eugene	Sports	USA	Football Player - HF
Sayles	John	Movie Production	USA	Director
Scacchi	Gretta	Performing Arts	Italy	Actress
Scaggs	Boz	Performing Arts	USA	Singer
Scala	Gia	Performing Arts	England	Actress
Scalia	Antonin	Law & Order	USA	Justice - Supreme Court
Scanderbeg	George Castriota	Politics	Albania	Leader/National Hero
Scanlon	Fredrick	Sports	Canada	Hockey Player - HF
Scarlatti	Alessandro	Creative Works	Italy	Composer
	Giuseppe	Creative Works	Italy	Composer
Scarpa	Afra e Tobia	Architecture	Italy	Architect
	Carlo	Architecture	Italy	Architect
Scarron	Paul	Creative Works	France	Poet/Dramatist
Scarwid	Diana	Performing Arts	USA	Actress - Acad Award Nom
Schaffner	Franklin J.	Movie Production	Japan	Director - Academy Award
Schalk	Raymond William (Ray)	Sports	USA	Baseball Player - HF
Schaller	Willy	Sports	Germany	Soccer Player - HF
Schallert	William	Performing Arts	USA	Actor
Schally	Andrew V.	Science	USA	Medicine - Nobel Laureate
Scharoun	Hans	Architecture	Germany	Architect
Schawlow	Arthur Leonard	Science	USA	Physics - Nobel Laureate
Schayes	Adolph (Dolph)	Sports	USA	Basketball Player - HF
Scheckter	Jody	Sports	South Africa	Race Car Driver
Scheider	Roy	Performing Arts	USA	Actor - Acad Award Nom
Schell	Maria	Performing Arts	Austria	Actress
	Maximilian	Performing Arts	Austria	Actor - Academy Award
Schelling	Friedrich Wilhelm Joseph von	Arts	Germany	Philosopher
	Thomas C.	Arts	USA	Economics - Nobel Laureate
Schenkel	Chris	Creative Works	USA	Journalist - Television
Schenkkan	Robert	Creative Works	USA	Dramatist - Pulitzer
Schertzinger	Victor	Movie Production	USA	Director - Acad Award Nom
Schiaparelli	Elsa	Works of Art	Italy	Painter - Surrealist
	Giovanni Virginio	Science	Italy	Astronomer
Schiff	Jacob	Business	USA	Financier
	Stacy	Creative Works	USA	Author - Pulitzer
Schiffer	Claudia	Performing Arts	Germany	Super Model
Schifrin	Lalo	Creative Works	Argentina	Composer/Pianist
Schildkraut	Joseph	Performing Arts	Austria	Actor - Academy Award
Schiller	Johann Christoph Friedrich von	Creative Works	Germany	Poet/Dramatist
Schindler	Rudolph Michael	Architecture	USA	Architect
Schinkel	Karl Friedrich	Architecture	Germany	Architect
Schipa	Tito	Performing Arts	Italy	Singer - Opera
Schirra	Walter Marty	Aviation	USA	Astronaut
Schlegel	August Wilhelm von	Creative Works	Germany	Poet/Critic
	Hans Wilhelm	Aviation	Germany	Astronaut
	Karl Wilhelm Friedrich von	Arts	Germany	Philosopher/Critic
Schleiermacher	Friedrich Ernest Daniel	Arts	Germany	Philosopher/Theologian
Schlesinger	Arthur Meier	Arts	USA	Historian
	Arthur Meier Jr.	Arts	USA	Historian
	John	Movie Production	England	Director - Academy Award
Schlesinger Jr.	Arthur Meier	Creative Works	USA	Author - Pulitzer
Schlick	Friedrich Albert Moritz	Arts	Germany	Philosopher
Schliemann	Heinrich	Arts	Germany	Archaeologist
Schlüter	Andreas	Architecture	Germany	Architect/Sculptor

LAST NAME	FIRST NAME	CATEGORY	COUNTRY	FAME
Schmeling	Max	Sports	Germany	Boxer - HF
Schmidt	Earnest J. (Ernie)	Sports	USA	Basketball Player - HF
	Hans	Architecture	Switzerland	Architect
	Joseph Paul (Joe)	Sports	USA	Football Player - HF
	Michael Jack (Mike)	Sports	USA	Baseball Player - HF
	Milton Conrad (Milt)	Sports	Canada	Hockey Player - HF
Schmit	Timothy B.	Performing Arts	USA	Rock & Roll - HF - The Eagles
Schmitt	Bernadotte E.	Creative Works	USA	Author - Pulitzer
	Harrison Hagan	Aviation	USA	Astronaut
Schnabel	Artur	Creative Works	Austria	Composer/Pianist
Schneider	Jean	Creative Works	USA	Author - Pulitzer
Schnitzler	Arthur	Creative Works	Austria	Novelist/Playwright
Schoendienst	Albert Fred (Red)	Sports	USA	Baseball Player - HF
Scholes	Myron S.	Arts	USA	Economics - Nobel Laureate
Scholz	Tom	Performing Arts	USA	Singer/Guitarist
Schommer	John J.	Sports	USA	Basketball Player - HF
Schönberg	Arnold	Creative Works	USA	Composer
Schopehauer	Arthur	Arts	Germany	Philosopher/Pessimist
Schorske	Carl E.	Creative Works	USA	Author - Pulitzer
Schramm Jr.	Texas Earnest (Tex)	Sports	USA	Football General Manager - HF
Schrieffer	John Robert	Science	USA	Physics - Nobel Laureate
Schriner	David (Sweeney)	Sports	Russia	Hockey Player - HF
Schrock	Richard R.	Science	USA	Chemistry - Nobel Laureate
Schroder	Rick	Performing Arts	USA	Actor
Schrödinger	Erwin	Science	Austria	Physics - Nobel Laureate
Schroeder	Barbet	Movie Production	Iran	Director - Acad Award Nom
	Frederick Rudolph (Ted)	Sports	USA	Tennis Player - HF
Schubert	Franz Peter	Creative Works	Austria	Composer
Schultz	Theodore W.	Arts	USA	Economics - Nobel Laureate
Schulz	Charles Monroe	Creative Works	USA	Cartoonist - Peanuts
Schumacher	Michael	Sports	Germany	Race Car Driver - HF
Schuman	William Howard	Creative Works	USA	Composer
Schumann	Robert Alexander	Creative Works	Germany	Composer
Schumann-Heink	Ernestine	Performing Arts	USA	Singer - Opera
Schurz	Carl	Politics	USA	Statesman/Journalist
Schutz	Heinrich	Creative Works	Germany	Composer
Schuyler	James	Creative Works	USA	Poet - Pulitzer
	Phillip John	War & Peace	USA	General - Revolutionary War
Schwartz	Melvin	Science	USA	Physics - Nobel Laureate
Schwarz	Rudolph	Architecture	Germany	Architect
Schwarzenegger	Arnold	Performing Arts	Austria	Actor
	Arnold Alois	Politics	USA	Governor - California
Schwarzkopf Jr.	Herbert Norman	War & Peace	USA	General - Army
Schweickart	Russell Luis	Aviation	USA	Astronaut
Schweitzer	Albert	Arts	France	Philosopher/Missionary/Theologian
	Albert	War & Peace	France	Peace - Nobel Laureate
Schwinger	Julian	Science	USA	Physics - Nobel Laureate
Scobee	Francis Richard	Aviation	USA	Astronaut
Scofield	Paul	Performing Arts	England	Actor - Academy Award
Scolari	Peter	Performing Arts	USA	Actor
Scorsese	Martin	Movie Production	USA	Director - Acad Award Nom
Scott	David Randolph	Aviation	USA	Astronaut
	Dred	Arts	USA	Negro Slave
	George C.	Performing Arts	USA	Actor - Academy Award
	George Gilbert	Architecture	England	Architect
	Lizabeth	Performing Arts	USA	Actress
	Martha	Performing Arts	USA	Actress - Acad Award Nom
	Randolph	Performing Arts	USA	Actor
	Ridley	Movie Production	England	Director - Acad Award Nom
	Robert Falcon	Exploration	England	Explorer - Antarctic
	Ronald	Performing Arts	Scotland	Rock & Roll - HF - AC/DC
	Sherry	Performing Arts	USA	Rock & Roll - HF - Earth Wind & Fire
	Walter	Creative Works	Scotland	Poet/Novelist

LAST NAME	FIRST NAME	CATEGORY	COUNTRY	FAME
Scott	Wendell	Sports	USA	Race Car Driver - HF
	Winfield	War & Peace	USA	General
	Winston Elliot	Aviation	USA	Astronaut
	Zachary	Performing Arts	USA	Actor
Scott (Warnow)	Harry (Raymond)	Performing Arts	USA	Band Leader - Big Band/Jazz - HF
Scotto	Renata	Performing Arts	Italy	Singer - Opera
Scotus	John Duns	Arts	Scotland	Theologian/Philosopher
Scowcroft	Brent	Politics	USA	National Security Advisor
Scriabin	Aleksandr Nikolayevich	Creative Works	Russia	Composer/Pianist
Scribe	Augustin Eugène	Creative Works	France	Dramatist/Librettist
Scripps	Edward Wyllis	Business	USA	Publishing - Newspaper
Scruggs	Earl Eugene	Performing Arts	USA	Country Music - HF - Foggy Mountain Boys
Scully	Vincent Edward (Vin)	Creative Works	USA	Journalist - Television
	Vincent J.	Architecture	USA	Architect - Jefferson Medal
Scully-Power	Paul Desmond	Aviation	USA	Astronaut
Seaborg	Glenn Theodore	Science	USA	Chemistry - Nobel Laureate
Seals	Dan	Performing Arts	USA	Singer
	Jim	Performing Arts	USA	Singer
Searfoss	Richard Alan	Aviation	USA	Astronaut
Searle	John	Arts	USA	Philosopher
Sears	Eleonora Randolph (Eleo)	Sports	USA	Tennis Player - HF
	Richard Dudley (Dick)	Sports	USA	Tennis Player - HF
Seaton	George	Movie Production	USA	Director - Acad Award Nom
Seau	Junior	Sports	USA	Football Player
Seaver	George Thomas (Tom)	Sports	USA	Baseball Player - HF
Sebastian	John	Performing Arts	USA	Singer
Seberg	Jean	Performing Arts	USA	Actress
Sedaka	Neil	Performing Arts	USA	Singer
Seddon	Margaret Rhea	Aviation	USA	Astronaut
Sedgman	Frank Allen	Sports	Australia	Tennis Player - HF
Sedgwick	Edie	Performing Arts	USA	Actress
	Kyra	Performing Arts	USA	Actress
Sedran	Barney	Sports	USA	Basketball Player - HF
See Jr.	Elliot McKay	Aviation	USA	Astronaut
Seeger	Pete	Performing Arts	USA	Singer - Rock & Roll - HF
Seferis	Giorgos	Creative Works	Greece	Literature - Nobel Laureate
Sega	Ronald Michael	Aviation	USA	Astronaut
Segal	Erich	Creative Works	USA	Author
	George	Performing Arts	USA	Actor - Acad Award Nom
Segar	Elzie Crisler	Creative Works	USA	Cartoonist - Popeye
Seger	Bob	Performing Arts	USA	Singer - Rock & Roll - HF
Segovia	Andrés	Performing Arts	Spain	Guitarist
Segrè	Emilio Gino	Science	USA	Physics - Nobel Laureate
Segura	Francisco Olegario (Pancho)	Sports	Ecuador	Tennis Player - HF
Seibert	Earl Walter	Sports	Canada	Hockey Player - HF
	Oliver Levi	Sports	Canada	Hockey Player - HF
Seidelman	Susan	Movie Production	USA	Director
Seifert	Jaroslav	Creative Works	Czechoslovakia	Literature - Nobel Laureate
Seigmeister	Elie	Creative Works	USA	Composer
Seinfeld	Jerry	Performing Arts	USA	Comedian
Seixas Jr.	Elias Victor	Sports	USA	Tennis Player - HF
Seko	Mobutu Sese	Politics	Zaire	President
Selassie	Haile	Politics	Ethiopia	Emperor
Selden	John	Politics	England	Politician/Historian
Selee	Frank Gibson	Sports	USA	Baseball Manager - HF
Seles	Monica	Sports	Yugoslavia	Tennis Player
Seligman	Joseph	Business	USA	Banking
Sellars	Wilfrid Stalker	Arts	USA	Philosopher
Sellecca	Connie	Performing Arts	USA	Actress
Selleck	Tom	Performing Arts	USA	Actor
Sellers	Peter	Performing Arts	England	Actor - Acad Award Nom
Selmon	Lee Roy	Sports	USA	Football Player - HF
Selten	Reinhard	Arts	Germany	Economics - Nobel Laureate

SOLVER SERIES: NAME FINDER

LAST NAME	FIRST NAME	CATEGORY	COUNTRY	FAME
Selznick	David O	Movie Production	USA	Director
Semenov	Nikolay	Science	Russia	Chemistry - Nobel Laureate
Semjonova	Uljana	Sports	Latvia	Basketball Player - HF
Semper	Gottfried	Architecture	Germany	Architect
Sen	Amartya	Arts	India	Economics - Nobel Laureate
Sendak	Maurice	Creative Works	USA	Author/Artist - Children's Books
Senna	Ayrton	Sports	Brazil	Race Car Driver - HF
Sennett	Mack	Movie Production	USA	Director/Producer
Serkin	Peter	Performing Arts	USA	Pianist
	Rudolf	Performing Arts	USA	Pianist
Serlio	Sebastiano	Architecture	Italy	Architect
Serra	Junípero	Exploration	Spain	Explorer/Missionary - Mexico
Sert	Jose Luis	Architecture	USA	Architect - AIA/Jefferson Gold Medal
Servetus	Michael	Science	Spain	Physician/Theologian
Service	Robert William	Creative Works	Canada	Writer
Sesno	Frank	Creative Works	USA	Journalist - Television
Sessions	Roger Huntington	Creative Works	USA	Composer
Seton	Anya	Creative Works	USA	Author
	Ernest Thompson	Creative Works	USA	Writer/Naturalist/Illustrator
Seurat	Georges Pierre	Works of Art	France	Painter - Pointillism
Sevastyanov	Vitali Ivanovich	Aviation	Russia	Astronaut
Severinsen	Doc	Performing Arts	USA	Band Leader/Conductor
Seversky	Alexander Procofieff de	Business	USA	Aviation Industry - Aeronautical Engineer
Sévigné	Marie de Rabutin-Chantal	Creative Works	France	Writer
Sevigny	Chloe	Performing Arts	USA	Actress - Acad Award Nom
Seville	David	Performing Arts	USA	Actor
Sewall	Samuel	Law & Order	USA	Jurist
Seward	William Henry	Politics	USA	Statesman/Secretary of State
Sewell	Anna	Creative Works	England	Author - Black Beauty
	Joseph Wheeler (Joe)	Sports	USA	Baseball Player - HF
	Rufus	Performing Arts	England	Actor
Sexton	Anne	Creative Works	USA	Poet - Pulitzer
Seymour	Jane	Performing Arts	England	Actress
	Stephanie	Performing Arts	USA	Super Model
Seynhaeve	Ingrid	Performing Arts	Belgium	Super Model
Shaara	Michael	Creative Works	USA	Novelist - Pulitzer
Shackelford	Ted	Performing Arts	USA	Actor
Shackleton	Henry Ernest	Exploration	England	Explorer - Antarctic
Shaffer	Paul	Performing Arts	Canada	Band Leader
Shaftesbury	Anthony Ashley Cooper	Politics	England	Statesman
Shahn	Benjamin	Works of Art	USA	Painter
Shakespeare	William	Creative Works	USA	Poet/Dramatist
Shalit	Gene	Creative Works	USA	Journalist - Television
Shamir	Yitzhak	Politics	Israel	Prime Minister
Shan	Eda Le	Creative Works	USA	Author
Shandling	Garry	Performing Arts	USA	Comedian
Shankar	Ravi	Performing Arts	Bangladesh	Sitarist
Shanley	John Patrick	Creative Works	USA	Dramatist - Pulitzer
Shannon	Del	Performing Arts	USA	Singer
	Fred Albert	Creative Works	USA	Author - Pulitzer
	Jackie De	Performing Arts	USA	Singer
Shannon (Westover)	Charles Weedon (Del)	Performing Arts	USA	Singer - Rock & Roll - HF
Shapiro	Karl	Creative Works	USA	Poet - Pulitzer
Shapley	Harlow	Science	USA	Astronomer
Sharif	Omar	Games	Egypt	Bridge Expert
	Omar	Performing Arts	Egypt	Actor - Acad Award Nom
Sharman	William W. (Bill)	Sports	USA	Basketball Player - HF
Sharon	Ariel	Politics	Israel	Prime Minister
Sharp	Alexander	Performing Arts	USA	Rock & Roll - HF - The Orioles
	Anthony	Performing Arts	England	Actor
	Dee Dee	Performing Arts	USA	Singer
	Phillip A.	Science	USA	Medicine - Nobel Laureate
Sharpe	William F.	Arts	USA	Economics - Nobel Laureate

LAST NAME	FIRST NAME	CATEGORY	COUNTRY	FAME
Sharpless	Karl Barry	Science	USA	Chemistry - Nobel Laureate
Shatalov	Vladimir Aleksandrovich	Aviation	Russia	Astronaut
Shatner	William	Performing Arts	Canada	Actor
Shavers	Charles James (Charlie)	Performing Arts	USA	Jazz Trumpeter - Big Band/Jazz - HF
Shaw	Artie	Performing Arts	USA	Band Leader/Clarinetist
	George Bernard	Creative Works	England	Literature - Nobel Laureate
	Henry Wheeler	Creative Works	USA	Humourist
	Howard Van Doren	Architecture	USA	Architect - AIA Gold Medal
	Irwin	Movie Production	USA	Producer/Writer
	Reta	Performing Arts	USA	Actress
	Robert	Performing Arts	England	Actor - Acad Award Nom
	Thomas Edward	Creative Works	England	Writer/Adventurer
	Wilbur	Sports	USA	Race Car Driver - HF
	William Lewis (Billy)	Sports	USA	Football Player - HF
Shaw (Arshawsky)	Arthur Jacob (Artie)	Performing Arts	USA	Band Leader - Big Band/Jazz - HF
Shaw Jr.	Brewster Hopkinson	Aviation	USA	Astronaut
Shawn	Ted	Performing Arts	USA	Dancer/Choreographer
Shays	Daniel	War & Peace	USA	Revolutionary Soldier
Shea	John	Performing Arts	USA	Actor
Sheaffer	Louis	Creative Works	USA	Author - Pulitzer
Shearer	Alan	Sports	England	Soccer Player
	Moira	Performing Arts	Scotland	Dancer/Actress
	Norma	Performing Arts	Canada	Actress - Academy Award
Shearing	George	Performing Arts	England	Jazz Pianist
Sheedy	Ally	Performing Arts	USA	Actress
Sheehan	Cornelius Mahoney (Neil)	Creative Works	USA	Author - Pulitzer
	Patty	Sports	USA	Golfer - HF
	Susan	Creative Works	USA	Author - Pulitzer
Sheen	Charlie	Performing Arts	USA	Actor
	Martin	Performing Arts	USA	Actor
Shelby	Carroll	Sports	USA	Race Car Driver - HF
Shell	Arthur (Art)	Sports	USA	Football Player - HF
Shelley	Mary Wollstonecraft	Creative Works	England	Novelist
	Percy Bysshe	Creative Works	England	Poet
Shepard	Odel	Creative Works	USA	Author - Pulitzer
	Sam	Performing Arts	USA	Actor - Acad Award Nom
	Samuel (Sam)	Creative Works	USA	Dramatist - Pulitzer
Shepard Jr.	Alan Bartlett	Aviation	USA	Astronaut
Shepherd	Cybil	Performing Arts	USA	Actress/Model
	Jean Parker	Creative Works	USA	Writer - Short Stories
	William McMichael	Aviation	USA	Astronaut
	Delia	Performing Arts	Denmark	Actress
Sheridan	Ann	Performing Arts	USA	Actress
	Brinsley	Creative Works	England	Dramatist/Politician
	Jim	Movie Production	Ireland	Director - Acad Award Nom
	Philip Henry	War & Peace	USA	Union General - Civil War
	Richard Brinsley	Creative Works	Ireland	Playwright
Sherman	Allan	Performing Arts	USA	Singer
	Bobby	Performing Arts	USA	Singer
	James S.	Politics	USA	Vice-President
	John	Politics	USA	Statesman
	Roger	Politics	USA	Statesman
	William Tecumseh	War & Peace	USA	Union General - Civil War
Sherrington	Charles Scott	Science	England	Medicine - Nobel Laureate
Sherwood	Robert Emmet	Creative Works	USA	Dramatist - Pulitzer
Shields	Brooke	Performing Arts	USA	Actress
	Carol	Creative Works	Canada	Author - Pulitzer
	Francis Xavier (Frank)	Sports	USA	Tennis Player - HF
Shipler	David K.	Creative Works	USA	Author - Pulitzer
Shirakawa	Hideki	Science	Japan	Chemistry - Nobel Laureate
Shire	Talia	Performing Arts	USA	Actress - Acad Award Nom
Shirley	Anne	Performing Arts	USA	Actress - Acad Award Nom
	James	Creative Works	England	Dramatist

SOLVER SERIES: NAME FINDER

LAST NAME	FIRST NAME	CATEGORY	COUNTRY	FAME
Shockley	William Bradford	Science	USA	Physics - Nobel Laureate
Sholokhov	Mikhail Aleksandrovich	Creative Works	Russia	Literature - Nobel Laureate
Sholom	Aleichem	Creative Works	Russia	Dramatist
Shonin	Georgi Stepanovich	Aviation	Russia	Astronaut
Shor	Bernard (Toots)	Sports	USA	Baseball Player
Shore	Dinah	Performing Arts	USA	Singer
	Dinah	Sports	USA	Golfer - HF
	Edward William (Eddie)	Sports	Canada	Hockey Player - HF
Short	Bobby	Performing Arts	USA	Singer/Pianist
	Martin	Performing Arts	Canada	Comedian
Shorter	Frank	Sports	Germany	Olympic Marathoner
	Wayne	Performing Arts	USA	Jazz Saxophonist - Big Band/Jazz - HF
Shostakovich	Dmitri	Creative Works	Russia	Composer
Shrimpton	Jean	Performing Arts	England	Super Model
Shriver	Loren James	Aviation	USA	Astronaut
	Maria	Creative Works	USA	Journalist - Television
	Pam	Sports	USA	Tennis Player - HF
Shue	Andrew	Performing Arts	USA	Actor
	Elisabeth	Performing Arts	USA	Actress - Acad Award Nom
Shula	Donald Francis (Don)	Sports	USA	Football Coach - HF
Shull	Clifford G.	Science	USA	Physics - Nobel Laureate
Shute	Nevil	Creative Works	England	Novelist
Shutt	Stephen John	Sports	Canada	Hockey Player - HF
Shyamalan	Manoj Night	Movie Production	India	Director - Acad Award Nom
Sibelius	Jean	Creative Works	Finland	Composer
Sica	Vittorio De	Movie Production	Italy	Director
	Vittorio De	Performing Arts	Italy	Actor - Acad Award Nom
Sidgwick	Henry	Arts	England	Philosopher
Sidney	Philip	Creative Works	England	Poet/Statesman
	Sylvia	Performing Arts	USA	Actress - Acad Award Nom
Siebert	Albert Charles (Babe)	Sports	Canada	Hockey Player - HF
Siegbahn	Kai M.	Science	Sweden	Physics - Nobel Laureate
	Karl Manne Georg	Science	Sweden	Physics - Nobel Laureate
Siegel	Benjamin (Bugsy)	Law & Order	USA	Mafia
	Robert	Architecture	USA	Architect
Siemens	William	Science	England	Inventor/Engineer
Sienkiewicz	Henryk	Creative Works	Poland	Literature - Nobel Laureate
Siepi	Cesare	Performing Arts	Italy	Singer - Opera
Sierra	Ruben	Sports	USA	Baseball Player
Sifford	Charlie	Sports	USA	Golfer - HF
Signoret	Simone	Performing Arts	Germany	Actress - Academy Award
Sikorsky	Igor Ivanovich	Business	USA	Aviation Industry - Aeronautical Engineer
Sillanpää	Frans Eemil	Creative Works	Finland	Literature - Nobel Laureate
Sillitoe	Alan	Creative Works	England	Author/Playwright
Sills	Beverly	Performing Arts	USA	Singer - Opera
Silone	Ignazio	Creative Works	Italy	Writer
Silver	Abba Hillel	Arts	USA	Rabbi
	Horace Ward Martin Tavares	Performing Arts	USA	Jazz Pianist/Composer - Big Band/Jazz - HF
	Ron	Performing Arts	USA	Actor
Silverberg	Robert	Creative Works	USA	Author - SciFi
Silverman	Kenneth	Creative Works	USA	Author - Pulitzer
Silvers	Phil	Performing Arts	USA	Comedian
Silverstein	Sheldon Allan (Shel)	Creative Works	USA	Poet/Composer
Sim	Alastair	Performing Arts	Scotland	Actor
Simic	Charles	Creative Works	Yugoslavia	Poet - Pulitzer
Simmons	Aloysius Harry (Al)	Sports	USA	Baseball Player - HF
	Jean	Performing Arts	England	Actress - Acad Award Nom
	Kimora Lee	Business	USA	Fashion Designer
Simms	Phil	Sports	USA	Football Player
Simon	Carly	Performing Arts	USA	Singer
	Claude	Creative Works	France	Literature - Nobel Laureate
	Herbert A.	Arts	USA	Economics - Nobel Laureate
	Neil	Creative Works	USA	Dramatist - Pulitzer

LAST NAME	FIRST NAME	CATEGORY	COUNTRY	FAME
Simon	Paul Frederic	Performing Arts	USA	Rock & Roll - HF - Simon & Garfunkel
	Paul Frederic	Performing Arts	USA	Singer/Composer
Simone (Waymon)	Eunice Kathleen (Nina)	Performing Arts	USA	Singer/Pianist - Big Band/Jazz - HF
Simonon	Paul	Performing Arts	England	Rock & Roll - HF - The Clash
Simpson	Adele	Business	USA	Designer - Fashion
	Harold Joseph (Bullet Joe)	Sports	Canada	Hockey Player - HF
	Louis	Creative Works	Jamaica	Poet - Pulitzer
	Orenthal James (The Juice)	Sports	USA	Football Player - HF
	Scott	Sports	USA	Golfer
Sims	John Haley (Zoot)	Performing Arts	USA	Jazz Saxaphonist - Big Band/Jazz - HF
	William Sowden	Creative Works	Canada	Author - Pulitzer
Sinan	Mimar (the Great)	Architecture	Turkey	Architect
Sinatra	Frank	Performing Arts	USA	Actor - Academy Award
	Frank	Performing Arts	USA	Singer - Big Band/Jazz - HF
Sinclair	Gord	Performing Arts	Canada	Canadian Music - HF - The Tragically Hip
	Harry F.	Business	USA	Oil Industry
	Upton Beall Jr.	Creative Works	USA	Novelist - Pulitzer
Singer	Isaac Bashevis	Creative Works	USA	Literature - Nobel Laureate
	Isaac Merritt	Science	USA	Inventor - Sewing Machine
	Lori	Performing Arts	USA	Actress
Singh	Vijay	Sports	Fiji	Golfer
Singletary	Michael (Mike)	Sports	USA	Football Player
Singleton	John	Movie Production	USA	Director - Acad Award Nom
Sinlse	Gary	Performing Arts	USA	Actor - Acad Award Nom
Siodmak	Robert	Movie Production	Germany	Director - Acad Award Nom
Siqueiros	José David Alfaro	Works of Art	Mexico	Painter - Murals
Sirtis	Marina	Performing Arts	England	Actress
Siskel	Gene	Creative Works	USA	Journalist - Newspaper
Sisler	George Harold	Sports	USA	Baseball Player - HF
Sisley	Alfred	Works of Art	France	Painter
Sismondi	Jean Charles Léonard	Arts	Switzerland	Historian/Economist
Sitter	Willem de	Science	Netherlands	Astronomer
Sittler	Darryl Glen	Sports	Canada	Hockey Player - HF
Sitwell	Edith	Creative Works	England	Poet/Critic
	Sacheverell	Creative Works	England	Poet/Critic
Siza	Alvaro Vieira	Architecture	Portugal	Architect - Pritzker Laureate
Skala	Lillia	Performing Arts	Austria	Actress - Acad Award Nom
Skeat	Walter William	Arts	England	Lexicographer/Philologist
Skelton	John	Creative Works	England	Poet
	Red	Performing Arts	USA	Comedian
Skerritt	Tom	Performing Arts	USA	Actor
Skidmore	Louis	Architecture	USA	Architect - AIA Gold Medal
Skinner	Burrhus Frederic	Arts	USA	Psychologist
Sklenarikova	Adriana	Performing Arts	Slovakia	Super Model
Skou	Jens C.	Science	Denmark	Chemistry - Nobel Laureate
Skye	Ione	Performing Arts	England	Actress
Slater	Helen	Performing Arts	USA	Actress
	Jackie Ray	Sports	USA	Football Player
Slaughter	Enos Bradsher	Sports	USA	Baseball Player - HF
Slayton	Donald Kent	Aviation	USA	Astronaut
Sledge	Percy	Performing Arts	USA	Singer - Rock & Roll - HF
Slezak	Erika	Performing Arts	USA	Actress
	Leo	Performing Arts	Czechoslovakia	Singer - Opera
Sloan	John	Works of Art	USA	Painter/Etcher
Sloane	Everett	Performing Arts	USA	Actor
Slocum	Henry Warner	Sports	USA	Tennis Player - HF
Slone	Philip	Sports	USA	Soccer Player - HF
Sluman	Jeff	Sports	USA	Golfer
Slyke	Andy Van	Sports	USA	Baseball Player
Smalley	Richard E.	Science	USA	Chemistry - Nobel Laureate
Smetana	Bedřich	Creative Works	Czechoslovakia	Composer
Smiley	Jane	Creative Works	USA	Novelist - Pulitzer
Smirke	Robert	Architecture	England	Architect

SOLVER SERIES: NAME FINDER

LAST NAME	FIRST NAME	CATEGORY	COUNTRY	FAME
Smith	Adam	Arts	Scotland	Philosopher/Economist
	Alexis	Performing Arts	Canada	Actress
	Alfred E. (Alf)	Sports	Canada	Hockey Player - HF
	Alfred Emanuel	Politics	USA	Politician
	Bessie	Performing Arts	USA	Singer - Big Band/Jazz - HF
	Bruce	Sports	USA	Football Player
	Bubba	Sports	USA	Football Player
	Buffalo Bob	Performing Arts	USA	Actor
	Carl	Performing Arts	USA	Singer - Country Music - HF
	Clinton James	Sports	Canada	Hockey Player - HF
	David	Works of Art	USA	Painter - Abstract Expressionist
	Elizabeth (Bessie)	Performing Arts	USA	Singer - Rock & Roll - HF
	Gregory White	Creative Works	USA	Author - Pulitzer
	Hamilton O.	Science	USA	Medicine - Nobel Laureate
	Hezekiah Leroy Gordon (Stuff)	Performing Arts	USA	Jazz Violinist - Big Band/Jazz - HF
	Hilton	Sports	USA	Baseball Player - HF
	Horton	Sports	USA	Golfer - HF
	Jackie Larue	Sports	USA	Football Player - HF
	Jaclyn	Performing Arts	USA	Actress
	Jedediah	Exploration	USA	Frontiersman - California
	John	Exploration	England	Colonist - America
	Joseph	Arts	USA	Founder - Mormon Church
	Justin H.	Creative Works	USA	Author - Pulitzer
	Kate	Performing Arts	USA	Singer
	Keely	Performing Arts	USA	Singer
	Kim	Performing Arts	USA	Super Model
	Liz	Creative Works	USA	Journalist - Newspaper
	Louise	Sports	USA	Race Car Driver - HF
	Maggie	Performing Arts	England	Actress - Academy Award
	Michael	Science	Canada	Chemistry - Nobel Laureate
	Michael John	Aviation	USA	Astronaut
	Osborne Earl (Ozzie)	Sports	USA	Baseball Player - HF
	Patti	Performing Arts	USA	Singer - Rock & Roll - HF
	Phil	Performing Arts	USA	Rock & Roll - HF - Lovin' Spoonful
	Reginald (Hooley)	Sports	Canada	Hockey Player - HF
	Stanley Roger (Stan)	Sports	USA	Tennis Player - HF
	Sydney	Creative Works	England	Essayist/Clergyman
	Thomas J.	Sports	Canada	Hockey Player - HF
	Vernon L.	Arts	USA	Economics - Nobel Laureate
	Walter (Red)	Creative Works	USA	Journalist - Newspaper
	Wilbur	Creative Works	Africa	Author
	Will	Performing Arts	USA	Actor - Acad Award Nom
	William	Science	England	Geologist
	William Henry (WillieThe Lion)	Performing Arts	USA	Jazz Pianist - Big Band/Jazz - HF
	William John (Bill)	Sports	Canada	Hockey Player - HF
Smith (Hogan)	Vicki Lynn (Anna Nicole)	Performing Arts	USA	Super Model
Smith-Court	Margaret	Sports	Australia	Tennis Player - HF
Smits	Jimmy	Performing Arts	USA	Actor
Smollett	Tobias George	Creative Works	England	Novelist
Smothers	Dick	Performing Arts	USA	Comedian
	Tom	Performing Arts	USA	Comedian
Smuts	Jan Christiaan	Politics	South Africa	Prime Minster
Smyslov	Vasily	Games	Russia	Chess Player
Snead	Jesse Carlye (JC)	Sports	USA	Golfer
	Norm	Sports	USA	Football Player
	Sam	Sports	USA	Golfer - HF
Snell	George D.	Science	USA	Medicine - Nobel Laureate
	Peter	Sports	New Zealand	Olympic Runner
Sneva	Tom	Sports	USA	Race Car Driver
Snider	Edwin Donald (Duke)	Sports	USA	Baseball Player - HF
Snipes	Wesley	Performing Arts	USA	Actor
Snodgrass	William DeWitt	Creative Works	USA	Poet - Pulitzer
	Carrie	Performing Arts	USA	Actress - Acad Award Nom

LAST NAME	FIRST NAME	CATEGORY	COUNTRY	FAME
Snorri	Sturluson	Creative Works	Iceland	Poet/Ice Historian
Snow	Charles Percy	Creative Works	England	Novelist/Physicist
	Clarence Eugene (Hank)	Performing Arts	Canada	Singer - Canadian Music - HF
	Clarence Eugene (Hank)	Performing Arts	Canada	Singer - Country Music - HF
	Phoebe	Performing Arts	USA	Singer
Snozzi	Luigi	Architecture	Switzerland	Architect
Snyder	Gary	Creative Works	USA	Poet - Pulitzer
	Tom	Creative Works	USA	Journalist - Television
Soane	John	Architecture	England	Architect
Sobieski	John	Politics	Poland	King
Socinus	Faustus	Politics	Italy	Reformer - Religious
Soddy	Frederick	Science	England	Chemistry - Nobel Laureate
Soderbergh	Steven	Movie Production	USA	Director - Academy Award
Söderblom	Lars Olof Jonathan Nathan	War & Peace	Sweden	Peace - Nobel Laureate
Sola-Morales	Manuel de	Architecture	Spain	Architect
Soleri	Paolo	Architecture	Italy	Architect
Soles	Linden	Creative Works	Canada	Journalist - Television
Solheim	Karstein	Business	USA	Manufacturing Industry
	Karsten	Sports	Norway	Golf Club Designer - HF
Solow	Robert M.	Arts	USA	Economics - Nobel Laureate
Solti	Georg	Performing Arts	Hungary	Conductor/Composer
Solvay	Ernest	Science	Belgium	Chemist
Solzhenitsyn	Aleksander Isaevich	Creative Works	Russia	Literature - Nobel Laureate
Somers	Suzanne	Performing Arts	USA	Actress
Sommer	Elke	Performing Arts	Germany	Actress
Sommerville	Dave	Performing Arts	Canada	Canadian Music - HF - The Diamonds
Sondergaard	Gale	Performing Arts	USA	Actress - Academy Award
Sondheim	Stephen	Creative Works	USA	Composer
Sontag	Susan	Creative Works	USA	Novelist
Soo	Jack	Performing Arts	USA	Comedian
Sorel	Edward	Creative Works	USA	Artist
	Georges	Creative Works	France	Writer/Philosopher
Sörenstam	Annika	Sports	Sweden	Golfer - HF
Sorkin	Arlene	Performing Arts	USA	Actress
Sorvino	Mira	Performing Arts	USA	Actress - Academy Award
	Paul	Performing Arts	USA	Actor
Sothern	Ann	Performing Arts	USA	Actress - Acad Award Nom
	Edward Hugh	Performing Arts	USA	Actor
Soto	Hernando de	Exploration	Spain	Explorer - Mississippi River
Sottsass	Ettore	Architecture	Austria	Architect
Soufflot	Jaques Germain	Architecture	France	Architect
Soul	David	Performing Arts	USA	Actor
Sousa	John Phillip	Creative Works	USA	Composer/Band Master
	Sammy	Sports	USA	Baseball Player
Souter	David Hackett	Law & Order	USA	Justice - Supreme Court
Southey	Robert	Creative Works	England	Poet Laureate/Writer
Souza	Edward Neto (Ed)	Sports	USA	Soccer Player - HF
	John Benevides (Clarkie)	Sports	USA	Soccer Player - HF
Soyer	Moses	Works of Art	USA	Painter
	Raphael	Works of Art	USA	Painter
Soyinka	Wole	Creative Works	Nigeria	Literature - Nobel Laureate
Spacek	Sissy	Performing Arts	USA	Actress - Academy Award
Spacey	Kevin	Performing Arts	USA	Actor - Academy Award
Spade	David	Performing Arts	USA	Comedian
Spader	James	Performing Arts	USA	Actor
Spahn	Warren Edward	Sports	USA	Baseball Player - HF
Spalding	Albert Goodwill	Sports	USA	Baseball Executive - HF
	Charles H. (Dick)	Sports	USA	Soccer Player - HF
Spano	Joe	Performing Arts	USA	Actor
	Vincent	Performing Arts	USA	Actor
Spark	Muriel Sarah	Creative Works	Scotland	Novelist
Sparks	Ned	Performing Arts	Canada	Comedian
Spassky	Boris	Games	Russia	Chess Player

SOLVER SERIES: NAME FINDER

LAST NAME	FIRST NAME	CATEGORY	COUNTRY	FAME
Speaker	Tristram E. (Tris)	Sports	USA	Baseball Player - HF
Speck	Richard Benjamin	Law & Order	USA	Serial Killer
Specter	Arlen	Politics	USA	Senator - Pennsylvania
Spector	Harvey Philip (Phil)	Creative Works	USA	Song Writer/Producer
	Ronnie	Performing Arts	USA	Singer - Rock & Roll - HF
Spee	Maximilan	War & Peace	Germany	Admiral
Speer	Albert	Architecture	Germany	Architect
Spelling	Aaron	Movie Production	USA	Director
	Tori	Performing Arts	USA	Actress
Speman	Hans	Science	Germany	Medicine - Nobel Laureate
Spence	Michael	Arts	USA	Economics - Nobel Laureate
Spencer	Herbert	Arts	England	Philosopher
	Timothy	Performing Arts	USA	Country Music - HF - Sons of the Pioneers
	Tom	Business	England	Confection Industry
Spender	Jeremy	Performing Arts	England	Rock & Roll - HF - Fleetwood Mac
	Stephen	Creative Works	England	Poet/Critic
Spengler	Oswald	Arts	Germany	Philosopher
Spenser	Edmund	Creative Works	England	Poet
Sperry	Elmer Ambrose	Science	USA	Inventor/Electrical Engineer
	Roger W.	Science	USA	Medicine - Nobel Laureate
Speyer	Leonora	Creative Works	USA	Poet - Pulitzer
Spielberg	Steven	Movie Production	USA	Director - Academy Award
Spillane	Frank Morrison (Mickey)	Creative Works	USA	Author - Crime Fiction
Spiner	Brent	Performing Arts	USA	Actor
Spinks	Leon	Sports	USA	Boxer
	Michael	Sports	USA	Boxer - HF
Spinoza	Baruch Benedict	Arts	Netherlands	Philosopher
Spitteler	Carl Friedrich Georg	Creative Works	Switzerland	Literature - Nobel Laureate
Spitz	Mark	Sports	USA	Olympic Swimmer
Spock	Benjamin McLane	Science	USA	Pediatrician/Writer
Spring	Sherwood Clark (Woody)	Aviation	USA	Astronaut
Springer	Robert Clyde	Aviation	USA	Astronaut
Springfield	Rick	Performing Arts	Australia	Singer/Actor
Springfield (O'Brien)	Mary Isobel (Dusty)	Performing Arts	England	Singer - Rock & Roll - HF
Springsteen	Bruce Frederic	Performing Arts	USA	Singer - Rock & Roll - HF
Spyri	Johanna Louise	Creative Works	Switzerland	Author
St. Clair	Robert Bruce (Bob) (Geek)	Sports	USA	Football Player - HF
St. Denis	Ruth	Performing Arts	USA	Dancer/Choreographer
St. James	Susan	Performing Arts	USA	Actress
St. John	Adela Rogers	Creative Works	USA	Journalist - Newspaper
	Jill	Performing Arts	USA	Actress
St. Laurent	Louis Stephen	Politics	Canada	Prime Minster
Stabler	Ken	Sports	USA	Football Player
Stack	Robert	Performing Arts	USA	Actor - Acad Award Nom
Stacy	Hollis	Sports	USA	Golfer
Stadler	Craig	Sports	USA	Golfer
Staël	Anne Louise Germaine Necker	Creative Works	France	Writer
Stafford	Jean	Creative Works	USA	Novelist - Pulitzer
	Jim	Performing Arts	USA	Singer - Pops/Country
	Jo Elizabeth	Performing Arts	USA	Singer - Big Band/Jazz - HF
	Thomas Patten	Aviation	USA	Astronaut
Stahl	Lesley	Creative Works	USA	Journalist - Television
Stalin	Joseph	Politics	Russia	Premier
Stallone	Sylvestor	Performing Arts	USA	Actor - Acad Award Nom
Stallworth	John Lee (Johnny)	Sports	USA	Football Player - HF
Stamos	John	Performing Arts	USA	Actor
Stamp	Terence	Performing Arts	England	Actor - Acad Award Nom
Stander	Lionel	Performing Arts	USA	Actor
Standish	Miles	War & Peace	England	Military Leader - Plymouth
Stang	Arnold	Performing Arts	USA	Comedian
Stanhope	Philip Dormer	Politics	England	Statesman
Stanislavsky	Konstantin	Performing Arts	Russia	Actor
Stanley	Allan Herbert	Sports	Canada	Hockey Player - HF

LAST NAME	FIRST NAME	CATEGORY	COUNTRY	FAME
Stanley	Henry Morton	Exploration	England	Explorer - Africa
	Kim	Performing Arts	USA	Actress - Acad Award Nom
	Russell (Barney)	Sports	Canada	Hockey Player - HF
	Wendell Meredith	Science	USA	Chemistry - Nobel Laureate
Stanton	Edwin McMasters	Politics	USA	Statesman/Secretary of War
	Elizabeth Cady	Politics	USA	Reformer/Suffragist
	Harry Dean	Performing Arts	USA	Actor
Stanwyck	Barbara	Performing Arts	USA	Actress - Acad Award Nom
Stapledon	William Olaf	Creative Works	England	Author - SciFi
Staples	Mavis	Performing Arts	USA	Rock & Roll - HF - The Staple Singers
	Roebuck (Pops)	Performing Arts	USA	Rock & Roll - HF - The Staple Singers
Stapleton	Jean	Performing Arts	USA	Actress
	Maureen	Performing Arts	USA	Actress - Academy Award
Star (Shirley)	Myra Belle	Law & Order	USA	Outlaw
Stargell	Wilver Dornel (Willie)	Sports	USA	Baseball Player - HF
Stark	Archibald MacPherson (Archie)	Sports	Scotland	Soccer Player - HF
	Johannes	Science	Germany	Physics - Nobel Laureate
Starr	Bryan Bartlett (Bart)	Sports	USA	Football Player - HF
	Kay	Performing Arts	USA	Singer - Pops
	Paul	Creative Works	USA	Author - Pulitzer
Starr (Starkey)	Richard (Ringo)	Performing Arts	England	Rock & Roll - HF - The Beatles
Stastny	Peter	Sports	Slovakia	Hockey Player - HF
Staub	Rusty	Sports	USA	Baseball Player
Staubach	Roger Thomas	Sports	USA	Football Player - HF
Staudinger	Hermann	Science	Germany	Chemistry - Nobel Laureate
Staunton	Imelda	Performing Arts	England	Actress - Acad Award Nom
Stauss	Peter	Performing Arts	USA	Actor
Stautner	Ernest Alfred (Ernie)	Sports	Bavaria	Football Player - HF
Stearnes	Norman Thomas (Turkey)	Sports	USA	Baseball Player - HF
Steele	John	Performing Arts	England	Rock & Roll - HF - The Animals
	Richard	Creative Works	England	Dramatist/Essayist
Steen	Jan	Works of Art	Netherlands	Painter
Steenburgen	Mary	Performing Arts	USA	Actress - Academy Award
Stefani	Gwen	Performing Arts	USA	Singer - Pops
Stefano	Alfredo Di	Sports	Argentina	Soccer Player - HF
Stefansson	Vilhjalmur	Exploration	Canada	Explorer - Arctic
Steffens	Joseph Lincoln	Creative Works	USA	Author/Journalist
Stegner	Wallace Earle	Creative Works	USA	Novelist - Pulitzer
Steichen	Edward	Arts	USA	Photographer
Steiger	Rod	Performing Arts	USA	Actor - Academy Award
Stein	Clarence S.	Architecture	USA	Architect - AIA Gold Medal
	Gertrude	Creative Works	USA	Writer
	Seymour	Performing Arts	USA	Promoter - Rock & Roll - HF
	William H.	Science	USA	Chemistry - Nobel Laureate
Steinbeck	John Ernst	Creative Works	USA	Literature - Nobel/Pulitzer
Steinberg	David	Performing Arts	Canada	Comedian
Steinberger	Jack	Science	USA	Physics - Nobel Laureate
Steinbrecher	Hank	Sports	USA	Soccer Promoter - HF
Steinbrenner	George	Business	USA	Baseball Owner
Steinem	Gloria	Creative Works	USA	Journalist - Magazine
Steinitz	Wilhelm	Games	Czechoslovakia	Chess Player
Steinmetz	Charles Proteus	Science	USA	Inventor/Electrical Engineer
	Christian	Sports	USA	Basketball Player - HF
Steinway	Heinrich	Business	USA	Manufacturing Industry - Pianos
Stella	Ettore	Architecture	Italy	Architect
Stendhal	Marie Henri	Creative Works	France	Novelist/Essayist
Stenerud	Jan	Sports	Norway	Football Player - HF
Stengel	Charles Dillon (Casey)	Sports	USA	Baseball Manager - HF
Stenmark	Ingemar	Sports	Sweden	Olympic Skier
Stenn	Anna	Performing Arts	Ukraine	Actress
Stephen	Leslie	Arts	England	Philosopher/Critic
Stephens	Alexander Hamilton	Politics	USA	Vice-President - Confederacy
	James	Creative Works	Ireland	Poet/Novelist

SOLVER SERIES: NAME FINDER

LAST NAME	FIRST NAME	CATEGORY	COUNTRY	FAME
Stephenson	Dwight Eugene	Sports	USA	Football Player - HF
	George	Science	England	Engineer - Steam Locomotive
	James	Performing Arts	England	Actor - Acad Award Nom
	Jan Lynne	Sports	Australia	Golfer
	Robert	Science	England	Engineer - Bridge Builder
Sterling	Jan	Performing Arts	USA	Actress - Acad Award Nom
	Ross Shaw	Business	USA	Railway Magnate
Stern	Howard	Performing Arts	USA	Show Host
	Isaac	Performing Arts	Russia	Violinist
	Otto	Science	USA	Physics - Nobel Laureate
	Robert Arthur Morton	Architecture	USA	Architect
Sternberg	Josef Von	Movie Production	Austria	Director - Acad Award Nom
Sterne	Laurence	Creative Works	England	Novelist
Sternhagen	Frances	Performing Arts	USA	Actress
Steuben	Frederick William Augustus von	War & Peace	USA	General - American Revolution
Stevens	Andrew	Performing Arts	USA	Actor
	Cat	Performing Arts	England	Singer - Pops
	Connie	Performing Arts	USA	Actress
	Dodie	Performing Arts	USA	Singer - Doo Whop
	George	Movie Production	USA	Director - Academy Award
	Inger	Performing Arts	Sweden	Actress
	John Paul	Law & Order	USA	Justice - Supreme Court
	Mark	Creative Works	USA	Author - Pulitzer
	Ray	Performing Arts	USA	Singer - Pops
	Stella	Performing Arts	USA	Actress
	Thaddeus	Politics	USA	Statesman/Abolitionist
	Wallace	Creative Works	USA	Poet - Pulitzer
Stevenson	Adlai E.	Politics	USA	Vice-President
	McLean	Performing Arts	USA	Actor
	Parker	Performing Arts	USA	Actor
	Robert	Movie Production	England	Director - Acad Award Nom
	Robert Louis Ballfour	Creative Works	Scotland	Poet/Novelist/Essayist
	Teofilo	Sports	USA	Boxer
Stewart	Al	Performing Arts	Scotland	Singer - Folk
	Gene	Performing Arts	USA	Rock & Roll - HF - The Soul Stirrers
	Jackie (The Flyng Scott)	Sports	Scotland	Race Car Driver - HF
	James	Performing Arts	USA	Actor - Academy Award
	John Sherratt (Black Jack)	Sports	Canada	Hockey Player - HF
	Nelson (Old Poison)	Sports	Canada	Hockey Player - HF
	Patrick	Performing Arts	England	Actor
	Payne William	Sports	USA	Golfer - HF
	Potter	Law & Order	USA	Justice - Supreme Court
	Rex	Performing Arts	USA	Jazz Cornetist - Big Band/Jazz - HF
	Robert Lee	Aviation	USA	Astronaut
	Rod (Roderick David)	Performing Arts	England	Singer - Rock & Roll - HF
	Sly (Sylvester)	Performing Arts	USA	Rock & Roll - HF - Sly & The Family Stone
Stieb	Dave	Sports	USA	Baseball Player
Stieglitz	Alfred	Works of Art	USA	Photographer
Stiers	David Ogden	Performing Arts	USA	Actor
Stigler	George J.	Arts	USA	Economics - Nobel Laureate
Stiglitz	Joseph E.	Arts	USA	Economics - Nobel Laureate
Stignani	Ebe	Performing Arts	Italy	Singer - Opera
Stiller	Jerry	Performing Arts	USA	Actor
Stills	Stephen Arthur	Performing Arts	USA	Rock & Roll - HF - Buffalo Springfield
Stimson	Henry Lewis	Politics	USA	Statesman/Secretary of State
Stipes	Michael	Performing Arts	USA	Singer/Composer
Stirling	James	Architecture	England	Architect - Pritzker/Jefferson Medal
Stitt	Edward (Sonny)	Performing Arts	USA	Jazz Saxophonist - Big Band/Jazz - HF
Stockton	Dave	Sports	USA	Golfer
	John	Sports	USA	Basketball Player
Stockwell	Dean	Performing Arts	USA	Actor - Acad Award Nom
Stoddard	Alexandra	Arts	USA	Philosopher/Writer
Stoitchkov	Hristo	Sports	Bulgaria	Soccer Player

LAST NAME	FIRST NAME	CATEGORY	COUNTRY	FAME
Stoker	Abraham (Bram)	Creative Works	Ireland	Author
	Hugh Gordon	Performing Arts	USA	Country Music - HF - The Jordonaires
Stokes	Maurice	Sports	USA	Basketball Player - HF
Stokowski	Leopold	Performing Arts	USA	Conductor - Orchestra
Stolle	Frederick Sydney (Fiery Fred)	Sports	Australia	Tennis Player - HF
Stoltz	Eric	Performing Arts	USA	Actor
Stone	Dee Wallace	Performing Arts	USA	Actress
	Edward Durell	Architecture	USA	Architect
	Harlan Fiske	Law & Order	USA	Chief Justice
	Irving	Creative Works	USA	Novelist
	Lewis	Performing Arts	USA	Actor - Acad Award Nom
	Lucy	Politics	USA	Reformer/Suffragist
	Milburn	Performing Arts	USA	Actor
	Oliver	Movie Production	USA	Director - Academy Award
	Richard	Arts	England	Economics - Nobel Laureate
	Sharon	Performing Arts	USA	Actress - Acad Award Nom
	Sylvester (Sly)	Performing Arts	USA	Singer
Stones	Dwight	Sports	USA	Olympic High Jumper
Stookey	Paul	Performing Arts	USA	Singer - Folk
Stoppard	Tom	Creative Works	England	Playwright
Storch	Larry	Performing Arts	USA	Actor
Storey	David	Creative Works	England	Author/Playwright
Storm	Gale	Performing Arts	USA	Actress/Singer
Störmer	Horst L.	Science	Germany	Physics - Nobel Laureate
Story	Joseph	Law & Order	USA	Justice - Supreme Court
Stottlemyre	Mel	Sports	USA	Baseball Player
Stout	Rex Todhunter	Creative Works	USA	Author
Stowe	Harriet Elizabeth Beecher	Creative Works	USA	Novelist
Strachey	Giles Lytton	Arts	England	Biographer
Stradivari	Antonio	Arts	Italy	Violin Maker
Strafford	Thomas Wentworth	Politics	England	Statesman
Straight	Beatrice	Performing Arts	USA	Actress - Academy Award
Strain	Sammy	Performing Arts	USA	Rock & Roll - HF - The O'Jays
Strait	George	Performing Arts	USA	Singer - Country & Western
Stram	Henry Louis (Hank)	Sports	USA	Football Coach - HF
Strand	Mark	Creative Works	Canada	Poet - Pulitzer
Strange	Curtis	Sports	USA	Golfer
Strasberg	Lee	Performing Arts	Ukraine	Actor - Acad Award Nom
Strasberg	Susan	Performing Arts	USA	Actress
Stratas	Teresa	Performing Arts	Canada	Singer - Opera
Straus	Oscar	Creative Works	Austria	Composer
Strauss	Isidor	Business	USA	Drygoods
	Johann	Creative Works	Austria	Composer - Waltzes
	Peter	Performing Arts	USA	Actor
	Richard	Creative Works	Germany	Composer/Conductor
	Robert	Performing Arts	USA	Actor - Acad Award Nom
Stravinsky	Igor Fedorovich	Creative Works	USA	Composer/Conductor
Strawberry	Darryl	Sports	USA	Baseball Player
Strayhorn	Billy	Performing Arts	USA	Jazz Pianist/Composer - Big Band/Jazz - HF
Streep	Meryl	Performing Arts	USA	Actress - Academy Award
Streisand	Barbra	Performing Arts	USA	Actress/Singer - Acad Award
Streit	Marlene Stewart	Sports	Canada	Golfer - HF
Stresemann	Gustav	War & Peace	Germany	Peace - Nobel Laureate
Stribling	Thomas Sigismund	Creative Works	USA	Novelist - Pulitzer
Strindberg	Johan August	Creative Works	Sweden	Novelist/Dramatist
Stritch	Elaine	Performing Arts	USA	Actress
Stroheim	Erich von	Performing Arts	Austria	Actor - Acad Award Nom
Strong Jr.	Elmer Kenneth (Ken)	Sports	USA	Football Player - HF
Strummer (Mellor)	John Graham (Joe)	Performing Arts	Turkey	Rock & Roll - HF - The Clash
Struthers	Sally	Performing Arts	USA	Actress
Strutt	Jedediah	Business	England	Textile Industry
	John William	Science	England	Physics - Nobel Laureate
Strzelecki	Paul Edmund de	Exploration	Poland	Explorer - Australia Mountains

SOLVER SERIES: NAME FINDER

LAST NAME	FIRST NAME	CATEGORY	COUNTRY	FAME
Stuart	Bruce	Sports	Canada	Hockey Player - HF
	Gilbert Charles	Works of Art	USA	Painter - Portrait
	James Ewell Brown	War & Peace	USA	General - Confederate
	Gloria	Performing Arts	USA	Actress - Acad Award Nom
Stuarti	Enzio	Performing Arts	Italy	Singer - Opera
Stubbins	Hugh A.	Architecture	USA	Architect - Jefferson Medal
Stubbs	Levi	Performing Arts	USA	Rock & Roll - HF - The Four Tops
Sturges	Preston	Movie Production	USA	Director - Acad Award Nom
	Peter	Exploration	Netherlands	Explorer - New York
	Peter	Politics	Netherlands	Governor
Stydahar	Joseph Lee (Joe)	Sports	USA	Football Player - HF
Styne	Jule	Creative Works	England	Composer
Styron	William	Creative Works	USA	Author - Pulitzer
Suckling	John	Creative Works	England	Poet
Sue	Eugene	Creative Works	France	Novelist
Suggs	Louise	Sports	USA	Golfer - HF
Sukova	Helena	Sports	Czechoslovakia	Tennis Player
Sullavan	Margaret	Performing Arts	USA	Actress - Acad Award Nom
Sullivan	Arthur Seymour	Creative Works	England	Composer
	Barry	Performing Arts	USA	Actor
	Danny	Sports	USA	Race Car Driver
	Ed	Performing Arts	USA	Show Host
	John Lawrence	Sports	USA	Boxer
	Kathryn Dwyer	Aviation	USA	Astronaut
	Louis Henry	Architecture	USA	Architect - AIA Gold Medal
	Susan	Performing Arts	USA	Actress
Sully	Maximilien de Béthune	Politics	France	Statesman
	Thomas	Works of Art	USA	Painter
Sully-Prudhomme	René François Armand	Creative Works	France	Poet/Critic
Sulston	John E.	Science	England	Medicine - Nobel Laureate
Sumac	Yma	Performing Arts	Peru	Singer - Folk
Summer	Donna	Performing Arts	USA	Singer - Disco
Summers (Somers)	Andrew (Andy)	Performing Arts	England	Rock & Roll - HF - The Police
Summerville	Slim	Performing Arts	USA	Comedian
Sumner	Charles	Politics	USA	Statesman/Abolitionist
	Gordon Matthew (Sting)	Performing Arts	England	Singer - Rock & Roll - HF
	James Batchellor	Science	USA	Chemistry - Nobel Laureate
	Rosalyn	Sports	USA	Olympic Skater
	William Graham	Arts	USA	Economist/Sociologist
Sun	Yatsen	Politics	China	Political & Revoltionary Leader
Sunday	Billy	Arts	USA	Evangilist - WW I
Sung	Alfred	Business	Japan	Fashion Designer
Sununu	John Edward	Politics	USA	Senator - New Hampshire
Surrey	Henry Howard	Creative Works	England	Poet/Courtier
Surtees	John	Sports	England	Race Car Driver - HF
Susann	Jacqueline	Creative Works	USA	Novelistt
Sutcliffe	Stu	Performing Arts	Scotland	Guitarist
Suter	Johann August	Business	USA	Gold Mining
Sutherland	Donald	Performing Arts	Canada	Actor
	Joan	Performing Arts	Australia	Singer - Opera
	Kiefer	Performing Arts	England	Actor
Sutherland Jr.	Earl W.	Science	USA	Medicine - Nobel Laureate
Suttner	Bertha von	War & Peace	Austria	Peace - Nobel Laureate
Sutton	Donald Howard (Don)	Sports	USA	Baseball Player - HF
Sutton-Bundy	May Godfray	Sports	USA	Tennis Player - HF
Suvorov	Aleksandr Vasilievich	War & Peace	Russia	Field Marshall
Suzman	Janet	Performing Arts	South Africa	Actress - Acad Award Nom
Svedberg	Theodore	Science	Sweden	Chemistry - Nobel Laureate
Swan	Annalyn	Creative Works	USA	Author - Pulitzer
Swanberg	William Andrew	Creative Works	USA	Author - Pulitzer
Swank	Hilary	Performing Arts	USA	Actress - Academy Award
Swann	Lynn Curtis	Sports	USA	Football Player - HF
Swanson	Gloria	Performing Arts	USA	Actress - Acad Award Nom

LAST NAME	FIRST NAME	CATEGORY	COUNTRY	FAME
Swayze	Patrick	Performing Arts	USA	Actor
Swedenborg	Emanuel	Arts	Sweden	Philosopher/Scientist/Mystic
Sweet	Henry	Arts	England	Linguist
Swenson	Inga	Performing Arts	USA	Actress
Swift	Jonathan	Creative Works	England	Satirist
Swigert	John Leonard	Aviation	USA	Astronaut
Swinburne	Algernon Charles	Creative Works	England	Poet/Critic
Swit	Loretta	Performing Arts	USA	Actress
Swords	Thomas	Sports	USA	Soccer Player - HF
Sydow	Max von	Performing Arts	Sweden	Actor - Acad Award Nom
Symonds	John Addington	Creative Works	England	Poet/Writer/Scholar
Synge	John Millington	Creative Works	Ireland	Dramatist
	Richard Laurence Millington	Science	England	Chemistry - Nobel Laureate
Syngman	Rhee	Politics	South Korea	Head of State
Szell	George	Performing Arts	USA	Conductor - Orchestra/Pianist
Szent-Györgyi	Albert von	Science	Hungary	Medicine - Nobel Laureate
Szold	Henrietta	Politics	USA	Zionist Leader
Szymborska	Wislawa	Creative Works	Poland	Literature - Nobel Laureate
Taft	Helen	Politics	USA	First Lady
	Lorado	Works of Art	USA	Sculptor
	William Howard	Politics	USA	President
Tagoré	Rabindranath	Creative Works	India	Literature - Nobel Laureate
Taine	Hippolyte Adolphe	Arts	France	Literary Critic/Historian
Takamine	Jokichi	Science	USA	Chemist
Tal	Mikhail Nekhemievich	Games	Latvia	Chess Player
	Shiraz	Performing Arts	Israel	Super Model
Talbert	William Franklin (Bill)	Sports	USA	Tennis Player - HF
Talbot	Nita	Performing Arts	USA	Actress
Tallis	Thomas	Creative Works	England	Composer
Talmadge	Norma	Performing Arts	USA	Actress
Tamblyn	Russ	Performing Arts	USA	Actor - Acad Award Nom
Tambor	Jeffrey	Performing Arts	USA	Actor
Tami	Rino	Architecture	Switzerland	Architect
Tamiroff	Akim	Performing Arts	Russia	Actor - Acad Award Nom
Tamm	Igor Evgenyevich	Science	Russia	Physics - Nobel Laureate
Tan	Amy	Creative Works	USA	Author
Tanaka	Koichi	Science	Japan	Chemistry - Nobel Laureate
Tandy	Jessica	Performing Arts	England	Actress - Academy Award
Taney	Roger Brooke	Law & Order	USA	Chief Justice
Tange	Kenzo	Architecture	Japan	Architect - Pritzker/ AIA Gold
Tanguy	Yves	Works of Art	France	Painter
Taniguchi	Yoshio	Architecture	Japan	Architect
Tanner	Paul	Performing Arts	USA	Jazz Trombonist - Big Band/Jazz - HF
	Roscoe	Sports	USA	Tennis Player
Tappan	Arthur	Business	USA	Drygoods
	Lewis	Business	USA	Drygoods
Tarantino	Quentin	Movie Production	USA	Director - Acad Award Nom
Tarbell	Ida Minerva	Creative Works	USA	Journalist/Author
Tarkenton	Francis Asbury (Fran)	Sports	USA	Football Player - HF
Tarkington	Newton Booth	Creative Works	USA	Novelist
Tartini	Giuseppe	Creative Works	Italy	Composer/Violinist
Tashlin	Frank	Movie Production	USA	Director
Tashman	Lilyan	Performing Arts	USA	Actress
Tasman	Abel Janszoon	Exploration	Netherlands	Explorer - Tasmania
Tasso	Torquato	Creative Works	Italy	Poet - Epic
Tate	Henry	Business	England	Entrepreneur
	James	Creative Works	USA	Poet - Pulitzer
	Jeffrey	Performing Arts	England	Conductor
	John Orley Allen	Creative Works	USA	Poet/Critic
	Nahum	Creative Works	England	Poet Laureate/Dramatist
Tatlin	Vladimir	Architecture	Russia	Architect/Painter/Sculptor
Tatum	Art	Performing Arts	USA	Jazz Pianist - Big Band/Jazz - HF
	Edward Lawrie	Science	USA	Medicine - Nobel Laureate

SOLVER SERIES: NAME FINDER

LAST NAME	FIRST NAME	CATEGORY	COUNTRY	FAME
Taube	Henry	Science	USA	Chemistry - Nobel Laureate
Taubman	William	Creative Works	USA	Author - Pulitzer
Taurog	Norman	Movie Production	USA	Director - Academy Award
Taussig	Frank William	Arts	USA	Political Economist
Taut	Bruno	Architecture	Turkey	Architect
Tawney	Richard Henry	Arts	England	Economist - Historian
Taylor	Alan	Creative Works	USA	Author - Pulitzer
	Billy (Doctor)	Performing Arts	USA	Jazz Pianist/Composer - Big Band/Jazz - HF
	Brook	Science	England	Mathematician
	Charles Robert (Charley)	Sports	USA	Football Player - HF
	Elizabeth	Performing Arts	England	Actress - Academy Award
	Frederick (Cyclone)	Sports	Canada	Hockey Player - HF
	Henry	Creative Works	USA	Poet - Pulitzer
	James	Performing Arts	USA	Singer - Rock & Roll - HF
	James Bayard	Creative Works	USA	Poet/Journalist
	James Charles (Jim)	Sports	USA	Football Player - HF
	Jeremy	Arts	England	Bishop/Theologian
	John	Arts	USA	Philosopher
	John Edward	Business	England	Publishing
	John H.	Sports	Scotland	Golfer - HF
	Joseph Deems	Creative Works	USA	Composer/Music Critic
	Joseph H.	Science	USA	Physics - Nobel Laureate
	Lawrence Julius	Sports	USA	Football Player - HF
	Lili	Performing Arts	USA	Actress
	Margaret	Politics	USA	First Lady
	Niki	Performing Arts	USA	Super Model
	Peter	Creative Works	USA	Novelist - Pulitzer
	Renee	Performing Arts	USA	Actress
	Richard E.	Science	Canada	Physics - Nobel Laureate
	Rip	Performing Arts	USA	Comedian
	Robert	Performing Arts	USA	Actor
	Robert Lewis	Creative Works	USA	Author - Pulitzer
	Rod	Performing Arts	Australia	Actor
	Roger	Performing Arts	England	Rock & Roll - HF - Queen
	Zachary	Politics	USA	President
	Zola	Performing Arts	USA	Rock & Roll - HF - The Platters
Tchaikovsky	Peter Ilyich	Creative Works	Russia	Composer
Teagarden	Weldon Leo (Jack)	Performing Arts	USA	Jazz Trombonist - Big Band/Jazz - HF
Teale	Edwin Way	Creative Works	USA	Author - Pulitzer
Teasdale	Sara	Creative Works	USA	Poet - Pulitzer
Tebaldi	Renata	Performing Arts	Italy	Singer - Opera
Tedesko	Anton	Architecture	USA	Architect
Teilhard de Chardin	Pierre	Arts	France	Paleontologist/Geologist
Telemann	Georg Philipp	Creative Works	Germany	Composer
Teller	Edward	Science	USA	Physicist - Nuclear
Temin	Howard Martin	Science	USA	Medicine - Nobel Laureate
Temple	Shirley	Performing Arts	USA	Actress - Academy Award
	William	Creative Works	England	Writer/Diplomat
Templeton	Alec	Performing Arts	USA	Pianist
Templewood	Samuel John Gurney Hoare	Politics	England	Statesman
Tench	Benmont	Performing Arts	USA	Rock & Roll - HF - Heart Breakers
Teniers	David	Works of Art	Italy	Painter
Tennant	Victoria	Performing Arts	England	Actress
Tenniel	John	Works of Art	England	Illustrator/Caricaturist
Tennille	Toni	Performing Arts	USA	Singer - Pops
Tennyson	Alfred	Creative Works	England	Poet Laureate
Ter Borch	Gerard	Works of Art	Netherlands	Painter
Teresa	Mother	War & Peace	India	Peace - Nobel Laureate
Tereshkova	Vanlentina Vladimirovna	Aviation	Russia	Astronaut
Terkel	Louis (Studs)	Creative Works	USA	Author - Pulitzer
Terman	Louis Madison	Arts	USA	Psychologist
Terragni	Giuseppe	Architecture	Italy	Architect
Terry	Clark	Performing Arts	USA	Jazz Trumpeter - Big Band/Jazz - HF

LAST NAME	FIRST NAME	CATEGORY	COUNTRY	FAME
Terry	Ellen	Performing Arts	England	Actress
	William Harold (Bill)	Sports	USA	Baseball Player - HF
Tesh	John	Creative Works	USA	Composer/Pianist
Teshigahara	Hiroshi	Movie Production	Japan	Director - Acad Award Nom
Tesla	Nikola	Science	USA	Inventor
Tessenow	Heinrich	Architecture	Germany	Architect
Testa	Clorindo	Architecture	Italy	Architect
Tetrazzini	Luisa	Performing Arts	Italy	Singer - Opera
Tevis	Walter Stone	Creative Works	USA	Author
Tex	Joe	Performing Arts	USA	Singer
Tey	Josephine	Creative Works	Scotland	Author
Thackeray	William Makepeace	Creative Works	England	Novelist
Thagard	Norman Earl	Aviation	USA	Astronaut
Thant	U	Politics	Burma	Secretary-General UN
Tharp	Twyla	Creative Works	USA	Choreographer
Thatcher	Margaret	Politics	England	Prime Minster
Thaves	Bob	Creative Works	USA	Cartoonist - Frank & Ernest
Theiler	Max	Science	South Africa	Medicine - Nobel Laureate
Theismann	Joe	Sports	USA	Football Player
Theorell	Axel Hugo Theodor	Science	Sweden	Medicine - Nobel Laureate
Thermes	Laura	Architecture	Italy	Architect
Theron	Charlize	Performing Arts	South Africa	Actress - Academy Award
Theroux	Paul Edward	Creative Works	USA	Novelist
Thicke	Alan	Performing Arts	Canada	Actor
Thiele	Gerhard Julius Paul	Aviation	Germany	Astronaut
Thiers	Louis Adolphe	Politics	France	Statesman/Historian
Thill	Georges	Performing Arts	France	Singer - Opera
Thirsk	Robert Brent	Aviation	Canada	Astronaut
Tho	Le Duc	War & Peace	Vietnam	Peace - Nobel Laureate
Thomas	Billy Joe (BJ)	Performing Arts	USA	Singer - Pops
	Cal	Creative Works	USA	Author/Journalist
	Carla	Performing Arts	USA	Singer
	Clarence	Law & Order	USA	Justice - Supreme Court
	Danny	Performing Arts	USA	Comedian
	Debi	Sports	USA	Olympic Skater
	Dylan Marlais	Creative Works	Wales	Poet
	Edward Donnall	Science	USA	Medicine - Nobel Laureate
	George Henry	War & Peace	USA	Union General - Civil War
	Herb	Sports	USA	Race Car Driver - HF
	Isiah	Sports	USA	Basketball Player - HF
	Jay	Performing Arts	USA	Actor
	Jess	Performing Arts	USA	Singer - Opera
	John Charles	Performing Arts	USA	Singer - Opera
	John Michael	Performing Arts	USA	Rock & Roll - HF - Jefferson Airplane
	Kristin Scott	Performing Arts	England	Actress - Acad Award Nom
	Kurt	Sports	USA	Basketball Player
	Marlo	Performing Arts	USA	Actress
	Norman Mattoon	Politics	USA	Socialist Leader
	Richard	Performing Arts	USA	Actor
	Rufus	Performing Arts	USA	Singer
	Seth	Science	USA	Inventor/Manufacturer
Thompson	Benjamin	Architecture	USA	Architect - AIA Gold Medal
	Benjamin	Politics	England	Statesman/Scientist
	Cecil R. (Tiny)	Sports	Canada	Hockey Player - HF
	Daley	Sports	England	Olympic Decathlete
	David	Exploration	Canada	Explorer - America West
	David	Sports	USA	Basketball Player - HF
	Dorothy	Creative Works	USA	Journalist - Newspaper
	Emma	Performing Arts	England	Actress - Academy Award
	Francis	Creative Works	England	Poet
	Henry Wilson (Hank)	Performing Arts	USA	Singer - Country Music - HF
	James Walter	Business	USA	Advertising
	Jim	Creative Works	USA	Novelist - Pulp Fiction

SOLVER SERIES: NAME FINDER

LAST NAME	FIRST NAME	CATEGORY	COUNTRY	FAME
Thompson	John A. (Cat)	Sports	USA	Basketball Player - HF
	John Lee	Movie Production	England	Director - Acad Award Nom
	John Sparrow David	Politics	Canada	Prime Minster
	Lawrance	Creative Works	USA	Author - Pulitzer
	Lea	Performing Arts	USA	Actress
	Marian Lee (Mickey)	Sports	USA	Race Car Driver - HF
	Roy	Business	England	Publishing
	Sada	Performing Arts	USA	Actress
	Samuel Luther (Sam)	Sports	USA	Baseball Player - HF
Thomson	Alexander	Architecture	Scotland	Architect
	George Paget	Science	England	Physics - Nobel Laureate
	James	Creative Works	Scotland	Poet
	John Arthur	Creative Works	Scotland	Writer/Naturalist
	Joseph John	Science	England	Physics - Nobel Laureate
	Peter	Sports	Australia	Golfer - HF
	Virgil	Creative Works	USA	Composer
	William	Science	England	Physicist/Mathematician
Thoreau	Henry David	Arts	USA	Philosopher/Poet/Author
Thorndike	Edward Lee	Arts	USA	Psychologist/Lexicographer
	Sybil	Performing Arts	England	Actress
Thorne	Stephen Douglas	Aviation	USA	Astronaut
Thornhill	Claude	Performing Arts	USA	Band Leader - Big Band/Jazz - HF
Thornton	Billy Bob	Performing Arts	USA	Actor - Acad Award Nom
	Kathryn Ryan Cordell	Aviation	USA	Astronaut
	William Edgar	Aviation	USA	Astronaut
Thorpe	James Francis (Jim)	Sports	USA	Football Player/Olympic Runner - HF
Thorvaldson	Eric (The Red)	Exploration	Norway	Explorer - Greenland
Thuot	Pierre Joseph	Aviation	USA	Astronaut
Thurber	James Grover	Creative Works	USA	Writer/Humorist/Cartoonist
Thurman	Uma	Performing Arts	USA	Actress - Acad Award Nom
Thurmond	James Strom	Politics	USA	Senator - South Carolina
	Nate	Sports	USA	Basketball Player - HF
Thurston	Scott	Performing Arts	USA	Rock & Roll - HF - Heart Breakers
Tiant	Luis	Sports	USA	Baseball Player
Tibbett	Lawrence	Performing Arts	USA	Actor - Acad Award Nom
Tiegs	Cheryl	Performing Arts	USA	Super Model
Tiepolo	Giovanni Battista	Works of Art	Italy	Painter
Tierney	Gene	Performing Arts	USA	Actress - Acad Award Nom
Tiffany	Charles L.	Works of Art	USA	Jeweller
	Louis Comfort	Works of Art	USA	Artist - Stained Glass
Tiger	Richard (Dick)	Sports	Nigeria	Boxer - HF
Til (Tilghman)	Earlington (Sonny)	Performing Arts	USA	Rock & Roll - HF - The Orioles
Tilden	Samuel Jones	Politics	USA	Politician
	William Taten (Big Bill)	Sports	USA	Tennis Player - HF
Tilghman	William (Bill)	Law & Order	USA	Lawman
Tillich	Paul	Arts	Germany	Philosopher/Theologian
Tillis	Mel	Performing Arts	USA	Singer - Country & Western
Tillman	Floyd	Performing Arts	USA	Singer - Country Music - HF
Tillotson	Johnny	Performing Arts	USA	Singer - Country & Western
Tilly	Meg	Performing Arts	Canada	Actress - Acad Award Nom
Tilton	Martha	Performing Arts	USA	Singer - Big Band/Jazz - HF
Tinbergen	Jan	Arts	Netherlands	Economics - Nobel Laureate
	Nikolaas	Science	England	Medicine - Nobel Laureate
Ting	Samuel Chao Chung	Science	USA	Physics - Nobel Laureate
Tingay	Lance	Sports	England	Tennis Reporter - HF
Tinker	Grant A.	Business	USA	Television Industry
	Joseph Bert (Joe)	Sports	USA	Baseball Player - HF
Tinling	Cuthbert Collingwood	Sports	England	Tennis Player - HF
Tintle	George Joseph	Sports	USA	Soccer Player - HF
Tintoretto	Il	Works of Art	Italy	Painter
Tiselius	Arne Wilhelm Kaurin	Science	Sweden	Chemistry - Nobel Laureate
Tito	Josip Broz	Politics	Yugoslavia	President/Prime Minister
Titov	Gherman Stepanovich	Aviation	Russia	Astronaut

LAST NAME	FIRST NAME	CATEGORY	COUNTRY	FAME
Tittle	Yelberton Abraham (YA)	Sports	USA	Football Player - HF
Tjader	Cal	Performing Arts	USA	Vibraphonist
Tobey	Mark	Works of Art	USA	Painter
Tobin	Brian	Sports	Australia	Tennis Player - HF
	James	Arts	USA	Economics - Nobel Laureate
Tocqueville	Alexis de	Creative Works	France	Author/Statesman
Todd	Alexander R.	Science	England	Chemistry - Nobel Laureate
	Michael	Performing Arts	USA	Actor
	Richard	Movie Production	Ireland	Director
	Richard	Performing Arts	Ireland	Actor - Acad Award Nom
Tognazzi	Ugo	Movie Production	Italy	Director
Tognini	Michel	Aviation	France	Astronaut
Toklas	Alice Babette	Creative Works	USA	Author
Toland	John	Creative Works	USA	Author
Toledo	Juan Bautista	Architecture	Spain	Architect
Toler	Sidney	Performing Arts	USA	Actor
Tolkien	John Ronald Reuel	Creative Works	England	Novelist/Scholar/Linguist
Toller	Ernst	Creative Works	Germany	Playwright
Tolstoy	Leo Nikolayevich	Creative Works	Russia	Novelist/Social Theorist
Tomei	Marisa	Performing Arts	USA	Actress - Academy Award
Tomlin	Lily	Performing Arts	USA	Actress - Acad Award Nom
Tomonaga	Sin-Itiro	Science	Japan	Physics - Nobel Laureate
Tompkins	Daniel D.	Politics	USA	Vice-President
Tone	Franchot	Performing Arts	USA	Actor - Acad Award Nom
Tonegawa	Susumu	Science	Japan	Medicine - Nobel Laureate
Toole	John Kennedy	Creative Works	USA	Novelist - Pulitzer
	Ottis	Law & Order	USA	Serial Killer
Toomey	William (Bill)	Sports	USA	Olympic Decathlete
Toorish	John Bernard (Bernie)	Performing Arts	Canada	Canadian Music - HF - The Four Lads
Topol	Chaim	Performing Arts	Palestine	Actor - Acad Award Nom
Torian	Reggie	Performing Arts	USA	Rock & Roll - HF - The Impressions
Torme	Melvin Howard (Mel)	Performing Arts	USA	Singer - Big Band/Jazz - HF
Torn	Rip	Performing Arts	USA	Actor - Acad Award Nom
Toro	Benicio Del	Performing Arts	Puerto Rico	Actor - Academy Award
Torquato	Tasso	Creative Works	Italy	Poet
Torquemada	Tomás de	Arts	Spain	Dominican Monk
Torre	Joe	Sports	USA	Baseball Player
	Susana	Architecture	USA	Architect
Torrence	Gwen	Sports	USA	Olympic Runner
Torrens	Robert	Politics	Australia	Statesman
Torres	Carlos Alberto	Sports	Brazil	Soccer Player - HF
	Jose	Sports	USA	Boxer - HF
Torricelli	Evangelista	Science	Italy	Physicist/Mathematician
Torrio	John (Little Johnny)	Law & Order	Italy	Mafia
Toscanini	Arturo	Performing Arts	Italy	Conductor - Orchestra
Toulouse-Lautrec	Henri Marie Raymond de	Works of Art	France	Painter/Lithographer
Toussaint	Pierre François Dominique	Politics	Haiti	General/Negro Liberator
Tovey	Donald Francis	Creative Works	England	Musicologist/Critic
Townes	Charles Hard	Science	USA	Physics - Nobel Laureate
Townsend	Bertha Louise (Birdie)	Sports	USA	Tennis Player - HF
	Robert	Movie Production	USA	Director
Townshend (The Who)	Peter	Performing Arts	England	Rock & Roll - HF - The Who
Toynbee	Arnold Joseph	Arts	England	Philosopher/Historian
Trabert	Marion Anthony (Tony)	Sports	USA	Tennis Player - HF
Tracey	Raphael (Ralph)	Sports	USA	Soccer Player - HF
Tracy	Lee	Performing Arts	USA	Actor - Acad Award Nom
	Spencer	Performing Arts	USA	Actor - Academy Award
Trafton	George Edward	Sports	USA	Football Player - HF
Tralle	Antemio di	Architecture	Italy	Architect
Travanti	Daniel J.	Performing Arts	USA	Actor
Travers	Henry	Performing Arts	England	Actor - Acad Award Nom
	Jerome D. (Jerry)	Sports	USA	Golfer - HF
	Mary	Performing Arts	USA	Singer - Folk

SOLVER SERIES: NAME FINDER

LAST NAME	FIRST NAME	CATEGORY	COUNTRY	FAME
Travis	Merle Robert	Performing Arts	USA	Singer - Country Music - HF
	Randy	Performing Arts	USA	Singer - Country & Western
	Walter	Sports	Australia	Golfer - HF
Travolta	John	Performing Arts	USA	Actor - Acad Award Nom
Traynor	Harold Joseph (Pie)	Sports	USA	Baseball Player - HF
Treacher	Arthur	Performing Arts	England	Actor
Trebek	Alex	Performing Arts	Canada	Show Host
Tree	Herbert Beerbohm	Performing Arts	England	Actor/Theatrical Manager
Treitschke	Heinrich von	Arts	Germany	Historian
Tresh	Tom	Sports	USA	Baseball Player
Tretiak	Vladislav Aleksandrovich	Sports	Russia	Hockey Player - HF
Trevelyan	George Macaulay	Arts	England	Historian
	George Otto	Arts	England	Historian/Politician
Trevino	Lee	Sports	USA	Golfer - HF
Trevor	Claire	Performing Arts	USA	Actress - Academy Award
Trezzini	Domenico	Architecture	Russia	Architect
Trickle	Dick	Sports	USA	Race Car Driver
Trihey	Henry Judah (Harry)	Sports	Canada	Hockey Player - HF
Trillin	Calvin	Creative Works	USA	Journalist - Newspaper
Trimble	David	War & Peace	England	Peace - Nobel Laureate
Trinh	Eugene Hau-Chau	Aviation	USA	Astronaut
Trippi	Charles Louis (Charley)	Sports	USA	Football Player - HF
Tristano	Lennie (Leonard Joseph)	Performing Arts	USA	Jazz Pianist/Composer - Big Band/Jazz - HF
Troell	Jan	Movie Production	Sweden	Director - Acad Award Nom
Troiana	Domenic	Performing Arts	Italy	Guitarist - Canadian Music - HF
Troisi	Massimo	Performing Arts	Italy	Actor - Acad Award Nom
Trollope	Anthony	Creative Works	England	Novelist
	Frances Milton	Creative Works	England	Writer
Trotsky	Leon	Politics	Russia	Revolutionist
Trottier	Bryan John	Sports	Canada	Hockey Player - HF
Trudeau	Garry	Creative Works	USA	Cartoonist - Doonesbury
	Pierre Elliott	Politics	Canada	Prime Minster
Trueblood	David Elton	Arts	USA	Philosopher/Author/Theologist
Truex	Ernest	Performing Arts	USA	Actor
Truffaut	Francois	Movie Production	France	Director - Acad Award Nom
Truly	Richard Harrison	Aviation	USA	Astronaut
Truman	Elizabeth (Bess)	Politics	USA	First Lady
	Harry S.	Politics	USA	President
Trumbull	John	Works of Art	USA	Painter
Trump	Donald	Business	USA	Real Estate
Truth	Sojourner	Politics	USA	Abolitionist
Tryggvason	Bjarni Valdimar	Aviation	Canada	Astronaut
Tryon	Thomas	Creative Works	USA	Novelist
Tschetter	Kris	Sports	USA	Golfer
Tschumi	Bernard	Architecture	Switzerland	Architect
Tse-Tung	Mao	Politics	China	Head of State
Tsien	Billie	Architecture	USA	Architect - Jefferson Medal
Tsui	Daniel C.	Science	USA	Physics - Nobel Laureate
Tubb	Ernest	Performing Arts	USA	Singer - Country Music - HF
Tubman	Harriet	Politics	USA	Abolitionist
	William Vacanarat Shadrach	Politics	Liberia	President
Tuchman	Barbara Wertheim	Creative Works	USA	Author - Pulitzer
Tucker	Forrest	Performing Arts	USA	Actor
	Michael	Performing Arts	USA	Actor
	Sophie	Performing Arts	Russia	Singer
	Tanya	Performing Arts	USA	Singer - Country & Western
Tudor	Anthony	Creative Works	England	Composer - Ballet
Tufts	Richard	Sports	USA	Golf Promoter - HF
Tully	Tom	Performing Arts	USA	Actor - Acad Award Nom
Tum	Rigoberta Menchú	War & Peace	Guatemala	Peace - Nobel Laureate
Tune	Tommy	Creative Works	USA	Choreographer
Tunnell	Emlen Lewis	Sports	USA	Football Player - HF
Tunney	Gene	Sports	USA	Boxer - HF

LAST NAME	FIRST NAME	CATEGORY	COUNTRY	FAME
Tupper	Charles	Politics	Canada	Prime Minster
Turgenev	Ivan Sergeevich	Creative Works	Russia	Novelist
Turgot	Anne Robertson Jacques	Politics	France	Statesman/Economist
Turlington	Christy	Performing Arts	USA	Super Model
Turnblad	Swan	Business	USA	Publishing
Turner	Clyde Douglas (Bulldog)	Sports	USA	Football Player - HF
	Curtis	Sports	USA	Race Car Driver - HF
	Frederick Jackson	Creative Works	USA	Author - Pulitzer
	Ike	Performing Arts	USA	Singer - Rock & Roll - HF
	Janine	Performing Arts	USA	Actress
	Joe Lynn	Performing Arts	USA	Singer - Rock & Roll - HF
	John Napier	Politics	Canada	Prime Minster
	Joseph Mallord William	Works of Art	England	Painter
	Kathleen	Performing Arts	USA	Actress - Acad Award Nom
	Lana	Performing Arts	USA	Actress - Acad Award Nom
	Nat	Politics	USA	Revolutionist - Negro
	Ted	Business	USA	Broadcasting
Turner (Bullock)	Anna Mae (Tina)	Performing Arts	USA	Singer - Rock & Roll - HF
Turow	Scott	Creative Works	USA	Author
Turpin	Ben	Performing Arts	USA	Actor
	Dick	Law & Order	England	Highwayman
	Randy	Sports	England	Boxer - HF
Turrell	James	Architecture	USA	Architect - Jefferson Medal
Turturro	Nicholas (Nick)	Performing Arts	USA	Actor
Tushingham	Rita	Performing Arts	England	Actress
Tussaud	Marie Gresholtz	Works of Art	Switzerland	Waxworks Exhibitor
Tutu	Desmond Mplio	Politics	South Africa	Activist - Human Rights
	Desmond Mplio	War & Peace	South Africa	Peace - Nobel Laureate
Twain	Mark	Creative Works	USA	Author/Journalist
Tway	Bob	Sports	USA	Golfer
Tweed	William	Business	USA	Manufacturing Industry
	William Marcy (Boss)	Politics	USA	Politician
Twelvetrees	Helen	Performing Arts	USA	Actress
Twitty (Jenkins)	Harold Lloyd (Conway)	Performing Arts	USA	Singer - Country Music - HF
Twyman	John K. (Jack)	Sports	USA	Basketball Player - HF
Tyler	Anne	Creative Works	USA	Author - Pulitzer
	John	Politics	USA	President
	Julia	Politics	USA	First Lady
	Letitia	Politics	USA	First Lady
	Wat	Politics	England	Rebellion Leader
Tyler (Tallarico)	Steven	Performing Arts	USA	Rock & Roll - HF - Aerosmith
Tylor	Edward Burnett	Arts	England	Anthropologist
Tyndale	William	Arts	England	Religious Reformer
Tyndall	John	Science	England	Physicist
Tyne	Claude Halstead Va	Creative Works	USA	Author - Pulitzer
Tyner	Alfred (McCoy)	Performing Arts	USA	Jazz Pianist - Big Band/Jazz - HF
Tyrrell	Susan	Performing Arts	USA	Actress - Acad Award Nom
Tyson	Cicely	Performing Arts	USA	Actress - Acad Award Nom
	Ian	Performing Arts	Canada	Canadian Music - HF - Ian and Sylvia
	Mike	Sports	USA	Boxer
	Sylvia	Performing Arts	Canada	Canadian Music - HF - Ian and Sylvia
Tyus	Wyomia	Sports	USA	Olympic Runner
Tzara	Tristan	Creative Works	Romania	Poet/Editor
Tzu	Lao	Arts	China	Philosopher
Uccello	Paolo	Works of Art	Italy	Painter - Early Renaissance
Udall	Nicholas	Creative Works	England	Playwright/Translator
Ueberroth	Peter Victor	Business	USA	Travel/Baseball
Uecker	Bob	Sports	USA	Baseball Player
Uggams	Leslie	Performing Arts	USA	Singer - Musicals
Uhland	Johann Ludwig	Creative Works	Germany	Poet/Literary Historian
Uhry	Alfred	Creative Works	USA	Dramatist - Pulitzer
Ulanova	Galina Sergeyevna	Performing Arts	Russia	Dancer - Ballerina
Ulbricht	Walter	Politics	Germany	Chief of State

SOLVER SERIES: NAME FINDER

LAST NAME	FIRST NAME	CATEGORY	COUNTRY	FAME
Ullman	Norman Victor (Norm)	Sports	Canada	Hockey Player - HF
	Tracey	Performing Arts	England	Actress
Ullmann	Liv	Performing Arts	Norway	Actress - Acad Award Nom
Ulrich	Lars	Performing Arts	Denmark	Rock & Roll - Metallica
	Laurel Thatcher	Creative Works	USA	Author - Pulitzer
	William Richard (Bud)	Sports	Canada	Golfer/Carpenter
Umberto	Eco	Creative Works	Italy	Novelist
Umeki	Miyoshi	Performing Arts	Japan	Actress - Academy Award
Unamuno	Miguel de	Arts	Spain	Philosopher/Writer
Underwood	Blair	Performing Arts	USA	Actor
Undset	Sigrid	Creative Works	Norway	Literature - Nobel Laureate
Ungaro	Emanuel	Business	France	Fashion Designer
Unger	Irwin	Creative Works	USA	Author - Pulitzer
Ungers	Oswald Mathias	Architecture	Germany	Architect
Unitas	John Constantine (Johnny)	Sports	USA	Football Player - HF
Unseld	Wesley S. (Wes)	Sports	USA	Basketball Player - HF
Unser	Bobby	Sports	USA	Race Car Driver - HF
Unser Sr.	Al	Sports	USA	Race Car Driver - HF
Untermeyer	Louis	Creative Works	USA	Poet/Anthologist/Critic
Updike	John	Creative Works	USA	Novelist - Pulitzer
Upshaw Jr.	Eugene Thurman (Gene)	Sports	USA	Football Player - HF
Urdaneta	Andres de	Exploration	Spain	Explorer - Phillipines
Ure	Mary	Performing Arts	Scotland	Actress - Acad Award Nom
Uresti	Omar	Sports	USA	Golfer
Urey	Harold Clayton	Science	USA	Chemistry - Nobel Laureate
Urich	Robert	Performing Arts	USA	Actor
Uris	Leon	Creative Works	USA	Novelist
Urquhart	Thomas	Creative Works	Scotland	Writer/Translator
Ussher	James	Arts	Ireland	Archbishop/Theologian
Ustinov	Peter	Performing Arts	England	Actor - Academy Award
Utrillo	Maurice	Works of Art	France	Painter
Utzon	Jørn	Architecture	Denmark	Architect - Pritzker Laureate
Uvedale	Nicholas	Creative Works	England	Playwright/Translator
Vaca	Alvar Nuñez Cabeza de	Exploration	Spain	Explorer - Texas
Vaccaro	Brenda	Performing Arts	USA	Actress - Acad Award Nom
Vacchini	Livio	Architecture	Switzerland	Architect
Vadi	Tibère	Architecture	Switzerland	Architect
Valachi	Joseph M.	Law & Order	USA	Mafia
Vale	Jerry	Performing Arts	USA	Singer - Pops
Valens (Valenzuela)	Richard Steven (Richie)	Performing Arts	USA	Singer - Rock & Roll - HF
Valentine	Hilton	Performing Arts	England	Rock & Roll - HF - The Animals
Valentino	Garavani	Business	Italy	Fashion Designer
	Rudolph	Performing Arts	Italy	Actor
Valenzuela	Fernando	Sports	USA	Baseball Player
Valera	Eamon De	Politics	Ireland	President
Valéry	Paul Ambroise	Creative Works	France	Poet/Essayist
Valle	Gino	Architecture	Italy	Architect
Vallee	Rudy	Performing Arts	USA	Singer - Big Band
Valletta	Amber	Performing Arts	USA	Super Model
Valli	Alida	Performing Arts	Italy	Actress
Valli (Castelluccio)	Frank (Frankie)	Performing Arts	USA	Rock & Roll - HF - The Four Seasons
	Frank (Frankie)	Performing Arts	USA	Singer - Rock & Roll - HF
Vanbrugh	John	Creative Works	England	Dramatist/Architect
Vance	Clarence Arthur (Dazzy)	Sports	USA	Baseball Player - HF
	Vivian	Performing Arts	USA	Actress
Vancouver	George	Exploration	England	Explorer - Canada West Coast
Vanderbilt	Cornelius	Business	USA	Industrialist/Capitalist
	Gloria	Business	USA	Fashion Designer
Vandivier	Robert P. (Fuzzy)	Sports	USA	Basketball Player - HF
Vandross	Luther Ronzoni	Performing Arts	USA	Singer - Rhythm & Blues
Vane	Henry	Politics	England	Statesman - Puritan
	John R.	Science	England	Medicine - Nobel Laureate
Vanzetti	Bartolomeo	Politics	Italy	Anarchist

LAST NAME	FIRST NAME	CATEGORY	COUNTRY	FAME
Vardon	Harry	Sports	USA	Golfer - HF
Vare	Glenna Collette	Sports	USA	Golfer - HF
Varley	John Herbert	Creative Works	USA	Author - SciFi
Varmus	Harold E.	Science	USA	Medicine - Nobel Laureate
Varsi	Diane	Performing Arts	USA	Actress - Acad Award Nom
	Achille	Sports	Italy	Race Car Driver - HF
Vasari	Georgio	Works of Art	Italy	Painter/Architect/Biographer
	Giogio	Architecture	Italy	Architect
Vau	Louis le	Architecture	France	Architect
Vauban	Sébastien le Prestre	War & Peace	France	Engineer
Vaughan	Henry	Creative Works	England	Poet/Metaphysician
	Sarah	Performing Arts	USA	Singer - Big Band/Jazz - HF
	Sarah	Performing Arts	USA	Singer - Rock & Roll - HF
Vaughan Williams	Ralph	Creative Works	England	Composer
Vaughn	Frank	Sports	USA	Soccer Player - HF
	Joseph Floyd (Arky)	Sports	USA	Baseball Player - HF
	Robert	Performing Arts	USA	Actor - Acad Award Nom
Veach	Charles Lacy	Aviation	USA	Astronaut
Veblen	Thorstein Bunde	Arts	USA	Economist - Political
Vee	Bobby	Performing Arts	USA	Singer - Rock & Roll - HF
Veeck Jr.	William Lewis (Bill)	Sports	USA	Baseball Executive - HF
Veidt	Conrad	Performing Arts	Germany	Actor
Velasquez	Patricia	Performing Arts	Venezuela	Super Model
Velázquez	Diego Rodríguez de Silva	Works of Art	Spain	Painter
Velde	Henry van de	Architecture	Belgium	Architect
Velez	Lupe	Performing Arts	Mexico	Actress
Veltman	Martinus J.G.	Science	Netherlands	Physics - Nobel Laureate
Vender	Claudio	Architecture	Italy	Architect
Vendome	Louis Joseph de	War & Peace	France	General/Marshall
Venn	John	Science	England	Mathematician
Ventura	Robin	Sports	USA	Baseball Player
Venturi	Ken	Sports	USA	Golfer
	Robert	Architecture	USA	Architect - Pritzker/Jefferson Medal
Venuti	Guiseppe (Joe)	Performing Arts	USA	Jazz Violinist - Big Band/Jazz - HF
Vérandrye	Pierre de la	Exploration	Canada	Explorer - Canada West
Verdi	Giuseppe Fortunino Francisco	Creative Works	Italy	Composer - Opera
Verdon	Gwen	Performing Arts	USA	Actress
Verdugo	Elena	Performing Arts	USA	Actress
Vereen	Ben	Performing Arts	USA	Actor - Musical
Verlaine	Paul	Creative Works	France	Poet
Vermeer	Jan	Works of Art	Netherlands	Painter
Verne	Jules	Creative Works	France	Novelist
Verner	Karl	Arts	Denmark	Philologist
Vernon	Edward	War & Peace	England	Admiral
Veronese	Paolo	Works of Art	Italy	Painter
Verrazano	Giovanni da	Exploration	Italy	Explorer - America East Coast
Verrocchio	Andrea del	Works of Art	Italy	Painter/Sculptor
Versace	Donatella	Business	Italy	Fashion Designer
	Gianni	Business	Italy	Fashion Designer
Vesalius	Andreas	Science	Italy	Anatomist
Vespucci	Americo	Exploration	Italy	Explorer - Amazon Region
Vezina	George	Sports	Canada	Hockey Player - HF
Vicenzo	Roberto De	Sports	Brazil	Golfer - HF
Vickery	William	Arts	USA	Economics - Nobel Laureate
Vidal	Eugene Luther Gore	Creative Works	USA	Novelist/Playwright
Vidor	King	Movie Production	USA	Director - Acad Award Nom
Vidov	Oleg	Performing Arts	Russia	Actor
Viereck	Peter Robert Edwin	Creative Works	USA	Poet - Pulitzer
Viganò	Vittoriano	Architecture	Italy	Architect
Vigneaud	Vincent du	Science	USA	Chemistry - Nobel Laureate
Vignola	Giacomo Barozzi da	Architecture	Italy	Architect
Vigny	Alfred Victor	Creative Works	France	Poet/Man of Letters
Vigoda	Abe	Performing Arts	USA	Actor

SOLVER SERIES: NAME FINDER

LAST NAME	FIRST NAME	CATEGORY	COUNTRY	FAME
Vilas	Guillermo	Sports	Argentina	Tennis Player - HF
Villa	Francisco	War & Peace	Mexico	Revolutionary Leader
	Francisco (Pancho)	Sports	Philippines	Boxer - HF
	José Doroteo (Pancho)	Politics	Mexico	Revolutionist
Villa-Lobos	Heitor	Creative Works	Brazil	Composer
Villanueva	Carlos Raúl	Architecture	Venezuela	Architect
Villard	Henry	Business	USA	Railway/Publishing
	Oswald Garrison	Business	USA	Publishing
Villella	Edward	Performing Arts	USA	Dancer - Ballet
Villeneuve	Gilles	Sports	Canada	Race Car Driver - HF
Villon	Francois	Creative Works	France	Poet
Vincent	Jan-Michael	Performing Arts	USA	Actor
Vincent (Craddock)	Vincent Eugene (Gene)	Performing Arts	USA	Singer - Rock & Roll - HF
Vinci	Leonardo da	Works of Art	Italy	Painter/Sculptor/Architect
Vines	Henry Ellsworth	Sports	USA	Tennis Player - HF
Vinge	Joan D.	Creative Works	USA	Author - SciFi
Vinson	Frederick Moore	Law & Order	USA	Chief Justice
	William	Business	USA	Oil Industry
	Bobby	Performing Arts	USA	Singer - Pops
Viollet le Duc	Eugène Emmanuel	Architecture	France	Architect
Viren	Lasse	Sports	Finland	Olympic Runner
Virtanen	Artturi Ilmari	Science	Finland	Chemistry - Nobel Laureate
Visconti	Luchino	Movie Production	Italy	Director
Vito	Danny De	Performing Arts	USA	Actor
	Tommy De	Performing Arts	USA	Rock & Roll - HF - The Four Seasons
Vitruvius	Marco Pollione	Architecture	Italy	Architect
Vittori	Roberto	Aviation	Italy	Astronaut
Vittorini	Elio	Creative Works	Italy	Novelist/Literary Critic
Vivaldi	Antonio	Creative Works	Italy	Composer/Violinist
Vizcaíno	Sebastián	Exploration	Spain	Explorer - Mexico West Coast
Vizquel	Omar	Sports	USA	Baseball Player
Vlaminck	Maurice de	Works of Art	France	Painter
Vleck	John Hasbrouck van	Science	USA	Physics - Nobel Laureate
Vogel	Paula	Creative Works	USA	Dramatist - Pulitzer
Voight	Jon	Performing Arts	USA	Actor - Academy Award
Volkov	Vladislav Nikolavevich	Aviation	Russia	Astronaut
Volta	Alessandro	Science	Italy	Physicist
Voltaire	François Marie Arouet de	Arts	France	Philosopher/Writer
Volynov	Boris Valentinovich	Aviation	Russia	Astronaut
Vonnegut Jr.	Kurt	Creative Works	USA	Novelist
Voss	James Shelton	Aviation	USA	Astronaut
Voto	Bernard De	Creative Works	USA	Author - Pulitzer
Vries	Hugo De	Science	Netherlands	Botanist
Vries	Peter De	Creative Works	USA	Novelist
Vuillard	Jean Édouard	Works of Art	France	Painter
Vukovich	Billy (Bill)	Sports	USA	Race Car Driver - HF
Waals	Johannes Diderik Van der	Science	Netherlands	Physics - Nobel Laureate
Waart	Edo de	Performing Arts	Netherlands	Conductor - Orchestra
Wachter	Edward A.	Sports	USA	Basketball Player - HF
Waddell	George Edward (Rube)	Sports	USA	Baseball Player - HF
Wade	Sarah Virginia (Ginny)	Sports	England	Tennis Player - HF
Wadkins	Lanny	Sports	USA	Golfer
Waggoner	Lyle	Performing Arts	USA	Actor
	Porter	Performing Arts	USA	Singer - Country Music - HF
Wagner	John Peter (Honus)	Sports	USA	Baseball Player - HF
	Lindsay	Performing Arts	USA	Actress
	Marie	Sports	USA	Tennis Player - HF
	Otto	Architecture	Austria	Architect
	Robert	Performing Arts	USA	Actor
	Wilhelm Richard	Creative Works	Germany	Composer
Wagner-Jauregg	Julius	Science	Austria	Medicine - Nobel Laureate
Waismann	Friedrich	Arts	Austria	Philosopher
Waite	John	Performing Arts	England	Singer - Rock & Roll - HF

LAST NAME	FIRST NAME	CATEGORY	COUNTRY	FAME
Waite	Morrison Remick	Law & Order	USA	Chief Justice
	Ralph	Performing Arts	USA	Actor
Waits	Tom	Performing Arts	USA	Singer - Contemporary
Waitz	Grete	Sports	Norway	Olympic Marathoner
Wakata	Koichi	Aviation	Japan	Astronaut
Waksman	Selman Abraham	Science	USA	Medicine - Nobel Laureate
Wal	Frederique Van Der	Performing Arts	Netherlands	Super Model
Walcott	Derek	Creative Works	Saint Lucia	Literature - Nobel Laureate
	Joseph (Jersey Joe)	Sports	USA	Boxer - HF
Wald	George	Science	USA	Medicine - Nobel Laureate
Walden	Robert	Performing Arts	USA	Actor
Waldheim	Kurt	Politics	Austria	Secretary-General UN
Walesa	Lech	Politics	Poland	President
	Lech	War & Peace	Poland	Peace - Nobel Laureate
Walken	Christopher	Performing Arts	USA	Actor - Academy Award
Walker	Aaron Thibeaux (T-Bone)	Performing Arts	USA	Guitarist/Songwriter - Big Band/Jazz - HF
	Aaron Thibeaux (T-Bone)	Performing Arts	USA	Singer - Rock & Roll - HF
	Alice Malsenior	Creative Works	USA	Author - Pulitzer
	Charles David	Aviation	USA	Astronaut
	David Mathieson	Aviation	USA	Astronaut
	Herschel	Sports	USA	Football Player
	John E.	Science	England	Chemistry - Nobel Laureate
	John Phillip (Jack)	Sports	Canada	Hockey Player - HF
	Mort	Creative Works	USA	Cartoonist - Beetle Bailey
	Nancy	Performing Arts	USA	Actress
	Peter	Architecture	USA	Architect - Jefferson Medal
	Ralph	Architecture	USA	Architect - AIA Gold Medal
	Ray	Performing Arts	USA	Country Music - HF - Sons of the Pioneers
	Robert	Performing Arts	USA	Actor
Walker Jr.	Ewell Doak	Sports	USA	Football Player - HF
Wallace	Alfred Russel	Arts	England	Naturalist
	Frank (Pee Wee)	Sports	USA	Soccer Player - HF
	George Corley	Politics	USA	Governor - Alabama
	Henry Agard	Politics	USA	Vice-President
	Lewis	Creative Works	USA	Novelist/General
	Lila Acheson	Creative Works	Canada	Author
	Myron Leon (Mike)	Creative Works	USA	Author/Journalist - Pulitzer
	Rhoderick John (Bobby)	Sports	USA	Baseball Player - HF
	Rusty	Sports	USA	Race Car Driver
	William	Politics	Scotland	Patriot
Wallach	Eli	Performing Arts	USA	Actor
	Otto	Science	Germany	Chemistry - Nobel Laureate
Wallenberg	Raoul	Arts	Sweden	Humanitarian/Diplomat
Wallenstein	Albrecht Eusebius Wenzel von	War & Peace	Austria	General
Waller	Edmund	Creative Works	England	Poet
	Fats (Thomas Wright)	Performing Arts	USA	Singer/Composer - Big Band/Jazz - HF
Wallis	Shani	Performing Arts	England	Actress
Walpole	Horace	Creative Works	England	Writer
	Robert	Politics	England	Prime Minster
Walsh	Edward Augustine (Ed)	Sports	USA	Baseball Player - HF
	Joe	Performing Arts	USA	Rock & Roll - HF - The Eagles
	Joe	Performing Arts	USA	Singer/Guitarist
	Martin (Marty)	Sports	Canada	Hockey Player - HF
	Raoul	Movie Production	USA	Director
	William Ernest (Bill)	Sports	USA	Football Coach - HF
Walsingham	Francis	Politics	England	Statesman
Walston	Ray	Performing Arts	USA	Actor
Walter	John	Business	England	Publishing
	Ulrich Hans	Aviation	Germany	Astronaut
Walter II	John	Business	England	Publishing
Walters	Barbara	Creative Works	USA	Journalist - Television
	Charles	Movie Production	USA	Director - Acad Award Nom
	Julie	Performing Arts	England	Actress - Acad Award Nom

SOLVER SERIES: NAME FINDER

LAST NAME	FIRST NAME	CATEGORY	COUNTRY	FAME
Walton	Ernest Thomas Sinton	Science	Ireland	Physics - Nobel Laureate
	Izaak	Creative Works	England	Writer
	Samuel Moore	Business	USA	Founder - Walmart
	William T. (Bill)	Sports	USA	Basketball Player - HF
	William Turner	Creative Works	England	Composer
Waltrip	Darrell	Sports	USA	Race Car Driver - HF
Walworth	Arthur	Creative Works	USA	Author - Pulitzer
Wambaugh	Joseph	Creative Works	USA	Author
Wanamaker	John	Business	USA	Merchant
	Sam	Performing Arts	USA	Actor
Waner	Lloyd James	Sports	USA	Baseball Player - HF
	Paul Glee	Sports	USA	Baseball Player - HF
Wang	Taylor Gun-Jin	Aviation	USA	Astronaut
	Vera	Business	USA	Fashion Designer
Wankel	Felix	Science	Germany	Inventor/Engineer
Wanzer	Robert (Bobby)	Sports	USA	Basketball Player - HF
Warburg	Otto Heinrich	Science	Germany	Medicine - Nobel Laureate
	Paul	Business	USA	Financier
Ward	Anita	Performing Arts	USA	Singer - Rock & Roll - HF
	Artemus	Creative Works	USA	Humorist
	Barbara	Creative Works	England	Writer
	Fred	Performing Arts	USA	Actor
	Holcombe	Sports	USA	Tennis Player - HF
	John Montgomery	Sports	USA	Baseball Player - HF
	Mary Augusta Arnold	Creative Works	England	Novelist
	Maxwell William	Business	Canada	Aviation Industry
	Rachel	Performing Arts	England	Actress
	Rodger	Sports	USA	Race Car Driver - HF
	Sela	Performing Arts	USA	Actress
	Simon	Performing Arts	England	Actor
Warden	Jack	Performing Arts	USA	Actor - Acad Award Nom
Warfield	Paul Dryden	Sports	USA	Football Player - HF
Warhol	Andy	Works of Art	USA	Artist
Warner	Curt	Sports	USA	Football Player
	Harry Byron	Performing Arts	England	Actor - Acad Award Nom
	Malcolm-Jamal	Performing Arts	USA	Actor
	William W.	Creative Works	USA	Author - Pulitzer
Warr	Thomas West De La	Politics	England	Governor - Virginia
Warren	Charles	Creative Works	USA	Author - Pulitzer
	Earl	Law & Order	USA	Chief Justice
	Estelle	Performing Arts	Canada	Super Model
	Lesley Anne	Performing Arts	USA	Actress - Acad Award Nom
	Robert Penn	Creative Works	USA	Novelist - Pulitzer
	Robert Penn	Creative Works	USA	Poet - Pulitzer
	Robin	Science	Australia	Medicine - Nobel Laureate
Warwick	Dionne	Performing Arts	USA	Singer - Rock & Roll - HF
	Richard Neville	Politics	England	Statesman/Military Leader
Washburn	Mona	Performing Arts	England	Actress
	Watson (Watty)	Sports	USA	Tennis Player - HF
Washington	Booker Taliaferro	Creative Works	USA	Author/Educator
	Denzel	Performing Arts	USA	Actor - Academy Award
	George	Politics	USA	President
	George	War & Peace	USA	General
	Martha Dandridge	Politics	USA	First Lady
Washington (Jones)	Ruth Lee (Dinah)	Performing Arts	USA	Singer - Big Band/Jazz - HF
Washington (Jones)	Ruth Lee (Dinah)	Performing Arts	USA	Singer - Rock & Roll - HF
Wassermann	August von	Science	Germany	Bacteriologist
	Jakob	Creative Works	Germany	Novelist
Wasserstein	Wendy	Creative Works	USA	Dramatist - Pulitzer
Watanabe	Ken	Performing Arts	Japan	Actor - Acad Award Nom
Waterfield	Robert Stanton (Bob)	Sports	USA	Football Player - HF
Waters	Ethel	Performing Arts	USA	Actress - Acad Award Nom
	George Roger	Performing Arts	England	Rock & Roll - HF - Pink Floyd

LAST NAME	FIRST NAME	CATEGORY	COUNTRY	FAME
Waters	George Roger	Performing Arts	England	Singer/Guitarist
	John	Movie Production	USA	Director
Waters (Morganfield)	McKinley (Muddy)	Performing Arts	USA	Singer - Rock & Roll - HF
Waterston	Sam	Performing Arts	USA	Actor - Acad Award Nom
Watson	AJ	Sports	USA	Race Car Designer - HF
	Deek	Performing Arts	USA	Rock & Roll - HF - The Ink Spots
	Emily	Performing Arts	England	Actress - Acad Award Nom
	Harry E. (Moose)	Sports	Canada	Hockey Player - HF
	Harry Percival	Sports	Canada	Hockey Player - HF
	James Dewey	Science	USA	Medicine - Nobel Laureate
	John Broadus	Arts	USA	Psychologist
	Lucile	Performing Arts	Canada	Actress - Acad Award Nom
	Tom	Sports	USA	Golfer - HF
Watt	James	Science	Scotland	Inventor/Engineer
Watteau	Jean-Antoine	Works of Art	France	Painter - Genre
Watterson II	William B. (Bill)	Creative Works	USA	Cartoonist - Calvin & Hobbes
Watts	André	Performing Arts	Germany	Pianist
	Charles Robert (Charlie)	Performing Arts	England	Rock & Roll - HF - Rolling Stones
	George Frederic	Works of Art	England	Painter/Sculptor - Symbolist
	Isaac	Arts	England	Clergyman/Writer - Hymns
	Naomi	Performing Arts	England	Actress - Acad Award Nom
Waugh	Alexander Raban (Alec)	Creative Works	England	Novelist
	Evelyn Arthur St. John	Creative Works	England	Novelist
Wavell	Archibald Percival	War & Peace	England	Field Marshall
Wayans	Damon	Performing Arts	USA	Comedian
	Keenan Ivory	Performing Arts	USA	Comedian
Wayne	Anthony	War & Peace	USA	General - Revolutionary War
	David	Performing Arts	USA	Actor
	John	Performing Arts	USA	Actor - Academy Award
Weah	George	Sports	Liberia	Soccer Player
Weatherly	Joseph Herbert (Joe)	Sports	USA	Race Car Driver - HF
Weathers	Carl	Performing Arts	USA	Actor
Weaver	Dennis	Performing Arts	USA	Actor
	Earl Sidney	Sports	USA	Baseball Manager - HF
	Fritz	Performing Arts	USA	Actor
	Sigourney	Performing Arts	USA	Actress - Acad Award Nom
Webb	Aston	Architecture	England	Architect - AIA Gold Medal
	Beatrice Potter	Arts	England	Economist/Social Reformer
	Clifton	Performing Arts	USA	Actor - Acad Award Nom
	Jack	Performing Arts	USA	Actor
	Jimmy	Creative Works	USA	Composer
	Phillip	Architecture	England	Architect/Designer
	Sidney James	Arts	England	Economist/Social Reformer
	William Henry (Chick)	Performing Arts	USA	Band Leader - Big Band/Jazz - HF
Webber	Andrew Lloyd	Creative Works	England	Composer
Weber	Carl Maria von	Creative Works	Germany	Composer
	Ernst Heinrich	Science	Germany	Physiologist/Anatomist
	Mary Ellen	Aviation	USA	Astronaut
	Max	Arts	Germany	Sociologist/Political Economist
	Wilhelm Edouard	Science	Germany	Physicist
Webern	Anton	Creative Works	Austria	Composer
Webster	Ben	Performing Arts	USA	Jazz Saxophonist - Big Band/Jazz - HF
	Daniel	Politics	USA	Statesman/Orator
	Michael Lewis (Mike)	Sports	USA	Football Player - HF
	Noah	Arts	USA	Lexicographer
Weddell	James	Exploration	England	Explorer - Antarctic
Wedgwood	Josiah	Business	England	Entrepreneur
Weekley	Ernest	Arts	England	Lexicographer/Etymologist
Weems	Mason Locke	Creative Works	USA	Writer/Clergyman
	Ted	Performing Arts	USA	Band Leader - Big Band/Jazz - HF
Weidemeyer	Carl	Architecture	Switzerland	Architect
Weidman	Jerome	Creative Works	USA	Dramatist - Pulitzer
Weil	Cynthia	Creative Works	USA	Composer/Song Writer

SOLVER SERIES: NAME FINDER

LAST NAME	FIRST NAME	CATEGORY	COUNTRY	FAME
Weil	Simone	Arts	France	Philosopher/Mystic
Weiland	Ralph (Cooney)	Sports	Canada	Hockey Player - HF
Weill	Kurt	Creative Works	USA	Composer
Weinberg	Steven	Science	USA	Physics - Nobel Laureate
Weiner	Jonathan	Creative Works	USA	Author - Pulitzer
Weininger	Otto	Arts	Austria	Philosopher
Weinmeister	Arnold George (Arnie)	Sports	Canada	Football Player - HF
Weir	Alexander (Alex)	Sports	Ireland	Soccer Player - HF
	Peter	Movie Production	Australia	Director - Acad Award Nom
Weiskopf	Tom	Sports	USA	Golfer
Weismann	August	Science	Germany	Biologist
Weiss	George Martin	Sports	USA	Baseball Executive -HF
Weissmuller	Johnny	Performing Arts	Romania	Actor
	Johnny	Sports	USA	Olympic Swimmer
Weitz	Bruce	Performing Arts	USA	Actor
	Paul Joseph	Aviation	USA	Astronaut
Weizmann	Chaim	Politics	Israel	President
Welch	Michael Francis (Mickey)	Sports	USA	Baseball Player - HF
	Raquel	Performing Arts	USA	Actress
Weld	Tuesday	Performing Arts	USA	Actress - Acad Award Nom
Welk	Lawrence	Performing Arts	USA	Band Leader - Big Band/Jazz - HF
Weller	Thomas Huckle	Science	USA	Medicine - Nobel Laureate
Welles	George Orson	Movie Production	USA	Director - Acad Award Nom
	George Orson	Performing Arts	USA	Actor - Acad Award Nom
	Sumner	Politics	USA	Diplomat
Wellington	Arthur Wellesley	Politics	England	Prime Minster
Wellman	William	Movie Production	USA	Director - Acad Award Nom
Wells	Herbert George	Creative Works	England	Novelist/Historian
	Kitty	Performing Arts	USA	Singer - Country & Western
	Mary	Creative Works	USA	Author - Pulitzer
	Mary	Performing Arts	USA	Singer - Motown
	Willie James	Sports	USA	Baseball Player - HF
Wells (Deason)	Muriel Ellen (Kitty)	Performing Arts	USA	Singer - Country Music - HF
Wells-Barnett	Ida Bell	Creative Works	USA	Journalist - Newspaper
Welty	Eudora	Creative Works	USA	Novelist - Pulitzer
Wen	Sun	Sports	China	Soccer Player
Wenders	Wim	Movie Production	Germany	Director
Wendt	George	Performing Arts	USA	Actor
Wenge	Ralph	Creative Works	USA	Journalist - Television
Wenner	Jann S.	Creative Works	USA	Journalist - Magazine
Werfel	Franz	Creative Works	Austria	Poet/Novelist/Playwright
Werner	Alfred	Science	Switzerland	Chemistry - Nobel Laureate
	Oskar	Performing Arts	Austria	Actor - Acad Award Nom
Wertmuller	Lina	Movie Production	Italy	Director - Acad Award Nom
Wesley	Charles	Arts	England	Clergyman/Writer - Hymns
	John	Arts	England	Clergyman/Evangelist
Wesson	Amy	Performing Arts	USA	Super Model
West	Adam	Performing Arts	USA	Actor
	Benjamin	Works of Art	USA	Painter
	Jerry A.	Sports	USA	Basketball Player - HF
	Mae	Performing Arts	USA	Actress
	Mary Jane (Mae)	Performing Arts	USA	Actress
	Nathanael	Creative Works	USA	Novelist
	Rebecca	Creative Works	England	Novelist/Critic
Westermarck	Edward Alexander	Arts	Finland	Anthropologist
Westheimer	Ruth	Creative Works	USA	Journalist - Television
Westinghouse	George	Business	USA	Manufacturer/Inventor
Weston	Jack	Performing Arts	USA	Actor
Westwick	Harry (Rat)	Sports	Canada	Hockey Player - HF
Westwood	Vivienne	Business	England	Fashion Designer
Wethered	Joyce	Sports	England	Golfer - HF
Weyerhauser	Frederick	Business	USA	Lumber Industry
Weymoiuth	Martina (Tina)	Performing Arts	USA	Rock & Roll - HF - Talking Heads

LAST NAME	FIRST NAME	CATEGORY	COUNTRY	FAME
Wharton	Edith	Creative Works	USA	Novelist - Pulitzer
Wheat	Zachary Davis (Zack)	Sports	USA	Baseball Player - HF
Wheatley	Phillis	Creative Works	USA	Poet
Wheaton	Wil	Performing Arts	USA	Actor
Wheatstone	Charles	Science	England	Physicist
Wheeler	Humpy	Sports	USA	Race Car Promoter - HF
	William A.	Politics	USA	Vice-President
Whelan	Arleen	Performing Arts	USA	Actress
Whichcote	Benjamin	Arts	England	Philosopher
Whipple	George Hoyt	Science	USA	Medicine - Nobel Laureate
Whistler	James Abbott McNiell	Works of Art	USA	Painter/Etcher
Whitaker	Pernell	Sports	USA	Boxer
Whitbread	Samuel	Business	England	Retail Trade
Whitcroft	Frederick	Sports	Canada	Hockey Player - HF
White	Barry	Performing Arts	USA	Singer/Composer
	Betty	Performing Arts	USA	Actress
	Byron Raymond	Law & Order	USA	Justice - Supreme Court
	Clarence	Performing Arts	USA	Rock & Roll - HF - The Bryds
	Edward Douglas	Law & Order	USA	Chief Justice
	Elwyn Brooks	Creative Works	USA	Humorist
	Fred (Freddie)	Performing Arts	USA	Rock & Roll - HF - Earth Wind & Fire
	Gilbert	Arts	England	Naturalist
	Leonard D.	Creative Works	USA	Author - Pulitzer
	Nera D.	Sports	USA	Basketball Player - HF
	Patrick	Creative Works	Australia	Literature - Nobel Laureate
	Randy Lee	Sports	USA	Football Player - HF
	Reggie	Sports	USA	Football Player
	Stanford	Architecture	USA	Architect
	Terence Hanbury	Creative Works	India	Novelist
	Theodore Harold	Creative Works	USA	Author - Pulitzer
	Vanna	Performing Arts	USA	Show Host
	Walter Francis	Politics	USA	Negro Leader
	William Allen	Creative Works	USA	Author - Pulitzer
	William S.	Creative Works	USA	Author - Pulitzer
White II	Edward Higgins	Aviation	USA	Astronaut
White III	Edmund Valentine	Creative Works	USA	Author
Whitefield	George	Arts	England	Evangilist - Methodist
Whitehead	Alfred North	Arts	England	Philosopher/Mathematician
Whiteley	Jon	Performing Arts	Scotland	Actor - Academy Award
Whiteman	Paul	Performing Arts	USA	Conductor - Big Band/Jazz - HF
Whitford	Brad	Performing Arts	USA	Rock & Roll - HF - Aerosmith
Whitman	Malcolm Douglass (Mal)	Sports	USA	Tennis Player - HF
	Marcus	Exploration	USA	Frontiersman - America
	Stuart	Performing Arts	USA	Actor - Acad Award Nom
	Walter	Creative Works	USA	Poet
Whitmore	James	Performing Arts	USA	Actor - Acad Award Nom
Whitney	Eli	Science	USA	Inventor - Cotton Gin
Whittier	John Greenleaf	Creative Works	USA	Poet
Whittington	Richard	Business	England	Merchant
Whittle	Frank	Science	England	Inventor/Engineer
Whitty	May	Performing Arts	England	Actress - Acad Award Nom
Whitworth	Kathy	Sports	USA	Golfer - HF
Wickman	Carl Eric	Business	USA	Transportation Industry
Widdemer	Margaret	Creative Works	USA	Poet - Pulitzer
Widmark	Richard	Performing Arts	USA	Actor - Acad Award Nom
Wieland	Christopher Martin	Creative Works	Germany	Poet/Novelist/Translator
	Heinrich Otto	Science	Germany	Chemistry - Nobel Laureate
Wieman	Carl E.	Science	USA	Physics - Nobel Laureate
Wien	Wilhelm	Science	Germany	Physics - Nobel Laureate
Wiener	Norbert	Science	USA	Mathematician
Wieschaus	Eric F.	Science	USA	Medicine - Nobel Laureate
Wiesel	Eliezer (Elie)	Creative Works	USA	Author
	Eliezer (Elie)	War & Peace	USA	Peace - Nobel Laureate

SOLVER SERIES: NAME FINDER

LAST NAME	FIRST NAME	CATEGORY	COUNTRY	FAME
Wiesel	Torsten N.	Science	Sweden	Medicine - Nobel Laureate
Wiest	Dianne	Performing Arts	USA	Actress - Academy Award
Wiggin	Kate Douglas	Creative Works	USA	Writer/Educator
Wigner	Eugene Paul	Science	USA	Physics - Nobel Laureate
Wilander	Mats	Sports	Sweden	Tennis Player - HF
Wilberforce	William	Politics	England	Statesman
Wilbur	Richard	Creative Works	USA	Poet - Pulitzer
Wilcox	David (Dave)	Sports	USA	Football Player - HF
	Ella Wheeler	Creative Works	USA	Poet
Wilczek	Frank	Science	USA	Physics - Nobel Laureate
Wild	Jack	Performing Arts	England	Actor - Acad Award Nom
Wilde	Brandon De	Performing Arts	USA	Actor - Acad Award Nom
Wilde	Cornel	Performing Arts	USA	Actor - Acad Award Nom
	Oscar	Creative Works	England	Poet/Novelist/Playwright
	Ted	Movie Production	USA	Director - Acad Award Nom
Wilder	Billy	Movie Production	Hungary	Director - Academy Award
	Gene	Performing Arts	USA	Actor - Acad Award Nom
	Laura Ingalls	Creative Works	USA	Author - Children's Books
	Thornton Niven	Creative Works	USA	Dramatist - Pulitzer
Wilding	Anthony Frederick (Tony)	Sports	New Zealand	Tennis Player - HF
	Michael	Performing Arts	England	Actor
Wilhelm	James Hoyt	Sports	USA	Baseball Player - HF
	Kate	Creative Works	USA	Author
Wilkens	Leonard (Lenny)	Sports	USA	Basketball Player - HF
Wilkes	Charles	Exploration	USA	Explorer - Antarctic
	John	Politics	England	Reformer - Political
Wilkins	George Hubert	Exploration	Australia	Explorer - Polar
	Maurice Hugh Frederick	Science	England	Medicine - Nobel Laureate
Wilkinson	Geoffrey	Science	England	Chemistry - Nobel Laureate
	Tom	Performing Arts	England	Actor - Acad Award Nom
Will	George	Creative Works	USA	Journalist - Newspaper - Pulitzer
Willard	Francis Elizabeth Caroline	Politics	USA	Temperance Leader
	Jess	Sports	USA	Boxer - HF
Willey	Alan	Sports	England	Soccer Player - HF
Williams	Andy	Performing Arts	USA	Singer - Contemporary
	Betty	War & Peace	England	Peace - Nobel Laureate
	Billy Dee	Performing Arts	USA	Actor
	Billy Leo	Sports	USA	Baseball Player - HF
	Cara	Performing Arts	USA	Actress - Acad Award Nom
	Charles Kenneth	Creative Works	USA	Poet - Pulitzer
	Charles Melvin (Cootie)	Performing Arts	USA	Jazz Trumpeter - Big Band/Jazz - HF
	Cindy	Performing Arts	USA	Actress
	Clarence	Performing Arts	USA	Jazz Pianist/Composer - Big Band/Jazz - HF
	Cliff	Performing Arts	England	Rock & Roll - HF - AC/DC
	Daffydd Rhys	Aviation	Canada	Astronaut
	Don	Performing Arts	USA	Singer - Country & Western
	Donald Edward	Aviation	USA	Astronaut
	Edy	Performing Arts	USA	Actress
	Esther	Performing Arts	USA	Actress
	Isiah (Ike)	Sports	USA	Boxer - HF
	Jesse Lynch	Creative Works	USA	Dramatist - Pulitzer
	JoBeth	Performing Arts	USA	Actress
	John Christopher	Performing Arts	Australia	Guitarist/Classical
	John Towner	Creative Works	USA	Composer
	Joseph (Joe)	Sports	USA	Baseball Player - HF
	Joseph Goreed (Joe)	Performing Arts	USA	Singer - Big Band/Jazz - HF
	Mary Lou	Performing Arts	USA	Jazz Pianist/Composer - Big Band/Jazz - HF
	Mason	Performing Arts	USA	Guitarist/Classical
	Matt	Sports	USA	Baseball Player
	Paul	Architecture	USA	Architect
	Paul	Performing Arts	USA	Rock & Roll - HF - The Temptations
	Robin	Performing Arts	USA	Actor - Academy Award
	Robin	Performing Arts	USA	Comedian

LAST NAME	FIRST NAME	CATEGORY	COUNTRY	FAME
Williams	Roger	Arts	England	Clergyman/Colonist
	Roger	Performing Arts	USA	Pianist
	Samuel Anthony (Tony)	Performing Arts	USA	Jazz Drummer - Big Band/Jazz - HF
	Samuel Anthony (Tony)	Performing Arts	USA	Rock & Roll - HF - The Platters
	Tennessee	Creative Works	USA	Dramatist - Pulitzer
	Theodore Samuel (Ted)	Sports	USA	Baseball Player - HF
	Thomas Harry	Creative Works	USA	Author - Pulitzer
	Tod	Architecture	USA	Architect - Jefferson Medal
	Treat	Performing Arts	USA	Actor
	Vanessa	Performing Arts	USA	Actress
	Vanessa Lynn	Performing Arts	USA	Singer - Musicals
	Walter	Performing Arts	USA	Rock & Roll - HF - The O'Jays
	Wayne	Law & Order	USA	Serial Killer
	William Carlos	Creative Works	USA	Poet - Pulitzer
Williams (Miles)	Otis	Performing Arts	USA	Rock & Roll - HF - The Temptations
Williams Jr.	Clifton Curtis	Aviation	USA	Astronaut
	Randall (Hank)	Performing Arts	USA	Singer - Rock & Roll - HF
Williams II	Richard Norris (Dick)	Sports	USA	Tennis Player - HF
Williams Sr.	Hiram King (Hank)	Performing Arts	USA	Singer - Country Music - HF
	Hiram King (Hank)	Performing Arts	USA	Singer - Rock & Roll - HF
	Walter	Performing Arts	USA	Rock & Roll - HF - The O'Jays
Williams-Ellis	Clough	Architecture	England	Architect
Williamson	Michael	Creative Works	USA	Author - Pulitzer
	Nicol	Performing Arts	Scotland	Actor
Willis	Bruce	Performing Arts	Germany	Actor
	Victor Gazaway (Vic)	Sports	USA	Baseball Player - HF
	William Karnet (Bill)	Sports	USA	Football Player - HF
Willkie	Wendell Lewis	Politics	USA	Political Leader/Lawyer
Wills	Chill	Performing Arts	USA	Actor - Acad Award Nom
	Gary	Creative Works	USA	Author - Pulitzer
	James Robert (Bob)	Performing Arts	USA	Country Music - HF - Texas Playboys
	William John	Exploration	Australia	Explorer - Central Australia
Wills-Moody	Helen Newington	Sports	USA	Tennis Player - HF
Willstätter	Richard Martin	Science	Germany	Chemistry - Nobel Laureate
Wilson	Alexander	Arts	USA	Ornithologist
	Angus Frank Johnstone	Creative Works	England	Novelist/Short Story Writer
	Ann	Performing Arts	USA	Singer - Rock & Roll - HF
	August	Creative Works	USA	Dramatist - Pulitzer
	Brian	Performing Arts	USA	Rock & Roll - HF - The Beach Boys
	Brian Douglas	Creative Works	USA	Composer/Arranger
	Bruce	Sports	Canada	Soccer Player - HF
	Carl	Performing Arts	USA	Rock & Roll - HF - The Beach Boys
	Charles Thomson Rees	Science	England	Physics - Nobel Laureate
	Demond	Performing Arts	USA	Actor
	Dennis	Performing Arts	USA	Rock & Roll - HF - The Beach Boys
	Edith Bolling	Politics	USA	First Lady
	Edmund	Creative Works	USA	Writer/Critic
	Edward Osborne	Creative Works	USA	Author - Pulitzer
	Ellen Louise	Politics	USA	First Lady
	Flip	Performing Arts	USA	Comedian
	Forrest	Creative Works	USA	Author - Pulitzer
	Gahan	Creative Works	USA	Cartoonist - Magazines
	Gerald	Performing Arts	USA	Band Leader/Composer - Big Band/Jazz - HF
	Gordon Allan (Phat)	Sports	Canada	Hockey Player - HF
	Henry	Politics	USA	Vice-President
	Jack Leroy (Jackie)	Performing Arts	USA	Singer - Rock & Roll - HF
	James Harold	Politics	England	Prime Minster
	Kenneth G.	Science	USA	Physics - Nobel Laureate
	Lanford	Creative Works	USA	Dramatist - Pulitzer
	Lawrence Frank (Larry)	Sports	USA	Football Player - HF
	Lewis Robert (Hack)	Sports	USA	Baseball Player - HF
	Margaret	Creative Works	USA	Novelist - Pulitzer
	Marie	Performing Arts	USA	Actress

SOLVER SERIES: NAME FINDER

LAST NAME	FIRST NAME	CATEGORY	COUNTRY	FAME
Wilson	Mary	Performing Arts	USA	Rock & Roll - HF - The Supremes
	Nancy	Performing Arts	USA	Singer - Big Band/Jazz - HF
	Nancy	Performing Arts	USA	Singer - Rock & Roll - HF
	Paul	Performing Arts	USA	Rock & Roll - HF - The Flamingos
	Peter	Sports	Scotland	Soccer Player - HF
	Peter Barton (Pete)	Politics	USA	Senator - California
	Robert Woodrow	Science	USA	Physics - Nobel Laureate
	Theodore Shaw (Teddy)	Performing Arts	USA	Jazz Pianist - Big Band/Jazz - HF
	Thomas Woodrow	Politics	USA	President
	Thomas Woodrow	War & Peace	USA	Peace - Nobel Laureate
	Tom	Creative Works	USA	Cartoonist - Ziggy
	Trey	Performing Arts	USA	Actor
Wimille	Jean Pierre	Sports	France	Race Car Driver - HF
Winchell	Walter	Creative Works	USA	Journalist - Newspaper
Winckelmann	Johann Joachim	Arts	Germany	Archaeologist/Art Historian
Windaus	Adolf Otto	Science	Germany	Chemistry - Nobel Laureate
Winding	Kai Chresten	Performing Arts	Denmark	Jazz Trombonist
Windischmann	Michael	Sports	Germany	Soccer Player - HF
Windom	William	Performing Arts	USA	Actor
Winfield	David Mark (Dave)	Sports	USA	Baseball Player - HF
	Paul	Performing Arts	USA	Actor - Acad Award Nom
Winfrey	Oprah	Performing Arts	USA	Actress - Acad Award Nom
	Oprah	Performing Arts	USA	Show Host
Wing (Slick)	Grace Barnett	Performing Arts	USA	Rock & Roll - HF - Jefferson Airplane
Winger	Debra	Performing Arts	USA	Actress - Acad Award Nom
Wingfield	Walter Clopton	Sports	Wales	Tennis Inventor - HF
Winkler	Henry	Performing Arts	USA	Actor
Winningham	Mare	Performing Arts	USA	Actress - Acad Award Nom
Winslet	Kate	Performing Arts	England	Actress - Acad Award Nom
Winslow	Edward	Exploration	England	Colonist - Plymouth
	Kellen Boswell	Sports	USA	Football Player - HF
	Ola Elizabeth	Creative Works	USA	Author - Pulitzer
Winter	Vincent	Performing Arts	Scotland	Actor - Academy Award
Winters	Jonathon	Performing Arts	USA	Comedian
	Shelley	Performing Arts	USA	Actress - Academy Award
Winthrop	John	Exploration	England	Colonist - Massachusetts
Winwood	Estelle	Performing Arts	England	Actress
	Steven (Stevie)	Performing Arts	England	Rock & Roll - HF - Traffic
Wirtz	Alvin	Business	USA	Electricity
Wise	Robert	Movie Production	USA	Director - Academy Award
	Stephen Samuel	Arts	USA	Rabbi/Jewish Leader
Wisoff	Peter Jeffry Karl	Aviation	USA	Astronaut
Wister	Owen	Creative Works	USA	Novelist
Withers	Jane	Performing Arts	USA	Actress
Witherspoon	John	Arts	USA	Clergyman/Educator
Witt	Joyce De	Performing Arts	USA	Actress
	Katarina	Sports	Germany	Olympic Skater
Wittgenstein	Ludwig Josef Johann	Arts	England	Philosopher
Wittig	Georg	Science	England	Chemistry - Nobel Laureate
Wodehouse	Pelham Grenville	Creative Works	England	Novelist
Woffington	Peg	Performing Arts	Ireland	Actress
Wojciechowicz	Alexander Francis (Alex)	Sports	USA	Football Player - HF
Wolanin	Adam	Sports	Poland	Soccer Player - HF
Wolf	Friedrich August	Arts	Germany	Scholar - Classical
	Hugo	Creative Works	Austria	Composer
	Peter	Performing Arts	USA	Singer
Wolfe	Billy De	Performing Arts	USA	Actor
	James	War & Peace	England	General
	Linnie Marsh	Creative Works	USA	Author - Pulitzer
	Thomas Clayton	Creative Works	USA	Novelist
Wolf-Ferrari	Ermano	Creative Works	Italy	Composer
Wolfram	Von Eschenbach	Creative Works	Germany	Poet - Epic
Wollstonecraft	Mary	Creative Works	England	Writer

LAST NAME	FIRST NAME	CATEGORY	COUNTRY	FAME
Wolsey	Thomas	Politics	England	Statesman
Womack	Bobby	Performing Arts	USA	Singer - Rhythm & Blues
Wonder (Hardaway)	Steveland Judkins (Stevie)	Performing Arts	USA	Singer - Rock & Roll - HF
Wong	Anna May	Performing Arts	USA	Actress
Wood	Alexander (Sandy)	Sports	Scotland	Soccer Player - HF
	Chris	Performing Arts	England	Rock & Roll - HF - Traffic
	Glen	Sports	USA	Race Car Driver - HF
	Gordon S.	Creative Works	USA	Author - Pulitzer
	Grant	Works of Art	USA	Painter
	John	Architecture	England	Architect
	John	Business	England	Textile Industry
	Lana	Performing Arts	USA	Actress
	Leonard	War & Peace	USA	General/Political Administrator
	Natalie	Performing Arts	USA	Actress - Acad Award Nom
	Peggy	Performing Arts	USA	Actress - Acad Award Nom
	Robert W.	Science	USA	Physicist
	Ron	Performing Arts	England	Singer/Guitarist
	Samuel	Movie Production	USA	Director - Acad Award Nom
	Sydney Burr Beardsley	Sports	USA	Tennis Player - HF
	William Vernell (Willie)	Sports	USA	Football Player - HF
Woodard	Alfre	Performing Arts	USA	Actress - Acad Award Nom
	Lynette	Sports	USA	Basketball Player - HF
Wooden	John R.	Sports	USA	Basketball Player - HF
Woods	James	Performing Arts	USA	Actor - Acad Award Nom
	Tiger	Sports	USA	Golfer
Woodson (Creggett)	Ollie (Ali)	Performing Arts	USA	Rock & Roll - HF - The Temptations
Woodward	Comer Vann	Creative Works	USA	Author - Pulitzer
	Edward	Performing Arts	England	Actor
	Joanne	Performing Arts	USA	Actress - Academy Award
	Robert Burns	Science	USA	Chemistry - Nobel Laureate
Woolf	Leonard Sidney	Creative Works	England	Writer/Publisher
	Virginia	Creative Works	England	Author
Woolfolk	Andrew	Performing Arts	USA	Rock & Roll - HF - Earth Wind & Fire
Woollcott	Alexander Humphreys	Creative Works	USA	Writer/Critic
Woolley	Monty	Performing Arts	USA	Actor - Acad Award Nom
Woolworth	Frank Winfield	Business	USA	Merchant
Woosnam	Ian	Sports	Wales	Golfer
Worcester	Joseph Emerson	Arts	USA	Lexicographer
Worden	Alfred Merrill	Aviation	USA	Astronaut
Wordsworth	William	Creative Works	England	Poet Laureate
Worsley	Lorne John (Gump)	Sports	Canada	Hockey Player - HF
Worters	Roy (Shrimp)	Sports	Canada	Hockey Player - HF
Worth	Irene	Performing Arts	USA	Actress
Wortham	Gus Sessions	Business	USA	Insurance Industry
Worthy	James	Sports	USA	Basketball Player - HF
Wouk	Herman	Creative Works	USA	Author - Pulitzer
Wournos	Aileen	Law & Order	USA	Serial Killer
Wray	Fay	Performing Arts	Canada	Actress
Wren	Christopher	Architecture	England	Architect
Wrenn	Robert Duffield (Bob)	Sports	USA	Tennis Player - HF
Wright	Albert (Chalky)	Sports	Mexico	Boxer - HF
	Beals Coleman	Sports	USA	Tennis Player
	Billy	Sports	England	Soccer Player - HF
	Charles	Creative Works	USA	Poet - Pulitzer
	Douglas	Creative Works	USA	Dramatist - Pulitzer
	Frank Lloyd	Architecture	USA	Architect - AIA Gold Medal
	Franz	Creative Works	USA	Poet - Pulitzer
	George	Sports	USA	Baseball Executive -HF
	James Arlington	Creative Works	USA	Poet - Pulitzer
	Joseph	Arts	England	Lexicographer/Linguist
	Mary Kathryn (Mickey)	Sports	USA	Golfer - HF
	Max	Performing Arts	USA	Actor
	Orville	Aviation	USA	Inventor - Airplane

SOLVER SERIES: NAME FINDER

LAST NAME	FIRST NAME	CATEGORY	COUNTRY	FAME
Wright	Richard	Creative Works	USA	Novelist
	Richard William	Performing Arts	England	Rock & Roll - HF - Pink Floyd
	Simon	Performing Arts	England	Rock & Roll - HF - AC/DC
	Steven	Performing Arts	USA	Comedian
	Teresa	Performing Arts	USA	Actress - Academy Award
	Wilbur	Aviation	USA	Inventor - Airplane
	William Henry (Harry)	Sports	England	Baseball Executive -HF
Wundt	Wilhelm	Arts	Germany	Psychologist/Physiologist
Wurdemann	Audrey	Creative Works	USA	Poet - Pulitzer
Wurster	William Wilson	Architecture	USA	Architect - AIA Gold Medal
Wüthrich	Kurt	Science	Switzerland	Chemistry - Nobel Laureate
Wyatt	Jane	Performing Arts	USA	Actress
	Thomas	Creative Works	England	Poet/Diplomat
Wycherley	William	Creative Works	England	Dramatist
Wycherly	Margaret	Performing Arts	England	Actress - Acad Award Nom
Wycliffe	John	Arts	England	Reformer - Religious
Wyeth	Andrew Newell	Works of Art	USA	Painter
	Newell Convers	Works of Art	USA	Painter/Illustrator
Wyld	Henry Cecil Kennedy	Arts	England	Lexicographer/Linguist
Wyler	Gretchen	Performing Arts	USA	Actress
	William	Movie Production	Germany	Director - Academy Award
Wylie	Eleanor	Creative Works	USA	Poet
	Philip Gordon	Creative Works	USA	Author
Wyman	Bill	Performing Arts	England	Singer/Guitarist
	Jane	Performing Arts	USA	Actress - Academy Award
Wyman (Perks)	William George (Bill)	Performing Arts	England	Rock & Roll - HF - Rolling Stones
Wynalda	Eric	Sports	USA	Soccer Player - HF
Wyndham	John	Creative Works	England	Author - SciFi
Wynette	Tammy	Performing Arts	USA	Singer - Country Music - HF
Wynn	Early	Sports	USA	Baseball Player - HF
	Ed	Performing Arts	USA	Actor - Acad Award Nom
	Keenan	Performing Arts	USA	Actor
Wynter	Dana	Performing Arts	Germany	Actress
Wynyard	Diana	Performing Arts	England	Actress - Acad Award Nom
Wythe	George	Law & Order	USA	Jurist/Patriot
Xingjian	Gao	Creative Works	France	Literature - Nobel Laureate
Yalow	Rosalyn	Science	USA	Medicine - Nobel Laureate
Yamamoto	Isoroku	War & Peace	Japan	Naval Commander
Yang	Chen Ning	Science	China	Physics - Nobel Laureate
Yankovic	Al (Weird)	Performing Arts	USA	Singer
Yanovsky	Zal	Performing Arts	Canada	Singer/Guitarist - Canadian Music - HF
Yarborough	Glenn	Performing Arts	USA	Singer
	William Caleb (Cale)	Sports	USA	Race Car Driver - HF
Yard	Molly	Politics	USA	Activist - Feminism
Yardley	George	Sports	USA	Basketball Player - HF
Yarnell	Lorene	Performing Arts	USA	Dancer/Mime
Yarrow	Peter	Performing Arts	USA	Singer - Folk
Yary	Anthony Ronald (Ron)	Sports	USA	Football Player - HF
Yashin	Lev	Sports	Russia	Soccer Player - HF
Yastrzemski	Carl Michael	Sports	USA	Baseball Player - HF
Yates	Peter	Movie Production	England	Director - Acad Award Nom
Yat-Sen	Sun	Politics	China	Revolutionist
Yawkey	Thomas Austin (Tom)	Sports	USA	Baseball Executive - HF
Yeager	Chuck Elwood	Aviation	USA	Pilot - Sound Barrier
Yeats	William Butler	Creative Works	Ireland	Literature - Nobel Laureate
Yegorov	Boris Borisovich	Aviation	Russia	Astronaut
Yeliseyev	Aleksei Stanislavovich	Aviation	Russia	Astronaut
Yeltsin	Boris Nikolayevich	Politics	Russia	President
	Naina	Politics	Russia	First Lady
Yepremian	Garo	Sports	USA	Football Player
Yergin	Daniel	Creative Works	USA	Author - Pulitzer
Yester	Jerry	Performing Arts	USA	Rock & Roll - HF - Lovin' Spoonful
York	Michael	Performing Arts	England	Actor

LAST NAME	FIRST NAME	CATEGORY	COUNTRY	FAME
York	Susannah	Performing Arts	England	Actress - Acad Award Nom
Yost	Eddie	Sports	USA	Baseball Player
Yothers	Tina	Performing Arts	USA	Actress
Young	Angus	Performing Arts	Scotland	Rock & Roll - HF - AC/DC
	Arthur Henry	Creative Works	USA	Cartoonist - Satiric
	Brigham	Arts	USA	Mormon Leader
	Burt	Performing Arts	USA	Actor - Acad Award Nom
	Denton True (Cy)	Sports	USA	Baseball Player - HF
	Edward	Creative Works	England	Poet
	Faron	Performing Arts	USA	Singer - Country Music - HF
	Gig	Performing Arts	USA	Actor - Academy Award
	John Watts	Aviation	USA	Astronaut
	Jon Steven (Steve)	Sports	USA	Football Player - HF
	Lester	Performing Arts	USA	Jazz Saxophonist - Big Band/Jazz - HF
	Loretta	Performing Arts	USA	Actress - Academy Award
	Malcolm	Performing Arts	Scotland	Rock & Roll - HF - AC/DC
	Murat Bernard (Chic)	Creative Works	USA	Cartoonist - Blondie
	Neil	Performing Arts	Canada	Rock & Roll - HF - Buffalo Springfield
	Otis	Performing Arts	USA	Actor
	Robert	Performing Arts	USA	Actor
	Roland	Performing Arts	England	Actor - Acad Award Nom
	Thomas	Science	England	Physicist/Physician/Linguist
	Trummy	Performing Arts	USA	Jazz Saxophonist - Big Band/Jazz - HF
	Verne	Performing Arts	USA	Rock & Roll - HF - The Drifters
Young Jr.	Andrew Jackson	Politics	USA	Politician/Activist - Civil Rights
Youngblood III	Herbert Jackson (Jack)	Sports	USA	Football Player - HF
Younghusband	Francis	Exploration	England	Explorer - Himalayas
Youngman	Henny	Performing Arts	England	Comedian
Youngs	Ross Middlebrook	Sports	USA	Baseball Player - HF
Yount	Robin Rachel	Sports	USA	Baseball Player - HF
Ypsilanti	Alexander	War & Peace	Greece	Revolutionary Leader
	Demetrios	War & Peace	Greece	Revolutionary Leader
Yukawa	Hideki	Science	Japan	Physics - Nobel Laureate
Yunick	Henry (Smokey)	Sports	USA	Race Car Designer - HF
Yuro	Timi	Performing Arts	USA	Singer
Zadora	Pia	Performing Arts	USA	Actress
Zaharias	Mildred Didrikson (Babe)	Sports	USA	Golfer - HF
Zale	Anthony Florian (Tony)	Sports	USA	Boxer - HF
Zander	Robin	Performing Arts	USA	Singer - Rock & Roll - HF
Zangwill	Israel	Creative Works	England	Novelist/Playwright
Zanuck	Darryl F.	Movie Production	USA	Director
Zanuso	Marco	Architecture	Italy	Architect
Zapata	Emiliano	Politics	Mexico	Revolutionist
Zapotek	Emil	Sports	Czechoslovakia	Olympic Marathoner
Zappa	Frank Vincent	Performing Arts	USA	Singer - Rock & Roll - HF
Zaragoza	Daniel	Sports	Mexico	Boxer - HF
Zarate	Carlos	Sports	Mexico	Boxer - HF
Zarley	Kermit	Sports	USA	Golfer
Zaturenska	Marya	Creative Works	Russia	Poet - Pulitzer
Zedong	Mao (Chairman Mao)	War & Peace	China	Military Leader
Zeeman	Peter	Science	Netherlands	Physics - Nobel Laureate
Zeffirelli	Franco	Movie Production	Italy	Director - Acad Award Nom
Zell	Harry von	Performing Arts	USA	Actor
Zellweger	Renee	Performing Arts	USA	Actress - Academy Award
Zemeckis	Robert	Movie Production	USA	Director - Academy Award
Zenger	John Peter	Creative Works	USA	Journalist/Publisher
Zerbe	Anthony	Performing Arts	USA	Actor
Zerhusen	Albert (Al)	Sports	USA	Soccer Player - HF
Zermani	Paolo	Architecture	Italy	Architect
Zernike	Frits Frederik	Science	Netherlands	Physics - Nobel Laureate
Zeta-Jones	Catherine	Performing Arts	Wales	Actress - Academy Award
Zetterling	Mai	Performing Arts	Sweden	Actress
Zevon	Warren	Performing Arts	USA	Singer

SOLVER SERIES: NAME FINDER

LAST NAME	FIRST NAME	CATEGORY	COUNTRY	FAME
Zewail	Ahmed Hassan	Science	USA	Chemistry - Nobel Laureate
Zhukov	Georgi Konstantinovich	War & Peace	Russia	Soviet Marshall
Ziegfeld	Florenz	Movie Production	USA	Producer - Theatrical
Ziegler	Karl	Science	Germany	Chemistry - Nobel Laureate
	Ronald Louis (Ron)	Politics	USA	Press Secretary
Ziemba	Karen	Performing Arts	USA	Actress
Ziering	Ian	Performing Arts	USA	Actor
Zimbalist	Efrem	Performing Arts	USA	Violinist
Zimbalist Jr.	Efrem	Performing Arts	USA	Actor
Zimmerman	Dominikus	Architecture	Germany	Architect
Zindane	Zinédine	Sports	France	Soccer Player
Zindel	Paul	Creative Works	USA	Dramatist - Pulitzer
Zinkernagel	Rolf M.	Science	Switzerland	Medicine - Nobel Laureate
Zinneman	Fred	Movie Production	Austria	Director - Academy Award
Zinsser	Hans	Science	USA	Bacteriologist
Zivic	Fritzie	Sports	USA	Boxer - HF
Žižka	Jan	War & Peace	Bohemia	General
Zoeller	Fuzzy	Sports	USA	Golfer
Zoff	Dino	Sports	Italy	Soccer Player - HF
Zola	Emile Édouard Charles Antoine	Creative Works	France	Novelist
Zorach	William	Works of Art	USA	Painter/Sculptor
Zorn	Anders Leonard	Works of Art	Sweden	Painter/Sculptor/Etcher
Zorrilla	José	Creative Works	Spain	Poet/Playwright
Zsigmondy	Richard Adolf	Science	Germany	Chemistry - Nobel Laureate
Zuckerman	Pinchas	Performing Arts	Israel	Conductor/Violinist
Zukor	Adolph	Movie Production	Hungary	Producer
Zulu	Shaka	War & Peace	South Africa	Military Leader
Zumthor	Peter	Architecture	Switzerland	Architect
Zumwalt Jr.	Elmo Russell	War & Peace	USA	Admiral
Zurbarán	Francisco de	Works of Art	Spain	Painter
Zweig	Arnold	Creative Works	Germany	Novelist/Playwright/Essayist
	Stefan	Creative Works	Austria	Novelist/Playwright
Zwingli	Ulrich	Arts	Switzerland	Reformer - Protestant

FIRST NAME	LAST NAME	CATEGORY	COUNTRY	FAME
Aage Niels Henrik David	Bohr	Science	Denmark	Physics - Nobel Laureate
Aalbert	Cuyp	Works of Art	Netherlands	Painter
Aaron	Burr	Politics	USA	Vice-President
	Ciechanover	Science	Israel	Chemistry - Nobel Laureate
	Copland	Creative Works	USA	Composer
	Klug	Science	England	Chemistry - Nobel Laureate
	Pryor	Sports	USA	Boxer - HF
	Spelling	Movie Production	USA	Director
Aaron Thibeaux (T-Bone)	Walker	Performing Arts	USA	Guitarist/Songwriter - Big Band/Jazz - HF
	Walker	Performing Arts	USA	Singer - Rock & Roll - HF
Abba Hillel	Silver	Arts	USA	Rabbi
Abbie	Hoffman	Creative Works	USA	Journalist - Magazine
Abbott Lawrence	Lowell	Arts	USA	Educator
Abby	Dalton	Performing Arts	USA	Actress
Abd al-Salam	Faraj	Creative Works	Egypt	Writer
Abdul (Duke)	Fakir	Performing Arts	USA	Rock & Roll - HF - The Four Tops
Abdus	Salam	Science	Pakistan	Physics - Nobel Laureate
Abe	Fortas	Law & Order	USA	Justice - Supreme Court
	Kobo	Creative Works	Japan	Novelist/Playwright
	Lyman	Performing Arts	USA	Orchestra Leader
	Vigoda	Performing Arts	USA	Actor
Abel Janszoon	Tasman	Exploration	Netherlands	Explorer - Tasmania
Abigail	Adams	Politics	USA	First Lady
	Fillmore	Politics	USA	First Lady
Abigail Van	Buren	Creative Works	USA	Journalist - Newspaper
Abner	Doubleday	Sports	USA	Inventor - Baseball
Abraham	Cowley	Creative Works	England	Poet/Essayist
	Flexner	Arts	USA	Educator
	Lincoln	Politics	USA	President
Abraham (Bram)	Stoker	Creative Works	Ireland	Author
Abraham Alfonse	Gallatin	Business	USA	Financier/Statesman
Abraham Arden	Brill	Arts	USA	Psychoanalyst
Abraham Harold	Maslow	Arts	USA	Philosopher
Abraham Joshua	Heschel	Arts	USA	Philosopher/Scholar/Rabbi
Abram S. (Abe)	Burrows	Creative Works	USA	Dramatist - Pulitzer
Abu	Bakr	Politics	Saudi Arabia	Calif
Abu Abdulla Ibn	Battuta	Exploration	Morocco	Explorer - Africa
Achille	Varzi	Sports	Italy	Race Car Driver - HF

SOLVER SERIES: NAME FINDER

FIRST NAME	LAST NAME	CATEGORY	COUNTRY	FAME
Achille Charles Léonce	Broglie	Politics	France	Statesman
Achille Émile Othon	Friesz	Works of Art	France	Painter
Ada	Maris	Performing Arts	USA	Actress
	Rehan	Performing Arts	Ireland	Actress
Ada Louise	Huxtable	Architecture	USA	Architect - Jefferson Medal
Adah Isaacs	Menken	Performing Arts	USA	Actress/Poet
Adalberto	Libera	Architecture	Italy	Architect
Adam	Ant	Performing Arts	England	Singer
	Arkin	Performing Arts	USA	Actor
	Faith	Performing Arts	England	Singer/Actor
	Mickiewicz	Creative Works	Poland	Poet
	Smith	Arts	Scotland	Philosopher/Economist
	West	Performing Arts	USA	Actor
	Wolanin	Sports	Poland	Soccer Player - HF
	Clayton	Performing Arts	England	Rock & Roll - HF - U2
Addison	Mizner	Architecture	USA	Architect
Adela Rogers	St. John	Creative Works	USA	Journalist - Newspaper
	Astaire	Performing Arts	USA	Dancer
	Simpson	Business	USA	Designer - Fashion
Adelina	Patti	Performing Arts	Italy	Singer - Opera
Adelino (Billy)	Gonsalves	Sports	USA	Soccer Player - HF
Adlai E.	Stevenson	Politics	USA	Vice-President
Adolf	Hitler	War & Peace	Germany	Military Leader
	Loos	Architecture	Austria	Architect
	Meyer	Architecture	Germany	Architect
Adolf F.	Brix	Science	Germany	Chemist
Adolf Friedrich Johann	Butenandt	Science	Germany	Chemistry - Nobel Laureate
Adolf Otto	Windaus	Science	Germany	Chemistry - Nobel Laureate
Adolfo Pérez	Esquivel	War & Peace	Argentina	Peace - Nobel Laureate
Adolph	Bachmeier	Sports	Romania	Soccer Player - HF
	Caesar	Performing Arts	USA	Actor - Acad Award Nom
	Green	Creative Works	USA	Composer
	Zukor	Movie Production	Hungary	Producer
Adolph (Dolph)	Schayes	Sports	USA	Basketball Player - HF
Adolph Simon	Ochs	Creative Works	USA	Publisher - Newspaper
Adolphe	Menjou	Performing Arts	USA	Actor - Acad Award Nom
Adolphus	Busch	Business	USA	Breweries
Adrian	Dantley	Sports	USA	Basketball Player
	Lyne	Movie Production	England	Director - Acad Award Nom
Adrian (Addie)	Joss	Sports	USA	Baseball Player - HF
Adrian Constantine (Cap)	Anson	Sports	USA	Baseball Player - HF
Adrian Francis	Rollini	Performing Arts	USA	Jazz Saxophonist - Big Band/Jazz - HF
Adrian Karl	Quist	Sports	Australia	Tennis Player - HF
Adriana	Karembeu	Performing Arts	Czechoslovakia	Super Model
	Lima	Performing Arts	Brazil	Super Model
	Sklenarikova	Performing Arts	Slovakia	Super Model
Adrianne Shirley Ann	Hayden-Jones	Sports	England	Tennis Player - HF
Adrien	Brody	Performing Arts	USA	Actor - Academy Award
Adrien Marie	Legendre	Science	France	Mathematician
Adrienne	Barbeau	Performing Arts	USA	Actress
Afra e Tobia	Scarpa	Architecture	Italy	Architect
Aga	Khan	Architecture	France	Architect - Jefferson Medal
Agatha	Christie	Creative Works	England	Writer
Agnes	Moorehead	Performing Arts	USA	Actress - Acad Award Nom
Agnes George De	Mille	Performing Arts	USA	Dancer/Choreographer
Aguinaldo	Emilio	Politics	Philippines	Leader
Ahmad	Rashad	Sports	USA	Football Player
Ahmed Hassan	Zewail	Science	USA	Chemistry - Nobel Laureate
Aidan	Quinn	Performing Arts	USA	Actor
Aileen	Quinn	Performing Arts	USA	Actress
	Wournos	Law & Order	USA	Serial Killer
AJ	Watson	Sports	USA	Race Car Designer - HF
Akim	Tamiroff	Performing Arts	Russia	Actor - Acad Award Nom

FIRST NAME	LAST NAME	CATEGORY	COUNTRY	FAME
Akira	Endo	Performing Arts	Japan	Conductor
	Kurosawa	Movie Production	Japan	Director - Acad Award Nom
Al	Albert	Creative Works	USA	Journalist - Television
	Capp	Creative Works	USA	Cartoonist - Lil Abner
	Geiberger	Sports	USA	Golfer
	Hirschfeld	Creative Works	USA	Cartoonist - NY Times
	Holbert	Sports	USA	Race Car Driver - HF
	Jarreau	Performing Arts	USA	Singer
	Martino	Performing Arts	USA	Singer
	Molinaro	Performing Arts	USA	Actor
	Oerter	Sports	USA	Olympic Runner
	Pacino	Performing Arts	USA	Actor - Academy Award
	Ritz	Performing Arts	USA	Comedian
	Stewart	Performing Arts	Scotland	Singer - Folk
	Unser Sr.	Sports	USA	Race Car Driver - HF
Al (Scarface)	Capone	Law & Order	USA	Mafia
Al (Weird)	Yankovic	Performing Arts	USA	Singer
Alain	Delon	Performing Arts	France	Actor
	Lombard	Performing Arts	USA	Conductor
Alain (The Professor)	Prost	Sports	France	Race Car Driver - HF
Alain René	Lesage	Creative Works	France	Novelist/Dramatist
Alain René Le	Sage	Creative Works	.France	Novelist
Alan	Alda	Performing Arts	USA	Actor Acad Award Nom
	Arkin	Performing Arts	USA	Actor - Acad Award Nom
	Bates	Performing Arts	England	Actor - Acad Award Nom
	Cranston	Politics	USA	Senator
	Dugan	Creative Works	USA	Poet - Pulitzer
	Hale Jr	Performing Arts	USA	Actor
	Heeger	Science	USA	Chemistry - Nobel Laureate
	King	Performing Arts	USA	Comedian
	Kulwicki	Sports	USA	Race Car Driver - HF
	Ladd	Performing Arts	USA	Actor
	Lomax	Arts	USA	Collector - American Folk Songs
	Mowbray	Performing Arts	England	Actor
	Osmond	Performing Arts	USA	Singer
	Rachins	Performing Arts	USA	Actor
	Shearer	Sports	England	Soccer Player
	Sillitoe	Creative Works	England	Author/Playwright
	Taylor	Creative Works	USA	Author - Pulitzer
	Thicke	Performing Arts	Canada	Actor
	Willey	Sports	England	Soccer Player - HF
	Price	Performing Arts	England	Rock & Roll - HF - The Animals
Alan Alexander	Milne	Creative Works	England	Playwright/Novelist/Writer
Alan Bartlett	Shepard Jr.	Aviation	USA	Astronaut
Alan Cedric	Page	Sports	USA	Football Player - HF
Alan G.	MacDiarmid	Science	New Zealand	Chemistry - Nobel Laureate
Alan J.	Pakula	Movie Production	USA	Director - Acad Award Nom
	Parker	Movie Production	England	Director - Acad Award Nom
Alan LaVerne	Bean	Aviation	USA	Astronaut
Alan Lloyd	Hodgkin	Science	England	Medicine - Nobel Laureate
Alan Richard	Michaels	Creative Works	USA	Journalist - Television
Alan Scott	Berg	Creative Works	USA	Author - Pulitzer
Alan Stewart	Paton	Creative Works	South Africa	Author
Alastair	Sim	Performing Arts	Scotland	Actor
Alastair Bradley	Martin	Sports	USA	Tennis Player - HF
Alban Maria Johannes	Berg	Creative Works	Austria	Composer/Opera
Alben W.	Barkley	Politics	USA	Vice-President
Albert	Anastasia	Law & Order	Italy	Mafia
	Basserman	Performing Arts	Germany	Actor - Acad Award Nom
	Brooks	Performing Arts	USA	Actor - Acad Award Nom
	Camus	Creative Works	France	Literature - Nobel Laureate
	Claude	Science	Belgium	Medicine - Nobel Laureate
	Einstein	Science	USA	Physics - Nobel Laureate

SOLVER SERIES: NAME FINDER

FIRST NAME	LAST NAME	CATEGORY	COUNTRY	FAME
Albert	Ellis	Arts	USA	Psychologist
	Finney	Performing Arts	England	Actor - Acad Award Nom
	Fish	Law & Order	USA	Serial Killer - Hannibal Lector
	Gobat	War & Peace	Switzerland	Peace - Nobel Laureate
	Gore	Politics	USA	Vice-President
	Hackett	Creative Works	USA	Dramatist - Pulitzer
	Kahn	Architecture	USA	Architect
	Lebrun	Politics	France	President
	Reichman	Business	Canada	Real Estate
	Reynolds	Politics	Ireland	Prime Minister
	Sacco Jr.	Aviation	USA	Astronaut
	Schweitzer	Arts	France	Philosopher/Missionary/Theologian
	Schweitzer	War & Peace	France	Peace - Nobel Laureate
	Speer	Architecture	Germany	Architect
Albert (Al)	Green	Performing Arts	USA	Singer - Rock & Roll - HF
	Harker	Sports	USA	Soccer Player - HF
	Zerhusen	Sports	USA	Soccer Player - HF
Albert (Chalky)	Wright	Sports	Mexico	Boxer - HF
Albert Abraham	Michelson	Science	USA	Physics - Nobel Laureate
Albert Benjamin (Happy)	Chandler	Sports	USA	Baseball Commissioner - HF
Albert Bruce	Sabin	Science	USA	Physician - Polio Vaccine
Albert Charles (Babe)	Siebert	Sports	Canada	Hockey Player - HF
Albert De	Salvo	Law & Order	USA	Serial Killer - Boston Strangler
Albert Edwin (Eddie)	Condon	Performing Arts	USA	Band Leader - Big Band/Jazz - HF
Albert Fred (Red)	Schoendienst	Sports	USA	Baseball Player - HF
Albert Gillis	Laney	Sports	USA	Tennis Writer - HF
Albert Glen (Turk)	Edwards	Sports	USA	Football Player - HF
Albert Goodwill	Spalding	Sports	USA	Baseball Executive - HF
Albert Jeremiah	Beveridge	Creative Works	USA	Author - Pulitzer
Albert Jeremiah	Beveridge	Politics	USA	Statesman/Historian
Albert John	Lutuli	War & Peace	South Africa	Peace - Nobel Laureate
Albert Joseph (Al)	Barlick	Sports	USA	Baseball Umpire - HF
Albert Phillip	McKay	Performing Arts	USA	Rock & Roll - HF - Earth Wind & Fire
Albert Pinkham	Ryder	Works of Art	USA	Painter
Albert Sidney	Johnston	War & Peace	USA	Confederate General
Albert von	Szent-Györgyi	Science	Hungary	Medicine - Nobel Laureate
Albert William (Al)	Kaline	Sports	USA	Baseball Player - HF
Alberta	Hunter	Performing Arts	USA	Singer - Big Band/Jazz - HF
Alberto	Ascari	Sports	Italy	Race Car Driver - HF
	Erede	Performing Arts	Italy	Conductor
	Giacometti	Works of Art	Switzerland	Painter/Sculptor
	Moravia	Creative Works	Italy	Novelist
	Sartoris	Architecture	Italy	Architect
Albrecht	Dürer	Works of Art	Germany	Painter/Engraver
	Kossel	Science	Germany	Medicine - Nobel Laureate
Albrecht Eusebius Wenzel von	Wallenstein	War & Peace	Austria	General
Aldo	Moro	Politics	Italy	Head of State
	Morris	Movie Production	USA	Director
	Ray	Performing Arts	USA	Actor
	Rossi	Architecture	Italy	Architect - Pritzker/Jefferson Medal
Aldo Teo (Buff)	Donelli	Sports	USA	Soccer Player - HF
Aldo van	Eyck	Architecture	Netherlands	Architect
Aldous Leonard	Huxley	Creative Works	England	Novelist/Essayist
Alec	Baldwin	Performing Arts	USA	Actor - Acad Award Nom
	Douglas-Home	Politics	England	Prime Minister
	Guiness	Performing Arts	England	Actor - Academy Award
	Templeton	Performing Arts	USA	Pianist
Aleichem	Sholom	Creative Works	Russia	Dramatist
Aleister	Crowley	Science	England	Writer/Poet/Occultist
Alejandre Rodrigues (Alex)	Olmedo	Sports	Peru	Tennis Player - HF
Alejandro	Rey	Performing Arts	Argentina	Actor
Aleksander Isaevich	Solzhenitsyn	Creative Works	Russia	Literature - Nobel Laureate
Aleksandr Feodorovich	Kerensky	Politics	Russia	Prime Minister

FIRST NAME	LAST NAME	CATEGORY	COUNTRY	FAME
Aleksandr Konstantinovich	Glazunov	Creative Works	Russia	Composer
Aleksandr Mikhailovich	Prokhorov	Science	Russia	Physics - Nobel Laureate
Aleksandr Nikolayevich	Scriabin	Creative Works	Russia	Composer/Pianist
Aleksandr Porfirevich	Borodin	Creative Works	Russia	Composer
Aleksandr Sergeyevich	Pushkin	Creative Works	Russia	Poet
Aleksandr Vasilievich	Suvorov	War & Peace	Russia	Field Marshall
Aleksei Nikolaevich	Kosygin	Politics	Russia	Premier - U.S.S.R.
Aleksei Stanislavovich	Yeliseyev	Aviation	Russia	Astronaut
Alesandro di	Cagliostro	Science	Sicily	Alchemist
Alessandro	Antonelli	Architecture	Italy	Architect
	Manzoni	Creative Works	Italy	Poet/Novelist
	Mendini	Architecture	Italy	Architect
	Scarlatti	Creative Works	Italy	Composer
	Volta	Science	Italy	Physicist
Alex	Connell	Sports	Canada	Hockey Player - HF
	Cord	Performing Arts	USA	Actor
	Ely	Sports	Brazil	Soccer Player - HF
	English	Sports	USA	Basketball Player - HF
	Haley	Creative Works	USA	Author
	McNab	Sports	Scotland	Soccer Player - HF
	Raymond	Creative Works	USA	Cartoonist - Blondie
	Trebek	Performing Arts	Canada	Show Host
Alexander	Alekhine	Games	Russia	Chess Player
	Archipenko	Works of Art	USA	Sculptor
	Bain	Arts	Scotland	Philosopher
	Calder	Works of Art	USA	Abstract Sculptor
	Campbell	Arts	USA	Clergyman
	Fleming	Science	England	Medicine - Nobel Laureate
	Graves	Performing Arts	USA	Rock & Roll - HF - The Moonglows
	Hall	Movie Production	USA	Director - Acad Award Nom
	Hamilton	Politics	USA	Statesman
	Khalifman	Games	Russia	Chess Player
	Klein	Architecture	USA	Architect
	Knox	Performing Arts	Canada	Actor - Acad Award Nom
	Lifeson	Performing Arts	Canada	Canadian Music - HF - Rush
	Mackenzie	Exploration	Canada	Explorer - Canada West
	MacKenzie	Politics	Canada	Prime Minister
	Meiklejohn	Arts	USA	Philosopher
	Payne	Movie Production	USA	Director - Acad Award Nom
	Pope	Creative Works	England	Poet
	Sharp	Performing Arts	USA	Rock & Roll - HF - The Orioles
	Thomson	Architecture	Scotland	Architect
	Wilson	Arts	USA	Ornithologist
	Ypsilanti	War & Peace	Greece	Revolutionary Leader
Alexander (Alex)	Weir	Sports	Ireland	Soccer Player - HF
Alexander (Sandy)	Wood	Sports	Scotland	Soccer Player - HF
Alexander Francis (Alex)	Wojciechowicz	Sports	USA	Football Player - HF
Alexander Franklin (Frank)	James	Law & Order	USA	Outlaw
Alexander Graham	Bell	Business	USA	Telephones
	Bell	Science	USA	Inventor - Telephone
Alexander Hamilton	Stephens	Politics	USA	Vice-President - Confederacy
Alexander Humphreys	Woollcott	Creative Works	USA	Writer/Critic
Alexander Joy	Cartwright	Sports	USA	Baseball Pioneer - HF
Alexander Meigs	Haig Jr.	War & Peace	USA	General - Army
Alexander Peter (Alex)	Delvecchio	Sports	Canada	Hockey Player - HF
Alexander Procofieff de	Seversky	Business	USA	Aviation Industry - Aeronautical Engineer
Alexander R.	Todd	Science	England	Chemistry - Nobel Laureate
Alexander Raban (Alec)	Waugh	Creative Works	England	Novelist
Alexander Stirling	Calder	Works of Art	USA	Sculptor
Alexander Von	Humboldt	Exploration	Prussia	Explorer - South America
Alexander Walter (Sandy)	Lyle	Sports	England	Golfer
Alexandr Alexandrovich	Blok	Creative Works	Russia	Poet
Alexandra	Stoddard	Arts	USA	Philosopher/Writer

SOLVER SERIES: NAME FINDER

FIRST NAME	LAST NAME	CATEGORY	COUNTRY	FAME
Alexandre	Dumas	Creative Works	France	Novelist/Dramatist/Playwright
Alexandre Edmond	Becquerel	Science	France	Physicist
Alexei	Kovalev	Sports	Russia	Hockey Player
Alexei A.	Abrikosov	Science	USA	Physics - Nobel Laureate
Alexei Arkhipovich	Leonov	Aviation	Russia	Astronaut
Alexis	Carrel	Science	France	Medicine - Nobel Laureate
	Smith	Performing Arts	Canada	Actress
Alexis de	Tocqueville	Creative Works	France	Author/Statesman
Alfonse	D'Amato	Politics	USA	Senator
Alfonso	Reyes	Creative Works	Mexico	Author
Alfonso Garcia	Robles	War & Peace	Mexico	Peace - Nobel Laureate
Alfre	Woodard	Performing Arts	USA	Actress - Acad Award Nom
Alfred	Adler	Science	Austria	Psychiatrist
	Drake	Performing Arts	USA	Actor - Musical
	Dreyfus	War & Peace	France	Army Officer
	Hitchcock	Movie Production	England	Director - Acad Award Nom
	Kastler	Science	France	Physics - Nobel Laureate
	Krupp	Business	Germany	Industrialist
	Lunt	Performing Arts	USA	Actor - Acad Award Nom
	Neubauer	Sports	Czechoslovakia	Race Car Driver - HF
	Noyes	Creative Works	England	Poet
	Sisley	Works of Art	France	Painter
	Stieglitz	Works of Art	USA	Photographer
	Sung	Business	Japan	Fashion Designer
	Tennyson	Creative Works	England	Poet Laureate
	Uhry	Creative Works	USA	Dramatist - Pulitzer
	Werner	Science	Switzerland	Chemistry - Nobel Laureate
	Austin	Creative Works	England	Poet
Alfred (McCoy)	Tyner	Performing Arts	USA	Jazz Pianist - Big Band/Jazz - HF
Alfred Abraham	Knopf	Business	USA	Publishing
Alfred Bernhard	Nobel	Business	Sweden	Industrialist/Philanthropist
Alfred Bertram	Guthrie	Creative Works	USA	Novelist - Pulitzer
Alfred Charles	Kinsey	Science	USA	Zoologist - Sexual Behavior
Alfred Charles Bernard	Lovell	Science	England	Astronomer
Alfred Charles William	Harmsworth	Arts	England	Newspaper Publisher
	Northcliffe	Arts	England	Publisher - Newspaper
Alfred D.	Chandler	Creative Works	USA	Author - Pulitzer
	Hershey	Science	USA	Medicine - Nobel Laureate
Alfred Damon	Runyon	Creative Works	USA	Journalist/Short Story Writer
Alfred E. (Aif)	Smith	Sports	Canada	Hockey Player - HF
Alfred Earle (Greasy)	Neale	Sports	USA	Football Coach - HF
Alfred Edward	Housman	Creative Works	England	Poet
Alfred Emanuel	Smith	Politics	USA	Politician
Alfred G.	Gilman	Science	USA	Medicine - Nobel Laureate
Alfred Habdank	Korzybski	Creative Works	USA	Writer/Semanticist
Alfred Hermann	Fried	War & Peace	Austria	Peace - Nobel Laureate
Alfred Joyce	Kilmer	Creative Works	USA	Poet
Alfred Jules	Ayer	Arts	England	Philosopher
Alfred Louis	Kroeber	Arts	USA	Anthropologist
Alfred Merrill	Worden	Aviation	USA	Astronaut
Alfred Mossman (Alf)	Landon	Politics	USA	Governor - Kansas
Alfred N. (Al)	Cervi	Sports	USA	Basketball Player - HF
Alfred North	Whitehead	Arts	England	Philosopher/Mathematician
Alfred Russel	Wallace	Arts	England	Naturalist
Alfred Thayer	Mahan	War & Peace	USA	Naval Officer/Historian
Alfred Victor	Vigny	Creative Works	France	Poet/Man of Letters
Alfredo Di	Stefano	Sports	Argentina	Soccer Player - HF
Alger	Hiss	Politics	USA	Government Official/Lawyer
Algernon Charles	Swinburne	Creative Works	England	Poet/Critic
Ali	Abd al-Raziq	Arts	Egypt	Philosopher
	MacGraw	Performing Arts	USA	Actress - Acad Award Nom
	Mehemet	Politics	Egypt	Viceroy
Alice	Brady	Performing Arts	USA	Actress - Academy Award

FIRST NAME	LAST NAME	CATEGORY	COUNTRY	FAME
Alice	Cooper	Performing Arts	USA	Singer
	Dodd	Performing Arts	England	Super Model
	Faye	Performing Arts	USA	Actress
	Ghostley	Performing Arts	USA	Actress
	Marble	Sports	USA	Tennis Player - HF
Alice Babette	Toklas	Creative Works	USA	Author
Alice Boyd	Adams	Creative Works	USA	Novelist/Short Story Writer
Alice Hathaway	Roosevelt	Politics	USA	First Lady
Alice Malsenior	Walker	Creative Works	USA	Author - Pulitzer
Alicia	Bridges	Performing Arts	USA	Singer
Alida	Valli	Performing Arts	Italy	Actress
Aline	MacMahon	Performing Arts	USA	Actress - Acad Award Nom
Alison	Lurie	Creative Works	USA	Author - Pulitzer
Alistair	Cooke	Creative Works	England	Journalist - Television
Alla	Nazimova	Performing Arts	Ukraine	Actress
Allan	Cunningham	Exploration	England	Explorer - Brazil/Australia
	Nevins	Creative Works	USA	Author - Pulitzer
	Pinkerton	Law & Order	USA	Private Detective
	Robertson	Sports	Scotland	Golfer - HF
	Sherman	Performing Arts	USA	Singer
Allan Herbert	Stanley	Sports	Canada	Hockey Player - HF
Allan M.	Cormack	Science	USA	Medicine - Nobel Laureate
Allan M. (Scotty)	Davidson	Sports	Canada	Hockey Player - HF
Allen	Davis	Sports	USA	Football Commissioner - HF
	Drury	Creative Works	USA	Author - Pulitzer
	Ginsberg	Creative Works	USA	Poet
	Jenkins	Performing Arts	USA	Actor
	Ramsay	Creative Works	Scotland	Poet/Bookseller
Allison (Al)	Danzig	Sports	USA	Tennis Player - HF
Allison Lee	Merriweather	Works of Art	USA	Painter
Allvar	Gullstrand	Science	Sweden	Medicine - Nobel Laureate
Ally	Sheedy	Performing Arts	USA	Actress
Allyce	Beasley	Performing Arts	USA	Actress
Alma	Gluck	Performing Arts	USA	Singer - Opera
	Kruger	Performing Arts	USA	Actress
	Reville	Creative Works	England	Writer
Almudena	Fernandes	Performing Arts	Spain	Super Model
Alonso Alvarez de	Pineda	Exploration	Spain	Explorer - Gulf of Mexico
Alonzo	Mourning	Sports	USA	Basketball Player
Aloysius Harry (Al)	Simmons	Sports	USA	Baseball Player - HF
Alphonse Emil (Tuffy)	Leemans	Sports	USA	Football Player - HF
Alphonse Marie Louis de	Lamartine	Creative Works	France	Poet
Alphonso de	Albuquerque	Exploration	Portugal	Explorer - Spice Islands
Alphonso Ramón (Al)	López	Sports	USA	Baseball Manager - HF
Alponse François de	Sade	Creative Works	France	Novelist/Soldier
Althea	Gibson	Sports	USA	Tennis Player - HF
Althea Louise	Brough	Sports	USA	Tennis Player - HF
Alton	Delmore	Performing Arts	USA	Country Music - HF - Delmore Brothers
Alton Glenn	Miller	Performing Arts	USA	Band Leader - Big Band/Jazz - HF
Alva	Myrdal	War & Peace	Sweden	Peace - Nobel Laureate
Alvar	Aalto	Architecture	Finland	Architect - AIA/Jefferson Gold Medal
Alvar Nuñez Cabeza de	Vaca	Exploration	Spain	Explorer - Texas
Alvaro	Obregón	Politics	Mexico	President
Alvaro Vieira	Siza	Architecture	Portugal	Architect - Pritzker Laureate
Alvin	Ailey	Performing Arts	USA	Actor
	Wirtz	Business	USA	Electricity
Alvin Pleasant (A.P.)	Carter	Performing Arts	USA	Country Music - HF - Carter Family
Alvin Ray (Pete)	Rozelle	Sports	USA	Football Commissioner - HF
Alvino	Rey	Performing Arts	USA	Guitarist/Singer
Alvis Edgar (Buck)	Owens	Performing Arts	USA	Singer - Country Music - HF
Alvis Forrest	Gregg	Sports	USA	Football Player - HF
Alvise Da	Cadamosto	Exploration	Italy	Explorer - West Africa
Amanda	Holden	Performing Arts	England	Actress

SOLVER SERIES: NAME FINDER

FIRST NAME	LAST NAME	CATEGORY	COUNTRY	FAME
Amanda	Plummer	Performing Arts	USA	Actress
Amartya	Sen	Arts	India	Economics - Nobel Laureate
Amber	Valletta	Performing Arts	USA	Super Model
Ambroise	Paré	Science	France	Surgeon
Ambrose Everett	Burnside	War & Peace	USA	General
Ambrose Gwinett	Bierce	Creative Works	USA	Writer/Satire
Amedeo	Avogadro	Science	Italy	Chemist/Physicist
	Modigliani	Works of Art	Italy	Painter
Amelia	Earhart	Aviation	USA	Pioneer Aviator
Amelia Jenks	Bloomer	Politics	USA	Social Reformist
Amelita	Galli-Curci	Performing Arts	USA	Singer - Opera
Americo	Vespucci	Exploration	Italy	Explorer - Amazon Region
Amery Hare (Hobey)	Baker	Sports	USA	Hockey Player - HF
Amilcare	Ponchielli	Creative Works	Italy	Composer - Opera
Amos	Oz	Creative Works	Israel	Journalist/Novelist
Amos Bronson	Alcott	Arts	USA	Philosopher
Amos Wilson	Rusie	Sports	USA	Baseball Player - HF
Amy	Alcott	Sports	USA	Golfer - HF
	Irving	Performing Arts	USA	Actress - Acad Award Nom
	Lowell	Creative Works	USA	Poet - Pulitzer
	Madigan	Performing Arts	USA	Actress - Acad Award Nom
	Tan	Creative Works	USA	Author
	Grant	Performing Arts	USA	Singer
	Wesson	Performing Arts	USA	Super Model
Ana	Alicia	Performing Arts	Mexico	Actress
Ana Claudia	Michels	Performing Arts	Brazil	Super Model
Ana Paula	Arosio	Performing Arts	Brazil	Super Model
Anatal	Dorati	Performing Arts	USA	Conductor
Anatole	France	Creative Works	France	Literature - Nobel Laureate
	Litvak	Movie Production	Ukraine	Director - Acad Award Nom
Anatoli Vassilyevich	Filipchenko	Aviation	Russia	Astronaut
Anatoly	Karpov	Games	Russia	Chess Player
Anders	Celsius	Science	Sweden	Inventor - Astronomer
Anders Borje	Salming	Sports	Sweden	Hockey Player - HF
Anders Jöns	Angström	Science	Sweden	Physicist
Anders Leonard	Zorn	Works of Art	Sweden	Painter/Sculptor/Etcher
Andie	MacDowell	Performing Arts	USA	Actress
Ando	Hiroshige	Works of Art	Japan	Painter
André	Agassi	Sports	USA	Tennis Player
	Breton	Creative Works	France	Poet/Critic
	Chénier	Creative Works	France	Poet
	Dawson	Sports	USA	Baseball Player
	Derain	Works of Art	France	Painter
	Kostelanetz	Performing Arts	Russia	Conductor/Arranger
	Lwoff	Science	France	Medicine - Nobel Laureate
	Malraux	Creative Works	France	Writer/Politician
	Masséna	War & Peace	France	Marshall
	Maurois	Arts	France	Biographer
	Previn	Performing Arts	Germany	Conductor/Composer
	Watts	Performing Arts	Germany	Pianist
André Alice	Norton	Creative Works	USA	Author - SciFi
Andre Frédéric	Cournand	Science	USA	Medicine - Nobel Laureate
André Hercule	Fleury	Politics	France	Statesman/Cardinal
André le	Nôtre	Architecture	France	Architect - Landscape Design
André Marie	Ampere	Science	France	Physicist
André Paul Guillaume	Gide	Creative Works	France	Literature - Nobel Laureate
Andrea	Doria	War & Peace	Italy	Admiral
	Leeds	Performing Arts	USA	Actress - Acad Award Nom
	Mantegna	Works of Art	Italy	Painter/Engraver
	Martin	Performing Arts	USA	Actress
	McArdle	Performing Arts	USA	Actress
	Mitchell	Creative Works	USA	Journalist - Television
	Palladio	Architecture	Italy	Architect

FIRST NAME	LAST NAME	CATEGORY	COUNTRY	FAME
Andrea del	Sarto	Works of Art	Italy	Painter
	Sarto	Works of Art	Italy	Painter
	Verrocchio	Works of Art	Italy	Painter/Sculptor
Andreas	Schlüter	Architecture	Germany	Architect/Sculptor
	Vesalius	Science	Italy	Anatomist
Andrei Andreevich	Gromyko	Politics	Russia	Diplomat
Andrei Dmitrievich	Sakharov	War & Peace	Russia	Peace - Nobel Laureate
Andrei Romanovich	Chikatilo	Law & Order	Ukraine	Serial Killer
Andres	Duany	Architecture	USA	Architect - Jefferson Medal
Andrés	Segovia	Performing Arts	Spain	Guitarist
Andres de	Urdaneta	Exploration	Spain	Explorer - Phillipines
Andrew	Carnegie	Business	USA	Industialist/Philanthropist
	Cohen	Arts	USA	Philosopher
	Gaines	Arts	USA	Philosopher
	Jackson	Politics	USA	President
	Johnson	Politics	USA	President
	Marvell	Creative Works	England	Poet
	McCarthy	Performing Arts	USA	Actor
	Shue	Performing Arts	USA	Actor
	Stevens	Performing Arts	USA	Actor
	Woolfolk	Performing Arts	USA	Rock & Roll - HF - Earth Wind & Fire
Andrew (Andy)	Auld	Sports	Scotland	Soccer Player - HF
	Summers (Somers)	Performing Arts	England	Rock & Roll - HF - The Police
Andrew (Rube)	Foster	Sports	USA	Baseball Executive - HF
Andrew Bonar	Law	Politics	England	Prime Minister
Andrew Cecil	Bradley	Arts	England	Educator/Critic
Andrew Cunningham	McLaughlin	Creative Works	USA	Author - Pulitzer
Andrew Fielding	Huxley	Science	England	Medicine - Nobel Laureate
Andrew Jackson	Young Jr.	Politics	USA	Politician/Activist - Civil Rights
Andrew James (Andy)	Bathgate	Sports	Canada	Hockey Player - HF
Andrew Lloyd	Webber	Creative Works	England	Composer
Andrew Michael	Allen	Aviation	USA	Astronaut
Andrew Newell	Wyeth	Works of Art	USA	Painter
Andrew Philip	Cunanan	Law & Order	USA	Serial Killer
Andrew Richard (Andy)	Robustelli	Sports	USA	Football Player - HF
Andrew V.	Schally	Science	USA	Medicine - Nobel Laureate
Andrew William	Mellon	Business	USA	Financier/Mining Industry
Andrian Grigoryevich	Nikolaev	Aviation	Russia	Astronaut
Andy	Devine	Performing Arts	USA	Actor
	Garcia	Performing Arts	Cuba	Actor - Acad Award Nom
	Gibb	Performing Arts	England	Singer
	Granatelli	Sports	USA	Race Car Driver - HF
	Griffith	Performing Arts	USA	Actor
	Kirk	Performing Arts	USA	Jazz Saxophonist - Big Band/Jazz - HF
	Phillip	Sports	USA	Basketball Player - HF
	Rooney	Creative Works	USA	Journalist - Newspaper
	Warhol	Works of Art	USA	Artist
	Williams	Performing Arts	USA	Singer - Contempory
	North	Sports	USA	Golfer
Andy Van	Slyke	Sports	USA	Baseball Player
Aneurin	Bevan	Politics	Wales	Minister
Ang	Lee	Movie Production	Taiwan	Director - Acad Award Nom
Angela	Bassett	Performing Arts	USA	Actress - Acad Award Nom
	Bassett	Performing Arts	USA	Singer
	Lansbury	Performing Arts	England	Actress - Acad Award Nom
	Lindvall	Performing Arts	USA	Super Model
Angela Yvonne	Davis	Politics	USA	Activist/Abolutionist
Angelina	Jolie	Performing Arts	USA	Actress - Academy Award
Angelo	Buono	Law & Order	USA	Serial Killer - Hillside Strangler
Angelo (Hank)	Luisetti	Sports	USA	Basketball Player - HF
Angie	Dickinson	Performing Arts	USA	Actress
	Everhart	Performing Arts	USA	Super Model
Angus	Young	Performing Arts	Scotland	Rock & Roll - HF - AC/DC

SOLVER SERIES: NAME FINDER

FIRST NAME	LAST NAME	CATEGORY	COUNTRY	FAME
Angus Frank Johnstone	Wilson	Creative Works	England	Novelist/Short Story Writer
Ani Di	Franco	Performing Arts	USA	Singer
Aniello (The Hat)	Dellacroce	Law & Order	USA	Mafia
Anita	Baker	Performing Arts	USA	Singer
	Brookner	Creative Works	England	Writer/Art Critic
	Ekberg	Performing Arts	Sweden	Actress
	Gillette	Performing Arts	USA	Actress
	Loos	Creative Works	USA	Screenwriter/Playwright
	O'Day	Performing Arts	USA	Singer
	Pointer	Performing Arts	USA	Singer
	Ward	Performing Arts	USA	Singer - Rock & Roll - HF
Anjelica	Huston	Performing Arts	USA	Actress - Academy Award
Ann	Beattie	Creative Works	USA	Author
	Blyth	Performing Arts	USA	Actress - Acad Award Nom
	Harding	Performing Arts	USA	Actress - Acad Award Nom
	Jillian	Performing Arts	USA	Actress
	Landers	Creative Works	USA	Journalist - Newspaper
	Lee	Arts	England	Mystic - Shakers Founder
	Miller	Performing Arts	USA	Actress/Dancer
	Radcliffe	Creative Works	England	Author
	Reinking	Performing Arts	USA	Actress
	Sheridan	Performing Arts	USA	Actress
	Sothern	Performing Arts	USA	Actress - Acad Award Nom
	Wilson	Performing Arts	USA	Singer - Rock & Roll - HF
Ann B	Davis	Performing Arts	USA	Singer
Ann De	Salvo	Performing Arts	USA	Actress
Ann Willis	Richards	Politics	USA	Governor - Texas
Anna	Freud	Science	Austria	Psychiatrist
	Harrison	Politics	USA	First Lady
	Magnani	Performing Arts	Italy	Actress - Academy Award
	Moffo	Performing Arts	Italy	Singer - Opera
	Neagle	Performing Arts	USA	Actress
	Paquin	Performing Arts	Canada	Actress - Academy Award
	Pavlova	Performing Arts	Russia	Dancer - Ballerina
	Quindland	Creative Works	USA	Author
	Sewell	Creative Works	England	Author - Black Beauty
	Stenn	Performing Arts	Ukraine	Actress
Anna Eleanor	Roosevelt	Politics	USA	First Lady
Anna Mae (Tina)	Turner (Bullock)	Performing Arts	USA	Singer - Rock & Roll - HF
Anna Margarethe (Molla)	Mallory	Sports	Norway	Tennis Player - HF
Anna Maria	Alberghetti	Performing Arts	Italy	Actress
Anna Mary Robertson	Moses	Works of Art	USA	Painter - Primitive
Anna May	Wong	Performing Arts	USA	Actress
Annalyn	Swan	Creative Works	USA	Author - Pulitzer
Anne	Applebaum	Creative Works	USA	Author - Pulitzer
	Archer	Performing Arts	USA	Actress - Acad Award Nom
	Bancroft	Performing Arts	USA	Actress - Academy Award
	Baxter	Performing Arts	USA	Actress - Academy Award
	Boleyn	Politics	England	King's Wife
	Bradstreet	Creative Works	USA	Poet
	Brontë	Creative Works	England	Novelist
	Donovan	Sports	USA	Basketball Player - HF
	Francis	Performing Arts	USA	Actress
	Hutchinson	Arts	USA	Founder of Rhode Island
	Jackson	Performing Arts	USA	Actress
	Jeffreys	Performing Arts	USA	Actress
	Klein	Business	USA	Fashion Designer
	Meara	Performing Arts	USA	Actress
	Murray	Performing Arts	Canada	Singer - Canadian Music - HF
	Ramsey	Performing Arts	USA	Actress - Acad Award Nom
	Revere	Performing Arts	USA	Actress - Academy Award
	Sexton	Creative Works	USA	Poet - Pulitzer
	Shirley	Performing Arts	USA	Actress - Acad Award Nom

FIRST NAME	LAST NAME	CATEGORY	COUNTRY	FAME
Anne	Tyler	Creative Works	USA	Author - Pulitzer
Anne E.	Meyers	Sports	USA	Basketball Player - HF
Anne Frances Robbins	Reagan	Politics	USA	First Lady
Anne Louise Germaine Necker	Staël	Creative Works	France	Writer
Anne Morrow	Lindbergh	Creative Works	USA	Author
Anne Robertson Jacques	Turgot	Politics	France	Statesman/Economist
Annette	Bening	Performing Arts	USA	Actress - Acad Award Nom
	Funicello	Performing Arts	USA	Actress
	O'Toole	Performing Arts	USA	Actress
Annie	Besant	Politics	England	Theosophist
	Dillard	Creative Works	USA	Author - Pulitzer
	Lennox	Performing Arts	Scotland	Singer
	Oakley	Law & Order	USA	Hunter/Sure Shot
	Potts	Performing Arts	USA	Actress
Annika	Sörenstam	Sports	Sweden	Golfer - HF
Ann-Margret	Olsson	Performing Arts	Sweden	Actress - Acad Award Nom
Annunzio	Mantovani	Performing Arts	England	Conductor/Composer
Anouk	Aimee	Performing Arts	France	Actress - Acad Award Nom
Ansel	Adams	Works of Art	USA	Photography
Antanasio (Tony)	Pérez	Sports	Cuba	Baseball Player - HF
Antemio di	Tralle	Architecture	Italy	Architect
Anthelme	Brillat-Savarin	Arts	France	Food Expert
Anthony	Andrews	Performing Arts	England	Actor
	Edwards	Performing Arts	USA	Actor
	Franciosa	Performing Arts	USA	Actor - Acad Award Nom
	Harvey	Movie Production	England	Director - Acad Award Nom
	Hecht	Creative Works	USA	Poet - Pulitzer
	Hope	Creative Works	England	Novelist
	Hopkins	Performing Arts	Wales	Actor - Academy Award
	Minghella	Movie Production	England	Director - Academy Award
	Newly	Performing Arts	England	Singer
	Perkins	Performing Arts	USA	Actor - Acad Award Nom
	Quayle	Performing Arts	England	Actor - Acad Award Nom
	Quinn	Performing Arts	Mexico	Actor - Academy Award
	Trollope	Creative Works	England	Novelist
	Tudor	Creative Works	England	Composer - Ballet
	Wayne	War & Peace	USA	General - Revolutionary War
	Zerbe	Performing Arts	USA	Actor
	Sharp	Performing Arts	England	Actor
Anthony Ashley Cooper	Shaftesbury	Politics	England	Statesman
Anthony Colin Bruce	Chapman	Sports	England	Race Car Designer - HF
Anthony Dalton (Tony)	Roche	Sports	Australia	Tennis Player - HF
Anthony Dominick (Tony)	Bennett (Benedetto)	Performing Arts	USA	Singer - Big Band/Jazz - HF
Anthony Drew (Tony)	Dorsett Sr.	Sports	USA	Football Player - HF
Anthony Florian (Tony)	Zale	Sports	USA	Boxer - HF
Anthony Frederick (Tony)	Wilding	Sports	New Zealand	Tennis Player - HF
Anthony Herman Gerard	Fokker	Aviation	USA	Aircraft Designer
Anthony J.	Leggett	Science	England	Physics - Nobel Laureate
Anthony James (Tony)	Esposito	Sports	Canada	Hockey Player - HF
Anthony Joseph (AJ)	Foyt	Sports	USA	Race Car Driver - HF
Anthony Joseph (Joe)	Perry (Pereira)	Performing Arts	USA	Rock & Roll - HF - Aerosmith
Anthony McLeod	Kennedy	Law & Order	USA	Justice - Supreme Court
Anthony Michael (Tony)	Lazzeri	Sports	USA	Baseball Player - HF
Anthony Robert (Tony)	Canadeo	Sports	USA	Football Player - HF
Anthony Ronald (Ron)	Yary	Sports	USA	Football Player - HF
Anthony Van	Dyck	Works of Art	Italy	Painter
Anthony Wayne	England	Aviation	USA	Astronaut
Antoine	Pevsner	Works of Art	Russia	Sculptor/Painter
	Predock	Architecture	USA	Architect
Antoine (Fats)	Domino	Performing Arts	USA	Singer - Rock & Roll - HF
Antoine César	Becquerel	Science	France	Physicist
Antoine de	Sainte-Exupéry	Creative Works	France	Writer/Aviator
Antoine de la Mothe	Cadillac	Exploration	France	Explorer - Detroit

SOLVER SERIES: NAME FINDER

FIRST NAME	LAST NAME	CATEGORY	COUNTRY	FAME
Antoine Henri	Becquerel	Science	France	Physics - Nobel Laureate
Antoine Jean	Gros	Works of Art	France	Painter
Antoine Quatremère de	Quincy	Architecture	France	Architect
Antoine-Laurent de	Lavoisier	Science	France	Chemist
Anton	Bruckner	Creative Works	Austria	Composer
	Tedesko	Architecture	USA	Architect
	Webern	Creative Works	Austria	Composer
Anton (Tony)	Hulman Jr.	Sports	USA	Race Car Promoter - HF
Anton Grigorevich	Rubinstein	Creative Works	Russia	Composer/Pianist
Anton Pavlovich	Chekhov	Creative Works	Russia	Writer/Dramatist
Anton van	Leeuwenhoek	Arts	Netherlands	Naturalist
Antoni	Gaudi	Architecture	Spain	Architect
Antonín	Dvořák	Creative Works	Czechoslovakia	Composer
	Scalia	Law & Order	USA	Justice - Supreme Court
Antonio	Canaletto	Works of Art	Italy	Painter
	Canova	Works of Art	Italy	Sculptor
	Cervantes	Sports	Columbia	Boxer - HF
	Croci	Architecture	Switzerland	Architect
	Moro	Works of Art	Netherlands	Painter - Portrait
	Salieri	Creative Works	Austria	Composer
	Sant'Elia	Architecture	Italy	Architect
	Stradivari	Arts	Italy	Violin Maker
	Vivaldi	Creative Works	Italy	Composer/Violinist
Antonio Allegri de	Correggio	Works of Art	Italy	Painter
Antonio Caetano Egas	Moniz	Science	Portugal	Medicine - Nobel Laureate
Antonio da il Giovane	Sangallo	Architecture	Italy	Architect
Antonio da il Vecchio	Sangallo	Architecture	Italy	Architect
Antonio de Oliveira	Salazar	Politics	Portugal	Prime Minister
Antonio López de	Santa Anna	Politics	Mexico	President
Antony	Hewish	Science	England	Physics - Nobel Laureate
Anwar al	Sadat	Politics	Egypt	Head of State
	Sadat	War & Peace	Egypt	Peace - Nobel Laureate
Anya	Seton	Creative Works	USA	Author
Aphonse	Daudet	Creative Works	France	Novelist
April	Heinrichs	Sports	USA	Soccer Player - HF
Ara	Parseghian	Sports	USA	Football Player
Aram	Khachaturian	Creative Works	Russia	Composer
Arata	Isozaki	Architecture	Japan	Architect
Arcangelo	Corelli	Creative Works	Italy	Composer/Violinist
Archer John Porter	Martin	Science	England	Chemistry - Nobel Laureate
Archibald	Geikie	Science	Scotland	Geologist
	MacLeish	Creative Works	USA	Dramatist - Pulitzer
	MacLeish	Creative Works	USA	Poet - Pulitzer
	Prentice	Business	England	Publishing
Archibald MacPherson (Archie)	Stark	Sports	Scotland	Soccer Player - HF
Archibald Percival	Wavell	War & Peace	England	Field Marshall
Archibald Vivian	Hill	Science	England	Medicine - Nobel Laureate
Archie	Moore	Sports	USA	Boxer - HF
Archivio Piero	Bottoni	Architecture	Italy	Architect
Aretha Louise	Franklin	Performing Arts	USA	Singer - Rock & Roll - HF
Ari	Meyers	Performing Arts	Puerto Rico	Actress
Arie	Luyendyk	Sports	Netherlands	Race Car Driver
Ariel	Durant	Creative Works	USA	Author - Pulitzer
	Sharon	Politics	Israel	Prime Minister
Aristide	Briand	Politics	France	Statesman
	Briand	War & Peace	France	Peace - Nobel Laureate
Aristide Joseph Bonaventure	Maillol	Works of Art	France	Sculptor
Aristotle	Onassis	Business	Greece	Shipping Magnate
Arleen	Whelan	Performing Arts	USA	Actress
Arlen	Specter	Politics	USA	Senator - Pennsylvania
Arlene	Dahl	Performing Arts	USA	Actress
	Francis	Performing Arts	USA	Actress
	Sorkin	Performing Arts	USA	Actress

FIRST NAME	LAST NAME	CATEGORY	COUNTRY	FAME
Arlo	Allen	Performing Arts	USA	Pianist/Trombonist
	Guthrie	Performing Arts	USA	Singer
Armand	Assante	Performing Arts	USA	Actor
	Hammer	Business	USA	Oil Industry
Armand Jean du Plessis	Richelieu	Politics	France	Statesman
Armando	Brasini	Architecture	Italy	Architect
Armando Anthony (Chick)	Corea	Performing Arts	USA	Jazz Pianist
Armin	Mueller-Stahl	Performing Arts	Russia	Actor - Acad Award Nom
Arne	Jacobsen	Architecture	Denmark	Architect
Arne Christer	Fuglesang	Aviation	Sweden	Astronaut
Arne Wilhelm Kaurin	Tiselius	Science	Sweden	Chemistry - Nobel Laureate
Arnie	Mausser	Sports	USA	Soccer Player - HF
Arno Allan	Penzias	Science	USA	Physics - Nobel Laureate
Arnold	Rothstein	Law & Order	USA	Underworld - Jewish
	Schönberg	Creative Works	USA	Composer
	Schwarzenegger	Performing Arts	Austria	Actor
	Stang	Performing Arts	USA	Comedian
	Zweig	Creative Works	Germany	Novelist/Playwright/Essayist
Arnold (Arnie)	Oliver	Sports	USA	Soccer Player - HF
	Palmer	Sports	USA	Golfer - HF
	Risen	Sports	USA	Basketball Player - HF
Arnold Alois	Schwarzenegger	Politics	USA	Governor - California
Arnold Charles (Arnie)	Herber	Sports	USA	Football Player - HF
Arnold George (Arnie)	Weinmeister	Sports	Canada	Football Player - HF
Arnold Joseph	Toynbee	Arts	England	Philosopher/Historian
Arnold Lucius	Gesell	Arts	USA	Psychologist
Arnolfo di	Cambio	Architecture	Italy	Architect/Sculptor
Arsenio	Hall	Performing Arts	USA	Comedian
Arshile	Gorky	Works of Art	USA	Painter - Abstract Expressionist
Art	Carney	Performing Arts	USA	Actor - Academy Award
	Linkletter	Performing Arts	Canada	Comedian
	Monk	Sports	USA	Football Player
	Tatum	Performing Arts	USA	Jazz Pianist - Big Band/Jazz - HF
Arte	Johnson	Performing Arts	USA	Comedian
Artemus	Ward	Creative Works	USA	Humorist
Arthur	Balfour	Politics	England	Prime Minster
	Buchwald	Creative Works	USA	Journalist - Newspaper
	Fiedler	Performing Arts	USA	Conductor
	Godfrey	Performing Arts	USA	Comedian
	Hailey	Creative Works	England	Author
	Harden	Science	England	Chemistry - Nobel Laureate
	Henderson	War & Peace	England	Peace - Nobel Laureate
	Hiller	Movie Production	Canada	Director - Acad Award Nom
	Honegger	Creative Works	Switzerland	Composer
	Hunnicutt	Performing Arts	USA	Actor - Acad Award Nom
	Keith	Arts	England	Antropologist/Writer
	Kennedy	Performing Arts	USA	Actor - Acad Award Nom
	Kent	Creative Works	Canada	Journalist - Television
	Kornberg	Science	USA	Medicine - Nobel Laureate
	Lewis	Arts	England	Economics - Nobel Laureate
	Liberty	Business	England	Retail Trade
	Meighen	Politics	Canada	Prime Minister
	Miller	Creative Works	USA	Dramatist - Pulitzer
	O'Connell	Performing Arts	USA	Actor - Acad Award Nom
	Penn	Movie Production	USA	Director - Acad Award Nom
	Phillip	Exploration	England	Explorer - Australia
	Rackham	Creative Works	England	Illustrator
	Rubinstein	Performing Arts	USA	Pianist
	Schnitzler	Creative Works	Austria	Novelist/Playwright
	Schopehauer	Arts	Germany	Philosopher/Pessimist
	Tappan	Business	USA	Drygoods
	Treacher	Performing Arts	England	Actor
	Walworth	Creative Works	USA	Author - Pulitzer

SOLVER SERIES: NAME FINDER

FIRST NAME	LAST NAME	CATEGORY	COUNTRY	FAME
Arthur	Brooks	Performing Arts	USA	Rock & Roll - HF - The Impressions
Arthur (Art)	Blakey	Performing Arts	USA	Jazz Drummer - Big Band/Jazz - HF
	Shell	Sports	USA	Football Player - HF
Arthur (Harpo)	Marx	Performing Arts	USA	Comedian
Arthur Charles	Clarke	Creative Works	England	Author - SciFi
	Erickson	Architecture	Canada	Architect - AIA Gold Medal
	Nielson	Sports	USA	Tennis Player - HF
Arthur Conan	Doyle	Creative Works	England	Novelist/Physician
Arthur Darcy (Bobby)	Locke	Sports	South Africa	Golfer - HF
Arthur David (Tappy)	Larsen	Sports	USA	Tennis Player - HF
Arthur Edmund (Art)	Coulter	Sports	Canada	Hockey Player - HF
Arthur Edward (Art)	Pepper Jr.	Performing Arts	USA	Jazz Saxophonist - Big Band/Jazz - HF
Arthur F.	Farrel	Sports	Canada	Hockey Player - HF
Arthur Garfield	Hays	Law & Order	USA	Lawyer/Civil Libertarian
Arthur Henry	Young	Creative Works	USA	Cartoonist - Satiric
Arthur Holly	Compton	Science	USA	Physics - Nobel Laureate
Arthur Howie (Art)	Ross	Sports	Canada	Hockey Player - HF
Arthur Hugh	Clough	Creative Works	England	Poet
Arthur Ira (Art)	Garfunkel	Performing Arts	USA	Rock & Roll - HF - Simon & Garfunkel
Arthur Jacob (Artie)	Shaw (Arshawsky)	Performing Arts	USA	Band Leader - Big Band/Jazz - HF
Arthur James (Art)	Donovan Jr.	Sports	USA	Football Player - HF
Arthur John	Evans	Arts	England	Archaeologist
Arthur Joseph (Art)	Rooney Sr.	Sports	USA	Football Founder - HF
Arthur Leonard	Schawlow	Science	USA	Physics - Nobel Laureate
Arthur Meier	Schlesinger	Arts	USA	Historian
	Schlesinger Jr.	Creative Works	USA	Author - Pulitzer
Arthur Meier Jr.	Schlesinger	Arts	USA	Historian
Arthur Neville	Chamberlain	Politics	England	Prime Minister
Arthur Robert	Ashe Jr.	Sports	USA	Tennis Player - HF
Arthur Seymour	Sullivan	Creative Works	England	Composer
Arthur Stanley	Eddington	Science	England	Astronomer/Astrophysicist
Arthur Stewart (Art)	Farmer	Performing Arts	USA	Jazz Trumpeter - Big Band/Jazz - HF
Arthur Thomas	Quiller-Couch	Creative Works	England	Writer
Arthur Wellesley	Wellington	Politics	England	Prime Minster
Arthur Wing	Pinero	Creative Works	England	Playwright
Arthur Worth (Bud)	Collins Jr.	Sports	USA	Tennis Player - HF
Artie	Shaw	Performing Arts	USA	Band Leader/Clarinetist
Artis	Gilmore	Sports	USA	Basketball Player
Artturi Ilmari	Virtanen	Science	Finland	Chemistry - Nobel Laureate
Artur	Schnabel	Creative Works	Austria	Composer/Pianist
Artur Antunes (Zico)	Coimbra	Sports	Brazil	Soccer Player - HF
Arturo	Toscanini	Performing Arts	Italy	Conductor - Orchestra
Arvid	Carlsson	Science	Sweden	Medicine - Nobel Laureate
Asa	Gray	Science	USA	Botanist
Asa (Al)	Jolson (Yoelson)	Performing Arts	Lithuania	Singer
Asa Griggs	Candler	Business	USA	Coca Cola Founder
Asher Brown	Durand	Works of Art	USA	Painter
Ashley John	Cooper	Sports	Australia	Tennis Player - HF
Asta	Nielson	Performing Arts	Germany	Actress
Aston	Webb	Architecture	England	Architect - AIA Gold Medal
Astrid	Munoz	Performing Arts	Puerto Rico	Super Model
Astrud	Gilberto	Performing Arts	Brazil	Singer
Athol	Fugard	Creative Works	South Africa	Playwright
Atom	Egoyan	Movie Production	Egypt	Director - Acad Award Nom
Aubrey V. (Dit)	Clapper	Sports	Canada	Hockey Player - HF
Aubrey Vincent	Beardsley	Works of Art	England	Painter
Audie	Murphy	Performing Arts	USA	Actor
Audrey	Hepburn	Performing Arts	Belgium	Actress - Academy Award
	Meadows	Performing Arts	China	Actress
	Wurdemann	Creative Works	USA	Poet - Pulitzer
August	Belmont	Business	USA	Banking
	Chouteau	Business	USA	Fur Trade
	Weismann	Science	Germany	Biologist

FIRST NAME	LAST NAME	CATEGORY	COUNTRY	FAME
August	Wilson	Creative Works	USA	Dramatist - Pulitzer
August Friedrich Ferdinand	Kotzebue	Creative Works	Germany	Playwright
August Mike	Michalske	Sports	USA	Football Player - HF
August von	Wassermann	Science	Germany	Bacteriologist
August Wilhelm von	Schlegel	Creative Works	Germany	Poet/Critic
Augusta	Gregory	Creative Works	Ireland	Playwright
Auguste	Comte	Arts	France	Philosopher
	Escoffier	Creative Works	France	Writer - Cooking
	Perret	Architecture	France	Architect - AIA Gold Medal
	Piccard	Science	Switzerland	Physicist
Auguste Marie François	Beernaert	War & Peace	Belgium	Peace - Nobel Laureate
Augustin Eugène	Scribe	Creative Works	France	Dramatist/Librettist
Augustin Jean	Fresnel	Science	France	Physicist
Augusto Romano	Burelli	Architecture	Italy	Architect
Augustus	Sainte-Gaudens	Works of Art	USA	Sculptor
Aung San Suu	Kyi	War & Peace	Burma	Peace - Nobel Laureate
Aurel Emile	Joliat	Sports	Canada	Hockey Player - HF
Aurelie	Claudel	Performing Arts	France	Super Model
Aurelio	Galfetti	Architecture	Switzerland	Architect
Ava	Gardner	Performing Arts	USA	Actress - Acad Award Nom
Avram	Hershko	Science	Israel	Chemistry - Nobel Laureate
Avram Noam	Chomsky	Arts	USA	Linguist
Avril Phaedra Douglas (Kim)	Campbell	Politics	Canada	Prime Minister
Axel Hugo Theodor	Theorell	Science	Sweden	Medicine - Nobel Laureate
Ayn	Rand	Creative Works	USA	Novelist/Philosopher
Ayrton	Senna	Sports	Brazil	Race Car Driver - HF
Azumah	Nelson	Sports	Ghana	Boxer - HF
Bailey	Howell	Sports	USA	Basketball Player - HF
Baldassare	Castiglione	Creative Works	Italy	Writer/Diplomat
Baldassarre	Longhena	Architecture	Italy	Architect
	Peruzzi	Architecture	Italy	Architect
Ballington	Booth	Arts	England	Revivalist
Baltasar	Gracián	Arts	Spain	Philosopher/Jesuit
Balthasar Johann	Neumann	Architecture	Germany	Architect
Barbara	Barrie	Performing Arts	USA	Actress - Acad Award Nom
	Bel Geddes	Performing Arts	USA	Actress - Acad Award Nom
	Bosson	Performing Arts	USA	Actress
	Bush	Politics	USA	First Lady
	Eden	Performing Arts	USA	Actress
	Feldon	Performing Arts	USA	Actress
	Hale	Performing Arts	USA	Actress
	Harris	Performing Arts	USA	Actress - Acad Award Nom
	Hershey	Performing Arts	USA	Actress - Acad Award Nom
	Mandrell	Performing Arts	USA	Singer
	McClintock	Science	USA	Medicine - Nobel Laureate
	O'Neil	Performing Arts	USA	Actress - Acad Award Nom
	Rush	Performing Arts	USA	Actress
	Stanwyck	Performing Arts	USA	Actress - Acad Award Nom
	Walters	Creative Works	USA	Journalist - Television
	Ward	Creative Works	England	Writer
Barbara Levy	Boxer	Politics	USA	Senator
Barbara Wertheim	Tuchman	Creative Works	USA	Author - Pulitzer
Barbet	Schroeder	Movie Production	Iran	Director - Acad Award Nom
Barbra	Streisand	Performing Arts	USA	Actress/Singer - Acad Award
Barnard	Hughes	Performing Arts	USA	Actor
Barney	Kessell	Performing Arts	USA	Jazz Guitarist - Big Band/Jazz - HF
	Sedran	Sports	USA	Basketball Player - HF
Barry	Bonds	Sports	USA	Baseball Player
	Bostwick	Performing Arts	USA	Actor - Musical
	Fitzgerald	Performing Arts	Ireland	Actor - Academy Award
	Gibb	Performing Arts	England	Rock & Roll - HF - The Bee Gees
	Levinson	Movie Production	USA	Director - Academy Award
	Manilow	Performing Arts	USA	Singer

SOLVER SERIES: NAME FINDER

FIRST NAME	LAST NAME	CATEGORY	COUNTRY	FAME
Barry	Mann	Creative Works	USA	Song Writer
	Sullivan	Performing Arts	USA	Actor
	White	Performing Arts	USA	Singer/Composer
Barry David	Sanders	Sports	USA	Football Player - HF
Barry J.	Marshall	Science	Australia	Medicine - Nobel Laureate
Barry Morris	Goldwater	Politics	USA	Senator - Arizona
Bart	Conner	Sports	USA	Olympic Gymnast
	McGhee	Sports	Scotland	Soccer Player - HF
Bartolomé	Las Casas	Arts	Spain	Historian/Missionary
Bartolomé Esteban	Murillo	Works of Art	Spain	Painter
Bartolomeo	Vanzetti	Politics	Italy	Anarchist
Bartolomeu	Dias	Exploration	Portugal	Explorer - Africa West Coast
Baruch Benedict	Spinoza	Arts	Netherlands	Philosopher
Baruch S.	Blumberg	Science	USA	Medicine - Nobel Laureate
Baruj	Benacerraf	Science	USA	Medicine - Nobel Laureate
Basil	Rathbone	Performing Arts	South Africa	Actor - Acad Award Nom
Bea	Benaderet	Performing Arts	USA	Actress
Beah	Richards	Performing Arts	USA	Actress - Acad Award Nom
Beals Coleman	Wright	Sports	USA	Tennis Player
Beatrice	Arthur	Performing Arts	USA	Actress/Comedian
	Campbell	Performing Arts	England	Actress
	Lillie	Performing Arts	Canada	Comedian
	Straight	Performing Arts	USA	Actress - Academy Award
Beatrice Potter	Webb	Arts	England	Economist/Social Reformer
Beatrix	Potter	Creative Works	England	Writer/Illustrator - Children's Books
Beau	Bridges	Performing Arts	USA	Actor
Bebe	Daniels	Performing Arts	USA	Actress
	Neuwirth	Performing Arts	USA	Actress
Bedřich	Smetana	Creative Works	Czechoslovakia	Composer
Bel	Kaufman	Creative Works	Russia	Author
Bela	Bartók	Creative Works	Hungary	Composer
	Lugosi	Performing Arts	Hungary	Actor
Béla	Fleck	Performing Arts	USA	Band Leader
	Kun	Politics	Hungary	Communist Leader
Belinda	Carlisle	Performing Arts	USA	Singer
Bella	Karoly	Sports	Romania	Olympic Gymnast Coach
Bella Savitsky	Abzug	Politics	USA	Stateswoman
Ben	Blue	Performing Arts	Canada	Comedian
	Bradlee	Creative Works	USA	Journalist - Newspaper
	Crenshaw	Sports	USA	Golfer - HF
	Cross	Performing Arts	England	Actor
	Gazzara	Performing Arts	USA	Actor
	Hecht	Creative Works	USA	Screenwriter
	Hogan	Sports	USA	Golfer - HF
	Johnson	Performing Arts	USA	Actor - Academy Award
	Kingsley	Performing Arts	England	Actor - Academy Award
	Pollack	Performing Arts	USA	Band Leader - Big Band/Jazz - HF
	Turpin	Performing Arts	USA	Actor
	Vereen	Performing Arts	USA	Actor - Musical
	Webster	Performing Arts	USA	Jazz Saxophonist - Big Band/Jazz - HF
Ben Nighthorse	Campbell	Politics	USA	Senator
Ben Roy	Mottelson	Science	Denmark	Physics - Nobel Laureate
Benedetto	Croce	Arts	Italy	Philosopher/Critic
Benedict	Arnold	War & Peace	USA	Revolutionist
Bengt I.	Samuelsson	Science	Sweden	Medicine - Nobel Laureate
Beniamino	Gigli	Performing Arts	Italy	Singer - Opera
Benicio Del	Toro	Performing Arts	Puerto Rico	Actor - Academy Award
Benito	Mussolini	Politics	Italy	Dictator
Benito Pablo	Juárez	Politics	Mexico	President
Benjamin	Constant	Creative Works	France	Writer/Politician
	Disraeli	Politics	England	Prime Minister
	Franklin	Science	USA	Inventor/Statesman/Writer
	Harrison	Politics	USA	President

FIRST NAME	LAST NAME	CATEGORY	COUNTRY	FAME
Benjamin	Hotchkis	Business	USA	Firearms
	Jowett	Arts	England	Classical Scholar
	Odom	Performing Arts	USA	Rock & Roll - HF - The Soul Stirrers
	Orr (Orzechowski)	Performing Arts	USA	Bassist - The Cars
	Rush	Science	USA	Physician
	Shahn	Works of Art	USA	Painter
	Thompson	Architecture	USA	Architect - AIA Gold Medal
	Thompson	Politics	England	Statesman/Scientist
	West	Works of Art	USA	Painter
	Whichcote	Arts	England	Philosopher
BenJamin (Ben)	Jonson	Creative Works	England	Poet/Dramatist
Benjamin (Benny)	Friedman	Sports	USA	Football Player - HF
Benjamin (Bugsy)	Siegel	Law & Order	USA	Mafia
Benjamin (Whitey)	Ford (Duke of Palucah)	Performing Arts	USA	Comedian - Country Music - HF
Benjamin David (Benny)	Goodman	Performing Arts	USA	Band Leader - Big Band/Jazz - HF
Benjamin Henry	Latrobe	Architecture	USA	Architect
Benjamin Lawrence	Reid	Creative Works	USA	Author - Pulitzer
Benjamin McLane	Spock	Science	USA	Pediatrician/Writer
Benjamin Nathan	Cardozo	Law & Order	USA	Justice/Supreme Court
Benjamin S.	Kline	Science	USA	Pathologist
Benmont	Tench	Performing Arts	USA	Rock & Roll - HF - Heart Breakers
Bennett Alfred	Cerf	Business	USA	Publishing
	Cerf	Creative Works	USA	Author
Bennett Lester (Benny)	Carter	Performing Arts	USA	Band Leader - Big Band/Jazz - HF
Benny	Parsons	Sports	USA	Race Car Driver - HF
Benny (Papa Zita) (William)	Benjamin	Performing Arts	USA	Drummer - Rock & Roll - HF
Benoit Constant	Coquelin	Performing Arts	France	Actor
Benvenuto	Cellini	Works of Art	Italy	Sculpture/Goldsmith
Berend Tobia	Boeyinga	Architecture	Netherlands	Architect - Churches
Berke	Breathed	Creative Works	USA	Cartoonist - Pulitzer
Berlin Guy	Chamberlin	Sports	USA	Football Player - HF
Bern Eli (Bernie)	Oldfield	Sports	USA	Race Car Driver - HF
Bernadette	Peters	Performing Arts	USA	Singer
Bernadotte E.	Schmitt	Creative Works	USA	Author - Pulitzer
Bernal Diaz Del	Castillo	Exploration	Spain	Explorer - Mexico
Bernard	Bailyn	Creative Works	USA	Author - Pulitzer
	Berenson	Creative Works	USA	Art Critic
	Katz	Science	England	Medicine - Nobel Laureate
	King	Sports	USA	Basketball Player
	Kliban	Creative Works	USA	Cartoonist - Playboy
	Malamud	Creative Works	USA	Novelist - Pulitzer
	Pares	Arts	England	Historian
	Tschumi	Architecture	Switzerland	Architect
Bernard (Bennie)	Borgman	Sports	USA	Basketball Player - HF
Bernard (Benny)	McLaughlin	Sports	USA	Soccer Player - HF
Bernard (Buddy)	Rich	Performing Arts	USA	Band Leader - Big Band/Jazz - HF
Bernard (Toots)	Shor	Sports	USA	Baseball Player
Bernard Allan	Federko	Sports	Canada	Hockey Player - HF
Bernard Andrew	Harris Jr.	Aviation	USA	Astronaut
Bernard de	Mandeville	Creative Works	England	Satirist
Bernard De	Voto	Creative Works	USA	Author - Pulitzer
Bernard Joseph Andre (Bernie)	Geoffrion	Sports	Canada	Hockey Player - HF
Bernard Law	Montgomery	War & Peace	England	Field Marshall
Bernard Mannes	Baruch	Business	USA	Financier/Statesman
Bernard Marcel (Bernie)	Parent	Sports	Canada	Hockey Player - HF
Bernard Ralph	Maybeck	Architecture	USA	Architect - AIA Gold Medal
Bernardo	Bertolucci	Movie Production	Italy	Director - Acad Award Nom
	O'Higgins	Politics	Chile	President
Bernardo Alberto	Houssay	Science	Argentina	Medicine - Nobel Laureate
Bernd	Rosemeyer	Sports	Netherlands	Race Car Driver - HF
Bernhard	Langer	Sports	Germany	Golfer - HF
Bernhard von	Bülow	Politics	Germany	Chancellor
Bernie	Kopell	Performing Arts	USA	Actor

SOLVER SERIES: NAME FINDER

FIRST NAME	LAST NAME	CATEGORY	COUNTRY	FAME
Bernie	Leadon	Performing Arts	USA	Rock & Roll - HF - The Eagles
Berry	Oakley	Performing Arts	USA	Rock & Roll - HF - Allmann Brothers Band
Bert	Blyleven	Sports	USA	Baseball Player
	Holldobler	Creative Works	Germany	Author - Pulitzer
	Lahr	Performing Arts	USA	Actor
	Parks	Performing Arts	USA	Actor
	Sakmann	Science	Germany	Medicine - Nobel Laureate
Bertha Louise (Birdie)	Townsend	Sports	USA	Tennis Player - HF
Bertha von	Suttner	War & Peace	Austria	Peace - Nobel Laureate
Bertie	Ahern	Politics	Ireland	Prime Minster
Bertil	Ohlin	Arts	Sweden	Economics - Nobel Laureate
Bertolt	Brecht	Creative Works	Germany	Playwright
Bertram	Goodhue	Architecture	USA	Architect - AIA Gold Medal
Bertram Albert (Bert)	Patenaude	Sports	USA	Soccer Player - HF
Bertram N.	Brockhouse	Science	Canada	Physics - Nobel Laureate
Bess	Armstrong	Performing Arts	USA	Actress
	Myerson	Performing Arts	USA	Actress
Bessie	Love	Performing Arts	USA	Actress - Acad Award Nom
	Smith	Performing Arts	USA	Singer - Big Band/Jazz - HF
Beth	Daniel	Sports	USA	Golfer - HF
	Henley	Creative Works	USA	Dramatist - Pulitzer
Betsey	Johnson	Business	USA	Fashion Designer
Betsy	Blair	Performing Arts	USA	Actress - Acad Award Nom
	King	Sports	USA	Golfer - HF
	Palmer	Performing Arts	USA	Actress
	Rawls	Sports	USA	Golfer - HF
	Ross	Arts	USA	Flag Maker
Bette	Davis	Performing Arts	USA	Actress - Academy Award
	Midler	Performing Arts	USA	Actress - Acad Award Nom
	Midler	Performing Arts	USA	Singer
Betty	Buckley	Performing Arts	USA	Actress
	Compson	Performing Arts	USA	Actress - Acad Award Nom
	Friedan	Creative Works	USA	Writer
	Grable	Performing Arts	USA	Actor
	Hutton	Performing Arts	USA	Actress
	Jameson	Sports	USA	Golfer - HF
	Kelley	Performing Arts	USA	Rock & Roll - HF - Martha & The Vandellas
	White	Performing Arts	USA	Actress
	Williams	War & Peace	England	Peace - Nobel Laureate
Betty Kay	Nuthall-Shoemaker	Sports	England	Tennis Player - HF
Beulah	Bondi	Performing Arts	USA	Actress - Acad Award Nom
Beverley	Lee	Performing Arts	USA	Rock & Roll - HF - The Shirelles
Beverly	D'Angelo	Performing Arts	USA	Actress
	Sills	Performing Arts	USA	Singer - Opera
Bibi	Andersson	Performing Arts	Sweden	Actress
	Besch	Performing Arts	Austria	Actress
Bil	Baird	Performing Arts	USA	Puppeteer
	Keane	Creative Works	USA	Cartoonist - Family Circle
Bill	Anderson	Performing Arts	USA	Singer - Country Music - HF
	Bixby	Performing Arts	USA	Actor
	Cosby	Performing Arts	USA	Comedian
	Elliott	Sports	USA	Race Car Driver
	Gates	Business	USA	Microsoft
	Kenny	Performing Arts	USA	Rock & Roll - HF - The Ink Spots
	Kreutzmann	Performing Arts	USA	Rock & Roll - HF - Grateful Dead
	Murray	Performing Arts	USA	Actor - Acad Award Nom
	Murray	Performing Arts	USA	Comedian
	Pinkney	Performing Arts	USA	Rock & Roll - HF - The Drifters
	Ripken	Sports	USA	Baseball Player
	Wyman	Performing Arts	England	Singer/Guitarist
	Evans	Performing Arts	USA	Jazz Pianist - Big Band/Jazz - HF
Billie	Burke	Performing Arts	USA	Actress - Acad Award Nom
	Tsien	Architecture	USA	Architect - Jefferson Medal

FIRST NAME	LAST NAME	CATEGORY	COUNTRY	FAME
Billie Jean Moffitt	King	Sports	USA	Tennis Player - HF
Billings Learned	Hand	Law & Order	USA	Jurist
Billy	Barty	Performing Arts	USA	Actor
	Casper	Sports	USA	Golfer - HF
	Conn	Sports	USA	Boxer - HF
	Crystal	Performing Arts	USA	Actor/Comedian
	Daniels	Performing Arts	USA	Singer
	Eckstine	Performing Arts	USA	Band Leader - Big Band/Jazz - HF
	Gibbons	Performing Arts	USA	Rock & Roll - HF - ZZ Top
	Idol	Performing Arts	England	Singer
	Johnson	Performing Arts	USA	Rock & Roll - HF - The Moonglows
	Ocean	Performing Arts	West Indies	Singer
	Preston	Performing Arts	USA	Pianist/Writer
	Strayhorn	Performing Arts	USA	Jazz Pianist/Composer - Big Band/Jazz - HF
	Sunday	Arts	USA	Evangilist - WW I
	Wilder	Movie Production	Hungary	Director - Academy Award
	Wright	Sports	England	Soccer Player - HF
Billy (Bill)	Vukovich	Sports	USA	Race Car Driver - HF
Billy (Doctor)	Taylor	Performing Arts	USA	Jazz Pianist/Composer - Big Band/Jazz - HF
Billy Bob	Thornton	Performing Arts	USA	Actor - Acad Award Nom
Billy De	Wolfe	Performing Arts	USA	Actor
Billy Dee	Williams	Performing Arts	USA	Actor
Billy Joe (BJ)	Thomas	Performing Arts	USA	Singer - Pops
Billy Leo	Williams	Sports	USA	Baseball Player - HF
Billy Sol	Estes	Business	USA	Cotton Industry
Bing	Crosby	Sports	USA	Golfer - HF
Birch Evans (Evan)	Bayh III	Politics	USA	Senator
Birgit	Nilsson	Performing Arts	Sweden	Singer - Opera
Bjarni	Herjulfsson	Exploration	Iceland	Explorer - America East Coast
Bjarni Valdimar	Tryggvason	Aviation	Canada	Astronaut
Björn Rune	Borg	Sports	Sweden	Tennis Player - HF
Björnstjerne Martinus	Björnson	Creative Works	Norway	Literature - Nobel Laureate
Blair	Brown	Performing Arts	USA	Actress
	Russel	Sports	Canada	Hockey Player - HF
	Underwood	Performing Arts	USA	Actor
Blaise	Pascal	Science	France	Mathematician/Philsopher
	Pascal	Science	France	Physicist/Mathematician
Blake	Edwards	Movie Production	USA	Director
Blythe	Danner	Performing Arts	USA	Actress
Bo	Derek	Performing Arts	USA	Actress
	Diddley	Performing Arts	USA	Singer/Song Writer
	Jackson	Sports	USA	Football Player
Bob	Beamon	Sports	USA	Olympic Long Jumper
	Cain	Creative Works	USA	Journalist - Radio
	Costas	Creative Works	USA	Journalist - Television
	Crane	Performing Arts	USA	Actor
	Crewe	Performing Arts	USA	Rock & Roll - HF - The Four Seasons
	Dalton	Law & Order	USA	Outlaw
	Denver	Performing Arts	USA	Actor
	Elliott	Performing Arts	USA	Comedian
	Estes	Sports	USA	Golfer
	Ezrin	Performing Arts	Canada	Musician/Producer - Canadian Music - HF
	Fosse	Movie Production	USA	Director - Academy Award
	Foster	Sports	USA	Boxer - HF
	Glidden	Sports	USA	Race Car Driver - HF
	Greene	Creative Works	USA	Journalist - Newspaper
	Hope	Performing Arts	England	Comedian
	Hope	Sports	USA	Golfer - HF
	Hoskins	Performing Arts	England	Actor - Acad Award Nom
	Keeshan	Performing Arts	USA	Show Host
	Mackie	Business	USA	Fashion Designer
	Mathias	Sports	USA	Olympic Decathlon
	Montana	Creative Works	USA	Cartoonist - Archie

SOLVER SERIES: NAME FINDER

FIRST NAME	LAST NAME	CATEGORY	COUNTRY	FAME
Bob	Montgomery	Sports	USA	Boxer - HF
	Newhart	Performing Arts	USA	Comedian
	Nolan	Performing Arts	Canada	Country Music - HF - Sons of the Pioneers
	Richards	Sports	USA	Olympic Pole Vaulter
	Saget	Performing Arts	USA	Actor
	Seger	Performing Arts	USA	Singer - Rock & Roll - HF
	Thaves	Creative Works	USA	Cartoonist - Frank & Ernest
	Tway	Sports	USA	Golfer
	Uecker	Sports	USA	Baseball Player
	Charles	Sports	New Zealand	Golfer
	Guadio	Performing Arts	USA	Rock & Roll - HF - The Four Seasons
Bob (Bullet)	Hayes	Sports	USA	Olympic Sprinter
Bob (Fleetwood)	Mac (Brunning)	Performing Arts	England	Rock & Roll - HF - Fleetwood Mac
Bobby	Allison	Sports	USA	Race Car Driver - HF
	Bonds	Sports	USA	Baseball Player
	Chacon	Sports	USA	Boxer - HF
	Charlton	Sports	England	Soccer Player - HF
	Driscoll	Performing Arts	USA	Actor - Academy Award
	Fischer	Games	USA	Chess Player
	Goldsboro	Performing Arts	USA	Singer
	Hebert	Sports	USA	Football Player
	Isaac	Sports	USA	Race Car Driver - HF
	Lenarduzzi	Sports	Canada	Soccer Player - HF
	Lester	Performing Arts	USA	Rock & Roll - HF - The Moonglows
	Massey	Performing Arts	USA	Rock & Roll - HF - The O'Jays
	McFerrin	Performing Arts	USA	Singer
	Moore	Sports	England	Soccer Player - HF
	Rahal	Sports	USA	Race Car Driver - HF
	Rydell	Performing Arts	USA	Singer
	Sherman	Performing Arts	USA	Singer
	Short	Performing Arts	USA	Singer/Pianist
	Unser	Sports	USA	Race Car Driver - HF
	Vee	Performing Arts	USA	Singer - Rock & Roll - HF
	Vinton	Performing Arts	USA	Singer - Pops
	Womack	Performing Arts	USA	Singer - Rhythm & Blues
Bonaventure	Elzevir	Arts	Netherlands	Printer
Bondleaux	Bryant	Performing Arts	USA	Violinist - Country Music - HF
Bonita	Granville	Performing Arts	USA	Actress - Acad Award Nom
Bonnie	Franklin	Performing Arts	USA	Actress
	Parker	Law & Order	USA	Outlaw
	Pointer	Performing Arts	USA	Singer
	Raitt	Performing Arts	USA	Singer - Rock & Roll - HF
Booker T.	Jones	Performing Arts	USA	Rock & Roll - HF - Booker T & The Mg's
Booker Taliaferro	Washington	Creative Works	USA	Author/Educator
Boomer	Esiason	Sports	USA	Football Player
Boris	Becker	Sports	Germany	Tennis Player - HF
	Karloff	Performing Arts	England	Actor
	Podrecca	Architecture	Yugoslavia	Architect
	Spassky	Games	Russia	Chess Player
Boris Borisovich	Yegorov	Aviation	Russia	Astronaut
Boris Fëdorovich	Godunov	Politics	Russia	Czar
Boris Leonidovich	Pasternak	Creative Works	Russia	Literature - Nobel Laureate
Boris Nikolayevich	Yeltsin	Politics	Russia	President
Boris Valentinovich	Volynov	Aviation	Russia	Astronaut
Bowie Kent	Kuhn	Sports	USA	Baseball Commissioner
Boz	Scaggs	Performing Arts	USA	Singer
Brad	Dourif	Performing Arts	USA	Actor - Acad Award Nom
	Faxon	Sports	USA	Golfer
	Pitt	Performing Arts	USA	Actor - Acad Award Nom
	Whitford	Performing Arts	USA	Rock & Roll - HF - Aerosmith
Bradford	Dillman	Performing Arts	USA	Actor
Branch	McCracken	Sports	USA	Basketball Player - HF
Brandon De	Wilde	Performing Arts	USA	Actor - Acad Award Nom

FIRST NAME	LAST NAME	CATEGORY	COUNTRY	FAME
Branford	Marsalis	Performing Arts	USA	Jazz Saxaphonist
Braxton	Bragg	War & Peace	USA	General
Bray	Hammond	Creative Works	USA	Author - Pulitzer
Brenda	Blethyn	Performing Arts	England	Actress - Acad Award Nom
	Fricker	Performing Arts	Ireland	Actress - Academy Award
	Vaccaro	Performing Arts	USA	Actress - Acad Award Nom
Brenda Mae	Lee (Tarpley)	Performing Arts	USA	Singer - Country Music - HF
	Lee (Tarpley)	Performing Arts	USA	Singer - Rock & Roll - HF
Brendan	Behan	Creative Works	Ireland	Playwright/Author
Brent	Musburger	Creative Works	USA	Journalist - Television
	Mydland	Performing Arts	Germany	Rock & Roll - HF - Grateful Dead
	Scowcroft	Politics	USA	National Security Advisor
	Spiner	Performing Arts	USA	Actor
Bret	Harte	Creative Works	USA	Writer - Short Stories
	Saberhagen	Sports	USA	Baseball Player
Brett	Hull	Sports	Canada	Hockey Player
	Ogle	Sports	Australia	Golfer
Brewster Hopkinson	Shaw Jr.	Aviation	USA	Astronaut
Brian	Aherne	Performing Arts	England	Actor - Acad Award Nom
	Benben	Performing Arts	USA	Actor
	Boitano	Sports	USA	Olympic Skater
	Boru	Politics	Ireland	King
	Dennehy	Performing Arts	USA	Actor
	Donlevy	Performing Arts	Northern Ireland	Actor - Acad Award Nom
	Duffy	Aviation	USA	Astronaut
	Eno	Creative Works	England	Composer/Producer
	Holland	Creative Works	USA	Composer
	Hyland	Performing Arts	USA	Singer
	Jones	Performing Arts	England	Rock & Roll - HF - Rolling Stones
	Keith	Performing Arts	USA	Actor
	Tobin	Sports	Australia	Tennis Player - HF
	Wilson	Performing Arts	USA	Rock & Roll - HF - The Beach Boys
	Johnson	Performing Arts	England	Rock & Roll - HF - AC/DC
Brian David	Josephson	Science	England	Physics - Nobel Laureate
Brian De	Palma	Movie Production	USA	Director
Brian Douglas	Wilson	Creative Works	USA	Composer/Arranger
Brian Doyle	Murray	Performing Arts	USA	Comedian
Brian Francis Wynne	Garfield	Creative Works	USA	Author
Brian Harold	May	Performing Arts	England	Rock & Roll - HF - Queen
Brian Todd	O'Leary	Aviation	USA	Astronaut
Brian Wilson	Aldiss	Creative Works	England	Author - SciFi
Bridget	Fonda	Performing Arts	USA	Actress
	Hall	Performing Arts	USA	Super Model
Briggs Swift	Cunningham Jr.	Sports	USA	Race Car Driver - HF
Brigham	Young	Arts	USA	Mormon Leader
Brigitte	Bardot	Performing Arts	France	Actress
	Nielson	Performing Arts	Denmark	Actress
Brinsley	Sheridan	Creative Works	England	Dramatist/Politician
Britt	Ekland	Performing Arts	Sweden	Actress
Broderick	Crawford	Performing Arts	USA	Actor - Academy Award
Bronislaw (Bronko)	Nagurski	Sports	Canada	Football Player - HF
Bronislaw Kaspar	Malinowski	Arts	Poland	Anthropologist
Bronson	Pinchot	Performing Arts	USA	Actor
Brook	Benton	Performing Arts	USA	Singer
	Taylor	Science	England	Mathematician
Brooke	Adams	Performing Arts	USA	Actress
	Shields	Performing Arts	USA	Actress
Brooke Russell	Astor	Creative Works	USA	Writer/Philanthropist
Brooks Calbert	Robinson	Sports	USA	Baseball Player - HF
Bruce	Beresford	Movie Production	Australia	Director - Acad Award Nom
	Boxleitner	Performing Arts	USA	Actor
	Cabot	Performing Arts	USA	Actor
	Crampton	Sports	Australia	Golfer

SOLVER SERIES: NAME FINDER

FIRST NAME	LAST NAME	CATEGORY	COUNTRY	FAME
Bruce	Davison	Performing Arts	USA	Actor - Acad Award Nom
	Dern	Performing Arts	USA	Actor - Acad Award Nom
	Goff	Architecture	USA	Architect
	Graham	Architecture	USA	Architect - High Rise
	Jenner	Sports	USA	Olympic Decathlete
	Lee	Performing Arts	USA	Actor
	McCandless II	Aviation	USA	Astronaut
	McLaren	Sports	New Zealand	Race Car Driver - HF
	Merrifield	Science	USA	Chemistry - Nobel Laureate
	Smith	Sports	USA	Football Player
	Stuart	Sports	Canada	Hockey Player - HF
	Weitz	Performing Arts	USA	Actor
	Willis	Performing Arts	Germany	Actor
	Cockburn	Performing Arts	Canada	Singer/Guitarist - Canadian Music - HF
	Fairbairn	Performing Arts	Canada	Musician/Producer - Canadian Music - HF
	Palmer	Performing Arts	Canada	Rock & Roll - HF - Buffalo Springfield
	Rogers	Arts	USA	Typographer/Book Designer
	Wilson	Sports	Canada	Soccer Player - HF
Bruce (Charles)	Catton	Creative Works	USA	Author - Pulitzer
Bruce Edward	Melnick	Aviation	USA	Astronaut
Bruce Frederic	Springsteen	Performing Arts	USA	Singer - Rock & Roll - HF
Bruno	Bettelheim	Arts	USA	Psychologist
	Kirby	Performing Arts	USA	Actor
	Minardi	Architecture	Italy	Architect
	Reichlin	Architecture	Switzerland	Architect
	Taut	Architecture	Turkey	Architect
Bryan	Adams	Performing Arts	Canada	Singer
	Brown	Performing Arts	Australia	Actor
	Ferry	Performing Arts	England	Singer
Bryan Aldwyn	Hextall	Sports	Canada	Hockey Player - HF
Bryan Bartlett (Bart)	Starr	Sports	USA	Football Player - HF
Bryan James (Chas)	Chandler	Performing Arts	England	Rock & Roll - HF - The Animals
Bryan John	Trottier	Sports	Canada	Hockey Player - HF
Bryan Moral (Bitsy)	Grant Jr.	Sports	USA	Tennis Player - HF
Bryant	Gumble	Creative Works	USA	Journalist - Television
Bryce	Courtenay	Creative Works	South Africa	Author
Bubba	Smith	Sports	USA	Football Player
Buck	Henry	Movie Production	USA	Director - Acad Award Nom
	Henry	Performing Arts	USA	Comedian
	Johnson	Performing Arts	USA	Jazz Trumpeter - Big Band/Jazz - HF
Bud	Abbott	Performing Arts	USA	Comedian
	Powell	Performing Arts	USA	Jazz Pianist - Big Band/Jazz - HF
Buddy	Bolden	Performing Arts	USA	Jazz Trumpeter - Big Band/Jazz - HF
	Ebsen	Performing Arts	USA	Actor
	Greco	Performing Arts	USA	Singer
	Guy	Performing Arts	USA	Guitarist - Rock & Roll - HF
	Hackett	Performing Arts	USA	Comedian
	Rosar	Sports	USA	Baseball Player
Buddy De	Franco	Performing Arts	USA	Jazz Clarinetist - Big Band/Jazz - HF
Buffalo Bob	Smith	Performing Arts	USA	Actor
Buffy	Sainte-Marie	Performing Arts	Canada	Singer - Canadian Music - HF
Buonarroti	Michelangelo	Architecture	Italy	Architect/Sculptor/Painter/Author
Burgess	Meredith	Performing Arts	USA	Actor - Acad Award Nom
Burl	Ives	Performing Arts	USA	Actor/Singer - Academy Award
Burleigh Arland	Grimes	Sports	USA	Baseball Player - HF
Burrhus Frederic	Skinner	Arts	USA	Psychologist
Burt	Bacharach	Creative Works	USA	Composer/Pianist
	Lancaster	Performing Arts	USA	Actor - Academy Award
	Reynolds	Performing Arts	USA	Actor - Acad Award Nom
	Young	Performing Arts	USA	Actor - Acad Award Nom
Burton	Cummings	Performing Arts	Canada	Canadian Music - HF - The Guess Who
	Richter	Science	USA	Physics - Nobel Laureate
Burton J.	Hendrick	Creative Works	USA	Author - Pulitzer

FIRST NAME	LAST NAME	CATEGORY	COUNTRY	FAME
Busby	Berkely	Movie Production	USA	Director
Buster	Crabbe	Performing Arts	USA	Actor
	Keaton	Performing Arts	USA	Actor
Butterfly	McQueen	Performing Arts	USA	Actress
Button	Gwinett	Politics	USA	Patriot
Byron	Nelson	Sports	USA	Golfer - HF
Byron Bancroft (Ban)	Johnson	Sports	USA	Baseball Executive - HF
Byron Kurt	Lichtenberg	Aviation	USA	Astronaut
Byron Raymond	White	Law & Order	USA	Justice - Supreme Court
C. Thomas	Howell	Performing Arts	USA	Actor
Cabell (Cab)	Calloway III	Performing Arts	USA	Band Leader - Big Band/Jazz - HF
Cal	Ripken Jr.	Sports	USA	Baseball Player
	Thomas	Creative Works	USA	Author/Journalist
	Tjader	Performing Arts	USA	Vibraphonist
Caleb	Cushing	Politics	USA	Diplomat
Calista	Flockhart	Performing Arts	USA	Actress
Calvin	Klein	Business	USA	Fashion Designer
	Peete	Sports	USA	Golfer
	Trillin	Creative Works	USA	Journalist - Newspaper
Calvin J.	Murphy	Sports	USA	Basketball Player - HF
Cam	Neely	Sports	Canada	Hockey Player - HF
Cameron	Mitchell	Performing Arts	USA	Actor
Camille	Flammarion	Science	France	Astronomer
	Pissarro	Works of Art	France	Painter
Camillo	Golgi	Science	Italy	Medicine - Nobel Laureate
Camilo José	Cela	Creative Works	Spain	Literature - Nobel Laureate
Candice	Bergen	Performing Arts	USA	Actress - Acad Award Nom
Candy	Clark	Performing Arts	USA	Actress - Acad Award Nom
Cara	Williams	Performing Arts	USA	Actress - Acad Award Nom
Carin	Jennings-Gabarra	Sports	USA	Soccer Player - HF
Carl	Barth	Arts	Switzerland	Theologian
	Bernstein	Creative Works	USA	Journalist - Newspaper
	Betz	Performing Arts	USA	Actor
	Bosch	Science	Germany	Chemistry - Nobel Laureate
	Dennis	Creative Works	USA	Poet - Pulitzer
	Ichan	Business	USA	Entrepreneur
	Lewis	Sports	USA	Olympic Runner
	Milles	Works of Art	USA	Sculptor
	Orff	Creative Works	Germany	Composer
	Panzram	Law & Order	USA	Serial Killer
	Reiner	Performing Arts	USA	Comedian
	Sagan	Science	USA	Astronomer
	Sandburg	Creative Works	USA	Author - Pulitzer
	Sandburg	Creative Works	USA	Poet - Pulitzer
	Schurz	Politics	USA	Statesman/Journalist
	Smith	Performing Arts	USA	Singer - Country Music - HF
	Weathers	Performing Arts	USA	Actor
	Weidemeyer	Architecture	Switzerland	Architect
	Wilson	Performing Arts	USA	Rock & Roll - HF - The Beach Boys
Carl (Bobo)	Olson	Sports	USA	Boxer - HF
Carl Clinton Van	Doren	Creative Works	USA	Author - Pulitzer
Carl David	Anderson	Science	USA	Physics - Nobel Laureate
Carl E.	Schorske	Creative Works	USA	Author - Pulitzer
	Wieman	Science	USA	Physics - Nobel Laureate
Carl Edward	Sagan	Creative Works	USA	Author - Pulitzer
Carl Eric	Wickman	Business	USA	Transportation Industry
Carl Ferdinand	Cori	Science	USA	Medicine - Nobel Laureate
Carl Franz	Bally	Business	Switzerland	Fashion Designer
Carl Friedrich Georg	Spitteler	Creative Works	Switzerland	Literature - Nobel Laureate
Carl Gotthard	Langhans	Architecture	Germany	Architect
Carl Gustaf Verner von	Heidenstam	Creative Works	Sweden	Literature - Nobel Laureate
Carl Gustav	Jung	Science	Switzerland	Psychiatrist/Psychologist
Carl Joseph	Meade	Aviation	USA	Astronaut

SOLVER SERIES: NAME FINDER

FIRST NAME	LAST NAME	CATEGORY	COUNTRY	FAME
Carl Lee	Eller	Sports	USA	Football Player - HF
	Perkins (Perkings)	Performing Arts	USA	Singer - Rock & Roll - HF
Carl Maria von	Weber	Creative Works	Germany	Composer
Carl Michael	Yastrzemski	Sports	USA	Baseball Player - HF
Carl N.	Degler	Creative Works	USA	Author - Pulitzer
Carl Owen	Hubbell	Sports	USA	Baseball Player - HF
Carl von	Ossietzky	Creative Works	Germany	Journalist/Pacifist
	Ossietzky	War & Peace	Germany	Peace - Nobel Laureate
Carla	Bruni	Performing Arts	Italy	Super Model
	Thomas	Performing Arts	USA	Singer
Carla Anderson	Hills	Politics	USA	Assistant Attorney-General
Carlo	Aymonino	Architecture	Italy	Architect
	Gambino	Law & Order	Sicily	Mafia
	Goldoni	Creative Works	Italy	Dramatist
	Maderno	Architecture	Italy	Architect
	Mollino	Architecture	Italy	Architect
	Ponti	Movie Production	Italy	Director
	Rubbia	Science	Italy	Physics - Nobel Laureate
	Scarpa	Architecture	Italy	Architect
Carlos	Monzon	Sports	Argentina	Boxer - HF
	Ortiz	Sports	Puerto Rico	Boxer - HF
	Palomino	Sports	USA	Boxer - HF
	Santana	Performing Arts	Mexico	Guitarist
	Santana	Performing Arts	Mexico	Singer - Rock & Roll - HF
	Zarate	Sports	Mexico	Boxer - HF
Carlos Alberto	Torres	Sports	Brazil	Soccer Player - HF
Carlos Filipe Ximenes	Belo	War & Peace	East Timor	Peace - Nobel Laureate
Carlos Raúl	Villanueva	Architecture	Venezuela	Architect
Carlos Saavedra	Lamas	War & Peace	Argentina	Peace - Nobel Laureate
Carlotta	Patti	Performing Arts	Italy	Singer - Opera
Carlton	Mabee	Creative Works	USA	Author - Pulitzer
Carlton Ernest	Fisk	Sports	USA	Baseball Player - HF
Carlton Joseph Huntley	Hayes	Arts	USA	Historian
Carly	Simon	Performing Arts	USA	Singer
Carmen	Miranda	Performing Arts	Portugal	Actress
Carmine (The Cigar)	Galante	Law & Order	Sicily	Mafia
Carol	Alt	Performing Arts	USA	Super Model
	Blazejowski	Sports	USA	Basketball Player - HF
	Burnett	Performing Arts	USA	Comedian
	Channing	Performing Arts	USA	Actress - Acad Award Nom
	Heiss	Sports	USA	Olympic Skater
	Kane	Performing Arts	USA	Actress - Acad Award Nom
	Lawrence	Performing Arts	USA	Actress
	Mann	Sports	USA	Golfer - HF
	Reed	Movie Production	England	Director - Academy Award
	Shields	Creative Works	Canada	Author - Pulitzer
Carole	King	Performing Arts	USA	Singer
	Landis	Performing Arts	USA	Actress
	Lombard	Performing Arts	USA	Actress - Acad Award Nom
Caroline	Miller	Creative Works	USA	Novelist - Pulitzer
Caroline Carmichael	Fillmore	Politics	USA	First Lady
Caroline Lavinia	Harrison	Politics	USA	First Lady
Carolus	Linnaeus	Science	Sweden	Botanist
Carolyn	Jones	Performing Arts	USA	Actress - Acad Award Nom
	Kizer	Creative Works	USA	Poet - Pulitzer
Carre	Otis	Performing Arts	USA	Super Model
Carrie	Fisher	Performing Arts	USA	Actress
	Snodgress	Performing Arts	USA	Actress - Acad Award Nom
Carrie Chapman	Catt	Politics	USA	Leader - Women's Suffrage
Carroll	Baker	Performing Arts	USA	Actress - Acad Award Nom
	O'Connor	Performing Arts	USA	Actor
	Shelby	Sports	USA	Race Car Driver - HF
Carry	Nation	Politics	USA	Agitator - Temperance

FIRST NAME	LAST NAME	CATEGORY	COUNTRY	FAME
Carson	McCullers	Creative Works	USA	Novelist
Cary	Elwes	Performing Arts	England	Actor
	Grant	Performing Arts	England	Actor - Acad Award Nom
	Middlecoff	Sports	USA	Golfer - HF
Caryn Elaine (Whoopi)	Goldberg	Performing Arts	USA	Actress - Academy Award
Casey	Kasem	Performing Arts	USA	Show Host - Radio
Casimir	Pulaski	War & Peace	Poland	General - Am. Revolutionary Army
Cass	Elliot	Performing Arts	USA	Singer
	Gilbert	Architecture	USA	Architect
Cassidy	Rae	Performing Arts	USA	Actress
Cat	Stevens	Performing Arts	England	Singer - Pops
Catalina Sandino	Moreno	Performing Arts	Columbia	Actress - Acad Award Nom
Cate	Blanchett	Performing Arts	Australia	Actress - Academy Award
Catherine	Burns	Performing Arts	USA	Actress - Acad Award Nom
	Deneuve	Performing Arts	France	Actress - Acad Award Nom
	Keener	Performing Arts	USA	Actress - Acad Award Nom
	Zeta-Jones	Performing Arts	Wales	Actress - Academy Award
Cathy	Guisewite	Creative Works	USA	Cartoonist - Cathy
	Moriarty	Performing Arts	USA	Actress
	Rigby	Sports	USA	Olympic Gymnast
Caudette	Colbert	Performing Arts	France	Actress - Academy Award
Cazzie	Russell	Sports	USA	Basketball Player
Cearbhall	O'Dalaigh	Politics	Ireland	President
Cecil	Beaton	Works of Art	England	Photographer
	Fielder	Sports	USA	Baseball Player
	Kellaway	Performing Arts	South Africa	Actor - Acad Award Nom
	King	Business	England	Publishing
Cecil Blount De	Mille	Movie Production	USA	Director - Acad Award Nom
Cecil Day	Lewis	Creative Works	England	Poet Laureate/Novelist
Cecil Frank	Powell	Science	England	Physics - Nobel Laureate
Cecil Henry (Babe)	Dye	Sports	Canada	Hockey Player - HF
Cecil John	Rhodes	Business	England	Financier/Administrator
Cecil R. (Tiny)	Thompson	Sports	Canada	Hockey Player - HF
Cecil Scott	Forester	Creative Works	England	Novelist
Cedric	Hardwicke	Performing Arts	England	Actor
Celeste	Holm	Performing Arts	USA	Actress - Academy Award
Celia	Johnson	Performing Arts	England	Actress - Acad Award Nom
Cesar	Romero	Performing Arts	USA	Actor
César	Franck	Creative Works	France	Composer/Organist
	Milstein	Science	England	Medicine - Nobel Laureate
	Pelli	Architecture	Argentina	Architect - AIA Gold Medal
Cesar Estrada	Chavez	Business	USA	Union Leader
Cesare	Borgia	War & Peace	Italy	Cardinal
	Lombroso	Science	Italy	Physician/Criminologist
	Siepi	Performing Arts	Italy	Singer - Opera
Cesare di Lorenzo	Cesariano	Architecture	Italy	Architect
Chad	Everett	Performing Arts	USA	Actor
Chaim	Herzog	Politics	Israel	President
	Potok	Creative Works	USA	Author
	Topol	Performing Arts	Palestine	Actor - Acad Award Nom
	Weizmann	Politics	Israel	President
Chaing	Kai-shek	War & Peace	China	Military Leader
Chaka	Kahn	Performing Arts	USA	Singer
Chandrasekhara Venkata	Raman	Science	India	Physics - Nobel Laureate
Chang	Ch'ien	Exploration	China	Explorer - Central Asia
Charles	Addams	Creative Works	USA	Cartoonist - Addams Family
	Aznavour	Performing Arts	France	Singer
	Barkley	Sports	USA	Basketball Player
	Barry	Architecture	England	Architect/Designer
	Bickford	Performing Arts	USA	Actor - Acad Award Nom
	Boyer	Performing Arts	France	Actor - Acad Award Nom
	Bronson	Performing Arts	USA	Actor
	Brown	Performing Arts	USA	Singer - Rock & Roll - HF

SOLVER SERIES: NAME FINDER

FIRST NAME	LAST NAME	CATEGORY	COUNTRY	FAME
Charles	Bulfinch	Architecture	USA	Architect - Government Buildings
	Carroll	War & Peace	USA	Revolutionary Leader
	Chaplin	Movie Production	England	Director - Academy Award
	Coburn	Performing Arts	USA	Actor - Academy Award
	Cornwallis	War & Peace	England	General
	Crichton	Movie Production	England	Director - Acad Award Nom
	Curtis	Politics	USA	Vice-President
	Dickens	Creative Works	England	Novelist
	Durning	Performing Arts	USA	Actor - Acad Award Nom
	Frohman	Movie Production	USA	Producer/Theatrical Manager
	Fuller	Creative Works	USA	Dramatist - Pulitzer
	Fuqua	Performing Arts	USA	Rock & Roll - HF - The Ink Spots
	Garnier	Architecture	France	Architect
	Goodyear	Science	USA	Inventor - Vulcanizing Rubber
	Gordone	Creative Works	USA	Dramatist - Pulitzer
	Grey	Politics	England	Prime Minister
	Grodin	Performing Arts	USA	Actor
	Gwathmey	Architecture	USA	Architect
	Haid	Performing Arts	USA	Actor
	Harrod	Business	England	Retail Trade
	Kingsley	Creative Works	England	Novelist/Clergyman
	Kuralt	Creative Works	USA	Journalist - Television
	Lamb	Creative Works	England	Essayist/Critic
	Laughton	Performing Arts	England	Actor - Academy Award
	Lebrun	Works of Art	France	Painter - Historical
	Lee	War & Peace	USA	General - Revolutionary War
	Lindbergh	Aviation	USA	Aviator
	Lyell	Science	England	Geologist
	Mantoux	Science	France	Physician
	Olson	Creative Works	USA	Poet
	Pathé	Movie Production	France	Director
	Perrault	Creative Works	France	Writer/Compiler - Fairy Tales
	Reade	Creative Works	England	Novelist
	Simic	Creative Works	Yugoslavia	Poet - Pulitzer
	Sumner	Politics	USA	Statesman/Abolitionist
	Tupper	Politics	Canada	Prime Minster
	Walters	Movie Production	USA	Director - Acad Award Nom
	Warren	Creative Works	USA	Author - Pulitzer
	Wheatstone	Science	England	Physicist
	Wilkes	Exploration	USA	Explorer - Antarctic
	Wright	Creative Works	USA	Poet - Pulitzer
	Wesley	Arts	England	Clergyman/Writer - Hymns
Charles (Charlie)	Joiner Jr.	Sports	USA	Football Player - HF
Charles (Chick)	Evans	Sports	USA	Golfer - HF
Charles (Lucky)	Luciano	Law & Order	Sicily	Mafia
Charles (Red)	Farmer	Sports	USA	Race Car Driver - HF
Charles A.	Lindbergh	Creative Works	USA	Author - Pulitzer
Charles Albert (Charlie)	Comiskey	Sports	USA	Baseball Executive -HF
Charles Albert (Chief)	Bender	Sports	USA	Baseball Player - HF
Charles Anderson	Dana	Arts	USA	Newspaper Editor
Charles Andre Joseph de	Gaulle	Politics	France	President
Charles André Marie de	Gaulle	War & Peace	France	General
Charles Arthur	Bassett II	Aviation	USA	Astronaut
Charles Augustin	Sainte-Beuve	Creative Works	France	Writer/Literary Critic
Charles Augustus (Kid)	Nichols	Sports	USA	Baseball Player - HF
Charles Benjamin (Babe)	Adams	Sports	USA	Baseball Player
Charles Brenton	Huggins	Science	USA	Medicine - Nobel Laureate
Charles Brockden	Brown	Creative Works	USA	Novelist
Charles C. (Stretch)	Murphy	Sports	USA	Basketball Player - HF
Charles Camille	Saint-Saëns	Creative Works	France	Composer
Charles Cotes-worth	Pinckney	Politics	USA	Statesman/Diplomat
Charles D.	Hyatt	Sports	USA	Basketball Player - HF
Charles Daly	Barnet	Performing Arts	USA	Band Leader - Big Band/Jazz - HF

FIRST NAME	LAST NAME	CATEGORY	COUNTRY	FAME
Charles Dana	Gibson	Creative Works	USA	Journalist - Newspaper
Charles David	Walker	Aviation	USA	Astronaut
Charles de	Montesquieu	Arts	France	Philosopher
Charles Dillon (Casey)	Stengel	Sports	USA	Baseball Manager - HF
Charles Dion (Deanie)	O'Banion	Law & Order	USA	Mafia
Charles Donagh	Maginnis	Architecture	USA	Architect - AIA Gold Medal
Charles Donald	Gemar	Aviation	USA	Astronaut
Charles Edouard	Guillaume	Science	Switzerland	Physics - Nobel Laureate
Charles Edouard le	Corbusier	Architecture	Switzerland	Architect - AIA Gold Medal
Charles Edward	Ives	Creative Works	USA	Composer
	Russell	Creative Works	USA	Author - Pulitzer
Charles Edward (Chuck)	Berry	Performing Arts	USA	Singer - Rock & Roll - HF
Charles Edward (Joe)	Greene	Sports	USA	Football Player - HF
Charles Edwin	Markham	Creative Works	USA	Poet
Charles Eldon	Brady Jr.	Aviation	USA	Astronaut
Charles Elsworth (PeeWee)	Russell	Performing Arts	USA	Jazz Clarinetist - Big Band/Jazz - HF
Charles Evans	Hughes	Law & Order	USA	Jurist/Statesman
Charles Everett	Koop	Politics	USA	Surgeon General
Charles Farrar	Browne	Creative Works	USA	Humorist
Charles Follen	McKim	Architecture	USA	Architect - AIA Gold Medal
Charles Francis	Adams	Politics	USA	Statesman
Charles François	Daubigny	Works of Art	France	Painter - Landscapes
	Gounod	Creative Works	France	Composer
Charles Frank	Bolden Jr.	Aviation	USA	Astronaut
Charles Franklin	Kettering	Science	USA	Inventor/Electrical Engineer
Charles Gardner (Old Hoss)	Radbourn	Sports	USA	Baseball Player - HF
Charles Gates	Dawes	Politics	USA	Vice-President
	Dawes	War & Peace	USA	Peace - Nobel Laureate
Charles George	Gordon	War & Peace	England	General
Charles Glover	Barkla	Science	England	Physics - Nobel Laureate
Charles Graham	Drinkwater	Sports	Canada	Hockey Player - HF
Charles Greeley	Abbot	Science	USA	Astrophysicist
Charles H. (Dick)	Spalding	Sports	USA	Soccer Player - HF
Charles Hard	Townes	Science	USA	Physics - Nobel Laureate
Charles Hardin (Buddy)	Holly (Holley)	Performing Arts	USA	Singer - Rock & Roll - HF
Charles Henri de Rouvroy	Saint-Simon	Politics	France	Reformer - Social
Charles Henry	Goren	Games	USA	Bridge Expert
Charles Henry (Charlie)	Christian	Performing Arts	USA	Jazz Guitarist - Big Band/Jazz - HF
	Christian	Performing Arts	USA	Singer - Rock & Roll - HF
Charles Henry (Chuck)	Noll	Sports	USA	Football Coach - HF
Charles Herbert (Chuck)	Klein	Sports	USA	Baseball Player - HF
Charles Herbert (Red)	Ruffing	Sports	USA	Baseball Player - HF
Charles Horace	Mayo	Science	USA	Physician
Charles Howard	McIlwain	Creative Works	USA	Author - Pulitzer
Charles J.	Pedersen	Science	USA	Chemistry - Nobel Laureate
Charles James	Fox	Politics	England	Statesman/Orator
	Haughey	Politics	Ireland	Prime Minister
	Napier	War & Peace	England	General
Charles James (Charlie)	Shavers	Performing Arts	USA	Jazz Trumpeter - Big Band/Jazz - HF
Charles James (Chick)	Hafey	Sports	USA	Baseball Player - HF
Charles Joseph	Clark	Politics	Canada	Prime Minister
Charles Joseph Sylvanus (Syl)	Apps	Sports	Canada	Hockey Player - HF
Charles Jules Henri	Nicolle	Science	France	Medicine - Nobel Laureate
Charles Kay	Ogden	Arts	England	Educator/Linguist
Charles Kenneth	Williams	Creative Works	USA	Poet - Pulitzer
Charles L.	Tiffany	Works of Art	USA	Jeweller
Charles Lacy	Veach	Aviation	USA	Astronaut
Charles Leo (Gabby)	Hartnett	Sports	USA	Baseball Player - HF
Charles Leonard (Charlie)	Gehringer	Sports	USA	Baseball Player - HF
Charles Louis (Charley)	Trippi	Sports	USA	Football Player - HF
Charles Louis Alphonse	Laveran	Science	France	Medicine - Nobel Laureate
Charles Lutwidge	Dodgson	Creative Works	England	Author/Mathematician
Charles Marie de la	Condamine	Exploration	France	Explorer - Amazon Region

SOLVER SERIES: NAME FINDER

FIRST NAME	LAST NAME	CATEGORY	COUNTRY	FAME
Charles Marie René	Leconte de Lisle	Creative Works	England	Poet
Charles Martin	Hall	Science	USA	Chemist
Charles Martin (Charlie)	Colombo	Sports	USA	Soccer Player - HF
Charles Marting (Chuck)	Jones	Creative Works	USA	Cartoonist - Road Runner
Charles McLean	Andrews	Creative Works	USA	Author - Pulitzer
Charles Melvin (Cootie)	Williams	Performing Arts	USA	Jazz Trumpeter - Big Band/Jazz - HF
Charles Milles	Manson	Law & Order	USA	Serial Killer
Charles Monroe	Schulz	Creative Works	USA	Cartoonist - Peanuts
Charles Montagu	Doughty	Creative Works	England	Poet/Travel Writer
Charles Moss	Duke Jr.	Aviation	USA	Astronaut
Charles Ormond	Eames Jr.	Business	USA	Designer - Chairs
Charles Percy	Snow	Creative Works	England	Novelist/Physicist
Charles Peter	Conrad Jr.	Aviation	USA	Astronaut
Charles Philip (Chuck)	Bednarik	Sports	USA	Football Player - HF
Charles Proteus	Steinmetz	Science	USA	Inventor/Electrical Engineer
Charles Rennie	Mackintosh	Architecture	England	Architect
Charles Robert	Darwin	Science	England	Naturalist
	Richet	Science	France	Medicine - Nobel Laureate
Charles Robert (Charley)	Taylor	Sports	USA	Football Player - HF
Charles Robert (Charlie)	Watts	Performing Arts	England	Rock & Roll - HF - Rolling Stones
Charles Robert (Chuck)	Gardiner	Sports	Scotland	Hockey Player - HF
	McKinley	Sports	USA	Tennis Player - HF
Charles Rudolf	Friml	Creative Works	USA	Composer
Charles Sanders	Peirce	Science	USA	Mathematician/Philosopher
	Pierce	Arts	USA	Philosopher
Charles Scott	Sherrington	Science	England	Medicine - Nobel Laureate
Charles Spittal (Chuck)	Robb	Politics	USA	Senator - Virginia
Charles Stedman (Chuck)	Garland	Sports	USA	Tennis Player - HF
Charles Stewart	Parnell	Politics	Ireland	Nationalist Leader
Charles T. (Tarzan)	Cooper	Sports	USA	Basketball Player - HF
Charles Talbut	Onions	Arts	England	Lexicographer
Charles Thomas (Tom)	Hooper	Sports	Canada	Hockey Player - HF
Charles Thomson Rees	Wilson	Science	England	Physics - Nobel Laureate
Charles W.	Bidwell Sr.	Sports	USA	Football Owner - HF
	Fairbanks	Politics	USA	Vice-President
Charles Wakefield	Cadman	Creative Works	USA	Composer
Charles Weedon (Del)	Shannon (Westover)	Performing Arts	USA	Singer - Rock & Roll - HF
Charles Willard	Moore	Architecture	USA	Architect - AIA Gold Medal
Charles William	Beebe	Creative Works	USA	Writer/Naturalist
	Eliot	Arts	USA	Educator
Charles William (Charlie)	Conacher	Sports	Canada	Hockey Player - HF
Charles Willson	Peale	Works of Art	USA	Painter - Portrait
Charley Frank	Pride	Performing Arts	USA	Singer - Country Music - HF
Charlie	Daniels	Performing Arts	USA	Singer
	Foxx	Performing Arts	USA	Singer
	Mingus	Performing Arts	USA	Band Leader - Big Band/Jazz - HF
	Parker	Performing Arts	USA	Jazz Saxophonist - Big Band/Jazz - HF
	Rich	Performing Arts	USA	Singer
	Rose	Creative Works	USA	Journalist - Television
	Ruggles	Performing Arts	USA	Actor
	Sheen	Performing Arts	USA	Actor
	Sifford	Sports	USA	Golfer - HF
Charlie Bird	Parker	Performing Arts	USA	Jazz Saxophonist
Charlie Elzer	Loudermilk	Performing Arts	USA	Country Music - HF - Louvin Brothers
Charlize	Theron	Performing Arts	South Africa	Actress - Academy Award
Charlotte	Brontë	Creative Works	England	Novelist
	Rae	Performing Arts	USA	Actress
Charlotte (Lottie)	Dod	Sports	England	Tennis Player - HF
Charlton	Heston	Performing Arts	USA	Actor - Academy Award
Charlton Christopher	Frantz	Performing Arts	USA	Rock & Roll - HF - The Talking Heads
Charly (Charles)	Chaplin	Performing Arts	England	Actor - Academy Award
Chazz	Palminteri	Performing Arts	USA	Actor - Acad Award Nom
Cheech	Marin	Performing Arts	USA	Comedian

FIRST NAME	LAST NAME	CATEGORY	COUNTRY	FAME
Chen Ning	Yang	Science	China	Physics - Nobel Laureate
Cheri	Oteri	Performing Arts	USA	Actress
Cherilyn (Cher)	LaPierre	Performing Arts	USA	Actress/Singer - Acad Award
Cheryl	Ladd	Performing Arts	USA	Actress
	Miller	Sports	USA	Basketball Player - HF
	Tiegs	Performing Arts	USA	Super Model
Chester	Gould	Creative Works	USA	Cartoonist - Dick Tracy
	Morris	Performing Arts	USA	Actor - Acad Award Nom
Chester Alan	Arthur	Politics	USA	President
Chester Burton (Chet)	Atkins	Performing Arts	USA	Singer/Guitarist - Country Music - HF
	Atkins	Performing Arts	USA	Singer/Guitarist - Rock & Roll - HF
Chester Trent	Lotte Jr.	Politics	USA	Senator - Mississippi
Chester William	Nimitz	War & Peace	USA	Admiral
Chet	Huntley	Creative Works	USA	Journalist - Television
Chet (Chesney Henry)	Baker Jr.	Performing Arts	USA	Jazz Trumpeter - Big Band/Jazz - HF
Chevy	Chase	Performing Arts	USA	Actor/Comedian
Chiaki	Naito-Mukai	Aviation	Japan	Astronaut
Chill	Wills	Performing Arts	USA	Actor - Acad Award Nom
Chip	Hanauer	Sports	USA	Hydro Plane Driver - HF
Chita	Rivera	Performing Arts	USA	Singer
Chloe	Sevigny	Performing Arts	USA	Actress - Acad Award Nom
Chris	Berman	Creative Works	USA	Journalist - Television
	Elliott	Performing Arts	USA	Comedian
	Hillman	Performing Arts	USA	Rock & Roll - HF - The Bryds
	Mullin	Sports	USA	Basketball Player
	Noonan	Movie Production	Australia	Director - Acad Award Nom
	Rea	Performing Arts	England	Singer
	Rock	Performing Arts	USA	Comedian
	Sarandon	Performing Arts	USA	Actor - Acad Award Nom
	Schenkel	Creative Works	USA	Journalist - Television
	Dreja	Performing Arts	England	Rock & Roll - HF - The Yardbirds
	Jasper	Performing Arts	USA	Rock & Roll - HF - Isley Brothers
	Wood	Performing Arts	England	Rock & Roll - HF - Traffic
	Cooper	Performing Arts	USA	Actor - Academy Award
Chris Austin	Hadfield	Aviation	Canada	Astronaut
Chrissie	Hynde	Performing Arts	USA	Rock & Roll - HF - The Pretenders
Christiaan	Eijkman	Science	Netherlands	Medicine - Nobel Laureate
Christian	Dior	Business	France	Fashion Designer
	Doppler	Science	Austria	Physicist/Mathematician
	Huygens	Science	Netherlands	Physicist/Astronomer
	Lacroix	Business	France	Fashion Designer
	Menn	Architecture	Switzerland	Architect
	Steinmetz	Sports	USA	Basketball Player - HF
Christian Adolph (Sonny)	Jurgensen III	Sports	USA	Football Player - HF
Christian B.	Anfinsen	Science	USA	Chemistry - Nobel Laureate
Christian de	Duve	Science	Belgium	Medicine - Nobel Laureate
	Portzamparc	Architecture	France	Architect - Pritzker Laureate
Christian Friedrich	Hebbel	Creative Works	Germany	Poet/Playwright
Christian Friedrich Samuel	Hahnemann	Science	Germany	Physician - Homeopathy
Christian Lous	Lange	War & Peace	Norway	Peace - Nobel Laureate
Christian Matthias	Mommsen	Creative Works	Germany	Literature - Nobel Laureate
Christiane	Nüsslein-Volhard	Science	Germany	Medicine - Nobel Laureate
Christie	Brinkley	Performing Arts	USA	Super Model
Christina	Applegate	Performing Arts	USA	Actress
Christina Georgina	Rossetti	Creative Works	England	Poet
Christine	Lahti	Performing Arts	USA	Actress - Acad Award Nom
Christine Ann	McVie (Perfect)	Performing Arts	England	Rock & Roll - HF - Fleetwood Mac
Christine Marie (Chris)	Evert	Sports	USA	Tennis Player - HF
Christoph Willibald	Gluck	Creative Works	Germany	Composer
Christopher	Alexander	Architecture	Austria	Architect/Writer/Teacher
	Columbus	Exploration	Italy	Explorer - Caribbean
	Cross	Performing Arts	USA	Singer/Composer
	Fry	Creative Works	England	Playwright

SOLVER SERIES: NAME FINDER

FIRST NAME	LAST NAME	CATEGORY	COUNTRY	FAME
Christopher	Lee	Performing Arts	England	Actor
	Lloyd	Performing Arts	USA	Actor
	Marlowe	Creative Works	England	Poet/Dramatist
	Newport	Exploration	England	Explorer - Jamestown
	Plummer	Performing Arts	Canada	Actor
	Reeve	Performing Arts	USA	Actor
	Walken	Performing Arts	USA	Actor - Academy Award
	Wren	Architecture	England	Architect
Christopher (Christy)	Mathewson	Sports	USA	Baseball Player - HF
Christopher Houston (Kit)	Carson	Exploration	USA	Frontiersman - America
Christopher J. (Chris)	Dodd	Politics	USA	Senator - Connecticut
Christopher Martin	Wieland	Creative Works	Germany	Poet/Novelist/Translator
Christopher William Bradshaw	Isherwood	Creative Works	USA	Writer
Christy	Turlington	Performing Arts	USA	Super Model
Chubby	Checker	Performing Arts	USA	Singer
Chuck	Barksdale	Performing Arts	USA	Rock & Roll - HF - The Dells
	Cockerham	Performing Arts	USA	Rock & Roll - HF - The Drifters
	Connors	Performing Arts	USA	Actor
	Mangione	Performing Arts	USA	Jazz Flugel Horn
	Norris	Performing Arts	USA	Actor
Chuck Elwood	Yeager	Aviation	USA	Pilot - Sound Barrier
Chung Chen	Chiang Kaishek	Politics	China	Head of Government
Cicely	Tyson	Performing Arts	USA	Actress - Acad Award Nom
Cifford O.	Hagen	Sports	USA	Basketball Player - HF
Cilla	Black	Performing Arts	England	Singer
Cimabue	Giovanni	Works of Art	Italy	Painter
Cindy	Birdsong	Performing Arts	USA	Rock & Roll - HF - The Supremes
	Crawford	Performing Arts	USA	Super Model
	Williams	Performing Arts	USA	Actress
Cissy	Houston	Performing Arts	USA	Singer
Claes	Oldenburg	Works of Art	Sweden	Sculptor - Pop
Claiborne de Borda	Pell	Politics	USA	Senator - Rhode Island
Claire	Bloom	Performing Arts	England	Actress
	Trevor	Performing Arts	USA	Actress - Academy Award
Clara	Barton	Business	USA	Philanthropist - Red Cross
	Bow	Performing Arts	USA	Actress
Clarence	Brown	Movie Production	USA	Director - Acad Award Nom
	Thomas	Law & Order	USA	Justice - Supreme Court
	White	Performing Arts	USA	Rock & Roll - HF - The Bryds
	Williams	Performing Arts	USA	Jazz Pianist/Composer - Big Band/Jazz - HF
Clarence (Happy)	Day	Sports	Canada	Hockey Player - HF
Clarence Arthur (Dazzy)	Vance	Sports	USA	Baseball Player - HF
Clarence Charles	Beck	Creative Works	USA	Cartoonist - Captain Marvel
Clarence Eugene (Hank)	Snow	Performing Arts	Canada	Singer - Canadian Music - HF
	Snow	Performing Arts	Canada	Singer - Country Music - HF
Clarence James (Peck)	Griffin	Sports	USA	Tennis Player - HF
Clarence McKay (Ace)	Parker	Sports	USA	Football Player - HF
Clarence Munroe	Clark	Sports	USA	Tennis Player - HF
Clarence S.	Stein	Architecture	USA	Architect - AIA Gold Medal
Clarence Seward	Darrow	Law & Order	USA	Lawyer
Clarens William	Nelson	Aviation	USA	Astronaut
Clark	Gable	Performing Arts	USA	Actor - Academy Award
	Gillies	Sports	Canada	Hockey Player - HF
	Terry	Performing Arts	USA	Jazz Trumpeter - Big Band/Jazz - HF
Clark Calvin	Griffith	Sports	USA	Baseball Executive -HF
Claude	Bernard	Science	France	Physiologist
	Cohen-Tannoudji	Science	France	Physics - Nobel Laureate
	Debussy	Creative Works	France	Composer
	Jarman Jr	Performing Arts	USA	Actor - Academy Award
	Lelouch	Movie Production	France	Director - Acad Award Nom
	Levi-Strauss	Arts	France	Anthropologist
	Monet	Works of Art	France	Painter
	Nicollier	Aviation	Switzerland	Astronaut

FIRST NAME	LAST NAME	CATEGORY	COUNTRY	FAME
Claude	Rains	Performing Arts	England	Actor - Acad Award Nom
	Simon	Creative Works	France	Literature - Nobel Laureate
	Thornhill	Performing Arts	USA	Band Leader - Big Band/Jazz - HF
Claude Adrien	Helvétius	Arts	France	Philosopher
Claude Driskett	Hopkins	Performing Arts	USA	Band Leader - Big Band/Jazz - HF
Claude Earl (Chuck)	Rayner	Sports	Canada	Hockey Player - HF
Claude Fayette	Bragdon	Architecture	USA	Architect/Painter/Author
Claude Halstead Va	Tyne	Creative Works	USA	Author - Pulitzer
Claude Joseph Rouget de	Lisle	Creative Works	France	Composer/Army Officer
Claude Nicholas	Ledoux	Architecture	France	Architect
Claudia	Schiffer	Performing Arts	Germany	Super Model
Claudia (Ladybird) Alta	Johnson	Politics	USA	First Lady
Claudio	Arrau	Performing Arts	Chile	Pianist
	Vender	Architecture	Italy	Architect
Claudio Giovanni Antonio	Monteverdi	Creative Works	Italy	Composer
Claudius	Galen	Science	Greece	Writer/Physician
Clayton	Moore	Performing Arts	USA	Actor
Clea	Lewis	Performing Arts	USA	Actress
Cleavon	Little	Performing Arts	USA	Actor
Clement Clarke	Moore	Creative Works	USA	Poet
Clément Philibert Léo	Delibes	Creative Works	France	Composer
Clement Richard	Attlee	Politics	England	Prime Minster
Cleo	Laine	Performing Arts	England	Singer
Clete	Boyer	Sports	USA	Baseball Player
Cleveland	Amory	Creative Works	USA	Author
Cliff	Arquette	Performing Arts	USA	Actor/Comedian
	Drysdale	Sports	South Africa	Tennis Player
	Richard	Performing Arts	India	Singer
	Robertson	Performing Arts	USA	Actor - Academy Award
	Williams	Performing Arts	England	Rock & Roll - HF - AC/DC
Clifford	Brown	Performing Arts	USA	Jazz Trumpeter - Big Band/Jazz - HF
	Odets	Creative Works	USA	Playwright
	Roberts	Sports	USA	Golf Promoter - HF
Clifford Franklin (Cliff)	Battles	Sports	USA	Football Player - HF
Clifford G.	Shull	Science	USA	Physics - Nobel Laureate
Clifton	Webb	Performing Arts	USA	Actor - Acad Award Nom
Clifton Curtis	Williams Jr.	Aviation	USA	Astronaut
Clint	Black	Performing Arts	USA	Singer
	Eastwood	Performing Arts	USA	Actor - Acad Award Nom
	Murchison	Business	USA	Publishing/Oil Industry
	Eastwood	Movie Production	USA	Director - Academy Award
Clinton James	Smith	Sports	Canada	Hockey Player - HF
Clinton Joseph	Davisson	Science	USA	Physics - Nobel Laureate
Clinton S. (Clint)	Benedict	Sports	Canada	Hockey Player - HF
Clive	Barker	Creative Works	England	Author
	Barker	Movie Production	England	Director
	Barnes	Creative Works	USA	Journalist - Newspaper
	Owen	Performing Arts	England	Actor - Acad Award Nom
Clive Staples	Lewis	Creative Works	England	Writer
Clive W.J.	Granger	Arts	England	Economics - Nobel Laureate
Clorindo	Testa	Architecture	Italy	Architect
Cloris	Leachman	Performing Arts	USA	Actress - Academy Award
Clough	Williams-Ellis	Architecture	England	Architect
Clu	Gulager	Performing Arts	USA	Actor
Clyde	Drexler	Sports	USA	Basketball Player - HF
Clyde Champion	Barrow	Law & Order	USA	Outlaw
Clyde Douglas (Bulldog)	Turner	Sports	USA	Football Player - HF
Clyde E.	Lovellette	Sports	USA	Basketball Player
Clyde Jackson	Browne	Performing Arts	Germany	Singer - Rock & Roll - HF
Clyde Julian (Red)	Foley	Performing Arts	USA	Singer - Country Music - HF
Clyde Lensley	McPhatter	Performing Arts	USA	Singer - Rock & Roll - HF
Coco	Chanel	Business	France	Fashion Designer
Cokie	Roberts	Creative Works	USA	Journalist - Television

SOLVER SERIES: NAME FINDER

FIRST NAME	LAST NAME	CATEGORY	COUNTRY	FAME
Cola di	Rienzi	Politics	Italy	Patriot/Political Reformer
Cole	Porter	Creative Works	USA	Composer - Popular Songs
Coleman Randolph	Hawkins	Performing Arts	USA	Jazz Saxophonist - Big Band/Jazz - HF
Colette	Marchand	Performing Arts	France	Actress - Acad Award Nom
Colin Luther	Powell	Politics	USA	Secretary of State
	Powell	War & Peace	USA	General
Collis Potter	Huntington	Business	USA	Railway Magnate
Colm	Meany	Performing Arts	Ireland	Actor
Comer Vann	Woodward	Creative Works	USA	Author - Pulitzer
Conchata	Ferrell	Performing Arts	USA	Actress
Condé Montrose	Nast	Business	USA	Publishing/Magazine
Connie	Chung	Creative Works	USA	Journalist - Television
	Francis	Performing Arts	USA	Singer
	Sellecca	Performing Arts	USA	Actress
	Stevens	Performing Arts	USA	Actress
Conrad	Bain	Performing Arts	Canada	Actor
	Black	Business	Canada	Media Magnate
	Hilton	Business	USA	Hotelier
	Nagel	Performing Arts	USA	Actor
	Richter	Creative Works	USA	Novelist - Pulitzer
	Veidt	Performing Arts	Germany	Actor
Conrad Potter	Aiken	Creative Works	USA	Poet - Pulitzer
Constance	Bennett	Performing Arts	USA	Actress
	Garnett	Arts	England	Translator
Constance McLaughlin	Green	Creative Works	USA	Author - Pulitzer
Constantin	Brancusi	Works of Art	Romania	Sculptor
Constantine Gene	Mako	Sports	Hungary	Tennis Player - HF
Constantinos Apostolou	Doxiadis	Architecture	Greece	Architect
Conte Giacomo	Leopardi	Arts	Italy	Philosopher/Poet
Cora	Baird	Performing Arts	USA	Puppeteer
Corbin	Bernsen	Performing Arts	USA	Actor
Cordell	Hull	Politics	USA	Statesman
	Hull	War & Peace	USA	Peace - Nobel Laureate
Coretta Scott	King	Politics	USA	Wife - Martin Luther King
Corey	Feldman	Performing Arts	USA	Actor
	Haim	Performing Arts	Canada	Actor
	Pavin	Sports	USA	Golfer
Corinne	Griffith	Performing Arts	USA	Actress - Acad Award Nom
Corneille Jean François	Heymans	Science	Belgium	Medicine - Nobel Laureate
Cornel	Wilde	Performing Arts	USA	Actor - Acad Award Nom
Cornelis	Floris de Vriend	Architecture	Belgium	Architect
	Jansen	Arts	Netherlands	Theologian
Cornelius	Vanderbilt	Business	USA	Industrialist/Capitalist
"Cornelius (Connie, The Hawk)"	Hawkins	Sports	USA	Basketball Player - HF
Cornelius Alexander (Connie)	Mack	Sports	USA	Baseball Manager - HF
Cornelius Mahoney (Neil)	Sheehan	Creative Works	USA	Author - Pulitzer
Corrado (Connie)	Codarini	Performing Arts	Canada	Canadian Music - HF - The Four Lads
Costa	Gavras	Movie Production	Greece	Director - Acad Award Nom
Cotton	Mather	Creative Works	USA	Writer/Clergyman
Count (William)	Basie	Performing Arts	USA	Band Leader - Big Band/Jazz - HF
Countee	Cullen	Creative Works	USA	Poet
Courtenay	Cox	Performing Arts	USA	Actress
Coventry Kersey Dighton	Patmore	Creative Works	England	Poet
Cozy	Cole	Performing Arts	USA	Jazz Drummer
Craig	Breedlove	Sports	USA	Race Car Driver - HF
	Stadler	Sports	USA	Golfer
Creighton Williams	Abrams Jr.	War & Peace	USA	General - Army
Cristiano	Ronaldo	Sports	Brazil	Soccer Player
Crystal	Gayle	Performing Arts	USA	Singer
Cuba	Gooding Jr.	Performing Arts	USA	Actor - Academy Award
Curly	Howard	Performing Arts	USA	Comedian
Curt	Gowdy	Creative Works	USA	Journalist - Television
	Warner	Sports	USA	Football Player

FIRST NAME	LAST NAME	CATEGORY	COUNTRY	FAME
Curtis	Cokes	Sports	USA	Boxer - HF
	Hanson	Movie Production	USA	Director - Acad Award Nom
	Mayfield	Performing Arts	USA	Rock & Roll - HF - The Impressions
	Strange	Sports	USA	Golfer
	Turner	Sports	USA	Race Car Driver - HF
Curtis Emerson Le	May	War & Peace	USA	General - Air Force
Curtis Lee	Brown Jr.	Aviation	USA	Astronaut
Cuthbert Collingwood	Tinling	Sports	England	Tennis Player - HF
Cy	Coleman	Creative Works	USA	Composer
Cybil	Shepherd	Performing Arts	USA	Actress/Model
Cyd	Charisse	Performing Arts	USA	Actress/Dancer
Cyndi	Lauper	Performing Arts	USA	Singer
Cynthia	Weil	Creative Works	USA	Composer/Song Writer
Cyrano de	Bergerac	Creative Works	France	Writer/Soldier
Cyril	Cusack	Performing Arts	South Africa	Actor
	Pearson	Business	England	Publishing
	Ritchard	Performing Arts	Australia	Comedian
Cyril Joseph (Cy)	Denneny	Sports	Canada	Hockey Player - HF
Cyril Norman	Hinshelwood	Science	England	Chemistry - Nobel Laureate
Cyrus	Adler	Creative Works	USA	Writer
	Clark	Business	USA	Entrepreneur
	Eaton	Business	USA	Industrialist
Cyrus Hall	McCormick	Science	USA	Inventor - Reaping Machine
Cyrus West	Field	Business	USA	Industrialist
Czeslaw	Milosz	Creative Works	Poland	Literature - Nobel Laureate
Dabney	Coleman	Performing Arts	USA	Actor
Daffydd Rhys	Williams	Aviation	Canada	Astronaut
Dag Hjalmar Agne Carl	Hammarskjöld	Politics	Sweden	Secretary - United Nations
	Hammarskjöld	War & Peace	Sweden	Peace - Nobel Laureate
Dale	Earnhardt	Sports	USA	Race Car Driver - HF
	Evans	Performing Arts	USA	Actress
	Maharidge	Works of Art	USA	Photographer - Pulitzer
	Murphy	Sports	USA	Baseball Player
	Robertson	Performing Arts	USA	Actor
	Douglass	Sports	USA	Golfer
Dale (Ducky)	Hawerchuk	Sports	Canada	Hockey Player - HF
Dale Allan	Gardner	Aviation	USA	Astronaut
Dale Leon	Bumpers	Politics	USA	Senator
Daley	Thompson	Sports	England	Olympic Decathlete
Dámaso Peréz (Mambo King)	Prado	Performing Arts	Cuba	Pianist
Damon	Wayans	Performing Arts	USA	Comedian
Dan	Aykroyd	Performing Arts	Canada	Actor - Acad Award Nom
	Blocker	Performing Arts	USA	Actor
	Dailey	Performing Arts	USA	Actor - Acad Award Nom
	Duryea	Performing Arts	USA	Actor
	Fogelberg	Performing Arts	USA	Singer
	Hill	Performing Arts	Canada	Singer
	Kiley	Architecture	USA	Architect - Jefferson Medal
	Maskell	Sports	England	Tennis Player - HF
	O'Herlihy	Performing Arts	Ireland	Actor - Acad Award Nom
	Rostenkowski	Politics	USA	Congressman - Illinois
	Rowan	Performing Arts	USA	Comedian
	Seals	Performing Arts	USA	Singer
Dan (Chief)	George	Performing Arts	Canada	Actor - Acad Award Nom
Dana	Andrews	Performing Arts	USA	Actor
	Carvey	Performing Arts	USA	Comedian
	Delany	Performing Arts	USA	Actress
	Wynter	Performing Arts	Germany	Actress
Dane	Clark	Performing Arts	USA	Actor
Daniel	Barenboim	Performing Arts	Argentina	Conductor/Pianist
	Bernoulli	Science	Switzerland	Physicist
	Boone	Exploration	USA	Frontiersman - Kentucky
	Bovet	Science	Italy	Medicine - Nobel Laureate

SOLVER SERIES: NAME FINDER

FIRST NAME	LAST NAME	CATEGORY	COUNTRY	FAME
Daniel	Day-Lewis	Performing Arts	England	Actor - Academy Award
	Defoe	Creative Works	England	Writer
	Guggenheim	Business	USA	Industrialist/Philanthropist
	Jones	Arts	England	Phonetician
	Kahneman	Arts	USA	Economics - Nobel Laureate
	Lanois	Performing Arts	Canada	Musician/Producer - Canadian Music - HF
	Libeskind	Architecture	Poland	Architect
	Massey	Performing Arts	England	Actor - Acad Award Nom
	Morgan	War & Peace	USA	Revolutionary General
	Nathans	Science	USA	Medicine - Nobel Laureate
	O'Connell	Politics	Ireland	Nationalist Leader
	Shays	War & Peace	USA	Revolutionary Soldier
	Webster	Politics	USA	Statesman/Orator
	Yergin	Creative Works	USA	Author - Pulitzer
	Zaragoza	Sports	Mexico	Boxer - HF
Daniel C.	Tsui	Science	USA	Physics - Nobel Laureate
Daniel Carleton	Gajdusek	Science	USA	Medicine - Nobel Laureate
Daniel Charles	Brandenstein	Aviation	USA	Astronaut
Daniel Chester	French	Works of Art	USA	Sculptor
Daniel Constantine (Dan)	Marino Jr.	Sports	USA	Football Player - HF
Daniel D.	Tompkins	Politics	USA	Vice-President
Daniel Farrell (Dan)	Reeves	Sports	USA	Football Owner - HF
Daniel Francis (Dan)	Fouts	Sports	USA	Football Player - HF
Daniel Francois Esprit	Auber	Creative Works	France	Composer/Opera
Daniel Hudson	Burnham	Architecture	USA	Architect
Daniel Irving (Dan)	Rather	Creative Works	USA	Journalist - Television
Daniel J.	Boorstein	Creative Works	USA	Author - Pulitzer
	Travanti	Performing Arts	USA	Actor
Daniel John	Fortmann	Sports	USA	Football Player - HF
Daniel Ken	Inouye	Politics	USA	Senator - Hawaii
Daniel L.	McFadden	Arts	USA	Economics - Nobel Laureate
Daniel Lee (Dan)	Dierdorf	Sports	USA	Football Player - HF
Daniel M. (Dan)	Rooney	Sports	USA	Football Team President
Daniel Oliver (Dan)	Hampton	Sports	USA	Football Player - HF
Daniel P. (Dan)	Issel	Sports	USA	Basketball Player - HF
Daniel Patrick	Moynihan	Architecture	USA	Architect - Jefferson Medal
Daniel Patrick (Pat)	Moynihan	Politics	USA	Senator - New York
Daniel Robert (Bob)	Graham	Politics	USA	Senator - Florida
Daniel Sexton (Dan)	Gurney	Sports	USA	Race Car Driver - HF
Daniela	Pestova	Performing Arts	Czechoslovakia	Super Model
Danny	Aiello	Performing Arts	USA	Actor - Acad Award Nom
	Ainge	Sports	USA	Basketball Player
	Glover	Performing Arts	USA	Actor
	Kaye	Performing Arts	USA	Actor
	Kirwan	Performing Arts	England	Rock & Roll - HF - Fleetwood Mac
	Sullivan	Sports	USA	Race Car Driver
	Thomas	Performing Arts	USA	Comedian
Danny De	Vito	Performing Arts	USA	Actor
Dante	Alighieri	Creative Works	Italy	Poet
Dante Bert Joseph	Lavelli	Sports	USA	Football Player - HF
Dante Gabriel	Rossetti	Creative Works	England	Poet/Painter
Daphne du	Maurier	Creative Works	England	Author/Playwright
Dario	Fo	Creative Works	Italy	Literature - Nobel Laureate
Darius	Milhaud	Creative Works	France	Composer
Darlene	Love	Performing Arts	USA	Singer
Darlene Ruth	Hard	Sports	USA	Tennis Player - HF
Darrell	Evans	Sports	USA	Baseball Player
	Waltrip	Sports	USA	Race Car Driver - HF
Darren	McGavin	Performing Arts	USA	Actor
Darryl	Ponicsan	Creative Works	USA	Screenwriter
	Strawberry	Sports	USA	Baseball Player
Darryl F.	Zanuck	Movie Production	USA	Director
Darryl Glen	Sittler	Sports	Canada	Hockey Player - HF

FIRST NAME	LAST NAME	CATEGORY	COUNTRY	FAME
Daryl	Hall	Performing Arts	USA	Singer
	Hannah	Performing Arts	USA	Actress
Dashiell	Hammett	Creative Works	USA	Author
Dave	Barry	Creative Works	USA	Journalist - Newspaper
	Brubeck	Performing Arts	USA	Jazz Pianist - Big Band/Jazz - HF
	Hill	Sports	USA	Golfer
	Kingman	Sports	USA	Baseball Player
	Marr	Sports	USA	Golfer
	Matthews	Performing Arts	South Africa	Singer/Guitarist
	Prater	Performing Arts	USA	Rock & Roll - HF - Sam & Dave
	Sommerville	Performing Arts	Canada	Canadian Music - HF - The Diamonds
	Stieb	Sports	USA	Baseball Player
	Stockton	Sports	USA	Golfer
Dave (The Edge)	Evans	Performing Arts	Ireland	Rock & Roll - HF - U2
Davey	Allison	Sports	USA	Race Car Driver - HF
	Brown	Sports	USA	Soccer Player - HF
	Johnson	Sports	USA	Baseball Player
David	Auburn	Creative Works	USA	Dramatist - Pulitzer
	Baltimore	Science	USA	Medicine - Nobel Laureate
	Beatty	War & Peace	England	Admiral
	Beckham	Sports	England	Soccer Player
	Belasco	Creative Works	USA	Playwright/Actor
	Ben-Gurion	Politics	Israel	Prime Minster
	Birney	Performing Arts	USA	Actor
	Brenner	Performing Arts	USA	Comedian
	Broder	Creative Works	USA	Journalist - Newspaper
	Byrne	Performing Arts	Scotland	Rock & Roll - HF - The Talking Heads
	Carradine	Performing Arts	USA	Actor
	Cassidy	Performing Arts	USA	Singer/Actor
	Cone	Sports	USA	Baseball Player
	Crosby	Performing Arts	USA	Rock & Roll - HF - Crosby Stills & Nash
	Crosby	Performing Arts	USA	Rock & Roll - HF - The Bryds
	Dale	Business	England	Textile Industry
	Doyle	Performing Arts	USA	Actor
	Dukes	Performing Arts	USA	Actor
	Duval	Sports	USA	Golfer
	Essex	Performing Arts	England	Singer
	Farragut	War & Peace	USA	Naval Commander
	Foster	Performing Arts	Canada	Musician/Composer - Canadian Music - HF
	Frost	Creative Works	England	Journalist - Television
	Garrick	Performing Arts	England	Actor/Theatrical Manager
	Gates	Performing Arts	USA	Singer
	Graham	Sports	Australia	Golfer
	Gray	Sports	England	Tennis Reporter - HF
	Grayson	Creative Works	USA	Author
	Groh	Performing Arts	USA	Actor
	Halberstam	Creative Works	USA	Journalist - Pulitzer
	Hartman	Creative Works	USA	Journalist - Television
	Hemmings	Performing Arts	England	Actor
	Hockney	Works of Art	England	Painter/Photographer
	Hume	Arts	Scotland	Philosopher/Historian
	Janssen	Performing Arts	USA	Actor
	Keith	Performing Arts	USA	Actor
	Lean	Movie Production	England	Director - Academy Award
	Leisure	Performing Arts	USA	Comedian
	Letterman	Performing Arts	USA	Show Host/Comedian
	Levine	Creative Works	USA	Cartoonist - Political
	Livingstone	Exploration	Scotland	Explorer - Africa
	Lloyd George	Politics	England	Prime Minister
	Low	Creative Works	England	Cartoonist - Political
	Lynch	Movie Production	USA	Director - Acad Award Nom
	Lynch	Performing Arts	USA	Rock & Roll - HF - The Platters
	Mamet	Creative Works	USA	Dramatist - Pulitzer

225

SOLVER SERIES: NAME FINDER

FIRST NAME	LAST NAME	CATEGORY	COUNTRY	FAME
David	McCallum	Performing Arts	Scotland	Actor
	McCullough	Creative Works	USA	Author - Pulitzer
	Merrick	Movie Production	USA	Director
	Nelson	Performing Arts	USA	Actor/Producer
	Niven	Performing Arts	England	Actor - Academy Award
	Paymer	Performing Arts	USA	Actor - Acad Award Nom
	Pearson	Sports	USA	Race Car Driver - HF
	Rabe	Creative Works	USA	Screenwriter/Playwright
	Remnick	Creative Works	USA	Author - Pulitzer
	Ricardo	Arts	England	Economist
	Rizzio	Performing Arts	Italy	Violinist
	Seville	Performing Arts	USA	Actor
	Smith	Works of Art	USA	Painter - Abstract Expressionist
	Soul	Performing Arts	USA	Actor
	Spade	Performing Arts	USA	Comedian
	Steinberg	Performing Arts	Canada	Comedian
	Storey	Creative Works	England	Author/Playwright
	Teniers	Works of Art	Italy	Painter
	Thompson	Exploration	Canada	Explorer - America West
	Thompson	Sports	USA	Basketball Player - HF
	Trimble	War & Peace	England	Peace - Nobel Laureate
	Wayne	Performing Arts	USA	Actor
David (Dave)	Bing	Sports	USA	Basketball Player - HF
	Debusschere	Sports	USA	Basketball Player - HF
	Wilcox	Sports	USA	Football Player - HF
David (Davie)	Crockett	Exploration	USA	Frontiersman - America
David (Robert David)	Bowie (Hayward-Jones)	Performing Arts	England	Singer - Rock & Roll - HF
David (Son of Sam)	Berkowitz	Law & Order	USA	Serial Killer
David (Sweeney)	Schriner	Sports	Russia	Hockey Player - HF
David Brion	Davis	Creative Works	USA	Author - Pulitzer
David Carl	Hilmers	Aviation	USA	Astronaut
David D. (Deacon)	Jones	Sports	USA	Football Player - HF
David Dean	Rusk	Politics	USA	Secretary of State
David Dixon	Porter	War & Peace	USA	Union Admiral - Civil War
David Elton	Trueblood	Arts	USA	Philosopher/Author/Theologian
David Frederick	Attenborough	Arts	England	Anthropologist
David Friedrich	Gilly	Architecture	Germany	Architect
David Fyodorovich	Oistrakh	Performing Arts	Russia	Violinist
David H.	Hubel	Science	USA	Medicine - Nobel Laureate
David Hackett	Fischer	Creative Works	USA	Author - Pulitzer
	Souter	Law & Order	USA	Justice - Supreme Court
David Henry	Clayton-Thomas	Performing Arts	England	Singer - Canadian Music - HF
David Herbert	Donald	Creative Works	USA	Author - Pulitzer
	Lawrence	Creative Works	England	Poet/Novelist
David J.	Garrow	Creative Works	USA	Author - Pulitzer
	Gross	Science	USA	Physics - Nobel Laureate
	Mays	Creative Works	USA	Author - Pulitzer
David James (Dave)	Bancroft	Sports	USA	Baseball Player - HF
David John	Gilmour	Performing Arts	England	Rock & Roll - HF - Pink Floyd
David John (Dave)	Casper	Sports	USA	Football Player - HF
David K.	Shipler	Creative Works	USA	Author - Pulitzer
David Lee	Roth	Performing Arts	USA	Singer
David Levering	Lewis	Creative Works	USA	Author - Pulitzer
David Lewelyn	Griffith	Movie Production	USA	Director/Producer
David Lloyd	George	Politics	England	Prime Minister
David M.	Lee	Science	USA	Physics - Nobel Laureate
	Potter	Creative Works	USA	Author - Pulitzer
David Mark (Dave)	Winfield	Sports	USA	Baseball Player - HF
David Mathieson	Walker	Aviation	USA	Astronaut
David Matthew	Kennedy	Creative Works	USA	Author - Pulitzer
David McClure	Brinkley	Creative Works	USA	Journalist - Television
David McDowell	Brown	Aviation	USA	Astronaut
David Michael (Dave)	Keon	Sports	Canada	Hockey Player - HF

FIRST NAME	LAST NAME	CATEGORY	COUNTRY	FAME
David Norman	Dinkins	Politics	USA	Mayor - New York City
David O	Selznick	Movie Production	USA	Director
David Ogden	Stiers	Performing Arts	USA	Actor
David Randolph	Scott	Aviation	USA	Astronaut
David Russell Gordon (Dave)	Davies	Performing Arts	England	Rock & Roll - HF - The Kinks
David W. (Dave)	Cowens	Sports	USA	Basketball Player - HF
Davis	Love III	Sports	USA	Golfer
Davis Eli (David)	Ruffin	Performing Arts	USA	Rock & Roll - HF - The Temptations
Davy	Jones	Performing Arts	England	Singer
Dawn	Fraser	Sports	Australia	Olympic Swimmer
De Benneville (Bert)	Bell	Sports	USA	Football Commissioner - HF
De Ford	Bailey	Performing Arts	USA	Singer - Country Music - HF
Dean	Chance	Sports	USA	Baseball Player
	Jagger	Performing Arts	USA	Actor - Academy Award
	Stockwell	Performing Arts	USA	Actor - Acad Award Nom
	Jones	Performing Arts	USA	Actor
	Martin	Performing Arts	USA	Singer
Dean Gooderham	Acheson	Creative Works	USA	Author - Pulitzer
	Acheson	Politics	USA	Secretary of State
Dean Ray	Koontz	Creative Works	USA	Author
Deane	Beman	Sports	USA	Golfer - HF
Deanna	Durbin	Performing Arts	Canada	Actress - Academy Award
Deanne	Fitzmaurice	Works of Art	USA	Photographer - Pulitzer
Debbie	Allen	Performing Arts	USA	Actress
	Gibson	Performing Arts	USA	Singer
	Reynolds	Performing Arts	USA	Actress - Acad Award Nom
Debby	Boone	Performing Arts	USA	Singer
Debi	Thomas	Sports	USA	Olympic Skater
Deborah	Adair	Performing Arts	USA	Actress
	Harry	Performing Arts	USA	Singer
	Kerr	Performing Arts	Scotland	Actress - Acad Award Nom
Debra	Messing	Performing Arts	USA	Actress
	Winger	Performing Arts	USA	Actress - Acad Award Nom
Declan Patrick (Elvis)	Costello (MacManus)	Performing Arts	England	Rock & Roll - HF - The Attractions
Dee Dee	Sharp	Performing Arts	USA	Singer
Dee Wallace	Stone	Performing Arts	USA	Actress
Deek	Watson	Performing Arts	USA	Rock & Roll - HF - The Ink Spots
DeForest	Kelley	Performing Arts	USA	Actor
Deidre	Hall	Performing Arts	USA	Actress
Deion	Sanders	Sports	USA	Baseball Player
Del	Shannon	Performing Arts	USA	Singer
Delbert	Mann	Movie Production	USA	Director - Academy Award
Delia	Ephron	Performing Arts	USA	Actress
	Sheppard	Performing Arts	Denmark	Actress
Della	Reese	Performing Arts	USA	Actress/Singer
Delta	Burke	Performing Arts	USA	Actress
Demetri	Porphyrios	Architecture	Greece	Architect
Demetrios	Ypsilanti	War & Peace	Greece	Revolutionary Leader
Demi	Moore	Performing Arts	USA	Actress
Demond	Wilson	Performing Arts	USA	Actor
Denholm	Elliott	Performing Arts	England	Actor - Acad Award Nom
Denis	Diderot	Arts	France	Philosopher/Encyclopedist
	Hulme	Sports	New Zealand	Race Car Driver - HF
	Savard	Sports	Canada	Hockey Player - HF
Denis Charles	Potvin	Sports	Canada	Hockey Player - HF
Denise	Curry	Sports	USA	Basketball Player - HF
Denise Scott	Brown	Architecture	USA	Architect
Dennis	Bergkamp	Sports	Netherlands	Soccer Player
	Gabor	Science	England	Physics - Nobel Laureate
	Hopper	Performing Arts	USA	Actor - Acad Award Nom
	Miller	Performing Arts	USA	Comedian
	O'Keefe	Performing Arts	USA	Actor
	Quaid	Performing Arts	USA	Actor

SOLVER SERIES: NAME FINDER

FIRST NAME	LAST NAME	CATEGORY	COUNTRY	FAME
Dennis	Rodman	Sports	USA	Basketball Player
	Weaver	Performing Arts	USA	Actor
	Wilson	Performing Arts	USA	Rock & Roll - HF - The Beach Boys
	Edwards	Performing Arts	USA	Rock & Roll - HF - The Temptations
Dennis (Denny) Gerrard	Doherty	Performing Arts	Canada	Canadian Music - HF - Mamas & Papas
	Doherty	Performing Arts	Canada	Rock & Roll - HF - Mamas & Papas
Dennis Joseph (Dan)	Brouthers	Sports	USA	Baseball Player - HF
Dennis Lee	Eckersley	Sports	USA	Baseball Player - HF
Denton True (Cy)	Young	Sports	USA	Baseball Player - HF
Denzel	Washington	Performing Arts	USA	Actor - Academy Award
Derek	Jacobi	Performing Arts	England	Actor
	Walcott	Creative Works	Saint Lucia	Literature - Nobel Laureate
Derek H.R.	Barton	Science	England	Chemistry - Nobel Laureate
Des	O'Connor	Performing Arts	England	Singer
Desi	Arnaz	Performing Arts	Cuba	Actor/Musician
Desiderius	Erasmus	Arts	Netherlands	Humanist/Theologian
Desmond Mplio	Tutu	Politics	South Africa	Activist - Human Rights
	Tutu	War & Peace	South Africa	Peace - Nobel Laureate
DeWayne Louis (Tiny)	Lund	Sports	USA	Race Car Driver - HF
Dewey	Martin	Performing Arts	Canada	Rock & Roll - HF - Buffalo Springfield
DeWitt	Clinton	Politics	USA	Governor - New York
Dexter	Gordon	Performing Arts	USA	Actor - Acad Award Nom
	Gordon	Performing Arts	USA	Jazz Saxophonist - Big Band/Jazz - HF
Diahann	Carroll	Performing Arts	USA	Actress - Acad Award Nom
Dian	Fossey	Science	USA	Ethologist
Diana	Dors	Performing Arts	England	Actress
	Muldaur	Performing Arts	USA	Actress
	Rigg	Performing Arts	England	Actress
	Scarwid	Performing Arts	USA	Actress - Acad Award Nom
	Wynyard	Performing Arts	England	Actress - Acad Award Nom
Diane	Arbus	Works of Art	USA	Photographer
	Cilento	Performing Arts	New Guinea	Actress - Acad Award Nom
	Keaton	Performing Arts	USA	Actress - Academy Award
	Ladd	Performing Arts	USA	Actress - Acad Award Nom
	Lane	Performing Arts	USA	Actress - Acad Award Nom
	McBain	Performing Arts	USA	Actress
	McWhorter	Creative Works	USA	Author - Pulitzer
	Sawyer	Creative Works	USA	Journalist - Television
	Varsi	Performing Arts	USA	Actress - Acad Award Nom
Diane Ersnastine (Diana)	Ross	Performing Arts	USA	Actress - Acad Award Nom
	Ross	Performing Arts	USA	Rock & Roll - HF - The Supremes
Dianne	Wiest	Performing Arts	USA	Actress - Academy Award
Dianne Goldman Berman	Feinstein	Politics	USA	Senator - California
Dick	Button	Sports	USA	Olympic Skater
	Cavett	Performing Arts	USA	Show Host/Comedian
	Clark	Performing Arts	USA	Producer
	Fosbury	Sports	USA	Olympic High Jumper
	Gregory	Performing Arts	USA	Comedian/Politician
	Martin	Performing Arts	USA	Comedian
	Nicolosi	Arts	USA	Philosopher
	Powell	Performing Arts	USA	Actor
	Smothers	Performing Arts	USA	Comedian
	Trickle	Sports	USA	Race Car Driver
Dick	Turpin	Law & Order	England	Highwayman
Dick Van	Dyke	Performing Arts	USA	Actor
Dickey (Forrest Richard)	Betts	Performing Arts	USA	Rock & Roll - HF - Allmann Brothers Band
Dickinson W.	Richards	Science	USA	Medicine - Nobel Laureate
Diderik	Buxtehude	Creative Works	Denmark	Composer/Organist
Didi	Conn	Performing Arts	USA	Actress
Didier	Pitre	Sports	Canada	Hockey Player - HF
Diego	Rivera	Works of Art	Mexico	Painter
Diego Armando	Maradona	Sports	Italy	Soccer Player
Diego Rodríguez de Silva	Velázquez	Works of Art	Spain	Painter

FIRST NAME	LAST NAME	CATEGORY	COUNTRY	FAME
Dimitris	Pikionis	Architecture	Greece	Architect
Dina	Merrill	Performing Arts	USA	Actress
Dinah	Shore	Performing Arts	USA	Singer
	Shore	Sports	USA	Golfer - HF
Dino	Danelli	Performing Arts	USA	Rock & Roll - HF - The Young Rascals
	Meneghin	Sports	Italy	Basketball Player - HF
	Zoff	Sports	Italy	Soccer Player - HF
Diogo	Dias	Exploration	Portugal	Explorer - Madagascar
Dion	Boucicault	Performing Arts	England	Actor/Playwright
Dion Di	Mucci	Performing Arts	USA	Singer - Rock & Roll - HF
Dionne	Warwick	Performing Arts	USA	Singer - Rock & Roll - HF
Dirck	Hartog	Exploration	Netherlands	Explorer - Australia West Coast
Dirk	Benedict	Performing Arts	USA	Actor
	Bogarde	Performing Arts	England	Actor
Dirk Dries David Damian	Frimout	Aviation	Belgium	Astronaut
Django	Reinhardt	Performing Arts	Belgium	Jazz Guitarist - Big Band/Jazz - HF
Djimon	Hounsou	Performing Arts	Africa	Actor - Acad Award Nom
Dmitri	Shostakovich	Creative Works	Russia	Composer
Dmitri Ivanovich	Mendeleev	Science	Russia	Chemist
Doc	Severinsen	Performing Arts	USA	Band Leader/Conductor
Dodie	Stevens	Performing Arts	USA	Singer - Doo Whop
Dody	Goodman	Performing Arts	USA	Actress
Dolly Rebecca	Parton	Performing Arts	USA	Singer - Country Music - HF
Dolores Del	Rio	Performing Arts	Mexico	Actress
Dom	Deluise	Performing Arts	USA	Actor
Dom Di	Maggio	Sports	USA	Baseball Player
Domenic	Troiana	Performing Arts	Italy	Guitarist - Canadian Music - HF
Domenico	Dolce	Business	Italy	Fashion Designer
	Ghirlandaio	Works of Art	Italy	Painter
	Trezzini	Architecture	Russia	Architect
Domenico da	Cortona	Architecture	Italy	Architect
Domenikos El	Greco	Works of Art	Italy	Painter
Dominikus	Zimmerman	Architecture	Germany	Architect
Don	Adams	Performing Arts	USA	Actor
	Ameche	Performing Arts	USA	Actor - Academy Award
	Carlos	Politics	Spain	Pretender to Throne
	Defore	Performing Arts	USA	Actor
	Felder	Performing Arts	USA	Rock & Roll - HF - The Eagles
	Garlits	Sports	USA	Race Car Driver - HF
	Henley	Performing Arts	USA	Rock & Roll - HF - The Eagles
	Ho	Performing Arts	USA	Singer
	January	Sports	USA	Golfer
	Johnson	Performing Arts	USA	Actor
	Knotts	Performing Arts	USA	Comedian
	Larsen	Sports	USA	Baseball Player
	Mattingly	Sports	USA	Baseball Player
	McLean	Performing Arts	USA	Singer
	Murray	Performing Arts	USA	Actor - Acad Award Nom
	Myrick	Performing Arts	USA	Rock & Roll - HF - Earth Wind & Fire
	Novello	Performing Arts	USA	Comedian
	Rickles	Performing Arts	USA	Comedian
	Williams	Performing Arts	USA	Singer - Country & Western
	Cheadle	Performing Arts	USA	Actor - Acad Award Nom
	Cherry	Performing Arts	USA	Jazz Trumpeter - Big Band/Jazz - HF
Don (The Snake)	Prudhomme	Sports	USA	Race Car Driver - HF
Don E.	Fehrenbacher	Creative Works	USA	Author - Pulitzer
Don Leslie	Lind	Aviation	USA	Astronaut
Don Richard (Richie)	Ashburn	Sports	USA	Baseball Player - HF
Don Vitone (Vito)	Genovese	Law & Order	Italy	Mafia
Donald	Crisp	Performing Arts	England	Actor - Academy Award
	Fagen	Performing Arts	USA	Rock & Roll - HF - Steely Dan
	Justice	Creative Works	USA	Poet - Pulitzer
	Margulies	Creative Works	USA	Dramatist - Pulitzer

SOLVER SERIES: NAME FINDER

FIRST NAME	LAST NAME	CATEGORY	COUNTRY	FAME
Donald	Meek	Performing Arts	Scotland	Actor
	O'Connor	Performing Arts	USA	Actor
	Pleasence	Performing Arts	England	Actor
	Ross	Sports	Scotland	Golfer/Course Designer - HF
	Sutherland	Performing Arts	Canada	Actor
	Trump	Business	USA	Real Estate
	Dunn	Performing Arts	USA	Rock & Roll - HF - Booker T & The Mg's
Donald Arthur	Glaser	Science	USA	Physics - Nobel Laureate
Donald Baxter	MacMillan	Exploration	USA	Explorer - Arctic
Donald Edward	Williams	Aviation	USA	Astronaut
Donald Eugene (Don)	Gibson	Performing Arts	USA	Singer - Country Music - HF
Donald Francis	Tovey	Creative Works	England	Musicologist/Critic
Donald Francis (Don)	Shula	Sports	USA	Football Coach - HF
Donald Henderson (Dan)	Bain	Sports	Canada	Hockey Player - HF
Donald Herod	Peterson	Aviation	USA	Astronaut
Donald Howard (Don)	Sutton	Sports	USA	Baseball Player - HF
Donald J.	Cram	Science	USA	Chemistry - Nobel Laureate
Donald Kent	Slayton	Aviation	USA	Astronaut
Donald L.	Coburn	Creative Works	USA	Dramatist - Pulitzer
Donald Lee	Holmquest	Aviation	USA	Astronaut
Donald Matthew (Don)	Redman	Performing Arts	USA	Jazz Clarinetist - Big Band/Jazz - HF
Donald Mitchell	Healey	Sports	England	Race Car Driver - HF
Donald Montgomery (Don)	Hutson	Sports	USA	Football Player - HF
Donald Neil	Johnston	Sports	USA	Basketball Player - HF
Donald Ray	McMonagle	Aviation	USA	Astronaut
Donald Robert Perry	Marquis	Creative Works	USA	Humorist/Journalist
Donald Rogers (Don)	Maynard	Sports	USA	Football Player - HF
Donald Scott (Don)	Drysdale	Sports	USA	Baseball Player - HF
Donatella	Versace	Business	Italy	Fashion Designer
Donato d'Agnolo	Bramante	Architecture	Italy	Architect/Painter
Donn Fulton	Eisele	Aviation	USA	Astronaut
Donna	Caponi	Sports	USA	Golfer - HF
	Dixon	Performing Arts	USA	Actress
	Fargo	Performing Arts	USA	Singer
	Karan	Business	USA	Fashion Designer
	Kelley	Creative Works	USA	Journalist - Television
	Mills	Performing Arts	USA	Actress
	Reed	Performing Arts	USA	Actress - Academy Award
	Summer	Performing Arts	USA	Singer - Disco
	Godchaux	Performing Arts	USA	Rock & Roll - HF - Grateful Dead
Donny	Osmond	Performing Arts	USA	Singer
Dorian	Harewood	Performing Arts	USA	Actor
Doris	Day	Performing Arts	USA	Actress - Acad Award Nom
	Day	Performing Arts	USA	Singer
	Kenner-Jackson	Performing Arts	USA	Rock & Roll - HF - The Shirelles
	Roberts	Performing Arts	USA	Actress
Doris Jane	Hart	Sports	USA	Tennis Player - HF
Doris Kearns	Goodwin	Creative Works	USA	Author - Pulitzer
Doris May	Lessing	Creative Works	Iran	Novelist
Dorothea (Dolley) Payne	Madison	Politics	USA	First Lady
Dorothy	Dandridge	Performing Arts	USA	Actress - Acad Award Nom
	Gish	Performing Arts	USA	Actress
	Lamour	Performing Arts	USA	Actress
	Loudon	Performing Arts	USA	Actress
	Malone	Performing Arts	USA	Actress - Academy Award
	McGuire	Performing Arts	USA	Actress - Acad Award Nom
	Parker	Creative Works	USA	Poet/Writer
	Thompson	Creative Works	USA	Journalist - Newspaper
Dorothy (Dodo)	Cheney	Sports	USA	Tennis Player - HF
Dorothy Campbell Hurd	Howe	Sports	Scotland	Golfer - HF
Dorothy Canfield	Fisher	Creative Works	USA	Writer
Dorothy Crowfoot	Hodgkin	Science	England	Chemistry - Nobel Laureate
Dorothy Edith	Round-Little	Sports	England	Tennis Player - HF

FIRST NAME	LAST NAME	CATEGORY	COUNTRY	FAME
Dorothy L.	Sayers	Creative Works	England	Author
Dorthea Katherine	Douglass-Chambers	Sports	USA	Tennis Player - HF
Dottie (Pepper)	Mochrie	Sports	USA	Golfer
Doug	Henning	Performing Arts	Canada	Magician
	McClure	Performing Arts	USA	Actor
Douglas	Fairbanks	Performing Arts	USA	Actor
	Fairbanks Jr.	Performing Arts	USA	Actor
	Haig	War & Peace	England	Commander in Chief
	Hyde	Politics	Ireland	President
	Kiker	Creative Works	USA	Journalist - Television
	MacArthur	War & Peace	USA	Commander in Chief
	Mawson	Exploration	Australia	Explorer - Antarctica
	Wright	Creative Works	USA	Dramatist - Pulitzer
Douglas Bradford (Brad)	Park	Sports	Canada	Hockey Player - HF
Douglas D.	Osheroff	Science	USA	Physics - Nobel Laureate
Douglas Glenn (Dee Dee)	Colvin	Performing Arts	Germany	Rock & Roll - HF - The Ramones
Douglas Leon (Doug)	Atkins	Sports	USA	Football Player - HF
Douglas Noël	Adams	Creative Works	England	Author
Douglas Norman (Doug)	Harvey	Sports	Canada	Hockey Player - HF
Douglas Richard	Hofstadter	Creative Works	USA	Author - Pulitzer
Douglas S.	Freeman	Creative Works	USA	Author - Pulitzer
Douglas Wagner (Doug)	Bentley	Sports	Canada	Hockey Player - HF
Douglass C.	North	Arts	USA	Economics - Nobel Laureate
Drazen	Dalipagic	Sports	Yugoslavia	Basketball Player - HF
	Petrovic	Sports	Croatia	Basketball Player - HF
Dred	Scott	Arts	USA	Negro Slave
Drew	Barrymore	Performing Arts	USA	Actress
Duane	Allman	Performing Arts	USA	Singer/Guitarist
	Eddy	Performing Arts	USA	Guitarist
Duane Edgar	Graveline	Aviation	USA	Astronaut
Duane Gene (Digger)	Carey	Aviation	USA	Astronaut
Dudley	Moore	Performing Arts	England	Actor - Acad Award Nom
Dudley R.	Herschbach	Science	USA	Chemistry - Nobel Laureate
Duilio	Loi	Sports	Italy	Boxer - HF
Dumas	Malone	Creative Works	USA	Author - Pulitzer
Duncan	Edwards	Sports	England	Soccer Player - HF
Duncan McMillan (Mickey)	MacKay	Sports	Canada	Hockey Player - HF
Durward	Kirby	Performing Arts	USA	Actor
Dustin	Hoffman	Performing Arts	USA	Actor - Academy Award
Dusty	Hill	Performing Arts	USA	Rock & Roll - HF - ZZ Top
Dwight	Evans	Sports	USA	Baseball Player
	Gooden	Sports	USA	Baseball Player
	Stones	Sports	USA	Olympic High Jumper
Dwight David (Ike)	Eisenhower	Politics	USA	President
	Eisenhower	War & Peace	USA	General - Army
Dwight Eugene	Stephenson	Sports	USA	Football Player - HF
Dwight Filley	Davis	Sports	USA	Tennis Player - HF
Dwight Lyman	Moody	Arts	USA	Evangelist
Dwight Muhammad	Qawi	Sports	USA	Boxer - HF
Dyan	Cannon	Performing Arts	USA	Actress - Acad Award Nom
Dylan Marlais	Thomas	Creative Works	Wales	Poet
Eamon De	Valera	Politics	Ireland	President
Earl	Grey	Politics	England	Prime Minister
	Holliman	Performing Arts	USA	Actor
	Morrall	Sports	USA	Football Player
	Warren	Law & Order	USA	Chief Justice
Earl (Butch)	Buchholz Jr.	Sports	USA	Tennis Player - HF
Earl Bertrand Arthur William	Russell	Creative Works	England	Literature - Nobel Laureate
Earl Christian	Campbell	Sports	USA	Football Player - HF
Earl Derr	Biggars	Creative Works	USA	Writer - Mystery
Earl Eugene	Scruggs	Performing Arts	USA	Country Music - HF - Foggy Mountain Boys
Earl Harry (Dutch)	Clark	Sports	USA	Football Player - HF
Earl Kenneth (Fatha)	Hines	Performing Arts	USA	Jazz Pianist - Big Band/Jazz - HF

FIRST NAME	LAST NAME	CATEGORY	COUNTRY	FAME
Earl Louis (Curly)	Lambeau	Sports	USA	Football Coach - HF
Earl Sidney	Weaver	Sports	USA	Baseball Manager - HF
Earl W.	Sutherland Jr.	Science	USA	Medicine - Nobel Laureate
Earl Walter	Seibert	Sports	Canada	Hockey Player - HF
Earle	Coombs	Sports	USA	Baseball Player
Earle Bryan	Combs	Sports	USA	Baseball Player - HF
Earlington (Sonny)	Til (Tilghman)	Performing Arts	USA	Rock & Roll - HF - The Orioles
Early	Wynn	Sports	USA	Baseball Player - HF
Earnest	Byner	Sports	USA	Football Player
Earnest J. (Ernie)	Schmidt	Sports	USA	Basketball Player - HF
Eartha	Kitt	Performing Arts	USA	Singer
Earvin (Magic)	Johnson	Sports	USA	Basketball Player - HF
Ebe	Stignani	Performing Arts	Italy	Singer - Opera
Ebenezer Ralston (Ebbie)	Goodfellow	Sports	Canada	Hockey Player - HF
Eco	Umberto	Creative Works	Italy	Novelist
Ed	Ames	Performing Arts	USA	Singer/Actor
	Asner	Performing Arts	USA	Actor
	Begley	Performing Arts	USA	Actor - Academy Award
	Begley, Jr.	Performing Arts	USA	Actor
	Bradley	Creative Works	USA	Journalist - Television
	Harris	Performing Arts	USA	Actor - Acad Award Nom
	McBain	Creative Works	USA	Novelist - Crime Fiction
	McMahon	Performing Arts	USA	Show Host/Comedian
	Nelson	Performing Arts	USA	Actor
	O'Neill	Performing Arts	USA	Actor
	Sullivan	Performing Arts	USA	Show Host
	Wynn	Performing Arts	USA	Actor - Acad Award Nom
Ed (Too Tall)	Jones	Sports	USA	Football Player
Eda Le	Shan	Creative Works	USA	Author
Edd J.	Roush	Sports	USA	Baseball Player - HF
Eddie	Albert	Performing Arts	USA	Actor - Acad Award Nom
	Bracken	Performing Arts	USA	Actor
	Brigati	Performing Arts	USA	Rock & Roll - HF - The Young Rascals
	Cantor	Performing Arts	USA	Singer/Actor
	Fisher	Performing Arts	USA	Singer
	Foy	Performing Arts	USA	Actor
	Foy Jr	Performing Arts	USA	Actor
	Izzard	Performing Arts	Ireland	Comedian
	Levert	Performing Arts	USA	Rock & Roll - HF - The O'Jays
	Money	Performing Arts	USA	Singer
	Murphy	Performing Arts	USA	Comedian
	Rabbitt	Performing Arts	USA	Singer
	Yost	Sports	USA	Baseball Player
Eddie Clarence	Murray	Sports	USA	Baseball Player - HF
Eddie James	Kendricks	Performing Arts	USA	Rock & Roll - HF - The Temptations
Eddy (Richard Edward)	Arnold	Performing Arts	USA	Singer - Country Music - HF
Eder	Jofre	Sports	Brazil	Boxer - HF
Edgar	Bergen	Performing Arts	USA	Comedian
	Buchanan	Performing Arts	USA	Actor
	Guest	Creative Works	England	Poet
	Quinet	Arts	France	Philosopher/Poet/Historian
Edgar Allan	Poe	Creative Works	USA	Poet/Short Story Writer/Critic
Edgar Charles (Sam)	Rice	Sports	USA	Baseball Player - HF
Edgar Dean	Mitchell	Aviation	USA	Astronaut
Edgar Douglas	Adrian	Science	USA	Medicine - Nobel Laureate
Edgar Lawrence	Doctorow	Creative Works	USA	Novelist
Edgar Lee	Masters	Creative Works	USA	Poet
Edgar Louis	Laprade	Sports	Canada	Hockey Player - HF
Edgar Rice	Burroughs	Creative Works	USA	Writer
Edgar Wilson	Nye	Creative Works	USA	Humorist
Edie	Adams	Performing Arts	USA	Actress
	Brickell	Performing Arts	USA	Singer
	Falco	Performing Arts	USA	Actress

FIRST NAME	LAST NAME	CATEGORY	COUNTRY	FAME
Edie	McClurg	Performing Arts	USA	Actress
	Sedgwick	Performing Arts	USA	Actress
Edita	Gruberova	Performing Arts	Slovakia	Singer - Opera
Edith	Evans	Performing Arts	England	Actress - Acad Award Nom
	Piaf	Performing Arts	France	Singer
	Sitwell	Creative Works	England	Poet/Critic
	Wharton	Creative Works	USA	Novelist - Pulitzer
Edith Bolling	Wilson	Politics	USA	First Lady
Edith Kermit	Roosevelt	Politics	USA	First Lady
Edith Louisa	Cavell	Science	England	Nurse
Edmond	O'Brien	Performing Arts	USA	Actor - Academy Award
	Rostand	Creative Works	France	Poet/Dramatist
Edmond Charles Edouard	Genêt	Politics	France	Diplomat
Edmond H.	Fischer	Science	Switzerland	Medicine - Nobel Laureate
Edmond Louis Huot de	Goncourt	Creative Works	France	Novelist/Art Critic
Edmund	Burke	Arts	England	Philosopher/Writer/Statesman
	Cartwright	Science	England	Inventor - Power Loom
	Gunter	Science	England	Mathematician
	Gwenn	Performing Arts	Wales	Actor - Academy Award
	Halley	Science	England	Astronomer/Mathematician
	Kean	Performing Arts	England	Actor
	Kemper	Law & Order	USA	Serial Killer
	Kennedy	Exploration	Australia	Explorer - Australia
	Lowe	Performing Arts	USA	Actor
	Malone	Arts	Ireland	Literary Critic/Editor
	Morris	Creative Works	USA	Author - Pulitzer
	Spenser	Creative Works	England	Poet
	Waller	Creative Works	England	Poet
	Wilson	Creative Works	USA	Writer/Critic
Edmund Gustav Albrecht	Husserl	Arts	Germany	Philosopher
Edmund Henry Hynman	Allenby	War & Peace	England	Commander
Edmund Percival	Hillary	Exploration	New Zealand	Explorer - Antarctic
Edmund Sixtus	Muskie	Politics	USA	Senator - Maine
Edmund Valentine	White III	Creative Works	USA	Author
Edmund William	Gosse	Creative Works	England	Poet/Critic/Biographer
Edna	Ferber	Creative Works	USA	Author - Pulitzer
	O'Brien	Creative Works	Ireland	Author
Edna Annie	Proulx	Creative Works	USA	Author - Novelist
Edna May	Oliver	Performing Arts	USA	Actress - Acad Award Nom
Edna St. Vincent	Millay	Creative Works	USA	Poet - Pulitzer
Edo de	Waart	Performing Arts	Netherlands	Conductor - Orchestra
Edoardo	Persico	Architecture	Italy	Architect
Edouard	Manet	Works of Art	France	Painter - Impressionist
	Molinaro	Movie Production	France	Director - Acad Award Nom
Edouard (Newsy)	Lalonde	Sports	Canada	Hockey Player - HF
Édouard Victor Antoine	Lalo	Creative Works	France	Composer
Edson Arantes	Pelé	Sports	Brazil	Soccer Player - HF
Eduard	Beneš	Politics	Czechoslovakia	President
	Buchner	Science	Germany	Chemistry - Nobel Laureate
Eduardo Souto de	Moura	Architecture	Portugal	Architect
Edvard	Munch	Works of Art	Norway	Painter/Print Maker
Edvard Hagerup	Grieg	Creative Works	Norway	Composer
Edwar Coley	Burne-Jones	Works of Art	England	Painter/Designer
Edward	Albee	Creative Works	USA	Dramatist - Pulitzer
	Baines	Business	England	Publishing
	Bellamy	Creative Works	USA	Writer/Theorist
	Braddock	War & Peace	England	General
	Canning	Creative Works	USA	Author - Pulitzer
	Coke	Politics	England	Statesman/Jurist
	Dmytryk	Movie Production	Canada	Director - Acad Award Nom
	Dowden	Arts	Ireland	Biographer/Critic
	Eggleston	Creative Works	USA	Novelist/Historian
	Everett	Politics	USA	Statesman/Orator

SOLVER SERIES: NAME FINDER

FIRST NAME	LAST NAME	CATEGORY	COUNTRY	FAME
Edward	Fitzgerald	Creative Works	England	Poet/Translator
	Fox	Performing Arts	England	Actor
	Gibbon	Arts	England	Historian
	Grey	Politics	England	Statesman
	Herrmann	Performing Arts	USA	Actor
	Hopper	Works of Art	USA	Painter - Realist
	Hulton	Business	England	Publishing
	Jenner	Science	England	Physician
	Lear	Works of Art	England	Painter/Illustrator/Humorist
	Lloyd	Business	England	Publishing
	Pease	Business	England	Railway Magnate
	Rutledge	Politics	USA	Statesman
	Sapir	Arts	USA	Linguist/Anthropologist
	Sorel	Creative Works	USA	Artist
	Steichen	Works of Art	USA	Photographer
	Teller	Science	USA	Physicist - Nuclear
	Vernon	War & Peace	England	Admiral
	Villella	Performing Arts	USA	Dancer - Ballet
	Winslow	Exploration	England	Colonist - Plymouth
	Woodward	Performing Arts	England	Actor
	Young	Creative Works	England	Poet
	Norton	Performing Arts	USA	Actor - Acad Award Nom
Edward (Ed)	Murphy	Sports	Scotland	Soccer Player - HF
Edward (Eddie)	Holland	Creative Works	USA	Composer
	Rickenbacker	Sports	USA	Race Car Driver - HF
Edward (Fast Eddie)	Giacomin	Sports	Canada	Hockey Player - HF
Edward (Kid)	Ory	Performing Arts	USA	Band Leader - Big Band/Jazz - HF
Edward (Sonny)	Stitt	Performing Arts	USA	Jazz Saxophonist - Big Band/Jazz - HF
Edward (Teddy)	Glover	Sports	England	Soccer Player - HF
Edward A.	Wachter	Sports	USA	Basketball Player - HF
Edward Adelbert	Doisy	Science	USA	Medicine - Nobel Laureate
Edward Alexander	MacDowell	Creative Works	USA	Composer/Pianist
	Westermarck	Arts	Finland	Anthropologist
Edward Augustine (Ed)	Walsh	Sports	USA	Baseball Player - HF
Edward B.	Lewis	Science	USA	Medicine - Nobel Laureate
Edward Benjamin	Britten	Creative Works	England	Composer
Edward Burnett	Tylor	Arts	England	Anthropologist
Edward C.	Prescott	Arts	USA	Economics - Nobel Laureate
Edward C. (Ed)	Macauley	Sports	USA	Basketball Player - HF
Edward Calvin	Kendall	Science	USA	Medicine - Nobel Laureate
Edward Charles	Pickering	Science	USA	Physicist/Astronomer
Edward Charles (Whitey)	Ford	Sports	USA	Baseball Player - HF
Edward Donnall	Thomas	Science	USA	Medicine - Nobel Laureate
Edward Douglas	White	Law & Order	USA	Chief Justice
Edward Durell	Stone	Architecture	USA	Architect
Edward Estlin	Cummings	Creative Works	USA	Poet
Edward Evan	Evans-Pritchard	Arts	England	Anthropologist
Edward Everett	Hale	Arts	USA	Clergyman/Writer
	Horton	Performing Arts	USA	Comedian
Edward Francis (Ed)	Healey	Sports	USA	Football Player - HF
Edward G.	Robinson	Performing Arts	Romania	Actor
Edward Galen	Givens Jr.	Aviation	USA	Astronaut
Edward George	Gibson	Aviation	USA	Astronaut
Edward George (Eddie)	Gerard	Sports	Canada	Hockey Player - HF
Edward George Earl	Bulwer-Lytton	Creative Works	England	Playwright/Novelist
Edward Grant	Barrow	Sports	USA	Baseball Executive - HF
Edward Henry	Harriman	Business	USA	Financier/Railroad Magnate
Edward Higgins	White II	Aviation	USA	Astronaut
Edward Hugh	Sothern	Performing Arts	USA	Actor
Edward Hugh (Ned)	Hanlon	Sports	USA	Baseball Manager - HF
Edward Irving (Ed)	Koch	Politics	USA	Mayor - New York City
Edward J.	Larson	Creative Works	USA	Author - Pulitzer
Edward James	Olmos	Performing Arts	USA	Actor - Acad Award Nom

FIRST NAME	LAST NAME	CATEGORY	COUNTRY	FAME
Edward James (Ed)	Delahanty	Sports	USA	Baseball Player - HF
Edward James (Ted)	Hughes	Creative Works	England	Poet
Edward John	Eyre	Exploration	Australia	Explorer - South Australia
Edward John (Ed)	McIlvenny	Sports	Scotland	Soccer Player - HF
Edward John Moreton	Dunsany	Creative Works	Ireland	Poet/Playwright
Edward Kennedy (Duke)	Ellington	Performing Arts	USA	Band Leader - Big Band/Jazz - HF
Edward Larrabee	Barnes	Architecture	USA	Architect - Jefferson Medal
Edward Lawrie	Tatum	Science	USA	Medicine - Nobel Laureate
Edward Lee	Thorndike	Arts	USA	Psychologist/Lexicographer
Edward Levy	Lawson	Business	England	Publishing
Edward Mandell	House	Politics	USA	Diplomat
Edward Mills	Purcell	Science	USA	Physics - Nobel Laureate
Edward Moore (Ted)	Kennedy	Politics	USA	Senator - Massachusetts
Edward Morgan	Forster	Creative Works	England	Novelist
Edward Neto (Ed)	Souza	Sports	USA	Soccer Player - HF
Edward Osborne	Wilson	Creative Works	USA	Author - Pulitzer
Edward P.	Jones	Creative Works	USA	Novelist - Pulitzer
Edward Phillips	Oppenheim	Creative Works	England	Novelist
Edward Ray (Eddie)	Cochran	Performing Arts	USA	Singer - Rock & Roll - HF
Edward Reginald (Reg)	Noble	Sports	Canada	Hockey Player - HF
Edward Richard George	Heath	Politics	England	Prime Minister
Edward Robert	Bulwer	Creative Works	England	Poet
Edward Roscoe	Murrow	Creative Works	USA	Journalist - Radio
Edward Stewart (Eddie)	Plank	Sports	USA	Baseball Player - HF
Edward Theodore (Ed)	Gein	Law & Order	USA	Serial Killer
Edward Trowbridge (Eddie)	Collins Sr.	Sports	USA	Baseball Player - HF
Edward Uhler	Condon	Science	USA	Physicist
Edward Vernon	Rickenbacker	Aviation	USA	Aviator/Aviation Executive
Edward Victor	Appleton	Science	England	Physics - Nobel Laureate
Edward W. (Moose)	Krause	Sports	USA	Basketball Player - HF
Edward William	Bok	Creative Works	USA	Author - Pulitzer
	Brooke III	Politics	USA	Senator
	Elgar	Creative Works	England	Composer
Edward William (Eddie)	Shore	Sports	Canada	Hockey Player - HF
Edward Wyllis	Scripps	Business	USA	Publishing - Newspaper
Edwin	Arnold	Creative Works	England	Poet/Journalist
	O'Connor	Creative Works	USA	Novelist/Journalist - Pulitzer
Edwin Arlington	Robinson	Creative Works	USA	Poet - Pulitzer
Edwin C.	Moses	Sports	USA	Olympic Hurdler
Edwin Donald (Duke)	Snider	Sports	USA	Baseball Player - HF
Edwin Eugene (Buzz)	Aldrin	Aviation	USA	Astronaut
Edwin Frank (Eddy)	Duchin	Performing Arts	USA	Pianist
Edwin G.	Burrows	Creative Works	USA	Author - Pulitzer
	Krebs	Science	USA	Medicine - Nobel Laureate
Edwin Henry	Landseer	Works of Art	England	Painter - Animals
Edwin Herbert	Land	Science	USA	Inventor - Land Camera
Edwin Jacob (Jake)	Garn	Aviation	USA	Astronaut
	Garn	Politics	USA	Senator - Utah
Edwin Keith (Banjo)	Matthews	Sports	USA	Race Car Driver - HF
Edwin Landseer	Lutyens	Architecture	England	Architect - AIA Gold Medal
Edwin Lee (Eddie)	Mathews	Sports	USA	Baseball Player
Edwin Mattison	McMillan	Science	USA	Chemistry - Nobel Laureate
Edwin McMasters	Stanton	Politics	USA	Statesman/Secretary of War
Edwin Powell	Hubble	Science	USA	Astronomer
Edwin Thomas	Booth	Performing Arts	USA	Actor
Edwin Way	Teale	Creative Works	USA	Author - Pulitzer
Edy	Williams	Performing Arts	USA	Actress
Eero	Saarinen	Architecture	USA	Architect - AIA Gold Medal
Efrain (Chico)	Chacurian	Sports	Argentina	Soccer Player - HF
Efrem	Zimbalist	Performing Arts	USA	Violinist
	Zimbalist Jr.	Performing Arts	USA	Actor
Ehud	Barak	Politics	Israel	Prime Minister
Eileen	Brennan	Performing Arts	USA	Actress - Acad Award Nom

SOLVER SERIES: NAME FINDER

FIRST NAME	LAST NAME	CATEGORY	COUNTRY	FAME
Eileen	Heckart	Performing Arts	USA	Actress - Academy Award
Eisaku	Sato	War & Peace	Japan	Peace - Nobel Laureate
El	Greco	Works of Art	Spain	Painter
Eladio	Dieste	Architecture	Uruguay	Architect
Elaine	May	Performing Arts	USA	Actress/Director
	Stritch	Performing Arts	USA	Actress
Elayne	Boosler	Performing Arts	USA	Comedian
Elbridge	Gerry	Politics	USA	Vice-President
Eldra De	Barge	Performing Arts	USA	Singer
Eleanor	Parker	Performing Arts	USA	Actress - Acad Award Nom
	Powell	Performing Arts	USA	Actress/Dancer
	Wylie	Creative Works	USA	Poet
Eleanora (Billie)	Holiday (Fagan)	Performing Arts	USA	Singer - Big Band/Jazz - HF
	Holiday (Fagan)	Performing Arts	USA	Singer - Rock & Roll - HF
Elena	Gerhardt	Performing Arts	Germany	Singer - Opera
	Nikolaidi	Performing Arts	Greece	Singer - Opera
	Verdugo	Performing Arts	USA	Actress
Eleonora	Duse	Performing Arts	Italy	Actress
Eleonora Randolph (Eleo)	Sears	Sports	USA	Tennis Player - HF
Éleuthère Irénée du	Pont	Business	USA	Industrialist
Elfriede	Jelinek	Creative Works	Austria	Literature - Nobel Laureate
Elgin	Baylor	Sports	USA	Basketball Player - HF
Eli	Wallach	Performing Arts	USA	Actor
	Whitney	Science	USA	Inventor - Cotton Gin
Elia	Kazan	Creative Works	Turkey	Screenwriter
	Kazan	Movie Production	Turkey	Director - Academy Award
Elias	Canetti	Creative Works	Bulgaria	Literature - Nobel Laureate
	Holl	Architecture	Germany	Architect
	Howe	Science	USA	Inventor - Sewing Machine
Elias James	Corey	Science	USA	Chemistry - Nobel Laureate
Elias Victor	Seixas Jr.	Sports	USA	Tennis Player - HF
Elie	Ducommun	War & Peace	Switzerland	Peace - Nobel Laureate
	Seigmeister	Creative Works	USA	Composer
Élie	Metchnikoff	Science	Russia	Biologist/Bacteriologist
Eliezer (Elie)	Wiesel	Creative Works	USA	Author
	Wiesel	War & Peace	USA	Peace - Nobel Laureate
Elihu	Root	Politics	USA	Statesman
	Root	War & Peace	USA	Peace - Nobel Laureate
Elinor	Donahue	Performing Arts	USA	Actress
	Glyn	Creative Works	England	Novelist
Elio	Fiorucci	Business	Italy	Fashion Designer
	Vittorini	Creative Works	Italy	Novelist/Literary Critic
Eliot	Ness	Law & Order	USA	Treasury Agent
Elisabeth	Bergner	Performing Arts	Ukraine	Actress - Acad Award Nom
	Shue	Performing Arts	USA	Actress - Acad Award Nom
Elisabeth Holmes (Bessie)	Moore	Sports	USA	Tennis Player - HF
Elisha Graves	Otis	Science	USA	Inventor - Elevator
Elissa	Landi	Performing Arts	Italy	Actress/Author
Eliza	Johnson	Politics	USA	First Lady
Elizabeth	Arden	Business	USA	Designing
	Ashley	Performing Arts	USA	Actress
	Bishop	Creative Works	USA	Poet - Pulitzer
	Blackwell	Science	USA	Physician
	Frank	Creative Works	USA	Author - Pulitzer
	Hartman	Performing Arts	USA	Actress - Acad Award Nom
	Hurley	Performing Arts	England	Super Model
	McGovern	Performing Arts	USA	Actress - Acad Award Nom
	Monroe	Politics	USA	First Lady
	Montgomery	Performing Arts	USA	Actress
	Perkins	Performing Arts	USA	Actress
	Plater-Zyberk	Architecture	USA	Architect - Jefferson Medal
	Taylor	Performing Arts	England	Actress - Academy Award
Elizabeth (Bess)	Truman	Politics	USA	First Lady

FIRST NAME	LAST NAME	CATEGORY	COUNTRY	FAME
Elizabeth (Bessie)	Smith	Performing Arts	USA	Singer - Rock & Roll - HF
Elizabeth Ann (Betty)	Ford	Politics	USA	First Lady
Elizabeth Barrett	Browning	Creative Works	England	Poet
Elizabeth Cady	Stanton	Politics	USA	Reformer/Suffragist
Elizabeth Cleghorn	Gaskell	Creative Works	England	Novelist
Elizabeth Hanford (Liddy)	Dole	Politics	USA	Senator - North Carolina
Elizabeth Montague (Bunny)	Ryan	Sports	USA	Tennis Player - HF
Elke	Sommer	Performing Arts	Germany	Actress
Ella	Logan	Performing Arts	Scotland	Singer
Ella Jane	Fitzgerald	Performing Arts	USA	Singer - Big Band/Jazz - HF
Ella Rose Tambussi	Grasso	Politics	USA	Governor - Connecticut
Ella Wheeler	Wilcox	Creative Works	USA	Poet
Elle	MacPherson	Performing Arts	Australia	Super Model
Ellen	Barkin	Performing Arts	USA	Actress
	Burstyn	Performing Arts	USA	Actress - Academy Award
	Corby	Performing Arts	USA	Actress - Acad Award Nom
	Drew	Performing Arts	USA	Actress
	Terry	Performing Arts	England	Actress
Ellen Anderson Gholson	Glasgow	Creative Works	USA	Novelist - Pulitzer
Ellen Crosby	Roosevelt	Sports	USA	Tennis Player - HF
Ellen Forde	Hansell	Sports	USA	Tennis Player - HF
Ellen Lewis	Arthur	Politics	USA	First Lady
Ellen Louise	Wilson	Politics	USA	First Lady
Ellen Naomi (Mama Cass)	Elliott (Cohen)	Performing Arts	USA	Rock & Roll - HF - Mamas & Papas
Ellie	Greenwich	Performing Arts	USA	Singer
Elliot Lee	Richardson	Politics	USA	Politician
Elliot McKay	See Jr.	Aviation	USA	Astronaut
Elliott	Abrams	Politics	USA	Assistant Secretary of State
	Gould	Performing Arts	USA	Actor - Acad Award Nom
Ellis	Havelock	Creative Works	England	Author
Ellis (Bo)	Didley (Bates)	Performing Arts	USA	Singer - Rock & Roll - HF
Ellison Shoji	Onizuka	Aviation	USA	Astronaut
Elly	Ameling	Performing Arts	Netherlands	Singer - Opera
Elmer	Bernstein	Creative Works	USA	Composer/Movie Music
Elmer Ambrose	Sperry	Science	USA	Inventor/Electrical Engineer
Elmer Harrison	Flick	Sports	USA	Baseball Player - HF
Elmer James	Lach	Sports	Canada	Hockey Player - HF
Elmer Kenneth (Ken)	Strong Jr.	Sports	USA	Football Player - HF
Elmer L.	Rice	Creative Works	USA	Dramatist - Pulitzer
Elmo	Lincoln	Performing Arts	USA	Actor
Elmo Russell	Zumwalt Jr.	War & Peace	USA	Admiral
Elmore	James	Performing Arts	USA	Singer - Rock & Roll - HF
	Leonard	Creative Works	USA	Novelist
Elroy Leon (Crazy Legs)	Hirsch	Sports	USA	Football Player - HF
Elsa	Benitez	Performing Arts	Mexico	Super Model
	Lanchester	Performing Arts	England	Actress - Acad Award Nom
	Martinelli	Performing Arts	Italy	Actress
	Peretti	Business	Italy	Designer - Jewelry
	Schiaparelli	Works of Art	Italy	Painter - Surrealist
Elsie	Janis	Performing Arts	USA	Actress
Elvin E.	Hayes	Sports	USA	Basketball Player - HF
Elvin Lamont	Bethea	Sports	USA	Football Player - HF
Elvis Aaron	Presley	Performing Arts	USA	Singer - Country Music - HF
	Presley	Performing Arts	USA	Singer - Rock & Roll - HF
Elwyn Brooks	White	Creative Works	USA	Humorist
Ely	Culbertson	Games	USA	Bridge Expert
Elzie Crisler	Segar	Creative Works	USA	Cartoonist - Popeye
Elzie Wylie (Buck)	Baker Sr.	Sports	USA	Race Car Driver - HF
Emanuel	Lasker	Games	Germany	Chess Player
	Swedenborg	Arts	Sweden	Philosopher/Scientist/Mystic
	Ungaro	Business	France	Fashion Designer
Emeril	Lagasse	Performing Arts	USA	Actor - Chef
Emerson	Fittipaldi	Sports	Brazil	Race Car Driver - HF

SOLVER SERIES: NAME FINDER

FIRST NAME	LAST NAME	CATEGORY	COUNTRY	FAME
Emil	Jannings	Performing Arts	Switzerland	Actor - Academy Award
	Kraepelin	Science	Germany	Psychiatrist
	Zapotek	Sports	Czechoslovakia	Olympic Marathoner
Emil (Butch)	Bouchard	Sports	Canada	Hockey Player - HF
Emil Adolf von	Behring	Science	Germany	Medicine - Nobel Laureate
Emil Grigoryevich	Gilels	Performing Arts	Ukraine	Pianist - Classical
Emil Theodor	Kocher	Science	Switzerland	Medicine - Nobel Laureate
Emile	Griffith	Sports	USA	Boxer - HF
Émile	Gaboriau	Creative Works	France	Writer - Detective Stories
	Jaques-Dalcroze	Creative Works	Switzerland	Composer
Emile Édouard Charles Antoine	Zola	Creative Works	France	Novelist
Émile Léon	Cammaerts	Creative Works	Belgium	Poet
Émile Michel	Cioran	Arts	France	Philosopher
Emile Percy (The Cat)	Francis	Sports	Canada	Hockey Player
Emiliano	Zapata	Politics	Mexico	Revolutionist
Emilio	Ambasz	Architecture	USA	Architect
	Estevez	Performing Arts	USA	Actor
	Pucci	Business	Italy	Fashion Designer
Emilio Gino	Segrè	Science	USA	Physics - Nobel Laureate
Emily	Brontë	Creative Works	England	Novelist/Poet
	Post	Creative Works	USA	Author
	Watson	Performing Arts	England	Actress - Acad Award Nom
Emily Elizabeth	Dickinson	Creative Works	USA	Poet
Emily Greene	Balche	War & Peace	USA	Peace - Nobel Laureate
Emlen Lewis	Tunnell	Sports	USA	Football Player - HF
Emma	Calvé	Performing Arts	France	Singer - Opera
	Lazarus	Creative Works	USA	Poet
	Samms	Performing Arts	England	Actress
	Thompson	Performing Arts	England	Actress - Academy Award
Emmeline	Pankhurst	Politics	England	Suffragist
Emmett	Dalton	Law & Order	USA	Outlaw
	Kelly	Performing Arts	USA	Comedian
Emmy	Destinn	Performing Arts	Czechoslovakia	Singer - Opera
Emmylou	Harris	Performing Arts	USA	Singer
Emo	Phillips	Performing Arts	USA	Comedian
Emory	Holloway	Creative Works	USA	Author - Pulitzer
Endre	Ady	Creative Works	Hungary	Poet
Engelbert	Humperdinck	Creative Works	Germany	Composer
	Humperdink	Performing Arts	India	Singer
Enid	Bagnold	Creative Works	England	Novelist
	Markey	Performing Arts	USA	Actress
Enid Mary	Blyton	Creative Works	England	Author
En-Lai	Chou	Politics	China	Prime Minister
Enoch Arnold	Bennett	Creative Works	England	Novelist
Enos	Cabell	Sports	USA	Baseball Player
Enos Bradsher	Slaughter	Sports	USA	Baseball Player - HF
Enrico	Caruso	Performing Arts	Italy	Singer - Opera
	Fermi	Science	Italy	Physics - Nobel Laureate
	Iglesias	Performing Arts	Spain	Singer
Enzio	Stuarti	Performing Arts	Italy	Singer - Opera
Enzo Anselmo	Ferrari	Sports	Italy	Race Car Driver - HF
Eppa	Rixey	Sports	USA	Baseball Player - HF
Erasmus	Darwin	Science	England	Naturalist/Physician
Eric	Ambler	Creative Works	England	Author
	Blore	Performing Arts	England	Actor
	Carmen	Performing Arts	USA	Singer/Composer
	Coates	Creative Works	England	Composer
	Heiden	Sports	USA	Olympic Speed Skater
	Hoffer	Arts	USA	Philosopher
	Idle	Performing Arts	England	Comedian
	Roberts	Performing Arts	USA	Actor - Acad Award Nom
	Rohmer	Movie Production	France	Director
	Stoltz	Performing Arts	USA	Actor

FIRST NAME	LAST NAME	CATEGORY	COUNTRY	FAME
Eric	Wynalda	Sports	USA	Soccer Player - HF
	Burden	Performing Arts	England	Rock & Roll - HF - The Animals
Eric (The Red)	Thorvaldson	Exploration	Norway	Explorer - Greenland
Eric A.	Cornell	Science	USA	Physics - Nobel Laureate
Eric Allan	Dolphy	Performing Arts	USA	Jazz Saxophonist - Big Band/Jazz - HF
Eric Demetric	Dickerson	Sports	USA	Football Player - HF
Eric F.	Wieschaus	Science	USA	Medicine - Nobel Laureate
Eric Hilliard (Ricky)	Nelson	Performing Arts	USA	Singer - Rock & Roll - HF
Eric Honeywood	Partridge	Arts	England	Lexicographer/Writer
Eric Nolan	Grant	Performing Arts	USA	Rock & Roll - HF - The O'Jays
Eric Owen	Moss	Architecture	USA	Architect
Eric Patrick	Clapton	Performing Arts	England	"Rock & Roll - HF - Cream,Yardbirds"
Eric R.	Kandel	Science	USA	Medicine - Nobel Laureate
Eric Russell	Bentley	Creative Works	USA	Drama Critic/Director
Erica	Jong	Creative Works	USA	Author
	Morini	Performing Arts	Austria	Violinist
Erich	Fromm	Arts	Germany	Philosopher/Psychologist
	Leinsdorf	Performing Arts	Austria	Conductor
	Mendelsohn	Architecture	USA	Architect
	Segal	Creative Works	USA	Author
Erich Maria	Remarque	Creative Works	USA	Novelist
Erich von	Stroheim	Performing Arts	Austria	Actor - Acad Award Nom
Erie	Mills	Performing Arts	USA	Singer - Opera
Erik	Estrada	Performing Arts	USA	Actor
	Kramer	Sports	USA	Football Player
Erik Alfred Leslie	Satie	Creative Works	France	Composer
Erik Axel	Karlfeldt	Creative Works	Sweden	Literature - Nobel Laureate
Erik Gunnar	Asplund	Architecture	Sweden	Architect
Erik Homburger	Erikson	Creative Works	USA	Author - Pulitzer
Erika	Slezak	Performing Arts	USA	Actress
Erin	Gray	Performing Arts	USA	Actress
	Moran	Performing Arts	USA	Actress
Erle Stanley	Gardner	Creative Works	USA	Author
Erma	Bombeck	Creative Works	USA	Journalist - Newspaper
Ermano	Wolf-Ferrari	Creative Works	Italy	Composer
Ernest	Becker	Creative Works	USA	Author - Pulitzer
	Bevin	Politics	England	Labor Leader
	Bloch	Creative Works	USA	Composer Classical
	Borgnine	Performing Arts	USA	Actor - Academy Award
	Jones	Arts	England	Psychoanalyst
	Nagel	Arts	USA	Philosopher
	Poole	Creative Works	USA	Novelist - Pulitzer
	Rutherford	Science	England	Chemistry - Nobel Laureate
	Samuels	Creative Works	USA	Author - Pulitzer
	Solvay	Science	Belgium	Chemist
	Truex	Performing Arts	USA	Actor
	Weekley	Arts	England	Lexicographer/Etymologist
	Tubb	Performing Arts	USA	Singer - Country Music - HF
Ernest (Ernie)	Banks	Sports	USA	Baseball Player - HF
	Russell	Sports	Canada	Hockey Player - HF
Ernest (Moose)	Johnson	Sports	Canada	Hockey Player - HF
Ernest (Tennessee Ernie)	Ford	Performing Arts	USA	Singer - Country Music - HF
Ernest Alfred (Ernie)	Stautner	Sports	Bavaria	Football Player - HF
Ernest Alonzo (Ernie)	Nevers	Sports	USA	Football Player - HF
Ernest Christopher	Dowson	Creative Works	England	Poet - Lyric
Ernest Loring (Red)	Nichols	Performing Arts	USA	Jazz Cornetist - Big Band/Jazz - HF
Ernest Miller	Hemingway	Creative Works	USA	Literature - Nobel/Pulitzer
Ernest Orlando	Lawrence	Science	USA	Physics - Nobel Laureate
Ernest Taylor (Ernie)	Pyle	Creative Works	USA	Journalist - Newspaper
Ernest Thomas Sinton	Walton	Science	Ireland	Physics - Nobel Laureate
Ernest Thompson	Seton	Creative Works	USA	Writer/Naturalist/Illustrator
Ernestine	Schumann-Heink	Performing Arts	USA	Singer - Opera
Ernesto	Basile	Architecture	Italy	Architect

SOLVER SERIES: NAME FINDER

FIRST NAME	LAST NAME	CATEGORY	COUNTRY	FAME
Ernesto	Sabato	Creative Works	Argentina	Author
Ernesto Natali (Ernie)	Lombardi	Sports	USA	Baseball Player - HF
Ernesto Rafael (Che)	Guevara	War & Peace	Cuba	Revolutionist/Guerilla Leader
Ernesto Teodoro	Moneta	War & Peace	Italy	Peace - Nobel Laureate
Ernie	Bushmiller	Creative Works	USA	Cartoonist - Nancy
	Els	Sports	South Africa	Golfer
	Irvan	Sports	USA	Race Car Driver
	Isley	Performing Arts	USA	Rock & Roll - HF - Isley Brothers
	Kovacs	Performing Arts	USA	Comedian
	Maresca	Performing Arts	USA	Singer/Composer
Erno	Rapée	Performing Arts	Hungary	Band Leader/Composer
Ernö	Dohnányi	Creative Works	Hungary	Composer/Pianist
Ernõ	Rubik	Science	Hungary	Inventor/Sculptor - Rubik's Cube
Ernst	Bloch	Arts	Germany	Philosopher
	Cassirer	Arts	Germany	Philosopher
	Lubitsch	Movie Production	Germany	Director - Acad Award Nom
	Mach	Arts	Austria	Philosopher/Physicist
	May	Architecture	Germany	Architect
	Ruska	Science	Germany	Physics - Nobel Laureate
	Toller	Creative Works	Germany	Playwright
Ernst Boris	Chain	Science	England	Medicine - Nobel Laureate
Ernst Heinrich	Haeckel	Science	Germany	Biologist/Philosopher
	Weber	Science	Germany	Physiologist/Anatomist
Ernst Otto	Fischer	Science	Germany	Chemistry - Nobel Laureate
Ernst Theodor Amadeus	Hoffmann	Creative Works	Germany	Composer/Writer
Ernst Willi	Messerschmid	Aviation	Germany	Astronaut
Errol	Flynn	Performing Arts	Australia	Actor
Erroll Louis	Garner	Performing Arts	USA	Jazz Pianist - Big Band/Jazz - HF
Erskine	Caldwell	Creative Works	USA	Novelist
Erskine Hamilton	Childers	Politics	Ireland	President
Erwin	Neher	Science	Germany	Medicine - Nobel Laureate
	Piscator	Movie Production	USA	Director/Producer- Theatrical
	Schrödinger	Science	Austria	Physics - Nobel Laureate
Erwin Johannes Eugen	Rommel	War & Peace	Germany	Field Marshall
Esai	Morales	Performing Arts	USA	Actor
Estee	Lauder	Business	USA	Cosmetics Industry
Estelle	Getty	Performing Arts	USA	Actress
	Parsons	Performing Arts	USA	Actress - Academy Award
	Warren	Performing Arts	Canada	Super Model
	Winwood	Performing Arts	England	Actress
Estes	Kefauver	Politics	USA	Senator - Tennessee
Esther	Forbes	Creative Works	USA	Author - Pulitzer
	Rolle	Performing Arts	USA	Actress
	Williams	Performing Arts	USA	Actress
Ethan	Allen	War & Peace	USA	Revolutionist
	Coen	Movie Production	USA	Director
	Hawke	Performing Arts	USA	Actor - Acad Award Nom
Ethel	Barrymore	Performing Arts	USA	Actress - Academy Award
	Merman	Performing Arts	USA	Singer
	Waters	Performing Arts	USA	Actress - Acad Award Nom
Ethel Skakel	Kennedy	Politics	USA	Wife - Robert Kennedy
Étienne	Gaboury	Architecture	Canada	Architect
Étienne Bonnot de	Condillac	Arts	France	Philosopher
Etienne Louis	Boulée	Architecture	France	Architect
Ettore	Bugatti	Sports	Italy	Race Car Designer - HF
	Sottsass	Architecture	Austria	Architect
	Stella	Architecture	Italy	Architect
Eudora	Welty	Creative Works	USA	Novelist - Pulitzer
Eugene	Field	Creative Works	USA	Poet/Journalist
	Ionesco	Creative Works	France	Playwright
	Ormandy	Performing Arts	Hungary	Conductor/Violinist
	Sue	Creative Works	France	Novelist
Eugene Andrew	Cernan	Aviation	USA	Astronaut

FIRST NAME	LAST NAME	CATEGORY	COUNTRY	FAME
Eugene Benjamin	Germany	Business	USA	Oil Industry
Eugène Emmanuel	Viollet le Duc	Architecture	France	Architect
Eugene Gladstone	O'Neill	Creative Works	USA	Literature - Nobel/Pulitzer
Eugène Hau-Chau	Trinh	Aviation	USA	Astronaut
Eugène Henri Paul	Gauguin	Works of Art	France	Painter
Eugene Joseph (Gene)	McCarthy	Politics	USA	Senator - Minnesota
Eugene Luther Gore	Vidal	Creative Works	USA	Novelist/Playwright
Eugene Paul	Wigner	Science	USA	Physics - Nobel Laureate
Eugene Thurman (Gene)	Upshaw Jr.	Sports	USA	Football Player - HF
Eugene Victor	Debs	Business	USA	Labor Leader
Eugenio	Montale	Creative Works	Italy	Literature - Nobel Laureate
Euine Fay	Jones	Architecture	USA	Architect - AIA Gold Medal
Eunice Kathleen (Nina)	Simone (Waymon)	Performing Arts	USA	Singer/Pianist - Big Band/Jazz - HF
Eusebio	Pedroza	Sports	Panama	Boxer - HF
Eusebio Ferreria	Da Silva	Sports	Mozambique	Soccer Player - HF
Eusebio Francisco	Kino	Exploration	Spain	Explorer - Mexico
Eva	Gabor	Performing Arts	Hungary	Actress
	Herzigova	Performing Arts	Czechoslovakia	Super Model
	Marton	Performing Arts	Hungary	Singer - Opera
Eva Le	Gallienne	Performing Arts	England	Actress
	Gallienne	Performing Arts	England	Actress - Acad Award Nom
Eva Marie	Saint	Performing Arts	USA	Actress - Academy Award
Evan	Fischer	Performing Arts	USA	Canadian Music - HF - The Diamonds
	Hunter	Creative Works	USA	Author
Evander	Holyfield	Sports	USA	Boxer
Evangeline Cory	Booth	Arts	England	Revivalist
Evangelista	Torricelli	Science	Italy	Physicist/Mathematician
Evariste	Galois	Science	France	Mathematician
Eve	Arden	Performing Arts	USA	Actress - Acad Award Nom
	Plumb	Performing Arts	USA	Actress
Eve Rabin	Queler	Performing Arts	USA	Conductor
Evelyn	Ashford	Sports	USA	Olympic Runner
	Keyes	Performing Arts	USA	Actress
Evelyn Arthur St. John	Waugh	Creative Works	England	Novelist
Everett	Sloane	Performing Arts	USA	Actor
Everett Grunz	Marshall	Performing Arts	USA	Actor
Everett McKinley	Dirksen	Politics	USA	Senator
Evita (Eva)	Peron	Politics	Argentina	First Lady
Evonne Fay	Goolagong	Sports	Australia	Tennis Player - HF
Ewa	Aulin	Performing Arts	Sweden	Actress
Ewan	McGregor	Performing Arts	Scotland	Actor
Ewell Doak	Walker Jr.	Sports	USA	Football Player - HF
Eydie	Gorme	Performing Arts	USA	Singer
Eyvind	Johnson	Creative Works	Sweden	Literature - Nobel Laureate
Ezekiel	Carey	Performing Arts	USA	Rock & Roll - HF - The Flamingos
Ezio	Pinza	Performing Arts	Italy	Singer - Opera
Ezra	Cornell	Business	USA	Capitalist/Philanthropist
Ezra Loomis	Pound	Creative Works	USA	Poet
Ezra Taft	Benson	Politics	USA	Secretary of Agriculture
Ezzard	Charles	Sports	USA	Boxer - HF
Fabio	Reinhart	Architecture	Switzerland	Architect
Fabri	Salcedo	Sports	Spain	Soccer Player - HF
Fahrid Murray	Abraham	Performing Arts	USA	Actor - Academy Award
Fanny	Brice	Performing Arts	USA	Comedian
	Burney	Creative Works	England	Novelist/Diarist
	Kemble	Performing Arts	England	Actress
Farley	Granger	Performing Arts	USA	Actor
Faron	Young	Performing Arts	USA	Singer - Country Music - HF
Farrah	Fawcett	Performing Arts	USA	Actress
Farrokh (Freddie)	Mercury (Bulsara)	Performing Arts	Tanzania	Rock & Roll - HF - Queen
Fats (Thomas Wright)	Waller	Performing Arts	USA	Singer/Composer - Big Band/Jazz - HF
Fatty	Arbuckle	Performing Arts	USA	Comedian
Faustus	Socinus	Politics	Italy	Reformer - Religious

SOLVER SERIES: NAME FINDER

FIRST NAME	LAST NAME	CATEGORY	COUNTRY	FAME
Fay	Bainter	Performing Arts	USA	Actress - Academy Award
	Wray	Performing Arts	Canada	Actress
Faye	Dunaway	Performing Arts	USA	Actress - Academy Award
Federico	Fellini	Movie Production	Italy	Director - Acad Award Nom
	Garcia Lorca	Creative Works	Spain	Poet/Playwright
Federico Garcia	Lorca	Creative Works	Spain	Poet
Felipe	Alou	Sports	USA	Baseball Player
Felix	Adler	Arts	USA	Philosopher/Educator
	Bloch	Science	USA	Physics - Nobel Laureate
	Candela	Architecture	Spain	Architect
	Cavaliere	Performing Arts	USA	Rock & Roll - HF - The Young Rascals
	Frankfurter	Law & Order	USA	Justice - Supreme Court
	Mendelssohn	Creative Works	Germany	Composer
	Wankel	Science	Germany	Inventor/Engineer
Feodor	Lynen	Science	Germany	Medicine - Nobel Laureate
Feodor Ivanovich	Chaliapin	Performing Arts	Russia	Singer - Opera
Feodor Mikhailovich	Dostoyevsky	Creative Works	Russia	Novelist
Ferde	Grofé	Creative Works	USA	Composer/Pianist
Ferdinand	Buisson	War & Peace	France	Peace - Nobel Laureate
	Foch	War & Peace	France	Marshall
	Lassalle	Arts	Germany	Socialist/Writer
	Magellan	Exploration	Spain	Explorer - Circumnavigation
	Marcos	Politics	Philippines	President
	Porsche	Sports	Bohemia	Race Car Designer - HF
Ferdinand (Jelly Roll)	Morton (Lemothe)	Performing Arts	USA	Singer - Big Band/Jazz - HF
	Morton (Lemothe)	Performing Arts	USA	Singer - Rock & Roll - HF
Ferdinand August	Bebel	Arts	Germany	Socialist/Writer
Ferdinand Charles (Fernie)	Flaman	Sports	Canada	Hockey Player - HF
Ferdinand de	Saussure	Arts	Switzerland	Linguist
Ferdinand Julius	Cohn	Science	Germany	Botanist/Bacteriologist
Ferdinand Marie de	Lesseps	Politics	France	Diplomat/Engineer - Suez
Ferdinand Victor Eugene	Delacroix	Works of Art	France	Painter
Ferenc	Molnár	Creative Works	Hungary	Playwright/Novelist
	Puskas	Sports	Hungary	Soccer Player - HF
Ferguson Arthur (Fergie)	Jenkins	Sports	Canada	Baseball Player - HF
Ferid	Murad	Science	USA	Medicine - Nobel Laureate
Fernand	Léger	Works of Art	France	Painter
	Pouillon	Architecture	France	Architect
Fernanda	Montenegro	Performing Arts	Brazil	Actress - Acad Award Nom
Fernando	Clavijo	Sports	Uruguay	Soccer Player - HF
	Lamas	Performing Arts	Argentina	Actor
	Meirelles	Movie Production	Brazil	Director - Acad Award Nom
	Rey	Performing Arts	Spain	Actor
	Valenzuela	Sports	USA	Baseball Player
Ferruccido Benvenuto	Busoni	Creative Works	Italy	Composer
Fess	Parker	Performing Arts	USA	Actor
Fidel Alejandro	Castro	War & Peace	Cuba	Revolutionary Leader - President
Filippino	Lippi	Works of Art	Italy	Painter
Fillipo	Brunelleschi	Architecture	Italy	Architect
Fillippo	Juvarra	Architecture	Italy	Architect
Finbar Patrick (Barry)	McGuigan	Sports	Ireland	Boxer - HF
Finley Peter	Dunne	Creative Works	USA	Humorist/Journalist
Finn E.	Kydland	Arts	Norway	Economics - Nobel Laureate
Fiorello Henry La	Guardia	Politics	USA	Lawyer/Political Leader
Fletcher	Henderson	Performing Arts	USA	Band Leader - Big Band/Jazz - HF
Fletcher Joseph (Joe)	Perry	Sports	USA	Football Player - HF
Flip	Wilson	Performing Arts	USA	Comedian
Flora	Robson	Performing Arts	England	Actress - Acad Award Nom
Florence	Henderson	Performing Arts	USA	Actress
	Nightingale	Science	England	Nurse - Crimean War
Florence Angela Margaret	Mortimer-Barrett	Sports	England	Tennis Player - HF
Florence Glenda (Flo)	Ballard	Performing Arts	USA	Rock & Roll - HF - The Supremes
Florence Kling	Harding	Politics	USA	First Lady

FIRST NAME	LAST NAME	CATEGORY	COUNTRY	FAME
Florenz	Ziegfeld	Movie Production	USA	Producer - Theatrical
Floyd	Cramer	Performing Arts	USA	Singer - Country Music - HF
	Cramer	Performing Arts	USA	Singer - Rock & Roll - HF
	Patterson	Sports	USA	Boxer - HF
	Tillman	Performing Arts	USA	Singer - Country Music - HF
Ford Christopher	Frick	Sports	USA	Baseball Commissioner - HF
Ford Madox	Ford	Creative Works	England	Writer/Editor
Forrest	Tucker	Performing Arts	USA	Actor
	Wilson	Creative Works	USA	Author - Pulitzer
Forrest S. (Red)	Debernardy	Sports	USA	Basketball Player - HF
Fra	Angelico	Works of Art	Italy	Painter
Fra Filippo	Lippi	Works of Art	Italy	Painter
Frances	Alda	Performing Arts	USA	Singer - Opera
	Cleveland	Politics	USA	First Lady
	Farmer	Performing Arts	USA	Actress
	Goodrich	Creative Works	USA	Dramatist - Pulitzer
	McDormand	Performing Arts	USA	Actress - Academy Award
	Perkins	Arts	USA	Social Worker
	Sternhagen	Performing Arts	USA	Actress
Frances Charles (Frank)	Brimsek	Sports	Canada	Hockey Player - HF
Frances Hodgson	Burnett	Creative Works	USA	Writer
Frances Milton	Trollope	Creative Works	England	Writer
Frances Xavier	Cabrini	Arts	USA	Nun
Francesco	Borromini	Architecture	Italy	Architect
	Cellini	Architecture	Italy	Architect
	Cilea	Performing Arts	Italy	Singer/Composer
	Crispi	Politics	Italy	Prime Minister
	Petrarch	Creative Works	Italy	Poet/Scholar
Francesco (Frank)	Costello	Law & Order	Italy	Mafia
Francesco di Giorgio	Martini	Architecture	Italy	Architect
Franchot	Tone	Performing Arts	USA	Actor - Acad Award Nom
Francis	Asbury	Arts	USA	Bishop
	Bacon	Politics	England	Essayist/Statesman/Philosopher
	Beaumont	Creative Works	England	Dramatist
	Drake	Exploration	England	Explorer - Circumnavigation
	Galton	Science	England	Writer/Pioneer - Eugenics
	Hutcheson	Arts	Ireland	Philosopher
	Lai	Performing Arts	France	Singer
	Lieber	Arts	USA	Philosopher
	Marion	War & Peace	USA	General - Revolutionary War
	Ouimet	Sports	USA	Golfer - HF
	Parkman	Arts	USA	Historian
	Quarles	Creative Works	England	Poet
	Thompson	Creative Works	England	Poet
	Walsingham	Politics	England	Statesman
	Younghusband	Exploration	England	Explorer - Himalayas
Francis (Frank)	McGee	Sports	Canada	Hockey Player - HF
Francis Andrew	Gaffney	Aviation	USA	Astronaut
Francis Asbury (Fran)	Tarkenton	Sports	USA	Football Player - HF
Francis Elizabeth Caroline	Willard	Politics	USA	Temperance Leader
Francis Ford	Coppola	Movie Production	USA	Director - Academy Award
Francis Harry Compton	Crick	Science	England	Medicine - Nobel Laureate
Francis James	Childers	Arts	USA	Scholar
Francis Jean Marcel	Poulenc	Creative Works	France	Composer
Francis John (Hun)	Ryan	Sports	USA	Soccer Player - HF
Francis M. (King)	Clancy	Sports	Canada	Hockey Player - HF
Francis Richard	Scobee	Aviation	USA	Astronaut
Francis Scott	Key	Creative Works	USA	Poet
Francis Scott Ley	Fitzgerald	Creative Works	USA	Author - Pulitzer
Francis Townsend (Frank)	Hunter	Sports	USA	Tennis Player - HF
Francis Turner	Palgrave	Creative Works	England	Poet/Anthologist
Francis William	Aston	Science	England	Chemistry - Nobel Laureate
Francis William (Frank)	Mahovolich	Sports	Canada	Hockey Player - HF

SOLVER SERIES: NAME FINDER

FIRST NAME	LAST NAME	CATEGORY	COUNTRY	FAME
Francis X.	Bushman	Performing Arts	USA	Actor
Francis Xavier (Frank)	Shields	Sports	USA	Tennis Player - HF
Francisco	Franco	Politics	Spain	Dictator
	Pizarro	Exploration	Spain	Explorer - South America
	Pizarro	War & Peace	Spain	Conquistador
	Villa	War & Peace	Mexico	Revolutionary Leader
Francisco (Pancho)	Villa	Sports	Philippines	Boxer - HF
Francisco de	Herrera	Works of Art	Spain	Painter
	Zurbarán	Works of Art	Spain	Painter
Francisco Fernández de	Córdoba	Exploration	Spain	Explorer - Mexico
Francisco Indalecio	Madero	Politics	Mexico	President
Francisco José de	Goya	Works of Art	Spain	Painter
Francisco Olegario (Pancho)	Segura	Sports	Ecuador	Tennis Player - HF
Francisco Tomás	Garcés	Exploration	Spain	Explorer - South/West America
Francisco Vásquez de	Coronado	Exploration	Spain	Explorer - Mexico
Franciszek Andrew (Frank)	Parker	Sports	USA	Tennis Player - HF
Franco	Albini	Architecture	Italy	Architect/Furniture Designer
	Harris	Sports	USA	Football Player - HF
	Modigliani	Arts	USA	Economics - Nobel Laureate
	Ponti	Architecture	Switzerland	Architect
	Purini	Architecture	Italy	Architect
	Zeffirelli	Movie Production	Italy	Director - Acad Award Nom
Franco Egidio	Malerba	Aviation	France	Astronaut
Francois	Mitterrand	Politics	France	President
	Truffaut	Movie Production	France	Director - Acad Award Nom
	Villon	Creative Works	France	Poet
François	Boucher	Works of Art	France	Painter
	Clouet	Works of Art	France	Painter - Portraits
	Couperin	Creative Works	France	Composer/Organist
	Jacob	Science	France	Medicine - Nobel Laureate
	Mauriac	Creative Works	France	Literature - Nobel Laureate
	Quesnay	Science	France	Physician/Economist
	Rabelais	Creative Works	France	Satirist/Humorist
François (Papa Doc)	Duvalier	Politics	Haiti	President
François Auguste René	Rodin	Works of Art	France	Sculptor
François de La	Rochefoucauld	Arts	France	Moralist/Writer
François de Lorraine	Guise	Politics	France	Statesman/General
François de Salignac	Fénelon	Arts	France	Clergyman/Writer
François Marie Arouet de	Voltaire	Arts	France	Philosopher/Writer
François Marie Charles	Fourier	Politics	France	Socialist Reformer
François Pierre Guillaume	Guizot	Politics	France	Statesman/Historian
Francois X. (Frank)	Boucher	Sports	Canada	Hockey Player - HF
Francoise (Frankie)	Durr	Sports	France	Tennis Player - HF
Frank	Borghi	Sports	USA	Soccer Player - HF
	Borzage	Movie Production	USA	Director - Academy Award
	Busseri	Performing Arts	Canada	Canadian Music - HF - The Four Lads
	Capra	Movie Production	Italy	Director - Academy Award
	Deford	Creative Works	USA	Journalist - Newspaper
	Finlay	Performing Arts	England	Actor - Acad Award Nom
	Fredrickson	Sports	Canada	Hockey Player - HF
	Gatski	Sports	USA	Football Player - HF
	Gorshin	Performing Arts	USA	Comedian
	Herbert	Creative Works	USA	Author
	Howard	Sports	USA	Baseball Player
	Israel	Architecture	USA	Architect
	Langella	Performing Arts	USA	Actor
	Lloyd	Movie Production	Scotland	Director - Academy Award
	Loesser	Creative Works	USA	Dramatist - Pulitzer
	Lorenzo	Business	USA	Aviation Industry
	McCourt	Creative Works	USA	Author - Pulitzer
	Morgan	Performing Arts	USA	Actor - Acad Award Nom
	Muir	Creative Works	England	Writer - Comedy
	Nighbor	Sports	Canada	Hockey Player - HF

FIRST NAME	LAST NAME	CATEGORY	COUNTRY	FAME
Frank	Norris	Creative Works	USA	Novelist
	Perry	Movie Production	USA	Director - Acad Award Nom
	Rankin	Sports	Canada	Hockey Player - HF
	Robinson	Sports	USA	Baseball Player - HF
	Sesno	Creative Works	USA	Journalist - Television
	Shorter	Sports	Germany	Olympic Marathoner
	Sinatra	Performing Arts	USA	Actor - Academy Award
	Tashlin	Movie Production	USA	Director
	Vaughn	Sports	USA	Soccer Player - HF
	Whittle	Science	England	Inventor/Engineer
	Wilczek	Science	USA	Physics - Nobel Laureate
	Barsalona	Performing Arts	USA	Promoter - Rock & Roll - HF
	Beard	Performing Arts	USA	Rock & Roll - HF - ZZ Top
	Sinatra	Performing Arts	USA	Singer - Big Band/Jazz - HF
Frank (Frankie)	Valli (Castelluccio)	Performing Arts	USA	Rock & Roll - HF - The Four Seasons
	Valli (Castelluccio)	Performing Arts	USA	Singer - Rock & Roll - HF
Frank (Pee Wee)	Wallace	Sports	USA	Soccer Player - HF
Frank (The Enforcer)	Nitti	Law & Order	Italy	Mafia
Frank Allen	Sedgman	Sports	Australia	Tennis Player - HF
Frank Billings	Kellogg	War & Peace	USA	Peace - Nobel Laureate
Frank C.	Foyston	Sports	Canada	Hockey Player - HF
Frank Curtis	Michel	Aviation	USA	Astronaut
Frank Daniel	Gilroy	Creative Works	USA	Dramatist - Pulitzer
Frank Francis (Frankie)	Frisch	Sports	USA	Baseball Player - HF
Frank Frederick	Borman	Aviation	USA	Astronaut
Frank Gelett	Burgess	Creative Works	USA	Humorist/Illustrator
Frank Gibson	Selee	Sports	USA	Baseball Manager - HF
Frank Julius (Pee Wee)	King (Kuczynski)	Performing Arts	USA	Musician - Country Music - HF
Frank Lee	Culbertson Jr.	Aviation	USA	Astronaut
Frank Leroy	Chance	Sports	USA	Baseball Player - HF
Frank Lloyd	Wright	Architecture	USA	Architect - AIA Gold Medal
Frank Luther	Mott	Creative Works	USA	Author - Pulitzer
Frank Macfarlane	Burnet	Science	Australia	Medicine - Nobel Laureate
Frank Manning (Bruiser)	Kinard	Sports	USA	Football Player - HF
Frank Morrison (Mickey)	Spillane	Creative Works	USA	Author - Crime Fiction
Frank Newton	Gifford	Sports	USA	Football Player - HF
Frank O.	Gehry	Architecture	USA	Architect - Pritzker/ AIA Gold
Frank Sherwood	Rowland	Science	USA	Chemistry - Nobel Laureate
Frank V.	Ramsey	Sports	USA	Basketball Player - HF
Frank Vincent	Zappa	Performing Arts	USA	Singer - Rock & Roll - HF
Frank William	Taussig	Arts	USA	Political Economist
Frank Winfield	Woolworth	Business	USA	Merchant
Frank Xavier (Moose)	Goheen	Sports	USA	Hockey Player - HF
Frankie	Avalon	Performing Arts	USA	Singer/Actor
	Laine	Performing Arts	USA	Singer
	Rayder	Performing Arts	USA	Super Model
Franklin	Gowen	Business	USA	Railway Magnate
	Pierce	Politics	USA	President
Franklin (Frankie)	Lymon	Performing Arts	USA	Singer - Rock & Roll - HF
Franklin Delano	Roosevelt	Politics	USA	President
Franklin J.	Schaffner	Movie Production	Japan	Director - Academy Award
Franklin Story	Musgrave	Aviation	USA	Astronaut
Frans	Hals	Works of Art	Netherlands	Painter
Frans Eemil	Sillanpää	Creative Works	Finland	Literature - Nobel Laureate
Frantz	Fanon	Science	France	Psychiatrist
Franz	Beckenbauer	Sports	Germany	Soccer Player - HF
	Boas	Arts	USA	Anthropologist
	Bopp	Arts	Germany	Philologist
	Grillparzer	Creative Works	Austria	Dramatist
	Kafka	Creative Works	Austria	Writer
	Kline	Works of Art	USA	Painter - Abstract Expressionist
	Lehár	Creative Works	Hungary	Composer - Operettas
	Liszt	Creative Works	Hungary	Composer/Pianist

SOLVER SERIES: NAME FINDER

FIRST NAME	LAST NAME	CATEGORY	COUNTRY	FAME
Franz	Marc	Works of Art	Germany	Painter
	Werfel	Creative Works	Austria	Poet/Novelist/Playwright
	Wright	Creative Works	USA	Poet – Pulitzer
Franz Joseph	Haydn	Creative Works	Austria	Composer
Franz Peter	Schubert	Creative Works	Austria	Composer
Fred	Allen	Performing Arts	USA	Actor/Comedian
	Astaire	Performing Arts	USA	Actor – Acad Award Nom
	Beardsworth	Sports	England	Soccer Player – HF
	Black	Business	USA	Aviation Industry
	Cash	Performing Arts	USA	Rock & Roll – HF – The Impressions
	Corcoran	Sports	USA	Golfer – HF
	Couples	Sports	USA	Golfer
	Dryer	Performing Arts	USA	Actor
	Dryer	Sports	USA	Football Player
	Gwynne	Performing Arts	USA	Actor
	Korth	Business	USA	Banking
	Lorenzen	Sports	USA	Race Car Driver – HF
	MacMurray	Performing Arts	USA	Actor
	McGriff	Sports	USA	Baseball Player
	Offenhauser	Sports	USA	Race Car Designer – HF
	Rogers	Performing Arts	USA	Show Host
	Savage	Performing Arts	USA	Actor
	Ward	Performing Arts	USA	Actor
	Zinneman	Movie Production	Austria	Director – Academy Award
Fred (Freddie)	White	Performing Arts	USA	Rock & Roll – HF – Earth Wind & Fire
Fred Albert	Shannon	Creative Works	USA	Author – Pulitzer
Fred Clifford	Clarke	Sports	USA	Baseball Player – HF
Fred G. (Steamer)	Maxwell	Sports	Canada	Hockey Player – HF
Fred Wallace	Haise Jr.	Aviation	USA	Astronaut
Fred Weldon	Leslie	Aviation	USA	Astronaut
Freda	Payne	Performing Arts	USA	Singer
Freddie	Keppard	Performing Arts	USA	Jazz Cornetist – Big Band/Jazz – HF
	Prinze	Performing Arts	USA	Actor
	Prinze Jr.	Performing Arts	USA	Actor
Freddie (Frederick DeWayne)	Hubbard	Performing Arts	USA	Jazz Trumpeter – Big Band/Jazz –HF
Freddy	Cannon	Performing Arts	USA	Singer
	Fender	Performing Arts	USA	Singer
Frederic	Forrest	Performing Arts	USA	Actor – Acad Award Nom
	Remington	Works of Art	USA	Painter/Sculptor/Illustrator
Frédéric	Mistral	Creative Works	France	Literature – Nobel Laureate
	Passy	Arts	France	Economist
	Passy	War & Peace	France	Peace – Nobel Laureate
Frédéric Auguste	Bartholdi	Works of Art	France	Sculptor
Frédéric François	Chopin	Creative Works	Poland	Composer
Frederic L.	Paxson	Creative Works	USA	Author – Pulitzer
Frederic William	Goudy	Arts	USA	Print Designer
	Maitland	Law & Order	England	Jurist/Legal Historian
Frederick	Church	Works of Art	USA	Painter – Landscape
	Delius	Creative Works	England	Composer
	Douglass	Creative Works	USA	Journalist – Newspaper
	Douglass	Politics	USA	Statesman/Journalist
	Marryat	Creative Works	England	Novelist/Naval Officer
	North	Politics	England	Prime Minister
	Pohl	Creative Works	USA	Author – SciFi
	Pollock	Law & Order	England	Jurist/Writer
	Reins	Science	USA	Physics – Nobel Laureate
	Sanger	Science	England	Chemistry – Nobel Laureate
	Soddy	Science	England	Chemistry – Nobel Laureate
	Weyerhauser	Business	USA	Lumber Industry
	Whitcroft	Sports	Canada	Hockey Player – HF
Frederick (Cyclone)	Taylor	Sports	Canada	Hockey Player – HF
Frederick Bean (Tex)	Avery	Creative Works	USA	Cartoonist – Animated Movies
Frederick Beasley	Alexander	Sports	USA	Tennis Player – HF

FIRST NAME	LAST NAME	CATEGORY	COUNTRY	FAME
Frederick Chapman	Robbins	Science	USA	Medicine - Nobel Laureate
Frederick Charles (Fred)	Lindstrom	Sports	USA	Baseball Player - HF
Frederick Childe	Hassam	Works of Art	USA	Painter/Etcher
Frederick Douglass (Fritz)	Pollard	Sports	USA	Football Player - HF
Frederick Gowland	Hopkins	Science	England	Medicine - Nobel Laureate
Frederick Grant	Banting	Science	Canada	Medicine - Nobel Laureate
Frederick Hamilton	Hauck	Aviation	USA	Astronaut
Frederick Howard (Fred)	Hovey	Sports	USA	Tennis Player - HF
Frederick Hugh (Hughie)	Lehman	Sports	Canada	Hockey Player - HF
Frederick Jackson	Turner	Creative Works	USA	Author - Pulitzer
Frederick James	Furnivall	Arts	England	Philologist/Editor
Frederick John (Fred)	Perry	Sports	England	Tennis Player - HF
Frederick Joseph (Bun)	Cook	Sports	Canada	Hockey Player - HF
Frederick Law	Olmsted	Architecture	USA	Architect - Landscape Design
Frederick Moore	Vinson	Law & Order	USA	Chief Justice
Frederick Rudolph (Ted)	Schroeder	Sports	USA	Tennis Player - HF
Frederick S. (Fred)	Biletnikoff	Sports	USA	Football Player - HF
Frederick Sydney (Fiery Fred)	Stolle	Sports	Australia	Tennis Player - HF
Frederick William Augustus von	Steuben	War & Peace	USA	General - American Revolution
Frederik Willem de	Klerk	War & Peace	South Africa	Peace - Nobel Laureate
Frederique Van Der	Wal	Performing Arts	Netherlands	Super Model
Fredric	March	Performing Arts	USA	Actor - Academy Award
Fredrick	Scanlon	Sports	Canada	Hockey Player - HF
Fredrik	Bajer	War & Peace	Denmark	Peace - Nobel Laureate
Freeman	Gosden	Performing Arts	USA	Comedian
Frei	Otto	Architecture	Germany	Architect - Jefferson Medal
Frew Donald	McMillan	Sports	South Africa	Tennis Player - HF
Fridtjof	Nansen	Exploration	Norway	Explorer - Arctic
	Nansen	War & Peace	Norway	Peace - Nobel Laureate
Friedensreich	Hundertwasser	Architecture	Austria	Architect
Friedrich	Bergius	Science	Germany	Chemistry - Nobel Laureate
	Engels	Arts	Germany	Philosopher/Socialist/Writer
	Waismann	Arts	Austria	Philosopher
Friedrich Albert Moritz	Schlick	Arts	Germany	Philosopher
Friedrich August	Wolf	Arts	Germany	Scholar - Classical
Friedrich August von	Hayek	Arts	Austria	Economics - Nobel Laureate
Friedrich Ernest Daniel	Schleiermacher	Arts	Germany	Philosopher/Theologian
Friedrich Gustav Emil Martin	Niemöller	Arts	Germany	Protestant Leader
Friedrich Heinrich	Humboldt	Exploration	Germany	Explorer- Orinoco River
Friedrich Max	Müller	Arts	England	Philologist/Mythologist
Friedrich von	Flotow	Creative Works	Germany	Composer - Opera
Friedrich Wilhelm	Nietzsche	Arts	Germany	Philosopher
Friedrich Wilhelm August	Froebel	Arts	Germany	Educator
Friedrich Wilhelm Joseph von	Schelling	Arts	Germany	Philosopher
Frits Frederik	Zernike	Science	Netherlands	Physics - Nobel Laureate
Fritz	Haber	Science	Germany	Chemistry - Nobel Laureate
	Kreisler	Creative Works	USA	Composer/Violinist
	Lang	Movie Production	Austria	Director
	Pregl	Science	Austria	Chemistry - Nobel Laureate
	Weaver	Performing Arts	USA	Actor
Fritz Albert	Lipmann	Science	USA	Medicine - Nobel Laureate
Fritz Reuter	Leiber Jr.	Creative Works	USA	Author - SciFi
Fritzie	Zivic	Sports	USA	Boxer - HF
Fumihiko	Maki	Architecture	Japan	Architect - Pritzker/Jefferson Medal
Fuzzy	Zoeller	Sports	USA	Golfer
Gabby	Hayes	Performing Arts	USA	Actor
Gabe	Kaplan	Performing Arts	USA	Comedian
Gabriel	Batistuta	Sports	Argentina	Soccer Player
	Fahrenheit	Science	Germany	Physicist
	Lippmann	Science	France	Physics - Nobel Laureate
	Marcel	Arts	France	Philosopher
Gabriel (Flash)	Elorde	Sports	Philippines	Boxer - HF
Gabriel Garcia	Márquez	Creative Works	Colombia	Literature - Nobel Laureate

SOLVER SERIES: NAME FINDER

FIRST NAME	LAST NAME	CATEGORY	COUNTRY	FAME
Gabriel Tirso de	Molina	Creative Works	Spain	Dramatist
Gabriel Urbain	Fauré	Creative Works	France	Composer
Gabriela	Mistral	Creative Works	Chile	Literature - Nobel Laureate
	Sabatini	Sports	Argentina	Tennis Player
Gabriele	D'Annunzio	Creative Works	Italy	Poet
Gabrielle	Chanel	Business	France	Fashion Designer
Gae	Aulenti	Architecture	Italy	Architect
Gaetano	Donizetti	Creative Works	Italy	Composer - Opera
Gaetano Alberto (Guy)	Lombardo	Performing Arts	Canada	Band Leader - Big Band/Jazz - HF
	Lombardo	Performing Arts	Canada	Band Leader - Canadian Music - HF
Gahan	Wilson	Creative Works	USA	Cartoonist - Magazines
Gail	Devers	Sports	USA	Olympic Runner
	Godwin	Creative Works	USA	Novelist
	Goodrich	Sports	USA	Basketball Player - HF
Gaius Julius	Caesar	War & Peace	Italy	Dictator/Military Leader
Gale	Gordon	Performing Arts	USA	Actor
	Sondergaard	Performing Arts	USA	Actress - Academy Award
	Storm	Performing Arts	USA	Actress/Singer
Gale Eugene	Sayers	Sports	USA	Football Player - HF
Galileo	Galilei	Science	Italy	Astronomer/Physicist
Galina Sergeyevna	Ulanova	Performing Arts	Russia	Dancer - Ballerina
Galway	Kinnell	Creative Works	USA	Poet - Pulitzer
Gamal Abdel	Nasser	Politics	Saudi Arabia	President
Gamaliel	Bradford	Arts	USA	Biographer
Gao	Hong	Sports	China	Soccer Player
	Xingjian	Creative Works	France	Literature - Nobel Laureate
Garavani	Valentino	Business	Italy	Fashion Designer
Gardnar Putnam (Gar)	Mulloy	Sports	USA	Tennis Player - HF
Gardner	Rea	Creative Works	USA	Cartoonist
Garo	Yepremian	Sports	USA	Football Player
Garret A.	Hobart	Politics	USA	Vice-President
Garrett	Fitzgerald	Politics	Ireland	Prime Minister
Garrison	Keillor	Creative Works	USA	Journalist - Radio
Garry	Shandling	Performing Arts	USA	Comedian
	Trudeau	Creative Works	USA	Cartoonist - Doonesbury
Garth	Brooks	Performing Arts	USA	Singer/Composer
Garth (Eric)	Hudson	Performing Arts	Canada	Rock & Roll - HF - The Band
Gary	Burghoff	Performing Arts	USA	Actor
	Busey	Performing Arts	USA	Actor - Acad Award Nom
	Clark	Sports	USA	Football Player
	Coleman	Performing Arts	USA	Actor
	Cooper	Performing Arts	USA	Actor - Academy Award
	Kasparov	Games	Russia	Chess Player
	Larson	Creative Works	USA	Cartoonist - Far Side
	Lineker	Sports	England	Soccer Player
	Merrill	Performing Arts	USA	Actor
	Oldman	Performing Arts	England	Actor
	Player	Sports	South Africa	Golfer - HF
	Sandy	Performing Arts	USA	Actor
	Sinise	Performing Arts	USA	Actor - Acad Award Nom
	Snyder	Creative Works	USA	Poet - Pulitzer
	Wills	Creative Works	USA	Author - Pulitzer
Gary Edmund	Carter	Sports	USA	Baseball Player - HF
Gary Eugene	Payton	Aviation	USA	Astronaut
Gary S.	Becker	Arts	USA	Economics - Nobel Laureate
Gary Warren	Hart	Politics	USA	Senator - Colorado
Gaspar	Corte Real	Exploration	Portugal	Explorer - Greenland
Gaspar de	Portolá	Exploration	Spain	Explorer - California
Gaspard de	Coligny	War & Peace	France	Admiral
Gaston	Bachelard	Arts	France	Philosopher
	Lachaise	Works of Art	USA	Sculptor
Gates	McFadden	Performing Arts	USA	Actress
Gavin	MacLeod	Performing Arts	USA	Actor

FIRST NAME	LAST NAME	CATEGORY	COUNTRY	FAME
Gaylord Jackson	Perry	Sports	USA	Baseball Player - HF
Gebhard Leberecht von	Blücher	War & Peace	Germany	Field Marshall
Geddy	Lee	Performing Arts	Canada	Canadian Music - HF - Rush
Geena	Davis	Performing Arts	USA	Actress - Academy Award
Gena	Rowlands	Performing Arts	USA	Actress - Acad Award Nom
Gena Lee	Nolan	Performing Arts	USA	Actress
Gene	Barry	Performing Arts	USA	Actor
	Chandler	Performing Arts	USA	Singer
	Cornish	Performing Arts	Canada	Rock & Roll - HF - The Young Rascals
	Fullmer	Sports	USA	Boxer - HF
	Hackman	Performing Arts	USA	Actor - Academy Award
	Kelly	Performing Arts	USA	Actor - Acad Award Nom
	Krupa	Performing Arts	USA	Jazz Drummer - Big Band/Jazz - HF
	Littler	Sports	USA	Golfer - HF
	Lockhart	Performing Arts	Canada	Actor - Acad Award Nom
	Olaff	Sports	USA	Soccer Player - HF
	Pitney	Performing Arts	USA	Singer - Rock & Roll - HF
	Saks	Movie Production	USA	Director
	Sarazen	Sports	USA	Golfer - HF
	Shalit	Creative Works	USA	Journalist - Television
	Siskel	Creative Works	USA	Journalist - Newspaper
	Stewart	Performing Arts	USA	Rock & Roll - HF - The Soul Stirrers
	Tierney	Performing Arts	USA	Actress - Acad Award Nom
	Tunney	Sports	USA	Boxer - HF
	Wilder	Performing Arts	USA	Actor - Acad Award Nom
Gene (Harold Eugene)	Clark	Performing Arts	USA	Rock & Roll - HF - The Bryds
Gene (Orvon)	Autry	Performing Arts	USA	Actor/Singer - Country Music - HF
Genevieve	Bujold	Performing Arts	Canada	Actress - Acad Award Nom
Genghis	Khan	War & Peace	Mongolia	Military Leader
Gentile	Bellini	Works of Art	Italy	Painter
Geoff	Coombes	Sports	England	Soccer Player - HF
Geoffrey	Chaucer	Creative Works	England	Poet
	Holder	Performing Arts	Trinidad	Actor
	Rush	Performing Arts	Australia	Actor - Academy Award
	Wilkinson	Science	England	Chemistry - Nobel Laureate
Georg	Solti	Performing Arts	Hungary	Conductor/Composer
	Wittig	Science	England	Chemistry - Nobel Laureate
Georg Morris	Brandes	Arts	Denmark	Literary Critic
Georg Philipp	Telemann	Creative Works	Germany	Composer
Georg Simon	Ohm	Science	Germany	Physicist
Georg von	Békésy	Science	USA	Medicine - Nobel Laureate
Georg Wilhelm Frederich	Hegel	Arts	Germany	Philosopher
George	Ade	Creative Works	USA	Humorist
	Archer	Sports	USA	Golfer
	Arliss	Performing Arts	England	Actor - Academy Award
	Baker	Creative Works	USA	Cartoonist - Sad Sack
	Balanchine	Creative Works	USA	Choreographer
	Bancroft	Performing Arts	USA	Actor - Acad Award Nom
	Bancroft	Politics	USA	Statesman
	Barr	Sports	Scotland	Soccer Player - HF
	Benson	Performing Arts	USA	Jazz Guitarist/Singer
	Berkely	Arts	Ireland	Philosopher
	Best	Sports	Northern Ireland	Soccer Player - HF
	Bignotti	Sports	USA	Race Car Driver - HF
	Bradshaw	Business	England	Railway Magnate
	Brent	Creative Works	France	Poet/Art Critic
	Brown	Business	USA	Ship Building
	Brown	Sports	Scotland	Soccer Player - HF
	Burns	Performing Arts	USA	Actor - Academy Award
	Cadbury	Business	England	Confection Industry
	Canning	Politics	England	Prime Minister
	Carlin	Performing Arts	USA	Comedian
	Catlin	Works of Art	USA	Artist/Ethnologist

SOLVER SERIES: NAME FINDER

FIRST NAME	LAST NAME	CATEGORY	COUNTRY	FAME
George	Chakiris	Performing Arts	USA	Actor - Academy Award
	Chapman	Creative Works	England	Playwright
	Clinton	Politics	USA	Vice-President
	Clooney	Performing Arts	USA	Actor
	Courtauld	Business	England	Textile Industry
	Crabbe	Creative Works	England	Poet
	Cruikshank	Creative Works	England	Caricaturist/Illustrator
	Cukor	Movie Production	USA	Director - Academy Award
	Dangerfield	Creative Works	USA	Author - Pulitzer
	Dewey	War & Peace	USA	Admiral
	Dillon	Creative Works	USA	Poet - Pulitzer
	Dzundza	Performing Arts	Germany	Actor
	Eastman	Business	USA	Kodak Film Company
	Eliot (Marian Evans)	Creative Works	England	Novelist
	Etherege	Creative Works	England	Playwright
	Farquar	Creative Works	England	Playwright
	Fox	Arts	England	Religious Leader
	Gershwin	Creative Works	USA	Composer
	Gervin	Sports	USA	Basketball Player - HF
	Grenville	Politics	England	Prime Minister
	Grizzard	Performing Arts	USA	Actor
	Grosz	Works of Art	USA	Painter/Caricaturist
	Grote	Arts	England	Historian
	Hainsworth	Sports	Canada	Hockey Player - HF
	Hamilton	Performing Arts	USA	Actor
	Harrison	Performing Arts	England	Rock & Roll - HF - The Beatles
	Hepplewhite	Arts	England	Cabinetmaker
	Hudson	Business	England	Railway Magnate
	Inness	Works of Art	USA	Painter
	Jessel	Performing Arts	USA	Comedian
	Kelly	Creative Works	USA	Dramatist - Pulitzer
	Kennedy	Performing Arts	USA	Actor - Academy Award
	Lucas	Movie Production	USA	Director - Acad Award Nom
	Macdonald	Creative Works	Scotland	Poet/Novelist
	McNamara	Sports	Canada	Hockey Player - HF
	Meany	Business	USA	Labor Leader
	Meredith	Creative Works	England	Poet/Novelist
	Michael	Performing Arts	England	Singer
	Monk	War & Peace	England	General/Politician
	Moorhouse	Sports	England	Soccer Player - HF
	Murphy	Performing Arts	USA	Actor
	Nelson	Performing Arts	USA	Rock & Roll - HF - The Orioles
	Oppen	Creative Works	USA	Poet - Pulitzer
	Orwell	Creative Works	England	Writer
	Peabody	Business	USA	Merchant/Philanthropist
	Peele	Creative Works	England	Dramatist
	Peppard	Performing Arts	USA	Actor
	Porter	Science	England	Chemistry - Nobel Laureate
	Raft	Performing Arts	USA	Actor
	Rawlinson	Arts	England	Historian/Orientalist
	Reeves	Performing Arts	USA	Actor
	Richardson	Sports	Canada	Hockey Player - HF
	Sanders	Performing Arts	Russia	Actor - Academy Award
	Santayana	Arts	Spain	Philosopher/Writer
	Seaton	Movie Production	USA	Director - Acad Award Nom
	Segal	Performing Arts	USA	Actor - Acad Award Nom
	Shearing	Performing Arts	England	Jazz Pianist
	Steinbrenner	Business	USA	Baseball Owner
	Stephenson	Science	England	Engineer - Steam Locomotive
	Stevens	Movie Production	USA	Director - Academy Award
	Strait	Performing Arts	USA	Singer - Country & Western
	Szell	Performing Arts	USA	Conductor - Orchestra/Pianist
	Vancouver	Exploration	England	Explorer - Canada West Coast

FIRST NAME	LAST NAME	CATEGORY	COUNTRY	FAME
George	Vezina	Sports	Canada	Hockey Player - HF
	Wald	Science	USA	Medicine - Nobel Laureate
	Washington	Politics	USA	President
	Washington	War & Peace	USA	General
	Weah	Sports	Liberia	Soccer Player
	Wendt	Performing Arts	USA	Actor
	Westinghouse	Business	USA	Manufacturer/Inventor
	Whitefield	Arts	England	Evangilist - Methodist
	Will	Creative Works	USA	Journalist - Newspaper - Pulitzer
	Wright	Sports	USA	Baseball Executive -HF
	Wythe	Law & Order	USA	Jurist/Patriot
	Yardley	Sports	USA	Basketball Player - HF
George (Buck)	Boucher	Sports	Canada	Hockey Player - HF
George (Spanky)	McFarland	Performing Arts	USA	Actor
George A.	Akerlof	Arts	USA	Economics - Nobel Laureate
	Olah	Science	USA	Chemistry - Nobel Laureate
George Alfred	Henty	Creative Works	England	Writer
George Anderson	McAfee	Sports	USA	Football Player - HF
George Armstrong	Custer	War & Peace	USA	Army Officer
George Augustus	Moore	Creative Works	Ireland	Novelist/Playwright/Critic
George Bernard	Shaw	Creative Works	England	Literature - Nobel Laureate
George Brinton	McClellan	War & Peace	USA	General - Civil War
George Brown	Post	Architecture	USA	Architect - AIA Gold Medal
George C.	Scott	Performing Arts	USA	Actor - Academy Award
George Caleb	Bingham	Works of Art	USA	Painter - Realist
George Castriota	Scanderbeg	Politics	Albania	Leader/National Hero
George Catlett	Marshall	Politics	USA	Statesman/General
	Marshall	War & Peace	USA	Peace - Nobel Laureate
George Clyde	Kell	Sports	USA	Baseball Player - HF
George Corley	Wallace	Politics	USA	Governor - Alabama
George D.	Snell	Science	USA	Medicine - Nobel Laureate
George David	Low	Aviation	USA	Astronaut
George de	Hevesy	Science	Hungary	Chemistry - Nobel Laureate
George Driver (Pinky)	Nelson	Aviation	USA	Astronaut
George E.	Palade	Science	USA	Medicine - Nobel Laureate
George Edward	Foreman	Sports	USA	Boxer - HF
	Moore	Arts	England	Philosopher
	Pickett	War & Peace	USA	Confederate General
	Trafton	Sports	USA	Football Player - HF
George Edward (Chief)	Armstrong	Sports	Canada	Hockey Player - HF
George Edward (Rube)	Waddell	Sports	USA	Baseball Player - HF
George Edward Bateman	Saintsbury	Arts	England	Critic - Literary
George Eugène	Haussmann	Architecture	France	Architect
George Francis	Abbott	Creative Works	USA	Dramatist - Pulitzer
	Musso	Sports	USA	Football Player - HF
George Frederic	Watts	Works of Art	England	Painter/Sculptor - Symbolist
George Frederick	Blanda	Sports	USA	Football Player - HF
	Handel	Creative Works	England	Composer
George Frost	Kennan	Creative Works	USA	Author - Pulitzer
George Gilbert	Murray	Arts	England	Scholar - Classical
	Scott	Architecture	England	Architect
George Glen	Jones	Performing Arts	USA	Singer - Country Music - HF
George Gordon	Meade	War & Peace	USA	General - Civil War
George Gray	Barnard	Works of Art	USA	Sculptor
George H.	Hitchings	Science	USA	Medicine - Nobel Laureate
George Harold	Sisler	Sports	USA	Baseball Player - HF
George Henry	Borrow	Creative Works	England	Writer/Linguist
	Dalziel	Business	England	Publishing
	Lewes	Creative Works	England	Writer/Critic
	Thomas	War & Peace	USA	Union General - Civil War
George Herbert	Allen	Sports	USA	Football Player - HF
George Herbert Walker	Bush	Politics	USA	President
George Herman (Babe)	Ruth	Sports	USA	Baseball Player - HF

FIRST NAME	LAST NAME	CATEGORY	COUNTRY	FAME
George Howard	Brett	Sports	USA	Baseball Player - HF
George Hoyt	Whipple	Science	USA	Medicine - Nobel Laureate
George Hubert	Wilkins	Exploration	Australia	Explorer - Polar
George J.	Stigler	Arts	USA	Economics - Nobel Laureate
George Joseph	Tintle	Sports	USA	Soccer Player - HF
George L.	Mikan	Sports	USA	Basketball Player - HF
George Lange	Kelly	Sports	USA	Baseball Player - HF
George Lee (Sparky)	Anderson	Sports	USA	Baseball Manager - HF
George Leo	Connor	Sports	USA	Football Player - HF
George Louis Palmella du	Maurier	Creative Works	England	Novelist/Illustrator
George Lyman	Kittredge	Arts	USA	Scholar/Educator
George M.	Dallas	Politics	USA	Vice-President
George Macaulay	Trevelyan	Arts	England	Historian
George Martin	Lott	Sports	USA	Tennis Player - HF
	Weiss	Sports	USA	Baseball Executive -HF
George Michael	Cohan	Performing Arts	USA	Actor/Playwright/Producer
George Mortimer	Pullman	Business	USA	Manufacturing - Pullman Car
George Murphy	Foster	Performing Arts	USA	Jazz Bassist - Big Band/Jazz - HF
George Nathaniel	Curzon	Politics	England	Viceroy
George Norman	Douglas	Creative Works	England	Novelist/Essayist
George Orson	Welles	Movie Production	USA	Director - Acad Award Nom
	Welles	Performing Arts	USA	Actor - Acad Award Nom
George Otto	Trevelyan	Arts	England	Historian/Politician
George Paget	Thomson	Science	England	Physics - Nobel Laureate
George Pierce	Baker	Creative Works	USA	Author
George Plimpton	Adams	Arts	USA	Philosopher
George Preston	Marshall	Sports	USA	Football Founder - HF
George Reginald (Red)	Horner	Sports	Canada	Hockey Player - HF
George Richards	Minot	Science	USA	Medicine - Nobel Laureate
George Robert	Gissing	Creative Works	England	Novelist
George Roger	Waters	Performing Arts	England	Rock & Roll - HF - Pink Floyd
	Waters	Performing Arts	England	Singer/Guitarist
George Rogers	Clark	War & Peace	USA	Revolutionary Leader
George Roy	Hill	Movie Production	USA	Director - Academy Award
George S	Patton	War & Peace	USA	General
George Simon	Kaufman	Creative Works	USA	Dramatist - Pulitzer
George Stacey	Davis	Sports	USA	Baseball Player - HF
George Stanley	Halas	Sports	USA	Football Coach - HF
	McGovern	Politics	USA	Senator - South Dakota
George T.	Delacorte	Business	USA	Publishing - Dell
George Thomas (Tom)	Seaver	Sports	USA	Baseball Player - HF
George Townsend	Adee	Sports	USA	Tennis Player - HF
George W.	Bush	Politics	USA	President
George Washington	Cable	Creative Works	USA	Novelist
	Carver	Science	USA	Botanist/Chemist
	Goethals	War & Peace	USA	Army Officer/Engineer
George Wells	Beadle	Science	USA	Medicine - Nobel Laureate
George Wesley	Bellows	Works of Art	USA	Painter
George White	Chadwick	Creative Works	USA	Composer
George William	Hay	Sports	Canada	Hockey Player - HF
	Norris	Politics	USA	Senator
	Russell	Creative Works	Ireland	Poet/Essayist
Georges	Bizet	Creative Works	France	Composer/Opera
	Braque	Works of Art	France	Painter
	Charpak	Science	France	Physics - Nobel Laureate
	Duhamel	Creative Works	France	Poet/Novelist/Dramatist
	Enesco	Creative Works	Romania	Composer/Violinist/Conductor
	Pire	War & Peace	Belgium	Peace - Nobel Laureate
	Rouault	Works of Art	France	Painter - Fauvist Expressionist
	Sorel	Creative Works	France	Writer/Philosopher
	Thill	Performing Arts	France	Singer - Opera
Georges Benjamin Eugéne	Clemenceau	Politics	France	Premier
Georges J.F.	Köhler	Science	Germany	Medicine - Nobel Laureate

FIRST NAME	LAST NAME	CATEGORY	COUNTRY	FAME
Georges Jacques	Danton	Politics	France	Revolutionary Leader
Georges Léopold	Cuvier	Arts	France	Naturalist
Georges Louis Leclerc	Buffon	Arts	France	Naturalist
Georges Pierre	Seurat	Works of Art	France	Painter - Pointillism
Georgi Konstantinovich	Zhukov	War & Peace	Russia	Soviet Marshall
Georgi Stepanovich	Shonin	Aviation	Russia	Astronaut
Georgi Timofeyevich	Beregovoi	Aviation	Russia	Astronaut
Georgia	O'Keefe	Works of Art	USA	Painter
Georgina	Grenville	Performing Arts	South Africa	Super Model
Georgio	Armani	Business	Italy	Fashion Designer
	Vasari	Works of Art	Italy	Painter/Architect/Biographer
Georgius	Agricola	Science	Germany	Scholar
Geraint	Evans	Performing Arts	Wales	Singer - Opera
Gerald	McRaney	Performing Arts	USA	Actor
	Wilson	Performing Arts	USA	Band Leader/Composer - Big Band/Jazz - HF
Gerald (Jerry)	Herman	Creative Works	USA	Composer
Gerald Joseph (Gerry)	Mulligan	Performing Arts	USA	Jazz Saxophonist - Big Band/Jazz - HF
Gerald Leighton	Patterson	Sports	Australia	Tennis Player - HF
Gerald M.	Edelman	Science	USA	Medicine - Nobel Laureate
Gerald Michael (Gerry)	Cheevers	Sports	Canada	Hockey Player - HF
Gerald Paul	Carr	Aviation	USA	Astronaut
Gerald Rudolph	Ford	Politics	USA	President
Geraldine	Farrar	Performing Arts	USA	Singer - Opera
	Fitzgerald	Performing Arts	Ireland	Actress - Acad Award Nom
	Page	Performing Arts	USA	Actress - Academy Award
Geraldo	Rivera	Creative Works	USA	Journalist - Television
Gerard	Debreu	Arts	USA	Economics - Nobel Laureate
	Depardieu	Performing Arts	France	Actor - Acad Award Nom
	Dou	Works of Art	Netherlands	Painter
	Ter Borch	Works of Art	Netherlands	Painter
Gerard Manley	Hopkins	Creative Works	England	Poet/Jesuit Priest
Gerardo (Kid)	Gavilan	Sports	Cuba	Boxer - HF
Gerd	Binnig	Science	Germany	Physics - Nobel Laureate
	Muller	Sports	Germany	Soccer Player - HF
Gerhard	Domagk	Science	Germany	Medicine - Nobel Laureate
	Herzberg	Science	Canada	Chemistry - Nobel Laureate
Gerhard Julius Paul	Thiele	Aviation	Germany	Astronaut
Gerhardus	Mercator	Arts	Italy	Geographer/Cartographer
Gerhardus 't	Hooft	Science	Netherlands	Physics - Nobel Laureate
Gerhart Johann Robert	Hauptmann	Creative Works	Germany	Literature - Nobel Laureate
Geri (Ginger)	Halliwell	Performing Arts	England	Rock & Roll - Spice Girls
Gerrit	Rietveld	Architecture	Netherlands	Architect
Gerry	Rafferty	Performing Arts	Scotland	Singer
Gertrude	Astor	Performing Arts	USA	Actress
	Berg	Performing Arts	USA	Comedian
	Ederle	Sports	USA	Swimmer - English Channel
	Lawrence	Performing Arts	England	Actress
	Stein	Creative Works	USA	Writer
Gertrude (Ma)	Rainey (Pridgett)	Performing Arts	USA	Singer - Big Band/Jazz - HF
	Rainey (Pridgett)	Performing Arts	USA	Singer - Rock & Roll - HF
Gertrude B.	Elion	Science	USA	Medicine - Nobel Laureate
Gerty	Cori	Science	USA	Medicine - Nobel Laureate
Gherman Stepanovich	Titov	Aviation	Russia	Astronaut
Gia	Scala	Performing Arts	England	Actress
Giacomo	Meyerbeer	Creative Works	Germany	Composer - Opera
	Moraglia	Architecture	Italy	Architect
	Puccini	Creative Works	Italy	Composer - Opera
Giacomo Barozzi da	Vignola	Architecture	Italy	Architect
Giambattista	Bodoni	Arts	Italy	Print Designer
Gian Lorenzo	Bemini	Works of Art	Italy	Artist
	Bernini	Architecture	Italy	Architect
Giancarlo	Giannini	Performing Arts	Italy	Actor - Acad Award Nom
Gian-Carlo	Menotti	Creative Works	USA	Composer - Opera

SOLVER SERIES: NAME FINDER

FIRST NAME	LAST NAME	CATEGORY	COUNTRY	FAME
Giancarlo de	Carlo	Architecture	Italy	Architect
Gianni	Versace	Business	Italy	Fashion Designer
Gig	Young	Performing Arts	USA	Actor - Academy Award
Gigi	Fernandez	Sports	USA	Tennis Player
Gil	Eannes	Exploration	Portugal	Explorer - North Africa
	Hodges	Sports	USA	Baseball Player
Gilbert	Cass	Architecture	USA	Architect - Skyscraper
	Parker	Creative Works	Canada	Novelist
	Roland	Performing Arts	Mexico	Actor
	Ryle	Arts	England	Philosopher
	White	Arts	England	Naturalist
Gilbert (Gil)	Perreault	Sports	Canada	Hockey Player - HF
Gilbert Charles	Stuart	Works of Art	USA	Painter - Portrait
Gilbert Keith	Chesterton	Creative Works	England	Writer
Gilda	Radner	Performing Arts	USA	Comedian
Giles Lytton	Strachey	Arts	England	Biographer
Gilles	Villeneuve	Sports	Canada	Race Car Driver - HF
Gillo	Pontecorvo	Movie Production	Italy	Director - Acad Award Nom
Gilorma (Sam) (Momo)	Giancana	Law & Order	USA	Mafia
Gina	Gershon	Performing Arts	USA	Actress
	Lollobrigida	Performing Arts	Italy	Actress
Ginger	Baker	Performing Arts	England	Rock & Roll - HF - Cream
	Rogers	Performing Arts	USA	Actress - Academy Award
Gino	Cappelletti	Sports	USA	Football Player
	Gard (Gardassanich)	Sports	Croatia	Soccer Player - HF
	Pariani	Sports	USA	Soccer Player - HF
	Valle	Architecture	Italy	Architect
Gino John	Marchetti	Sports	USA	Football Player - HF
Gio	Ponti	Architecture	Italy	Architect
Gioacchino Antonio	Rossini	Creative Works	Italy	Composer
Giogio	Vasari	Architecture	Italy	Architect
Giordano	Bruno	Arts	Italy	Philosopher
Giorgio	Chinaglia	Sports	Italy	Soccer Player - HF
	Chirico	Works of Art	Italy	Painter
	Grassi	Architecture	Italy	Architect
Giorgos	Seferis	Creative Works	Greece	Literature - Nobel Laureate
Giosuè	Carducci	Creative Works	Italy	Literature - Nobel Laureate
Giovanni	Bellini	Works of Art	Italy	Painter
	Boccaccio	Creative Works	Italy	Author/Poet
	Cimabue	Works of Art	Italy	Painter/Artist
	Martinelli	Performing Arts	USA	Singer - Opera
Giovanni Battista	Pergolesi	Creative Works	Italy	Composer
	Piranesi	Architecture	Italy	Architect
	Quadrio	Architecture	Italy	Architect
	Tiepolo	Works of Art	Italy	Painter
Giovanni da	Fiesole	Works of Art	Italy	Painter
	Verrazano	Exploration	Italy	Explorer - America East Coast
Giovanni Jacopo	Casanova	Arts	Italy	Adventurer
Giovanni Lorenzo	Bernini	Works of Art	Italy	Sculptor/Painter
Giovanni Pico della	Mirandola	Arts	Italy	Philosopher/Humanist
Giovanni Virginio	Schiaparelli	Science	Italy	Astronomer
Gisele	Bundchen	Performing Arts	Brazil	Super Model
	MacKenzie	Performing Arts	Canada	Singer
Giuliano da	Sangallo	Architecture	Italy	Architect
Giulio	Natta	Science	Italy	Chemistry - Nobel Laureate
	Romano	Architecture	Italy	Architect
Giuseppe	Garibaldi	War & Peace	Italy	General/Patriot
	Mazzini	Politics	Italy	Patriot/Revolutionist
	Pagano	Architecture	Austria	Architect
	Samonà	Architecture	Italy	Architect
	Scarlatti	Creative Works	Italy	Composer
	Tartini	Creative Works	Italy	Composer/Violinist
	Terragni	Architecture	Italy	Architect

FIRST NAME	LAST NAME	CATEGORY	COUNTRY	FAME
Giuseppe Antonio	Guarneri	Arts	Italy	Violin Maker
Giuseppe Fortunino Francisco	Verdi	Creative Works	Italy	Composer - Opera
Gladys	Cooper	Performing Arts	England	Actress - Acad Award Nom
	George	Performing Arts	USA	Actress - Acad Award Nom
Gladys Marie	Knight	Performing Arts	USA	Rock & Roll - HF - The Pips
Gladys Medalie	Heldman	Sports	USA	Tennis Player - HF
Glen	Campbell	Performing Arts	USA	Singer - Country Music - HF
	Wood	Sports	USA	Race Car Driver - HF
Glenda	Jackson	Performing Arts	England	Actress - Academy Award
Glenn	Close	Performing Arts	USA	Actress - Acad Award Nom
	Ford	Performing Arts	USA	Actor
	Frey	Performing Arts	USA	Rock & Roll - HF - The Eagles
	McCarthy	Business	USA	Oil Industry
	Murcutt	Architecture	Australia	Architect - Pritzker/Jefferson Medal
	Yarborough	Performing Arts	USA	Singer
Glenn (Fireball)	Roberts	Sports	USA	Race Car Driver - HF
Glenn Hammond	Curtis	Aviation	USA	Aircraft Construction
Glenn Henry	Hall	Sports	Canada	Hockey Player - HF
Glenn Herbert	Gould	Performing Arts	Canada	Pianist - Canadian Music - HF
Glenn Theodore	Seaborg	Science	USA	Chemistry - Nobel Laureate
Glenna Collette	Vare	Sports	USA	Golfer - HF
Gloria	Estefan	Performing Arts	Cuba	Singer
	Grahame	Performing Arts	USA	Actress - Academy Award
	Loring	Performing Arts	USA	Actress/Singer
	Steinem	Creative Works	USA	Journalist - Magazine
	Stuart	Performing Arts	USA	Actress - Acad Award Nom
	Swanson	Performing Arts	USA	Actress - Acad Award Nom
	Vanderbilt	Business	USA	Fashion Designer
Gloria De	Haven	Performing Arts	USA	Actress
Glynis	Johns	Performing Arts	South Africa	Actress - Acad Award Nom
Godfrey N.	Hounsfield	Science	England	Medicine - Nobel Laureate
Golda	Meir	Politics	Israel	Prime Minister
Goldie	Hawn	Performing Arts	USA	Actress - Acad Award Nom
Gord	Sinclair	Performing Arts	Canada	Canadian Music - HF - The Tragically Hip
Gordon	Banks	Sports	England	Soccer Player - HF
	Bunshaft	Architecture	USA	Architect - Pritzker Laureate
	Downie	Performing Arts	Canada	Canadian Music - HF - The Tragically Hip
	Jump	Performing Arts	USA	Actor
	Lightfoot	Performing Arts	Canada	Singer - Folk - Canadian Music - HF
	MacRae	Performing Arts	USA	Singer
	Pinsent	Performing Arts	Canada	Actor
	Roberts	Sports	Canada	Hockey Player - HF
Gordon (Gordie)	Johncock	Sports	USA	Race Car Driver - HF
Gordon (Gordie) (Mr. Hockey)	Howe	Sports	Canada	Hockey Player - HF
Gordon (Specs)	Powell	Performing Arts	USA	Jazz Trombonist - Big Band/Jazz - HF
Gordon (Tex)	Beneke	Performing Arts	USA	Band Leader/Saxophonist
Gordon Allan (Phat)	Wilson	Sports	Canada	Hockey Player - HF
Gordon Arthur	Drillon	Sports	Canada	Hockey Player - HF
Gordon Blanchard (Duke)	Keats	Sports	Canada	Hockey Player - HF
Gordon Matthew (Sting)	Sumner	Performing Arts	England	Singer - Rock & Roll - HF
Gordon S.	Wood	Creative Works	USA	Author - Pulitzer
Gordon Stanley (Mickey)	Cochrane	Sports	USA	Baseball Player - HF
Gordon Willard	Allport	Arts	USA	Psychologist
Gottfried	Boehm	Architecture	Germany	Architect - Pritzker Laureate
	Semper	Architecture	Germany	Architect
Gottfried Von (The Baron)	Cramm	Sports	Germany	Tennis Player - HF
Gottfried Wilhelm von	Leibniz	Arts	Germany	Philosopher/Mathematician
Gotthold	Ephraim	Creative Works	Germany	Dramatist/Critic
Gottlieb	Daimler	Business	Germany	Automobile Industy
Gottlieb Eliel	Saarinen	Architecture	Finland	Architect - AIA Gold Medal
Gouverneur	Morris	Politics	USA	Statesman/Diplomat
Gower	Champion	Creative Works	USA	Choreographer
Grace	Jones	Performing Arts	Jamaica	Singer/Model

SOLVER SERIES: NAME FINDER

FIRST NAME	LAST NAME	CATEGORY	COUNTRY	FAME
Grace	Kelly	Performing Arts	USA	Actress - Academy Award
	Moore	Performing Arts	USA	Actress - Acad Award Nom
Grace Anna	Coolidge	Politics	USA	First Lady
Grace Barnett	Wing (Slick)	Performing Arts	USA	Rock & Roll - HF - Jefferson Airplane
Gracie	Allen	Performing Arts	USA	Actress/Comedian
	Fields	Performing Arts	England	Singer
Graham	Chapman	Performing Arts	England	Comedian
	Greene	Creative Works	England	Novelist
	Greene	Performing Arts	Canada	Actor - Acad Award Nom
	Nash	Performing Arts	England	Rock & Roll - HF - Crosby Stills & Nash
	Parker	Performing Arts	England	Singer
Graig	Nettles	Sports	USA	Baseball Player
Grandpa (Louis Marshall)	Jones	Performing Arts	USA	Singer - Country Music - HF
Grant	Fuhr	Sports	Canada	Hockey Player - HF
	Wood	Works of Art	USA	Painter
Grant A.	Tinker	Business	USA	Television Industry
Granville Stanley	Hall	Arts	USA	Psychologist/Educator
Gratton	Dalton	Law & Order	USA	Outlaw
Grayson	Hall	Performing Arts	USA	Actress - Acad Award Nom
Grazia	Deledda	Creative Works	Italy	Literature - Nobel Laureate
Greer	Garson	Performing Arts	England	Actress - Academy Award
Greg	Kinnear	Performing Arts	USA	Actor - Acad Award Nom
	Lake	Performing Arts	England	Singer
	Louganis	Sports	USA	Olympic
	Morris	Performing Arts	USA	Actor
	Norman	Sports	Australia	Golfer - HF
Gregg	Allmann	Performing Arts	USA	Rock & Roll - HF - Allmann Brothers Band
Gregor Johann	Mendel	Science	Austria	Botanist - Founder of Genetics
Gregory	Ain	Architecture	USA	Architect
	Harrison	Performing Arts	USA	Actor
	Hines	Performing Arts	USA	Actor/Dancer
	Peck	Performing Arts	USA	Actor - Academy Award
Gregory Bruce	Jarvis	Aviation	USA	Astronaut
Gregory Jordan	Harbaugh	Aviation	USA	Astronaut
Gregory La	Cava	Movie Production	USA	Director - Acad Award Nom
Gregory Thomas	Linteris	Aviation	USA	Astronaut
Gregory White	Smith	Creative Works	USA	Author - Pulitzer
Greta	Garbo	Performing Arts	Sweden	Actress - Acad Award Nom
Gretchen	Wyler	Performing Arts	USA	Actress
Grete	Waitz	Sports	Norway	Olympic Marathoner
Gretta	Scacchi	Performing Arts	Italy	Actress
Griffin	Dunne	Performing Arts	USA	Actor
Grigori Efimovich	Rasputin	Science	Russia	Faith Healer/Religious Mystic
Grover Cleveland (Pete)	Alexander	Sports	USA	Baseball Player - HF
Guarino	Guarini	Architecture	Italy	Architect
Guccio	Gucci	Business	Italy	Fashion Designer
Guglielmo	Marconi	Science	Italy	Physics - Nobel Laureate
Guido	Canella	Architecture	Italy	Architect
	d'Arezzo	Arts	Italy	Musical Theorist
	Reni	Works of Art	Italy	Painter - Baroque
Guillaume	Appollinaire	Creative Works	France	Poet/Essayist
Guillaume Victor Emile	Augier	Creative Works	France	Playwright
Guillermo	Vilas	Sports	Argentina	Tennis Player - HF
Guion Steward	Bluford	Aviation	USA	Astronaut
Guiseppe (Joe)	Venuti	Performing Arts	USA	Jazz Violinist - Big Band/Jazz - HF
Gunnar	Birkerts	Architecture	USA	Architect
	Nelson	Performing Arts	USA	Singer
Günter	Blobel	Science	USA	Medicine - Nobel Laureate
	Grass	Creative Works	Germany	Literature - Nobel Laureate
Gus	Bell	Sports	USA	Baseball Player
Gus Sessions	Wortham	Business	USA	Insurance Industry
Gus Van	Sant	Movie Production	USA	Director - Acad Award Nom
Gustav	Klimt	Works of Art	Austria	Painter - Art Nouveau

FIRST NAME	LAST NAME	CATEGORY	COUNTRY	FAME
Gustav	Mahler	Creative Works	Austria	Composer
	Stresemann	War & Peace	Germany	Peace - Nobel Laureate
Gustav Ludwig	Hertz	Science	Germany	Physics - Nobel Laureate
Gustav Robert	Kirchhoff	Science	Germany	Physicist
Gustav Theodor	Fechner	Science	Germany	Physicist/Philosopher
Gustave	Charpentier	Creative Works	France	Composer
	Courbet	Works of Art	France	Painter
	Flaubert	Creative Works	France	Novelist
Gustavus	Adolphus	War & Peace	Sweden	Military Leader - King
Gustavus Theodore Von	Holst	Creative Works	England	Composer
Guy	Fawkes	War & Peace	England	Conspirator
	Forget	Sports	Morocco	Tennis Player
	Kibbee	Performing Arts	USA	Actor
	Laroche	Business	France	Fashion Designer
Guy Damien La	Fleur	Sports	Canada	Hockey Player - HF
Guy Gerard	Lapointe	Sports	Canada	Hockey Player - HF
Guy Pene du	Bois	Works of Art	USA	Painter/Art Critic
Guy Spencer	Gardner	Aviation	USA	Astronaut
Gwen	Stefani	Performing Arts	USA	Singer - Pops
	Torrence	Sports	USA	Olympic Runner
	Verdon	Performing Arts	USA	Actress
Gwendolyn	Brooks	Creative Works	USA	Poet - Pulitzer
Gwyneth	Paltrow	Performing Arts	USA	Actress - Academy Award
Gypsy Rose	Lee	Performing Arts	USA	Dancer
Gyula	Andrássy	Politics	Hungary	Prime Minister
Habib ben Ali	Bourguiba	Politics	Tunisia	President
Hafez	al Assad	Politics	Syria	President
Haile	Selassie	Politics	Ethiopia	Emperor
Haing .S	Ngor	Performing Arts	Cambodia	Actor - Academy Award
Hakeem	Olajuwon	Sports	USA	Basketball Player
Hal	Holbrook	Performing Arts	USA	Actor
	Linden	Performing Arts	USA	Actor
	Prince	Movie Production	USA	Director
	Ashby	Movie Production	USA	Director - Acad Award Nom
Haldan Keffer	Hartline	Science	USA	Medicine - Nobel Laureate
Hale	Irwin	Sports	USA	Golfer - HF
Haley Joel	Osment	Performing Arts	USA	Actor - Acad Award Nom
Halldór Kiljan	Laxness	Creative Works	Iceland	Literature - Nobel Laureate
Halle	Berry	Performing Arts	USA	Actress - Academy Award
Hamilton	Camp	Performing Arts	England	Actor
	Fish	Politics	USA	Statesman
	Hume	Exploration	Australia	Explorer - Australia
Hamilton Livingston (Billy)	Gilmour	Sports	Canada	Hockey Player - HF
Hamilton O.	Smith	Science	USA	Medicine - Nobel Laureate
Hana	Mandlíková	Sports	Czechoslovakia	Tennis Player - HF
Hank	Jones	Performing Arts	USA	Pianist - Big Band/Jazz -HF
	Steinbrecher	Sports	USA	Soccer Promoter - HF
Hannah	Arendt	Politics	Germany	Philosopher/Political Theorist
	More	Creative Works	England	Writer - Religious Tracts
Hannah Van	Buren	Politics	USA	First Lady
Hannes	Meyer	Architecture	Switzerland	Architect
Hannes Olof Gösta	Alfvén	Science	Sweden	Physics - Nobel Laureate
Hannibal	Barca	War & Peace	Carthage	Military Commander
	Hamlin	Politics	USA	Vice-President
Hannibal Hamlin	Garland	Creative Works	USA	Author - Pulitzer
Hans	Bernoulli	Architecture	Switzerland	Architect
	Conried	Performing Arts	USA	Actor
	Fischer	Science	Germany	Chemistry - Nobel Laureate
	Hofmann	Works of Art	Germany	Painter
	Holbein	Works of Art	Germany	Painter - Portrait
	Hollein	Architecture	Austria	Architect - Pritzker Laureate
	Kollhoff	Architecture	Germany	Architect
	Memling	Works of Art	Germany	Painter

SOLVER SERIES: NAME FINDER

FIRST NAME	LAST NAME	CATEGORY	COUNTRY	FAME
Hans	Poelzig	Architecture	Germany	Architect
	Sachs	Performing Arts	Germany	Singer - Meister
	Scharoun	Architecture	Germany	Architect
	Schmidt	Architecture	Switzerland	Architect
	Speman	Science	Germany	Medicine - Nobel Laureate
	Zinsser	Science	USA	Bacteriologist
Hans Adolf	Krebs	Science	England	Medicine - Nobel Laureate
Hans Albrecht	Bethe	Science	USA	Physics - Nobel Laureate
Hans Christian	Andersen	Creative Works	Denmark	Writer/Poet
Hans Dom van der	Laan	Architecture	Netherlands	Architect
Hans G.	Dehmelt	Science	USA	Physics - Nobel Laureate
Hans Karl August Simon von	Euler-Chelpin	Science	Sweden	Chemistry - Nobel Laureate
Hans Wilhelm	Schlegel	Aviation	Germany	Astronaut
Har Gobind	Khorana	Science	USA	Medicine - Nobel Laureate
Harlan	Ellison	Creative Works	USA	Author
Harlan Fiske	Stone	Law & Order	USA	Chief Justice
Harlan O.	Page	Sports	USA	Basketball Player - HF
Harley	Granville-Barker	Creative Works	England	Playwright/Critic/Actor
Harlow	Shapley	Science	USA	Astronomer
Harmensz van Rijn	Rembrandt	Works of Art	Netherlands	Painter/Etcher
Harmon Clayton	Killebrew	Sports	USA	Baseball Player - HF
Harold	Arlen	Creative Works	USA	Composer
	Bauer	Performing Arts	USA	Pianist
	Harmsworth	Business	England	Publishing
	Hilton	Sports	England	Golfer - HF
	Johnson	Sports	USA	Boxer - HF
	Kroto	Science	England	Chemistry - Nobel Laureate
	Lloyd	Performing Arts	USA	Comedian
	MacMillan	Politics	England	Prime Minister
	Melvin	Performing Arts	USA	Singer (Blue Notes)
	Pinter	Creative Works	England	Literature - Nobel Laureate
	Pinter	Movie Production	England	Director
	Ramis	Performing Arts	USA	Actor
	Rosenberg	Arts	USA	Philosopher/Writer/Educator
	Russell	Performing Arts	Canada	Actor - Academy Award
Harold (Hal)	Newhouser	Sports	USA	Baseball Player - HF
Harold (Harry)	Oliver	Sports	Canada	Hockey Player - HF
Harold Clayton	Urey	Science	USA	Chemistry - Nobel Laureate
Harold E.	Foster	Sports	USA	Basketball Player - HF
	Varmus	Science	USA	Medicine - Nobel Laureate
Harold E. (Hal)	Greer	Sports	USA	Basketball Player - HF
Harold Edward (Red)	Grange	Sports	USA	Football Player - HF
Harold Hart	Crane	Creative Works	USA	Poet
Harold Henry (Pee Wee)	Reese	Sports	USA	Baseball Player - HF
Harold Hugh (Harry)	Cameron	Sports	Canada	Hockey Player - HF
Harold Humphrey	Hackett	Sports	USA	Tennis Player - HF
Harold Jacob	Rome	Creative Works	USA	Composer/Songwriter
Harold Joseph	Laski	Politics	England	Political Scientist/Socialist
Harold Joseph (Bullet Joe)	Simpson	Sports	Canada	Hockey Player - HF
Harold Joseph (Pie)	Traynor	Sports	USA	Baseball Player - HF
Harold Lenoir	Davis	Creative Works	USA	Novelist - Pulitzer
Harold Lloyd (Conway)	Twitty (Jenkins)	Performing Arts	USA	Singer - Country Music - HF
Harold Pemberton	Brittan	Sports	England	Soccer Player - HF
Harold Peter (Bud)	Grant Jr.	Sports	USA	Football Coach - HF
Harold Rupert	Alexander	Politics	England	Statesman
Harold Wallace	Ross	Business	USA	Magazine Editor
Haroldson L.	Hunt	Business	USA	Oil Industry
Harper	Lee	Creative Works	USA	Novelist - Pulitzer
Harriet	Martineau	Arts	England	Theologian
	Nelson	Performing Arts	USA	Actress
	Tubman	Politics	USA	Abolitionist
Harriet Elizabeth Beecher	Stowe	Creative Works	USA	Novelist
Harrison	Ford	Performing Arts	USA	Actor - Acad Award Nom

FIRST NAME	LAST NAME	CATEGORY	COUNTRY	FAME
Harrison Hagan	Schmitt	Aviation	USA	Astronaut
Harrold M. (Harry)	Hyland	Sports	Canada	Hockey Player - HF
Harry	Anderson	Performing Arts	USA	Actor
	Beaumont	Movie Production	USA	Director - Acad Award Nom
	Belafonte	Performing Arts	USA	Singer
	Bridges	Business	USA	Labor Leader
	Carey	Performing Arts	USA	Actor - Acad Award Nom
	Carney	Performing Arts	USA	Jazz Saxophonist - Big Band/Jazz - HF
	Chapin	Performing Arts	USA	Singer
	Connick Jr.	Performing Arts	USA	Singer
	Cooper	Sports	England	Golfer - HF
	Gant	Sports	USA	Race Car Driver - HF
	Guardino	Performing Arts	USA	Actor
	Hamlin	Performing Arts	USA	Actor
	Harper	Sports	USA	Baseball Player
	Houdini	Performing Arts	USA	Magician
	Hyde	Sports	USA	Race Car Promoter - HF
	Lauder	Performing Arts	Scotland	Comedian/Singer
	Martinson	Creative Works	Sweden	Literature - Nobel Laureate
	Morgan	Performing Arts	USA	Actor
	Nilsson	Performing Arts	USA	Singer
	Reasoner	Creative Works	USA	Journalist - Television
	Ritz	Performing Arts	USA	Comedian
	Vardon	Sports	USA	Golfer - HF
Harry (Apple Cheeks)	Lumley	Sports	Canada	Hockey Player - HF
Harry (Buddy)	Jeanette	Sports	USA	Basketball Player - HF
Harry (Hap)	Holmes	Sports	Canada	Hockey Player - HF
Harry (Rat)	Westwick	Sports	Canada	Hockey Player - HF
Harry (Raymond)	Scott (Warnow)	Performing Arts	USA	Band Leader - Big Band/Jazz - HF
Harry (Sweets)	Edison	Performing Arts	USA	Trumpeter - Big Band/Jazz - HF
Harry Alonzo (Sundance Kid)	Longabaugh	Law & Order	USA	Outlaw
Harry Andrew	Blackmun	Law & Order	USA	Justice/Supreme Court
Harry Bartholomew	Hooper	Sports	USA	Baseball Player - HF
Harry Byron	Warner	Performing Arts	England	Actor - Acad Award Nom
Harry Dean	Stanton	Performing Arts	USA	Actor
Harry E. (Moose)	Watson	Sports	Canada	Hockey Player - HF
Harry Edwin	Heilmann	Sports	USA	Baseball Player - HF
	Helmsley	Law & Order	USA	Fraud Artist
Harry F.	Sinclair	Business	USA	Oil Industry
Harry Haag	James	Performing Arts	USA	Band Leader - Big Band/Jazz - HF
Harry J.	Gallatin	Sports	USA	Basketball Player - HF
Harry Joseph	Keough	Sports	USA	Soccer Player - HF
Harry L. (Punch)	Broadbent	Sports	Canada	Hockey Player - HF
Harry Lillis (Bing)	Crosby	Performing Arts	USA	Actor/Singer - Academy Award
	Crosby	Performing Arts	USA	Singer - Big Band/Jazz - HF
Harry M.	Markowitz	Arts	USA	Economics - Nobel Laureate
Harry Percival	Watson	Sports	Canada	Hockey Player - HF
Harry S.	Truman	Politics	USA	President
Harry von	Zell	Performing Arts	USA	Actor
Hart	Moss	Creative Works	USA	Playwright
Hartmut	Michel	Science	Germany	Chemistry - Nobel Laureate
Harvey	Cushing	Creative Works	USA	Author - Pulitzer
	Fuqua	Performing Arts	USA	Rock & Roll - HF - The Moonglows
	Keitel	Performing Arts	USA	Actor - Acad Award Nom
	Korman	Performing Arts	USA	Actor
	Penick	Sports	USA	Golf Teacher - HF
	Pulford	Sports	Canada	Hockey Player - HF
Harvey (Busher)	Jackson	Sports	Canada	Hockey Player - HF
Harvey Philip (Phil)	Spector	Creative Works	USA	Song Writer/Producer
Harvey Williams	Cushing	Science	USA	Neurosurgeon
Hassan	Fathy	Architecture	Egypt	Architect
Hatcher	Hughes	Creative Works	USA	Dramatist - Pulitzer
Hattie	McDaniel	Performing Arts	USA	Actress - Academy Award

SOLVER SERIES: NAME FINDER

FIRST NAME	LAST NAME	CATEGORY	COUNTRY	FAME
Hayley	Mills	Performing Arts	England	Actress - Academy Award
Haym	Salomon	Business	USA	Financier
Hazel Virginia (Lady Tennis)	Hotchkiss-Wightman	Sports	USA	Tennis Player - HF
Hazen	Pingree	Business	USA	Manufacturing Industry
Hazen Shirley (Kiki)	Cuyler	Sports	USA	Baseball Player - HF
Heather	Locklear	Performing Arts	USA	Actress
Hector	Babenco	Movie Production	Argentina	Director - Acad Award Nom
	Berlioz	Creative Works	France	Composer Classical
	Camacho	Sports	USA	Boxer
	Guimard	Architecture	France	Architect
Hector (Toe)	Blake	Sports	Canada	Hockey Player - HF
Hector Hugh (Saki)	Munro	Creative Works	England	Author
Hedy	Lamarr	Performing Arts	Austria	Actress
Heidi	Bohay	Performing Arts	USA	Actress
	Klum	Performing Arts	Germany	Super Model
Heike Kamerlingh	Onnes	Science	Netherlands	Physics - Nobel Laureate
Heinrich	Böll	Creative Works	Germany	Literature - Nobel Laureate
	Heine	Creative Works	Germany	Poet/Essayist
	Rohrer	Science	Switzerland	Physics - Nobel Laureate
	Schliemann	Arts	Germany	Archaeologist
	Schutz	Creative Works	Germany	Composer
	Steinway	Business	USA	Manufacturing Industry - Pianos
	Tessenow	Architecture	Germany	Architect
Heinrich Otto	Wieland	Science	Germany	Chemistry - Nobel Laureate
Heinrich Rudolph	Hertz	Science	Germany	Physicist
Heinrich von	Treitschke	Arts	Germany	Historian
Heinz Wilhelm	Guderian	War & Peace	Germany	General
Heitor	Villa-Lobos	Creative Works	Brazil	Composer
Helen	Hayes	Performing Arts	USA	Actress - Academy Award
	Hunt	Performing Arts	USA	Actress - Academy Award
	Menken	Performing Arts	USA	Actress
	Mirren	Performing Arts	England	Actress - Acad Award Nom
	Reddy	Performing Arts	Australia	Singer
	Slater	Performing Arts	USA	Actress
	Taft	Politics	USA	First Lady
	Twelvetrees	Performing Arts	USA	Actress
Helen Adams	Keller	Creative Works	USA	Writer/Lecturer
Helen Gurley	Brown	Creative Works	USA	Journalist - Magazine
Helen Hull	Jacobs	Sports	USA	Tennis Player - HF
Helen Newington	Wills-Moody	Sports	USA	Tennis Player - HF
Helen Oakley	Dance	Performing Arts	USA	Arranger - Big Band/Jazz - HF
Helena	Blavatsky	Arts	Russia	Theosophist
	Bonham-Carter	Performing Arts	England	Actress - Acad Award Nom
	Christensen	Performing Arts	Denmark	Super Model
	Modjeska	Performing Arts	Poland	Actress
	Sukova	Sports	Czechoslovakia	Tennis Player
Helene	Elliott	Sports	USA	Hockey Journalist - HF
Helmut	Jahn	Architecture	Germany	Architect
	Kohl	Politics	Germany	Chancellor
Helmuth Johannes Ludwig von	Moltke	War & Peace	Germany	General
Helmuth Karl Bernard	Moltke	War & Peace	Germany	Field Marshall
Hendrick Petrus	Berlage	Architecture	Netherlands	Architect
Hendrik Antoon	Lorentz	Science	Netherlands	Physics - Nobel Laureate
Heneage	Ogilvie	Science	England	Physician/Surgeon
Henny	Youngman	Performing Arts	England	Comedian
Henri	Barbusse	Creative Works	France	Novelist/Journalist
	Bergson	Creative Works	France	Literature - Nobel Laureate
	Christophe	Politics	Haiti	King
	Labrouste	Architecture	France	Architect
	Matisse	Works of Art	France	Painter
	Moissan	Science	France	Chemistry - Nobel Laureate
	Rousseau	Works of Art	France	Painter - Primitive
	Sauvage	Architecture	France	Architect

FIRST NAME	LAST NAME	CATEGORY	COUNTRY	FAME
Henri Carl Peter	Dam	Science	Denmark	Medicine - Nobel Laureate
Henri de Lorranine	Guise	Politics	France	Statesman/General
Henri Frédéric	Amiel	Creative Works	Switzerland	Writer
Henri Jean	Cochet	Sports	France	Tennis Player - HF
Henri Marie Raymond de	Toulouse-Lautrec	Works of Art	France	Painter/Lithographer
Henri Millon de	Montherlant	Creative Works	France	Novelist/Playwright
Henri Philippe	Pétain	Politics	France	Premier
Henri René Albert Guy de	Maupassant	Creative Works	France	Novelist/Short Story Writer
Henrietta	Szold	Politics	USA	Zionist Leader
Henrik	Ibsen	Creative Works	Norway	Poet/Playwright
	Pontoppidan	Creative Works	Denmark	Literature - Nobel Laureate
Henry	Bacon	Architecture	USA	Architect - AIA Gold Medal
	Bacon	Works of Art	USA	Painter
	Bessemer	Science	England	Engineer
	Booth	Business	England	Railway Magnate
	Bradley	Arts	England	Lexicographer
	Campbell-Bannerman	Politics	England	Prime Minister
	Cavendish	Science	England	Physicist/Chemist
	Chadwick	Sports	England	Baseball Pioneer - HF
	Clay	Politics	USA	Statesman/Orator
	Clews	Business	USA	Financier
	Cotton	Sports	England	Golfer - HF
	Draper	Science	USA	Astronomer
	Fielding	Creative Works	England	Novelist
	Fonda	Performing Arts	USA	Actor - Academy Award
	Ford	Business	USA	Manufacturer - Automobiles
	Ford	Sports	USA	Race Car Designer - HF
	Gibson	Performing Arts	USA	Comedian
	Gratton	Politics	Ireland	Statesman
	Hallam	Arts	England	Historian
	Hathaway	Movie Production	USA	Director - Acad Award Nom
	Hetherington	Business	England	Publishing
	Hudson	Exploration	England	Explorer - America
	James	Creative Works	USA	Author - Pulitzer
	Kelsey	Exploration	England	Explorer - Canada Inland
	King	Movie Production	USA	Director - Acad Award Nom
	Koster	Movie Production	Germany	Director - Acad Award Nom
	Lee	War & Peace	USA	General - Revolutionary War
	Lomb	Business	USA	Optical Industry
	Mancini	Performing Arts	USA	Conductor/Composer
	Miller	Creative Works	USA	Writer
	Moore	Works of Art	England	Sculptor
	Morgan	Performing Arts	USA	Comedian
	Morgan	War & Peace	Wales	Buccaneer
	Morgenthau	Politics	USA	Secretary of the Treasury
	Percy	War & Peace	England	Soldier/Rebel
	Purcell	Creative Works	England	Composer
	Raeburn	Works of Art	Scotland	Painter
	Sidgwick	Arts	England	Philosopher
	Sweet	Arts	England	Linguist
	Tate	Business	England	Entrepreneur
	Taube	Science	USA	Chemistry - Nobel Laureate
	Taylor	Creative Works	USA	Poet - Pulitzer
	Travers	Performing Arts	England	Actor - Acad Award Nom
	Vane	Politics	England	Statesman - Puritan
	Vaughan	Creative Works	England	Poet/Metaphysician
	Villard	Business	USA	Railway/Publishing
	Wilson	Politics	USA	Vice-President
	Winkler	Performing Arts	USA	Actor
Henry (Harry)	Ratican	Sports	USA	Soccer Player - HF
Henry (Professor Roy)	Longhair (Byrd)	Performing Arts	USA	Singer - Rock & Roll - HF
Henry (Red)	Allen	Performing Arts	USA	Jazz Trumpeter - Big Band/Jazz - HF
Henry (Smokey)	Yunick	Sports	USA	Race Car Designer - HF

SOLVER SERIES: NAME FINDER

FIRST NAME	LAST NAME	CATEGORY	COUNTRY	FAME
Henry Agard	Wallace	Politics	USA	Vice-President
Henry Alfred	Kissinger	Politics	USA	Secretary of State
	Kissinger	War & Peace	USA	Peace - Nobel Laureate
Henry Austin	Dobson	Creative Works	England	Poet
Henry Benjamin (Hank)	Greenberg	Sports	USA	Baseball Player - HF
Henry Brooks	Adams	Creative Works	USA	Author - Pulitzer
Henry Cabot	Lodge	Politics	USA	Senator
Henry Cecil Kennedy	Wyld	Arts	England	Lexicographer/Linguist
Henry Christian (Harry)	Hopman	Sports	Australia	Tennis Player - HF
Henry Clay	Frick	Business	USA	Industrialist
Henry Creswicke	Rawlinson	Arts	England	Orientalist/Statesman
Henry D.	Dakin	Science	USA	Chemist
Henry David	Thoreau	Arts	USA	Philosopher/Poet/Author
Henry Dixon	Cowell	Creative Works	USA	Composer
Henry Doyle (Homer)	Haynes	Performing Arts	USA	Country Music - HF - Homer & Jethro
Henry Ellsworth	Vines	Sports	USA	Tennis Player - HF
Henry Elmer	Barnes	Arts	USA	Historian/Sociologist
Henry Emmett (Heinie)	Manush	Sports	USA	Baseball Player - HF
Henry Ernest	Shackleton	Exploration	England	Explorer - Antarctic
Henry F.	Pringle	Creative Works	USA	Author - Pulitzer
Henry Fairfield	Osborn	Science	USA	Paleontologist/Biologist
Henry Hallett	Dale	Science	England	Medicine - Nobel Laureate
Henry Handel	Richardson	Creative Works	Australia	Novelist
Henry Havelock	Ellis	Creative Works	England	Writer/Psychologist
Henry Hobson	Richardson	Architecture	USA	Architect
Henry Howard	Surrey	Creative Works	England	Poet/Courtier
Henry J. (Dutch)	Dehnert	Sports	USA	Basketball Player - HF
Henry John	Kaiser	Business	USA	Industrialist
Henry John Temple	Palmerston	Politics	England	Prime Minister
Henry Judah (Harry)	Trihey	Sports	Canada	Hockey Player - HF
Henry La	Fontaine	War & Peace	Belgium	Peace - Nobel Laureate
Henry Lee	Lucas	Law & Order	USA	Serial Killer
Henry Lewis	Stimson	Politics	USA	Statesman/Secretary of State
Henry Louis	Mencken	Creative Works	USA	Journalist - Newspaper
Henry Louis (Hank)	Aaron	Sports	USA	Baseball Player - HF
	Stram	Sports	USA	Football Coach - HF
Henry Louis (Lou)	Gehrig	Sports	USA	Baseball Player - HF
Henry Morton	Stanley	Exploration	England	Explorer - Africa
Henry Robinson	Luce	Business	USA	Publisher/Editor
Henry Ross	Perot	Business	USA	Computer Industry
	Perot	Politics	USA	Presidential Candidate
Henry Ryder	Haggard	Creative Works	England	Novelist
Henry Thomas	Buckle	Arts	England	Historian
Henry van de	Velde	Architecture	Belgium	Architect
Henry Vernon (Harry)	Howell	Sports	Canada	Hockey Player - HF
Henry W.	Kendall	Science	USA	Physics - Nobel Laureate
	Lawton	War & Peace	USA	Major General
Henry W. (Bunny)	Austin	Sports	England	Tennis Player - HF
Henry Wadsworth	Longfellow	Creative Works	USA	Poet
Henry Ward	Beecher	Arts	USA	Clergyman
Henry Warner	Slocum	Sports	USA	Tennis Player - HF
Henry Warren	Hartsfield Jr.	Aviation	USA	Astronaut
Henry Watson	Fowler	Arts	England	Lexicographer/Arbiter
Henry Wendell	Jordan	Sports	USA	Football Player - HF
Henry Wheeler	Shaw	Creative Works	USA	Humourist
Henry Wilson (Hank)	Thompson	Performing Arts	USA	Singer - Country Music - HF
Henryk	Sienkiewicz	Creative Works	Poland	Literature - Nobel Laureate
Herb	Alpert	Performing Arts	USA	Band Leader/Trumpeter
	Block	Creative Works	USA	Cartoonist - Pulitzer
	Caen	Creative Works	USA	Journalist
	Graffis	Sports	USA	Golf Promoter - HF
	Reed	Performing Arts	USA	Rock & Roll - HF - The Platters
	Thomas	Sports	USA	Race Car Driver - HF

FIRST NAME	LAST NAME	CATEGORY	COUNTRY	FAME
Herbert	Brenon	Movie Production	Ireland	Director - Acad Award Nom
	Feis	Creative Works	USA	Author - Pulitzer
	Hauptman	Science	USA	Chemistry - Nobel Laureate
	Kroemer	Science	Germany	Physics - Nobel Laureate
	Lom	Performing Arts	Hungary	Actor
	Marcuse	Arts	Germany	Philosopher
	Marshall	Performing Arts	England	Actor
	Ross	Movie Production	USA	Director - Acad Award Nom
	Spencer	Arts	England	Philosopher
Herbert (Herbie)	Lewis	Sports	Canada	Hockey Player - HF
Herbert (Zeppo)	Marx	Performing Arts	USA	Comedian
Herbert A.	Simon	Arts	USA	Economics - Nobel Laureate
Herbert A. (Herb)	Adderly	Sports	USA	Football Player - HF
Herbert Beerbohm	Tree	Performing Arts	England	Actor/Theatrical Manager
Herbert C.	Brown	Science	USA	Chemistry - Nobel Laureate
Herbert Clark	Hoover	Politics	USA	President
Herbert Edward	Read	Creative Works	England	Poet/Art Critic
Herbert Ernst (Willy)	Brandt	Politics	Germany	Chancellor
Herbert George	Wells	Creative Works	England	Novelist/Historian
Herbert Henry	Asquith	Politics	England	Prime Minister
Herbert Jackson (Jack)	Youngblood III	Sports	USA	Football Player - HF
Herbert Jay (Herbie)	Mann	Performing Arts	USA	Jazz Flutist
Herbert Jefferis (Herb)	Pennock	Sports	USA	Baseball Player - HF
Herbert Jeffrey (Herbie)	Hancock	Performing Arts	USA	Jazz Pianist/Composer - Big Band/Jazz - HF
Herbert Marshall	McLuhan	Creative Works	Canada	Writer/Educator
Herbert Martin (Herb)	Gardiner	Sports	Canada	Hockey Player - HF
Herbert Norman	Schwarzkopf Jr.	War & Peace	USA	General - Army
Herbert P.	Bix	Creative Works	USA	Author - Pulitzer
Herbert Sebastian	Agar	Creative Works	England	Author - Pulitzer
Herbert Spencer	Gasser	Science	USA	Medicine - Nobel Laureate
Herbert William (Buddy)	O'Connor	Sports	Canada	Hockey Player - HF
Herman	Brown	Business	USA	Ship Building
	Melville	Creative Works	USA	Novelist
	Wouk	Creative Works	USA	Author - Pulitzer
Herman Francis	David	Sports	England	Tennis Player - HF
Herman Poole (Sun)	Ra (Blount)	Performing Arts	USA	Band Leader - Big Band/Jazz - HF
Hermann	Hesse	Creative Works	Switzerland	Literature - Nobel Laureate
	Prey	Performing Arts	Germany	Singer - Opera
	Rorschach	Arts	Switzerland	Psychologist
	Staudinger	Science	Germany	Chemistry - Nobel Laureate
Hermann Emil	Fischer	Science	Germany	Chemistry - Nobel Laureate
Hermann Joseph	Muller	Science	USA	Medicine - Nobel Laureate
Hermann Ludwig Ferdinand von	Helmholtz	Science	Germany	Physicist/Physiologist
Hermann Wilhelm	Goering	War & Peace	Germany	Nazi Field Marshall
Hermione	Baddeley	Performing Arts	England	Actress - Acad Award Nom
	Gingold	Performing Arts	England	Actress
Hernán	Cortés	Exploration	Spain	Explorer - Mexico
Hernando	Cortés	War & Peace	Spain	Military Leader
Hernando de	Soto	Exploration	Spain	Explorer - Mississippi River
Herschel	Bernardi	Performing Arts	USA	Actor
	Walker	Sports	USA	Football Player
Hezekiah Leroy Gordon (Stuff)	Smith	Performing Arts	USA	Jazz Violinist - Big Band/Jazz - HF
Hideki	Shirakawa	Science	Japan	Chemistry - Nobel Laureate
	Yukawa	Science	Japan	Physics - Nobel Laureate
Hideyo	Noguchi	Science	Japan	Bacteriologist
Hieronymus	Bosch	Works of Art	Netherlands	Painter
Hilaire Germain Edgar	Degas	Works of Art	France	Painter
Hilary	Swank	Performing Arts	USA	Actress - Academy Award
Hillary	Clinton	Politics	USA	First Lady
Hilton	Smith	Sports	USA	Baseball Player - HF
	Valentine	Performing Arts	England	Rock & Roll - HF - The Animals
Hippolyte Adolphe	Taine	Arts	France	Literary Critic/Historian
Hippolyte Jean	Giraudoux	Creative Works	France	Novelist/Playwright

SOLVER SERIES: NAME FINDER

FIRST NAME	LAST NAME	CATEGORY	COUNTRY	FAME
Hippolyte Paul	Delaroche	Works of Art	France	Painter
Hiram King (Hank)	Williams Sr.	Performing Arts	USA	Singer - Country Music - HF
	Williams Sr.	Performing Arts	USA	Singer - Rock & Roll - HF
Hiram Stevens	Maxim	Business	England	Engineer/Inventor - Firearms
Hiroshi	Teshigahara	Movie Production	Japan	Director - Acad Award Nom
Hisako (Chako)	Higuchi	Sports	Japan	Golfer - HF
Hoagland Howard (Hoagy)	Carmichael	Creative Works	USA	Composer
Holcombe	Ward	Sports	USA	Tennis Player - HF
Hollis	Stacy	Sports	USA	Golfer
Holly	Hunter	Performing Arts	USA	Actress - Acad Award Nom
Holly Michelle	Phillips	Performing Arts	USA	Rock & Roll - HF - Mamas & Papas
Holmes Sterling	Morrison	Performing Arts	USA	Rock & Roll - HF - Velvet Underground
Honor	Blackman	Performing Arts	England	Actress
Honore	Daumier	Works of Art	France	Painter/Lithographer
Honoré de	Balzac	Creative Works	France	Novelist
Honoré Gabriel Riqueti	Mirabeau	Politics	France	Revolutionist/Statesman
Hoot	Gibson	Performing Arts	USA	Actor
Hope	Lange	Performing Arts	USA	Actress - Acad Award Nom
	Emerson	Performing Arts	USA	Actress - Acad Award Nom
Hoppy (Orville)	Jones	Performing Arts	USA	Rock & Roll - HF - The Ink Spots
Horace	Greeley	Politics	USA	Political Leader/Journalist
	Greely	Creative Works	USA	Journalist - Newspaper
	Mann	Arts	USA	Educator
	Walpole	Creative Works	England	Writer
Horace Howard	Furness	Arts	USA	Scholar - Shakespear
Horace Ward Martin Tavares	Silver	Performing Arts	USA	Jazz Pianist/Composer - Big Band/Jazz - HF
Horatio	Alger	Creative Works	USA	Writer
	Gates	War & Peace	USA	General
	Greenough	Works of Art	USA	Sculptor
	Nelson	War & Peace	England	Admiral
Horatio Herbert	Kitchener	War & Peace	England	Statesman/Military Officer
Horst	Buchholz	Performing Arts	Germany	Actor
Horst L.	Störmer	Science	Germany	Physics - Nobel Laureate
Hortense	Calisher	Creative Works	USA	Author
Horton	Foote	Creative Works	USA	Dramatist - Pulitzer
	Smith	Sports	USA	Golfer - HF
Howard	Cosell	Creative Works	USA	Journalist - Television
	Engel	Creative Works	Canada	Author
	Hanson	Creative Works	USA	Composer
	Hesseman	Performing Arts	USA	Actor
	Johnson	Business	USA	Hotelier
	Johnson	Sports	USA	Baseball Player
	Jones	Performing Arts	England	Singer
	Keel	Performing Arts	USA	Actor - Musical
	Lindsay	Creative Works	USA	Dramatist - Pulitzer
	Nemerov	Creative Works	USA	Poet - Pulitzer
	Pyle	Creative Works	USA	Writer/Illustrator
	Sackler	Creative Works	USA	Dramatist - Pulitzer
	Stern	Performing Arts	USA	Show Host
	Hawks	Movie Production	USA	Director - Acad Award Nom
Howard (Duane)	Allmann	Performing Arts	USA	Rock & Roll - HF - Allmann Brothers Band
Howard Chandler	Christy	Works of Art	USA	Painter/Illustrator
Howard E.	Rollins Jr.	Performing Arts	USA	Actor - Acad Award Nom
Howard Earl	Averill	Sports	USA	Baseball Player - HF
Howard Henry	Baker Jr.	Politics	USA	Senator
Howard Martin	Temin	Science	USA	Medicine - Nobel Laureate
Howard Michael (Howie)	Long	Sports	USA	Football Coach - HF
Howard Mumford	Jones	Arts	USA	Educator/Critic
	Jones	Creative Works	USA	Author - Pulitzer
Howard Robard	Hughes	Business	USA	Industrialist
Howard Van Doren	Shaw	Architecture	USA	Architect - AIA Gold Medal
Howard Walter	Florey	Science	Australia	Medicine - Nobel Laureate
Howarth William (Howie)	Morenz	Sports	Canada	Hockey Player - HF

FIRST NAME	LAST NAME	CATEGORY	COUNTRY	FAME
Howie	Epstein	Performing Arts	USA	Rock & Roll - HF - Heart Breakers
	Mandel	Performing Arts	Canada	Comedian
Howlin Wolf (Chester)	Burnett	Performing Arts	USA	Singer - Rock & Roll - HF
Hoyt	Axton	Performing Arts	USA	Singer/Composer
	Hawkings	Performing Arts	USA	Country Music - HF - The Jordonaires
Hristo	Stoitchkov	Sports	Bulgaria	Soccer Player
Hubert	Green	Sports	USA	Golfer
	Laws	Performing Arts	USA	Jazz Flutist
Hubert de	Givenchy	Business	France	Fashion Designer
Hubert George (Bill)	Quackenbush	Sports	Canada	Hockey Player - HF
Hubert H.	Humphrey	Politics	USA	Vice-President
Huddie William	Ledbetter	Performing Arts	USA	Rock & Roll - HF - Lead Belly
Hudson	Maxim	Science	USA	Chemist/Inventor - Explosives
Huey	Lewis	Performing Arts	USA	Singer
Huey Pierce (The Kingfish)	Long	Politics	USA	Senator - Louisiana
Hug Edward (The king)	McElhenny Jr.	Sports	USA	Football Player - HF
Hugh	Capet	Politics	France	King
	Downs	Creative Works	USA	Journalist - Television
	Duffy	Sports	USA	Baseball Player - HF
	Farr	Performing Arts	USA	Country Music - HF - Sons of the Pioneers
	Griffith	Performing Arts	Wales	Actor - Academy Award
	Hudson	Movie Production	England	Director - Acad Award Nom
	Latimer	Arts	England	Protestant Bishop/Reformer
	Masekela	Performing Arts	South Africa	Flugel Horn Player
	O'Brian	Performing Arts	USA	Actor
Hugh A.	Stubbins	Architecture	USA	Architect - Jefferson Medal
Hugh Ambrose (Hughie)	Jennings	Sports	USA	Baseball Player - HF
Hugh David	Politzer	Science	USA	Physics - Nobel Laureate
Hugh Gordon	Stoker	Performing Arts	USA	Country Music - HF - The Jordonaires
Hugh John	Lofting	Creative Works	USA	Writer/Illustrator
Hugh L. (Shorty)	Ray	Sports	USA	Football Advisor - HF
Hugh Laurence (Little Do)	Doherty	Sports	England	Tennis Player - HF
Hugh Marston	Hefner	Business	USA	Publishing
Hugh Roy	Cullen	Business	USA	Oil Industry
Hugo	Boss	Business	Germany	Fashion Designer
	Grotius	Politics	Netherlands	Statesman/Jurist/Scholar
	Häring	Architecture	Germany	Architect
	Wolf	Creative Works	Austria	Composer
Hugo De	Vries	Science	Netherlands	Botanist
Hugo La Fayette	Black	Law & Order	USA	Jurist
Hugo von	Hofmannsthal	Creative Works	Austria	Poet/Playwright
Hume	Cronyn	Performing Arts	Canada	Actor - Acad Award Nom
Humphrey	Bogart	Performing Arts	USA	Actor - Academy Award
	Gilbert	Exploration	England	Explorer - Canada East Coast
Humphry	Davy	Science	England	Chemist
Humpy	Wheeler	Sports	USA	Race Car Promoter - HF
Hung-chang	Li	Politics	China	Prime Minister
Huntz	Hall	Performing Arts	USA	Actor
Huybrecht Van	Eyck	Works of Art	Belgium	Painter
Hyman George	Rickover	War & Peace	USA	Admiral
Ian	Anderson	Performing Arts	Scotland	Flutist
	Baker-Finch	Sports	Australia	Golfer
	Bannen	Performing Arts	Scotland	Actor - Acad Award Nom
	Carmichael	Performing Arts	England	Actor
	Fleming	Creative Works	England	Author
	Holm	Performing Arts	England	Actor - Acad Award Nom
	Hunter	Performing Arts	England	Singer
	McHarg	Architecture	USA	Architect - Jefferson Medal
	McKellen	Performing Arts	England	Actor - Acad Award Nom
	McShane	Performing Arts	England	Actor
	Richardson	Performing Arts	Scotland	Actor
	Tyson	Performing Arts	Canada	Canadian Music - HF - Ian and Sylvia
	Woosnam	Sports	Wales	Golfer

SOLVER SERIES: NAME FINDER

FIRST NAME	LAST NAME	CATEGORY	COUNTRY	FAME
Ian	Ziering	Performing Arts	USA	Actor
Ian Ernest Gilmore (Gil)	Evans (Green)	Performing Arts	Canada	Jazz Pianist - Big Band/Jazz - HF
	Evans (Green)	Performing Arts	Canada	Jazz Pianist - Canadian Music - HF
Ibn-Rusjd	Averroes	Arts	Spain	Philosopher
Ida	Kaminska	Performing Arts	Ukraine	Actress - Acad Award Nom
	Lupino	Performing Arts	England	Actress
	McKinley	Politics	USA	First Lady
Ida Bell	Wells-Barnett	Creative Works	USA	Journalist - Newspaper
Ida Minerva	Tarbell	Creative Works	USA	Journalist/Author
Idi	Amin	Politics	Uganda	President
Ieoh Ming	Pei	Architecture	USA	Architect - Pritzker/ AIA Gold
Ignace Jan	Paderewski	Creative Works	Poland	Composer/Pianist
	Paderewski	Politics	Poland	Prime Minister
Ignazio	Gardella	Architecture	Italy	Architect
	Silone	Creative Works	Italy	Writer
Igor Davidovich	Oistrakh	Performing Arts	Russia	Violinist
Igor Evgenyevich	Tamm	Science	Russia	Physics - Nobel Laureate
Igor Fedorovich	Stravinsky	Creative Works	USA	Composer/Conductor
Igor Ivanovich	Sikorsky	Business	USA	Aviation Industry - Aeronautical Engineer
Ike	Turner	Performing Arts	USA	Singer - Rock & Roll - HF
Il	Giorgione	Works of Art	Italy	Painter
	Perugino	Works of Art	Italy	Painter
	Tintoretto	Works of Art	Italy	Painter
Ilan	Ramon	Aviation	Israel	Astronaut
Ilene	Graff	Performing Arts	USA	Actress/Singer
Ilie (Bucharest Bufoon)	Nastase	Sports	Romania	Tennis Player - HF
Il'ja Mikhailovich	Frank	Science	Russia	Physics - Nobel Laureate
Ilka	Chase	Performing Arts	USA	Actress
Ilona	Massey	Performing Arts	Hungary	Actress/Singer
Ilya	Prigogine	Science	Belgium	Chemistry - Nobel Laureate
Ilya Grigorievich	Ehrenburg	Creative Works	Russia	Writer
Ilya Ilyich	Mechnikov	Science	Russia	Medicine - Nobel Laureate
Ima	Hogg	Business	USA	Philanthropist/Pianist
Imelda	Marcos	Politics	Philippines	First Lady
	Staunton	Performing Arts	England	Actress - Acad Award Nom
Immanuel	Kant	Arts	Germany	Philosopher
Immanuel Hermass von	Fichte	Arts	Germany	Philosopher
Imogene	Coca	Performing Arts	USA	Actress
Imre	Kertész	Creative Works	Hungary	Literature - Nobel Laureate
	Lakatos	Arts	Hungary	Philosopher/Mathematician
	Makovecz	Architecture	Hungary	Architect
	Nagy	Politics	Hungary	Prime Minister
Ina	Balin	Performing Arts	USA	Actress
	Claire	Performing Arts	USA	Actress
Increase	Mather	Creative Works	USA	Writer/Clergyman
Indira Nehru	Gandi	Politics	India	Prime Minister
Inez	Foxx	Performing Arts	USA	Singer
	Rivero	Performing Arts	Argentina	Super Model
	Sastre	Performing Arts	Spain	Super Model
Inga	Swenson	Performing Arts	USA	Actress
Ingemar	Johansson	Sports	Sweden	Boxer - HF
	Stenmark	Sports	Sweden	Olympic Skier
Inger	Stevens	Performing Arts	Sweden	Actress
Ingmar	Bergman	Movie Production	Sweden	Director - Acad Award Nom
Ingrid	Bergman	Performing Arts	Sweden	Actress - Academy Award
	Seynhaeve	Performing Arts	Belgium	Super Model
Inigo	Jones	Architecture	England	Architect/Stage Designer
Ione	Skye	Performing Arts	England	Actress
Ira	Gershwin	Creative Works	USA	Dramatist - Pulitzer
	Levin	Creative Works	USA	Author/Playwright
Ira Lonnie	Loudermilk	Performing Arts	USA	Country Music - HF - Louvin Brothers
Irene	Cara	Performing Arts	USA	Singer/Actress
	Castle	Performing Arts	USA	Actress

FIRST NAME	LAST NAME	CATEGORY	COUNTRY	FAME
Irene	Dunne	Performing Arts	USA	Actress - Acad Award Nom
	Papas	Performing Arts	Greece	Actress
	Ryan	Performing Arts	USA	Actress
	Worth	Performing Arts	USA	Actress
Irène	Joliot-Curie	Science	France	Chemistry - Nobel Laureate
Iris	Murdoch	Creative Works	England	Author
Irvine Wallace (Ace)	Bailey	Sports	Canada	Hockey Player - HF
Irving	Babbitt	Arts	USA	Educator/Critic
	Berlin	Creative Works	USA	Composer Music
	Cummings	Movie Production	USA	Director - Acad Award Nom
	Langmuir	Science	USA	Chemistry - Nobel Laureate
	Stone	Creative Works	USA	Novelist
Irving (Irv)	Gotti	Performing Arts	USA	Music Producer
Irving R.	Levine	Creative Works	USA	Journalist - Television
Irwin	Edman	Arts	USA	Philosopher
	Rose	Science	USA	Chemistry - Nobel Laureate
	Unger	Creative Works	USA	Author - Pulitzer
	Shaw	Movie Production	USA	Producer/Writer
Isaac	Albéniz	Creative Works	Spain	Composer/Pianist
	Asimov	Creative Works	Russia	Author - SciFi
	Babel	Creative Works	Russia	Writer
	Brock	Politics	Canada	Lieutenant Governor
	Casaubon	Arts	France	Theologian
	Hayes	Performing Arts	USA	Singer - Rock & Roll - HF
	Newton	Science	England	Mathematician/Philosopher
	Pitman	Science	England	Inventor - Shorthand
	Stern	Performing Arts	Russia	Violinist
	Watts	Arts	England	Clergyman/Writer - Hymns
Isaac Bashevis	Singer	Creative Works	USA	Literature - Nobel Laureate
Isaac Donald (Don)	Everly	Performing Arts	USA	Country Music - HF - Everly Brothers
	Everly	Performing Arts	USA	Rock & Roll - HF - Everly Brothers
Isaac Merritt	Singer	Science	USA	Inventor - Sewing Machine
Isaak	Mizrahi	Business	USA	Fashion Designer
Isabel	Sanford	Performing Arts	USA	Actress
Isabella	Eberhardt	Exploration	Switzerland	Explorer - North Africa
	Rossellini	Performing Arts	Italy	Actress
Isabelle	Adjani	Performing Arts	France	Actress - Acad Award Nom
Isadora	Duncan	Performing Arts	USA	Dancer
Isadore (Friz)	Freleng	Creative Works	USA	Cartoonist - Warner Bros.
Isaiah	Berlin	Arts	England	Philosopher
Isak	Dinesen	Creative Works	Denmark	Author
Isamu	Noguchi	Works of Art	Japan	Sculptor
Isao	Aoki	Sports	Japan	Golfer - HF
Isham	Jones	Performing Arts	USA	Band Leader - Big Band/Jazz - HF
Isiah	Thomas	Sports	USA	Basketball Player - HF
Isiah (Ike)	Williams	Sports	USA	Boxer - HF
Isidor	Strauss	Business	USA	Drygoods
Isidor Isaac	Rabi	Science	USA	Physics - Nobel Laureate
Isidoro di	Mileto	Architecture	Italy	Architect
Ismael	Laguna	Sports	Panama	Boxer - HF
Ismet	Inönü	Politics	Turkey	Prime Minister
Isola	Jones	Performing Arts	USA	Singer - Opera
Isoroku	Yamamoto	War & Peace	Japan	Naval Commander
Israel	Putnam	War & Peace	USA	General - Revolutionary War
	Zangwill	Creative Works	England	Novelist/Playwright
Israel (Ira)	Gershwin	Creative Works	USA	Composer
Israel Harold (Izzy)	Asper	Business	Canada	Communications
Israel Isidore (Irving)	Berlin (Baline)	Performing Arts	Siberia	Composer/Lyricist - Big Band/Jazz - HF
Italo	Calvino	Creative Works	Italy	Author
Ito	Midori	Sports	Japan	Olympic Skater
Itzhak	Perlman	Performing Arts	Israel	Violinist
Ivan	Dixon	Performing Arts	USA	Director
	Jandl	Performing Arts	Czechoslovakia	Actor - Academy Award

SOLVER SERIES: NAME FINDER

FIRST NAME	LAST NAME	CATEGORY	COUNTRY	FAME
Ivan	Lendl	Sports	Czechoslovakia	Tennis Player - HF
	Leonidov	Architecture	Russia	Architect
	Meštrovic	Works of Art	Yugoslavia	Sculptor
	Nagy	Performing Arts	Hungary	Dancer/Composer - Ballet
	Reitman	Movie Production	Czechoslovakia	Director
Ivan Alekseyevich	Bunin	Creative Works	Russia	Literature - Nobel Laureate
Ivan Petrovich	Pavlov	Science	Russia	Medicine - Nobel Laureate
Ivan Sergeevich	Turgenev	Creative Works	Russia	Novelist
Ivan Wilfred (Ching)	Johnson	Sports	Canada	Hockey Player - HF
Ivar	Giaever	Science	USA	Physics - Nobel Laureate
Ivo	Andric	Creative Works	Yugoslavia	Literature - Nobel Laureate
Ivor	Novello	Performing Arts	Wales	Actor
Ivor Armstrong	Richards	Arts	England	Critic - Literary
Ivy	Compton-Burnett	Creative Works	England	Novelist
Izaak	Walton	Creative Works	England	Writer
Jacinto	Benavente	Creative Works	Spain	Literature - Nobel Laureate
Jack	Albertson	Performing Arts	USA	Actor - Academy Award
	Anderson	Creative Works	USA	Journalist - Newspaper - Pulitzer
	Benny	Performing Arts	USA	Comedian
	Bruce	Performing Arts	Scotland	Rock & Roll - HF - Cream
	Burke Jr.	Sports	USA	Golfer - HF
	Cardiff	Movie Production	England	Director - Acad Award Nom
	Carson	Performing Arts	Canada	Actor
	Carter	Performing Arts	USA	Comedian
	Casady	Performing Arts	USA	Rock & Roll - HF - Jefferson Airplane
	Clayton	Movie Production	England	Director - Acad Award Nom
	Delaney	Sports	Canada	Boxer - HF
	Dempsey	Sports	USA	Boxer - HF
	Elam	Performing Arts	USA	Actor
	Gilford	Performing Arts	USA	Actor - Acad Award Nom
	Haley	Performing Arts	USA	Actor
	Hawkins	Performing Arts	England	Actor
	Holt	Performing Arts	USA	Actor
	Jones	Performing Arts	USA	Singer
	Kerouac	Creative Works	USA	Novelist/Poet
	Klugman	Performing Arts	USA	Actor
	Kruschen	Performing Arts	Canada	Actor - Acad Award Nom
	Lemmon	Performing Arts	USA	Actor - Academy Award
	London	Creative Works	USA	Novelist/Short Story Writer
	Lord	Performing Arts	USA	Actor
	Miles	Creative Works	USA	Author - Pulitzer
	Nicholson	Performing Arts	USA	Actor - Academy Award
	Nicklaus	Sports	USA	Golfer - HF
	Oakie	Performing Arts	USA	Actor - Acad Award Nom
	Paar	Performing Arts	USA	Show Host
	Palance	Performing Arts	USA	Actor - Academy Award
	Roush	Sports	USA	Race Car Designer - HF
	Soo	Performing Arts	USA	Comedian
	Steinberger	Science	USA	Physics - Nobel Laureate
	Warden	Performing Arts	USA	Actor - Acad Award Nom
	Webb	Performing Arts	USA	Actor
	Weston	Performing Arts	USA	Actor
	Wild	Performing Arts	England	Actor - Acad Award Nom
Jack (JC)	Higinbotham	Performing Arts	USA	Jazz Trombonist - Big Band/Jazz - HF
Jack (Jumping Jack)	McCracken	Sports	USA	Basketball Player - HF
Jack D.	Ruttan	Sports	Canada	Hockey Player - HF
Jack French	Kemp	Politics	USA	Congressman
Jack La (Jake)	Motta	Sports	USA	Boxer - HF
Jack Leroy (Jackie)	Wilson	Performing Arts	USA	Singer - Rock & Roll - HF
Jack N.	Rakove	Creative Works	USA	Author - Pulitzer
Jack R	Salamanca	Creative Works	USA	Author
Jack Raphael	Ham Jr.	Sports	USA	Football Player - HF
Jack Robert	Lousma	Aviation	USA	Astronaut

FIRST NAME	LAST NAME	CATEGORY	COUNTRY	FAME
Jack Roosevelt (Jackie)	Robinson	Sports	USA	Baseball Player - HF
Jack S.	Kilby	Science	USA	Physics - Nobel Laureate
Jack W.	Germond	Creative Works	USA	Journalist - Newspaper
Jackie	Collins	Creative Works	England	Novelist
	Coogan	Performing Arts	USA	Actor
	Cooper	Performing Arts	USA	Actor - Acad Award Nom
	Gleason	Performing Arts	USA	Actor - Acad Award Nom
	Ickx	Sports	Belgium	Race Car Driver - HF
	Jackson	Performing Arts	USA	Rock & Roll - HF - The Jackson Five
	Mahon	Creative Works	Canada	Journalist - Television
	Mason	Performing Arts	USA	Comedian
Jackie (The Flyng Scott)	Stewart	Sports	Scotland	Race Car Driver - HF
Jackie De	Shannon	Performing Arts	USA	Singer
Jackie Larue	Smith	Sports	USA	Football Player - HF
Jackie Ray	Slater	Sports	USA	Football Player
Jackson	Pollock	Works of Art	USA	Painter - Abstract
Jaclyn	Smith	Performing Arts	USA	Actress
Jacob	Abbott	Creative Works	USA	Author
	Burckhardt	Arts	Switzerland	Historian/Critic
	Carey	Performing Arts	USA	Rock & Roll - HF - The Flamingos
	Riis	Creative Works	USA	Journalist/Social Reformer
	Schiff	Business	USA	Financier
Jacob Nelson (Nellie)	Fox	Sports	USA	Baseball Player - HF
Jacob Peter (Jake)	Beckley	Sports	USA	Baseball Player - HF
Jacob Van	Artevelde	Politics	USA	Statesman
Jacob van	Ruisdael	Works of Art	Netherlands	Painter - Landscape
Jacobus	Arminius	Arts	Netherlands	Theologian
Jacobus Henricus Van't	Hoff	Science	Netherlands	Chemistry - Nobel Laureate
Jacobus Johannes Pieter	Oud	Architecture	Netherlands	Architect
Jacog	Epstein	Works of Art	England	Sculptor
Jacopo	Bellini	Works of Art	Italy	Painter
Jacopo Tatti	Sansovino	Architecture	Italy	Architect
Jacqueline	Bisset	Performing Arts	England	Actress
	Susann	Creative Works	USA	Novelistt
Jacqueline Lee	Kennedy	Politics	USA	First Lady
Jacques	Bernoulli	Science	Switzerland	Mathematician
	Cartier	Exploration	France	Explorer - St. Lawrence River
	Halévy	Creative Works	France	Composer
	Herzog	Architecture	Switzerland	Architect - Pritzker Laureate
	Lipchitz	Works of Art	USA	Sculptor
	Loeb	Science	USA	Biologist/Physiologist
	Maritain	Arts	France	Philosopher
	Marquette	Exploration	France	Explorer - Mississippi River
	Monod	Science	France	Medicine - Nobel Laureate
	Necker	Business	France	Financier/Statesman
	Offenbach	Creative Works	France	Composer - Operettas
	Piccard	Exploration	Switzerland	Explorer - Marine
Jacques (Toto)	Brugnon	Sports	France	Tennis Player - HF
Jacques Bénigne	Bossuet	Arts	France	Bishop/Orator
Jacques Gerard	Lemaire	Sports	Canada	Hockey Player - HF
Jacques Henri	Bernardin de Saint-Pierre	Creative Works	France	Writer
Jacques la	Ramie	Exploration	Canada	Explorer - Colorado River
Jacques René	Hébert	War & Peace	France	Revolutionary Leader
Jacques-Louis	David	Works of Art	France	Painter
Jada	Pinkett-Smith	Performing Arts	USA	Actress
Jagadis Chandra	Bose	Science	India	Physicist
Jaime	King	Performing Arts	USA	Super Model
	Lerner	Architecture	Brazil	Architect - Jefferson Medal
Jaime Robert (Robbie)	Robertson	Performing Arts	Canada	Rock & Roll - HF - The Band
Jair Ventura Jairzinho	Filho	Sports	Brazil	Soccer Player - HF
Jake (Greasy Thumb)	Guzik	Law & Order	Russia	Mafia
Jakob	Böhme	Arts	Germany	Philosopher/Mystic
Jakob	Grimm	Creative Works	Germany	Philologist - Fairy Tales

SOLVER SERIES: NAME FINDER

FIRST NAME	LAST NAME	CATEGORY	COUNTRY	FAME
Jakob	Prandtauer	Architecture	Austria	Architect
	Wassermann	Creative Works	Germany	Novelist
James	Abercrombie	Business	USA	Oil Industry
	Agee	Creative Works	USA	Novelist/Poet - Pulitzer
	Arness	Performing Arts	USA	Actor
	Boswell	Creative Works	Scotland	Writer/Lawyer
	Braid	Sports	Scotland	Golfer - HF
	Broderick	Performing Arts	USA	Actor
	Brolin	Performing Arts	USA	Actor
	Buchanan	Politics	USA	President
	Caan	Performing Arts	USA	Actor - Acad Award Nom
	Cagney	Performing Arts	USA	Actor - Academy Award
	Callaghan	Politics	England	Prime Minister
	Cameron	Movie Production	Canada	Director - Academy Award
	Chadwick	Science	England	Physics - Nobel Laureate
	Coburn	Performing Arts	USA	Actor - Academy Award
	Coco	Performing Arts	USA	Actor - Acad Award Nom
	Cook	Exploration	England	Explorer - Arctic/Australia
	Cromwell	Performing Arts	USA	Actor - Acad Award Nom
	Dean	Performing Arts	USA	Actor - Acad Award Nom
	Dickey	Creative Works	USA	Poet
	Douglas	War & Peace	Scotland	Military Leader
	Dunn	Performing Arts	USA	Actor - Acad Award Nom
	Dwight	Sports	France	Tennis Player - HF
	Elkin	Business	USA	Oil Industry
	Farentino	Performing Arts	USA	Actor
	Feibleman	Creative Works	USA	Author/Philosopher
	Fox	Performing Arts	England	Actor
	Franck	Science	Germany	Physics - Nobel Laureate
	Gadsden	Politics	USA	Diplomat
	Galway	Performing Arts	Ireland	Flutist
	Garner	Performing Arts	USA	Actor - Acad Award Nom
	Gentle	Sports	USA	Soccer Player - HF
	Gibbs	Architecture	England	Architect
	Gleason	Performing Arts	USA	Actor - Acad Award Nom
	Goldman	Creative Works	USA	Playwright/Novelist
	Hargreaves	Science	England	Inventor - Spinning Jenny
	Hoban	Architecture	USA	Architect
	Hogg	Creative Works	Scotland	Poet
	Honeyman-Scott	Performing Arts	England	Rock & Roll - HF - The Pretenders
	Ingram	Performing Arts	USA	Singer
	Ivory	Movie Production	USA	Director - Acad Award Nom
	Jones	Creative Works	USA	Author
	Kent	Law & Order	USA	Jurist
	Kirkwood	Creative Works	USA	Dramatist - Pulitzer
	Lapine	Creative Works	USA	Dramatist - Pulitzer
	Levine	Performing Arts	USA	Conductor
	Loeb	Business	USA	Banking/Philanthropist
	Longstreet	War & Peace	USA	Confederate General
	Macpherson	Creative Works	Scotland	Poet
	Madison	Politics	USA	President
	Martineau	Arts	England	Philosopher/Theologian
	Mason	Performing Arts	England	Actor - Acad Award Nom
	Merrill	Creative Works	USA	Poet - Pulitzer
	Mill	Arts	Scotland	Philosoper/Historian
	Monroe	Politics	USA	President
	Moody	Performing Arts	USA	Jazz Saxophonist - Big Band/Jazz - HF
	Otis	Politics	USA	Advocate - Civil Rights
	Parkinson	Science	England	Physician
	Patterson	Creative Works	USA	Author
	Phelan	Business	USA	Banking
	Polk	Politics	USA	President
	Schuyler	Creative Works	USA	Poet - Pulitzer

FIRST NAME	LAST NAME	CATEGORY	COUNTRY	FAME
James	Shirley	Creative Works	England	Dramatist
	Spader	Performing Arts	USA	Actor
	Stephens	Creative Works	Ireland	Poet/Novelist
	Stephenson	Performing Arts	England	Actor - Acad Award Nom
	Stewart	Performing Arts	USA	Actor - Academy Award
	Stirling	Architecture	England	Architect - Pritzker/Jefferson Medal
	Tate	Creative Works	USA	Poet - Pulitzer
	Taylor	Performing Arts	USA	Singer - Rock & Roll - HF
	Thomson	Creative Works	Scotland	Poet
	Tobin	Arts	USA	Economics - Nobel Laureate
	Turrell	Architecture	USA	Architect - Jefferson Medal
	Ussher	Arts	Ireland	Archbishop/Theologian
	Watt	Science	Scotland	Inventor/Engineer
	Weddell	Exploration	England	Explorer - Antarctic
	Whitmore	Performing Arts	USA	Actor - Acad Award Nom
	Wolfe	War & Peace	England	General
	Woods	Performing Arts	USA	Actor - Acad Award Nom
	Worthy	Sports	USA	Basketball Player - HF
	Basekett	Performing Arts	USA	Actor - Academy Award
	Belushi	Performing Arts	USA	Actor
James (Diamond Jim)	Brady	Business	USA	Financier/Philanthropy
James (Jesse)	Owens	Sports	USA	Olympic
James (Jim)	Brown	Sports	Scotland	Soccer Player - HF
	Nance	Creative Works	USA	Journalist - Television
James (Jim) Douglas	Morrison	Performing Arts	USA	Rock & Roll - HF - The Doors
James (Jimmy)	Arnold	Performing Arts	Canada	Canadian Music - HF - The Four Lads
	Clark Jr.	Sports	Scotland	Race Car Driver - HF
	Dorsey	Performing Arts	USA	Band Leader - Big Band/Jazz - HF
	Gallagher	Sports	Scotland	Soccer Player - HF
James (Jimmy) Earl	Carter	Politics	USA	President
	Carter	War & Peace	USA	Peace - Nobel Laureate
James A.	Baker	Politics	USA	Secretary of State
	Michener	Creative Works	USA	Author - Pulitzer
	Mirrlees	Arts	England	Economics - Nobel Laureate
James A. Van	Allen	Science	USA	Physicist
James Abbott McNiell	Whistler	Works of Art	USA	Painter/Etcher
James Abram	Garfield	Politics	USA	President
James Alan	McPherson	Creative Works	USA	Novelist - Pulitzer
James Alton	McDivitt	Aviation	USA	Astronaut
James Alvin (Jim)	Palmer	Sports	USA	Baseball Player - HF
James Andrew (Jimmy)	Rushing	Performing Arts	USA	Singer - Big Band/Jazz - HF
James Anthony	Froude	Arts	England	Historian
	Pawelczyk	Aviation	USA	Astronaut
James Arlington	Wright	Creative Works	USA	Poet - Pulitzer
James Arthur	Lovell Jr.	Aviation	USA	Astronaut
James Augustine Aloysius	Joyce	Creative Works	Ireland	Poet/Novelist
James Augustus (Catfish)	Hunter	Sports	USA	Baseball Player - HF
James Augustus Henry	Murray	Arts	England	Lexicographer
James Barrett	Reston	Creative Works	USA	Journalist - Newspaper
James Batchellor	Sumner	Science	USA	Chemistry - Nobel Laureate
James Bayard	Taylor	Creative Works	USA	Poet/Journalist
James Benson	Irwin	Aviation	USA	Astronaut
James Branch	Cabell	Creative Works	USA	Novelist
James Brander	Matthews	Creative Works	USA	Writer/Scholar/Critic
James Bryant	Conant	Science	USA	Chemist/Educator
James Buchanan	Eads	Science	USA	Engineer
James Butler (Wild Bill)	Hickok	Law & Order	USA	Lawman
James C.	Pollard	Sports	USA	Basketball Player - HF
James Cecil (Little Jimmy)	Dickens	Performing Arts	USA	Singer - Country Music - HF
James Charles (Jim)	Taylor	Sports	USA	Football Player - HF
James Charles (Jimmie)	Rodgers	Performing Arts	USA	Country Music - HF - Singing Brakeman
James Clark	Ross	Exploration	England	Explorer - Polar
James Clerk	Maxwell	Science	Scotland	Physicist

SOLVER SERIES: NAME FINDER

FIRST NAME	LAST NAME	CATEGORY	COUNTRY	FAME
James Columbus (Jay)	McShann	Performing Arts	USA	Band Leader - Big Band/Jazz - HF
James Craig	Adamson	Aviation	USA	Astronaut
James Danforth	Quayle	Politics	USA	Vice-President
James David	Lofton	Sports	USA	Football Player - HF
James Dewey	Watson	Science	USA	Medicine - Nobel Laureate
James Dickenson (Dick)	Irvin	Sports	Canada	Hockey Player - HF
James Douglas Van (Ox)	Hoften	Aviation	USA	Astronaut
James du Maresqu	Clavell	Creative Works	Australia	Author
James Dwight	Dana	Science	USA	Geologist/Mineralogist
James E.	Meade	Arts	England	Economics - Nobel Laureate
James Earl	Jones	Performing Arts	USA	Actor - Acad Award Nom
James Earl (Jimmy)	Johnson	Sports	USA	Football Player - HF
James Edward (Jim)	Finks	Sports	USA	Football Administrator - HF
	Kelly	Sports	USA	Football Player - HF
James Edwin (Jim)	Otto	Sports	USA	Football Player - HF
James Emory (Jimmy)	Foxx	Sports	USA	Baseball Player - HF
James Ernest	Renshaw	Sports	England	Tennis Player - HF
James Ewell Brown	Stuart	War & Peace	USA	General - Confederate
James Fenimore	Cooper	Creative Works	USA	Novelist
James Ford	Rhodes	Creative Works	USA	Author - Pulitzer
James Francis (Jim)	Thorpe	Sports	USA	Football Player/Olympic Runner - HF
James Francis (Pud)	Galvin	Sports	USA	Baseball Player - HF
James Frank	Dobie	Creative Works	USA	Writer/Scholar
James Frederick	Buchli	Aviation	USA	Astronaut
James George	Frazer	Arts	Scotland	Antropologist
James Gillespie	Blaine	Politics	USA	Secretary of State
James Gleason (Jimmy)	Conzelman	Sports	USA	Football Player - HF
James Gordon	Bennett	Creative Works	USA	Journalist
James Gould	Cozzens	Creative Works	USA	Novelist - Pulitzer
James Graham	Ballard	Creative Works	England	Novelist
James Grover	Thurber	Creative Works	USA	Writer/Humorist/Cartoonist
James Harold	Wilson	Politics	England	Prime Minster
James Harvey	Robinson	Arts	USA	Historian
James Henry (Jim)	O'Rourke	Sports	USA	Baseball Player - HF
James Henry (Jimmy)	Gardner	Sports	Canada	Hockey Player - HF
James Henry Leigh	Hunt	Creative Works	England	Poet/Essayist/Critic
James Henry Van (Tie-Breaker)	Alen	Sports	USA	Tennis Player - HF
James Herbert (Eubie)	Blake	Performing Arts	USA	Jazz Pianist/Composer - Big Band/Jazz - HF
James Hopwood	Jeans	Science	England	Physicist/Astronomer
James Hoyt	Wilhelm	Sports	USA	Baseball Player - HF
James J.	Corbett	Sports	USA	Boxer - HF
	Heckman	Arts	USA	Economics - Nobel Laureate
James Jerome	Hill	Business	USA	Railway Magnate
James John (Jim)	Langer	Sports	USA	Football Player - HF
James Joseph (Jimmy)	Collins	Sports	USA	Baseball Player - HF
James Joseph (Roger)	McGuinn	Performing Arts	USA	Rock & Roll - HF - The Bryds
James L.	Brooks	Movie Production	USA	Director - Academy Award
James Langston	Hughes	Creative Works	USA	Poet/Writer
James Leroy (Jim)	Bottomley	Sports	USA	Baseball Player - HF
James Louis (JJ)	Johnson	Performing Arts	USA	Jazz Trombonist - Big Band/Jazz - HF
James M.	Buchanan Jr.	Arts	USA	Economics - Nobel Laureate
	Ives	Works of Art	USA	Lithographer
	McPherson	Creative Works	USA	Author - Pulitzer
James MacGregor	Burns	Creative Works	USA	Author - Pulitzer
James Mallahan	Cain	Creative Works	USA	Novelist - Crime Fiction
James Mark	Baldwin	Arts	USA	Psychologist
James Matthew	Barrie	Creative Works	England	Playwright/Novelist
James Melvin (Jimmie)	Lunceford	Performing Arts	USA	Band Leader - Big Band/Jazz - HF
James Montgomery	Flagg	Creative Works	USA	Illustrator
James Nathaniel (Jim)	Brown	Sports	USA	Football Player - HF
James P.	Johnson	Performing Arts	USA	Jazz Pianist - Big Band/Jazz - HF
James Patrick	Donleavy	Creative Works	USA	Novelist
James Patrick (Jimmy)	Page	Performing Arts	England	Rock & Roll - HF - Led Zepplin

FIRST NAME	LAST NAME	CATEGORY	COUNTRY	FAME
James Paul	McCartney	Performing Arts	England	Rock & Roll - HF - The Beatles
James Paul David (Jim)	Bunning	Sports	USA	Baseball Player - HF
James Philip	Bagian	Aviation	USA	Astronaut
James Phinney	Baxter III	Creative Works	USA	Author - Pulitzer
James Ramsay	MacDonald	Politics	England	Prime Minister
James Riddle (Jimmy)	Hoffa	Business	USA	Labor Leader
James Robert	Mann	Politics	USA	Congressman
James Robert (Bob)	Wills	Performing Arts	USA	Country Music - HF - Texas Playboys
James Ronald (Jim)	Ryun	Sports	USA	Olympic Runner
James Rowland	Angell	Arts	USA	Psychologist
James Russell	Lowell	Creative Works	USA	Poet/Essayist
James S.	Sherman	Politics	USA	Vice-President
James Scott (Jimmy)	Connors	Sports	USA	Tennis Player - HF
James Shelton	Voss	Aviation	USA	Astronaut
James Stanley (Jim)	Hall	Performing Arts	USA	Jazz Guitarist - Big Band/Jazz - HF
James Stephen (Jim)	Ringo	Sports	USA	Football Player - HF
James Strom	Thurmond	Politics	USA	Senator - South Carolina
James Thomas	Farrell	Creative Works	USA	Novelist
James Thomas (Cool Papa)	Bell	Sports	USA	Baseball Player - HF
James Thomas (Jim)	Parker	Sports	USA	Football Player - HF
James Travis	Reeves	Performing Arts	USA	Singer - Country Music - HF
James Truslow	Adams	Creative Works	USA	Author - Pulitzer
James W.	Black	Science	England	Medicine - Nobel Laureate
James Walter	Thompson	Business	USA	Advertising
James Watson	Cronin	Science	USA	Physics - Nobel Laureate
James Weldon	Johnson	Creative Works	USA	Writer/Diplomat
James Whitcomb	Riley	Creative Works	USA	Poet
James William	Fulbright	Politics	USA	Senator
Jamesetta (Etta)	James (Hawkins)	Performing Arts	USA	Singer - Rock & Roll - HF
Jameson	Parker	Performing Arts	USA	Actor
Jamie	Farr	Performing Arts	USA	Actor
	Foxx	Performing Arts	USA	Actor - Academy Award
Jamie Lee	Curtis	Performing Arts	USA	Actress
Jan	Bruegel	Works of Art	Italy	Painter
	Hammer	Creative Works	Czechoslovakia	Composer
	Hooks	Performing Arts	USA	Comedian
	Kiepura	Performing Arts	Poland	Singer - Opera
	Kodes	Sports	Czechoslovakia	Tennis Player - HF
	Masaryk	Politics	Czechoslovakia	Statesman
	Peerce	Performing Arts	USA	Singer - Opera
	Steen	Works of Art	Netherlands	Painter
	Stenerud	Sports	Norway	Football Player - HF
	Sterling	Performing Arts	USA	Actress - Acad Award Nom
	Tinbergen	Arts	Netherlands	Economics - Nobel Laureate
	Troell	Movie Production	Sweden	Director - Acad Award Nom
	Vermeer	Works of Art	Netherlands	Painter
	Žižka	War & Peace	Bohemia	General
Jan Christiaan	Smuts	Politics	South Africa	Prime Minster
Jan Lynne	Stephenson	Sports	Australia	Golfer
Jan Nepomuk	Neruda	Creative Works	Czechoslovakia	Poet/Writer
Jan Van	Eyck	Works of Art	Belgium	Painter
Jan van Olden	Barneveldt	Politics	Netherlands	Statesman/Patriot
Jana	Novotna	Sports	Czechoslovakia	Tennis Player - HF
Jane	Addams	Creative Works	USA	Social Worker
	Addams	War & Peace	USA	Peace - Nobel Laureate
	Alexander	Performing Arts	USA	Actress - Acad Award Nom
	Austen	Creative Works	England	Novelist
	Brody	Creative Works	USA	Journalist - Newspaper
	Campion	Movie Production	New Zealand	Director - Acad Award Nom
	Curtin	Performing Arts	USA	Actress
	Darwell	Performing Arts	USA	Actress - Academy Award
	Fonda	Performing Arts	USA	Actress - Academy Award
	Grey	Politics	England	Queen

SOLVER SERIES: NAME FINDER

FIRST NAME	LAST NAME	CATEGORY	COUNTRY	FAME
Jane	Jacobs	Architecture	Canada	Architect - Jefferson Medal
	Powell	Performing Arts	USA	Actress
	Russell	Performing Arts	USA	Actress
	Seymour	Performing Arts	England	Actress
	Smiley	Creative Works	USA	Novelist - Pulitzer
	Withers	Performing Arts	USA	Actress
	Wyatt	Performing Arts	USA	Actress
	Wyman	Performing Arts	USA	Actress - Academy Award
Jane Bryant	Quinn	Creative Works	USA	Journalist - Newspaper
Jane Mears	Pierce	Politics	USA	First Lady
Janet	Evans	Sports	USA	Olympic Swimmer
	Gaynor	Performing Arts	USA	Actress - Acad Award Nom
	Guthrie	Sports	USA	Race Car Driver - HF
	Jackson	Performing Arts	USA	Singer
	Leigh	Performing Arts	USA	Actress - Acad Award Nom
	Margolin	Performing Arts	USA	Actress
	McTeer	Performing Arts	England	Actress - Acad Award Nom
	Reno	Politics	USA	Attorney General
	Suzman	Performing Arts	South Africa	Actress - Acad Award Nom
Janine	Turner	Performing Arts	USA	Actress
Janis	Ian	Performing Arts	USA	Singer
	Paige	Performing Arts	USA	Actress
Janis Lyn	Joplin	Performing Arts	USA	Singer - Rock & Roll - HF
Jan-Michael	Vincent	Performing Arts	USA	Actor
Jann S.	Wenner	Creative Works	USA	Journalist - Magazine
János	Hunyadi	War & Peace	Hungary	General
Jaquelin T.	Robertson	Architecture	USA	Architect - Jefferson Medal
Jaques	Cousteau	Exploration	France	Explorer - Marine
Jaques Germain	Soufflot	Architecture	France	Architect
Jared	Diamond	Creative Works	USA	Author - Pulitzer
	Leto	Performing Arts	USA	Actor
Jari Pekka	Kurri	Sports	Finland	Hockey Player - HF
Jaroslav	Drobny	Sports	Czechoslovakia	Tennis Player - HF
	Heyrovsky	Science	Czechoslovakia	Chemistry - Nobel Laureate
	Seifert	Creative Works	Czechoslovakia	Literature - Nobel Laureate
Jascha	Heifetz	Performing Arts	USA	Violinist
Jasmine	Guy	Performing Arts	USA	Actress
Jason	Alexander	Performing Arts	USA	Actor
	Bateman	Performing Arts	USA	Actor
	Miller	Creative Works	USA	Dramatist - Pulitzer
	Miller	Performing Arts	USA	Actor - Acad Award Nom
	Robards Jr.	Performing Arts	USA	Actor - Academy Award
Jasper	Johns	Works of Art	USA	Painter/Sculptor
Javier	Bardem	Performing Arts	Spain	Actor - Acad Award Nom
Jawaharlal	Nehru	Politics	India	Prime Minister
Jay	Gould	Business	USA	Financier
	Greenberg	Creative Works	USA	Composer Pianist
	Leno	Performing Arts	USA	Show Host/Comedian
	Thomas	Performing Arts	USA	Actor
	Osmond	Performing Arts	USA	Singer
Jay Anthony	Lukas	Creative Works	USA	Author - Pulitzer
Jay Clark	Buckey Jr.	Aviation	USA	Astronaut
Jay Hanna (Dizzy)	Dean	Sports	USA	Baseball Player - HF
Jaye	Davidson	Performing Arts	USA	Actor - Acad Award Nom
Jayne	Kennedy	Performing Arts	USA	Actress
	Mansfield	Performing Arts	USA	Actress
	Meadows	Performing Arts	China	Actress
Jayne Anne	Phillips	Creative Works	USA	Author
Jean	Anouilh	Creative Works	France	Playwright
	Arthur	Performing Arts	USA	Actress - Acad Award Nom
	Auel	Creative Works	USA	Author
	Baudrillard	Arts	France	Philosopher/Sociologist
	Bernoulli	Science	Switzerland	Mathematician

FIRST NAME	LAST NAME	CATEGORY	COUNTRY	FAME
Jean	Bodin	Arts	France	Philosopher/Jurist
	Clouet	Works of Art	France	Painter - Portraits
	Cocteau	Creative Works	France	Poet/Novelist/Playwright
	Cocteau	Movie Production	France	Director
	Dausset	Science	France	Medicine - Nobel Laureate
	Froissart	Creative Works	France	Poet/Chronicler
	Genêt	Creative Works	France	Novelist/Playwright
	Hagen	Performing Arts	USA	Actress - Acad Award Nom
	Harlow	Performing Arts	USA	Actress
	Labatut	Architecture	USA	Architect - Jefferson Medal
	Lafitte	Law & Order	France	Pirate
	Marsh	Performing Arts	England	Actress
	Muir	Business	England	Fashion Designer
	Negulesco	Movie Production	Romania	Director - Acad Award Nom
	Nicollet	Exploration	France	Explorer - Great Lakes
	Nouvel	Architecture	France	Architect
	Patou	Business	France	Fragrance Designer
	Peltier	Science	France	Physicist
	Piaget	Arts	Switzerland	Psychologist
	Renoir	Movie Production	France	Director - Acad Award Nom
	Schneider	Creative Works	USA	Author - Pulitzer
	Seberg	Performing Arts	USA	Actress
	Shrimpton	Performing Arts	England	Super Model
	Sibelius	Creative Works	Finland	Composer
	Simmons	Performing Arts	England	Actress - Acad Award Nom
	Stafford	Creative Works	USA	Novelist - Pulitzer
	Stapleton	Performing Arts	USA	Actress
Jean (Hans)	Arp	Works of Art	France	Painter/Sculptor
Jean Arthur	Beliveau	Sports	Canada	Hockey Player - HF
Jean Auguste Dominique	Ingres	Works of Art	France	Painter
Jean Baptiste	Colbert	Politics	France	Statesman
	Greuze	Works of Art	France	Painter
	Lully	Creative Works	France	Composer - Opera
	Molière	Creative Works	France	Dramatist
	Perrin	Science	France	Physics - Nobel Laureate
	Racine	Creative Works	France	Poet/Dramatist
Jean Baptiste (Jack)	Laviolette	Sports	Canada	Hockey Player - HF
Jean Baptiste de	Rochambeau	War & Peace	France	General - Revolutionary War
Jean Baptiste de la	Harpe	Exploration	France	Explorer - America South
Jean Baptiste Joseph	Fourier	Science	France	Physicist/Mathematician
Jean Baptiste Jules	Bernadotte	War & Peace	France	Marshall
Jean Baptiste Siméon	Chardin	Works of Art	France	Painter
Jean Bernard Léon	Foucault	Science	France	Physicist
Jean Charles Léonard	Sismondi	Arts	Switzerland	Historian/Economist
Jean de	Joinville	Arts	France	Chronicler
	Reszke	Performing Arts	Poland	Singer - Opera
Jean de La	Bruyère	Creative Works	France	Essayist/Moralist
	Fontaine	Creative Works	France	Poet/Writer
Jean Édouard	Vuillard	Works of Art	France	Painter
Jean Félix	Piccard	Science	Switzerland	Physicist
Jean François	Champollion	Arts	France	Egyptologist
	Millet	Works of Art	France	Painter
Jean François Casimir	Delavigne	Creative Works	France	Poet/Playwright
Jean Françoise Julie	Récamier	Politics	France	Social Leader
Jean Frédéric	Joliot-Curie	Science	France	Chemistry - Nobel Laureate
Jean Henri	Fabre	Science	France	Entomologist
Jean Henry	Dunant	Business	Switzerland	Philanthropist - Red Cross
	Dunant	War & Peace	Switzerland	Peace - Nobel Laureate
Jean Jacques	Lequeu	Architecture	France	Architect
	Rousseau	Arts	France	Philosopher/Writer
Jean Joseph Charles Louis	Blanc	Arts	France	Socialist/Historian
Jean Joseph Jacques	Chrétien	Politics	Canada	Prime Minister
Jean Jules	Jusserand	Creative Works	USA	Author - Pulitzer

SOLVER SERIES: NAME FINDER

FIRST NAME	LAST NAME	CATEGORY	COUNTRY	FAME
Jean Léon	Jaurès	Politics	France	Socialist Leader/Journalist
Jean Louis	Pascal	Architecture	France	Architect - AIA Gold Medal
Jean Louis Ernest	Meissonier	Works of Art	France	Painter
Jean Martin	Charcot	Science	France	Neurologist
Jean Nicolas Arthur	Rimbaud	Creative Works	France	Poet
Jean Nicolas Louis	Durand	Architecture	France	Architect
Jean Parker	Shepherd	Creative Works	USA	Writer - Short Stories
Jean Paul	Getty	Business	USA	Oil Industry
	Marat	Politics	France	Revolutionary Leader
	Richter	Creative Works	Germany	Writer
Jean Philippe	Rameau	Creative Works	France	Composer/Organist
Jean Pierre	Wimille	Sports	France	Race Car Driver - HF
Jean René (The Crocodile)	Lacoste	Sports	France	Tennis Player - HF
Jean Robert	Borotra	Sports	France	Tennis Player - HF
Jean Victor	Moreau	War & Peace	France	General
Jean-Antoine	Watteau	Works of Art	France	Painter - Genre
Jean-Baptiste (Illinois)	Jacquet	Performing Arts	USA	Jazz Saxophonist - Big Band/Jazz - HF
Jean-Baptiste Camille	Corot	Works of Art	France	Painter
Jean-Baptiste-Point du	Sable	Exploration	France	Explorer - Chicago
Jean-Claude	Killy	Sports	France	Olympic - Skier
Jean-Claude Van	Damme	Performing Arts	Belgium	Actor
Jeane Jordan	Kirkpatrick	Politics	USA	Politician
Jeanette	MacDonald	Performing Arts	USA	Actress - Musical
Jean-François André	Clervoy	Aviation	France	Astronaut
Jean-François de la	Perouse	Exploration	France	Explorer - Hawaii
Jean-Jacques	Favier	Aviation	France	Astronaut
Jean-Loup Jacques Marie	Chrétien	Aviation	France	Astronaut
Jean-Luc	Godard	Movie Production	France	Director
Jean-Marie	Lehn	Science	France	Chemistry - Nobel Laureate
Jeanne	Crain	Performing Arts	USA	Actress - Acad Award Nom
	Eagels	Performing Arts	USA	Actress - Acad Award Nom
	Moreau	Performing Arts	France	Actress
Jeanne (Joan of Arc)	D'Arc	War & Peace	France	Heroine/Military Leader
Jeannie	Berlin	Performing Arts	USA	Actress - Acad Award Nom
Jean-Paul	Belmondo	Performing Arts	France	Actor
	Gaultier	Business	France	Fashion Designer
	Sartre	Creative Works	France	Literature - Nobel Laureate
Jean-Pierre	Aumont	Performing Arts	France	Actor
	Pepin	Sports	France	Soccer Player
	Rampal	Performing Arts	France	Flutist
Jedediah	Smith	Exploration	USA	Frontiersman - California
	Strutt	Business	England	Textile Industry
Jeff	Beck	Performing Arts	England	Guitarist
	Bridges	Performing Arts	USA	Actor - Acad Award Nom
	Chandler	Performing Arts	USA	Actor - Academy Award
	Chandler	Sports	USA	Boxer - HF
	Cook	Performing Arts	USA	Country Music - HF - Alabama
	Daniels	Performing Arts	USA	Actor
	Fahey	Performing Arts	USA	Actor
	Fenech	Sports	Australia	Boxer - HF
	Goldblum	Performing Arts	USA	Actor
	Greenfield	Creative Works	USA	Journalist - Television
	Lynne	Performing Arts	England	Singer/Guitarist
	Sluman	Sports	USA	Golfer
Jefferson	Davis	Politics	USA	President - Confederacy
Jeffery Kenneth (Jeff)	MacNelly	Creative Works	USA	Cartoonist - Editorial
Jeffrey	Amherst	War & Peace	England	General
	Dahmer	Law & Order	USA	Serial Killer
	Eugenides	Creative Works	USA	Novelist - Pulitzer
	Hunter	Performing Arts	USA	Actor
	Tambor	Performing Arts	USA	Actor
	Tate	Performing Arts	England	Conductor
Jeffrey Alan	Hoffman	Aviation	USA	Astronaut

FIRST NAME	LAST NAME	CATEGORY	COUNTRY	FAME
Jeffry Ross (Joey)	Ramone (Hyman)	Performing Arts	USA	Rock & Roll - HF - The Ramones
Jenna	Elfman	Performing Arts	USA	Actress
Jennifer	Beals	Performing Arts	USA	Actress
	Capriati	Sports	USA	Tennis Player
	Connelly	Performing Arts	USA	Actress - Academy Award
	Grey	Performing Arts	USA	Actress
	Jones	Performing Arts	USA	Actress - Academy Award
	O'Neill	Performing Arts	Brazil	Actress
Jennifer Jason	Leigh	Performing Arts	USA	Actress
Jenny	Agutter	Performing Arts	England	Actress
	Lind	Performing Arts	Sweden	Singer - Opera
Jens C.	Skou	Science	Denmark	Chemistry - Nobel Laureate
Jens Otto Harry	Jesperson	Arts	Denmark	Linguist
Jeremiah (Jerry)	Harrison	Performing Arts	USA	Rock & Roll - HF - The Talking Heads
Jeremy	Bentham	Arts	England	Philosopher/Economist
	Irons	Performing Arts	England	Actor - Academy Award
	Spender	Performing Arts	England	Rock & Roll - HF - Fleetwood Mac
	Taylor	Arts	England	Bishop/Theologian
Jermaine	Jackson	Performing Arts	USA	Rock & Roll - HF - The Jackson Five
Jerome	Hines	Performing Arts	USA	Singer - Opera
	Karle	Science	USA	Chemistry - Nobel Laureate
	Robbins	Movie Production	USA	Director - Academy Award
	Weidman	Creative Works	USA	Dramatist - Pulitzer
Jerome D. (Jerry)	Travers	Sports	USA	Golfer - HF
Jerome David	Kern	Creative Works	USA	Composer
	Salinger	Creative Works	USA	Novelist/Short Story Writer
Jerome I.	Friedman	Science	USA	Physics - Nobel Laureate
Jerome Jay	Apt III	Aviation	USA	Astronaut
Jerome John	Garcia	Performing Arts	USA	Rock & Roll - HF - Grateful Dead
Jerry	Adler	Performing Arts	USA	Harmonica Musician - Classical Soloist
	Bock	Creative Works	USA	Composer - Musicals
	Butler	Performing Arts	USA	Rock & Roll - HF - The Impressions
	Lewis	Performing Arts	USA	Comedian
	Orbach	Performing Arts	USA	Actor
	Pate	Sports	USA	Golfer
	Reed	Performing Arts	USA	Singer
	Rice	Sports	USA	Football Player
	Seinfeld	Performing Arts	USA	Comedian
	Stiller	Performing Arts	USA	Actor
	Vale	Performing Arts	USA	Singer - Pops
	Yester	Performing Arts	USA	Rock & Roll - HF - Lovin' Spoonful
Jerry A.	West	Sports	USA	Basketball Player - HF
Jerry Lee	Lewis	Performing Arts	USA	Singer - Rock & Roll - HF
Jerry Michael	Linenger	Aviation	USA	Astronaut
Jerry R.	Lucas	Sports	USA	Basketball Player - HF
Jerry Van	Dyke	Performing Arts	USA	Actor
Jess	Thomas	Performing Arts	USA	Singer - Opera
	Willard	Sports	USA	Boxer - HF
Jesse Alexander	Helms	Politics	USA	Senator - North Carolina
Jesse Cail	Burkett	Sports	USA	Baseball Player - HF
Jesse Carlye (JC)	Snead	Sports	USA	Golfer
Jesse Holman	Jones	Business	USA	Construction Industry
Jesse Joseph	Haines	Sports	USA	Baseball Player - HF
Jesse Louis	Jackson Sr.	Politics	USA	Activist - Civil Rights
Jesse Lynch	Williams	Creative Works	USA	Dramatist - Pulitzer
Jesse Woodson	James	Law & Order	USA	Outlaw
Jessi	Colter	Performing Arts	USA	Actor
Jessi (Duane)	Eddy (Colter)	Performing Arts	USA	Singer - Rock & Roll - HF
Jessica	Harper	Performing Arts	USA	Actress
	Lange	Performing Arts	USA	Actress - Academy Award
	Mitford	Creative Works	England	Author
	Tandy	Performing Arts	England	Actress - Academy Award
Jessie	Booth	Business	England	Retail Trade

SOLVER SERIES: NAME FINDER

FIRST NAME	LAST NAME	CATEGORY	COUNTRY	FAME
Jesus	Alou	Sports	USA	Baseball Player
Jethro (Kenneth)	Burns	Performing Arts	USA	Country Music - HF - Homer & Jethro
Jhumpa	Lahiri	Creative Works	USA	Novelist - Pulitzer
Jill	Clayburgh	Performing Arts	USA	Actress - Acad Award Nom
	Eikenberry	Performing Arts	USA	Actress
	St. John	Performing Arts	USA	Actress
Jim	Backus	Performing Arts	USA	Actor
	Berry	Creative Works	USA	Cartoonist - Berry's World
	Capaldi (Traffic)	Performing Arts	England	Rock & Roll - HF - Traffic
	Colbert	Sports	USA	Golfer
	Courier	Sports	USA	Tennis Player - HF
	Croce	Performing Arts	USA	Singer
	Dale	Performing Arts	England	Actor
	Davis	Creative Works	USA	Cartoonist - Garfield
	Dent	Sports	USA	Golfer
	Hall	Sports	USA	Race Car Driver - HF
	Hutton	Performing Arts	USA	Actor
	Kaat	Sports	USA	Baseball Player
	Lehrer	Creative Works	USA	Journalist - Television
	McCarty	Performing Arts	England	Rock & Roll - HF - The Yardbirds
	McMahon	Sports	USA	Football Player
	Messina	Performing Arts	USA	Rock & Roll - HF - Buffalo Springfield
	Nabors	Performing Arts	USA	Actor
	Nance	Sports	USA	Football Player
	Plunkett	Sports	USA	Football Player
	Rice	Sports	USA	Baseball Player
	Seals	Performing Arts	USA	Singer
	Sheridan	Movie Production	Ireland	Director - Acad Award Nom
	Stafford	Performing Arts	USA	Singer - Pops/Country
	Thompson	Creative Works	USA	Novelist - Pulp Fiction
Jim (Long Jim)	Barnes	Sports	England	Golfer - HF
Jimi	Hendrix	Performing Arts	USA	Singer - Rock & Roll - HF
Jimmie	Noone	Performing Arts	USA	Jazz Clarinetist - Big Band/Jazz - HF
	Rodgers	Performing Arts	USA	Singer - Rock & Roll - HF
Jimmie (James Houston)	Davis	Performing Arts	USA	Singer - Country Music - HF
Jimmy	Blanton	Performing Arts	USA	Jazz Bassist - Big Band/Jazz - HF
	Breslin	Creative Works	USA	Journalist - Newspaper - Pulitzer
	Broadbent	Performing Arts	England	Actor - Academy Award
	Buffett	Performing Arts	USA	Singer/Composer
	Carter	Sports	USA	Boxer - HF
	Demaret	Sports	USA	Golfer - HF
	Douglas	Sports	USA	Soccer Player - HF
	Dunn	Sports	USA	Soccer Player - HF
	Durante	Performing Arts	USA	Comedian
	Osmond	Performing Arts	USA	Singer
	Ritz	Performing Arts	USA	Comedian
	Roe	Sports	USA	Soccer Player - HF
	Smits	Performing Arts	USA	Actor
	Webb	Creative Works	USA	Composer
Jimmy (Cowboy)	Bryan	Sports	USA	Race Car Driver - HF
Jo Elizabeth	Stafford	Performing Arts	USA	Singer - Big Band/Jazz - HF
Jo Van	Fleet	Performing Arts	USA	Actress - Academy Award
Joachim	Murat	War & Peace	France	Marshal
Joachim Fritz (John)	Kay (Krauledat)	Performing Arts	Germany	Singer - Canadian Music - HF
Joan	Allen	Performing Arts	USA	Actress - Acad Award Nom
	Baez	Performing Arts	USA	Singer/Composer
	Bennett	Performing Arts	USA	Actress
	Benoit	Sports	USA	Olympic Marathoner
	Blondell	Performing Arts	USA	Actress - Acad Award Nom
	Collins	Performing Arts	England	Actress
	Crawford	Performing Arts	USA	Actress - Academy Award
	Crawfprd	Sports	USA	Basketball Player - HF
	Cusack	Performing Arts	USA	Actress - Acad Award Nom

FIRST NAME	LAST NAME	CATEGORY	COUNTRY	FAME
Joan	Davis	Performing Arts	USA	Actress
	Didion	Creative Works	USA	Journalist - Magazine
	Fontaine	Performing Arts	Japan	Actress - Academy Award
	Hackett	Performing Arts	USA	Actress - Acad Award Nom
	Jett	Performing Arts	USA	Singer
	Kroc	Business	USA	Philanthropy
	Lorring	Performing Arts	China	Actress - Acad Award Nom
	Miró	Works of Art	Spain	Painter/Sculptor - Surrealist
	Plowright	Performing Arts	England	Actress - Acad Award Nom
	Rivers	Performing Arts	USA	Comedian
	Sutherland	Performing Arts	Australia	Singer - Opera
Joan D.	Vinge	Creative Works	USA	Author - SciFi
Joan Van	Ark	Performing Arts	USA	Actress
Joanna	Kerns	Performing Arts	USA	Actress
Joanne	Dru	Performing Arts	USA	Actress
	Woodward	Performing Arts	USA	Actress - Academy Award
Joanne Gunderson	Carner	Sports	USA	Golfer - HF
João Batista Villanova	Artigas	Architecture	Brazil	Architect
Joaquin	Alvarez Quintero	Creative Works	Spain	Playwright
	Miller	Creative Works	USA	Poet
	Phoenix	Performing Arts	Puerto Rico	Actor - Acad Award Nom
JoBeth	Williams	Performing Arts	USA	Actress
Jocelyne	Lagarde	Performing Arts	Tahiti	Actress - Acad Award Nom
Jochen	Rindt	Sports	Germany	Race Car Driver - HF
Jodie	Foster	Performing Arts	USA	Actress - Academy Award
Jody	Scheckter	Sports	South Africa	Race Car Driver
Joe	Amato	Sports	USA	Race Car Driver - HF
	Butler	Performing Arts	USA	Rock & Roll - HF - Lovin' Spoonful
	Carter	Sports	USA	Baseball Player
	Cocker	Performing Arts	England	Singer
	Dumars	Sports	USA	Basketball Player
	Flynn	Performing Arts	USA	Actor
	Franklin	Creative Works	USA	Journalist - Television
	Jackson	Performing Arts	England	Singer
	Lapchick	Sports	USA	Basketball Player - HF
	Mantell	Performing Arts	USA	Actor - Acad Award Nom
	Miller	Performing Arts	England	Comedian
	Pesci	Performing Arts	USA	Actor - Academy Award
	Piscopo	Performing Arts	USA	Comedian
	Spano	Performing Arts	USA	Actor
	Tex	Performing Arts	USA	Singer
	Theismann	Sports	USA	Football Player
	Torre	Sports	USA	Baseball Player
	Walsh	Performing Arts	USA	Rock & Roll - HF - The Eagles
	Walsh	Performing Arts	USA	Singer/Guitarist
	Barbera	Creative Works	USA	Cartoonist
Joe (King)	Oliver	Performing Arts	USA	Band Leader - Big Band/Jazz - HF
Joe (Smokin Joe)	Frazier	Sports	USA	Boxer - HF
Joe Don	Baker	Performing Arts	USA	Actor
Joe E.	Brown	Performing Arts	USA	Comedian
	Lewis	Performing Arts	USA	Singer
Joe Frank	Edwards Jr.	Aviation	USA	Astronaut
Joe Henry	Engle	Aviation	USA	Astronaut
Joe Jackson	Gibbs	Sports	USA	Football Coach - HF
Joe Leonard	Morgan	Sports	USA	Baseball Player - HF
Joe Lynn	Turner	Performing Arts	USA	Singer - Rock & Roll - HF
Joel	Barlow	Creative Works	USA	Poet/Diplomat
	Coen	Movie Production	USA	Director - Acad Award Nom
	Grey	Performing Arts	USA	Actor - Academy Award
	McCrea	Performing Arts	USA	Actor
Joel Chandler	Harris	Creative Works	USA	Author
Joey	Bishop	Performing Arts	USA	Actor/Comedian
	Dee	Performing Arts	USA	Rock & Roll - HF - The Young Rascals

SOLVER SERIES: NAME FINDER

FIRST NAME	LAST NAME	CATEGORY	COUNTRY	FAME
Joey	Maxim	Sports	USA	Boxer - HF
Joey (Joseph)	Kramer	Performing Arts	USA	Rock & Roll - HF - Aerosmith
Johan	Bojer	Creative Works	Norway	Novelist/Playwright
	Cruyff	Sports	Netherlands	Soccer Player - HF
Johan August	Strindberg	Creative Works	Sweden	Novelist/Dramatist
Johan Bernhard	Fischer von Erlach	Architecture	Austria	Architect
Johann	Deisenhofer	Science	Germany	Chemistry - Nobel Laureate
	Froben	Arts	Germany	Printer
	Goethe	Creative Works	Germany	Poet/Dramatist
	Gutenberg	Arts	Germany	Printer
	Reuchlin	Arts	Germany	Scholar - Humanist
	Strauss	Creative Works	Austria	Composer - Waltzes
Johann August	Suter	Business	USA	Gold Mining
Johann Christian	Bach	Creative Works	Germany	Composer/Organist
Johann Christoph Friedrich von	Schiller	Creative Works	Germany	Poet/Dramatist
Johann De	Kalb	War & Peace	France	General
Johann Fredrich	Herbart	Arts	Germany	Philosopher/Educator
Johann Friedrich Adolf von	Baeyer	Science	Germany	Chemistry - Nobel Laureate
Johann Gottfried von	Herder	Arts	Germany	Philosopher/Poet
Johann Gottlieb	Fichte	Arts	Germany	Philosopher
Johann Heinrich	Pestalozzi	Arts	Switzerland	Educational Reformer
Johann Joachim	Winckelmann	Arts	Germany	Archaeologist/Art Historian
Johann Ludwig	Uhland	Creative Works	Germany	Poet/Literary Historian
Johann Maier von	Eck	Arts	Germany	Theologian
Johann Sebastian	Bach	Creative Works	Germany	Composer/Organist
Johanna Louise	Spyri	Creative Works	Switzerland	Author
Johannes	Brahms	Creative Works	Germany	Composer
	Eckhart	Arts	Germany	Theologian/Mystic
	Kepler	Science	Germany	Astronomer/Mathematician
	Stark	Science	Germany	Physics - Nobel Laureate
Johannes Diderik Van der	Waals	Science	Netherlands	Physics - Nobel Laureate
Johannes Georg	Bednorz	Science	Germany	Physics - Nobel Laureate
Johannes Hans Daniel	Jensen	Science	Germany	Physics - Nobel Laureate
Johannes Scotus	Erigena	Arts	Ireland	Theologian/Philosopher
Johannes Vilhelm	Jensen	Creative Works	Denmark	Literature - Nobel Laureate
John	Adams	Politics	USA	President
	Agar	Performing Arts	USA	Actor
	Amos	Performing Arts	USA	Actor
	Anderson	Arts	Scotland	Philosopher
	Andre	War & Peace	England	Major
	Arbuthnot	Creative Works	Scotland	Writer/Physician
	Ashbery	Creative Works	USA	Poet - Pulitzer
	Astin	Performing Arts	USA	Actor
	Austin	Arts	England	Legal Philosopher
	Ball	Arts	England	Priest
	Ball	Sports	England	Golfer - HF
	Bardeen	Science	USA	Physics - Nobel Laureate
	Barrymore	Performing Arts	USA	Actor
	Bartlett	Creative Works	USA	Editor/Publisher
	Baskerville	Arts	England	Printer/Designer
	Beckman	Sports	USA	Basketball Player - HF
	Belushi	Performing Arts	USA	Actor
	Berryman	Creative Works	USA	Poet - Pulitzer
	Betjeman	Creative Works	England	Poet Laureate
	Biddle	Arts	England	Theologian
	Boorman	Movie Production	England	Director - Acad Award Nom
	Bradshaw	Arts	USA	Philosopher/Lecturer/Author
	Bright	Politics	England	Statesman
	Brodie	Sports	USA	Football Player
	Brown	Politics	USA	Abolitionist
	Bruton	Politics	Ireland	Prime Minister
	Buchan	Creative Works	Scotland	Novelist/Statesman
	Bunyan	Creative Works	England	Writer/Preacher

FIRST NAME	LAST NAME	CATEGORY	COUNTRY	FAME
John	Burgoyne	War & Peace	England	General
	Burroughs	Creative Works	USA	Writer/Naturalist
	Cabot	Exploration	England	Explorer - Canada
	Cale	Performing Arts	Wales	Rock & Roll - HF - Velvet Underground
	Candy	Performing Arts	Canada	Actor/Comedian
	Carradine	Performing Arts	USA	Actor
	Carteret	Politics	England	Statesman/Diplomat
	Cartwright	Politics	England	Reformer
	Carver	Politics	USA	Governor - Plymouth Colony
	Cassavetes	Movie Production	USA	Director - Acad Award Nom
	Cassavetes	Performing Arts	USA	Actor - Acad Award Nom
	Chancellor	Creative Works	USA	Journalist - Television
	Charles	Sports	Wales	Soccer Player - HF
	Cheever	Creative Works	USA	Author - Pulitzer
	Churchill	Politics	England	Duke
	Ciardi	Creative Works	USA	Poet
	Cleave	Business	England	Publishing
	Cleese	Performing Arts	England	Actor
	Colette	Arts	England	Theologian
	Coltrane	Performing Arts	USA	Jazz Saxophonist - Big Band/Jazz - HF
	Constable	Works of Art	England	Painter - Landscapes
	Cook	Sports	USA	Golfer
	Cotton	Arts	USA	Clergyman - Puritan
	Cusack	Performing Arts	USA	Actor
	Dall	Performing Arts	USA	Actor - Acad Award Nom
	Dalton	Science	England	Chemist/Physicist
	Daly	Sports	USA	Golfer
	Davidson	Performing Arts	USA	Singer
	Deacon	Performing Arts	England	Rock & Roll - HF - Queen
	Densmore	Performing Arts	USA	Rock & Roll - HF - The Doors
	Denver	Performing Arts	USA	Singer
	Derek	Performing Arts	USA	Actor
	Dewey	Arts	USA	Philosopher/Educator
	Dickinson	Politics	USA	Statesman
	Donne	Creative Works	England	Poet
	Dowland	Creative Works	England	Composer/Lutanist
	Downey	Business	USA	Oil Industry
	Drew	Performing Arts	USA	Actor
	Dryden	Creative Works	England	Poet Laureate
	Eliot	Arts	USA	Clergyman
	Endecott	Politics	England	Governor - Massachusetts
	Entwistle	Performing Arts	England	Rock & Roll - HF - The Who
	Ericson	War & Peace	USA	Naval Engineer
	Erskine	Arts	Scotland	Religious Reformer
	Erskine	Creative Works	USA	Writer/Educator
	Erskine	Law & Order	Scotland	Jurist
	Farrow	Movie Production	Australia	Director - Acad Award Nom
	Felton	Performing Arts	USA	Canadian Music - HF - The Diamonds
	Fielden	Business	England	Textile Industry
	Fiske	Arts	USA	Philosopher/Historian
	Fitch	Science	USA	Inventor - Steam Boat
	Flaxman	Arts	England	Sculptor
	Florio	Creative Works	England	Writer/Lexicographer
	Ford	Creative Works	England	Dramatist
	Ford	Movie Production	USA	Director - Academy Award
	Forsythe	Performing Arts	USA	Actor
	Fowles	Creative Works	England	Author
	Frankenheimer	Movie Production	USA	Director
	Franklin	Exploration	England	Explorer - Arctic
	Galsworthy	Creative Works	England	Literature - Nobel Laureate
	Garfield	Performing Arts	USA	Actor - Acad Award Nom
	Gay	Creative Works	England	Dramatist/Poet
	Gay	Creative Works	England	Poet/Playwright

SOLVER SERIES: NAME FINDER

FIRST NAME	LAST NAME	CATEGORY	COUNTRY	FAME
John	Gielgud	Performing Arts	England	Actor - Academy Award
	Gilbert	Performing Arts	USA	Actor
	Goodman	Performing Arts	USA	Actor
	Gower	Creative Works	England	Poet
	Grisham	Creative Works	USA	Author
	Hall	Performing Arts	USA	Singer
	Hampden	Politics	England	Statesman/Parlimentarian
	Hancock	Politics	USA	President - Continental Congress
	Harkes	Sports	USA	Soccer Player - HF
	Harvard	Arts	England	Clergyman
	Hawkins	Exploration	England	Explorer - Caribbean
	Hawkins	War & Peace	England	Naval Officer/Slave Trader
	Hejduk	Architecture	USA	Architect
	Hersey	Creative Works	USA	Author - Pulitzer
	Hillerman	Performing Arts	USA	Actor
	Hodiak	Performing Arts	USA	Actor
	Horrocks	Business	England	Textile Industry
	Houseman	Performing Arts	Romania	Actor - Academy Award
	Hume	War & Peace	England	Peace - Nobel Laureate
	Hunter	Science	England	Surgeon/Physiologist
	Hurt	Performing Arts	England	Actor - Acad Award Nom
	Huston	Movie Production	USA	Director - Academy Award
	Huston	Performing Arts	USA	Actor - Acad Award Nom
	Ireland	Performing Arts	Canada	Actor - Acad Award Nom
	Irving	Creative Works	USA	Writer
	Jacobs	Sports	England	Golfer - HF
	Japp	Sports	Scotland	Soccer Player - HF
	Jasper	Arts	USA	Philosopher/Clergyman
	Jay	Politics	USA	Justice - Supreme Court
	Kander	Creative Works	USA	Composer
	Keats	Creative Works	England	Poet
	Kerr	Performing Arts	USA	Actor
	Knowles	Creative Works	USA	Novelist
	Knox	Arts	Scotland	Clergyman/Religious Reformer
	Landis	Movie Production	USA	Director
	Lansing	Law & Order	USA	Jurist
	Larroquette	Performing Arts	USA	Actor
	Leguizamo	Performing Arts	Colombia	Actor
	Lithgow	Performing Arts	USA	Actor - Acad Award Nom
	Locke	Arts	England	Philosopher
	Lyly	Creative Works	England	Author/Dramatist
	Mackey	Sports	USA	Football Player - HF
	Madden	Movie Production	England	Director - Acad Award Nom
	Madden	Sports	USA	Football Player/Coach/Commentator
	Major	Politics	England	Prime Minister
	Malkovich	Performing Arts	USA	Actor - Acad Award Nom
	Mandeville	Creative Works	England	Author
	Marcum	Sports	USA	Race Car Driver - HF
	Marin	Works of Art	USA	Painter
	Marley	Performing Arts	USA	Actor - Acad Award Nom
	Marshall	Business	England	Textile Industry
	Marshall	Law & Order	USA	Chief Justice
	Marston	Creative Works	England	Dramatist/Satirist
	Masefield	Creative Works	England	Poet Laureate/Writer
	McCormack	Performing Arts	USA	Singer - Opera
	McGuire	Sports	Scotland	Soccer Player - HF
	McIntosh	Science	Canada	Inventor - McIntosh Apple
	McPhee	Creative Works	USA	Author - Pulitzer
	Menzies	Business	England	Retail Trade
	Mills	Performing Arts	England	Actor - Academy Award
	Milton	Creative Works	England	Poet
	Muir	Science	USA	Naturalist/Writer
	Napier	Science	Scotland	Mathematician - Logarithms

FIRST NAME	LAST NAME	CATEGORY	COUNTRY	FAME
John	Nash	Architecture	England	Architect
	Nelson	Sports	Scotland	Soccer Player - HF
	Ogilvie	Arts	Scotland	Lexicographer
	Oldcastle	Politics	England	Lollard Leader
	Olerud	Sports	USA	Baseball Player
	Owens	Business	England	Textile Industry
	Patrick	Creative Works	USA	Dramatist - Pulitzer
	Perkins	Performing Arts	Canada	Canadian Music - HF - The Crew Cuts
	Pope	War & Peace	USA	Union General - Civil War
	Pym	Politics	England	Parliamentary Leader
	Rae	Exploration	Scotland	Explorer - Arctic
	Raitt	Performing Arts	USA	Singer
	Randolph	Politics	USA	Statesman/Orator
	Ratzenberger	Performing Arts	USA	Actor
	Rawls	Arts	USA	Philosopher
	Reed	Creative Works	USA	Journalist/Radical
	Ritter	Performing Arts	USA	Comedian
	Roberts	Creative Works	Canada	Journalist - Television
	Romains	Creative Works	France	Poet/Novelist/Playwright
	Ross	Exploration	England	Explorer - Arctic
	Ruskin	Architecture	England	Architect/Writer/Poet/Artist
	Ruskin	Creative Works	England	Writer/Art Critic/Social Reformer
	Russell	Politics	England	Prime Minister
	Rutledge	Politics	USA	Statesman
	Sainsbury	Business	England	Confection Industry
	Saxon	Performing Arts	USA	Actor
	Sayles	Movie Production	USA	Director
	Schlesinger	Movie Production	England	Director - Academy Award
	Searle	Arts	USA	Philosopher
	Sebastian	Performing Arts	USA	Singer
	Selden	Politics	England	Politician/Historian
	Shea	Performing Arts	USA	Actor
	Sherman	Politics	USA	Statesman
	Singleton	Movie Production	USA	Director - Acad Award Nom
	Skelton	Creative Works	England	Poet
	Sloan	Works of Art	USA	Painter/Etcher
	Smith	Exploration	England	Colonist - America
	Soane	Architecture	England	Architect
	Sobieski	Politics	Poland	King
	Stamos	Performing Arts	USA	Actor
	Stockton	Sports	USA	Basketball Player
	Suckling	Creative Works	England	Poet
	Surtees	Sports	England	Race Car Driver - HF
	Taylor	Arts	USA	Philosopher
	Tenniel	Works of Art	England	Illustrator/Caricaturist
	Tesh	Creative Works	USA	Composer/Pianist
	Toland	Creative Works	USA	Author
	Travolta	Performing Arts	USA	Actor - Acad Award Nom
	Trumbull	Works of Art	USA	Painter
	Tyler	Politics	USA	President
	Tyndall	Science	England	Physicist
	Updike	Creative Works	USA	Novelist - Pulitzer
	Vanbrugh	Creative Works	England	Dramatist/Architect
	Venn	Science	England	Mathematician
	Waite	Performing Arts	England	Singer - Rock & Roll - HF
	Walter	Business	England	Publishing
	Walter II	Business	England	Publishing
	Wanamaker	Business	USA	Merchant
	Waters	Movie Production	USA	Director
	Wayne	Performing Arts	USA	Actor - Academy Award
	Wesley	Arts	England	Clergyman/Evangelist
	Wilkes	Politics	England	Reformer - Political
	Winthrop	Exploration	England	Colonist - Massachusetts

SOLVER SERIES: NAME FINDER

FIRST NAME	LAST NAME	CATEGORY	COUNTRY	FAME
John	Witherspoon	Arts	USA	Clergyman/Educator
	Wood	Architecture	England	Architect
	Wood	Business	England	Textile Industry
	Wycliffe	Arts	England	Reformer - Religious
	Wyndham	Creative Works	England	Author - SciFi
	Steele	Performing Arts	England	Rock & Roll - HF - The Animals
	Oates	Performing Arts	USA	Singer
John (Dapper Don)	Gotti	Law & Order	USA	Mafia
John (Frenchy)	Boulos	Sports	Haiti	Soccer Player - HF
John (Hondo)	Havlicek	Sports	USA	Basketball Player - HF
John (Jackie)	Hynes	Sports	Scotland	Soccer Player - HF
John (Jock)	Ferguson	Sports	Scotland	Soccer Player - HF
John (Johnny Appleseed)	Chapman	Exploration	USA	Frontiersman - America
John (Johnny)	Ramone (Cummings)	Performing Arts	USA	Rock & Roll - HF - The Ramones
John (Jukey)	Nanoski	Sports	USA	Soccer Player - HF
John (Little Johnny)	Torrio	Law & Order	Italy	Mafia
John (Papa)	Creach	Performing Arts	USA	Rock & Roll - HF - Jefferson Airplane
John A.	Pople	Science	England	Chemistry - Nobel Laureate
John A. (Cat)	Thompson	Sports	USA	Basketball Player - HF
John Aaron	Lewis	Performing Arts	USA	Jazz Pianist/Composer - Big Band/Jazz - HF
John Addington	Symonds	Creative Works	England	Poet/Writer/Scholar
John Albert	Elway	Sports	USA	Football Player - HF
John Albert (Jack)	Kramer	Sports	USA	Tennis Player - HF
John Alden	Carpenter	Creative Works	USA	Composer
John Alexander	Carroll	Creative Works	USA	Author - Pulitzer
	Macdonald	Politics	Canada	Prime Minister
John Alexander (Bid)	McPhee	Sports	USA	Baseball Player - HF
John Allen	Hannah	Sports	USA	Football Player - HF
John Anthony	Burgess	Creative Works	England	Author
	Llewellyn	Aviation	USA	Astronaut
John Arthur	Thomson	Creative Works	Scotland	Writer/Naturalist
John Arthur (Black Jack)	Brabham	Sports	Australia	Race Car Driver - HF
John Augustin	Daly	Creative Works	USA	Playwright
John Augustus	Roebling	Architecture	USA	Bridge Designer/Civil Engineer
John B.	Fenn	Science	USA	Chemistry - Nobel Laureate
John Bell	Hood	War & Peace	USA	Confederate General
John Benevides (Clarkie)	Souza	Sports	USA	Soccer Player - HF
John Bernard (Bernie)	Toorish	Performing Arts	Canada	Canadian Music - HF - The Four Lads
John Bertrand (Jocko)	Conlan	Sports	USA	Baseball Umpire - HF
John Birks (Dizzy)	Gillespie	Performing Arts	USA	Band Leader - Big Band/Jazz - HF
John Bower (Bouse)	Hutton	Sports	Canada	Hockey Player - HF
John Boyd	Orr	War & Peace	England	Peace - Nobel Laureate
John Boynton	Priestley	Creative Works	England	Novelist/Playwright/Critic
John Broadus	Watson	Arts	USA	Psychologist
John Burdon	Haldane	Science	England	Biologist/Writer
John C.	Harsanyi	Arts	USA	Economics - Nobel Laureate
	Polanyi	Science	Canada	Chemistry - Nobel Laureate
	Reilly	Performing Arts	USA	Actor - Acad Award Nom
John C. (Jack)	Marshall	Sports	Canada	Hockey Player - HF
John Cabell	Breckenridge	Politics	USA	Vice-President
John Caldwell	Calhoun	Politics	USA	Vice-President
John Calvin	Coolidge	Politics	USA	President
John Cameron	Fogerty	Performing Arts	USA	Rock & Roll - HF - Creed. Clearwater Revival
John Carew	Eccles	Science	Australia	Medicine - Nobel Laureate
John Charles	Frémont	War & Peace	USA	Union General
	Thomas	Performing Arts	USA	Singer - Opera
John Christopher	Williams	Performing Arts	Australia	Guitarist/Classical
John Constantine (Johnny)	Unitas	Sports	USA	Football Player - HF
John Cornelius (Johnny)	Hodges	Performing Arts	USA	Saxophonist - Big Band/Jazz - HF
John Cougar	Mellencamp	Performing Arts	USA	Singer
John Cowdery	Kendrew	Science	England	Chemistry - Nobel Laureate
John Cowper	Powys	Creative Works	England	Novelist/Critic
John Crowe	Ransom	Creative Works	USA	Poet/Critic

FIRST NAME	LAST NAME	CATEGORY	COUNTRY	FAME
John D. (Honey)	Russell	Sports	USA	Basketball Player - HF
John Dann	MacDonald	Creative Works	USA	Author
John David	Newcombe	Sports	Australia	Tennis Player - HF
John David Francis	Bartoe	Aviation	USA	Astronaut
John Davison	Rockefeller	Business	USA	Industrialist/Philanthropist
John Davison Jr.	Rockefeller	Business	USA	Industrialist/Philanthropist
John Dickson	Carr	Creative Works	USA	Novelist - Crime Fiction
John Donald (Don)	Budge	Sports	USA	Tennis Player - HF
John Douglas	Cockcroft	Science	England	Physics - Nobel Laureate
John Duns	Scotus	Arts	Scotland	Theologian/Philosopher
John Dwight (Happy Jack)	Chesbro	Sports	USA	Baseball Player - HF
John E.	Carter	Performing Arts	USA	"Rock & Roll - HF - The Flamingos,The Dells"
	Mack	Creative Works	USA	Author - Pulitzer
	Sulston	Science	England	Medicine - Nobel Laureate
	Walker	Science	England	Chemistry - Nobel Laureate
John Edgar	Hoover	Law & Order	USA	Director - FBI
John Edmund	Phillips	Performing Arts	USA	Rock & Roll - HF - Mamas & Papas
	Bromwich	Sports	Australia	Tennis Player - HF
	Sununu	Politics	USA	Senator - New Hampshire
	Taylor	Business	England	Publishing
John Edward (Budge)	Patty	Sports	USA	Tennis Player - HF
John Edward Dalberg	Acton	Arts	England	Philosopher/Historian
John Elmer	Blaha	Aviation	USA	Astronaut
John Ely	Burchard	Architecture	USA	Architect - Jefferson Medal
John Ernst	Steinbeck	Creative Works	USA	Literature - Nobel/Pulitzer
John Everett	Millais	Works of Art	England	Painter
John F.	Kennedy	Creative Works	USA	Author - Pulitzer
	Nash	Arts	USA	Economics - Nobel Laureate
John Fitzgerald	Kennedy	Politics	USA	President
John Foster	Dulles	Politics	USA	Secretary of State
John Franklin	Enders	Science	USA	Medicine - Nobel Laureate
John Franklin (Frank)	Baker	Sports	USA	Baseball Player - HF
John Frederick William	Herschel	Science	England	Physicist/Chemist/Astronomer
John G.	Avildsen	Movie Production	USA	Director - Academy Award
John George	Diefenbaker	Politics	Canada	Prime Minister
John Gerard	Dinkeloo	Architecture	USA	Architect
John Gibson	Clarkson	Sports	USA	Baseball Player - HF
John Gould	Fletcher	Creative Works	England	Poet/Playwright - Pulitzer
John Graham	McVie	Performing Arts	England	Rock & Roll - HF - Fleetwood Mac
John Graham (Joe)	Strummer (Mellor)	Performing Arts	Turkey	Rock & Roll - HF - The Clash
John Greenleaf	Whittier	Creative Works	USA	Poet
John Greer	Ervine	Creative Works	England	Novelist/Playwright
John Gregory	Dunne	Creative Works	USA	Novelist
John Gutzon	Borglum	Works of Art	USA	Sculptor/Painter
John H.	Taylor	Sports	Scotland	Golfer - HF
John H. (Doc)	Holliday	Law & Order	USA	Outlaw
John Haley (Zoot)	Sims	Performing Arts	USA	Jazz Saxaphonist - Big Band/Jazz - HF
John Harold (Jack)	Lambert	Sports	USA	Football Player - HF
John Hasbrouck van	Vleck	Science	USA	Physics - Nobel Laureate
John Haynes	Holmes	Arts	USA	Clergyman/Reformer
John Henry	Bonham	Performing Arts	England	Rock & Roll - HF - Led Zepplin
	Johnson	Sports	USA	Football Player - HF
	Newman	Arts	England	Theologian/Writer
	O'Hara	Creative Works	USA	Author
John Henry (Hank)	Ballard (Kendricks)	Performing Arts	USA	Singer - Rock & Roll - HF
John Henry (Pop)	Lloyd	Sports	USA	Baseball Player - HF
John Herbert	Varley	Creative Works	USA	Author - SciFi
John Herbert (Gentleman Jack)	Crawford	Sports	Australia	Tennis Player - HF
John Herbert (Johnathan)	Frid	Performing Arts	Canada	Actor
John Herschel	Glenn	Aviation	USA	Astronaut
	Glenn Jr.	Politics	USA	Senator - Ohio
John Howard	Northrop	Science	USA	Chemistry - Nobel Laureate
John Hunt	Morgan	War & Peace	USA	Confederate General

SOLVER SERIES: NAME FINDER

FIRST NAME	LAST NAME	CATEGORY	COUNTRY	FAME
John J.	Schommer	Sports	USA	Basketball Player - HF
John Jacob	Astor	Business	USA	Financier
	Bausch	Business	USA	Optical Industry
John James	Audubon	Science	USA	Ornithologist
	Audubon	Works of Art	USA	Painter
	Osborne	Creative Works	England	Playwright
John James (Jack)	Adams	Sports	Canada	Hockey Player - HF
John James Richard	Macleod	Science	Canada	Medicine - Nobel Laureate
John Joseph	McGraw	Sports	USA	Baseball Manager - HF
	Pershing	Creative Works	USA	Author - Pulitzer
	Pershing	War & Peace	USA	General
John Joseph (Johnny)	Evers	Sports	USA	Baseball Player - HF
John Joseph Caldwell	Abbott	Politics	Canada	Prime Minister
John Joseph Molesworth	Oxley	Exploration	Australia	Explorer - Tasmania
John K. (Jack)	Twyman	Sports	USA	Basketball Player - HF
John Kennedy	Toole	Creative Works	USA	Novelist - Pulitzer
	Galbraith	Creative Works	Canada	Economist
John Kilian Houston	Brunner	Creative Works	England	Novelist
John Kingsley (Joe)	Orton	Creative Works	England	Playwright
John L.	Hall	Science	USA	Physics - Nobel Laureate
John L.H.	Down	Science	England	Physician - Down's Syndrome
John La	Farge	Works of Art	USA	Artist/Writer
John Lawrence	Sullivan	Sports	USA	Boxer
John Le	Carré	Creative Works	England	Author
John Lee	Thompson	Movie Production	England	Director - Acad Award Nom
John Lee (Johnny)	Stallworth	Sports	USA	Football Player - HF
John Leonard	Swigert	Aviation	USA	Astronaut
John Leroy (Jack)	Christiansen	Sports	USA	Football Player - HF
John Livingston	Lowes	Arts	USA	Educator/Scholar/Critic
John Llewellyn	Lewis	Business	USA	Labor Leader
John Lothrop	Motley	Politics	USA	Diplomat/Historian
John M.	Coetzee	Creative Works	South Africa	Literature - Nobel Laureate
John Marshall	Harlan	Law & Order	USA	Justice - Supreme Court
John Mary	Lynch	Politics	Ireland	Prime Minister
John Maynard	Keyes	Creative Works	England	Writer/Economist
	Keynes	Arts	England	Economist
John McCreary	Fabian	Aviation	USA	Astronaut
John Michael	Bishop	Science	USA	Medicine - Nobel Laureate
	Lounge	Aviation	USA	Astronaut
	Thomas	Performing Arts	USA	Rock & Roll - HF - Jefferson Airplane
John Millington	Synge	Creative Works	Ireland	Dramatist
John Milton	Cage	Creative Works	USA	Composer
	Hay	Politics	USA	Statesman/Writer
John Montgomery	Ward	Sports	USA	Baseball Player - HF
John Moses	Browning	Science	USA	Inventor - Firearms
John Nance	Garner	Politics	USA	Vice-President
John Napier	Turner	Politics	Canada	Prime Minster
John Oliver	Creighton	Aviation	USA	Astronaut
John Orley Allen	Tate	Creative Works	USA	Poet/Critic
John Patrick	McEnroe	Sports	USA	Tennis Player - HF
	Shanley	Creative Works	USA	Dramatist - Pulitzer
John Paul	Jones	War & Peace	USA	Naval Officer - Revolutionary War
	Stevens	Law & Order	USA	Justice - Supreme Court
John Paul (Johnny)	Bucyk	Sports	Canada	Hockey Player - HF
John Peter	Altgeld	Politics	USA	Governor
	Zenger	Creative Works	USA	Journalist/Publisher
John Peter (Honus)	Wagner	Sports	USA	Baseball Player - HF
John Phillip	Kemble	Performing Arts	England	Actor
	Sousa	Creative Works	USA	Composer/Band Master
John Phillip (Jack)	Walker	Sports	Canada	Hockey Player - HF
John Phillips	Marquand	Creative Works	USA	Novelist - Pulitzer
John Pierpont	Morgan	Business	USA	Financier
John Proctor (Jack)	Darragh	Sports	Canada	Hockey Player - HF

FIRST NAME	LAST NAME	CATEGORY	COUNTRY	FAME
John Quincy	Adams	Politics	USA	President
John R.	Hicks	Arts	England	Economics - Nobel Laureate
	Vane	Science	England	Medicine - Nobel Laureate
	Wooden	Sports	USA	Basketball Player - HF
John Raleigh	Mott	War & Peace	USA	Peace - Nobel Laureate
John Richard	Green	Arts	England	Historian
John Robert	Schrieffer	Science	USA	Physics - Nobel Laureate
John Robert (Johnny)	Mize	Sports	USA	Baseball Player - HF
John Roderigo Dos	Passos	Creative Works	USA	Novelist/Artist
	Passos	Creative Works	USA	Writer
John Ronald Reuel	Tolkien	Creative Works	England	Novelist/Scholar/Linguist
John Rushworth	Jellicoe	War & Peace	England	Admiral
John S.	Roosma	Sports	USA	Basketball Player - HF
John Samuel	Kenyon	Arts	USA	Phonetician/Educator
John Sherratt (Black Jack)	Stewart	Sports	Canada	Hockey Player - HF
John Simmons	Barth	Creative Works	USA	Novelist/Short Story Writer
John Singer	Sargent	Works of Art	USA	Painter
John Singleton	Copley	Works of Art	USA	Painter
John Sparrow David	Thompson	Politics	Canada	Prime Minster
John Steuart	Curry	Works of Art	USA	Painter - Regionalist
John Stuart	Mill	Arts	England	Philosopher/Political Economist
John Sumter	Bull	Aviation	USA	Astronaut
John Thomas	Morgan	Performing Arts	USA	Singer - Country Music - HF
John Thomas Godfray Hope	Doeg	Sports	USA	Tennis Player - HF
John Towner	Williams	Creative Works	USA	Composer
John V.	Lindsay	Architecture	USA	Architect - Jefferson Medal
John Van	Ryn	Sports	USA	Tennis Player - HF
John Victor (Blood)	McNally	Sports	USA	Football Player - HF
John W.	Dower	Creative Works	USA	Author - Pulitzer
John Warcup	Cornforth	Science	Australia	Chemistry - Nobel Laureate
John Watts	Young	Aviation	USA	Astronaut
John Wayne	Gacy	Law & Order	USA	Serial Killer - Killer Clown
John Wellborn	Root	Architecture	USA	Architect - AIA Gold Medal
John Wesley	Powell	Exploration	USA	Explorer - America Deserts
John Wesley (Wes)	Montgomery	Performing Arts	USA	Jazz Guitarist - Big Band/Jazz - HF
John Wilkes	Booth	Performing Arts	USA	Actor/Assassin
John William	Dawson	Arts	Canada	Geologist/Naturalist
	Draper	Science	USA	Scientist/Historian
	Strutt	Science	England	Physics - Nobel Laureate
John William (Johnny)	Bower	Sports	Canada	Hockey Player - HF
John William Strutt	Rayleigh	Science	England	Physicist
John Winston	Lennon	Performing Arts	England	Rock & Roll - HF - The Beatles
Johnathon	Edwards	Arts	USA	Philosopher/Theologian
Johnnie	Ray	Performing Arts	USA	Singer
Johnny	Carson	Performing Arts	USA	Show Host/Comedian
	Depp	Performing Arts	USA	Actor - Acad Award Nom
	Dodds	Performing Arts	USA	Jazz Clarinetist - Big Band/Jazz - HF
	Faye	Performing Arts	Canada	Canadian Music - HF - The Tragically Hip
	Graham	Performing Arts	USA	Rock & Roll - HF - Earth Wind & Fire
	Hart	Creative Works	USA	Cartoonist - BC
	Mathis	Performing Arts	USA	Singer
	Miller	Sports	USA	Golfer - HF
	Moore	Sports	Scotland	Soccer Player - HF
	Paycheck	Performing Arts	USA	Singer
	Reed	Performing Arts	USA	Rock & Roll - HF - The Orioles
	Rivers	Performing Arts	USA	Singer
	Rutherford	Sports	USA	Race Car Driver - HF
	Tillotson	Performing Arts	USA	Singer - Country & Western
	Weissmuller	Performing Arts	Romania	Actor
	Weissmuller	Sports	USA	Olympic Swimmer
Johnny (Cyrus Whitfield)	Bond	Performing Arts	USA	Singer - Country Music - HF
Johnny (John R.)	Cash	Performing Arts	USA	Singer - Country Music - HF
	Cash	Performing Arts	USA	Singer - Rock & Roll - HF

SOLVER SERIES: NAME FINDER

FIRST NAME	LAST NAME	CATEGORY	COUNTRY	FAME
Johnny Lee	Bench	Sports	USA	Baseball Player - HF
	Hooker	Performing Arts	USA	Singer - Rock & Roll - HF
Johns	Hopkins	Creative Works	USA	Financier/Philanthropist
Johnston	Forbes-Robertson	Performing Arts	England	Actor
Jokichi	Takamine	Science	USA	Chemist
Jomo	Kenyatta	Politics	Africa	President/Kenya
Jon	Anderson	Performing Arts	England	Singer
	Bon Jovi	Performing Arts	USA	Singer/Composer
	Lovitz	Performing Arts	USA	Comedian
	Voight	Performing Arts	USA	Actor - Academy Award
	Whiteley	Performing Arts	Scotland	Actor - Academy Award
Jon Andrew	McBride	Aviation	USA	Astronaut
Jon Steven (Steve)	Young	Sports	USA	Football Player - HF
Jonas Edward	Salk	Science	USA	Physician - Polio Vaccine
Jonathan	Demme	Movie Production	USA	Director - Academy Award
	Larson	Creative Works	USA	Dramatist - Pulitzer
	Swift	Creative Works	England	Satirist
	Weiner	Creative Works	USA	Author - Pulitzer
Jonathon	Frakes	Performing Arts	USA	Actor
	Miller	Creative Works	England	Producer/Author
	Miller	Movie Production	England	Director
	Pryce	Performing Arts	Wales	Actor
	Winters	Performing Arts	USA	Comedian
Jons	Berzelius	Science	Sweden	Chemist
Jorge	Amado	Creative Works	Brazil	Author
	Bolet	Performing Arts	Cuba	Conductor/Pianist
	Posada	Sports	Puerto Rica	Baseball Player
Jorge Luis	Borges	Creative Works	Argentina	Poet/Writer
Jorie	Graham	Creative Works	USA	Poet - Pulitzer
Jorma	Kaukonen	Performing Arts	USA	Rock & Roll - HF - Jefferson Airplane
Jørn	Utzon	Architecture	Denmark	Architect - Pritzker Laureate
Jose	Napoles	Sports	Cuba	Boxer - HF
	Torres	Sports	USA	Boxer - HF
José	Canseco	Sports	USA	Baseball Player
	Carreras	Performing Arts	Spain	Singer - Opera
	Echegaray	Creative Works	Spain	Literature - Nobel Laureate
	Feliciano	Performing Arts	Puerto Rico	Singer
	Ferrer	Performing Arts	Puerto Rico	Actor - Academy Award
	Limón	Performing Arts	Mexico	Dancer
	Ortega y Gasset	Creative Works	Spain	Essayist/Philosopher
	Ramos-Horta	War & Peace	East Timor	Peace - Nobel Laureate
	Ribera	Works of Art	Spain	Painter
	Saramago	Creative Works	Portugal	Literature - Nobel Laureate
	Zorrilla	Creative Works	Spain	Poet/Playwright
José Clemente	Orozco	Works of Art	Mexico	Painter
José David Alfaro	Siqueiros	Works of Art	Mexico	Painter - Murals
José de	San Martín	War & Peace	Argentina	Revolutionary Leader
José de la Cruz Porfirio	Díaz	Politics	Mexico	President
José Doroteo (Pancho)	Villa	Politics	Mexico	Revolutionist
José Julian	Martí	Creative Works	Cuba	Poet/Essayist/Revolutionary
Jose Luis	Sert	Architecture	USA	Architect - AIA/Jefferson Gold Medal
José Mercado	Rizal	Creative Works	Philippines	Poet/Novelist/Patriot
José Ortega y	Gasset	Arts	Spain	Philosopher/Essayist
José Raúl	Capablanca	Games	Cuba	Chess Player
Josef	Hofmann	Creative Works	USA	Composer/Pianist
	Muggenast	Architecture	Austria	Architect
Josef Von	Sternberg	Movie Production	Austria	Director - Acad Award Nom
Joseph	Addison	Creative Works	England	Essayist/Poet
	Banks	Science	England	Botanist
	Brant	War & Peace	USA	Mowhawk Chief
	Brodsky	Creative Works	USA	Literature - Nobel Laureate
	Campanella	Performing Arts	USA	Actor
	Campbell	Arts	USA	Philosopher/Author/Editor

FIRST NAME	LAST NAME	CATEGORY	COUNTRY	FAME
Joseph	Carenza	Sports	USA	Soccer Player - HF
	Colombo	Law & Order	USA	Mafia
	Conrad	Creative Works	Ukraine	Novelist/Short Story Writer
	Cotton	Performing Arts	USA	Actor
	Damien	Arts	Belgium	Priest/Missionary
	Davidson	Works of Art	USA	Sculptor
	Eichler	Architecture	USA	Architect/Developer
	Esherick	Architecture	USA	Architect - AIA Gold Medal
	Fry	Business	England	Confection Industry
	Gurney	Business	USA	Railway Magnate
	Hall	Arts	England	Philosopher/Theologian
	Heller	Creative Works	USA	Novelist
	Hoffman	Architecture	Austria	Architect
	Hooker	War & Peace	USA	Union General
	Jefferson	Performing Arts	USA	Actor
	Joachim	Creative Works	Hungary	Composer/Violinist
	Johnson	Business	England	Publishing
	Kramm	Creative Works	USA	Dramatist - Pulitzer
	Lelyveld	Creative Works	USA	Author - Pulitzer
	Lister	Science	England	Surgeon
	Maca	Sports	Belgium	Soccer Player - HF
	Papp	Movie Production	USA	Director
	Paxton	Architecture	England	Architect
	Pennel	Works of Art	USA	Etcher/Illustrator/Writer
	Priestley	Science	England	Scientist/Theologian
	Pulitzer	Business	USA	Publishing/Philanthropist
	Pulitzer	Creative Works	USA	Journalist - Newspaper
	Rowntree	Business	England	Confection Industry
	Sandars	Business	England	Railway Magnate
	Schildkraut	Performing Arts	Austria	Actor - Academy Award
	Seligman	Business	USA	Banking
	Smith	Arts	USA	Founder - Mormon Church
	Stalin	Politics	Russia	Premier
	Story	Law & Order	USA	Justice - Supreme Court
	Wambaugh	Creative Works	USA	Author
	Wright	Arts	England	Lexicographer/Linguist
	Erlanger	Science	USA	Medicine - Nobel Laureate
Joseph (Bananas)	Bonnano	Law & Order	Sicily	Mafia
Joseph (Hammer)	Profaci	Law & Order	Italy	Mafia
Joseph (Jersey Joe)	Walcott	Sports	USA	Boxer - HF
Joseph (Joe)	Gryzik	Sports	Poland	Soccer Player - HF
	Lando	Performing Arts	USA	Actor
	Louis	Sports	USA	Boxer - HF
	Mullen	Sports	USA	Hockey Player - HF
	Primeau	Sports	Canada	Hockey Player - HF
	Williams	Sports	USA	Baseball Player - HF
Joseph Anthony (Joe)	Pass (Passalaqua)	Performing Arts	USA	Jazz Guitarist - Big Band/Jazz - HF
Joseph Austen	Chamberlain	Politics	England	Statesman
	Chamberlain	War & Peace	England	Peace - Nobel Laureate
Joseph Bert (Joe)	Tinker	Sports	USA	Baseball Player - HF
Joseph C.	Dey	Sports	USA	Golf Promoter - HF
Joseph Carrol	Naish	Performing Arts	USA	Actor - Acad Award Nom
Joseph Clifford (Joe)	Montana	Sports	USA	Football Player - HF
Joseph Deems	Taylor	Creative Works	USA	Composer/Music Critic
Joseph E.	Murray	Science	USA	Medicine - Nobel Laureate
	Stiglitz	Arts	USA	Economics - Nobel Laureate
Joseph Eduard (Joe)	Gaetjens	Sports	Haiti	Soccer Player - HF
	Cronin	Sports	USA	Baseball Player - HF
Joseph Eggleston	Johnston	War & Peace	USA	Confederate General
Joseph Emerson	Worcester	Arts	USA	Lexicographer
Joseph Ernest	Renan	Arts	France	Historian/Essayist
	Rotblat	War & Peace	England	Peace - Nobel Laureate
Joseph F.	Fulks	Sports	USA	Basketball Player - HF

SOLVER SERIES: NAME FINDER

FIRST NAME	LAST NAME	CATEGORY	COUNTRY	FAME
Joseph F. (Joe)	Carr	Sports	USA	Football League Administrator - HF
Joseph Floyd (Arky)	Vaughn	Sports	USA	Baseball Player - HF
Joseph Frederick	Cullman III	Sports	USA	Tennis Player - HF
Joseph Gilbert Yvon (Jean)	Ratelle	Sports	Canada	Hockey Player - HF
Joseph Goreed (Joe)	Williams	Performing Arts	USA	Singer - Big Band/Jazz - HF
Joseph Gurney	Cannon	Politics	USA	Congressman
Joseph H.	Taylor	Science	USA	Physics - Nobel Laureate
Joseph Henri (Pocket Rocket)	Richard	Sports	Canada	Hockey Player - HF
Joseph Henri Maurice (Rocket)	Richard	Sports	Canada	Hockey Player - HF
Joseph Henry	Garagiola	Creative Works	USA	Journalist - Television
Joseph Henry (Joe)	Hall	Sports	England	Hockey Player - HF
Joseph Herbert (Joe)	Weatherly	Sports	USA	Race Car Driver - HF
Joseph Hillaire Pierre	Belloc	Creative Works	England	Writer
Joseph J.	Ellis	Creative Works	USA	Author - Pulitzer
Joseph Jacques	Plante	Sports	Canada	Hockey Player - HF
Joseph Jacques Césaire	Joffre	War & Peace	France	Commander in Chief
Joseph Jacques Hughes	Laperriere	Sports	Canada	Hockey Player - HF
Joseph James (Joe)	Kelley	Sports	USA	Baseball Player - HF
Joseph Jean-Pierre Marc	Garneau	Aviation	Canada	Astronaut
Joseph Jerome (Joe)	McGinnity	Sports	USA	Baseball Player - HF
Joseph John	Thomson	Science	England	Physics - Nobel Laureate
Joseph L.	Goldstein	Science	USA	Medicine - Nobel Laureate
	Mankiewicz	Movie Production	USA	Director - Academy Award
Joseph Lane	Kirkland	Business	USA	Labor Leader
Joseph Lee (Joe)	Stydahar	Sports	USA	Football Player - HF
Joseph Lincoln	Steffens	Creative Works	USA	Author/Journalist
Joseph Louis	Gay-Lussac	Science	France	Chemist/Physicist
	Lagrange	Science	France	Astronomer/Mathematician
Joseph Lynn	Patrick	Sports	Canada	Hockey Player - HF
Joseph M.	Valachi	Law & Order	USA	Mafia
Joseph Mallord William	Turner	Works of Art	England	Painter
Joseph Maria	Olbrick	Architecture	Germany	Architect
Joseph Marie de	Maistre	Arts	France	Philosopher/Writer
Joseph Michael (Joe)	Medwick	Sports	USA	Baseball Player - HF
Joseph Michael De (Joe)	Lamielleure	Sports	USA	Football Player - HF
Joseph Napoleon (Joe)	Guyon	Sports	USA	Football Player - HF
Joseph Nathaniel De (Joe)	Loach	Sports	USA	Olympic - Sprinter
Joseph P.	Lash	Creative Works	USA	Author - Pulitzer
Joseph Paul	Goebbels	Politics	Germany	Nazi Propagandist
Joseph Paul (Joe)	Schmidt	Sports	USA	Football Player - HF
Joseph Paul Di (Joe)	Maggio	Sports	USA	Baseball Player - HF
Joseph Percival	Allen	Aviation	USA	Astronaut
Joseph Peter	Kerwin	Aviation	USA	Astronaut
Joseph R.	Brennan	Sports	USA	Basketball Player - HF
Joseph Raphael	Hunt	Sports	USA	Tennis Player - HF
Joseph Raymond	McCarthy	Politics	USA	Senator - Wisconsin
Joseph Robinette	Biden Jr.	Politics	USA	Senator
Joseph Rudyard	Kipling	Creative Works	England	Literature - Nobel Laureate
Joseph Sill	Clark	Sports	USA	Tennis Player - HF
Joseph Vincent (Joe)	McCarthy	Sports	USA	Baseball Manager - HF
Joseph von	Fraunhofer	Science	Bavaria	Optician
Joseph Wheeler (Joe)	Sewell	Sports	USA	Baseball Player - HF
Joseph William (Joe)	Namath	Sports	USA	Football Player - HF
Joseph Wood	Krutch	Creative Works	USA	Essayist/Naturalist/Critic
Josephine	Baker	Performing Arts	USA	Actress
	Tey	Creative Works	Scotland	Author
	Hull	Performing Arts	USA	Actress - Academy Award
Josephine Winslow	Johnson	Creative Works	USA	Novelist - Pulitzer
Josephus	Daniels	Politics	USA	Statesman
Josh	Billings	Performing Arts	USA	Humorist
	Mostel	Performing Arts	USA	Actor
Joshua	Fielden	Business	England	Textile Industry
	Lederberg	Science	USA	Medicine - Nobel Laureate

FIRST NAME	LAST NAME	CATEGORY	COUNTRY	FAME
Joshua	Logan	Creative Works	USA	Dramatist - Pulitzer
	Logan	Movie Production	USA	Director - Acad Award Nom
	Reynolds	Works of Art	England	Painter - Portrait
Joshua (Josh)	Gibson	Sports	USA	Baseball Player - HF
Josiah	Quincy	War & Peace	USA	Patriot - Revolutionary
	Royce	Arts	USA	Philosopher/Educator
	Wedgwood	Business	England	Entrepreneur
Josiah Willard	Gibbs	Science	USA	Physicist/Mathematician
Josie	Maran	Performing Arts	USA	Super Model
Josip Broz	Tito	Politics	Yugoslavia	President/Prime Minister
Joyce	Brothers	Creative Works	USA	Journalist/Psychologist - Newspaper
	Randolph	Performing Arts	USA	Actress
	Redman	Performing Arts	Ireland	Actress - Acad Award Nom
	Wethered	Sports	England	Golfer - HF
Joyce Carol	Oates	Creative Works	USA	Novelist
Joyce De	Witt	Performing Arts	USA	Actress
Joze	Plecnik	Architecture	Slovenia	Architect
Juan	Belmonte	Sports	Spain	Bull Fighter
	Gris	Works of Art	Spain	Painter
	Perez	Exploration	Spain	Explorer - America East Coast
Juan (Chi Chi)	Rodriquez	Sports	Puerto Rico	Golfer - HF
Juan Antonio	Marichal	Sports	Dominican Rep	Baseball Player - HF
Juan Bautista	Toledo	Architecture	Spain	Architect
Juan Bautista de	Anza	Exploration	Mexico	Explorer - California
Juan Caramuel de	Lobkowitz	Architecture	Italy	Architect
Juan Carlos	Onetti	Creative Works	Paraguay	Novelist/Short Story Writer
Juan de	Fuca	Exploration	Greece	Explorer - West America
	Oñate	Exploration	Spain	Explorer - New Mexico
Juan Domingo	Perón Sosa	Politics	Argentina	President
Juan Navarro	Baldeweg	Architecture	Spain	Architect
Juan Ponce de	Leon	Exploration	Spain	Explorer - Florida
	León	Exploration	Spain	Explorer - Florida
Juan Ramón	Jiménez	Creative Works	Spain	Literature - Nobel Laureate
Juan Rodriguez	Cabrillo	Exploration	Spain	Explorer - California
Juanita	Moore	Performing Arts	USA	Actress - Acad Award Nom
Juan-Manuel	Fangio	Sports	Argentina	Race Car Driver - HF
Jubal Anderson	Early	War & Peace	USA	Confederate General
Judd	Hirsch	Performing Arts	USA	Actor - Acad Award Nom
	Nelson	Performing Arts	USA	Actor
Jude	Law	Performing Arts	England	Actor - Acad Award Nom
Judge	Reinhold	Performing Arts	USA	Actor
Judi	Dench	Performing Arts	England	Actress - Academy Award
Judith	Anderson	Performing Arts	Australia	Actress - Acad Award Nom
	Crist	Creative Works	USA	Journalist - Newspaper
	Ivey	Performing Arts	USA	Actress
	Krantz	Creative Works	USA	Novelist
	Light	Performing Arts	USA	Actress
Judy	Bell	Sports	USA	Golfer - HF
	Blume	Creative Works	USA	Author
	Carne	Performing Arts	USA	Comedian
	Collins	Performing Arts	USA	Singer
	Davis	Performing Arts	Australia	Actress - Acad Award Nom
	Garland	Performing Arts	USA	Actress/Singer - Acad Award
	Holliday	Performing Arts	USA	Actress - Academy Award
	Rankin	Sports	USA	Golfer - HF
Juice	Newton	Performing Arts	USA	Singer
Jule	Styne	Creative Works	England	Composer
Jules	Bordet	Science	Belgium	Medicine - Nobel Laureate
	Dassin	Movie Production	USA	Director - Acad Award Nom
	Feiffer	Creative Works	USA	Cartoonist - Political
	Mazarin	Politics	France	Statesman/Prelate
	Michelet	Arts	France	Historian
	Verne	Creative Works	France	Novelist

SOLVER SERIES: NAME FINDER

FIRST NAME	LAST NAME	CATEGORY	COUNTRY	FAME
Jules Alfred Huot de	Goncourt	Creative Works	France	Novelist/Art Critic
Jules Émile Frédéric	Massenet	Creative Works	France	Composer
Jules Hardouin	Mansart	Architecture	France	Architect
Jules Henri	Poincaré	Science	France	Mathematician
Juli	Inkster	Sports	USA	Golfer - HF
Julia	Duffy	Performing Arts	USA	Actress
	Grant	Politics	USA	First Lady
	Louis-Dreyfus	Performing Arts	USA	Actress
	Marlowe	Performing Arts	USA	Actress
	Morgan	Architecture	USA	Architect
	Ormond	Performing Arts	England	Actress
	Peterkin	Creative Works	USA	Novelist - Pulitzer
	Roberts	Performing Arts	USA	Actress - Acad Award Nom
	Tyler	Politics	USA	First Lady
Julia Ward	Howe	Creative Works	USA	Poet/Social Reformer
Julian	Dubuque	Exploration	France	Explorer - Mississippi River
	Lennon	Performing Arts	England	Singer
	Schwinger	Science	USA	Physics - Nobel Laureate
Julian (Cannonball)	Adderley	Performing Arts	USA	Jazz Saxophonist - Big Band/Jazz - HF
Julian Hedworth George	Byng	Politics	England	General
Julian Sorrell	Huxley	Science	England	Biologist/Writer
Julian Southall (Uncle Mike)	Myrick	Sports	USA	Tennis Promoter - HF
Julianne	Moore	Performing Arts	USA	Actress - Acad Award Nom
Julie	Andrews	Performing Arts	England	Actress - Academy Award
	Christie	Performing Arts	India	Actress - Academy Award
	Harris	Performing Arts	USA	Actress - Acad Award Nom
	Kavner	Performing Arts	USA	Actor
	London	Performing Arts	USA	Singer
	Payette	Aviation	Canada	Astronaut
	Walters	Performing Arts	England	Actress - Acad Award Nom
Juliette	Binoche	Performing Arts	France	Actress - Academy Award
	Lewis	Performing Arts	USA	Actress - Acad Award Nom
	Low	Arts	USA	Founder - Girl Scouts
Juliette Paxton	Atkinson	Sports	USA	Tennis Player - HF
Julio	Iglesias	Performing Arts	Spain	Singer
Julio Cesar	Chavez	Sports	USA	Boxer
Julius	Axelrod	Science	USA	Medicine - Nobel Laureate
	Boros	Sports	USA	Golfer - HF
	LaRosa	Performing Arts	USA	Singer
	Wagner-Jauregg	Science	Austria	Medicine - Nobel Laureate
Julius (Groucho)	Marx	Performing Arts	USA	Comedian
Julius Andreas Grib	Fibiger	Science	Denmark	Medicine - Nobel Laureate
Julius Robert	Oppenheimer	Science	USA	Physicist - Nuclear
Julius Timothy (Tim)	Flock	Sports	USA	Race Car Driver - HF
Julius W.	Erving	Sports	USA	Basketball Player - HF
June	Allyson	Performing Arts	USA	Actress
	Carter	Performing Arts	USA	Singer
	Haver	Performing Arts	USA	Actress
	Havoc	Performing Arts	Canada	Actress
	Lockhart	Performing Arts	USA	Actress
	Pointer	Performing Arts	USA	Singer
Junior	Seau	Sports	USA	Football Player
Junious (Buck)	Buchanan	Sports	USA	Football Player - HF
Junípero	Serra	Exploration	Spain	Explorer/Missionary - Mexico
Junius Brutus	Booth	Performing Arts	USA	Actor
Jürgen	Habermas	Arts	Germany	Philosopher/Social Theorist
	Klinsman	Sports	Germany	Soccer Player
Justin	Hayward	Performing Arts	England	Singer
	Henry	Performing Arts	USA	Actor - Acad Award Nom
	Kaplan	Creative Works	USA	Author - Pulitzer
Justin Brooks	Atkinson	Creative Works	USA	Journalist
Justin H.	Smith	Creative Works	USA	Author - Pulitzer
Justine	Bateman	Performing Arts	USA	Actress

FIRST NAME	LAST NAME	CATEGORY	COUNTRY	FAME
Justus von	Liebig	Science	Germany	Chemist
K.D.	Lang	Performing Arts	Canada	Singer
Kadeem	Hardison	Performing Arts	USA	Actor
Kahlil	Gibran	Creative Works	Lebanon	Poet
Kai Chresten	Winding	Performing Arts	Denmark	Jazz Trombonist
Kai M.	Siegbahn	Science	Sweden	Physics - Nobel Laureate
Kalpana	Chawla	Aviation	USA	Astronaut
Kareem	Abdul-Jabbar	Sports	USA	Basketball Player - HF
Karel	Čapek	Creative Works	Czechoslovakia	Playwright/Novelist
Karen	Allen	Performing Arts	USA	Actress
	Black	Performing Arts	USA	Actress - Acad Award Nom
	Carpenter	Performing Arts	USA	Singer
	Horney	Science	Germany	Psychoanalyist
	Mulder	Performing Arts	Netherlands	Super Model
	Ziemba	Performing Arts	USA	Actress
Karl	Czerny	Creative Works	Austria	Composer
	Doenitz	War & Peace	Germany	Grand Admiral
	Farr	Performing Arts	USA	Country Music - HF - Sons of the Pioneers
	Goldmark	Creative Works	Hungary	Composer
	Jaspers	Arts	Germany	Philosopher
	Lagerfeld	Business	Germany	Fashion Designer
	Landsteiner	Science	Austria	Medicine - Nobel Laureate
	Liebknecht	Politics	Germany	Socialist Leader
	Malden	Performing Arts	USA	Actor - Academy Award
	Malone	Sports	USA	Basketball Player
	Moser	Architecture	Switzerland	Architect
	Shapiro	Creative Works	USA	Poet - Pulitzer
	Verner	Arts	Denmark	Philologist
	Ziegler	Science	Germany	Chemistry - Nobel Laureate
Karl Adolph	Gjellerup	Creative Works	Denmark	Literature - Nobel Laureate
Karl Alex	Müller	Science	Switzerland	Physics - Nobel Laureate
Karl Augustus	Menninger	Science	USA	Psychiatrist
Karl B.	Mollweide	Science	Germany	Mathematician
Karl Barry	Sharpless	Science	USA	Chemistry - Nobel Laureate
Karl Ferdinand	Braun	Science	Germany	Physics - Nobel Laureate
Karl Friedrich	Schinkel	Architecture	Germany	Architect
Karl Gordon	Henize	Aviation	USA	Astronaut
Karl Gunner	Myrdal	Arts	Sweden	Economics - Nobel Laureate
Karl Heirich	Marx	Politics	Germany	Revolutionary Leader
Karl Hjalmar	Branting	War & Peace	Sweden	Peace - Nobel Laureate
Karl Howell	Behr	Sports	USA	Tennis Player - HF
Karl Manne Georg	Siegbahn	Science	Sweden	Physics - Nobel Laureate
Karl Phillipp Emanuel	Bach	Creative Works	Germany	Composer
Karl Raimund	Popper	Arts	Austria	Philosopher
Karl Robert	Nesselrode	Politics	Russia	Statesman/Diplomat
Karl Taylor	Compton	Science	USA	Physicist
Karl von	Frisch	Science	Germany	Medicine - Nobel Laureate
Karl Wilhelm Friedrich von	Schlegel	Arts	Germany	Philosopher/Critic
Karl-Heinz	Granitza	Sports	Germany	Soccer Player - HF
Karol Joseph	Bobko	Aviation	USA	Astronaut
Karolina	Kurkova	Performing Arts	Czechoslovakia	Super Model
Karstein	Solheim	Business	USA	Manufacturing Industry
Karsten	Solheim	Sports	Norway	Golf Club Designer - HF
Kary B.	Mullis	Science	USA	Chemistry - Nobel Laureate
Kasim	Abul	Science	Saudi Arabia	Surgeon
Katarina	Witt	Sports	Germany	Olympic Skater
Kate	Hudson	Performing Arts	USA	Actress - Acad Award Nom
	Jackson	Performing Arts	USA	Actress
	Moss	Performing Arts	England	Super Model
	Mulgrew	Performing Arts	USA	Actress
	Nelligan	Performing Arts	Canada	Actress - Acad Award Nom
	O'Mara	Performing Arts	England	Actress
	Reid	Performing Arts	England	Actress

SOLVER SERIES: NAME FINDER

FIRST NAME	LAST NAME	CATEGORY	COUNTRY	FAME
Kate	Smith	Performing Arts	USA	Singer
	Wilhelm	Creative Works	USA	Author
	Winslet	Performing Arts	England	Actress - Acad Award Nom
Kate Douglas	Wiggin	Creative Works	USA	Writer/Educator
Katharine	Cornell	Performing Arts	USA	Actress
	Graham	Creative Works	USA	Author - Pulitzer
	Hepburn	Performing Arts	USA	Actress - Academy Award
	Ross	Performing Arts	USA	Actress - Acad Award Nom
Käthe	Kollwitz	Works of Art	Germany	Painter/Etcher/Lithographer
Katherine	Helmond	Performing Arts	USA	Actress
	Mansfield	Creative Works	England	Writer - Short Stories
Katherine Anne	Porter	Creative Works	USA	Novelist - Pulitzer
Kathleen	Turner	Performing Arts	USA	Actress - Acad Award Nom
Kathleen (Kitty)	McKane-Godfree	Sports	England	Tennis Player - HF
Kathlees	Quinlan	Performing Arts	USA	Actress - Acad Award Nom
Kathryn	Grayson	Performing Arts	USA	Actress
Kathryn Dwyer	Sullivan	Aviation	USA	Astronaut
Kathryn Ryan Cordell	Thornton	Aviation	USA	Astronaut
Kathy	Bates	Performing Arts	USA	Actress - Academy Award
	Ireland	Performing Arts	USA	Super Model
	Mattea	Performing Arts	USA	Singer
	Whitworth	Sports	USA	Golfer - HF
Katie	Couric	Creative Works	USA	Journalist - Television
Katina	Paxinou	Performing Arts	Greece	Actress - Academy Award
Katsushika	Hokusai	Works of Art	Japan	Painter/Engraver
Katy	Jurado	Performing Arts	Mexico	Actress - Acad Award Nom
Kay	Kyser	Performing Arts	USA	Band Leader
	Lenz	Performing Arts	USA	Actress
	Medford	Performing Arts	USA	Actress - Acad Award Nom
	Starr	Performing Arts	USA	Singer - Pops
Kay Toinette (KT)	Oslin	Performing Arts	USA	Singer
Kaye	Ballard	Performing Arts	USA	Singer
KC	Jones	Sports	USA	Basketball Player - HF
Keanu	Reeves	Performing Arts	Lebanon	Actor
Keely	Smith	Performing Arts	USA	Singer
Keenan	Wynn	Performing Arts	USA	Actor
Keenan Ivory	Wayans	Performing Arts	USA	Comedian
Keene	Curtis	Performing Arts	USA	Actor
Keir	Dullea	Performing Arts	USA	Actor
Keisha	Castle-Hughes	Performing Arts	Australia	Actress - Acad Award Nom
Keith	Carradine	Performing Arts	USA	Actor
	Godchaux	Performing Arts	USA	Rock & Roll - HF - Grateful Dead
	Haring	Works of Art	USA	Painter
	Hernandez	Sports	USA	Baseball Player
	Jarrett	Performing Arts	USA	Jazz Pianist
	Moon	Performing Arts	England	Rock & Roll - HF - The Who
	Relf	Performing Arts	England	Rock & Roll - HF - The Yardbirds
	Richards	Performing Arts	England	Rock & Roll - HF - Rolling Stones
Keith Rupert	Murdoch	Business	USA	Media Magnate
Kellen Boswell	Winslow	Sports	USA	Football Player - HF
Kelly	McGillis	Performing Arts	USA	Actress
Kelsey	Grammer	Performing Arts	Virgin Islands	Actor
Ken	Berry	Performing Arts	USA	Actor
	Howard	Performing Arts	USA	Actor
	Kercheval	Performing Arts	USA	Actor
	Kesey	Creative Works	USA	Author
	McGregor	Sports	Australia	Tennis Player - HF
	Norton	Sports	USA	Boxer - HF
	Olin	Performing Arts	USA	Actor
	Osmond	Performing Arts	USA	Actor
	Russell	Movie Production	England	Director - Acad Award Nom
	Stabler	Sports	USA	Football Player
	Venturi	Sports	USA	Golfer

FIRST NAME	LAST NAME	CATEGORY	COUNTRY	FAME
Ken	Watanabe	Performing Arts	Japan	Actor - Acad Award Nom
Kenesaw Mountain	Landis	Law & Order	USA	Jurist
	Landis	Sports	USA	Baseball Commissioner - HF
Kenichi	Fukui	Science	Japan	Chemistry - Nobel Laureate
Kenneth	Bianchi	Law & Order	USA	Serial Killer - Hillside Strangler
	Branagh	Movie Production	Ireland	Director - Acad Award Nom
	Branagh	Performing Arts	Ireland	Actor - Acad Award Nom
	Cole	Business	USA	Fashion Designer
	Silverman	Creative Works	USA	Author - Pulitzer
Kenneth (Ken)	Buchanan	Sports	Scotland	Boxer - HF
Kenneth (Kenny)	Ball	Performing Arts	England	Jazz Trumpeter/Band Leader
Kenneth (Knute)	Rockne	Sports	USA	Football Coach
Kenneth (Red)	Norville (Norvo)	Performing Arts	USA	Jazz Vibraphonist - Big Band/Jazz - HF
Kenneth Earl (Kenny)	Burrrell	Performing Arts	USA	Jazz Guitarist - Big Band/Jazz - HF
Kenneth G.	Wilson	Science	USA	Physics - Nobel Laureate
Kenneth J.	Arrow	Arts	USA	Economics - Nobel Laureate
Kenneth Joseph (Kenny)	Reardon	Sports	Canada	Hockey Player - HF
Kenneth Ray (Ken)	Houston	Sports	USA	Football Player - HF
Kenneth Robert (Ken)	Rosewall	Sports	Australia	Tennis Player - HF
Kenneth Stanley	Reightler	Aviation	USA	Astronaut
Kenneth Wayne (Ken)	Dryden	Sports	Canada	Hockey Player - HF
Kenny	Dalglish	Sports	Scotland	Soccer Player - HF
	Loggins	Performing Arts	USA	Singer
	Roberts	Sports	USA	Motor Cycle Race Driver - HF
	Rogers	Performing Arts	USA	Singer
Kenny (Kenneth)	Clarke (Spearman)	Performing Arts	USA	Band Leader - Big Band/Jazz - HF
Kenzaburo	Oe	Creative Works	Japan	Literature - Nobel Laureate
Kenzo	Tange	Architecture	Japan	Architect - Pritzker/ AIA Gold
Kermit	Zarley	Sports	USA	Golfer
Ketti	Frings	Creative Works	USA	Dramatist - Pulitzer
Kevin	Bacon	Performing Arts	USA	Actor
	Costner	Movie Production	USA	Director - Academy Award
	Costner	Performing Arts	USA	Actor - Acad Award Nom
	Dobson	Performing Arts	USA	Actor
	Kline	Performing Arts	USA	Actor - Academy Award
	McCarthy	Performing Arts	USA	Actor - Acad Award Nom
	McHale	Sports	USA	Basketball Player - HF
	Mitchell	Sports	USA	Baseball Player
	Nealon	Performing Arts	USA	Comedian
	Roche	Architecture	USA	Architect - Pritzker/ AIA Gold
	Spacey	Performing Arts	USA	Actor - Academy Award
Kevin Patrick (Chili)	Chilton	Aviation	USA	Astronaut
Kevin Richard	Kregel	Aviation	USA	Astronaut
Khaosai (The Thai Tyson)	Galaxy	Sports	Thailand	Boxer - HF
Kiefer	Sutherland	Performing Arts	England	Actor
Kiki	Dee	Performing Arts	England	Singer
Kim	Alexis	Performing Arts	USA	Super Model
	Basinger	Performing Arts	USA	Actress - Academy Award
	Carnes	Performing Arts	USA	Singer
	Dae-jung	War & Peace	South Korea	Peace - Nobel Laureate
	Darby	Performing Arts	USA	Actress
	Hunter	Performing Arts	USA	Actress - Academy Award
	Novak	Performing Arts	USA	Actress
	Smith	Performing Arts	USA	Super Model
	Stanley	Performing Arts	USA	Actress - Acad Award Nom
Kim Dae	Jung	Politics	South Korea	President
Kimora Lee	Simmons	Business	USA	Fashion Designer
King	Hussein	Politics	Jordan	King
	Vidor	Movie Production	USA	Director - Acad Award Nom
King (Mr.G)	Gustav V	Sports	Sweden	Tennis Player - HF
Kingsley	Amis	Creative Works	England	Author
Kirby	Puckett	Sports	USA	Baseball Player - HF
Kiri Te	Kanawa	Performing Arts	New Zealand	Singer - Opera

FIRST NAME	LAST NAME	CATEGORY	COUNTRY	FAME
Kirk	Cameron	Performing Arts	USA	Actor
	Douglas	Performing Arts	USA	Actor - Acad Award Nom
Kirsten	Flagstad	Performing Arts	Norway	Singer - Opera
Kirstie	Alley	Performing Arts	USA	Actress
Kirsty	Hume	Performing Arts	Scotland	Super Model
Kisho	Kurokawa	Architecture	Japan	Architect
Kitty	Carlisle	Performing Arts	USA	Singer
	Wells	Performing Arts	USA	Singer - Country & Western
Klas Pontus	Arnoldson	War & Peace	Sweden	Peace - Nobel Laureate
Klaus Maria	Brandauer	Performing Arts	Austria	Actor - Acad Award Nom
Klaus von	Klitzing	Science	Germany	Physics - Nobel Laureate
Klemens Wenzel von	Metternich	Politics	Austria	Statesman/Diplomat
Knud Johan Victor	Rasmussen	Exploration	Denmark	Explorer - Arctic
Knut Pedersen	Hamsun	Creative Works	Norway	Literature - Nobel Laureate
Kofi Atta	Annan	War & Peace	Ghana	Peace - Nobel Laureate
Koichi	Tanaka	Science	Japan	Chemistry - Nobel Laureate
	Wakata	Aviation	Japan	Astronaut
Konrad	Adenauer	Politics	Germany	Chancellor
	Bloch	Science	USA	Medicine - Nobel Laureate
Konrad Zacharias	Lorenz	Science	Austria	Medicine - Nobel Laureate
Konstantin	Melnikov	Architecture	Austria	Architect
	Stanislavsky	Performing Arts	Russia	Actor
Konstantin Petrovich	Feoktistov	Aviation	Russia	Astronaut
Kresimir	Cosic	Sports	Croatia	Basketball Player - HF
Kris	Kristofferson	Performing Arts	USA	Actor/Singer - Country Music - HF
	Tschetter	Sports	USA	Golfer
Kristin Scott	Thomas	Performing Arts	England	Actress - Acad Award Nom
Kristy	McNichol	Performing Arts	USA	Actress
Krzysztof	Kieslowski	Movie Production	Poland	Director - Acad Award Nom
Kurt	Alder	Science	Germany	Chemistry - Nobel Laureate
	Gödel	Arts	USA	Philosopher/Mathematician
	Koffka	Arts	USA	Psychologist
	Russell	Performing Arts	USA	Actor
	Thomas	Sports	USA	Basketball Player
	Vonnegut Jr.	Creative Works	USA	Novelist
	Waldheim	Politics	Austria	Secretary-General UN
	Weill	Creative Works	USA	Composer
	Wüthrich	Science	Switzerland	Chemistry - Nobel Laureate
Kyle	MacLachlan	Performing Arts	USA	Actor
	Petty	Sports	USA	Race Car Driver
	Rote	Sports	USA	Football Player
	Sedgwick	Performing Arts	USA	Actress
Laetitia	Casta	Performing Arts	France	Super Model
Lafayette Ronald	Hubbard	Creative Works	USA	Author - SciFi
Lafcadio	Hearn	Creative Works	USA	Writer
Lainie	Kazan	Performing Arts	USA	Singer
Lalo	Schifrin	Creative Works	Argentina	Composer/Pianist
Lamar	Hunt	Sports	USA	Football Owner - HF
	Hunt	Sports	USA	Tennis Founder - HF
Lamont	Dozier	Creative Works	USA	Composer
Lamoral	Egmont	Politics	Italy	Statesman
Lana	Cantrell	Performing Arts	Australia	Singer
	Turner	Performing Arts	USA	Actress - Acad Award Nom
	Wood	Performing Arts	USA	Actress
Lance	Ito	Law & Order	USA	Judge - Simpson Case
	Tingay	Sports	England	Tennis Reporter - HF
Lance Dwight	Alworth	Sports	USA	Football Player - HF
Lancelot	Andrewes	Arts	England	Theologian
Lanford	Wilson	Creative Works	USA	Dramatist - Pulitzer
Lani	Guinier	Politics	USA	Proponent - Civil Rights
Lanny	Wadkins	Sports	USA	Golfer
Lanny King	McDonald	Sports	Canada	Hockey Player - HF
Lao	Tzu	Arts	China	Philosopher

FIRST NAME	LAST NAME	CATEGORY	COUNTRY	FAME
Lara Flynn	Boyle	Performing Arts	USA	Actress
Laraine	Day	Performing Arts	USA	Actress
Larry	Adler	Performing Arts	USA	Harmonica Musician
	Bird	Sports	USA	Basketball Player - HF
	Drake	Performing Arts	USA	Actor
	Fine	Performing Arts	USA	Comedian
	Hagman	Performing Arts	USA	Actor
	Holmes	Sports	USA	Boxer
	King	Creative Works	USA	Journalist - Television
	McMurtry	Creative Works	USA	Novelist - Pulitzer
	Mize	Sports	USA	Golfer
	Mullen Jr.	Performing Arts	Ireland	Rock & Roll - HF - U2
	Niven	Creative Works	USA	Author - SciFi
	Parks	Performing Arts	USA	Actor - Acad Award Nom
	Robinson	Sports	Canada	Hockey Player - HF
	Storch	Performing Arts	USA	Actor
Larry Thomas	Murphy	Sports	Canada	Hockey Player - HF
Lars	Onsager	Science	USA	Chemistry - Nobel Laureate
	Ulrich	Performing Arts	Denmark	Rock & Roll - Metallica
Lars Olof Jonathan Nathan	Söderblom	War & Peace	Sweden	Peace - Nobel Laureate
Lasse	Hallstrom	Movie Production	Sweden	Director - Acad Award Nom
	Viren	Sports	Finland	Olympic Runner
Laszlo	Papp	Sports	Hungary	Boxer - HF
Laura	Ashley	Business	England	Designing
	Branigan	Performing Arts	USA	Singer
	Bush	Politics	USA	First Lady
	Davies	Sports	England	Golfer
	Dern	Performing Arts	USA	Actress - Acad Award Nom
	Linney	Performing Arts	USA	Actress - Acad Award Nom
	Thermes	Architecture	Italy	Architect
	Ponte	Performing Arts	Spain	Super Model
Laura Elizabeth	Richards	Creative Works	USA	Author - Pulitzer
Laura Ingalls	Wilder	Creative Works	USA	Author - Children's Books
Laurel Blair Salton	Clark	Aviation	USA	Astronaut
Laurel Thatcher	Ulrich	Creative Works	USA	Author - Pulitzer
Lauren	Bacall	Performing Arts	USA	Actress - Acad Award Nom
	Hutton	Performing Arts	USA	Actress
Lauren (Laddie)	Gale	Sports	USA	Basketball Player - HF
Laurence	Harvey	Performing Arts	Lithuania	Actor - Acad Award Nom
	Olivier	Movie Production	England	Director - Acad Award Nom
	Olivier	Performing Arts	England	Actor - Academy Award
	Sterne	Creative Works	England	Novelist
Laurie	Metcalf	Performing Arts	USA	Actress
Lauritz Lebrecht Hommel	Melchior	Performing Arts	USA	Singer - Opera
LaVern	Baker	Performing Arts	USA	Singer - Rock & Roll - HF
Laverne	Allison	Performing Arts	USA	Rock & Roll - HF - The Dells
LaVerne	Andrews	Performing Arts	USA	Singer
Lawrance	Thompson	Creative Works	USA	Author - Pulitzer
Lawrence	Alma-Tadema	Works of Art	England	Painter
	Durrell	Creative Works	England	Author
	Fishburne	Performing Arts	USA	Actor - Acad Award Nom
	Halprin	Architecture	USA	Architect - Jefferson Medal
	Kasdan	Movie Production	USA	Director
	Payton	Performing Arts	USA	Rock & Roll - HF - The Four Tops
	Sanders	Creative Works	USA	Author
	Tibbett	Performing Arts	USA	Actor - Acad Award Nom
	Welk	Performing Arts	USA	Band Leader - Big Band/Jazz - HF
	Brown	Performing Arts	USA	Jazz Trombonist - Big Band/Jazz - HF
Lawrence (Larry)	Dunn (Dunhill)	Performing Arts	USA	Rock & Roll - HF - Earth Wind & Fire
Lawrence A.	Cremin	Creative Works	USA	Author - Pulitzer
Lawrence Adams	Baker Sr.	Sports	USA	Tennis Player - HF
Lawrence Ari	Fleischer	Politics	USA	Federal Press Secretary
Lawrence Chatmon (Larry)	Little	Sports	USA	Football Player - HF

SOLVER SERIES: NAME FINDER

FIRST NAME	LAST NAME	CATEGORY	COUNTRY	FAME
Lawrence Dale	Bell	Business	USA	Aviation - Helecopters
Lawrence Eugene (Larry)	Doby	Sports	USA	Baseball Player - HF
Lawrence Frank (Larry)	Wilson	Sports	USA	Football Player - HF
Lawrence H.	Gibson	Creative Works	USA	Author - Pulitzer
Lawrence James	Delucas	Aviation	USA	Astronaut
Lawrence Julius	Taylor	Sports	USA	Football Player - HF
Lawrence Peter (Yogi)	Berra	Sports	USA	Baseball Player - HF
Lawrence R.	Klein	Arts	USA	Economics - Nobel Laureate
Lawrence Richard (Larry)	Csonka	Sports	USA	Football Player - HF
Lawson	Little	Sports	USA	Golfer - HF
Lazare Nicolas Marguerite	Carnot	Politics	France	Statesman
Lázaro	Cárdenas	Politics	Mexico	President
Le Duc	Tho	War & Peace	Vietnam	Peace - Nobel Laureate
Lea	Thompson	Performing Arts	USA	Actress
Leanne	Rimes	Performing Arts	USA	Singer - Country Music
Lech	Walesa	Politics	Poland	President
	Walesa	War & Peace	Poland	Peace - Nobel Laureate
Lee	Grant	Performing Arts	USA	Actress - Academy Award
	Harper	Creative Works	USA	Author
	Horsley	Performing Arts	USA	Actor
	Majors	Performing Arts	USA	Actor
	Marvin	Performing Arts	USA	Actor - Academy Award
	Petty	Sports	USA	Race Car Driver - HF
	Remick	Performing Arts	USA	Actress - Acad Award Nom
	Salk	Arts	USA	Psychologist
	Strasberg	Performing Arts	Ukraine	Actor - Acad Award Nom
	Tracy	Performing Arts	USA	Actor - Acad Award Nom
	Trevino	Sports	USA	Golfer - HF
Lee A.	Iacocca	Business	USA	Automobile Industy
Lee De	Forest	Science	USA	Inventor - Radio Equipment
Lee J.	Cobb	Performing Arts	USA	Actor - Acad Award Nom
Lee Mack	Ritenour	Performing Arts	USA	Jazz Guitarist
Lee Roy	Selmon	Sports	USA	Football Player - HF
Lehmen	Engel	Creative Works	USA	Author
Leif	Ericson	Exploration	Iceland	Explorer - East Coast America
Leigh	Hunt	Business	England	Publishing
Leland H.	Hartwell	Science	USA	Medicine - Nobel Laureate
Leland Standford (Larry) Sr.	MacPhail	Sports	USA	Baseball Pioneer - HF
Leland Standford (Lee) Jr.	MacPhail	Sports	USA	Baseball Executive - HF
Lemuel Jackson (Lem)	Barney	Sports	USA	Football Player - HF
Len	Berman	Creative Works	USA	Journalist - Television
	Cariou	Performing Arts	Canada	Actor/Singer
	Deighton	Creative Works	England	Author
	Dykstra	Sports	USA	Baseball Player
	Oliver	Sports	USA	Soccer Player - HF
Lena	Horne	Performing Arts	USA	Singer - Big Band/Jazz - HF
	Olin	Performing Arts	Sweden	Actress - Acad Award Nom
Lennie (Leonard Joseph)	Tristano	Performing Arts	USA	Jazz Pianist/Composer - Big Band/Jazz - HF
Lenny	Breau	Performing Arts	USA	Guitarist - Canadian Music - HF
	Bruce	Performing Arts	USA	Comedian
Leo	Carrilo	Performing Arts	USA	Actor
	Diegel	Sports	USA	Golfer - HF
	Esaki	Science	Japan	Physics - Nobel Laureate
	Genn	Performing Arts	England	Actor - Acad Award Nom
	Gorcey	Performing Arts	USA	Comedian
	Rosten	Creative Works	USA	Writer
	Sayer	Performing Arts	England	Singer
	Slezak	Performing Arts	Czechoslovakia	Singer - Opera
	McCarey	Movie Production	USA	Director - Academy Award
Leo Ernest (The Lip)	Durocher	Sports	USA	Baseball Manager - HF
Leo G.	Carroll	Performing Arts	England	Actor
Leo James	Rainwater	Science	USA	Physics - Nobel Laureate
Leo Joseph	Boivin	Sports	Canada	Hockey Player - HF

FIRST NAME	LAST NAME	CATEGORY	COUNTRY	FAME
Leo Joseph	Nomellini	Sports	Italy	Football Player - HF
Leo Nikolayevich	Tolstoy	Creative Works	Russia	Novelist/Social Theorist
Leo von	Klenze	Architecture	Germany	Architect/Painter/Writer
Leon	Ames	Performing Arts	USA	Actor
	Day	Sports	USA	Baseball Player - HF
	Edel	Creative Works	USA	Author - Pulitzer
	Errol	Performing Arts	Australia	Comedian
	Krier	Architecture	England	Architect - Jefferson Medal
	Russell	Performing Arts	USA	Singer
	Spinks	Sports	USA	Boxer
	Trotsky	Politics	Russia	Revolutionist
	Uris	Creative Works	USA	Novelist
Léon	Daudet	Politics	France	Politician/Journalist
	Gambetta	Politics	France	Premier
	Jouhaux	War & Peace	France	Peace - Nobel Laureate
Leon (Bix)	Beiderbecke	Performing Arts	USA	Jazz Cornetist - Big Band/Jazz - HF
Leon Allen (Goose)	Goslin	Sports	USA	Baseball Player - HF
Leon Battista	Alberti	Architecture	Italy	Architect/Painter/Sculptor
Leon F.	Litwack	Creative Works	USA	Author - Pulitzer
Leon M.	Lederman	Science	USA	Physics - Nobel Laureate
Leon Neil	Cooper	Science	USA	Physics - Nobel Laureate
Leon Nikolaevich	Bakst	Works of Art	Russia	Painter
Léon Victor Auguste	Bourgeois	War & Peace	France	Peace - Nobel Laureate
Leona	Helmsley	Law & Order	USA	Fraud Artist
	Mitchell	Performing Arts	USA	Singer - Opera
Leonard	Bacon	Creative Works	USA	Poet - Pulitzer
	Baker	Creative Works	USA	Author - Pulitzer
	Bernstein	Creative Works	USA	Composer/Conductor
	Bloomfield	Arts	USA	Linguist
	Cohen	Creative Works	Canada	Poet/Song Writer
	Cohen	Performing Arts	Canada	Singer/Composer - Canadian Music - HF
	Frey	Performing Arts	USA	Actor - Acad Award Nom
	Maltin	Creative Works	Canada	Journalist - Television
	Nimoy	Performing Arts	USA	Actor
	Wood	War & Peace	USA	General/Political Administrator
Leonard (Chico)	Marx	Performing Arts	USA	Comedian
Leonard (Len)	Barry (Borisoff)	Performing Arts	USA	Singer
Leonard (Lenny)	Wilkens	Sports	USA	Basketball Player - HF
Leonard (Roy)	Rogers (Slye)	Performing Arts	USA	Country Music - HF - Sons of the Pioneers
Leonard D.	White	Creative Works	USA	Author - Pulitzer
Leonard Edward (Lenny)	Moore	Sports	USA	Football Player - HF
Leonard Guy (Len)	Ford Jr.	Sports	USA	Football Player - HF
Leonard Patrick (Red)	Kelly	Sports	Canada	Hockey Player - HF
Leonard Ray (Len)	Dawson	Sports	USA	Football Player - HF
Leonard Sidney	Woolf	Creative Works	England	Writer/Publisher
Leonard Williams	Levy	Creative Works	USA	Author - Pulitzer
Leonardo da	Vinci	Works of Art	Italy	Painter/Sculptor/Architect
Leonardo Di	Caprio	Performing Arts	USA	Actor - Acad Award Nom
Leonhard	Euler	Science	Switzerland	Mathematician
Leonid	Brezhnev	Politics	Russia	General Secretary
Leonid Konstantinovich	Kadenyuk	Aviation	Ukraine	Astronaut
Leonid Nikolayevich	Andreyev	Creative Works	Russia	Playwright/Novelist
Leonid Vitaliyevich	Kantorovich	Arts	Russia	Economics - Nobel Laureate
Léonide	Massine	Performing Arts	USA	Ballet Dancer/Choreographer
Leonie	Rysanek	Performing Arts	Austria	Singer - Opera
Leonora	Speyer	Creative Works	USA	Poet - Pulitzer
Leopold	Auer	Performing Arts	Hungary	Violinist
	Ruzicka	Science	Switzerland	Chemistry - Nobel Laureate
	Stokowski	Performing Arts	USA	Conductor - Orchestra
Léopold	Eyharts	Aviation	France	Astronaut
Leopold von	Ranke	Arts	Germany	Historian
Leora	Dana	Performing Arts	USA	Actress
Leoš	Janáček	Creative Works	Czechoslovakia	Composer

SOLVER SERIES: NAME FINDER

FIRST NAME	LAST NAME	CATEGORY	COUNTRY	FAME
Leroy	Anderson	Creative Works	USA	Composer
	Kelly	Sports	USA	Football Player - HF
LeRoy	Neiman	Works of Art	USA	Artist
Leroy Gordon	Cooper	Aviation	USA	Astronaut
Leroy Robert (Satchel)	Paige	Sports	USA	Baseball Player - HF
Lesley	Gore	Performing Arts	USA	Singer
	Stahl	Creative Works	USA	Journalist - Television
Lesley Anne	Warren	Performing Arts	USA	Actress - Acad Award Nom
Lesley Rosemary Turner	Bowrey	Sports	Australia	Tennis Player - HF
Lesley-Anne	Down	Performing Arts	England	Actress
Leslie	Browne	Performing Arts	USA	Actress - Acad Award Nom
	Caron	Performing Arts	France	Actress - Acad Award Nom
	Howard	Performing Arts	England	Actor - Acad Award Nom
	Nielson	Performing Arts	Canada	Actor
	Stephen	Arts	England	Philosopher/Critic
	Uggams	Performing Arts	USA	Singer - Musicals
Leslie (Les)	Aspin	Politics	USA	Secretary of Defense
Lester	Holt	Creative Works	USA	Journalist - Television
	Lanin	Performing Arts	USA	Band Leader
	Patrick	Sports	Canada	Hockey Player - HF
	Young	Performing Arts	USA	Jazz Saxophonist - Big Band/Jazz - HF
Lester (Les) Raymond	Brown	Performing Arts	USA	Band Leader - Big Band/Jazz - HF
Lester Bowles	Pearson	Politics	Canada	Prime Minister
	Pearson	War & Peace	Canada	Peace - Nobel Laureate
Lester Raymond	Flatt	Performing Arts	USA	Country Music - HF - Foggy Mountain Boys
Lester William (Les)	Paul (Polfuss)	Performing Arts	USA	Guitarist - Big Band/Jazz - HF
	Paul (Polfuss)	Performing Arts	USA	Rock & Roll - HF - Les Paul & Mary Ford
Letitia	Tyler	Politics	USA	First Lady
Lev	Yashin	Sports	Russia	Soccer Player - HF
Lev Davidivich	Landau	Science	Russia	Physics - Nobel Laureate
Levar	Burton	Performing Arts	Germany	Actor
Levi	Stubbs	Performing Arts	USA	Rock & Roll - HF - The Four Tops
Levi P.	Morton	Politics	USA	Vice-President
Lew	Ayres	Performing Arts	USA	Actor - Acad Award Nom
	Jenkins	Sports	USA	Boxer - HF
	Lehr	Performing Arts	USA	Comedian
Lewis	Carroll	Creative Works	England	Author/Mathematician
	Cass	Politics	USA	Statesman
	Milestone	Movie Production	Russia	Director - Academy Award
	Mumford	Architecture	USA	Architect - Jefferson Medal
	Mumford	Arts	USA	Philosopher - Social
	Stone	Performing Arts	USA	Actor - Acad Award Nom
	Tappan	Business	USA	Drygoods
	Wallace	Creative Works	USA	Novelist/General
Lewis Alan (Lew)	Hoad	Sports	Australia	Tennis Player - HF
Lewis Allan (Lou)	Reed	Performing Arts	USA	Rock & Roll - HF - Velvet Underground
Lewis Bernstein	Namier	Arts	England	Historian
Lewis Burwell	Puller Jr.	Creative Works	USA	Author - Pulitzer
Lewis Franklin	Powell	Law & Order	USA	Justice - Supreme Court
Lewis Henry	Morgan	Arts	USA	Anthropologist
Lewis Robert (Hack)	Wilson	Sports	USA	Baseball Player - HF
Liam	Cosgrave	Politics	Ireland	Prime Minister
	Neeson	Performing Arts	Northern Ireland	Actor - Acad Award Nom
	O'Flaherty	Creative Works	Ireland	Author
Licia	Albanese	Performing Arts	USA	Singer - Opera
Lila	Kedrova	Performing Arts	Russia	Actress - Academy Award
Lila Acheson	Wallace	Creative Works	Canada	Author
Lili	Taylor	Performing Arts	USA	Actress
	Lehmann	Performing Arts	Germany	Singer - Opera
	Palmer	Performing Arts	Poland	Actress
Lillia	Skala	Performing Arts	Austria	Actress - Acad Award Nom
Lillian	Armstrong (Hardin)	Performing Arts	USA	Jazz Pianist/Composer - Big Band/Jazz - HF
	Gish	Performing Arts	USA	Actress - Acad Award Nom

FIRST NAME	LAST NAME	CATEGORY	COUNTRY	FAME
Lillian	Hellman	Creative Works	USA	Playwright
	Russell	Performing Arts	USA	Actress/Singer
Lillie	Langtry	Performing Arts	England	Actress
Lillie Mae (Betty)	Carter (Jones)	Performing Arts	USA	Jazz Singer - Big Band/Jazz - HF
Lilly	Reich	Architecture	Germany	Architect
Lily	Pons	Performing Arts	France	Singer - Opera
	Tomlin	Performing Arts	USA	Actress - Acad Award Nom
Lilyan	Tashman	Performing Arts	USA	Actress
Lin	Biao	War & Peace	China	General - Communist
Lina	Bo Bardi	Architecture	Brazil	Architect/Furniture Designer
	Wertmuller	Movie Production	Italy	Director - Acad Award Nom
Lincoln	Ellsworth	Exploration	USA	Explorer - Polar
Linda	Blair	Performing Arts	USA	Actress - Acad Award Nom
	Darnell	Performing Arts	USA	Actress
	Evangelista	Performing Arts	Canada	Super Model
	Evans	Performing Arts	USA	Actress
	Gray	Performing Arts	USA	Actress
	Hamilton	Performing Arts	USA	Actress
	Hunt	Performing Arts	USA	Actress - Academy Award
	Lavin	Performing Arts	USA	Actress
	Ronstadt	Performing Arts	USA	Singer
Linda B.	Buck	Science	USA	Medicine - Nobel Laureate
Linden	Soles	Creative Works	Canada	Journalist - Television
Lindley	Murray	Arts	England	Grammarian
Lindley Armstrong (Spike)	Jones	Performing Arts	USA	Drummer/Comedian
Lindsay	Anderson	Movie Production	India	Director
	Crouse	Performing Arts	USA	Actress - Acad Award Nom
	Wagner	Performing Arts	USA	Actress
Lindsey	Buckingham	Performing Arts	USA	Rock & Roll - HF - Fleetwood Mac
Linnie Marsh	Wolfe	Creative Works	USA	Author - Pulitzer
Linus Carl	Pauling	Science	USA	Chemistry - Nobel Laureate
	Pauling	War & Peace	USA	Peace - Nobel Laureate
Lion	Feuchtwanger	Creative Works	Germany	Novelist
Lionel	Atwill	Performing Arts	England	Actor
	Barrymore	Movie Production	USA	Director - Acad Award Nom
	Barrymore	Performing Arts	USA	Actor - Academy Award
	Richie	Performing Arts	USA	Singer
	Stander	Performing Arts	USA	Actor
Lionel (Hamps)	Hampton	Performing Arts	USA	Band Leader - Big Band/Jazz - HF
Lionel Pretoria	Conacher	Sports	Canada	Hockey Player - HF
Lisa	Alther	Creative Works	USA	Author
	Bonet	Performing Arts	USA	Actress
	Eichhorn	Performing Arts	USA	Actress
	Hartman	Performing Arts	USA	Actress
	Noor	Politics	Jordan	Queen
Lise	Meitner	Science	Austria	Nuclear Physicist
Lisel	Mueller	Creative Works	Germany	Poet - Pulitzer
Lita	Ford	Performing Arts	England	Singer
	Grey	Performing Arts	USA	Actress
Liu	Ailing	Sports	China	Soccer Player
Liv	Ullmann	Performing Arts	Norway	Actress - Acad Award Nom
Livio	Vacchini	Architecture	Switzerland	Architect
Liz	Claiborne	Business	USA	Fashion Designer
	Smith	Creative Works	USA	Journalist - Newspaper
Liza	Minnelli	Performing Arts	USA	Actress - Academy Award
	Minnelli	Performing Arts	USA	Singer
Lizabeth	Scott	Performing Arts	USA	Actress
Llewelyn	Powys	Creative Works	England	Author
Lloyd	Bridges	Performing Arts	USA	Actor
	Mangrum	Sports	USA	Golfer - HF
	Monsen	Sports	USA	Soccer Player - HF
	Nolan	Performing Arts	USA	Actor
	Price	Performing Arts	USA	Singer - Rock & Roll - HF

SOLVER SERIES: NAME FINDER

FIRST NAME	LAST NAME	CATEGORY	COUNTRY	FAME
Lloyd	Robertson	Creative Works	Canada	Journalist - Television
Lloyd (Big Finger)	Moore	Performing Arts	USA	Rock & Roll - HF - The Soul Stirrers
Lloyd Blaine	Hammond Jr.	Aviation	USA	Astronaut
Lloyd James	Waner	Sports	USA	Baseball Player - HF
Lloyd Millard	Bentsen Jr.	Politics	USA	Senator
Lodewijk Van Den	Berg	Aviation	USA	Astronaut
Lodovico	Ariosto	Creative Works	Italy	Poet/Author
Lois	Chiles	Performing Arts	USA	Actress
	Gould	Creative Works	USA	Author
	Nettleton	Performing Arts	USA	Actress
Lola	Falana	Performing Arts	USA	Singer
Lon	Chaney	Performing Arts	USA	Actor
	Chaney Jr.	Performing Arts	USA	Actor
	Nol	War & Peace	Vietnam	Cambodian General
Loni	Anderson	Performing Arts	USA	Actress
Lonnie	Donegan	Performing Arts	Scotland	Singer
Lorado	Taft	Works of Art	USA	Sculptor
Loreena	McKennitt	Performing Arts	Canada	Singer
Loren Corey	Eiseley	Arts	USA	Philosopher/Essayist/Naturalist
Loren D.	Estleman	Creative Works	USA	Author
Loren James	Shriver	Aviation	USA	Astronaut
Loren Wilbur	Acton	Aviation	USA	Astronaut
Lorene	Yarnell	Performing Arts	USA	Dancer/Mime
Lorenzo	Ghiberti	Architecture	Italy	Architect
	Ghiberti	Works of Art	Italy	Sculptor
	Lamas	Performing Arts	USA	Actor
Lorenzo da	Ponte	Creative Works	Italy	Poet/Librettist
Loretta	Lynn(Webb)	Performing Arts	USA	Singer - Country Music - HF
	Swit	Performing Arts	USA	Actress
	Young	Performing Arts	USA	Actress - Academy Award
Lori	McKenna	Performing Arts	USA	Singer
	Petty	Performing Arts	USA	Actress
	Singer	Performing Arts	USA	Actress
Lorin	Maazel	Performing Arts	France	Conductor - Orchestra
Lorna	Luft	Performing Arts	USA	Singer
Lorne	Greene	Performing Arts	Canada	Actor
	Michaels	Movie Production	Canada	Director
Lorne John (Gump)	Worsley	Sports	Canada	Hockey Player - HF
Lorraine	Bracco	Performing Arts	USA	Actress - Acad Award Nom
Lothar	Matthäus	Sports	Germany	Soccer Player
Lotte	Lehmann	Performing Arts	Germany	Singer - Opera
	Lenya	Performing Arts	Austria	Actress - Acad Award Nom
Lou	Christie	Performing Arts	USA	Singer
	Costello	Performing Arts	USA	Comedian
	Ferrigno	Performing Arts	USA	Actor
	Gramm	Performing Arts	USA	Singer
	Hoover	Politics	USA	First Lady
	Rawls	Performing Arts	USA	Singer
Lou Diamond	Phillips	Performing Arts	Philippines	Actor
Louie (Luigi Paulino)	Bellson (Balassoni)	Performing Arts	USA	Jazz Drummer - Big Band/Jazz - HF
Louis	Althusser	Arts	Algeria	Philosopher
	Auchincloss	Creative Works	USA	Novelist
	Blériot	Aviation	France	Aeronautical Engineer
	Botha	Politics	South Africa	Prime Minister
	Braille	Arts	France	Printing/Writing
	Bromfield	Creative Works	USA	Author - Pulitzer
	Calhern	Performing Arts	USA	Actor - Acad Award Nom
	Chevrolet	Sports	Switzerland	Race Car Driver - HF
	Elzevir	Arts	Netherlands	Printer
	Gossett Jr.	Performing Arts	USA	Actor - Academy Award
	Joliet	Exploration	Canada	Explorer - Mississippi River
	Jourdan	Performing Arts	USA	Actor
	MacNeice	Creative Works	England	Poet/Classical Scholar

FIRST NAME	LAST NAME	CATEGORY	COUNTRY	FAME
Louis	Malle	Movie Production	France	Director - Acad Award Nom
	Menand	Creative Works	USA	Author - Pulitzer
	Meyer	Sports	USA	Race Car Driver - HF
	Mountbatten	War & Peace	England	Admiral
	Nye	Performing Arts	USA	Actor
	Pasteur	Science	France	Chemist/Bacteriologist
	Prima	Performing Arts	USA	Band Leader - Big Band/Jazz - HF
	Renault	War & Peace	France	Peace - Nobel Laureate
	Rukeyser	Creative Works	USA	Journalist - Television
	Sheaffer	Creative Works	USA	Author - Pulitzer
	Simpson	Creative Works	Jamaica	Poet - Pulitzer
	Skidmore	Architecture	USA	Architect - AIA Gold Medal
	Untermeyer	Creative Works	USA	Poet/Anthologist/Critic
Louis (Lou)	Boudreau	Sports	USA	Baseball Player - HF
	Creekmur	Sports	USA	Football Player - HF
Louis (Satchmo)	Armstrong	Performing Arts	USA	Jazz Trumpeter - Big Band/Jazz -HF
Louis (Studs)	Terkel	Creative Works	USA	Author - Pulitzer
Louis Adolphe	Thiers	Politics	France	Statesman/Historian
Louis Antoine Léon de	Sainte-Just	War & Peace	France	Revolutionist
Louis Antoinne de	Bougainville	Exploration	France	Explorer - Falkland Islands
Louis B.	Mayer	Movie Production	Russia	Director
Louis César Victor Maurice	Broglie	Science	France	Physicist
Louis Charles Alfred de	Musset	Creative Works	France	Poet/Writer
Louis Clark (Lou)	Brock	Sports	USA	Baseball Player - HF
Louis Comfort	Tiffany	Works of Art	USA	Artist - Stained Glass
Louis de Buade	Frontenac	Politics	France	Colonial Governor
Louis Dembitz	Brandeis	Law & Order	USA	Justice/Supreme Court
Louis Eugène Félix	Néel	Science	France	Physics - Nobel Laureate
Louis Henry	Sullivan	Architecture	USA	Architect - AIA Gold Medal
Louis Isadore	Kahn	Architecture	USA	Architect - AIA Gold Medal
Louis J.	Ignarro	Science	USA	Medicine - Nobel Laureate
Louis Joseph de	Montcalm	War & Peace	France	General
	Vendome	War & Peace	France	General/Marshall
Louis le	Vau	Architecture	France	Architect
Louis Madison	Terman	Arts	USA	Psychologist
Louis Phillipe Joseph	Orléans	Politics	France	Revolutionist
Louis R.	Harlan	Creative Works	USA	Author - Pulitzer
Louis Roy (Lou)	Groza	Sports	USA	Football Player - HF
Louis Seymour Bazett	Leakey	Arts	England	Anthropologist
Louis Stephen	St. Laurent	Politics	Canada	Prime Minster
Louis Thomas	Jordan	Performing Arts	USA	Singer - Rock & Roll - HF
Louis Victor Pierre Raymond de	Broglie	Science	France	Physics - Nobel Laureate
Louisa May	Alcott	Creative Works	USA	Novelist
Louise	Dresser	Performing Arts	USA	Actress - Acad Award Nom
	Fletcher	Performing Arts	USA	Actress - Academy Award
	Gluck	Creative Works	USA	Poet - Pulitzer
	Lasser	Performing Arts	USA	Actress
	Pound	Arts	USA	Linguist/Folklorist
	Smith	Sports	USA	Race Car Driver - HF
	Suggs	Sports	USA	Golfer - HF
Louise Arner	Boyd	Exploration	USA	Explorer - Arctic
Louise Catherine	Adams	Politics	USA	First Lady
Luca della	Robbia	Works of Art	Italy	Sculptor - Early Renaissance
Lucas	Cranach	Works of Art	Germany	Painter/Engraver
Lucas Vázquez de	Ayllón	Exploration	Spain	Explorer - North Carolina
Luchino	Visconti	Movie Production	Italy	Director
Luciano	Baldessari	Architecture	Italy	Architect
	Pavarotti	Performing Arts	Italy	Singer - Opera
	Plamondon	Performing Arts	Canada	Francophone Lyricist - Canadian Music - HF
Lucie	Arnaz	Performing Arts	USA	Actress
Lucie Simplice Camille	Desmoulins	Creative Works	France	Journalist/Pamphleteer
Lucile	Watson	Performing Arts	Canada	Actress - Acad Award Nom
Lucille	Ball (Arnaz)	Performing Arts	USA	Comedian/Actress

SOLVER SERIES: NAME FINDER

FIRST NAME	LAST NAME	CATEGORY	COUNTRY	FAME
Lucine	Amara	Performing Arts	USA	Singer - Opera
Lucio	Costa	Architecture	Brazil	Architect/Planner/Author
Lucius Benjamin (Luke)	Appling	Sports	USA	Baseball Player - HF
Lucius Venable (Lucky)	Millinder	Performing Arts	USA	Band Leader - Big Band/Jazz - HF
Lucretia	Borgia	Politics	Italy	Duchess
	Bori	Performing Arts	USA	Singer - Opera
	Garfield	Politics	USA	First Lady
	Mott	Politics	USA	Abolitionist/Rights Advocate
Lucy	Stone	Politics	USA	Reformer/Suffragist
Lucy Ware	Hayes	Politics	USA	First Lady
Ludovico	Quaroni	Architecture	Italy	Architect
Ludwig	Hiberseimer	Architecture	Germany	Architect
	Quidde	War & Peace	Germany	Peace - Nobel Laureate
Ludwig Andreas	Feuerbach	Arts	Germany	Philosopher/Materialist
Ludwig Josef Johann	Wittgenstein	Arts	England	Philosopher
Ludwig Miès van der Rohe	Rohe	Architecture	USA	Architect - AIA/Jefferson Gold Medal
Ludwig van	Beethoven	Creative Works	Germany	Composer
Ludwig Van	Beethoven	Creative Works	Austria	Composer
Luigi	Boccherini	Creative Works	Italy	Composer
	Cherubini	Creative Works	Italy	Composer
	Galvani	Science	Italy	Physicist/Physiologist
	Moretti	Architecture	Italy	Architect
	Pirandello	Creative Works	Italy	Literature - Nobel Laureate
	Snozzi	Architecture	Switzerland	Architect
Luigi Ernesto	Alva	Performing Arts	Peru	Singer - Opera
Luis	Barragan	Architecture	Mexico	Architect - Pritzker Laureate
	Bunuel	Movie Production	France	Director
	Figo	Sports	Portugal	Soccer Player
	Rodriquez	Sports	Cuba	Boxer - HF
	Tiant	Sports	USA	Baseball Player
Luis Ernesto	Aparicio	Sports	Venezuela	Baseball Player - HF
Luis F.	Leloir	Science	Argentina	Chemistry - Nobel Laureate
Luis Walter	Alvarez	Science	USA	Physics - Nobel Laureate
Luisa	Tetrazzini	Performing Arts	Italy	Singer - Opera
	Rainer	Performing Arts	Germany	Actress - Academy Award
Luiz Vaz de	Camões	Creative Works	England	Poet
Lukas	Foss	Creative Works	USA	Composer
Luke	Perry	Performing Arts	USA	Actor
Lupe	Velez	Performing Arts	Mexico	Actress
Lusia	Harris-Stewart	Sports	USA	Basketball Player - HF
Luther	Burbank	Science	USA	Horticulturalist
Luther Ronzoni	Vandross	Performing Arts	USA	Singer - Rhythm & Blues
Lydia Kamekeha	Liliuokalani	Politics	USA	Queen - Hawaiian Islands
Lyle	Lovett	Performing Arts	USA	Singer
	Waggoner	Performing Arts	USA	Actor
Lyle Russell Cedric (Skitch)	Henderson	Performing Arts	USA	Conductor/Composer/Pianist
Lyman	Abbott	Creative Works	USA	Author
	Beecher	Arts	USA	Theologian/Clergyman
Lyman Frank	Baum	Creative Works	USA	Writer
Lynda	Carter	Performing Arts	USA	Actress
Lyndon Baines	Johnson	Politics	USA	President
Lynette	Woodard	Sports	USA	Basketball Player - HF
Lynn	Anderson	Performing Arts	USA	Actress
	Carlin	Performing Arts	USA	Actress - Acad Award Nom
	Fontanne	Performing Arts	England	Actress - Acad Award Nom
	Johnston	Creative Works	Canada	Cartoonist
	Redgrave	Performing Arts	England	Actress - Acad Award Nom
Lynn Curtis	Swann	Sports	USA	Football Player - HF
Lynn Morley	Martin	Politics	USA	Congressman
Lynn Nolan	Ryan	Sports	USA	Baseball Player - HF
Lyonel Charles Adrian	Feininger	Works of Art	USA	Painter
Mabel	Normand	Performing Arts	USA	Actress
Mabel Esmonde	Cahill	Sports	Ireland	Tennis Player - HF

FIRST NAME	LAST NAME	CATEGORY	COUNTRY	FAME
Mac	Davis	Performing Arts	USA	Singer
Macaulay	Culkin	Performing Arts	USA	Actor
MacDonald	Carey	Performing Arts	USA	Actor
Mack	Sennett	Movie Production	USA	Director/Producer
Mackenzie	Bowell	Politics	Canada	Prime Minister
MacKenzie	Phillips	Performing Arts	USA	Singer
Mackinlay	Kantor	Creative Works	USA	Novelist - Pulitzer
Madeline	Kahn	Performing Arts	USA	Actress - Acad Award Nom
Mae	Clarke	Performing Arts	USA	Actress
	Murray	Performing Arts	USA	Actress
	Questel	Performing Arts	USA	Singer
	West	Performing Arts	USA	Actress
Mae Carol	Jemison	Aviation	USA	Astronaut
Magaret Ayer	Barnes	Creative Works	USA	Novelist - Pulitzer
Magda	Gabor	Performing Arts	Hungary	Actress
Maggie	McNamara	Performing Arts	USA	Actress - Acad Award Nom
	Smith	Performing Arts	England	Actress - Academy Award
Magnus	Albertus	Arts	Germany	Philosopher
Mahalia	Jackson	Performing Arts	USA	Singer - Rock & Roll - HF
Mai	Zetterling	Performing Arts	Sweden	Actress
Mairead	Corrigan	War & Peace	England	Peace - Nobel Laureate
Makoto "Mako"	Iwamatsu	Performing Arts	Japan	Actor - Acad Award Nom
Malcolm	Campbell	Sports	USA	Race Car Driver - HF
	Forbes	Business	USA	Publishing
	McDowell	Performing Arts	England	Actor
	Young	Performing Arts	Scotland	Rock & Roll - HF - AC/DC
Malcolm (Mal)	Anderson	Sports	USA	Tennis Player - HF
Malcolm Douglass (Mal)	Whitman	Sports	USA	Tennis Player - HF
Malcolm Greene	Chance	Sports	USA	Tennis Player - HF
Malcolm Scott	Carpenter	Aviation	USA	Astronaut
Malcolm X.	Little	Politics	USA	Activist
Malcolm-Jamal	Warner	Performing Arts	USA	Actor
Mamie Geneva	Eisenhower	Politics	USA	First Lady
Mamie Van	Doren	Performing Arts	USA	Actress
Mamoru	Mohri	Aviation	Japan	Astronaut
Man	Ray	Works of Art	USA	Painter/Photographer
Mandy	Patinkin	Performing Arts	USA	Actor
Manfred	Elgen	Science	Germany	Chemistry - Nobel Laureate
Manley Lanier (Sonny)	Carter Jr.	Aviation	USA	Astronaut
Manly Palmer	Hall	Arts	Canada	Philosopher
Manoj Night	Shyamalan	Movie Production	India	Director - Acad Award Nom
Manolo (Manuel)	Alonso	Sports	Spain	Tennis Player - HF
Manon von	Gerkan	Performing Arts	Germany	Super Model
Manuel	Falla	Creative Works	Spain	Composer
	Ortiz	Sports	USA	Boxer - HF
Manuel De	Falla	Creative Works	Spain	Composer - Classical
Manuel de	Sola-Morales	Architecture	Spain	Architect
Manuel Dos (Garrincha)	Santos	Sports	Brazil	Soccer Player - HF
Manuel Luis	Quezon	Politics	Philippines	President
Manuel Martinez (Manolo)	Santana	Sports	Spain	Tennis Player - HF
Manuel Rodriguez	Manolete	Sports	Spain	Matador
Mao	Tse-Tung	Politics	China	Head of State
Mao (Chairman Mao)	Zedong	War & Peace	China	Military Leader
Marc	Chagall	Works of Art	France	Painter/Stained Glass Artist
	Cohn	Performing Arts	USA	Singer/Song Writer
Marc Antoine	Laugier	Architecture	France	Architect
Marcel	Breuer	Architecture	USA	Architect - AIA/Jefferson Gold Medal
	Duchamp	Works of Art	USA	Painter
	Dupré	Creative Works	France	Composer
	Marceau	Performing Arts	France	Pantomimist
	Pronovost	Sports	Canada	Hockey Player - HF
	Proust	Creative Works	France	Novelist
Marcel (Casablanca Clouter)	Cerdan	Sports	Algeria	Boxer - HF

SOLVER SERIES: NAME FINDER

FIRST NAME	LAST NAME	CATEGORY	COUNTRY	FAME
Marcel Elphege	Dionne	Sports	Canada	Hockey Player - HF
Marcello	Malpighi	Science	Italy	Physiologist - Micro Anatomy
	Mastroianni	Performing Arts	Italy	Actor - Acad Award Nom
	Piacentini	Architecture	Italy	Architect
Marcelo (Iron Man)	Balboa	Sports	USA	Soccer Player - HF
Marcia Gay	Harden	Performing Arts	USA	Actress - Academy Award
Marco	Polo	Exploration	Italy	Explorer - East Asia
	Zanuso	Architecture	Italy	Architect
Marco Pollione	Vitruvius	Architecture	Italy	Architect
Marco Van	Basten	Sports	Netherlands	Soccer Player - HF
Marcos	Pontes	Aviation	Brazil	Astronaut
Marcos de	Niza	Exploration	Italy	Explorer - Mexico/New Mexico
Marcus	Diener	Architecture	Switzerland	Architect
	Garvey	Politics	West Indies	Leader - Negro
	Hanna	Business	USA	Financier/Politician
	Whitman	Exploration	USA	Frontiersman - America
Marcus Lee	Hansen	Creative Works	USA	Author - Pulitzer
Marcus LeMarr	Allen	Sports	USA	Football Player - HF
Mare	Winningham	Performing Arts	USA	Actress - Acad Award Nom
Marg	Helgenberger	Performing Arts	USA	Actress
Margaret	Atwood	Creative Works	Canada	Author
	Avery	Performing Arts	USA	Actress - Acad Award Nom
	Bourke-White	Works of Art	USA	Photographer
	Clapp	Creative Works	USA	Author - Pulitzer
	Drabble	Creative Works	England	Novelist
	Dumont	Performing Arts	USA	Actress
	Edson	Creative Works	USA	Dramatist - Pulitzer
	Hamilton	Performing Arts	USA	Actress
	Leech	Creative Works	USA	Author - Pulitzer
	Leighton	Performing Arts	England	Actress - Acad Award Nom
	Mead	Arts	USA	Anthropologist/Writer
	O'Brien	Performing Arts	USA	Actress - Academy Award
	Rutherford	Performing Arts	England	Actress - Academy Award
	Sanger	Science	USA	Nurse
	Smith-Court	Sports	Australia	Tennis Player - HF
	Sullavan	Performing Arts	USA	Actress - Acad Award Nom
	Taylor	Politics	USA	First Lady
	Thatcher	Politics	England	Prime Minster
	Widdemer	Creative Works	USA	Poet - Pulitzer
	Wilson	Creative Works	USA	Novelist - Pulitzer
	Wycherly	Performing Arts	England	Actress - Acad Award Nom
Margaret Evelyn Osborne du	Pont	Sports	USA	Tennis Player - HF
Margaret Jane	Pauley	Creative Works	USA	Journalist - Television
Margaret Louise	Coit	Creative Works	USA	Author - Pulitzer
Margaret Marian	McPartland (Turner)	Performing Arts	England	Jazz Pianist - Big Band/Jazz - HF
Margaret Munnerlyn	Mitchell	Creative Works	USA	Author - Pulitzer
Margaret Rhea	Seddon	Aviation	USA	Astronaut
Margaret Rumer	Godden	Creative Works	England	Novelist
Margaret Smith	Court	Sports	Australia	Tennis Player
Margaux	Hemingway	Performing Arts	USA	Actress
Marge	Champion	Performing Arts	USA	Actress/Dancer
	Piercy	Creative Works	USA	Poet
Margot	Fonteyn	Performing Arts	England	Dancer - Ballerina
	Kidder	Performing Arts	Canada	Actress
Maria	Charo	Performing Arts	Spain	Singer
	Edgeworth	Creative Works	England	Novelist
	Goeppert-Mayer	Science	USA	Physics - Nobel Laureate
	Mitchell	Science	USA	Astronomer
	Montessori	Arts	Italy	Educator
	Ouspenskaya	Performing Arts	Russia	Actress - Acad Award Nom
	Schell	Performing Arts	Austria	Actress
	Shriver	Creative Works	USA	Journalist - Television
Maria Conchita	Alonso	Performing Arts	Cuba	Actress

FIRST NAME	LAST NAME	CATEGORY	COUNTRY	FAME
Maria Esther Andion	Bueno	Sports	Brazil	Tennis Player - HF
Maria Meneghini	Callas	Performing Arts	Germany	Singer - Opera
Mariah	Carey	Performing Arts	USA	Singer
Marian	Anderson	Performing Arts	USA	Singer
	Mercer	Performing Arts	USA	Actress
Marian Lee (Mickey)	Thompson	Sports	USA	Race Car Driver - HF
Marianne	Faithful	Performing Arts	England	Singer
	Jean-Baptiste	Performing Arts	England	Actress - Acad Award Nom
Marianne Craig	Moore	Creative Works	USA	Poet - Pulitzer
Marie	Curie	Science	France	Chemistry - Nobel Laureate
	Curie	Science	France	Physics - Nobel Laureate
	Dressler	Performing Arts	Canada	Actress - Academy Award
	Osmond	Performing Arts	USA	Singer
	Wagner	Sports	USA	Tennis Player - HF
	Wilson	Performing Arts	USA	Actress
Marie Anne Charlotte	Corday	Politics	France	Girondist
Marie de Rabutin-Chantal	Sévigné	Creative Works	France	Writer
Marie Edmé Maurice de	MacMahon	Politics	France	President
Marie Francois Sadi	Carnot	Politics	France	President
Marie Gresholtz	Tussaud	Works of Art	Switzerland	Waxworks Exhibitor
Marie Henri	Beyle	Creative Works	France	Novelist/Essayist
	Stendhal	Creative Works	France	Novelist/Essayist
Marie-Christine	Barrault	Performing Arts	France	Actress - Acad Award Nom
Mariel	Hemingway	Performing Arts	USA	Actress - Acad Award Nom
Mariette	Hartley	Performing Arts	USA	Actress
Marilu	Henner	Performing Arts	USA	Actress
Marilyn	French	Creative Works	USA	Author
	Horne	Performing Arts	USA	Singer
	Monroe	Performing Arts	USA	Actress
Marilynne	Robinson	Creative Works	USA	Novelist - Pulitzer
Marina	Sirtis	Performing Arts	England	Actress
Mario	Andretti	Sports	Italy	Race Car Driver - HF
	Asnago	Architecture	Italy	Architect
	Botta	Architecture	Switzerland	Architect
	Chiattone	Architecture	Switzerland	Architect/Painter
	Cuomo	Politics	USA	Governor - New York
	Lanza	Performing Arts	USA	Singer
	Lemieux	Sports	Canada	Hockey Player - HF
	Puzo	Creative Works	USA	Author
	Ridolfi	Architecture	Italy	Architect
Mario J.	Molina	Science	USA	Chemistry - Nobel Laureate
Mario Van	Peebles	Performing Arts	Mexico	Actor
Marion	Motley	Sports	USA	Football Player - HF
	Ross	Performing Arts	USA	Actress
Marion Anthony (Tony)	Trabert	Sports	USA	Tennis Player - HF
Marisa	Pavan	Performing Arts	Italy	Actress - Acad Award Nom
	Tomei	Performing Arts	USA	Actress - Academy Award
Marjorie	Main	Performing Arts	USA	Actress - Acad Award Nom
	Rambeau	Performing Arts	USA	Actress - Acad Award Nom
Marjorie Kinnan	Rawlings	Creative Works	USA	Novelist - Pulitzer
Mark	Calcavecchia	Sports	USA	Golfer
	Carrier	Sports	USA	Football Player
	Clayton	Sports	USA	Football Player
	Donohue	Sports	USA	Race Car Driver - HF
	Duper	Sports	USA	Football Player
	Gastineau	Sports	USA	Football Player
	Hamill	Performing Arts	USA	Actor
	Harmon	Performing Arts	USA	Actor
	Hopkins	Arts	USA	Educator
	Knopfler	Performing Arts	Scotland	Singer
	Lemon	Business	USA	Publishing
	Linn-Baker	Performing Arts	USA	Actor
	McGwire	Sports	USA	Baseball Player

SOLVER SERIES: NAME FINDER

FIRST NAME	LAST NAME	CATEGORY	COUNTRY	FAME
Mark	Messier	Sports	Canada	Hockey Player
	O'Meara	Sports	USA	Golfer
	Robson	Movie Production	Canada	Director - Acad Award Nom
	Rothko	Works of Art	Latvia	Painter - Abstract Expressionist
	Russell	Performing Arts	USA	Comedian/Pianist
	Rydell	Movie Production	USA	Director - Acad Award Nom
	Rypien	Sports	USA	Football Player
	Spitz	Sports	USA	Olympic Swimmer
	Stevens	Creative Works	USA	Author - Pulitzer
	Strand	Creative Works	Canada	Poet - Pulitzer
	Tobey	Works of Art	USA	Painter
	Twain	Creative Works	USA	Author/Journalist
Mark (Marky)	Ramone (Bell)	Performing Arts	USA	Rock & Roll - HF - The Ramones
Mark Albert Van	Doren	Creative Works	USA	Poet - Pulitzer
Mark Antony DeWolfe	Howe	Creative Works	USA	Author - Pulitzer
Mark Charles	Lee	Aviation	USA	Astronaut
Mark E.	Neely Jr.	Creative Works	USA	Author - Pulitzer
Mark Joel	Herdon	Performing Arts	USA	Country Music - HF - Alabama
Mark Levon	Helm	Performing Arts	USA	Rock & Roll - HF - The Band
Mark Neil	Brown	Aviation	USA	Astronaut
Markie	Post	Performing Arts	USA	Actress
Markus Cook (Marc)	Connelly	Creative Works	USA	Dramatist - Pulitzer
Marla	Gibbs	Performing Arts	USA	Actress
Marlee	Matlin	Performing Arts	USA	Actress - Academy Award
Marlene	Dietrich	Performing Arts	Germany	Actress - Acad Award Nom
Marlene Bauer	Hagge	Sports	USA	Golfer - HF
Marlene Stewart	Streit	Sports	Canada	Golfer - HF
Marlo	Thomas	Performing Arts	USA	Actress
Marlon	Brando	Performing Arts	USA	Actor - Academy Award
	Jackson	Performing Arts	USA	Rock & Roll - HF - The Jackson Five
Marques	Haynes	Sports	USA	Basketball Player - HF
Marquis	James	Creative Works	USA	Author - Pulitzer
Marsha	Mason	Performing Arts	USA	Actress - Acad Award Nom
	Norman	Creative Works	USA	Dramatist - Pulitzer
Martha	Graham	Performing Arts	USA	Dancer
	Grimes	Creative Works	USA	Author
	Hyer	Performing Arts	USA	Actress - Acad Award Nom
	Reeves	Performing Arts	USA	Rock & Roll - HF - Martha & The Vandellas
	Tilton	Performing Arts	USA	Singer - Big Band/Jazz - HF
	Scott	Performing Arts	USA	Actress - Acad Award Nom
Martha (Calamity) Jane	Canarray	Law & Order	USA	Hunter
Martha Dandridge	Washington	Politics	USA	First Lady
Martha Wayles	Jefferson	Politics	USA	First Lady
Martin	Amis	Creative Works	England	Novelist
	Balsam	Performing Arts	USA	Actor - Academy Award
	Behaim	Exploration	Portugal	Explorer - West Africa
	Brest	Movie Production	USA	Director - Acad Award Nom
	Buber	Arts	Israel	Philosopher/Theologian
	Chambers	Performing Arts	England	Rock & Roll - HF - The Pretenders
	Flavin	Creative Works	USA	Novelist - Pulitzer
	Frobisher	Exploration	England	Explorer - North West Passage
	Heidegger	Arts	Germany	Philosopher/Existentialist
	Knudsen	Science	Denmark	Chemist
	Landau	Performing Arts	USA	Actor - Academy Award
	Lawrence	Performing Arts	Germany	Comedian
	Luther	Arts	Germany	Theologian
	Milner	Performing Arts	USA	Actor
	Mull	Performing Arts	USA	Comedian
	Rodbell	Science	USA	Medicine - Nobel Laureate
	Ryle	Science	England	Physics - Nobel Laureate
	Scorsese	Movie Production	USA	Director - Acad Award Nom
	Sheen	Performing Arts	USA	Actor
	Short	Performing Arts	Canada	Comedian

FIRST NAME	LAST NAME	CATEGORY	COUNTRY	FAME
Martin	Ritt	Movie Production	USA	Director - Acad Award Nom
Martin (Marty)	Walsh	Sports	Canada	Hockey Player - HF
Martin A. (Marty)	Barry	Sports	Canada	Hockey Player - HF
Martin Alonso	Pinzón	Exploration	Spain	Explorer - Caribbean
Martin Andersen	Nexo	Creative Works	Denmark	Novelist
Martin Brian	Mulroney	Politics	Canada	Prime Minister
Martin David (Marty)	Robbins(Robinson)	Performing Arts	USA	Singer - Country Music - HF
Martin Joseph	Fettman	Aviation	USA	Astronaut
Martin L.	Perl	Science	USA	Physics - Nobel Laureate
Martin Luther	King Jr.	Politics	USA	Clergyman
	King Jr.	War & Peace	USA	Peace - Nobel Laureate
Martín Magdaleno	Dihigo	Sports	Cuba	Baseball Player - HF
Martin Van	Buren	Politics	USA	President
Martina	Arroyo	Performing Arts	USA	Singer - Opera
	Klein	Performing Arts	Argentina	Super Model
	Navrátilová	Sports	Czechoslovakia	Tennis Player - HF
Martina (Tina)	Weymoiuth	Performing Arts	USA	Rock & Roll - HF - Talking Heads
Martinus J.G.	Veltman	Science	Netherlands	Physics - Nobel Laureate
Marty	Feldman	Performing Arts	England	Comedian
Marty (Martyn)	Balin (Buckwald)	Performing Arts	USA	Rock & Roll - HF - Jefferson Airplane
Marv Philip	Albert	Creative Works	USA	Journalist - Television
Marvin	Hagler	Sports	USA	Boxer - HF
	Hamlisch	Creative Works	USA	Composer
	Isley	Performing Arts	USA	Rock & Roll - HF - Isley Brothers
	Junior	Performing Arts	USA	Rock & Roll - HF - The Dells
Marvin Daniel (Marv)	Levy	Sports	USA	Football Coach - HF
Marvin Pentz	Gaye Jr.	Performing Arts	USA	Singer - Rock & Roll - HF
Mary	Astor	Performing Arts	USA	Actress - Academy Award
	Badham	Performing Arts	USA	Actress - Acad Award Nom
	Cassatt	Works of Art	USA	Painter
	Chase	Creative Works	USA	Dramatist - Pulitzer
	Frann	Performing Arts	USA	Actress
	Gross	Performing Arts	USA	Comedian
	Lincoln	Politics	USA	First Lady
	Lyon	Arts	USA	Educator
	Martin	Performing Arts	USA	Actress
	McAleese	Politics	Ireland	President
	McCarthy	Creative Works	USA	Novelist
	McDonnell	Performing Arts	USA	Actress - Acad Award Nom
	Oliver	Creative Works	USA	Poet - Pulitzer
	Pickford	Performing Arts	Canada	Actress - Academy Award
	Robinson	Politics	Ireland	President
	Steenburgen	Performing Arts	USA	Actress - Academy Award
	Travers	Performing Arts	USA	Singer - Folk
	Ure	Performing Arts	Scotland	Actress - Acad Award Nom
	Wells	Creative Works	USA	Author - Pulitzer
	Wells	Performing Arts	USA	Singer - Motown
	Wilson	Performing Arts	USA	Rock & Roll - HF - The Supremes
	Wollstonecraft	Creative Works	England	Writer
Mary Ann	Evans	Performing Arts	USA	Actress
	Lamb	Creative Works	England	Writer
Mary Augusta Arnold	Ward	Creative Works	England	Novelist
Mary Baker	Eddy	Arts	USA	Founder - Christian Science
Mary Beth	Hurt	Performing Arts	USA	Actress
Mary Elizabeth	Mastrantonio	Performing Arts	USA	Actress - Acad Award Nom
Mary Elizabeth (Tipper)	Gore	Politics	USA	Second Lady
Mary Ellen	Weber	Aviation	USA	Astronaut
Mary Ewing (Mother of Tennis)	Outerbridge	Sports	USA	Tennis Player - HF
Mary Flannery	O'Connor	Creative Works	USA	Author
Mary Henrietta	Kingsley	Exploration	England	Explorer - Africa West/North
Mary Higgins	Clark	Creative Works	USA	Novelist
Mary Isobel (Dusty)	Springfield (O'Brien)	Performing Arts	England	Singer - Rock & Roll - HF
Mary Jane (Mae)	West	Performing Arts	USA	Actress

SOLVER SERIES: NAME FINDER

FIRST NAME	LAST NAME	CATEGORY	COUNTRY	FAME
Mary Joe	Fernandez	Sports	USA	Tennis Player
Mary Kathryn (Mickey)	Wright	Sports	USA	Golfer - HF
Mary Kendall	Browne	Sports	USA	Tennis Player - HF
Mary Leontyne	Price	Performing Arts	USA	Singer - Opera
Mary Lou	Retton	Sports	USA	Olympic Gymnast
	Williams	Performing Arts	USA	Jazz Pianist/Composer - Big Band/Jazz - HF
Mary Roberts	Rinehart	Creative Works	USA	Playwright/Writer - Mysteries
Mary Scott Lord	Harrison	Politics	USA	First Lady
Mary Stuart	Masterson	Performing Arts	USA	Actress
Mary Tyler	Moore	Performing Arts	USA	Actress - Acad Award Nom
Mary Wollstonecraft	Shelley	Creative Works	England	Novelist
Mary Wortley	Montagu	Creative Works	England	Writer
Marya	Zaturenska	Creative Works	Russia	Poet - Pulitzer
Masahiko (Fighting)	Harada	Sports	Japan	Boxer - HF
Masatoshi	Koshiba	Science	Japan	Physics - Nobel Laureate
Mason	Adams	Performing Arts	USA	Actor
	Williams	Performing Arts	USA	Guitarist/Classical
Mason Locke	Weems	Creative Works	USA	Writer/Clergyman
Massimiliano	Fuksas	Architecture	Italy	Architect
Massimo	Troisi	Performing Arts	Italy	Actor - Acad Award Nom
Mateo	Alemán	Creative Works	Spain	Novelist
Matha	Raye	Performing Arts	USA	Comedian
Mathis James (Jimmy)	Reed	Performing Arts	USA	Singer - Rock & Roll - HF
Mats	Wilander	Sports	Sweden	Tennis Player - HF
Matt	Bahr	Sports	USA	Football Player
	Biondi	Sports	USA	Olympic Swimmer
	Damon	Performing Arts	USA	Actor - Acad Award Nom
	Dillon	Performing Arts	USA	Actor
	Groening	Creative Works	USA	Cartoonist - The Simpsons
	Williams	Sports	USA	Baseball Player
Matt Le	Blanc	Performing Arts	USA	Actor
Matteo Maria	Boiardo	Creative Works	Italy	Poet
Matthew	Arnold	Creative Works	England	Poet/Essayist
	Broderick	Performing Arts	USA	Actor
	Flinders	Exploration	England	Explorer - Australia
	Modine	Performing Arts	USA	Actor
	Perry	War & Peace	USA	Naval Officer
	Prior	Creative Works	England	Poet
Matthew Alexander	Henson	Exploration	USA	Explorer - Arctic
Matthew B.	Brady	Works of Art	USA	Photographer
Matthew Saad	Mohammad	Sports	USA	Boxer - HF
Matthias	Grünewald	Works of Art	Germany	Painter
Matty	Alou	Sports	USA	Baseball Player
Maud	Barger-Wallach	Sports	USA	Tennis Player - HF
Maude	Adams	Performing Arts	Sweden	Actress
Maude Howe	Elliott	Creative Works	USA	Author - Pulitzer
Maureen	Forrester	Performing Arts	Canada	Singer - Opera - Canadian Music - HF
	McGovern	Performing Arts	USA	Singer
	O'Hara	Performing Arts	Ireland	Actress
	O'Sullivan	Performing Arts	Ireland	Actress
	Stapleton	Performing Arts	USA	Actress - Academy Award
Maureen Catherine (Little Mo)	Connolly	Sports	USA	Tennis Player - HF
Mauri	Rose	Sports	USA	Race Car Driver - HF
Maurice	Allais	Arts	France	Economics - Nobel Laureate
	Barrymore	Performing Arts	USA	Actor
	Béjart	Creative Works	France	Composer
	Chevalier	Performing Arts	France	Actor - Acad Award Nom
	Gibb	Performing Arts	England	Rock & Roll - HF - The Bee Gees
	Sendak	Creative Works	USA	Author/Artist - Children's Books
	Stokes	Sports	USA	Basketball Player - HF
	Utrillo	Works of Art	France	Painter
Maurice de	Vlaminck	Works of Art	France	Painter
Maurice Evans (Red)	McLoughlin	Sports	USA	Tennis Player - HF

FIRST NAME	LAST NAME	CATEGORY	COUNTRY	FAME
Maurice Hugh Frederick	Wilkins	Science	England	Medicine - Nobel Laureate
Maurice Joseph	Ravel	Creative Works	France	Composer
Maurice Joseph (Joe)	Malone	Sports	Canada	Hockey Player - HF
Maurice Polidore Bernhard	Maeterlinck	Creative Works	Belgium	Literature - Nobel Laureate
Maurits Cornelis	Escher	Works of Art	Netherlands	Illustrator
Maurizio	Cheli	Aviation	Italy	Astronaut
Maurus	Jókai	Creative Works	Hungary	Novelist
Mavis	Staples	Performing Arts	USA	Rock & Roll - HF - The Staple Singers
Max	Abramovitz	Architecture	USA	Architect
	Baer	Sports	USA	Boxer - HF
	Beckmann	Works of Art	Germany	Painter - Expressionist
	Beerbohm	Creative Works	England	Essayist/Novelist
	Born	Science	Germany	Physics - Nobel Laureate
	Bruch	Creative Works	Germany	Composer
	Delbrück	Science	USA	Medicine - Nobel Laureate
	Ernst	Works of Art	Germany	Painter - Surrealist
	Euwe	Games	Netherlands	Chess Player
	Gail	Performing Arts	USA	Actor
	Horkheimer	Arts	Germany	Philosopher
	Rasser	Architecture	Germany	Architect
	Roach	Performing Arts	USA	Jazz Drummer - Big Band/Jazz - HF
	Schmeling	Sports	Germany	Boxer - HF
	Theiler	Science	South Africa	Medicine - Nobel Laureate
	Weber	Arts	Germany	Sociologist/Political Economist
	Wright	Performing Arts	USA	Actor
Max (Marty)	Friedman	Sports	USA	Basketball Player - HF
Max Ferdinand	Perutz	Science	England	Chemistry - Nobel Laureate
Max George	Carey	Sports	USA	Baseball Player - HF
Max Karl Ernst Ludwig	Planck	Science	Germany	Physicist - Nobel Prize
Max Simon	Nordau	Science	Germany	Physician/Writer
Max von	Laue	Science	Germany	Physics - Nobel Laureate
	Sydow	Performing Arts	Sweden	Actor - Acad Award Nom
Maxene	Andrews	Performing Arts	USA	Singer
Maxey	Rosenbloom	Sports	USA	Boxer - HF
Maxfield	Parrish	Works of Art	USA	Painter/Illustrator
Maxim	Gorki	Creative Works	Russia	Novelist/Playwright
Maximilan	Spee	War & Peace	Germany	Admiral
Maximilian	Schell	Performing Arts	Austria	Actor - Academy Award
Maximilien de Béthune	Sully	Politics	France	Statesman
Maximovitch	Litvinov	Politics	Russia	Statesman
Maxine	Kumin	Creative Works	USA	Poet - Pulitzer
Maxmilien	Robespierre	War & Peace	France	Revolutionist
Maxwell	Anderson	Creative Works	USA	Dramatist - Pulitzer
	Bodenheim	Creative Works	USA	Poet/Novelist
Maxwell Herbert Lloyd	Bentley	Sports	Canada	Hockey Player - HF
Maxwell William	Ward	Business	Canada	Aviation Industry
May	Robson	Performing Arts	Australia	Actress - Acad Award Nom
	Whitty	Performing Arts	England	Actress - Acad Award Nom
May Godfray	Sutton-Bundy	Sports	USA	Tennis Player - HF
Maya	Angelou	Creative Works	USA	Poet/Historian
	Lin	Architecture	Thailand	Architect
Maybelle Addington	Carter	Performing Arts	USA	Country Music - HF - Carter Family
Maynarad	Ferguson	Performing Arts	Canada	Jazz Trumpeter - Canadian Music - HF
McKinley (Muddy)	Waters (Morganfield)	Performing Arts	USA	Singer - Rock & Roll - HF
McLean	Stevenson	Performing Arts	USA	Actor
Meade Anderson (Lux)	Lewis	Performing Arts	USA	Pianist/Composer - Big Band/Jazz - HF
Meg	Mallon	Sports	USA	Golfer
	Ryan	Performing Arts	USA	Actress
	Tilly	Performing Arts	Canada	Actress - Acad Award Nom
Megan	Follows	Performing Arts	Canada	Actress
	Gallagher	Performing Arts	USA	Actress
Meindert	Hobbema	Works of Art	Netherlands	Painter
Meinhard von	Gerkan	Architecture	Germany	Architect

SOLVER SERIES: NAME FINDER

FIRST NAME	LAST NAME	CATEGORY	COUNTRY	FAME
Mel	Allen	Creative Works	USA	Journalist - Television
	Blanc	Performing Arts	USA	Comedian
	Brooks	Movie Production	USA	Director
	Brooks	Performing Arts	USA	Actor
	Ferrer	Performing Arts	USA	Actor
	Gibson	Movie Production	USA	Director - Academy Award
	Gibson	Performing Arts	USA	Actor
	Kenyon	Sports	USA	Race Car Driver - HF
	Stottlemyre	Sports	USA	Baseball Player
	Tillis	Performing Arts	USA	Singer - Country & Western
Melanie	Griffith	Performing Arts	USA	Actress - Acad Award Nom
	Mayron	Performing Arts	USA	Actress
Melba	Moore	Performing Arts	USA	Singer
Melina	Mercouri	Performing Arts	Greece	Actress - Acad Award Nom
Melinda	Dillon	Performing Arts	USA	Actress - Acad Award Nom
Melissa	Gilbert	Performing Arts	USA	Actress
	Manchester	Performing Arts	USA	Singer
Melville	Dewey	Arts	USA	Educator/Librarian
Melville Weston	Fuller	Law & Order	USA	Justice - Supreme Court
Melvin	Calvin	Science	USA	Chemistry - Nobel Laureate
	Schwartz	Science	USA	Physics - Nobel Laureate
Melvin (Donald Melvin)	Franklin (English)	Performing Arts	USA	Rock & Roll - HF - The Temptations
Melvin (Mel)	Powell (Epstein)	Performing Arts	USA	Jazz Pianist - Big Band/Jazz - HF
Melvin (Sy)	Oliver	Performing Arts	USA	Arranger - Big Band/Jazz - HF
Melvin (Tony)	Bettenhausen	Sports	USA	Race Car Driver - HF
Melvin Cornell (Mel)	Blount	Sports	USA	Football Player - HF
Melvin Howard (Mel)	Torme	Performing Arts	USA	Singer - Big Band/Jazz - HF
Melvin Jack (Mel)	Hein	Sports	USA	Football Player - HF
Melvin Lacy (Mel)	Renfro	Sports	USA	Football Player - HF
Melvin Thomas (Mel)	Ott	Sports	USA	Baseball Player - HF
Melvyn	Douglas	Performing Arts	USA	Actor - Academy Award
Menachem	Begin	Politics	Israel	Prime Minister
	Begin	War & Peace	Israel	Peace - Nobel Laureate
Merce	Cunningham	Creative Works	USA	Choreographer
Mercedes	McCambridge	Performing Arts	USA	Actress - Academy Award
	Ruehl	Performing Arts	USA	Actress - Academy Award
Meridith	Baxter	Performing Arts	USA	Actress
Meriwether	Lewis	Exploration	USA	Explorer - Missouri River
Merle	Oberon	Performing Arts	India	Actress - Acad Award Nom
Merle E.	Curti	Creative Works	USA	Author - Pulitzer
Merle Robert	Travis	Performing Arts	USA	Singer - Country Music - HF
Merle Ronald	Haggard	Performing Arts	USA	Singer - Country Music - HF
Merlin Jay	Olsen	Sports	USA	Football Player - HF
Merlo J.	Pusey	Creative Works	USA	Author - Pulitzer
Merrill	Osmond	Performing Arts	USA	Singer
Merton H.	Miller	Arts	USA	Economics - Nobel Laureate
Merv	Griffin	Performing Arts	USA	Show Host/Singer
Mervyn	Leroy	Movie Production	USA	Director - Acad Award Nom
	Rose	Sports	Australia	Tennis Player - HF
Mervyn (Red)	Dutton	Sports	Canada	Hockey Player - HF
Meryl	Streep	Performing Arts	USA	Actress - Academy Award
Meyer (The Brain)	Lansky	Law & Order	Russia	Mafia
Meyer Anselm	Rothschild	Business	Germany	Founder - Bank
Mia	Farrow	Performing Arts	USA	Actress
	Hamm	Sports	USA	Soccer
	Sara	Performing Arts	USA	Actress
Michael	Anderson	Movie Production	England	Director - Acad Award Nom
	Ansara	Performing Arts	Syria	Actor
	Bass	Business	England	Retail Trade
	Bonallack	Sports	England	Golfer - HF
	Cacoyannis	Movie Production	Cyprus	Director - Acad Award Nom
	Caine	Performing Arts	England	Actor - Academy Award
	Chabon	Creative Works	USA	Author - Pulitzer

FIRST NAME	LAST NAME	CATEGORY	COUNTRY	FAME
Michael	Chang	Sports	USA	Tennis Player
	Chekhov	Performing Arts	Russia	Actor - Acad Award Nom
	Cimino	Movie Production	USA	Director - Academy Award
	Collins	Aviation	USA	Astronaut
	Collins	War & Peace	Ireland	Revolutionary Leader
	Crawford	Performing Arts	England	Actor
	Crichton	Creative Works	USA	Author
	Cristofer	Creative Works	USA	Dramatist - Pulitzer
	Cudahy	Business	USA	Livestock
	Cunningham	Creative Works	USA	Novelist - Pulitzer
	Curtiz	Movie Production	Hungary	Director - Academy Award
	Dorn	Performing Arts	USA	Actor
	Douglas	Performing Arts	USA	Actor - Academy Award
	Drayton	Creative Works	England	Poet
	Dunn	Performing Arts	USA	Actor - Acad Award Nom
	Faraday	Science	England	Scientist - Electricity
	Graves	Architecture	USA	Architect - AIA Gold Medal
	Gross	Performing Arts	USA	Actor
	Hopkins	Architecture	England	Architect
	Jackson	Performing Arts	USA	Rock & Roll - HF - The Jackson Five
	Jackson	Performing Arts	USA	Singer - Rock & Roll - HF
	Jordan	Sports	USA	Basketball Player
	Kammen	Creative Works	USA	Author - Pulitzer
	Keaton	Performing Arts	USA	Actor
	Landon	Performing Arts	USA	Actor
	Learned	Performing Arts	USA	Actress
	Lerner	Performing Arts	USA	Actor - Acad Award Nom
	Mann	Movie Production	USA	Director - Acad Award Nom
	Marks	Business	England	Retail Trade
	McDonald	Performing Arts	USA	Singer
	McGill	Performing Arts	USA	Rock & Roll - HF - The Dells
	McKean	Performing Arts	USA	Actor
	Moriarty	Performing Arts	USA	Actor
	Nader	Performing Arts	USA	Actor
	Nesmith	Creative Works	USA	Song Writer
	O'Keefe	Performing Arts	USA	Actor - Acad Award Nom
	Ontkean	Performing Arts	Canada	Actor
	Palin	Performing Arts	England	Comedian
	Radford	Movie Production	India	Director - Acad Award Nom
	Redgrave	Performing Arts	England	Actor - Acad Award Nom
	Rennie	Performing Arts	England	Actor
	Richards	Performing Arts	USA	Actor
	Schumacher	Sports	Germany	Race Car Driver - HF
	Servetus	Science	Spain	Physician/Theologian
	Shaara	Creative Works	USA	Novelist - Pulitzer
	Smith	Science	Canada	Chemistry - Nobel Laureate
	Spence	Arts	USA	Economics - Nobel Laureate
	Spinks	Sports	USA	Boxer - HF
	Stipes	Performing Arts	USA	Singer/Composer
	Todd	Performing Arts	USA	Actor
	Tucker	Performing Arts	USA	Actor
	Wilding	Performing Arts	England	Actor
	Williamson	Creative Works	USA	Author - Pulitzer
	Windischmann	Sports	Germany	Soccer Player - HF
	York	Performing Arts	England	Actor
	Grady Jr.	Performing Arts	USA	Rock & Roll - HF - The Soul Stirrers
Michael (Mick)	Jones	Performing Arts	England	Rock & Roll - HF - The Clash
Michael (Mike)	Bossy	Sports	Canada	Hockey Player - HF
	Clarke	Performing Arts	USA	Rock & Roll - HF - The Bryds
	Grant	Sports	Canada	Hockey Player - HF
	Singletary	Sports	USA	Football Player
Michael Alfred	Gartner	Sports	Canada	Hockey Player - HF
Michael Anthony	Muñoz	Sports	USA	Football Player - HF

SOLVER SERIES: NAME FINDER

FIRST NAME	LAST NAME	CATEGORY	COUNTRY	FAME
Michael Anthony (Mike)	Munchak	Sports	USA	Football Player - HF
Michael C.	Mahon	Performing Arts	USA	Actor
Michael Clarke	Duncan	Performing Arts	USA	Actor - Acad Award Nom
Michael Dammann	Eisner	Business	USA	Disney Film Head
Michael Francis (Mickey)	Welch	Sports	USA	Baseball Player - HF
Michael Gordon (Mike)	Oldfield	Performing Arts	England	Musician/Composer
Michael Idvorsky	Pupin	Creative Works	USA	Author - Pulitzer
	Pupin	Science	USA	Physicist/Inventor
Michael Ivanovich	Rostovtzeff	Arts	USA	Historian
Michael J.	Fox	Performing Arts	Canada	Actor
	Pollard	Performing Arts	USA	Actor - Acad Award Nom
Michael Jack (Mike)	Schmidt	Sports	USA	Baseball Player - HF
Michael James	McCulley	Aviation	USA	Astronaut
	McDonald	Performing Arts	USA	Comedian
Michael James (Mike)	Haynes	Sports	USA	Football Player - HF
Michael John	Smith	Aviation	USA	Astronaut
Michael John (Mike)	Fleetwood	Performing Arts	England	Rock & Roll - HF - Fleetwood Mac
	Rutherford	Performing Arts	England	Singer/Guitarist
Michael Joseph (King)	Kelly	Sports	USA	Baseball Player - HF
Michael Joseph (Mike)	McCormack Jr.	Sports	USA	Football Player - HF
Michael Keller (Mike)	Ditka	Sports	USA	Football Player - HF
Michael Lewis (Mike)	Webster	Sports	USA	Football Player - HF
Michael Lloyd	Coats	Aviation	USA	Astronaut
Michael McKenzie (Mike)	McCallum	Sports	Jamaica	Boxer - HF
Michael Phillip	Anderson	Aviation	USA	Astronaut
Michael Phillip (Mick)	Jagger	Performing Arts	England	Rock & Roll - HF - Rolling Stones
Michael Richard Uram	Clifford	Aviation	USA	Astronaut
Michael S.	Brown	Science	USA	Medicine - Nobel Laureate
Michael Stanley	Dukakis	Politics	USA	Governor - Massachusetts
Michael V.	Gazzo	Performing Arts	USA	Actor - Acad Award Nom
Michael Webb	Pierce	Performing Arts	USA	Singer - Country Music - HF
Michael William	Balfe	Creative Works	England	Composer/Opera
Michaelangelo	Antonioni	Movie Production	Italy	Director - Acad Award Nom
Michaelangelo Amerighi da	Caravaggio	Works of Art	Italy	Painter
Michel	Fokine	Creative Works	USA	Choreographer
	Foucault	Arts	France	Philosopher
	Goulet	Sports	Canada	Hockey Player - HF
	Legrand	Performing Arts	France	Jazz Pianist
	Ney	War & Peace	France	Military Leader
	Platini	Sports	France	Soccer Player - HF
	Tognini	Aviation	France	Astronaut
Michel de	Klerk	Architecture	Netherlands	Architect
Michel de l'	Epee	Creative Works	France	Writer - Sign Language
Michel Eyquem de	Montaigne	Arts	France	Philosopher/Writer
Michel Guillaume Jean de	Crèvecoeur	Creative Works	France	Essayist
Michelangelo	Buonarroti	Works of Art	Italy	Sculptor/Painter/Poet/Architect
Michele	Greene	Performing Arts	USA	Actress
	Lee	Performing Arts	USA	Actress
Michelle	Akers	Sports	USA	Soccer Player - HF
	Behennah	Performing Arts	Singapore	Super Model
	Pfeiffer	Performing Arts	USA	Actress - Acad Award Nom
Michelozzo di Bartolomeo	Michelozzi	Architecture	Italy	Architect
Michiel Adriaanszoon de	Ruysdael	War & Peace	Netherlands	Admiral
Mick	Avory	Performing Arts	England	Rock & Roll - HF - The Kinks
	Fleetwood	Performing Arts	England	Band Leader/Drummer
Mickey	Gilley	Performing Arts	USA	Singer
	Hart	Performing Arts	USA	Rock & Roll - HF - Grateful Dead
	Rooney	Performing Arts	USA	Actor - Academy Award
	Rourke	Performing Arts	USA	Actor
Mickey Charles	Mantle	Sports	USA	Baseball Player - HF
Micki	Harris	Performing Arts	USA	Rock & Roll - HF - The Shirelles
Miguel	Alemán	Politics	Mexico	President
	Canto	Sports	USA	Boxer - HF

FIRST NAME	LAST NAME	CATEGORY	COUNTRY	FAME
Miguel Angel	Asturias	Creative Works	Guatemala	Literature - Nobel Laureate
Miguel de	Cervantes	Creative Works	Spain	Poet/Novelist/Playwright
	Unamuno	Arts	Spain	Philosopher/Writer
Mihály	Károlyi	Politics	Hungary	President
Mike	Arturi	Performing Arts	USA	Rock & Roll - HF - Lovin' Spoonful
	Bookie	Sports	USA	Soccer Player - HF
	Campbell	Performing Arts	USA	Rock & Roll - HF - Heart Breakers
	Connors	Performing Arts	USA	Actor
	Douglas	Performing Arts	Canada	Canadian Music - HF - The Diamonds
	Farrell	Performing Arts	USA	Actor
	Figgis	Movie Production	England	Director - Acad Award Nom
	Hill	Sports	USA	Golfer
	Hulbert	Sports	USA	Golfer
	Kinsley	Creative Works	USA	Journalist - Newspaper
	Leigh	Movie Production	England	Director - Acad Award Nom
	Myers	Performing Arts	Canada	Comedian
	Nichols	Movie Production	Germany	Director - Academy Award
	Post	Creative Works	USA	Composer
	Tyson	Sports	USA	Boxer
Mike (The Bike)	Hailwood	Sports	England	Race Car Driver - HF
Mikhail	Baryshnikov	Performing Arts	Latvia	Actor - Acad Award Nom
	Baryshnikov	Performing Arts	Latvia	Dancer
	Botvinnik	Games	Russia	Chess Player
Mikhail Aleksandrovich	Bakunin	Politics	Russia	Philosopher/Anarchist
	Sholokhov	Creative Works	Russia	Literature - Nobel Laureate
Mikhail Feodorovich	Romanov	Politics	Russia	Czar
Mikhail Ilarionovich	Kutuzov	War & Peace	Russia	Field Marshall
Mikhail Ivanovich	Glinka	Creative Works	Russia	Composer
Mikhail Nekhemievich	Tal	Games	Latvia	Chess Player
Mikhail Sergeyevich	Gorbachev	Politics	Russia	Head of State
	Gorbachev	War & Peace	Russia	Peace - Nobel Laureate
Mikhail Yurievich	Lermontov	Creative Works	Russia	Poet/Novelist
Milan	Kundera	Creative Works	Czechoslovakia	Author
Milburn	Stone	Performing Arts	USA	Actor
Mildred	Bailer	Performing Arts	USA	Singer - Big Band/Jazz - HF
	Dunnock	Performing Arts	USA	Actress - Acad Award Nom
	Natwick	Performing Arts	USA	Actress - Acad Award Nom
Mildred (Babe)	Didrikson	Sports	USA	Olympic Javelin/Hurdles
Mildred Didrikson (Babe)	Zaharias	Sports	USA	Golfer - HF
Miles	Standish	War & Peace	England	Military Leader - Plymouth
	Coverdale	Arts	England	Clergyman - Translator
	Davis	Performing Arts	USA	Jazz Trumpeter - Big Band/Jazz - HF
Miles Gilbert (Tim)	Horton	Sports	Canada	Hockey Player - HF
Miliza	Korjus	Performing Arts	Poland	Actress - Acad Award Nom
Milla	Jovovich	Performing Arts	Ukraine	Super Model
Millard	Fillmore	Politics	USA	President
Millard Tuttle (Millar)	Lang	Sports	USA	Soccer Player - HF
Miller James (Mighty Mite)	Huggins	Sports	USA	Baseball Manager - HF
Millie Elizabeth	Hughes-Fulford	Aviation	USA	Astronaut
Milo	O'Shea	Performing Arts	Ireland	Actor
Milos	Forman	Movie Production	Czechoslovakia	Director - Academy Award
Milton	Ager	Creative Works	USA	Composer/Pianist/Songwriter
	Berle	Performing Arts	USA	Comedian
	Caniff	Creative Works	USA	Cartoonist - Terry and the Pirates
	Friedman	Arts	USA	Economics - Nobel Laureate
Milton (Gummo)	Marx	Performing Arts	USA	Comedian
Milton (Milt)	Jackson	Performing Arts	USA	Jazz Vibraphonist - Big Band/Jazz - HF
Milton Bennett	Medary	Architecture	USA	Architect - AIA Gold Medal
Milton Conrad (Milt)	Schmidt	Sports	Canada	Hockey Player - HF
Mimar (the Great)	Sinan	Architecture	Turkey	Architect
Mimi	Rogers	Performing Arts	USA	Actress
Mini (Susanna)	Anden	Performing Arts	Sweden	Super Model
Minnie	Riperton	Performing Arts	USA	Singer

SOLVER SERIES: NAME FINDER

FIRST NAME	LAST NAME	CATEGORY	COUNTRY	FAME
Minnie	Driver	Performing Arts	England	Actress - Acad Award Nom
Minnie Jocelyn	Elders	Politics	USA	Surgeon General
Minnie Maddern	Fiske	Performing Arts	USA	Actress
Mira	Nair	Movie Production	India	Director
	Sorvino	Performing Arts	USA	Actress - Academy Award
Miranda	Richardson	Performing Arts	England	Actress - Acad Award Nom
Mircea	Eliade	Arts	USA	Theologian
Mirella	Freni	Performing Arts	Italy	Singer - Opera
Miriam	Hopkins	Performing Arts	USA	Actress - Acad Award Nom
	Makeba	Performing Arts	South Africa	Singer
Mischa	Auer	Performing Arts	Russia	Actor - Acad Award Nom
	Elman	Performing Arts	USA	Violinist
Misty	Rowe	Performing Arts	USA	Actress
Mitchell William (Mitch)	Miller	Performing Arts	USA	Choir Leader
Mitford McLeod	Mathews	Arts	USA	Lexicographer/Educator
Mitzi	Gaynor	Performing Arts	USA	Actress - Musical
Miyoshi	Umeki	Performing Arts	Japan	Actress - Academy Award
Mobutu Sese	Seko	Politics	Zaire	President
Modest Petrovich	Moussorgsky	Creative Works	Russia	Composer
	Mussorgsky	Creative Works	Russia	Composer
Moe	Berg	Sports	USA	Baseball Player/Spy
	Drabowsky	Sports	Poland	Baseball Player
	Howard	Performing Arts	USA	Comedian
Mohammed El	Baradei	War & Peace	Egypt	Peace - Nobel Laureate
Mohammed Reza	Pahlavi	Politics	Iran	Shah
Mohandas Karamchand	Gandi	Politics	India	Leader - Hindu Nationalist
Moira	Shearer	Performing Arts	Scotland	Dancer/Actress
Moisej	Ginzburg	Architecture	Russia	Architect
Molly	Ringwald	Performing Arts	USA	Actress
	Yard	Politics	USA	Activist - Feminism
Mona	Charen	Creative Works	USA	Jounalist - Newspaper
	Washburn	Performing Arts	England	Actress
Mona Jane Van	Duyn	Creative Works	USA	Poet - Pulitzer
Monford (Monte)	Irvin	Sports	USA	Baseball Player - HF
Monica	Bellucci	Performing Arts	Italy	Super Model
	Seles	Sports	Yugoslavia	Tennis Player
Montgomery	Clift	Performing Arts	USA	Actor - Acad Award Nom
Monty	Hall	Performing Arts	Canada	Show Host
	Woolley	Performing Arts	USA	Actor - Acad Award Nom
Mordecai Peter Centennial	Brown	Sports	USA	Baseball Player - HF
Morey	Amsterdam	Performing Arts	USA	Comedian
Morgan	Fairchild	Performing Arts	USA	Actress
	Freeman	Performing Arts	USA	Actor - Academy Award
Morgan Gardner	Bulkeley	Sports	USA	Baseball Executive - HF
Morley	Safer	Creative Works	Canada	Journalist - Television
Morrie	Ryskind	Creative Works	USA	Dramatist - Pulitzer
Morris (Moe)	Koffman	Performing Arts	Canada	Jazz Flutist - Canadian Music - HF
Morris Hiram (Red)	Badgro	Sports	USA	Football Player - HF
Morris Raphael	Cohen	Arts	USA	Philosopher
Morrison Remick	Waite	Law & Order	USA	Chief Justice
Mort	Drucker	Creative Works	USA	Cartoonist - Mad Magazine
	Sahl	Performing Arts	Canada	Comedian
	Walker	Creative Works	USA	Cartoonist - Beetle Bailey
Mortimer Jerome	Adler	Arts	USA	Philosopher
Moses	Malone	Sports	USA	Basketball Player - HF
	Mendelssohn	Arts	Germany	Philosopher - Jewish
	Soyer	Works of Art	USA	Painter
Moses Jacob	Ezekiel	Works of Art	USA	Sculptor
Moshe	Arens	Politics	Israel	Foreign Minister
	Dayan	War & Peace	Israel	Military Leader
	Safdie	Architecture	Israel	Architect
Moss	Hart	Creative Works	USA	Dramatist - Pulitzer
Mother	Teresa	War & Peace	India	Peace - Nobel Laureate

FIRST NAME	LAST NAME	CATEGORY	COUNTRY	FAME
Muammar Abu Minyar al	Qaddafi	Politics	Libya	Head of State
Muhammad	Abduh	Arts	Egypt	Philosopher
Muhammad (Casius Clay)	Ali	Sports	USA	Boxer - HF
Muhammad Hosni Said	Mubarak	Politics	Egypt	President
Mundell	Lowe	Performing Arts	USA	Jazz Guitarist - Big Band/Jazz - HF
Mungo	Park	Exploration	Scotland	Explorer - Africa
Murat Bernard (Chic)	Young	Creative Works	USA	Cartoonist - Blondie
Muriel Ellen (Kitty)	Wells (Deason)	Performing Arts	USA	Singer - Country Music - HF
Muriel Sarah	Spark	Creative Works	Scotland	Novelist
Murillo	Bartolomé	Works of Art	Spain	Painter
Murray	Costello	Sports	Canada	Hockey Player - HF
	Gell-Mann	Science	USA	Physics - Nobel Laureate
Murray Bert	Olmstead	Sports	Canada	Hockey Player - HF
Mustafa	Kemal	Politics	Egypt	Patriot - Revolutionary
Myer	Guggenheim	Business	USA	Mining Industry
Myra	Hess	Performing Arts	England	Pianist
Myra Belle	Star (Shirley)	Law & Order	USA	Outlaw
Myrna	Loy	Performing Arts	USA	Actress
Myron	Cohen	Performing Arts	Poland	Comedian
Myron Leon (Mike)	Wallace	Creative Works	USA	Author/Journalist - Pulitzer
Myron S.	Scholes	Arts	USA	Economics - Nobel Laureate
Nadia	Comaneci	Sports	Romania	Olympic Gymnast
Nadia Juliette	Boulanger	Performing Arts	France	Conductor/Teacher
Nadine	Berger	Creative Works	Canada	Journalist - Television
	Gordimer	Creative Works	South Africa	Literature - Nobel Laureate
Nadja	Auermann	Performing Arts	Germany	Super Model
Naguib	Mahfouz	Creative Works	Egypt	Literature - Nobel Laureate
Nahum	Tate	Creative Works	England	Poet Laureate/Dramatist
Naina	Yeltsin	Politics	Russia	First Lady
Nan	Merriman	Performing Arts	USA	Singer - Opera
Nancy	Allen	Performing Arts	USA	Actress
	Carroll	Performing Arts	USA	Actress - Acad Award Nom
	Dussault	Performing Arts	USA	Actress - Musical
	Kelly	Performing Arts	USA	Actress - Acad Award Nom
	Kulp	Performing Arts	USA	Actress
	Lieberman	Sports	USA	Basketball Player - HF
	Lopez	Sports	USA	Golfer - HF
	Marchand	Performing Arts	USA	Actress
	Mitford	Creative Works	England	Novelist
	Olson	Performing Arts	USA	Actress - Acad Award Nom
	Richey	Sports	USA	Tennis Player - HF
	Walker	Performing Arts	USA	Actress
	Wilson	Performing Arts	USA	Singer - Big Band/Jazz - HF
	Wilson	Performing Arts	USA	Singer - Rock & Roll - HF
Nanette	Fabray	Performing Arts	USA	Actress
Naomi	Campbell	Performing Arts	England	Super Model
	Judd	Performing Arts	USA	Singer
	Watts	Performing Arts	England	Actress - Acad Award Nom
Napoléon	Bonaparte	War & Peace	France	General
Napoleon (Nap)	Lajoie	Sports	USA	Baseball Player - HF
Nastassia	Kinski	Performing Arts	Germany	Actress
Nat	Adderley	Performing Arts	USA	Jazz Trumpeter
	Holman	Sports	USA	Basketball Player - HF
	Turner	Politics	USA	Revolutionist - Negro
Natalie	Cole	Performing Arts	USA	Singer
	Portman	Performing Arts	Israel	Actress - Acad Award Nom
	Wood	Performing Arts	USA	Actress - Acad Award Nom
Nate	Thurmond	Sports	USA	Basketball Player - HF
Nathan	Hale	War & Peace	USA	Soldier - Revolutionary War
	Meyer	Business	Germany	Banking
	Milstein	Performing Arts	USA	Violinist
Nathan Ernesto	Rogers	Architecture	Italy	Architect
Nathanael	Greene	War & Peace	USA	General - Revolutionary War

SOLVER SERIES: NAME FINDER

FIRST NAME	LAST NAME	CATEGORY	COUNTRY	FAME
Nathanael	West	Creative Works	USA	Novelist
Nathaniel	Bacon	Exploration	USA	Colonist - Virginia
	Bailey	Creative Works	England	Lexicographer
	Bowditch	Science	USA	Mathematician/Astronomer
	Currier	Works of Art	USA	Lithographer
	Hawthorne	Creative Works	USA	Novelist/Short Story Writer
	Nelson	Performing Arts	USA	Rock & Roll - HF - The Flamingos
Nathaniel (Nat King)	Cole	Performing Arts	USA	Singer - Rock & Roll - HF
	Cole	Performing Arts	USA	Singer/Musician - Big Band/Jazz - HF
Nathaniel (Nate) (Tiny)	Archibald	Sports	USA	Basketball Player - HF
Nathaniel Alexander	Owings	Architecture	USA	Architect - AIA Gold Medal
Navarre Scott	Momaday	Creative Works	USA	Novelist - Pulitzer
Neal	Hefti	Performing Arts	USA	Jazz Trumpeter
	Matthews Jr.	Performing Arts	USA	Country Music - HF - The Jordonaires
Neale Andrew	Fraser	Sports	Australia	Tennis Player - HF
Ned	Beatty	Performing Arts	USA	Actor - Acad Award Nom
	Brooks	Creative Works	USA	Author
	Rorem	Creative Works	USA	Composer/Pianist
	Sparks	Performing Arts	Canada	Comedian
Ned (Gentleman)	Jarrett	Sports	USA	Race Car Driver - HF
Nehemiah	Persoff	Performing Arts	Israel	Actor
Neil	Bonnett	Sports	USA	Race Car Driver - HF
	Coles	Sports	England	Golfer - HF
	Diamond	Performing Arts	USA	Singer
	Jordan	Movie Production	England	Director - Acad Award Nom
	Peart	Performing Arts	Canada	Canadian Music - HF - Rush
	Sedaka	Performing Arts	USA	Singer
	Simon	Creative Works	USA	Dramatist - Pulitzer
	Young	Performing Arts	Canada	Rock & Roll - HF - Buffalo Springfield
Neil Alden	Armstrong	Aviation	USA	Astronaut
Neil McNeil	Colville	Sports	Canada	Hockey Player - HF
Nell	Carter	Performing Arts	USA	Actress
	Gwyn	Performing Arts	England	Actress
Nellie	Bly	Creative Works	USA	Journalist - Newspaper
	Melba	Performing Arts	Australia	Singer - Opera
	Sachs	Creative Works	Sweden	Literature - Nobel Laureate
Nello	Santi	Performing Arts	Italy	Conductor
Nelson	Eddy	Performing Arts	USA	Singer
	Mandela	War & Peace	South Africa	Peace - Nobel Laureate
	Piquet	Sports	Brazil	Race Car Driver - HF
	Riddle	Performing Arts	USA	Conductor/Composer
Nelson (Old Poison)	Stewart	Sports	Canada	Hockey Player - HF
Nelson Aldrich	Rockefeller	Politics	USA	Vice-President
Nelson De	Mille	Creative Works	USA	Author
Nera D.	White	Sports	USA	Basketball Player - HF
Nesta Robert (Bob)	Marley	Performing Arts	Jamaica	Singer - Rock & Roll - HF
Nestor	Chylak Jr.	Sports	USA	Baseball Umpire - HF
Neve	Campbell	Performing Arts	Canada	Actress
Nevil	Shute	Creative Works	England	Novelist
Nevill Francis	Mott	Science	England	Physics - Nobel Laureate
Neville	Marriner	Performing Arts	England	Conductor/Violinist
Newell Convers	Wyeth	Works of Art	USA	Painter/Illustrator
Newton Booth	Tarkington	Creative Works	USA	Novelist
Newton Diehl	Baker	Politics	USA	Statesman
Newton Leroy (Newt)	Gingrich	Politics	USA	Speaker of the House
Ngaio	Marsh	Creative Works	New Zealand	Novelist - Crime Fiction
Ngo Dinh	Diem	Politics	South Vietnam	President
Nguyen Van	Ho Chi Minh	Politics	North Vietnam	President
Nia	Long	Performing Arts	USA	Actress
	Peeples	Performing Arts	USA	Actress
Nia Nicole	Abdallah	Sports	USA	Olympic Taekwondo
Niccolo	Amati	Arts	Italy	Violin Maker
	Machiavelli	Creative Works	Italy	Writer/Statesman

FIRST NAME	LAST NAME	CATEGORY	COUNTRY	FAME
Niccolò	Paganini	Creative Works	Italy	Composer/Violinist
Nicholas	Baudin	Exploration	France	Explorer - Tasmania
	Biddle	Business	USA	Financier
	Boileau-Despréaux	Creative Works	France	Poet/Critic
	Copernicus	Science	Poland	Astronomer
	Dante	Creative Works	USA	Dramatist - Pulitzer
	Gage	Creative Works	Greece	Author
	Kropfelder	Sports	USA	Soccer Player - HF
	Ridley	Arts	England	Bishop/Protestant Reformer
	Rowe	Performing Arts	Scotland	Actor
	Udall	Creative Works	England	Playwright/Translator
	Uvedale	Creative Works	England	Playwright/Translator
Nicholas (Nick)	Massi (Macioci)	Performing Arts	USA	Rock & Roll - HF - The Four Seasons
	Turturro	Performing Arts	USA	Actor
Nicholas Anthony (Nick)	Buoniconti	Sports	USA	Football Player - HF
Nicholas Di (Nick)	Orio	Sports	USA	Soccer Player - HF
Nicholas Murray	Butler	War & Peace	USA	Peace - Nobel Laureate
Nicholas Vachel	Lindsay	Creative Works	USA	Poet
Nick	Adams	Performing Arts	USA	Actor - Acad Award Nom
	Faldo	Sports	England	Golfer - HF
	Lowe	Performing Arts	England	Singer
	Nolte	Performing Arts	USA	Actor - Acad Award Nom
	Price	Sports	South Africa	Golfer - HF
Nicky	Headon	Performing Arts	England	Rock & Roll - HF - The Clash
Nicol	Williamson	Performing Arts	Scotland	Actor
Nicola	Pagliara	Architecture	Italy	Architect
	Pisano	Works of Art	Italy	Sculptor/Architect
	Sacco	Politics	Italy	Anarchist
Nicola (Nicky)	Pietrangeli	Sports	Italy	Tennis Player - HF
Nicolaas	Bloembergen	Science	USA	Physics - Nobel Laureate
Nicolai	Gedda	Performing Arts	Sweden	Singer - Opera
Nicolas	Cage	Performing Arts	USA	Actor - Academy Award
	Malebranche	Arts	France	Philosopher
	Poussin	Works of Art	France	Painter
	Roeg	Movie Production	England	Director
Nicolas (Nick)	Mason	Performing Arts	England	Rock & Roll - HF - Pink Floyd
Nicolas Léonard Sadi	Carnot	Science	France	Physicist
Nicolay Gennadiyevich	Basov	Science	Russia	Physics - Nobel Laureate
Nicole	Kidman	Performing Arts	USA	Actress - Academy Award
	Miller	Business	USA	Fashion Designer
Nicolino	Locche	Sports	Argentina	Boxer - HF
Niels K.	Jerne	Science	Denmark	Medicine - Nobel Laureate
Niels Ryberg	Finsen	Science	Denmark	Medicine - Nobel Laureate
Nigel	Bruce	Performing Arts	Mexico	Actor
	Havers	Performing Arts	England	Actor
	Hawthorne	Performing Arts	England	Actor - Acad Award Nom
	Mansell	Sports	England	Race Car Driver - HF
Niki	Taylor	Performing Arts	USA	Super Model
Niki van	Lauda	Sports	Austria	Race Car Driver - HF
Nikita Sergeyevich	Khrushchev	Politics	Russia	Premier
Nikola	Tesla	Science	USA	Inventor
Nikolaas	Tinbergen	Science	England	Medicine - Nobel Laureate
Nikolai Alexsandrovich	Berdyaev	Arts	Russia	Philosopher
Nikolai Andreyevich	Rimsky-Korsakov	Creative Works	Russia	Composer
Nikolai Ivanovich	Lobachevski	Science	Russia	Mathematician
Nikolai Vasillevich	Gogol	Creative Works	Russia	Novelist/Dramatist
Nikolaus	Pevsner	Architecture	England	Architect - Jefferson Medal
Nikolay	Semenov	Science	Russia	Chemistry - Nobel Laureate
Nikos	Kazantzakis	Creative Works	Greece	Novelist
Nilo	Cruz	Creative Works	USA	Dramatist - Pulitzer
Nils Adolf Erik	Nordenskjöld	Exploration	Sweden	Explorer - Arctic
Nils Gustaf	Dalén	Science	Sweden	Physics - Nobel Laureate
Nin	Anaïs	Creative Works	France	Novelist/Short Story Writer

SOLVER SERIES: NAME FINDER

FIRST NAME	LAST NAME	CATEGORY	COUNTRY	FAME
Nina	Brosh	Performing Arts	Israel	Super Model
	Foch	Performing Arts	Netherlands	Actress - Acad Award Nom
	Ricci	Business	France	Fashion Designer
Nino	Benvenuti	Sports	USA	Boxer - HF
	Cerruti	Business	Italy	Fashion Designer
	Rota	Creative Works	Italy	Composer
Nipsey	Russell	Performing Arts	USA	Comedian
Nita	Naldi	Performing Arts	USA	Actor
	Talbot	Performing Arts	USA	Actress
Noah	Beery	Performing Arts	USA	Actor
	Webster	Arts	USA	Lexicographer
Noel	Coward	Performing Arts	England	Actor/Playwright
	Gallagher	Performing Arts	England	Rock & Roll - Oasis
	Harrison	Performing Arts	England	Singer
Nora	Ephron	Creative Works	USA	Novelist
	Kaye	Performing Arts	USA	Dancer - Ballerina
Nora (Dora)	Bayes (Goldberg)	Performing Arts	USA	Actress
Norbert	Wiener	Science	USA	Mathematician
Noriyuki (Pat)	Morita	Performing Arts	USA	Actor - Acad Award Nom
Norm	Crosby	Performing Arts	USA	Comedian
	Snead	Sports	USA	Football Player
Norma	Shearer	Performing Arts	Canada	Actress - Academy Award
	Talmadge	Performing Arts	USA	Actress
	Aleandro	Performing Arts	Argentina	Actress - Acad Award Nom
Norma Delores (Peggy)	Lee (Engstrom)	Performing Arts	USA	Actress/Singer - Acad Award Nom
	Lee (Engstrom)	Performing Arts	USA	Singer - Big Band/Jazz - HF
Norman	Angell	Creative Works	England	Economist/Writer
	Angell	War & Peace	England	Peace - Nobel Laureate
	Cousins	Creative Works	USA	Journalist - Magazine
	Fell	Performing Arts	USA	Actor
	Foster	Architecture	England	Architect - Pritzker/ AIA Gold
	Granz	Performing Arts	Switzerland	Jazz Impresario - Big Band/Jazz - HF
	Jewison	Movie Production	Canada	Director - Acad Award Nom
	Rockwell	Works of Art	USA	Illustrator
	Taurog	Movie Production	USA	Director - Academy Award
Norman Bel	Geddes	Arts	USA	"Designer - Theatrical, Industrial"
Norman Colin	Dexter	Creative Works	England	Author
Norman E.	Borlaug	War & Peace	USA	Peace - Nobel Laureate
Norman Earl	Thagard	Aviation	USA	Astronaut
Norman Everard	Brookes	Sports	Australia	Tennis Player - HF
Norman F.	Ramsey	Science	USA	Physics - Nobel Laureate
Norman Graham	Hill	Sports	England	Race Car Driver - HF
Norman Kingsley	Mailer	Creative Works	USA	Author - Pulitzer
Norman Mack Van (Norm)	Brocklin	Sports	USA	Football Player - HF
Norman Mattoon	Thomas	Politics	USA	Socialist Leader
Norman Thomas (Turkey)	Stearnes	Sports	USA	Baseball Player - HF
Norman Victor (Norm)	Ullman	Sports	Canada	Hockey Player - HF
Octavio	Paz	Creative Works	Mexico	Literature - Nobel Laureate
Odd	Hassel	Science	Norway	Chemistry - Nobel Laureate
Odel	Shepard	Creative Works	USA	Author - Pulitzer
Odilon	Redon	Works of Art	France	Painter/Lithographer
Odysseus	Elytis	Creative Works	Greece	Literature - Nobel Laureate
Ogden	Nash	Creative Works	USA	Poet
O'Kelly	Isley	Performing Arts	USA	Rock & Roll - HF - Isley Brothers
Ola Elizabeth	Winslow	Creative Works	USA	Author - Pulitzer
Ole	Bull	Performing Arts	Norway	Violinist
	Evinrude	Business	USA	Outboard Engine Designer
	Olsen	Performing Arts	USA	Comedian
Ole Edvart	Rolvaag	Creative Works	USA	Novelist
Oleg	Cassini	Business	USA	Designer - Fashions
	Vidov	Performing Arts	Russia	Actor
Olga	Korbut	Sports	Russia	Olympic Gymnast
Olin	Dutra	Sports	USA	Golfer

FIRST NAME	LAST NAME	CATEGORY	COUNTRY	FAME
Oliver	Cromwell	Politics	England	Revolutionary Leader
	Cromwell	War & Peace	England	Military Leader
	Ellsworth	Law & Order	USA	Justice - Supreme Court
	Goldsmith	Creative Works	Ireland	Poet/Playwright/Novelist
	Hardy	Performing Arts	USA	Comedian
	Heaviside	Science	England	Physicist
	Kahn	Sports	Germany	Soccer Player
	Reed	Performing Arts	England	Actor
	Stone	Movie Production	USA	Director - Academy Award
Oliver Hazard	Perry	War & Peace	USA	Naval Officer
Oliver Joseph	Lodge	Science	England	Physicist/Writer
Oliver La	Farge	Creative Works	USA	Novelist - Pulitzer
Oliver Laurence	North	War & Peace	USA	Colonel
Oliver Levi	Seibert	Sports	Canada	Hockey Player - HF
Oliver Samuel	Campbell	Sports	USA	Tennis Player - HF
Oliver Waterman	Larkin	Creative Works	USA	Author - Pulitzer
Oliver Wendell	Holmes	Science	USA	Physician/Writer
Olivia	Newton-John	Performing Arts	England	Singer
Olivia De	Havilland	Performing Arts	Japan	Actress - Academy Award
Ollie (Ali)	Woodson (Creggett)	Performing Arts	USA	Rock & Roll - HF - The Temptations
Ollie Genoa	Matson	Sports	USA	Football Player - HF
Olympia	Dukakis	Performing Arts	USA	Actress - Academy Award
Omar	Khayyám	Creative Works	Persia	Poet
	Sharif	Games	Egypt	Bridge Expert
	Sharif	Performing Arts	Egypt	Actor - Acad Award Nom
	Uresti	Sports	USA	Golfer
	Vizquel	Sports	USA	Baseball Player
Omar Hashim	Epps	Performing Arts	USA	Actor
Omar Nelson	Bradley	War & Peace	USA	General
Omar Palqu	Olivares	Sports	Puerto Rico	Baseball Player
Ona	Munson	Performing Arts	USA	Actress
Oona	Chaplin (O'Neill)	Performing Arts	USA	Actress
Oprah	Winfrey	Performing Arts	USA	Actress - Acad Award Nom
	Winfrey	Performing Arts	USA	Show Host
Orel	Hershiser	Sports	USA	Baseball Player
Orenthal James (The Juice)	Simpson	Sports	USA	Football Player - HF
Oriana	Fallaci	Creative Works	Italy	Author/Journalist
Orlando	Gibbons	Creative Works	England	Composer/Organist
Orlando Manuel	Cepeda	Sports	Puerto Rico	Baseball Player - HF
Ornette	Coleman	Performing Arts	USA	Jazz Saxophonist - Big Band/Jazz - HF
Orrin Grant	Hatch	Politics	USA	Senator - Utah
Orson	Bean	Performing Arts	USA	Actor
Orville	Moody	Sports	USA	Golfer
	Wright	Aviation	USA	Inventor - Airplane
Osa	Massen	Performing Arts	Denmark	Actress
Osborne Earl (Ozzie)	Smith	Sports	USA	Baseball Player - HF
Oscar	Hammerstein	Business	USA	Tobacco Industry
	Hammerstein	Creative Works	USA	Librettist/Lyricist
	Hammerstein II	Creative Works	USA	Dramatist - Pulitzer
	Handlin	Creative Works	USA	Author - Pulitzer
	Hijuelos	Creative Works	USA	Author - Pulitzer
	Levant	Performing Arts	USA	Pianist/Composer
	Niemeyer	Architecture	Brazil	Architect - Pritzker Laureate
	Pettiford	Performing Arts	USA	Bassist/Cellist - Big Band/Jazz - HF
	Straus	Creative Works	Austria	Composer
	Wilde	Creative Works	England	Poet/Novelist/Playwright
Oscar Arias	Sánchez	Politics	Costa Rica	President
	Sánchez	War & Peace	Costa Rica	Peace - Nobel Laureate
Oscar Carlyle	Buley	Creative Works	USA	Author - Pulitzer
Oscar de la	Renta	Business	France	Fashion Designer
Oscar Emmanuel	Peterson	Performing Arts	Canada	Jazz Pianist - Big Band/Jazz - HF -
	Peterson	Performing Arts	Canada	Jazz Pianist - Canadian Music - HF
Oscar McKinley	Charleston	Sports	USA	Baseball Player - HF

SOLVER SERIES: NAME FINDER

FIRST NAME	LAST NAME	CATEGORY	COUNTRY	FAME
Oscar P.	Robertson	Sports	USA	Basketball Player - HF
Oskar	Homolka	Performing Arts	Austria	Actor - Acad Award Nom
	Kokoschka	Works of Art	England	Painter
	Werner	Performing Arts	Austria	Actor - Acad Award Nom
Ossie	Davis	Performing Arts	USA	Actor
Oswald	Spengler	Arts	Germany	Philosopher
Oswald Garrison	Villard	Business	USA	Publishing
Oswald Mathias	Ungers	Architecture	Germany	Architect
Otis	Carré	Performing Arts	USA	Super Model
	Nixon	Sports	USA	Baseball Player
	Redding	Performing Arts	USA	Singer - Rock & Roll -HF
	Williams (Miles)	Performing Arts	USA	Rock & Roll - HF - The Temptations
	Young	Performing Arts	USA	Actor
	Anderson	Sports	USA	Football Player
	Toole	Law & Order	USA	Serial Killer
Ottmar	Mergenthaler	Science	USA	Inventor - Linotype
Otto	Hahn	Science	Germany	Chemistry - Nobel Laureate
	Harbach	Creative Works	USA	Lyricist
	Kahn	Business	USA	Financier
	Klemperer	Performing Arts	Germany	Conductor/Composer
	Kruger	Performing Arts	USA	Actor
	Loewi	Science	Austria	Medicine - Nobel Laureate
	Preminger	Movie Production	Austria	Director - Acad Award Nom
	Stern	Science	USA	Physics - Nobel Laureate
	Wagner	Architecture	Austria	Architect
	Wallach	Science	Germany	Chemistry - Nobel Laureate
	Weininger	Arts	Austria	Philosopher
Otto Eduard Leopold von	Bismarck	Politics	Germany	Chancellor
Otto Everett	Graham Jr.	Sports	USA	Football Player - HF
Otto Fritz	Meyerhof	Science	Germany	Medicine - Nobel Laureate
Otto Heinrich	Warburg	Science	Germany	Medicine - Nobel Laureate
Otto Paul Hermann	Diels	Science	Germany	Chemistry - Nobel Laureate
Ottorino	Respighi	Creative Works	Italy	Composer
Owen	Chamberlain	Science	USA	Physics - Nobel Laureate
	Davis	Creative Works	USA	Dramatist - Pulitzer
	Glendower	War & Peace	Wales	Chieftain
	Meredith	Creative Works	England	Poet/Diplomat
	Wister	Creative Works	USA	Novelist
Owen Kay	Garriott	Aviation	USA	Astronaut
Owen Willans	Richardson	Science	England	Physics - Nobel Laureate
Ozzie	Nelson	Performing Arts	USA	Actor
	Newsome Jr.	Sports	USA	Football Player - HF
Ozzy	Osbourne	Performing Arts	England	Singer
Paavo	Nurmi	Sports	Finland	Olympic Runner
Pablo	Casals	Creative Works	Spain	Composer/Cellist
	Neruda	Creative Works	Chile	Literature - Nobel Laureate
	Picasso	Works of Art	Spain	Sculptor/Painter - Cubist
Paco	Rabanne	Business	France	Fashion Designer
Padraic	Columbo	Creative Works	Ireland	Poet/Playwright
Pam	Dawber	Performing Arts	USA	Actress
	Grier	Performing Arts	USA	Actress
	Shriver	Sports	USA	Tennis Player - HF
Pamela Sue	Martin	Performing Arts	USA	Actress
Panfilo de	Narvaez	Exploration	Spain	Explorer - Cuba
Paolo	Maldini	Sports	Italy	Soccer Player
	Portoghesi	Architecture	Italy	Architect
	Soleri	Architecture	Italy	Architect
	Uccello	Works of Art	Italy	Painter - Early Renaissance
	Veronese	Works of Art	Italy	Painter
	Zermani	Architecture	Italy	Architect
Paolo Angelo	Nespoli	Aviation	Italy	Astronaut
Pär Fabian	Lagerkvist	Creative Works	Sweden	Literature - Nobel Laureate
Parker	Stevenson	Performing Arts	USA	Actor

FIRST NAME	LAST NAME	CATEGORY	COUNTRY	FAME
Pascual	Perez	Sports	Argentina	Boxer - HF
Pasha	Ali	Politics	Turkey	Governor
Pat	Barrett	Performing Arts	Canada	Canadian Music - HF - The Crew Cuts
	Benatar	Performing Arts	USA	Singer
	Boone	Performing Arts	USA	Singer/Actor
	Bradley	Sports	USA	Golfer - HF
	Buchanan	Creative Works	USA	Journalist - Newspaper
	Carroll	Performing Arts	USA	Actress
	Conroy	Creative Works	USA	Novelist
	Garrett	Law & Order	USA	Lawman
	Harrington Jr.	Performing Arts	USA	Actor
	McBride	Sports	USA	Soccer Player - HF
	O'Brien	Performing Arts	USA	Actor
	Riley	Sports	USA	Basketball Player
	Sajak	Performing Arts	USA	Show Host
Pat La	Fontaine	Sports	USA	Hockey Player - HF
Patricia	Clarkson	Performing Arts	USA	Actress - Acad Award Nom
	Collinge	Performing Arts	Ireland	Actress - Acad Award Nom
	Neal	Performing Arts	USA	Actress - Academy Award
	Velasquez	Performing Arts	Venezuela	Super Model
Patricia Consolatrix Hilliard	Robertson	Aviation	USA	Astronaut
Patrick	Abercrombie	Architecture	England	Architect - AIA Gold Medal
	Duffy	Performing Arts	USA	Actor
	Ewing	Sports	USA	Basketball Player
	Henry	Politics	USA	Statesman/Orator
	MacNee	Performing Arts	England	Actor
	McGoohan	Performing Arts	USA	Actor
	O'Neal	Performing Arts	USA	Actor
	Stewart	Performing Arts	England	Actor
	Swayze	Performing Arts	USA	Actor
	White	Creative Works	Australia	Literature - Nobel Laureate
Patrick (Ace)	Ntsoelengoe	Sports	South Africa	Soccer Player - HF
Patrick John	Hillary	Politics	Ireland	President
Patrick Joseph	Kennedy	Business	USA	Importer
Patrick Joseph (Paddy)	Moran	Sports	Canada	Hockey Player - HF
Patrick Maynard Stuart	Blackett	Science	England	Physics - Nobel Laureate
Patrick Pierre Roger	Baudry	Aviation	France	Astronaut
Patsy (Ruby)	Montana (Blevins)	Performing Arts	USA	Singer - Country Music - HF
Patti	Andrews	Performing Arts	USA	Singer
	Austin	Performing Arts	USA	Singer
	Lupone	Performing Arts	USA	Actress
	Page	Performing Arts	USA	Singer
	Reagan (Davis)	Performing Arts	USA	Actress
	Smith	Performing Arts	USA	Singer - Rock & Roll - HF
Patti La	Belle	Performing Arts	USA	Singer
Patty	Berg	Sports	USA	Golfer - HF
	Duke	Performing Arts	USA	Actress - Academy Award
	McCormack	Performing Arts	USA	Actress - Acad Award Nom
	Sheehan	Sports	USA	Golfer - HF
Paul	Anka	Performing Arts	Canada	Singer/Composer - Canadian Music - HF
	Berg	Science	USA	Chemistry - Nobel Laureate
	Caligiuri	Sports	USA	Soccer Player - HF
	Cézanne	Works of Art	France	Painter - Impressionist
	Child	Sports	England	Soccer Player - HF
	Douglas	Performing Arts	USA	Actor
	Ehrlich	Science	Germany	Medicine - Nobel Laureate
	Éluard	Creative Works	France	Poet
	Endacott	Sports	USA	Basketball Player - HF
	Greengard	Science	USA	Medicine - Nobel Laureate
	Hankar	Architecture	Belgium	Architect
	Harvey	Creative Works	USA	Journalist - Radio
	Hindemith	Creative Works	USA	Composer
	Hogan	Performing Arts	Australia	Actor

SOLVER SERIES: NAME FINDER

FIRST NAME	LAST NAME	CATEGORY	COUNTRY	FAME
Paul	Horgan	Creative Works	USA	Author - Pulitzer
	Kantner	Creative Works	USA	Song Writer/Guitarist
	Kantner	Performing Arts	USA	Rock & Roll - HF - Jefferson Airplane
	Karrer	Science	Switzerland	Chemistry - Nobel Laureate
	Klee	Works of Art	Switzerland	Painter - Abstract
	Kruger	Politics	South Africa	President
	Langois	Performing Arts	Canada	Canadian Music - HF - The Tragically Hip
	Lukas	Performing Arts	Hungary	Actor - Academy Award
	Lynde	Performing Arts	USA	Comedian
	Manship	Works of Art	USA	Sculptor
	Mazursky	Movie Production	USA	Director
	Mellon	Architecture	USA	Architect - Jefferson Medal
	Muldoon	Creative Works	Ireland	Poet - Pulitzer
	Muni	Performing Arts	Ukraine	Actor - Academy Award
	Newman	Performing Arts	USA	Actor - Academy Award
	Potter	Works of Art	Netherlands	Painter
	Reichman	Business	Canada	Real Estate
	Revere	Politics	USA	Patriot/Silversmith
	Reynaud	Politics	France	Premier
	Robeson	Performing Arts	USA	Actor/Singer
	Robi (Roby)	Performing Arts	USA	Rock & Roll - HF - The Platters
	Rodgers	Performing Arts	England	Singer
	Rudolph	Architecture	USA	Architect
	Sabatier	Science	France	Chemistry - Nobel Laureate
	Scarron	Creative Works	France	Poet/Dramatist
	Scofield	Performing Arts	England	Actor - Academy Award
	Shaffer	Performing Arts	Canada	Band Leader
	Simonon	Performing Arts	England	Rock & Roll - HF - The Clash
	Sorvino	Performing Arts	USA	Actor
	Starr	Creative Works	USA	Author - Pulitzer
	Stookey	Performing Arts	USA	Singer - Folk
	Tanner	Performing Arts	USA	Jazz Trombonist - Big Band/Jazz - HF
	Tillich	Arts	Germany	Philosopher/Theologian
	Verlaine	Creative Works	France	Poet
	Warburg	Business	USA	Financier
	Whiteman	Performing Arts	USA	Conductor - Big Band/Jazz - HF
	Williams	Architecture	USA	Architect
	Williams	Performing Arts	USA	Rock & Roll - HF - The Temptations
	Wilson	Performing Arts	USA	Rock & Roll - HF - The Flamingos
	Winfield	Performing Arts	USA	Actor - Acad Award Nom
	Zindel	Creative Works	USA	Dramatist - Pulitzer
	Desmond	Performing Arts	USA	Jazz Saxophonist - Big Band/Jazz - HF
	Gonsalves	Performing Arts	USA	Jazz Saxophonist - Big Band/Jazz - HF
Paul (Big Pauly)	Castellano	Law & Order	USA	Mafia
Paul (Duts)	Danilo	Sports	USA	Soccer Player - HF
Paul (Little Poison)	Runyan	Sports	USA	Golfer - HF
Paul A.	Samuelson	Arts	USA	Economics - Nobel Laureate
Paul Adrien Maurice	Dirac	Science	England	Physics - Nobel Laureate
Paul Ambroise	Valéry	Creative Works	France	Poet/Essayist
Paul Andrew (Andy)	Richter	Performing Arts	USA	Comedian
Paul C.	Lauterbur	Science	USA	Medicine - Nobel Laureate
Paul Charles Joseph	Bourget	Creative Works	France	Novelist/Essayist
Paul D.	Boyer	Science	USA	Chemistry - Nobel Laureate
Paul David (Bono)	Hewson	Performing Arts	Ireland	Rock & Roll - HF - U2
Paul Desmond	Scully-Power	Aviation	USA	Astronaut
Paul Douglas	Coffey	Sports	Canada	Hockey Player - HF
Paul Dryden	Warfield	Sports	USA	Football Player - HF
Paul Edgar Phillipe	Martin	Politics	Canada	Prime Minister
Paul Edmund de	Strzelecki	Exploration	Poland	Explorer - Australia Mountains
Paul Édouard	Passy	Arts	France	Phonetician
Paul Edward	Theroux	Creative Works	USA	Novelist
Paul Eliot	Green	Creative Works	USA	Dramatist - Pulitzer
Paul Eugene	Brown	Sports	USA	Football Coach - HF

FIRST NAME	LAST NAME	CATEGORY	COUNTRY	FAME
Paul Frederic	Simon	Performing Arts	USA	Rock & Roll - HF - Simon & Garfunkel
	Simon	Performing Arts	USA	Singer/Composer
Paul Glee	Waner	Sports	USA	Baseball Player - HF
Paul Gustave	Doré	Works of Art	France	Painter/Illustrator
Paul Henri d'Estournelles de	Constant	War & Peace	France	Peace - Nobel Laureate
Paul Henry de	Kruif	Science	USA	Bacteriologist/Writer
Paul Herman	Buck	Creative Works	USA	Author - Pulitzer
Paul Hermann	Müller	Science	Switzerland	Medicine - Nobel Laureate
Paul J.	Arizin	Sports	USA	Basketball Player - HF
	Crutzen	Science	Netherlands	Chemistry - Nobel Laureate
	Flory	Science	USA	Chemistry - Nobel Laureate
Paul James	Krause	Sports	USA	Football Player - HF
Paul Johann Ludwig	Heyse	Creative Works	Germany	Literature - Nobel Laureate
Paul Joseph	Weitz	Aviation	USA	Astronaut
Paul Laurence	Chambers	Performing Arts	USA	Jazz Bassist - Big Band/Jazz - HF
	Dunbar	Creative Works	USA	Poet
Paul Le	Mat	Performing Arts	USA	Actor
Paul Leo	Molitor	Sports	USA	Baseball Player - HF
Paul Louis Charles	Claudel	Creative Works	France	Poet/Playwright
Paul M.	Nurse	Science	England	Medicine - Nobel Laureate
Paul Michael Nikolaus	Bonatz	Architecture	Germany	Architect
Paul Phillippe	Cret	Architecture	USA	Architect - AIA Gold Medal
Paul Vernon	Hornung	Sports	USA	Football Player - HF
Paul von	Hindenburg	War & Peace	Germany	Field Marshall
Paula	Abdul	Performing Arts	USA	Singer/Choreographer
	Poundstone	Performing Arts	USA	Comedian
	Prentiss	Performing Arts	USA	Actress
	Vogel	Creative Works	USA	Dramatist - Pulitzer
Paulette	Goddard	Performing Arts	USA	Actress - Acad Award Nom
Pauline	Collins	Performing Arts	England	Actress - Acad Award Nom
	Kael	Creative Works	USA	Journalist - Newspaper
Pauline May	Betz-Addie	Sports	USA	Tennis Player - HF
Pavel Aleksevevich	Cherenkov	Science	Russia	Physics - Nobel Laureate
Pavel Ivanovich	Belyayev	Aviation	Russia	Astronaut
Pavel Romanovich	Popovich	Aviation	Russia	Astronaut
Payne William	Stewart	Sports	USA	Golfer - HF
Peabo	Bryson	Performing Arts	USA	Singer
Pearl	Bailey	Performing Arts	USA	Singer/Composer
Pearl Sydenstricker	Buck	Creative Works	USA	Literature - Nobel/Pulitzer
Pedro	Almodovar	Movie Production	Spain	Director - Acad Award Nom
Pedro Alvares	Cabral	Exploration	Portugal	Explorer - Brazil
Pedro de	Alvarado	War & Peace	Spain	General
Pedro Fernandez de	Quiros	Exploration	Portugal	Explorer - South Pacific
Pedro Francisco	Duque	Aviation	Spain	Astronaut
Pedro Menendez de	Aviles	Exploration	Spain	Explorer - Florida
Pee Wee	Herman	Performing Arts	USA	Comedian
Peg	Woffington	Performing Arts	Ireland	Actress
Peggy	Ashcroft	Performing Arts	England	Actress - Academy Award
	Cass	Performing Arts	USA	Actress - Acad Award Nom
	Fleming	Sports	USA	Olympic Skater
	Rea	Performing Arts	USA	Actress
	Wood	Performing Arts	USA	Actress - Acad Award Nom
Peggy Ann	Garner	Performing Arts	USA	Actress - Academy Award
Pelham Grenville	Wodehouse	Creative Works	England	Novelist
Penelope	Milford	Performing Arts	USA	Actress - Acad Award Nom
Penny	Marshall	Performing Arts	USA	Actress
Percival	Lowell	Science	USA	Astronomer
Percy	Kilbride	Performing Arts	USA	Actor
	LeSueur	Sports	Canada	Hockey Player - HF
	Sledge	Performing Arts	USA	Singer - Rock & Roll - HF
Percy Aldridge	Grainger	Creative Works	USA	Composer/Pianist
Percy Bysshe	Shelley	Creative Works	England	Poet
Percy Williams	Bridgman	Science	USA	Physics - Nobel Laureate

SOLVER SERIES: NAME FINDER

FIRST NAME	LAST NAME	CATEGORY	COUNTRY	FAME
Percy Wyndham	Lewis	Creative Works	England	Author/Painter
Perle	Mesta	Politics	USA	Political Supporter
Pernell	Roberts	Performing Arts	USA	Actor
	Whitaker	Sports	USA	Boxer
Perry	Ellis	Business	USA	Fashion Designer
	King	Performing Arts	USA	Actor
	Miller	Creative Works	USA	Author - Pulitzer
Perry Thomas (Mr. Tennis)	Jones	Sports	USA	Tennis Promoter - HF
Pete	Farndon	Performing Arts	England	Rock & Roll - HF - The Pretenders
	Rose	Sports	USA	Baseball Player
	Sampras	Sports	USA	Tennis Player
	Seeger	Performing Arts	USA	Singer - Rock & Roll - HF
	Postlethwaite	Performing Arts	England	Actor - Acad Award Nom
Peter	Agre	Science	USA	Chemistry - Nobel Laureate
	Arno	Creative Works	USA	Cartoonist - New Yorker
	Asher	Performing Arts	England	Singer
	Behrens	Architecture	Germany	Architect
	Benchley	Creative Works	USA	Author - Jaws
	Bogdanovich	Movie Production	USA	Director - Acad Award Nom
	Boyle	Performing Arts	USA	Actor
	Brook	Movie Production	England	Director
	Cattaneo	Movie Production	England	Director - Acad Award Nom
	Cetera	Performing Arts	USA	Singer
	Cook	Performing Arts	England	Comedian
	Cooper	Business	USA	Steel Industry/Philanthropy
	Cushing	Performing Arts	England	Actor
	Dollond	Business	England	Retail Trade
	Dominick	Architecture	USA	Architect
	Falk	Performing Arts	USA	Actor - Acad Award Nom
	Finch	Performing Arts	England	Actor - Academy Award
	Firth	Performing Arts	England	Actor - Acad Award Nom
	Fonda	Performing Arts	USA	Actor - Acad Award Nom
	Frampton	Performing Arts	England	Singer
	Gabriel	Performing Arts	England	Singer
	Glenville	Movie Production	England	Director - Acad Award Nom
	Graves	Performing Arts	USA	Actor
	Haskell	Performing Arts	USA	Actor
	Jennings	Creative Works	Canada	Journalist - Television
	Kent	Creative Works	Canada	Journalist - Television
	Kurten	Law & Order	Germany	Serial Killer - Dusseldorf Vampire
	Lawford	Performing Arts	England	Actor
	Lorre	Performing Arts	Slovakia	Actor
	Maas	Creative Works	USA	Novelist
	Mansbridge	Creative Works	Canada	Journalist - Television
	Mansfield	Science	England	Medicine - Nobel Laureate
	Marshall	Performing Arts	USA	Comedian
	Minuit	Exploration	Netherlands	Explorer - Manhattan
	Minuit	Politics	Netherlands	Director General
	Mitchell	Science	England	Chemistry - Nobel Laureate
	Noone	Performing Arts	England	Singer
	O'Toole	Performing Arts	Ireland	Actor - Acad Award Nom
	Pears	Performing Arts	England	Singer - Opera
	Quaife (The Kinks)	Performing Arts	England	Rock & Roll - HF - The Kinks
	Renzulli	Sports	USA	Soccer Player - HF
	Scolari	Performing Arts	USA	Actor
	Sellers	Performing Arts	England	Actor - Acad Award Nom
	Serkin	Performing Arts	USA	Pianist
	Snell	Sports	New Zealand	Olympic Runner
	Stastny	Sports	Slovakia	Hockey Player - HF
	Stauss	Performing Arts	USA	Actor
	Strauss	Performing Arts	USA	Actor
	Stuyvesant	Exploration	Netherlands	Explorer - New York
	Stuyvesant	Politics	Netherlands	Governor

FIRST NAME	LAST NAME	CATEGORY	COUNTRY	FAME
Peter	Taylor	Creative Works	USA	Novelist - Pulitzer
	Thomson	Sports	Australia	Golfer - HF
	Townshend (The Who)	Performing Arts	England	Rock & Roll - HF - The Who
	Ustinov	Performing Arts	England	Actor - Academy Award
	Walker	Architecture	USA	Architect - Jefferson Medal
	Weir	Movie Production	Australia	Director - Acad Award Nom
	Wilson	Sports	Scotland	Soccer Player - HF
	Wolf	Performing Arts	USA	Singer
	Yarrow	Performing Arts	USA	Singer - Folk
	Yates	Movie Production	England	Director - Acad Award Nom
	Zeeman	Science	Netherlands	Physics - Nobel Laureate
	Zumthor	Architecture	Switzerland	Architect
	Jackson	Movie Production	New Zealand	Director - Academy Award
Peter Allan	Green (Greenbaum)	Performing Arts	England	Rock & Roll - HF - Fleetwood Mac
Peter Barton (Pete)	Wilson	Politics	USA	Senator - California
Peter Brian	Medawar	Science	England	Medicine - Nobel Laureate
Peter C.	Doherty	Science	Australia	Medicine - Nobel Laureate
Peter De	Vries	Creative Works	USA	Novelist
Peter Dewey (Pete)	Fountain Jr.	Performing Arts	USA	Jazz Clarinetist - Big Band/Jazz - HF
Peter Holden	Gregg	Sports	USA	Race Car Driver - HF
Peter Ilyich	Tchaikovsky	Creative Works	Russia	Composer
Peter Jeffry Karl	Wisoff	Aviation	USA	Astronaut
Peter Josef	Lenné	Architecture	Germany	Architect - Landscape Design
Peter Joseph William	Debye	Science	USA	Chemistry - Nobel Laureate
Peter Louis (Pete)	Pihos	Sports	USA	Football Player - HF
Peter Mark	Roget	Science	England	Physician/Compiler - Thesaurus
Peter P. (Pete)	Maravich	Sports	USA	Basketball Player - HF
Peter Paul	Rubens	Works of Art	Netherlands	Painter
Peter Robert Edwin	Viereck	Creative Works	USA	Poet - Pulitzer
Peter Victor	Ueberroth	Business	USA	Travel/Baseball
Pëtr Leonidovich	Kapitza	Science	Russia	Physics - Nobel Laureate
Petroleum V.	Nasby	Creative Works	USA	Humorist
Petula	Clark	Performing Arts	England	Singer
Peyton	Rous	Science	USA	Medicine - Nobel Laureate
Phil	Collins	Performing Arts	England	Singer/Composer
	Donahue	Creative Works	USA	Journalist - Television
	Harris	Performing Arts	USA	Comedian
	Hartman	Performing Arts	Canada	Comedian
	Hill	Sports	USA	Race Car Driver - HF
	Mahre	Sports	USA	Olympic Skier
	Ochs	Performing Arts	USA	Singer
	Silvers	Performing Arts	USA	Comedian
	Simms	Sports	USA	Football Player
	Smith	Performing Arts	USA	Rock & Roll - HF - Lovin' Spoonful
Philibert	Delorme	Architecture	France	Architect - Renaissance
Philip	Glass	Creative Works	USA	Composer
	Larkin	Creative Works	England	Poet/Novelist
	Levine	Creative Works	USA	Poet - Pulitzer
	Roth	Creative Works	USA	Novelist - Pulitzer
	Sidney	Creative Works	England	Poet/Statesman
	Slone	Sports	USA	Soccer Player - HF
Philip Anthony (Phil)	Esposito	Sports	Canada	Hockey Player - HF
Philip Cortelyou	Johnson	Architecture	USA	Architect - Pritzker/ AIA Gold
Philip Dormer	Stanhope	Politics	England	Statesman
Philip Francis (Phil)	Rizzuto	Sports	USA	Baseball Player - HF
Philip Gordon	Wylie	Creative Works	USA	Author
Philip Henry	Sheridan	War & Peace	USA	Union General - Civil War
Philip Henry (Phil)	Niekro	Sports	USA	Baseball Player - HF
Philip J.	Noel-Baker	War & Peace	England	Peace - Nobel Laureate
Philip José	Farmer	Creative Works	USA	Author
Philip Kenyon	Chapman	Aviation	USA	Astronaut
Philip Showalter	Hench	Science	USA	Medicine - Nobel Laureate
Philip Warren	Anderson	Science	USA	Physics - Nobel Laureate

FIRST NAME	LAST NAME	CATEGORY	COUNTRY	FAME
Philippe	Chartrier	Sports	France	Tennis Player - HF
	Perrin	Aviation	France	Astronaut
Philippus Aurelus	Paracelsus	Science	Switzerland	Physician/Alchemist
Phillip	Henslowe	Arts	England	Theater Manager
	Lesh (Chapman)	Performing Arts	USA	Rock & Roll - HF - Grateful Dead
	Massinger	Creative Works	England	Dramatist
	Melanchthon	Politics	Germany	Reformer - Protestant
	Webb	Architecture	England	Architect/Designer
Phillip (Phil)	Everly	Performing Arts	USA	Country Music - HF - Everly Brothers
	Everly	Performing Arts	USA	Rock & Roll - HF - Everly Brothers
	Rudd (Norman)	Performing Arts	Australia	Rock & Roll - HF - AC/DC
Phillip A.	Sharp	Science	USA	Medicine - Nobel Laureate
Phillip John	Schuyler	War & Peace	USA	General - Revolutionary War
Phillip Morin	Freneau	Creative Works	USA	Poet/Journalist
Phillip Van	Artevelde	Politics	USA	Statesman
Phillipe de	Comines	Arts	France	Historian/Diplomat
	Mornay	Politics	France	Diplomat
Phillipp Eduard Anton von	Lenard	Science	Germany	Physics - Nobel Laureate
Phillips	Brooks	Creative Works	USA	Writer/Clergyman
Phillis	Wheatley	Creative Works	USA	Poet
Philo	Judaeus	Arts	Greece	Philosopher
Phineas Taylor	Barnum	Arts	USA	Showman
Phoebe	Cates	Performing Arts	USA	Actress
	Snow	Performing Arts	USA	Singer
Phylicia	Rashad	Performing Arts	USA	Actress
Phyllis	Diller	Performing Arts	USA	Comedian
	McGinley	Creative Works	USA	Poet - Pulitzer
Pia	Lindstrom	Performing Arts	Sweden	Actress
	Zadora	Performing Arts	USA	Actress
Pier Luigi	Nervi	Architecture	Italy	Architect - AIA Gold Medal
Pier Paolo	Pasolini	Movie Production	Italy	Director
Pierce	Brosnan	Performing Arts	Ireland	Actor
Pierino Ronald (Perry)	Como	Performing Arts	USA	Singer - Big Band/Jazz - HF
Piero	Portaluppi	Architecture	Italy	Architect
Pierre	Abelard	Arts	France	Theologian/Philosopher
	Bayle	Arts	France	Philosopher/Critic
	Bonnard	Works of Art	France	Painter
	Cardin	Business	France	Fashion Designer
	Corneille	Creative Works	France	Dramatist
	Curie	Science	France	Physics - Nobel Laureate
	Etchebaster	Sports	France	Tennis Player - HF
	Laval	Politics	France	Premier
	Lescot	Architecture	France	Architect
	Loti	Creative Works	France	Novelist
	Louÿs	Creative Works	France	Poet/Novelist
	Monteux	Performing Arts	USA	Conductor - Orchestra
	Teilhard de Chardin	Arts	France	Paleontologist/Geologist
Pierre Antoine	Delamair	Architecture	France	Architect
Pierre Athanase La	Rochelle	Arts	France	Lexicographer/Grammarian
Pierre Auguste	Renoir	Works of Art	France	Painter
Pierre Charles	Baudelaire	Creative Works	France	Poet
	L'Enfant	Architecture	France	Architect/Engineer
Pierre de	Meuron	Architecture	Switzerland	Architect - Pritzker Laureate
	Montreuil	Architecture	France	Architect
	Ronsard	Creative Works	France	Poet
Pierre de la	Vérandrye	Exploration	Canada	Explorer - Canada West
Pierre Elliott	Trudeau	Politics	Canada	Prime Minster
Pierre Emil George	Salinger	Politics	USA	Senator/Press Secretary
Pierre Esprit	Radisson	Exploration	France	Explorer - Minnesota
Pierre ÉtienneThéodore	Rousseau	Works of Art	France	Painter - Landscape
Pierre François Dominique	Toussaint	Politics	Haiti	General/Negro Liberator
Pierre François-Xavier	Charlevoix	Exploration	France	Explorer - Mississippi River
Pierre Gustave Toutant de	Beauregard	War & Peace	USA	General

FIRST NAME	LAST NAME	CATEGORY	COUNTRY	FAME
Pierre Jean de	Béranger	Creative Works	France	Lyric Poet
Pierre Joseph	Proudhon	Arts	France	Socialist/Writer
	Thuot	Aviation	USA	Astronaut
Pierre Marie Félix	Janet	Arts	France	Psychologist
Pierre Paul	Pilote	Sports	Canada	Hockey Player - HF
	Prud'hon	Works of Art	France	Painter/Draftsman
Pierre Puvis de	Chavannes	Works of Art	France	Painter
Pierre Simon de	Laplace	Science	France	Astronomer/Mathematician
Pierre Teilhard de	Chardin	Arts	France	Philosopher/Geologist/Jesuit
Pierre-Gilles de	Gennes	Science	France	Physics - Nobel Laureate
Pierre-Jean David	D'Angers	Works of Art	France	Sculptor
Piet	Mondrian	Works of Art	Netherlands	Painter
Pieter	Bruegel	Works of Art	Italy	Painter
Pieter de	Hooch	Works of Art	Netherlands	Painter
Pieter Lodewijk	Kramer	Architecture	Netherlands	Architect
Pietro	Aretino	Creative Works	Italy	Writer
	Belluschi	Architecture	Italy	Architect - AIA Gold Medal
	Germi	Movie Production	Italy	Director - Acad Award Nom
	Mascagni	Creative Works	Italy	Composer - Opera
Pietro da	Cortona	Architecture	Italy	Architect
Pinchas	Zuckerman	Performing Arts	Israel	Conductor/Violinist
Pio	Baroja	Creative Works	Spain	Novelist
Piper	Laurie	Performing Arts	USA	Actress - Acad Award Nom
Pipino	Cuevas	Sports	Mexico	Boxer - HF
Placido	Domingo	Performing Arts	Spain	Singer - Opera
Plutarco Elías	Calles	Politics	Mexico	President
Pola	Negri	Performing Arts	Poland	Actress
Polly	Bergen	Performing Arts	USA	Actress
	Holliday	Performing Arts	USA	Actress
Polykarp	Kusch	Science	USA	Physics - Nobel Laureate
Porter	Waggoner	Performing Arts	USA	Singer - Country Music - HF
Potter	Stewart	Law & Order	USA	Justice - Supreme Court
Prentiss	Barnes	Performing Arts	USA	Rock & Roll - HF - Moonglows
Preston	Foster	Performing Arts	USA	Actor
	Sturges	Movie Production	USA	Director - Acad Award Nom
Primo	Carnera	Sports	Italy	Boxer
Prince Rogers	Nelson	Performing Arts	USA	Singer - Rock & Roll - HF
Priscilla	Presley	Performing Arts	USA	Actress
Prosper	Ménière	Science	France	Physician
	Mérimée	Creative Works	France	Novelist/Essayist/Historian
Pyotr (Peter the Great)	Alekseyvich	Politics	Russia	Emperor
Queen	Latifah	Performing Arts	USA	Actress - Acad Award Nom
Quentin	Crisp	Creative Works	England	Author
	Tarantino	Movie Production	USA	Director - Acad Award Nom
Quincy Delight	Jones	Performing Arts	USA	Musician/Producer - Big Band/Jazz - HF
Quinn	Cummings	Performing Arts	USA	Actress - Acad Award Nom
Rabindranath	Tagoré	Creative Works	India	Literature - Nobel Laureate
Rabon	Delmore	Performing Arts	USA	Country Music - HF - Delmore Brothers
Rachael	Griffiths	Performing Arts	Australia	Actress - Acad Award Nom
Rachel	Crothers	Creative Works	USA	Playwright
	Hunter	Performing Arts	New Zealand	Super Model
	Roberts	Performing Arts	Wales	Actress - Acad Award Nom
	Ward	Performing Arts	England	Actress
Rachel Donelson	Jackson	Politics	USA	First Lady
Rachel Louise	Carson	Science	USA	Biologist/Writer
Radu	Lupu	Performing Arts	Romania	Pianist
Rae Dawn	Chong	Performing Arts	Canada	Actress
Rafael	Moneo	Architecture	Spain	Architect - Pritzker Laureate
Rafaël	Kubelik	Performing Arts	Czechoslovakia	Orchestra Conductor
Rafael Herrera (Rafe)	Osuna	Sports	Mexico	Tennis Player - HF
Rafer Lewis	Johnson	Sports	USA	Olympic Runner
Ragnar	Frisch	Arts	Norway	Economics - Nobel Laureate
	Granit	Science	Sweden	Medicine - Nobel Laureate

SOLVER SERIES: NAME FINDER

FIRST NAME	LAST NAME	CATEGORY	COUNTRY	FAME
Ragnar	Ostberg	Architecture	Sweden	Architect - AIA Gold Medal
Rahman Khan	Abdur	Politics	Afghanistan	Amir
Rainer Maria	Rilke	Creative Works	Austria	Poet - Lyric
Raisa	Gorbachev	Politics	Russia	First Lady
Rajiv	Ghandi	Politics	India	Prime Minister
Ralph	Bellamy	Performing Arts	USA	Actor - Acad Award Nom
	Capone	Law & Order	Italy	Mafia
	Carrafi	Sports	USA	Soccer Player - HF
	Earnhardt	Sports	USA	Race Car Driver - HF
	Ellison	Creative Works	USA	Author
	Fiennes	Performing Arts	England	Actor - Acad Award Nom
	Gudahl	Sports	USA	Golfer - HF
	Lauren	Business	USA	Fashion Designer
	Macchio	Performing Arts	USA	Actor
	Moody Jr.	Sports	USA	Race Car Driver - HF
	Nader	Politics	USA	Lawyer/Reformer
	Reichman	Business	Canada	Real Estate
	Richardson	Performing Arts	England	Actor - Acad Award Nom
	Vaughan Williams	Creative Works	England	Composer
	Waite	Performing Arts	USA	Actor
	Walker	Architecture	USA	Architect - AIA Gold Medal
	Wenge	Creative Works	USA	Journalist - Television
Ralph (Cooney)	Weiland	Sports	Canada	Hockey Player - HF
Ralph Adams	Cram	Architecture	USA	Architect/Writer
Ralph Barton	Perry	Creative Works	USA	Author - Pulitzer
Ralph De	Palma	Sports	Italy	Race Car Driver - HF
Ralph Johnson	Bunche	Politics	USA	Statesman/Educator
	Bunche	War & Peace	USA	Peace - Nobel Laureate
Ralph McPherran	Kiner	Sports	USA	Baseball Player - HF
Ralph Waldo	Emerson	Creative Works	USA	Poet/Essayist/Philosopher
Ramana	Maharshi	Arts	India	Philosopher /Sage
Ramon	Novarro	Performing Arts	Mexico	Actor
Ramon Grau San	Martin	Politics	Cuba	President
Ramsey	Lewis	Creative Works	USA	Composer/Pianist
Randall (Hank)	Williams Jr.	Performing Arts	USA	Singer - Rock & Roll - HF
Randolph	Scott	Performing Arts	USA	Actor
Randolph Henry Spencer	Churchill	Politics	England	Statesman
Randy	Meisner	Performing Arts	USA	Rock & Roll - HF - The Eagles
	Newman	Creative Works	USA	Composer
	Quaid	Performing Arts	USA	Actor - Acad Award Nom
	Travis	Performing Arts	USA	Singer - Country & Western
	Turpin	Sports	England	Boxer - HF
Randy Lee	White	Sports	USA	Football Player - HF
Randy Yeuell	Owen	Performing Arts	USA	Country Music - HF - Alabama
Ransom Eli	Olds	Business	USA	Automobile Industy
Ranulf	Fiennes	Exploration	England	Explorer - Polar Explorer
Raoul	Wallenberg	Arts	Sweden	Humanitarian/Diplomat
	Walsh	Movie Production	USA	Director
Raoul Ernest Joseph	Dufy	Works of Art	France	Painter
Raphael	Holinshed	Arts	England	Chronicler
	Santi	Works of Art	Italy	Painter/Architect
	Soyer	Works of Art	USA	Painter
Raphael (Ralph)	Tracey	Sports	USA	Soccer Player - HF
Raquel	Welch	Performing Arts	USA	Actress
Rasmus Christian	Rasht	Arts	Denmark	Philologist
Raul	Julia	Performing Arts	Puerto Rico	Actor
Raül Gonzalez	Blanco	Sports	Spain	Soccer Player
Ravi	Shankar	Performing Arts	Bangladesh	Sitarist
Ray	Bolger	Performing Arts	USA	Actor
	Bradbury	Creative Works	USA	Author - SciFi
	Charles (Robinson)	Performing Arts	USA	Singer - Rock & Roll - HF
	Charles (Robinson)	Performing Arts	USA	Singer/Pianist - Big Band/Jazz - HF
	Conniff	Performing Arts	USA	Band Leader/Trombonist

FIRST NAME	LAST NAME	CATEGORY	COUNTRY	FAME
Ray	Fox	Sports	USA	Race Car Designer - HF
	Kroc	Business	USA	McDonalds Restaurants
	Liotta	Performing Arts	USA	Actor
	Manzarek	Performing Arts	USA	Rock & Roll - HF - The Doors
	Mercer	Sports	USA	Boxer
	Milland	Performing Arts	Wales	Actor - Academy Award
	Noble	Performing Arts	England	Band Leader - Big Band/Jazz - HF
	Satyajit	Movie Production	India	Director
	Stevens	Performing Arts	USA	Singer - Pops
	Walker	Performing Arts	USA	Country Music - HF - Sons of the Pioneers
	Walston	Performing Arts	USA	Actor
	Perkins	Performing Arts	Canada	Canadian Music - HF - The Crew Cuts
Ray (Raymond Matthews)	Brown	Performing Arts	USA	Jazz Bassist - Big Band/Jazz - HF
Ray Noble	Price	Performing Arts	USA	Singer - Country Music - HF
Ray Stannard	Baker	Creative Works	USA	Author - Pulitzer
Ray Willis	Nance	Performing Arts	USA	Jazz Trumpeter - Big Band/Jazz - HF
Raymond	Bernabei	Sports	USA	Soccer Player - HF
	Burr	Performing Arts	Canada	Actor
	Chandler	Creative Works	USA	Novelist - Crime Fiction
	Davis Jr.	Science	USA	Physics - Nobel Laureate
	Floyd	Sports	USA	Golfer - HF
	Massey	Performing Arts	Canada	Actor - Acad Award Nom
	Poincaré	Politics	France	President
Raymond (Sugar Ray)	Leonard	Sports	USA	Boxer - HF
	Robinson	Sports	USA	Boxer - HF
Raymond Douglas (Ray)	Davies	Performing Arts	England	Rock & Roll - HF - The Kinks
Raymond Emmett -	Berry	Sports	USA	Football Player - HF
Raymond Emmitt (Ray)	Dandridge	Sports	USA	Baseball Player - HF
Raymond Ernest (Ray)	Nitschke	Sports	USA	Football Player - HF
Raymond Ferdinand	Loewy	Business	USA	Industrial Designer
Raymond Jean (Ray)	Bourque	Sports	Canada	Hockey Player - HF
Raymond Lee	Ditmars	Arts	USA	Naturalist/Zoo Curator
Raymond Paul (Ray)	Flaherty	Sports	USA	Football Coach - HF
Raymond William (Ray)	Schalk	Sports	USA	Baseball Player - HF
Reba	McEntire	Performing Arts	USA	Singer
Rebecca	Romijn-Stamos	Performing Arts	USA	Actress/Super Model
	West	Creative Works	England	Novelist/Critic
Rebecca De	Mornay	Performing Arts	USA	Actress
Red	Auerbach	Sports	USA	Basketball Player
	Buttons	Performing Arts	USA	Actor - Academy Award
	Skelton	Performing Arts	USA	Comedian
Redd	Foxx	Performing Arts	USA	Comedian
Reggie	Roby	Sports	USA	Football Player
	Torian	Performing Arts	USA	Rock & Roll - HF - The Impressions
	White	Sports	USA	Football Player
Regina	King	Performing Arts	USA	Actress
	Resnik	Performing Arts	USA	Singer
Reginald	Denny	Performing Arts	England	Actor
	Marsh	Works of Art	USA	Painter
	Owen	Performing Arts	England	Actor
	Pole	Arts	England	Archbishop of Canterbury
Reginald (Hooley)	Smith	Sports	Canada	Hockey Player - HF
Reginald Frank (Reggie)	Doherty	Sports	England	Tennis Player - HF
Reginald K. (Elton)	John (Dwight)	Performing Arts	England	Singer - Rock & Roll - HF
Reginald Martinez (Reggie)	Jackson	Sports	USA	Baseball Player - HF
Reima	Pietilä	Architecture	Finland	Architect
Reinhard	Selten	Arts	Germany	Economics - Nobel Laureate
Reinhard Alfred	Furrer	Aviation	Germany	Astronaut
Rem	Koolhaas	Architecture	Netherlands	Architect - Pritzker Laureate
Rembrandt	Peale	Works of Art	USA	Painter - Neoclassical
Rembrandt Van	Rijn	Works of Art	Netherlands	Painter/Engraver
Rémy de	Gourmont	Arts	France	Philosopher/Poet/Novelist/Critic
Rena	Rowan	Business	Poland	Fashion Designer

FIRST NAME	LAST NAME	CATEGORY	COUNTRY	FAME
Renaldo	Benson	Performing Arts	USA	Rock & Roll - HF - The Four Tops
Renata	Scotto	Performing Arts	Italy	Singer - Opera
	Tebaldi	Performing Arts	Italy	Singer - Opera
Renato	Dulbecco	Science	USA	Medicine - Nobel Laureate
Rene	Russo	Performing Arts	USA	Actress
René	Auberjonois	Performing Arts	USA	Actor
	Cassin	War & Peace	France	Peace - Nobel Laureate
	Clair	Movie Production	France	Director
	Coty	Politics	France	President
	Descartes	Arts	France	Philosopher/Mathematician
	Magritte	Works of Art	Belgium	Painter - Surrealist
René François Armand	Sully-Prudhomme	Creative Works	France	Poet/Critic
René Jules	Dubos	Creative Works	USA	Author - Pulitzer
Renee	Adoree	Performing Arts	France	Actress
	Taylor	Performing Arts	USA	Actress
	Zellweger	Performing Arts	USA	Actress - Academy Award
Renée	Fleming	Performing Arts	USA	Singer - Opera
Réne-Robert Cavelier de la	Salle	Exploration	France	Explorer - Mississippi River
Renzo	Piano	Architecture	Italy	Architect - Pritzker Laureate
Reri	Grist	Performing Arts	USA	Singer - Opera
Respighi	Ottorino	Creative Works	Italy	Composer
Reta	Shaw	Performing Arts	USA	Actress
Reuben Lucius (Rube)	Goldberg	Creative Works	USA	Cartoonist - Pulitzer
Rex	Harrison	Performing Arts	England	Actor - Academy Award
	Mays	Sports	USA	Race Car Driver - HF
	Reed	Creative Works	USA	Journalist - Newspaper
	Stewart	Performing Arts	USA	Jazz Cornetist - Big Band/Jazz - HF
Rex Todhunter	Stout	Creative Works	USA	Author
Rhea	Perlman	Performing Arts	USA	Actress
Rhee	Syngman	Politics	South Korea	Head of State
Rhoderick John (Bobby)	Wallace	Sports	USA	Baseball Player - HF
Rhonda	Fleming	Performing Arts	USA	Actress
Rhys L.	Isaac	Creative Works	USA	Author - Pulitzer
Ric	Ocasek	Performing Arts	USA	Singer
Ricardo	Legorreta	Architecture	Mexico	Architect - AIA Gold Medal
	Montalban	Performing Arts	Mexico	Actor
	Muti	Performing Arts	Italy	Conductor
	Porro	Architecture	Cuba	Architect
Riccardo	Bofill	Architecture	Spain	Architect
	Giacconi	Science	USA	Physics - Nobel Laureate
Rich	Little	Performing Arts	Canada	Comedian
Richard	Arkwright	Business	England	Textile Industry
	Arkwright	Science	England	Inventor
	Attenborough	Movie Production	England	Director - Academy Award
	Axel	Science	USA	Medicine - Nobel Laureate
	Barthelmess	Performing Arts	USA	Actor - Acad Award Nom
	Basehart	Performing Arts	USA	Actor
	Benjamin	Movie Production	USA	Director
	Benjamin	Performing Arts	USA	Actor
	Bentley	Creative Works	England	Scholar/Critic
	Boone	Performing Arts	USA	Actor
	Branson	Business	England	Aviation - Virgin Blue
	Bright	Performing Arts	USA	Actor
	Brooks	Movie Production	USA	Director - Acad Award Nom
	Burton	Performing Arts	Wales	Actor - Acad Award Nom
	Cameron	Arts	Scotland	Minister/Covenanter
	Carlile	Business	England	Publishing
	Castellano	Performing Arts	USA	Actor - Acad Award Nom
	Chamberlain	Performing Arts	USA	Actor
	Cheney	Politics	USA	Vice-President
	Conte	Performing Arts	USA	Actor
	Crashaw	Creative Works	England	Poet - Religion
	Crenna	Performing Arts	USA	Actor

FIRST NAME	LAST NAME	CATEGORY	COUNTRY	FAME
Richard	Cromwell	Politics	England	Protector - Commonwealth
	Cumberland	Arts	England	Philosopher/Bishop
	Dawson	Performing Arts	England	Actor
	Dent	Sports	USA	Football Player
	Dix	Performing Arts	USA	Actor - Acad Award Nom
	Dreyfuss	Performing Arts	USA	Actor - Academy Award
	Dunbar	Performing Arts	USA	Rock & Roll - HF - The Drifters
	Dysart	Performing Arts	USA	Actor
	Eberhart	Creative Works	USA	Poet - Pulitzer
	Ellmann	Creative Works	USA	Author - Pulitzer
	Farnsworth	Performing Arts	USA	Actor - Acad Award Nom
	Ford	Creative Works	USA	Author - Pulitzer
	Gere	Performing Arts	USA	Actor
	Grenville	War & Peace	England	Naval Commander
	Hakluyt	Arts	England	Geographer/Chronicler
	Harris	Performing Arts	Ireland	Actor - Acad Award Nom
	Hooker	Arts	England	Clergyman/Writer
	Howard	Creative Works	USA	Poet - Pulitzer
	Jaeckel	Performing Arts	USA	Actor - Acad Award Nom
	Jordan	Performing Arts	USA	Actor
	Kiley	Performing Arts	USA	Singer
	Kluger	Creative Works	USA	Author - Pulitzer
	Kuhn	Science	Germany	Chemistry - Nobel Laureate
	Lewis	Performing Arts	USA	Comedian
	Long	Performing Arts	USA	Actor
	Lovelace	Creative Works	England	Poet
	Mansfield	Performing Arts	USA	Actor
	Manuel	Performing Arts	Canada	Rock & Roll - HF - The Band
	Meier	Architecture	USA	Architect - Pritzker/ AIA Gold
	Moll	Performing Arts	USA	Actor
	Mulligan	Performing Arts	USA	Actor
	Porson	Arts	England	Scholar - Classical
	Pryor	Performing Arts	USA	Comedian
	Ramirez	Law & Order	USA	Serial Killer - Night Stalker
	Rhodes	Creative Works	USA	Author - Pulitzer
	Rodgers	Creative Works	USA	Composer - Musicals
	Rodgers	Creative Works	USA	Dramatist - Pulitzer
	Rogers	Architecture	England	Architect - Jefferson Medal
	Rorty	Arts	USA	Philosopher
	Rush	Movie Production	USA	Director - Acad Award Nom
	Russo	Creative Works	USA	Novelist - Pulitzer
	Steele	Creative Works	England	Dramatist/Essayist
	Stone	Arts	England	Economics - Nobel Laureate
	Strauss	Creative Works	Germany	Composer/Conductor
	Thomas	Performing Arts	USA	Actor
	Todd	Movie Production	Ireland	Director
	Todd	Performing Arts	Ireland	Actor - Acad Award Nom
	Tufts	Sports	USA	Golf Promoter - HF
	Whittington	Business	England	Merchant
	Widmark	Performing Arts	USA	Actor - Acad Award Nom
	Wilbur	Creative Works	USA	Poet - Pulitzer
	Wright	Creative Works	USA	Novelist
	Brooks	Performing Arts	USA	Rock & Roll - HF - The Impressions
Richard (Dick)	Savitt	Sports	USA	Tennis Player - HF
	Tiger	Sports	Nigeria	Boxer - HF
Richard (Dick) (Night Train)	Lane	Sports	USA	Football Player - HF
Richard (Ringo)	Starr (Starkey)	Performing Arts	England	Rock & Roll - HF - The Beatles
Richard (The King)	Petty	Sports	USA	Race Car Driver - HF
Richard Adolf	Zsigmondy	Science	Germany	Chemistry - Nobel Laureate
Richard Alan	Searfoss	Aviation	USA	Astronaut
Richard Alonzo (Pancho)	Gonzales	Sports	USA	Tennis Player - HF
Richard Andrew	Gephardt	Politics	USA	Congressman - Missouri
Richard Arthur (Dik)	Browne	Creative Works	USA	Cartoonist - Hagar

SOLVER SERIES: NAME FINDER

FIRST NAME	LAST NAME	CATEGORY	COUNTRY	FAME
Richard Bedford	Bennett	Politics	Canada	Prime Minster
Richard Benjamin	Speck	Law & Order	USA	Serial Killer
Richard Benjamin (Rick)	Ferrell	Sports	USA	Baseball Player - HF
Richard Brinsley	Sheridan	Creative Works	Ireland	Playwright
Richard Buckminster	Fuller	Architecture	USA	Architect - AIA Gold Medal
Richard Burdon	Haldane	Politics	Scotland	Statesman/Philosopher
Richard Couer de	Lion	War & Peace	England	Military Leader
Richard Dean	Anderson	Performing Arts	USA	Actor
Richard Dennis (Denny)	Ralston	Sports	USA	Tennis Player - HF
Richard Dudley (Dick)	Sears	Sports	USA	Tennis Player - HF
Richard E.	Smalley	Science	USA	Chemistry - Nobel Laureate
	Taylor	Science	Canada	Physics - Nobel Laureate
Richard Evelyn	Byrd	Exploration	USA	Explorer - Antarctic
Richard F. (Rick)	Barry	Sports	USA	Basketball Player - HF
Richard Francis	Burton	Exploration	England	Explorer/Writer - Africa
	Gordon Jr.	Aviation	USA	Astronaut
Richard Green (Dick)	Lugar	Politics	USA	Senator - Indiana
Richard Harding	Davis	Creative Works	USA	Novelist/Journalist/Editor
Richard Harrison	Truly	Aviation	USA	Astronaut
Richard Henry	Dana	Creative Works	USA	Writer/Lawyer
	Tawney	Arts	England	Economist - Historian
Richard J.	Roberts	Science	England	Medicine - Nobel Laureate
Richard James	Hieb	Aviation	USA	Astronaut
Richard Jordan	Gatling	Business	USA	Firearms
Richard Joseph	Daley	Politics	USA	Mayor - Chicago
	Neutra	Architecture	Austria	Architect - AIA Gold Medal
Richard Laurence Millington	Synge	Science	England	Chemistry - Nobel Laureate
Richard Lemon	Landers	Exploration	England	Explorer - Africa West
Richard M.	Johnson	Politics	USA	Vice-President
Richard Martin	Willstätter	Science	Germany	Chemistry - Nobel Laureate
Richard Marvin (Dick)	Butkus	Sports	USA	Football Player - HF
Richard Mervyn	Hare	Arts	England	Philosopher
Richard Michael	Daley	Politics	USA	Mayor - Chicago
	Mullane	Aviation	USA	Astronaut
Richard Milhous	Nixon	Politics	USA	President
Richard Morris	Hunt	Architecture	USA	Architect
Richard Neville	Warwick	Politics	England	Statesman/Military Leader
Richard Noel	Richards	Aviation	USA	Astronaut
Richard Norris (Dick)	Williams II	Sports	USA	Tennis Player - HF
Richard Oswalt	Covey	Aviation	USA	Astronaut
Richard P.	Feynman	Science	USA	Physics - Nobel Laureate
Richard R.	Ernst	Science	Switzerland	Chemistry - Nobel Laureate
	Schrock	Science	USA	Chemistry - Nobel Laureate
Richard R. (Dickie)	Boon	Sports	Canada	Hockey Player - HF
Richard S. (Dick)	McGuire	Sports	USA	Basketball Player - HF
Richard Stanley (Dick)	Francis	Creative Works	Wales	Author
Richard Steven (Richie)	Valens (Valenzuela)	Performing Arts	USA	Singer - Rock & Roll - HF
Richard Stoddert	Ewell	War & Peace	USA	Confederate General
Richard Warrington Baldwin	Lewis	Creative Works	USA	Author - Pulitzer
Richard Wayne (Little Richard)	Richard (Penniman)	Performing Arts	USA	Singer - Rock & Roll - HF
Richard William	Wright	Performing Arts	England	Rock & Roll - HF - Pink Floyd
Richard William (Rube)	Marquard	Sports	USA	Baseball Player - HF
Richard Winston (Dickie)	Moore	Sports	Canada	Hockey Player - HF
Richie	Evans	Sports	USA	Race Car Driver - HF
	Furay	Performing Arts	USA	Rock & Roll - HF - Buffalo Springfield
	Havens	Performing Arts	USA	Singer
Rick	Atkinson	Creative Works	USA	Author - Pulitzer
	Danko	Performing Arts	Canada	Rock & Roll - HF - The Band
	Mears	Sports	USA	Race Car Driver - HF
	Moranis	Performing Arts	Canada	Actor
	Schroder	Performing Arts	USA	Actor
	Springfield	Performing Arts	Australia	Singer/Actor
Rick (Ricky)	Davis	Sports	USA	Soccer Player - HF

FIRST NAME	LAST NAME	CATEGORY	COUNTRY	FAME
Rick Douglas	Husband	Aviation	USA	Astronaut
Rickey	Henderson	Sports	USA	Baseball Player
Rickie Lee	Jones	Performing Arts	USA	Singer
Ricky	Bell	Sports	USA	Football Player
Riddick	Bowe	Sports	USA	Boxer
Ridley	Scott	Movie Production	England	Director - Acad Award Nom
Rigoberta Menchú	Tum	War & Peace	Guatemala	Peace - Nobel Laureate
Riley B. (BB)	King	Performing Arts	USA	Guitarist/Songwriter - Big Band/Jazz - HF
	King	Performing Arts	USA	Singer - Rock & Roll - HF
Ringgold Wilmer	Lardner	Creative Works	USA	Humorist/Sports Reporter
Rino	Tami	Architecture	Switzerland	Architect
Rip	Taylor	Performing Arts	USA	Comedian
	Torn	Performing Arts	USA	Actor - Acad Award Nom
Rita	Coolidge	Performing Arts	USA	Singer
	Dove	Creative Works	USA	Poet - Pulitzer
	Gam	Performing Arts	USA	Actress
	Hayworth	Performing Arts	USA	Actress
	Moreno	Performing Arts	Puerto Rico	Actress - Academy Award
	Rudner	Performing Arts	USA	Comedian
	Tushingham	Performing Arts	England	Actress
Rivaldo Vito Barbosa	Ferreria	Sports	Brazil	Soccer Player
River	Phoenix	Performing Arts	USA	Actor - Acad Award Nom
Roald	Amunsden	Exploration	Norway	Explorer - Polar
	Dahl	Creative Works	Wales	Writer
	Hoffmann	Science	USA	Chemistry - Nobel Laureate
Rob	Lowe	Performing Arts	USA	Actor
	Marshall	Movie Production	USA	Director - Acad Award Nom
	McConnell	Performing Arts	Canada	Trombonist/Arranger - Canadian Music - HF
	Reiner	Movie Production	USA	Director
	Reiner	Performing Arts	USA	Comedian
Robb	Nen	Sports	USA	Baseball Player
Robbie	McIntosh	Performing Arts	England	Rock & Roll - HF - The Pretenders
Robby	Baker	Performing Arts	Canada	Canadian Music - HF - The Tragically Hip
	Benson	Performing Arts	USA	Actor
	Krieger	Performing Arts	USA	Rock & Roll - HF - The Doors
Robert	Alda	Performing Arts	USA	Actor
	Altman	Movie Production	USA	Director - Acad Award Nom
	Ballard	Exploration	USA	Explorer - Marine/Titanic
	Bárány	Science	Austria	Medicine - Nobel Laureate
	Barnard	Creative Works	England	Author
	Bateman	Works of Art	Canada	Painter
	Benton	Movie Production	USA	Director - Academy Award
	Blake	Performing Arts	USA	Actor
	Blake	War & Peace	England	Admiral
	Bly	Creative Works	USA	Author/Poet
	Boyle	Science	England	Chemist/Physicist
	Brown	Science	England	Botanist
	Browning	Creative Works	England	Poet
	Bruce	Creative Works	USA	Author - Pulitzer
	Bruce	Politics	Scotland	King
	Burns	Creative Works	Scotland	Poet
	Burton	Creative Works	England	Writer/Clergyman
	Clary	Performing Arts	France	Actor
	Clive	Politics	England	Statesman
	Coles	Creative Works	USA	Author - Pulitzer
	Conrad	Performing Arts	USA	Actor
	Crumb	Creative Works	USA	Cartoonist - Fritz the Cat
	Culp	Performing Arts	USA	Actor
	Cummings	Performing Arts	USA	Actor
	Dinwiddie	Politics	England	Governor - Virginia
	Donat	Performing Arts	England	Actor - Academy Award
	Downey	Movie Production	USA	Director
	"Downey, Jr"	Performing Arts	USA	Actor - Acad Award Nom

SOLVER SERIES: NAME FINDER

FIRST NAME	LAST NAME	CATEGORY	COUNTRY	FAME
Robert	Dudley	Politics	England	Courtier
	Duvall	Performing Arts	USA	Actor - Academy Award
	Englund	Performing Arts	USA	Actor
	Evans	Creative Works	USA	Journalist - Television
	Forster	Performing Arts	USA	Actor - Acad Award Nom
	Foxworth	Performing Arts	USA	Actor
	Fulton	Science	USA	Inventor - Steam Boat
	Goulet	Performing Arts	USA	Singer
	Gray	Exploration	USA	Explorer - Circumnavigation
	Greene	Creative Works	England	Poet/Dramatist/Pamphleteer
	Guillaume	Performing Arts	USA	Actor - Musical
	Hays	Performing Arts	USA	Actor
	Herrick	Creative Works	England	Poet
	Hillyer	Creative Works	USA	Poet - Pulitzer
	Hofstadter	Science	USA	Physics - Nobel Laureate
	Hooke	Science	England	Inventor/Physicist
	Hooks	Performing Arts	USA	Actor
	Horvitz	Science	USA	Medicine - Nobel Laureate
	Huber	Science	Germany	Chemistry - Nobel Laureate
	Ito	Performing Arts	Canada	Actor
	Joffrey	Performing Arts	USA	Dancer - Ballet
	Klein	Performing Arts	USA	Actor - Musical
	Koch	Science	Germany	Medicine - Nobel Laureate
	Lansing	Performing Arts	USA	Actor
	Leonard	Movie Production	USA	Director - Acad Award Nom
	Loggia	Performing Arts	USA	Actor - Acad Award Nom
	Ludlum	Creative Works	USA	Author - Spy Novels
	MacNeil	Creative Works	Canada	Journalist - Television
	Maillart	Architecture	Switzerland	Architect
	Maplethorpe	Works of Art	USA	Photographer
	Merrill	Performing Arts	USA	Singer - Opera
	Mitchum	Performing Arts	USA	Actor - Acad Award Nom
	Montgomery	Performing Arts	USA	Actor - Acad Award Nom
	Morley	Performing Arts	England	Actor - Acad Award Nom
	Morris	Business	USA	Financier/Patriot
	Morrison	Sports	Scotland	Soccer Player - HF
	Morse	Performing Arts	USA	Actor
	Motherwell	Works of Art	USA	Painter - Abstract Expressionist
	Mulligan	Movie Production	USA	Director - Acad Award Nom
	Novak	Creative Works	USA	Journalist - Newspaper
	Nozick	Arts	USA	Philosopher
	Owen	Architecture	England	Architect
	Owen	Business	England	Textile Industry
	Palmer	Performing Arts	England	Singer
	Parish	Sports	USA	Basketball Player - HF
	Peel	Politics	England	Prime Minister
	Peel Sr.	Business	England	Textile Industry
	Preston	Performing Arts	USA	Actor - Acad Award Nom
	Prosky	Performing Arts	USA	Actor
	Rauschenberg	Works of Art	USA	Painter - Pop
	Redford	Movie Production	USA	Director - Academy Award
	Redford	Performing Arts	USA	Actor - Acad Award Nom
	Reed	Performing Arts	USA	Actor
	Robinson	Science	England	Chemistry - Nobel Laureate
	Rossen	Movie Production	USA	Director - Acad Award Nom
	Ryan	Performing Arts	USA	Actor - Acad Award Nom
	Schenkkan	Creative Works	USA	Dramatist - Pulitzer
	Shaw	Performing Arts	England	Actor - Acad Award Nom
	Siegel	Architecture	USA	Architect
	Silverberg	Creative Works	USA	Author - SciFi
	Siodmak	Movie Production	Germany	Director - Acad Award Nom
	Smirke	Architecture	England	Architect
	Southey	Creative Works	England	Poet Laureate/Writer

FIRST NAME	LAST NAME	CATEGORY	COUNTRY	FAME
Robert	Stack	Performing Arts	USA	Actor - Acad Award Nom
	Stephenson	Science	England	Engineer - Bridge Builder
	Stevenson	Movie Production	England	Director - Acad Award Nom
	Strauss	Performing Arts	USA	Actor - Acad Award Nom
	Taylor	Performing Arts	USA	Actor
	Torrens	Politics	Australia	Statesman
	Townsend	Movie Production	USA	Director
	Urich	Performing Arts	USA	Actor
	Vaughn	Performing Arts	USA	Actor - Acad Award Nom
	Venturi	Architecture	USA	Architect - Pritzker/Jefferson Medal
	Wagner	Performing Arts	USA	Actor
	Walden	Performing Arts	USA	Actor
	Walker	Performing Arts	USA	Actor
	Walpole	Politics	England	Prime Minster
	Wise	Movie Production	USA	Director - Academy Award
	Young	Performing Arts	USA	Actor
	Zemeckis	Movie Production	USA	Director - Academy Award
	Johnson	Performing Arts	USA	Singer - Rock & Roll HF
Robert (Bob)	Brookmeyer	Performing Arts	USA	Jazz Trombonist - Big Band/Jazz - HF
	Falkenburg	Sports	USA	Tennis Player - HF
	Gibson	Sports	USA	Baseball Player - HF
	Gormley	Sports	USA	Soccer Player - HF
	Hall (Weir)	Performing Arts	USA	Rock & Roll - HF - Grateful Dead
	Harlow	Sports	USA	Golf Promoter - HF
	McAdoo	Sports	USA	Basketball Player - HF
	Millar	Sports	Scotland	Soccer Player - HF
Robert (Bobby)	McDermott	Sports	USA	Basketball Player - HF
	Wanzer	Sports	USA	Basketball Player - HF
Robert (Cal)	Hubbard	Sports	USA	Baseball Umpire - HF
Robert (Kool)	Bell	Performing Arts	USA	Singer/Composer
Robert A.	Mundell	Arts	Canada	Economics - Nobel Laureate
Robert A. (Bob)	Kurland	Sports	USA	Basketball Player - HF
Robert Alan (Bob)	Dylan (Zimmerman)	Performing Arts	USA	Singer - Rock & Roll - HF
Robert Alexander	Schumann	Creative Works	Germany	Composer
Robert Allan	Caro	Creative Works	USA	Author - Pulitzer
Robert Allen (Bob)	Griese	Sports	USA	Football Player - HF
Robert Andrews	Millikan	Science	USA	Physics - Nobel Laureate
Robert Anson	Heinlein	Creative Works	USA	Author - SciFi
Robert Anthony	Eden	Politics	England	Prime Minister
	Plant	Performing Arts	England	Rock & Roll - HF - Led Zepplin
Robert Anthony (Bob)	Hewitt	Sports	Australia	Tennis Player - HF
Robert Arthur Morton	Stern	Architecture	USA	Architect
Robert Arthur Talbot	Gascoyne-Cecil	Politics	England	Prime Minister
Robert B.	Laughlin	Science	USA	Physics - Nobel Laureate
Robert Blake Theodore (Ted)	Lindsay	Sports	Canada	Hockey Player - HF
Robert Brent	Thirsk	Aviation	Canada	Astronaut
Robert Bruce (Bob) (Geek)	St. Clair	Sports	USA	Football Player - HF
Robert Burns	Woodward	Science	USA	Chemistry - Nobel Laureate
Robert C.	Merton	Arts	USA	Economics - Nobel Laureate
	Richardson	Science	USA	Physics - Nobel Laureate
Robert Calvin (Bobby) (Blue)	Bland	Performing Arts	USA	Singer - Rock & Roll - HF
Robert Calvin (Cal)	Hubbard	Sports	USA	Football Player - HF
Robert Charles	Benchley	Creative Works	USA	Humorist
Robert Clyde	Springer	Aviation	USA	Astronaut
Robert Cornelius (Bobby)	Mitchell	Sports	USA	Football Player - HF
Robert De	Niro	Performing Arts	USA	Actor - Academy Award
Robert Dudley	Leicester	Arts	England	Courtier
Robert Duffield (Bob)	Wrenn	Sports	USA	Tennis Player - HF
Robert E.	Davies	Sports	USA	Basketball Player - HF
	Lucas Jr.	Arts	USA	Economics - Nobel Laureate
Robert Earle (Bobby)	Clarke	Sports	Canada	Hockey Player - HF
Robert Edward	Lee	War & Peace	USA	Commander in Chief
Robert Edwin	Peary	Exploration	USA	Explorer - North Pole

FIRST NAME	LAST NAME	CATEGORY	COUNTRY	FAME
Robert Emmet	Sherwood	Creative Works	USA	Dramatist - Pulitzer
Robert F.	Curl Jr.	Science	USA	Chemistry - Nobel Laureate
	Engle III	Arts	USA	Economics - Nobel Laureate
	Furchgott	Science	USA	Medicine - Nobel Laureate
Robert F. (Ace)	Gruenig	Sports	USA	Basketball Player - HF
Robert Falcon	Scott	Exploration	England	Explorer - Antarctic
Robert Francis (Bobby)	Kennedy	Politics	USA	Senator - New York
Robert Franklin	Overmyer	Aviation	USA	Astronaut
Robert Gascoyne	Cecil	War & Peace	England	Peace - Nobel Laureate
Robert Glenn (Junior)	Johnson	Sports	USA	Race Car Driver - HF
Robert Gordon	Menzies	Politics	Australia	Prime Minister
Robert Gordon (Bobby)	Orr	Sports	Canada	Hockey Player - HF
Robert Granville (Bob)	Lemon	Sports	USA	Baseball Player - HF
Robert Green	Ingersoll	Law & Order	USA	Lawyer/Lecturer
Robert H.	Grubbs	Science	USA	Chemistry - Nobel Laureate
Robert Houghwout	Jackson	Law & Order	USA	Justice - Supreme Court
Robert Hyde	Greg	Business	England	Textile Industry
Robert J.	Aumann	Arts	Germany	Economics - Nobel Laureate
	Kelleher	Sports	USA	Tennis Player - HF
Robert J. (Bob)	Cousy	Sports	USA	Basketball Player - HF
	Houbregs	Sports	Canada	Basketball Player - HF
	Lanier	Sports	USA	Basketball Player - HF
Robert J. Van de	Graaff	Science	USA	Physicist
Robert Jesse (Bob)	Pulford	Sports	Canada	Hockey Player - HF
Robert John	Riggins	Sports	USA	Football Player - HF
Robert Joseph	Annis	Sports	USA	Soccer Player - HF
	Cenker	Aviation	USA	Astronaut
	Flaherty	Movie Production	USA	Director - Documentaries
Robert Joseph (Bob)	Dole	Politics	USA	Senator - Kansas
Robert K.	Massie	Creative Works	USA	Author - Pulitzer
Robert L.	Pettit	Sports	USA	Basketball Player - HF
Robert Laird	Borden	Politics	Canada	Prime Minster
Robert Larimore (Bobby)	Riggs	Sports	USA	Tennis Player - HF
Robert Laurel	Crippen	Aviation	USA	Astronaut
Robert Lawrence (Bobby)	Layne	Sports	USA	Football Player - HF
Robert Lee	Frost	Creative Works	USA	Poet - Pulitzer
	Stewart	Aviation	USA	Astronaut
Robert Lee (Bobby)	Bell Jr.	Sports	USA	Football Player - HF
	Hatfield	Performing Arts	USA	Rock & Roll - HF - Righteous Brothers
Robert Lee (Hoot)	Gibson	Aviation	USA	Astronaut
Robert Lee (Sam)	Huff	Sports	USA	Football Player - HF
Robert Leo (Bobby)	Hackett	Performing Arts	USA	Cornetist/Guitarist - Big Band/Jazz - HF
Robert Leroy	Parker	Law & Order	USA	Outlaw - Butch Cassidy
Robert Lewis	Taylor	Creative Works	USA	Author - Pulitzer
Robert Lewis (Bob)	Lilly	Sports	USA	Football Player - HF
Robert Lindley	Murray	Sports	USA	Tennis Player - HF
Robert Louis Ballfour	Stevenson	Creative Works	Scotland	Poet/Novelist/Essayist
Robert M.	Solow	Arts	USA	Economics - Nobel Laureate
Robert Marion La	Follette	Politics	USA	Legislator/Reformer
Robert Marvin (Bobby)	Hull	Sports	Canada	Hockey Player - HF
Robert Maynard	Hutchins	Arts	USA	Educator
Robert Michael (Bob)	Gainey	Sports	Canada	Hockey Player - HF
Robert Moses (Lefty)	Grove	Sports	USA	Baseball Player - HF
Robert N.	Butler	Creative Works	USA	Author - Pulitzer
Robert O'Hara	Burke	Exploration	Australia	Explorer - Central Australia
Robert Olen	Butler	Creative Works	USA	Author - Pulitzer
Robert P. (Fuzzy)	Vandivier	Sports	USA	Basketball Player - HF
Robert P. Tristram	Coffin	Creative Works	USA	Poet - Pulitzer
Robert Penn	Warren	Creative Works	USA	Novelist - Pulitzer
	Warren	Creative Works	USA	Poet - Pulitzer
Robert Pershing (Bobby)	Doerr	Sports	USA	Baseball Player - HF
Robert R.	Livingston	Politics	USA	Statesman
Robert Ranke	Graves	Creative Works	England	Poet/Novelist/Critic

FIRST NAME	LAST NAME	CATEGORY	COUNTRY	FAME
Robert S.	Mulliken	Science	USA	Chemistry - Nobel Laureate
Robert Samuel	Kerr	Business	USA	Oil Industry
Robert Seymour	Bridges	Creative Works	England	Poet Laureate
Robert Stanford (Bob Boomer)	Brown	Sports	USA	Football Player - HF
Robert Stanton (Bob)	Waterfield	Sports	USA	Football Player - HF
Robert Stephenson Smyth	Baden-Powell	War & Peace	England	General
Robert Theodore (Bobby)	Bauer	Sports	Canada	Hockey Player - HF
Robert Trail Spence Jr.	Lowell	Creative Works	USA	Poet - Pulitzer
Robert Treat	Paine	Politics	USA	Jurist/Statesman
Robert Trent	Jones Sr.	Sports	England	Golf Course Designer - HF
Robert Tyre (Bobby)	Jones Jr.	Sports	USA	Golfer - HF
Robert W.	Craddock	Sports	USA	Soccer Player - HF
	Fogel	Arts	USA	Economics - Nobel Laureate
	Holley	Science	USA	Medicine - Nobel Laureate
	Wood	Science	USA	Physicist
Robert Wilhelm	Bunsen	Science	Germany	Chemist/Inventor
Robert William	Service	Creative Works	Canada	Writer
Robert William (Bob)	Packwood	Politics	USA	Senator - Oregon
Robert William Andrew (Bob)	Feller	Sports	USA	Baseball Player - HF
Robert Woodrow	Wilson	Science	USA	Physics - Nobel Laureate
Robert Yale	Lary Jr.	Sports	USA	Football Player - HF
Roberta	Flack	Performing Arts	USA	Singer
	Peters	Performing Arts	USA	Singer - Opera
Roberta Joan (Joni)	Mitchell	Performing Arts	Canada	Singer - Rock & Roll - Canadian Music HF
	Mitchell	Performing Arts	Canada	Singer - Rock & Roll - HF
Roberta Lynn	Bodnar	Aviation	Canada	Astronaut
Roberto	Alomar	Sports	USA	Baseball Player
	Baggio	Sports	Brazil	Soccer Player
	Benigni	Movie Production	Italy	Director - Acad Award Nom
	Benigni	Performing Arts	Italy	Actor - Academy Award
	Carlos	Sports	Brazil	Soccer Player
	Clemente	Sports	Puerto Rico	Baseball Player - HF
	Duran	Sports	USA	Boxer
	Ortiz	Sports	USA	Baseball Player
	Rivelino	Sports	Brazil	Soccer Player - HF
	Rossellini	Movie Production	Italy	Director
	Vittori	Aviation	Italy	Astronaut
Roberto De	Vicenzo	Sports	Brazil	Golfer - HF
Robin	Gibb	Performing Arts	England	Rock & Roll - HF - The Bee Gees
	Givens	Performing Arts	USA	Actress
	Leach	Creative Works	England	Journalist - Television
	Ventura	Sports	USA	Baseball Player
	Warren	Science	Australia	Medicine - Nobel Laureate
	Williams	Performing Arts	USA	Actor - Academy Award
	Williams	Performing Arts	USA	Comedian
	Zander	Performing Arts	USA	Singer - Rock & Roll - HF
Robin Evan	Roberts	Sports	USA	Baseball Player - HF
Robin George	Collingwood	Arts	England	Philosopher/Historian
Robin Rachel	Yount	Sports	USA	Baseball Player - HF
Rocco Scott La	Faro	Performing Arts	USA	Jazz Bassist - Big Band/Jazz - HF
Rock	Hudson	Performing Arts	USA	Actor - Acad Award Nom
Rockwell	Kent	Works of Art	USA	Artist
Rocky	Marciano	Sports	USA	Boxer - HF
Rod	Steiger	Performing Arts	USA	Actor - Academy Award
	Taylor	Performing Arts	Australia	Actor
Rod (Roderick David)	Stewart	Performing Arts	England	Singer - Rock & Roll - HF
Rod Corry	Langway	Sports	Taiwan	Hockey Player - HF
Roddy	McDowall	Performing Arts	England	Actor
Roderick	MacKinnon	Science	USA	Chemistry - Nobel Laureate
Rodger	Ward	Sports	USA	Race Car Driver - HF
Rodney	Crowell	Creative Works	USA	Composer
	Dangerfield	Performing Arts	USA	Comedian
	Porter	Science	England	Medicine - Nobel Laureate

SOLVER SERIES: NAME FINDER

FIRST NAME	LAST NAME	CATEGORY	COUNTRY	FAME
Rodney Cline (Rod)	Carew	Sports	Panama	Baseball Player - HF
Rodney George (Rocket)	Laver	Sports	Australia	Tennis Player - HF
Rodney Leon	Brasfield	Performing Arts	USA	Comedian - Country Music - HF
Rodolfo	Neri Vela	Aviation	Mexico	Astronaut
Rodriquez Gabriel (Rod)	Gilbert	Sports	Canada	Hockey Player
Roebuck (Pops)	Staples	Performing Arts	USA	Rock & Roll - HF - The Staple Singers
Roger	Ascham	Creative Works	England	Writer
	Bacon	Arts	England	Philosopher
	Bannister	Sports	USA	Olympic Runner
	Clemens	Sports	USA	Baseball Player
	Connor	Sports	USA	Baseball Player - HF
	Corman	Movie Production	USA	Director
	Craig	Sports	USA	Football Player
	Daltrey	Performing Arts	England	Rock & Roll - HF - The Who
	Diener	Architecture	Switzerland	Architect
	Ebert	Creative Works	USA	Journalist - Newspaper
	Guillemin	Science	USA	Medicine - Nobel Laureate
	Kingdom	Sports	USA	Olympic Hurdler
	Maris	Sports	USA	Baseball Player
	Moore	Performing Arts	England	Actor
	Mudd	Creative Works	USA	Journalist - Television
	Penrose	Science	England	Physicist/Mathematician
	Penske	Sports	USA	Race Car Driver - HF
	Rees	Performing Arts	Wales	Actor
	Sherman	Politics	USA	Statesman
	Williams	Arts	England	Clergyman/Colonist
	Williams	Performing Arts	USA	Pianist
	Taylor	Performing Arts	England	Rock & Roll - HF - Queen
Roger Brooke	Taney	Law & Order	USA	Chief Justice
Roger Bruce	Chaffee	Aviation	USA	Astronaut
Roger David	Casement	Politics	Ireland	Nationalist
Roger Dean	Miller	Performing Arts	USA	Singer - Country Music - HF
Roger Eliot	Fry	Works of Art	England	Art Critic
Roger Huntington	Sessions	Creative Works	USA	Composer
Roger Keith	Crouch	Aviation	USA	Astronaut
Roger Keith (Syd)	Barrett	Performing Arts	England	Rock & Roll - HF - Pink Floyd
Roger Martin du	Gard	Creative Works	France	Literature - Nobel Laureate
Roger Philip	Bresnahan	Sports	USA	Baseball Player - HF
Roger Thomas	Staubach	Sports	USA	Football Player - HF
Roger W.	Sperry	Science	USA	Medicine - Nobel Laureate
Rogers	Hornsby	Sports	USA	Baseball Player - HF
Roland	Joffe	Movie Production	England	Director - Acad Award Nom
	Petit	Creative Works	France	Choreographer
	Young	Performing Arts	England	Actor - Acad Award Nom
Roland Glen (Rollie)	Fingers	Sports	USA	Baseball Player - HF
Rolf M.	Zinkernagel	Science	Switzerland	Medicine - Nobel Laureate
Romain	Roland	Creative Works	France	Literature - Nobel Laureate
Romaldo	Giurgola	Architecture	USA	Architect - AIA/Jefferson Gold Medal
Roman	Polanski	Movie Production	France	Director - Academy Award
Romario Da Souza	Faria	Sports	Brazil	Soccer Player
Ron	Carter	Performing Arts	USA	Jazz Bassist - Big Band/Jazz - HF
	Ely	Performing Arts	USA	Actor
	Howard	Movie Production	USA	Director - Academy Award
	Howard	Performing Arts	USA	Actor
	Leibman	Performing Arts	USA	Actor
	McKernan	Performing Arts	USA	Rock & Roll - HF - Grateful Dead
	McPhatter	Performing Arts	USA	Rock & Roll - HF - The Drifters
	Moody	Performing Arts	England	Actor - Acad Award Nom
	Nessen	Creative Works	USA	Journalist - Newspaper
	Perlman	Performing Arts	USA	Actor
	Silver	Performing Arts	USA	Actor
	Wood	Performing Arts	England	Singer/Guitarist
Rona	Jaffe	Creative Works	USA	Author

FIRST NAME	LAST NAME	CATEGORY	COUNTRY	FAME
Ronald	Colman	Performing Arts	England	Actor - Academy Award
	Reagan	Politics	USA	President
	Ross	Science	England	Medicine - Nobel Laureate
	Scott	Performing Arts	Scotland	Rock & Roll - HF - AC/DC
	Isley	Performing Arts	USA	Rock & Roll - HF - Isley Brothers
Ronald Anthony	Parise	Aviation	USA	Astronaut
Ronald Arbuthnott	Knox	Arts	England	Priest/Translator
Ronald David	Laing	Science	Scotland	Psychiatrist
Ronald Ellwin	Evans	Aviation	USA	Astronaut
Ronald Erwin	McNair	Aviation	USA	Astronaut
Ronald George Wreyford	Norrish	Science	England	Chemistry - Nobel Laureate
Ronald H.	Coase	Arts	England	Economics - Nobel Laureate
Ronald Harmon (Ron)	Brown	Politics	USA	Secretary of Commerce
Ronald Jack (Ron)	Mix	Sports	USA	Football Player - HF
Ronald John	Grabe	Aviation	USA	Astronaut
Ronald Louis (Ron)	Ziegler	Politics	USA	Press Secretary
Ronald Mandel (Ronnie)	Lott	Sports	USA	Football Player - HF
Ronald Michael	Sega	Aviation	USA	Astronaut
Ronald Vernie (Ron)	Dellums	Politics	USA	Senator
Ronaldo de Assis (Ronaldinho)	Moreira	Sports	Brazil	Soccer Player
Ronee	Blakely	Performing Arts	USA	Singer - Country & Western
	Blakley	Performing Arts	USA	Actress - Acad Award Nom
Ronnie	Milsap	Performing Arts	USA	Singer
	Peterson	Sports	Sweden	Race Car Driver - HF
	Spector	Performing Arts	USA	Singer - Rock & Roll - HF
Ronnie Walter	Cunningham	Aviation	USA	Astronaut
Roone	Arledge	Business	USA	Television
Roosevelt	Brown Jr.	Sports	USA	Football Player - HF
Rory	Calhoun	Performing Arts	USA	Actor
Rosa	Bonheur	Works of Art	France	Painter
	Ponselle	Performing Arts	USA	Singer - Opera
Rosalind	Ashford	Performing Arts	USA	Rock & Roll - HF - Martha & The Vandellas
	Chao	Performing Arts	USA	Actress
	Russell	Performing Arts	USA	Actress - Acad Award Nom
Rosalyn	Sumner	Sports	USA	Olympic Skater
	Yalow	Science	USA	Medicine - Nobel Laureate
Rosalynn	Carter	Politics	USA	First Lady
Rosanna	Arquette	Performing Arts	USA	Actress
Rosanne	Cash	Performing Arts	USA	Singer
Roscoe	Ates	Performing Arts	USA	Actor
	Pound	Arts	USA	Educator/Legal Scholar
	Tanner	Sports	USA	Tennis Player
Roscoe Lee	Browne	Performing Arts	USA	Actor
Rose	Macaulay	Creative Works	England	Novelist
Roseanne	Arnold	Performing Arts	USA	Actress/Comedian
Rosemary	Clooney	Performing Arts	USA	Singer/Actress
	Harris	Performing Arts	England	Actress - Acad Award Nom
Rosemary (Roma)	Downey	Performing Arts	Ireland	Actress
Rosemary (Rosie)	Casals	Sports	USA	Tennis Player - HF
Rosemary De	Camp	Performing Arts	USA	Actress
Rosie	Grier	Sports	USA	Football Player
	Perez	Performing Arts	USA	Actress - Acad Award Nom
Ross	Hunter	Movie Production	USA	Director
	Macdonald	Creative Works	USA	Author
	Martin	Performing Arts	Poland	Actor
Ross Middlebrook	Youngs	Sports	USA	Baseball Player - HF
Ross Shaw	Sterling	Business	USA	Railway Magnate
Rossano	Brazzi	Performing Arts	Italy	Actor
Rowland (Bunny)	Berigan (Bernart)	Performing Arts	USA	Jazz Trumpeter - Big Band/Jazz -HF
Roy	Acuff	Performing Arts	USA	Singer - Country Music - HF
	Beane	Law & Order	USA	Judge
	Campanella	Sports	USA	Baseball Player - HF
	Clark	Performing Arts	USA	Singer

SOLVER SERIES: NAME FINDER

FIRST NAME	LAST NAME	CATEGORY	COUNTRY	FAME
Roy	Cohn	Law & Order	USA	Lawyer - Mafia
	Dotrice	Performing Arts	England	Actor
	Scheider	Performing Arts	USA	Actor - Acad Award Nom
	Thompson	Business	England	Publishing
Roy (David)	Eldridge	Performing Arts	USA	Jazz Trumpeter - Big Band/Jazz -HF
Roy (Shrimp)	Worters	Sports	Canada	Hockey Player - HF
Roy Chapman	Andrews	Exploration	USA	Explorer - Mongolia
Roy Ellsworth	Harris	Creative Works	USA	Composer
Roy Franklin	Nichols	Creative Works	USA	Author - Pulitzer
Roy Gordon	Conacher	Sports	Canada	Hockey Player - HF
Roy J.	Glauber	Science	USA	Physics - Nobel Laureate
Roy Kelton	Orbison	Performing Arts	USA	Singer - Rock & Roll - HF
Roy Stanley	Emerson	Sports	Australia	Tennis Player - HF
Roy Wilson	Howard	Arts	USA	Newspaper Publisher/Editor
Roz	Chast	Creative Works	USA	Cartoonist - New Yorker
Rtia	Levi-Montalcini	Science	Italy	Medicine - Nobel Laureate
Ruben	Blades	Performing Arts	Panama	Actor/Composer
	Olivares	Sports	Mexico	Boxer - HF
	Sierra	Sports	USA	Baseball Player
Ruby	Dee	Performing Arts	USA	Actress
	Keeler	Performing Arts	Canada	Actress
Rudi	Gernreich	Business	Austria	Designer - Fashions
	Maugeri	Performing Arts	Canada	Canadian Music - HF - The Crew Cuts
Rudolf	Akermann	Business	England	Publishing
	Bing	Performing Arts	Austria	Singer - Opera
	Carnap	Arts	Germany	Philosopher
	Serkin	Performing Arts	USA	Pianist
Rudolf (Rudi)	Caracciola	Sports	Germany	Race Car Driver - HF
Rudolf Christoph	Eucken	Creative Works	Germany	Literature - Nobel Laureate
Rudolf Karl	Bultmann	Arts	Germany	Theologian
Rudolf Ludwig	Mössbauer	Science	Germany	Physics - Nobel Laureate
Rudolph	Diesel	Science	Germany	Inventor - Diesel Engine
	Isley	Performing Arts	USA	Rock & Roll - HF - Isley Brothers
	Nureyev	Performing Arts	Russia	Dancer - Ballet
	Otto	Arts	Germany	Philosopher/Theologian
	Schwarz	Architecture	Germany	Architect
	Valentino	Performing Arts	Italy	Actor
Rudolph (Rudy)	Kuntner	Sports	Vienna	Soccer Player - HF
Rudolph A.	Marcus	Science	USA	Chemistry - Nobel Laureate
Rudolph Michael	Schindler	Architecture	USA	Architect
Rudy	Getzinger	Sports	Yugoslavia	Soccer Player - HF
	Vallee	Performing Arts	USA	Singer - Big Band
Rue	McClanahan	Performing Arts	USA	Actress
Rufus	Choate	Law & Order	USA	Lawyer
	Sewell	Performing Arts	England	Actor
	Thomas	Performing Arts	USA	Singer
Rufus Parnell (Parnelli)	Jones	Sports	USA	Race Car Driver - HF
Ruggiero	Leoncavallo	Creative Works	Italy	Composer - Opera
Rula	Lenska	Performing Arts	England	Actress
Rupert	Brooke	Creative Works	England	Poet
	Crosse	Performing Arts	West Indies	Actor - Acad Award Nom
Ruslan	Ponomariov	Games	Ukraine	Chess Player
Russ	Columbo	Performing Arts	USA	Singer/Violinist/Actor
	Tamblyn	Performing Arts	USA	Actor - Acad Award Nom
Russell	Baker	Creative Works	USA	Journalist/Author - Pulitzer
	Crouse	Creative Works	USA	Dramatist - Pulitzer
	Crowe	Performing Arts	New Zealand	Actor - Academy Award
	Sage	Business	USA	Financier
Russell (Barney)	Stanley	Sports	Canada	Hockey Player - HF
Russell (Dubbie)	Bowie	Sports	Canada	Hockey Player - HF
Russell A.	Hulse	Science	USA	Physics - Nobel Laureate
Russell Blaine	Nye	Creative Works	USA	Author - Pulitzer
Russell Luis	Schweickart	Aviation	USA	Astronaut

FIRST NAME	LAST NAME	CATEGORY	COUNTRY	FAME
Rustam	Kasimdzhanov	Games	Uzbekistan	Chess Player
Rusty	Staub	Sports	USA	Baseball Player
	Wallace	Sports	USA	Race Car Driver
Rutger	Hauer	Performing Arts	Netherlands	Actor
Ruth	Brown	Performing Arts	USA	Singer - Rock & Roll - HF
	Buzzi	Performing Arts	USA	Comedian
	Chatterton	Performing Arts	USA	Actress - Acad Award Nom
	Gordon	Performing Arts	USA	Actress - Academy Award
	Hussey	Performing Arts	USA	Actress - Acad Award Nom
	Pointer	Performing Arts	USA	Singer
	Roman	Performing Arts	USA	Actress
	St. Denis	Performing Arts	USA	Dancer/Choreographer
	Westheimer	Creative Works	USA	Journalist - Television
Ruth Barbara	Rendell	Creative Works	England	Author - Crime Fiction
Ruth Fulton	Benedict	Arts	USA	Anthropologist
Ruth Joan Bader	Ginsburg	Law & Order	USA	Justice - Supreme Court
Ruth Lee (Dinah)	Washington (Jones)	Performing Arts	USA	Singer - Big Band/Jazz - HF
	Washington (Jones)	Performing Arts	USA	Singer - Rock & Roll - HF
Rutherford Birchard	Hayes	Politics	USA	President
Ryan	O'Neal	Performing Arts	USA	Actor - Acad Award Nom
Ryne	Sandberg	Sports	USA	Baseball Player - HF
Ryoji	Noyori	Science	Japan	Chemistry - Nobel Laureate
Sacha	Guitry	Creative Works	France	Playwright/Actor
Sacheverell	Sitwell	Creative Works	England	Poet/Critic
Sada	Thompson	Performing Arts	USA	Actress
Saddam	Hussein	Politics	Iraq	President/Military Leader
Saint-John	Perse	Creative Works	France	Literature - Nobel Laureate
Sal	Bando	Sports	USA	Baseball Player
	Messina	Sports	USA	Hockey Broadcaster - HF
	Mineo	Performing Arts	USA	Actor - Acad Award Nom
Sally	Field	Performing Arts	USA	Actress - Academy Award
	Kellerman	Performing Arts	USA	Actress - Acad Award Nom
	Kirkland	Performing Arts	USA	Actress - Acad Award Nom
	Rand	Performing Arts	USA	Actress
	Struthers	Performing Arts	USA	Actress
Sally Ann	Howes	Performing Arts	England	Actress
Sally Kristen	Ride	Aviation	USA	Astronaut
Salma	Hayek	Performing Arts	Mexico	Actress - Acad Award Nom
Salman Abdel-Aziz	Al-Saud	Aviation	Saudi Arabia	Astronaut
Salmon Portland	Chase	Law & Order	USA	Chief Justice
Salvador	Dali	Works of Art	Spain	Painter
	Pániker	Arts	Spain	Philosopher/Writer
Salvador E.	Luria	Science	USA	Medicine - Nobel Laureate
Salvadore	Sanchez	Sports	Mexico	Boxer - HF
Salvatore	Quasimodo	Creative Works	Italy	Literature - Nobel Laureate
Salvatore (Bill)	Bonnano	Law & Order	USA	Mafia
Salvatore (Eddie)	Lang (Massaro)	Performing Arts	USA	Jazz Guitarist - Big Band/Jazz - HF
Salvatore (Frank)	Capone	Law & Order	USA	Mafia
Salvatore (Sammy the Bull)	Gravano	Law & Order	USA	Mafia
Sam	Donaldson	Creative Works	USA	Journalist - Television
	Elliott	Performing Arts	USA	Actor
	Jaffe	Performing Arts	USA	Actor - Acad Award Nom
	Moore	Performing Arts	USA	Rock & Roll - HF - Sam & Dave
	Neill	Performing Arts	Northern Ireland	Actor
	Shepard	Performing Arts	USA	Actor - Acad Award Nom
	Snead	Sports	USA	Golfer - HF
	Wanamaker	Performing Arts	USA	Actor
	Waterston	Performing Arts	USA	Actor - Acad Award Nom
	Mendes	Movie Production	England	Director - Academy Award
Samantha	Eggar	Performing Arts	England	Actress - Acad Award Nom
	Morton	Performing Arts	England	Actress - Acad Award Nom
	Power	Creative Works	Ireland	Author - Pulitzer
Sammy	Davis Jr.	Performing Arts	USA	Singer

SOLVER SERIES: NAME FINDER

FIRST NAME	LAST NAME	CATEGORY	COUNTRY	FAME
Sammy	Hagar	Performing Arts	USA	Singer
	Kahn	Performing Arts	USA	Actor
	Nestico	Performing Arts	USA	Composer/Arranger - Big Band/Jazz - HF
	Sousa	Sports	USA	Baseball Player
	Strain	Performing Arts	USA	Rock & Roll - HF - The O'Jays
Sammy (The Clutch)	Angott	Sports	USA	Boxer - HF
Sammy Adrian	Baugh	Sports	USA	Football Player - HF
Sampson	Lloyd II	Business	England	Entrepreneur
Samuel	Adams	Politics	USA	Statesman
	Barber	Creative Works	USA	Composer
	Beckett	Creative Works	Ireland	Literature - Nobel Laureate
	Butler	Creative Works	England	Author
	Butler	Creative Works	England	Composer
	Butler	Works of Art	England	Painter
	Chase	Law & Order	USA	Justice/Supreme Court
	Colt	Science	USA	Inventor - Revolver
	Cooke	Performing Arts	USA	Singer - Rock & Roll - HF
	Courtauld	Business	England	Textile Industry
	Crompton	Science	England	Inventor - Spinning Mule
	Cunard	Business	Canada	Shipping Magnate
	Fielden	Business	England	Textile Industry
	Goldwyn	Movie Production	Poland	Director
	Gooden	Performing Arts	USA	Rock & Roll - HF - The Impressions
	Greg	Business	England	Textile Industry
	Houston	Politics	USA	Senator
	Houston	War & Peace	USA	General - Texas Army
	Huntington	Politics	USA	Statesman
	Johnson	Creative Works	England	Writer/Lexicographer/Critic
	Laing	Business	England	Railway Magnate
	McClure	Business	USA	Publishing
	Pepys	Creative Works	England	Writer - Diary
	Richardson	Creative Works	England	Novelist
	Sewall	Law & Order	USA	Jurist
	Whitbread	Business	England	Retail Trade
	Wood	Movie Production	USA	Director - Acad Award Nom
Samuel (Sam)	Jones	Sports	USA	Basketball Player - HF
	Shepard	Creative Works	USA	Dramatist - Pulitzer
Samuel (Sambo)	Mockbee	Architecture	USA	Architect - AIA Gold Medal
Samuel (Sammy)	Fain	Creative Works	USA	Composer
	Kaye (Zarnokay)	Performing Arts	USA	Band Leader - Big Band/Jazz - HF
Samuel Anthony (Tony)	Williams	Performing Arts	USA	Jazz Drummer - Big Band/Jazz - HF
	Williams	Performing Arts	USA	Rock & Roll - HF - The Platters
Samuel Augustus (Sam)	Nunn	Politics	USA	Senator - Georgia
Samuel Chao Chung	Ting	Science	USA	Physics - Nobel Laureate
Samuel de	Champlain	Exploration	France	Explorer - Quebec
Samuel Earl (Sam)	Crawford	Sports	USA	Baseball Player - HF
Samuel Eliot	Morison	Creative Works	USA	Author - Pulitzer
Samuel Finley Breese	Morse	Science	USA	Inventor - Telegraph
Samuel Flagg	Bemis	Creative Works	USA	Author - Pulitzer
Samuel John Gurney Hoare	Templewood	Politics	England	Statesman
Samuel Jones	Tilden	Politics	USA	Politician
Samuel L.	Jackson	Performing Arts	USA	Actor - Acad Award Nom
Samuel Langhorne	Clemens	Creative Works	USA	Writer/Humorist
Samuel Luther (Sam)	Thompson	Sports	USA	Baseball Player - HF
Samuel Milton	Jones	Business	USA	Manufacturing Industry
Samuel Moore	Walton	Business	USA	Founder - Walmart
Samuel Pierpoint	Langley	Science	USA	Physicist/Astronomer
Samuel Rawson	Gardiner	Arts	England	Historian
Samuel Ray	Delany	Creative Works	USA	Author - SciFi
Samuel Russell (Rusty)	Crawford	Sports	Canada	Hockey Player - HF
Samuel Taliaferro (Sam)	Rayburn	Politics	USA	Congressman
Samuel Taylor	Coleridge	Arts	England	Philosopher/Lyrical Poet/Critic
Samuel Thorton	Durrance	Aviation	USA	Astronaut

FIRST NAME	LAST NAME	CATEGORY	COUNTRY	FAME
Sándor	Petöfi	Creative Works	Hungary	Poet/Patriot
Sandra	Bernhard	Performing Arts	USA	Comedian
	Dee	Performing Arts	USA	Actress
	Haynie	Sports	USA	Golfer - HF
	Palmer	Sports	USA	Golfer
Sandra Day	O'Connor	Law & Order	USA	Justice - Supreme Court
Sandro	Botticelli	Works of Art	Italy	Painter
Sandy	Alomar	Sports	USA	Baseball Player
	Dennis	Performing Arts	USA	Actress - Academy Award
	Denny	Performing Arts	England	Singer
	Duncan	Performing Arts	USA	Actress
	Saddler	Sports	USA	Boxer - HF
Sanford (Sandy)	Koufax	Sports	USA	Baseball Player - HF
Santiago	Calatrava	Architecture	Spain	Architect
Santiago Ramón y	Cajal	Science	Spain	Medicine - Nobel Laureate
Sanzio	Raffaello	Architecture	Italy	Architect
Sara	Allgood	Performing Arts	Ireland	Actress - Acad Award Nom
	Gilbert	Performing Arts	USA	Actress
	Paretsky	Creative Works	USA	Author - Crime Fiction
	Teasdale	Creative Works	USA	Poet - Pulitzer
Sara Dougherty	Carter	Performing Arts	USA	Country Music - HF - Carter Family
Sarah	Bernhardt	Performing Arts	France	Actress
	Caldwell	Creative Works	USA	Screenwriter
	Miles	Performing Arts	England	Actress - Acad Award Nom
	Polk	Politics	USA	First Lady
	Purcell	Performing Arts	USA	Actress
	Vaughan	Performing Arts	USA	Singer - Big Band/Jazz - HF
	Vaughan	Performing Arts	USA	Singer - Rock & Roll - HF
	O'Hare	Performing Arts	England	Super Model
Sarah Flower	Adams	Creative Works	England	Author/Poet
Sarah Hammond	Palfrey	Sports	USA	Tennis Player - HF
Sarah Jessica	Parker	Performing Arts	USA	Actress
Sarah Margaret	Fuller	Creative Works	USA	Writer/Social Reformer
Sarah Ophelia (Minnie)	Pearl (Colley)	Performing Arts	USA	Comedian - Country Music - HF
Sarah Orne	Jewett	Creative Works	USA	Writer
Sarah Virginia (Ginny)	Wade	Sports	England	Tennis Player - HF
Sasha	Cohen	Sports	USA	Olympic Skater
Satchmo (Louis Daniel)	Armstrong	Performing Arts	USA	Singer - Rock & Roll - HF
Saul	Bellow	Creative Works	USA	Literature - Nobel/Pulitzer
Saverio	Muratori	Architecture	Italy	Architect
Scatman	Crothers	Performing Arts	USA	Singer/Composer
Schack August Steenberg	Krogh	Science	Denmark	Medicine - Nobel Laureate
Schuyler	Colfax	Politics	USA	Vice-President
Scott	Baio	Performing Arts	USA	Actor
	Bakula	Performing Arts	USA	Actor
	Glenn	Performing Arts	USA	Actor
	Hamilton	Sports	USA	Olympic Skater
	Hicks	Movie Production	Uganda	Director - Acad Award Nom
	Joplin	Performing Arts	USA	Pianist/Composer - Big Band/Jazz - HF
	Simpson	Sports	USA	Golfer
	Thurston	Performing Arts	USA	Rock & Roll - HF - Heart Breakers
	Turow	Creative Works	USA	Author
Scott Jay (Doc)	Horowitz	Aviation	USA	Astronaut
Scottie	Pippen	Sports	USA	Basketball Player
Seamus	Heaney	Creative Works	Ireland	Literature - Nobel Laureate
Sean	Astin	Performing Arts	USA	Actor
	Connery	Performing Arts	Scotland	Actor - Academy Award
	MacBride	War & Peace	Ireland	Peace - Nobel Laureate
	O'Casey	Creative Works	Ireland	Playwright
	O'Grady	Sports	USA	Boxer
	Penn	Performing Arts	USA	Actor - Academy Award
Sean Thomas	O'Kelly	Politics	Ireland	President
Sebastian	Cabot	Exploration	England	Explorer - North West Passage

SOLVER SERIES: NAME FINDER

FIRST NAME	LAST NAME	CATEGORY	COUNTRY	FAME
Sebastian	Cabot	Performing Arts	England	Actor
	Cermenho	Exploration	Spain	Explorer - California
Sebastián	Vizcaíno	Exploration	Spain	Explorer - Mexico West Coast
Sebastian de	Grazia	Creative Works	USA	Author - Pulitzer
Sebastian Newbold	Coe	Sports	England	Olympic Runner
Sebastiano	Serlio	Architecture	Italy	Architect
Sébastien le Prestre	Vauban	War & Peace	France	Engineer
Seebohm	Rowntree	Business	England	Confection Industry
Seiji	Ozawa	Performing Arts	Japan	Conductor
Sela	Ward	Performing Arts	USA	Actress
Selassie	Haile	Politics	Ethiopia	Emperor
Selma	Diamond	Performing Arts	Canada	Actress
Selma Ottillana Lovisa	Lagerlöf	Creative Works	Sweden	Literature - Nobel Laureate
Selman Abraham	Waksman	Science	USA	Medicine - Nobel Laureate
Senta	Berger	Performing Arts	Austria	Actress
Serafin	Alvarez Quintero	Creative Works	Spain	Playwright
Serge	Koussevitzky	Performing Arts	Russia	Conductor
Sergei	Belov	Sports	Russia	Basketball Player - HF
	Prokofiev	Creative Works	Russia	Composer
Sergei Mikhailovich	Eisenstein	Movie Production	Russia	Director/Producer
Sergei Pavlovich	Diaghilev	Performing Arts	Russia	Ballet Producer
Serger Aubrey	Savard	Sports	Canada	Hockey Player - HF
Sergi Vassilievich	Rachmaninoff	Creative Works	Russia	Composer/Conductor/Violinist
Sergio	Leone	Movie Production	Italy	Director
	Mendes	Performing Arts	Brazil	Jazz Pianist/Arranger
Sessue	Hayakawa	Performing Arts	Japan	Actor - Acad Award Nom
Seth	Low	Business	USA	Importer
	Thomas	Science	USA	Inventor/Manufacturer
Seve	Ballesteros	Sports	Spain	Golfer - HF
Severo	Ochoa	Science	USA	Medicine - Nobel Laureate
Seymour	Cassel	Performing Arts	USA	Actor - Acad Award Nom
	Stein	Performing Arts	USA	Promoter - Rock & Roll - HF
Shahbanu Farah	Pahlavi	Politics	Iran	Empress
Shaka	Zulu	War & Peace	South Africa	Military Leader
Shalom	Harlow	Performing Arts	Canada	Super Model
Shana	Alexander	Creative Works	USA	Journalist - Magazine
Shane	Gould	Sports	Australia	Olympic Swimmer
Shani	Wallis	Performing Arts	England	Actress
Shannon	Higgins-Cirovski	Sports	USA	Soccer Player - HF
Shaquille	O'Neal	Sports	USA	Basketball Player
Shari	Belafonte	Performing Arts	USA	Actress
	Lewis	Performing Arts	USA	Puppeteer
Sharon	Gless	Performing Arts	USA	Actress
	Stone	Performing Arts	USA	Actress - Acad Award Nom
Sharon Christa Corrigan	McAuliffe	Aviation	USA	Astronaut
Shaun	Cassidy	Performing Arts	USA	Actor
Shecky	Greene	Performing Arts	USA	Comedian
Sheena	Easton	Performing Arts	Scotland	Singer
Sheldon	Govier	Sports	Scotland	Soccer Player - HF
	Leonard	Performing Arts	USA	Actor/Comedian
Sheldon (Shelly)	Manne	Performing Arts	USA	Jazz Drummer - Big Band/Jazz - HF
Sheldon Allan (Shel)	Silverstein	Creative Works	USA	Poet/Composer
Sheldon Lee	Glashow	Science	USA	Physics - Nobel Laureate
Shelley	Berman	Performing Arts	USA	Comedian
	Duvall	Performing Arts	USA	Actress
	Fabares	Performing Arts	USA	Actress/Singer
	Long	Performing Arts	USA	Actress
	Winters	Performing Arts	USA	Actress - Academy Award
Shemp	Howard	Performing Arts	USA	Comedian
Shere	Hite	Creative Works	USA	Author
Sheree	North	Performing Arts	USA	Actress
Sherman	Hemsley	Performing Arts	USA	Comedian
Sherry	Scott	Performing Arts	USA	Rock & Roll - HF - Earth Wind & Fire

FIRST NAME	LAST NAME	CATEGORY	COUNTRY	FAME
Sherwood	Anderson	Creative Works	USA	Novelist
Sherwood Clark (Woody)	Spring	Aviation	USA	Astronaut
Shigeru	Ban	Architecture	Japan	Architect - Jefferson Medal
Shikibu	Murasaki	Creative Works	Japan	Poet/Novelist
Shimon	Peres	Politics	Israel	Prime Minister
	Peres	War & Peace	Israel	Peace - Nobel Laureate
Shiraz	Tal	Performing Arts	Israel	Super Model
Shirin	Ebadi	War & Peace	Iran	Peace - Nobel Laureate
Shirley	Bassey	Performing Arts	Wales	Singer
	Booth	Performing Arts	USA	Actress - Academy Award
	Eaton	Performing Arts	England	Actress
	Ellis	Performing Arts	USA	Singer
	Horne	Performing Arts	USA	Singer/Pianist - Big Band/Jazz - HF
	Jones	Performing Arts	USA	Actress - Academy Award
	Knight	Performing Arts	USA	Actress - Acad Award Nom
	MacLaine	Performing Arts	USA	Actress - Academy Award
	Muldowney	Sports	USA	Race Car Driver - HF
	Temple	Performing Arts	USA	Actress - Academy Award
Shirley Ann	Grau	Creative Works	USA	Author - Pulitzer
Shirley June	Fry-Irvin	Sports	USA	Tennis Player - HF
Shmuel Yosef	Agnon	Creative Works	Israel	Literature - Nobel Laureate
Shohreh	Aghdashloo	Performing Arts	Iran	Actress - Acad Award Nom
Sholem	Asch	Creative Works	USA	Playwright/Novelist
Sid	Breame	Sports	USA	Baseball Player
	Caesar	Performing Arts	USA	Comedian
Sid Williams	Richardson	Business	USA	Oil Industry
Sidney	Altman	Science	Canada	Chemistry - Nobel Laureate
	Bechet	Performing Arts	USA	Jazz Saxaphonist - Big Band/Jazz - HF
	Franklin	Movie Production	USA	Director - Acad Award Nom
	Hook	Arts	USA	Philosopher
	Howard	Creative Works	USA	Dramatist - Pulitzer
	Kingsley	Creative Works	USA	Dramatist - Pulitzer
	Lanier	Creative Works	USA	Poet
	Lumet	Movie Production	USA	Director - Acad Award Nom
	Poitier	Performing Arts	USA	Actor - Academy Award
	Toler	Performing Arts	USA	Actor
Sidney (Beau)	Jack	Sports	USA	Boxer - HF
Sidney (Sid)	Gillman	Sports	USA	Football Coach - HF
	Luckman	Sports	USA	Football Player - HF
Sidney Gerald (Sid)	Abel	Sports	Canada	Hockey Player - HF
Sidney James	Webb	Arts	England	Economist/Social Reformer
Sidney Joseph	Perelman	Creative Works	USA	Humorist
Sidney McNeil	Gutierrez	Aviation	USA	Astronaut
Sidonie Gabrielle Claudine	Colette	Creative Works	France	Novelist
Siegfried Lorraine	Sassoon	Creative Works	England	Poet/Writer
Sigmund	Freud	Science	Austria	Psychiatrist/Physician
Signe	Hasso	Performing Arts	Sweden	Actress
Sigourney	Weaver	Performing Arts	USA	Actress - Acad Award Nom
Sigrid	Undset	Creative Works	Norway	Literature - Nobel Laureate
Silas	Deane	Politics	USA	Revolutionary Patriot
Silas Seth (Si)	Griffis	Sports	USA	Hockey Player - HF
Simon	Estes	Performing Arts	USA	Singer - Opera
	Flexner	Science	USA	Pathologist
	Fraser	Exploration	Canada	Explorer - Alberta
	Guggenheim	Business	USA	Industrialist/Philanthropist
	Kuznets	Arts	USA	Economics - Nobel Laureate
	Ward	Performing Arts	England	Actor
	Wright	Performing Arts	England	Rock & Roll - HF - AC/DC
Simon de	Montfort	War & Peace	France	Crusader
Simón José	Bolivar	War & Peace	Venezuela	General/Revolutionary
Simon Le	Bon	Performing Arts	England	Singer
Simon van der	Meer	Science	Netherlands	Physics - Nobel Laureate
Simone	Cantoni	Architecture	Switzerland	Architect

FIRST NAME	LAST NAME	CATEGORY	COUNTRY	FAME
Simone	Signoret	Performing Arts	Germany	Actress - Academy Award
	Weil	Arts	France	Philosopher/Mystic
Simone de	Beauvoir	Creative Works	France	Novelist/Essayist/Philosopher
Sinclair	Lewis	Creative Works	USA	Literature - Nobel Laureate
Sinead	O'Connor	Performing Arts	Ireland	Singer
Sin-Itiro	Tomonaga	Science	Japan	Physics - Nobel Laureate
Sissela	Bok	Arts	Sweden	Philosopher
Sissy	Spacek	Performing Arts	USA	Actress - Academy Award
Skeeter	Davis	Performing Arts	USA	Singer
Slater N. (Dugie)	Martin	Sports	USA	Basketball Player - HF
Slim	Summerville	Performing Arts	USA	Comedian
Sly (Sylvester)	Stewart	Performing Arts	USA	Rock & Roll - HF - Sly & The Family Stone
Sofia	Coppola	Movie Production	USA	Director - Acad Award Nom
Soichi	Noguchi	Aviation	Japan	Astronaut
Sojourner	Truth	Politics	USA	Abolitionist
Sol	Hurok	Movie Production	USA	Impresario
Sollie	McElroy	Performing Arts	USA	Rock & Roll - HF - The Flamingos
Solomon	Burke	Performing Arts	USA	Singer - Rock & Roll - HF
	Loeb	Business	USA	Drygoods
Solomon R.	Guggenheim	Business	USA	Industrialist/Philanthropist
Sondra	Locke	Performing Arts	USA	Actress - Acad Award Nom
Sonia	Braga	Performing Arts	Brazil	Actress
Sonja	Henie	Sports	Norway	Olympic Skater
Sonny	Bono	Performing Arts	USA	Singer
	Liston	Sports	USA	Boxer - HF
	Rollins	Performing Arts	USA	Jazz Saxophonist - Big Band/Jazz - HF
Sophia	Loren	Performing Arts	Italy	Actress - Academy Award
Sophie	Okonedo	Performing Arts	England	Actress - Acad Award Nom
	Tucker	Performing Arts	Russia	Singer
Soren Aabye	Kierkegaard	Arts	Denmark	Philosopher/Theologian
Soupy	Sales	Performing Arts	USA	Comedian
Sparky	Lyle	Sports	USA	Baseball Player
Spencer	Tracy	Performing Arts	USA	Actor - Academy Award
Spike	Jonze	Movie Production	USA	Director - Acad Award Nom
	Lee	Movie Production	USA	Director
Spiro T.	Agnew	Politics	USA	Vice-President
Sprague	Cleghorn	Sports	Canada	Hockey Player - HF
Spring	Byington	Performing Arts	USA	Actress - Acad Award Nom
Sri	Aurobindo	Arts	India	Philosopher
Stacey	Dash	Performing Arts	USA	Actress
	Keach	Performing Arts	USA	Actor
Stacy	Schiff	Creative Works	USA	Author - Pulitzer
Stan	Kenton	Performing Arts	USA	Jazz Pianist
	Laurel	Performing Arts	England	Comedian
Stanford	Moore	Science	USA	Chemistry - Nobel Laureate
	White	Architecture	USA	Architect
Stanley	Baldwin	Politics	England	Prime Minster
	Cohen	Science	USA	Medicine - Nobel Laureate
	Holloway	Performing Arts	England	Actor - Acad Award Nom
	Karnow	Creative Works	USA	Author - Pulitzer
	Kramer	Movie Production	USA	Director - Acad Award Nom
	Kubrick	Movie Production	USA	Director - Acad Award Nom
	Kunitz	Creative Works	USA	Poet - Pulitzer
	Milgram	Arts	USA	Philosopher
	Chesney	Sports	USA	Soccer Player - HF
	Matthews	Sports	England	Soccer Player - HF
Stanley (Stan)	Barstow	Creative Works	England	Author
	Getz (Gayetzby)	Performing Arts	USA	Jazz Saxophonist - Big Band/Jazz - HF
	Mikita	Sports	Czechoslovakia	Hockey Player - HF
Stanley Anthony (Stan)	Coveleski	Sports	USA	Baseball Player - HF
Stanley B.	Prusiner	Science	USA	Medicine - Nobel Laureate
Stanley David	Griggs	Aviation	USA	Astronaut
Stanley Frank (Stan)	Musial	Sports	USA	Baseball Player - HF

FIRST NAME	LAST NAME	CATEGORY	COUNTRY	FAME
Stanley Martin (Stan)	Lee	Creative Works	USA	Cartoonist - Spiderman
Stanley Melbourne	Bruce	Politics	Australia	Prime Minister
Stanley Newcomb (Stan)	Kenton	Performing Arts	USA	Band Leader - Big Band/Jazz - HF
Stanley Paul (Stan)	Jones	Sports	USA	Football Player - HF
Stanley Raymond (Bucky)	Harris	Sports	USA	Baseball Manager - HF
Stanley Roger (Stan)	Smith	Sports	USA	Tennis Player - HF
Stefan	Edberg	Sports	Sweden	Tennis Player - HF
	Zweig	Creative Works	Austria	Novelist/Playwright
Stefannie	Powers	Performing Arts	USA	Actress
Stefano	Gabbana	Business	Italy	Fashion Designer
Steffi	Graf	Sports	Germany	Tennis Player - HF
Stella	McCartney	Business	England	Fashion Designer
	Stevens	Performing Arts	USA	Actress
Stephane	Grappelli	Performing Arts	France	Jazz Violinist - Big Band/Jazz - HF
Stéphane	Mallarmé	Creative Works	France	Poet - Symbolist
Stephanie	Seymour	Performing Arts	USA.	Super Model
Stephanie Lynn (Stevie)	Nicks	Performing Arts	USA	Rock & Roll - HF - Fleetwood Mac
Stephen	Becker	Creative Works	USA	Novelist
	Bishop	Performing Arts	USA	Singer/Composer
	Bonsal	Creative Works	USA	Author - Pulitzer
	Boyd	Performing Arts	Northern Ireland	Actor
	Crane	Creative Works	USA	Novelist
	Daldry	Movie Production	England	Director - Acad Award Nom
	Decatur	War & Peace	USA	Naval Officer
	Dunn	Creative Works	USA	Poet - Pulitzer
	Frears	Movie Production	England	Director - Acad Award Nom
	Girard	Business	USA	Financier/Philanthropist
	Phillips	Creative Works	England	Dramatist - Poetic
	Rea	Performing Arts	Northern Ireland	Actor - Acad Award Nom
	Sondheim	Creative Works	USA	Composer
	Spender	Creative Works	England	Poet/Critic
Stephen Arnold	Douglas	Politics	USA	Politician
Stephen Arthur	Stills	Performing Arts	USA	Rock & Roll - HF - Buffalo Springfield
Stephen Butler	Leacock	Arts	Canada	Humorist/Political Economist
Stephen Collins	Foster	Creative Works	USA	Composer - Songs
Stephen Douglas	Thorne	Aviation	USA	Astronaut
Stephen Edwin	King	Creative Works	USA	Novelist - Horror
Stephen Fuller	Austin	Exploration	USA	Frontiersman - America
Stephen Grover	Cleveland	Politics	USA	President
Stephen James (Steve)	Howe	Performing Arts	England	Guitarist
Stephen John	Shutt	Sports	Canada	Hockey Player - HF
Stephen Joseph (Steve)	Owen	Sports	USA	Football Player - HF
Stephen Michael (Steve)	Largent	Sports	USA	Football Player - HF
Stephen Samuel	Wise	Arts	USA	Rabbi/Jewish Leader
Stephen Scott	Oswald	Aviation	USA	Astronaut
Stephen Van	Rensselaer	Politics	USA	Politician/General
Stephen Vincent	Benét	Creative Works	USA	Poet - Pulitzer
Stephen W. Van (Steve)	Buren	Sports	USA	Football Player - HF
Stephen William	Hawking	Science	England	Physicist
Stepin	Fetchit	Performing Arts	USA	Comedian
Sterling	Holloway	Performing Arts	USA	Actor
Steve	Albert	Creative Works	USA	Journalist - Television
	Allen	Performing Arts	USA	Actor/Comedian
	Bartowski	Sports	USA	Football Player
	Boone	Performing Arts	USA	Rock & Roll - HF - Lovin' Spoonful
	Coll	Creative Works	USA	Novelist - Pulitzer
	Douglas	Performing Arts	USA	Singer - Rock & Roll - HF
	Elkington	Sports	Australia	Golfer
	Ferrone	Performing Arts	England	Rock & Roll - HF - Heart Breakers
	Garvey	Sports	USA	Baseball Player
	Guttenberg	Performing Arts	USA	Actor
	Kanaly	Performing Arts	USA	Actor
	Lawrence	Performing Arts	USA	Singer

SOLVER SERIES: NAME FINDER

FIRST NAME	LAST NAME	CATEGORY	COUNTRY	FAME
Steve	Martin	Performing Arts	USA	Actor
	McQueen	Performing Arts	USA	Actor - Acad Award Nom
	Miller	Performing Arts	USA	Band Leader/Guitarist
	Pate	Sports	USA	Golfer
	Perry	Performing Arts	USA	Singer
	Saxon	Sports	USA	Base Ball Player
	Cropper	Performing Arts	USA	Rock & Roll - HF - Booker T & The Mg's
Steve De	Berg	Sports	USA	Football Player
Steveland Judkins (Stevie)	Wonder (Hardaway)	Performing Arts	USA	Singer - Rock & Roll - HF
Steven	Chu	Science	USA	Physics - Nobel Laureate
	Hahn	Creative Works	USA	Author - Pulitzer
	Holl	Architecture	USA	Architect
	Millhauser	Creative Works	USA	Novelist - Pulitzer
	Naifeh	Creative Works	USA	Author - Pulitzer
	Soderbergh	Movie Production	USA	Director - Academy Award
	Spielberg	Movie Production	USA	Director - Academy Award
	Tyler (Tallarico)	Performing Arts	USA	Rock & Roll - HF - Aerosmith
	Weinberg	Science	USA	Physics - Nobel Laureate
	Wright	Performing Arts	USA	Comedian
Steven (Steve)	Nieve(Nason)	Performing Arts	England	Rock & Roll - HF- Costello & The Attractions
Steven (Stevie)	Winwood	Performing Arts	England	Rock & Roll - HF - Traffic
Steven Glenwood	MacLean	Aviation	Canada	Astronaut
Steven Michael James (Steve)	Ovett	Sports	England	Olympic Runner
Steven Norman (Steve)	Carlton	Sports	USA	Baseball Player - HF
Stewart	Copeland	Performing Arts	USA	Rock & Roll - HF - The Police
	Granger	Performing Arts	England	Actor
Stirling	Moss	Sports	England	Race Car Driver - HF
Stockard	Channing	Performing Arts	USA	Actress - Acad Award Nom
Stu	Erwin	Performing Arts	USA	Actor - Acad Award Nom
	Sutcliffe	Performing Arts	Scotland	Guitarist
Stuart	Whitman	Performing Arts	USA	Actor - Acad Award Nom
Stuart Allen	Roosa	Aviation	USA	Astronaut
Stubby	Kaye	Performing Arts	USA	Actor - Musical
Sturluson	Snorri	Creative Works	Iceland	Poet/Ice Historian
Subramanyan	Chandrasekhar	Science	USA	Physics - Nobel Laureate
Sue	Grafton	Creative Works	USA	Author
	Miller	Creative Works	USA	Author
Sue Ane	Langdon	Performing Arts	USA	Actress
Sully	Prudhomme	Creative Works	France	Literature - Nobel Laureate
Sumner	Welles	Politics	USA	Diplomat
Sumner Chilton	Powell	Creative Works	USA	Author - Pulitzer
Sun	Wen	Sports	China	Soccer Player
	Yat-Sen	Politics	China	Revolutionist
Sune K.	Bergström	Science	Sweden	Medicine - Nobel Laureate
Susan	Anspach	Performing Arts	USA	Actress
	Anton	Performing Arts	USA	Actress
	Blakely	Performing Arts	Germany	Actress
	Clark	Performing Arts	Canada	Actress
	Dey	Performing Arts	USA	Actress
	Glaspell	Creative Works	USA	Dramatist - Pulitzer
	Hayward	Performing Arts	USA	Actress - Academy Award
	Kohner	Performing Arts	USA	Actress - Acad Award Nom
	Lucci	Performing Arts	USA	Actress
	Peters	Performing Arts	USA	Actress - Acad Award Nom
	Ruttan	Performing Arts	USA	Actress
	Sarandon	Performing Arts	USA	Actress - Academy Award
	Seidelman	Movie Production	USA	Director
	Sheehan	Creative Works	USA	Author - Pulitzer
	Sontag	Creative Works	USA	Novelist
	St. James	Performing Arts	USA	Actress
	Strasberg	Performing Arts	USA	Actress
	Sullivan	Performing Arts	USA	Actress
	Tyrrell	Performing Arts	USA	Actress - Acad Award Nom

FIRST NAME	LAST NAME	CATEGORY	COUNTRY	FAME R
Susan B.	Anthony	Politics	USA	Women's Rights Proponent
Susan Eloise	Hinton	Creative Works	USA	Author
Susan Jane	Helms	Aviation	USA	Astronaut
Susan Katherina	Langer	Arts	USA	Philosopher
Susan Leigh	Kilrain	Aviation	USA	Astronaut
Susana	Torre	Architecture	USA	Architect
Susannah	York	Performing Arts	England	Actress - Acad Award Nom
Susumu	Tonegawa	Science	Japan	Medicine - Nobel Laureate
Suzan-Lori	Parks	Creative Works	USA	Dramatist - Pulitzer
Suzanne	Pleshette	Performing Arts	USA	Actress
	Somers	Performing Arts	USA	Actress
Suzanne Rachel Flore	Lenglen	Sports	France	Tennis Player - HF
Svante August	Arrhenius	Science	Sweden	Chemistry - Nobel Laureate
Sven	Nater	Sports	USA	Basketball Player
Sven Anders	Hedin	Exploration	Sweden	Explorer- Central Asia
Sven Olof Joachim	Palme	Politics	Sweden	Prime Minister
Sverre	Fehn	Architecture	Norway	Architect - Pritzker Laureate
Swan	Turnblad	Business	USA	Publishing
Swoosie	Kurtz	Performing Arts	USA	Actress
Sybil	Leek	Science	England	Astrologer/Witch
	Thorndike	Performing Arts	England	Actress
Sydney	Brenner	Science	England	Medicine - Nobel Laureate
	Greenstreet	Performing Arts	England	Actor - Acad Award Nom
	Pollack	Movie Production	USA	Director - Acad Award Nom
	Ringer	Science	England	Physiologist
	Smith	Creative Works	England	Essayist/Clergyman
Sydney Burr Beardsley	Wood	Sports	USA	Tennis Player - HF
Sydney Harris (Syd)	Howe	Sports	Canada	Hockey Player - HF
Sylvester (Sly)	Stone	Performing Arts	USA	Singer
Sylvestor	Stallone	Performing Arts	USA	Actor - Acad Award Nom
Sylvia	Miles	Performing Arts	USA	Actress
	Plath	Creative Works	USA	Poet - Pulitzer
	Sidney	Performing Arts	USA	Actress - Acad Award Nom
	Tyson	Performing Arts	Canada	Canadian Music - HF - Ian and Sylvia
Sylvia Alice	Earle	Exploration	USA	Explorer - Marine
Sylvio	Mantha	Sports	Canada	Hockey Player - HF
Syngman	Rhee	Politics	South Korea	President
Tab	Hunter	Performing Arts	USA	Singer
	Ramos	Sports	Uruguay	Soccer Player - HF
Tad	Mosel	Creative Works	USA	Dramatist - Pulitzer
Tadao	Ando	Architecture	Japan	Architect - Pritzker/ AIA Gold
Tadd (Tadley Ewing)	Dameron (Peake)	Performing Arts	USA	Jazz Pianist/Composer - Big Band/Jazz - HF
Tadeus	Reichstein	Science	Switzerland	Medicine - Nobel Laureate
Tai	Babilonia	Sports	USA	Olympic Skater
Taina	Elg	Performing Arts	Finland	Actress
Takao	Doi	Aviation	Japan	Astronaut
Tal	Farrow	Performing Arts	USA	Jazz Guitarist - Big Band/Jazz - HF
Talbot Faulkner	Hamlin	Creative Works	USA	Author - Pulitzer
Talcott	Parsons	Arts	USA	Sociologist
Talia	Shire	Performing Arts	USA	Actress - Acad Award Nom
Tallulah	Bankhead	Performing Arts	USA	Actress
Tamara Elizabeth	Jernigan	Aviation	USA	Astronaut
Tammy	Grimes	Performing Arts	USA	Actress
	Wynette	Performing Arts	USA	Singer - Country Music - HF
Tanya	Roberts	Performing Arts	USA	Actress
	Tucker	Performing Arts	USA	Singer - Country & Western
Tara	Lipinski	Sports	USA	Olympic Skater
	Reid	Performing Arts	USA	Actress
Tasso	Torquato	Creative Works	Italy	Poet
Tatjana	Patitz	Performing Arts	Sweden	Super Model
Tatum	O'Neal	Performing Arts	USA	Actress - Academy Award
Taylor	Branch	Creative Works	USA	Author - Pulitzer
	Hackford	Movie Production	USA	Director - Acad Award Nom

SOLVER SERIES: NAME FINDER

FIRST NAME	LAST NAME	CATEGORY	COUNTRY	FAME
Taylor Gun-Jin	Wang	Aviation	USA	Astronaut
Tazio	Nuvolari	Sports	Italy	Race Car Driver - HF
Tea	Leoni	Performing Arts	USA	Actress
Ted	Danson	Performing Arts	USA	Actor
	Key	Creative Works	USA	Cartoonist - Political
	Knight	Performing Arts	USA	Actor
	Kooser	Creative Works	USA	Poet - Pulitzer
	Koppel	Creative Works	USA	Journalist - Television
	Lapidus	Business	France	Designer - Fashion/Fragrances
	Levine	Performing Arts	USA	Actor
	Lewis	Performing Arts	USA	Clarinetist/Jazz Musician
	Lewis	Performing Arts	USA	Comedian
	Mack	Performing Arts	USA	Show Host - Television
	Shackelford	Performing Arts	USA	Actor
	Shawn	Performing Arts	USA	Dancer/Choreographer
	Turner	Business	USA	Broadcasting
	Weems	Performing Arts	USA	Band Leader - Big Band/Jazz - HF
	Wilde	Movie Production	USA	Director - Acad Award Nom
Ted (The Nuge)	Nugent	Performing Arts	USA	Band Leader/Guitarist
Teddy	Pendergrass	Performing Arts	USA	Singer
Teddy Wayne	Gentry	Performing Arts	USA	Country Music - HF - Alabama
Teena	Marie	Performing Arts	USA	Singer
Telly	Savalas	Performing Arts	USA	Actor - Acad Award Nom
Tempestt	Bledsoe	Performing Arts	USA	Actress
Tennessee	Williams	Creative Works	USA	Dramatist - Pulitzer
Tenzin	Gyatso	War & Peace	Tibet	Peace - Nobel Laureate
Tenzing	Norgay	Exploration	Nepal	Explorer - Mount Everest
Teofilo	Stevenson	Sports	USA	Boxer
Terence	Stamp	Performing Arts	England	Actor - Acad Award Nom
Terence Hanbury	White	Creative Works	India	Novelist
Terence Thomas	Henricks	Aviation	USA	Astronaut
Teresa	Brewer	Performing Arts	USA	Singer
	Lourenco	Performing Arts	Trinidad	Super Model
	Stratas	Performing Arts	Canada	Singer - Opera
	Wright	Performing Arts	USA	Actress - Academy Award
Teressa	Graves	Performing Arts	USA	Actress
Teri	Garr	Performing Arts	USA	Actress - Acad Award Nom
Terrance Gordon (Terry)	Sawchuk	Sports	Canada	Hockey Player - HF
Terrence	Malick	Movie Production	USA	Director - Acad Award Nom
Terri	Clark	Performing Arts	Canada	Singer - Country Music
Terry	Chimes	Performing Arts	England	Rock & Roll - HF - The Clash
	Gibbs	Performing Arts	USA	Jazz Vibraphonist - Big Band/Jazz - HF
	Gilliam	Performing Arts	USA	Actor
	Johnson	Performing Arts	USA	Rock & Roll - HF - The Flamingos
	Jones	Performing Arts	Wales	Comedian
	Moore	Performing Arts	USA	Actress - Acad Award Nom
Terry Jonathon	Hart	Aviation	USA	Astronaut
Terry Paxton	Bradshaw	Sports	USA	Football Player - HF
Terry Wayne	Norris	Sports	USA	Boxer - HF
Tess	Harper	Performing Arts	USA	Actress - Acad Award Nom
Tessie	O'Shea	Performing Arts	Wales	Actress
Texas Earnest (Tex)	Schramm Jr.	Sports	USA	Football General Manager - HF
Thad	Mumford	Creative Works	USA	Screenwriter - Mash
Thaddeus	Stevens	Politics	USA	Statesman/Abolitionist
Thaddeus Joseph (Thad)	Jones	Performing Arts	USA	Jazz Trumpeter - Big Band/Jazz - HF
Thadeus	Kosciusko	War & Peace	Poland	General/Patriot
Thalia	Assuras	Creative Works	Canada	Journalist - Television
Theda	Bara	Performing Arts	USA	Actress
Thelma	Ritter	Performing Arts	USA	Actress - Acad Award Nom
Thelma Catherine Patricia	Nixon	Politics	USA	First Lady
Thelonious Sphere	Monk	Performing Arts	USA	Jazz Pianist - Big Band/Jazz - HF
Theo van	Doesburg	Architecture	Netherlands	Architect
Theobald von	Bethmann-Hollweg	Politics	Germany	Chancellor

FIRST NAME	LAST NAME	CATEGORY	COUNTRY	FAME
Theodor	Herzl	Creative Works	Austria	Writer
	Leschetizky	Creative Works	Poland	Composer/Pianist/Teacher
Theodor Ludwig Wiesengrund	Adorno	Arts	Germany	Philosopher/Sociologist
Theodore	Bikel	Performing Arts	Austria	Actor - Acad Award Nom
	Hänsch	Science	Germany	Physics - Nobel Laureate
	Link	Architecture	USA	Architect
	Roethke	Creative Works	USA	Poet - Pulitzer
	Roosevelt	Politics	USA	President
	Roosevelt	War & Peace	USA	Peace - Nobel Laureate
	Rroethke	Creative Works	USA	Poet
	Svedberg	Science	Sweden	Chemistry - Nobel Laureate
Theodore (Fats)	Navarro	Performing Arts	USA	Jazz Trumpeter - Big Band/Jazz - HF
Theodore Amar (Ted)	Lyons	Sports	USA	Baseball Player - HF
Theodore Cordy	Freeman	Aviation	USA	Astronaut
Theodore Francis	Powys	Creative Works	England	Novelist
Theodore Harold	White	Creative Works	USA	Author - Pulitzer
Theodore Herman Albert	Dreiser	Creative Works	USA	Novelist
Theodore Paul (Ted)	Hendricks	Sports	Guatemala	Football Player - HF
Theodore Robert (Ted)	Bundy	Law & Order	USA	Serial Killer
Theodore Roosevelt	Pell	Sports	USA	Tennis Player - HF
Theodore Samuel (Ted)	Williams	Sports	USA	Baseball Player - HF
Theodore Shaw (Teddy)	Wilson	Performing Arts	USA	Jazz Pianist - Big Band/Jazz - HF
Theodore W.	Schultz	Arts	USA	Economics - Nobel Laureate
Theodore William	Richards	Science	USA	Chemistry - Nobel Laureate
Theodosius Grigorievich	Dobzhansky	Science	USA	Geneticist
Theodre Samuel (Ted Teeter)	Kennedy	Sports	Canada	Hockey Player - HF
Théophile	Gautier	Creative Works	France	Poet/Novelist
Theresa	Russell	Performing Arts	USA	Actress
Thierry	Hermes	Business	France	Fashion Designer
Thom	Mayne	Architecture	USA	Architect
Thomas	Addison	Science	England	Physician
	Allinson	Business	England	Entrepreneur
	Aquinas	Arts	Italy	Philosopher
	Arnold	Arts	England	Educator
	Ashton	Business	England	Textile Industry
	Bayes	Science	England	Mathematician/Clergyman
	Beecham	Performing Arts	England	Conductor
	Berger	Creative Works	USA	Novelist
	Betterton	Performing Arts	England	Actor
	Bodley	Politics	England	Statesman/Scholar
	Brassey	Business	England	Railway Magnate
	Browne	Science	England	Physician/Writer
	Bulfinch	Creative Works	USA	Writer/Mythologist
	Burberry	Business	England	Fashion Designer
	Campbell	Creative Works	Scotland	Poet
	Campion	Creative Works	England	Poet/Composer
	Carew	Creative Works	England	Poet
	Carlyle	Creative Works	England	Writer
	Chatterton	Creative Works	England	Poet
	Chippendale	Arts	England	Furniture Designer
	Cole	Works of Art	USA	Painter
	Cook	Business	England	Travel Industry
	Coryate	Creative Works	England	Writer
	Costain	Creative Works	Canada	Novelist - Historical
	Coutts	Business	England	Entrepreneur
	Cranmer	Arts	England	Archbishop
	Cromwell	Politics	England	Statesman
	Dale	Politics	England	Governor - Virginia
	Dekker	Creative Works	England	Playwright
	Duggan	Sports	England	Soccer Player - HF
	Eakins	Works of Art	USA	Painter/Sculptor
	Elyot	Creative Works	England	Writer/Diplomat
	Erastus	Arts	Germany	Theologian

SOLVER SERIES: NAME FINDER

FIRST NAME	LAST NAME	CATEGORY	COUNTRY	FAME
Thomas	Fielden	Business	England	Textile Industry
	Gage	War & Peace	England	General
	Gainsborough	Works of Art	England	Painter
	Gomez	Performing Arts	USA	Actor - Acad Award Nom
	Gray	Creative Works	England	Poet
	Hardy	Creative Works	England	Poet/Novelist
	Hässler	Sports	Germany	Soccer Player
	Hearns	Sports	USA	Boxer
	Hendricks	Politics	USA	Vice-President
	Hobbes	Arts	England	Philosopher/Author
	Hodgkin	Science	England	Physician
	Hood	Creative Works	England	Poet/Humorist
	Hooker	Arts	England	Clergyman
	Hughes	Creative Works	England	Writer/Social Reformer
	Hutchinson	Politics	USA	Governor of Massachusetts
	Jefferson	Architecture	USA	Architect - AIA Gold Medal
	Jefferson	Politics	USA	President
	Kuhn	Arts	USA	Philosopher/Historian
	Kyd	Creative Works	England	Dramatist
	Lawrence	Works of Art	England	Painter - Portrait
	Malory	Creative Works	England	Compiler - Arthurian Tales
	Mann	Creative Works	Germany	Literature - Nobel Laureate
	Middleton	Creative Works	England	Dramatist
	Mitchell	Performing Arts	USA	Actor - Academy Award
	Moore	Creative Works	Ireland	Poet
	More	Creative Works	England	Writer/Statesman
	Nashe	Creative Works	England	Satirist/Pamphleteer
	Nast	Creative Works	USA	Cartoonist - Newspaper
	Otway	Creative Works	England	Dramatist
	Paine	Creative Works	USA	Writer/Revolutionary Patriot
	Percy	Arts	England	Collector - Ballads
	Pride	War & Peace	England	Army Officer
	Rowlandson	Works of Art	England	Painter/Caricaturist
	Ryan	Business	USA	Railway Magnate
	Sackville	Creative Works	England	Poet/Statesman
	Sully	Works of Art	USA	Painter
	Swords	Sports	USA	Soccer Player - HF
	Tallis	Creative Works	England	Composer
	Tryon	Creative Works	USA	Novelist
	Urquhart	Creative Works	Scotland	Writer/Translator
	Wolsey	Politics	England	Statesman
	Wyatt	Creative Works	England	Poet/Diplomat
	Young	Science	England	Physicist/Physician/Linguist
Thomas (Tom)	Florie	Sports	USA	Soccer Player - HF
	Hamilton	Performing Arts	USA	Rock & Roll - HF - Aerosmith
	Pettitt	Sports	England	Tennis Player - HF
Thomas (Tommy)	Dorsey	Performing Arts	USA	Band Leader - Big Band/Jazz - HF
	Dunderdale	Sports	Australia	Hockey Player - HF
Thomas à	Kempis	Arts	Germany	Scholar/Monk
Thomas Alva	Edison	Science	USA	Inventor - Electrical Devices
Thomas Anthony	Dooley	Science	USA	Medical Doctor
Thomas Augustine	Arne	Creative Works	England	Composer/Violinist
Thomas Austin (Tom)	Yawkey	Sports	USA	Baseball Executive - HF
Thomas B.	Barlow	Sports	USA	Basketball Player - HF
Thomas Babington	Macaulay	Politics	England	Statesman/Essayist
Thomas Bailey	Aldrich	Creative Works	USA	Poet/Novelist
Thomas Boone	Pickens	Business	USA	Oil Industry
Thomas C.	Schelling	Arts	USA	Economics - Nobel Laureate
Thomas Charles (Tommy)	Lasorda	Sports	USA	Baseball Manager - HF
Thomas Christian (Tom)	Johnson	Sports	Canada	Hockey Player - HF
Thomas Chrowder	Chamberlin	Science	USA	Geologist
Thomas Clayton	Wolfe	Creative Works	USA	Novelist
Thomas Dale	Akers	Aviation	USA	Astronaut

FIRST NAME	LAST NAME	CATEGORY	COUNTRY	FAME
Thomas David	Jones	Aviation	USA	Astronaut
Thomas De	Quincey	Creative Works	England	Essayist/Critic
Thomas Edmund	Dewey	Law & Order	USA	Lawyer
	Dewey	Politics	USA	Governor - New York
Thomas Edward	Lawrence	Creative Works	England	Writer/Adventurer
	Shaw	Creative Works	England	Writer/Adventurer
Thomas Franklin (Tommy)	McDonald	Sports	USA	Football Player - HF
Thomas Haden	Church	Performing Arts	USA	Actor - Acad Award Nom
Thomas Harry	Williams	Creative Works	USA	Author - Pulitzer
Thomas Hart	Benton	Politics	USA	Senator
	Benton	Works of Art	USA	Painter
Thomas Henry	Huxley	Science	England	Biologist/Writer
Thomas Henry (Tom)	Connolly	Sports	USA	Baseball Umpire - HF
Thomas Huckle	Weller	Science	USA	Medicine - Nobel Laureate
Thomas Hunt	Morgan	Science	USA	Medicine - Nobel Laureate
Thomas J.	Gola	Sports	USA	Basketball Player - HF
	Smith	Sports	Canada	Hockey Player - HF
Thomas Jacob	Hilfiger	Business	USA	Fashion Designer
Thomas Jesse (Tom)	Fears	Sports	USA	Football Player - HF
Thomas John	Hennen	Aviation	USA	Astronaut
Thomas Jonathon (Stonewall)	Jackson	War & Peace	USA	Confederate General
Thomas K.	McGraw	Creative Works	USA	Author - Pulitzer
Thomas Kenneth	Mattingly II	Aviation	USA	Astronaut
Thomas L. (Tom)	Clancy Jr.	Creative Works	USA	Author
Thomas Lee (Tom)	Mack	Sports	USA	Football Player - HF
Thomas Livingstone	Mitchell	Exploration	Australia	Explorer - Australia South East
Thomas Love	Peacock	Creative Works	England	Poet/Novelist
Thomas Lovell	Beddoes	Creative Works	England	Poet/Playwright
Thomas Michael	Disch	Creative Works	USA	Author - SciFi
Thomas Michael (Tommy)	McCarthy	Sports	USA	Baseball Player - HF
Thomas Mott	Osborne	Law & Order	USA	Reformer - Prison
Thomas N. (Tommy)	Phillips	Sports	Canada	Hockey Player - HF
Thomas O. (Tom)	Kite	Sports	USA	Golfer - HF
Thomas Patten	Stafford	Aviation	USA	Astronaut
Thomas Power	O'Connor	Politics	Ireland	Nationalist Leader
Thomas R.	Cech	Science	USA	Chemistry - Nobel Laureate
	Marshall	Politics	USA	Vice-President
Thomas Robert	Malthus	Arts	England	Political Economist
Thomas Rocco (Rocky)	Graziano	Sports	USA	Boxer - HF
Thomas Ruggles	Pynchon Jr.	Creative Works	USA	Novelist
Thomas Sigismund	Stribling	Creative Works	USA	Novelist - Pulitzer
Thomas Stearns	Eliot	Creative Works	England	Literature - Nobel Laureate
Thomas Stephen	Foley	Politics	USA	Congressman
Thomas W. (Tom)	Heinsohn	Sports	USA	Basketball Player - HF
Thomas Wade (Tom)	Landry	Sports	USA	Football Player - HF
Thomas Wentworth	Higginson	Creative Works	USA	Writer/Social Reformer
	Strafford	Politics	England	Statesman
Thomas West De La	Warr	Politics	England	Governor - Virginia
Thomas Woodrow	Wilson	Politics	USA	President
	Wilson	War & Peace	USA	Peace - Nobel Laureate
Thor	Heyerdahl	Exploration	Norway	Explorer - South Pacific
Thornton Niven	Wilder	Creative Works	USA	Dramatist - Pulitzer
Thorstein Bunde	Veblen	Arts	USA	Economist - Political
Thurgood	Marshall	Politics	USA	Justice - Supreme Court
Tia	Carrere	Performing Arts	USA	Actress
Tia Dashon	Mowry	Performing Arts	Germany	Actress
Tibère	Vadi	Architecture	Switzerland	Architect
Tige	Andrews	Performing Arts	USA	Actor
Tiger	Woods	Sports	USA	Golfer
Tigran	Petrosian	Games	Armenia	Chess Player
Tim	Conway	Performing Arts	USA	Comedian
	Curry	Performing Arts	England	Actor
	Holt	Performing Arts	USA	Actor

SOLVER SERIES: NAME FINDER

FIRST NAME	LAST NAME	CATEGORY	COUNTRY	FAME
Tim	Hunt	Science	England	Medicine - Nobel Laureate
	Matheson	Performing Arts	USA	Actor
	McCarver	Sports	USA	Baseball Player
	Raines	Sports	USA	Baseball Player
	Reid	Performing Arts	USA	Actor
	Richmond	Sports	USA	Race Car Driver - HF
	Robbins	Movie Production	USA	Director - Acad Award Nom
	Robbins	Performing Arts	USA	Actor - Academy Award
	Roth	Performing Arts	England	Actor - Acad Award Nom
	Russert	Performing Arts	USA	Show Host/Political Analyst
Timi	Yuro	Performing Arts	USA	Singer
Timothy	Bottoms	Performing Arts	USA	Actor
	Busfield	Performing Arts	USA	Actor
	Dalton	Performing Arts	Wales	Actor
	Eaton	Business	Canada	Retail Trade
	Hutton	Performing Arts	USA	Actor - Academy Award
	Spencer	Performing Arts	USA	Country Music - HF - Sons of the Pioneers
Timothy (Tim)	Burton	Movie Production	USA	Director
Timothy B.	Schmit (The Eagles)	Performing Arts	USA	Singer - Rock & Roll - HF
Timothy James (Tim)	Mara	Sports	USA	Football Founder - HF
Timothy John (Tim)	Keefe	Sports	USA	Baseball Player - HF
Timur (Tamerlane)	Lang	War & Peace	Mongolia	Military Leader
Tina	Louise	Performing Arts	USA	Actress
	Rosenberg	Creative Works	USA	Author - Pulitzer
	Yothers	Performing Arts	USA	Actress
Tino	Martinez	Sports	USA	Baseball Player
Tippi	Hedren	Performing Arts	USA	Actress
Tisa	Farrow	Performing Arts	USA	Actress
Tito	Jackson	Performing Arts	USA	Rock & Roll - HF - The Jackson Five
	Puente	Performing Arts	Puerto Rica	Jazz Drummer - Big Band/Jazz - HF
	Schipa	Performing Arts	Italy	Singer - Opera
Titus	Oates	Politics	England	Conspirator
	Salt	Business	England	Textile Industry
Titus Lucretius Carus	Lucretius	Arts	Italy	Philosopher
Tjalling C.	Koopmans	Arts	USA	Economics - Nobel Laureate
Tobe	Hooper	Movie Production	USA	Director
Tobias George	Smollett	Creative Works	England	Novelist
Tobias Michael Carl	Asser	War & Peace	Netherlands	Peace - Nobel Laureate
Tod	Browning	Movie Production	USA	Director
	Williams	Architecture	USA	Architect - Jefferson Medal
Todd	Christensen	Sports	USA	Football Player
Todd Harry	Rundgren	Performing Arts	USA	Singer/Guitarist
Tom	Arnold	Performing Arts	USA	Actor
	Berenger	Performing Arts	USA	Actor - Acad Award Nom
	Bosley	Performing Arts	USA	Actor
	Brokaw	Creative Works	USA	Journalist - Television
	Carvel	Business	USA	Confection Industry - Soft Ice Cream
	Cochrane	Performing Arts	Canada	Singer/Song Writer - Canadian Music - HF
	Conti	Performing Arts	Scotland	Actor - Acad Award Nom
	Courtenay	Performing Arts	England	Actor - Acad Award Nom
	Cruise	Performing Arts	USA	Actor - Acad Award Nom
	Ewell	Performing Arts	USA	Actor
	Finney	Sports	England	Soccer Player - HF
	Fogerty	Performing Arts	USA	Rock & Roll - HF - Creed. Clearwater Revival
	Glavine	Sports	USA	Baseball Player
	Harmon	Sports	USA	Football Player
	Hulce	Performing Arts	USA	Actor - Acad Award Nom
	Jones	Performing Arts	Wales	Singer
	Lehman	Sports	USA	Golfer
	Mix	Performing Arts	USA	Actor
	Morris Jr.	Sports	Scotland	Golfer - HF
	Morris Sr.	Sports	Scotland	Golfer - HF
	Okker	Sports	Netherlands	Tennis Player

FIRST NAME	LAST NAME	CATEGORY	COUNTRY	FAME
Tom	Petty	Performing Arts	USA	Rock & Roll - HF - Heart Breakers
	Poston	Performing Arts	USA	Comedian
	Scholz	Performing Arts	USA	Singer/Guitarist
	Selleck	Performing Arts	USA	Actor
	Skerritt	Performing Arts	USA	Actor
	Smothers	Performing Arts	USA	Comedian
	Sneva	Sports	USA	Race Car Driver
	Snyder	Creative Works	USA	Journalist - Television
	Spencer	Business	England	Confection Industry
	Stoppard	Creative Works	England	Playwright
	Tresh	Sports	USA	Baseball Player
	Tully	Performing Arts	USA	Actor - Acad Award Nom
	Waits	Performing Arts	USA	Singer - Contempory
	Watson	Sports	USA	Golfer - HF
	Weiskopf	Sports	USA	Golfer
	Wilkinson	Performing Arts	England	Actor - Acad Award Nom
	Wilson	Creative Works	USA	Cartoonist - Ziggy
	Hanks	Performing Arts	USA	Actor - Academy Award
Tom (Whitey)	Fleming	Sports	Scotland	Soccer Player - HF
Tom Campbell	Clark	Law & Order	USA	Justice/Supreme Court
Tom T.	Hall	Performing Arts	USA	Singer
Tomás de	Torquemada	Arts	Spain	Dominican Monk
Tomáš Garoque	Masaryk	Politics	Czechoslovakia	President
Tommy	Armour	Sports	Scotland	Golfer - HF
	Bolt	Sports	USA	Golfer - HF
	Chong	Performing Arts	Canada	Comedian
	Gaither	Performing Arts	USA	Rock & Roll - HF - The Orioles
	Hunt	Performing Arts	USA	Rock & Roll - HF - The Flamingos
	James	Performing Arts	USA	Singer
	Tune	Creative Works	USA	Choreographer
Tommy De	Vito	Performing Arts	USA	Rock & Roll - HF - The Four Seasons
Tommy Lee	Jones	Performing Arts	USA	Actor - Academy Award
Toni	Collette	Performing Arts	Australia	Actress - Acad Award Nom
	Morrison	Creative Works	USA	Literature - Nobel/Pulitzer
	Tennille	Performing Arts	USA	Singer - Pops
Tony	Banks	Creative Works	England	Song Writer/Keyboarder
	Blair	Politics	England	Prime Minster
	Curtis	Performing Arts	USA	Actor - Acad Award Nom
	Danza	Performing Arts	USA	Actor
	Dow	Performing Arts	USA	Actor
	Garnier	Architecture	France	Architect
	Gwynn	Sports	USA	Baseball Player
	Jacklin	Sports	England	Golfer - HF
	Kubek	Sports	USA	Baseball Player
	Kushner	Creative Works	USA	Dramatist - Pulitzer
	Lema	Sports	USA	Golfer
	Martin	Performing Arts	USA	Singer
	Musante	Performing Arts	USA	Actor
	Oliva	Sports	USA	Baseball Player
	Orlando	Performing Arts	USA	Singer
	Peña	Sports	USA	Baseball Player
	Randall	Performing Arts	USA	Actor
	Richardson	Movie Production	England	Director - Academy Award
	Roberts	Performing Arts	USA	Actor
	Sarg	Performing Arts	Guatemala	Puppeteer
Tori	Amos	Performing Arts	USA	Singer/Song Writer
	Spelling	Performing Arts	USA	Actress
Torquato	Tasso	Creative Works	Italy	Poet - Epic
Torsten N.	Wiesel	Science	Sweden	Medicine - Nobel Laureate
Toshiko	Akiyoshi	Performing Arts	Manchuria	Jazz Pianist - Big Band/Jazz - HF
Toshiro	Mifune	Performing Arts	China	Actor
Totie	Fields	Performing Arts	USA	Comedian
Toyo	Ito	Architecture	Japan	Architect

FIRST NAME	LAST NAME	CATEGORY	COUNTRY	FAME
Toyohiko	Kagawa	Politics	Japan	Social Reformer/Writer
Tracey	Ullman	Performing Arts	England	Actress
Traci	Bingham	Performing Arts	USA	Actress/Model
Tracy	Chapman	Performing Arts	USA	Singer
	Kidder	Creative Works	USA	Author - Pulitzer
Tracy Ann	Austin	Sports	USA	Tennis Player - HF
Travis Calvin	Jackson	Sports	USA	Baseball Player - HF
Treat	Williams	Performing Arts	USA	Actor
Trevor	Howard	Performing Arts	England	Actor - Acad Award Nom
Trey	Wilson	Performing Arts	USA	Actor
Trini	Alvarado	Performing Arts	USA	Actress
	Lopez	Performing Arts	USA	Singer
Trish Van	Devere	Performing Arts	USA	Actress
Tristan	Tzara	Creative Works	Romania	Poet/Editor
Tristram E. (Tris)	Speaker	Sports	USA	Baseball Player - HF
Troy	Aikman	Sports	USA	Football Player
	Donahue	Performing Arts	USA	Actor
Truman	Capote	Creative Works	USA	Author
Trummy	Young	Performing Arts	USA	Jazz Saxophonist - Big Band/Jazz - HF
Trygve	Haavelmo	Arts	Norway	Economics - Nobel Laureate
Tsung-Dao	Lee	Science	China	Physics - Nobel Laureate
Tuesday	Weld	Performing Arts	USA	Actress - Acad Award Nom
Tug	McGraw	Sports	USA	Baseball Player
Twyla	Tharp	Creative Works	USA	Choreographer
Tycho	Brahe	Science	Denmark	Astronomer
Tyler	Dennett	Creative Works	USA	Author - Pulitzer
Tyne	Daly	Performing Arts	USA	Actress
Tyra	Banks	Performing Arts	USA	Super Model
	Ferrel	Performing Arts	USA	Actress
Tyrone	Power	Performing Arts	USA	Actor
Tyrus Raymond (Ty)	Cobb	Sports	USA	Baseball Player - HF
U	Thant	Politics	Burma	Secretary-General UN
Ugo	Foscolo	Creative Works	Italy	Poet
	Tognazzi	Movie Production	Italy	Director
Ulf Dietrich	Merbold	Aviation	Germany	Astronaut
Ulf von	Euler	Science	Sweden	Medicine - Nobel Laureate
Uljana	Semjonova	Sports	Latvia	Basketball Player - HF
Ulrich	Zwingli	Arts	Switzerland	Reformer - Protestant
Ulrich Hans	Walter	Aviation	Germany	Astronaut
Ultiminio (Sugar)	Ramos	Sports	Cuba	Boxer - HF
Ulu	Grosbard	Movie Production	Belgium	Director
Ulysses Simpson	Grant	Politics	USA	President
	Grant	War & Peace	USA	General
Uma	Thurman	Performing Arts	USA	Actress - Acad Award Nom
Umberto	Boccioni	Works of Art	Italy	Painter/Sculptor
	Eco	Creative Works	Italy	Author
	Guidoni	Aviation	Italy	Astronaut
Una	Merkel	Performing Arts	USA	Actress - Acad Award Nom
	O'Connor	Performing Arts	Northern Ireland	Actress
Uncle Dave (David)	Macon	Performing Arts	USA	Singer - Country Music - HF
Upton Beall Jr.	Sinclair	Creative Works	USA	Novelist - Pulitzer
Urban Charles (Red)	Faber	Sports	USA	Baseball Player - HF
Uri	Geller	Performing Arts	Israel	Magician
Ursula	Andress	Performing Arts	Switzerland	Actress
Ursula Kroeber Le	Guin	Creative Works	USA	Novelist
Uta	Hagen	Performing Arts	Germany	Actress
Val	Kilmer	Performing Arts	USA	Actor
Val Logsdon	Fitch	Science	USA	Physics - Nobel Laureate
Valentina	Cortese	Performing Arts	Italy	Actress - Acad Award Nom
Valeri	Kharlamov	Sports	Russia	Hockey Player - HF
Valeri Fyodorovich	Bykovskiy	Aviation	Russia	Astronaut
Valeri Nikolayevich	Kubasov	Aviation	Russia	Astronaut
Valeria	Mazza	Performing Arts	Argentina	Super Model

FIRST NAME	LAST NAME	CATEGORY	COUNTRY	FAME
Valerie	Bertinelli	Performing Arts	USA	Actress
	Harper	Performing Arts	USA	Actress
	Perrine	Performing Arts	USA	Actress - Acad Award Nom
Valery	Borzov	Sports	Russia	Olympic Runner
Van	Cliburn	Performing Arts	USA	Pianist
	Heflin	Performing Arts	USA	Actor - Academy Award
	Johnson	Performing Arts	USA	Actor
	Morrison	Performing Arts	Northern Ireland	Singer
Van Wyck	Brooks	Creative Works	USA	Author - Pulitzer
Vanessa	Lorenzo	Performing Arts	Spain	Super Model
	Mae	Performing Arts	China	Violinist
	Redgrave	Performing Arts	England	Actress - Academy Award
	Williams	Performing Arts	USA	Actress
Vanessa Lynn	Williams	Performing Arts	USA	Singer - Musicals
Vanlentina Vladimirovna	Tereshkova	Aviation	Russia	Astronaut
Vanna	White	Performing Arts	USA	Show Host
Vannevar	Bush	Science	USA	Engineer/Administrator
Vasco da	Gama	Exploration	Portugal	Explorer - Africa Coast
Vasco Núñez de	Balboa	Exploration	Spain	Explorer - Panama
Vasily	Smyslov	Games	Russia	Chess Player
Vaslav	Nijinsky	Performing Arts	Russia	Dancer - Ballet
Vaughn	Monroe	Performing Arts	USA	Singer
Venustiano	Carranza	Politics	Mexico	President
Vera	Miles	Performing Arts	USA	Actress
	Wang	Business	USA	Fashion Designer
Vera Helena Hruba	Ralston	Sports	Czechoslovakia	Olympic Skater
Vern	Mikkelsen	Sports	USA	Basketball Player - HF
Verne	Young	Performing Arts	USA	Rock & Roll - HF - The Drifters
Vernon	Castle	Creative Works	England	Writer
Vernon (Marion Try)	Dalhart (Slaughter)	Performing Arts	USA	Singer - Country Music - HF
Vernon Earl (The Pearl)	Monroe	Sports	USA	Basketball Player - HF
Vernon L.	Smith	Arts	USA	Economics - Nobel Laureate
Vernon Louis	Parrington	Creative Works	USA	Author - Pulitzer
Vernon Louis (Lefty)	Gómez	Sports	USA	Baseball Player - HF
Veronica	Hamel	Performing Arts	USA	Actress
	Lake	Performing Arts	USA	Actress
Viacheslav	Fetisov	Sports	Russia	Hockey Player - HF
Vic	Damone	Performing Arts	USA	Singer
	Morrow	Performing Arts	USA	Actor
Vicki	Lawrence	Performing Arts	USA	Actress
Vicki Lynn (Anna Nicole)	Smith (Hogan)	Performing Arts	USA	Super Model
Vico	Magistretti	Architecture	Italy	Architect
Victor	Borge	Performing Arts	Denmark	Pianist/Entertainer
	Buono	Performing Arts	USA	Actor - Acad Award Nom
	Cousin	Arts	France	Philosopher
	Fleming	Movie Production	USA	Director - Academy Award
	Galindez	Sports	Argentina	Boxer - HF
	Grignard	Science	France	Chemistry - Nobel Laureate
	Herbert	Creative Works	Ireland	Composer - Light Opera
	Horta	Architecture	Belgium	Architect
	Jory	Performing Arts	Canada	Actor
	Laloux	Architecture	France	Architect - AIA Gold Medal
	Mature	Performing Arts	USA	Actor
	McLaglen	Performing Arts	England	Actor - Academy Award
	Schertzinger	Movie Production	USA	Director - Acad Award Nom
Victor (Vic)	Dana	Performing Arts	USA	Singer
Victor A.	Hansen	Sports	USA	Basketball Player - HF
Victor Franz	Hess	Science	Austria	Physics - Nobel Laureate
Victor Gazaway (Vic)	Willis	Sports	USA	Baseball Player - HF
Victor Marie	Hugo	Creative Works	England	Poet/Novelist/Playwright
Victoria	Jackson	Performing Arts	USA	Comedian
	Principal	Performing Arts	Japan	Actress
	Tennant	Performing Arts	England	Actress

SOLVER SERIES: NAME FINDER

FIRST NAME	LAST NAME	CATEGORY	COUNTRY	FAME
Victorien	Sardou	Creative Works	France	Dramatist
Vida	Blue	Sports	USA	Baseball Player
Vidiadhar Surajprasad	Naipaul	Creative Works	England	Literature - Nobel Laureate
Vijay	Singh	Sports	Fiji	Golfer
Vikki	Carr	Performing Arts	USA	Singer
Viktor Vassilyevich	Gorbatko	Aviation	Russia	Astronaut
Vilfredo	Pareto	Arts	Switzerland	Economist/Sociologist
Vilhjalmur	Stefansson	Exploration	Canada	Explorer - Arctic
Vin	Diesel	Performing Arts	USA	Actor
Vincent	Canby	Creative Works	USA	Journalist - Newspaper
	Gardenia	Performing Arts	Italy	Actor - Acad Award Nom
	Price	Performing Arts	USA	Actor
	Spano	Performing Arts	USA	Actor
	Winter	Performing Arts	Scotland	Actor - Academy Award
Vincent (Vinnie)	Richards	Sports	USA	Tennis Player - HF
Vincent du	Vigneaud	Science	USA	Chemistry - Nobel Laureate
Vincent Edward (Vin)	Scully	Creative Works	USA	Journalist - Television
Vincent Eugene (Gene)	Vincent (Craddock)	Performing Arts	USA	Singer - Rock & Roll - HF
Vincent J.	Scully	Architecture	USA	Architect - Jefferson Medal
Vincent Thomas (Vince)	Lombardi	Sports	USA	Football Coach - HF
Vincent Van	Gogh	Works of Art	Netherlands	Painter
Vincente	Aleixandre	Creative Works	Spain	Literature - Nobel Laureate
	Blasco Ibáñez	Creative Works	Spain	Novelist
	Minnelli	Movie Production	USA	Director - Academy Award
	Saldivar	Sports	Mexico	Boxer - HF
Vincente Yáñez	Pinzón	Exploration	Spain	Explorer - Caribbean
Vincenzo	Bellini	Creative Works	Italy	Composer/Opera
Virgil	Thomson	Creative Works	USA	Composer
Virgil Ivan (Gus)	Grissom	Aviation	USA	Astronaut
Virginia	Bruce	Performing Arts	USA	Actress
	Dare	Arts	USA	First American Child
	Graham	Performing Arts	USA	Actress
	Madsen	Performing Arts	USA	Actress - Acad Award Nom
	Mayo	Performing Arts	USA	Actress
	Woolf	Creative Works	England	Author
Virginia Patterson (Patsy)	Cline (Hensley)	Performing Arts	USA	Singer - Country Music - HF
Virna	Lisi	Performing Arts	Italy	Actress
Viswanathan	Anand	Games	India	Chess Player
Vitali Ivanovich	Sevastyanov	Aviation	Russia	Astronaut
Vitaly L.	Ginzburg	Science	Russia	Physics - Nobel Laureate
Vitas	Gerulaitis	Sports	USA	Tennis Player
Vittoriano	Viganò	Architecture	Italy	Architect
Vittorio	Alfieri	Creative Works	Italy	Dramatist/Poet
	Gregotti	Architecture	Italy	Architect
	Jano	Sports	Italy	Race Car Driver - HF
Vittorio De	Sica	Movie Production	Italy	Director
	Sica	Performing Arts	Italy	Actor - Acad Award Nom
Vittorio Emanuele	Orlando	Politics	Italy	Premier
Vitus Jonassen	Bering	Exploration	Denmark	Explorer - Siberia
Viveca	Lindfors	Performing Arts	Sweden	Actress
Vivian	Blaine	Performing Arts	USA	Singer/Comedian
	Vance	Performing Arts	USA	Actress
Vivien	Leigh	Performing Arts	India	Actress - Academy Award
	Merchant	Performing Arts	England	Actress - Acad Award Nom
Vivienne	Westwood	Business	England	Fashion Designer
Vladimir	Horowitz	Performing Arts	Russia	Pianist
	Kramnik	Games	Russia	Chess Player
	Nabokov	Creative Works	USA	Writer/Teacher
	Prelog	Science	Switzerland	Chemistry - Nobel Laureate
	Tatlin	Architecture	Russia	Architect/Painter/Sculptor
Vladimir Aleksandrovich	Shatalov	Aviation	Russia	Astronaut
Vladimir Ilyich	Lenin	Politics	Russia	Premier - U.S.S.R.
Vladimir Mikhailovich	Komarov	Aviation	Russia	Astronaut

FIRST NAME	LAST NAME	CATEGORY	COUNTRY	FAME
Vladimirovich	Mayakovsky	Creative Works	Russia	Poet
Vladislav (Bogie)	Bogicevic	Sports	Yugoslavia	Soccer Player - HF
Vladislav Aleksandrovich	Tretiak	Sports	Russia	Hockey Player - HF
Vladislav Nikolavevich	Volkov	Aviation	Russia	Astronaut
Vo Nguyen	Giap	War & Peace	Vietnam	General - Four Star
Von Eschenbach	Wolfram	Creative Works	Germany	Poet - Epic
Vyacheslav Mikhailovich	Molotov	Politics	Russia	Statesman
Wade	Boggs	Sports	USA	Baseball Player - HF
Waite Charles	Hoyt	Sports	USA	Baseball Player - HF
Waldemar	Cierpinski	Sports	Germany	Olympic Marathoner
Walden Roberto (Bobby)	Darin (Cossotto)	Performing Arts	USA	Actor - Acad Award Nom
	Darin (Cossotto)	Performing Arts	USA	Singer - Rock & Roll - HF
Walker	Percy	Creative Works	USA	Author
Wallace	Beery	Performing Arts	USA	Actor - Academy Award
	Stevens	Creative Works	USA	Poet - Pulitzer
Wallace Earle	Stegner	Creative Works	USA	Novelist - Pulitzer
Wallace Kirkman	Harrison	Architecture	USA	Architect - AIA Gold Medal
Wally	Cox	Performing Arts	USA	Comedian
	Parks	Sports	USA	Race Car Promoter - HF
Walt	Kelly	Creative Works	USA	Animator
Walter	Bagehot	Arts	England	Economist/Journalist
	Benjamin	Creative Works	Germany	Writer/Critic
	Brennan	Performing Arts	USA	Actor - Academy Award
	Cronkite	Creative Works	USA	Journalist - Newspaper
	Dick	Sports	Scotland	Soccer Player - HF
	Frazier	Sports	USA	Basketball Player - HF
	Gilbert	Science	USA	Chemistry - Nobel Laureate
	Gropius	Architecture	Germany	Architect - AIA Gold Medal
	Hagen	Sports	USA	Golfer - HF
	Hampden	Performing Arts	USA	Actor
	Huston	Performing Arts	Canada	Actor - Academy Award
	Kohn	Science	USA	Chemistry - Nobel Laureate
	Lanz	Creative Works	USA	Cartoonist - Woody Woodpecker
	Lippmann	Arts	USA	Journalist
	Map	Creative Works	Wales	Poet/Satirist
	Matthau	Performing Arts	USA	Actor - Academy Award
	Mondale	Politics	USA	Vice-President
	Pidgeon	Performing Arts	Canada	Actor - Acad Award Nom
	Piston	Creative Works	USA	Composer
	Raleigh	Politics	England	Statesman/Explorer/Poet
	Reed	Science	USA	Surgeon/Bacteriologist
	Reuther	Business	USA	Labor Leader
	Scott	Creative Works	Scotland	Poet/Novelist
	Travis	Sports	Australia	Golfer - HF
	Ulbricht	Politics	Germany	Chief of State
	Whitman	Creative Works	USA	Poet
	Williams	Performing Arts	USA	Rock & Roll - HF - The O'Jays
	Winchell	Creative Works	USA	Journalist - Newspaper
	Lang	Movie Production	USA	Director - Acad Award Nom
	Williams Sr.	Performing Arts	USA	Rock & Roll - HF - The O'Jays
Walter (Babe)	Pratt	Sports	Canada	Hockey Player - HF
Walter (Red)	Barber	Creative Works	USA	Journalist - Television
	Smith	Creative Works	USA	Journalist - Newspaper
Walter (Walt)	Bellamy	Sports	USA	Basketball Player - HF
Walter A.	McDougall	Creative Works	USA	Author - Pulitzer
Walter Alfred	Bahr	Sports	USA	Soccer Player - HF
Walter Andrew (Walt)	Kiesling	Sports	USA	Football Player - HF
Walter Carl	Becker	Performing Arts	USA	Rock & Roll - HF - Steely Dan
Walter Chauncey	Camp	Sports	USA	Football Coach
Walter Clopton	Wingfield	Sports	Wales	Tennis Inventor - HF
Walter de la	Mare	Creative Works	England	Poet/Novelist
Walter Edward (Turk)	Broda	Sports	Canada	Hockey Player - HF
Walter Elias	Disney	Movie Production	USA	Producer

SOLVER SERIES: NAME FINDER

FIRST NAME	LAST NAME	CATEGORY	COUNTRY	FAME
Walter Emmonds	Alston	Sports	USA	Baseball Manager - HF
Walter Fenner (Buck)	Leonard	Sports	USA	Baseball Player - HF
Walter Francis	White	Politics	USA	Negro Leader
Walter Hermann	Nernst	Science	Germany	Chemistry - Nobel Laureate
Walter Hines	Page	Creative Works	USA	Journalist/Editor/Diplomat
Walter Horatio	Pater	Creative Works	England	Essayist/Critic
Walter Houser	Brattain	Science	USA	Physics - Nobel Laureate
Walter Hubert	Annenberg	Business	USA	Media Magnate
Walter Jackson	Bate	Creative Works	USA	Author - Pulitzer
Walter James (Rabbit)	Maranville	Sports	USA	Baseball Player - HF
Walter Jerry	Payton	Sports	USA	Football Player - HF
Walter Johannes	Damrosch	Creative Works	USA	Composer/Conductor
Walter Marty	Schirra	Aviation	USA	Astronaut
Walter Norman	Haworth	Science	England	Chemistry - Nobel Laureate
Walter Perry	Johnson	Sports	USA	Baseball Player - HF
Walter Rudolf	Hess	Science	Switzerland	Medicine - Nobel Laureate
Walter Savage	Landor	Creative Works	England	Poet/Writer
Walter Stone	Tevis	Creative Works	USA	Author
Walter William	Skeat	Arts	England	Lexicographer/Philologist
Walther	Bothe	Science	Germany	Physics - Nobel Laureate
	Rathenau	Business	Germany	Industrialist/Statesman
Wanda	Landowska	Performing Arts	Poland	Harpsichordist
Wangari	Maathai	War & Peace	Kenya	Peace - Nobel Laureate
Ward	Bond	Performing Arts	USA	Actor
Warner	Baxter	Performing Arts	USA	Actor - Academy Award
	Oland	Performing Arts	Sweden	Actor
Warren	Beatty	Performing Arts	USA	Actor - Acad Award Nom
	Christopher	Politics	USA	Secretary of State
	Hastings	Politics	England	Statesman
	Moon	Sports	USA	Football Player
	Oates	Performing Arts	USA	Actor
	Zevon	Performing Arts	USA	Singer
	Beatty	Movie Production	USA	Director - Academy Award
Warren (Baby)	Dodds	Performing Arts	USA	Jazz Drummer - Big Band/Jazz - HF
Warren Crandall	Giles	Sports	USA	Baseball Executive - HF
Warren Earl	Burger	Law & Order	USA	Chief Justice
Warren Edward	Spahn	Sports	USA	Baseball Player - HF
Warren Gamaliel	Harding	Politics	USA	President
Washington	Irving	Creative Works	USA	Author
Wassily	Kandinsky	Works of Art	Russia	Painter
	Leontief	Arts	USA	Economics - Nobel Laureate
Wat	Tyler	Politics	England	Rebellion Leader
Watson (Watty)	Washburn	Sports	USA	Tennis Player - HF
Waylon	Jennings	Performing Arts	USA	Singer - Country Music - HF
Wayne	Newton	Performing Arts	USA	Singer
	Osmond	Performing Arts	USA	Singer
	Shorter	Performing Arts	USA	Jazz Saxophonist - Big Band/Jazz - HF
	Williams	Law & Order	USA	Serial Killer
Wayne Douglas (Great One)	Gretzky	Sports	Canada	Hockey Player - HF
Wayne Vernal	Millner	Sports	USA	Football Player - HF
Weldon Leo (Jack)	Teagarden	Performing Arts	USA	Jazz Trombonist - Big Band/Jazz - HF
Wellington Timothy	Mara	Sports	USA	Football Owner - HF
Wendell	Corey	Performing Arts	USA	Actor
	Phillips	Politics	USA	Abolitionist
	Scott	Sports	USA	Race Car Driver - HF
Wendell Lewis	Willkie	Politics	USA	Political Leader/Lawyer
Wendell Meredith	Stanley	Science	USA	Chemistry - Nobel Laureate
Wendy	Hiller	Performing Arts	England	Actress - Academy Award
	Wasserstein	Creative Works	USA	Dramatist - Pulitzer
Werner	Arber	Science	Switzerland	Medicine - Nobel Laureate
	Forssmann	Science	Germany	Medicine - Nobel Laureate
	Herzog	Movie Production	Germany	Director
	Klemperer	Performing Arts	Germany	Actor

FIRST NAME	LAST NAME	CATEGORY	COUNTRY	FAME
Werner	Nilsen	Sports	Norway	Soccer Player - HF
	Fricker	Sports	Yugoslavia	Soccer Player - HF
	Roth	Sports	Yugoslavia	Soccer Player - HF
Werner E.	Mieth	Sports	Germany	Soccer Player - HF
Werner Karl	Heisenberg	Science	Germany	Physics - Nobel Laureate
Wernher von	Braun	Aviation	USA	Engineer - Rocket
Wes	Craven	Creative Works	USA	Novelist
	Parker	Sports	USA	Baseball Player
Wesley	Ruggles	Movie Production	USA	Director - Acad Award Nom
	Snipes	Performing Arts	USA	Actor
Wesley Branch	Rickey	Sports	USA	Baseball Executive -HF
Wesley S. (Wes)	Unseld	Sports	USA	Basketball Player - HF
Whitelaw	Reid	Creative Works	USA	Journalist - Newspaper
Whitney	Houston	Performing Arts	USA	Singer
Wifred	Grenfell	Science	England	Physician/Writer
Wil	Wheaton	Performing Arts	USA	Actor
Wilber Joe (Bullet)	Rogan	Sports	USA	Baseball Player - HF
Wilbert	Robinson	Sports	USA	Baseball Manager - HF
Wilbur	Shaw	Sports	USA	Race Car Driver - HF
	Smith	Creative Works	Africa	Author
	Wright	Aviation	USA	Inventor - Airplane
Wilbur (Will)	Bradley (Schwichtenberg)	Performing Arts	USA	Band Leader - Big Band/Jazz - HF
Wilbur Charles (Weeb)	Ewbank	Sports	USA	Football Coach - HF
Wilbur Francis (Pete)	Henry	Sports	USA	Football Player - HF
Wiley	Post	Aviation	USA	Pilot - Around the World
Wilf (Montana Slim)	Carter	Performing Arts	Canada	Singer - Canadian Music - HF
Wilford	Brimley	Performing Arts	USA	Actor
Wilfred	Laurier	Politics	Canada	Prime Minister
	Owen	Creative Works	England	Poet
Wilfred Thomas (Shorty)	Green	Sports	Canada	Hockey Player - HF
Wilfredo	Gómez	Sports	Puerto Rico	Boxer - HF
Wilfrid Stalker	Sellars	Arts	USA	Philosopher
Wilhelm	Grimm	Creative Works	Germany	Philologist - Fairy Tales
	Ostwald	Science	Germany	Chemistry - Nobel Laureate
	Steinitz	Games	Czechoslovakia	Chess Player
	Wien	Science	Germany	Physics - Nobel Laureate
	Wundt	Arts	Germany	Psychologist/Physiologist
Wilhelm Conrad	Röntgen	Science	Germany	Physics - Nobel Laureate
Wilhelm Edouard	Weber	Science	Germany	Physicist
Wilhelm Konrad	Roentgen	Science	Germany	Physicist - X-Ray Discoverer
Wilhelm Richard	Wagner	Creative Works	Germany	Composer
Will	Clark	Sports	USA	Baseball Player
	Durant	Creative Works	USA	Author - Pulitzer
	Eisner	Creative Works	USA	Cartoonist
	Geer	Performing Arts	USA	Actor
	Rogers	Performing Arts	USA	Actor/Humorist
	Smith	Performing Arts	USA	Actor - Acad Award Nom
Willa Sibert	Cather	Creative Works	USA	Novelist - Pulitzer
Willard Frank	Libby	Science	USA	Chemistry - Nobel Laureate
Willard Van Orman	Quine	Arts	USA	Philosopher
Willem	Dafoe	Performing Arts	USA	Actor - Acad Award Nom
	Einthoven	Science	Netherlands	Medicine - Nobel Laureate
	Jantszoon	Exploration	Netherlands	Explorer - Australia
Willem de	Kooning	Works of Art	USA	Painter
	Sitter	Science	Netherlands	Astronomer
William	Archer	Creative Works	Scotland	Playwright
	Arrol	Business	England	Railway Magnate
	Atherton	Performing Arts	USA	Actor
	Baffin	Exploration	England	Explorer - Arctic
	Baldwin	Performing Arts	USA	Actor
	Beebe	Exploration	USA	Explorer - Deep Sea
	Bendix	Performing Arts	USA	Actor - Acad Award Nom
	Benton	Business	USA	Advertising

SOLVER SERIES: NAME FINDER

FIRST NAME	LAST NAME	CATEGORY	COUNTRY	FAME
William	Berkely	Politics	England	Governor
	Blackstone	Law & Order	England	Jurist
	Blake	Creative Works	England	Poet/Artist
	Bligh	War & Peace	England	Commander
	Booth	Arts	England	Revivalist
	Bradford	Politics	USA	Governor
	Brewster	Exploration	England	Pilgrim - Plymounth
	Bruder	Architecture	USA	Architect
	Byrd	Creative Works	England	Composer
	Caslon	Arts	England	Type Designer
	Caxton	Arts	England	Printer
	Christopher	Performing Arts	USA	Actor
	Clark	Exploration	USA	Explorer - Missouri River
	Cobbett	Business	England	Publishing
	Cobbett	Creative Works	England	Journalist/Reformer
	Colgate	Business	USA	Industrialist - Soap
	Collins	Creative Works	England	Poet
	Congreve	Creative Works	England	Playwright
	Conrad	Performing Arts	USA	Actor
	Cowper	Creative Works	England	Poet
	Crookes	Science	England	Chemist/Physicist
	Dampier	Exploration	England	Explorer - Caribbean
	Daniels	Performing Arts	USA	Actor
	D'Avenant	Creative Works	England	Poet/Playwright
	Demarest	Performing Arts	USA	Actor - Acad Award Nom
	Devane	Performing Arts	USA	Actor
	Dieterle	Movie Production	Germany	Director - Acad Award Nom
	Duer	Politics	USA	Statesman
	Dunbar	Creative Works	Scotland	Poet
	Faulkner	Creative Works	USA	Literature - Nobel/Pulitzer
	Frawley	Performing Arts	USA	Actor
	Gaddis	Creative Works	USA	Novelist
	Gargan	Performing Arts	USA	Actor - Acad Award Nom
	Godwin	Creative Works	England	Writer/Political Philosopher
	Golding	Creative Works	England	Literature - Nobel Laureate
	Grace	Business	USA	Shipping Magnate
	Green	Business	USA	Labor Leader
	Harvey	Science	England	Physician
	Hazlitt	Creative Works	England	Essayist
	Herschel	Science	England	Astronomer
	Hickey	Performing Arts	USA	Actor - Acad Award Nom
	Hobby	Business	USA	Newspaper Industry
	Hogarth	Works of Art	England	Painter/Engraver
	Holabird	Architecture	USA	Architect - Skyscraper
	Holden	Performing Arts	USA	Actor - Academy Award
	Hone	Business	England	Publishing
	Hovell	Exploration	England	Explorer - Australia
	Howe	War & Peace	England	Commander in Chief
	Hulton	Business	England	Railway Magnate
	Hurt	Performing Arts	USA	Actor - Academy Award
	Inge	Creative Works	Ireland	Dramatist - Pulitzer
	James	Arts	USA	Philosopher/Psychologist
	James	Business	England	Railway Magnate
	Jenner	Science	England	Physician
	Kennedy	Creative Works	USA	Novelist - Pulitzer
	Kidd	Law & Order	England	Privateer/Pirate
	Langland	Creative Works	England	Poet
	Laud	Arts	England	Prelate/Archbishop
	Lever	Business	England	Entrepreneur
	McKinley	Politics	USA	President
	Meredith	Creative Works	USA	Poet - Pulitzer
	Mitchell	War & Peace	USA	Army Officer/Aviation Pioneer
	Morris	Architecture	England	Architect

FIRST NAME	LAST NAME	CATEGORY	COUNTRY	FAME
William	Morris	Business	England	Entrepreneur
	Morris	Works of Art	England	Artist/Craftsman/Poet
	Ockham	Arts	England	Philosopher
	Osler	Science	Canada	Physician
	Paley	Arts	England	Theologian/Philosopher
	Pawley	Business	USA	Transportation Industry
	Penn	Exploration	England	Leader - Quakers
	Pitt	Politics	England	Prime Minister
	Powell	Performing Arts	USA	Actor - Acad Award Nom
	Powell	Performing Arts	USA	Rock & Roll - HF - The O'Jays
	Powell	Performing Arts	USA	Rock & Roll - HF - The O'Jays
	Radcliffe	Business	England	Textile Industry
	Ramsay	Science	England	Chemistry - Nobel Laureate
	Safire	Creative Works	USA	Journalist - Newspaper - Pulitzer
	Saroyan	Creative Works	USA	Dramatist - Pulitzer
	Schallert	Performing Arts	USA	Actor
	Shakespeare	Creative Works	USA	Poet/Dramatist
	Shatner	Performing Arts	Canada	Actor
	Siemens	Science	England	Inventor/Engineer
	Smith	Science	England	Geologist
	Styron	Creative Works	USA	Author - Pulitzer
	Taubman	Creative Works	USA	Author - Pulitzer
	Temple	Creative Works	England	Writer/Diplomat
	Thomson	Science	England	Physicist/Mathematician
	Tweed	Business	USA	Manufacturing Industry
	Tyndale	Arts	England	Religious Reformer
	Vickery	Arts	USA	Economics - Nobel Laureate
	Vinson	Business	USA	Oil Industry
	Wallace	Politics	Scotland	Patriot
	Wellman	Movie Production	USA	Director - Acad Award Nom
	Wilberforce	Politics	England	Statesman
	Windom	Performing Arts	USA	Actor
	Wordsworth	Creative Works	England	Poet Laureate
	Wycherley	Creative Works	England	Dramatist
	Wyler	Movie Production	Germany	Director - Academy Award
	Zorach	Works of Art	USA	Painter/Sculptor
	McKinney	Performing Arts	USA	Jazz Drummer - Big Band/Jazz - HF
William (Bill)	Cook	Sports	Canada	Hockey Player - HF
	Dana	Performing Arts	USA	Actor
	France Jr.	Sports	USA	Race Car Promoter - HF
	Gadsby	Sports	Canada	Hockey Player - HF
	Hanna	Creative Works	USA	Cartoonist - Tom and Jerry
	Klem	Sports	USA	Baseball Umpire - HF
	Looby	Sports	USA	Soccer Player - HF
	Mosienko	Sports	Canada	Hockey Player - HF
	Moyers	Creative Works	USA	Journalist - Television
	Muncey	Sports	USA	Hydroplane Race Driver - HF
	Tilghman	Law & Order	USA	Lawman
	Toomey	Sports	USA	Olympic Decathlete
William (Billy)	Burch	Sports	USA	Hockey Player - HF
	Connolly	Performing Arts	Scotland	Comedian
William (Buck)	Ewing	Sports	USA	Baseball Player - HF
William (Buffalo Bill)	Cody	Law & Order	USA	Hunter/Scout/Indian Fighter
William (Hopalong)	Cassidy (Boyd)	Performing Arts	USA	Actor
William (Little Willie John)	John	Performing Arts	USA	Singer - Rock & Roll - HF
William (Pop)	Gates	Sports	USA	Basketball Player - HF
William (Smokey)	Robinson	Performing Arts	USA	Singer - Rock & Roll - HF
William (Tucker)	Fryer	Sports	England	Soccer Player - HF
William (Will)	Harridge	Sports	USA	Baseball Executive - HF
William A.	Wheeler	Politics	USA	Vice-President
William Adams	Delano	Architecture	USA	Architect - AIA Gold Medal
William Alexander	Craigie	Arts	England	Lexicographer
William Alfred	Fowler	Science	USA	Physics - Nobel Laureate

SOLVER SERIES: NAME FINDER

FIRST NAME	LAST NAME	CATEGORY	COUNTRY	FAME
William Alison	Anders	Aviation	USA	Astronaut
William Allan	Neilson	Arts	USA	Educator/Editor
William Allen	White	Creative Works	USA	Author - Pulitzer
William Aloysius (Bill)	McGowan	Sports	USA	Baseball Umpire - HF
William Ambrose	Hulbert	Sports	USA	Baseball Executive - HF
William Andrew	Swanberg	Creative Works	USA	Author - Pulitzer
William Arthur	Pailes	Aviation	USA	Astronaut
William Arthur (Candy)	Cummings	Sports	USA	Baseball Executive - HF
William Augustus (Bill)	Larned	Sports	USA	Tennis Player - HF
William Averell	Harriman	Business	USA	Financier/Industrialist
William B. (Bill)	Watterson II	Creative Works	USA	Cartoonist - Calvin & Hobbes
William Barclay	Masterson	Law & Order	USA	Lawman
William Benjamin	Lenoir	Aviation	USA	Astronaut
William Bliss	Carman	Creative Works	Canada	Poet/Journalist
William Boyd (Bill)	McKechnie	Sports	USA	Baseball Manager - HF
William Bradford	Shockley	Science	USA	Physics - Nobel Laureate
William Butler	Yeats	Creative Works	Ireland	Literature - Nobel Laureate
William C. (Bill)	Campbell	Sports	USA	Golfer - HF
William C. (Skinny)	Johnson	Sports	USA	Basketball Player - HF
William Cabell	Bruce	Creative Works	USA	Author - Pulitzer
William Caleb (Cale)	Yarborough	Sports	USA	Race Car Driver - HF
William Cameron	McCool	Aviation	USA	Astronaut
William Carlos	Williams	Creative Works	USA	Poet - Pulitzer
William Charles	Macready	Performing Arts	England	Actor
William Charles (Bill)	Barber	Sports	Canada	Hockey Player - HF
William Charles (Willie)	Renshaw	Sports	England	Tennis Player - HF
William Christopher	Handy	Performing Arts	USA	Band Leader - Big Band/Jazz - HF
William Clarke	Hinkle	Sports	USA	Football Player - HF
William Claude (WC)	Fields (Dukenfield)	Performing Arts	USA	Comedian
William Clyde	Fitch	Creative Works	USA	Playwright
William Cornelius Van	Horne	Business	Canada	Railway Magnate
William Crawford	Grogas	War & Peace	USA	Medical Officer
William Cullen	Bryant	Creative Works	USA	Poet
William D.	Phillips	Science	USA	Physics - Nobel Laureate
William Dean	Howells	Creative Works	USA	Novelist/Critic/Editor
William Delford (Willie)	Davis	Sports	USA	Football Player - HF
William DeWitt	Snodgrass	Creative Works	USA	Poet - Pulitzer
William Donald (Don)	McNeill	Sports	USA	Tennis Player - HF
William E. (Billy)	May	Performing Arts	USA	Composer/Arranger - Big Band/Jazz - HF
William Edgar	Thornton	Aviation	USA	Astronaut
William Edward	Parry	Exploration	England	Explorer - Arctic
William Edward Burghardt du	Bois	Arts	USA	Historian/Educator
William Edward Hartpole	Lecky	Arts	England	Historian
William Ellery	Channing	Politics	USA	Social Critic
William Ernest	Henley	Creative Works	England	Poet/Editor/Critic
	Hewitt	Sports	USA	Football Player - HF
	Hocking	Arts	USA	Philosopher
William Ernest (Bill)	Walsh	Sports	USA	Football Coach - HF
William Ewart	Gladstone	Politics	England	Prime Minister
William Ewing (Slew)	Hester	Sports	USA	Tennis Player - HF
William F.	Buckley	Creative Works	USA	Journalist - Newspaper
	Sharpe	Arts	USA	Economics - Nobel Laureate
William F. (Bill)	Russell	Sports	USA	Basketball Player - HF
William Ferdie (Willie)	Brown	Sports	USA	Football Player - HF
William Francis	Giauque	Science	USA	Chemistry - Nobel Laureate
William Franklin (Bill)	Talbert	Sports	USA	Tennis Player - HF
William Frederick	Cody	Exploration	USA	Frontiersman - America
	Fisher	Aviation	USA	Astronaut
William George	Evans	Sports	USA	Baseball Umpire - HF
	Gregory	Aviation	USA	Astronaut
William George (Bill)	McGimsie	Sports	Canada	Hockey Player - HF
	Wyman (Perks)	Performing Arts	England	Rock & Roll - HF - Rolling Stones
William Graham	Sumner	Arts	USA	Economist/Sociologist

FIRST NAME	LAST NAME	CATEGORY	COUNTRY	FAME
William H.	Goetzmann	Creative Works	USA	Author - Pulitzer
	Macy	Performing Arts	USA	Actor - Acad Award Nom
	Stein	Science	USA	Chemistry - Nobel Laureate
William H. (Billy the Kid)	Bonney	Law & Order	USA	Outlaw
William Harold (Bill)	Terry	Sports	USA	Baseball Player - HF
William Hendrick (Bill)	Foster	Sports	USA	Baseball Player - HF
William Henry	Beveridge	Science	England	Economist
	Bragg	Science	England	Physics - Nobel Laureate
	Harrison	Politics	USA	President
	Hudson	Arts	England	Naturalist/Writer
	Pickering	Science	USA	Astronomer
	Seward	Politics	USA	Statesman/Secretary of State
William Henry (Chick)	Webb	Performing Arts	USA	Band Leader - Big Band/Jazz - HF
William Henry (Harry)	Wright	Sports	England	Baseball Executive -HF
William Henry (Willie)	Keeler	Sports	USA	Baseball Player - HF
William Henry (WillieThe Lion)	Smith	Performing Arts	USA	Jazz Pianist - Big Band/Jazz - HF
William Henry Getty (Bill)	France Sr.	Sports	USA	Race Car Promoter - HF
William Hickling	Prescott	Arts	USA	Historian
William Holman	Hunt	Works of Art	England	Painter
William Holmes	McGuffey	Arts	USA	Educator/Editor
William Hooker	Gillette	Performing Arts	USA	Actor
William Howard	Schuman	Creative Works	USA	Composer
	Taft	Politics	USA	President
William Hubbs	Rehnquist	Politics	USA	Chief Justice
William J. (Bill)	George	Sports	USA	Football Player - HF
William J. (Billy)	Cunningham	Sports	USA	Basketball Player - HF
William Jackson	Clothier	Sports	USA	Tennis Player - HF
William James	Mayo	Science	USA	Physician
William James (Willie)	Dixon	Performing Arts	USA	Singer - Rock & Roll - HF
William Jefferson	Clinton	Politics	USA	President
William Jennings	Bryan	Politics	USA	Politician/Orator
William Jennings Bryan (Billy)	Herman	Sports	USA	Baseball Player - HF
William John	Wills	Exploration	Australia	Explorer - Central Australia
William John (Bill)	Smith	Sports	Canada	Hockey Player - HF
William John Clifton (Bill)	Haley	Performing Arts	USA	Band Leader - Rock & Roll - HF
	Haley	Performing Arts	USA	Singer - Rock & Roll - HF
William Joseph	Brennan	Law & Order	USA	Justice/Supreme Court
William Jullius (Judy)	Johnson	Sports	USA	Baseball Player - HF
William K.	Clifford	Arts	England	Philosopher/Mathematician
William Karnet (Bill)	Willis	Sports	USA	Football Player - HF
William Lamb	Melbourne	Politics	England	Prime Minister
William Lawrence	Bragg	Science	England	Physics - Nobel Laureate
William le Baron	Jenney	Architecture	USA	Architect - Skyscraper
William Levise (Mitch)	Ryder	Performing Arts	USA	Singer
William Lewis (Bill)	Veeck Jr.	Sports	USA	Baseball Executive - HF
William Lewis (Billy)	Shaw	Sports	USA	Football Player - HF
William Lloyd	Garrison	Arts	USA	Editor/Lecturer/Abolitionist
William Lyon Mackenzie	King	Politics	Canada	Prime Minister
William M. (Little Bill)	Johnston	Sports	USA	Tennis Player - HF
William Mailes (Bill)	Cowley	Sports	Canada	Hockey Player - HF
William Makepeace	Thackeray	Creative Works	England	Novelist
William Malcolm	Dickey	Sports	USA	Baseball Player - HF
William Marcy (Boss)	Tweed	Politics	USA	Politician
William Marinus Dudok	Hilversum	Architecture	Netherlands	Architect - AIA Gold Medal
William Martin (Billy)	Joel	Performing Arts	USA	Singer - Rock & Roll - HF
William Matthew Flinders	Petrie	Arts	England	Archaeologist/Egyptologist
William Maxwell	Aitken	Business	England	Publishing
William Maxwell Aitkin	Beaverbrook	Creative Works	England	Publisher
William McChesney	Martin	Sports	USA	Tennis Promoter - HF
William McGarvey	Dudley	Sports	USA	Football Player - HF
William McMichael	Shepherd	Aviation	USA	Astronaut
William Milton (Riley)	Hern	Sports	Canada	Hockey Player - HF
William N.	Lipscomb	Science	USA	Chemistry - Nobel Laureate

SOLVER SERIES: NAME FINDER

FIRST NAME	LAST NAME	CATEGORY	COUNTRY	FAME
William Olaf	Stapledon	Creative Works	England	Author - SciFi
William Orville	Douglas	Law & Order	USA	Justice - Supreme Court
William Orville (Lefty)	Frizzell	Performing Arts	USA	Singer - Country Music - HF
William Owen	Bradley	Performing Arts	USA	Singer - Country Music - HF
William Parry	Murphy	Science	USA	Medicine - Nobel Laureate
William Payne	Alston	Arts	USA	Philosopher
William Philip (Phil)	Gramm	Politics	USA	Senator - Texas
William R.	King	Politics	USA	Vice-President
William Ralph	Blass	Business	USA	Fashion Designer
	Inge	Arts	England	Theologian
William Randal	Cremer	War & Peace	England	Peace - Nobel Laureate
William Randolph	Hearst	Business	USA	Newspaper Publisher
William Reid	Pogue	Aviation	USA	Astronaut
William Richard (Bud)	Ulrich	Sports	Canada	Golfer/Carpenter
William Robert (Billy)	Hamilton	Sports	USA	Baseball Player - HF
William Ronald (Bill)	Durnan	Sports	Canada	Hockey Player - HF
William Rose	Benét	Creative Works	USA	Poet - Pulitzer
William Roy (Link)	Lyman	Sports	USA	Football Player - HF
William S.	Cohen	Politics	USA	Secretary of Defense
	Hart	Performing Arts	USA	Actor
	Knowles	Science	USA	Chemistry - Nobel Laureate
	McFeely	Creative Works	USA	Author - Pulitzer
	White	Creative Works	USA	Author - Pulitzer
William Samuel	Paley	Business	USA	Media Magnate
William Schwenck	Gilbert	Creative Works	England	Poet/Librettist
William Shamus	O'Brien	Sports	Scotland	Soccer Player - HF
William Smith (Bill)	Monroe	Performing Arts	USA	Country Music - HF - Blue Grass Boys
William Somerset	Maugham	Creative Works	England	Novelist/Playwright
William Sowden	Sims	Creative Works	Canada	Author - Pulitzer
William Stanley	Merwin	Creative Works	USA	Poet - Pulitzer
William Stanley (Bill)	Mazeroski	Sports	USA	Baseball Player - HF
William Starke	Rosecrans	War & Peace	USA	General - Civil War
William T. (Bill)	Walton	Sports	USA	Basketball Player - HF
William Taten (Big Bill)	Tilden	Sports	USA	Tennis Player - HF
William Tecumseh	Sherman	War & Peace	USA	Union General - Civil War
William Thomas (Bill)	Medley	Performing Arts	USA	Rock & Roll - HF - Righteous Brothers
William Thomas Green	Morton	Science	USA	Dentist
William Toliver (Bill)	Carlisle	Performing Arts	USA	Singer - Country Music - HF
William Turner	Walton	Creative Works	England	Composer
William Tyrone	Guthrie	Movie Production	England	Director
William Vacanarat Shadrach	Tubman	Politics	Liberia	President
William Vaughn	Moody	Creative Works	USA	Poet/Playwright
William Vernell (Willie)	Wood	Sports	USA	Football Player - HF
William W.	Warner	Creative Works	USA	Author - Pulitzer
William W. (Bill)	Bradley	Sports	USA	Basketball Player - HF
	Sharman	Sports	USA	Basketball Player - HF
William Warren (Bill)	Bradley	Politics	USA	Senator
William Wayne	Caudill	Architecture	USA	Architect - AIA Gold Medal
William Wilkie	Collins	Creative Works	England	Novelist
William Wilson	Wurster	Architecture	USA	Architect - AIA Gold Medal
William Zebulon	Foster	Politics	USA	Political Leader - Communist
Willie	Anderson	Sports	Scotland	Golfer - HF
	McGee	Sports	USA	Baseball Player
	Pastrano	Sports	USA	Boxer - HF
	Rogers	Performing Arts	USA	Rock & Roll - HF - The Soul Stirrers
Willie (Will O' the Wisp)	Pep	Sports	USA	Boxer - HF
Willie Edward	Lanier	Sports	USA	Football Player - HF
Willie Howard	Mays	Sports	USA	Baseball Player - HF
Willie Hugh	Nelson	Performing Arts	USA	Singer - Country Music - HF
Willie James	Wells	Sports	USA	Baseball Player - HF
Willie Lee	McCovey	Sports	USA	Baseball Player - HF
Willis	Reed Jr.	Sports	USA	Basketball Player - HF
Willis Eugene	Lamb	Science	USA	Physics - Nobel Laureate

FIRST NAME	LAST NAME	CATEGORY	COUNTRY	FAME
Willy	Brandt	War & Peace	Germany	Peace - Nobel Laureate
	Roy	Sports	Germany	Soccer Player - HF
	Schaller	Sports	Germany	Soccer Player - HF
Wilma Glodean	Rudolph	Sports	USA	Olympic Runner
Wilmer Lawson	Allison Jr.	Sports	USA	Tennis Player - HF
Wilson	Pickett	Performing Arts	USA	Singer - Rock & Roll - HF
Wilton M. (Wilt)	Chamberlain	Sports	USA	Basketball Player - HF
Wilver Dornel (Willie)	Stargell	Sports	USA	Baseball Player - HF
Wim	Wenders	Movie Production	Germany	Director
Winfield	Scott	War & Peace	USA	General
Winfield Scott	Hancock	War & Peace	USA	Union General
Winona	Ryder	Performing Arts	USA	Actress - Acad Award Nom
Winslow	Homer	Works of Art	USA	Painter
Winston	Churchill	Creative Works	USA	Novelist
Winston Elliot	Scott	Aviation	USA	Astronaut
Winston Leonard Spencer	Churchill	Creative Works	England	Literature - Nobel Laureate
	Churchill	Politics	England	Prime Minister
Wislawa	Szymborska	Creative Works	Poland	Literature - Nobel Laureate
Wladyslaw Stanislaw	Reymont	Creative Works	Poland	Literature - Nobel Laureate
Wlliam	Friedkin	Movie Production	USA	Director - Academy Award
Wole	Soyinka	Creative Works	Nigeria	Literature - Nobel Laureate
Wolf	Blitzer	Creative Works	USA	Journalist - Television
Wolfgang	Ketterie	Science	Germany	Physics - Nobel Laureate
	Köhler	Arts	Germany	Psychologist
	Paul	Science	Germany	Physics - Nobel Laureate
	Pauli	Science	Austria	Physics - Nobel Laureate
	Peterson	Movie Production	Germany	Director - Acad Award Nom
Wolfgang Amadeus	Mozart	Creative Works	Austria	Composer
Woodbridge Strong Van	Dyke	Movie Production	USA	Director - Acad Award Nom
Woodrow Charles (Woody)	Herman (Wilson)	Performing Arts	USA	Band Leader - Big Band/Jazz - HF
Woodrow Clarence (Woody)	Dumart	Sports	Canada	Hockey Player - HF
Woodrow Wilson (Woody)	Guthrie	Performing Arts	USA	Singer - Rock & Roll - HF
Woodward Morris (Tex)	Ritter	Performing Arts	USA	Singer - Country Music - HF
Woody	Allen	Movie Production	USA	Director - Academy Award
	Allen	Performing Arts	USA	Actor - Acad Award Nom
	Harrelson	Performing Arts	USA	Actor - Acad Award Nom
Wubbo Johannes	Ockels	Aviation	Netherlands	Astronaut
Wyatt	Earp	Law & Order	USA	Lawman
Wylie (Buddy)	Baker	Sports	USA	Race Car Driver - HF
Wynonna	Judd	Performing Arts	USA	Singer
Wynton	Marsalis	Performing Arts	USA	Jazz Trumpeter - Big Band/Jazz - HF
Wyomia	Tyus	Sports	USA	Olympic Runner
Wystan Hugh	Auden	Creative Works	England	Poet - Pulitzer
Xavier	Cugat	Performing Arts	Cuba	Band Leader
Yamila	Diaz	Performing Arts	Argentina	Super Model
Yannick	Noah	Sports	France	Tennis Player - HF
Yaphet	Kotto	Performing Arts	USA	Actor
Yasir	Arafat	Politics	Palestine	President
	Arafat	War & Peace	Palestine	Peace - Nobel Laureate
Yasmeen	Ghauri	Performing Arts	Canada	Super Model
Yasmin Le	Bon	Performing Arts	England	Super Model
Yasunari	Kawabata	Creative Works	Japan	Literature - Nobel Laureate
Yatsen	Sun	Politics	China	Political & Revoltionary Leader
Yehudl	Menuhin	Performing Arts	USA	Violinist
Yelberton Abraham (YA)	Tittle	Sports	USA	Football Player - Ht
Yeugeni Vassilyevich	Khrunov	Aviation	Russia	Astronaut
Yitzhak	Rabin	Politics	Israel	Prime Minister
	Rabin	War & Peace	Israel	Peace - Nobel Laureate
	Shamir	Politics	Israel	Prime Minister
Yma	Sumac	Performing Arts	Peru	Singer - Folk
Yoko	Ono	Performing Arts	Japan	Singer
	Ono	Works of Art	Japan	Painter
Yoshio	Taniguchi	Architecture	Japan	Architect

SOLVER SERIES: NAME FINDER

FIRST NAME	LAST NAME	CATEGORY	COUNTRY	FAME
Yuan T.	Lee	Science	USA	Chemistry - Nobel Laureate
Yukio	Mishima	Creative Works	Japan	Author
Yul	Brynner	Performing Arts	USA	Actor - Academy Award
Yuri Alekseyevich	Gagarin	Aviation	Russia	Cosmonaut
Yusef	Komunyakaa	Creative Works	USA	Poet - Pulitzer
Yvan Serge (Roadrunner)	Cournoyer	Sports	Canada	Hockey Player - HF
Yves	Chauvin	Science	France	Chemistry - Nobel Laureate
	Saint Laurent	Business	France	Fashion Designer
	Tanguy	Works of Art	France	Painter
Yvette	Mimieux	Performing Arts	USA	Actress
Yvonne	Elliman	Performing Arts	USA	Singer
Yvonne De	Carlo	Performing Arts	Canada	Actress
Zachary	Scott	Performing Arts	USA	Actor
	Taylor	Politics	USA	President
Zachary Davis (Zack)	Wheat	Sports	USA	Baseball Player - HF
Zaha	Hadid	Architecture	England	Architect - Pritzker Laureate
Zal	Yanovsky	Performing Arts	Canada	Singer/Guitarist - Canadian Music - HF
Zane	Grey	Creative Works	USA	Novelist
Zasu	Pitts	Performing Arts	USA	Actress
Zebulon Montgomery	Pike	Exploration	USA	Explorer - Mississippi River
Zero	Mostel	Performing Arts	USA	Actor
Zhang	Quian	Exploration	China	Explorer - Central Asia
Zhores I.	Alferov	Science	Russia	Physics - Nobel Laureate
Zhou	En-Lai	Politics	China	Premier
Zinédine	Zindane	Sports	France	Soccer Player
Zoe	Akins	Creative Works	USA	Dramatist - Pulitzer
	Caldwell	Performing Arts	Australia	Actress
Zola	Budd	Sports	South Africa	Olympic Runner
	Taylor	Performing Arts	USA	Rock & Roll - HF - The Platters
Zoltan	Kodály	Creative Works	Hungary	Composer
Zona	Gale	Creative Works	USA	Dramatist - Pulitzer
Zsa Zsa	Gabor	Performing Arts	Hungary	Actress
Zubin	Mehta	Performing Arts	India	Conductor

FAME	LAST NAME	FIRST NAME	COUNTRY
ARCHITECTURE:			
Architect	Abramovitz	Max	USA
	Ain	Gregory	USA
	Ambasz	Emilio	USA
	Antonelli	Alessandro	Italy
	Artigas	João Batista Villanova	Brazil
	Asnago	Mario	Italy
	Asplund	Erik Gunnar	Sweden
	Aulenti	Gae	Italy
	Aymonino	Carlo	Italy
	Baldessari	Luciano	Italy
	Baldeweg	Juan Navarro	Spain
	Basile	Ernesto	Italy
	Behrens	Peter	Germany
	Berlage	Hendrick Petrus	Netherlands
	Bernini	Gian Lorenzo	Italy
	Bernoulli	Hans	Switzerland
	Birkerts	Gunnar	USA
	Bofill	Riccardo	Spain
	Bonatz	Paul Michael Nikolaus	Germany
	Borromini	Francesco	Italy
	Botta	Mario	Switzerland
	Bottoni	Archivio Piero	Italy
	Boulée	Etienne Louis	France
	Brasini	Armando	Italy
	Brown	Denise Scott	USA
	Bruder	William	USA
	Brunelleschi	Fillipo	Italy
	Burelli	Augusto Romano	Italy
	Burnham	Daniel Hudson	USA
	Calatrava	Santiago	Spain
	Candela	Felix	Spain
	Canella	Guido	Italy
	Cantoni	Simone	Switzerland

SOLVER SERIES: NAME FINDER

FAME	LAST NAME	FIRST NAME	COUNTRY
Architect	Carlo	Giancarlo de	Italy
	Cellini	Francesco	Italy
	Cesariano	Cesare di Lorenzo	Italy
	Cortona	Domenico da	Italy
	Cortona	Pietro da	Italy
	Croci	Antonio	Switzerland
	Delamair	Pierre Antoine	France
	Diener	Marcus	Switzerland
	Diener	Roger	Switzerland
	Dieste	Eladio	Uruguay
	Dinkeloo	John Gerard	USA
	Doesburg	Theo van	Netherlands
	Dominick	Peter	USA
	Doxiadis	Constantinos Apostolou	Greece
	Durand	Jean Nicolas Louis	France
	Eyck	Aldo van	Netherlands
	Fathy	Hassan	Egypt
	Fischer von Erlach	Johan Bernhard	Austria
	Floris de Vriend	Cornelis	Belgium
	Fuksas	Massimiliano	Italy
	Gaboury	Étienne	Canada
	Galfetti	Aurelio	Switzerland
	Gardella	Ignazio	Italy
	Garnier	Charles	France
	Garnier	Tony	France
	Gaudi	Antoni	Spain
	Gerkan	Meinhard von	Germany
	Ghiberti	Lorenzo	Italy
	Gibbs	James	England
	Gilbert	Cass	USA
	Gilly	David Friedrich	Germany
	Ginzburg	Moisej	Russia
	Goff	Bruce	USA
	Grassi	Giorgio	Italy
	Gregotti	Vittorio	Italy
	Guarini	Guarino	Italy
	Guimard	Hector	France
	Gwathmey	Charles	USA
	Hankar	Paul	Belgium
	Häring	Hugo	Germany
	Haussmann	George Eugène	France
	Hejduk	John	USA
	Hiberseimer	Ludwig	Germany
	Hoban	James	USA
	Hoffman	Joseph	Austria
	Holl	Elias	Germany
	Holl	Steven	USA
	Hopkins	Michael	England
	Horta	Victor	Belgium
	Hundertwasser	Friedensreich	Austria
	Hunt	Richard Morris	USA
	Isozaki	Arata	Japan
	Israel	Frank	USA
	Ito	Toyo	Japan
	Jacobsen	Arne	Denmark
	Jahn	Helmut	Germany
	Juvarra	Fillippo	Italy
	Kahn	Albert	USA

FAME	LAST NAME	FIRST NAME	COUNTRY
Architect	Klein	Alexander	USA
	Klerk	Michel de	Netherlands
	Kollhoff	Hans	Germany
	Kramer	Pieter Lodewijk	Netherlands
	Kurokawa	Kisho	Japan
	Laan	Hans Dom van der	Netherlands
	Labrouste	Henri	France
	Langhans	Carl Gotthard	Germany
	Latrobe	Benjamin Henry	USA
	Laugier	Marc Antoine	France
	Ledoux	Claude Nicholas	France
	Leonidov	Ivan	Russia
	Lequeu	Jean Jacques	France
	Lescot	Pierre	France
	Libera	Adalberto	Italy
	Libeskind	Daniel	Poland
	Lin	Maya	Thailand
	Link	Theodore	USA
	Lobkowitz	Juan Caramuel de	Italy
	Longhena	Baldassarre	Italy
	Loos	Adolf	Austria
	Mackintosh	Charles Rennie	England
	Maderno	Carlo	Italy
	Magistretti	Vico	Italy
	Maillart	Robert	Switzerland
	Makovecz	Imre	Hungary
	Mansart	Jules Hardouin	France
	Martini	Francesco di Giorgio	Italy
	May	Ernst	Germany
	Mayne	Thom	USA
	Melnikov	Konstantin	Austria
	Mendelsohn	Erich	USA
	Mendini	Alessandro	Italy
	Menn	Christian	Switzerland
	Meyer	Adolf	Germany
	Meyer	Hannes	Switzerland
	Michelozzi	Michelozzo di Bartolomeo	Italy
	Mileto	Isidoro di	Italy
	Minardi	Bruno	Italy
	Mizner	Addison	USA
	Mollino	Carlo	Italy
	Montreuil	Pierre de	France
	Moraglia	Giacomo	Italy
	Moretti	Luigi	Italy
	Morgan	Julia	USA
	Morris	William	England
	Moser	Karl	Switzerland
	Moss	Eric Owen	USA
	Moura	Eduardo Souto de	Portugal
	Muggenast	Josef	Austria
	Muratori	Saverio	Italy
	Nash	John	England
	Neumann	Balthasar Johann	Germany
	Nouvel	Jean	France
	Olbrick	Joseph Maria	Germany
	Oud	Jacobus Johannes Pieter	Netherlands
	Owen	Robert	England
	Pagano	Giuseppe	Austria

SOLVER SERIES: NAME FINDER

FAME	LAST NAME	FIRST NAME	COUNTRY
Architect	Pagliara	Nicola	Italy
	Palladio	Andrea	Italy
	Paxton	Joseph	England
	Persico	Edoardo	Italy
	Peruzzi	Baldassarre	Italy
	Piacentini	Marcello	Italy
	Pietilä	Reima	Finland
	Pikionis	Dimitris	Greece
	Piranesi	Giovanni Battista	Italy
	Plecnik	Joze	Slovenia
	Podrecca	Boris	Yugoslavia
	Poelzig	Hans	Germany
	Ponti	Franco	Switzerland
	Ponti	Gio	Italy
	Porphyrios	Demetri	Greece
	Porro	Ricardo	Cuba
	Portaluppi	Piero	Italy
	Portoghesi	Paolo	Italy
	Pouillon	Fernand	France
	Prandtauer	Jakob	Austria
	Predock	Antoine	USA
	Purini	Franco	Italy
	Quadrio	Giovanni Battista	Italy
	Quaroni	Ludovico	Italy
	Quincy	Antoine Quatremère de	France
	Raffaello	Sanzio	Italy
	Rasser	Max	Germany
	Reich	Lilly	Germany
	Reichlin	Bruno	Switzerland
	Reinhart	Fabio	Switzerland
	Richardson	Henry Hobson	USA
	Ridolfi	Mario	Italy
	Rietveld	Gerrit	Netherlands
	Rogers	Nathan Ernesto	Italy
	Romano	Giulio	Italy
	Rudolph	Paul	USA
	Safdie	Moshe	Israel
	Samonà	Giuseppe	Italy
	Sangallo	Antonio da il Giovane	Italy
	Sangallo	Antonio da il Vecchio	Italy
	Sangallo	Giuliano da	Italy
	Sansovino	Jacopo Tatti	Italy
	Sant'Elia	Antonio	Italy
	Sartoris	Alberto	Italy
	Sauvage	Henri	France
	Scarpa	Afra e Tobia	Italy
	Scarpa	Carlo	Italy
	Scharoun	Hans	Germany
	Schindler	Rudolph Michael	USA
	Schinkel	Karl Friedrich	Germany
	Schmidt	Hans	Switzerland
	Schwarz	Rudolph	Germany
	Scott	George Gilbert	England
	Semper	Gottfried	Germany
	Serlio	Sebastiano	Italy
	Siegel	Robert	USA
	Sinan	Mimar (the Great)	Turkey
	Smirke	Robert	England

FAME	LAST NAME	FIRST NAME	COUNTRY
Architect	Snozzi	Luigi	Switzerland
	Soane	John	England
	Sola-Morales	Manuel de	Spain
	Soleri	Paolo	Italy
	Sottsass	Ettore	Austria
	Soufflot	Jaques Germain	France
	Speer	Albert	Germany
	Stella	Ettore	Italy
	Stern	Robert Arthur Morton	USA
	Stone	Edward Durell	USA
	Tami	Rino	Switzerland
	Taniguchi	Yoshio	Japan
	Taut	Bruno	Turkey
	Tedesko	Anton	USA
	Terragni	Giuseppe	Italy
	Tessenow	Heinrich	Germany
	Testa	Clorindo	Italy
	Thermes	Laura	Italy
	Thomson	Alexander	Scotland
	Toledo	Juan Bautista	Spain
	Torre	Susana	USA
	Tralle	Antemio di	Italy
	Trezzini	Domenico	Russia
	Tschumi	Bernard	Switzerland
	Ungers	Oswald Mathias	Germany
	Vacchini	Livio	Switzerland
	Vadi	Tibère	Switzerland
	Valle	Gino	Italy
	Vasari	Giogio	Italy
	Vau	Louis le	France
	Velde	Henry van de	Belgium
	Vender	Claudio	Italy
	Viganò	Vittoriano	Italy
	Vignola	Giacomo Barozzi da	Italy
	Villanueva	Carlos Raúl	Venezuela
	Viollet le Duc	Eugène Emmanuel	France
	Vitruvius	Marco Pollione	Italy
	Wagner	Otto	Austria
	Weidemeyer	Carl	Switzerland
	White	Stanford	USA
	Williams	Paul	USA
	Williams-Ellis	Clough	England
	Wood	John	England
	Wren	Christopher	England
	Zanuso	Marco	Italy
	Zermani	Paolo	Italy
	Zimmerman	Dominikus	Germany
	Zumthor	Peter	Switzerland
Architect - AIA Gold Medal	Abercrombie	Patrick	England
	Bacon	Henry	USA
	Belluschi	Pietro	Italy
	Caudill	William Wayne	USA
	Corbusier	Charles Edouard le	Switzerland
	Cret	Paul Phillippe	USA
	Delano	William Adams	USA
	Erickson	Arthur Charles	Canada
	Esherick	Joseph	USA
	Fuller	Richard Buckminster	USA

SOLVER SERIES: NAME FINDER

FAME	LAST NAME	FIRST NAME	COUNTRY
Architect - AIA Gold Medal	Goodhue	Bertram	USA
	Graves	Michael	USA
	Gropius	Walter	Germany
	Harrison	Wallace Kirkman	USA
	Hilversum	William Marinus Dudok	Netherlands
	Jefferson	Thomas	USA
	Jones	Euine Fay	USA
	Kahn	Louis Isadore	USA
	Laloux	Victor	France
	Legorreta	Ricardo	Mexico
	Lutyens	Edwin Landseer	England
	Maginnis	Charles Donagh	USA
	Maybeck	Bernard Ralph	USA
	McKim	Charles Follen	USA
	Medary	Milton Bennett	USA
	Mockbee	Samuel (Sambo)	USA
	Moore	Charles Willard	USA
	Nervi	Pier Luigi	Italy
	Neutra	Richard Joseph	Austria
	Ostberg	Ragnar	Sweden
	Owings	Nathaniel Alexander	USA
	Pascal	Jean Louis	France
	Pelli	César	Argentina
	Perret	Auguste	France
	Post	George Brown	USA
	Root	John Wellborn	USA
	Saarinen	Eero	USA
	Saarinen	Gottlieb Eliel	Finland
	Shaw	Howard Van Doren	USA
	Skidmore	Louis	USA
	Stein	Clarence S.	USA
	Sullivan	Louis Henry	USA
	Thompson	Benjamin	USA
	Walker	Ralph	USA
	Webb	Aston	England
	Wright	Frank Lloyd	USA
	Wurster	William Wilson	USA
Architect - AIA/Jefferson Gold Medal	Aalto	Alvar	Finland
	Breuer	Marcel	USA
	Giurgola	Romaldo	USA
	Rohe	Ludwig Miës van der Rohe	USA
	Sert	Jose Luis	USA
Architect - Churches	Boeyinga	Berend Tobia	Netherlands
Architect - Government Buildings	Bulfinch	Charles	USA
Architect - High Rise	Graham	Bruce	USA
Architect - Jefferson Medal	Ban	Shigeru	Japan
	Barnes	Edward Larrabee	USA
	Burchard	John Ely	USA
	Duany	Andres	USA
	Halprin	Lawrence	USA
	Huxtable	Ada Louise	USA
	Jacobs	Jane	Canada
	Khan	Aga	France
	Kiley	Dan	USA
	Krier	Leon	England
	Labatut	Jean	USA
	Lerner	Jaime	Brazil
	Lindsay	John V.	USA

FAME	LAST NAME	FIRST NAME	COUNTRY
Architect - Jefferson Medal	McHarg	Ian	USA
	Mellon	Paul	USA
	Moynihan	Daniel Patrick	USA
	Mumford	Lewis	USA
	Otto	Frei	Germany
	Pevsner	Nikolaus	England
	Plater-Zyberk	Elizabeth	USA
	Robertson	Jaquelin T.	USA
	Rogers	Richard	England
	Scully	Vincent J.	USA
	Stubbins	Hugh A.	USA
	Tsien	Billie	USA
	Turrell	James	USA
	Walker	Peter	USA
Architect - Jefferson Medal	Williams	Tod	USA
Architect - Landscape Design	Lenné	Peter Josef	Germany
	Nôtre	André le	France
	Olmsted	Frederick Law	USA
Architect - Pritzker Laureate	Barragan	Luis	Mexico
	Boehm	Gottfried	Germany
	Bunshaft	Gordon	USA
	Fehn	Sverre	Norway
	Hadid	Zaha	England
	Herzog	Jacques	Switzerland
	Hollein	Hans	Austria
	Koolhaas	Rem	Netherlands
	Meuron	Pierre de	Switzerland
	Moneo	Rafael	Spain
	Niemeyer	Oscar	Brazil
	Piano	Renzo	Italy
	Portzamparc	Christian de	France
	Siza	Alvaro Vieira	Portugal
	Utzon	Jørn	Denmark
Architect - Pritzker/ AIA Gold	Ando	Tadao	Japan
	Foster	Norman	England
	Gehry	Frank O.	USA
	Johnson	Philip Cortelyou	USA
	Meier	Richard	USA
	Pei	Ieoh Ming	USA
	Roche	Kevin	USA
	Tange	Kenzo	Japan
Architect - Pritzker/Jefferson Medal	Maki	Fumihiko	Japan
	Murcutt	Glenn	Australia
	Rossi	Aldo	Italy
	Stirling	James	England
	Venturi	Robert	USA
Architect - Renaissance	Delorme	Philibert	France
	Cass	Gilbert	USA
	Holabird	William	USA
	Jenney	William le Baron	USA
Architect/Designer	Barry	Charles	England
	Webb	Phillip	England
Architect/Developer	Eichler	Joseph	USA
Architect/Engineer	L'Enfant	Pierre Charles	France
Architect/Furniture Designer	Albini	Franco	Italy
Architect/Furniture Designer	Bo Bardi	Lina	Brazil
Architect/Painter	Bramante	Donato d'Agnolo	Italy
	Chiattone	Mario	Switzerland

FAME	LAST NAME	FIRST NAME	COUNTRY
Architect/Painter/Author	Bragdon	Claude Fayette	USA
Architect/Painter/Sculptor	Alberti	Leon Battista	Italy
	Tatlin	Vladimir	Russia
Architect/Painter/Writer	Klenze	Leo von	Germany
Architect/Planner/Author	Costa	Lucio	Brazil
Architect/Sculptor	Cambio	Arnolfo di	Italy
	Schlüter	Andreas	Germany
Architect/Sculptor/Painter/Author	Michelangelo	Buonarroti	Italy
Architect/Stage Designer	Jones	Inigo	England
Architect/Writer	Cram	Ralph Adams	USA
Architect/Writer/Poet/Artist	Ruskin	John	England
Architect/Writer/Teacher	Alexander	Christopher	Austria
Bridge Designer/Civil Engineer	Roebling	John Augustus	USA

ARTS:

FAME	LAST NAME	FIRST NAME	COUNTRY
Adventurer	Casanova	Giovanni Jacopo	Italy
Anthropologist	Attenborough	David Frederick	England
	Benedict	Ruth Fulton	USA
	Boas	Franz	USA
	Evans-Pritchard	Edward Evan	England
	Kroeber	Alfred Louis	USA
	Leakey	Louis Seymour Bazett	England
	Levi-Strauss	Claude	France
	Malinowski	Bronislaw Kaspar	Poland
	Morgan	Lewis Henry	USA
	Tylor	Edward Burnett	England
	Westermarck	Edward Alexander	Finland
Anthropologist/Writer	Mead	Margaret	USA
	Frazer	James George	Scotland
	Keith	Arthur	England
Archaeologist	Evans	Arthur John	England
	Schliemann	Heinrich	Germany
Archaeologist/Art Historian	Winckelmann	Johann Joachim	Germany
Archaeologist/Egyptologist	Petrie	William Matthew Flinders	England
Archbishop	Cranmer	Thomas	England
Archbishop of Canterbury	Pole	Reginald	England
Archbishop/Theologian	Ussher	James	Ireland
Biographer	Bradford	Gamaliel	USA
	Maurois	André	France
	Strachey	Giles Lytton	England
Biographer/Critic	Dowden	Edward	Ireland
Bishop	Asbury	Francis	USA
Bishop/Orator	Bossuet	Jacques Bénigne	France
Bishop/Protestant Reformer	Ridley	Nicholas	England
Bishop/Theologian	Taylor	Jeremy	England
Cabinetmaker	Hepplewhite	George	England
Chronicler	Holinshed	Raphael	England
	Joinville	Jean de	France
Classical Scholar	Jowett	Benjamin	England
Clergyman	Beecher	Henry Ward	USA
	Campbell	Alexander	USA
	Eliot	John	USA
	Harvard	John	England
	Hooker	Thomas	England
Clergyman/Puritan	Cotton	John	USA
Clergyman/Translator	Coverdale	Miles	England
Clergyman/Colonist	Williams	Roger	England

FAME	LAST NAME	FIRST NAME	COUNTRY
Clergyman/Educator	Witherspoon	John	USA
Clergyman/Evangelist	Wesley	John	England
Clergyman/Reformer	Holmes	John Haynes	USA
Clergyman/Religious Reformer	Knox	John	Scotland
	Fénelon	François de Salignac	France
	Hale	Edward Everett	USA
	Hooker	Richard	England
Clergyman/Writer - Hymns	Watts	Isaac	England
	Wesley	Charles	England
Collector - American Folk Songs	Lomax	Alan	USA
Collector - Ballads	Percy	Thomas	England
Courtier	Leicester	Robert Dudley	England
Critic - Literary	Richards	Ivor Armstrong	England
	Saintsbury	George Edward Bateman	England
"Designer - Theatrical, Industrial"	Geddes	Norman Bel	USA
Dominican Monk	Torquemada	Tomás de	Spain
Economics - Nobel Laureate	Akerlof	George A.	USA
	Allais	Maurice	France
	Arrow	Kenneth J.	USA
	Aumann	Robert J.	Germany
	Becker	Gary S.	USA
	Buchanan Jr.	James M.	USA
	Coase	Ronald H.	England
	Debreu	Gerard	USA
	Engle III	Robert F.	USA
	Fogel	Robert W.	USA
	Friedman	Milton	USA
	Frisch	Ragnar	Norway
	Granger	Clive W.J.	England
	Haavelmo	Trygve	Norway
	Harsanyi	John C.	USA
	Hayek	Friedrich August von	Austria
	Heckman	James J.	USA
	Hicks	John R.	England
	Kahneman	Daniel	USA
	Kantorovich	Leonid Vitaliyevich	Russia
	Klein	Lawrence R.	USA
	Koopmans	Tjalling C.	USA
	Kuznets	Simon	USA
	Kydland	Finn E.	Norway
	Leontief	Wassily	USA
	Lewis	Arthur	England
	Lucas Jr.	Robert E.	USA
	Markowitz	Harry M.	USA
	McFadden	Daniel L.	USA
	Meade	James E.	England
	Merton	Robert C.	USA
	Miller	Merton H.	USA
	Mirrlees	James A.	England
	Modigliani	Franco	USA
	Mundell	Robert A.	Canada
	Myrdal	Karl Gunnar	Sweden
	Nash	John F.	USA
	North	Douglass C.	USA
	Ohlin	Bertil	Sweden
	Prescott	Edward C.	USA
	Samuelson	Paul A.	USA
	Schelling	Thomas C.	USA

SOLVER SERIES: NAME FINDER

FAME	LAST NAME	FIRST NAME	COUNTRY
Economics - Nobel Laureate	Scholes	Myron S.	USA
	Schultz	Theodore W.	USA
	Selten	Reinhard	Germany
	Sen	Amartya	India
	Sharpe	William F.	USA
	Simon	Herbert A.	USA
	Smith	Vernon L.	USA
	Solow	Robert M.	USA
	Spence	Michael	USA
	Stigler	George J.	USA
	Stiglitz	Joseph E.	USA
	Stone	Richard	England
	Tinbergen	Jan	Netherlands
	Tobin	James	USA
	Vickery	William	USA
Economist	Keynes	John Maynard	England
	Passy	Frédéric	France
	Ricardo	David	England
Economist/Historian	Tawney	Richard Henry	England
Economist/Political	Veblen	Thorstein Bunde	USA
Economist/Journalist	Bagehot	Walter	England
Economist/Social Reformer	Webb	Beatrice Potter	England
	Webb	Sidney James	England
Economist/Sociologist	Pareto	Vilfredo	Switzerland
	Sumner	William Graham	USA
Editor/Lecturer/Abolitionist	Garrison	William Lloyd	USA
Educational Reformer	Pestalozzi	Johann Heinrich	Switzerland
Educator	Arnold	Thomas	England
	Eliot	Charles William	USA
	Flexner	Abraham	USA
	Froebel	Friedrich Wilhelm August	Germany
	Hopkins	Mark	USA
	Hutchins	Robert Maynard	USA
	Lowell	Abbott Lawrence	USA
	Lyon	Mary	USA
	Mann	Horace	USA
	Montessori	Maria	Italy
Educator/Critic	Babbitt	Irving	USA
	Bradley	Andrew Cecil	England
	Jones	Howard Mumford	USA
Educator/Editor	McGuffey	William Holmes	USA
Educator/Editor	Neilson	William Allan	USA
Educator/Legal Scholar	Pound	Roscoe	USA
Educator/Librarian	Dewey	Melville	USA
Educator/Linguist	Ogden	Charles Kay	England
Educator/Scholar/Critic	Lowes	John Livingston	USA
Egyptologist	Champollion	Jean François	France
Evangelist	Moody	Dwight Lyman	USA
Evangilist - Methodist	Whitefield	George	England
Evangilist - WW I	Sunday	Billy	USA
First American Child	Dare	Virginia	USA
Flag Maker	Ross	Betsy	USA
Food Expert	Brillat-Savarin	Anthelme	France
Founder - Christian Science	Eddy	Mary Baker	USA
Founder - Girl Scouts	Low	Juliette	USA
Founder - Mormon Church	Smith	Joseph	USA
Founder of Rhode Island	Hutchinson	Anne	USA
Furniture Designer	Chippendale	Thomas	England

FAME	LAST NAME	FIRST NAME	COUNTRY
Geographer/Cartographer	Mercator	Gerhardus	Italy
Geographer/Chronicler	Hakluyt	Richard	England
Geologist/Naturalist	Dawson	John William	Canada
Grammarian	Murray	Lindley	England
Historian	Buckle	Henry Thomas	England
	Froude	James Anthony	England
	Gardiner	Samuel Rawson	England
	Gibbon	Edward	England
	Green	John Richard	England
	Grote	George	England
	Hallam	Henry	England
	Hayes	Carlton Joseph Huntley	USA
	Lecky	William Edward Hartpole	England
	Michelet	Jules	France
	Namier	Lewis Bernstein	England
	Pares	Bernard	England
	Parkman	Francis	USA
	Prescott	William Hickling	USA
	Ranke	Leopold von	Germany
	Robinson	James Harvey	USA
	Rostovtzeff	Michael Ivanovich	USA
	Schlesinger	Arthur Meier	USA
	Schlesinger	Arthur Meier Jr.	USA
	Treitschke	Heinrich von	Germany
	Trevelyan	George Macaulay	England
Historian/Critic	Burckhardt	Jacob	Switzerland
Historian/Diplomat	Comines	Phillipe de	France
Historian/Economist	Sismondi	Jean Charles Léonard	Switzerland
Historian/Educator	Bois	William Edward Burghardt du	USA
Historian/Essayist	Renan	Joseph Ernest	France
Historian/Missionary	Las Casas	Bartolomé	Spain
Historian/Orientalist	Rawlinson	George	England
Historian/Politician	Trevelyan	George Otto	England
Historian/Sociologist	Barnes	Henry Elmer	USA
Humanist/Theologian	Erasmus	Desiderius	Netherlands
Humanitarian/Diplomat	Wallenberg	Raoul	Sweden
Humorist/Political Economist	Leacock	Stephen Butler	Canada
Journalist	Lippmann	Walter	USA
Legal Philosopher	Austin	John	England
Lexicographer	Bradley	Henry	England
	Craigie	William Alexander	England
	Murray	James Augustus Henry	England
	Ogilvie	John	Scotland
	Onions	Charles Talbut	England
	Webster	Noah	USA
	Worcester	Joseph Emerson	USA
Lexicographer/Arbiter	Fowler	Henry Watson	England
Lexicographer/Educator	Mathews	Mitford McLeod	USA
Lexicographer/Etymologist	Weekley	Ernest	England
Lexicographer/Grammarian	Rochelle	Pierre Athanase La	France
Lexicographer/Linguist	Wright	Joseph	England
	Wyld	Henry Cecil Kennedy	England
Lexicographer/Philologist	Skeat	Walter William	England
Lexicographer/Writer	Partridge	Eric Honeywood	England
Linguist	Bloomfield	Leonard	USA
	Chomsky	Avram Noam	USA
	Jesperson	Jens Otto Harry	Denmark
	Saussure	Ferdinand de	Switzerland

SOLVER SERIES: NAME FINDER

FAME	LAST NAME	FIRST NAME	COUNTRY
Linguist	Sweet	Henry	England
Linguist/Anthropologist	Sapir	Edward	USA
Linguist/Folklorist	Pound	Louise	USA
Literary Critic	Brandes	Georg Morris	Denmark
Literary Critic/Editor	Malone	Edmund	Ireland
Literary Critic/Historian	Taine	Hippolyte Adolphe	France
Minister/Covenanter	Cameron	Richard	Scotland
Moralist/Writer	Rochefoucauld	François de La	France
Mormon Leader	Young	Brigham	USA
Musical Theorist	d'Arezzo	Guido	Italy
Mystic - Shakers Founder	Lee	Ann	England
Naturalist	Buffon	Georges Louis Leclerc	France
	Cuvier	Georges Léopold	France
	Leeuwenhoek	Anton van	Netherlands
	Wallace	Alfred Russel	England
	White	Gilbert	England
Naturalist/Writer	Hudson	William Henry	England
Naturalist/Zoo Curator	Ditmars	Raymond Lee	USA
Negro Slave	Scott	Dred	USA
Newspaper Editor	Dana	Charles Anderson	USA
Newspaper Publisher	Harmsworth	Alfred Charles William	England
Newspaper Publisher/Editor	Howard	Roy Wilson	USA
Nun	Cabrini	Frances Xavier	USA
Orientalist/Statesman	Rawlinson	Henry Creswicke	England
Ornithologist	Wilson	Alexander	USA
Paleontologist/Geologist	Teilhard de Chardin	Pierre	France
Philologist	Bopp	Franz	Germany
	Rasht	Rasmus Christian	Denmark
	Verner	Karl	Denmark
Philologist/Editor	Furnivall	Frederick James	England
Philologist/Mythologist	Müller	Friedrich Max	England
Philosoper/Historian	Mill	James	Scotland
Philosopher	Abd al-Raziq	Ali	Egypt
	Abduh	Muhammad	Egypt
	Adams	George Plimpton	USA
	Adler	Mortimer Jerome	USA
	Albertus	Magnus	Germany
	Alcott	Amos Bronson	USA
	Alston	William Payne	USA
	Althusser	Louis	Algeria
	Anderson	John	Scotland
	Aquinas	Thomas	Italy
	Aurobindo	Sri	India
	Averroes	Ibn-Rusjd	Spain
	Ayer	Alfred Jules	England
	Bachelard	Gaston	France
	Bacon	Roger	England
	Bain	Alexander	Scotland
	Berdyaev	Nikolai Alexsandrovich	Russia
	Berkely	George	Ireland
	Berlin	Isaiah	England
	Bloch	Ernst	Germany
	Bok	Sissela	Sweden
	Bruno	Giordano	Italy
	Carnap	Rudolf	Germany
	Cassirer	Ernst	Germany
	Cioran	Émile Michel	France

FAME	LAST NAME	FIRST NAME	COUNTRY
Philosopher	Cohen	Andrew	USA
	Cohen	Morris Raphael	USA
	Comte	Auguste	France
	Condillac	Étienne Bonnot de	France
	Cousin	Victor	France
	Edman	Irwin	USA
	Fichte	Immanuel Hermass von	Germany
	Fichte	Johann Gottlieb	Germany
	Foucault	Michel	France
	Gaines	Andrew	USA
	Hall	Manly Palmer	Canada
	Hare	Richard Mervyn	England
	Hegel	Georg Wilhelm Frederich	Germany
	Helvétius	Claude Adrien	France
	Hocking	William Ernest	USA
	Hoffer	Eric	USA
	Hook	Sidney	USA
	Horkheimer	Max	Germany
	Husserl	Edmund Gustav Albrecht	Germany
	Hutcheson	Francis	Ireland
	Jaspers	Karl	Germany
	Judaeus	Philo	Greece
	Kant	Immanuel	Germany
	Langer	Susan Katherina	USA
	Lieber	Francis	USA
	Locke	John	England
	Lucretius	Titus Lucretius Carus	Italy
	Malebranche	Nicolas	France
	Marcel	Gabriel	France
	Marcuse	Herbert	Germany
	Maritain	Jacques	France
	Maslow	Abraham Harold	USA
	Meiklejohn	Alexander	USA
	Milgram	Stanley	USA
	Montesquieu	Charles de	France
	Moore	George Edward	England
	Nagel	Ernest	USA
	Nicolosi	Dick	USA
	Nietzsche	Friedrich Wilhelm	Germany
	Nozick	Robert	USA
	Ockham	William	England
	Pierce	Charles Sanders	USA
	Popper	Karl Raimund	Austria
	Quine	Willard Van Orman	USA
	Rawls	John	USA
	Rorty	Richard	USA
	Ryle	Gilbert	England
	Schelling	Friedrich Wilhelm Joseph von	Germany
	Schlick	Friedrich Albert Moritz	Germany
	Searle	John	USA
	Sellars	Wilfrid Stalker	USA
	Sidgwick	Henry	England
	Spencer	Herbert	England
	Spengler	Oswald	Germany
	Spinoza	Baruch Benedict	Netherlands
	Taylor	John	USA
	Tzu	Lao	China
	Waismann	Friedrich	Austria

SOLVER SERIES: NAME FINDER

FAME	LAST NAME	FIRST NAME	COUNTRY
Philosopher	Weininger	Otto	Austria
	Whichcote	Benjamin	England
	Wittgenstein	Ludwig Josef Johann	England
Philosopher/Jewish	Mendelssohn	Moses	Germany
Philosopher/Social	Mumford	Lewis	USA
Philosopher /Sage	Maharshi	Ramana	India
Philosopher/Author	Hobbes	Thomas	England
Philosopher/Author/Editor	Campbell	Joseph	USA
Philosopher/Author/Theologist	Trueblood	David Elton	USA
Philosopher/Bishop	Cumberland	Richard	England
Philosopher/Clergyman	Jasper	John	USA
Philosopher/Critic	Bayle	Pierre	France
	Croce	Benedetto	Italy
	Schlegel	Karl Wilhelm Friedrich von	Germany
	Stephen	Leslie	England
Philosopher/Economist	Bentham	Jeremy	England
	Smith	Adam	Scotland
Philosopher/Educator	Adler	Felix	USA
	Dewey	John	USA
	Herbart	Johann Fredrich	Germany
	Royce	Josiah	USA
Philosopher/Encyclopedist	Diderot	Denis	France
Philosopher/Essayist	Gasset	José Ortega y	Spain
Philosopher/Essayist/Naturalist	Eiseley	Loren Corey	USA
Philosopher/Existentialist	Heidegger	Martin	Germany
Philosopher/Geologist/Jesuit	Chardin	Pierre Teilhard de	France
Philosopher/Historian	Acton	John Edward Dalberg	England
	Collingwood	Robin George	England
	Fiske	John	USA
	Hume	David	Scotland
	Kuhn	Thomas	USA
	Toynbee	Arnold Joseph	England
Philosopher/Humanist	Mirandola	Giovanni Pico della	Italy
Philosopher/Jesuit	Gracián	Baltasar	Spain
Philosopher/Jurist	Bodin	Jean	France
Philosopher/Lecturer/Author	Bradshaw	John	USA
Philosopher/Lyrical Poet/Critic	Coleridge	Samuel Taylor	England
Philosopher/Materialist	Feuerbach	Ludwig Andreas	Germany
Philosopher/Mathematician	Clifford	William K.	England
	Descartes	René	France
	Gödel	Kurt	USA
	Lakatos	Imre	Hungary
	Leibniz	Gottfried Wilhelm von	Germany
	Whitehead	Alfred North	England
Philosopher/Missionary/Theologian	Schweitzer	Albert	France
Philosopher/Mystic	Böhme	Jakob	Germany
	Weil	Simone	France
Philosopher/Pessimist	Schopehauer	Arthur	Germany
Philosopher/Physicist	Mach	Ernst	Austria
Philosopher/Poet	Herder	Johann Gottfried von	Germany
Philosopher/Poet	Leopardi	Conte Giacomo	Italy
Philosopher/Poet/Author	Thoreau	Henry David	USA
Philosopher/Poet/Historian	Quinet	Edgar	France
Philosopher/Poet/Novelist/Critic	Gourmont	Rémy de	France
Philosopher/Political Economist	Mill	John Stuart	England
Philosopher/Psychologist	Fromm	Erich	Germany
	James	William	USA
Philosopher/Scholar/Rabbi	Heschel	Abraham Joshua	USA

FAME	LAST NAME	FIRST NAME	COUNTRY
Philosopher/Scientist/Mystic	Swedenborg	Emanuel	Sweden
Philosopher/Social Theorist	Habermas	Jürgen	Germany
Philosopher/Socialist/Writer	Engels	Friedrich	Germany
Philosopher/Sociologist	Adorno	Theodor Ludwig Wiesengrund	Germany
	Baudrillard	Jean	France
Philosopher/Theologian	Buber	Martin	Israel
	Edwards	Johnathon	USA
	Hall	Joseph	England
	Kierkegaard	Soren Aabye	Denmark
	Martineau	James	England
	Otto	Rudolph	Germany
	Schleiermacher	Friedrich Ernest Daniel	Germany
	Tillich	Paul	Germany
Philosopher/Writer	Maistre	Joseph Marie de	France
	Montaigne	Michel Eyquem de	France
	Pániker	Salvador	Spain
	Rousseau	Jean Jacques	France
	Santayana	George	Spain
	Stoddard	Alexandra	USA
	Unamuno	Miguel de	Spain
	Voltaire	François Marie Arouet de	France
Philosopher/Writer/Educator	Rosenberg	Harold	USA
Philosopher/Writer/Statesman	Burke	Edmund	England
Phonetician	Jones	Daniel	England
	Passy	Paul Édouard	France
Phonetician/Educator	Kenyon	John Samuel	USA
Political Economist	Malthus	Thomas Robert	England
	Taussig	Frank William	USA
Prelate/Archbishop	Laud	William	England
Priest	Ball	John	England
Priest/Missionary	Damien	Joseph	Belgium
Priest/Translator	Knox	Ronald Arbuthnott	England
Print Designer	Bodoni	Giambattista	Italy
	Goudy	Frederic William	USA
Printer	Caxton	William	England
	Elzevir	Bonaventure	Netherlands
	Elzevir	Louis	Netherlands
	Froben	Johann	Germany
	Gutenberg	Johann	Germany
Printer/Designer	Baskerville	John	England
Printing/Writing	Braille	Louis	France
Protestant Bishop/Reformer	Latimer	Hugh	England
Protestant Leader	Niemöller	Friedrich Gustav Emil Martin	Germany
Psychoanalyst	Brill	Abraham Arden	USA
	Jones	Ernest	England
Psychologist	Allport	Gordon Willard	USA
	Angell	James Rowland	USA
	Baldwin	James Mark	USA
	Bettelheim	Bruno	USA
	Ellis	Albert	USA
	Gesell	Arnold Lucius	USA
	Janet	Pierre Marie Félix	France
	Koffka	Kurt	USA
	Köhler	Wolfgang	Germany
	Piaget	Jean	Switzerland
	Rorschach	Hermann	Switzerland
Psychologist	Salk	Lee	USA
	Skinner	Burrhus Frederic	USA

SOLVER SERIES: NAME FINDER

FAME	LAST NAME	FIRST NAME	COUNTRY
Psychologist	Terman	Louis Madison	USA
	Watson	John Broadus	USA
Psychologist/Educator	Hall	Granville Stanley	USA
Psychologist/Lexicographer	Thorndike	Edward Lee	USA
Psychologist/Physiologist	Wundt	Wilhelm	Germany
Publisher - Newspaper	Northcliffe	Alfred Charles William	England
Rabbi	Silver	Abba Hillel	USA
Rabbi/Jewish Leader	Wise	Stephen Samuel	USA
Reformer - Protestant	Zwingli	Ulrich	Switzerland
Reformer - Religious	Wycliffe	John	England
Religious Leader	Fox	George	England
Religious Reformer	Erskine	John	Scotland
	Tyndale	William	England
Revivalist	Booth	Ballington	England
	Booth	Evangeline Cory	England
	Booth	William	England
Scholar	Childers	Francis James	USA
Scholar - Classical	Murray	George Gilbert	England
	Porson	Richard	England
	Wolf	Friedrich August	Germany
Scholar - Humanist	Reuchlin	Johann	Germany
Scholar - Shakespear	Furness	Horace Howard	USA
Scholar/Educator	Kittredge	George Lyman	USA
Scholar/Monk	Kempis	Thomas à	Germany
Sculptor	Flaxman	John	England
Showman	Barnum	Phineas Taylor	USA
Social Worker	Perkins	Frances	USA
Socialist/Historian	Blanc	Jean Joseph Charles Louis	France
Socialist/Writer	Bebel	Ferdinand August	Germany
	Lassalle	Ferdinand	Germany
	Proudhon	Pierre Joseph	France
Sociologist	Parsons	Talcott	USA
Sociologist/Political Economist	Weber	Max	Germany
Theater Manager	Henslowe	Phillip	England
Theologian	Andrewes	Lancelot	England
	Arminius	Jacobus	Netherlands
	Barth	Carl	Switzerland
	Biddle	John	England
	Bultmann	Rudolf Karl	Germany
	Casaubon	Isaac	France
	Colette	John	England
	Eck	Johann Maier von	Germany
	Eliade	Mircea	USA
	Erastus	Thomas	Germany
	Inge	William Ralph	England
	Jansen	Cornelis	Netherlands
	Luther	Martin	Germany
	Martineau	Harriet	England
Theologian/Clergyman	Beecher	Lyman	USA
Theologian/Mystic	Eckhart	Johannes	Germany
Theologian/Philosopher	Abelard	Pierre	France
	Erigena	Johannes Scotus	Ireland
	Paley	William	England
	Scotus	John Duns	Scotland
Theologian/Writer	Newman	John Henry	England
Theosophist	Blavatsky	Helena	Russia
Translator	Garnett	Constance	England

FAME	LAST NAME	FIRST NAME	COUNTRY
Type Designer	Caslon	William	England
Typographer/Book Designer	Rogers	Bruce	USA
Violin Maker	Amati	Niccolo	Italy
	Guarneri	Giuseppe Antonio	Italy
	Stradivari	Antonio	Italy

AVIATION:

Aeronautical Engineer	Blériot	Louis	France
Aircraft Construction	Curtis	Glenn Hammond	USA
Aircraft Designer	Fokker	Anthony Herman Gerard	USA
Astronaut	Acton	Loren Wilbur	USA
	Adamson	James Craig	USA
	Akers	Thomas Dale	USA
	Aldrin	Edwin Eugene (Buzz)	USA
	Allen	Andrew Michael	USA
	Allen	Joseph Percival	USA
	Al-Saud	Salman Abdel-Aziz	Saudi Arabia
	Anders	William Alison	USA
	Anderson	Michael Phillip	USA
	Apt III	Jerome Jay	USA
	Armstrong	Neil Alden	USA
	Bagian	James Philip	USA
	Bartoe	John David Francis	USA
	Bassett II	Charles Arthur	USA
	Baudry	Patrick Pierre Roger	France
	Bean	Alan LaVerne	USA
	Belyayev	Pavel Ivanovich	Russia
	Beregovoi	Georgi Timofeyevich	Russia
	Berg	Lodewijk Van Den	USA
	Blaha	John Elmer	USA
	Bluford	Guion Steward	USA
	Bobko	Karol Joseph	USA
	Bodnar	Roberta Lynn	Canada
	Bolden Jr.	Charles Frank	USA
	Borman	Frank Frederick	USA
	Brady Jr.	Charles Eldon	USA
	Brandenstein	Daniel Charles	USA
	Brown	David McDowell	USA
	Brown	Mark Neil	USA
	Brown Jr.	Curtis Lee	USA
	Buchli	James Frederick	USA
	Buckey Jr.	Jay Clark	USA
	Bull	John Sumter	USA
	Bykovskiy	Valeri Fyodorovich	Russia
	Carey	Duane Gene (Digger)	USA
	Carpenter	Malcolm Scott	USA
	Carr	Gerald Paul	USA
	Carter Jr.	Manley Lanier (Sonny)	USA
	Cenker	Robert Joseph	USA
	Cernan	Eugene Andrew	USA
	Chaffee	Roger Bruce	USA
	Chapman	Philip Kenyon	USA
	Chawla	Kalpana	USA
	Cheli	Maurizio	Italy
	Chilton	Kevin Patrick (Chili)	USA
	Chrétien	Jean-Loup Jacques Marie	France

SOLVER SERIES: NAME FINDER

FAME	LAST NAME	FIRST NAME	COUNTRY
Astronaut	Clark	Laurel Blair Salton	USA
	Clervoy	Jean-François André	France
	Clifford	Michael Richard Uram	USA
	Coats	Michael Lloyd	USA
	Collins	Michael	USA
	Conrad Jr.	Charles Peter	USA
	Cooper	Leroy Gordon	USA
	Covey	Richard Oswalt	USA
	Creighton	John Oliver	USA
	Crippen	Robert Laurel	USA
	Crouch	Roger Keith	USA
	Culbertson Jr.	Frank Lee	USA
	Cunningham	Ronnie Walter	USA
	Delucas	Lawrence James	USA
	Doi	Takao	Japan
	Duffy	Brian	USA
	Duke Jr.	Charles Moss	USA
	Duque	Pedro Francisco	Spain
	Durrance	Samuel Thorton	USA
	Edwards Jr.	Joe Frank	USA
	Eisele	Donn Fulton	USA
	England	Anthony Wayne	USA
	Engle	Joe Henry	USA
	Evans	Ronald Ellwin	USA
	Eyharts	Léopold	France
	Fabian	John McCreary	USA
	Favier	Jean-Jacques	France
	Feoktistov	Konstantin Petrovich	Russia
	Fettman	Martin Joseph	USA
	Filipchenko	Anatoli Vassilyevich	Russia
	Fisher	William Frederick	USA
	Freeman	Theodore Cordy	USA
	Frimout	Dirk Dries David Damian	Belgium
	Fuglesang	Arne Christer	Sweden
	Furrer	Reinhard Alfred	Germany
	Gaffney	Francis Andrew	USA
	Gardner	Dale Allan	USA
	Gardner	Guy Spencer	USA
	Garn	Edwin Jacob (Jake)	USA
	Garneau	Joseph Jean-Pierre Marc	Canada
	Garriott	Owen Kay	USA
	Gemar	Charles Donald	USA
	Gibson	Edward George	USA
	Gibson	Robert Lee (Hoot)	USA
	Givens Jr.	Edward Galen	USA
	Glenn	John Herschel	USA
	Gorbatko	Viktor Vassilyevich	Russia
	Gordon Jr.	Richard Francis	USA
	Grabe	Ronald John	USA
	Graveline	Duane Edgar	USA
	Gregory	William George	USA
	Griggs	Stanley David	USA
	Grissom	Virgil Ivan (Gus)	USA
	Guidoni	Umberto	Italy
	Gutierrez	Sidney McNeil	USA
	Hadfield	Chris Austin	Canada
	Haise Jr.	Fred Wallace	USA
	Hammond Jr.	Lloyd Blaine	USA

FAME	LAST NAME	FIRST NAME	COUNTRY
Astronaut	Harbaugh	Gregory Jordan	USA
	Harris Jr.	Bernard Andrew	USA
	Hart	Terry Jonathon	USA
	Hartsfield Jr.	Henry Warren	USA
	Hauck	Frederick Hamilton	USA
	Helms	Susan Jane	USA
	Henize	Karl Gordon	USA
	Hennen	Thomas John	USA
	Henricks	Terence Thomas	USA
	Hieb	Richard James	USA
	Hilmers	David Carl	USA
	Hoffman	Jeffrey Alan	USA
	Hoften	James Douglas Van (Ox)	USA
	Holmquest	Donald Lee	USA
	Horowitz	Scott Jay (Doc)	USA
	Hughes-Fulford	Millie Elizabeth	USA
	Husband	Rick Douglas	USA
	Irwin	James Benson	USA
	Jarvis	Gregory Bruce	USA
	Jemison	Mae Carol	USA
	Jernigan	Tamara Elizabeth	USA
	Jones	Thomas David	USA
	Kadenyuk	Leonid Konstantinovich	Ukraine
	Kerwin	Joseph Peter	USA
	Khrunov	Yeugeni Vassilyevich	Russia
	Kilrain	Susan Leigh	USA
	Komarov	Vladimir Mikhailovich	Russia
	Kregel	Kevin Richard	USA
	Kubasov	Valeri Nikolayevich	Russia
	Lee	Mark Charles	USA
	Lenoir	William Benjamin	USA
	Leonov	Alexei Arkhipovich	Russia
	Leslie	Fred Weldon	USA
	Lichtenberg	Byron Kurt	USA
	Lind	Don Leslie	USA
	Linenger	Jerry Michael	USA
	Linteris	Gregory Thomas	USA
	Llewellyn	John Anthony	USA
	Lounge	John Michael	USA
	Lousma	Jack Robert	USA
	Lovell Jr.	James Arthur	USA
	Low	George David	USA
	MacLean	Steven Glenwood	Canada
	Malerba	Franco Egidio	France
	Mattingly II	Thomas Kenneth	USA
	McAuliffe	Sharon Christa Corrigan	USA
	McBride	Jon Andrew	USA
	McCandless II	Bruce	USA
	McCool	William Cameron	USA
	McCulley	Michael James	USA
	McDivitt	James Alton	USA
	McMonagle	Donald Ray	USA
	McNair	Ronald Erwin	USA
	Meade	Carl Joseph	USA
	Melnick	Bruce Edward	USA
	Merbold	Ulf Dietrich	Germany
	Messerschmid	Ernst Willi	Germany
	Michel	Frank Curtis	USA

SOLVER SERIES: NAME FINDER

FAME	LAST NAME	FIRST NAME	COUNTRY
Astronaut	Mitchell	Edgar Dean	USA
	Mohri	Mamoru	Japan
	Mullane	Richard Michael	USA
	Musgrave	Franklin Story	USA
	Naito-Mukai	Chiaki	Japan
	Nelson	Clarens William	USA
	Nelson	George Driver (Pinky)	USA
	Neri Vela	Rodolfo	Mexico
	Nespoli	Paolo Angelo	Italy
	Nicollier	Claude	Switzerland
	Nikolaev	Andrian Grigoryevich	Russia
	Noguchi	Soichi	Japan
	Ockels	Wubbo Johannes	Netherlands
	O'Leary	Brian Todd	USA
	Onizuka	Ellison Shoji	USA
	Oswald	Stephen Scott	USA
	Overmyer	Robert Franklin	USA
	Pailes	William Arthur	USA
	Parise	Ronald Anthony	USA
	Pawelczyk	James Anthony	USA
	Payette	Julie	Canada
	Payton	Gary Eugene	USA
	Perrin	Philippe	France
	Peterson	Donald Herod	USA
	Pogue	William Reid	USA
	Pontes	Marcos	Brazil
	Popovich	Pavel Romanovich	Russia
	Ramon	Ilan	Israel
	Reightler	Kenneth Stanley	USA
	Richards	Richard Noel	USA
	Ride	Sally Kristen	USA
	Robertson	Patricia Consolatrix Hilliard	USA
	Roosa	Stuart Allen	USA
	Sacco Jr.	Albert	USA
	Schirra	Walter Marty	USA
	Schlegel	Hans Wilhelm	Germany
	Schmitt	Harrison Hagan	USA
	Schweickart	Russell Luis	USA
	Scobee	Francis Richard	USA
	Scott	David Randolph	USA
	Scott	Winston Elliot	USA
	Scully-Power	Paul Desmond	USA
	Searfoss	Richard Alan	USA
	Seddon	Margaret Rhea	USA
	See Jr.	Elliot McKay	USA
	Sega	Ronald Michael	USA
	Sevastyanov	Vitali Ivanovich	Russia
	Shatalov	Vladimir Aleksandrovich	Russia
	Shaw Jr.	Brewster Hopkinson	USA
	Shepard Jr.	Alan Bartlett	USA
	Shepherd	William McMichael	USA
	Shonin	Georgi Stepanovich	Russia
	Shriver	Loren James	USA
	Slayton	Donald Kent	USA
	Smith	Michael John	USA
	Spring	Sherwood Clark (Woody)	USA
	Springer	Robert Clyde	USA
	Stafford	Thomas Patten	USA

FAME	LAST NAME	FIRST NAME	COUNTRY
Astronaut	Stewart	Robert Lee	USA
	Sullivan	Kathryn Dwyer	USA
	Swigert	John Leonard	USA
	Tereshkova	Vanlentina Vladimirovna	Russia
	Thagard	Norman Earl	USA
	Thiele	Gerhard Julius Paul	Germany
	Thirsk	Robert Brent	Canada
	Thorne	Stephen Douglas	USA
	Thornton	Kathryn Ryan Cordell	USA
	Thornton	William Edgar	USA
	Thuot	Pierre Joseph	USA
	Titov	Gherman Stepanovich	Russia
	Tognini	Michel	France
	Trinh	Eugene Hau-Chau	USA
	Truly	Richard Harrison	USA
	Tryggvason	Bjarni Valdimar	Canada
	Veach	Charles Lacy	USA
	Vittori	Roberto	Italy
	Volkov	Vladislav Nikolavevich	Russia
	Volynov	Boris Valentinovich	Russia
	Voss	James Shelton	USA
	Wakata	Koichi	Japan
	Walker	Charles David	USA
	Walker	David Mathieson	USA
	Walter	Ulrich Hans	Germany
	Wang	Taylor Gun-Jin	USA
	Weber	Mary Ellen	USA
	Weitz	Paul Joseph	USA
	White II	Edward Higgins	USA
	Williams	Daffydd Rhys	Canada
	Williams	Donald Edward	USA
	Williams Jr.	Clifton Curtis	USA
	Wisoff	Peter Jeffry Karl	USA
	Worden	Alfred Merrill	USA
	Yegorov	Boris Borisovich	Russia
	Yeliseyev	Aleksei Stanislavovich	Russia
	Young	John Watts	USA
Aviator	Lindbergh	Charles	USA
Aviator/Aviation Executive	Rickenbacker	Edward Vernon	USA
Cosmonaut	Gagarin	Yuri Alekseyevich	Russia
Engineer - Rocket	Braun	Wernher von	USA
Inventor - Airplane	Wright	Orville	USA
	Wright	Wilbur	USA
Pilot - Around the World	Post	Wiley	USA
Pilot - Sound Barrier	Yeager	Chuck Elwood	USA
Pioneer Aviator	Earhart	Amelia	USA

BUSINESS:

Advertising	Benton	William	USA
	Thompson	James Walter	USA
Automobile Industy	Daimler	Gottlieb	Germany
	Iacocca	Lee A.	USA
	Olds	Ransom Eli	USA
Aviation - Helecopters	Bell	Lawrence Dale	USA
Aviation - Virgin Blue	Branson	Richard	England
Aviation Industry	Black	Fred	USA
	Lorenzo	Frank	USA

SOLVER SERIES: NAME FINDER

FAME	LAST NAME	FIRST NAME	COUNTRY
Aviation Industry	Ward	Maxwell William	Canada
Aviation Industry - Aeronautical Engineer	Seversky	Alexander Procofieff de	USA
	Sikorsky	Igor Ivanovich	USA
Banking	Belmont	August	USA
	Korth	Fred	USA
	Meyer	Nathan	Germany
	Phelan	James	USA
	Seligman	Joseph	USA
Banking/Philanthropist	Loeb	James	USA
Baseball Owner	Steinbrenner	George	USA
Breweries	Busch	Adolphus	USA
Broadcasting	Turner	Ted	USA
Capitalist/Philanthropist	Cornell	Ezra	USA
Coca Cola Founder	Candler	Asa Griggs	USA
Communications	Asper	Israel Harold (Izzy)	Canada
Computer Industry	Perot	Henry Ross	USA
Confection Industry	Cadbury	George	England
	Fry	Joseph	England
	Rowntree	Joseph	England
	Rowntree	Seebohm	England
	Sainsbury	John	England
	Spencer	Tom	England
Confection Industry - Soft Ice Cream	Carvel	Tom	USA
Construction Industry	Jones	Jesse Holman	USA
Cosmetics Industry	Lauder	Estee	USA
Cotton Industry	Estes	Billy Sol	USA
Designer - Chairs	Eames Jr.	Charles Ormond	USA
Disney Film Head	Eisner	Michael Dammann	USA
Drygoods	Loeb	Solomon	USA
	Strauss	Isidor	USA
	Tappan	Arthur	USA
	Tappan	Lewis	USA
Electricity	Wirtz	Alvin	USA
Engineer/Inventor - Firearms	Maxim	Hiram Stevens	England
Entrepreneur	Allinson	Thomas	England
	Clark	Cyrus	USA
	Coutts	Thomas	England
	Ichan	Carl	USA
	Lever	William	England
	Lloyd II	Sampson	England
	Morris	William	England
	Tate	Henry	England
	Wedgwood	Josiah	England
Fashion Designer	Arden	Elizabeth	USA
	Armani	Georgio	Italy
	Ashley	Laura	England
	Bally	Carl Franz	Switzerland
	Blass	William Ralph	USA
	Boss	Hugo	Germany
	Burberry	Thomas	England
	Cardin	Pierre	France
	Cassini	Oleg	USA
	Cerruti	Nino	Italy
	Chanel	Coco	France
	Chanel	Gabrielle	France
	Claiborne	Liz	USA
	Cole	Kenneth	USA
	Dior	Christian	France

FAME	LAST NAME	FIRST NAME	COUNTRY
Fashion Designer	Dolce	Domenico	Italy
	Ellis	Perry	USA
	Fiorucci	Elio	Italy
	Gabbana	Stefano	Italy
	Gaultier	Jean-Paul	France
	Gernreich	Rudi	Austria
	Givenchy	Hubert de	France
	Gucci	Guccio	Italy
	Hermes	Thierry	France
	Hilfiger	Thomas Jacob	USA
	Johnson	Betsey	USA
	Karan	Donna	USA
	Klein	Anne	USA
	Klein	Calvin	USA
	Lacroix	Christian	France
	Lagerfeld	Karl	Germany
	Laroche	Guy	France
	Lauren	Ralph	USA
	Mackie	Bob	USA
	McCartney	Stella	England
	Miller	Nicole	USA
	Mizrahi	Isaak	USA
	Muir	Jean	England
	Pucci	Emilio	Italy
	Rabanne	Paco	France
	Renta	Oscar de la	France
	Ricci	Nina	France
	Rowan	Rena	Poland
	Saint Laurent	Yves	France
	Simmons	Kimora Lee	USA
	Simpson	Adele	USA
	Sung	Alfred	Japan
	Ungaro	Emanuel	France
	Valentino	Garavani	Italy
	Vanderbilt	Gloria	USA
	Versace	Donatella	Italy
	Versace	Gianni	Italy
	Wang	Vera	USA
	Westwood	Vivienne	England
Fashion/Fragrance Designer	Lapidus	Ted	France
Fashion/Jewelery Designer	Peretti	Elsa	Italy
Financier	Astor	John Jacob	USA
	Biddle	Nicholas	USA
	Clews	Henry	USA
	Gould	Jay	USA
	Kahn	Otto	USA
	Morgan	John Pierpont	USA
	Sage	Russell	USA
	Salomon	Haym	USA
	Schiff	Jacob	USA
	Warburg	Paul	USA
Financier/Administrator	Rhodes	Cecil John	England
Financier/Industrialist	Harriman	William Averell	USA
Financier/Mining Industry	Mellon	Andrew William	USA
Financier/Patriot	Morris	Robert	USA
Financier/Philanthropist	Girard	Stephen	USA
	Brady	James (Diamond Jim)	USA
Financier/Politician	Hanna	Marcus	USA

SOLVER SERIES: NAME FINDER

FAME	LAST NAME	FIRST NAME	COUNTRY
Financier/Railroad Magnate	Harriman	Edward Henry	USA
Financier/Statesman	Baruch	Bernard Mannes	USA
	Gallatin	Abraham Alfonse	USA
	Necker	Jacques	France
Firearms	Gatling	Richard Jordan	USA
	Hotchkis	Benjamin	USA
Founder - Bank	Rothschild	Meyer Anselm	Germany
Founder - Walmart	Walton	Samuel Moore	USA
Fragrance Designer	Patou	Jean	France
Fur Trade	Chouteau	August	USA
Gold Mining	Suter	Johann August	USA
Hotelier	Hilton	Conrad	USA
Hotelier	Johnson	Howard	USA
Importer	Kennedy	Patrick Joseph	USA
	Low	Seth	USA
Industialist/Philanthropist	Carnegie	Andrew	USA
Industrial Designer	Loewy	Raymond Ferdinand	USA
Industrialist	Eaton	Cyrus	USA
	Field	Cyrus West	USA
	Frick	Henry Clay	USA
	Hughes	Howard Robard	USA
	Kaiser	Henry John	USA
	Krupp	Alfred	Germany
	Pont	Éleuthère Irénée du	USA
Industrialist - Soap	Colgate	William	USA
Industrialist/Capitalist	Vanderbilt	Cornelius	USA
Industrialist/Philanthropist	Guggenheim	Daniel	USA
	Guggenheim	Simon	USA
	Guggenheim	Solomon R.	USA
	Nobel	Alfred Bernhard	Sweden
	Rockefeller	John Davison	USA
	Rockefeller	John Davison Jr.	USA
Industrialist/Statesman	Rathenau	Walther	Germany
Insurance Industry	Wortham	Gus Sessions	USA
Kodak Film Company	Eastman	George	USA
Labor Leader	Bridges	Harry	USA
	Debs	Eugene Victor	USA
	Green	William	USA
	Hoffa	James Riddle (Jimmy)	USA
	Kirkland	Joseph Lane	USA
	Lewis	John Llewellyn	USA
	Meany	George	USA
	Reuther	Walter	USA
Livestock	Cudahy	Michael	USA
Lumber Industry	Weyerhauser	Frederick	USA
Magazine Editor	Ross	Harold Wallace	USA
Manufacturer - Automobiles	Ford	Henry	USA
Manufacturer/Inventor	Westinghouse	George	USA
Manufacturing - Pullman Car	Pullman	George Mortimer	USA
Manufacturing Industry	Jones	Samuel Milton	USA
	Pingree	Hazen	USA
	Solheim	Karstein	USA
	Tweed	William	USA
Manufacturing - Pianos	Steinway	Heinrich	USA
McDonalds Restaurants	Kroc	Ray	USA
Media Magnate	Annenberg	Walter Hubert	USA
	Black	Conrad	Canada
	Murdoch	Keith Rupert	USA

FAME	LAST NAME	FIRST NAME	COUNTRY
Media Magnate	Paley	William Samuel	USA
Merchant	Wanamaker	John	USA
	Whittington	Richard	England
	Woolworth	Frank Winfield	USA
Merchant/Philanthropist	Peabody	George	USA
Microsoft	Gates	Bill	USA
Mining Industry	Guggenheim	Myer	USA
Newspaper Industry	Hobby	William	USA
Newspaper Publisher	Hearst	William Randolph	USA
Oil Industry	Abercrombie	James	USA
	Cullen	Hugh Roy	USA
	Downey	John	USA
	Elkin	James	USA
	Germany	Eugene Benjamin	USA
	Getty	Jean Paul	USA
	Hammer	Armand	USA
	Hunt	Haroldson L.	USA
	Kerr	Robert Samuel	USA
	McCarthy	Glenn	USA
	Pickens	Thomas Boone	USA
	Richardson	Sid Williams	USA
	Sinclair	Harry F.	USA
	Vinson	William	USA
Optical Industry	Bausch	John Jacob	USA
	Lomb	Henry	USA
Outboard Engine Designer	Evinrude	Ole	USA
Philanthropist - Red Cross	Barton	Clara	USA
	Dunant	Jean Henry	Switzerland
Philanthropist/Pianist	Hogg	Ima	USA
Philanthropy	Kroc	Joan	USA
Publisher/Editor	Luce	Henry Robinson	USA
Publishing	Aitken	William Maxwell	England
	Akermann	Rudolf	England
	Baines	Edward	England
	Carlile	Richard	England
	Cerf	Bennett Alfred	USA
	Cleave	John	England
	Cobbett	William	England
	Dalziel	George Henry	England
	Forbes	Malcolm	USA
	Harmsworth	Harold	England
	Hefner	Hugh Marston	USA
	Hetherington	Henry	England
	Hone	William	England
	Hulton	Edward	England
	Hunt	Leigh	England
	Johnson	Joseph	England
	King	Cecil	England
	Knopf	Alfred Abraham	USA
	Lawson	Edward Levy	England
	Lemon	Mark	USA
	Lloyd	Edward	England
	McClure	Samuel	USA
	Pearson	Cyril	England
	Prentice	Archibald	England
	Taylor	John Edward	England
	Thompson	Roy	England
	Turnblad	Swan	USA

SOLVER SERIES: NAME FINDER

FAME	LAST NAME	FIRST NAME	COUNTRY
Publishing	Villard	Oswald Garrison	USA
	Walter	John	England
	Walter II	John	England
Publishing - Dell	Delacorte	George T.	USA
Publishing - Newspaper	Scripps	Edward Wyllis	USA
Publishing/Magazine	Nast	Condé Montrose	USA
Publishing/Oil Industry	Murchison	Clint	USA
Publishing/Philanthropist	Pulitzer	Joseph	USA
Railway Magnate	Arrol	William	England
	Booth	Henry	England
	Bradshaw	George	England
	Brassey	Thomas	England
	Gowen	Franklin	USA
	Gurney	Joseph	USA
	Hill	James Jerome	USA
	Horne	William Cornelius Van	Canada
	Hudson	George	England
	Hulton	William	England
	Huntington	Collis Potter	USA
	James	William	England
	Laing	Samuel	England
	Pease	Edward	England
	Ryan	Thomas	USA
	Sandars	Joseph	England
	Sterling	Ross Shaw	USA
Railway/Publishing	Villard	Henry	USA
Real Estate	Reichman	Albert	Canada
	Reichman	Paul	Canada
	Reichman	Ralph	Canada
	Trump	Donald	USA
Retail Trade	Bass	Michael	England
	Booth	Jessie	England
	Dollond	Peter	England
	Eaton	Timothy	Canada
	Harrod	Charles	England
	Liberty	Arthur	England
	Marks	Michael	England
	Menzies	John	England
	Whitbread	Samuel	England
Ship Building	Brown	George	USA
	Brown	Herman	USA
Shipping Magnate	Cunard	Samuel	Canada
	Grace	William	USA
	Onassis	Aristotle	Greece
Steel Industry/Philanthropy	Cooper	Peter	USA
Telephones	Bell	Alexander Graham	USA
Television Industry	Arledge	Roone	USA
	Tinker	Grant A.	USA
Textile Industry	Arkwright	Richard	England
	Ashton	Thomas	England
	Courtauld	George	England
	Courtauld	Samuel	England
	Dale	David	England
	Fielden	John	England
	Fielden	Joshua	England
	Fielden	Samuel	England
	Fielden	Thomas	England
	Greg	Robert Hyde	England

FAME	LAST NAME	FIRST NAME	COUNTRY
Textile Industry	Greg	Samuel	England
	Horrocks	John	England
	Marshall	John	England
	Owen	Robert	England
	Owens	John	England
	Peel Sr.	Robert	England
	Radcliffe	William	England
	Salt	Titus	England
	Strutt	Jedediah	England
	Wood	John	England
Tobacco Industry	Hammerstein	Oscar	USA
Transportation Industry	Pawley	William	USA
	Wickman	Carl Eric	USA
Travel Industry	Cook	Thomas	England
Travel/Baseball	Ueberroth	Peter Victor	USA
Union Leader	Chavez	Cesar Estrada	USA

CREATIVE WORKS:

Animator	Kelly	Walt	USA
Art Critic	Berenson	Bernard	USA
Artist	Sorel	Edward	USA
Author	Abbott	Jacob	USA
	Abbott	Lyman	USA
	Adams	Douglas Noël	England
	Alther	Lisa	USA
	Amado	Jorge	Brazil
	Ambler	Eric	England
	Amis	Kingsley	England
	Amory	Cleveland	USA
	Atwood	Margaret	Canada
	Auel	Jean	USA
	Baker	George Pierce	USA
	Barker	Clive	England
	Barnard	Robert	England
	Barstow	Stanley (Stan)	England
	Beattie	Ann	USA
	Blume	Judy	USA
	Blyton	Enid Mary	England
	Brooks	Ned	USA
	Burgess	John Anthony	England
	Butler	Samuel	England
	Calisher	Hortense	USA
	Calvino	Italo	Italy
	Capote	Truman	USA
	Carré	John Le	England
	Cerf	Bennett Alfred	USA
	Clancy Jr.	Thomas L. (Tom)	USA
	Clavell	James du Maresqu	Australia
	Courtenay	Bryce	South Africa
	Crichton	Michael	USA
	Crisp	Quentin	England
	Deighton	Len	England
	Dexter	Norman Colin	England
	Dinesen	Isak	Denmark
	Durrell	Lawrence	England
	Eco	Umberto	Italy
	Ellison	Harlan	USA

SOLVER SERIES: NAME FINDER

FAME	LAST NAME	FIRST NAME	COUNTRY
Author	Ellison	Ralph	USA
	Engel	Howard	Canada
	Engel	Lehmen	USA
	Estleman	Loren D.	USA
	Farmer	Philip José	USA
	Fleming	Ian	England
	Fowles	John	England
	Francis	Richard Stanley (Dick)	Wales
	French	Marilyn	USA
	Gage	Nicholas	Greece
	Gardner	Erle Stanley	USA
	Garfield	Brian Francis Wynne	USA
	Gould	Lois	USA
	Grafton	Sue	USA
	Grayson	David	USA
	Grimes	Martha	USA
	Grisham	John	USA
	Hailey	Arthur	England
	Haley	Alex	USA
	Hammett	Dashiell	USA
	Harper	Lee	USA
	Harris	Joel Chandler	USA
	Havelock	Ellis	England
	Herbert	Frank	USA
	Hinton	Susan Eloise	USA
	Hite	Shere	USA
	Hunter	Evan	USA
	Irving	Washington	USA
	Jaffe	Rona	USA
	Jones	James	USA
	Jong	Erica	USA
	Kaufman	Bel	Russia
	Kesey	Ken	USA
	Koontz	Dean Ray	USA
	Kundera	Milan	Czechoslovakia
	Lindbergh	Anne Morrow	USA
	MacDonald	John Dann	USA
	Macdonald	Ross	USA
	Mandeville	John	England
	Mille	Nelson De	USA
	Miller	Sue	USA
	Mishima	Yukio	Japan
	Mitford	Jessica	England
	Munro	Hector Hugh (Saki)	England
	Murdoch	Iris	England
	O'Brien	Edna	Ireland
	O'Connor	Mary Flannery	USA
	O'Flaherty	Liam	Ireland
	O'Hara	John Henry	USA
	Paton	Alan Stewart	South Africa
	Patterson	James	USA
	Percy	Walker	USA
	Phillips	Jayne Anne	USA
	Post	Emily	USA
	Potok	Chaim	USA
	Powys	Llewelyn	England
	Puzo	Mario	USA
	Quindland	Anna	USA

FAME	LAST NAME	FIRST NAME	COUNTRY
Author	Radcliffe	Ann	England
	Reyes	Alfonso	Mexico
	Sabato	Ernesto	Argentina
	Salamanca	Jack R	USA
	Sanders	Lawrence	USA
	Sayers	Dorothy L.	England
	Segal	Erich	USA
	Seton	Anya	USA
	Shan	Eda Le	USA
	Smith	Wilbur	Africa
	Spyri	Johanna Louise	Switzerland
	Stoker	Abraham (Bram)	Ireland
	Stout	Rex Todhunter	USA
	Tan	Amy	USA
	Tevis	Walter Stone	USA
	Tey	Josephine	Scotland
	Toklas	Alice Babette	USA
	Toland	John	USA
	Turow	Scott	USA
	Wallace	Lila Acheson	Canada
	Wambaugh	Joseph	USA
	White III	Edmund Valentine	USA
	Wiesel	Eliezer (Elie)	USA
	Wilhelm	Kate	USA
	Woolf	Virginia	England
	Wylie	Philip Gordon	USA
Author - Black Beauty	Sewell	Anna	England
Author - Children's Books	Wilder	Laura Ingalls	USA
Author - Crime Fiction	Paretsky	Sara	USA
	Rendell	Ruth Barbara	England
	Spillane	Frank Morrison (Mickey)	USA
Author - Jaws	Benchley	Peter	USA
Author/Novelist	Proulx	Edna Annie	USA
Author - Pulitzer	Acheson	Dean Gooderham	USA
	Adams	Henry Brooks	USA
	Adams	James Truslow	USA
	Agar	Herbert Sebastian	England
	Andrews	Charles McLean	USA
	Applebaum	Anne	USA
	Atkinson	Rick	USA
	Bailyn	Bernard	USA
	Baker	Leonard	USA
	Baker	Ray Stannard	USA
	Bate	Walter Jackson	USA
	Baxter III	James Phinney	USA
	Becker	Ernest	USA
	Bemis	Samuel Flagg	USA
	Berg	Alan Scott	USA
	Beveridge	Albert Jeremiah	USA
	Bix	Herbert P.	USA
	Bok	Edward William	USA
	Bonsal	Stephen	USA
	Boorstein	Daniel J.	USA
	Branch	Taylor	USA
	Bromfield	Louis	USA
	Brooks	Van Wyck	USA
	Bruce	Robert	USA
	Bruce	William Cabell	USA

SOLVER SERIES: NAME FINDER

FAME	LAST NAME	FIRST NAME	COUNTRY
Author - Pulitzer	Buck	Paul Herman	USA
	Buley	Oscar Carlyle	USA
	Burns	James MacGregor	USA
	Burrows	Edwin G.	USA
	Butler	Robert N.	USA
	Butler	Robert Olen	USA
	Canning	Edward	USA
	Caro	Robert Allan	USA
	Carroll	John Alexander	USA
	Catton	Bruce (Charles)	USA
	Chabon	Michael	USA
	Chandler	Alfred D.	USA
	Cheever	John	USA
	Clapp	Margaret	USA
	Coit	Margaret Louise	USA
	Coles	Robert	USA
	Cremin	Lawrence A.	USA
	Curti	Merle E.	USA
	Cushing	Harvey	USA
	Dangerfield	George	USA
	Davis	David Brion	USA
	Degler	Carl N.	USA
	Dennett	Tyler	USA
	Diamond	Jared	USA
	Dillard	Annie	USA
	Donald	David Herbert	USA
	Doren	Carl Clinton Van	USA
	Dower	John W.	USA
	Drury	Allen	USA
	Dubos	René Jules	USA
	Durant	Ariel	USA
	Durant	Will	USA
	Edel	Leon	USA
	Elliott	Maude Howe	USA
	Ellis	Joseph J.	USA
	Ellmann	Richard	USA
	Erikson	Erik Homburger	USA
	Fehrenbacher	Don E.	USA
	Feis	Herbert	USA
	Ferber	Edna	USA
	Fischer	David Hackett	USA
	Fitzgerald	Francis Scott Ley	USA
	Forbes	Esther	USA
	Ford	Richard	USA
	Frank	Elizabeth	USA
	Freeman	Douglas S.	USA
	Garland	Hannibal Hamlin	USA
	Garrow	David J.	USA
	Gibson	Lawrence H.	USA
	Goetzmann	William H.	USA
	Goodwin	Doris Kearns	USA
	Graham	Katharine	USA
	Grau	Shirley Ann	USA
	Grazia	Sebastian de	USA
	Green	Constance McLaughlin	USA
	Hahn	Steven	USA
	Hamlin	Talbot Faulkner	USA
	Hammond	Bray	USA

FAME	LAST NAME	FIRST NAME	COUNTRY
Author - Pulitzer	Handlin	Oscar	USA
	Hansen	Marcus Lee	USA
	Harlan	Louis R.	USA
	Hendrick	Burton J.	USA
	Hersey	John	USA
	Hijuelos	Oscar	USA
	Hofstadter	Douglas Richard	USA
	Holldobler	Bert	Germany
	Holloway	Emory	USA
	Horgan	Paul	USA
	Howe	Mark Antony DeWolfe	USA
	Isaac	Rhys L.	USA
	James	Henry	USA
	James	Marquis	USA
	Jones	Howard Mumford	USA
	Jusserand	Jean Jules	USA
	Kammen	Michael	USA
	Kaplan	Justin	USA
	Karnow	Stanley	USA
	Kennan	George Frost	USA
	Kennedy	David Matthew	USA
	Kennedy	John F.	USA
	Kidder	Tracy	USA
	Kluger	Richard	USA
	Larkin	Oliver Waterman	USA
	Larson	Edward J.	USA
	Lash	Joseph P.	USA
	Leech	Margaret	USA
	Lelyveld	Joseph	USA
	Levy	Leonard Williams	USA
	Lewis	David Levering	USA
	Lewis	Richard Warrington Baldwin	USA
	Lindbergh	Charles A.	USA
	Litwack	Leon F.	USA
	Lukas	Jay Anthony	USA
	Lurie	Alison	USA
	Mabee	Carlton	USA
	Mack	John E.	USA
	Mailer	Norman Kingsley	USA
	Malone	Dumas	USA
	Massie	Robert K.	USA
	Mays	David J.	USA
	McCourt	Frank	USA
	McCullough	David	USA
	McDougall	Walter A.	USA
	McFeely	William S.	USA
	McGraw	Thomas K.	USA
	McIlwain	Charles Howard	USA
	McLaughlin	Andrew Cunningham	USA
	McPhee	John	USA
	McPherson	James M.	USA
	McWhorter	Diane	USA
	Menand	Louis	USA
	Michener	James A.	USA
	Miles	Jack	USA
	Miller	Perry	USA
	Mitchell	Margaret Munnerlyn	USA
	Morison	Samuel Eliot	USA

SOLVER SERIES: NAME FINDER

FAME	LAST NAME	FIRST NAME	COUNTRY
Author - Pulitzer	Morris	Edmund	USA
	Mott	Frank Luther	USA
	Naifeh	Steven	USA
	Neely Jr.	Mark E.	USA
	Nevins	Allan	USA
	Nichols	Roy Franklin	USA
	Nye	Russell Blaine	USA
	Parrington	Vernon Louis	USA
	Paxson	Frederic L.	USA
	Perry	Ralph Barton	USA
	Pershing	John Joseph	USA
	Potter	David M.	USA
	Powell	Sumner Chilton	USA
	Power	Samantha	Ireland
	Pringle	Henry F.	USA
	Puller Jr.	Lewis Burwell	USA
	Pupin	Michael Idvorsky	USA
	Pusey	Merlo J.	USA
	Rakove	Jack N.	USA
	Reid	Benjamin Lawrence	USA
	Remnick	David	USA
	Rhodes	James Ford	USA
	Rhodes	Richard	USA
	Richards	Laura Elizabeth	USA
	Rosenberg	Tina	USA
	Russell	Charles Edward	USA
	Sagan	Carl Edward	USA
	Samuels	Ernest	USA
	Sandburg	Carl	USA
	Schiff	Stacy	USA
	Schlesinger Jr.	Arthur Meier	USA
	Schmitt	Bernadotte E.	USA
	Schneider	Jean	USA
	Schorske	Carl E.	USA
	Shannon	Fred Albert	USA
	Sheaffer	Louis	USA
	Sheehan	Cornelius Mahoney (Neil)	USA
	Sheehan	Susan	USA
	Shepard	Odel	USA
	Shields	Carol	Canada
	Shipler	David K.	USA
	Silverman	Kenneth	USA
	Sims	William Sowden	Canada
	Smith	Gregory White	USA
	Smith	Justin H.	USA
	Starr	Paul	USA
	Stevens	Mark	USA
	Styron	William	USA
	Swan	Annalyn	USA
	Swanberg	William Andrew	USA
	Taubman	William	USA
	Taylor	Alan	USA
	Taylor	Robert Lewis	USA
	Teale	Edwin Way	USA
	Terkel	Louis (Studs)	USA
	Thompson	Lawrance	USA
	Tuchman	Barbara Wertheim	USA
	Turner	Frederick Jackson	USA

FAME	LAST NAME	FIRST NAME	COUNTRY
Author - Pulitzer	Tyler	Anne	USA
	Tyne	Claude Halstead Va	USA
	Ulrich	Laurel Thatcher	USA
	Unger	Irwin	USA
	Voto	Bernard De	USA
	Walker	Alice Malsenior	USA
	Walworth	Arthur	USA
	Warner	William W.	USA
	Warren	Charles	USA
	Weiner	Jonathan	USA
	Wells	Mary	USA
	White	Leonard D.	USA
	White	Theodore Harold	USA
	White	William Allen	USA
	White	William S.	USA
	Williams	Thomas Harry	USA
	Williamson	Michael	USA
	Wills	Gary	USA
	Wilson	Edward Osborne	USA
	Wilson	Forrest	USA
	Winslow	Ola Elizabeth	USA
	Wolfe	Linnie Marsh	USA
	Wood	Gordon S.	USA
	Woodward	Comer Vann	USA
	Wouk	Herman	USA
	Yergin	Daniel	USA
Author - SciFi	Aldiss	Brian Wilson	England
	Asimov	Isaac	Russia
	Bradbury	Ray	USA
	Clarke	Arthur Charles	England
	Delany	Samuel Ray	USA
	Disch	Thomas Michael	USA
	Heinlein	Robert Anson	USA
	Hubbard	Lafayette Ronald	USA
	Leiber Jr.	Fritz Reuter	USA
	Niven	Larry	USA
	Norton	André Alice	USA
	Pohl	Frederick	USA
	Silverberg	Robert	USA
	Stapledon	William Olaf	England
	Varley	John Herbert	USA
	Vinge	Joan D.	USA
	Wyndham	John	England
Author - Spy Novels	Ludlum	Robert	USA
Author/Artist - Children's Books	Sendak	Maurice	USA
Author/Dramatist	Lyly	John	England
Author/Educator	Washington	Booker Taliaferro	USA
Author/Journalist	Fallaci	Oriana	Italy
	Steffens	Joseph Lincoln	USA
	Thomas	Cal	USA
	Twain	Mark	USA
Author/Journalist - Pulitzer	Wallace	Myron Leon (Mike)	USA
Author/Mathematician	Carroll	Lewis	England
	Dodgson	Charles Lutwidge	England
Author/Painter	Lewis	Percy Wyndham	England
Author/Philosopher	Feibleman	James	USA
Author/Playwright	Levin	Ira	USA
	Maurier	Daphne du	England

SOLVER SERIES: NAME FINDER

FAME	LAST NAME	FIRST NAME	COUNTRY
Author - Pulitzer	Sillitoe	Alan	England
	Storey	David	England
Author/Poet	Adams	Sarah Flower	England
	Bly	Robert	USA
	Boccaccio	Giovanni	Italy
Author/Statesman	Tocqueville	Alexis de	France
Caricaturist/Illustrator	Cruikshank	George	England
Cartoonist	Barbera	Joe	USA
	Eisner	Will	USA
	Johnston	Lynn	Canada
	Rea	Gardner	USA
Cartoonist - Addams Family	Addams	Charles	USA
Cartoonist - Animated Movies	Avery	Frederick Bean (Tex)	USA
Cartoonist - Archie	Montana	Bob	USA
Cartoonist - BC	Hart	Johnny	USA
Cartoonist - Beetle Bailey	Walker	Mort	USA
Cartoonist - Berry's World	Berry	Jim	USA
Cartoonist - Blondie	Raymond	Alex	USA
Cartoonist - Blondie	Young	Murat Bernard (Chic)	USA
Cartoonist - Calvin & Hobbes	Watterson II	William B. (Bill)	USA
Cartoonist - Captain Marvel	Beck	Clarence Charles	USA
Cartoonist - Cathy	Guisewite	Cathy	USA
Cartoonist - Dick Tracy	Gould	Chester	USA
Cartoonist - Doonesbury	Trudeau	Garry	USA
Cartoonist - Editorial	MacNelly	Jeffery Kenneth (Jeff)	USA
Cartoonist - Family Circle	Keane	Bil	USA
Cartoonist - Far Side	Larson	Gary	USA
Cartoonist - Frank & Ernest	Thaves	Bob	USA
Cartoonist - Fritz the Cat	Crumb	Robert	USA
Cartoonist - Garfield	Davis	Jim	USA
Cartoonist - Hagar	Browne	Richard Arthur (Dik)	USA
Cartoonist - Lil Abner	Capp	Al	USA
Cartoonist - Mad Magazine	Drucker	Mort	USA
Cartoonist - Magazines	Wilson	Gahan	USA
Cartoonist - Nancy	Bushmiller	Ernie	USA
Cartoonist - New Yorker	Arno	Peter	USA
	Chast	Roz	USA
Cartoonist - Newspaper	Nast	Thomas	USA
Cartoonist - NY Times	Hirschfeld	Al	USA
Cartoonist - Peanuts	Schulz	Charles Monroe	USA
Cartoonist - Playboy	Kliban	Bernard	USA
Cartoonist - Political	Feiffer	Jules	USA
	Key	Ted	USA
	Levine	David	USA
	Low	David	England
Cartoonist - Popeye	Segar	Elzie Crisler	USA
Cartoonist - Pulitzer	Block	Herb	USA
	Breathed	Berke	USA
	Goldberg	Reuben Lucius (Rube)	USA
Cartoonist - Road Runner	Jones	Charles Marting (Chuck)	USA
Cartoonist - Sad Sack	Baker	George	USA
Cartoonist - Satiric	Young	Arthur Henry	USA
Cartoonist - Spiderman	Lee	Stanley Martin (Stan)	USA
Cartoonist - Terry and the Pirates	Caniff	Milton	USA
Cartoonist - The Simpsons	Groening	Matt	USA
Cartoonist - Tom and Jerry	Hanna	William (Bill)	USA
Cartoonist - Warner Bros.	Freleng	Isadore (Friz)	USA
Cartoonist - Woody Woodpecker	Lanz	Walter	USA

FAME	LAST NAME	FIRST NAME	COUNTRY
Cartoonist - Ziggy	Wilson	Tom	USA
Choreographer	Balanchine	George	USA
	Champion	Gower	USA
	Cunningham	Merce	USA
	Fokine	Michel	USA
	Petit	Roland	France
	Tharp	Twyla	USA
	Tune	Tommy	USA
Compiler - Arthurian Tales	Malory	Thomas	England
Composer	Anderson	Leroy	USA
	Arlen	Harold	USA
	Bach	Karl Phillipp Emanuel	Germany
	Barber	Samuel	USA
	Bartók	Bela	Hungary
	Beethoven	Ludwig van	Germany
	Beethoven	Ludwig Van	Austria
	Béjart	Maurice	France
	Boccherini	Luigi	Italy
	Borodin	Aleksandr Porfirevich	Russia
	Brahms	Johannes	Germany
	Britten	Edward Benjamin	England
	Bruch	Max	Germany
	Bruckner	Anton	Austria
	Busoni	Ferruccido Benvenuto	Italy
	Butler	Samuel	England
	Byrd	William	England
	Cadman	Charles Wakefield	USA
	Cage	John Milton	USA
	Carmichael	Hoagland Howard (Hoagy)	USA
	Carpenter	John Alden	USA
	Chadwick	George White	USA
	Charpentier	Gustave	France
	Cherubini	Luigi	Italy
	Chopin	Frederic François	Poland
	Coates	Eric	England
	Coleman	Cy	USA
	Copland	Aaron	USA
	Cowell	Henry Dixon	USA
	Crowell	Rodney	USA
	Czerny	Karl	Austria
	Debussy	Claude	France
	Delibes	Clément Philibert Léo	France
	Delius	Frederick	England
	Dozier	Lamont	USA
	Dupré	Marcel	France
	Dvořák	Antonín	Czechoslovakia
	Elgar	Edward William	England
	Fain	Samuel (Sammy)	USA
	Falla	Manuel	Spain
	Fauré	Gabriel Urbain	France
	Foss	Lukas	USA
	Friml	Charles Rudolf	USA
	Gershwin	George	USA
	Gershwin	Israel (Ira)	USA
	Glass	Philip	USA
	Glazunov	Aleksandr Konstantinovich	Russia
	Glinka	Mikhail Ivanovich	Russia
	Gluck	Christoph Willibald	Germany

SOLVER SERIES: NAME FINDER

FAME	LAST NAME	FIRST NAME	COUNTRY
Composer	Goldmark	Karl	Hungary
	Gounod	Charles François	France
	Green	Adolph	USA
	Grieg	Edvard Hagerup	Norway
	Halévy	Jacques	France
	Hamlisch	Marvin	USA
	Hammer	Jan	Czechoslovakia
	Handel	George Frederick	England
	Hanson	Howard	USA
	Harris	Roy Ellsworth	USA
	Haydn	Franz Joseph	Austria
	Herman	Gerald (Jerry)	USA
	Hindemith	Paul	USA
	Holland	Brian	USA
	Holland	Edward (Eddie)	USA
	Holst	Gustavus Theodore Von	England
	Honegger	Arthur	Switzerland
	Humperdinck	Engelbert	Germany
	Ives	Charles Edward	USA
	Janáček	Leoš	Czechoslovakia
	Jaques-Dalcroze	Émile	Switzerland
	Kander	John	USA
	Kern	Jerome David	USA
	Khachaturian	Aram	Russia
	Kodály	Zoltan	Hungary
	Lalo	Édouard Victor Antoine	France
	Mahler	Gustav	Austria
	Massenet	Jules Émile Frédéric	France
	Mendelssohn	Felix	Germany
	Milhaud	Darius	France
	Monteverdi	Claudio Giovanni Antonio	Italy
	Moussorgsky	Modest Petrovich	Russia
	Mozart	Wolfgang Amadeus	Austria
	Mussorgsky	Modest Petrovich	Russia
	Newman	Randy	USA
	Orff	Carl	Germany
	Ottorino	Respighi	Italy
	Pergolesi	Giovanni Battista	Italy
	Piston	Walter	USA
	Post	Mike	USA
	Poulenc	Francis Jean Marcel	France
	Prokofiev	Sergei	Russia
	Purcell	Henry	England
	Ravel	Maurice Joseph	France
	Respighi	Ottorino	Italy
	Rimsky-Korsakov	Nikolai Andreyevich	Russia
	Rossini	Gioacchino Antonio	Italy
	Rota	Nino	Italy
	Saint-Saëns	Charles Camille	France
	Salieri	Antonio	Austria
	Satie	Erik Alfred Leslie	France
	Scarlatti	Alessandro	Italy
	Scarlatti	Giuseppe	Italy
	Schönberg	Arnold	USA
	Schubert	Franz Peter	Austria
	Schuman	William Howard	USA
	Schumann	Robert Alexander	Germany
	Schutz	Heinrich	Germany

FAME	LAST NAME	FIRST NAME	COUNTRY
Composer	Seigmeister	Elie	USA
	Sessions	Roger Huntington	USA
	Shostakovich	Dmitri	Russia
	Sibelius	Jean	Finland
	Smetana	Bed_ich	Czechoslovakia
	Sondheim	Stephen	USA
	Straus	Oscar	Austria
	Styne	Jule	England
	Sullivan	Arthur Seymour	England
	Tallis	Thomas	England
	Tchaikovsky	Peter Ilyich	Russia
	Telemann	Georg Philipp	Germany
	Thomson	Virgil	USA
	Vaughan Williams	Ralph	England
	Villa-Lobos	Heitor	Brazil
	Wagner	Wilhelm Richard	Germany
	Walton	William Turner	England
	Webb	Jimmy	USA
	Webber	Andrew Lloyd	England
	Weber	Carl Maria von	Germany
	Webern	Anton	Austria
	Weill	Kurt	USA
	Williams	John Towner	USA
	Wolf	Hugo	Austria
	Wolf-Ferrari	Ermano	Italy
Composer - Ballet	Tudor	Anthony	England
Composer - Classical	Falla	Manuel De	Spain
Composer - Light Opera	Herbert	Victor	Ireland
Composer - Musicals	Bock	Jerry	USA
	Rodgers	Richard	USA
Composer - Opera	Donizetti	Gaetano	Italy
	Flotow	Friedrich von	Germany
	Leoncavallo	Ruggiero	Italy
	Lully	Jean Baptiste	France
	Mascagni	Pietro	Italy
	Menotti	Gian-Carlo	USA
	Meyerbeer	Giacomo	Germany
	Ponchielli	Amilcare	Italy
	Puccini	Giacomo	Italy
	Verdi	Giuseppe Fortunino Francisco	Italy
Composer - Operettas	Lehár	Franz	Hungary
	Offenbach	Jacques	France
Composer - Popular Songs	Porter	Cole	USA
Composer - Songs	Foster	Stephen Collins	USA
Composer - Waltzes	Strauss	Johann	Austria
Composer Classical	Berlioz	Hector	France
	Bloch	Ernest	USA
Composer Music	Berlin	Irving	USA
Composer Pianist	Greenberg	Jay	USA
Composer/Army Officer	Lisle	Claude Joseph Rouget de	France
Composer/Arranger	Wilson	Brian Douglas	USA
Composer/Band Master	Sousa	John Phillip	USA
Composer/Cellist	Casals	Pablo	Spain
Composer/Conductor	Bernstein	Leonard	USA
	Damrosch	Walter Johannes	USA
	Strauss	Richard	Germany
	Stravinsky	Igor Fedorovich	USA
Composer/Conductor/Violinist	Rachmaninoff	Sergi Vassilievich	Russia

SOLVER SERIES: NAME FINDER

FAME	LAST NAME	FIRST NAME	COUNTRY
Composer/Lutanist	Dowland	John	England
Composer/Movie Music	Bernstein	Elmer	USA
Composer/Music Critic	Taylor	Joseph Deems	USA
Composer/Opera	Auber	Daniel Francois Esprit	France
	Balfe	Michael William	England
	Bellini	Vincenzo	Italy
	Berg	Alban Maria Johannes	Austria
	Bizet	Georges	France
Composer/Organist	Bach	Johann Christian	Germany
	Bach	Johann Sebastian	Germany
	Buxtehude	Diderik	Denmark
	Couperin	François	France
	Franck	César	France
	Gibbons	Orlando	England
	Rameau	Jean Philippe	France
Composer/Pianist	Albéniz	Isaac	Spain
	Bacharach	Burt	USA
	Dohnányi	Ernö	Hungary
	Grainger	Percy Aldridge	USA
	Grofé	Ferde	USA
	Hofmann	Josef	USA
	Lewis	Ramsey	USA
	Liszt	Franz	Hungary
	MacDowell	Edward Alexander	USA
	Paderewski	Ignace Jan	Poland
	Rorem	Ned	USA
	Rubinstein	Anton Grigorevich	Russia
	Schifrin	Lalo	Argentina
	Schnabel	Artur	Austria
	Scriabin	Aleksandr Nikolayevich	Russia
	Tesh	John	USA
Composer/Pianist/Songwriter	Ager	Milton	USA
Composer/Pianist/Teacher	Leschetizky	Theodor	Poland
Composer/Producer	Eno	Brian	England
Composer/Song Writer	Weil	Cynthia	USA
Composer/Songwriter	Rome	Harold Jacob	USA
Composer/Violinist	Arne	Thomas Augustine	England
	Corelli	Arcangelo	Italy
	Joachim	Joseph	Hungary
	Kreisler	Fritz	USA
	Paganini	Niccolò	Italy
	Tartini	Giuseppe	Italy
	Vivaldi	Antonio	Italy
Composer/Violinist/Conductor	Enesco	Georges	Romania
Composer/Writer	Hoffmann	Ernst Theodor Amadeus	Germany
Drama Critic/Director	Bentley	Eric Russell	USA
	Beaumont	Francis	England
	Corneille	Pierre	France
	Ford	John	England
	Goldoni	Carlo	Italy
	Grillparzer	Franz	Austria
	Kyd	Thomas	England
	Massinger	Phillip	England
	Middleton	Thomas	England
	Molière	Jean Baptiste	France
	Molina	Gabriel Tirso de	Spain
	Otway	Thomas	England
	Peele	George	England

FAME	LAST NAME	FIRST NAME	COUNTRY
Drama Critic/Director	Sardou	Victorien	France
	Shirley	James	England
	Sholom	Aleichem	Russia
	Synge	John Millington	Ireland
	Wycherley	William	England
Dramatist - Poetic	Phillips	Stephen	England
Dramatist - Pulitzer	Abbott	George Francis	USA
	Akins	Zoe	USA
	Albee	Edward	USA
	Anderson	Maxwell	USA
	Auburn	David	USA
	Burrows	Abram S. (Abe)	USA
	Chase	Mary	USA
	Coburn	Donald L.	USA
	Connelly	Markus Cook (Marc)	USA
	Cristofer	Michael	USA
	Crouse	Russell	USA
	Cruz	Nilo	USA
	Dante	Nicholas	USA
	Davis	Owen	USA
	Edson	Margaret	USA
	Foote	Horton	USA
	Frings	Ketti	USA
	Fuller	Charles	USA
	Gale	Zona	USA
	Gershwin	Ira	USA
	Gilroy	Frank Daniel	USA
	Glaspell	Susan	USA
	Goodrich	Frances	USA
	Gordone	Charles	USA
	Green	Paul Eliot	USA
	Hackett	Albert	USA
	Hammerstein II	Oscar	USA
	Hart	Moss	USA
	Henley	Beth	USA
	Howard	Sidney	USA
	Hughes	Hatcher	USA
	Inge	William	Ireland
	Kaufman	George Simon	USA
	Kelly	George	USA
	Kingsley	Sidney	USA
	Kirkwood	James	USA
	Kramm	Joseph	USA
	Kushner	Tony	USA
	Lapine	James	USA
	Larson	Jonathan	USA
	Lindsay	Howard	USA
	Loesser	Frank	USA
	Logan	Joshua	USA
	MacLeish	Archibald	USA
	Mamet	David	USA
	Margulies	Donald	USA
	Miller	Arthur	USA
	Miller	Jason	USA
	Mosel	Tad	USA
	Norman	Marsha	USA
	Parks	Suzan-Lori	USA
	Patrick	John	USA

SOLVER SERIES: NAME FINDER

FAME	LAST NAME	FIRST NAME	COUNTRY
Dramatist - Pulitzer	Rice	Elmer L.	USA
	Rodgers	Richard	USA
	Ryskind	Morrie	USA
	Sackler	Howard	USA
	Saroyan	William	USA
	Schenkkan	Robert	USA
	Shanley	John Patrick	USA
	Shepard	Samuel (Sam)	USA
	Sherwood	Robert Emmet	USA
	Simon	Neil	USA
	Uhry	Alfred	USA
	Vogel	Paula	USA
	Wasserstein	Wendy	USA
	Weidman	Jerome	USA
	Wilder	Thornton Niven	USA
	Williams	Jesse Lynch	USA
	Williams	Tennessee	USA
	Wilson	August	USA
	Wilson	Lanford	USA
	Wright	Douglas	USA
	Zindel	Paul	USA
Dramatist/Architect	Vanbrugh	John	England
Dramatist/Critic	Ephraim	Gotthold	Germany
Dramatist/Essayist	Steele	Richard	England
Dramatist/Librettist	Scribe	Augustin Eugène	France
Dramatist/Poet	Alfieri	Vittorio	Italy
	Gay	John	England
Dramatist/Politician	Sheridan	Brinsley	England
Dramatist/Satirist	Marston	John	England
Economist	Galbraith	John Kenneth	Canada
Economist/Writer	Angell	Norman	England
Editor/Publisher	Bartlett	John	USA
Essayist	Crèvecoeur	Michel Guillaume Jean de	France
	Hazlitt	William	England
Essayist/Clergyman	Smith	Sydney	England
Essayist/Critic	Lamb	Charles	England
	Pater	Walter Horatio	England
	Quincey	Thomas De	England
Essayist/Moralist	Bruyère	Jean de La	France
Essayist/Naturalist/Critic	Krutch	Joseph Wood	USA
Essayist/Novelist	Beerbohm	Max	England
Essayist/Philosopher	Ortega y Gasset	José	Spain
Essayist/Poet	Addison	Joseph	England
Financier/Philanthropist	Hopkins	Johns	USA
Humorist	Ade	George	USA
	Benchley	Robert Charles	USA
	Browne	Charles Farrar	USA
	Nasby	Petroleum V.	USA
	Nye	Edgar Wilson	USA
	Perelman	Sidney Joseph	USA
	Shaw	Henry Wheeler	USA
	Ward	Artemus	USA
	White	Elwyn Brooks	USA
Humorist/Illustrator	Burgess	Frank Gelett	USA
Humorist/Journalist	Dunne	Finley Peter	USA
	Marquis	Donald Robert Perry	USA
Humorist/Sports Reporter	Lardner	Ringgold Wilmer	USA
Illustrator	Flagg	James Montgomery	USA

FAME	LAST NAME	FIRST NAME	COUNTRY
Illustrator	Rackham	Arthur	England
Journalist	Atkinson	Justin Brooks	USA
	Bennett	James Gordon	USA
	Caen	Herb	USA
Journalist - Magazine	Alexander	Shana	USA
	Brown	Helen Gurley	USA
	Cousins	Norman	USA
	Didion	Joan	USA
	Hoffman	Abbie	USA
	Steinem	Gloria	USA
	Wenner	Jann S.	USA
Journalist - Newspaper	Barnes	Clive	USA
	Barry	Dave	USA
	Bernstein	Carl	USA
	Bly	Nellie	USA
	Bombeck	Erma	USA
	Bradlee	Ben	USA
	Broder	David	USA
	Brody	Jane	USA
	Buchanan	Pat	USA
	Buchwald	Arthur	USA
	Buckley	William F.	USA
	Buren	Abigail Van	USA
	Canby	Vincent	USA
	Charen	Mona	USA
	Crist	Judith	USA
	Cronkite	Walter	USA
	Deford	Frank	USA
	Douglass	Frederick	USA
	Ebert	Roger	USA
	Germond	Jack W.	USA
	Gibson	Charles Dana	USA
	Greely	Horace	USA
	Greene	Bob	USA
	Kael	Pauline	USA
	Kinsley	Mike	USA
	Landers	Ann	USA
	Mencken	Henry Louis	USA
	Nessen	Ron	USA
	Novak	Robert	USA
	Pulitzer	Joseph	USA
	Pyle	Ernest Taylor (Ernie)	USA
	Quinn	Jane Bryant	USA
	Reed	Rex	USA
	Reid	Whitelaw	USA
	Reston	James Barrett	USA
	Rooney	Andy	USA
	Siskel	Gene	USA
	Smith	Liz	USA
	Smith	Walter (Red)	USA
	St. John	Adela Rogers	USA
	Thompson	Dorothy	USA
	Trillin	Calvin	USA
	Wells-Barnett	Ida Bell	USA
	Winchell	Walter	USA
Journalist - Newspaper - Pulitzer	Anderson	Jack	USA
	Breslin	Jimmy	USA

SOLVER SERIES: NAME FINDER

FAME	LAST NAME	FIRST NAME	COUNTRY
Journalist - Newspaper - Pulitzer	Safire	William	USA
	Will	George	USA
Journalist - Pulitzer	Halberstam	David	USA
Journalist - Radio	Cain	Bob	USA
	Harvey	Paul	USA
	Keillor	Garrison	USA
	Murrow	Edward Roscoe	USA
Journalist - Television	Albert	Al	USA
	Albert	Marv Philip	USA
	Albert	Steve	USA
	Allen	Mel	USA
	Assuras	Thalia	Canada
	Barber	Walter (Red)	USA
	Berger	Nadine	Canada
	Berman	Chris	USA
	Berman	Len	USA
	Blitzer	Wolf	USA
	Bradley	Ed	USA
	Brinkley	David McClure	USA
	Brokaw	Tom	USA
	Chancellor	John	USA
	Chung	Connie	USA
	Cooke	Alistair	England
	Cosell	Howard	USA
	Costas	Bob	USA
	Couric	Katie	USA
	Donahue	Phil	USA
	Donaldson	Sam	USA
	Downs	Hugh	USA
	Evans	Robert	USA
	Franklin	Joe	USA
	Frost	David	England
	Garagiola	Joseph Henry	USA
	Gowdy	Curt	USA
	Greenfield	Jeff	USA
	Gumble	Bryant	USA
	Hartman	David	USA
	Holt	Lester	USA
	Huntley	Chet	USA
	Jennings	Peter	Canada
	Kelley	Donna	USA
	Kent	Arthur	Canada
	Kent	Peter	Canada
	Kiker	Douglas	USA
	King	Larry	USA
	Koppel	Ted	USA
	Kuralt	Charles	USA
	Leach	Robin	England
	Lehrer	Jim	USA
	Levine	Irving R.	USA
	MacNeil	Robert	Canada
	Mahon	Jackie	Canada
	Maltin	Leonard	Canada
	Mansbridge	Peter	Canada
	Michaels	Alan Richard	USA
	Mitchell	Andrea	USA
	Moyers	William (Bill)	USA
	Mudd	Roger	USA

FAME	LAST NAME	FIRST NAME	COUNTRY
Journalist - Television	Musburger	Brent	USA
	Nance	James (Jim)	USA
	Pauley	Margaret Jane	USA
	Rather	Daniel Irving (Dan)	USA
	Reasoner	Harry	USA
	Rivera	Geraldo	USA
	Roberts	Cokie	USA
	Roberts	John	Canada
	Robertson	Lloyd	Canada
	Rose	Charlie	USA
	Rukeyser	Louis	USA
	Safer	Morley	Canada
	Sawyer	Diane	USA
	Schenkel	Chris	USA
	Scully	Vincent Edward (Vin)	USA
	Sesno	Frank	USA
	Shalit	Gene	USA
	Shriver	Maria	USA
	Snyder	Tom	USA
	Soles	Linden	Canada
	Stahl	Lesley	USA
	Walters	Barbara	USA
	Wenge	Ralph	USA
	Westheimer	Ruth	USA
Journalist/Author	Tarbell	Ida Minerva	USA
Journalist/Author - Pulitzer	Baker	Russell	USA
Journalist/Editor/Diplomat	Page	Walter Hines	USA
Journalist/Novelist	Oz	Amos	Israel
Journalist/Pacifist	Ossietzky	Carl von	Germany
Journalist/Pamphleteer	Desmoulins	Lucie Simplice Camille	France
Journalist/Psychologist - Newspaper	Brothers	Joyce	USA
Journalist/Publisher	Zenger	John Peter	USA
Journalist/Radical	Reed	John	USA
Journalist/Reformer	Cobbett	William	England
Journalist/Short Story Writer	Runyon	Alfred Damon	USA
Journalist/Social Reformer	Riis	Jacob	USA
Lexicographer	Bailey	Nathaniel	England
Librettist/Lyricist	Hammerstein	Oscar	USA
Literature - Nobel/Pulitzer	Hemingway	Ernest Miller	USA
Literature - Nobel Laureate	Agnon	Shmuel Yosef	Israel
	Aleixandre	Vincente	Spain
	Andric	Ivo	Yugoslavia
	Asturias	Miguel Angel	Guatemala
	Beckett	Samuel	Ireland
	Benavente	Jacinto	Spain
	Bergson	Henri	France
	Björnson	Björnstjerne Martinus	Norway
	Böll	Heinrich	Germany
	Brodsky	Joseph	USA
	Bunin	Ivan Alekseyevich	Russia
	Camus	Albert	France
	Canetti	Elias	Bulgaria
	Carducci	Giosuè	Italy
	Cela	Camilo José	Spain
	Churchill	Winston Leonard Spencer	England
	Coetzee	John M.	South Africa
	Deledda	Grazia	Italy
	Echegaray	José	Spain

FAME	LAST NAME	FIRST NAME	COUNTRY
Literature - Nobel Laureate	Eliot	Thomas Stearns	England
	Elytis	Odysseus	Greece
	Eucken	Rudolf Christoph	Germany
	Fo	Dario	Italy
	France	Anatole	France
	Galsworthy	John	England
	Gard	Roger Martin du	France
	Gide	André Paul Guillaume	France
	Gjellerup	Karl Adolph	Denmark
	Golding	William	England
	Gordimer	Nadine	South Africa
	Grass	Günter	Germany
	Hamsun	Knut Pedersen	Norway
	Hauptmann	Gerhart Johann Robert	Germany
	Heaney	Seamus	Ireland
	Heidenstam	Carl Gustaf Verner von	Sweden
	Hesse	Hermann	Switzerland
	Heyse	Paul Johann Ludwig	Germany
	Jelinek	Elfriede	Austria
	Jensen	Johannes Vilhelm	Denmark
	Jiménez	Juan Ramón	Spain
	Johnson	Eyvind	Sweden
	Karlfeldt	Erik Axel	Sweden
	Kawabata	Yasunari	Japan
	Kertész	Imre	Hungary
	Kipling	Joseph Rudyard	England
	Lagerkvist	Pär Fabian	Sweden
	Lagerlöf	Selma Ottillana Lovisa	Sweden
	Laxness	Halldór Kiljan	Iceland
	Lewis	Sinclair	USA
	Maeterlinck	Maurice Polidore Bernhard	Belgium
	Mahfouz	Naguib	Egypt
	Mann	Thomas	Germany
	Márquez	Gabriel Garcia	Colombia
	Martinson	Harry	Sweden
	Mauriac	François	France
	Milosz	Czeslaw	Poland
	Mistral	Frédéric	France
	Mistral	Gabriela	Chile
	Mommsen	Christian Matthias	Germany
	Montale	Eugenio	Italy
	Naipaul	Vidiadhar Surajprasad	England
	Neruda	Pablo	Chile
	Oe	Kenzaburo	Japan
	Pasternak	Boris Leonidovich	Russia
	Paz	Octavio	Mexico
	Perse	Saint-John	France
	Pinter	Harold	England
	Pirandello	Luigi	Italy
	Pontoppidan	Henrik	Denmark
	Prudhomme	Sully	France
	Quasimodo	Salvatore	Italy
	Reymont	Wladyslaw Stanislaw	Poland
	Roland	Romain	France
	Russell	Earl Bertrand Arthur William	England
	Sachs	Nellie	Sweden
	Saramago	José	Portugal
	Sartre	Jean-Paul	France

FAME	LAST NAME	FIRST NAME	COUNTRY
Literature - Nobel Laureate	Seferis	Giorgos	Greece
	Seifert	Jaroslav	Czechoslovakia
	Shaw	George Bernard	England
	Sholokhov	Mikhail Aleksandrovich	Russia
	Sienkiewicz	Henryk	Poland
	Sillanpää	Frans Eemil	Finland
	Simon	Claude	France
	Singer	Isaac Bashevis	USA
	Solzhenitsyn	Aleksander Isaevich	Russia
	Soyinka	Wole	Nigeria
	Spitteler	Carl Friedrich Georg	Switzerland
	Szymborska	Wislawa	Poland
	Tagoré	Rabindranath	India
	Undset	Sigrid	Norway
	Walcott	Derek	Saint Lucia
	White	Patrick	Australia
	Xingjian	Gao	France
	Yeats	William Butler	Ireland
Literature - Nobel/Pulitzer	Bellow	Saul	USA
Literature - Nobel/Pulitzer	Buck	Pearl Sydenstricker	USA
Literature - Nobel/Pulitzer	Faulkner	William	USA
Literature - Nobel/Pulitzer	Morrison	Toni	USA
Literature - Nobel/Pulitzer	O'Neill	Eugene Gladstone	USA
Literature - Nobel/Pulitzer	Steinbeck	John Ernst	USA
Lyric Poet	Béranger	Pierre Jean de	France
Lyricist	Harbach	Otto	USA
Musicologist/Critic	Tovey	Donald Francis	England
Novelist	Alcott	Louisa May	USA
	Alemán	Mateo	Spain
	Amis	Martin	England
	Anderson	Sherwood	USA
	Auchincloss	Louis	USA
	Austen	Jane	England
	Bagnold	Enid	England
	Ballard	James Graham	England
	Balzac	Honoré de	France
	Baroja	Pio	Spain
	Becker	Stephen	USA
	Bennett	Enoch Arnold	England
	Berger	Thomas	USA
	Blasco Ibáñez	Vincente	Spain
	Brontë	Anne	England
	Brontë	Charlotte	England
	Brown	Charles Brockden	USA
	Brunner	John Kilian Houston	England
	Cabell	James Branch	USA
	Cable	George Washington	USA
	Caldwell	Erskine	USA
	Churchill	Winston	USA
	Clark	Mary Higgins	USA
	Colette	Sidonie Gabrielle Claudine	France
	Collins	Jackie	England
	Collins	William Wilkie	England
	Compton-Burnett	Ivy	England
	Conroy	Pat	USA
	Cooper	James Fenimore	USA
	Crane	Stephen	USA
	Craven	Wes	USA

SOLVER SERIES: NAME FINDER

FAME	LAST NAME	FIRST NAME	COUNTRY
Novelist	Daudet	Aphonse	France
	Dickens	Charles	England
	Doctorow	Edgar Lawrence	USA
	Donleavy	James Patrick	USA
	Dostoyevsky	Feodor Mikhailovich	Russia
	Drabble	Margaret	England
	Dreiser	Theodore Herman Albert	USA
	Dunne	John Gregory	USA
	Edgeworth	Maria	England
	Eliot (Marian Evans)	George	England
	Ephron	Nora	USA
	Farrell	James Thomas	USA
	Feuchtwanger	Lion	Germany
	Fielding	Henry	England
	Flaubert	Gustave	France
	Forester	Cecil Scott	England
	Forster	Edward Morgan	England
	Gaddis	William	USA
	Gaskell	Elizabeth Cleghorn	England
	Gissing	George Robert	England
	Glyn	Elinor	England
	Godden	Margaret Rumer	England
	Godwin	Gail	USA
	Greene	Graham	England
	Grey	Zane	USA
	Guin	Ursula Kroeber Le	USA
	Haggard	Henry Ryder	England
	Heller	Joseph	USA
	Hope	Anthony	England
	Jókai	Maurus	Hungary
	Kazantzakis	Nikos	Greece
	Knowles	John	USA
	Krantz	Judith	USA
	Leonard	Elmore	USA
	Lessing	Doris May	Iran
	Loti	Pierre	France
	Maas	Peter	USA
	Macaulay	Rose	England
	McCarthy	Mary	USA
	McCullers	Carson	USA
	Melville	Herman	USA
	Mitford	Nancy	England
	Moravia	Alberto	Italy
	Nexo	Martin Andersen	Denmark
	Norris	Frank	USA
	Oates	Joyce Carol	USA
	Oppenheim	Edward Phillips	England
	Parker	Gilbert	Canada
	Powys	Theodore Francis	England
	Proust	Marcel	France
	Pynchon Jr.	Thomas Ruggles	USA
	Reade	Charles	England
	Remarque	Erich Maria	USA
	Richardson	Henry Handel	Australia
	Richardson	Samuel	England
	Rolvaag	Ole Edvart	USA
	Sage	Alain René Le	France
	Shelley	Mary Wollstonecraft	England

FAME	LAST NAME	FIRST NAME	COUNTRY
Novelist	Shute	Nevil	England
	Smollett	Tobias George	England
	Sontag	Susan	USA
	Spark	Muriel Sarah	Scotland
	Sterne	Laurence	England
	Stone	Irving	USA
	Stowe	Harriet Elizabeth Beecher	USA
	Sue	Eugene	France
	Tarkington	Newton Booth	USA
	Thackeray	William Makepeace	England
	Theroux	Paul Edward	USA
	Trollope	Anthony	England
	Tryon	Thomas	USA
	Turgenev	Ivan Sergeevich	Russia
	Umberto	Eco	Italy
	Uris	Leon	USA
	Verne	Jules	France
	Vonnegut Jr.	Kurt	USA
	Vries	Peter De	USA
	Ward	Mary Augusta Arnold	England
	Wassermann	Jakob	Germany
	Waugh	Alexander Raban (Alec)	England
	Waugh	Evelyn Arthur St. John	England
	West	Nathanael	USA
	White	Terence Hanbury	India
	Wister	Owen	USA
	Wodehouse	Pelham Grenville	England
	Wolfe	Thomas Clayton	USA
	Wright	Richard	USA
	Zola	Emile Édouard Charles Antoine	France
Novelist - Crime Fiction	Cain	James Mallahan	USA
	Carr	John Dickson	USA
	Chandler	Raymond	USA
	Marsh	Ngaio	New Zealand
	McBain	Ed	USA
Novelist - Historical	Costain	Thomas	Canada
Novelist - Horror	King	Stephen Edwin	USA
Novelist - Pulitzer	Barnes	Magaret Ayer	USA
	Cather	Willa Sibert	USA
	Coll	Steve	USA
	Cozzens	James Gould	USA
	Cunningham	Michael	USA
	Davis	Harold Lenoir	USA
	Eugenides	Jeffrey	USA
	Farge	Oliver La	USA
	Flavin	Martin	USA
	Glasgow	Ellen Anderson Gholson	USA
	Guthrie	Alfred Bertram	USA
	Johnson	Josephine Winslow	USA
	Jones	Edward P.	USA
	Kantor	Mackinlay	USA
	Kennedy	William	USA
	Lahiri	Jhumpa	USA
	Lee	Harper	USA
	Malamud	Bernard	USA
	Marquand	John Phillips	USA
	McMurtry	Larry	USA
	McPherson	James Alan	USA

SOLVER SERIES: NAME FINDER

FAME	LAST NAME	FIRST NAME	COUNTRY
Novelist - Pulitzer	Miller	Caroline	USA
	Millhauser	Steven	USA
	Momaday	Navarre Scott	USA
	Peterkin	Julia	USA
	Poole	Ernest	USA
	Porter	Katherine Anne	USA
	Rawlings	Marjorie Kinnan	USA
	Richter	Conrad	USA
	Robinson	Marilynne	USA
	Roth	Philip	USA
	Russo	Richard	USA
	Shaara	Michael	USA
	Sinclair	Upton Beall Jr.	USA
	Smiley	Jane	USA
	Stafford	Jean	USA
	Stegner	Wallace Earle	USA
	Stribling	Thomas Sigismund	USA
	Taylor	Peter	USA
	Toole	John Kennedy	USA
	Updike	John	USA
	Warren	Robert Penn	USA
	Welty	Eudora	USA
	Wharton	Edith	USA
	Wilson	Margaret	USA
Novelist - Pulp Fiction	Thompson	Jim	USA
Novelist/Art Critic	Goncourt	Edmond Louis Huot de	France
	Goncourt	Jules Alfred Huot de	France
Novelist/Artist	Passos	John Roderigo Dos	USA
Novelist/Clergyman	Kingsley	Charles	England
Novelist/Critic	Powys	John Cowper	England
	West	Rebecca	England
Novelist/Critic/Editor	Howells	William Dean	USA
Novelist/Diarist	Burney	Fanny	England
Novelist/Dramatist	Gogol	Nikolai Vasillevich	Russia
	Lesage	Alain René	France
	Strindberg	Johan August	Sweden
Novelist/Dramatist/Playwright	Dumas	Alexandre	France
Novelist/Essayist	Beyle	Marie Henri	France
	Bourget	Paul Charles Joseph	France
	Douglas	George Norman	England
	Huxley	Aldous Leonard	England
	Stendhal	Marie Henri	France
Novelist/Essayist/Historian	Mérimée	Prosper	France
Novelist/Essayist/Philosopher	Beauvoir	Simone de	France
Novelist/General	Wallace	Lewis	USA
Novelist/Historian	Eggleston	Edward	USA
	Wells	Herbert George	England
Novelist/Illustrator	Maurier	George Louis Palmella du	England
Novelist/Journalist	Barbusse	Henri	France
Novelist/Journalist - Pulitzer	O'Connor	Edwin	USA
Novelist/Journalist/Editor	Davis	Richard Harding	USA
Novelist/Literary Critic	Vittorini	Elio	Italy
Novelist/Naval Officer	Marryat	Frederick	England
Novelist/Philosopher	Rand	Ayn	USA
Novelist/Physician	Doyle	Arthur Conan	England
Novelist/Physicist	Snow	Charles Percy	England
Novelist/Playwright	Bojer	Johan	Norway
	Ervine	John Greer	England

FAME	LAST NAME	FIRST NAME	COUNTRY
Novelist/Playwright	Genêt	Jean	France
	Giraudoux	Hippolyte Jean	France
	Gorki	Maxim	Russia
	Kobo	Abe	Japan
	Maugham	William Somerset	England
	Montherlant	Henri Millon de	France
	Schnitzler	Arthur	Austria
	Vidal	Eugene Luther Gore	USA
	Zangwill	Israel	England
	Zweig	Stefan	Austria
Novelist/Playwright/Critic	Moore	George Augustus	Ireland
	Priestley	John Boynton	England
Novelist/Playwright/Essayist	Zweig	Arnold	Germany
Novelist/Poet	Brontë	Emily	England
	Kerouac	Jack	USA
Novelist/Poet - Pulitzer	Agee	James	USA
Novelist/Scholar/Linguist	Tolkien	John Ronald Reuel	England
Novelist/Short Story Writer	Adams	Alice Boyd	USA
	Anaïs	Nin	France
	Barth	John Simmons	USA
	Conrad	Joseph	Ukraine
	Hawthorne	Nathaniel	USA
	London	Jack	USA
	Maupassant	Henri René Albert Guy de	France
	Onetti	Juan Carlos	Paraguay
	Salinger	Jerome David	USA
	Wilson	Angus Frank Johnstone	England
Novelist/Social Theorist	Tolstoy	Leo Nikolayevich	Russia
Novelist/Soldier	Sade	Alponse François de	France
Novelist/Statesman	Buchan	John	Scotland
Novelistt	Susann	Jacqueline	USA
Philologist - Fairy Tales	Grimm	Jakob	Germany
	Grimm	Wilhelm	Germany
Playwright	Alvarez Quintero	Joaquin	Spain
	Alvarez Quintero	Serafin	Spain
	Anouilh	Jean	France
	Archer	William	Scotland
	Augier	Guillaume Victor Emile	France
	Brecht	Bertolt	Germany
	Chapman	George	England
	Congreve	William	England
	Crothers	Rachel	USA
	Daly	John Augustin	USA
	Dekker	Thomas	England
	Etherege	George	England
	Farquar	George	England
	Fitch	William Clyde	USA
	Fry	Christopher	England
	Fugard	Athol	South Africa
	Gregory	Augusta	Ireland
	Hellman	Lillian	USA
	Ionesco	Eugene	France
	Kotzebue	August Friedrich Ferdinand	Germany
	Moss	Hart	USA
	O'Casey	Sean	Ireland
	Odets	Clifford	USA
	Orton	John Kingsley (Joe)	England
	Osborne	John James	England

SOLVER SERIES: NAME FINDER

FAME	LAST NAME	FIRST NAME	COUNTRY
Playwright	Pinero	Arthur Wing	England
	Sheridan	Richard Brinsley	Ireland
	Stoppard	Tom	England
	Toller	Ernst	Germany
Playwright/Actor	Belasco	David	USA
	Guitry	Sacha	France
Playwright/Author	Behan	Brendan	Ireland
Playwright/Critic/Actor	Granville-Barker	Harley	England
Playwright/Novelist	Andreyev	Leonid Nikolayevich	Russia
	Asch	Sholem	USA
	Barrie	James Matthew	England
	Bulwer-Lytton	Edward George Earl	England
	Čapek	Karel	Czechoslovakia
	Goldman	James	USA
	Molnár	Ferenc	Hungary
Playwright/Novelist/Writer	Milne	Alan Alexander	England
Playwright/Translator	Udall	Nicholas	England
	Uvedale	Nicholas	England
Playwright/Writer - Mysteries	Rinehart	Mary Roberts	USA
Poet	Ady	Endre	Hungary
	Alighieri	Dante	Italy
	Austin	Alfred	England
	Baudelaire	Pierre Charles	France
	Blok	Alexandr Alexandrovich	Russia
	Boiardo	Matteo Maria	Italy
	Bradstreet	Anne	USA
	Brooke	Rupert	England
	Browning	Elizabeth Barrett	England
	Browning	Robert	England
	Bryant	William Cullen	USA
	Bulwer	Edward Robert	England
	Burns	Robert	Scotland
	Cammaerts	Émile Léon	Belgium
	Camões	Luiz Vaz de	England
	Campbell	Thomas	Scotland
	Carew	Thomas	England
	Chatterton	Thomas	England
	Chaucer	Geoffrey	England
	Chénier	André	France
	Ciardi	John	USA
	Clough	Arthur Hugh	England
	Collins	William	England
	Cowper	William	England
	Crabbe	George	England
	Crane	Harold Hart	USA
	Cullen	Countee	USA
	Cummings	Edward Estlin	USA
	D'Annunzio	Gabriele	Italy
	Dickey	James	USA
	Dickinson	Emily Elizabeth	USA
	Dobson	Henry Austin	England
	Donne	John	England
	Drayton	Michael	England
	Dunbar	Paul Laurence	USA
	Dunbar	William	Scotland
	Éluard	Paul	France
	Foscolo	Ugo	Italy
	Gibran	Kahlil	Lebanon

FAME	LAST NAME	FIRST NAME	COUNTRY
Poet	Ginsberg	Allen	USA
	Gower	John	England
	Gray	Thomas	England
	Guest	Edgar	England
	Herrick	Robert	England
	Hogg	James	Scotland
	Housman	Alfred Edward	England
	Hughes	Edward James (Ted)	England
	Keats	John	England
	Key	Francis Scott	USA
	Khayyám	Omar	Persia
	Kilmer	Alfred Joyce	USA
	Lamartine	Alphonse Marie Louis de	France
	Langland	William	England
	Lanier	Sidney	USA
	Lazarus	Emma	USA
	Leconte de Lisle	Charles Marie René	England
	Lindsay	Nicholas Vachel	USA
	Longfellow	Henry Wadsworth	USA
	Lorca	Federico Garcia	Spain
	Lovelace	Richard	England
	Macpherson	James	Scotland
	Markham	Charles Edwin	USA
	Marvell	Andrew	England
	Masters	Edgar Lee	USA
	Mayakovsky	Vladimirovich	Russia
	Mickiewicz	Adam	Poland
	Miller	Joaquin	USA
	Milton	John	England
	Moore	Clement Clarke	USA
	Moore	Thomas	Ireland
	Nash	Ogden	USA
	Noyes	Alfred	England
	Olson	Charles	USA
	Owen	Wilfred	England
	Patmore	Coventry Kersey Dighton	England
	Piercy	Marge	USA
	Pope	Alexander	England
	Pound	Ezra Loomis	USA
	Prior	Matthew	England
	Pushkin	Aleksandr Sergeyevich	Russia
	Quarles	Francis	England
	Riley	James Whitcomb	USA
	Rimbaud	Jean Nicolas Arthur	France
	Ronsard	Pierre de	France
	Rossetti	Christina Georgina	England
	Rroethke	Theodore	USA
	Shelley	Percy Bysshe	England
	Skelton	John	England
	Spenser	Edmund	England
	Suckling	John	England
	Thomas	Dylan Marlais	Wales
	Thompson	Francis	England
	Thomson	James	Scotland
	Torquato	Tasso	Italy
	Verlaine	Paul	France
	Villon	Francois	France
	Waller	Edmund	England

SOLVER SERIES: NAME FINDER

FAME	LAST NAME	FIRST NAME	COUNTRY
Poet	Wheatley	Phillis	USA
	Whitman	Walter	USA
	Whittier	John Greenleaf	USA
	Wilcox	Ella Wheeler	USA
	Wylie	Eleanor	USA
	Young	Edward	England
Poet – Epic	Tasso	Torquato	Italy
	Wolfram	Von Eschenbach	Germany
Poet – Lyric	Dowson	Ernest Christopher	England
	Rilke	Rainer Maria	Austria
Poet – Pulitzer	Aiken	Conrad Potter	USA
	Ashbery	John	USA
	Auden	Wystan Hugh	England
	Bacon	Leonard	USA
	Benét	Stephen Vincent	USA
	Benét	William Rose	USA
	Berryman	John	USA
	Bishop	Elizabeth	USA
	Brooks	Gwendolyn	USA
	Coffin	Robert P. Tristram	USA
	Dennis	Carl	USA
	Dillon	George	USA
	Doren	Mark Albert Van	USA
	Dove	Rita	USA
	Dugan	Alan	USA
	Dunn	Stephen	USA
	Duyn	Mona Jane Van	USA
	Eberhart	Richard	USA
	Frost	Robert Lee	USA
	Gluck	Louise	USA
	Graham	Jorie	USA
	Hecht	Anthony	USA
	Hillyer	Robert	USA
	Howard	Richard	USA
	Justice	Donald	USA
	Kinnell	Galway	USA
	Kizer	Carolyn	USA
	Komunyakaa	Yusef	USA
	Kooser	Ted	USA
	Kumin	Maxine	USA
	Kunitz	Stanley	USA
	Levine	Philip	USA
	Lowell	Amy	USA
	Lowell	Robert Trail Spence Jr.	USA
	MacLeish	Archibald	USA
	McGinley	Phyllis	USA
	Meredith	William	USA
	Merrill	James	USA
	Merwin	William Stanley	USA
	Millay	Edna St. Vincent	USA
	Moore	Marianne Craig	USA
	Mueller	Lisel	Germany
	Muldoon	Paul	Ireland
	Nemerov	Howard	USA
	Oliver	Mary	USA
	Oppen	George	USA
	Plath	Sylvia	USA
	Robinson	Edwin Arlington	USA

FAME	LAST NAME	FIRST NAME	COUNTRY
Poet - Pulitzer	Roethke	Theodore	USA
	Sandburg	Carl	USA
	Schuyler	James	USA
	Sexton	Anne	USA
	Shapiro	Karl	USA
	Simic	Charles	Yugoslavia
	Simpson	Louis	Jamaica
	Snodgrass	William DeWitt	USA
	Snyder	Gary	USA
	Speyer	Leonora	USA
	Stevens	Wallace	USA
	Strand	Mark	Canada
	Tate	James	USA
	Taylor	Henry	USA
	Teasdale	Sara	USA
	Viereck	Peter Robert Edwin	USA
	Warren	Robert Penn	USA
	Widdemer	Margaret	USA
	Wilbur	Richard	USA
	Williams	Charles Kenneth	USA
	Williams	William Carlos	USA
	Wright	Charles	USA
	Wright	Franz	USA
	Wright	James Arlington	USA
	Wurdemann	Audrey	USA
	Zaturenska	Marya	Russia
Poet - Religion	Crashaw	Richard	England
Poet - Symbolist	Mallarmé	Stéphane	France
Poet Laureate	Betjeman	John	England
	Bridges	Robert Seymour	England
	Dryden	John	England
	Tennyson	Alfred	England
	Wordsworth	William	England
Poet Laureate/Dramatist	Tate	Nahum	England
Poet Laureate/Novelist	Lewis	Cecil Day	England
Poet Laureate/Writer	Masefield	John	England
	Southey	Robert	England
Poet/Anthologist	Palgrave	Francis Turner	England
Poet/Anthologist/Critic	Untermeyer	Louis	USA
Poet/Art Critic	Brent	George	France
	Read	Herbert Edward	England
Poet/Artist	Blake	William	England
Poet/Author	Ariosto	Lodovico	Italy
Poet/Bookseller	Ramsay	Allen	Scotland
Poet/Chronicler	Froissart	Jean	France
Poet/Classical Scholar	MacNeice	Louis	England
Poet/Composer	Campion	Thomas	England
	Silverstein	Sheldon Allan (Shel)	USA
Poet/Courtier	Surrey	Henry Howard	England
Poet/Critic	Boileau-Despréaux	Nicholas	France
	Breton	André	France
	Ransom	John Crowe	USA
	Schlegel	August Wilhelm von	Germany
	Sitwell	Edith	England
	Sitwell	Sacheverell	England
	Spender	Stephen	England
	Sully-Prudhomme	René François Armand	France
	Swinburne	Algernon Charles	England

SOLVER SERIES: NAME FINDER

FAME	LAST NAME	FIRST NAME	COUNTRY
Poet/Critic	Tate	John Orley Allen	USA
Poet/Critic/Biographer	Gosse	Edmund William	England
Poet/Diplomat	Barlow	Joel	USA
	Meredith	Owen	England
	Wyatt	Thomas	England
Poet/Dramatist	Goethe	Johann	Germany
	Jonson	BenJamin (Ben)	England
	Marlowe	Christopher	England
	Racine	Jean Baptiste	France
	Rostand	Edmond	France
	Scarron	Paul	France
	Schiller	Johann Christoph Friedrich von	Germany
	Shakespeare	William	USA
Poet/Dramatist/Pamphleteer	Greene	Robert	England
Poet/Editor	Tzara	Tristan	Romania
Poet/Editor/Critic	Henley	William Ernest	England
Poet/Essayist	Appollinaire	Guillaume	France
	Arnold	Matthew	England
	Cowley	Abraham	England
	Heine	Heinrich	Germany
	Lowell	James Russell	USA
	Russell	George William	Ireland
	Valéry	Paul Ambroise	France
Poet/Essayist/Critic	Hunt	James Henry Leigh	England
Poet/Essayist/Philosopher	Emerson	Ralph Waldo	USA
Poet/Essayist/Revolutionary	Martí	José Julian	Cuba
Poet/Historian	Angelou	Maya	USA
Poet/Humorist	Hood	Thomas	England
Poet/Ice Historian	Snorri	Sturluson	Iceland
Poet/Jesuit Priest	Hopkins	Gerard Manley	England
Poet/Journalist	Arnold	Edwin	England
	Carman	William Bliss	Canada
	Field	Eugene	USA
	Freneau	Phillip Morin	USA
	Taylor	James Bayard	USA
Poet/Librettist	Gilbert	William Schwenck	England
	Ponte	Lorenzo da	Italy
Poet/Literary Historian	Uhland	Johann Ludwig	Germany
Poet/Man of Letters	Vigny	Alfred Victor	France
Poet/Metaphysician	Vaughan	Henry	England
Poet/Novelist	Aldrich	Thomas Bailey	USA
	Bodenheim	Maxwell	USA
	Gautier	Théophile	France
	Hardy	Thomas	England
	Joyce	James Augustine Aloysius	Ireland
	Larkin	Philip	England
	Lawrence	David Herbert	England
	Lermontov	Mikhail Yurievich	Russia
	Louÿs	Pierre	France
	Macdonald	George	Scotland
	Manzoni	Alessandro	Italy
	Mare	Walter de la	England
	Meredith	George	England
	Murasaki	Shikibu	Japan
	Peacock	Thomas Love	England
	Scott	Walter	Scotland
	Stephens	James	Ireland
Poet/Novelist/Critic	Graves	Robert Ranke	England

FAME	LAST NAME	FIRST NAME	COUNTRY
Poet/Novelist/Dramatist	Duhamel	Georges	France
Poet/Novelist/Essayist	Stevenson	Robert Louis Ballfour	Scotland
Poet/Novelist/Patriot	Rizal	José Mercado	Philippines
Poet/Novelist/Playwright	Cervantes	Miguel de	Spain
	Cocteau	Jean	France
	Hugo	Victor Marie	England
	Romains	John	France
	Werfel	Franz	Austria
	Wilde	Oscar	England
Poet/Novelist/Translator	Wieland	Christopher Martin	Germany
Poet/Painter	Rossetti	Dante Gabriel	England
Poet/Patriot	Petöfi	Sándor	Hungary
Poet/Playwright	Beddoes	Thomas Lovell	England
	Claudel	Paul Louis Charles	France
	Columbo	Padraic	Ireland
	D'Avenant	William	England
	Delavigne	Jean François Casimir	France
	Dunsany	Edward John Moreton	Ireland
	Garcia Lorca	Federico	Spain
	Gay	John	England
	Hebbel	Christian Friedrich	Germany
	Hofmannsthal	Hugo von	Austria
	Ibsen	Henrik	Norway
	Moody	William Vaughn	USA
	Zorrilla	José	Spain
Poet/Playwright - Pulitzer	Fletcher	John Gould	England
Poet/Playwright/Novelist	Goldsmith	Oliver	Ireland
Poet/Satirist	Map	Walter	Wales
Poet/Scholar	Petrarch	Francesco	Italy
Poet/Short Story Writer/Critic	Poe	Edgar Allan	USA
Poet/Social Reformer	Howe	Julia Ward	USA
Poet/Song Writer	Cohen	Leonard	Canada
Poet/Statesman	Sackville	Thomas	England
	Sidney	Philip	England
Poet/Translator	Fitzgerald	Edward	England
Poet/Travel Writer	Doughty	Charles Montagu	England
Poet/Writer	Borges	Jorge Luis	Argentina
	Fontaine	Jean de La	France
	Hughes	James Langston	USA
	Landor	Walter Savage	England
	Musset	Louis Charles Alfred de	France
	Neruda	Jan Nepomuk	Czechoslovakia
	Parker	Dorothy	USA
	Sassoon	Siegfried Lorraine	England
	Symonds	John Addington	England
Poet/Writer/Scholar	Miller	Jonathon	England
Producer/Author	Beaverbrook	William Maxwell Aitkin	England
Publisher	Ochs	Adolph Simon	USA
Publisher - Newspaper	Mandeville	Bernard de	England
Satirist	Swift	Jonathan	England
Satirist/Humorist	Rabelais	François	France
Satirist/Pamphleteer	Nashe	Thomas	England
Scholar/Critic	Bentley	Richard	England
Screenwriter	Caldwell	Sarah	USA
	Hecht	Ben	USA
	Kazan	Elia	Turkey
	Ponicsan	Darryl	USA
Screenwriter - Mash	Mumford	Thad	USA

SOLVER SERIES: NAME FINDER

FAME	LAST NAME	FIRST NAME	COUNTRY
Screenwriter/Playwright	Loos	Anita	USA
	Rabe	David	USA
Social Worker	Addams	Jane	USA
Song Writer	Mann	Barry	USA
	Nesmith	Michael	USA
Song Writer/Guitarist	Kantner	Paul	USA
Song Writer/Keyboarder	Banks	Tony	England
Song Writer/Producer	Spector	Harvey Philip (Phil)	USA
Writer	Adler	Cyrus	USA
	Alger	Horatio	USA
	Amiel	Henri Frédéric	Switzerland
	Aretino	Pietro	Italy
	Ascham	Roger	England
	Babel	Isaac	Russia
	Baum	Lyman Frank	USA
	Belloc	Joseph Hillaire Pierre	England
	Bernardin de Saint-Pierre	Jacques Henri	France
	Burnett	Frances Hodgson	USA
	Burroughs	Edgar Rice	USA
	Carlyle	Thomas	England
	Castle	Vernon	England
	Chesterton	Gilbert Keith	England
	Christie	Agatha	England
	Coryate	Thomas	England
	Dahl	Roald	Wales
	Defoe	Daniel	England
	Ehrenburg	Ilya Grigorievich	Russia
	Faraj	Abd al-Salam	Egypt
	Fisher	Dorothy Canfield	USA
	Friedan	Betty	USA
	Hearn	Lafcadio	USA
	Henty	George Alfred	England
	Herzl	Theodor	Austria
	Irving	John	USA
	Isherwood	Christopher William Bradshaw	USA
	Jewett	Sarah Orne	USA
	Kafka	Franz	Austria
	Lamb	Mary Ann	England
	Lewis	Clive Staples	England
	Miller	Henry	USA
	Montagu	Mary Wortley	England
	Orwell	George	England
	Passos	John Roderigo Dos	USA
	Quiller-Couch	Arthur Thomas	England
	Reville	Alma	England
	Richter	Jean Paul	Germany
	Rosten	Leo	USA
	Service	Robert William	Canada
	Sévigné	Marie de Rabutin-Chantal	France
	Silone	Ignazio	Italy
	Staël	Anne Louise Germaine Necker	France
	Stein	Gertrude	USA
	Trollope	Frances Milton	England
	Walpole	Horace	England
	Walton	Izaak	England
	Ward	Barbara	England
	Wollstonecraft	Mary	England
Writer - Comedy	Muir	Frank	England

FAME	LAST NAME	FIRST NAME	COUNTRY
Writer - Cooking	Escoffier	Auguste	France
Writer - Detective Stories	Gaboriau	Émile	France
Writer - Diary	Pepys	Samuel	England
Writer - Mystery	Biggars	Earl Derr	USA
Writer - Religious Tracts	More	Hannah	England
Writer - Short Stories	Harte	Bret	USA
	Mansfield	Katherine	England
	Shepherd	Jean Parker	USA
Writer - Sign Language	Epee	Michel de l'	France
Writer/Adventurer	Lawrence	Thomas Edward	England
	Shaw	Thomas Edward	England
Writer/Art Critic	Brookner	Anita	England
Writer/Art Critic/Social Reformer	Ruskin	John	England
Writer/Aviator	Sainte-Exupéry	Antoine de	France
Writer/Clergyman	Brooks	Phillips	USA
	Burton	Robert	England
	Mather	Cotton	USA
	Mather	Increase	USA
	Weems	Mason Locke	USA
Writer/Compiler - Fairy Tales	Perrault	Charles	France
Writer/Critic	Benjamin	Walter	Germany
	Lewes	George Henry	England
	Wilson	Edmund	USA
	Woollcott	Alexander Humphreys	USA
Writer/Diplomat	Castiglione	Baldassare	Italy
	Elyot	Thomas	England
	Johnson	James Weldon	USA
	Temple	William	England
Writer/Dramatist	Chekhov	Anton Pavlovich	Russia
Writer/Economist	Keyes	John Maynard	England
Writer/Editor	Ford	Ford Madox	England
Writer/Educator	Erskine	John	USA
	McLuhan	Herbert Marshall	Canada
	Wiggin	Kate Douglas	USA
Writer/Humorist	Clemens	Samuel Langhorne	USA
Writer/Humorist/Cartoonist	Thurber	James Grover	USA
Writer/Illustrator	Lofting	Hugh John	USA
	Pyle	Howard	USA
Writer/Illustrator - Children's Books	Potter	Beatrix	England
Writer/Lawyer	Boswell	James	Scotland
	Dana	Richard Henry	USA
Writer/Lecturer	Keller	Helen Adams	USA
Writer/Lexicographer	Florio	John	England
Writer/Lexicographer/Critic	Johnson	Samuel	England
Writer/Linguist	Borrow	George Henry	England
Writer/Literary Critic	Sainte-Beuve	Charles Augustin	France
Writer/Mythologist	Bulfinch	Thomas	USA
Writer/Naturalist	Beebe	Charles William	USA
	Burroughs	John	USA
	Thomson	John Arthur	Scotland
Writer/Naturalist/Illustrator	Seton	Ernest Thompson	USA
Writer/Philanthropist	Astor	Brooke Russell	USA
Writer/Philosopher	Sorel	Georges	France
Writer/Physician	Arbuthnot	John	Scotland
Writer/Poet	Andersen	Hans Christian	Denmark
Writer/Political Philosopher	Godwin	William	England
Writer/Politician	Constant	Benjamin	France
	Malraux	André	France

SOLVER SERIES: NAME FINDER

FAME	LAST NAME	FIRST NAME	COUNTRY
Writer/Preacher	Bunyan	John	England
Writer/Psychologist	Ellis	Henry Havelock	England
Writer/Publisher	Woolf	Leonard Sidney	England
Writer/Revolutionary Patriot	Paine	Thomas	USA
Writer/Satire	Bierce	Ambrose Gwinett	USA
Writer/Scholar	Dobie	James Frank	USA
Writer/Scholar/Critic	Matthews	James Brander	USA
Writer/Semanticist	Korzybski	Alfred Habdank	USA
Writer/Social Reformer	Fuller	Sarah Margaret	USA
	Higginson	Thomas Wentworth	USA
	Hughes	Thomas	England
Writer/Soldier	Bergerac	Cyrano de	France
Writer/Statesman	Machiavelli	Niccolo	Italy
	More	Thomas	England
Writer/Teacher	Nabokov	Vladimir	USA
Writer/Theorist	Bellamy	Edward	USA
Writer/Translator	Urquhart	Thomas	Scotland

EXPLORATION:

Colonist – America	Smith	John	England
Colonist – Massachusetts	Winthrop	John	England
Colonist – Plymouth	Winslow	Edward	England
Colonist – Virginia	Bacon	Nathaniel	USA
Explorer – Africa	Battuta	Abu Abdulla Ibn	Morocco
	Livingstone	David	Scotland
	Park	Mungo	Scotland
	Stanley	Henry Morton	England
Explorer – Africa Coast	Gama	Vasco da	Portugal
Explorer – Africa West	Landers	Richard Lemon	England
Explorer – Africa West Coast	Dias	Bartolomeu	Portugal
Explorer – Africa West/North	Kingsley	Mary Henrietta	England
Explorer – Alberta	Fraser	Simon	Canada
Explorer – Amazon Region	Condamine	Charles Marie de la	France
	Vespucci	Americo	Italy
Explorer – America	Hudson	Henry	England
Explorer – America Deserts	Powell	John Wesley	USA
Explorer – America East Coast	Herjulfsson	Bjarni	Iceland
	Perez	Juan	Spain
	Verrazano	Giovanni da	Italy
Explorer – America South	Harpe	Jean Baptiste de la	France
Explorer – America West	Thompson	David	Canada
Explorer – Antarctic	Byrd	Richard Evelyn	USA
	Hillary	Edmund Percival	New Zealand
	Mawson	Douglas	Australia
	Scott	Robert Falcon	England
	Shackleton	Henry Ernest	England
	Wilkes	Charles	USA
	Weddell	James	England
Explorer – Arctic	Baffin	William	England
	Boyd	Louise Arner	USA
	Franklin	John	England
	Henson	Matthew Alexander	USA
	MacMillan	Donald Baxter	USA
	Nansen	Fridtjof	Norway
	Nordenskjöld	Nils Adolf Erik	Sweden
	Parry	William Edward	England
	Rae	John	Scotland

FAME	LAST NAME	FIRST NAME	COUNTRY
Explorer - Arctic	Rasmussen	Knud Johan Victor	Denmark
	Ross	John	England
	Stefansson	Vilhjalmur	Canada
Explorer - Arctic/Australia	Cook	James	England
Explorer - Australia	Flinders	Matthew	England
	Hovell	William	England
	Hume	Hamilton	Australia
	Jantszoon	Willem	Netherlands
	Kennedy	Edmund	Australia
	Phillip	Arthur	England
Explorer - Australia Mountains	Strzelecki	Paul Edmund de	Poland
Explorer - Australia South East	Mitchell	Thomas Livingstone	Australia
Explorer - Australia West Coast	Hartog	Dirck	Netherlands
Explorer - Brazil	Cabral	Pedro Alvares	Portugal
Explorer - Brazil/Australia	Cunningham	Allan	England
Explorer - California	Anza	Juan Bautista de	Mexico
	Cabrillo	Juan Rodriguez	Spain
	Cermenho	Sebastian	Spain
	Portolá	Gaspar de	Spain
Explorer - Canada	Cabot	John	England
Explorer - Canada East Coast	Gilbert	Humphrey	England
Explorer - Canada Inland	Kelsey	Henry	England
Explorer - Canada West	Mackenzie	Alexander	Canada
	Vérandrye	Pierre de la	Canada
Explorer - Canada West Coast	Vancouver	George	England
Explorer - Caribbean	Columbus	Christopher	Italy
	Dampier	William	England
	Hawkins	John	England
	Pinzón	Martin Alonso	Spain
	Pinzón	Vincente Yáñez	Spain
Explorer - Central Asia	Ch'ien	Chang	China
	Quian	Zhang	China
Explorer - Central Australia	Burke	Robert O'Hara	Australia
	Wills	William John	Australia
Explorer - Chicago	Sable	Jean-Baptiste-Point du	France
Explorer - Circumnavigation	Drake	Francis	England
	Gray	Robert	USA
	Magellan	Ferdinand	Spain
Explorer - Colorado River	Ramie	Jacques la	Canada
Explorer - Cuba	Narvaez	Panfilo de	Spain
Explorer - Deep Sea	Beebe	William	USA
Explorer - Detroit	Cadillac	Antoine de la Mothe	France
Explorer - East Asia	Polo	Marco	Italy
Explorer - East Coast America	Ericson	Leif	Iceland
Explorer - Falkland Islands	Bougainville	Louis Antoinne de	France
Explorer - Florida	Aviles	Pedro Menendez de	Spain
	Leon	Juan Ponce de	Spain
	León	Juan Ponce de	Spain
Explorer - Great Lakes	Nicollet	Jean	France
Explorer - Greenland	Corte Real	Gaspar	Portugal
	Thorvaldson	Eric (The Red)	Norway
Explorer - Gulf of Mexico	Pineda	Alonso Alvarez de	Spain
Explorer - Hawaii	Perouse	Jean-François de la	France
Explorer - Himalayas	Younghusband	Francis	England
Explorer - Jamestown	Newport	Christopher	England
Explorer - Madagascar	Dias	Diogo	Portugal
Explorer - Manhattan	Minuit	Peter	Netherlands
Explorer - Marine	Cousteau	Jaques	France

SOLVER SERIES: NAME FINDER

FAME	LAST NAME	FIRST NAME	COUNTRY
Explorer - Marine	Earle	Sylvia Alice	USA
	Piccard	Jacques	Switzerland
Explorer - Marine/Titanic	Ballard	Robert	USA
Explorer - Mexico	Castillo	Bernal Diaz Del	Spain
	Córdoba	Francisco Fernández de	Spain
	Coronado	Francisco Vásquez de	Spain
	Cortés	Hernán	Spain
	Kino	Eusebio Francisco	Spain
Explorer - Mexico West Coast	Vizcaíno	Sebastián	Spain
Explorer - Mexico/New Mexico	Niza	Marcos de	Italy
Explorer - Minnesota	Radisson	Pierre Esprit	France
Explorer - Mississippi River	Charlevoix	Pierre François-Xavier	France
	Dubuque	Julian	France
	Joliet	Louis	Canada
	Marquette	Jacques	France
	Pike	Zebulon Montgomery	USA
	Salle	Réne-Robert Cavelier de la	France
	Soto	Hernando de	Spain
Explorer - Missouri River	Clark	William	USA
	Lewis	Meriwether	USA
Explorer - Mongolia	Andrews	Roy Chapman	USA
Explorer - Mount Everest	Norgay	Tenzing	Nepal
Explorer - New Mexico	Oñate	Juan de	Spain
Explorer - New York	Stuyvesant	Peter	Netherlands
Explorer - North Africa	Eannes	Gil	Portugal
	Eberhardt	Isabella	Switzerland
Explorer - North Carolina	Ayllón	Lucas Vázquez de	Spain
Explorer - North Pole	Peary	Robert Edwin	USA
Explorer - North West Passage	Cabot	Sebastian	England
	Frobisher	Martin	England
Explorer - Panama	Balboa	Vasco Núnez de	Spain
Explorer - Phillipines	Urdaneta	Andres de	Spain
Explorer - Polar	Amunsden	Roald	Norway
	Ellsworth	Lincoln	USA
	Fiennes	Ranulf	England
	Ross	James Clark	England
	Wilkins	George Hubert	Australia
Explorer - Quebec	Champlain	Samuel de	France
Explorer - Siberia	Bering	Vitus Jonassen	Denmark
Explorer - South America	Humboldt	Alexander Von	Prussia
	Pizarro	Francisco	Spain
Explorer - South Australia	Eyre	Edward John	Australia
Explorer - South Pacific	Heyerdahl	Thor	Norway
	Quiros	Pedro Fernandez de	Portugal
Explorer - South/West America	Garcés	Francisco Tomás	Spain
Explorer - Spice Islands	Albuquerque	Alphonso de	Portugal
Explorer - St. Lawrence River	Cartier	Jacques	France
Explorer - Tasmania	Baudin	Nicholas	France
	Oxley	John Joseph Molesworth	Australia
	Tasman	Abel Janszoon	Netherlands
Explorer - Texas	Vaca	Alvar Nuñez Cabeza de	Spain
Explorer - West Africa	Behaim	Martin	Portugal
	Cadamosto	Alvise Da	Italy
Explorer - West America	Fuca	Juan de	Greece
Explorer - Central Asia	Hedin	Sven Anders	Sweden
Explorer- Orinoco River	Humboldt	Friedrich Heinrich	Germany
Explorer/Missionary - Mexico	Serra	Junípero	Spain
Explorer/Writer - Africa	Burton	Richard Francis	England

FAME	LAST NAME	FIRST NAME	COUNTRY
Frontiersman - America	Austin	Stephen Fuller	USA
	Carson	Christopher Houston (Kit)	USA
	Chapman	John (Johnny Appleseed)	USA
	Cody	William Frederick	USA
	Crockett	David (Davie)	USA
	Whitman	Marcus	USA
Frontiersman - California	Smith	Jedediah	USA
Frontiersman - Kentucky	Boone	Daniel	USA
Leader - Quakers	Penn	William	England
Pilgrim - Plymounth	Brewster	William	England

GAMES:

Bridge Expert	Culbertson	Ely	USA
	Goren	Charles Henry	USA
	Sharif	Omar	Egypt
Chess Player	Alekhine	Alexander	Russia
	Anand	Viswanathan	India
	Botvinnik	Mikhail	Russia
	Capablanca	José Raúl	Cuba
	Euwe	Max	Netherlands
	Fischer	Bobby	USA
	Karpov	Anatoly	Russia
	Kasimdzhanov	Rustam	Uzbekistan
	Kasparov	Gary	Russia
	Khalifman	Alexander	Russia
	Kramnik	Vladimir	Russia
	Lasker	Emanuel	Germany
	Petrosian	Tigran	Armenia
	Ponomariov	Ruslan	Ukraine
	Smyslov	Vasily	Russia
	Spassky	Boris	Russia
	Steinitz	Wilhelm	Czechoslovakia
	Tal	Mikhail Nekhemievich	Latvia

LAW & ORDER:

Chief Justice	Burger	Warren Earl	USA
	Chase	Salmon Portland	USA
	Marshall	John	USA
	Stone	Harlan Fiske	USA
	Taney	Roger Brooke	USA
	Vinson	Frederick Moore	USA
	Waite	Morrison Remick	USA
	Warren	Earl	USA
	White	Edward Douglas	USA
Director - FBI	Hoover	John Edgar	USA
Fraud Artist	Helmsley	Harry Edwin	USA
	Helmsley	Leona	USA
Highwayman	Turpin	Dick	England
Hunter	Canarray	Martha (Calamity) Jane	USA
Hunter/Scout/Indian Fighter	Cody	William (Buffalo Bill)	USA
Hunter/Sure Shot	Oakley	Annie	USA
Judge	Beane	Roy	USA
Judge - Simpson Case	Ito	Lance	USA
Jurist	Black	Hugo La Fayette	USA
	Blackstone	William	England
	Erskine	John	Scotland

SOLVER SERIES: NAME FINDER

FAME	LAST NAME	FIRST NAME	COUNTRY
Jurist	Hand	Billings Learned	USA
	Kent	James	USA
	Landis	Kenesaw Mountain	USA
	Lansing	John	USA
	Sewall	Samuel	USA
Jurist/Legal Historian	Maitland	Frederic William	England
Jurist/Patriot	Wythe	George	USA
Jurist/Statesman	Hughes	Charles Evans	USA
Jurist/Writer	Pollock	Frederick	England
Justice - Supreme Court	Blackmun	Harry Andrew	USA
	Brandeis	Louis Dembitz	USA
	Brennan	William Joseph	USA
	Cardozo	Benjamin Nathan	USA
	Chase	Samuel	USA
	Clark	Tom Campbell	USA
	Douglas	William Orville	USA
	Ellsworth	Oliver	USA
	Fortas	Abe	USA
	Frankfurter	Felix	USA
	Fuller	Melville Weston	USA
	Ginsburg	Ruth Joan Bader	USA
	Harlan	John Marshall	USA
	Jackson	Robert Houghwout	USA
	Kennedy	Anthony McLeod	USA
	O'Connor	Sandra Day	USA
	Powell	Lewis Franklin	USA
	Scalia	Antonin	USA
	Souter	David Hackett	USA
	Stevens	John Paul	USA
	Stewart	Potter	USA
	Story	Joseph	USA
	Thomas	Clarence	USA
	White	Byron Raymond	USA
Lawman	Earp	Wyatt	USA
	Garrett	Pat	USA
	Hickok	James Butler (Wild Bill)	USA
	Masterson	William Barclay	USA
	Tilghman	William (Bill)	USA
Lawyer	Choate	Rufus	USA
	Darrow	Clarence Seward	USA
	Dewey	Thomas Edmund	USA
Lawyer - Mafia	Cohn	Roy	USA
Lawyer/Civil Libertarian	Hays	Arthur Garfield	USA
Lawyer/Lecturer	Ingersoll	Robert Green	USA
Mafia	Anastasia	Albert	Italy
	Bonnano	Joseph (Bananas)	Sicily
	Bonnano	Salvatore (Bill)	USA
	Capone	Al (Scarface)	USA
	Capone	Ralph	Italy
	Capone	Salvatore (Frank)	USA
	Castellano	Paul (Big Pauly)	USA
	Colombo	Joseph	USA
	Costello	Francesco (Frank)	Italy
	Dellacroce	Aniello (The Hat)	USA
	Galante	Carmine (The Cigar)	Sicily
	Gambino	Carlo	Sicily
	Genovese	Don Vitone (Vito)	Italy
	Giancana	Gilorma (Sam) (Momo)	USA

FAME	LAST NAME	FIRST NAME	COUNTRY
Mafia	Gotti	John (Dapper Don)	USA
	Gravano	Salvatore (Sammy the Bull)	USA
	Guzik	Jake (Greasy Thumb)	Russia
	Lansky	Meyer (The Brain)	Russia
	Luciano	Charles (Lucky)	Sicily
	Nitti	Frank (The Enforcer)	Italy
	O'Banion	Charles Dion (Deanie)	USA
	Profaci	Joseph (Hammer)	Italy
	Siegel	Benjamin (Bugsy)	USA
	Torrio	John (Little Johnny)	Italy
	Valachi	Joseph M.	USA
Outlaw	Barrow	Clyde Champion	USA
	Bonney	William H. (Billy the Kid)	USA
	Dalton	Bob	USA
	Dalton	Emmett	USA
	Dalton	Gratton	USA
	Holliday	John H. (Doc)	USA
	James	Alexander Franklin (Frank)	USA
	James	Jesse Woodson	USA
	Longabaugh	Harry Alonzo (Sundance Kid)	USA
	Parker	Bonnie	USA
	Star (Shirley)	Myra Belle	USA
Outlaw - Butch Cassidy	Parker	Robert Leroy	USA
Pirate	Lafitte	Jean	France
Private Detective	Pinkerton	Allan	USA
Privateer/Pirate	Kidd	William	England
Reformer - Prison	Osborne	Thomas Mott	USA
Serial Killer	Berkowitz	David (Son of Sam)	USA
	Bundy	Theodore Robert (Ted)	USA
	Chikatilo	Andrei Romanovich	Ukraine
	Cunanan	Andrew Philip	USA
	Dahmer	Jeffrey	USA
	Gein	Edward Theodore (Ed)	USA
	Kemper	Edmund	USA
	Lucas	Henry Lee	USA
	Manson	Charles Milles	USA
	Panzram	Carl	USA
	Speck	Richard Benjamin	USA
	Toole	Ottis	USA
	Williams	Wayne	USA
	Wournos	Aileen	USA
Serial Killer - Boston Strangler	Salvo	Albert De	USA
Serial Killer - Dusseldorf Vampire	Kurten	Peter	Germany
Serial Killer - Hannibal Lector	Fish	Albert	USA
Serial Killer - Hillside Strangler	Bianchi	Kenneth	USA
	Buono	Angelo	USA
Serial Killer - Killer Clown	Gacy	John Wayne	USA
Serial Killer - Night Stalker	Ramirez	Richard	USA
Treasury Agent	Ness	Eliot	USA
Underworld - Jewish	Rothstein	Arnold	USA

MOVIE PRODUCTION:

Director	Anderson	Lindsay	India
	Barker	Clive	England
	Benjamin	Richard	USA
	Brook	Peter	England
	Brooks	Mel	USA

SOLVER SERIES: NAME FINDER

FAME	LAST NAME	FIRST NAME	COUNTRY
Director	Browning	Tod	USA
	Bunuel	Luis	France
	Burton	Timothy (Tim)	USA
	Clair	René	France
	Cocteau	Jean	France
	Coen	Ethan	USA
	Corman	Roger	USA
	Downey	Robert	USA
	Edwards	Blake	USA
	Frankenheimer	John	USA
	Godard	Jean-Luc	France
	Goldwyn	Samuel	Poland
	Grosbard	Ulu	Belgium
	Guthrie	William Tyrone	England
	Herzog	Werner	Germany
	Hooper	Tobe	USA
	Hunter	Ross	USA
	Kasdan	Lawrence	USA
	Landis	John	USA
	Lang	Fritz	Austria
	Lee	Spike	USA
	Leone	Sergio	Italy
	Mayer	Louis B.	Russia
	Mazursky	Paul	USA
	Merrick	David	USA
	Michaels	Lorne	Canada
	Miller	Jonathon	England
	Morris	Aldo	USA
	Nair	Mira	India
	Palma	Brian De	USA
	Papp	Joseph	USA
	Pasolini	Pier Paolo	Italy
	Pathé	Charles	France
	Pinter	Harold	England
	Ponti	Carlo	Italy
	Prince	Hal	USA
	Reiner	Rob	USA
	Reitman	Ivan	Czechoslovakia
	Roeg	Nicolas	England
	Rohmer	Eric	France
	Rossellini	Roberto	Italy
	Saks	Gene	USA
	Satyajit	Ray	India
	Sayles	John	USA
	Seidelman	Susan	USA
	Selznick	David O	USA
	Sica	Vittorio De	Italy
	Spelling	Aaron	USA
	Tashlin	Frank	USA
	Todd	Richard	Ireland
	Tognazzi	Ugo	Italy
	Townsend	Robert	USA
	Visconti	Luchino	Italy
	Walsh	Raoul	USA
	Waters	John	USA
	Wenders	Wim	Germany
	Zanuck	Darryl F.	USA
	Berkely	Busby	USA

FAME	LAST NAME	FIRST NAME	COUNTRY
Director - Acad Award Nom	Almodovar	Pedro	Spain
	Altman	Robert	USA
	Anderson	Michael	England
	Antonioni	Michaelangelo	Italy
	Ashby	Hal	USA
	Babenco	Hector	Argentina
	Barrymore	Lionel	USA
	Beaumont	Harry	USA
	Benigni	Roberto	Italy
	Beresford	Bruce	Australia
	Bergman	Ingmar	Sweden
	Bertolucci	Bernardo	Italy
	Bogdanovich	Peter	USA
	Boorman	John	England
	Branagh	Kenneth	Ireland
	Brenon	Herbert	Ireland
	Brest	Martin	USA
	Brooks	Richard	USA
	Brown	Clarence	USA
	Cacoyannis	Michael	Cyprus
	Campion	Jane	New Zealand
	Cardiff	Jack	England
	Cassavetes	John	USA
	Cattaneo	Peter	England
	Cava	Gregory La	USA
	Clayton	Jack	England
	Coen	Joel	USA
	Coppola	Sofia	USA
	Crichton	Charles	England
	Cummings	Irving	USA
	Daldry	Stephen	England
	Dassin	Jules	USA
	Dieterle	William	Germany
	Dmytryk	Edward	Canada
	Dyke	Woodbridge Strong Van	USA
	Egoyan	Atom	Egypt
	Farrow	John	Australia
	Fellini	Federico	Italy
	Figgis	Mike	England
	Franklin	Sidney	USA
	Frears	Stephen	England
	Gavras	Costa	Greece
	Germi	Pietro	Italy
	Glenville	Peter	England
	Hackford	Taylor	USA
	Hall	Alexander	USA
	Hallstrom	Lasse	Sweden
	Hanson	Curtis	USA
	Harvey	Anthony	England
	Hathaway	Henry	USA
	Hawks	Howard	USA
	Henry	Buck	USA
	Hicks	Scott	Uganda
	Hiller	Arthur	Canada
	Hitchcock	Alfred	England
	Hudson	Hugh	England
	Ivory	James	USA
	Jewison	Norman	Canada

SOLVER SERIES: NAME FINDER

FAME	LAST NAME	FIRST NAME	COUNTRY
Director - Acad Award Nom	Joffe	Roland	England
	Jonze	Spike	USA
	Jordan	Neil	England
	Kieslowski	Krzysztof	Poland
	King	Henry	USA
	Koster	Henry	Germany
	Kramer	Stanley	USA
	Kubrick	Stanley	USA
	Kurosawa	Akira	Japan
	Lang	Walter	USA
	Lee	Ang	Taiwan
	Leigh	Mike	England
	Lelouch	Claude	France
	Leonard	Robert	USA
	Leroy	Mervyn	USA
	Litvak	Anatole	Ukraine
	Logan	Joshua	USA
	Lubitsch	Ernst	Germany
	Lucas	George	USA
	Lumet	Sidney	USA
	Lynch	David	USA
	Lyne	Adrian	England
	Madden	John	England
	Malick	Terrence	USA
	Malle	Louis	France
	Mann	Michael	USA
	Marshall	Rob	USA
	Meirelles	Fernando	Brazil
	Mille	Cecil Blount De	USA
	Molinaro	Edouard	France
	Mulligan	Robert	USA
	Negulesco	Jean	Romania
	Noonan	Chris	Australia
	Olivier	Laurence	England
	Pakula	Alan J.	USA
	Parker	Alan J.	England
	Payne	Alexander	USA
	Penn	Arthur	USA
	Perry	Frank	USA
	Peterson	Wolfgang	Germany
	Pollack	Sydney	USA
	Pontecorvo	Gillo	Italy
	Preminger	Otto	Austria
	Radford	Michael	India
	Renoir	Jean	France
	Ritt	Martin	USA
	Robbins	Tim	USA
	Robson	Mark	Canada
	Ross	Herbert	USA
	Rossen	Robert	USA
	Ruggles	Wesley	USA
	Rush	Richard	USA
	Russell	Ken	England
	Rydell	Mark	USA
	Sant	Gus Van	USA
	Schertzinger	Victor	USA
	Schroeder	Barbet	Iran
	Scorsese	Martin	USA

FAME	LAST NAME	FIRST NAME	COUNTRY
Director - Acad Award Nom	Scott	Ridley	England
	Seaton	George	USA
	Sheridan	Jim	Ireland
	Shyamalan	Manoj Night	India
	Singleton	John	USA
	Siodmak	Robert	Germany
	Sternberg	Josef Von	Austria
	Stevenson	Robert	England
	Sturges	Preston	USA
	Tarantino	Quentin	USA
	Teshigahara	Hiroshi	Japan
	Thompson	John Lee	England
	Troell	Jan	Sweden
	Truffaut	Francois	France
	Vidor	King	USA
	Walters	Charles	USA
	Weir	Peter	Australia
	Welles	George Orson	USA
	Wellman	William	USA
	Wertmuller	Lina	Italy
	Wilde	Ted	USA
	Wood	Samuel	USA
	Yates	Peter	England
	Zeffirelli	Franco	Italy
Director - Academy Award	Allen	Woody	USA
	Attenborough	Richard	England
	Avildsen	John G.	USA
	Beatty	Warren	USA
	Benton	Robert	USA
	Borzage	Frank	USA
	Brooks	James L.	USA
	Cameron	James	Canada
	Capra	Frank	Italy
	Chaplin	Charles	England
	Cimino	Michael	USA
	Coppola	Francis Ford	USA
	Costner	Kevin	USA
	Cukor	George	USA
	Curtiz	Michael	Hungary
	Demme	Jonathan	USA
	Eastwood	Clint	USA
	Fleming	Victor	USA
	Ford	John	USA
	Forman	Milos	Czechoslovakia
	Fosse	Bob	USA
	Friedkin	Wlliam	USA
	Gibson	Mel	USA
	Hill	George Roy	USA
	Howard	Ron	USA
	Huston	John	USA
	Jackson	Peter	New Zealand
	Kazan	Elia	Turkey
	Lean	David	England
	Levinson	Barry	USA
	Lloyd	Frank	Scotland
	Mankiewicz	Joseph L.	USA
	Mann	Delbert	USA
	McCarey	Leo	USA

SOLVER SERIES: NAME FINDER

FAME	LAST NAME	FIRST NAME	COUNTRY
Director - Academy Award	Mendes	Sam	England
	Milestone	Lewis	Russia
	Minghella	Anthony	England
	Minnelli	Vincente	USA
	Nichols	Mike	Germany
	Polanski	Roman	France
	Redford	Robert	USA
	Reed	Carol	England
	Richardson	Tony	England
	Robbins	Jerome	USA
	Schaffner	Franklin J.	Japan
	Schlesinger	John	England
	Soderbergh	Steven	USA
	Spielberg	Steven	USA
	Stevens	George	USA
	Stone	Oliver	USA
	Taurog	Norman	USA
	Wilder	Billy	Hungary
	Wise	Robert	USA
	Wyler	William	Germany
	Zemeckis	Robert	USA
	Zinneman	Fred	Austria
Director - Documentaries	Flaherty	Robert Joseph	USA
Director/Producer	Eisenstein	Sergei Mikhailovich	Russia
	Griffith	David Lewelyn	USA
	Sennett	Mack	USA
Director/Producer- Theatrical	Piscator	Erwin	USA
Impresario	Hurok	Sol	USA
Producer	Disney	Walter Elias	USA
	Zukor	Adolph	Hungary
Producer - Theatrical	Ziegfeld	Florenz	USA
Producer/Theatrical Manager	Frohman	Charles	USA
Producer/Writer	Shaw	Irwin	USA

PERFORMING ARTS:

Actor	Adams	Don	USA
	Adams	Mason	USA
	Agar	John	USA
	Ailey	Alvin	USA
	Alda	Robert	USA
	Alexander	Jason	USA
	Ames	Leon	USA
	Amos	John	USA
	Anderson	Harry	USA
	Anderson	Richard Dean	USA
	Andrews	Anthony	England
	Andrews	Dana	USA
	Andrews	Tige	USA
	Ansara	Michael	Syria
	Arkin	Adam	USA
	Arness	James	USA
	Arnold	Tom	USA
	Asner	Ed	USA
	Assante	Armand	USA
	Astin	John	USA
	Astin	Sean	USA
	Ates	Roscoe	USA

FAME	LAST NAME	FIRST NAME	COUNTRY
Actor	Atherton	William	USA
	Atwill	Lionel	England
	Auberjonois	René	USA
	Aumont	Jean-Pierre	France
	Backus	Jim	USA
	Bacon	Kevin	USA
	Bain	Conrad	Canada
	Baio	Scott	USA
	Baker	Joe Don	USA
	Bakula	Scott	USA
	Baldwin	William	USA
	Barry	Gene	USA
	Barrymore	John	USA
	Barrymore	Maurice	USA
	Barty	Billy	USA
	Basehart	Richard	USA
	Bateman	Jason	USA
	Bean	Orson	USA
	Beery	Noah	USA
	"Begley, Jr."	Ed	USA
	Belmondo	Jean-Paul	France
	Belushi	James	USA
	Belushi	John	USA
	Benben	Brian	USA
	Benedict	Dirk	USA
	Benjamin	Richard	USA
	Benson	Robby	USA
	Bernardi	Herschel	USA
	Bernsen	Corbin	USA
	Berry	Ken	USA
	Betterton	Thomas	England
	Betz	Carl	USA
	Birney	David	USA
	Bixby	Bill	USA
	Blake	Robert	USA
	Blanc	Matt Le	USA
	Blocker	Dan	USA
	Blore	Eric	England
	Bogarde	Dirk	England
	Bolger	Ray	USA
	Bond	Ward	USA
	Boone	Richard	USA
	Booth	Edwin Thomas	USA
	Booth	Junius Brutus	USA
	Bosley	Tom	USA
	Bottoms	Timothy	USA
	Boxleitner	Bruce	USA
	Boyd	Stephen	Northern Ireland
	Boyle	Peter	USA
	Bracken	Eddie	USA
	Brazzi	Rossano	Italy
	Bridges	Beau	USA
	Bridges	Lloyd	USA
	Bright	Richard	USA
	Brimley	Wilford	USA
	Broderick	James	USA
	Broderick	Matthew	USA
	Brolin	James	USA

SOLVER SERIES: NAME FINDER

FAME	LAST NAME	FIRST NAME	COUNTRY
Actor	Bronson	Charles	USA
	Brooks	Mel	USA
	Brosnan	Pierce	Ireland
	Brown	Bryan	Australia
	Browne	Roscoe Lee	USA
	Bruce	Nigel	Mexico
	Buchanan	Edgar	USA
	Buchholz	Horst	Germany
	Burghoff	Gary	USA
	Burr	Raymond	Canada
	Burton	Levar	Germany
	Busfield	Timothy	USA
	Bushman	Francis X.	USA
	Cabot	Bruce	USA
	Cabot	Sebastian	England
	Calhoun	Rory	USA
	Cameron	Kirk	USA
	Camp	Hamilton	England
	Campanella	Joseph	USA
	Carey	MacDonald	USA
	Carmichael	Ian	England
	Carradine	David	USA
	Carradine	John	USA
	Carradine	Keith	USA
	Carrilo	Leo	USA
	Carroll	Leo G.	England
	Carson	Jack	Canada
	Cassidy	Shaun	USA
	Cassidy (Boyd)	William (Hopalong)	USA
	Chamberlain	Richard	USA
	Chaney	Lon	USA
	Chaney Jr.	Lon	USA
	Christopher	William	USA
	Clark	Dane	USA
	Clary	Robert	France
	Cleese	John	England
	Clooney	George	USA
	Coleman	Dabney	USA
	Coleman	Gary	USA
	Colter	Jessi	USA
	Connors	Chuck	USA
	Connors	Mike	USA
	Conrad	Robert	USA
	Conrad	William	USA
	Conried	Hans	USA
	Conte	Richard	USA
	Coogan	Jackie	USA
	Coquelin	Benoit Constant	France
	Cord	Alex	USA
	Corey	Wendell	USA
	Cotton	Joseph	USA
	Crabbe	Buster	USA
	Crane	Bob	USA
	Crawford	Michael	England
	Crenna	Richard	USA
	Cross	Ben	England
	Culkin	Macaulay	USA
	Culp	Robert	USA

FAME	LAST NAME	FIRST NAME	COUNTRY
Actor	Cummings	Robert	USA
	Curry	Tim	England
	Curtis	Keene	USA
	Cusack	Cyril	South Africa
	Cusack	John	USA
	Cushing	Peter	England
	Dale	Jim	England
	Dalton	Timothy	Wales
	Damme	Jean-Claude Van	Belgium
	Dana	William (Bill)	USA
	Daniels	Jeff	USA
	Daniels	William	USA
	Danson	Ted	USA
	Danza	Tony	USA
	Davis	Ossie	USA
	Dawson	Richard	England
	Defore	Don	USA
	Delon	Alain	France
	Deluise	Dom	USA
	Dennehy	Brian	USA
	Denny	Reginald	England
	Denver	Bob	USA
	Derek	John	USA
	Devane	William	USA
	Devine	Andy	USA
	Diesel	Vin	USA
	Dillman	Bradford	USA
	Dillon	Matt	USA
	Dobson	Kevin	USA
	Donahue	Troy	USA
	Dorn	Michael	USA
	Dotrice	Roy	England
	Douglas	Paul	USA
	Dow	Tony	USA
	Doyle	David	USA
	Drake	Larry	USA
	Drew	John	USA
	Dryer	Fred	USA
	Duffy	Patrick	USA
	Dukes	David	USA
	Dullea	Keir	USA
	Dunne	Griffin	USA
	Duryea	Dan	USA
	Dyke	Dick Van	USA
	Dyke	Jerry Van	USA
	Dysart	Richard	USA
	Dzundza	George	Germany
	Ebsen	Buddy	USA
	Edwards	Anthony	USA
	Elam	Jack	USA
	Elliott	Sam	USA
	Elwes	Cary	England
	Ely	Ron	USA
	Englund	Robert	USA
	Epps	Omar Hashim	USA
	Estevez	Emilio	USA
	Estrada	Erik	USA
	Everett	Chad	USA

SOLVER SERIES: NAME FINDER

FAME	LAST NAME	FIRST NAME	COUNTRY
Actor	Ewell	Tom	USA
	Fahey	Jeff	USA
	Fairbanks	Douglas	USA
	Fairbanks Jr.	Douglas	USA
	Farentino	James	USA
	Farr	Jamie	USA
	Farrell	Mike	USA
	Feldman	Corey	USA
	Fell	Norman	USA
	Ferrer	Mel	USA
	Ferrigno	Lou	USA
	Flynn	Errol	Australia
	Flynn	Joe	USA
	Forbes-Robertson	Johnston	England
	Ford	Glenn	USA
	Forsythe	John	USA
	Foster	Preston	USA
	Fox	Edward	England
	Fox	James	England
	Fox	Michael J.	Canada
	Foxworth	Robert	USA
	Foy	Eddie	USA
	Foy Jr	Eddie	USA
	Frakes	Jonathon	USA
	Frawley	William	USA
	Frid	John Herbert (Johnathan)	Canada
	Gail	Max	USA
	Gazzara	Ben	USA
	Geer	Will	USA
	Gere	Richard	USA
	Gibson	Hoot	USA
	Gibson	Mel	USA
	Gilbert	John	USA
	Gillette	William Hooker	USA
	Gilliam	Terry	USA
	Glenn	Scott	USA
	Glover	Danny	USA
	Goldblum	Jeff	USA
	Goodman	John	USA
	Gordon	Gale	USA
	Grable	Betty	USA
	Grammer	Kelsey	Virgin Islands
	Granger	Farley	USA
	Granger	Stewart	England
	Graves	Peter	USA
	Greene	Lorne	Canada
	Griffith	Andy	USA
	Grizzard	George	USA
	Grodin	Charles	USA
	Groh	David	USA
	Gross	Michael	USA
	Guardino	Harry	USA
	Gulager	Clu	USA
	Guttenberg	Steve	USA
	Gwynne	Fred	USA
	Hagman	Larry	USA
	Haid	Charles	USA
	Haim	Corey	Canada

FAME	LAST NAME	FIRST NAME	COUNTRY
Actor	Hale Jr	Alan	USA
	Haley	Jack	USA
	Hall	Huntz	USA
	Hamill	Mark	USA
	Hamilton	George	USA
	Hamlin	Harry	USA
	Hampden	Walter	USA
	Hardison	Kadeem	USA
	Hardwicke	Cedric	England
	Harewood	Dorian	USA
	Harmon	Mark	USA
	Harrington Jr.	Pat	USA
	Harrison	Gregory	USA
	Hart	William S.	USA
	Haskell	Peter	USA
	Hauer	Rutger	Netherlands
	Havers	Nigel	England
	Hawkins	Jack	England
	Hayes	Gabby	USA
	Hays	Robert	USA
	Hemmings	David	England
	Herrmann	Edward	USA
	Hesseman	Howard	USA
	Hillerman	John	USA
	Hodiak	John	USA
	Hogan	Paul	Australia
	Holbrook	Hal	USA
	Holder	Geoffrey	Trinidad
	Holliman	Earl	USA
	Holloway	Sterling	USA
	Holt	Jack	USA
	Holt	Tim	USA
	Hooks	Robert	USA
	Horsley	Lee	USA
	Howard	Ken	USA
	Howard	Ron	USA
	Howell	C. Thomas	USA
	Hughes	Barnard	USA
	Hunter	Jeffrey	USA
	Hutton	Jim	USA
	Ito	Robert	Canada
	Jacobi	Derek	England
	Janssen	David	USA
	Jefferson	Joseph	USA
	Jenkins	Allen	USA
	Johnson	Don	USA
	Johnson	Van	USA
	Jones	Dean	USA
	Jordan	Richard	USA
	Jory	Victor	Canada
	Jourdan	Louis	USA
	Julia	Raul	Puerto Rico
	Jump	Gordon	USA
	Kahn	Sammy	USA
	Kanaly	Steve	USA
	Karloff	Boris	England
	Kavner	Julie	USA
	Kaye	Danny	USA

SOLVER SERIES: NAME FINDER

FAME	LAST NAME	FIRST NAME	COUNTRY
Actor	Keach	Stacey	USA
	Kean	Edmund	England
	Keaton	Buster	USA
	Keaton	Michael	USA
	Keith	Brian	USA
	Keith	David	USA
	Kelley	DeForest	USA
	Kemble	John Phillip	England
	Kercheval	Ken	USA
	Kerr	John	USA
	Kibbee	Guy	USA
	Kilbride	Percy	USA
	Kilmer	Val	USA
	King	Perry	USA
	Kirby	Bruno	USA
	Kirby	Durward	USA
	Klemperer	Werner	Germany
	Klugman	Jack	USA
	Knight	Ted	USA
	Kopell	Bernie	USA
	Korman	Harvey	USA
	Kotto	Yaphet	USA
	Kruger	Otto	USA
	Ladd	Alan	USA
	Lahr	Bert	USA
	Lamas	Fernando	Argentina
	Lamas	Lorenzo	USA
	Lando	Joseph (Joe)	USA
	Landon	Michael	USA
	Langella	Frank	USA
	Lansing	Robert	USA
	Larroquette	John	USA
	Lawford	Peter	England
	Lee	Bruce	USA
	Lee	Christopher	England
	Leguizamo	John	Colombia
	Leibman	Ron	USA
	Leto	Jared	USA
	Levine	Ted	USA
	Lincoln	Elmo	USA
	Linden	Hal	USA
	Linn-Baker	Mark	USA
	Liotta	Ray	USA
	Little	Cleavon	USA
	Lloyd	Christopher	USA
	Lom	Herbert	Hungary
	Long	Richard	USA
	Lord	Jack	USA
	Lorre	Peter	Slovakia
	Lowe	Edmund	USA
	Lowe	Rob	USA
	Lugosi	Bela	Hungary
	Macchio	Ralph	USA
	MacLachlan	Kyle	USA
	MacLeod	Gavin	USA
	MacMurray	Fred	USA
	MacNee	Patrick	England
	Macready	William Charles	England

FAME	LAST NAME	FIRST NAME	COUNTRY
Actor	Mahon	Michael C.	USA
	Majors	Lee	USA
	Mansfield	Richard	USA
	Marshall	Everett Grunz	USA
	Marshall	Herbert	England
	Martin	Ross	Poland
	Martin	Steve	USA
	Mat	Paul Le	USA
	Matheson	Tim	USA
	Mature	Victor	USA
	McCallum	David	Scotland
	McCarthy	Andrew	USA
	McClure	Doug	USA
	McCrea	Joel	USA
	McDowall	Roddy	England
	McDowell	Malcolm	England
	McFarland	George (Spanky)	USA
	McGavin	Darren	USA
	McGoohan	Patrick	USA
	McGregor	Ewan	Scotland
	McKean	Michael	USA
	McRaney	Gerald	USA
	McShane	Ian	England
	Meany	Colm	Ireland
	Meek	Donald	Scotland
	Merrill	Gary	USA
	Mifune	Toshiro	China
	Milner	Martin	USA
	Mitchell	Cameron	USA
	Mix	Tom	USA
	Modine	Matthew	USA
	Molinaro	Al	USA
	Moll	Richard	USA
	Montalban	Ricardo	Mexico
	Moore	Clayton	USA
	Moore	Roger	England
	Morales	Esai	USA
	Moranis	Rick	Canada
	Morgan	Harry	USA
	Moriarty	Michael	USA
	Morris	Greg	USA
	Morrow	Vic	USA
	Morse	Robert	USA
	Mostel	Josh	USA
	Mostel	Zero	USA
	Mowbray	Alan	England
	Mulligan	Richard	USA
	Murphy	Audie	USA
	Murphy	George	USA
	Musante	Tony	USA
	Nabors	Jim	USA
	Nader	Michael	USA
	Nagel	Conrad	USA
	Naldi	Nita	USA
	Neill	Sam	Northern Ireland
	Nelson	Ed	USA
	Nelson	Judd	USA
	Nelson	Ozzie	USA

SOLVER SERIES: NAME FINDER

FAME	LAST NAME	FIRST NAME	COUNTRY
Actor	Nielson	Leslie	Canada
	Nimoy	Leonard	USA
	Nolan	Lloyd	USA
	Norris	Chuck	USA
	Novarro	Ramon	Mexico
	Novello	Ivor	Wales
	Nye	Louis	USA
	Oates	Warren	USA
	O'Brian	Hugh	USA
	O'Brien	Pat	USA
	O'Connor	Carroll	USA
	O'Connor	Donald	USA
	O'Keefe	Dennis	USA
	Oland	Warner	Sweden
	Oldman	Gary	England
	Olin	Ken	USA
	O'Neal	Patrick	USA
	O'Neill	Ed	USA
	Ontkean	Michael	Canada
	Orbach	Jerry	USA
	O'Shea	Milo	Ireland
	Osmond	Ken	USA
	Owen	Reginald	England
	Parker	Fess	USA
	Parker	Jameson	USA
	Parks	Bert	USA
	Patinkin	Mandy	USA
	Peebles	Mario Van	Mexico
	Peppard	George	USA
	Perlman	Ron	USA
	Perry	Luke	USA
	Persoff	Nehemiah	Israel
	Phillips	Lou Diamond	Philippines
	Pinchot	Bronson	USA
	Pinsent	Gordon	Canada
	Pleasence	Donald	England
	Plummer	Christopher	Canada
	Powell	Dick	USA
	Power	Tyrone	USA
	Price	Vincent	USA
	Prinze	Freddie	USA
	Prinze Jr.	Freddie	USA
	Prosky	Robert	USA
	Pryce	Jonathon	Wales
	Quaid	Dennis	USA
	Quinn	Aidan	USA
	Rachins	Alan	USA
	Raft	George	USA
	Ramis	Harold	USA
	Randall	Tony	USA
	Ratzenberger	John	USA
	Ray	Aldo	USA
	Reed	Oliver	England
	Reed	Robert	USA
	Rees	Roger	Wales
	Reeve	Christopher	USA
	Reeves	George	USA
	Reeves	Keanu	Lebanon

FAME	LAST NAME	FIRST NAME	COUNTRY
Actor	Reid	Tim	USA
	Reinhold	Judge	USA
	Rennie	Michael	England
	Rey	Alejandro	Argentina
	Rey	Fernando	Spain
	Richards	Michael	USA
	Richardson	Ian	Scotland
	Roberts	Pernell	USA
	Roberts	Tony	USA
	Robertson	Dale	USA
	Robinson	Edward G.	Romania
	Roland	Gilbert	Mexico
	Romero	Cesar	USA
	Rourke	Mickey	USA
	Rowe	Nicholas	Scotland
	Ruggles	Charlie	USA
	Russell	Kurt	USA
	Saget	Bob	USA
	Sandy	Gary	USA
	Savage	Fred	USA
	Saxon	John	USA
	Schallert	William	USA
	Schroder	Rick	USA
	Schwarzenegger	Arnold	Austria
	Scolari	Peter	USA
	Scott	Randolph	USA
	Scott	Zachary	USA
	Selleck	Tom	USA
	Seville	David	USA
	Sewell	Rufus	England
	Shackelford	Ted	USA
	Sharp	Anthony	England
	Shatner	William	Canada
	Shea	John	USA
	Sheen	Charlie	USA
	Sheen	Martin	USA
	Shue	Andrew	USA
	Silver	Ron	USA
	Sim	Alastair	Scotland
	Skerritt	Tom	USA
	Sloane	Everett	USA
	Smith	Buffalo Bob	USA
	Smits	Jimmy	USA
	Snipes	Wesley	USA
	Sorvino	Paul	USA
	Sothern	Edward Hugh	USA
	Soul	David	USA
	Spader	James	USA
	Spano	Joe	USA
	Spano	Vincent	USA
	Spiner	Brent	USA
	Stamos	John	USA
	Stander	Lionel	USA
	Stanislavsky	Konstantin	Russia
	Stanton	Harry Dean	USA
	Stauss	Peter	USA
	Stevens	Andrew	USA
	Stevenson	McLean	USA

SOLVER SERIES: NAME FINDER

FAME	LAST NAME	FIRST NAME	COUNTRY
Actor	Stevenson	Parker	USA
	Stewart	Patrick	England
	Stiers	David Ogden	USA
	Stiller	Jerry	USA
	Stoltz	Eric	USA
	Stone	Milburn	USA
	Storch	Larry	USA
	Strauss	Peter	USA
	Sullivan	Barry	USA
	Sutherland	Donald	Canada
	Sutherland	Kiefer	England
	Swayze	Patrick	USA
	Tambor	Jeffrey	USA
	Taylor	Robert	USA
	Taylor	Rod	Australia
	Thicke	Alan	Canada
	Thomas	Jay	USA
	Thomas	Richard	USA
	Todd	Michael	USA
	Toler	Sidney	USA
	Travanti	Daniel J.	USA
	Treacher	Arthur	England
	Truex	Ernest	USA
	Tucker	Forrest	USA
	Tucker	Michael	USA
	Turpin	Ben	USA
	Turturro	Nicholas (Nick)	USA
	Underwood	Blair	USA
	Urich	Robert	USA
	Valentino	Rudolph	Italy
	Veidt	Conrad	Germany
	Vidov	Oleg	Russia
	Vigoda	Abe	USA
	Vincent	Jan-Michael	USA
	Vito	Danny De	USA
	Waggoner	Lyle	USA
	Wagner	Robert	USA
	Waite	Ralph	USA
	Walden	Robert	USA
	Walker	Robert	USA
	Wallach	Eli	USA
	Walston	Ray	USA
	Wanamaker	Sam	USA
	Ward	Fred	USA
	Ward	Simon	England
	Warner	Malcolm-Jamal	USA
	Wayne	David	USA
	Weathers	Carl	USA
	Weaver	Dennis	USA
	Weaver	Fritz	USA
	Webb	Jack	USA
	Weissmuller	Johnny	Romania
	Weitz	Bruce	USA
	Wendt	George	USA
	West	Adam	USA
	Weston	Jack	USA
	Wheaton	Wil	USA
	Wilding	Michael	England

FAME	LAST NAME	FIRST NAME	COUNTRY
Actor	Williams	Billy Dee	USA
	Williams	Treat	USA
	Williamson	Nicol	Scotland
	Willis	Bruce	Germany
	Wilson	Demond	USA
	Wilson	Trey	USA
	Windom	William	USA
	Winkler	Henry	USA
	Wolfe	Billy De	USA
	Woodward	Edward	England
	Wright	Max	USA
	Wynn	Keenan	USA
	York	Michael	England
	Young	Otis	USA
	Young	Robert	USA
	Zell	Harry von	USA
	Zerbe	Anthony	USA
	Ziering	Ian	USA
	Zimbalist Jr.	Efrem	USA
Actor - Acad Award Nom	Adams	Nick	USA
	Aherne	Brian	England
	Aiello	Danny	USA
	Albert	Eddie	USA
	Alda	Alan	USA
	Allen	Woody	USA
	Arkin	Alan	USA
	Astaire	Fred	USA
	Auer	Mischa	Russia
	Aykroyd	Dan	Canada
	Ayres	Lew	USA
	Baldwin	Alec	USA
	Bancroft	George	USA
	Bannen	Ian	Scotland
	Bardem	Javier	Spain
	Barthelmess	Richard	USA
	Baryshnikov	Mikhail	Latvia
	Basserman	Albert	Germany
	Bates	Alan	England
	Beatty	Ned	USA
	Beatty	Warren	USA
	Bellamy	Ralph	USA
	Bendix	William	USA
	Berenger	Tom	USA
	Bickford	Charles	USA
	Bikel	Theodore	Austria
	Boyer	Charles	France
	Branagh	Kenneth	Ireland
	Brandauer	Klaus Maria	Austria
	Bridges	Jeff	USA
	Brooks	Albert	USA
	Buono	Victor	USA
	Burton	Richard	Wales
	Busey	Gary	USA
	Caan	James	USA
	Caesar	Adolph	USA
	Calhern	Louis	USA
	Caprio	Leonardo Di	USA
	Carey	Harry	USA

SOLVER SERIES: NAME FINDER

FAME	LAST NAME	FIRST NAME	COUNTRY
Actor - Acad Award Nom	Cassavetes	John	USA
	Cassel	Seymour	USA
	Castellano	Richard	USA
	Cheadle	Don	USA
	Chekhov	Michael	Russia
	Chevalier	Maurice	France
	Church	Thomas Haden	USA
	Clift	Montgomery	USA
	Cobb	Lee J.	USA
	Coco	James	USA
	Conti	Tom	Scotland
	Cooper	Jackie	USA
	Costner	Kevin	USA
	Courtenay	Tom	England
	Cromwell	James	USA
	Cronyn	Hume	Canada
	Crosse	Rupert	West Indies
	Cruise	Tom	USA
	Curtis	Tony	USA
	Dafoe	Willem	USA
	Dailey	Dan	USA
	Dall	John	USA
	Damon	Matt	USA
	Darin (Cossotto)	Walden Roberto (Bobby)	USA
	Davidson	Jaye	USA
	Davison	Bruce	USA
	Dean	James	USA
	Demarest	William	USA
	Depardieu	Gerard	France
	Depp	Johnny	USA
	Dern	Bruce	USA
	Dix	Richard	USA
	Donlevy	Brian	Northern Ireland
	Douglas	Kirk	USA
	Dourif	Brad	USA
	"Downey, Jr"	Robert	USA
	Duncan	Michael Clarke	USA
	Dunn	James	USA
	Dunn	Michael	USA
	Durning	Charles	USA
	Eastwood	Clint	USA
	Elliott	Denholm	England
	Erwin	Stu	USA
	Falk	Peter	USA
	Farnsworth	Richard	USA
	Fiennes	Ralph	England
	Finlay	Frank	England
	Finney	Albert	England
	Firth	Peter	England
	Fishburne	Lawrence	USA
	Fonda	Peter	USA
	Ford	Harrison	USA
	Forrest	Frederic	USA
	Forster	Robert	USA
	Franciosa	Anthony	USA
	Frey	Leonard	USA
	Garcia	Andy	Cuba
	Gardenia	Vincent	Italy

FAME	LAST NAME	FIRST NAME	COUNTRY
Actor - Acad Award Nom	Garfield	John	USA
	Gargan	William	USA
	Garner	James	USA
	Gazzo	Michael V.	USA
	Genn	Leo	England
	George	Dan (Chief)	Canada
	Giannini	Giancarlo	Italy
	Gilford	Jack	USA
	Gleason	Jackie	USA
	Gleason	James	USA
	Gomez	Thomas	USA
	Gordon	Dexter	USA
	Gould	Elliott	USA
	Grant	Cary	England
	Greene	Graham	Canada
	Greenstreet	Sydney	England
	Harrelson	Woody	USA
	Harris	Ed	USA
	Harris	Richard	Ireland
	Harvey	Laurence	Lithuania
	Hawke	Ethan	USA
	Hawthorne	Nigel	England
	Hayakawa	Sessue	Japan
	Henry	Justin	USA
	Hickey	William	USA
	Hirsch	Judd	USA
	Holloway	Stanley	England
	Holm	Ian	England
	Homolka	Oskar	Austria
	Hopper	Dennis	USA
	Hoskins	Bob	England
	Hounsou	Djimon	Africa
	Howard	Leslie	England
	Howard	Trevor	England
	Hudson	Rock	USA
	Hulce	Tom	USA
	Hunnicutt	Arthur	USA
	Hurt	John	England
	Huston	John	USA
	Ireland	John	Canada
	Iwamatsu	Makoto "Mako"	Japan
	Jackson	Samuel L.	USA
	Jaeckel	Richard	USA
	Jaffe	Sam	USA
	Jones	James Earl	USA
	Keitel	Harvey	USA
	Kellaway	Cecil	South Africa
	Kelly	Gene	USA
	Kennedy	Arthur	USA
	Kinnear	Greg	USA
	Knox	Alexander	Canada
	Kruschen	Jack	Canada
	Law	Jude	England
	Lerner	Michael	USA
	Lithgow	John	USA
	Lockhart	Gene	Canada
	Loggia	Robert	USA
	Lunt	Alfred	USA

SOLVER SERIES: NAME FINDER

FAME	LAST NAME	FIRST NAME	COUNTRY
Actor - Acad Award Nom	Macy	William H.	USA
	Malkovich	John	USA
	Mantell	Joe	USA
	Marley	John	USA
	Mason	James	England
	Massey	Daniel	England
	Massey	Raymond	Canada
	Mastroianni	Marcello	Italy
	McCarthy	Kevin	USA
	McKellen	Ian	England
	McQueen	Steve	USA
	Menjou	Adolphe	USA
	Meredith	Burgess	USA
	Miller	Jason	USA
	Mineo	Sal	USA
	Mitchum	Robert	USA
	Montgomery	Robert	USA
	Moody	Ron	England
	Moore	Dudley	England
	Morgan	Frank	USA
	Morita	Noriyuki (Pat)	USA
	Morley	Robert	England
	Morris	Chester	USA
	Mueller-Stahl	Armin	Russia
	Murray	Bill	USA
	Murray	Don	USA
	Naish	Joseph Carrol	USA
	Neeson	Liam	Northern Ireland
	Nolte	Nick	USA
	Norton	Edward	USA
	Oakie	Jack	USA
	O'Connell	Arthur	USA
	O'Herlihy	Dan	Ireland
	O'Keefe	Michael	USA
	Olmos	Edward James	USA
	O'Neal	Ryan	USA
	Osment	Haley Joel	USA
	O'Toole	Peter	Ireland
	Owen	Clive	England
	Palminteri	Chazz	USA
	Parks	Larry	USA
	Paymer	David	USA
	Perkins	Anthony	USA
	Phoenix	Joaquin	Puerto Rico
	Phoenix	River	USA
	Pidgeon	Walter	Canada
	Pitt	Brad	USA
	Pollard	Michael J.	USA
	Postlethwaite	Pete	England
	Powell	William	USA
	Preston	Robert	USA
	Quaid	Randy	USA
	Quayle	Anthony	England
	Rains	Claude	England
	Rathbone	Basil	South Africa
	Rea	Stephen	Northern Ireland
	Redford	Robert	USA
	Redgrave	Michael	England

FAME	LAST NAME	FIRST NAME	COUNTRY
Actor - Acad Award Nom	Reilly	John C.	USA
	Reynolds	Burt	USA
	Richardson	Ralph	England
	Roberts	Eric	USA
	Rollins Jr.	Howard E.	USA
	Roth	Tim	England
	Ryan	Robert	USA
	Sarandon	Chris	USA
	Savalas	Telly	USA
	Scheider	Roy	USA
	Segal	George	USA
	Sellers	Peter	England
	Sharif	Omar	Egypt
	Shaw	Robert	England
	Shepard	Sam	USA
	Sica	Vittorio De	Italy
	Sinise	Gary	USA
	Smith	Will	USA
	Stack	Robert	USA
	Stallone	Sylvestor	USA
	Stamp	Terence	England
	Stephenson	James	England
	Stockwell	Dean	USA
	Stone	Lewis	USA
	Strasberg	Lee	Ukraine
	Strauss	Robert	USA
	Stroheim	Erich von	Austria
	Sydow	Max von	Sweden
	Tamblyn	Russ	USA
	Tamiroff	Akim	Russia
	Thornton	Billy Bob	USA
	Tibbett	Lawrence	USA
	Todd	Richard	Ireland
	Tone	Franchot	USA
	Topol	Chaim	Palestine
	Torn	Rip	USA
	Tracy	Lee	USA
	Travers	Henry	England
	Travolta	John	USA
	Troisi	Massimo	Italy
	Tully	Tom	USA
	Vaughn	Robert	USA
	Warden	Jack	USA
	Warner	Harry Byron	England
	Watanabe	Ken	Japan
	Waterston	Sam	USA
	Webb	Clifton	USA
	Welles	George Orson	USA
	Werner	Oskar	Austria
	Whitman	Stuart	USA
	Whitmore	James	USA
	Widmark	Richard	USA
	Wild	Jack	England
	Wilde	Brandon De	USA
	Wilde	Cornel	USA
	Wilder	Gene	USA
	Wilkinson	Tom	England
	Wills	Chill	USA

SOLVER SERIES: NAME FINDER

FAME	LAST NAME	FIRST NAME	COUNTRY
Actor - Acad Award Nom	Winfield	Paul	USA
	Woods	James	USA
	Woolley	Monty	USA
	Wynn	Ed	USA
	Young	Burt	USA
	Young	Roland	England
Actor - Academy Award	Abraham	Fahrid Murray	USA
	Albertson	Jack	USA
	Ameche	Don	USA
	Arliss	George	England
	Balsam	Martin	USA
	Barrymore	Lionel	USA
	Basekett	James	USA
	Baxter	Warner	USA
	Beery	Wallace	USA
	Begley	Ed	USA
	Benigni	Roberto	Italy
	Bogart	Humphrey	USA
	Borgnine	Ernest	USA
	Brando	Marlon	USA
	Brennan	Walter	USA
	Broadbent	Jimmy	England
	Brody	Adrien	USA
	Brynner	Yul	USA
	Burns	George	USA
	Buttons	Red	USA
	Cage	Nicolas	USA
	Cagney	James	USA
	Caine	Michael	England
	Carney	Art	USA
	Chakiris	George	USA
	Chandler	Jeff	USA
	Chaplin	Charly (Charles)	England
	Coburn	Charles	USA
	Coburn	James	USA
	Colman	Ronald	England
	Connery	Sean	Scotland
	Cooper	Chris	USA
	Cooper	Gary	USA
	Crawford	Broderick	USA
	Crisp	Donald	England
	Crowe	Russell	New Zealand
	Day-Lewis	Daniel	England
	Donat	Robert	England
	Douglas	Melvyn	USA
	Douglas	Michael	USA
	Dreyfuss	Richard	USA
	Driscoll	Bobby	USA
	Duvall	Robert	USA
	Ferrer	José	Puerto Rico
	Finch	Peter	England
	Fitzgerald	Barry	Ireland
	Fonda	Henry	USA
	Foxx	Jamie	USA
	Freeman	Morgan	USA
	Gable	Clark	USA
	Gielgud	John	England
	Gooding Jr.	Cuba	USA

FAME	LAST NAME	FIRST NAME	COUNTRY
Actor - Academy Award	Gossett Jr.	Louis	USA
	Grey	Joel	USA
	Griffith	Hugh	Wales
	Guiness	Alec	England
	Gwenn	Edmund	Wales
	Hackman	Gene	USA
	Hanks	Tom	USA
	Harrison	Rex	England
	Heflin	Van	USA
	Heston	Charlton	USA
	Hoffman	Dustin	USA
	Holden	William	USA
	Hopkins	Anthony	Wales
	Houseman	John	Romania
	Hurt	William	USA
	Huston	Walter	Canada
	Hutton	Timothy	USA
	Irons	Jeremy	England
	Jagger	Dean	USA
	Jandl	Ivan	Czechoslovakia
	Jannings	Emil	Switzerland
	Jarman Jr	Claude	USA
	Johnson	Ben	USA
	Jones	Tommy Lee	USA
	Kennedy	George	USA
	Kingsley	Ben	England
	Kline	Kevin	USA
	Lancaster	Burt	USA
	Landau	Martin	USA
	Laughton	Charles	England
	Lemmon	Jack	USA
	Lukas	Paul	Hungary
	Malden	Karl	USA
	March	Fredric	USA
	Marvin	Lee	USA
	Matthau	Walter	USA
	McLaglen	Victor	England
	Milland	Ray	Wales
	Mills	John	England
	Mitchell	Thomas	USA
	Muni	Paul	Ukraine
	Newman	Paul	USA
	Ngor	Haing .S	Cambodia
	Nicholson	Jack	USA
	Niro	Robert De	USA
	Niven	David	England
	O'Brien	Edmond	USA
	Olivier	Laurence	England
	Pacino	Al	USA
	Palance	Jack	USA
	Peck	Gregory	USA
	Penn	Sean	USA
	Pesci	Joe	USA
	Poitier	Sidney	USA
	Quinn	Anthony	Mexico
	Robards Jr.	Jason	USA
	Robbins	Tim	USA
	Robertson	Cliff	USA

SOLVER SERIES: NAME FINDER

FAME	LAST NAME	FIRST NAME	COUNTRY
Actor - Academy Award	Rooney	Mickey	USA
	Rush	Geoffrey	Australia
	Russell	Harold	Canada
	Sanders	George	Russia
	Schell	Maximilian	Austria
	Schildkraut	Joseph	Austria
	Scofield	Paul	England
	Scott	George C.	USA
	Sinatra	Frank	USA
	Spacey	Kevin	USA
	Steiger	Rod	USA
	Stewart	James	USA
	Toro	Benicio Del	Puerto Rico
	Tracy	Spencer	USA
	Ustinov	Peter	England
	Voight	Jon	USA
	Walken	Christopher	USA
	Washington	Denzel	USA
	Wayne	John	USA
	Whiteley	Jon	Scotland
	Williams	Robin	USA
	Winter	Vincent	Scotland
	Young	Gig	USA
Actor - Chef	Lagasse	Emeril	USA
Actor - Musical	Bostwick	Barry	USA
	Drake	Alfred	USA
	Guillaume	Robert	USA
	Kaye	Stubby	USA
	Keel	Howard	USA
	Klein	Robert	USA
	Vereen	Ben	USA
Actor/Assassin	Booth	John Wilkes	USA
Actor/Comedian	Allen	Fred	USA
	Allen	Steve	USA
	Arquette	Cliff	USA
	Bishop	Joey	USA
	Candy	John	Canada
	Chase	Chevy	USA
	Crystal	Billy	USA
	Leonard	Sheldon	USA
Actor/Composer	Blades	Ruben	Panama
Actor/Dancer	Hines	Gregory	USA
Actor/Humorist	Rogers	Will	USA
Actor/Musician	Arnaz	Desi	Cuba
Actor/Playwright	Boucicault	Dion	England
	Coward	Noel	England
Actor/Playwright/Producer	Cohan	George Michael	USA
Actor/Producer	Nelson	David	USA
Actor/Singer	Cariou	Len	Canada
	Robeson	Paul	USA
Actor/Singer - Academy Award	Crosby	Harry Lillis (Bing)	USA
	Ives	Burl	USA
Actor/Singer - Country Music - HF	Autry	Gene (Orvon)	USA
	Kristofferson	Kris	USA
Actor/Theatrical Manager	Garrick	David	England
	Tree	Herbert Beerbohm	England
Actress	Adair	Deborah	USA
	Adams	Brooke	USA

FAME	LAST NAME	FIRST NAME	COUNTRY
Actress	Adams	Edie	USA
	Adams	Maude	Sweden
	Adoree	Renee	France
	Agutter	Jenny	England
	Alberghetti	Anna Maria	Italy
	Alicia	Ana	Mexico
	Allen	Debbie	USA
	Allen	Karen	USA
	Allen	Nancy	USA
	Alley	Kirstie	USA
	Allyson	June	USA
	Alonso	Maria Conchita	Cuba
	Alvarado	Trini	USA
	Anderson	Loni	USA
	Anderson	Lynn	USA
	Andersson	Bibi	Sweden
	Andress	Ursula	Switzerland
	Anspach	Susan	USA
	Anton	Susan	USA
	Applegate	Christina	USA
	Ark	Joan Van	USA
	Armstrong	Bess	USA
	Arnaz	Lucie	USA
	Arquette	Rosanna	USA
	Ashley	Elizabeth	USA
	Astor	Gertrude	USA
	Aulin	Ewa	Sweden
	Baker	Josephine	USA
	Balin	Ina	USA
	Bankhead	Tallulah	USA
	Bara	Theda	USA
	Barbeau	Adrienne	USA
	Bardot	Brigitte	France
	Barkin	Ellen	USA
	Barrymore	Drew	USA
	Bateman	Justine	USA
	Baxter	Meridith	USA
	Bayes (Goldberg)	Nora (Dora)	USA
	Beals	Jennifer	USA
	Beasley	Allyce	USA
	Belafonte	Shari	USA
	Benaderet	Bea	USA
	Bennett	Constance	USA
	Bennett	Joan	USA
	Bergen	Polly	USA
	Berger	Senta	Austria
	Bernhardt	Sarah	France
	Bertinelli	Valerie	USA
	Besch	Bibi	Austria
	Bisset	Jacqueline	England
	Blackman	Honor	England
	Blakely	Susan	Germany
	Bledsoe	Tempestt	USA
	Bloom	Claire	England
	Bohay	Heidi	USA
	Bonet	Lisa	USA
	Bosson	Barbara	USA
	Bow	Clara	USA

SOLVER SERIES: NAME FINDER

FAME	LAST NAME	FIRST NAME	COUNTRY
Actress	Boyle	Lara Flynn	USA
	Braga	Sonia	Brazil
	Brown	Blair	USA
	Bruce	Virginia	USA
	Buckley	Betty	USA
	Burke	Delta	USA
	Caldwell	Zoe	Australia
	Camp	Rosemary De	USA
	Campbell	Beatrice	England
	Campbell	Neve	Canada
	Carlo	Yvonne De	Canada
	Carrere	Tia	USA
	Carroll	Pat	USA
	Carter	Lynda	USA
	Carter	Nell	USA
	Castle	Irene	USA
	Cates	Phoebe	USA
	Chaplin (O'Neill)	Oona	USA
	Chao	Rosalind	USA
	Chase	Ilka	USA
	Chiles	Lois	USA
	Chong	Rae Dawn	Canada
	Claire	Ina	USA
	Clark	Susan	Canada
	Clarke	Mae	USA
	Coca	Imogene	USA
	Collins	Joan	England
	Conn	Didi	USA
	Cornell	Katharine	USA
	Cox	Courtenay	USA
	Curtin	Jane	USA
	Curtis	Jamie Lee	USA
	Dahl	Arlene	USA
	Dalton	Abby	USA
	Daly	Tyne	USA
	Dana	Leora	USA
	D'Angelo	Beverly	USA
	Daniels	Bebe	USA
	Danner	Blythe	USA
	Darby	Kim	USA
	Darnell	Linda	USA
	Dash	Stacey	USA
	Davis	Joan	USA
	Dawber	Pam	USA
	Day	Laraine	USA
	Dee	Ruby	USA
	Dee	Sandra	USA
	Delany	Dana	USA
	Derek	Bo	USA
	Devere	Trish Van	USA
	Dey	Susan	USA
	Diamond	Selma	Canada
	Dickinson	Angie	USA
	Dixon	Donna	USA
	Donahue	Elinor	USA
	Doren	Mamie Van	USA
	Dors	Diana	England
	Down	Lesley-Anne	England

FAME	LAST NAME	FIRST NAME	COUNTRY
Actress	Downey	Rosemary (Roma)	Ireland
	Drew	Ellen	USA
	Dru	Joanne	USA
	Duffy	Julia	USA
	Dumont	Margaret	USA
	Duncan	Sandy	USA
	Duse	Eleonora	Italy
	Duvall	Shelley	USA
	Eaton	Shirley	England
	Eden	Barbara	USA
	Eichhorn	Lisa	USA
	Eikenberry	Jill	USA
	Ekberg	Anita	Sweden
	Ekland	Britt	Sweden
	Elfman	Jenna	USA
	Elg	Taina	Finland
	Ephron	Delia	USA
	Evans	Dale	USA
	Evans	Linda	USA
	Evans	Mary Ann	USA
	Fabray	Nanette	USA
	Fairchild	Morgan	USA
	Falco	Edie	USA
	Farmer	Frances	USA
	Farrow	Mia	USA
	Farrow	Tisa	USA
	Fawcett	Farrah	USA
	Faye	Alice	USA
	Feldon	Barbara	USA
	Ferrel	Tyra	USA
	Ferrell	Conchata	USA
	Fisher	Carrie	USA
	Fiske	Minnie Maddern	USA
	Fleming	Rhonda	USA
	Flockhart	Calista	USA
	Follows	Megan	Canada
	Fonda	Bridget	USA
	Francis	Anne	USA
	Francis	Arlene	USA
	Franklin	Bonnie	USA
	Frann	Mary	USA
	Funicello	Annette	USA
	Gabor	Eva	Hungary
	Gabor	Magda	Hungary
	Gabor	Zsa Zsa	Hungary
	Gallagher	Megan	USA
	Gallienne	Eva Le	England
	Gam	Rita	USA
	Gershon	Gina	USA
	Getty	Estelle	USA
	Ghostley	Alice	USA
	Gibbs	Marla	USA
	Gilbert	Melissa	USA
	Gilbert	Sara	USA
	Gillette	Anita	USA
	Gingold	Hermione	England
	Gish	Dorothy	USA
	Givens	Robin	USA

FAME	LAST NAME	FIRST NAME	COUNTRY
Singer	Mathis	Johnny	USA
	Mattea	Kathy	USA
	McDonald	Michael	USA
	McEntire	Reba	USA
	McFerrin	Bobby	USA
	McGovern	Maureen	USA
	McKenna	Lori	USA
	McKennitt	Loreena	Canada
	McLean	Don	USA
	Mellencamp	John Cougar	USA
	Merman	Ethel	USA
	Michael	George	England
	Midler	Bette	USA
	Milsap	Ronnie	USA
	Minnelli	Liza	USA
	Money	Eddie	USA
	Monroe	Vaughn	USA
	Moore	Melba	USA
	Morrison	Van	Northern Ireland
	Nelson	Gunnar	USA
	Newly	Anthony	England
	Newton	Juice	USA
	Newton	Wayne	USA
	Newton-John	Olivia	England
	Nilsson	Harry	USA
	Noone	Peter	England
	Oates	John	USA
	Ocasek	Ric	USA
	Ocean	Billy	West Indies
	Ochs	Phil	USA
	O'Connor	Des	England
	O'Connor	Sinead	Ireland
	O'Day	Anita	USA
	Ono	Yoko	Japan
	Orlando	Tony	USA
	Osbourne	Ozzy	England
	Oslin	Kay Toinette (KT)	USA
	Osmond	Alan	USA
	Osmond	Donny	USA
	Osmond	Jay	USA
	Osmond	Jimmy	USA
	Osmond	Marie	USA
	Osmond	Merrill	USA
	Osmond	Wayne	USA
	Page	Patti	USA
	Palmer	Robert	England
	Parker	Graham	England
	Paycheck	Johnny	USA
	Payne	Freda	USA
	Pendergrass	Teddy	USA
	Perry	Steve	USA
	Peters	Bernadette	USA
	Phillips	MacKenzie	USA
	Piaf	Edith	France
	Pointer	Anita	USA
	Pointer	Bonnie	USA
	Pointer	June	USA
	Pointer	Ruth	USA

FAME	LAST NAME	FIRST NAME	COUNTRY
Singer	Questel	Mae	USA
	Rabbitt	Eddie	USA
	Rafferty	Gerry	Scotland
	Raitt	John	USA
	Rawls	Lou	USA
	Ray	Johnnie	USA
	Rea	Chris	England
	Reddy	Helen	Australia
	Reed	Jerry	USA
	Resnik	Regina	USA
	Rich	Charlie	USA
	Richard	Cliff	India
	Richie	Lionel	USA
	Riperton	Minnie	USA
	Rivera	Chita	USA
	Rivers	Johnny	USA
	Rodgers	Paul	England
	Rogers	Kenny	USA
	Ronstadt	Linda	USA
	Roth	David Lee	USA
	Russell	Leon	USA
	Rydell	Bobby	USA
	Ryder *	William Levise (Mitch)	USA
	Sayer	Leo	England
	Scaggs	Boz	USA
	Seals	Dan	USA
	Seals	Jim	USA
	Sebastian	John	USA
	Sedaka	Neil	USA
	Shannon	Del	USA
	Shannon	Jackie De	USA
	Sharp	Dee Dee	USA
	Sherman	Allan	USA
	Sherman	Bobby	USA
	Shore	Dinah	USA
	Simon	Carly	USA
	Smith	Kate	USA
	Smith	Keely	USA
	Snow	Phoebe	USA
	Stone	Sylvester (Sly)	USA
	Tex	Joe	USA
	Thomas	Carla	USA
	Thomas	Rufus	USA
	Tucker	Sophie	Russia
	Wolf	Peter	USA
	Yankovic	Al (Weird)	USA
	Yarborough	Glenn	USA
	Yuro	Timi	USA
	Zevon	Warren	USA
Singer - Big Band	Vallee	Rudy	USA
Singer - Big Band/Jazz - HF	Bailer	Mildred	USA
	Bennett (Benedetto)	Anthony Dominick (Tony)	USA
	Como	Pierino Ronald (Perry)	USA
	Crosby	Harry Lillis (Bing)	USA
	Fitzgerald	Ella Jane	USA
	Holiday (Fagan)	Eleanora (Billie)	USA
	Horne	Lena	USA
	Hunter	Alberta	USA

FAME	LAST NAME	FIRST NAME	COUNTRY
Singer - Big Band/Jazz - HF	Lee (Engstrom)	Norma Delores (Peggy)	USA
	Morton (Lemothe)	Ferdinand (Jelly Roll)	USA
	Rainey (Pridgett)	Gertrude (Ma)	USA
	Rushing	James Andrew (Jimmy)	USA
	Sinatra	Frank	USA
	Smith	Bessie	USA
	Stafford	Jo Elizabeth	USA
	Tilton	Martha	USA
	Torme	Melvin Howard (Mel)	USA
	Vaughan	Sarah	USA
	Washington (Jones)	Ruth Lee (Dinah)	USA
	Williams	Joseph Goreed (Joe)	USA
	Wilson	Nancy	USA
Singer - Canadian Music - HF	Carter	Wilf (Montana Slim)	Canada
	Clayton-Thomas	David Henry	England
	Kay (Krauledat)	Joachim Fritz (John)	Germany
	Murray	Anne	Canada
	Sainte-Marie	Buffy	Canada
	Snow	Clarence Eugene (Hank)	Canada
Singer - Contempory	Waits	Tom	USA
	Williams	Andy	USA
Singer - Country & Western	Blakely	Ronee	USA
	Strait	George	USA
	Tillis	Mel	USA
	Tillotson	Johnny	USA
	Travis	Randy	USA
	Tucker	Tanya	USA
	Wells	Kitty	USA
	Williams	Don	USA
Singer - Country Music	Clark	Terri	Canada
	Rimes	Leanne	USA
Singer - Country Music - HF	Acuff	Roy	USA
	Anderson	Bill	USA
	Arnold	Eddy (Richard Edward)	USA
	Bailey	De Ford	USA
	Bond	Johnny (Cyrus Whitfield)	USA
	Bradley	William Owen	USA
	Campbell	Glen	USA
	Carlisle	William Toliver (Bill)	USA
	Cash	Johnny (John R.)	USA
	Cline (Hensley)	Virginia Patterson (Patsy)	USA
	Cramer	Floyd	USA
	Dalhart (Slaughter)	Vernon (Marion Try)	USA
	Davis	Jimmie (James Houston)	USA
	Dickens	James Cecil (Little Jimmy)	USA
	Foley	Clyde Julian (Red)	USA
	Ford	Ernest (Tennessee Ernie)	USA
	Frizzell	William Orville (Lefty)	USA
	Gibson	Donald Eugene (Don)	USA
	Haggard	Merle Ronald	USA
	Jennings	Waylon	USA
	Jones	George Glen	USA
	Jones	Grandpa (Louis Marshall)	USA
	Lee (Tarpley)	Brenda Mae	USA
	Lynn(Webb)	Loretta	USA
	Macon	Uncle Dave (David)	USA
	Miller	Roger Dean	USA
	Montana (Blevins)	Patsy (Ruby)	USA

SOLVER SERIES: NAME FINDER

FAME	LAST NAME	FIRST NAME	COUNTRY
Singer - Country Music - HF	Morgan	John Thomas	USA
	Nelson	Willie Hugh	USA
	Owens	Alvis Edgar (Buck)	USA
	Parton	Dolly Rebecca	USA
	Pierce	Michael Webb	USA
	Presley	Elvis Aaron	USA
	Price	Ray Noble	USA
	Pride	Charley Frank	USA
	Reeves	James Travis	USA
	Ritter	Woodward Morris (Tex)	USA
	Robbins(Robinson)	Martin David (Marty)	USA
	Smith	Carl	USA
	Snow	Clarence Eugene (Hank)	Canada
	Thompson	Henry Wilson (Hank)	USA
	Tillman	Floyd	USA
	Travis	Merle Robert	USA
	Tubb	Ernest	USA
	Twitty (Jenkins)	Harold Lloyd (Conway)	USA
	Waggoner	Porter	USA
	Wells (Deason)	Muriel Ellen (Kitty)	USA
	Williams Sr.	Hiram King (Hank)	USA
	Wynette	Tammy	USA
	Young	Faron	USA
Singer - Disco	Summer	Donna	USA
Singer - Doo Whop	Stevens	Dodie	USA
Singer - Folk	Stewart	Al	Scotland
	Stookey	Paul	USA
	Sumac	Yma	Peru
	Travers	Mary	USA
	Yarrow	Peter	USA
Singer - Folk - Canadian Music - HF	Lightfoot	Gordon	Canada
Singer - Meister	Sachs	Hans	Germany
Singer - Motown	Wells	Mary	USA
Singer - Musicals	Uggams	Leslie	USA
	Williams	Vanessa Lynn	USA
Singer - Opera	Albanese	Licia	USA
	Alda	Frances	USA
	Alva	Luigi Ernesto	Peru
	Amara	Lucine	USA
	Ameling	Elly	Netherlands
	Arroyo	Martina	USA
	Bing	Rudolf	Austria
	Bori	Lucretia	USA
	Callas	Maria Meneghini	Germany
	Calvé	Emma	France
	Carreras	José	Spain
	Caruso	Enrico	Italy
	Chaliapin	Feodor Ivanovich	Russia
	Destinn	Emmy	Czechoslovakia
	Domingo	Placido	Spain
	Estes	Simon	USA
	Evans	Geraint	Wales
	Farrar	Geraldine	USA
	Flagstad	Kirsten	Norway
	Fleming	Renée	USA
	Freni	Mirella	Italy
	Galli-Curci	Amelita	USA
	Gedda	Nicolai	Sweden

FAME	LAST NAME	FIRST NAME	COUNTRY
Singer - Opera	Gerhardt	Elena	Germany
	Gigli	Beniamino	Italy
	Gluck	Alma	USA
	Grist	Reri	USA
	Gruberova	Edita	Slovakia
	Hines	Jerome	USA
	Jones	Isola	USA
	Kanawa	Kiri Te	New Zealand
	Kiepura	Jan	Poland
	Lehmann	Lilli	Germany
	Lehmann	Lotte	Germany
	Lind	Jenny	Sweden
	Martinelli	Giovanni	USA
	Marton	Eva	Hungary
	McCormack	John	USA
	Melba	Nellie	Australia
	Melchior	Lauritz Lebrecht Hommel	USA
	Merrill	Robert	USA
	Merriman	Nan	USA
	Mills	Erie	USA
	Mitchell	Leona	USA
	Moffo	Anna	Italy
	Nikolaidi	Elena	Greece
	Nilsson	Birgit	Sweden
	Patti	Adelina	Italy
	Patti	Carlotta	Italy
	Pavarotti	Luciano	Italy
	Pears	Peter	England
	Peerce	Jan	USA
	Peters	Roberta	USA
	Pinza	Ezio	Italy
	Pons	Lily	France
	Ponselle	Rosa	USA
	Prey	Hermann	Germany
	Price	Mary Leontyne	USA
	Reszke	Jean de	Poland
	Rysanek	Leonie	Austria
	Schipa	Tito	Italy
	Schumann-Heink	Ernestine	USA
	Scotto	Renata	Italy
	Siepi	Cesare	Italy
	Sills	Beverly	USA
	Slezak	Leo	Czechoslovakia
	Stignani	Ebe	Italy
	Stratas	Teresa	Canada
	Stuarti	Enzio	Italy
	Sutherland	Joan	Australia
	Tebaldi	Renata	Italy
	Tetrazzini	Luisa	Italy
	Thill	Georges	France
	Thomas	Jess	USA
	Thomas	John Charles	USA
Singer - Opera - Canadian Music - HF	Forrester	Maureen	Canada
Singer - Pops	Starr	Kay	USA
	Stefani	Gwen	USA
	Stevens	Cat	England
	Stevens	Ray	USA
	Tennille	Toni	USA

SOLVER SERIES: NAME FINDER

FAME	LAST NAME	FIRST NAME	COUNTRY
Singer - Pops	Thomas	Billy Joe (BJ)	USA
	Vale	Jerry	USA
	Vinton	Bobby	USA
Singer - Pops/Country	Stafford	Jim	USA
Singer - Rhythm & Blues	Vandross	Luther Ronzoni	USA
	Womack	Bobby	USA
Singer - Rock & Roll - Canadian Music HF	Mitchell	Roberta Joan (Joni)	Canada
Singer - Rock & Roll - HF	Armstrong	Satchmo (Louis Daniel)	USA
	Baker	LaVern	USA
	Ballard (Kendricks)	John Henry (Hank)	USA
	Berry	Charles Edward (Chuck)	USA
	Bland	Robert Calvin (Bobby) (Blue)	USA
	Bowie (Hayward-Jones)	David (Robert David)	England
	Brown	Charles	USA
	Brown	Ruth	USA
	Browne	Clyde Jackson	Germany
	Burke	Solomon	USA
	Burnett	Howlin Wolf (Chester)	USA
	Cash	Johnny (John R.)	USA
	Charles (Robinson)	Ray	USA
	Christian	Charles Henry (Charlie)	USA
	Cochran	Edward Ray (Eddie)	USA
	Cole	Nathaniel (Nat King)	USA
	Cooke	Samuel	USA
	Cramer	Floyd	USA
	Darin (Cossotto)	Walden Roberto (Bobby)	USA
	Didley (Bates)	Ellis (Bo)	USA
	Dixon	William James (Willie)	USA
	Domino	Antoine (Fats)	USA
	Douglas	Steve	USA
	Dylan (Zimmerman)	Robert Alan (Bob)	USA
	Eddy (Colter)	Jessi (Duane)	USA
	Franklin	Aretha Louise	USA
	Gaye Jr.	Marvin Pentz	USA
	Green	Albert (Al)	USA
	Guthrie	Woodrow Wilson (Woody)	USA
	Haley	William John Clifton (Bill)	USA
	Hayes	Isaac	USA
	Hendrix	Jimi	USA
	Holiday (Fagan)	Eleanora (Billie)	USA
	Holly (Holley)	Charles Hardin (Buddy)	USA
	Hooker	Johnny Lee	USA
	Jackson	Mahalia	USA
	Jackson	Michael	USA
	James	Elmore	USA
	James (Hawkins)	Jamesetta (Etta)	USA
	Joel	William Martin (Billy)	USA
	John	William (Little Willie John)	USA
	John (Dwight)	Reginald K. (Elton)	England
	Johnson	Robert	USA
	Joplin	Janis Lyn	USA
	Jordan	Louis Thomas	USA
	King	Riley B. (BB)	USA
	Lee (Tarpley)	Brenda Mae	USA
	Lewis	Jerry Lee	USA
	Longhair (Byrd)	Henry (Professor Roy)	USA
	Lymon	Franklin (Frankie)	USA
	Marley	Nesta Robert (Bob)	Jamaica

FAME	LAST NAME	FIRST NAME	COUNTRY
Singer - Rock & Roll - HF	McPhatter	Clyde Lensley	USA
	Mitchell	Roberta Joan (Joni)	Canada
	Morton (Lemothe)	Ferdinand (Jelly Roll)	USA
	Mucci	Dion Di	USA
	Nelson	Eric Hilliard (Ricky)	USA
	Nelson	Prince Rogers	USA
	Orbison	Roy Kelton	USA
	Perkins (Perkings)	Carl Lee	USA
	Pickett	Wilson	USA
	Pitney	Gene	USA
	Presley	Elvis Aaron	USA
	Price	Lloyd	USA
	Rainey (Pridgett)	Gertrude (Ma)	USA
	Raitt	Bonnie	USA
	Redding	Otis	USA
	Reed	Mathis James (Jimmy)	USA
	Richard (Penniman)	Richard Wayne (Little Richard)	USA
	Robinson	William (Smokey)	USA
	Rodgers	Jimmie	USA
	Santana	Carlos	Mexico
	Schmit (The Eagles)	Timothy B.	USA
	Seeger	Pete	USA
	Seger	Bob	USA
	Shannon (Westover)	Charles Weedon (Del)	USA
	Sledge	Percy	USA
	Smith	Elizabeth (Bessie)	USA
	Smith	Patti	USA
	Spector	Ronnie	USA
	Springfield (O'Brien)	Mary Isobel (Dusty)	England
	Springsteen	Bruce Frederic	USA
	Stewart	Rod (Roderick David)	England
	Sumner	Gordon Matthew (Sting)	England
	Taylor	James	USA
	Turner	Ike	USA
	Turner	Joe Lynn	USA
	Turner (Bullock)	Anna Mae (Tina)	USA
	Valens (Valenzuela)	Richard Steven (Richie)	USA
	Valli (Castelluccio)	Frank (Frankie)	USA
	Vaughan	Sarah	USA
	Vee	Bobby	USA
	Vincent (Craddock)	Vincent Eugene (Gene)	USA
	Waite	John	England
	Walker	Aaron Thibeaux (T-Bone)	USA
	Ward	Anita	USA
	Warwick	Dionne	USA
	Washington (Jones)	Ruth Lee (Dinah)	USA
	Waters (Morganfield)	McKinley (Muddy)	USA
	Williams Jr.	Randall (Hank)	USA
	Williams Sr.	Hiram King (Hank)	USA
	Wilson	Ann	USA
	Wilson	Jack Leroy (Jackie)	USA
	Wilson	Nancy	USA
	Wonder (Hardaway)	Steveland Judkins (Stevie)	USA
	Zander	Robin	USA
	Zappa	Frank Vincent	USA
Singer (Blue Notes)	Melvin	Harold	USA
Singer/Actor	Ames	Ed	USA
	Avalon	Frankie	USA

SOLVER SERIES: NAME FINDER

FAME	LAST NAME	FIRST NAME	COUNTRY
Singer/Actor	Boone	Pat	USA
	Cantor	Eddie	USA
	Cassidy	David	USA
	Faith	Adam	England
	Springfield	Rick	Australia
Singer/Actress	Cara	Irene	USA
	Clooney	Rosemary	USA
Singer/Choreographer	Abdul	Paula	USA
Singer/Comedian	Blaine	Vivian	USA
Singer/Composer	Axton	Hoyt	USA
	Baez	Joan	USA
	Bailey	Pearl	USA
	Bell	Robert (Kool)	USA
	Bishop	Stephen	USA
	Bon Jovi	Jon	USA
	Brooks	Garth	USA
	Buffett	Jimmy	USA
	Carmen	Eric	USA
	Cilea	Francesco	Italy
	Collins	Phil	England
	Cross	Christopher	USA
	Crothers	Scatman	USA
	Maresca	Ernie	USA
	Simon	Paul Frederic	USA
	Stipes	Michael	USA
	White	Barry	USA
Singer/Composer - Big Band/Jazz - HF	Waller	Fats (Thomas Wright)	USA
Singer/Composer - Canadian Music - HF	Anka	Paul	Canada
	Cohen	Leonard	Canada
Singer/Guitarist	Allman	Duane	USA
	Lynne	Jeff	England
	Matthews	Dave	South Africa
	Rundgren	Todd Harry	USA
	Rutherford	Michael John (Mike)	England
	Scholz	Tom	USA
	Walsh	Joe	USA
	Waters	George Roger	England
	Wood	Ron	England
	Wyman	Bill	England
Singer/Guitarist - Canadian Music - HF	Cockburn	Bruce	Canada
	Yanovsky	Zal	Canada
Singer/Guitarist - Country Music - HF	Atkins	Chester Burton (Chet)	USA
Singer/Guitarist - Rock & Roll - HF	Atkins	Chester Burton (Chet)	USA
Singer/Model	Jones	Grace	Jamaica
Singer/Musician - Big Band/Jazz - HF	Cole	Nathaniel (Nat King)	USA
Singer/Pianist	Short	Bobby	USA
Singer/Pianist - Big Band/Jazz - HF	Charles (Robinson)	Ray	USA
	Horne	Shirley	USA
	Simone (Waymon)	Eunice Kathleen (Nina)	USA
Singer/Song Writer	Amos	Tori	USA
	Cohn	Marc	USA
	Diddley	Bo	USA
Singer/Song Writer - Canadian Music - HF	Cochrane	Tom	Canada
Singer/Violinist/Actor	Columbo	Russ	USA
Sitarist	Shankar	Ravi	Bangladesh
Super Model	Alexis	Kim	USA
	Alt	Carol	USA
	Anden	Mini (Susanna)	Sweden

FAME	LAST NAME	FIRST NAME	COUNTRY
Super Model	Arosio	Ana Paula	Brazil
	Auermann	Nadja	Germany
	Banks	Tyra	USA
	Behennah	Michelle	Singapore
	Bellucci	Monica	Italy
	Benitez	Elsa	Mexico
	Bon	Yasmin Le	England
	Brinkley	Christie	USA
	Brosh	Nina	Israel
	Bruni	Carla	Italy
	Bundchen	Gisele	Brazil
	Campbell	Naomi	England
	Carré	Otis	USA
	Casta	Laetitia	France
	Christensen	Helena	Denmark
	Claudel	Aurelie	France
	Crawford	Cindy	USA
	Diaz	Yamila	Argentina
	Dodd	Alice	England
	Evangelista	Linda	Canada
	Everhart	Angie	USA
	Fernandes	Almudena	Spain
	Gerkan	Manon von	Germany
	Ghauri	Yasmeen	Canada
	Grenville	Georgina	South Africa
	Hall	Bridget	USA
	Harlow	Shalom	Canada
	Herzigova	Eva	Czechoslovakia
	Hume	Kirsty	Scotland
	Hunter	Rachel	New Zealand
	Hurley	Elizabeth	England
	Ireland	Kathy	USA
	Jovovich	Milla	Ukraine
	Karembeu	Adriana	Czechoslovakia
	King	Jaime	USA
	Klein	Martina	Argentina
	Klum	Heidi	Germany
	Kurkova	Karolina	Czechoslovakia
	Lima	Adriana	Brazil
	Lindvall	Angela	USA
	Lorenzo	Vanessa	Spain
	Lourenco	Teresa	Trinidad
	MacPherson	Elle	Australia
	Maran	Josie	USA
	Mazza	Valeria	Argentina
	Michels	Ana Claudia	Brazil
	Moss	Kate	England
	Mulder	Karen	Netherlands
	Munoz	Astrid	Puerto Rico
	O'Hare	Sarah	England
	Otis	Carre	USA
	Patitz	Tatjana	Sweden
	Pestova	Daniela	Czechoslovakia
	Ponte	Laura	Spain
	Rayder	Frankie	USA
	Rivero	Inez	Argentina
	Sastre	Inez	Spain
	Schiffer	Claudia	Germany

SOLVER SERIES: NAME FINDER

FAME	LAST NAME	FIRST NAME	COUNTRY
Super Model	Seymour	Stephanie	USA
	Seynhaeve	Ingrid	Belgium
	Shrimpton	Jean	England
	Sklenarikova	Adriana	Slovakia
	Smith	Kim	USA
	Smith (Hogan)	Vicki Lynn (Anna Nicole)	USA
	Tal	Shiraz	Israel
	Taylor	Niki	USA
	Tiegs	Cheryl	USA
	Turlington	Christy	USA
	Valletta	Amber	USA
	Velasquez	Patricia	Venezuela
	Wal	Frederique Van Der	Netherlands
	Warren	Estelle	Canada
	Wesson	Amy	USA
Trombonist/Arranger - Canadian Music - HF	McConnell	Rob	Canada
Trumpeter - Big Band/Jazz - HF	Edison	Harry (Sweets)	USA
Vibraphonist	Tjader	Cal	USA
Violinist	Auer	Leopold	Hungary
	Bull	Ole	Norway
	Elman	Mischa	USA
	Heifetz	Jascha	USA
	Mae	Vanessa	China
	Menuhin	Yehudi	USA
	Milstein	Nathan	USA
	Morini	Erica	Austria
	Oistrakh	David Fyodorovich	Russia
	Oistrakh	Igor Davidovich	Russia
	Perlman	Itzhak	Israel
	Rizzio	David	Italy
	Stern	Isaac	Russia
	Zimbalist	Efrem	USA
Violinist - Country Music - HF	Bryant	Bondleaux	USA

POLITICS:

FAME	LAST NAME	FIRST NAME	COUNTRY
Abolitionist	Brown	John	USA
	Phillips	Wendell	USA
	Truth	Sojourner	USA
	Tubman	Harriet	USA
Abolitionist/Rights Advocate	Mott	Lucretia	USA
Activist	Little	Malcolm X.	USA
Activist - Civil Rights	Jackson Sr.	Jesse Louis	USA
Activist - Feminism	Yard	Molly	USA
Activist - Human Rights	Tutu	Desmond Mplio	South Africa
Activist/Abolitionist	Davis	Angela Yvonne	USA
Advocate - Civil Rights	Otis	James	USA
Agitator - Temperance	Nation	Carry	USA
Amir	Abdur	Rahman Khan	Afghanistan
Anarchist	Sacco	Nicola	Italy
	Vanzetti	Bartolomeo	Italy
Assistant Attorney-General	Hills	Carla Anderson	USA
Assistant Secretary of State	Abrams	Elliott	USA
Attorney General	Reno	Janet	USA
Calif	Bakr	Abu	Saudi Arabia
Chancellor	Adenauer	Konrad	Germany
	Bethmann-Hollweg	Theobald von	Germany
	Bismarck	Otto Eduard Leopold von	Germany

FAME	LAST NAME	FIRST NAME	COUNTRY
Chancellor	Brandt	Herbert Ernst (Willy)	Germany
	Bülow	Bernhard von	Germany
	Kohl	Helmut	Germany
Chief Justice	Rehnquist	William Hubbs	USA
Chief of State	Ulbricht	Walter	Germany
Clergyman	King Jr.	Martin Luther	USA
Colonial Governor	Frontenac	Louis de Buade	France
Communist Leader	Kun	Béla	Hungary
Congressman	Cannon	Joseph Gurney	USA
	Foley	Thomas Stephen	USA
	Kemp	Jack French	USA
	Mann	James Robert	USA
	Martin	Lynn Morley	USA
	Rayburn	Samuel Taliaferro (Sam)	USA
Congressman - Illinois	Rostenkowski	Dan	USA
Congressman - Missouri	Gephardt	Richard Andrew	USA
Conspirator	Oates	Titus	England
Courtier	Dudley	Robert	England
Czar	Godunov	Boris Fëdorovich	Russia
	Romanov	Mikhail Feodorovich	Russia
Dictator	Franco	Francisco	Spain
	Mussolini	Benito	Italy
Diplomat	Cushing	Caleb	USA
	Gadsden	James	USA
	Genêt	Edmond Charles Edouard	France
	Gromyko	Andrei Andreevich	Russia
	House	Edward Mandell	USA
	Mornay	Phillipe de	France
	Welles	Sumner	USA
Diplomat/Engineer - Suez	Lesseps	Ferdinand Marie de	France
Diplomat/Historian	Motley	John Lothrop	USA
Director General	Minuit	Peter	Netherlands
Duchess	Borgia	Lucretia	Italy
Duke	Churchill	John	England
Emperor	Alekseyvich	Pyotr (Peter the Great)	Russia
	Haile	Selassie	Ethiopia
	Selassie	Haile	Ethiopia
Empress	Pahlavi	Shahbanu Farah	Iran
Essayist/Statesman/Philosopher	Bacon	Francis	England
Federal Press Secretary	Fleischer	Lawrence Ari	USA
First Lady	Adams	Abigail	USA
	Adams	Louise Catherine	USA
	Arthur	Ellen Lewis	USA
	Buren	Hannah Van	USA
	Bush	Barbara	USA
	Bush	Laura	USA
	Carter	Rosalynn	USA
	Cleveland	Frances	USA
	Clinton	Hillary	USA
	Coolidge	Grace Anna	USA
	Eisenhower	Mamie Geneva	USA
	Fillmore	Abigail	USA
	Fillmore	Caroline Carmichael	USA
	Ford	Elizabeth Ann (Betty)	USA
	Garfield	Lucretia	USA
	Gorbachev	Raisa	Russia
	Grant	Julia	USA
	Harding	Florence Kling	USA

SOLVER SERIES: NAME FINDER

FAME	LAST NAME	FIRST NAME	COUNTRY
First Lady	Harrison	Anna	USA
	Harrison	Caroline Lavinia	USA
	Harrison	Mary Scott Lord	USA
	Hayes	Lucy Ware	USA
	Hoover	Lou	USA
	Jackson	Rachel Donelson	USA
	Jefferson	Martha Wayles	USA
	Johnson	Claudia (Ladybird) Alta	USA
	Johnson	Eliza	USA
	Kennedy	Jacqueline Lee	USA
	Lincoln	Mary	USA
	Madison	Dorothea (Dolley) Payne	USA
	Marcos	Imelda	Philippines
	McKinley	Ida	USA
	Monroe	Elizabeth	USA
	Nixon	Thelma Catherine Patricia	USA
	Peron	Evita (Eva)	Argentina
	Pierce	Jane Mears	USA
	Polk	Sarah	USA
	Reagan	Anne Frances Robbins	USA
	Roosevelt	Alice Hathaway	USA
	Roosevelt	Anna Eleanor	USA
	Roosevelt	Edith Kermit	USA
	Taft	Helen	USA
	Taylor	Margaret	USA
	Truman	Elizabeth (Bess)	USA
	Tyler	Julia	USA
	Tyler	Letitia	USA
	Washington	Martha Dandridge	USA
	Wilson	Edith Bolling	USA
	Wilson	Ellen Louise	USA
	Yeltsin	Naina	Russia
Foreign Minister	Arens	Moshe	Israel
General	Byng	Julian Hedworth George	England
General Secretary	Brezhnev	Leonid	Russia
General/Negro Liberator	Toussaint	Pierre François Dominique	Haiti
Girondist	Corday	Marie Anne Charlotte	France
Government Official/Lawyer	Hiss	Alger	USA
Governor	Ali	Pasha	Turkey
	Altgeld	John Peter	USA
	Berkely	William	England
	Bradford	William	USA
	Stuyvesant	Peter	Netherlands
Governor - Alabama	Wallace	George Corley	USA
Governor - California	Schwarzenegger	Arnold Alois	USA
Governor - Connecticut	Grasso	Ella Rose Tambussi	USA
Governor - Kansas	Landon	Alfred Mossman (Alf)	USA
Governor - Massachusetts	Dukakis	Michael Stanley	USA
	Endecott	John	England
Governor - New York	Clinton	DeWitt	USA
	Cuomo	Mario	USA
	Dewey	Thomas Edmund	USA
Governor - Plymouth Colony	Carver	John	USA
Governor - Texas	Richards	Ann Willis	USA
Governor - Virginia	Dale	Thomas	England
	Dinwiddle	Robert	England
	Warr	Thomas West De La	England
Governor of Massachusetts	Hutchinson	Thomas	USA

FAME	LAST NAME	FIRST NAME	COUNTRY
Head of Government	Chiang Kaishek	Chung Chen	China
Head of State	Gorbachev	Mikhail Sergeyevich	Russia
	Moro	Aldo	Italy
	Qaddafi	Muammar Abu Minyar al	Libya
	Sadat	Anwar al	Egypt
	Syngman	Rhee	South Korea
	Tse-Tung	Mao	China
Jurist/Statesman	Paine	Robert Treat	USA
Justice - Supreme Court	Jay	John	USA
	Marshall	Thurgood	USA
King	Boru	Brian	Ireland
	Bruce	Robert	Scotland
	Capet	Hugh	France
	Christophe	Henri	Haiti
	Hussein	King	Jordan
	Sobieski	John	Poland
King's Wife	Boleyn	Anne	England
Labor Leader	Bevin	Ernest	England
Lawyer/Political Leader	Guardia	Fiorello Henry La	USA
Lawyer/Reformer	Nader	Ralph	USA
Leader	Emilio	Aguinaldo	Philippines
Leader - Hindu Nationalist	Gandi	Mohandas Karamchand	India
Leader - Negro	Garvey	Marcus	West Indies
Leader - Women's Sufferage	Catt	Carrie Chapman	USA
Leader/National Hero	Scanderbeg	George Castriota	Albania
Legislator/Reformer	Follette	Robert Marion La	USA
Lieutenant Governor	Brock	Isaac	Canada
Lollard Leader	Oldcastle	John	England
Mayor - Chicago	Daley	Richard Joseph	USA
	Daley	Richard Michael	USA
Mayor - New York City	Dinkins	David Norman	USA
	Koch	Edward Irving (Ed)	USA
Minister	Bevan	Aneurin	Wales
National Security Advisor	Scowcroft	Brent	USA
Nationalist Leader	Casement	Roger David	Ireland
	O'Connell	Daniel	Ireland
	O'Connor	Thomas Power	Ireland
	Parnell	Charles Stewart	Ireland
Nazi Propagandist	Goebbels	Joseph Paul	Germany
Negro Leader	White	Walter Francis	USA
Parliamentary Leader	Pym	John	England
Patriot	Gwinett	Button	USA
	Wallace	William	Scotland
Patriot - Revolutionary	Kemal	Mustafa	Egypt
Patriot/Political Reformer	Rienzi	Cola di	Italy
Patriot/Revolutionist	Mazzini	Giuseppe	Italy
Patriot/Silversmith	Revere	Paul	USA
Philosopher/Anarchist	Bakunin	Mikhail Aleksandrovich	Russia
Philosopher/Political Theorist	Arendt	Hannah	Germany
Political & Revoltionary Leader	Sun	Yatsen	China
Political Leader - Communist	Foster	William Zebulon	USA
Political Leader/Journalist	Greeley	Horace	USA
Political Leader/Lawyer	Willkie	Wendell Lewis	USA
Political Scientist/Socialist	Laski	Harold Joseph	England
Political Supporter	Mesta	Perle	USA
Politician	Douglas	Stephen Arnold	USA
	Kirkpatrick	Jeane Jordan	USA
	Richardson	Elliot Lee	USA

SOLVER SERIES: NAME FINDER

FAME	LAST NAME	FIRST NAME	COUNTRY
Politician	Smith	Alfred Emanuel	USA
	Tilden	Samuel Jones	USA
	Tweed	William Marcy (Boss)	USA
Politician/Activist - Civil Rights	Young Jr.	Andrew Jackson	USA
Politician/General	Rensselaer	Stephen Van	USA
Politician/Historian	Selden	John	England
Politician/Journalist	Daudet	Léon	France
Politician/Orator	Bryan	William Jennings	USA
Premier	Clemenceau	Georges Benjamin Eugéne	France
	En-Lai	Zhou	China
	Gambetta	Léon	France
	Khrushchev	Nikita Sergeyevich	Russia
	Laval	Pierre	France
	Orlando	Vittorio Emanuele	Italy
	Pétain	Henri Philippe	France
	Reynaud	Paul	France
	Stalin	Joseph	Russia
Premier - U.S.S.R.	Kosygin	Aleksei Nikolaevich	Russia
	Lenin	Vladimir Ilyich	Russia
President	Adams	John	USA
	Adams	John Quincy	USA
	al Assad	Hafez	Syria
	Alemán	Miguel	Mexico
	Amin	Idi	Uganda
·	Arafat	Yasir	Palestine
	Arthur	Chester Alan	USA
	Bene_	Eduard	Czechoslovakia
	Bourguiba	Habib ben Ali	Tunisia
	Buchanan	James	USA
	Buren	Martin Van	USA
	Bush	George Herbert Walker	USA
	Bush	George W.	USA
	Calles	Plutarco Elías	Mexico
	Cárdenas	Lázaro	Mexico
	Carnot	Marie Francois Sadi	France
	Carranza	Venustiano	Mexico
	Carter	James (Jimmy) Earl	USA
	Childers	Erskine Hamilton	Ireland
	Cleveland	Stephen Grover	USA
	Clinton	William Jefferson	USA
	Coolidge	John Calvin	USA
	Coty	René	France
	Díaz	José de la Cruz Porfirio	Mexico
	Diem	Ngo Dinh	South Vietnam
	Duvalier	François (Papa Doc)	Haiti
	Eisenhower	Dwight David (Ike)	USA
	Fillmore	Millard	USA
	Ford	Gerald Rudolph	USA
	Garfield	James Abram	USA
	Gaulle	Charles Andre Joseph de	France
	Grant	Ulysses Simpson	USA
	Harding	Warren Gamaliel	USA
	Harrison	Benjamin	USA
	Harrison	William Henry	USA
	Hayes	Rutherford Birchard	USA
	Herzog	Chaim	Israel
	Hillary	Patrick John	Ireland
	Ho Chi Minh	Nguyen Van	North Vietnam

FAME	LAST NAME	FIRST NAME	COUNTRY
President	Hoover	Herbert Clark	USA
	Hyde	Douglas	Ireland
	Jackson	Andrew	USA
	Jefferson	Thomas	USA
	Johnson	Andrew	USA
	Johnson	Lyndon Baines	USA
	Juárez	Benito Pablo	Mexico
	Jung	Kim Dae	South Korea
	Károlyi	Mihály	Hungary
	Kennedy	John Fitzgerald	USA
	Kruger	Paul	South Africa
	Lebrun	Albert	France
	Lincoln	Abraham	USA
	MacMahon	Marie Edmé Maurice de	France
	Madero	Francisco Indalecio	Mexico
	Madison	James	USA
	Marcos	Ferdinand	Philippines
	Martin	Ramon Grau San	Cuba
	Masaryk	Tomá_Garogue	Czechoslovakia
	McAleese	Mary	Ireland
	McKinley	William	USA
	Mitterrand	Francois	France
	Monroe	James	USA
	Mubarak	Muhammad Hosni Said	Egypt
	Nasser	Gamal Abdel	Saudi Arabia
	Nixon	Richard Milhous	USA
	Obregón	Alvaro	Mexico
	O'Dalaigh	Cearbhall	Ireland
	O'Higgins	Bernardo	Chile
	O'Kelly	Sean Thomas	Ireland
	Perón Sosa	Juan Domingo	Argentina
	Pierce	Franklin	USA
	Poincaré	Raymond	France
	Polk	James	USA
	Quezon	Manuel Luis	Philippines
	Reagan	Ronald	USA
	Rhee	Syngman	South Korea
	Robinson	Mary	Ireland
	Roosevelt	Franklin Delano	USA
	Roosevelt	Theodore	USA
	Sánchez	Oscar Arias	Costa Rica
	Santa Anna	Antonio López de	Mexico
	Seko	Mobutu Sese	Zaire
	Taft	William Howard	USA
	Taylor	Zachary	USA
	Truman	Harry S.	USA
	Tubman	William Vacanarat Shadrach	Liberia
	Tyler	John	USA
	Valera	Eamon De	Ireland
	Walesa	Lech	Poland
	Washington	George	USA
	Weizmann	Chaim	Israel
	Wilson	Thomas Woodrow	USA
	Yeltsin	Boris Nikolayevich	Russia
President - Confederacy	Davis	Jefferson	USA
President - Continental Congress	Hancock	John	USA
President/Kenya	Kenyatta	Jomo	Africa
President/Military Leader	Hussein	Saddam	Iraq

SOLVER SERIES: NAME FINDER

FAME	LAST NAME	FIRST NAME	COUNTRY
President/Prime Minister	Tito	Josip Broz	Yugoslavia
Presidential Candidate	Perot	Henry Ross	USA
Press Secretary	Ziegler	Ronald Louis (Ron)	USA
Pretender to Throne	Carlos	Don	Spain
Prime Minister	Abbott	John Joseph Caldwell	Canada
	Ahern	Bertie	Ireland
	Andrássy	Gyula	Hungary
	Asquith	Herbert Henry	England
	Attlee	Clement Richard	England
	Baldwin	Stanley	England
	Balfour	Arthur	England
	Barak	Ehud	Israel
	Begin	Menachem	Israel
	Ben-Gurion	David	Israel
	Bennett	Richard Bedford	Canada
	Blair	Tony	England
	Borden	Robert Laird	Canada
	Botha	Louis	South Africa
	Bowell	Mackenzie	Canada
	Bruce	Stanley Melbourne	Australia
	Bruton	John	Ireland
	Callaghan	James	England
	Campbell	Avril Phaedra Douglas (Kim)	Canada
	Campbell-Bannerman	Henry	England
	Canning	George	England
	Chamberlain	Arthur Neville	England
	Chou	En-Lai	China
	Chrétien	Jean Joseph Jacques	Canada
	Churchill	Winston Leonard Spencer	England
	Clark	Charles Joseph	Canada
	Cosgrave	Liam	Ireland
	Crispi	Francesco	Italy
	Diefenbaker	John George	Canada
	Disraeli	Benjamin	England
	Douglas-Home	Alec	England
	Eden	Robert Anthony	England
	Fitzgerald	Garrett	Ireland
	Gandi	Indira Nehru	India
	Gascoyne-Cecil	Robert Arthur Talbot	England
	George	David Lloyd	England
	Ghandi	Rajiv	India
	Gladstone	William Ewart	England
	Grenville	George	England
	Grey	Charles	England
	Grey	Earl	England
	Haughey	Charles James	Ireland
	Heath	Edward Richard George	England
	Inönü	Ismet	Turkey
	Kerensky	Aleksandr Feodorovich	Russia
	King	William Lyon Mackenzie	Canada
	Laurier	Wilfred	Canada
	Law	Andrew Bonar	England
	Li	Hung-chang	China
	Lloyd George	David	England
	Lynch	John Mary	Ireland
	MacDonald	James Ramsay	England
	Macdonald	John Alexander	Canada
	MacKenzie	Alexander	Canada

FAME	LAST NAME	FIRST NAME	COUNTRY
Prime Minister	MacMillan	Harold	England
	Major	John	England
	Martin	Paul Edgar Phillipe	Canada
	Meighen	Arthur	Canada
	Meir	Golda	Israel
	Melbourne	William Lamb	England
	Menzies	Robert Gordon	Australia
	Mulroney	Martin Brian	Canada
	Nagy	Imre	Hungary
	Nehru	Jawaharlal	India
	North	Frederick	England
	Paderewski	Ignace Jan	Poland
	Palme	Sven Olof Joachim	Sweden
	Palmerston	Henry John Temple	England
	Pearson	Lester Bowles	Canada
	Peel	Robert	England
	Peres	Shimon	Israel
	Pitt	William	England
	Rabin	Yitzhak	Israel
	Reynolds	Albert	Ireland
	Russell	John	England
	Salazar	Antonio de Oliveira	Portugal
	Shamir	Yitzhak	Israel
	Sharon	Ariel	Israel
	Smuts	Jan Christiaan	South Africa
	St. Laurent	Louis Stephen	Canada
	Thatcher	Margaret	England
	Thompson	John Sparrow David	Canada
	Trudeau	Pierre Elliott	Canada
	Tupper	Charles	Canada
	Turner	John Napier	Canada
	Walpole	Robert	England
	Wellington	Arthur Wellesley	England
	Wilson	James Harold	England
Proponent - Civil Rights	Guinier	Lani	USA
Protector - Commonwealth	Cromwell	Richard	England
Queen	Grey	Jane	England
	Noor	Lisa	Jordan
Queen - Hawaiian Islands	Liliuokalani	Lydia Kamekeha	USA
Rebellion Leader	Tyler	Wat	England
Reformer	Cartwright	John	England
Reformer - Political	Wilkes	John	England
Reformer - Protestant	Melanchthon	Phillip	Germany
Reformer - Religious	Socinus	Faustus	Italy
Reformer - Social	Saint-Simon	Charles Henri de Rouvroy	France
Reformer/Suffragist	Stanton	Elizabeth Cady	USA
	Stone	Lucy	USA
Revolutionary Leader	Cromwell	Oliver	England
	Danton	Georges Jacques	France
	Marat	Jean Paul	France
	Marx	Karl Heirich	Germany
Revolutionary Patriot	Deane	Silas	USA
Revolutionist	Orléans	Louis Phillipe Joseph	France
	Trotsky	Leon	Russia
	Villa	José Doroteo (Pancho)	Mexico
	Yat-Sen	Sun	China
	Zapata	Emiliano	Mexico
Revolutionist - Negro	Turner	Nat	USA

SOLVER SERIES: NAME FINDER

FAME	LAST NAME	FIRST NAME	COUNTRY
Revolutionist/Statesman	Mirabeau	Honoré Gabriel Riqueti	France
Second Lady	Gore	Mary Elizabeth (Tipper)	USA
Secretary - United Nations	Hammarskjöld	Dag Hjalmar Agne Carl	Sweden
Secretary of Agriculture	Benson	Ezra Taft	USA
Secretary of Commerce	Brown	Ronald Harmon (Ron)	USA
Secretary of Defense	Aspin	Leslie (Les)	USA
	Cohen	William S.	USA
Secretary of State	Acheson	Dean Gooderham	USA
	Baker	James A.	USA
	Blaine	James Gillespie	USA
	Christopher	Warren	USA
	Dulles	John Foster	USA
	Kissinger	Henry Alfred	USA
	Powell	Colin Luther	USA
	Rusk	David Dean	USA
Secretary of the Treasury	Morgenthau	Henry	USA
Secretary-General UN	Thant	U	Burma
	Waldheim	Kurt	Austria
Senator	Baker Jr.	Howard Henry	USA
	Bayh III	Birch Evans (Evan)	USA
	Benton	Thomas Hart	USA
	Bentsen Jr.	Lloyd Millard	USA
	Biden Jr.	Joseph Robinette	USA
	Boxer	Barbara Levy	USA
	Bradley	William Warren (Bill)	USA
	Brooke III	Edward William	USA
	Bumpers	Dale Leon	USA
	Campbell	Ben Nighthorse	USA
	Cranston	Alan	USA
	D'Amato	Alfonse	USA
	Dellums	Ronald Vernie (Ron)	USA
	Dirksen	Everett McKinley	USA
	Fulbright	James William	USA
	Houston	Samuel	USA
	Lodge	Henry Cabot	USA
	Norris	George William	USA
Senator - Arizona	Goldwater	Barry Morris	USA
Senator - California	Feinstein	Dianne Goldman Berman	USA
	Wilson	Peter Barton (Pete)	USA
Senator - Colorado	Hart	Gary Warren	USA
Senator - Connecticut	Dodd	Christopher J. (Chris)	USA
Senator - Florida	Graham	Daniel Robert (Bob)	USA
Senator - Georgia	Nunn	Samuel Augustus (Sam)	USA
Senator - Hawaii	Inouye	Daniel Ken	USA
Senator - Indiana	Lugar	Richard Green (Dick)	USA
Senator - Kansas	Dole	Robert Joseph (Bob)	USA
Senator - Louisiana	Long	Huey Pierce (The Kingfish)	USA
Senator - Maine	Muskie	Edmund Sixtus	USA
Senator - Massachusetts	Kennedy	Edward Moore (Ted)	USA
Senator - Minnesota	McCarthy	Eugene Joseph (Gene)	USA
Senator - Mississippi	Lotte Jr.	Chester Trent	USA
Senator - New Hampshire	Sununu	John Edward	USA
Senator - New York	Kennedy	Robert Francis (Bobby)	USA
	Moynihan	Daniel Patrick (Pat)	USA
Senator - North Carolina	Dole	Elizabeth Hanford (Liddy)	USA
	Helms	Jesse Alexander	USA
Senator - Ohio	Glenn Jr.	John Herschel	USA
Senator - Oregon	Packwood	Robert William (Bob)	USA

FAME	LAST NAME	FIRST NAME	COUNTRY
Senator - Pennsylvania	Specter	Arlen	USA
Senator - Rhode Island	Pell	Claiborne de Borda	USA
Senator - South Carolina	Thurmond	James Strom	USA
Senator - South Dakota	McGovern	George Stanley	USA
Senator - Tennessee	Kefauver	Estes	USA
Senator - Texas	Gramm	William Philip (Phil)	USA
Senator - Utah	Garn	Edwin Jacob (Jake)	USA
	Hatch	Orrin Grant	USA
Senator - Virginia	Robb	Charles Spittal (Chuck)	USA
Senator - Wisconsin	McCarthy	Joseph Raymond	USA
Senator/Press Secretary	Salinger	Pierre Emil George	USA
Shah	Pahlavi	Mohammed Reza	Iran
Social Critic	Channing	William Ellery	USA
Social Leader	Récamier	Jean Françoise Julie	France
Social Reformer/Writer	Kagawa	Toyohiko	Japan
Social Reformist	Bloomer	Amelia Jenks	USA
Socialist Leader	Liebknecht	Karl	Germany
	Thomas	Norman Mattoon	USA
Socialist Leader/Journalist	Jaurès	Jean Léon	France
Socialist Reformer	Fourier	François Marie Charles	France
Speaker of the House	Gingrich	Newton Leroy (Newt)	USA
Statesman	Adams	Charles Francis	USA
	Adams	Samuel	USA
	Alexander	Harold Rupert	England
	Artevelde	Jacob Van	USA
	Artevelde	Phillip Van	USA
	Baker	Newton Diehl	USA
	Bancroft	George	USA
	Briand	Aristide	France
	Bright	John	England
	Broglie	Achille Charles Léonce	France
	Carnot	Lazare Nicolas Marguerite	France
	Cass	Lewis	USA
	Chamberlain	Joseph Austen	England
	Churchill	Randolph Henry Spencer	England
	Clive	Robert	England
	Colbert	Jean Baptiste	France
	Cromwell	Thomas	England
	Daniels	Josephus	USA
	Dickinson	John	USA
	Duer	William	USA
	Egmont	Lamoral	Italy
	Fish	Hamilton	USA
	Gratton	Henry	Ireland
	Grey	Edward	England
	Hamilton	Alexander	USA
	Hastings	Warren	England
	Hull	Cordell	USA
	Huntington	Samuel	USA
	Litvinov	Maximovitch	Russia
	Livingston	Robert R.	USA
	Masaryk	Jan	Czechoslovakia
	Molotov	Vyacheslav Mikhailovich	Russia
	Richelieu	Armand Jean du Plessis	France
	Root	Elihu	USA
	Rutledge	Edward	USA
	Rutledge	John	USA
	Shaftesbury	Anthony Ashley Cooper	England

SOLVER SERIES: NAME FINDER

FAME	LAST NAME	FIRST NAME	COUNTRY
Statesman	Sherman	John	USA
	Sherman	Roger	USA
	Stanhope	Philip Dormer	England
	Strafford	Thomas Wentworth	England
	Sully	Maximilien de Béthune	France
	Templewood	Samuel John Gurney Hoare	England
	Torrens	Robert	Australia
	Walsingham	Francis	England
	Wilberforce	William	England
	Wolsey	Thomas	England
Statesman - Puritan	Vane	Henry	England
Statesman/Abolitionist	Stevens	Thaddeus	USA
	Sumner	Charles	USA
Statesman/Cardinal	Fleury	André Hercule	France
Statesman/Diplomat	Carteret	John	England
	Metternich	Klemens Wenzel von	Austria
	Morris	Gouverneur	USA
	Nesselrode	Karl Robert	Russia
	Pinckney	Charles Cotes-worth	USA
Statesman/Economist	Turgot	Anne Robertson Jacques	France
Statesman/Educator	Bunche	Ralph Johnson	USA
Statesman/Essayist	Macaulay	Thomas Babington	England
Statesman/Explorer/Poet	Raleigh	Walter	England
Statesman/General	Guise	François de Lorraine	France
	Guise	Henri de Lorranine	France
	Marshall	George Catlett	USA
Statesman/Historian	Beveridge	Albert Jeremiah	USA
	Guizot	François Pierre Guillaume	France
	Thiers	Louis Adolphe	France
Statesman/Journalist	Douglass	Frederick	USA
	Schurz	Carl	USA
Statesman/Jurist	Coke	Edward	England
Statesman/Jurist/Scholar	Grotius	Hugo	Netherlands
Statesman/Military Leader	Warwick	Richard Neville	England
Statesman/Orator	Clay	Henry	USA
	Everett	Edward	USA
	Fox	Charles James	England
	Henry	Patrick	USA
	Randolph	John	USA
	Webster	Daniel	USA
Statesman/Parlimentarian	Hampden	John	England
Statesman/Patriot	Barneveldt	Jan van Olden	Netherlands
Statesman/Philosopher	Haldane	Richard Burdon	Scotland
Statesman/Prelate	Mazarin	Jules	France
Statesman/Scholar	Bodley	Thomas	England
Statesman/Scientist	Thompson	Benjamin	England
Statesman/Secretary of State	Seward	William Henry	USA
	Stimson	Henry Lewis	USA
Statesman/Secretary of War	Stanton	Edwin McMasters	USA
Statesman/Writer	Hay	John Milton	USA
Stateswoman	Abzug	Bella Savitsky	USA
Suffragist	Pankhurst	Emmeline	England
Surgeon General	Elders	Minnie Jocelyn	USA
	Koop	Charles Everett	USA
Temperance Leader	Willard	Francis Elizabeth Caroline	USA
Theosophist	Besant	Annie	England
Vice-President	Agnew	Spiro T.	USA
	Barkley	Alben W.	USA

FAME	LAST NAME	FIRST NAME	COUNTRY
Vice-President	Breckenridge	John Cabell	USA
	Burr	Aaron	USA
	Calhoun	John Caldwell	USA
	Cheney	Richard	USA
	Clinton	George	USA
	Colfax	Schuyler	USA
	Curtis	Charles	USA
	Dallas	George M.	USA
	Dawes	Charles Gates	USA
	Fairbanks	Charles W.	USA
	Garner	John Nance	USA
	Gerry	Elbridge	USA
	Gore	Albert	USA
	Hamlin	Hannibal	USA
	Hendricks	Thomas	USA
	Hobart	Garret A.	USA
	Humphrey	Hubert H.	USA
	Johnson	Richard M.	USA
	King	William R.	USA
	Marshall	Thomas R.	USA
	Mondale	Walter	USA
	Morton	Levi P.	USA
	Quayle	James Danforth	USA
	Rockefeller	Nelson Aldrich	USA
	Sherman	James S.	USA
	Stevenson	Adlai E.	USA
	Tompkins	Daniel D.	USA
	Wallace	Henry Agard	USA
	Wheeler	William A.	USA
	Wilson	Henry	USA
Vice-President - Confederacy	Stephens	Alexander Hamilton	USA
Viceroy	Curzon	George Nathaniel	England
	Mehemet	Ali	Egypt
Wife - Martin Luther King	King	Coretta Scott	USA
Wife - Robert Kennedy	Kennedy	Ethel Skakel	USA
Women's Rights Proponent	Anthony	Susan B.	USA
Zionist Leader	Szold	Henrietta	USA

SCIENCE:

Alchemist	Cagliostro	Alesandro di	Sicily
Anatomist	Vesalius	Andreas	Italy
Astrologer/Witch	Leek	Sybil	England
Astronomer	Brahe	Tycho	Denmark
	Copernicus	Nicholas	Poland
	Draper	Henry	USA
	Flammarion	Camille	France
	Herschel	William	England
	Hubble	Edwin Powell	USA
	Lovell	Alfred Charles Bernard	England
	Lowell	Percival	USA
	Mitchell	Maria	USA
	Pickering	William Henry	USA
	Sagan	Carl	USA
	Schiaparelli	Giovanni Virginio	Italy
	Shapley	Harlow	USA
	Sitter	Willem de	Netherlands
Astronomer/Astrophysicist	Eddington	Arthur Stanley	England

SOLVER SERIES: NAME FINDER

FAME	LAST NAME	FIRST NAME	COUNTRY
Astronomer/Mathematician	Halley	Edmund	England
	Kepler	Johannes	Germany
	Lagrange	Joseph Louis	France
	Laplace	Pierre Simon de	France
Astronomer/Physicist	Galilei	Galileo	Italy
Astrophysicist	Abbot	Charles Greeley	USA
Bacteriologist	Noguchi	Hideyo	Japan
	Wassermann	August von	Germany
	Zinsser	Hans	USA
Bacteriologist/Writer	Kruif	Paul Henry de	USA
Biologist	Weismann	August	Germany
Biologist/Bacteriologist	Metchnikoff	Élie	Russia
Biologist/Philosopher	Haeckel	Ernst Heinrich	Germany
Biologist/Physiologist	Loeb	Jacques	USA
Biologist/Writer	Carson	Rachel Louise	USA
	Haldane	John Burdon	England
	Huxley	Julian Sorrell	England
	Huxley	Thomas Henry	England
Botanist	Banks	Joseph	England
	Brown	Robert	England
	Gray	Asa	USA
	Linnaeus	Carolus	Sweden
	Vries	Hugo De	Netherlands
Botanist - Founder of Genetics	Mendel	Gregor Johann	Austria
Botanist/Bacteriologist	Cohn	Ferdinand Julius	Germany
Botanist/Chemist	Carver	George Washington	USA
Chemist	Berzelius	Jons	Sweden
	Brix	Adolf F.	Germany
	Dakin	Henry D.	USA
	Davy	Humphry	England
	Hall	Charles Martin	USA
	Knudsen	Martin	Denmark
	Lavoisier	Antoine-Laurent de	France
	Liebig	Justus von	Germany
	Mendeleev	Dmitri Ivanovich	Russia
	Solvay	Ernest	Belgium
	Takamine	Jokichi	USA
Chemist/Bacteriologist	Pasteur	Louis	France
Chemist/Educator	Conant	James Bryant	USA
Chemist/Inventor	Bunsen	Robert Wilhelm	Germany
Chemist/Inventor - Explosives	Maxim	Hudson	USA
Chemist/Physicist	Avogadro	Amedeo	Italy
	Boyle	Robert	England
	Crookes	William	England
	Dalton	John	England
	Gay-Lussac	Joseph Louis	France
Chemistry - Nobel Laureate	Agre	Peter	USA
	Alder	Kurt	Germany
	Altman	Sidney	Canada
	Anfinsen	Christian B.	USA
	Arrhenius	Svante August	Sweden
	Aston	Francis William	England
	Baeyer	Johann Friedrich Adolf von	Germany
	Barton	Derek H.R.	England
	Berg	Paul	USA
	Bergius	Friedrich	Germany
	Bosch	Carl	Germany
	Boyer	Paul D.	USA

FAME	LAST NAME	FIRST NAME	COUNTRY
Chemistry - Nobel Laureate	Brown	Herbert C.	USA
	Buchner	Eduard	Germany
	Butenandt	Adolf Friedrich Johann	Germany
	Calvin	Melvin	USA
	Cech	Thomas R.	USA
	Chauvin	Yves	France
	Ciechanover	Aaron	Israel
	Corey	Elias James	USA
	Cornforth	John Warcup	Australia
	Cram	Donald J.	USA
	Crutzen	Paul J.	Netherlands
	Curie	Marie	France
	Curl Jr.	Robert F.	USA
	Debye	Peter Joseph William	USA
	Deisenhofer	Johann	Germany
	Diels	Otto Paul Hermann	Germany
	Elgen	Manfred	Germany
	Ernst	Richard R.	Switzerland
	Euler-Chelpin	Hans Karl August Simon von	Sweden
	Fenn	John B.	USA
	Fischer	Ernst Otto	Germany
	Fischer	Hans	Germany
	Fischer	Hermann Emil	Germany
	Flory	Paul J.	USA
	Fukui	Kenichi	Japan
	Giauque	William Francis	USA
	Gilbert	Walter	USA
	Grignard	Victor	France
	Grubbs	Robert H.	USA
	Haber	Fritz	Germany
	Hahn	Otto	Germany
	Harden	Arthur	England
	Hassel	Odd	Norway
	Hauptman	Herbert	USA
	Haworth	Walter Norman	England
	Heeger	Alan	USA
	Herschbach	Dudley R.	USA
	Hershko	Avram	Israel
	Herzberg	Gerhard	Canada
	Hevesy	George de	Hungary
	Heyrovsky	Jaroslav	Czechoslovakia
	Hinshelwood	Cyril Norman	England
	Hodgkin	Dorothy Crowfoot	England
	Hoff	Jacobus Henricus Van't	Netherlands
	Hoffmann	Roald	USA
	Huber	Robert	Germany
	Joliot-Curie	Irène	France
	Joliot-Curie	Jean Frédéric	France
	Karle	Jerome	USA
	Karrer	Paul	Switzerland
	Kendrew	John Cowdery	England
	Klug	Aaron	England
	Knowles	William S.	USA
	Kohn	Walter	USA
	Kroto	Harold	England
	Kuhn	Richard	Germany
	Langmuir	Irving	USA
	Lee	Yuan T.	USA

SOLVER SERIES: NAME FINDER

FAME	LAST NAME	FIRST NAME	COUNTRY
Chemistry - Nobel Laureate	Lehn	Jean-Marie	France
	Leloir	Luis F.	Argentina
	Libby	Willard Frank	USA
	Lipscomb	William N.	USA
	MacDiarmid	Alan G.	New Zealand
	MacKinnon	Roderick	USA
	Marcus	Rudolph A.	USA
	Martin	Archer John Porter	England
	McMillan	Edwin Mattison	USA
	Merrifield	Bruce	USA
	Michel	Hartmut	Germany
	Mitchell	Peter	England
	Moissan	Henri	France
	Molina	Mario J.	USA
	Moore	Stanford	USA
	Mulliken	Robert S.	USA
	Mullis	Kary B.	USA
	Natta	Giulio	Italy
	Nernst	Walter Hermann	Germany
	Norrish	Ronald George Wreyford	England
	Northrop	John Howard	USA
	Noyori	Ryoji	Japan
	Olah	George A.	USA
	Onsager	Lars	USA
	Ostwald	Wilhelm	Germany
	Pauling	Linus Carl	USA
	Pedersen	Charles J.	USA
	Perutz	Max Ferdinand	England
	Polanyi	John C.	Canada
	Pople	John A.	England
	Porter	George	England
	Pregl	Fritz	Austria
	Prelog	Vladimir	Switzerland
	Prigogine	Ilya	Belgium
	Ramsay	William	England
	Richards	Theodore William	USA
	Robinson	Robert	England
	Rose	Irwin	USA
	Rowland	Frank Sherwood	USA
	Rutherford	Ernest	England
	Ruzicka	Leopold	Switzerland
	Sabatier	Paul	France
	Sanger	Frederick	England
	Schrock	Richard R.	USA
	Seaborg	Glenn Theodore	USA
	Semenov	Nikolay	Russia
	Sharpless	Karl Barry	USA
	Shirakawa	Hideki	Japan
	Skou	Jens C.	Denmark
	Smalley	Richard E.	USA
	Smith	Michael	Canada
	Soddy	Frederick	England
	Stanley	Wendell Meredith	USA
	Staudinger	Hermann	Germany
	Stein	William H.	USA
	Sumner	James Batchellor	USA
	Svedberg	Theodore	Sweden
	Synge	Richard Laurence Millington	England

FAME	LAST NAME	FIRST NAME	COUNTRY
Chemistry - Nobel Laureate	Tanaka	Koichi	Japan
	Taube	Henry	USA
	Tiselius	Arne Wilhelm Kaurin	Sweden
	Todd	Alexander R.	England
	Urey	Harold Clayton	USA
	Vigneaud	Vincent du	USA
	Virtanen	Artturi Ilmari	Finland
	Walker	John E.	England
	Wallach	Otto	Germany
	Werner	Alfred	Switzerland
	Wieland	Heinrich Otto	Germany
	Wilkinson	Geoffrey	England
	Willstätter	Richard Martin	Germany
	Windaus	Adolf Otto	Germany
	Wittig	Georg	England
	Woodward	Robert Burns	USA
	Wüthrich	Kurt	Switzerland
	Zewail	Ahmed Hassan	USA
	Ziegler	Karl	Germany
	Zsigmondy	Richard Adolf	Germany
Dentist	Morton	William Thomas Green	USA
Economist	Beveridge	William Henry	England
Engineer	Bessemer	Henry	England
	Eads	James Buchanan	USA
Engineer - Bridge Builder	Stephenson	Robert	England
Engineer - Steam Locomotive	Stephenson	George	England
Engineer/Administrator	Bush	Vannevar	USA
Entomologist	Fabre	Jean Henri	France
Ethologist	Fossey	Dian	USA
Faith Healer/Religious Mystic	Rasputin	Grigori Efimovich	Russia
Geneticist	Dobzhansky	Theodosius Grigorievich	USA
Geologist	Chamberlin	Thomas Chrowder	USA
	Geikie	Archibald	Scotland
	Lyell	Charles	England
	Smith	William	England
Geologist/Mineralogist	Dana	James Dwight	USA
Horticulturalist	Burbank	Luther	USA
Inventor	Arkwright	Richard	England
	Tesla	Nikola	USA
Inventor - Astronomer	Celsius	Anders	Sweden
Inventor - Cotton Gin	Whitney	Eli	USA
Inventor - Diesel Engine	Diesel	Rudolph	Germany
Inventor - Electrical Devices	Edison	Thomas Alva	USA
Inventor - Elevator	Otis	Elisha Graves	USA
Inventor - Firearms	Browning	John Moses	USA
Inventor - Land Camera	Land	Edwin Herbert	USA
Inventor - Linotype	Mergenthaler	Ottmar	USA
Inventor - McIntosh Apple	McIntosh	John	Canada
Inventor - Power Loom	Cartwright	Edmund	England
Inventor - Radio Equipment	Forest	Lee De	USA
Inventor - Reaping Machine	McCormick	Cyrus Hall	USA
Inventor - Revolver	Colt	Samuel	USA
Inventor - Sewing Machine	Howe	Elias	USA
	Singer	Isaac Merritt	USA
Inventor - Shorthand	Pitman	Isaac	England
Inventor - Spinning Jenny	Hargreaves	James	England
Inventor - Spinning Mule	Crompton	Samuel	England
Inventor - Steam Boat	Fitch	John	USA

SOLVER SERIES: NAME FINDER

FAME	LAST NAME	FIRST NAME	COUNTRY
Inventor - Steam Boat	Fulton	Robert	USA
Inventor - Telegraph	Morse	Samuel Finley Breese	USA
Inventor - Telephone	Bell	Alexander Graham	USA
Inventor - Vulcanizing Rubber	Goodyear	Charles	USA
Inventor/Electrical Engineer	Kettering	Charles Franklin	USA
	Sperry	Elmer Ambrose	USA
	Steinmetz	Charles Proteus	USA
Inventor/Engineer	Siemens	William	England
	Wankel	Felix	Germany
	Watt	James	Scotland
	Whittle	Frank	England
Inventor/Manufacturer	Thomas	Seth	USA
Inventor/Physicist	Hooke	Robert	England
Inventor/Sculptor - Rubik's Cube	Rubik	Ernő	Hungary
Inventor/Statesman/Writer	Franklin	Benjamin	USA
Mathametician	Galois	Evariste	France
	Bernoulli	Jacques	Switzerland
	Bernoulli	Jean	Switzerland
	Euler	Leonhard	Switzerland
	Gunter	Edmund	England
	Legendre	Adrien Marie	France
	Lobachevski	Nikolai Ivanovich	Russia
	Mollweide	Karl B.	Germany
	Poincaré	Jules Henri	France
	Taylor	Brook	England
	Venn	John	England
	Wiener	Norbert	USA
Mathematician - Logarithms	Napier	John	Scotland
Mathematician/Astronomer	Bowditch	Nathaniel	USA
Mathematician/Clergyman	Bayes	Thomas	England
Mathematician/Philosopher	Newton	Isaac	England
	Peirce	Charles Sanders	USA
	Pascal	Blaise	France
Medical Doctor	Dooley	Thomas Anthony	USA
Medicine - Nobel Laureate	Adrian	Edgar Douglas	USA
	Arber	Werner	Switzerland
	Axel	Richard	USA
	Axelrod	Julius	USA
	Baltimore	David	USA
	Banting	Frederick Grant	Canada
	Bárány	Robert	Austria
	Beadle	George Wells	USA
	Behring	Emil Adolf von	Germany
	Békésy	Georg von	USA
	Benacerraf	Baruj	USA
	Bergström	Sune K.	Sweden
	Bishop	John Michael	USA
	Black	James W.	England
	Blobel	Günter	USA
	Bloch	Konrad	USA
	Blumberg	Baruch S.	USA
	Bordet	Jules	Belgium
	Bovet	Daniel	Italy
	Brenner	Sydney	England
	Brown	Michael S.	USA
	Buck	Linda B.	USA
	Burnet	Frank Macfarlane	Australia
	Cajal	Santiago Ramón y	Spain

FAME	LAST NAME	FIRST NAME	COUNTRY
Medicine - Nobel Laureate	Carlsson	Arvid	Sweden
	Carrel	Alexis	France
	Chain	Ernst Boris	England
	Claude	Albert	Belgium
	Cohen	Stanley	USA
	Cori	Carl Ferdinand	USA
	Cori	Gerty	USA
	Cormack	Allan M.	USA
	Cournand	Andre Frédéric	USA
	Crick	Francis Harry Compton	England
	Dale	Henry Hallett	England
	Dam	Henri Carl Peter	Denmark
	Dausset	Jean	France
	Delbrück	Max	USA
	Doherty	Peter C.	Australia
	Doisy	Edward Adelbert	USA
	Domagk	Gerhard	Germany
	Dulbecco	Renato	USA
	Duve	Christian de	Belgium
	Eccles	John Carew	Australia
	Edelman	Gerald M.	USA
	Ehrlich	Paul	Germany
	Eijkman	Christiaan	Netherlands
	Einthoven	Willem	Netherlands
	Elion	Gertrude B.	USA
	Enders	John Franklin	USA
	Erlanger	Joseph	USA
	Euler	Ulf von	Sweden
	Fibiger	Julius Andreas Grib	Denmark
	Finsen	Niels Ryberg	Denmark
	Fischer	Edmond H.	Switzerland
	Fleming	Alexander	England
	Florey	Howard Walter	Australia
	Forssmann	Werner	Germany
	Frisch	Karl von	Germany
	Furchgott	Robert F.	USA
	Gajdusek	Daniel Carleton	USA
	Gasser	Herbert Spencer	USA
	Gilman	Alfred G.	USA
	Goldstein	Joseph L.	USA
	Golgi	Camillo	Italy
	Granit	Ragnar	Sweden
	Greengard	Paul	USA
	Guillemin	Roger	USA
	Gullstrand	Allvar	Sweden
	Hartline	Haldan Keffer	USA
	Hartwell	Leland H.	USA
	Hench	Philip Showalter	USA
	Hershey	Alfred D.	USA
	Hess	Walter Rudolf	Switzerland
	Heymans	Corneille Jean François	Belgium
	Hill	Archibald Vivian	England
	Hitchings	George H.	USA
	Hodgkin	Alan Lloyd	England
	Holley	Robert W.	USA
	Hopkins	Frederick Gowland	England
	Horvitz	Robert	USA
	Hounsfield	Godfrey N.	England

SOLVER SERIES: NAME FINDER

FAME	LAST NAME	FIRST NAME	COUNTRY
Medicine - Nobel Laureate	Houssay	Bernardo Alberto	Argentina
	Hubel	David H.	USA
	Huggins	Charles Brenton	USA
	Hunt	Tim	England
	Huxley	Andrew Fielding	England
	Ignarro	Louis J.	USA
	Jacob	François	France
	Jerne	Niels K.	Denmark
	Kandel	Eric R.	USA
	Katz	Bernard	England
	Kendall	Edward Calvin	USA
	Khorana	Har Gobind	USA
	Koch	Robert	Germany
	Kocher	Emil Theodor	Switzerland
	Köhler	Georges J.F.	Germany
	Kornberg	Arthur	USA
	Kossel	Albrecht	Germany
	Krebs	Edwin G.	USA
	Krebs	Hans Adolf	England
	Krogh	Schack August Steenberg	Denmark
	Landsteiner	Karl	Austria
	Lauterbur	Paul C.	USA
	Laveran	Charles Louis Alphonse	France
	Lederberg	Joshua	USA
	Levi-Montalcini	Rtia	Italy
	Lewis	Edward B.	USA
	Lipmann	Fritz Albert	USA
	Loewi	Otto	Austria
	Lorenz	Konrad Zacharias	Austria
	Luria	Salvador E.	USA
	Lwoff	André	France
	Lynen	Feodor	Germany
	Macleod	John James Richard	Canada
	Mansfield	Peter	England
	Marshall	Barry J.	Australia
	McClintock	Barbara	USA
	Mechnikov	Ilya Ilyich	Russia
	Medawar	Peter Brian	England
	Meyerhof	Otto Fritz	Germany
	Milstein	César	England
	Minot	George Richards	USA
	Moniz	Antonio Caetano Egas	Portugal
	Monod	Jacques	France
	Morgan	Thomas Hunt	USA
	Muller	Hermann Joseph	USA
	Müller	Paul Hermann	Switzerland
	Murad	Ferid	USA
	Murphy	William Parry	USA
	Murray	Joseph E.	USA
	Nathans	Daniel	USA
	Neher	Erwin	Germany
	Nicolle	Charles Jules Henri	France
	Nurse	Paul M.	England
	Nüsslein-Volhard	Christiane	Germany
	Ochoa	Severo	USA
	Palade	George E.	USA
	Pavlov	Ivan Petrovich	Russia
	Porter	Rodney	England

FAME	LAST NAME	FIRST NAME	COUNTRY
Medicine - Nobel Laureate	Prusiner	Stanley B.	USA
	Reichstein	Tadeus	Switzerland
	Richards	Dickinson W.	USA
	Richet	Charles Robert	France
	Robbins	Frederick Chapman	USA
	Roberts	Richard J.	England
	Rodbell	Martin	USA
	Ross	Ronald	England
	Rous	Peyton	USA
	Sakmann	Bert	Germany
	Samuelsson	Bengt I.	Sweden
	Schally	Andrew V.	USA
	Sharp	Phillip A.	USA
	Sherrington	Charles Scott	England
	Smith	Hamilton O.	USA
	Snell	George D.	USA
	Speman	Hans	Germany
	Sperry	Roger W.	USA
	Sulston	John E.	England
	Sutherland Jr.	Earl W.	USA
	Szent-Györgyi	Albert von	Hungary
	Tatum	Edward Lawrie	USA
	Temin	Howard Martin	USA
	Theiler	Max	South Africa
	Theorell	Axel Hugo Theodor	Sweden
	Thomas	Edward Donnall	USA
	Tinbergen	Nikolaas	England
	Tonegawa	Susumu	Japan
	Vane	John R.	England
	Varmus	Harold E.	USA
	Wagner-Jauregg	Julius	Austria
	Waksman	Selman Abraham	USA
	Wald	George	USA
	Warburg	Otto Heinrich	Germany
	Warren	Robin	Australia
	Watson	James Dewey	USA
	Weller	Thomas Huckle	USA
	Whipple	George Hoyt	USA
	Wieschaus	Eric F.	USA
	Wiesel	Torsten N.	Sweden
	Wilkins	Maurice Hugh Frederick	England
	Yalow	Rosalyn	USA
	Zinkernagel	Rolf M.	Switzerland
Naturalist	Darwin	Charles Robert	England
Naturalist/Physician	Darwin	Erasmus	England
Naturalist/Writer	Muir	John	USA
Neurologist	Charcot	Jean Martin	France
Neurosurgeon	Cushing	Harvey Williams	USA
Nuclear Physicist	Meitner	Lise	Austria
Nurse	Cavell	Edith Louisa	England
	Sanger	Margaret	USA
Nurse - Crimean War	Nightingale	Florence	England
Optician	Fraunhofer	Joseph von	Bavaria
Ornithologist	Audubon	John James	USA
Paleontologist/Biologist	Osborn	Henry Fairfield	USA
Pathologist	Flexner	Simon	USA
	Kline	Benjamin S.	USA
Pediatrician/Writer	Spock	Benjamin McLane	USA

SOLVER SERIES: NAME FINDER

FAME	LAST NAME	FIRST NAME	COUNTRY
Physician	Addison	Thomas	England
	Blackwell	Elizabeth	USA
	Harvey	William	England
	Hodgkin	Thomas	England
	Jenner	Edward	England
	Jenner	William	England
	Mantoux	Charles	France
	Mayo	Charles Horace	USA
	Mayo	William James	USA
	Ménière	Prosper	France
	Osler	William	Canada
	Parkinson	James	England
	Rush	Benjamin	USA
Physician - Down's Syndrome	Down	John L.H.	England
Physician - Homeopathy	Hahnemann	Christian Friedrich Samuel	Germany
Physician - Polio Vaccine	Sabin	Albert Bruce	USA
	Salk	Jonas Edward	USA
Physician/Alchemist	Paracelsus	Philippus Aurelus	Switzerland
Physician/Compiler - Thesaurus	Roget	Peter Mark	England
Physician/Criminologist	Lombroso	Cesare	Italy
Physician/Economist	Quesnay	François	France
Physician/Surgeon	Ogilvie	Heneage	England
Physician/Theologian	Servetus	Michael	Spain
Physician/Writer	Browne	Thomas	England
	Grenfell	Wifred	England
	Holmes	Oliver Wendell	USA
	Nordau	Max Simon	Germany
Physicist	Allen	James A. Van	USA
	Ampere	André Marie	France
	Angström	Anders Jöns	Sweden
	Becquerel	Alexandre Edmond	France
	Becquerel	Antoine César	France
	Bernoulli	Daniel	Switzerland
	Bose	Jagadis Chandra	India
	Broglie	Louis César Victor Maurice	France
	Carnot	Nicolas Léonard Sadi	France
	Compton	Karl Taylor	USA
	Condon	Edward Uhler	USA
	Fahrenheit	Gabriel	Germany
	Foucault	Jean Bernard Léon	France
	Fresnel	Augustin Jean	France
	Graaff	Robert J. Van de	USA
	Hawking	Stephen William	England
	Heaviside	Oliver	England
	Hertz	Heinrich Rudolph	Germany
	Kirchhoff	Gustav Robert	Germany
	Maxwell	James Clerk	Scotland
	Ohm	Georg Simon	Germany
	Peltier	Jean	France
	Piccard	Auguste	Switzerland
	Piccard	Jean Félix	Switzerland
	Rayleigh	John William Strutt	England
	Tyndall	John	England
	Volta	Alessandro	Italy
	Weber	Wilhelm Edouard	Germany
	Wheatstone	Charles	England
	Wood	Robert W.	USA
Physicist - Nobel Prize	Planck	Max Karl Ernst Ludwig	Germany

FAME	LAST NAME	FIRST NAME	COUNTRY
Physicist - Nuclear	Oppenheimer	Julius Robert	USA
	Teller	Edward	USA
Physicist - X-Ray Discoverer	Roentgen	Wilhelm Konrad	Germany
Physicist/Astronomer	Huygens	Christian	Netherlands
	Jeans	James Hopwood	England
	Langley	Samuel Pierpoint	USA
	Pickering	Edward Charles	USA
Physicist/Chemist	Cavendish	Henry	England
Physicist/Chemist/Astronomer	Herschel	John Frederick William	England
Physicist/Inventor	Pupin	Michael Idvorsky	USA
Physicist/Mathematician	Doppler	Christian	Austria
	Fourier	Jean Baptiste Joseph	France
	Gibbs	Josiah Willard	USA
	Pascal	Blaise	France
	Penrose	Roger	England
	Thomson	William	England
	Torricelli	Evangelista	Italy
Physicist/Philosopher	Fechner	Gustav Theodor	Germany
Physicist/Physician/Linguist	Young	Thomas	England
Physicist/Physiologist	Galvani	Luigi	Italy
	Helmholtz	Hermann Ludwig Ferdinand von	Germany
Physicist/Writer	Lodge	Oliver Joseph	England
Physics - Nobel Laureate	Abrikosov	Alexei A.	USA
	Alferov	Zhores I.	Russia
	Alfvén	Hannes Olof Gösta	Sweden
	Alvarez	Luis Walter	USA
	Anderson	Carl David	USA
	Anderson	Philip Warren	USA
	Appleton	Edward Victor	England
	Bardeen	John	USA
	Barkla	Charles Glover	England
	Basov	Nicolay Gennadiyevich	Russia
	Becquerel	Antoine Henri	France
	Bednorz	Johannes Georg	Germany
	Bethe	Hans Albrecht	USA
	Binnig	Gerd	Germany
	Blackett	Patrick Maynard Stuart	England
	Bloch	Felix	USA
	Bloembergen	Nicolaas	USA
	Bohr	Aage Niels Henrik David	Denmark
	Born	Max	Germany
	Bothe	Walther	Germany
	Bragg	William Henry	England
	Bragg	William Lawrence	England
	Brattain	Walter Houser	USA
	Braun	Karl Ferdinand	Germany
	Bridgman	Percy Williams	USA
	Brockhouse	Bertram N.	Canada
	Broglie	Louis Victor Pierre Raymond de	France
	Chadwick	James	England
	Chamberlain	Owen	USA
	Chandrasekhar	Subramanyan	USA
	Charpak	Georges	France
	Cherenkov	Pavel Aleksevevich	Russia
	Chu	Steven	USA
	Cockcroft	John Douglas	England
	Cohen-Tannoudji	Claude	France
	Compton	Arthur Holly	USA

SOLVER SERIES: NAME FINDER

FAME	LAST NAME	FIRST NAME	COUNTRY
Physics - Nobel Laureate	Cooper	Leon Neil	USA
	Cornell	Eric A.	USA
	Cronin	James Watson	USA
	Curie	Marie	France
	Curie	Pierre	France
	Dalén	Nils Gustaf	Sweden
	Davis Jr.	Raymond	USA
	Davisson	Clinton Joseph	USA
	Dehmelt	Hans G.	USA
	Dirac	Paul Adrien Maurice	England
	Einstein	Albert	USA
	Esaki	Leo	Japan
	Fermi	Enrico	Italy
	Feynman	Richard P.	USA
	Fitch	Val Logsdon	USA
	Fowler	William Alfred	USA
	Franck	James	Germany
	Frank	Il'ja Mikhailovich	Russia
	Friedman	Jerome I.	USA
	Gabor	Dennis	England
	Gell-Mann	Murray	USA
	Gennes	Pierre-Gilles de	France
	Giacconi	Riccardo	USA
	Giaever	Ivar	USA
	Ginzburg	Vitaly L.	Russia
	Glaser	Donald Arthur	USA
	Glashow	Sheldon Lee	USA
	Glauber	Roy J.	USA
	Goeppert-Mayer	Maria	USA
	Gross	David J.	USA
	Guillaume	Charles Edouard	Switzerland
	Hall	John L.	USA
	Hänsch	Theodore	Germany
	Heisenberg	Werner Karl	Germany
	Hertz	Gustav Ludwig	Germany
	Hess	Victor Franz	Austria
	Hewish	Antony	England
	Hofstadter	Robert	USA
	Hooft	Gerhardus 't	Netherlands
	Hulse	Russell A.	USA
	Jensen	Johannes Hans Daniel	Germany
	Josephson	Brian David	England
	Kapitza	Pëtr Leonidovich	Russia
	Kastler	Alfred	France
	Kendall	Henry W.	USA
	Ketterie	Wolfgang	Germany
	Kilby	Jack S.	USA
	Klitzing	Klaus von	Germany
	Koshiba	Masatoshi	Japan
	Kroemer	Herbert	Germany
	Kusch	Polykarp	USA
	Lamb	Willis Eugene	USA
	Landau	Lev Davidivich	Russia
	Laue	Max von	Germany
	Laughlin	Robert B.	USA
	Lawrence	Ernest Orlando	USA
	Lederman	Leon M.	USA
	Lee	David M.	USA

FAME	LAST NAME	FIRST NAME	COUNTRY
Physics - Nobel Laureate	Lee	Tsung-Dao	China
	Leggett	Anthony J.	England
	Lenard	Phillipp Eduard Anton von	Germany
	Lippmann	Gabriel	France
	Lorentz	Hendrik Antoon	Netherlands
	Marconi	Guglielmo	Italy
	Meer	Simon van der	Netherlands
	Michelson	Albert Abraham	USA
	Millikan	Robert Andrews	USA
	Mössbauer	Rudolf Ludwig	Germany
	Mott	Nevill Francis	England
	Mottelson	Ben Roy	Denmark
	Müller	Karl Alex	Switzerland
	Néel	Louis Eugène Félix	France
	Onnes	Heike Kamerlingh	Netherlands
	Osheroff	Douglas D.	USA
	Paul	Wolfgang	Germany
	Pauli	Wolfgang	Austria
	Penzias	Arno Allan	USA
	Perl	Martin L.	USA
	Perrin	Jean Baptiste	France
	Phillips	William D.	USA
	Politzer	Hugh David	USA
	Powell	Cecil Frank	England
	Prokhorov	Aleksandr Mikhailovich	Russia
	Purcell	Edward Mills	USA
	Rabi	Isidor Isaac	USA
	Rainwater	Leo James	USA
	Raman	Chandrasekhara Venkata	India
	Ramsey	Norman F.	USA
	Reins	Frederick	USA
	Richardson	Owen Willans	England
	Richardson	Robert C.	USA
	Richter	Burton	USA
	Rohrer	Heinrich	Switzerland
	Röntgen	Wilhelm Conrad	Germany
	Rubbia	Carlo	Italy
	Ruska	Ernst	Germany
	Ryle	Martin	England
	Salam	Abdus	Pakistan
	Schawlow	Arthur Leonard	USA
	Schrieffer	John Robert	USA
	Schrödinger	Erwin	Austria
	Schwartz	Melvin	USA
	Schwinger	Julian	USA
	Segrè	Emilio Gino	USA
	Shockley	William Bradford	USA
	Shull	Clifford G.	USA
	Siegbahn	Kai M.	Sweden
	Siegbahn	Karl Manne Georg	Sweden
	Stark	Johannes	Germany
	Steinberger	Jack	USA
	Stern	Otto	USA
	Störmer	Horst L.	Germany
	Strutt	John William	England
	Tamm	Igor Evgenyevich	Russia
	Taylor	Joseph H.	USA
	Taylor	Richard E.	Canada

SOLVER SERIES: NAME FINDER

FAME	LAST NAME	FIRST NAME	COUNTRY
Physics - Nobel Laureate	Thomson	George Paget	England
	Thomson	Joseph John	England
	Ting	Samuel Chao Chung	USA
	Tomonaga	Sin-Itiro	Japan
	Townes	Charles Hard	USA
	Tsui	Daniel C.	USA
	Veltman	Martinus J.G.	Netherlands
	Vleck	John Hasbrouck van	USA
	Waals	Johannes Diderik Van der	Netherlands
	Walton	Ernest Thomas Sinton	Ireland
	Weinberg	Steven	USA
	Wieman	Carl E.	USA
	Wien	Wilhelm	Germany
	Wigner	Eugene Paul	USA
	Wilczek	Frank	USA
	Wilson	Charles Thomson Rees	England
	Wilson	Kenneth G.	USA
	Wilson	Robert Woodrow	USA
	Yang	Chen Ning	China
	Yukawa	Hideki	Japan
	Zeeman	Peter	Netherlands
	Zernike	Frits Frederik	Netherlands
Physiologist	Bernard	Claude	France
	Ringer	Sydney	England
Physiologist - Micro Anatomy	Malpighi	Marcello	Italy
Physiologist/Anatomist	Weber	Ernst Heinrich	Germany
Psychiatrist	Adler	Alfred	Austria
	Fanon	Frantz	France
	Freud	Anna	Austria
	Kraepelin	Emil	Germany
	Laing	Ronald David	Scotland
	Menninger	Karl Augustus	USA
Psychiatrist/Physician	Freud	Sigmund	Austria
Psychiatrist/Psychologist	Jung	Carl Gustav	Switzerland
Psychoanalyist	Horney	Karen	Germany
Scholar	Agricola	Georgius	Germany
Scientist - Electricity	Faraday	Michael	England
Scientist/Historian	Draper	John William	USA
Scientist/Theologian	Priestley	Joseph	England
Surgeon	Abul	Kasim	Saudi Arabia
	Lister	Joseph	England
	Paré	Ambroise	France
Surgeon/Bacteriologist	Reed	Walter	USA
Surgeon/Physiologist	Hunter	John	England
Writer/Physician	Galen	Claudius	Greece
Writer/Pioneer - Eugenics	Galton	Francis	England
Writer/Poet/Occultist	Crowley	Aleister	England
Zoologist - Sexual Behavior	Kinsey	Alfred Charles	USA

SPORTS:

FAME	LAST NAME	FIRST NAME	COUNTRY
Base Ball Player	Saxon	Steve	USA
Baseball Commissioner	Kuhn	Bowie Kent	USA
Baseball Commissioner - HF	Chandler	Albert Benjamin (Happy)	USA
	Frick	Ford Christopher	USA
	Landis	Kenesaw Mountain	USA
Baseball Executive - HF	Barrow	Edward Grant	USA
	Bulkeley	Morgan Gardner	USA

FAME	LAST NAME	FIRST NAME	COUNTRY
Baseball Executive - HF	Cummings	William Arthur (Candy)	USA
	Foster	Andrew (Rube)	USA
	Giles	Warren Crandall	USA
	Harridge	William (Will)	USA
	Hulbert	William Ambrose	USA
	Johnson	Byron Bancroft (Ban)	USA
	MacPhail	Leland Standford (Lee) Jr.	USA
	Spalding	Albert Goodwill	USA
	Veeck Jr.	William Lewis (Bill)	USA
	Yawkey	Thomas Austin (Tom)	USA
	Comiskey	Charles Albert (Charlie)	USA
	Griffith	Clark Calvin	USA
	Rickey	Wesley Branch	USA
	Weiss	George Martin	USA
	Wright	George	USA
	Wright	William Henry (Harry)	England
Baseball Manager - HF	Alston	Walter Emmons	USA
	Anderson	George Lee (Sparky)	USA
	Durocher	Leo Ernest (The Lip)	USA
	Hanlon	Edward Hugh (Ned)	USA
	Harris	Stanley Raymond (Bucky)	USA
	Huggins	Miller James (Mighty Mite)	USA
	Lasorda	Thomas Charles (Tommy)	USA
	López	Alphonso Ramón (Al)	USA
	Mack	Cornelius Alexander (Connie)	USA
	McCarthy	Joseph Vincent (Joe)	USA
	McGraw	John Joseph	USA
	McKechnie	William Boyd (Bill)	USA
	Robinson	Wilbert	USA
	Selee	Frank Gibson	USA
	Stengel	Charles Dillon (Casey)	USA
	Weaver	Earl Sidney	USA
Baseball Pioneer - HF	Cartwright	Alexander Joy	USA
	Chadwick	Henry	England
	MacPhail	Leland Standford (Larry) Sr.	USA
Baseball Player	Adams	Charles Benjamin (Babe)	USA
	Alomar	Roberto	USA
	Alomar	Sandy	USA
	Alou	Felipe	USA
	Alou	Jesus	USA
	Alou	Matty	USA
	Bando	Sal	USA
	Bell	Gus	USA
	Blue	Vida	USA
	Blyleven	Bert	USA
	Bonds	Barry	USA
	Bonds	Bobby	USA
	Boyer	Clete	USA
	Breame	Sid	USA
	Cabell	Enos	USA
	Canseco	José	USA
	Carter	Joe	USA
	Chance	Dean	USA
	Clark	Will	USA
	Clemens	Roger	USA
	Cone	David	USA
	Coombs	Earle	USA
	Dawson	André	USA

SOLVER SERIES: NAME FINDER

FAME	LAST NAME	FIRST NAME	COUNTRY
Baseball Player	Drabowsky	Moe	Poland
	Dykstra	Len	USA
	Evans	Darrell	USA
	Evans	Dwight	USA
	Fielder	Cecil	USA
	Garvey	Steve	USA
	Glavine	Tom	USA
	Gooden	Dwight	USA
	Gwynn	Tony	USA
	Harper	Harry	USA
	Henderson	Rickey	USA
	Hernandez	Keith	USA
	Hershiser	Orel	USA
	Hodges	Gil	USA
	Howard	Frank	USA
	Johnson	Davey	USA
	Johnson	Howard	USA
	Kaat	Jim	USA
	Kingman	Dave	USA
	Kubek	Tony	USA
	Larsen	Don	USA
	Lyle	Sparky	USA
	Maggio	Dom Di	USA
	Maris	Roger	USA
	Martinez	Tino	USA
	Mathews	Edwin Lee (Eddie)	USA
	Mattingly	Don	USA
	McCarver	Tim	USA
	McGee	Willie	USA
	McGraw	Tug	USA
	McGriff	Fred	USA
	McGwire	Mark	USA
	Mitchell	Kevin	USA
	Murphy	Dale	USA
	Nen	Robb	USA
	Nettles	Graig	USA
	Nixon	Otis	USA
	Olerud	John	USA
	Oliva	Tony	USA
	Olivares	Omar Palqu	Puerto Rico
	Ortiz	Roberto	USA
	Parker	Wes	USA
	Peña	Tony	USA
	Posada	Jorge	Puerto Rica
	Raines	Tim	USA
	Rice	Jim	USA
	Ripken	Bill	USA
	Ripken Jr.	Cal	USA
	Rosar	Buddy	USA
	Rose	Pete	USA
	Saberhagen	Bret	USA
	Sanders	Deion	USA
	Shor	Bernard (Toots)	USA
	Sierra	Ruben	USA
	Slyke	Andy Van	USA
	Sousa	Sammy	USA
	Staub	Rusty	USA
	Stieb	Dave	USA

FAME	LAST NAME	FIRST NAME	COUNTRY
Baseball Player	Stottlemyre	Mel	USA
	Strawberry	Darryl	USA
	Tiant	Luis	USA
	Torre	Joe	USA
	Tresh	Tom	USA
	Uecker	Bob	USA
	Valenzuela	Fernando	USA
	Ventura	Robin	USA
	Vizquel	Omar	USA
	Williams	Matt	USA
	Yost	Eddie	USA
Baseball Player - HF	Aaron	Henry Louis (Hank)	USA
	Alexander	Grover Cleveland (Pete)	USA
	Anson	Adrian Constantine (Cap)	USA
	Aparicio	Luis Ernesto	Venezuela
	Appling	Lucius Benjamin (Luke)	USA
	Ashburn	Don Richard (Richie)	USA
	Averill	Howard Earl	USA
	Baker	John Franklin (Frank)	USA
	Bancroft	David James (Dave)	USA
	Banks	Ernest (Ernie)	USA
	Beckley	Jacob Peter (Jake)	USA
	Bell	James Thomas (Cool Papa)	USA
	Bench	Johnny Lee	USA
	Bender	Charles Albert (Chief)	USA
	Berra	Lawrence Peter (Yogi)	USA
	Boggs	Wade	USA
	Bottomley	James Leroy (Jim)	USA
	Boudreau	Louis (Lou)	USA
	Bresnahan	Roger Philip	USA
	Brett	George Howard	USA
	Brock	Louis Clark (Lou)	USA
	Brouthers	Dennis Joseph (Dan)	USA
	Brown	Mordecai Peter Centennial	USA
	Bunning	James Paul David (Jim)	USA
	Burkett	Jesse Cail	USA
	Campanella	Roy	USA
	Carew	Rodney Cline (Rod)	Panama
	Carey	Max George	USA
	Carlton	Steven Norman (Steve)	USA
	Carter	Gary Edmund	USA
	Cepeda	Orlando Manuel	Puerto Rico
	Chance	Frank Leroy	USA
	Charleston	Oscar McKinley	USA
	Chesbro	John Dwight (Happy Jack)	USA
	Clarke	Fred Clifford	USA
	Clarkson	John Gibson	USA
	Clemente	Roberto	Puerto Rico
	Cobb	Tyrus Raymond (Ty)	USA
	Cochrane	Gordon Stanley (Mickey)	USA
	Collins	James Joseph (Jimmy)	USA
	Collins Sr.	Edward Trowbridge (Eddie)	USA
	Combs	Earle Bryan	USA
	Connor	Roger	USA
	Coveleski	Stanley Anthony (Stan)	USA
	Crawford	Samuel Earl (Sam)	USA
	Cronin	Joseph Edward (Joe)	USA
	Cuyler	Hazen Shirley (Kiki)	USA

SOLVER SERIES: NAME FINDER

FAME	LAST NAME	FIRST NAME	COUNTRY
Baseball Player - HF	Dandridge	Raymond Emmitt (Ray)	USA
	Davis	George Stacey	USA
	Day	Leon	USA
	Dean	Jay Hanna (Dizzy)	USA
	Delahanty	Edward James (Ed)	USA
	Dickey	William Malcolm	USA
	Dihigo	Martín Magdaleno	Cuba
	Doby	Lawrence Eugene (Larry)	USA
	Doerr	Robert Pershing (Bobby)	USA
	Drysdale	Donald Scott (Don)	USA
	Duffy	Hugh	USA
	Eckersley	Dennis Lee	USA
	Evers	John Joseph (Johnny)	USA
	Ewing	William (Buck)	USA
	Faber	Urban Charles (Red)	USA
	Feller	Robert William Andrew (Bob)	USA
	Ferrell	Richard Benjamin (Rick)	USA
	Fingers	Roland Glen (Rollie)	USA
	Fisk	Carlton Ernest	USA
	Flick	Elmer Harrison	USA
	Ford	Edward Charles (Whitey)	USA
	Foster	William Hendrick (Bill)	USA
	Fox	Jacob Nelson (Nellie)	USA
	Foxx	James Emory (Jimmy)	USA
	Frisch	Frank Francis (Frankie)	USA
	Galvin	James Francis (Pud)	USA
	Gehrig	Henry Louis (Lou)	USA
	Gehringer	Charles Leonard (Charlie)	USA
	Gibson	Joshua (Josh)	USA
	Gibson	Robert (Bob)	USA
	Gómez	Vernon Louis (Lefty)	USA
	Goslin	Leon Allen (Goose)	USA
	Greenberg	Henry Benjamin (Hank)	USA
	Grimes	Burleigh Arland	USA
	Grove	Robert Moses (Lefty)	USA
	Hafey	Charles James (Chick)	USA
	Haines	Jesse Joseph	USA
	Hamilton	William Robert (Billy)	USA
	Hartnett	Charles Leo (Gabby)	USA
	Heilmann	Harry Edwin	USA
	Herman	William Jennings Bryan (Billy)	USA
	Hooper	Harry Bartholomew	USA
	Hornsby	Rogers	USA
	Hoyt	Waite Charles	USA
	Hubbell	Carl Owen	USA
	Hunter	James Augustus (Catfish)	USA
	Irvin	Monford (Monte)	USA
	Jackson	Reginald Martinez (Reggie)	USA
	Jackson	Travis Calvin	USA
	Jenkins	Ferguson Arthur (Fergie)	Canada
	Jennings	Hugh Ambrose (Hughie)	USA
	Johnson	Walter Perry	USA
	Johnson	William Jullius (Judy)	USA
	Joss	Adrian (Addie)	USA
	Kaline	Albert William (Al)	USA
	Keefe	Timothy John (Tim)	USA
	Keeler	William Henry (Willie)	USA
	Kell	George Clyde	USA

FAME	LAST NAME	FIRST NAME	COUNTRY
Baseball Player - HF	Kelley	Joseph James (Joe)	USA
	Kelly	George Lange	USA
	Kelly	Michael Joseph (King)	USA
	Killebrew	Harmon Clayton	USA
	Kiner	Ralph McPherran	USA
	Klein	Charles Herbert (Chuck)	USA
	Koufax	Sanford (Sandy)	USA
	Lajoie	Napoleon (Nap)	USA
	Lazzeri	Anthony Michael (Tony)	USA
	Lemon	Robert Granville (Bob)	USA
	Leonard	Walter Fenner (Buck)	USA
	Lindstrom	Frederick Charles (Fred)	USA
	Lloyd	John Henry (Pop)	USA
	Lombardi	Ernesto Natali (Ernie)	USA
	Lyons	Theodore Amar (Ted)	USA
	Maggio	Joseph Paul Di(Joe)	USA
	Mantle	Mickey Charles	USA
	Manush	Henry Emmett (Heinie)	USA
	Maranville	Walter James (Rabbit)	USA
	Marichal	Juan Antonio	Dominican Rep
	Marquard	Richard William (Rube)	USA
	Mathewson	Christopher (Christy)	USA
	Mays	Willie Howard	USA
	Mazeroski	William Stanley (Bill)	USA
	McCarthy	Thomas Michael (Tommy)	USA
	McCovey	Willie Lee	USA
	McGinnity	Joseph Jerome (Joe)	USA
	McPhee	John Alexander (Bid)	USA
	Medwick	Joseph Michael (Joe)	USA
	Mize	John Robert (Johnny)	USA
	Molitor	Paul Leo	USA
	Morgan	Joe Leonard	USA
	Murray	Eddie Clarence	USA
	Musial	Stanley Frank (Stan)	USA
	Newhouser	Harold (Hal)	USA
	Nichols	Charles Augustus (Kid)	USA
	Niekro	Philip Henry (Phil)	USA
	O'Rourke	James Henry (Jim)	USA
	Ott	Melvin Thomas (Mel)	USA
	Paige	Leroy Robert (Satchel)	USA
	Palmer	James Alvin (Jim)	USA
	Pennock	Herbert Jefferis (Herb)	USA
	Pérez	Antanasio (Tony)	Cuba
	Perry	Gaylord Jackson	USA
	Plank	Edward Stewart (Eddie)	USA
	Puckett	Kirby	USA
	Radbourn	Charles Gardner (Old Hoss)	USA
	Reese	Harold Henry (Pee Wee)	USA
	Rice	Edgar Charles (Sam)	USA
	Rixey	Eppa	USA
	Rizzuto	Philip Francis (Phil)	USA
	Roberts	Robin Evan	USA
	Robinson	Brooks Calbert	USA
	Robinson	Frank	USA
	Robinson	Jack Roosevelt (Jackie)	USA
	Rogan	Wilber Joe (Bullet)	USA
	Roush	Edd J.	USA
	Ruffing	Charles Herbert (Red)	USA

SOLVER SERIES: NAME FINDER

FAME	LAST NAME	FIRST NAME	COUNTRY
Baseball Player - HF	Rusie	Amos Wilson	USA
	Ruth	George Herman (Babe)	USA
	Ryan	Lynn Nolan	USA
	Sandberg	Ryne	USA
	Schalk	Raymond William (Ray)	USA
	Schmidt	Michael Jack (Mike)	USA
	Schoendienst	Albert Fred (Red)	USA
	Seaver	George Thomas (Tom)	USA
	Sewell	Joseph Wheeler (Joe)	USA
	Simmons	Aloysius Harry (Al)	USA
	Sisler	George Harold	USA
	Slaughter	Enos Bradsher	USA
	Smith	Hilton	USA
	Smith	Osborne Earl (Ozzie)	USA
	Snider	Edwin Donald (Duke)	USA
	Spahn	Warren Edward	USA
	Speaker	Tristram E. (Tris)	USA
	Stargell	Wilver Dornel (Willie)	USA
	Stearnes	Norman Thomas (Turkey)	USA
	Sutton	Donald Howard (Don)	USA
	Terry	William Harold (Bill)	USA
	Thompson	Samuel Luther (Sam)	USA
	Tinker	Joseph Bert (Joe)	USA
	Traynor	Harold Joseph (Pie)	USA
	Vance	Clarence Arthur (Dazzy)	USA
	Vaughn	Joseph Floyd (Arky)	USA
	Waddell	George Edward (Rube)	USA
	Wagner	John Peter (Honus)	USA
	Wallace	Rhoderick John (Bobby)	USA
	Walsh	Edward Augustine (Ed)	USA
	Waner	Lloyd James	USA
	Waner	Paul Glee	USA
	Ward	John Montgomery	USA
	Welch	Michael Francis (Mickey)	USA
	Wells	Willie James	USA
	Wheat	Zachary Davis (Zack)	USA
	Wilhelm	James Hoyt	USA
	Williams	Billy Leo	USA
	Williams	Joseph (Joe)	USA
	Williams	Theodore Samuel (Ted)	USA
	Willis	Victor Gazaway (Vic)	USA
	Wilson	Lewis Robert (Hack)	USA
	Winfield	David Mark (Dave)	USA
	Wynn	Early	USA
	Yastrzemski	Carl Michael	USA
	Young	Denton True (Cy)	USA
	Youngs	Ross Middlebrook	USA
	Yount	Robin Rachel	USA
Baseball Player/Spy	Berg	Moe	USA
Baseball Umpire - HF	Barlick	Albert Joseph (Al)	USA
	Chylak Jr.	Nestor	
	Conlan	John Bertrand (Jocko)	USA
	Connolly	Thomas Henry (Tom)	USA
	Evans	William George	USA
	Hubbard	Robert (Cal)	USA
	Klem	William (Bill)	USA
	McGowan	William Aloysius (Bill)	USA
Basketball Player	Ainge	Danny	USA

FAME	LAST NAME	FIRST NAME	COUNTRY
Basketball Player	Auerbach	Red	USA
	Barkley	Charles	USA
	Dantley	Adrian	USA
	Dumars	Joe	USA
	Ewing	Patrick	USA
	Gilmore	Artis	USA
	Jordan	Michael	USA
	King	Bernard	USA
	Lovellette	Clyde E.	USA
	Malone	Karl	USA
	Mourning	Alonzo	USA
	Mullin	Chris	USA
	Nater	Sven	USA
	Olajuwon	Hakeem	USA
	O'Neal	Shaquille	USA
	Pippen	Scottie	USA
	Riley	Pat	USA
	Rodman	Dennis	USA
	Russell	Cazzie	USA
	Stockton	John	USA
	Thomas	Kurt	USA
Basketball Player - HF	Abdul-Jabbar	Kareem	USA
	Archibald	Nathaniel (Nate) (Tiny)	USA
	Arizin	Paul J.	USA
	Barlow	Thomas B.	USA
	Barry	Richard F. (Rick)	USA
	Baylor	Elgin	USA
	Beckman	John	USA
	Bellamy	Walter (Walt)	USA
	Belov	Sergei	Russia
	Bing	David (Dave)	USA
	Bird	Larry	USA
	Blazejowski	Carol	USA
	Borgman	Bernard (Bennie)	USA
	Bradley	William W. (Bill)	USA
	Brennan	Joseph R.	USA
	Cervi	Alfred N. (Al)	USA
	Chamberlain	Wilton M. (Wilt)	USA
	Cooper	Charles T. (Tarzan)	USA
	Cosic	Kresimir	Croatia
	Cousy	Robert J. (Bob)	USA
	Cowens	David W. (Dave)	USA
	Crawfprd	Joan	USA
	Cunningham	William J. (Billy)	USA
	Curry	Denise	USA
	Dalipagic	Drazen	Yugoslavia
	Davies	Robert E.	USA
	Debernardy	Forrest S. (Red)	USA
	Debusschere	David (Dave)	USA
	Dehnert	Henry J. (Dutch)	USA
	Donovan	Anne	USA
	Drexler	Clyde	USA
	Endacott	Paul	USA
	English	Alex	USA
	Erving	Julius W.	USA
	Foster	Harold E.	USA
	Frazier	Walter	USA
	Friedman	Max (Marty)	USA

SOLVER SERIES: NAME FINDER

FAME	LAST NAME	FIRST NAME	COUNTRY
Basketball Player - HF	Fulks	Joseph F.	USA
	Gale	Lauren (Laddie)	USA
	Gallatin	Harry J.	USA
	Gates	William (Pop)	USA
	Gervin	George	USA
	Gola	Thomas J.	USA
	Goodrich	Gail	USA
	Greer	Harold E. (Hal)	USA
	Gruenig	Robert F. (Ace)	USA
	Hagen	Cifford O.	USA
	Hansen	Victor A.	USA
	Harris-Stewart	Lusia	USA
	Havlicek	John (Hondo)	USA
	Hawkins	"Cornelius (Connie, The Hawk)"	USA
	Hayes	Elvin E.	USA
	Haynes	Marques	USA
	Heinsohn	Thomas W. (Tom)	USA
	Holman	Nat	USA
	Houbregs	Robert J. (Bob)	Canada
	Howell	Bailey	USA
	Hyatt	Charles D.	USA
	Issel	Daniel P. (Dan)	USA
	Jeanette	Harry (Buddy)	USA
	Johnson	Earvin (Magic)	USA
	Johnson	William C. (Skinny)	USA
	Johnston	Donald Neil	USA
	Jones	KC	USA
	Jones	Samuel (Sam)	USA
	Krause	Edward W. (Moose)	USA
	Kurland	Robert A. (Bob)	USA
	Lanier	Robert J. (Bob)	USA
	Lapchick	Joe	USA
	Lieberman	Nancy	USA
	Lucas	Jerry R.	USA
	Luisetti	Angelo (Hank)	USA
	Macauley	Edward C. (Ed)	USA
	Malone	Moses	USA
	Maravich	Peter P. (Pete)	USA
	Martin	Slater N. (Dugie)	USA
	McAdoo	Robert (Bob)	USA
	McCracken	Branch	USA
	McCracken	Jack (Jumping Jack)	USA
	McDermott	Robert (Bobby)	USA
	McGuire	Richard S. (Dick)	USA
	McHale	Kevin	USA
	Meneghin	Dino	Italy
	Meyers	Anne E.	USA
	Mikan	George L.	USA
	Mikkelsen	Vern	USA
	Miller	Cheryl	USA
	Monroe	Vernon Earl (The Pearl)	USA
	Murphy	Calvin J.	USA
	Murphy	Charles C. (Stretch)	USA
	Page	Harlan O.	USA
	Parish	Robert	USA
	Petrovic	Drazen	Croatia
	Pettit	Robert L.	USA
	Phillip	Andy	USA

FAME	LAST NAME	FIRST NAME	COUNTRY
Basketball Player - HF	Pollard	James C.	USA
	Ramsey	Frank V.	USA
	Reed Jr.	Willis	USA
	Risen	Arnold (Arnie)	USA
	Robertson	Oscar P.	USA
	Roosma	John S.	USA
	Russell	John D. (Honey)	USA
	Russell	William F. (Bill)	USA
	Schayes	Adolph (Dolph)	USA
	Schmidt	Earnest J. (Ernie)	USA
	Schommer	John J.	USA
	Sedran	Barney	USA
	Semjonova	Uljana	Latvia
	Sharman	William W. (Bill)	USA
	Steinmetz	Christian	USA
	Stokes	Maurice	USA
	Thomas	Isiah	USA
	Thompson	David	USA
	Thompson	John A. (Cat)	USA
	Thurmond	Nate	USA
	Twyman	John K. (Jack)	USA
	Unseld	Wesley S. (Wes)	USA
	Vandivier	Robert P. (Fuzzy)	USA
	Wachter	Edward A.	USA
	Walton	William T. (Bill)	USA
	Wanzer	Robert (Bobby)	USA
	West	Jerry A.	USA
	White	Nera D.	USA
	Wilkens	Leonard (Lenny)	USA
	Woodard	Lynette	USA
	Wooden	John R.	USA
	Worthy	James	USA
	Yardley	George	USA
Boxer	Bowe	Riddick	USA
	Camacho	Hector	USA
	Carnera	Primo	Italy
	Chavez	Julio Cesar	USA
	Duran	Roberto	USA
	Hearns	Thomas	USA
	Holmes	Larry	USA
	Holyfield	Evander	USA
	Mercer	Ray	USA
	O'Grady	Sean	USA
	Spinks	Leon	USA
	Stevenson	Teofilo	USA
	Sullivan	John Lawrence	USA
	Tyson	Mike	USA
	Whitaker	Pernell	USA
Boxer - HF	Ali	Muhammad (Casius Clay)	USA
	Angott	Sammy (The Clutch)	USA
	Baer	Max	USA
	Benvenuti	Nino	USA
	Buchanan	Kenneth (Ken)	Scotland
	Canto	Miguel	USA
	Carter	Jimmy	USA
	Cerdan	Marcel (Casablanca Clouter)	Algeria
	Cervantes	Antonio	Columbia
	Chacon	Bobby	USA

SOLVER SERIES: NAME FINDER

FAME	LAST NAME	FIRST NAME	COUNTRY
Boxer - HF	Chandler	Jeff	USA
	Charles	Ezzard	USA
	Cokes	Curtis	USA
	Conn	Billy	USA
	Corbett	James J.	USA
	Cuevas	Pipino	Mexico
	Delaney	Jack	Canada
	Dempsey	Jack	USA
	Elorde	Gabriel (Flash)	Philippines
	Fenech	Jeff	Australia
	Foreman	George Edward	USA
	Foster	Bob	USA
	Frazier	Joe (Smokin Joe)	USA
	Fullmer	Gene	USA
	Galaxy	Khaosai (The Thai Tyson)	Thailand
	Galindez	Victor	Argentina
	Gavilan	Gerardo (Kid)	Cuba
	Gómez	Wilfredo	Puerto Rico
	Graziano	Thomas Rocco (Rocky)	USA
	Griffith	Emile	USA
	Hagler	Marvin	USA
	Harada	Masahiko (Fighting)	Japan
	Jack	Sidney (Beau)	USA
	Jenkins	Lew	USA
	Jofre	Eder	Brazil
	Johansson	Ingemar	Sweden
	Johnson	Harold	USA
	Laguna	Ismael	Panama
	Leonard	Raymond (Sugar Ray)	USA
	Liston	Sonny	USA
	Locche	Nicolino	Argentina
	Loi	Duilio	Italy
	Louis	Joseph (Joe)	USA
	Marciano	Rocky	USA
	Maxim	Joey	USA
	McCallum	Michael McKenzie (Mike)	Jamaica
	McGuigan	Finbar Patrick (Barry)	Ireland
	Mohammad	Matthew Saad	USA
	Montgomery	Bob	USA
	Monzon	Carlos	Argentina
	Moore	Archie	USA
	Motta	Jack La(Jake)	USA
	Napoles	Jose	Cuba
	Nelson	Azumah	Ghana
	Norris	Terry Wayne	USA
	Norton	Ken	USA
	Olivares	Ruben	Mexico
	Olson	Carl (Bobo)	USA
	Ortiz	Carlos	Puerto Rico
	Ortiz	Manuel	USA
	Palomino	Carlos	USA
	Papp	Laszlo	Hungary
	Pastrano	Willie	USA
	Patterson	Floyd	USA
	Pedroza	Eusebio	Panama
	Pep	Willie (Will O' the Wisp)	USA
	Perez	Pascual	Argentina
	Pryor	Aaron	USA

FAME	LAST NAME	FIRST NAME	COUNTRY
Boxer - HF	Qawi	Dwight Muhammad	USA
	Ramos	Ultiminio (Sugar)	Cuba
	Robinson	Raymond (Sugar Ray)	USA
	Rodriquez	Luis	Cuba
	Rosenbloom	Maxey	USA
	Saddler	Sandy	USA
	Saldivar	Vincente	Mexico
	Sanchez	Salvadore	Mexico
	Schmeling	Max	Germany
	Spinks	Michael	USA
	Tiger	Richard (Dick)	Nigeria
	Torres	Jose	USA
	Tunney	Gene	USA
	Turpin	Randy	England
	Villa	Francisco (Pancho)	Philippines
	Walcott	Joseph (Jersey Joe)	USA
	Willard	Jess	USA
	Williams	Isiah (Ike)	USA
	Wright	Albert (Chalky)	Mexico
	Zale	Anthony Florian (Tony)	USA
	Zaragoza	Daniel	Mexico
	Zarate	Carlos	Mexico
	Zivic	Fritzie	USA
Bull Fighter	Belmonte	Juan	Spain
Football Administrator - HF	Finks	James Edward (Jim)	USA
Football Advisor - HF	Ray	Hugh L. (Shorty)	USA
Football Coach	Camp	Walter Chauncey	USA
	Rockne	Kenneth (Knute)	USA
Football Coach - HF	Brown	Paul Eugene	USA
	Ewbank	Wilbur Charles (Weeb)	USA
	Flaherty	Raymond Paul (Ray)	USA
	Gibbs	Joe Jackson	USA
	Gillman	Sidney (Sid)	USA
	Grant Jr.	Harold Peter (Bud)	USA
	Halas	George Stanley	USA
	Lambeau	Earl Louis (Curly)	USA
	Levy	Marvin Daniel (Marv)	USA
	Lombardi	Vincent Thomas (Vince)	USA
	Long	Howard Michael (Howie)	USA
	Neale	Alfred Earle (Greasy)	USA
	Noll	Charles Henry (Chuck)	USA
	Shula	Donald Francis (Don)	USA
	Stram	Henry Louis (Hank)	USA
	Walsh	William Ernest (Bill)	USA
Football Commissioner - HF	Bell	De Benneville (Bert)	USA
	Davis	Allen	USA
	Rozelle	Alvin Ray (Pete)	USA
Football Founder - HF	Mara	Timothy James (Tim)	USA
	Marshall	George Preston	USA
	Rooney Sr.	Arthur Joseph (Art)	USA
Football General Manager - HF	Schramm Jr.	Texas Earnest (Tex)	USA
Football League Administrator - HF	Carr	Joseph F. (Joe)	USA
Football Owner - HF	Bidwell Sr.	Charles W.	USA
	Hunt	Lamar	USA
	Mara	Wellington Timothy	USA
	Reeves	Daniel Farrell (Dan)	USA
Football Player	Aikman	Troy	USA
	Anderson	Ottis	USA

SOLVER SERIES: NAME FINDER

FAME	LAST NAME	FIRST NAME	COUNTRY
Football Player	Bahr	Matt	USA
	Bartowski	Steve	USA
	Bell	Ricky	USA
	Berg	Steve De	USA
	Brodie	John	USA
	Byner	Earnest	USA
	Cappelletti	Gino	USA
	Carrier	Mark	USA
	Christensen	Todd	USA
	Clark	Gary	USA
	Clayton	Mark	USA
	Craig	Roger	USA
	Dent	Richard	USA
	Dryer	Fred	USA
	Duper	Mark	USA
	Esiason	Boomer	USA
	Gastineau	Mark	USA
	Grier	Rosie	USA
	Harmon	Tom	USA
	Hebert	Bobby	USA
	Jackson	Bo	USA
	Jones	Ed (Too Tall)	USA
	Kramer	Erik	USA
	McMahon	Jim	USA
	Monk	Art	USA
	Moon	Warren	USA
	Morrall	Earl	USA
	Nance	Jim	USA
	Parseghian	Ara	USA
	Plunkett	Jim	USA
	Rashad	Ahmad	USA
	Rice	Jerry	USA
	Roby	Reggie	USA
	Rote	Kyle	USA
	Rypien	Mark	USA
	Seau	Junior	USA
	Simms	Phil	USA
	Singletary	Michael (Mike)	USA
	Slater	Jackie Ray	USA
	Smith	Bruce	USA
	Smith	Bubba	USA
	Snead	Norm	USA
	Stabler	Ken	USA
	Theismann	Joe	USA
	Walker	Herschel	USA
	Warner	Curt	USA
	White	Reggie	USA
	Yepremian	Garo	USA
Football Player - HF	Adderly	Herbert A. (Herb)	USA
	Allen	George Herbert	USA
	Allen	Marcus LeMarr	USA
	Alworth	Lance Dwight	USA
	Atkins	Douglas Leon (Doug)	USA
	Badgro	Morris Hiram (Red)	USA
	Barney	Lemuel Jackson (Lem)	USA
	Battles	Clifford Franklin (Cliff)	USA
	Baugh	Sammy Adrian	USA
	Bednarik	Charles Philip (Chuck)	USA

FAME	LAST NAME	FIRST NAME	COUNTRY
Football Player - HF	Bell Jr.	Robert Lee (Bobby)	USA
	Berry	Raymond Emmett	USA
	Bethea	Elvin Lamont	USA
	Biletnikoff	Frederick S. (Fred)	USA
	Blanda	George Frederick	USA
	Blount	Melvin Cornell (Mel)	USA
	Bradshaw	Terry Paxton	USA
	Brocklin	Norman Mack Van (Norm)	USA
	Brown	James Nathaniel (Jim)	USA
	Brown	Robert Stanford (Bob Boomer)	USA
	Brown	William Ferdie (Willie)	USA
	Brown Jr.	Roosevelt	USA
	Buchanan	Junious (Buck)	USA
	Buoniconti	Nicholas Anthony (Nick)	USA
	Buren	Stephen W. Van (Steve)	USA
	Butkus	Richard Marvin (Dick)	USA
	Campbell	Earl Christian	USA
	Canadeo	Anthony Robert (Tony)	USA
	Casper	David John (Dave)	USA
	Chamberlin	Berlin Guy	USA
	Christiansen	John Leroy (Jack)	USA
	Clark	Earl Harry (Dutch)	USA
	Connor	George Leo	USA
	Conzelman	James Gleason (Jimmy)	USA
	Creekmur	Louis (Lou)	USA
	Csonka	Lawrence Richard (Larry)	USA
	Davis	William Delford (Willie)	USA
	Dawson	Leonard Ray (Len)	USA
	Dickerson	Eric Demetric	USA
	Dierdorf	Daniel Lee (Dan)	USA
	Ditka	Michael Keller (Mike)	USA
	Donovan Jr.	Arthur James (Art)	USA
	Dorsett Sr.	Anthony Drew (Tony)	USA
	Dudley	William McGarvey	USA
	Edwards	Albert Glen (Turk)	USA
	Eller	Carl Lee	USA
	Elway	John Albert	USA
	Fears	Thomas Jesse (Tom)	USA
	Ford Jr.	Leonard Guy (Len)	USA
	Fortmann	Daniel John	USA
	Fouts	Daniel Francis (Dan)	USA
	Friedman	Benjamin (Benny)	USA
	Gatski	Frank	USA
	George	William J. (Bill)	USA
	Gifford	Frank Newton	USA
	Graham Jr.	Otto Everett	USA
	Grange	Harold Edward (Red)	USA
	Greene	Charles Edward (Joe)	USA
	Gregg	Alvis Forrest	USA
	Griese	Robert Allen (Bob)	USA
	Groza	Louis Roy (Lou)	USA
	Guyon	Joseph Napoleon (Joe)	USA
	Ham Jr.	Jack Raphael	USA
	Hampton	Daniel Oliver (Dan)	USA
	Hannah	John Allen	USA
	Harris	Franco	USA
	Haynes	Michael James (Mike)	USA
	Healey	Edward Francis (Ed)	USA

SOLVER SERIES: NAME FINDER

FAME	LAST NAME	FIRST NAME	COUNTRY
Football Player - HF	Hein	Melvin Jack (Mel)	USA
	Hendricks	Theodore Paul (Ted)	Guatemala
	Henry	Wilbur Francis (Pete)	USA
	Herber	Arnold Charles (Arnie)	USA
	Hewitt	William Ernest	USA
	Hinkle	William Clarke	USA
	Hirsch	Elroy Leon (Crazy Legs)	USA
	Hornung	Paul Vernon	USA
	Houston	Kenneth Ray (Ken)	USA
	Hubbard	Robert Calvin (Cal)	USA
	Huff	Robert Lee (Sam)	USA
	Hutson	Donald Montgomery (Don)	USA
	Johnson	James Earl (Jimmy)	USA
	Johnson	John Henry	USA
	Joiner Jr.	Charles (Charlie)	USA
	Jones	David D. (Deacon)	USA
	Jones	Stanley Paul (Stan)	USA
	Jordan	Henry Wendell	USA
	Jurgensen III	Christian Adolph (Sonny)	USA
	Kelly	James Edward (Jim)	USA
	Kelly	Leroy	USA
	Kiesling	Walter Andrew (Walt)	USA
	Kinard	Frank Manning (Bruiser)	USA
	Krause	Paul James	USA
	Lambert	John Harold (Jack)	USA
	Lamielleure	Joseph Michael De (Joe)	USA
	Landry	Thomas Wade (Tom)	USA
	Lane	Richard (Dick) (Night Train)	USA
	Langer	James John (Jim)	USA
	Lanier	Willie Edward	USA
	Largent	Stephen Michael (Steve)	USA
	Lary Jr.	Robert Yale	USA
	Lavelli	Dante Bert Joseph	USA
	Layne	Robert Lawrence (Bobby)	USA
	Leemans	Alphonse Emil (Tuffy)	USA
	Lilly	Robert Lewis (Bob)	USA
	Little	Lawrence Chatmon (Larry)	USA
	Lofton	James David	USA
	Lott	Ronald Mandel (Ronnie)	USA
	Luckman	Sidney (Sid)	USA
	Lyman	William Roy (Link)	USA
	Mack	Thomas Lee (Tom)	USA
	Mackey	John	USA
	Marchetti	Gino John	USA
	Marino Jr.	Daniel Constantine (Dan)	USA
	Matson	Ollie Genoa	USA
	Maynard	Donald Rogers (Don)	USA
	McAfee	George Anderson	USA
	McCormack Jr.	Michael Joseph (Mike)	USA
	McDonald	Thomas Franklin (Tommy)	USA
	McElhenny Jr.	Hug Edward (The king)	USA
	McNally	John Victor (Blood)	USA
	Michalske	August Mike	USA
	Millner	Wayne Vernal	USA
	Mitchell	Robert Cornelius (Bobby)	USA
	Mix	Ronald Jack (Ron)	USA
	Montana	Joseph Clifford (Joe)	USA
	Moore	Leonard Edward (Lenny)	USA

FAME	LAST NAME	FIRST NAME	COUNTRY
Football Player - HF	Motley	Marion	USA
	Munchak	Michael Anthony (Mike)	USA
	Muñoz	Michael Anthony	USA
	Musso	George Francis	USA
	Nagurski	Bronislaw (Bronko)	Canada
	Namath	Joseph William (Joe)	USA
	Nevers	Ernest Alonzo (Ernie)	USA
	Newsome Jr.	Ozzie	USA
	Nitschke	Raymond Ernest (Ray)	USA
	Nomellini	Leo Joseph	Italy
	Olsen	Merlin Jay	USA
	Otto	James Edwin (Jim)	USA
	Owen	Stephen Joseph (Steve)	USA
	Page	Alan Cedric	USA
	Parker	Clarence McKay (Ace)	USA
	Parker	James Thomas (Jim)	USA
	Payton	Walter Jerry	USA
	Perry	Fletcher Joseph (Joe)	USA
	Pihos	Peter Louis (Pete)	USA
	Pollard	Frederick Douglass (Fritz)	USA
	Renfro	Melvin Lacy (Mel)	USA
	Riggins	Robert John	USA
	Ringo	James Stephen (Jim)	USA
	Robustelli	Andrew Richard (Andy)	USA
	Sanders	Barry David	USA
	Sayers	Gale Eugene	USA
	Schmidt	Joseph Paul (Joe)	USA
	Selmon	Lee Roy	USA
	Shaw	William Lewis (Billy)	USA
	Shell	Arthur (Art)	USA
	Simpson	Orenthal James (The Juice)	USA
	Smith	Jackie Larue	USA
	St. Clair	Robert Bruce (Bob) (Geek)	USA
	Stallworth	John Lee (Johnny)	USA
	Starr	Bryan Bartlett (Bart)	USA
	Staubach	Roger Thomas	USA
	Stautner	Ernest Alfred (Ernie)	Bavaria
	Stenerud	Jan	Norway
	Stephenson	Dwight Eugene	USA
	Strong Jr.	Elmer Kenneth (Ken)	USA
	Stydahar	Joseph Lee (Joe)	USA
	Swann	Lynn Curtis	USA
	Tarkenton	Francis Asbury (Fran)	USA
	Taylor	Charles Robert (Charley)	USA
	Taylor	James Charles (Jim)	USA
	Taylor	Lawrence Julius	USA
	Tittle	Yelberton Abraham (YA)	USA
	Trafton	George Edward	USA
	Trippi	Charles Louis (Charley)	USA
	Tunnell	Emlen Lewis	USA
	Turner	Clyde Douglas (Bulldog)	USA
	Unitas	John Constantine (Johnny)	USA
	Upshaw Jr.	Eugene Thurman (Gene)	USA
	Walker Jr.	Ewell Doak	USA
	Warfield	Paul Dryden	USA
	Waterfield	Robert Stanton (Bob)	USA
	Webster	Michael Lewis (Mike)	USA
	Weinmeister	Arnold George (Arnie)	Canada

SOLVER SERIES: NAME FINDER

FAME	LAST NAME	FIRST NAME	COUNTRY
Football Player - HF	White	Randy Lee	USA
	Wilcox	David (Dave)	USA
	Willis	William Karnet (Bill)	USA
	Wilson	Lawrence Frank (Larry)	USA
	Winslow	Kellen Boswell	USA
	Wojciechowicz	Alexander Francis (Alex)	USA
	Wood	William Vernell (Willie)	USA
	Yary	Anthony Ronald (Ron)	USA
	Young	Jon Steven (Steve)	USA
	Youngblood III	Herbert Jackson (Jack)	USA
Football Player/Coach/Commentator	Madden	John	USA
Football Player/Olympic Runner - HF	Thorpe	James Francis (Jim)	USA
Football Team President	Rooney	Daniel M. (Dan)	USA
Golf Club Designer - HF	Solheim	Karsten	Norway
Golf Course Designer - HF	Jones Sr.	Robert Trent	England
Golf Promoter - HF	Dey	Joseph C.	USA
	Graffis	Herb	USA
	Harlow	Robert (Bob)	USA
	Roberts	Clifford	USA
	Tufts	Richard	USA
Golf Teacher - HF	Penick	Harvey	USA
Golfer	Archer	George	USA
	Baker-Finch	Ian	Australia
	Calcavecchia	Mark	USA
	Charles	Bob	New Zealand
	Colbert	Jim	USA
	Cook	John	USA
	Couples	Fred	USA
	Crampton	Bruce	Australia
	Daly	John	USA
	Davies	Laura	England
	Dent	Jim	USA
	Douglass	Dale	USA
	Dutra	Olin	USA
	Duval	David	USA
	Elkington	Steve	Australia
	Els	Ernie	South Africa
	Estes	Bob	USA
	Faxon	Brad	USA
	Geiberger	Al	USA
	Graham	David	Australia
	Green	Hubert	USA
	Hill	Dave	USA
	Hill	Mike	USA
	Hulbert	Mike	USA
	January	Don	USA
	Lehman	Tom	USA
	Lema	Tony	USA
	Love 111	Davis	USA
	Lyle	Alexander Walter (Sandy)	England
	Mallon	Meg	USA
	Marr	Dave	USA
	Mize	Larry	USA
	Mochrie	Dottie (Pepper)	USA
	Moody	Orville	USA
	North	Andy	USA
	Ogle	Brett	Australia
	O'Meara	Mark	USA

FAME	LAST NAME	FIRST NAME	COUNTRY
Golfer	Palmer	Sandra	USA
	Pate	Jerry	USA
	Pate	Steve	USA
	Pavin	Corey	USA
	Peete	Calvin	USA
	Simpson	Scott	USA
	Singh	Vijay	Fiji
	Sluman	Jeff	USA
	Snead	Jesse Carlye (JC)	USA
	Stacy	Hollis	USA
	Stadler	Craig	USA
	Stephenson	Jan Lynne	Australia
	Stockton	Dave	USA
	Strange	Curtis	USA
	Tschetter	Kris	USA
	Tway	Bob	USA
	Uresti	Omar	USA
	Venturi	Ken	USA
	Wadkins	Lanny	USA
	Weiskopf	Tom	USA
	Woods	Tiger	USA
	Woosnam	Ian	Wales
	Zarley	Kermit	USA
	Zoeller	Fuzzy	USA
Golfer - HF	Alcott	Amy	USA
	Anderson	Willie	Scotland
	Aoki	Isao	Japan
	Armour	Tommy	Scotland
	Ball	John	England
	Ballesteros	Seve	Spain
	Barnes	Jim (Long Jim)	England
	Bell	Judy	USA
	Beman	Deane	USA
	Berg	Patty	USA
	Bolt	Tommy	USA
	Bonallack	Michael	England
	Boros	Julius	USA
	Bradley	Pat	USA
	Braid	James	Scotland
	Burke Jr.	Jack	USA
	Campbell	William C. (Bill)	USA
	Caponi	Donna	USA
	Carner	Joanne Gunderson	USA
	Casper	Billy	USA
	Coles	Neil	England
	Cooper	Harry	England
	Corcoran	Fred	USA
	Cotton	Henry	England
	Crenshaw	Ben	USA
	Crosby	Bing	USA
	Daniel	Beth	USA
	Demaret	Jimmy	USA
	Diegel	Leo	USA
	Evans	Charles (Chick)	USA
	Faldo	Nick	England
	Floyd	Raymond	USA
	Gudahl	Ralph	USA
	Hagen	Walter	USA

SOLVER SERIES: NAME FINDER

FAME	LAST NAME	FIRST NAME	COUNTRY
Golfer - HF	Hagge	Marlene Bauer	USA
	Haynie	Sandra	USA
	Higuchi	Hisako (Chako)	Japan
	Hilton	Harold	England
	Hogan	Ben	USA
	Hope	Bob	USA
	Howe	Dorothy Campbell Hurd	Scotland
	Inkster	Juli	USA
	Irwin	Hale	USA
	Jacklin	Tony	England
	Jacobs	John	England
	Jameson	Betty	USA
	Jones Jr.	Robert Tyre (Bobby)	USA
	King	Betsy	USA
	Kite	Thomas O. (Tom)	USA
	Langer	Bernhard	Germany
	Little	Lawson	USA
	Littler	Gene	USA
	Locke	Arthur Darcy (Bobby)	South Africa
	Lopez	Nancy	USA
	Mangrum	Lloyd	USA
	Mann	Carol	USA
	Middlecoff	Cary	USA
	Miller	Johnny	USA
	Morris Jr.	Tom	Scotland
	Morris Sr.	Tom	Scotland
	Nelson	Byron	USA
	Nicklaus	Jack	USA
	Norman	Greg	Australia
	Ouimet	Francis	USA
	Palmer	Arnold (Arnie)	USA
	Player	Gary	South Africa
	Price	Nick	South Africa
	Rankin	Judy	USA
	Rawls	Betsy	USA
	Robertson	Allan	Scotland
	Rodriquez	Juan (Chi Chi)	Puerto Rico
	Runyan	Paul (Little Poison)	USA
	Sarazen	Gene	USA
	Sheehan	Patty	USA
	Shore	Dinah	USA
	Sifford	Charlie	USA
	Smith	Horton	USA
	Snead	Sam	USA
	Sörenstam	Annika	Sweden
	Stewart	Payne William	USA
	Streit	Marlene Stewart	Canada
	Suggs	Louise	USA
	Taylor	John H.	Scotland
	Thomson	Peter	Australia
	Travers	Jerome D. (Jerry)	USA
	Travis	Walter	Australia
	Trevino	Lee	USA
	Vardon	Harry	USA
	Vare	Glenna Collette	USA
	Vicenzo	Roberto De	Brazil
	Watson	Tom	USA
	Wethered	Joyce	England

FAME	LAST NAME	FIRST NAME	COUNTRY
Golfer - HF	Whitworth	Kathy	USA
	Wright	Mary Kathryn (Mickey)	USA
	Zaharias	Mildred Didrikson (Babe)	USA
Golfer/Carpenter	Ulrich	William Richard (Bud)	Canada
Golfer/Course Designer - HF	Ross	Donald	Scotland
Hockey Broadcaster - HF	Messina	Sal	USA
Hockey Journalist - HF	Elliott	Helene	USA
Hockey Player	Francis	Emile Percy (The Cat)	Canada
	Gilbert	Rodriquez Gabriel (Rod)	Canada
	Hull	Brett	Canada
	Kovalev	Alexei	Russia
	Messier	Mark	Canada
Hockey Player - HF	Abel	Sidney Gerald (Sid)	Canada
	Adams	John James (Jack)	Canada
	Apps	Charles Joseph Sylvanus (Syl)	Canada
	Armstrong	George Edward (Chief)	Canada
	Bailey	Irvine Wallace (Ace)	Canada
	Bain	Donald Henderson (Dan)	Canada
	Baker	Amery Hare (Hobey)	USA
	Barber	William Charles (Bill)	Canada
	Barry	Martin A. (Marty)	Canada
	Bathgate	Andrew James (Andy)	Canada
	Bauer	Robert Theodore (Bobby)	Canada
	Beliveau	Jean Arthur	Canada
	Benedict	Clinton S. (Clint)	Canada
	Bentley	Douglas Wagner (Doug)	Canada
	Bentley	Maxwell Herbert Lloyd	Canada
	Blake	Hector (Toe)	Canada
	Boivin	Leo Joseph	Canada
	Boon	Richard R. (Dickie)	Canada
	Bossy	Michael (Mike)	Canada
	Bouchard	Emil (Butch)	Canada
	Boucher	Francois X. (Frank)	Canada
	Boucher	George (Buck)	Canada
	Bourque	Raymond Jean (Ray)	Canada
	Bower	John William (Johnny)	Canada
	Bowie	Russell (Dubbie)	Canada
	Brimsek	Frances Charles (Frank)	Canada
	Broadbent	Harry L. (Punch)	Canada
	Broda	Walter Edward (Turk)	Canada
	Bucyk	John Paul (Johnny)	Canada
	Burch	William (Billy)	USA
	Cameron	Harold Hugh (Harry)	Canada
	Cheevers	Gerald Michael (Gerry)	Canada
	Clancy	Francis M. (King)	Canada
	Clapper	Aubrey V. (Dit)	Canada
	Clarke	Robert Earle (Bobby)	Canada
	Cleghorn	Sprague	Canada
	Coffey	Paul Douglas	Canada
	Colville	Neil McNeil	Canada
	Conacher	Charles William (Charlie)	Canada
	Conacher	Lionel Pretoria	Canada
	Conacher	Roy Gordon	Canada
	Connell	Alex	Canada
	Cook	Frederick Joseph (Bun)	Canada
	Cook	William (Bill)	Canada
	Costello	Murray	Canada
	Coulter	Arthur Edmund (Art)	Canada

SOLVER SERIES: NAME FINDER

FAME	LAST NAME	FIRST NAME	COUNTRY
Hockey Player - HF	Cournoyer	Yvan Serge (Roadrunner)	Canada
	Cowley	William Mailes (Bill)	Canada
	Crawford	Samuel Russell (Rusty)	Canada
	Darragh	John Proctor (Jack)	Canada
	Davidson	Allan M. (Scotty)	Canada
	Day	Clarence (Happy)	Canada
	Delvecchio	Alexander Peter (Alex)	Canada
	Denneny	Cyril Joseph (Cy)	Canada
	Dionne	Marcel Elphege	Canada
	Drillon	Gordon Arthur	Canada
	Drinkwater	Charles Graham	Canada
	Dryden	Kenneth Wayne (Ken)	Canada
	Dumart	Woodrow Clarence (Woody)	Canada
	Dunderdale	Thomas (Tommy)	Australia
	Durnan	William Ronald (Bill)	Canada
	Dutton	Mervyn (Red)	Canada
	Dye	Cecil Henry (Babe)	Canada
	Esposito	Anthony James (Tony)	Canada
	Esposito	Philip Anthony (Phil)	Canada
	Farrel	Arthur F.	Canada
	Federko	Bernard Allan	Canada
	Fetisov	Viacheslav	Russia
	Flaman	Ferdinand Charles (Fernie)	Canada
	Fleur	Guy Damien La	Canada
	Fontaine	Pat La	USA
	Foyston	Frank C.	Canada
	Fredrickson	Frank	Canada
	Fuhr	Grant	Canada
	Gadsby	William (Bill)	Canada
	Gainey	Robert Michael (Bob)	Canada
	Gardiner	Charles Robert (Chuck)	Scotland
	Gardiner	Herbert Martin (Herb)	Canada
	Gardner	James Henry (Jimmy)	Canada
	Gartner	Michael Alfred	Canada
	Geoffrion	Bernard Joseph Andre (Bernie)	Canada
	Gerard	Edward George (Eddie)	Canada
	Giacomin	Edward (Fast Eddie)	Canada
	Gillies	Clark	Canada
	Gilmour	Hamilton Livingston (Billy)	Canada
	Goheen	Frank Xavier (Moose)	USA
	Goodfellow	Ebenezer Ralston (Ebbie)	Canada
	Goulet	Michel	Canada
	Grant	Michael (Mike)	Canada
	Green	Wilfred Thomas (Shorty)	Canada
	Gretzky	Wayne Douglas (Great One)	Canada
	Griffis	Silas Seth (Si)	USA
	Hainsworth	George	Canada
	Hall	Glenn Henry	Canada
	Hall	Joseph Henry (Joe)	England
	Harvey	Douglas Norman (Doug)	Canada
	Hawerchuk	Dale (Ducky)	Canada
	Hay	George William	Canada
	Hern	William Milton (Riley)	Canada
	Hextall	Bryan Aldwyn	Canada
	Holmes	Harry (Hap)	Canada
	Hooper	Charles Thomas (Tom)	Canada
	Horner	George Reginald (Red)	Canada
	Horton	Miles Gilbert (Tim)	Canada

FAME	LAST NAME	FIRST NAME	COUNTRY
Hockey Player - HF	Howe	Gordon (Gordie) (Mr. Hockey)	Canada
	Howe	Sydney Harris (Syd)	Canada
	Howell	Henry Vernon (Harry)	Canada
	Hull	Robert Marvin (Bobby)	Canada
	Hutton	John Bower (Bouse)	Canada
	Hyland	Harrold M. (Harry)	Canada
	Irvin	James Dickenson (Dick)	Canada
	Jackson	Harvey (Busher)	Canada
	Johnson	Ernest (Moose)	Canada
	Johnson	Ivan Wilfred (Ching)	Canada
	Johnson	Thomas Christian (Tom)	Canada
	Joliat	Aurel Emile	Canada
	Keats	Gordon Blanchard (Duke)	Canada
	Kelly	Leonard Patrick (Red)	Canada
	Kennedy	Theodre Samuel (Ted Teeter)	Canada
	Keon	David Michael (Dave)	Canada
	Kharlamov	Valeri	Russia
	Kurri	Jari Pekka	Finland
	Lach	Elmer James	Canada
	Lalonde	Edouard (Newsy)	Canada
	Langway	Rod Corry	Taiwan
	Laperriere	Joseph Jacques Hughes	Canada
	Lapointe	Guy Gerard	Canada
	Laprade	Edgar Louis	Canada
	Laviolette	Jean Baptiste (Jack)	Canada
	Lehman	Frederick Hugh (Hughie)	Canada
	Lemaire	Jacques Gerard	Canada
	Lemieux	Mario	Canada
	LeSueur	Percy	Canada
	Lewis	Herbert (Herbie)	Canada
	Lindsay	Robert Blake Theodore (Ted)	Canada
	Lumley	Harry (Apple Cheeks)	Canada
	MacKay	Duncan McMillan (Mickey)	Canada
	Mahovolich	Francis William (Frank)	Canada
	Malone	Maurice Joseph (Joe)	Canada
	Mantha	Sylvio	Canada
	Marshall	John C. (Jack)	Canada
	Maxwell	Fred G. (Steamer)	Canada
	McDonald	Lanny King	Canada
	McGee	Francis (Frank)	Canada
	McGimsie	William George (Bill)	Canada
	McNamara	George	Canada
	Mikita	Stanley (Stan)	Czechoslovakia
	Moore	Richard Winston (Dickie)	Canada
	Moran	Patrick Joseph (Paddy)	Canada
	Morenz	Howarth William (Howie)	Canada
	Mosienko	William (Bill)	Canada
	Mullen	Joseph (Joe)	USA
	Murphy	Larry Thomas	Canada
	Neely	Cam	Canada
	Nighbor	Frank	Canada
	Noble	Edward Reginald (Reg)	Canada
	O'Connor	Herbert William (Buddy)	Canada
	Oliver	Harold (Harry)	Canada
	Olmstead	Murray Bert	Canada
	Orr	Robert Gordon (Bobby)	Canada
	Parent	Bernard Marcel (Bernie)	Canada
	Park	Douglas Bradford (Brad)	Canada

SOLVER SERIES: NAME FINDER

FAME	LAST NAME	FIRST NAME	COUNTRY
Hockey Player - HF	Patrick	Joseph Lynn	Canada
	Patrick	Lester	Canada
	Perreault	Gilbert (Gil)	Canada
	Phillips	Thomas N. (Tommy)	Canada
	Pilote	Pierre Paul	Canada
	Pitre	Didier	Canada
	Plante	Joseph Jacques	Canada
	Potvin	Denis Charles	Canada
	Pratt	Walter (Babe)	Canada
	Primeau	Joseph (Joe)	Canada
	Pronovost	Marcel	Canada
	Pulford	Harvey	Canada
	Pulford	Robert Jesse (Bob)	Canada
	Quackenbush	Hubert George (Bill)	Canada
	Rankin	Frank	Canada
	Ratelle	Joseph Gilbert Yvon (Jean)	Canada
	Rayner	Claude Earl (Chuck)	Canada
	Reardon	Kenneth Joseph (Kenny)	Canada
	Richard	Joseph Henri (Pocket Rocket)	Canada
	Richard	Joseph Henri Maurice (Rocket)	Canada
	Richardson	George	Canada
	Roberts	Gordon	Canada
	Robinson	Larry	Canada
	Ross	Arthur Howie (Art)	Canada
	Russel	Blair	Canada
	Russell	Ernest (Ernie)	Canada
	Ruttan	Jack D.	Canada
	Salming	Anders Borje	Sweden
	Savard	Denis	Canada
	Savard	Serger Aubrey	Canada
	Sawchuk	Terrance Gordon (Terry)	Canada
	Scanlon	Fredrick	Canada
	Schmidt	Milton Conrad (Milt)	Canada
	Schriner	David (Sweeney)	Russia
	Seibert	Earl Walter	Canada
	Seibert	Oliver Levi	Canada
	Shore	Edward William (Eddie)	Canada
	Shutt	Stephen John	Canada
	Siebert	Albert Charles (Babe)	Canada
	Simpson	Harold Joseph (Bullet Joe)	Canada
	Sittler	Darryl Glen	Canada
	Smith	Alfred E. (Alf)	Canada
	Smith	Clinton James	Canada
	Smith	Reginald (Hooley)	Canada
	Smith	Thomas J.	Canada
	Smith	William John (Bill)	Canada
	Stanley	Allan Herbert	Canada
	Stanley	Russell (Barney)	Canada
	Stastny	Peter	Slovakia
	Stewart	John Sherratt (Black Jack)	Canada
	Stewart	Nelson (Old Poison)	Canada
	Stuart	Bruce	Canada
	Taylor	Frederick (Cyclone)	Canada
	Thompson	Cecil R. (Tiny)	Canada
	Tretiak	Vladislav Aleksandrovich	Russia
	Trihey	Henry Judah (Harry)	Canada
	Trottier	Bryan John	Canada
	Ullman	Norman Victor (Norm)	Canada

FAME	LAST NAME	FIRST NAME	COUNTRY
Hockey Player - HF	Vezina	George	Canada
	Walker	John Phillip (Jack)	Canada
	Walsh	Martin (Marty)	Canada
	Watson	Harry E. (Moose)	Canada
	Watson	Harry Percival	Canada
	Weiland	Ralph (Cooney)	Canada
	Westwick	Harry (Rat)	Canada
	Whitcroft	Frederick	Canada
	Wilson	Gordon Allan (Phat)	Canada
	Worsley	Lorne John (Gump)	Canada
	Worters	Roy (Shrimp)	Canada
Hydro Plane Driver - HF	Hanauer	Chip	USA
Hydroplane Race Driver - HF	Muncey	William (Bill)	USA
Inventor - Baseball	Doubleday	Abner	USA
Matador	Manolete	Manuel Rodriguez	Spain
Motor Cycle Race Driver - HF	Roberts	Kenny	USA
Olympic Decathlete	Jenner	Bruce	USA
	Thompson	Daley	England
	Toomey	William (Bill)	USA
	Mathias	Bob	USA
Olympic Gymnast	Comaneci	Nadia	Romania
	Conner	Bart	USA
	Korbut	Olga	Russia
	Retton	Mary Lou	USA
	Rigby	Cathy	USA
Olympic Gymnast Coach	Karoly	Bella	Romania
Olympic High Jumper	Fosbury	Dick	USA
	Stones	Dwight	USA
Olympic Hurdler	Kingdom	Roger	USA
	Moses	Edwin C.	USA
Olympic Javelin/Hurdles	Didrikson	Mildred (Babe)	USA
Olympic Long Jumper	Beamon	Bob	USA
Olympic Marathoner	Benoit	Joan	USA
	Cierpinski	Waldemar	Germany
	Shorter	Frank	Germany
	Waitz	Grete	Norway
	Zapotek	Emil	Czechoslovakia
Olympic Pole Vaulter	Richards	Bob	USA
Olympic Runner	Ashford	Evelyn	USA
	Bannister	Roger	USA
	Borzov	Valery	Russia
	Budd	Zola	South Africa
	Coe	Sebastian Newbold	England
	Devers	Gail	USA
	Johnson	Rafer Lewis	USA
	Lewis	Carl	USA
	Nurmi	Paavo	Finland
	Oerter	Al	USA
	Ovett	Steven Michael James (Steve)	England
	Owens	James (Jesse)	USA
	Rudolph	Wilma Glodean	USA
	Ryun	James Ronald (Jim)	USA
	Snell	Peter	New Zealand
	Torrence	Gwen	USA
	Tyus	Wyomia	USA
	Viren	Lasse	Finland
Olympic Skater	Babilonia	Tai	USA
	Boitano	Brian	USA

NAME	TYPE	ORGIN	CATEGORY
Adad	God	Babylonian	Oracles
			Storm
Aditi	Mother	Hindu	Of the Gods
Aeacus	Offspring	Greek	Of Zeus
Aeger	God	Norse	Sea
Aegina	Consort	Greek	Of Zeus
Aegir	God	Norse	Sea
Aegle	Offspring	Greek	Of Zeus
Aeolus	God	Greek	Winds
Aesir	God	Norse	Pantheon
Aestas	Goddess	Roman	Summer
Aglaia	Offspring	Greek	Of Zeus
"Aine (of Knockaine, Cliach, Cnoc)"	Goddess	Irish	Moon
Alceme	Consort	Greek	Of Zeus
Amaethon	God	Welsh	Agriculture
Ambika	Goddess	Hindu	Mangoes
Amen	God	Egyptian	Creation
Amen-Ra	God	Egyptian	Sun
Amon	God	Egyptian	Chief God
			Fertility
Amon-Re	God	Egyptian	Sun
Amor	God	Roman	Love
Amun	God	Egyptian	Chief God
Amun-Ra	God	Egyptian	Sun
Angus Mac Oc (Og)	God	Irish	Beauty
			Love
			Youth
Annona	Goddess	Roman	Crops
Antiope	Consort	Greek	Of Zeus
Anu	God	Babylonian	Heaven
Anu	Goddess	Irish	Earth
			Plenty
Anubis	God	Egyptian	Dead
			Embalming
Aoibhell	Goddess	Irish	Evil
Apet	Goddess	Egyptian	Protection (Childbirth)

SOLVER SERIES: NAME FINDER

NAME	TYPE	ORGIN	CATEGORY
Aphrodite	Goddess	Greek	Beauty
			Love
Apollo	Offspring	Greek	Of Zeus
Apollo	God	Greek	Sun
			Youth
Apollo	God	Roman	Music
			Sun
Ara	Goddess	Greek	Destruction
			Retribution
			Vengeance
Arawn	God	Welsh	Dead
			Underworld
Arcas	Offspring	Greek	Of Zeus
Ares	Offspring	Greek	Of Zeus
Ares	God	Greek	War
Ares	God	Roman	War
Argus	God	Greek	Sky
Arianrhod	Goddess	Welsh	Beauty
			Fertility
			Reincarnation
Artemis	Goddess	Greek	Agriculture
			Chase
			Goblins
			Hunting
			Moon
			Nature
Artemis	Goddess	Roman	Moon
Aruru	Goddess	Babylonian	Womb
Asclepius	God	Greek	Medicine
Asgard	Home	Norse	Of the Gods
Ashur	God	Assyrian	War
Astarte	Goddess	Greek	Moon
Astarte	Goddess	Phoenician	Fertility
Ate	Goddess	Greek	Criminal Folly
			Mischief
Ate	Offspring	Greek	Of Zeus
Ate	Goddess	Greek	Retribution
Aten	King	Egyptian	Of the Gods
Aten	God	Egyptian	Sun
Athena	Goddess	Greek	Arts
			War
			Wisdom
			Of Zeus
Atum	Creator	Egyptian	Of the Gods
Aurora	Goddess	Roman	Dawn
Bacchus	God	Greek	Revelry
Bacchus	God	Roman	Revelry
			Wine
"Badb (Badhbh, Badb Catha)"	Goddess	Irish	Enlightenment
			Inspiration
Baldur	God	Norse	Peace
Banba (Bandba)	Goddess	Irish	Fertility
Banba (Bandba)			War
Bast	Goddess	Egyptian	Cat
Bastet	Goddess	Egyptian	Protection
Bel	God	Greek	Earth
			Heaven(s)
"Bel (Belenus, Belinos, Beli Mawr)"	God	Irish	Cattle
			Crops

NAME	TYPE	ORGIN	CATEGORY
"Bel (Belenus, Belinos, Beli Mawr)"	God	Irish	Fertility
			Fire
			Healing
			Hot Springs
			Prosperity
			Purification
			Success
"Bel (Belenus, Belinos, Beli Mawr)"	God	Welsh	Cattle
			Crops
			Fertility
			Fire
			Healing
			Hot Springs
			Prosperity
			Purification
			Success
Bellona	Goddess	Greek	War
Bellona	Goddess	Roman	War
Belus	Offspring	Greek	Of Zeus
Bes	God	Egyptian	Pleasure
			Protection
			Protection (Evil & Misfortune)
"Blodeuwedd (Blodwin, Blancheflor)"	Goddess	Welsh	Flowers
			Moon
			Wisdom
"Boann (Boannan, Boyne)"	Goddess	Irish	River
Boreas	God	Greek	Wind - North
			Wind - North
Boreas	God	Roman	Wind - North
Bragi	God	Norse	Poetry
Brahama	Creator	Hindu	Of the Gods
Bran the Blessed (Benedigeidfran)	God	Welsh	Arts
			Music
			Prophecy
			War
			Writing
Branwen	Goddess	Welsh	Beauty
			Love
"Brigit (Brid, Brig, Brigid, Brighid)"	Goddess	Irish	Agriculture
			Fire
			Healing
			Inspiration
			Learning Divination
			Occult Knowledge
			Poetry
			Prophecy
			Smithcraft
Buto	Goddess	Egyptian	Serpent
Caer Ibormeith	Goddess	Irish	Dreams
			Sleep
Caillech	Goddess	Irish	Disease
			Plague
Calyce	Consort	Greek	Of Zeus
Ceres	Goddess	Roman	Agriculture
			Fertility
			Grain
			Vegetation
"Ceridwen (Caridwen, Ceridwen)"	Goddess	Welsh	Death
			Initiation

SOLVER SERIES: NAME FINDER

NAME	TYPE	ORGIN	CATEGORY
"Ceridwen (Caridwen, Ceridwen)"	Goddess	Welsh	Inspiration
			Magic
			Regeneration
"Cernunnos (Cerowain, Cernenus)"	God	Welsh	Animals
			Commerce
			Crossroads
			Fertility
			Reincarnation
			Virility
			Warriors
			Woodland
Chloris	Goddess	Greek	Flowers
Chons	God	Egyptian	Moon
Clotho	Offspring	Greek	Of Zeus
Comus	God	Greek	Festivity
			Mirth
Comus	God	Roman	Festivity
			Joy
			Mirth
Cora	Goddess	Greek	Vegetation
Cora	Goddess	Roman	Nether World
Cotys	Goddess	Greek	Vegetation
"Creiddylad (Creudylad, Cordelia)"	Goddess	Welsh	Flowers
			Love
Cronus	God	Greek	Harvest
Cupid	God	Roman	Love
Cynthia	Goddess	Roman	Moon
Dagan	God	Babylonian	Earth
Dagda	God	Irish	Arts
			Chief God
			Knowledge
			Magic
			Music
			Prophecy
			Prosperity
			Regeneration
Danae	Consort	Greek	Of Zeus
Danu (Dana)	Queen	Irish	Magic
			Of the Gods
			Plenty
			Rivers
			Wells
			Wisdom
Dea	Goddess	Roman	Growth
Demeter	Goddess	Greek	Agriculture
			Marriage
Demeter	Goddess	Roman	Fertility
Devi	Goddess	Hindu	Mother of Life
Dian	Goddess	Roman	Moon
Dian Cecht (Diancecht)	God	Irish	Healing
			Magic
			Medicine
Dian Cecht (Diancecht)			Regeneration
Diana	Goddess	Roman	Hunting
Dionysus	God	Greek	Revelry
			Wine
Dis	God	Roman	Hades
			Underworld
Don	Goddess	Irish	Air

NAME	TYPE	ORGIN	CATEGORY
Don	Goddess	Irish	Sea
Donar	God	Norse	Thunder
Donn	Goddess	Welsh	Sea
Doris	Goddess	Greek	Seas
Druantia	Goddess	Welsh	Queen of the Druids
Dua	God	Egyptian	Protection (Stomach of the Dead)
Durga	Goddess	Hindu	Beyond Reach
Dylan	God	Welsh	Sea
Ea	God	Babylonian	Incantations
			Water
			Wisdom
Eadon	Goddess	Irish	Nurse of the Poets
Eir	Goddess	Norse	Healing
Eiru (Erin)	Goddess	Irish	Ruler
Ellil	God	Babylonian	Air
			Sky
Eos	Goddess	Greek	Dawn
Epona	Goddess	Roman	Horses
Epona	Goddess	Welsh	Horses
Erda	Goddess	Norse	Earth
Ereshkigal	Goddess	Babylonian	Underworld
Ergane	Goddess	Greek	Weaving
Eridanus	God	Greek	River
Eris	Goddess	Greek	Discord
			Mischief
			Strife
Eros	God	Greek	Love
Europa	Consort	Greek	Of Zeus
Eurus	God	Greek	Wind - Southeast
Eurus	God	Roman	Wind - East
Faun	God	Roman	Fields
			Herds
Fauna	Goddess	Roman	Fertility
Faunus	God	Roman	Pastoral
Feronia	Goddess	Roman	Fountain
Fides	Goddess	Roman	Faith
			Virtue
Flidais	Goddess	Irish	Forests
			Wild Creatures
Flora	Goddess	Roman	Flowers
Forseti	God	Norse	Justice
			Order
Frey	God	Norse	Fertility
Freya	Goddess	Norse	Beauty
			Love
Frigg(a)	Goddess	Norse	Marriage
			Motherhood
Gaea	Goddess	Greek	Earth
Gaia	Goddess	Greek	Earth
			Marriage
Ganesha	God	Hindu	Prosperity
			Wisdom
Geb	God	Egyptian	Earth
Goibniu	God	Irish	Blacksmiths
			Brewing
			Weapon Makers
Goibniu	God	Welsh	Blacksmiths
			Brewing
			Weapon Makers

SOLVER SERIES: NAME FINDER

NAME	TYPE	ORGIN	CATEGORY
Gwethyr	God	Welsh	Upperworld
Gwydion	God	Welsh	Enchantmen
			Illusion
			Magic
Gwynn ap Nudd	God	Welsh	Underworld
Hades	God	Greek	Underworld
Hapi	God	Egyptian	Nile
Hapy	God	Egyptian	Innundation
Hathor	Goddess	Egyptian	Joy
			Love
			Protection
Hebe	Offspring	Greek	Of Zeus
Hebe	Goddess	Greek	Youth
Hecate	Goddess	Greek	Earth
			Ghosts
			Magic
			Moon
			Sorcery
			Witchcraft
Heimdall	Watchman	Norse	Of the Gods
Hel	Goddess	Norse	Underworld
Helen	Offspring	Greek	Of Zeus
Helios	God	Greek	Sun
			Sun
Hera	Goddess	Greek	Air
			Heavens
			Marriage
			Of the Gods
			Of Zeus
			Women
Hermes	Herald	Greek	Of the Gods
Hermes	Offspring	Greek	Of Zeus
Hestia	Goddess	Greek	Hearth
Hoder	God	Norse	Winter
Hodur	God	Norse	Darkness
			Winter
Hoenir	God	Norse	Asa-God
Horus	God	Egyptian	Protection (Hawk-Headed)
			Sky
Hygeia	Goddess	Greek	Health
Hymen	God	Greek	Marriage
Hypnos	God	Greek	Sleep
Hypnus	God	Greek	Sleep
Idun	Goddess	Norse	Immortality
			Spring
			Youth
Imhotep	God	Egyptian	Medicine
Ino	Goddess	Greek	Seas
			Sky
Irene	Goddess	Greek	Peace
Ishtar	Goddess	Babylonian	Love
Isis	Goddess	Egyptian	Protection
Janus	God	Roman	Gates
Jove	God	Roman	Chief God
Juno	Goddess	Roman	Marriage
Juno	Queen	Roman	Of the Gods
Jupiter	God	Roman	Chief God
			Lightning
Jupiter Pluvius	God	Roman	Rain

NAME	TYPE	ORGIN	CATEGORY
Kali	Goddess	Hindu	Evil
Kama	God	Hindu	Love
Kehpri	God	Egyptian	Creation
			Movement of the Sun
			Rebirth
Khafre	God	Egyptian	God-King
Khnum	God	Egyptian	Creation
Khonsu	God	Egyptian	Moon
Krishna	God	Hindu	Protection (Against Evil)
Lakshmi	Goddess	Hindu	Beauty
			Enjoyment
			Wealth
Lar	God	Roman	Tutelary
Lars	God	Roman	Household
Leda	Goddess	Greek	Night
Leda	Consort	Greek	Of Zeus
Leto	Goddess	Greek	Night
Leto	Consort	Greek	Of Zeus
Llew Llaw Gyffes	God	Welsh	Hero
Llud Llaw Ereint	God	Welsh	Harpers
			Healing
			Poetry
			Smithcraft
			Sorcery
			Water
Llyr	God	Irish	Sea
			Water
Loki	God	Norse	Discord
			Fire
			Mischief
Lucina	Goddess	Roman	Birth
			Light
"Lugh (Llew, Lug, Lugus)"	God	Irish	Arts
			Healing
			Journeys
			Prophecy
			Sun
"Lugh (Llew, Lug, Lugus)"	God	Welsh	Arts
			Healing
			Journeys
			Prophecy
			Sun
Luna	Goddess	Roman	Moon
Lupercus	God	Roman	Pastoral
Maat	Goddess	Egyptian	Harmony
			Justice
			Truth
"Macha (Mania, Mana, Mene, Minne)"	Goddess	Irish	Cunning
			Death
			Physical Force
			War
Maia	Consort	Greek	Of Zeus
Manannan Mac Lir	God	Welsh	Commerce
			Magic
			Navigation
			Rebirth
			Sea
			Storm
			Weather

SOLVER SERIES: NAME FINDER

NAME	TYPE	ORGIN	CATEGORY
Manawydan ap Llyr	God	Irish	Commerce
			Magic
			Navigation
			Rebirth
			Sea
			Storm
			Weather
Marduk	God	Babylonian	Sun
Mare	Goddess	Roman	Sea
Margawse	Mother	Welsh	Of the Gods
Mars	God	Roman	War
Math Mathonwy	God	Welsh	Enchantment
			Magic
Matuta	Goddess	Roman	Birth
			Dawn
Menkaure	God	Egyptian	God-King
Mercury	God	Roman	Patron
"Merlin (Merddin, Myrddin)"	God	Welsh	Arts
			Healing
			Illusion
			Magic
			Prophecy
Metis	Consort	Greek	Of Zeus
Min	God	Egyptian	Fertility
Minerva	Goddess	Roman	War
			Wisdom
Minos	Offspring	Greek	Of Zeus
Mnemosyne	Goddess	Greek	Memory
Mnevis	God	Egyptian	Black Bull of the Sun
Moira	Goddess	Greek	Fate
Momus	God	Greek	Mockery
			Ridicule
Morpheus	God	Roman	Sleep
"Morrigan (Morrigu, Morrighan, Morgan)"	Goddess	Irish	Lust
			Magic
			Prophecy
			War
"Morrigan (Morrigu, Morrighan, Morgan)"	Goddess	Welsh	Lust
			Magic
			Prophecy
			War
Mors	God	Roman	Death
Mut	Goddess	Egyptian	Sky
Neit	God	Irish	Battle
Nemesis	Goddess	Greek	Revenge
			Vengeance
Nephthys	Goddess	Egyptian	Protection (Of the Dead)
Neptune	God	Roman	Sea
Nergal	God	Babylonian	Underworld
Neureus	God	Greek	Sea
Niamh	Goddess	Irish	Beauty
			Brightness
Nike	Goddess	Greek	Victory
Ninurta	God	Babylonian	War
Norn	Goddess	Norse	Destiny
Norns	God	Norse	Fates
Notus	God	Roman	Wind - South
Nox	Goddess	Roman	Night
"Nuada (Nudd, Nodens, Lud, Ereint)"	God	Irish	Harpers

NAME	TYPE	ORGIN	CATEGORY
"Nuada (Nudd, Nodens, Lud, Ereint)"	God	Irish	Healing
			Historians
			Magic
			Poetry
			War
			Writing
"Nuada (Nudd, Nodens, Lud, Ereint)"	God	Welsh	Harpers
			Healing
			Historians
			Magic
			Poetry
			War
			Writing
Nut	Goddess	Egyptian	Heavens
			Sky
Nyx	Goddess	Greek	Night
Odin	God	Norse	Chief God
"Ogma (Oghma,Ogmios)"	God	Welsh	Eloquence
			Inspiration
			Language
			Magic
			Music
			Physical Force
			Poetry
			Writing
Oniros	God	Greek	Dream
Ops	Goddess	Roman	Agriculture
			Fertility
			Harvest
			Plenty
Orcus	God	Roman	Hades
			Lower World
			Underworld
Orion	God	Greek	Hunter
Osiris	God	Egyptian	Judge of the dead
			Underworld
			Vegetation
Pales	Goddess	Roman	Herds
Pallas	Goddess	Greek	Wisdom
Pan	God	Greek	Fields
			Flocks
			Forest
Pan	God	Roman	Herds
Parca	Goddess	Roman	Birth
Parcae	Goddess	Roman	Fates
Pax	Goddess	Roman	Peace
Penates	God	Roman	Household
Pepi	God	Egyptian	God-King
Phoebus	God	Greek	Sun
Picus	God	Roman	Agriculture
Pluto	God	Greek	Underworld
			Hades
Pluto			Underworld
Plutus	God	Greek	Wealth
Pollox	Offspring	Greek	Of Zeus
Pomona	Goddess	Roman	Fruits
Poseidon	God	Greek	Sea
Proserpina	Goddess	Roman	Nether World
Ptah	God	Egyptian	Craftsmen

SOLVER SERIES: NAME FINDER

NAME	TYPE	ORGIN	CATEGORY
Ptah	God	Egyptian	Creation/Bearer of the ankh
			Memphis
Pwyll (pen annwn)	God	Welsh	Cunning
			Virtue
Qetesh	Goddess	Egyptian	Beauty
			Love
Quirinus	God	Roman	War
Ra	God	Egyptian	Sun
Ragnarok	God	Norse	Destruction
Ra-Horakhty	God	Egyptian	Rising Sun
Ramses	God	Egyptian	God-King
Ran	Goddess	Norse	Sea
Re	God	Egyptian	Sun
Rhea	Mother	Greek	Of the Gods
Salus	Goddess	Roman	Health
			Prosperity
Sati	Goddess	Egyptian	Elephantine
Sati	Queen	Egyptian	Of the Gods
Saturn	God	Roman	Agriculture
Satyr	God	Greek	Demigod
"Scathach (Scota,Scatha,Scath)"	Goddess	Irish	Healing
			Magic
			Martial Arts
			Prophecy
Sekhet	Goddess	Egyptian	Protection (Women)
Sekhmet	Goddess	Egyptian	War
Selene	Goddess	Greek	Moon
Selene	Consort	Greek	Of Zeus
Selket	Goddess	Egyptian	Protection (Childbirth)
Semele	Consort	Greek	Of Zeus
Senusert	God	Egyptian	God-King
Serapis	God	Egyptian	Lower World
Serapis	God	Roman	Lower World
Seshat	Goddess	Egyptian	Measurement
			Writing
Set	God	Egyptian	Chaos
			Evil
Seth	God	Egyptian	Chaos
			Evil
Shamash	God	Babylonian	Sin
Shu	God	Egyptian	Air
Sif	Goddess	Norse	Corn
Sin	God	Babylonian	Moon
Skuld	Goddess	Norse	Future
Sobek	God	Egyptian	Nile (Crocodile)
Sol	God	Roman	Sun
Somnus	God	Roman	Night
			Sleep
Spes	Goddess	Roman	Hope
Sylvanus	God	Roman	Woods
Taliesin	God	Welsh	Magic
			Music
			Poetry
			Wisdom
			Writing
Tammuz	God	Babylonian	Fertility
			Vegetation
Taweret	Goddess	Egyptian	Protection (Childbirth)
Tefnut	Goddess	Egyptian	Moisture

SECTION 4 - GODS AND GODDESSES LISTED ALPHABETICALLY BY NAME

NAME	TYPE	ORGIN	CATEGORY
Tellus	Goddess	Roman	Earth
Tellus	Goddess	Roman	Fields
Terra	Goddess	Roman	Earth
			Fields
Thalia	Offspring	Greek	Of Zeus
Themis	Goddess	Greek	Justice
Themis	Consort	Greek	Of Zeus
Thor	God	Norse	Thunder
Thoth	God	Egyptian	Knowledge
			Magic
			Moon
			Wisdom
			Writing
Thutmose	God	Egyptian	God-King
Triton	God	Greek	Demigod
			Sea
Trivia	Goddess	Roman	Crossroads
Tyche	Goddess	Greek	Chance
Tyr	God	Norse	Sky
Ull	God	Norse	Frost Glitter
			Skiing
Uranus	God	Greek	Heaven(s)
Vacuna	Goddess	Roman	Hunting
Vali	God	Norse	Avenger
Vanir	God	Norse	Earlier Race
Venus	Goddess	Roman	Beauty
			Love
Verdandi	Goddess	Norse	Present
Vertumnus	God	Roman	Season
Vesta	Goddess	Roman	Fire
			Hearth
Vulcan	God	Greek	Fire
Vulcan	God	Roman	Fire
Wepwawet	God	Egyptian	Funerary Cult
			War
White Lady	Goddess	Irish	Death
			Destruction
White Lady	Goddess	Welsh	Death
			Destruction
Zephyr	God	Roman	Wind - West
Zethus	Offspring	Greek	Of Zeus
Zeus	God	Greek	Chief God
			Heaven(s)
			Rain
			Sky
			Supreme

CATEGORY	ORGIN	NAME	TYPE
Agriculture	Greek	Artemis	Goddess
	Greek	Demeter	Goddess
	Irish	"Brigit (Brid, Brig, Brigid, Brighid)"	Goddess
	Roman	Picus	God
	Roman	Saturn	God
	Roman	Ops	Goddess
	Roman	Ceres	Goddess
	Welsh	Amaethon	God
Air	Babylonian	Ellil	God
	Egyptian	Shu	God
	Greek	Hera	Goddess
	Irish	Don	Goddess
Animals	Welsh	"Cernunnos (Cerowain, Cernenus)"	God
Arts	Greek	Athena	Goddess
	Irish	Dagda	God
	Irish	"Lugh (Llew, Lug, Lugus)"	God
	Welsh	Bran the Blessed (Benedigeidfran)	God
	Welsh	"Lugh (Llew, Lug, Lugus)"	God
	Welsh	"Merlin (Merddin, Myrddin)"	God
Asa-God	Norse	Hoenir	God
Avenger	Norse	Vali	God
Battle	Irish	Neit	God
Beauty	Egyptian	Qetesh	Goddess
	Greek	Aphrodite	Goddess
	Hindu	Lakshmi	Goddess
	Irish	Angus Mac Oc (Og)	God
	Irish	Niamh	Goddess
	Norse	Freya	Goddess
	Roman	Venus	Goddess
	Welsh	Arianrhod	Goddess
	Welsh	Branwen	Goddess
Beyond Reach	Hindu	Durga	Goddess
Birth	Roman	Parca	Goddess
	Roman	Lucina	Goddess
	Roman	Matuta	Goddess
Black Bull of the Sun	Egyptian	Mnevis	God
Blacksmiths	Irish	Goibniu	God

SOLVER SERIES: NAME FINDER

CATEGORY	ORGIN	NAME	TYPE
Blacksmiths	Welsh	Goibniu	God
Brewing	Irish	Goibniu	God
	Welsh	Goibniu	God
Brightness	Irish	Niamh	Goddess
Cat	Egyptian	Bast	Goddess
Cattle	Irish	"Bel (Belenus, Belinos, Beli Mawr)"	God
	Welsh	"Bel (Belenus, Belinos, Beli Mawr)"	God
Chance	Greek	Tyche	Goddess
Chaos	Egyptian	Set	God
	Egyptian	Seth	God
Chase	Greek	Artemis	Goddess
Chief God	Egyptian	Amon	God
	Egyptian	Amun	God
	Greek	Zeus	God
	Irish	Dagda	God
	Norse	Odin	God
	Roman	Jove	God
	Roman	Jupiter	God
Commerce	Irish	Manawydan ap Llyr	God
	Welsh	"Cernunnos (Cerowain, Cernenus)"	God
	Welsh	Manannan Mac Lir	God
Corn	Norse	Sif	Goddess
Craftsmen	Egyptian	Ptah	God
Creation	Egyptian	Khnum	God
	Egyptian	Kehpri	God
	Egyptian	Amen	God
Creation/Bearer of the ankh	Egyptian	Ptah	God
Criminal Folly	Greek	Ate	Goddess
Crops	Irish	"Bel (Belenus, Belinos, Beli Mawr)"	God
	Roman	Annona	Goddess
	Welsh	"Bel (Belenus, Belinos, Beli Mawr)"	God
Crossroads	Roman	Trivia	Goddess
	Welsh	"Cernunnos (Cerowain, Cernenus)"	God
Cunning	Irish	"Macha (Mania, Mana, Mene, Minne)"	Goddess
	Welsh	Pwyll (pen annwn)	God
Darkness	Norse	Hodur	God
Dawn	Greek	Eos	Goddess
	Roman	Aurora	Goddess
	Roman	Matuta	Goddess
Dead	Egyptian	Anubis	God
	Welsh	Arawn	God
Death	Irish	"Macha (Mania, Mana, Mene, Minne)"	Goddess
Death	Irish	White Lady	Goddess
	Roman	Mors	God
	Welsh	"Ceridwen (Caridwen, Ceridwen)"	Goddess
	Welsh	White Lady	Goddess
Demigod	Greek	Satyr	God
	Greek	Triton	God
Destiny	Norse	Norn	Goddess
Destruction	Greek	Ara	Goddess
	Irish	White Lady	Goddess
	Norse	Ragnarok	God
	Welsh	White Lady	Goddess
Discord	Greek	Eris	Goddess
	Norse	Loki	God
Disease	Irish	Caillech	Goddess
Dreams	Greek	Oniros	God
	Irish	Caer Ibormeith	Goddess
Earlier Race	Norse	Vanir	God

CATEGORY	ORGIN	NAME	TYPE
Earth	Babylonian	Dagan	God
	Egyptian	Geb	God
	Greek	Bel	God
	Greek	Gaea	Goddess
	Greek	Gaia	Goddess
	Greek	Hecate	Goddess
	Irish	Anu	Goddess
	Norse	Erda	Goddess
	Roman	Terra	Goddess
	Roman	Tellus	Goddess
Elephantine	Egyptian	Sati	Goddess
Eloquence	Welsh	"Ogma (Oghma,Ogmios)"	God
Embalming	Egyptian	Anubis	God
Enchantmen	Welsh	Gwydion	God
	Welsh	Math Mathonwy	God
Enjoyment	Hindu	Lakshmi	Goddess
Enlightenment	Irish	"Badb (Badhbh, Badb Catha)"	Goddess
Evil	Egyptian	Set	God
	Egyptian	Seth	God
	Hindu	Kali	Goddess
	Irish	Aoibhell	Goddess
Faith	Roman	Fides	Goddess
Fate	Greek	Moira	Goddess
Fates	Norse	Norns	God
	Roman	Parcae	Goddess
Fertility	Babylonian	Tammuz	God
	Egyptian	Min	God
	Egyptian	Amon	God
	Irish	"Bel (Belenus, Belinos, Beli Mawr)"	God
	Irish	Banba (Bandba)	Goddess
	Norse	Frey	God
	Phoenician	Astarte	Goddess
	Roman	Ops	Goddess
	Roman	Ceres	Goddess
	Roman	Fauna	Goddess
	Roman	Demeter	Goddess
	Welsh	"Bel (Belenus, Belinos, Beli Mawr)"	God
	Welsh	"Cernunnos (Cerowain, Cernenus)"	God
	Welsh	Arianrhod	Goddess
Festivity	Greek	Comus	God
	Roman	Comus	God
Fields	Greek	Pan	God
Fields	Roman	Faun	God
	Roman	Terra	Goddess
	Roman	Tellus	Goddess
Fire	Greek	Vulcan	God
	Irish	"Bel (Belenus, Belinos, Beli Mawr)"	God
	Irish	"Brigit (Brid, Brig, Brigid, Brighid)"	Goddess
	Norse	Loki	God
	Roman	Vulcan	God
	Roman	Vesta	Goddess
	Welsh	"Bel (Belenus, Belinos, Beli Mawr)"	God
Flocks	Greek	Pan	God
Flowers	Greek	Chloris	Goddess
	Roman	Flora	Goddess
	Welsh	"Blodeuwedd (Blodwin, Blancheflor)"	Goddess
	Welsh	"Creiddylad (Creudylad, Cordelia)"	Goddess
Forests	Greek	Pan	God
	Irish	Flidais	Goddess

SOLVER SERIES: NAME FINDER

CATEGORY	ORGIN	NAME	TYPE
Fountain	Roman	Feronia	Goddess
Frost Glitter	Norse	Ull	God
Fruits	Roman	Pomona	Goddess
Funerary Cult	Egyptian	Wepwawet	God
Future	Norse	Skuld	Goddess
Gates	Roman	Janus	God
Ghosts	Greek	Hecate	Goddess
Goblins	Greek	Artemis	Goddess
God-King	Egyptian	Pepi	God
	Egyptian	Khafre	God
	Egyptian	Ramses	God
	Egyptian	Menkaure	God
	Egyptian	Senusert	God
	Egyptian	Thutmose	God
Grain	Roman	Ceres	Goddess
Growth	Roman	Dea	Goddess
Hades	Roman	Dis	God
	Roman	Orcus	God
	Roman	Pluto	God
Harmony	Egyptian	Maat	Goddess
Harpers	Irish	"Nuada (Nudd, Nodens, Lud, Ereint)"	God
	Welsh	Llud Llaw Ereint	God
	Welsh	"Nuada (Nudd, Nodens, Lud, Ereint)"	God
Harvest	Greek	Cronus	God
	Roman	Ops	Goddess
Healing	Irish	"Bel (Belenus, Belinos, Beli Mawr)"	God
	Irish	Dian Cecht (Diancecht)	God
	Irish	"Lugh (Llew, Lug, Lugus)"	God
	Irish	"Nuada (Nudd, Nodens, Lud, Ereint)"	God
	Irish	"Brigit (Brid, Brig, Brigid, Brighid)"	Goddess
	Irish	"Scathach (Scota,Scatha,Scath)"	Goddess
	Norse	Eir	Goddess
	Welsh	"Bel (Belenus, Belinos, Beli Mawr)"	God
	Welsh	Llud Llaw Ereint	God
	Welsh	"Lugh (Llew, Lug, Lugus)"	God
	Welsh	"Merlin (Merddin, Myrddin)"	God
	Welsh	"Nuada (Nudd, Nodens, Lud, Ereint)"	God
Health	Greek	Hygeia	Goddess
	Roman	Salus	Goddess
Hearth	Greek	Hestia	Goddess
	Roman	Vesta	Goddess
Heavens	Babylonian	Anu	God
Heavens	Greek	Bel	God
	Greek	Zeus	God
	Greek	Uranus	God
	Egyptian	Nut	Goddess
	Greek	Hera	Goddess
Herds	Roman	Faun	God
	Roman	Pan	God
	Roman	Pales	Goddess
Hero	Welsh	Llew Llaw Gyffes	God
Historians	Irish	"Nuada (Nudd, Nodens, Lud, Ereint)"	God
	Welsh	"Nuada (Nudd, Nodens, Lud, Ereint)"	God
Hope	Roman	Spes	Goddess
Horses	Roman	Epona	Goddess
	Welsh	Epona	Goddess
Hot Springs	Irish	"Bel (Belenus, Belinos, Beli Mawr)"	God
	Welsh	"Bel (Belenus, Belinos, Beli Mawr)"	God
Household	Roman	Lars	God

SECTION 5 - GODS AND GODDESSES LISTED ALPHABETICALLY BY CATEGORY

CATEGORY	ORGIN	NAME	TYPE
Household	Roman	Penates	God
Hunter	Greek	Orion	God
Hunting	Greek	Artemis	Goddess
	Roman	Diana	Goddess
	Roman	Vacuna	Goddess
Illusion	Welsh	Gwydion	God
	Welsh	"Merlin (Merddin, Myrddin)"	God
Immortality	Norse	Idun	Goddess
Incantations	Babylonian	Ea	God
Initiation	Welsh	"Ceridwen (Caridwen, Ceridwen)"	Goddess
Innundation	Egyptian	Hapy	God
Inspiration	Irish	"Badb (Badhbh, Badb Catha)"	Goddess
	Irish	"Brigit (Brid, Brig, Brigid, Brighid)"	Goddess
	Welsh	"Ogma (Oghma,Ogmios)"	God
	Welsh	"Ceridwen (Caridwen, Ceridwen)"	Goddess
Journeys	Irish	"Lugh (Llew, Lug, Lugus)"	God
	Welsh	"Lugh (Llew, Lug, Lugus)"	God
Joy	Egyptian	Hathor	Goddess
	Roman	Comus	God
Judge of the dead	Egyptian	Osiris	God
Justice	Egyptian	Maat	Goddess
	Greek	Themis	Goddess
	Norse	Forseti	God
Knowledge	Egyptian	Thoth	God
	Irish	Dagda	God
Language	Welsh	"Ogma (Oghma,Ogmios)"	God
Learning Divination	Irish	"Brigit (Brid, Brig, Brigid, Brighid)"	Goddess
Light	Roman	Lucina	Goddess
Lightning	Roman	Jupiter	God
Love	Babylonian	Ishtar	Goddess
	Egyptian	Hathor	Goddess
	Egyptian	Qetesh	Goddess
	Greek	Eros	God
	Greek	Aphrodite	Goddess
	Hindu	Kama	God
	Irish	Angus Mac Oc (Og)	God
	Norse	Freya	Goddess
	Roman	Amor	God
	Roman	Cupid	God
	Roman	Venus	Goddess
	Welsh	Branwen	Goddess
	Welsh	"Creiddylad (Creudylad, Cordelia)"	Goddess
Lower World	Egyptian	Serapis	God
	Roman	Orcus	God
	Roman	Serapis	God
Lust	Irish	"Morrigan (Morrigu, Morrighan, Morgan)"	Goddess
	Welsh	"Morrigan (Morrigu, Morrighan, Morgan)"	Goddess
Magic	Egyptian	Thoth	God
	Greek	Hecate	Goddess
	Irish	Dagda	God
	Irish	Dian Cecht (Diancecht)	God
	Irish	Manawydan ap Llyr	God
	Irish	"Nuada (Nudd, Nodens, Lud, Ereint)"	God
	Irish	"Morrigan (Morrigu, Morrighan, Morgan)"	Goddess
	Irish	"Scathach (Scota,Scatha,Scath)"	Goddess
	Irish	Danu (Dana)	Queen
	Welsh	Gwydion	God
	Welsh	Manannan Mac Lir	God
	Welsh	Math Mathonwy	God

SOLVER SERIES: NAME FINDER

CATEGORY	ORGIN	NAME	TYPE
Magic	Welsh	"Merlin (Merddin, Myrddin)"	God
	Welsh	"Nuada (Nudd, Nodens, Lud, Ereint)"	God
	Welsh	"Ogma (Oghma,Ogmios)"	God
	Welsh	Taliesin	God
	Welsh	"Ceridwen (Caridwen, Ceridwen)"	Goddess
	Welsh	"Morrigan (Morrigu, Morrighan, Morgan)"	Goddess
Mangoes	Hindu	Ambika	Goddess
Marriage	Greek	Hymen	God
	Greek	Gaia	Goddess
	Greek	Hera	Goddess
	Greek	Demeter	Goddess
	Norse	Frigg(a)	Goddess
	Roman	Juno	Goddess
Martial Arts	Irish	"Scathach (Scota,Scatha,Scath)"	Goddess
Measurement	Egyptian	Seshat	Goddess
Medicine	Egyptian	Imhotep	God
	Greek	Asclepius	God
	Irish	Dian Cecht (Diancecht)	God
Memory	Greek	Mnemosyne	Goddess
Memphis	Egyptian	Ptah	God
Mirth	Greek	Comus	God
Mirth	Roman	Comus	God
Mischief	Greek	Ate	Goddess
	Greek	Eris	Goddess
	Norse	Loki	God
Mockery	Greek	Momus	God
Moisture	Egyptian	Tefnut	Goddess
Moon	Babylonian	Sin	God
	Egyptian	Chons	God
	Egyptian	Thoth	God
	Egyptian	Khonsu	God
	Greek	Hecate	Goddess
	Greek	Selene	Goddess
	Greek	Artemis	Goddess
	Greek	Astarte	Goddess
	Irish	"Aine (of Knockaine, Cliach, Cnoc)"	Goddess
	Roman	Dian	Goddess
	Roman	Luna	Goddess
	Roman	Artemis	Goddess
	Roman	Cynthia	Goddess
	Welsh	"Blodeuwedd (Blodwin, Blancheflor)"	Goddess
Mother of Life	Hindu	Devi	Goddess
Motherhood	Norse	Frigg(a)	Goddess
Movement of the Sun	Egyptian	Kehpri	God
Music	Irish	Dagda	God
	Roman	Apollo	God
	Welsh	Bran the Blessed (Benedigeidfran)	God
	Welsh	"Ogma (Oghma,Ogmios)"	God
	Welsh	Taliesin	God
Nature	Greek	Artemis	Goddess
Navigation	Irish	Manawydan ap Llyr	God
	Welsh	Manannan Mac Lir	God
Nether World	Roman	Cora	Goddess
	Roman	Proserpina	Goddess
Night	Greek	Nyx	Goddess
	Greek	Leda	Goddess
	Greek	Leto	Goddess
	Roman	Somnus	God
	Roman	Nox	Goddess

CATEGORY	ORGIN	NAME	TYPE
Nile	Egyptian	Hapi	God
Nile (Crocodile)	Egyptian	Sobek	God
Nurse of the Poets	Irish	Eadon	Goddess
Occult Knowledge	Irish	"Brigit (Brid, Brig, Brigid, Brighid)"	Goddess
Of the Gods	Egyptian	Atum	Creator
	Egyptian	Aten	King
	Egyptian	Sati	Queen
	Greek	Hermes	Herald
	Greek	Rhea	Mother
	Greek	Hera	Queen
	Hindu	Brahama	Creator
	Hindu	Aditi	Mother
	Irish	Danu (Dana)	Queen
	Norse	Asgard	Home
	Norse	Heimdall	Watchman
	Roman	Juno	Queen
	Welsh	Margawse	Mother
Of Zeus	Greek	Hera	Consort
	Greek	Leda	Consort
	Greek	Leto	Consort
	Greek	Maia	Consort
	Greek	Danae	Consort
	Greek	Metis	Consort
	Greek	Aegina	Consort
	Greek	Calyce	Consort
	Greek	Europa	Consort
	Greek	Semele	Consort
	Greek	Selene	Consort
	Greek	Themis	Consort
	Greek	Alceme	Consort
	Greek	Antiope	Consort
	Greek	Ate	Offspring
	Greek	Ares	Offspring
	Greek	Hebe	Offspring
	Greek	Aegle	Offspring
	Greek	Arcas	Offspring
	Greek	Belus	Offspring
	Greek	Helen	Offspring
	Greek	Minos	Offspring
	Greek	Aeacus	Offspring
	Greek	Aglaia	Offspring
	Greek	Apollo	Offspring
Of Zeus	Greek	Athene	Offspring
	Greek	Clotho	Offspring
	Greek	Hermes	Offspring
	Greek	Pollox	Offspring
	Greek	Thalia	Offspring
	Greek	Zethus	Offspring
Oracles	Babylonian	Adad	God
Order	Norse	Forseti	God
Pantheon	Norse	Aesir	God
Pastoral	Roman	Faunus	God
	Roman	Lupercus	God
Patron	Roman	Mercury	God
Peace	Greek	Irene	Goddess
	Norse	Baldur	God
	Roman	Pax	Goddess
Physical Force	Irish	"Macha (Mania, Mana, Mene, Minne)"	Goddess
	Welsh	"Ogma (Oghma,Ogmios)"	God

SOLVER SERIES: NAME FINDER

CATEGORY	ORGIN	NAME	TYPE
Plague	Irish	Caillech	Goddess
Pleasure	Egyptian	Bes	God
Plenty	Irish	Anu	Goddess
	Irish	Danu (Dana)	Queen
	Roman	Ops	Goddess
Poetry	Irish	"Nuada (Nudd, Nodens, Lud, Ereint)"	God
	Irish	"Brigit (Brid, Brig, Brigid, Brighid)"	Goddess
	Norse	Bragi	God
	Welsh	Llud Llaw Ereint	God
	Welsh	"Nuada (Nudd, Nodens, Lud, Ereint)"	God
	Welsh	"Ogma (Oghma,Ogmios)"	God
	Welsh	Taliesin	God
Present	Norse	Verdandi	Goddess
Prophecy	Irish	Dagda	God
	Irish	"Lugh (Llew, Lug, Lugus)"	God
	Irish	"Brigit (Brid, Brig, Brigid, Brighid)"	Goddess
	Irish	"Morrigan (Morrigu, Morrighan, Morgan)"	Goddess
	Irish	"Scathach (Scota,Scatha,Scath)"	Goddess
	Welsh	Bran the Blessed (Benedigeidfran)	God
	Welsh	"Lugh (Llew, Lug, Lugus)"	God
	Welsh	"Merlin (Merddin, Myrddin)"	God
	Welsh	"Morrigan (Morrigu, Morrighan, Morgan)"	Goddess
Prosperity	Hindu	Ganesha	God
	Irish	Dagda	God
	Irish	"Bel (Belenus, Belinos, Beli Mawr)"	God
	Roman	Salus	Goddess
	Welsh	"Bel (Belenus, Belinos, Beli Mawr)"	God
Protection	Egyptian	Bes	God
	Egyptian	Bastet	Goddess
	Egyptian	Isis	Goddess
	Egyptian	Hathor	Goddess
Protection (Against Evil)	Hindu	Krishna	God
Protection (Childbirth)	Egyptian	Apet	Goddess
	Egyptian	Selket	Goddess
	Egyptian	Taweret	Goddess
Protection (Evil & Misfortune)	Egyptian	Bes	God
Protection (Hawk-Headed)	Egyptian	Horus	God
Protection (Of the Dead)	Egyptian	Nephthys	Goddess
Protection (Stomach of the Dead)	Egyptian	Dua	God
Protection (Women)	Egyptian	Sekhet	Goddess
Purification	Irish	"Bel (Belenus, Belinos, Beli Mawr)"	God
	Welsh	"Bel (Belenus, Belinos, Beli Mawr)"	God
Queen of the Druids	Welsh	Druantia	Goddess
Rain	Greek	Zeus	God
	Roman	Jupiter Pluvius	God
Rebirth	Egyptian	Kehpri	God
	Irish	Manawydan ap Llyr	God
	Welsh	Manannan Mac Lir	God
Regeneration	Irish	Dagda	God
	Irish	Dian Cecht (Diancecht)	God
	Welsh	"Ceridwen (Caridwen, Ceridwen)"	Goddess
Reincarnation	Welsh	"Cernunnos (Cerowain, Cernenus)"	God
	Welsh	Arianrhod	Goddess
Retribution	Greek	Ara	Goddess
	Greek	Ate	Goddess
Revelry	Greek	Dionysus	God
	Greek	Bacchus	God
	Roman	Bacchus	God
Revenge	Greek	Nemesis	Goddess

CATEGORY	ORGIN	NAME	TYPE
Ridicule	Greek	Momus	God
Rising Sun	Egyptian	Ra-Horakhty	God
Rivers	Greek	Eridanus	God
	Irish	"Boann (Boannan, Boyne)"	Goddess
	Irish	Danu (Dana)	Queen
Ruler	Irish	Eiru (Erin)	Goddess
Sea	Greek	Neureus	God
	Greek	Poseidon	God
	Greek	Triton	God
	Irish	Llyr	God
	Irish	Manawydan ap Llyr	God
	Irish	Don	Goddess
	Norse	Aeger	God
	Norse	Aegir	God
	Norse	Ran	Goddess
	Roman	Neptune	God
	Roman	Mare	Goddess
	Welsh	Dylan	God
	Welsh	Manannan Mac Lir	God
	Welsh	Donn	Goddess
	Greek	Ino	Goddess
	Greek	Doris	Goddess
Season	Roman	Vertumnus	God
Serpent	Egyptian	Buto	Goddess
Sin	Babylonian	Shamash	God
Skiing	Norse	Ull	God
Sky	Babylonian	Ellil	God
	Egyptian	Horus	God
	Egyptian	Mut	Goddess
	Egyptian	Nut	Goddess
	Greek	Zeus	God
	Greek	Argus	God
	Greek	Ino	Goddess
	Norse	Tyr	God
Sleep	Greek	Hypnos	God
	Greek	Hypnus	God
	Irish	Caer Ibormeith	Goddess
	Roman	Somnus	God
	Roman	Morpheus	God
Smithcraft	Irish	"Brigit (Brid, Brig, Brigid, Brighid)"	Goddess
	Welsh	Llud Llaw Ereint	God
Sorcery	Greek	Hecate	Goddess
Sorcery	Welsh	Llud Llaw Ereint	God
Spring	Norse	Idun	Goddess
Storm	Babylonian	Adad	God
	Irish	Manawydan ap Llyr	God
	Welsh	Manannan Mac Lir	God
Strife	Greek	Eris	Goddess
Success	Irish	"Bel (Belenus, Belinos, Beli Mawr)"	God
	Welsh	"Bel (Belenus, Belinos, Beli Mawr)"	God
Summer	Roman	Aestas	Goddess
Sun	Babylonian	Marduk	God
	Egyptian	Amen-Ra	God
	Egyptian	Amon-Re	God
	Egyptian	Amun-Ra	God
	Egyptian	Ra	God
	Egyptian	Re	God
	Egyptian	Aten	God
	Greek	Helios	God

SOLVER SERIES: NAME FINDER

CATEGORY	ORGIN	NAME	TYPE
Sun	Greek	Apollo	God
	Greek	Helios	God
	Greek	Phoebus	God
	Irish	"Lugh (Llew, Lug, Lugus)"	God
	Roman	Apollo	God
	Roman	Sol	God
	Welsh	"Lugh (Llew, Lug, Lugus)"	God
Supreme	Greek	Zeus	God
Thunder	Norse	Thor	God
	Norse	Donar	God
Truth	Egyptian	Maat	Goddess
Tutelary	Roman	Lar	God
Underworld	Babylonian	Nergal	God
	Babylonian	Ereshkigal	Goddess
	Egyptian	Osiris	God
	Greek	Hades	God
	Greek	Pluto	God
	Norse	Hel	Goddess
	Roman	Dis	God
	Roman	Orcus	God
	Roman	Pluto	God
	Welsh	Gwynn ap Nudd	God
	Welsh	Arawn	God
Upperworld	Welsh	Gwethyr	God
Vegetation	Babylonian	Tammuz	God
	Egyptian	Osiris	God
	Greek	Cora	Goddess
Vegetation	Greek	Cotys	Goddess
	Roman	Ceres	Goddess
Vengeance	Greek	Ara	Goddess
	Greek	Nemesis	Goddess
Victory	Greek	Nike	Goddess
Virility	Welsh	"Cernunnos (Cerowain, Cernenus)"	God
Virtue	Roman	Fides	Goddess
	Welsh	Pwyll (pen annwn)	God
War	Assyrian	Ashur	God
	Babylonian	Ninurta	God
	Egyptian	Wepwawet	God
	Egyptian	Sekhmet	Goddess
	Greek	Ares	God
	Greek	Athena	Goddess
	Greek	Bellona	Goddess
	Irish	"Nuada (Nudd, Nodens, Lud, Ereint)"	God
	Irish	Banba (Bandba)	Goddess
	Irish	"Macha (Mania, Mana, Mene, Minne)"	Goddess
	Irish	"Morrigan (Morrigu, Morrighan, Morgan)"	Goddess
	Roman	Ares	God
	Roman	Mars	God
	Roman	Quirinus	God
	Roman	Bellona	Goddess
	Roman	Minerva	Goddess
	Welsh	Bran the Blessed (Benedigeidfran)	God
	Welsh	"Nuada (Nudd, Nodens, Lud, Ereint)"	God
	Welsh	"Morrigan (Morrigu, Morrighan, Morgan)"	Goddess
Warriors	Welsh	"Cernunnos (Cerowain, Cernenus)"	God
Water	Babylonian	Ea	God
	Irish	Llyr	God
	Welsh	Llud Llaw Ereint	God
Wealth	Greek	Plutus	God
	Hindu	Lakshmi	Goddess

CATEGORY	ORGIN	NAME	TYPE
Weapon Makers	Irish	Goibniu	God
	Welsh	Goibniu	God
Weather	Irish	Manawydan ap Llyr	God
	Welsh	Manannan Mac Lir	God
Weaving	Greek	Ergane	Goddess
Wells	Irish	Danu (Dana)	Queen
Wild Creatures	Irish	Flidais	Goddess
Wind - East	Roman	Eurus	God
Wind - North	Greek	Boreas	God
	Greek	Boreas	God
	Roman	Boreas	God
Wind - South	Roman	Notus	God
Wind - Southeast	Greek	Eurus	God
Wind - West	Roman	Zephyr	God
Winds	Greek	Aeolus	God
Wine	Greek	Dionysus	God
	Roman	Bacchus	God
Winter	Norse	Hoder	God
	Norse	Hodur	God
Wisdom	Babylonian	Ea	God
	Egyptian	Thoth	God
	Greek	Athena	Goddess
	Greek	Pallas	Goddess
	Hindu	Ganesha	God
	Irish	Danu (Dana)	Queen
	Roman	Minerva	Goddess
Wisdom	Welsh	Taliesin	God
	Welsh	"Blodeuwedd (Blodwin, Blancheflor)"	Goddess
Witchcraft	Greek	Hecate	Goddess
Womb	Babylonian	Aruru	Goddess
Women	Greek	Hera	Goddess
Woodland	Welsh	"Cernunnos (Cerowain, Cernenus)"	God
Woods	Roman	Sylvanus	God
Writing	Egyptian	Thoth	God
	Egyptian	Seshat	Goddess
	Irish	"Nuada (Nudd, Nodens, Lud, Ereint)"	God
	Welsh	Bran the Blessed (Benedigeidfran)	God
	Welsh	"Nuada (Nudd, Nodens, Lud, Ereint)"	God
	Welsh	"Ogma (Oghma,Ogmios)"	God
	Welsh	Taliesin	God
Youth	Greek	Apollo	God
	Greek	Hebe	Goddess
	Irish	Angus Mac Oc (Og)	God
	Norse	Idun	Goddess

ORIGIN	TYPE	NAME	CATEGORY
Assyrian	God	Ashur	War
Babylonian	God	Ellil	Air
		Dagan	Earth
		Tammuz	Fertility
		Anu	Heaven
		Ea	Incantations
		Sin	Moon
		Adad	Oracles
		Shamash	Sin
		Ellil	Sky
		Adad	Storm
		Marduk	Sun
		Nergal	Underworld
		Tammuz	Vegetation
		Ninurta	War
		Ea	Water
		Ea	Wisdom
Babylonian	Goddess	Ishtar	Love
		Ereshkigal	Underworld
		Aruru	Womb
Egyptian	Creator	Atum	Of the Gods
		Shu	Air
		Mnevis	Black Bull of the Sun
		Set	Chaos
		Seth	Chaos
		Amon	Chief God
		Amun	Chief God
		Ptah	Craftsmen
Egyptian	Creator	Khnum	Creation
		Kehpri	Creation
		Amen	Creation
		Ptah	Creation/Bearer of the ankh
		Anubis	Dead
		Geb	Earth
		Anubis	Embalming

SOLVER SERIES: NAME FINDER

ORIGIN	TYPE	NAME	CATEGORY
Egyptian	Creator	Set	Evil
		Seth	Evil
		Min	Fertility
		Amon	Fertility
		Wepwawet	Funerary Cult
		Pepi	God-King
		Khafre	God-King
		Ramses	God-King
		Menkaure	God-King
		Senusert	God-King
		Thutmose	God-King
		Hapy	Innundation
		Osiris	Judge of the dead
		Thoth	Knowledge
		Serapis	Lower World
		Thoth	Magic
		Imhotep	Medicine
		Ptah	Memphis
		Chons	Moon
		Thoth	Moon
		Khonsu	Moon
		Kehpri	Movement of the Sun
		Hapi	Nile
		Sobek	Nile (Crocodile)
		Bes	Pleasure
		Bes	Protection
		Bes	Protection (Evil & Misfortune)
		Horus	Protection (Hawk-Headed)
		Dua	Protection (Stomach of the Dead)
		Kehpri	Rebirth
		Ra-Horakhty	Rising Sun
		Horus	Sky
		Amen-Ra	Sun
		Amon-Re	Sun
		Amun-Ra	Sun
		Ra	Sun
		Re	Sun
		Aten	Sun
		Osiris	Underworld
		Osiris	Vegetation
		Wepwawet	War
		Thoth	Wisdom
		Thoth	Writing
Egyptian	Goddess	Qetesh	Beauty
		Bast	Cat
		Sati	Elephantine
		Maat	Harmony
		Nut	Heavens
		Hathor	Joy
		Maat	Justice
Egyptian	Goddess	Hathor	Love
		Qetesh	Love
		Seshat	Measurement
		Tefnut	Moisture
		Bastet	Protection
		Isis	Protection
		Hathor	Protection

SECTION 6 - GODS AND GODDESSES LISTED ALPHABETICALLY BY ORIGIN

ORIGIN	TYPE	NAME	CATEGORY
Egyptian	Goddess	Apet	Protection (Childbirth)
		Selket	Protection (Childbirth)
		Taweret	Protection (Childbirth)
		Nephthys	Protection (Of the Dead)
		Sekhet	Protection (Women)
		Buto	Serpent
		Mut	Sky
		Nut	Sky
		Maat	Truth
		Sekhmet	War
		Seshat	Writing
Egyptian	King	Aten	Of the Gods
Egyptian	Queen	Sati	Of the Gods
Greek	Consort	Hera	Of Zeus
		Leda	Of Zeus
		Leto	Of Zeus
		Maia	Of Zeus
		Danae	Of Zeus
		Metis	Of Zeus
		Aegina	Of Zeus
		Calyce	Of Zeus
		Europa	Of Zeus
		Semele	Of Zeus
		Selene	Of Zeus
		Themis	Of Zeus
		Alceme	Of Zeus
		Antiope	Of Zeus
Greek	God	Zeus	Chief God
		Satyr	Demigod
		Triton	Demigod
		Oniros	Dream
		Bel	Earth
		Comus	Festivity
		Pan	Fields
		Vulcan	Fire
		Pan	Flocks
		Pan	Forest
		Cronus	Harvest
		Bel	Heaven(s)
		Zeus	Heaven(s)
		Uranus	Heaven(s)
		Orion	Hunter
		Eros	Love
		Hymen	Marriage
		Asclepius	Medicine
		Comus	Mirth
		Momus	Mockery
		Zeus	Rain
		Dionysus	Revelry
		Bacchus	Revelry
Greek	God	Momus	Ridicule
		Eridanus	River
		Neureus	Sea
		Poseidon	Sea
		Triton	Sea
		Zeus	Sky
		Argus	Sky

SOLVER SERIES: NAME FINDER

ORIGIN	TYPE	NAME	CATEGORY
Greek	God	Hypnos	Sleep
		Hypnus	Sleep
		Helios	Sun
		Apollo	Sun
		Helios	Sun
		Phoebus	Sun
		Zeus	Supreme
		Hades	Underworld
		Pluto	Underworld
		Ares	War
		Plutus	Wealth
		Boreas	Wind - North
		Boreas	Wind - North
		Eurus	Wind - Southeast
		Aeolus	Winds
		Dionysus	Wine
		Apollo	Youth
Greek	Goddess	Artemis	Agriculture
		Demeter	Agriculture
		Hera	Air
		Athena	Arts
		Aphrodite	Beauty
		Tyche	Chance
		Artemis	Chase
		Ate	Criminal Folly
		Eos	Dawn
		Ara	Destruction
		Eris	Discord
		Gaea	Earth
		Gaia	Earth
		Hecate	Earth
		Moira	Fate
		Chloris	Flowers
		Hecate	Ghosts
		Artemis	Goblins
		Hygeia	Health
		Hestia	Hearth
		Hera	Heavens
		Artemis	Hunting
		Themis	Justice
		Aphrodite	Love
		Hecate	Magic
		Gaia	Marriage
		Hera	Marriage
		Demeter	Marriage
		Mnemosyne	Memory
		Ate	Mischief
		Eris	Mischief
		Hecate	Moon
		Selene	Moon
Greek	Goddess	Artemis	Moon
		Astarte	Moon
		Artemis	Nature
		Nyx	Night
		Leda	Night
		Leto	Night
		Irene	Peace

ORIGIN	TYPE	NAME	CATEGORY
Greek	Goddess	Ara	Retribution
		Ate	Retribution
		Nemesis	Revenge
		Ino	Seas
		Doris	Seas
		Ino	Sky
		Hecate	Sorcery
		Eris	Strife
		Cora	Vegetation
		Cotys	Vegetation
		Ara	Vengeance
		Nemesis	Vengeance
		Nike	Victory
		Athena	War
		Bellona	War
		Ergane	Weaving
		Athena	Wisdom
		Pallas	Wisdom
		Hecate	Witchcraft
		Hera	Women
		Hebe	Youth
Greek	Herald	Hermes	Of the Gods
Greek	Mother	Rhea	Of the Gods
Greek	Offspring	Ate	Of Zeus
		Ares	Of Zeus
		Hebe	Of Zeus
		Aegle	Of Zeus
		Arcas	Of Zeus
		Belus	Of Zeus
		Helen	Of Zeus
		Minos	Of Zeus
		Aeacus	Of Zeus
		Aglaia	Of Zeus
		Apollo	Of Zeus
		Athene	Of Zeus
		Clotho	Of Zeus
		Hermes	Of Zeus
		Pollox	Of Zeus
		Thalia	Of Zeus
		Zethus	Of Zeus
Greek	Queen	Hera	Of the Gods
Hindu	Creator	Brahama	Of the Gods
Hindu	God	Kama	Love
		Ganesha	Prosperity
		Krishna	Protection (Against Evil)
		Ganesha	Wisdom
Hindu	Goddess	Lakshmi	Beauty
		Durga	Beyond Reach
		Lakshmi	Enjoyment
		Kali	Evil
Hindu	Goddess	Ambika	Mangoes
		Devi	Mother of Life
		Lakshmi	Wealth
Hindu	Mother	Aditi	Of the Gods
Irish	God	Dagda	Arts
		"Lugh (Llew, Lug, Lugus)"	Arts
		Neit	Battle

SOLVER SERIES: NAME FINDER

ORIGIN	TYPE	NAME	CATEGORY
Irish	God	Angus Mac Oc (Og)	Beauty
		Goibniu	Blacksmiths
		Goibniu	Brewing
		"Bel (Belenus, Belinos, Beli Mawr)"	Cattle
		Dagda	Chief God
		Manawydan ap Llyr	Commerce
		"Bel (Belenus, Belinos, Beli Mawr)"	Crops
		"Bel (Belenus, Belinos, Beli Mawr)"	Fertility
		"Bel (Belenus, Belinos, Beli Mawr)"	Fire
		"Nuada (Nudd, Nodens, Lud, Ereint)"	Harpers
		"Bel (Belenus, Belinos, Beli Mawr)"	Healing
		Dian Cecht (Diancecht)	Healing
		"Lugh (Llew, Lug, Lugus)"	Healing
		"Nuada (Nudd, Nodens, Lud, Ereint)"	Healing
		"Nuada (Nudd, Nodens, Lud, Ereint)"	Historians
		"Bel (Belenus, Belinos, Beli Mawr)"	Hot Springs
		"Lugh (Llew, Lug, Lugus)"	Journeys
		Dagda	Knowledge
		Angus Mac Oc (Og)	Love
		Dagda	Magic
		Dian Cecht (Diancecht)	Magic
		Manawydan ap Llyr	Magic
		"Nuada (Nudd, Nodens, Lud, Ereint)"	Magic
		Dian Cecht (Diancecht)	Medicine
		Dagda	Music
		Manawydan ap Llyr	Navigation
		"Nuada (Nudd, Nodens, Lud, Ereint)"	Poetry
		Dagda	Prophecy
		"Lugh (Llew, Lug, Lugus)"	Prophecy
		Dagda	Prosperity
		"Bel (Belenus, Belinos, Beli Mawr)"	Prosperity
		"Bel (Belenus, Belinos, Beli Mawr)"	Purification
		Manawydan ap Llyr	Rebirth
		Dagda	Regeneration
		Dian Cecht (Diancecht)	Regeneration
		Llyr	Sea
		Manawydan ap Llyr	Sea
		Manawydan ap Llyr	Storm
		"Bel (Belenus, Belinos, Beli Mawr)"	Success
		"Lugh (Llew, Lug, Lugus)"	Sun
		"Nuada (Nudd, Nodens, Lud, Ereint)"	War
		Llyr	Water
		Goibniu	Weapon Makers
		Manawydan ap Llyr	Weather
		"Nuada (Nudd, Nodens, Lud, Ereint)"	Writing
		Angus Mac Oc (Og)	Youth
Irish	Goddess	"Brigit (Brid, Brig, Brigid, Brighid)"	Agriculture
		Don	Air
		Niamh	Beauty
		Niamh	Brightness
Irish	Goddess	"Macha (Mania, Mana, Mene, Minne)"	Cunning
		"Macha (Mania, Mana, Mene, Minne)"	Death
		White Lady	Death
		White Lady	Destruction
		Caillech	Disease
		Caer Ibormeith	Dreams
		Anu	Earth

ORIGIN	TYPE	NAME	CATEGORY
Irish	Goddess	"Badb (Badhbh, Badb Catha)"	Enlightenment
		Aoibhell	Evil
		Banba (Bandba)	Fertility
		"Brigit (Brid, Brig, Brigid, Brighid)"	Fire
		Flidais	Forests
		"Brigit (Brid, Brig, Brigid, Brighid)"	Healing
		"Scathach (Scota,Scatha,Scath)"	Healing
		"Badb (Badhbh, Badb Catha)"	Inspiration
		"Brigit (Brid, Brig, Brigid, Brighid)"	Inspiration
		"Brigit (Brid, Brig, Brigid, Brighid)"	Learning Divination
		"Morrigan (Morrigu, Morrighan, Morgan)"	Lust
		"Morrigan (Morrigu, Morrighan, Morgan)"	Magic
		"Scathach (Scota,Scatha,Scath)"	Magic
		"Scathach (Scota,Scatha,Scath)"	Martial Arts
		"Aine (of Knockaine, Cliach, Cnoc)"	Moon
		Eadon	Nurse of the Poets
		"Brigit (Brid, Brig, Brigid, Brighid)"	Occult Knowledge
		"Macha (Mania, Mana, Mene, Minne)"	Physical Force
		Caillech	Plague
		Anu	Plenty
		"Brigit (Brid, Brig, Brigid, Brighid)"	Poetry
		"Brigit (Brid, Brig, Brigid, Brighid)"	Prophecy
		"Morrigan (Morrigu, Morrighan, Morgan)"	Prophecy
		"Scathach (Scota,Scatha,Scath)"	Prophecy
		"Boann (Boannan, Boyne)"	River
		Eiru (Erin)	Ruler
		Don	Sea
		Caer Ibormeith	Sleep
		"Brigit (Brid, Brig, Brigid, Brighid)"	Smithcraft
		Banba (Bandba)	War
		"Macha (Mania, Mana, Mene, Minne)"	War
		"Morrigan (Morrigu, Morrighan, Morgan)"	War
		Flidais	Wild Creatures
Irish	Queen	Danu (Dana)	Magic
		Danu (Dana)	Of the Gods
		Danu (Dana)	Plenty
		Danu (Dana)	Rivers
		Danu (Dana)	Wells
		Danu (Dana)	Wisdom
Norse	God	Hoenir	Asa-God
		Vali	Avenger
		Odin	Chief God
		Hodur	Darkness
		Ragnarok	Destruction
		Loki	Discord
		Vanir	Earlier Race
		Norns	Fates
		Frey	Fertility
		Loki	Fire
		Ull	Frost Glitter
Norse	God	Forseti	Justice
		Loki	Mischief
		Forseti	Order
		Aesir	Pantheon
		Baldur	Peace
		Bragi	Poetry
		Aeger	Sea

SOLVER SERIES: NAME FINDER

ORIGIN	TYPE	NAME	CATEGORY
Norse	God	Aegir	Sea
		Ull	Skiing
		Tyr	Sky
		Thor	Thunder
		Donar	Thunder
		Hoder	Winter
		Hodur	Winter
Norse	Goddess	Freya	Beauty
		Sif	Corn
		Norn	Destiny
		Erda	Earth
		Skuld	Future
		Eir	Healing
		Idun	Immortality
		Freya	Love
		Frigg(a)	Marriage
		Frigg(a)	Motherhood
		Verdandi	Present
		Ran	Sea
		Idun	Spring
		Hel	Underworld
		Idun	Youth
Norse	Home	Asgard	Of the Gods
Norse	Watchman	Heimdall	Of the Gods
Phoenician	Goddess	Astarte	Fertility
Roman	God	Picus	Agriculture
		Saturn	Agriculture
		Jove	Chief God
		Jupiter	Chief God
		Mors	Death
		Comus	Festivity
		Faun	Fields
		Vulcan	Fire
		Janus	Gates
		Dis	Hades
		Orcus	Hades
		Pluto	Hades
		Faun	Herds
		Pan	Herds
		Lars	Household
		Penates	Household
		Comus	Joy
		Jupiter	Lightning
		Amor	Love
		Cupid	Love
		Orcus	Lower World
		Serapis	Lower World
		Comus	Mirth
		Apollo	Music
		Somnus	Night
Roman	God	Faunus	Pastoral
		Lupercus	Pastoral
		Mercury	Patron
		Jupiter Pluvius	Rain
		Bacchus	Revelry
		Neptune	Sea
		Vertumnus	Season

SECTION 6 - GODS AND GODDESSES LISTED ALPHABETICALLY BY ORIGIN

ORIGIN	TYPE	NAME	CATEGORY
Roman	God	Somnus	Sleep
		Morpheus	Sleep
		Apollo	Sun
		Sol	Sun
		Lar	Tutelary
		Dis	Underworld
		Orcus	Underworld
		Pluto	Underworld
		Ares	War
		Mars	War
		Quirinus	War
		Eurus	Wind - East
		Boreas	Wind - North
		Notus	Wind - South
		Zephyr	Wind - West
		Bacchus	Wine
		Sylvanus	Woods
Roman	Goddess	Ops	Agriculture
		Ceres	Agriculture
		Venus	Beauty
		Parca	Birth
		Lucina	Birth
		Matuta	Birth
		Annona	Crops
		Trivia	Crossroads
		Aurora	Dawn
		Matuta	Dawn
		Terra	Earth
		Tellus	Earth
		Fides	Faith
		Parcae	Fates
		Ops	Fertility
		Ceres	Fertility
		Fauna	Fertility
		Demeter	Fertility
		Terra	Fields
		Tellus	Fields
		Vesta	Fire
		Flora	Flowers
		Feronia	Fountain
		Pomona	Fruits
		Ceres	Grain
		Dea	Growth
		Ops	Harvest
		Salus	Health
		Vesta	Hearth
		Pales	Herds
		Spes	Hope
		Epona	Horses
		Diana	Hunting
Roman	Goddess	Vacuna	Hunting
		Lucina	Light
		Venus	Love
		Juno	Marriage
		Dian	Moon
		Luna	Moon
		Artemis	Moon

SOLVER SERIES: NAME FINDER

ORIGIN	TYPE	NAME	CATEGORY
Roman	Goddess	Cynthia	Moon
		Cora	Nether World
		Proserpina	Nether World
		Nox	Night
		Pax	Peace
		Ops	Plenty
		Salus	Prosperity
		Mare	Sea
		Aestas	Summer
		Ceres	Vegetation
		Fides	Virtue
		Bellona	War
		Minerva	War
		Minerva	Wisdom
Roman	Queen	Juno	Of the Gods
Welsh	God	Amaethon	Agriculture
		"Cernunnos (Cerowain, Cernenus)"	Animals
		Bran the Blessed (Benedigeidfran)	Arts
		"Lugh (Llew, Lug, Lugus)"	Arts
		"Merlin (Merddin, Myrddin)"	Arts
		Goibniu	Blacksmiths
		Goibniu	Brewing
		"Bel (Belenus, Belinos, Beli Mawr)"	Cattle
		"Cernunnos (Cerowain, Cernenus)"	Commerce
		Manannan Mac Lir	Commerce
		"Bel (Belenus, Belinos, Beli Mawr)"	Crops
		"Cernunnos (Cerowain, Cernenus)"	Crossroads
		Pwyll (pen annwn)	Cunning
		Arawn	Dead
		"Ogma (Oghma,Ogmios)"	Eloquence
		Gwydion	Enchantmen
		Math Mathonwy	Enchantment
		"Bel (Belenus, Belinos, Beli Mawr)"	Fertility
		"Cernunnos (Cerowain, Cernenus)"	Fertility
		"Bel (Belenus, Belinos, Beli Mawr)"	Fire
		Llud Llaw Ereint	Harpers
		"Nuada (Nudd, Nodens, Lud, Ereint)"	Harpers
		"Bel (Belenus, Belinos, Beli Mawr)"	Healing
		Llud Llaw Ereint	Healing
		"Lugh (Llew, Lug, Lugus)"	Healing
		"Merlin (Merddin, Myrddin)"	Healing
		"Nuada (Nudd, Nodens, Lud, Ereint)"	Healing
		Llew Llaw Gyffes	Hero
		"Nuada (Nudd, Nodens, Lud, Ereint)"	Historians
		"Bel (Belenus, Belinos, Beli Mawr)"	Hot Springs
		Gwydion	Illusion
		"Merlin (Merddin, Myrddin)"	Illusion
		"Ogma (Oghma,Ogmios)"	Inspiration
		"Lugh (Llew, Lug, Lugus)"	Journeys
		"Ogma (Oghma,Ogmios)"	Language
Welsh	God	Gwydion	Magic
		Manannan Mac Lir	Magic
		Math Mathonwy	Magic
		"Merlin (Merddin, Myrddin)"	Magic
		"Nuada (Nudd, Nodens, Lud, Ereint)"	Magic
		"Ogma (Oghma,Ogmios)"	Magic
		Taliesin	Magic

ORIGIN	TYPE	NAME	CATEGORY
Welsh	God	Bran the Blessed (Benedigeidfran)	Music
		"Ogma (Oghma,Ogmios)"	Music
		Taliesin	Music
		Manannan Mac Lir	Navigation
		"Ogma (Oghma,Ogmios)"	Physical Force
		Llud Llaw Ereint	Poetry
		"Nuada (Nudd, Nodens, Lud, Ereint)"	Poetry
		"Ogma (Oghma,Ogmios)"	Poetry
		Taliesin	Poetry
		Bran the Blessed (Benedigeidfran)	Prophecy
		"Lugh (Llew, Lug, Lugus)"	Prophecy
		"Merlin (Merddin, Myrddin)"	Prophecy
		"Bel (Belenus, Belinos, Beli Mawr)"	Prosperity
		"Bel (Belenus, Belinos, Beli Mawr)"	Purification
		Manannan Mac Lir	Rebirth
		"Cernunnos (Cerowain, Cernenus)"	Reincarnation
		Dylan	Sea
		Manannan Mac Lir	Sea
		Llud Llaw Ereint	Smithcraft
		Llud Llaw Ereint	Sorcery
		Manannan Mac Lir	Storm
		"Bel (Belenus, Belinos, Beli Mawr)"	Success
		"Lugh (Llew, Lug, Lugus)"	Sun
		Gwynn ap Nudd	Underworld
		Arawn	Underworld
		Gwethyr	Upperworld
		"Cernunnos (Cerowain, Cernenus)"	Virility
		Pwyll (pen annwn)	Virtue
		Bran the Blessed (Benedigeidfran)	War
		"Nuada (Nudd, Nodens, Lud, Ereint)"	War
		"Cernunnos (Cerowain, Cernenus)"	Warriors
		Llud Llaw Ereint	Water
		Goibniu	Weapon Makers
		Manannan Mac Lir	Weather
		Taliesin	Wisdom
		"Cernunnos (Cerowain, Cernenus)"	Woodland
		Bran the Blessed (Benedigeidfran)	Writing
		"Nuada (Nudd, Nodens, Lud, Ereint)"	Writing
		"Ogma (Oghma,Ogmios)"	Writing
		Taliesin	Writing
Welsh	Goddess	Arianrhod	Beauty
		Branwen	Beauty
		"Ceridwen (Caridwen, Ceridwen)"	Death
		White Lady	Death
		White Lady	Destruction
		Arianrhod	Fertility
		"Blodeuwedd (Blodwin, Blancheflor)"	Flowers
		"Creiddylad (Creudylad, Cordelia)"	Flowers
		Epona	Horses
		"Ceridwen (Caridwen, Ceridwen)"	Initiation
Welsh	Goddess	"Ceridwen (Caridwen, Ceridwen)"	Inspiration
		Branwen	Love
		"Creiddylad (Creudylad, Cordelia)"	Love
		"Morrigan (Morrigu, Morrighan, Morgan)"	Lust
		"Ceridwen (Caridwen, Ceridwen)"	Magic
		"Morrigan (Morrigu, Morrighan, Morgan)"	Magic
		"Blodeuwedd (Blodwin, Blancheflor)"	Moon

ORIGIN	TYPE	NAME	CATEGORY
Welsh	Goddess	"Morrigan (Morrigu, Morrighan, Morgan)"	Prophecy
		Druantia	Queen of the Druids
		"Ceridwen (Caridwen, Ceridwen)"	Regeneration
		Arianrhod	Reincarnation
		Donn	Sea
		"Morrigan (Morrigu, Morrighan, Morgan)"	War
		"Blodeuwedd (Blodwin, Blancheflor)"	Wisdom
Welsh	Mother	Margawse	Of the Gods